marketing

McGRAW-HILL SERIES IN MARKETING

marketing
11TH EDITION

MICHAEL J. ETZEL
University of Notre Dame

BRUCE J. WALKER
University of Missouri–Columbia

WILLIAM J. STANTON
University of Colorado–Boulder

**Irwin
McGraw-Hill**

Boston, Massachusetts   Burr Ridge, Illinois   Dubuque, Iowa
Madison, Wisconsin   New York, New York   San Francisco, California   St. Louis, Missouri

Irwin/McGraw-Hill

A Division of The **McGraw·Hill** Companies

MARKETING

This book is printed on acid-free paper.

Text credits and photo credits appear beginning on page P-1 and on this page by reference.

3 4 5 6 7 8 9 0   DOW   DOW   9 0 9 8 7

ISBN 0-07-018954-4

This book was set in Times Roman by GTS Graphics, Inc.

The editors were Karen Westover, Dan Alpert, Richard Mason, and Bob Greiner.

The text designer was Francis Owens.

The cover designer was Deborah Chusid.

The production supervisors were Diane Renda and Rich DeVitto.

The photo editor was Stephen Forsling.

New drawings were rendered by Hadel Studio.

R. R. Donnelley & Sons Company was printer and binder.

Library of Congress Cataloging-in-Publication Data

Etzel, Michael J.
    Marketing / Michael J. Etzel, Bruce J. Walker, William J. Stanton.
    —11th ed.
       p.   cm.—(McGraw-Hill series in marketing)
    Rev. ed. of: Fundamentals of marketing / William J. Stanton,
Michael J. Etzel, Bruce J. Walker. 10th ed. c1994.
    Includes bibliographical references and indexes.
    ISBN 0-07-018954-4 (paper)
    1. Marketing.   I. Walker, Bruce J.   II. Stanton, William J.
III. Stanton, William J. Fundamentals of marketing.   IV. Title.
V. Series.
    HF5415.S745   1997   96-19807
    658.8—dc20   CIP

ABOUT THE AUTHORS

Michael J. Etzel received his Ph.D. in marketing from the University of Colorado in 1970. Since 1980, he has been a Professor of Marketing at the University of Notre Dame. He also has been on the faculties at Utah State University and the University of Kentucky. He has held visiting faculty positions at the University of South Carolina and the University of Hawaii. In 1990, he was a Fulbright Fellow at the University of Innsbruck, Austria, and in 1994 he directed and taught in the University of Notre Dame overseas program in Fremantle, Australia.

Professor Etzel has taught marketing courses from the introductory through the doctoral level. He is also a frequent presenter in executive training programs.

His research, primarily in marketing management and buyer behavior, has appeared in the *Journal of Marketing*, *Journal of Marketing Research*, *Journal of Consumer Research*, and other publications. He is the coauthor of another college-level text, *Retailing Today*.

He has been active in many aspects of the American Marketing Association at the local and national levels, most notably serving as Chairman of the Board in 1996–1997.

Bruce J. Walker is Professor of Marketing and Dean of the College of Business and Public Administration at the University of Missouri–Columbia. Professor Walker received his undergraduate degree in economics from Seattle University and his master's and Ph.D. degrees in business from the University of Colorado.

Professor Walker was a member of the marketing faculties at the University of Kentucky and then at Arizona State University. He moved to the University of Missouri in 1990.

Dr. Walker has taught a variety of courses, including principles of marketing. His research, focusing primarily on franchising, marketing channels, and survey-research methods, has been published in the *Journal of Marketing*, *California Management Review*, *Journal of Marketing Research*, and other periodicals. He has also coedited or coauthored conference proceedings and books, including *Retailing Today*.

Dr. Walker has been involved with both the American Marketing Association and the Western Marketing Educators Association. He served as vice president of AMA's Education Division and president of WMEA. Currently, he is a trustee for the International Franchise Association's Education Foundation.

William J. Stanton is Professor Emeritus of Marketing at the University of Colorado–Boulder. He received his Ph.D. in marketing from Northwestern University, where he was elected to Beta Gamma Sigma. He has worked in business and has taught in several management development programs for marketing executives. He has served as a consultant for various business organizations and has engaged in research projects for the federal government. Professor Stanton also has lectured at universities in Europe, Asia, Mexico, and New Zealand.

A coauthor of the leading text in sales management, Professor Stanton has also published several journal articles and monographs. *Marketing* has been translated into Spanish, and separate editions have been adapted (with coauthors) for Canada, Italy, Australia, and South Africa.

In a survey of marketing educators, Professor Stanton was voted one of the leaders in marketing thought. And he is listed in *Who's Who in America* and *Who's Who in the World*.

Mike Etzel
To my parents, Al and Audrey

Bruce Walker
To Pam, Therese, Brent, Steve, Scott, and Jennie

Bill Stanton
To Kelly and Little Joe

BRIEF CONTENTS

CONTENTS

PREFACE

To the Student

A recent ad placed by a corporate recruiter in the student newspaper on a college campus carried this headline:

> What does marketing have to do with public accounting? (The answer may surprise you.)

Well, we think the answer is "a lot," and it doesn't surprise us. More important, it shouldn't surprise you after reading this book.

Marketing is an integral part of all our lives. A large percentage of our waking hours is taken up by efforts to market something (a product or an idea, for example) or by the efforts of others marketing to us. Whether you are a student, professor, physician, small business owner, politician, or even a partner in a public accounting firm doesn't make any difference; you are engaged in marketing. The challenge is to do it well, and that requires an understanding of what marketing is and how to perform it.

But there is more to modern marketing than learning what it involves. Much of the excitement of marketing is created by the context in which it occurs. Take the field of communications, for example. Consider how recent developments in fiber optics, electronic mail, cellular phones, the Internet, and facsimile machines are changing our lives. Then multiply that impact by the changes in other areas such as manufacturing, agriculture, transportation, and entertainment. Technology appears to be expanding at an increasing rate, and every development creates new marketing opportunities.

The globalization of business is another development certain to continue. However, exactly what form this globalization will eventually take is far from clear. The world is trying to sort out several recent and ongoing events—the dismantling of the Soviet Union, the growth of private business in China, the possibility of a common currency in Europe, and reduced trade barriers among many countries of the world. Any one of these would dramatically affect world trade. All of them at the same time create unprecedented challenges. Virtually every business will be affected by increasing global competition, and many will see exciting international opportunities.

What does this mean for marketers? In some respects, we can say that their jobs won't change. They will still decide what products to offer, set prices they think customers will pay, provide products where customers can conveniently find them, and design promotional messages to inform and persuade potential buyers. However, in today's highly dynamic environment, these managers will be faced with more new situations than ever before. They will have access to more information than their predecessors, but will have to figure out how to avoid being buried under it and to use it effectively. They will have more strategic alternatives from which to select, but the cost of selecting the wrong one will be greater. They will be pursuing smaller markets, with products that have shorter lives, against a changing mix of competitors. In short, marketers will be operating in a faster-paced, higher-risk environment.

Fortunately, your career is commencing during this time of unprecedented environmental change and challenge—developments that can translate into successes for you. To make the most of this opportunity, you need an understanding of contemporary marketing and how it fits into our dynamic world. The objective of this new edition of *Marketing* is to help you gain that understanding.

Features of *Marketing*

This is the eleventh edition of *Marketing*. It has clearly passed the test of time. Our objective in this revision is to create a current, comprehensive, and involving book without detracting from its reputation as being highly readable.

We present marketing as a total system of business actions carried out by managers in individual organizations, in the context of the larger economy, and, indeed, in society as a whole. Regardless of whether managers are employed by a business or nonprofit organization, are providers of goods or services, or are doing business domestically or globally, they need to understand certain fundamentals of marketing.

We share those fundamentals with you through the framework of the marketing management process. An organization first sets objectives, taking into consideration the environmental forces that influence its efforts. The managers then select target markets and build a marketing program to achieve the objectives. The four elements integrated by managers in designing a marketing program—product, price, distribution, and promotion—are at the heart of marketing. Finally, an organization evaluates its performance and makes adjustments to its marketing strategy.

To help you understand and appreciate this process, we have provided explanations that are accompanied by many current, real-life examples of large and small firms, photo essays to illustrate concepts, and a variety of interesting boxed inserts to stimulate your thinking and challenge your mastery of the concepts. We have also included numerous international examples and illustrations to emphasize the global orientation that marketing is taking.

That's enough introduction. It's time to get started. Turn to Chapter 1 and begin your discovery of the world of marketing!

To the Instructor

Revising a successful book is a delicate process. On the one hand, it is essential that new developments and material be incorporated into a revised edition and the presentation be lively and engaging. On the other hand, the structure and format that has withstood the test of time should be retained. We have worked hard to maintain this balance by updating and revising the book, while preserving the organization, reader-friendly writing style, and extensive use of examples.

The book is divided into eight parts to reflect the marketing management process. They are:

- **Part One: Modern Marketing**
  An overview of what marketing is, the context in which it occurs, the process of marketing planning, and the marketing research effort that is so essential to support decision making.

- **Part Two: Target Markets**
  An examination of consumer and business markets, decision making by customers, the process of market segmentation, and demand forecasting.

- **Part Three: Product**
  An essential activity of marketing is translating needs of prospects into products that can be sold. The design, development, and testing of products are a part of the process, along with more visible features like brands and packaging.

- **Part Four: Price**
  The choice of a price and the adjustments made to that choice are governed by factors such as demand, costs, competition, and the broader strategy of the seller.

- **Part Five: Distribution**
  To appreciate the modern miracle of having products available when and where they are desired, one must examine both the institutions that conduct the transactions and those that transport goods.

- **Part Six: Promotion**
  Effective communications inform and persuade potential customers. Attractive promotions stimulate action. Formulating a message and transmitting it effectively are essential ingredients in a marketing effort.

- **Part Seven: Marketing in Special Fields**
  Two areas—services marketing (in for-profit and not-for-profit organizations) and international marketing—are sufficiently distinctive to warrant special coverage.

- **Part Eight: Managing the Marketing Effort**
  An effective marketing management process requires some guidance on implementing and evaluating the marketing effort and an examination of where marketing is headed.

What's New and Improved in This Edition
Because the reactions to the organization and presentation of the tenth edition were quite positive, the book has been fine-tuned rather than overhauled. The noteworthy changes are described below.

Coverage and Organization

- Discussions of the consumer market (Chapter 5) and the business market (Chapter 6) are now similarly structured. Each includes a description of the respective market as well as an overview of the buying process in each.
- Chapter 7 on market segmentation and target marketing now follows rather than precedes the

discussions of consumer and business markets. This arrangement gives the readers a basic familiarity with these markets before they begin thinking about how the markets can be subdivided.

- Demand forecasting has been moved from Chapter 3 to Chapter 7. Because adequate demand is a necessary condition for segmentation, linking it to segmentation and target marketing is logical.
- In order to reflect their shifting importance in the promotional mix, the amount of attention given to sales promotion in Chapter 18 has been expanded, whereas the discussion of advertising has been reduced.
- Emerging and evolving topics covered in this edition include:

Relationship marketing	Quality
Ethics	ISO 9000
Automatic replenishment	Generation X
On-line retailing	Decision support systems
Competitive intelligence	Brand equity
Product counterfeiting	Universal product design
Value pricing	Everyday low pricing
Slotting allowances	Retail supercenters
Global marketing	Market fragmentation
Reconsumption	Service encounters
Green marketing	Category-killer stores
Power centers	Market-response systems
Contract logistics	Efficient consumer response
Major-accounts organization	
Mass customization	

As this list would indicate, every chapter has been updated to reflect recent developments in marketing and the business environment.

- In recognition of the continuously growing importance of international marketing, this topic is integrated throughout the text and cases. In addition, a separate chapter on international marketing as well as a Global Perspective box in each chapter reflect the significance of this issue.
- Because of the positive response, this edition again combines wholesaling and physical distribution in one chapter, and integrates services marketing by for-profit and nonprofit organizations into a single chapter.
- This book includes two appendixes. The first, "Marketing Math," provides additional detail on price elasticity of demand, the basics of operat-

ing statements, markups, and return on investment as a measure of performance. We've found these topics to be a useful review for many students and essential concepts for students who have not been exposed to them previously. The second appendix, "Careers in Marketing," draws students' attention to the opportunities that exist in marketing. It begins by outlining a procedure for choosing a career, then goes on to describe a variety of marketing jobs and organizations that are heavily dependent on marketing. The last portion guides students through the job search process.

Chapter-Related Cases

- Each chapter begins with a contemporary case that introduces some of the concepts, strategies, and techniques covered in the chapter. At the conclusion of the chapter, the case is revisited and additional information is presented. By addressing the questions we present at the end of each case, students discover how they can apply what they have learned in the chapter to a marketing situation. Virtually all of these cases deal with highly recognizable companies and brands. Sixteen are entirely new to this edition, and six have been substantially revised. They are:

Harlem Globetrotters	McDonald's
Nordstrom	CBS pilot testing
Avon	Cessna
Black & Decker	General Motors electric car
General Motors' overlapping divisions	Levi's
Apple Computer	Boeing
Goodyear	J.C. Penney
Supervalu	Aleve
AGCO Corp.	Benetton
Enterprise Rent-A-Car	Toys "R" Us
Taco Bell	Bausch & Lomb

Part-Ending Cases

- Each of the eight parts of the text ends with two cases. All deal with familiar firms facing significant marketing challenges. Each case is designed to be realistic, yet the focus is on a relatively narrow aspect of marketing to prevent the beginning student from being overwhelmed by the complexity common to many marketing problems. An innovation in this edition is the inclusion of several cases that focus on competitive rivalries. An example of these "versus" cases is "Coke vs. Pepsi." This format allows students to examine intensely competitive situations in which marketing strategy often determines ultimate success. Twelve of the cases are new to this edition, and four are heavily revised from the last edition. The part-ending cases are:

Ben & Jerry's	Coke vs. Pepsi
American Express	The Gap
Estee	Gatorade vs. the
Southwest Airlines	Upstarts
Kmart	Home Depot
PowerBar	Federal Express
AT&T vs. MCI	Frito-Lay
vs. Sprint	Disney
Sears	Nike vs. Reebok

Pedagogical Support

- The book includes eight Commitment to Customer Satisfaction boxes that describe how real firms work to implement critical components of success. These boxes reinforce the importance of the marketing concept. They include:

  How annual colors for consumer and business products are selected.
  Award-winning "green" products.
  Real-time monitoring of products in transit.
  A money-back job guarantee offered by a college.

- Nineteen You Make the Decision boxes are interspersed throughout. These boxes present synopses of actual situations faced by marketers and ask students how they would respond. The boxes move the student from a passive observer of marketing to an active participant who makes decisions about marketing actions. Among the decisions are:

  How to appeal to Generation X.
  The viability of a wristwatch that monitors the wearer's media exposure.
  The optimal number of new-product introductions.
  Problems in marketing a new fragrance.
  Buying a retail franchise.
  The power of the media in creating perceptions about the European Union.
  Opportunities for women in sales.
  Whether or not on-line services violate consumers' privacy.

- Every chapter contains an Ethical Dilemma box. These boxes raise the student's awareness level of the nature and frequency of ethical challenges in marketing. Second, they help a student formulate an ethical perspective. A person's ethical sense is not developed by listening to advice; it comes from dealing with issues, making decisions, and then appraising those decisions. Topics covered include:

  How some administrators "fudge" statistics that appear in college guidebooks.
  Ambush marketing tactics at the Olympics.
  Airlines overbooking flights.
  Extreme market-skimming pricing by pharmaceutical firms.
  Participation in gray markets.
  "Free" offers that contain hidden charges.

- Each chapter is followed by two types of assignments. The first is a set of eight to ten questions that focus on applying the text material rather than simply reviewing terms or memorizing definitions. We call the second type Hands-On Marketing. These assignments require that students get out of the classroom and interact with customers and/or marketers. In carrying out these assignments, students will gather information firsthand or observe real marketing situations. As a result, they will develop a practical sense of how marketing is actually performed.

Teaching and Learning Supplements

The text is the primary element in a complete package of teaching and learning resources. The supporting items include:

- An *Instructor's Manual* that provides a complete outline of each chapter, lecture material in the form of additional examples and vignettes, and the material for one or two lectures for each chapter. The manual also includes commentaries on the chapter-related and part-ending cases; end-of-chapter questions; and Ethical Dilemma, Commitment to Customer Satisfaction, and You Make the Decision boxes.
- A *computer version of the instructor's manual* is available in ASCII files to facilitate modifying the original version to match your teaching style.
- A *Test Bank* of over 2,500 objective questions is available on disk. The questions are coded to indicate the type (definition, concept, application) and text location.

- A comprehensive *color transparency program* to enhance lectures and class discussions.
- Classroom presentation software using *Microsoft Powerpoint "slides"* available to adopters.
- A *video program* based on timely news footage that features a wide variety of organizations and complements text discussions.
- An *Internet supplement* consisting of an introduction to the use of the Internet as part of marketing strategy, exercises keyed to the text, and suggested Internet sites as sources of additional material for the cases.
- A student *Study Guide* that provides chapter outlines, test questions and real-world cases for each chapter, and exercises that involve students in practical marketing experiences.
- A *CD-ROM supplement* based on the strategic marketing planning tool CRUSH!

Watch for new developments in McGraw-Hill College Division product information and other services by visiting our World Wide Web site at:

http://www.mhcollege.com

Acknowledgments

We have benefited from the contributions of our students, past and present colleagues, other professors, and business executives in preparing this and previous editions of *Marketing*. To all these people, though too numerous to mention, we owe a debt of gratitude.

Several individuals have contributed significantly to the supplementary materials accompanying the text. The chapter-related and part-ending cases were written by Professor Craig A. Kelley of Sacramento State College. Professor Thomas J. Adams of Sacramento City College continues to do an outstanding job preparing the *Study Guide*. Professor Adams also worked with us and Professor Kelley in putting together a comprehensive *Instructor's Manual*. An extensive set of objective test questions were developed by Professors Tom and Betty Pritchett of Kennesaw State College.

We also received help with research from Grant Montgomery, Andy Smith, and Shifali Dhingra at various times during this revision. Melinda Mayfield also assisted in compiling the Glossary.

A number of professors examined the previous edition and reviewed early drafts of the current edition. Their advice and insights contributed to numerous improvements:

Ronald J. Adams, *University of North Florida*; Carol Bienstock, *Valdosta State University*; Roy Cabaniss, *Western Kentucky University*; Steven Engel, *University of Colorado–Boulder*; Mort Ettinger, *Salem State College*; Stephen Goodwin, *Illinois State University*; Craig A. Hollingshead, *Marshall University*; Denise M. Johnson, *University of Louisville*; Kenneth Laird, *Southern Connecticut State University*; Mary Lou Lockerby, *College of Du Page*; Irving Mason, *Herkimer County Community College*; Darryl W. Miller, *Washburn University*; Mark Mitchell, *University of South Carolina–Spartanburg*; Keith B. Murray, *Bryant College*; John Phillips, *University of San Francisco*; Charles Prohaska, *Central Connecticut State University*; Robert G. Roe, *University of Wyoming*; Louise Smith, *Towson State College*; Michael J. Swenson, *Brigham Young University*; Jack L. Taylor, *Portland State University*; Robert E. Thompson, *Indiana State University*; Timothy L. Wilson, *Clarion University*.

Finally, we would like to take this opportunity to thank the professionals within the College Division of The McGraw-Hill Companies, Inc., who did so much to make this book an effective and attractive teaching and learning resource. We especially want to thank our sponsoring editor, Karen Westover, for her energy, support, and patience. Dan Alpert, senior associate editor, offered his usual strong and steady guidance throughout the project. Editors Richard Mason and Bob Greiner ably managed the overall project on a day-to-day basis. Suzanne Olson, editorial assistant, was an important member of our team throughout the project and played a key role in coordinating our photo program. Gretlyn Cline proved to be a detailed, conscientious copyeditor. Francis Owens brought this book to life with his effective and contemporary design. Richard DeVitto and Diane Renda worked diligently to maintain quality as well as schedule. Stephen Forsling, photo editor, coordinated a complex photo program. Without the team effort of the editorial, design, and production departments, this textbook would not have materialized.

Michael J. Etzel
Bruce J. Walker
William J. Stanton

PART ONE

Modern Marketing

An introduction to marketing, the marketing environment, strategic planning in marketing, and marketing research

Marketing is many things. It is essential to the survival of most organizations; it is fast-paced and dynamic; it is highly visible; it is rewarding to its successful practitioners and frustrating to the less fortunate; and sometimes it is controversial. But one thing you can be sure of, it is never dull! Welcome to the place where an organization meets the public, where its ideas, planning, and execution are given the ultimate test of market acceptance or rejection.

To help you understand this activity, Chapter 1 explains what marketing is, how it has developed, and how it is continuing to develop. In Chapter 2 we examine the environmental forces that shape an organization's marketing program.

We'll see in Chapter 3 how an organization's marketing begins with strategic planning and includes specific marketing plans.

Chapter 4 explains the role of research in marketing and describes how marketing research is conducted and how demand is forecast.

CHAPTER 1

The Field of Marketing

What Will It Take for the
HARLEM GLOBETROTTERS
to Become Winners Again?

Why would a senior vice president at Honeywell, Inc., who had just been named one of the top-50 corporate strategists in the country by the *Journal of Business Strategy* and one of the 40 most powerful and influential black corporate executives by *Black Enterprise Magazine*, resign his position? If the answer is to gather a group of investors to spend $6 million for a bankrupt company that seemed to be going nowhere, you might wonder about his sanity, but that's what Mannie Jackson did. And now his skills as a marketer are being tested.

The Harlem Globetrotters, billed as the World's Greatest Basketball Show, have entertained audiences around the world for nearly 70 years with a mixture of outstanding basketball talent, ball-handling wizardry, and showmanship. But following the retirement of founder and promotional genius Abe Saperstein, a series of owners tried to take advantage of the Globetrotter legacy without making the investment in marketing that every product needs. The result was bankruptcy in 1991. Following the bankruptcy, the team continued to operate under court protection, but management seemed to lack direction and fan interest was declining. Mannie Jackson has set out to change that, but the challenge is daunting.

As a prospective owner, he discovered that the Globetrotters were well known and well liked around the world, but their show had become stale in the eyes of consumers. Many of the tricks developed by the team, such as behind-the-back passes and dribbling between the legs, had become commonplace in basketball. Further, given the competition for today's entertainment dollar, he felt the Globetrotters had to do more than just provide amusement. As a former Globetrotter team member, Jackson traveled around the world and met many prominent people including Fidel Castro, Nikita Khrushchev, and the pope. He saw firsthand that the Globetrotters are capable of bringing together people from many walks of life and different cultures to improve communications and understanding. He believes that with the right positioning and increased exposure the Globetrotters can become a force in raising social awareness, helping to restore trust in society, and increasing a sense of caring and concern.[1]

How can Mannie Jackson use marketing to restore the luster of this fabled team and achieve his objectives?

Marketing On-Line

The Internet can be a powerful marketing tool. We have included Uniform Resource Locators, or URLs (the technical term for Internet addresses), to help you find the "home pages" of many organizations covered in the text. However, not all companies have an Internet address, and so we occasionally substitute an address for a competing company or product. Space limitations occasionally require us to break URLs onto two lines; on actual Internet pages URLs always appear on one line.

http://www.harlemglobetrotters.com

The situation with the Harlem Globetrotters is an excellent example of the role marketing plays in an organization. On the one hand, deficient marketing nearly resulted in the team's demise. Now the hopes for the future are tied to a rejuvenated marketing effort. This is just one example of the role marketing plays in organizations. To begin to understand the topic, we need to address the question "What is marketing?" The answer is in Chapter 1, and it may surprise you. After studying this chapter, you should be able to explain:

CHAPTER GOALS

- The relationship between exchange and marketing.
- How marketing applies to business and nonbusiness situations.
- Marketing's evolution in the U.S.
- The difference between selling and marketing.
- The marketing concept.
- The impact of ethics and quality management in marketing.
- Marketing's role in the global economy, in the American socioeconomic system, in an individual organization, and in your life.

Nature and Scope of Marketing

Because marketing exists in so many forms, it is easy to underestimate how often it plays a role in our lives. Of course, we participate in the marketing process every time we buy goods and services. And you probably have had a job that included some aspect of dealing with customers. But did you realize that you also engage in a form of marketing when you vote, donate to charity, and prepare your résumé?

Exchange as the Focus

Marketing can occur any time one social unit (person or organization) strives to exchange something of value with another social unit. Thus, the essence of marketing is a transaction or exchange. In this broad sense, marketing consists of activities designed to generate and facilitate exchanges intended to satisfy human needs or wants.

Exchange is one of three ways we can satisfy our needs. If you want something, you can make it yourself, acquire it by theft or some form of coercion, or you can offer something of value (perhaps your money, your services, or another good) to a person who will exchange the desired item for what you offer. Only this last alternative is an exchange in the sense that marketing is occurring.

The following conditions must exist for a marketing exchange to take place:

- Two or more people or organizations must be involved, and each must have needs or wants to be satisfied. If you are totally self-sufficient in some area, there is no need for an exchange.
- The parties must be involved voluntarily.
- Each party must have something of value to contribute in the exchange, and each must believe that it will benefit from the exchange. In the case of an election, for example, the things of value are the votes of the electorate and the representation of the voters by the candidate.
- The parties must communicate with each other. The communication can take many forms and may even be through a third party, but without communication there can be no exchange.

These exchange conditions introduce a number of terms that deserve some elaboration. First there are the parties involved in the exchange. On one side of the

*A*n auction is one of the purest examples of a market and an exchange. It has buyers and sellers, something of value, and lots of communication. All sorts of products, from tobacco and thoroughbred horses to art, are sold at auction. Two of the most famous auction houses are Christie's (pictured here) and Sotheby's, both headquartered in London. These two firms each auction off over a billion dollars in goods yearly, mostly works of art but also unusual items such as an astronaut's space suit (for $225,500) and Elvis' costumes.

http://www.sirius.com/ ~christie/Christie.htm

http://www.worthinc.com/

exchange is the marketer. *Marketers* take the initiative in trying to stimulate and facilitate exchanges. They develop marketing plans and programs and implement them in hopes of creating an exchange. A college or university recruiting students, The American Cancer Society soliciting donors, and United Airlines seeking passengers are all marketers.

On the other side of the exchange is the *market*, made up of the persons or organizations to whom the marketing programs are directed and who will play a role in the acceptance or rejection of the offer. Markets are made up of *customers*, consisting of any person or group with whom an individual or organizational marketer has an existing or potential exchange relationship.

The people who comprise a market play a number of roles. First, there is the *decision maker*, the individual or organizational unit that has the authority to commit to the exchange. Then there are the *consumers*, those who actually use or consume the product. Another role is *purchaser*, the party who carries out the transaction. Finally, there are *influencers* who affect the decisions of others because of their expertise, position, or power. These are not simply semantic distinctions. Worth, Inc., the producer of a new, safer baseball for children's leagues, discovered that the different roles involved affect marketing decisions. Parents (influencers) love the ball, and kids (consumers) are more comfortable playing with it. Yet despite having the weight, feel, and bounce of a regular hardball, many coaches and youth league officials (decision makers) reject it as nontraditional. The problem for Worth's managers is deciding what its marketing effort should look like and how it should be directed to these different role players.[2]

Note also that an organization's markets encompass more than the customers for its primary product. For example, in addition to students who consume an education and the parents who frequently pay for all or some of it, a state university markets to the legislators to secure funds, to citizens living near the university who

WHY IS THE NUMBER OF FEMALE SKIERS DECREASING?

The number of women skiers has recently declined dramatically. Several possible explanations have been proposed. One is that ski equipment is designed for men and only slightly modified for women. As a result, it is not suited to women's smaller feet and lighter bodies. A second possibility is that ads for ski areas frequently depict skiers performing dramatic, high-risk stunts that don't appeal to most women. Still another factor may be the growing popularity of snowboarding. Snowboarders are viewed by many as undisciplined and reckless on the slopes, and as a re-

sult, their presence increases the fear of an accident. And then there is an issue of attitude. Men tend to be aggressive in their approach to skiing, while women are more interested in style and aesthetics. As a result, they are often incompatible on the slopes. Finally, for some women the dual pressures of maintaining a family and a career may simply not leave enough time for an activity such as skiing.

How much is marketing to blame for the decline in the number of women skiers?

Source: Marj Charlier, "Many Women Give Up Skiing; Resorts Shiver," *The Wall Street Journal*, Mar. 2, 1995, p. B1.

---

may be affected by its activities, and to alumni who support university programs. A firm's markets include government regulatory agencies, environmentalists, and stockholders.

In describing exchanges, we use the terms *needs* and *wants* interchangeably because marketing is relevant to both. Technically, needs can be viewed in a strict physiological sense (food, clothing, and shelter), with everything else defined as a want. However, from a customer's perspective the distinction is not as clear. For example, many people would consider a television or a personal computer a necessity.

Finally, the object of the exchange or what is being marketed is referred to generically as the *product*. It can be a good, service, idea, person, or place. All of these can be marketed, as we shall see.

Applications of Marketing

This book focuses on the activities carried out by organizations within our socio-economic system to facilitate mutually beneficial exchanges. These organizations may be profit-seeking business firms, or they may be what are called nonprofit organizations—a university, charity, church, police department, or museum, for example. (Marketing can also be performed by individuals. As you approach graduation, you can use marketing principles to maximize the effectiveness of your job search. We'll have more to say about this in the appendix, "Careers in Marketing.")

Both types of organizations face essentially the same marketing challenges and opportunities. As discussed in the chapter-opening case, Mannie Jackson is convinced that creative marketing can reinvigorate the Globetrotters. Similarly, the city of Pittsburgh recently undertook a multiyear marketing effort to revive the area's economy.[3] Consequently, we need a definition of marketing to guide executives in business and nonprofit organizations in managing their marketing efforts and to guide our examination of the subject.

http://www.pittsburgh.net/

Our definition of marketing—applicable in a business or a nonprofit organization—is as follows: **Marketing** is a total system of business activities designed to plan, price, promote, and distribute want-satisfying products to target markets to achieve organizational objectives. This definition has two significant implications:

- The entire system of business activities should be customer-oriented. Customers' wants must be recognized and satisfied.
- Marketing should start with an idea about a want-satisfying product and should not end until the customers' wants are completely satisfied, which may be some time after the exchange is made.

Evolution of Marketing

The foundations of marketing in America were laid in Colonial times, when the early settlers traded among themselves and with the Indians. Some settlers became retailers, wholesalers, and itinerant peddlers. However, large-scale marketing in the U.S. did not begin to take shape until the Industrial Revolution in the latter part of the 1800s. Since then, marketing has evolved through three successive stages of development: production orientation, sales orientation, and marketing orientation. But you should understand that these stages depict the general evolution of marketing and reflect a state of mind as much as they do a period of time. Thus, although many firms have progressed to the third stage, some are still in the first or second stage, as shown in Figure 1-1.

Production-Orientation Stage

Manufacturers in the **production-orientation stage** typically focused on increasing output while assuming that customers would seek out and buy reasonably priced, well-made products. Executives with backgrounds in manufacturing and engineering shaped the firm's strategy. In an era when the demand for goods generally exceeded the supply, the primary focus in business was to efficiently produce large quantities of products. Finding the customers was viewed as a relatively minor function.

The term marketing was not in use. Instead, producers had sales departments headed by executives whose sole job was to manage a sales force. The function of the sales department was simply to sell the company's output, at a price set by

FIGURE 1-1

Three stages of marketing evolution in the United States.

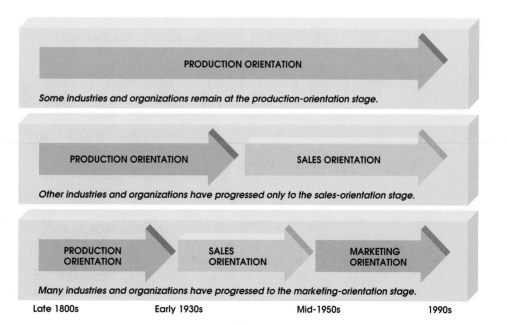

PRODUCTION ORIENTATION

Some industries and organizations remain at the production-orientation stage.

PRODUCTION ORIENTATION → SALES ORIENTATION

Other industries and organizations have progressed only to the sales-orientation stage.

PRODUCTION ORIENTATION → SALES ORIENTATION → MARKETING ORIENTATION

Many industries and organizations have progressed to the marketing-orientation stage.

| Late 1800s | Early 1930s | Mid-1950s | 1990s |

production and financial executives. The philosophy of the Pillsbury company in the late 1800s is characteristic of this stage: "Blessed with a supply of the finest North American Wheat, plenty of water power, and excellent milling machinery, we produce flour of the highest quality. Our basic function is to mill high-quality flour, and of course (and almost incidentally) we must hire salesmen to sell it, just as we hire accountants to keep our books."[4]

Manufacturers, wholesalers, and retailers operating in this stage emphasized internal operations and focused on efficiency and cost control. They felt that they knew what was best when it came to product assortments and customer services.

This emphasis on production and operations dominated until the Great Depression in the early 1930s. The approach is understandable when you consider that for generations the primary concern of business was how to produce and distribute an adequate quantity of acceptable products to meet the needs of a rapidly growing population.

Sales-Orientation Stage

The Depression changed perceptions. No longer was the main problem how to produce or grow enough, but rather it was how to sell the output. Just offering a good product was no assurance of market success. Managers began to realize that to sell their products in an environment where consumers had the opportunity to choose from among many alternatives required substantial promotional effort. Thus, the **sales-orientation stage** was characterized by a heavy reliance on promotional activity to sell the products the firm wanted to make. In this stage, selling-related activities and sales executives began to gain respect and responsibility from company management.

Along with responsibility came expectations for performance. Unfortunately, overly aggressive selling—the "hard sell"—and unscrupulous tactics also evolved during this period. As a result, selling developed an unsavory reputation in the eyes of many. Old habits die hard, and even now some organizations believe that they must use a hard-sell approach to prosper. In the United States the sales stage was common into the 1950s, when the marketing era began to emerge.

Marketing-Orientation Stage

At the end of World War II there was an enormous pent-up demand for consumer goods created by wartime shortages. As a result, manufacturing plants turned out tremendous quantities of goods that were quickly purchased. However, the postwar surge in consumer spending slowed down as supply caught up with demand, and many firms found that they had excess production capacity.

In an attempt to stimulate sales, firms reverted to the aggressive promotional and sales activities of the sales-orientation era. However, this time consumers were less willing to be persuaded. What the sellers discovered was that the war years had also changed the consumer. The thousands of service men and women who spent time overseas came home more sophisticated and worldly. In addition, the war effort brought many women out of the home and into the work force for the first time. Because of their experiences, consumers had become more knowledgeable, less naive, and less easily influenced. In addition, they had more choices. The technology that was developed during the war made it possible to produce a much greater variety of goods when converted to peacetime activity.

Thus the evolution of marketing continued. Many companies recognized that to put idle capacity to work they had to produce what consumers wanted. In the

marketing-orientation stage, companies identify what customers want and tailor all of the activities of the firm to satisfy those needs as efficiently as possible.

In this third stage, firms are marketing rather than merely selling. Several tasks that were once associated with other business functions became the responsibility of the top marketing executive, called the marketing manager or vice president of marketing. For instance, inventory control, warehousing, and some aspects of product planning are turned over to the head of marketing as a way of serving customers better. To increase effectiveness, input from the marketplace is sought at the beginning of a production cycle, as well as at the end. In addition, marketing is included in long-term as well as short-term company planning.

A marketing orientation requires that a firm's top executive have a favorable attitude toward marketing. Philip Knight, chairman and CEO of Nike, makes this point: "For years we thought of ourselves as a production-oriented company, meaning we put all our emphasis on designing and manufacturing the product. But now we understand that the most important thing we do is market the product."[5]

We are *not* saying that marketing executives should hold the top positions in a company. Nor are we saying that the president of a firm must come up through the marketing department. But it is necessary that the president understand the importance of marketing, that is, be *marketing-oriented*.

Many American business firms and nonprofit organizations are presently in this third stage in the evolution of marketing. Others may recognize the importance of a marketing orientation, but have difficulty implementing it. Implementation requires accepting the notion that the wants and needs of customers, not the desires of management, direct the organization. A leading business publication describes it this way: "Instead of choosing from what you have to offer, the new consumer tells you what he wants. You figure out how to supply it."[6]

A basic implication of placing customers first characterizes the way an organization describes what it does. Table 1-1 shows how some well-known organizations might define their businesses under a production orientation and how differently the business would be defined using a marketing orientation.

Note that not every organization needs to be marketing-oriented to prosper. A monopolist, such as a public utility, is virtually guaranteed of having customers. Therefore, its management should be much more concerned with low-cost, effi-

TABLE 1-1 What business are you in?

Company	Production-oriented answer	Marketing-oriented answer
AT&T	We operate a long-distance telephone company.	We provide reliable, efficient, and inexpensive telecommunications services.
Exxon	We produce oil and gasoline products.	We provide various types of safe and cost-effective energy.
Levi Strauss	We make blue jeans.	We offer comfort, fashion, and durability in wearing apparel.
Steelcase	We make office furniture.	We increase office productivity.
Kodak	We make cameras and film.	We help preserve beautiful memories.
Amtrak	We run railroads.	(See the "You Make the Decision" box on page 10.)

YOU MAKE THE DECISION

HAS AMTRAK CORRECTLY DEFINED THE BUSINESS IT IS IN?

Amtrak is in trouble. Long-distance trains run late 40 percent of the time, customer complaints are up every year (70,000 in 1994), and ridership is down. The reasons? Coaches are old and in disrepair, the food quality is poor, and the employees are often rude. In an attempt to reduce its operating deficit, the railroad recently lower the routes it travels by 20 percent. The result is that many important markets such as Atlanta to Chicago have no direct service, and many smaller cities and towns are left with no passenger rail service at all.

However, some routes are successful. For example, Metroliners between New York City and Washington, D.C., travel at 125 miles per hour and arrive on schedule 90 percent of the time. And trains do have their advantages. The seats are bigger and more comfortable than airline seats, business travelers can work more efficiently, and, of course, train riders get a nice view of the scenery.

If it is to survive, Amtrak needs a marketing-oriented description of what business it is in. What would you suggest?

http://www.amtrak.com/

Source: Daniel Machalba, "Poor and Shabby, Amtrak Plans to Shrink," *The Wall Street Journal*, Mar. 24, 1995, p. B1.

---

cient production than with marketing. There are also instances in which the potential customers consider the product to be so superior that they will seek it out. For example, the world's best heart surgeons or particularly popular artists find a market for their services regardless of their orientations.

Differences between Marketing and Selling

As marketing has evolved from a sales orientation to a marketing orientation, the terms *marketing* and *selling* are often used interchangeably. Some people even think they are synonymous. However, there are vast differences between the two activities. The basic difference is that selling is internally focused, while marketing is externally focused. Let's see what that means.

When a company makes a product and then tries to persuade customers to buy it, that's selling. In effect, the firm attempts to alter consumer demand to fit the firm's supply of the product. But when a firm finds out what the customer wants and develops a product that will satisfy that need and also yield a profit, that's marketing. In marketing, the company adjusts its supply to the will of consumer demand.

Some distinctions between selling and marketing are:

In selling	In marketing
Emphasis is on the product.	Emphasis is on customers' wants.
Company first makes the product and then figures out how to sell it.	Company first determines customers' wants and then figures out how to make and deliver a product to satisfy those wants.
Management is sales volume–oriented.	Management is profit-oriented.
Planning is short-run oriented, in terms of today's products and markets.	Planning is long-run oriented, in terms of new products, tomorrow's markets, and future growth.
Needs of sellers are stressed.	Wants of buyers are stressed.

The Marketing Concept

As businesspeople began to recognize that marketing is vital to the success of their organizations, a new philosophy of doing business developed. Called the **marketing concept**, it emphasizes customer orientation and coordination of marketing activities to achieve the organization's performance objectives. Sometimes the marketing concept is simply stated as a customer orientation, as expressed in these words of the late Sam Walton, founder of Wal-Mart, "There is only one boss: the customer."[7] As important as it is to stress customer satisfaction, however, this focus should not replace achievement of objectives as the fundamental rationale for the marketing concept.

Nature and Rationale

The marketing concept is based on three beliefs that are illustrated in Figure 1-2:

- All planning and operations should be *customer-oriented*. That is, every department and employee should be focused on contributing to the satisfaction of customers' needs. A customer orientation is demonstrated at Frito-Lay, a company that controls over 40 percent of the $2 billion potato chip business while charging the highest prices in the market.[8] Frito-Lay engineers have developed a simulated human mouth to measure the jaw effort needed to crunch a chip! By comparing taste preference results with test results from the simulated mouth, researchers found that 4 pounds per square inch of oral pressure is the ideal level of crunchiness. Now all chips are tested to meet this standard. As a company executive points out, "We have to be perfect; after all, no one really needs a potato chip."[9]

- All marketing activities in an organization should be *coordinated*. This means that marketing efforts (product planning, pricing, distribution, and promotion) should be designed and combined in a coherent, consistent way, and that one executive should have overall authority and responsibility for the complete set of marketing activities. Home Depot, Inc. has grown into a $16 billion home repair chain by bringing together the best feature of the neighborhood hardware store (advice and information), the attraction of a discount store (low prices), and a selection of products that exceeds both.[10]

- Customer-oriented, coordinated marketing is essential to achieve the *organization's performance objectives*. The primary objective for a business is typically a profitable sales volume. In nonprofit organizations the objective might be the number of people served or the variety of services offered. For example, to

FIGURE 1-2 Components and outcomes of the marketing concept.

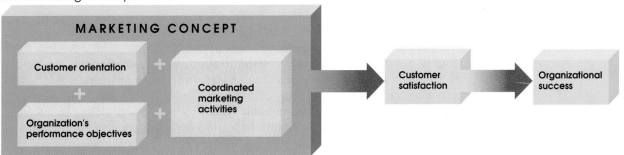

increase attendance some churches have more clearly defined the markets they hope to reach and increased their use of all forms of marketing. The results are often impressive. One church in Charlotte, North Carolina, targeted people with no connection to any religious institution. Following research on what had turned these "unchurched" people off, the services were made more contemporary, sermons on relevant topics such as parenting and financial management were introduced, fewer overt requests for money were made, and it was all communicated in highly focused advertising. As a result, in 16 months over 300 new members with no previous church affiliation were attracted.[11]

All ideas are subject to refinement and the marketing concept is no exception. The ability to effectively manage large amounts of information has allowed organizations to do an even better job of meeting customers' needs. Two of these developments are discussed below.

Relationship Marketing.   The initial notion of **relationship marketing** was that organizations should strive to build personal, long-term bonds with customers.[12] Identifying the needs of customers and satisfying them once can be profitable, but establishing a connection with customers such that the organization is regularly relied on for help is much more valuable. This relationship, more like being a partner than simply a participant in an exchange, only occurs if a sense of trust and commitment is established.

Firms go to great lengths to create relationships with customers. In France during the peak tourism season, Nestlé's baby food division provides rest stops along main highways for families with young children. Samples of Nestlé products are provided for babies, free diapers are available, and trained hostesses offer assistance to parents. In a 2-month period the company distributed 600,000 meals to 120,000 visitors. Motorcycle maker Harley-Davidson created a club for bike owners and offers the 200,000 members insurance, a travel agency, roadside emergency assistance, magazines, free safety courses, safe riding competitions, and 750 local chapters that hold regular meetings.[13] What do these companies hope to get in return? A feeling of goodwill, and a sense that the firm cares about more than making a sale. That is, they are seeking a long-term relationship with their customers.

More recently, the notion of establishing relationships has been extended beyond customers to all the groups an organization interacts with. These include suppliers, employees, the government, and even competitors. For example, IBM has forged strategic alliances with former rivals Toshiba and Siemens to develop memory chips.

Mass Customization.   The modern marketing system was built on identifying a need experienced by a large number of people (a mass market), and using mass production techniques and mass marketing (relying heavily on network television advertising) to satisfy that need. By producing and selling large quantities of standardized products, firms were able to keep the unit costs low and offer need-satisfying products at attractive prices. However, the market has changed. Mass marketing is being replaced by **mass customization**, that is, developing, producing, and delivering affordable products with enough variety and uniqueness that nearly every potential customer can have exactly what he or she wants.[14]

Mass customization is made possible by the tremendous advances in information technology. Firms are now able to learn a lot more about their current and prospective customers, and use that information in designing products, manufacturing, and distribution. They are also able to advertise to very specific audiences through cable television and the many special interest magazines now on newsstands. The result is a proliferation of products in many product categories. Consider, for example, the variety of dry breakfast cereals and soft drinks available to you. And mass customization is not limited to small items. Automobile buyers have so many makes, models, accessories, options, and colors to choose from in buying a new car that each one is nearly unique.[15]

The Societal Marketing Concept

Not long after the marketing concept became widely accepted by many firms, it came under fire. For more than 30 years critics have persistently charged that marketing ignores social responsibility. That is, although the marketing concept may help an organization achieve its goals, it may at the same time encourage actions that conflict with society's best interests.

From one point of view, these charges are true. A firm may totally satisfy its customers (and in the process achieve a hefty profit), while also adversely affecting society. To illustrate, a pulp and paper mill in the Pacific Northwest might be supplying its newspaper customers with quality newsprint at a reasonable price, but to do so it might be polluting the air and water near the mill.

However, this need not be the case. A firm's social responsibility can be quite compatible with the marketing concept. Compatibility depends on two things: how broadly a firm perceives its marketing goals, and how long it is willing to wait to achieve those goals. A firm that sufficiently extends the *breadth* and *time* dimensions of its marketing goals to fulfill its social responsibility is practicing what has become known as the **societal marketing concept**.

*A*s this ad suggests, Phillips Petroleum takes a proactive position with regard to the environment. In addition to developing cleaner burning fuels, Phillips recently doubled the capacity of its plastic recycling plant in Tulsa. It now can process 40 million pounds of plastic, the equivalent of 300 million one-gallon jugs. This may not be profitable in the short run, but it reflects a recognition that the company defines its market more broadly than just in terms of the people who buy its products.

When the marketing concept's breadth is extended, a company recognizes that its market includes not only the buyers of its products but also anyone directly affected by its operations. In our example, the paper mill has several markets to satisfy, including (1) the newspaper publishers, (2) the consumers of the air that contains impurities given off by the mill, and (3) the recreational users of the local river where the mill releases its waste matter.

Extending the time dimension of its marketing goals means that a firm should take a long-term view of customer satisfaction and performance objectives, rather than concentrate only on tomorrow. For a company to prosper in the long run, it must satisfy its customers' social needs as well as their economic needs.

Thus the marketing concept and a company's social responsibility are compatible if management strives over the long run to (1) satisfy the wants of its product-buying customers, (2) meet the societal needs of others affected by the firm's activities, and (3) achieve the company's performance objectives. The challenges of balancing these three often conflicting goals frequently place marketers in ethical predicaments. Thus, the issue of ethics in marketing deserves our consideration.

Ethics and Marketing

The task of marketers is to influence the behavior of customers. To accomplish this goal, marketers have a variety of tools at their disposal. Broadly speaking, these tools include the design of a product, the price at which it is offered, the message used to describe it, and the place in which it is made available.

Marketers are also responsible to a variety of groups. Certainly their customers depend on them to provide good products at reasonable prices. Also, their employers expect them to generate sales and profits, suppliers and distributors look to them for their continued business, and society expects them to be responsible citizens. The manner in which these marketing tools can be used, and the frequently divergent interests of the groups dependent on the marketer, create a wide variety of ethical challenges.

http://www.ama.org/

One response to the need for ethical guidance comes from the American Marketing Association, which has formulated a code of ethics for its members. It states:

> As a member of the American Marketing Association, I recognize the significance of my professional conduct and my responsibility to society and the other members of my profession:
> 1. By acknowledging my accountability to the organization for which I work.
> 2. By pledging my efforts to assure that all presentations of goods, services, and concepts be made honestly and clearly.
> 3. By striving to improve marketing knowledge and practice in order to better serve society.
> 4. By supporting free consumer choice in circumstances that are legal and consistent with generally accepted community standards.
> 5. By pledging to use the highest professional standards in my work and in my competitive activity.
> 6. By acknowledging the right of the American Marketing Association, through established procedure, to withdraw my membership if I am found to be in violation of ethical standards of professional conduct.

What Is Ethical Behavior?

A discussion of the philosophical underpinnings of ethics is beyond the scope of this book.[16] However, it is safe to say that there is considerable disagreement over what is and what is not ethical conduct. For example, ethics vary from society to society. Take bribery; though repugnant in most societies, it is an accepted and even necessary aspect of business behavior in many parts of the world. Thus, for our purposes it is sufficient to say that **ethics** are the rules we agree to play by. They are the standards of behavior generally accepted by a society.

Many U.S. organizations have discovered that employees do not necessarily develop a strong sense of ethical standards on their own. Embarrassing scandals and legal proceedings are frequent reminders that ethical behavior cannot be taken for granted. A recent court case revealed that in the late 1980s and early 1990s at least 16 Honda of America marketing executives accepted extravagant gifts from dealers in return for allocating extra cars that were in short supply. One executive admitted that before he was forced to resign he had received between $2 million and $5 million in bribes. He described the bribes as "gifts from friends."[17]

Instilling an Ethical Orientation

Organizations are not ignoring ethical issues. It is reported that 75 to 80 percent of major U.S. firms have codes of ethics for their employees.[18] In a study of 1,000 major U.S. corporations, 40 percent reported holding ethics workshops, and nearly one-third have set up ethics committees.[19] However, as long as there are conflicting goals and the opportunity for people to make judgments, ethical failures will occur. To relieve some of the pressure on employees faced with ethical challenges and perhaps reduce the frequency and severity of ethical problems, organizations have taken several steps.

One dimension of creating an ethical environment is to make sure that the demands on employees to perform are reasonable. Faced with unrealistic quotas and deadlines, people are much more likely to cut corners to accomplish their objectives. Citicorp fired several senior executives in a credit card–processing division for overstating revenues. The question is, Why did they feel compelled to falsify the information?

Another important facet of an ethical orientation is communicating clearly what the organization's standards are. Hewlett-Packard, for example, makes sure that all employees are completely familiar with its extensive code of conduct. To constantly remind employees of the importance of ethical behavior, Texas Instruments includes a weekly column on ethics in its international electronic news service. Included in the column are answers to specific issues raised by employees.

To help employees deal with ethical issues, some companies are creating a position for a full-time ethics officer. This high-level executive gives advice to senior management as well as responds to the complaints and questions of employees at all levels. At McDonnell Douglas Corp. all employees are informed about how to contact the ethics ombudsman whose responsibilities include protecting whistle-blowers.[20]

Organizations are also taking greater care to reward only ethical performance. It is important that employees see that success is the result of admirable behavior, not questionable practices.

The Benefits of Ethical Behavior

One could argue that ethical behavior should in itself be rewarding. However, there are tangible benefits as well. Business is built on relationships with suppliers, customers, employees, and other groups. The strength of those relationships is largely a function of the amount of trust the parties have in each other. Unethical behavior undermines trust and destroys relationships. It is not surprising that a list of companies noted for their attention to ethical standards—Johnson & Johnson,

http://www.hp.com/

http://www.ti.com/

http://www.mdc.com/

AN ETHICAL DILEMMA?

Guide books like *Barron's* and *Peterson's* as well as magazines such as *Money* and *U.S. News & World Report* publish information about colleges and universities that prospective students use in deciding where to apply. For a school with an attractive profile (high SATs, low acceptance rates, and high graduation rates) there are benefits in the form of increased applications and higher enrollments. Despite their popularity, some college administrators feel the ratings are misleading because they offer an incomplete picture of the schools. There are also suspicions that some schools submit "fudged" figures because the data are never checked. Despite these problems, schools par-

ticipate because they fear that not being represented could have serious negative consequences.

If you were the director of admissions at your school responsible for preparing the data for these publications, would you consider it unethical to exclude the verbal SAT scores for foreign students whose first language was not English? What about the scores of a group of economically disadvantaged students who were admitted under a special state-sponsored program?

Source: Steve Stecklow, "Colleges Inflate SATs and Graduation Rates in Popular Guidebooks," *The Wall Street Journal,* Apr. 5, 1995, p. A1.

Coca-Cola, Gerber, IBM, Kodak, 3M, Xerox, J.C. Penney, and Pitney Bowes—had annual growth rates between 1950 and 1990 nearly twice that of a sample of typical firms traded on the New York Stock Exchange.[21] Thus, ethics is a cornerstone of business success for many firms.

http://www.jnj.com/

However, there is a need for constant vigilance. Johnson & Johnson is probably the most often cited example of an ethical firm. Its corporate code of ethics is one of the oldest, written in 1932. And its handling of the Tylenol crisis in 1982, when eight people died as a result of products that had been tampered with, is considered a near-perfect example of ethical behavior. Yet, recently, Johnson & Johnson admitted that employees had intentionally destroyed documents sought by the government that dealt with its promotion of Retin-A.[22]

Issues related to ethics are often ambiguous. There are situations in which the behavior of a marketer might be judged inappropriate and unethical by some and totally acceptable by others. It is important for you to be aware of typical ethical challenges in marketing and to consider how you would respond to them. To help you in that regard, we have included Ethical Dilemma boxes throughout the book. In most, there are no absolutely right or wrong answers. That's why we call them dilemmas. We hope you find them interesting and helpful in refining your own sense of ethics.

Quality in Marketing

http://www.maytag.com/

Quality has always been important to consumers. The success of Maytag's "lonely repairman" television commercials is a good indication. The campaign, focusing on the dependability of Maytag appliances, has been running for 25 years and has contributed to 9 out of 10 U.S. consumers being familiar with the Maytag brand.[23] Rather than focus on quality, many U.S. businesses chose to maximize output through mass production and to minimize prices with cost controls. The objective was to have an "acceptable" level of quality, which meant being as good as the competition. This strategy was successful as long as quality remained fairly constant across competitors.

Some argue that American executives became complacent about quality, convincing themselves that even minor improvements would raise costs dramatically and thus make a firm uncompetitive. Meanwhile, the state-of-the-art manufacturing techniques that kept U.S. businesses ahead of the rest of the world were being adopted by firms overseas. Then these foreign firms added quality as a key ingredient of their strategies. The Japanese even created a national award for quality, called the Deming Prize, in 1951. Ironically, the award is named for W. Edwards Deming, an American quality consultant who for many years was much better received in Japan than in the U.S.

We now see from the success of foreign firms in automobiles, electronics, and computer hardware and software the benefits of a commitment to quality. Thus, improving quality became a high priority for U.S. organizations beginning in the 1980s.

What Is Quality?

http://www.boeing.com/

One component of quality is meeting and striving to exceed the requirements of the customer. This involves listening to the customer. The Boeing 777 is an example. It is the first commercial airliner based on a design that originated from customers' inputs. Airlines such as United and British Airways asked for greater flexibility in their aircraft, so the 777 incorporates modular construction that will permit it to be reconfigured from a multiple-class seating arrangement to a single class of service in just 3 days.[24]

A second component of quality is the absence of variation. That doesn't mean that a Chevrolet should perform as well as a Cadillac, or that the service at Motel 6 should be the same as the service at The Ritz Carlton. What it does mean is that a good or service should consistently deliver what it was designed to, without variation from one experience to another. Thus, every Chevrolet or every Motel 6 should provide consumers with an identical experience.

The most obvious application of variance control is in manufacturing. In fact, most manufacturers have had quality control departments for many years. However, the title "quality control" was misleading since the job was limited to inspecting finished products to prevent defective ones from leaving the plant. But meeting specifications in production did not ensure quality if the product was poorly designed or improperly serviced after it was sold. Thus, we discovered that the real indication of **quality** is how well a product meets the expectations of the customer.

The third component in improving quality is total organizational commitment. We've learned that quality control cannot be delegated to one department in an organization. It must permeate the entire organization. This is known as **total quality management** and it involves adopting the processes and procedures that will provide customers with the right product at the right place. One noted author describes the goals of total quality management as:

- Better, more appealing, less variable product quality.
- Quicker, less variable responses from design all the way to putting the product in the final user's hands.
- Greater flexibility in responding to customers' changing needs.
- Lower costs as a result of quality improvements, reductions in reworking, and waste elimination.[25]

The worldwide attention to quality is reflected in the development of the **ISO 9000 quality standards**. The International Organization for Standardization (ISO), a federation of national standards organizations, has created a certification process.

A firm seeking certification must conform to specific standards in its processes, procedures, operations, controls, and management. ISO 9000 is based on the assumption that if firms rigidly adhere to the same high standards, the output will be products of consistently high quality. Thus, certification allows a firm in one country to do business with suppliers or distributors anywhere in the world with confidence. Firms such as Xerox and IBM are demanding that suppliers become certified. In an even broader application, firms located in countries outside the European Union (EU) that want to sell to firms inside the EU are now required to be certified.[26]

For marketers, the best indication of quality is customer satisfaction. In a competitive environment, the ultimate measure of satisfaction is whether or not the customer returns to buy a product a second, third, or fourth time. However, a firm can't afford to gamble that its marketing decisions are correct and then wait for repeat purchases to confirm or reject those judgments. Instead, managers realize that satisfaction is determined by how closely *experience* with a product meets or exceeds a customer's *expectations*. Therefore, marketers must do two things:

http://www.whirlpool.com/

- Ensure that all marketing activities, such as the price of a product, the claims made for it in advertising, and the places in which it is sold, contribute to creating reasonable expectations on the part of the customer. Annually, Whirlpool Corp. mails a survey to 18,000 households asking consumers to rate Whirlpool appliances and to compare them to competitors' products. A slip in the ratings or an unfavorable evaluation relative to a competitor generates action to identify the cause and correct the problem.[27]
- Eliminate variations in customers' experiences in purchasing and consuming the product. This means, for example, that not only should every new Chevrolet you buy provide the same level of performance, but also every interaction you have with a Chevrolet dealer should be consistent and without surprises.

Instilling Quality

As managers have become more concerned about quality, a variety of quality-improvement programs have been developed. Though the programs have some differences, they typically involve:

- Studying competitors and noncompetitors to identify the highest standards of performance in such areas as delivery delays and eliminating defects. This process is called benchmarking.
- Management and labor working closely together in an atmosphere of trust and cooperation to improve performance.
- All employees making a commitment to constantly search for better ways of performing their functions.
- Forming partnerships with suppliers and customers so that their inputs for improvement can be incorporated into the operation.
- Measuring quality and the resulting customer satisfaction.

http://www.nist.gov/
quality_program/

To encourage greater effort in quality, the U.S. Congress created the Malcolm Baldrige Quality Award in 1987. Up to six winners are recognized each year among manufacturers, services firms, and small businesses. The Baldrige Award extends beyond manufacturing quality, to include quality levels and quality-improvement programs in all areas of companies. Just applying for the award is a difficult process. The application form contains 75 pages of questions. However, many firms have found that completing the questionnaire is a worthwhile exercise that leads to the discovery of quality weaknesses they are able to correct. Whatever the approach, it is clear that for U.S. firms to be competitive into the next century, the focus on quality must continue.

Importance of Marketing

Coca-Cola is sold in virtually every country in the world. Japanese autos continue to be popular in the U.S. Consumers choose from numerous brands of personal computers and airlines. Many students at your school obtained good jobs following graduation last term. Effective marketing is the common denominator in these diverse situations. And, as these examples suggest, marketing plays a major role in the global economy, in the American socioeconomic system, and in any individual organization. It also has significance for you personally—if not in business, then certainly in your role as a consumer.

Lufthansa is a good example of globalization. A few years ago it was the government-controlled airline of Germany, flying routes in Europe and overseas. However, faced with intense competitive pressure, Lufthansa became a private company and began exploring new market opportunities. As a result, it has formed strategic alliances with United Airlines, Scandinavian Airlines System (SAS), Thai International, and Varig that give it access to more routes and customers. In a joint venture with Air China, Lufthansa operates the largest airplane maintenance facility in China. And the catering division of Lufthansa provides 220 million meals a year to over 250 airlines around the world.

http://www.lufthansa.ch/

In the Global Economy

Until the late 1970s, American firms had a large and secure domestic market. The only significant foreign competition was in selected industries, such as agriculture, or for relatively narrow markets, such as luxury automobiles. But this changed dramatically through the 1980s as more foreign firms developed attractive products, honed their marketing expertise, and then successfully entered the U.S. market. Imported products in industries, such as office equipment, autos, apparel, watches, semiconductors, and consumer electronics, have been very successful. As a result, in recent years the United States has been importing more than it exports, creating large annual trade deficits.

In the not too distant future there will be new challenges. The dramatic changes taking place in the governments and economies of Eastern Europe and growing capitalism in China and the former Soviet Union will certainly create new competitors in international trade.

Trade agreements are also altering the global business picture. The European Union (EU), the North American Free Trade Agreement (NAFTA), and the Asia-Pacific Economic Cooperation (APEC) are reducing economic barriers and liberalizing trade between their members. However, as trade agreements increase the marketing opportunities for firms within the member countries, they often result in stiffened competition for firms from outside.

In response to these developments, more and more U.S. firms are looking abroad. They are concluding that their profit and growth objectives are most likely to be achieved through a combination of domestic and international marketing, not solely from domestic marketing. As shown in Table 1-2, many large U.S. firms derive a substantial percentage of their total revenues from exporting.

The move abroad is not limited to industrial giants. A recent survey of U.S. businesses found that 20 percent of companies with fewer than 500 employees exported goods or services in 1994, up from 16 percent in 1993.[28]

Although we don't yet know everything that will result from these developments, one thing is certain. We live in a global economy. World trade is growing three times faster than world production.[29] Most nations today—regardless of their degree of economic development or their political philosophy—recognize the

TABLE 1-2 The major U.S. exporters
The 10 U.S. companies with the most exports in 1994

Company	Exports (millions)	Percent of total sales	Best-selling products abroad
General Motors	$16,127	10	Motor vehicles and parts
Ford	11,892	9	Motor vehicles and parts
Boeing	11,844	54	Commercial and military aircraft
Chrysler	9,400	18	Motor vehicles and parts
General Electric	8,110	13	Jet engines, turbines
Motorola	7,370	33	Communications equipment
IBM	6,336	10	Computers
Philip Morris	4,942	9	Tobacco, beer, food
Archer Daniels Midland	4,675	41	Agricultural products
Hewlett-Packard	4,653	19	Measurement equipment

Source: "The Top 50 U.S. Exporters," *Fortune*, Nov. 13, 1995, p. 74. These figures do not reflect manufacturing operations in other countries by these U.S.-based firms.

importance of marketing beyond their own national borders. Indeed, economic growth in the less developed nations of the world depends greatly on their ability to design effective marketing systems to produce global customers for their raw materials and industrial output. We will explore these issues in more detail throughout the book.

In the American Socioeconomic System

Aggressive, effective marketing practices have been largely responsible for the high standard of living in the United States. The efficiency of mass marketing—extensive and rapid communication with customers through a wide variety of media and a distribution system that makes products readily available—combined with mass production has lowered the cost of many products. Now mass customization means even more products virtually tailored to our individual tastes. As a result, we enjoy things that once were considered luxuries and in many countries are still available only to people earning high incomes.

Since about 1920 (except during World War II), the available supply of products in the United States has far surpassed total demand. Making most products has been relatively easy; the real challenge has been marketing them.

Employment and Costs. We can get an idea of the significance of marketing in the U.S. economy by looking at how many of us are employed in some way in marketing and how much of what we spend covers the cost of marketing. *Between one-fourth and one-third of the U.S. civilian labor force is engaged in marketing activities.* This figure includes employees in retailing, wholesaling, transportation, warehousing, and communications industries, as well as people who work in marketing departments of manufacturers and those who work in marketing in agricultural, mining, and service industries. Furthermore, over the past century, jobs in marketing have increased at a much more rapid rate than jobs in production, reflecting marketing's expanded role in the economy. On the average, *about 50 cents of each dollar we spend as consumers goes to cover marketing costs.* The money pays for designing the products to meet our needs, making products readily available when and where we want them, and informing us about products. These activities add want-satisfying ability, or what is called utility, to products.

Creating Utility. A customer purchases a product because it provides satisfaction. The something that makes a product capable of satisfying wants is its **utility**. And it is through marketing that much of a product's utility is created.

Consider this example. Mannie Jackson decides to breathe new life into the Harlem Globetrotters basketball team. But a basketball team at its headquarters in Hollywood, California, is of little value to a person in Omaha, London, or Moscow who wants to be entertained. So the team must be transported to those cities (and hundreds of other places) and made available in arenas near potential customers. Then, potential buyers must be informed about the team's presence and the benefits it offers through various forms of promotion. Let's see what kinds of utility have been created in this process:

- *Form utility* is associated primarily with production—the physical or chemical changes that make a product more valuable. When lumber is made into furniture, form utility is created. This is production, not marketing. However, marketing contributes to decisions on the style, size, and color of the furniture. Similarly, marketing is involved in developing an entertainment product. In the case of the Globetrotters there are decisions about choreographing the show (including the performance of the opposing team), uniforms, and music, as well as the half-time entertainment. All of these contribute to the product's form utility.

- *Place utility* exists when a product is readily accessible to potential customers. A basketball team in Hollywood is of little value to potential spectators in Omaha or other parts of the world. So, physically moving the team to an arena near the customer adds to its value.
- *Time utility* means having a product available when you want it. In the case of the Globetrotters, customers like having entertainment available at times convenient to them. That means games are played in the evenings and on the weekends, not necessarily ideal for the players, but demanded by the customers.
- *Information utility* is created by informing prospective buyers that a product exists. Unless you know a product exists and where you can get it, the product has no value. Advertising that describes the team's scheduled appearance and provides some information about the show creates information utility. *Image utility* is a special type of information utility. It is the emotional or psychological value that a person attaches to a product or brand because of its reputation or social standing. Image utility is ordinarily associated with prestige or high-status products such as designer clothes, expensive foreign automobiles, or certain residential neighborhoods. However, the image-utility value of a given product may vary considerably depending on different consumers' perceptions. The Globetrotters, with their 70-year history, have an established

A GLOBAL PERSPECTIVE

IS THAT TOYOTA AN IMPORT?

The U.S. automobile market may appear to be three domestic producers—General Motors, Ford, and Chrysler, commonly called the "Big Three"—competing against several imported brands. But the situation is not this simple. Many "domestic" cars are manufactured abroad, and many "imports" are made in the U.S.

Take Toyota for example. A U.S. sales company was first established in 1957 to sell imported Toyotas. Since then the company's U.S. operation has grown considerably. Now there are two technical centers, a design center, and five manufacturing plants located in the U.S. The largest plant, in Georgetown, Kentucky, employs over 5,000 people. In Fremont, California, Toyota and General Motors jointly operate a plant that produces nearly 250,000 cars and trucks a year. Today, half the Toyota vehicles sold in the U.S. are built domestically, and in 1988 Toyota began *exporting* from the U.S. In 1993, 50,000 U.S.-built Toyotas were shipped to Europe, Canada, Taiwan, the Middle East, and . . . Japan!

This type of expansion is not limited to Toyota. Mercedes are made in Alabama, Mazdas are made in Michigan, and Hondas are made in Ohio. There are also numerous joint ventures. For example, Mazda manufactures Fords in Japan and Ford makes Mazdas in Europe. Joint ventures extend beyond manufacturing. For example, Chrysler sells Jeeps through Honda dealerships in Japan.

What drives the decisions to manufacture abroad and enter into joint ventures? Ultimately it is an attempt to implement the marketing concept. To satisfy customers' needs, a firm may seek lower production costs, increased product quality with a more sophisticated labor force, closer ties with suppliers, greater control over customer service, and/or a way to avoid import tariffs. Accomplishing these goals often requires new ways of operating.

http://www.toyota.com/

Sources: Jacqueline Mitchell, "Growing Movement to 'Buy American' Debates the Term," *The Wall Street Journal*, Jan. 24, 1992, p. A1; and "Toyota Update, Toyota Motor Sales," *U.S.A.*, Vol. 2, Summer 1994.

image for many consumers. The current owners have to hope that the last few years of poor performance have not tarnished the image.

- *Possession utility* is created when a customer buys the product—that is, ownership is transferred to the buyer. A customer outside an arena when the Globetrotters are playing inside doesn't experience any satisfaction. Thus, for a person to consume and enjoy the experience, a transaction must take place. This occurs when you exchange your money for tickets to a Globetrotters' game.

In Organizations

Marketing considerations should be an integral part of all short-range and long-range planning in any company. Here's why:

- The success of any business comes from satisfying the wants of its customers, which is the social and economic basis for the existence of all organizations.
- Although many activities are essential to a company's growth, marketing is the only one that produces revenue directly. (This is sometimes overlooked by the production managers who use these revenues and the financial executives who manage them.)

When managers are internally focused, products are designed by designers, manufactured by manufacturing people, priced by financial managers, and then given to sales managers to sell. This approach generally won't work in today's environment of intense competition and constant change. Just making a good product will not result in sales.

Service Marketers. The U.S. has gone from primarily a manufacturing economy to the world's first service economy. As opposed to goods, services are activities that are the object of a transaction. Examples are communications, entertainment, medical care, financial services, and repairs. Services account for over two-thirds of the nation's gross national product. Almost three-fourths of the country's nonfarm labor force is employed in service industries, and about one-half of all consumer expenditures are for the purchase of services. Projections for the year 2000 indicate that services' share of all these categories (gross national product, employment, expenditures) will be even greater.

Because the production of goods dominated our economy until recently, most of the marketing research and writing focused on concepts and strategies related to goods (such as groceries, clothing, machine tools, and automobiles) rather than on services. Now, some firms that are very marketing-oriented are in the services sector—for example, Federal Express, Disney, and Marriott Corp. Thus, we will investigate what makes services different from goods, and we will see how these differences affect marketing.

Nonprofit Marketers. During the 1980s and early 1990s many nonprofit organizations realized they needed effective marketing programs to make up for shrinking government subsidies, a decrease in charitable contributions, and other unfavorable economic conditions. Colleges with declining enrollments, hospitals with empty beds, and symphony orchestras playing to vacant seats all began to understand that marketing was essential to help them turn their situations around.

Today charities, museums, and even churches—all organizations that formerly rejected any thought of marketing—are embracing it as a means of growth and

*T*he marketing effort by a not-for-profit organization is similar to that performed by a traditional business firm, but it also has some unique features. For example, like an organization selling a product, The Art Institute of Chicago conducted an extensive advertising campaign to publicize the Monet exhibit. However, unlike a business firm, the campaign was financially supported by corporate sponsors, as you can see from this ad. This marketing effort was successful (though some of the credit should probably go to Monet!). Over 965,000 visitors passed through the Art Institute during the exhibit, and membership in the Art Institute increased by more than 50 percent.

http://www.artic.edu/aic/
firstpage.html

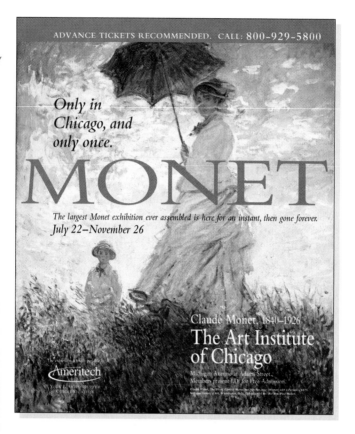

for some, survival. This trend is likely to accelerate during the remainder of the 1990s for two reasons:

- Increasing competition among nonprofit organizations. For example, the competition among colleges and universities for students is intensifying, and the search for donors has become more intense as the number of charities has increased.
- Nonprofit organizations need to improve their images and gain greater acceptance among donors, government agencies, news media, and of course, consumers, all of which collectively determine an organization's success.

In Your Life

Okay, so marketing is important globally, in our economy, and in an individual organization. But what's in it for you? Why should you study marketing? There are a number of reasons:

- Marketing pervades many daily activities. Consider how many marketers view you as part of their market. With people like you in mind, firms such as Nike, VISA, Microsoft, and Kellogg's have designed products, set prices, created advertisements, and chosen the best methods of making the product available to you. In response, you watch television with its commercials, buy various articles in different stores, and sometimes complain about prices or quality. Marketing occupies a large part of your daily life. If you doubt this, just imagine for a moment what it would be like if there were no marketing institu-

tions—no retail stores to buy from or no advertising to give you information, for example.
- Studying marketing will make you a better-informed consumer. You'll understand more about what underlies a seller's pricing and how brand names are selected, as well as the role of promotion and distribution.
- Last, marketing probably relates—directly or indirectly—to your career aspirations. If you are thinking about a marketing major and employment in a marketing position, you can develop a feel for what marketing managers do. (For an introduction to the many career opportunities in the field, we especially suggest you read the appendix, "Careers in Marketing.") If you're planning a career in accounting, finance, or some other business field, you can learn how marketing affects managerial decision making in these areas. Finally, if you are thinking about a career in a nonbusiness field such as health care, government, music, or education, you will learn how to use marketing in these organizations.

■ SUMMARY

The foundation of marketing is exchange, in which one party provides to another party something of value in return for something else of value. In a broad sense, marketing consists of all activities designed to generate or facilitate an exchange intended to satisfy human needs.

Business firms and nonprofit organizations engage in marketing. Products marketed include goods as well as services, ideas, people, and places. Marketing activities are targeted at markets consisting of product purchasers and also individuals and groups that influence the success of an organization.

In a business context, marketing is a total system of business activities designed to plan, price, promote, and distribute want-satisfying products to target markets to achieve organizational objectives. The main difference between marketing and selling is that in selling, the emphasis is on the seller's needs; in marketing, the emphasis is on customers' wants.

Marketing's evolution in the United States has gone through three stages: It began with the production orientation, passed through the sales orientation, and is now in the marketing orientation. In this third stage a company's efforts are focused on identifying and satisfying customers' needs. Recent refinements in the marketing orientation include relationship building and mass customization of products to meet the customer's individual needs.

Some organizations remain at the first or second stage, not progressing to the marketing-orientation stage, because they have monopoly power or because their products are in such great demand.

Other firms have difficulty implementing a marketing orientation.

A business philosophy called the marketing concept was developed to aid companies with supply capabilities that exceed consumer demand. According to the marketing concept, a firm is best able to achieve its performance objectives by adopting a customer orientation and coordinating all of its marketing activities. More recently, the societal marketing concept has been proposed as a philosophy by which a company can satisfy its customers and at the same time fulfill its social responsibility. Ethics, the standards of behavior accepted by society, and quality, as determined by the expectations of customers, are important concerns of marketing-oriented organizations.

Marketing is practiced today in all modern nations, regardless of their political philosophy. As international competition has heated up, the attention paid to marketing has increased. In the U.S. between one-fourth and one-third of the civilian work force is involved with marketing, and about one-half of consumer spending covers the cost of marketing. This investment in marketing is justified by the form, information, place, time, and possession utilities it creates.

Depending on circumstances, marketing can be vital to an organization's success. In recent years numerous service firms and nonprofit organizations have found marketing to be necessary and worthwhile. Marketing also can be useful to individual students, particularly in reference to career opportunities.

More about

THE HARLEM GLOBETROTTERS

The situation faced by Mannie Jackson and the Harlem Globetrotters illustrates the components of the marketing concept. First, there are the dual organizational objectives of operating a profitable business and contributing to the improvement of society. Next came the recognition that nothing happens unless the customer is satisfied. To do that the team must offer a good product. First, the show had to be more entertaining. Jackson achieved that by introducing new on-court routines and more-contemporary music. Next, he had to find great athletes with the stamina to play 300 nights a year. But being a good player isn't enough. To achieve Mannie Jackson's social objectives, the players must also be goodwill ambassadors. They have to act as role models on and off the court, by doing such things as enthusiastically talking to schoolchildren about the dangers of drugs or visiting hospitals. The players are prepared for this role with classes on everything from media relations to ethics.

Finally, there is the coordinated marketing program. To support the product, the Globetrotters must gain exposure and remind the public about the improved team. This will be accomplished through games televised on ABC's *Wide World of Sports*, serving as spokespersons in TV ads for Target Stores, and appearing on Wheaties cereal boxes. Future plans call for a feature-length movie with Columbia Pictures and a family entertainment complex that will include a Globetrotters variety show in Myrtle Beach, South Carolina. Also being organized are licensing and merchandising agreements to both capitalize on the Globetrotter image and increase exposure for the team. To meet demand, a second team has been created and the number of international engagements has been increased. Two years after Jackson took over, revenues are up over 30 percent and are still growing.[30]

1. What else should Mannie Jackson be doing to ensure that his marketing efforts will be successful?

■ KEY TERMS AND CONCEPTS

The numbers next to the terms refer to the pages on which the terms and concepts are defined. In addition, the glossary at the end of the book defines key terms and concepts.

Exchange (4)
Marketing (6)
Production-orientation
stage (7)
Sales-orientation stage (8)

Marketing-orientation
stage (9)
Marketing concept (11)
Relationship
marketing (12)

Mass customization (12)
Societal marketing
concept (13)
Ethics (15)
Quality (17)

Total quality
management (17)
ISO 9000 quality
standards (17)
Utility (21)

■ QUESTIONS AND PROBLEMS

1. Explain the concept of an exchange, including the conditions that must exist for an exchange to occur, and give an example of an exchange that does not involve money.
2. Name some companies that you believe are still in the production or sales stage in the evolution of marketing. Explain why you chose each of them.
3. Describe how each of the following could go beyond an exchange situation to establishing a relationship with customers.
    a. Hair stylist
    b. CPA firm
    c. Blood bank
    d. Automobile dealership
    e. University
    f. Appliance manufacturer
4. Describe how the actions of a shoe manufacturer engaged in "marketing" might be different from a show manufacturer engaged in "selling."
5. Explain the three elements that constitute the marketing concept.
6. "The marketing concept does not imply that marketing executives will run the firm. The concept requires only that whoever is in top management be marketing-oriented." Give examples of how a production manager, company treasurer, or personnel manager can be marketing-oriented.
7. For each of the following organizations, describe what is being marketed.
    a. Stardust hotel and casino in Las Vegas
    b. Airline Pilots Association labor union
    c. Professor teaching a first-year chemistry course
    d. Police department in your city
8. One way of explaining the utilities provided by market-

ing is to consider how we would live if there were no marketing facilities. Describe some of the ways in which your daily activities would be affected if there were no retail stores or advertising.

■ HANDS-ON MARKETING

1. Select an organizational unit at your school (for example, food service, placement office, intramural sports, library), observe the operation, and interview an administrator and some customers to identify (a) what is being exchanged; and (b) whether the unit is production-, sales-, or marketing-oriented.

9. Name two service firms that, in your opinion, do a good marketing job. Then name some that you think do a poor marketing job. Explain your reasoning in each case.

2. Visit a major supermarket and record all the alternative dry cereals that are available. Organize the list by the primary features of the cereals (for example, nutrition, taste, etc.) and any subcategories you can identify (taste might include sweet, fruity, and crispy). How do you explain this variety of products?

CHAPTER 2

The Dynamic Marketing Environment

Does
McDONALD'S
Have the Recipe for Success in a New Century?

For many years McDonald's has enjoyed success built on a few well-known ingredients. The company with the Golden Arches served a simple menu—featuring hamburgers, French fries, and soft drinks. The food was priced low, its quality was consistent, and it was served speedily from establishments that all looked alike and were extremely clean.

In recent years, however, McDonald's has seen its growth slow down in the U.S. and its dominant position challenged. Why? A major part of the answer lies in the changing environment in which McDonald's operates.

Let's start with the population picture. For many years, one of McDonald's main customer groups was young couples with several kids. Today, people are marrying at a much later age and families have fewer children, so part of McDonald's traditional customer base is eroding.

Then there are noteworthy cultural changes. As consumers have become more health conscious, their formerly huge consumption of beef has declined. Let's face it—burgers, fries, eggs, and sausage are not exactly at the top of dietitians' menu recommendations today. Michael Quinlan, the head of McDonald's, nevertheless contends that consumers "are more interested in taste, convenience, and value. . . . We're giving customers what they want."

True, consumers want convenience. In the past, many hopped in the car and drove to McDonald's. Today, they can pop something into the microwave oven or phone Domino's to have a pizza delivered.

McDonald's also faces stiff competition from many chains of fast-food restaurants. Taco Bell and Wendy's, among others, have cut their prices while trying to surpass McDonald's appealing menu items and speedy service. In late 1995, Edward Rensi, who oversees McDonald's operations in the U.S., even admitted, "We've got a lousy track record with quality, service, and cleanliness relative to our competition." To remedy the problem, McDonald's made improved service its top priority for 1996.

McDonald's "problems" shouldn't be exaggerated, however. Indeed, McDonald's is tremendously successful—in fact, it is the most profitable firm selling to retail customers in the U.S. over the past 10 years. And the enterprise is growing rapidly, opening an average of at least three units—and perhaps as many as eight—*per day* in domestic and foreign markets. To sustain its profitability and growth, however, McDonald's will need to adapt to a variety of significant environmental trends.[1]

What other changes are occurring in the environment that could have favorable or unfavorable effects on McDonald's?

http://www.mcdonalds.com/

As McDonald's situation illustrates, any organization must identify and then respond to numerous environmental forces. Some of these forces are external to the firm, while others come from within. Management can't do much about controlling the external forces, but it generally can control the internal ones.

Many of these forces influence what can and should be done in the area of marketing. Ultimately, a firm's ability to adapt to its operating environment determines, in large part, its level of business success. Thus McDonald's, like any organization, must manage its marketing program within its combined external and internal environment.

After studying this chapter, you should be able to explain:

CHAPTER GOALS

- The concept of environmental monitoring.
- How external environmental forces such as demographics, economic conditions, and social and cultural trends can affect an organization's marketing.
- How external factors such as markets as well as suppliers and intermediaries that are specific to a given firm can influence that firm's marketing.
- How nonmarketing resources within a firm can affect its marketing.

Environmental Monitoring

Environmental monitoring—also called *environmental scanning*—is the process of (1) gathering information regarding a company's external environment, (2) analyzing it, and (3) forecasting the impact of whatever trends the analysis suggests.

Today, much of the environmental discussion is about our physical environment—air quality, water pollution, disposal of solid waste, and conserving natural resources. However, we will use the term *environment* in a much broader sense in this chapter.

An organization operates within an *external* environment that it generally *cannot* control. At the same time, there are marketing and nonmarketing resources *within* the organization that generally *can* be controlled by its executives.

There are two levels of external forces:

- *Macro* influences (so called because they affect all firms), such as demographics, economic conditions, culture, and laws.
- *Micro* influences (so called because they affect a particular firm) consist of suppliers, marketing intermediaries, and customers. Micro influences, while external, are closely related to a specific company.

Successful marketing depends largely on a company's ability to manage its marketing programs within its environment. To do this, a firm's marketing executives must determine what makes up the firm's environment and then monitor it in a systematic, ongoing fashion. They must be alert to spot environmental trends that could be opportunities or problems for their organization.[2] Then marketing executives must be able to respond to these trends with the resources they control.

How important is environmental monitoring to business success? In a word, *very*. One study of about 100 large companies concluded, "Firms having advanced systems to monitor events in the external environment exhibited higher growth and greater profitability than firms that did not have such systems."[3]

External Macroenvironment

The following external forces have considerable influence on any organization's marketing opportunities and activities (see Figure 2-1). Therefore, they are *macroenvironmental forces*:

- Demographics
- Economic conditions
- Competition

- Social and cultural forces
- Political and legal forces
- Technology

A change in any one of them can cause changes in one or more of the others. Hence, they are interrelated. One thing they all have in common is that they are dynamic forces—that is, they are subject to change *and* at an increasing rate!

These forces are largely uncontrollable by management; but they are not *totally* uncontrollable. A company may be able to influence its external environment to some extent. For example, in international marketing a company can improve its competitive position by a joint venture with a foreign firm that markets a complementary product. Coca-Cola and Swiss-owned Nestlé, the world's largest food manufacturer, have joined forces to market ready-to-drink iced Nestea in the U.S. and chocolate, coffee, and tea drinks in Europe. A company may influence its political-legal environment by lobbying or by contributing to a legislator's campaign fund.

http://www.merck.com/

On the technological frontier, new-product research and development can strengthen a firm's competitive position. For instance, the Merck pharmaceutical company enjoyed a blockbuster success with two new products, Vasotec for treating high blood pressure and Mevacor for reducing cholesterol levels. At the same time, Merck's own technology became an external competitive force that affected other pharmaceutical companies.

Now let's take a look at these six external forces in more detail.

FIGURE 2-1

External macroenvironment of a company's marketing program.

Six largely uncontrollable external forces influence an organization's marketing activities.

Demographics

Demographics refer to the characteristics of human populations, including such factors as size, distribution, and growth. Because people constitute markets, demographics are of special interest to marketing executives. Demographics are considered in some detail in Chapter 5, so here we'll just cover a few examples of how demographic factors influence marketing programs.

Perhaps the most significant demographic trend is the aging of the U.S. population. More than one-quarter of the population is at least 50 years old now. During the past two decades, the 65-and-over age group expanded by more than 50 percent. This segment is projected to grow by another 70 percent by the year 2020; the 45-to-64 group will also swell considerably. During this same period, the under-25 segment is forecast to expand by a modest 20 percent and the 25-to-44 age group by a minuscule 3 percent. In fact, the number of 18- to 34-year-olds—which are very attractive to many marketers—will decline as we move into a new century.[4]

The marketing implications of this aging trend are substantial. Recognizing that the 50-and-over group possesses one-half the discretionary income in the U.S.,

The U. S. population is aging, to the point that the 50-and-over group is a particularly attractive target market for a variety of businesses and nonprofit organizations. The American Association of Retired Persons (AARP), a nonprofit entity, provides a range of services to its members, who must be at least age 50 but do not have to be retired. Over 30 million people belong to AARP. Key member benefits are travel-related discounts, the Modern Maturity *magazine, opportunities for service and friendship through local chapters, and even information about "grandparenting."*

http://www.aarp.org/

YOU MAKE THE DECISION

WHAT'S AN EFFECTIVE WAY TO APPEAL TO "GENERATION X"?

Perhaps you're a member of **Generation X**—sometimes termed *baby busters*, *twentysomethings*, or *boomerangers*. Whatever the label, this group of young people spends upwards of $125 billion annually. Consequently, Generation X is a market of considerable interest to some companies. However, developing effective marketing programs for this market has proved challenging, because it's difficult to describe Generation X precisely, much less understand its needs and behavior as consumers.

As distinguished from other groups such as *baby boomers*, Generation X refers to people born roughly between 1966 and 1976. More than 40 million people in the U.S. fall in this age range, comprising over 20 percent of the adult population. Marketers need to understand factors that influence the attitudes and behavior of Generation X. Specifically, this group is different than its predecessors in several important respects:

- They earn less and aren't optimistic about their financial prospects.
- Generation X believes education is vital to earning a decent living.
- They spend less time reading but devote more time to visual media (like TV) and arts (such as going to museums).
- Generation X members are less inclined to engage in physical exercise.
- They are much more likely to remain at home with their parents or to move back home after having left.

Another complication for marketers is that Generation X, often perceived as homogeneous, actually contains different segments. Research conducted by Saatchi & Saatchi identified four distinct segments within Generation X:

- *Cynical disclaimers*, who have received much attention from the press.
- *Traditional materialists*, who are quite positive and optimistic.
- *Hippies revisited*, who are intrigued by the 1960s.
- *Fifties machos*, who are ultraconservative.

Companies have tried various approaches to sell goods and services to Generation X. Saturn received high marks for a commercial showing a young woman treated respectfully in a dealer's showroom. Subaru was criticized for being too cool in an ad that said its Impreza model was "like punk rock." In a different category, Dewar's Scotch was praised for depicting young adults in realistic settings and then asking, "How about a real drink?" But Budweiser was disparaged for showing members of Generation X playing pool and talking about old-time TV comedies because it implied that young adults were unemployed and mindless. So the search for effective appeals continues.

What marketing strategies would you suggest to a company that wants to appeal to Generation X consumers? What strategies should be avoided?

Sources: Faye Rice, "Making Generational Marketing Come of Age," *Fortune*, June 26, 1995, pp. 110–112, 114; Nicholas Zill and John Robinson, "The Generation X Difference," *American Demographics*, April 1995, pp. 24–29, 32–33; and Jennifer Steinhauer, "How Do You Turn On the Twentysomething Market?" *The New York Times*, Apr. 17, 1994, p. F5.

---

investment firms such as Merrill Lynch, PaineWebber, and Shearson Lehman are especially targeting this segment of the population in their promotional campaigns. Movie theaters offer discounts to people over 65. Several Colorado ski resorts, such as Vail and Winter Park, offer reduced-price ski lift tickets for people 65 to 69 and free skiing for people 70 and over. Internationally, Best Western, a worldwide association of independently owned and operated motels and hotels, has used "dependable lodging on a retirement budget" as an advertising theme.

Another notable demographic trend is the rapid growth of minority markets—notably markets comprised of African Americans, persons of Hispanic origin, and

Asian Americans. Minorities now represent less than one-quarter of the total U.S. population; by the year 2020, the proportion will increase to about one-third. Over the next quarter century, particularly rapid growth is forecast for Asian Americans (over 200 percent) and Hispanics (about 125 percent). As a result, between now and 2020, Hispanics will surpass African Americans as the largest minority group in the U.S. Marketers are interested in these overall projections as well as the fact that there is a large and growing middle class in minority markets.[5]

None of these ethnic groups is homogeneous, however. The Hispanic market, for instance, really consists of separate markets built around subgroups of Cubans, Mexicans, Puerto Ricans, and other Latin Americans. A simple product such as beans illustrates the differences among subgroups. Cubans prefer black beans, Mexicans eat refried beans, and Puerto Ricans go for red beans.[6]

Many consumer-product companies are just beginning to realize that they must target their products and advertising at each of the Hispanic subgroups. Lacking funds to develop many new products, some companies are bringing popular brands from Latin America into the U.S. market. Examples include Colgate-Palmolive experimenting with its Mexican household cleaner, Fabuloso, in Los Angeles and Miami, and Nestlé marketing its Venezuelan breakfast cereal, Nestum, in selected areas within the U.S.[7] While these examples focus on Hispanic consumers, other ethnic groups in the U.S. also contain distinct subgroups with varied desires.

Economic Conditions

People alone do not make a market. They must have money to spend and be willing to spend it. Consequently, the **economic environment** is a significant force that affects the marketing activities of just about any organization. A marketing program is affected especially by such economic factors as the current and anticipated stage of the business cycle, as well as inflation and interest rates.

Stage of the Business Cycle. The traditional business cycle goes through four stages: prosperity, recession, depression, and recovery. However, economic strategies adopted by the federal government have averted the depression stage in the U.S. for about 60 years. Consequently, today we think in terms of a three-stage **business cycle**—prosperity, recession, and recovery—then returning full cycle to prosperity. Marketing executives need to know which stage of the business cycle the economy currently is in, because a company's marketing programs usually must be changed from one stage of the business cycle to another.

Prosperity is a period of economic growth. During this stage, organizations tend to expand their marketing programs as they add new products and enter new markets.

A *recession* is a period of retrenchment for consumers and businesses—we tighten our economic belts. People can become discouraged, scared, and angry. Naturally, these feelings affect their buying behavior, which, in turn, has major marketing implications for companies, often leading to economic losses. In a recession, consumers cut back on eating out and entertainment outside the home. As a result, firms catering to these needs face serious marketing challenges.[8]

For some companies, though, a recession can present profitable marketing opportunities. For example, during the recession in 1991, Campbell Soup spotted a trend away from the more expensive, ready-to-serve soups and toward lower-priced cook-at-home products. The company took its new cream of broccoli soup out of the higher-priced Gold Label can, cut the price, and put it in Campbell's

http://www.campbellsoups.com/

familiar red-and-white can. Furthermore, on the label they included recipes for using the soup as a base for homemade meals. The result: It became the first new soup since 1935 to be among the top-10 Campbell best-sellers.[9]

Recovery is the period when the economy is moving from recession to prosperity. The marketers' challenge is to determine how quickly prosperity will return and to what level. As unemployment declines and disposable income increases, companies expand their marketing efforts to improve sales and profits. As you read this, what stage of the business cycle do you think the U.S. economy is in currently?

Inflation. **Inflation** is a rise in the prices of goods and services. When prices rise at a faster rate than personal incomes, consumer buying power declines. Many countries today are plagued by extremely high rates of inflation—increases of 20, 30, or even 50 percent yearly. During the late 1970s and early 1980s, the U.S. experienced what for us was a high inflation rate of 10 to 14 percent. In contrast, during the early 1990s, inflation in the U.S. dropped below 5 percent.

Inflation rates affect government policies, consumer psychology, and also marketing programs. For instance, during periods of high inflation, consumers spend less as their buying power declines. At the same time, they may overspend today for fear that prices will be higher tomorrow. In turn, severe inflation presents real challenges in managing a marketing program—especially in determining the size of price increases.

Surprisingly, periods of low inflation—sometimes termed *disinflation*—also present challenges for marketers. In particular, it is very difficult for firms to raise prices because of consumer resistance. As a result, they need to cut their costs or else profits will evaporate. To do so, companies must take such steps as redesigning products to pare production costs and cutting back on coupons and other promotions that in effect lower prices.[10]

Interest Rates. **Interest rates** are another external economic factor that influences marketing programs. When interest rates are high, for instance, consumers tend not to make long-term purchases such as housing. Marketers sometimes offer below-market interest rates (a form of price cut) as a promotional device to increase business. Auto manufacturers used this tactic extensively in the late 1980s and early 1990s.

Competition

A company's competitive environment obviously is a major influence on its marketing programs.

Types of Competition. A firm generally faces three types of competition:

- *Brand competition* comes from marketers of directly similar products. Toys "R" Us is facing growing competition from discounters such as Wal-Mart and Target in selling toys.[11] VISA, MasterCard, and American Express compete internationally in the credit card field. And, yes, even Harvard and Massachusetts Institute of Technology compete with each other for charitable contributions from people who hold degrees from both schools.
- *Substitute products* satisfy the same need. During winter in Chicago, for example, the Bulls professional basketball team, the Blackhawks hockey team, the

DOES COMPETITION TRANSCEND NATIONAL BORDERS?

The answer to the preceding question is a resounding *Yes!* Indeed, the destiny of many American firms is affected by international competition. Foreign companies are selling their products in the U.S., and American firms are marketing in foreign countries.

In the early 1980s, the competition facing U.S. firms came primarily from Canadian, Mexican, Japanese, and Western European companies. More recently, enterprises from the four "Asian tigers" (Hong Kong, Korea, Taiwan, and Singapore) have added to the competitive pressures facing American firms.

Further, several developments on the international scene in the early 1990s present American marketers with profound challenges and attractive opportunities. One is the radical change from a government-controlled system to a relatively free-market economy in many countries—especially in Eastern Europe and Latin America. For example, to a large degree, prices have been decontrolled and government subsidies have been removed on many products in Poland, Russia, and Argentina. Furthermore, some major companies and industries, formerly 100 percent government-owned, have been sold in whole or in part to private interests.

Another development stems from an old saying, "If you can't lick 'em, join 'em." With that in mind, many U.S. and foreign firms have formed strategic alliances to compete in international markets. Some alliances involve past rivals. For example, Ford and

Volkswagen merged in Brazil and Argentina to create "Autolatina."

A firm typically forms a strategic alliance for one or more of three reasons: to enter a new geographic market, to gain added resources (ranging from new technology to skilled management), or to achieve economies of scale (which might provide more marketing "muscle"). Corning Glass Works, for example, penetrates foreign markets and gets infusions of technology through its alliances with companies in about 10 different countries.

Alliances that bring together firms from different countries are not a panacea, however. Problems can result. According to a study by the McKinsey & Co. consulting firm, only one-half of 150 alliances that were examined had been economically advantageous for both companies. Further, even those that are beneficial seem to have a limited life as the average length of strategic alliances is 7 years.

If not through strategic alliances, U.S. firms will seek other ways of coping with—and beating—foreign competition. Now that we have a global economy, U.S. companies will always face strong competition, both in domestic and foreign markets. These challenges will come not only from other American firms but also from increasingly strong, aggressive companies that are based in other countries.

Sources: Harvey D. Shapiro, "After NAFTA," *Hemispheres*, March 1995, pp. 74–79; Richard House, "Cross-Border Alliances: What Works, What Doesn't," *Institutional Investor*, May 1994, pp. 113–115+; and "Welcome to the Moscow Shopping Mall," *Business Week*, Aug. 19, 1991, p. 44.

Lyric Opera, the Chicago Symphony Orchestra, and stores selling or renting videos all compete for the entertainment dollar.

- In a third, more general type of competition, *every company* is a rival for the customer's limited buying power. So the competition faced by the maker of Prince tennis rackets might be several new pairs of Levi's Docker slacks, a Nissan repair bill, or a cash contribution to some charity.

Skillful marketing executives constantly monitor all aspects of competitors' marketing activities—their products, pricing, distribution systems, and promotional programs.

*V*IA Rail Canada represents an alternative to air or auto travel. As such, it illustrates competition from substitute products. However, if a couple decides to postpone a planned purchase of a home theater system and to take a trip on Rail Canada instead, this situation shows how many diverse organizations compete for consumers' discretionary funds.

http://www.viarail.ca/

Social and Cultural Forces

The task facing marketing executives is becoming more complex because our sociocultural patterns—life-styles, values, beliefs—are changing much more quickly than they used to. Here are a few changes in **social and cultural forces** that have significant marketing implications.

The Greening of America. In the 1990s, many Americans are placing a greater emphasis on the *quality* of life rather than on the *quantity* of goods consumed. The theme is "not more, but better." High on the list of what people consider integral to quality of life is the natural environment. Thus we hear more concerns expressed about air and water pollution, holes in the ozone layer, acid rain, solid waste disposal, and the destruction of rainforests and other natural resources. These concerns have raised the public's level of environmental consciousness—which is what we mean by the "greening of America."

The proportion of consumers who buy environmentally friendly products, at least occasionally, is growing gradually. At the start of this decade, about 48 percent of all consumers exhibited such behavior; in 3 years, the proportion of "green"

AN ETHICAL DILEMMA?

For a hefty fee, as much as $40 million, the International Olympic Committee grants worldwide sponsorship rights to many companies, but only to one firm in each product category. For the 1996 Summer Olympics, for example, VISA was the authorized credit card, Coca-Cola the official soft drink, and Kodak the sponsor for "imaging" products.

Some competing firms resort to *ambush marketing*, using the Olympic symbol or theme without authorization to imply they are connected with this prestigious sporting event. To minimize such unauthorized practices, the head of the 1996 Olympics sent a letter to hundreds of advertising agencies and public relations firms "appealing to the companies' patriotism to refrain from 'ambush' marketing." Still, competitors who are not sponsors devise promotions to capitalize on the popularity of the Olympics. Fuji Photo Film, for instance, is sponsoring a traveling exhibit, "Images of Excellence," that focuses on American successes in the sport of track and field. Not surprisingly, the exhibit's stop in Atlanta coincides with the 1996 Summer Olympics!

Is it ethical for a nonsponsoring competitor to use something that resembles the five-ring symbol of the Olympics in its advertising?

Sources: Wendy Bounds, "Fuji Move May Miff Kodak at Olympics," *The Wall Street Journal*, Oct. 31, 1995, p. B8; Bruce Horovitz, "'Ambush Marketers' May Be Disqualified," *USA Today*, July 19, 1995, p. 2B; and "Sportscene," *Columbia* (Missouri) *Daily Tribune*, May 27, 1995, p. 4B.

---

consumers rose to 55 percent.[12] Still, many people who hold favorable attitudes toward environmentally friendly products do not actually purchase them.[13]

Only a few consumers will purchase a product strictly because it is environmentally friendly. According to Roper Starch Worldwide, a market research firm, a common mistake by companies is neglecting to mention the product's benefit to the consumer, not just to the environment.[14] To satisfy "green consumers," a product must also be competitive with alternatives on such factors as price.

A growing number of businesses have noticed—and are responding to—consumers' environmental consciousness. To cite several examples:

- Many firms, such as Heinz, Anheuser-Busch, and Body Shop, not only are stressing their use of recyclable containers but also are promoting recycling.
- Ads for Revlon's New Age Naturals creams talk about their "nonanimal-tested formulas," but also emphasize that the products will lead to healthier skin.[15]
- During the 1980s, McDonald's was criticized for its polystyrene packaging. As a result, the company turned to paper containers. This action, along with an emphasis on recycling and consumer education, helped McDonald's earn a highly favorable environmental reputation in the eyes of consumers.[16]

Environmental consciousness is not limited to the U.S. In fact, it is greater in many other parts of the world—ranging from the European Union to Japan—than it is in the U.S. Closer to home, public concern about the environment is two and three times greater in Canada and Mexico, respectively, than in America.[17] As a result, a company must be environmentally sensitive in its marketing activities, especially product development, all around the world.

Changing Gender Roles. For many reasons, most notably the increasing number of two-income households, male-female roles related to families, jobs, recreation, and buying behavior are changing dramatically. For example, more men now shop for groceries, while more women buy gas and arrange for auto mainte-

environmental claims, and laws affecting door-to-door selling. All of these have been put in place by numerous states and municipalities.

Government agencies affect marketing in two other ways. First, they are an important *source of information* needed for effective marketing. The federal government is the largest source of published marketing information in the country. In this situation, instead of telling marketing executives what they must do or cannot do, the government is helping them. Second, government agencies are significant *buyers of products*. In fact, the government is the largest single buyer of goods and services in the U.S.

Technology

Technology has a tremendous impact on our life-styles, our consumption patterns, and our economic well-being. Just think of the effect of technological developments such as the airplane, plastics, television, computers, antibiotics, lasers, and—of course—video games. Except perhaps for the airplane, all these technologies reached their major markets in your lifetime or your parents' lifetime. Think how your life in the future might be affected by cures for the common cold, development of energy sources to replace fossil fuels, low-cost methods for making ocean water drinkable, or even commercial travel to the moon.

Consider some of the technological breakthroughs that are expanding our horizons as we near a new century. It's hard to grasp the fantastic possibilities in many fields ranging from pharmaceuticals to miniature electronics. For example, small handheld computers allow sales people to place orders directly from a customer's location.

Technological breakthroughs can affect markets in three ways:

- By starting entirely new industries, as computers, lasers, and robots have done.
- By radically altering, or virtually destroying, existing industries. When it first came out, television crippled the radio and movie industries. And computers all but replaced typewriters, sending Smith Corona Corp. into bankruptcy protection in mid-1995.
- By stimulating markets and industries not related to the new technology. New home appliances and microwavable foods give people additional time in which to engage in other activities.

Advances in technology also affect how marketing is carried out. For example, breakthroughs in communications now permit people and organizations to transact business from almost any location at any time of the day. In the near future, houses will be equipped with two-way TV signals.[25] Then consumers will be able to not only order up an incredible array of movies and video games but also scan electronic catalogs and place orders instantaneously.

To many observers, the Internet—a network of computers that was created to facilitate communications among scientists around the world—has enormous marketing ramifications. Just between 1990 and 1995, the number of people having access to the Internet increased tenfold, to 25 million; the number of businesses connected to this network grew twice as fast, to over 20,000.[26] With the Internet, a firm can present consumers with a combination of advertising, information, and entertainment related to its product. Consumers control whether they are exposed to a product and ultimately whether they want to learn more about it or even place an order. Currently, many marketers are intrigued by the Internet but are unsure about its role in their marketing programs. As one consultant said, "Right now, companies are pretty much still kicking the tires of the Internet."[27]

*L*ike many companies, Silicon Graphics (SG) has created a site on the Internet's World Wide Web. Silicon Surf, the name of SG's Web site, was established to allow current and prospective customers, as well as others with computer-graphics interests, to read the latest announcements about SG and learn about the company's technologies and products. Visitors to SG's site on the Internet can "surf" different sections, including: Who We Are; How Do I Buy; and Customer Support. Another section, Awesome Products, describes SG's hardware, software, and support products, as well as those of selected SG partners. A Serious Fun section displays graphics created by SG users and also contains games that can be downloaded by "surfers." By early 1996, there were more than 20,000 visitors to Silicon Surf daily, with almost one-half from outside the U.S.

http://www.sgi.com/

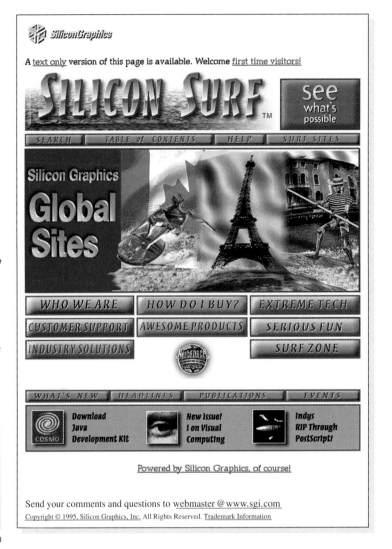

http://www.compaq.com/

We should also note that technology is a mixed blessing in some ways. A new technology may improve our lives in one area while creating environmental and social problems in other areas. Television provides built-in baby-sitters, but it's criticized for reducing family discussions and reading by children. The automobile makes life great in some ways, but it also creates traffic jams and air pollution. In turn, technology is expected to solve some problems it is criticized for having caused (air pollution, for example).

External Microenvironment

Three additional environmental forces are external to an organization and affect its marketing activities. These are the firm's market, suppliers, and marketing intermediaries. They represent *microenvironmental forces* for a company (see Figure 2-2). Dealing effectively with them is critical to business success. Recognizing that, Compaq Computer Corp. developed a complex computer simulation to help executives monitor the activities and attitudes of its customers, dealers, and suppliers.[28]

FIGURE 2-2 External microenvironment of a company's marketing program.

Three external forces, specific to a given company, shape its marketing activities. The company can influence these forces to some extent. The arrows reflect the interrelationships—flows of products, payments, information, and influence—between the company and its external environment.

While all three of these external forces are generally uncontrollable, they can be influenced in some situations. As such, they are different than the *macro*environmental forces discussed previously. A marketing organization, for example, may be able to exert pressure on its suppliers or middlemen. And, through its advertising, a firm should have some influence on its market.

The Market

The market really is what marketing is all about—how to reach it and serve it profitably and in a socially responsible manner. The market should be the focus of all marketing decisions in an organization. But just what is a market? A *market* may be defined as a place where buyers and sellers meet, goods or services are offered for sale, and transfers of ownership occur. A *market* may also be defined as the demand made by a certain group of potential buyers for a good or service. For instance, there is a farm *market* for petroleum products.

These definitions are not sufficiently precise to be useful to us here. For marketing purposes, we define a **market** as people or organizations with needs to satisfy, money to spend, and the willingness to spend it. Thus, in marketing any given good or service, three specific factors need to be considered:

- People or organizations with needs,
- Their purchasing power, and
- Their buying behavior.

When we consider *needs*, we do so from the perspective of the dictionary definition of need as the lack of anything that is required, desired, or useful. We do not limit needs to the physiological requirements of food, clothing, and shelter essential for survival. Recall from Chapter 1 that the words *needs* and *wants* are used interchangeably.

Suppliers

A business cannot sell a product without being able to make or buy it. That's why the people or firms that supply the goods or services required by a producer to make what it sells are critical to our marketing success. So too are the firms that provide the merchandise a wholesaler or retailer resells. And that's why we consider a firm's **suppliers** a vital part of its marketing environment.

Marketing executives often are not concerned enough with the supply side of marketing. But they do become very concerned when shortages occur. Shortages underscore the need for cooperative relationships with suppliers.

Marketing Intermediaries

Marketing intermediaries are independent business organizations that directly aid in the flow of goods and services between a marketing organization and its markets. There are two types of intermediaries: (1) the firms we call *middlemen*—wholesalers and retailers, and (2) various *facilitating organizations* furnishing such services as transportation, warehousing, and financing that are needed to complete exchanges between buyers and sellers.

These intermediaries operate between a company and its markets and between a company and its suppliers. Thus they are part of what we call *channels of distribution*.

In some cases, it may be more efficient for a company to not use marketing intermediaries. A producer can deal *directly* with its suppliers or sell *directly* to its customers and do its own shipping, financing, and so on. But marketing intermediaries are specialists in their respective fields. They often do a better job at a lower cost than the marketing organization can do by itself.

Organization's Internal Environment

An organization's marketing effort is also shaped by *internal* forces that are controllable by management. As shown in Figure 2-3, these internal influences include a firm's production, financial, and personnel activities. If the Dial Corporation is considering adding a new brand of soap, for example, it must determine whether existing production facilities and expertise can be used. If the new product requires a new plant or machinery, financial capability enters the picture.

Other nonmarketing forces are the company's location, its research and development (R&D) strength, and the overall image the firm projects to the public. Plant location often determines the geographic limits of a company's market, particularly if transportation costs are high or its products are perishable. The R&D factor may determine whether a company will lead or follow in its industry.

FIGURE 2-3

Internal environment affecting a company's marketing activities.

A company's internal, nonmarketing resources influence and support its marketing program.

Another thing we must consider in a firm's internal environment is the need to coordinate its marketing and nonmarketing activities. Sometimes this can be difficult because of conflicts in goals and executive personalities. Production people, for example, like to see long production runs of standardized items. However, marketing executives may want a variety of models, sizes, and colors to satisfy different market segments. Financial executives typically want tighter credit and expense limits than the marketing people consider necessary to be competitive.

To wrap up our discussion of the marketing environment, Figure 2-4 shows how all environmental forces combine to shape an organization's marketing program. Within the framework of these constraints, management should develop a marketing program to satisfy the needs of its markets. The strategic planning of marketing programs is the topic of the next chapter. Permeating the planning and operation of a marketing program is a company's marketing information system—a key marketing subsystem intended to aid management in solving its problems and making decisions. Chapter 4 is devoted to the subjects of marketing research and a company's flow of information.

FIGURE 2-4 The entire operating environment for a company's marketing program.

A marketing program must take into account both internal resources and external forces.

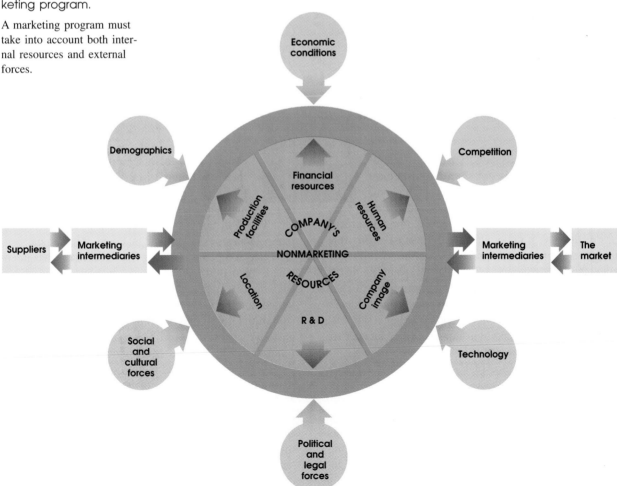

■ SUMMARY

Various environmental forces influence an organization's marketing activities. Some are external to the firm and are largely uncontrollable by the organization. Other forces are within the firm and are generally controllable by management. Successful marketing requires that a company develop and implement marketing programs that take into account its environment. To start with, management should set up a system for environmental monitoring—the process of gathering and evaluating environmental information.

Six broad variables constitute the external environment that generally cannot be controlled by an organization. Demographic factors are one of these macro influences. Another is economic conditions such as the business cycle, inflation, and interest rates. Management also must be aware of the various types of competition and the competitive structure within which its firm operates. Social and cultural forces, such as changes in life-styles, values, and beliefs, must be taken into account as marketing programs are developed. Four noteworthy sociocultural trends are the greening of America, changing gender roles, a greater premium on time, and added emphasis on physical fitness and health. Political and legal forces, ranging from monetary and fiscal policies to legislation, also affect marketing. As with the other external macroenvironmental influences, technology can present both opportunities and challenges for marketers.

Another set of environmental factors—suppliers, marketing intermediaries, and the market itself—is also external to the firm. But these forces can be controlled to some extent by the firm. While all three of these external forces are generally uncontrollable, they can be influenced in some situations. As such, these *micro*environmental forces are different from *macro*environmental forces such as economic conditions and technology.

At the same time, a set of nonmarketing resources *within* the firm—production facilities, personnel, finances, location, research and development, and company image—affects its marketing effort. These variables generally are controllable by management.

More about

McDONALD'S

*E*ven the world's largest fast-food company, McDonald's, is not immune to demographic trends, competitive pressures, and social and cultural influences. So under the leadership of Michael Quinlan, the company already has made several major changes to meet these environmental challenges. Recognizing customers' health consciousness, McDonald's has banned smoking in its company-owned restaurants. Responding to criticism from some consumers, the firm stopped using bleached white bags because some scientists believe they are harmful to the natural environment. More changes are under way and being planned.

Under the guidance of Ray Kroc, the company's founder, McDonald's was built on *standardization* as its key strategy. Today the strategy is *flexibility*, especially with respect to restaurant locations and design. Instead of free-standing locations, some McDonald's are now in buildings on university campuses and in office complexes; others can be found in Wal-Mart, Sears, and Incredible Universe stores. McDonald's—and its main competitors—also see opportunities in varied locations ranging from sports arenas to hospitals. Further, today there is variety in appearance and decor across the company's many outlets. The Wall Street McDonald's features a baby grand piano and a stock ticker tape machine, for example.

Price competition among fast-food chains has intensified. Taco Bell, in particular, emphasizes low prices. McDonald's responded with "Extra Value Meals," which combine several items at a lower price than the sum of the items' individual prices. The intent is to give customers good value while persuading them to spend more on each visit to McDonald's. These "combo" meals shave profit margins but boost sales volume. To maintain its profitability in the face of lower prices, McDonald's is pressing hard to reduce both start-up and operating costs. Toward that end, the firm switched to a sandwich bun that doesn't need toasting and also experimented with allowing customers to punch their own orders into a computer keyboard and to serve their own drinks.

Some observers think McDonald's should recognize the changing world conditions and concentrate on its foreign business. By the mid-1990s, McDonald's had over 4,300 restaurants in more than 70 countries (compared to 10,000 units in the U.S.). Two of its largest outlets are in the heart of Moscow and three blocks from Tiananmen Square in Beijing. McDonald's foreign operations generate about 45 percent of its operating income.

Still, McDonald's cannot afford to overlook its core market, the U.S. With that in mind, the company decided to pay more attention to its loyal customers. So-called superheavy users, typically males between the ages of 18 and 34, eat at McDonald's an average of four times per week. This group of loyal patrons accounts—almost incredibly—for more than three-quarters of the company's sales! Among the methods used to increase the number of visits by young adult males are promotions tied to the National Basketball Association and popular movies. In this way, McDonald's plans to boost domestic sales and profits at the same time it expands its foreign operations at an even faster pace.[29]

1. What other courses of action should McDonald's pursue in order to adapt to its changing operating environment?
2. Should the company concentrate more on foreign markets than on domestic ones?

KEY TERMS AND CONCEPTS

Environmental monitoring (44)
Demographics (46)
Generation X (47)
Economic environment (48)
Business cycle (48)
Inflation (49)
Interest rates (49)
Social and cultural forces (51)
Political and legal forces (54)
Technology (57)
Market (59)
Suppliers (59)
Marketing intermediaries (60)

QUESTIONS AND PROBLEMS

1. In some areas, the number of college-age students is still declining. What marketing measures should a school take to adjust to this trend?
2. For each of the following companies, give some examples of how its marketing program is likely to differ during periods of prosperity as contrasted with periods of recession:
   a. Campbell soups
   b. Schwinn bicycles
   c. General Cinema movie theaters
   d. Salvation Army
3. What would be the likely effect of high interest rates on the market for the following goods or services?
   a. Swatch watches
   b. Building materials
   c. Nursery school programs
4. Explain the three types of competition faced by a company. What marketing strategies or programs would you recommend to meet each type?
5. Name three U.S.-manufactured products you think would be highly acceptable to "green consumers" in European markets. Name three products you think would be environmentally unacceptable.
6. Give some examples of how the changing role of women has been reflected in American marketing.
7. What are some marketing implications of the increasing public interest in physical fitness and health?
8. Using examples other than those in this chapter, explain how a firm's marketing can be influenced by the environmental factor of technology.
9. Specify some external macroenvironmental forces affecting the marketing programs of:
   a. Pizza Hut
   b. Your school
   c. A local nightclub
   d. Clairol (hair-care products)
10. Explain how each of the following resources within a company might influence its marketing program:
   a. Plant location
   b. Company image
   c. Financial resources
   d. Personnel capability

HANDS-ON MARKETING

1. Identify two controversial social or cultural issues in the community where your school is located, and explain their impact on firms that market in the community.
2. After interviewing several consumers and businesspeople in your community, identify two products or companies at either the national or local levels that you think are doing very well regarding the physical environment. Identify two that you think are doing a poor job.

CHAPTER 3

Strategic
Marketing
Planning

Can
NORDSTROM
Continue to Succeed by Being Different?

I n many respects, Nordstrom has acted contrary to prevailing trends. Beginning as a shoe store in 1901, this Seattle-based retailer began to sell clothing in 1963, with other product lines added since then. During this same period, many retailers have reduced the number of product lines they carry. In a similar vein, Nordstrom has continued to add customer services. Other retailers, citing costs, have pruned services. Although aggressive in adding new merchandise and services, Nordstrom has been very cautious in adding new stores. Opening just several stores per year, the chain still has under 100 stores. In contrast, some successful retailers have been adding new stores almost weekly.

Nordstrom may ignore—or decide to counter—trends related to consumers and competition, but it has done so successfully. Its stores, featuring upscale apparel and shoes, generate sales exceeding $4 billion annually.

Further, Nordstrom has won a loyal following among shoppers, particularly within its target market of well-educated, middle-aged women in upper-income households. In fact, according to a *Consumer Reports* readers survey, it is top-ranked among all department stores in terms of overall customer satisfaction.

Nordstrom is well regarded for its merchandise, offering a broad assortment of high-quality brands. And the chain's prices, which some shoppers would regard as high, are acceptable to its target markets. As explained by one customer, "It's not an inexpensive store, but it is good value for the money."

It is in the area of customer service, however, where Nordstrom has attained legendary status. The retailer seeks to build lasting relationships with customers by treating them very well—even pampering them. Nordstrom's first step toward accomplishing this has been to have a large number of highly trained sales people. Perhaps even more impressive is its abundance of customer services, including valet parking, in-store restaurants, live piano music, free use of baby strollers, and liberal merchandise-return policies. It even offers "personal shoppers" who will take your list and pick suitable items for you. Some competitors, perhaps speaking out of jealousy, think Nordstrom does more in the area of customer service than is reasonable or cost-effective.[1]

Does Nordstrom have a sound plan for attracting shoppers and turning them into satisfied buyers and repeat customers?

http://directories.internetmci.com/marketplace/nordstrom/

In this chapter we'll examine how a company plans its total marketing program. After studying this chapter, you should be able to explain:

- The nature and scope of planning and how it fits within the management process.
- Similarities and differences among mission, objectives, strategies, and tactics.
- The essential difference between strategic company planning and strategic marketing planning.
- The steps involved in strategic marketing planning.
- The purpose and contents of an annual marketing plan.
- Similarities and differences as well as weaknesses and strengths across several models used in strategic planning.

As the Nordstrom case suggests, success for any organization requires skillful marketing management. The *marketing* part of the term *marketing management* was defined in Chapter 1, but what about the *management* part? **Management** is the process of planning, implementing, and evaluating the efforts of a group of people working toward a common goal. In this chapter we provide an overview of the management process and examine planning in some detail. Later, when you've learned more about the strategies and techniques of marketing, we will cover implementation and evaluation, the other two steps in the management process.

Planning as Part of Management

The management process, as applied to marketing, consists basically of (1) planning a marketing program, (2) implementing it, and (3) evaluating its performance. This process is illustrated in Figure 3-1.

The *planning* stage includes setting goals and designing strategies and tactics to reach these goals. The *implementation* stage entails forming and staffing the marketing organization and directing the actual operation of the organization according to the plan. The *evaluation* stage consists of analyzing past performance in relation to organizational goals.[2] This third stage indicates the interrelated, ongoing nature of the management process. That is, the results of this stage are used in *planning* goals and strategies for future periods. So the cycle continues.

The Nature of Planning

"If you don't know where you're going, any road will get you there." The point of this axiom is that all organizations need both general and specific plans to be successful. Management should first decide what it intends to accomplish as a total organization and develop a strategic plan to achieve these results. Based on this overall plan, each division of the organization should determine what its own plans will be. Of course, the role of marketing in these plans needs to be considered.

If planning is so important, exactly what is it? Quite simply, **planning** is deciding now what we are going to do later, including how and when we are going to do it. Without a plan, we cannot get things done effectively and efficiently, because we don't know what needs to be done or how to do it. In **strategic planning**, managers match an organization's resources with its market opportunities over the long run.

The fact that strategic planning has a long-run perspective does not mean that plans can be developed or executed in a sluggish manner. Many years ago, the term **strategic window** was suggested to describe the limited amount of time in

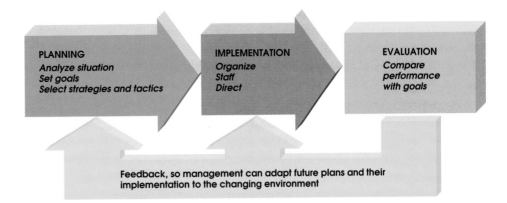

FIGURE 3-1
The management process in marketing.

which a firm's resources coincide with a particular market opportunity.[3] Typically, the "window" is open only temporarily. Thus a firm must be able to move rapidly and decisively when a strategic window opens. Netscape Communications Corp. did just that when the World Wide Web part of the Internet grew explosively. Almost overnight, there were tens of thousands of Websites, which are locations on the Internet that provide information and/or sell products. How could an Internet user sort through all of these Websites? Very quickly, Netscape developed— and is successfully selling—software to help users browse through Websites with some efficiency.[4]

http://www.netscape.com/

Key Planning Concepts

You need to become familiar with the basic terms used in discussing marketing management, especially in the planning phase.

Mission. An organization's **mission** states what customers it serves, what needs it satisfies, and what types of products it offers. A mission statement indicates, in general terms, the boundaries for an organization's activities.

A mission statement should be neither too broad and vague nor too narrow and specific. To say that a firm's mission is "to benefit American consumers" is too vague; to state that its purpose is "to make tennis balls" is too narrow. Neither statement outlines meaningful benefits for customers or provides much guidance to management. Unless the firm's purpose is clear to executives, strategic planning will likely result in disagreement and confusion.

Traditionally, companies stated their missions in production-oriented terms, such as "We make furnaces" (or telephones, or tennis rackets). Today, firms following the marketing concept express their mission in customer-oriented terms. Executives should think about the needs they are satisfying and the benefits they are providing. Thus, instead of "We make furnaces," Lennox Company's statement of mission should be "We provide home climate control." Recall that Table 1-1 illustrated marketing-oriented ways of stating a company's mission.

http://www.davelennox.com/

Objectives and Goals. We treat *objectives* and *goals* as synonyms. An **objective** is simply a desired outcome. Effective planning must begin with a set of objectives that are to be achieved by carrying out plans.

To be worthwhile and workable, objectives should be:

• Clear and specific.
• Stated in writing.

Marriott International states its mission quite simply: "We are committed to being the best lodging and management services company in the world by treating employees in ways that create extraordinary customer service and shareholder value." Two other groups are vital to Marriott— employees and shareholders. Marriott's products include several brands of lodging as well as management services, such as food and facilities management for business, education, and health-care clients, and management of retirement communities.

- Ambitious, but realistic.
- Consistent with one another.
- Quantitatively measurable wherever possible.
- Tied to a particular time period.

Consider these examples:

Weak (too general)		Workable
Increase our market share.	→	Increase our market share to 25% next year from its present 20% level.
Improve our company's public image.	→	Receive favorable recognition awards next year from at least three consumer or environmental groups.

Strategies and Tactics.   The term *strategy* was originally applied to the art of military generalship. In business, a **strategy** is a broad plan of action by which an organization intends to reach its objectives. In marketing, the relationship between objectives and strategies may be illustrated as follows:

Objectives		Possible strategies
Increase sales next year by 10% over this year's figure.	→	1. Intensify marketing efforts in domestic markets. 2. Expand into foreign markets.

http://www.marriott.com/

Room 851. Wants to have one foot in the ocean and the other in the office.

There's no such thing as pure play anymore. But that shouldn't stop you from lolling on a beach at a Marriott Resort. Work will feel a zillion miles away. But with our business services and your AT&T Calling Card, you can always dip a toe back into the office. Call your travel agent or 800-228-9290. It's not easy to get away, but we believe:

When you're comfortable you can do anything. **Marriott**
HOTELS · RESORTS · SUITES

KEY QUESTIONS FOR AN ORGANIZATION TO ANSWER

The concepts of mission, objectives, strategies, and tactics each raise an important question that must be answered by an organization seeking success in business or, more specifically, in marketing:

Concept		Question
Mission	→	What business are we in?
Objectives	→	What do we want to accomplish?
Strategies	→	In general terms, how are we going to get the job done?
Tactics	→	In specific terms, how are we going to get the job done?

Two organizations might have the same objective but use different strategies to reach it. For instance, both firms might aim to increase their market shares by 20 percent over the next 3 years. To do that, one firm might intensify its efforts in household markets, while the other might concentrate on expanding into institutional markets (for example, food-service organizations). Conversely, two organizations might have different objectives but select the same strategy to reach them.

A **tactic** is a means by which a strategy is implemented. A tactic is a more specific, detailed course of action than a strategy. Also, tactics generally cover shorter time periods than strategies. Here's an illustration:

Strategy		Tactics
Direct our promotion to males, ages 25–40.	→	1. Advertise in magazines read by this group of people. 2. Advertise on television programs watched by this group.

To be effective, a tactic must coincide with and support the strategy with which it is related.

Scope of Planning

Planning may cover long or short periods. Strategic planning is usually long range, covering 3, 5, 10, or (infrequently) 25 years. It requires the participation of top management and often involves a planning staff.

Long-range planning deals with company-wide issues such as expanding or contracting production, markets, and product lines. For example, all firms in the U.S. auto industry must look ahead to the next century to identify key markets, plan new products, and update production technologies.

Short-range planning typically covers 1 year or less and is the responsibility of middle- and lower-level managers. It focuses on such issues as determining which target markets will receive special attention and the specific composition of the marketing mix. Looking again at the auto industry, Chrysler Corporation annually decides which target markets it will concentrate on and whether its marketing mixes for each of these markets need to be changed. Naturally, short-range plans must be compatible with the organization's long-range intentions.

http://www.chrysler.com/

Planning the marketing strategies in a firm should be conducted on three different levels:

- *Strategic company planning.* At this level management defines an organization's mission, sets long-range goals, and formulates broad strategies to achieve these goals. These company-wide goals and strategies then become the framework for planning in the firm's different functional areas, such as production, finance, human resources, research and development, *and* marketing.

- *Strategic marketing planning.* The top marketing executives set goals and strategies for an organization's marketing effort. Strategic *marketing* planning obviously should be coordinated with *company-wide* planning.
- *Annual marketing planning.* Short-term plans should be prepared for a firm's major functions. Covering a specific period, usually 1 year, the annual marketing plan is based on the firm's strategic marketing planning.

Strategic Company Planning

Strategic company planning consists of four essential steps:

1. Define the organizational mission.
2. Analyze the situation.
3. Set organizational objectives.
4. Select strategies to achieve these objectives.

The process is shown in the top part of Figure 3-2. The first step, *defining the organizational mission*, influences all subsequent planning. For some firms, this step requires only reviewing the existing mission statement and confirming that it is still suitable. Still, this straightforward step is too often ignored.

Conducting a situation analysis, the second step, is vital because strategic planning is influenced by many factors beyond and within an organization. By **situa-**

FIGURE 3-2

Three levels of organizational planning.

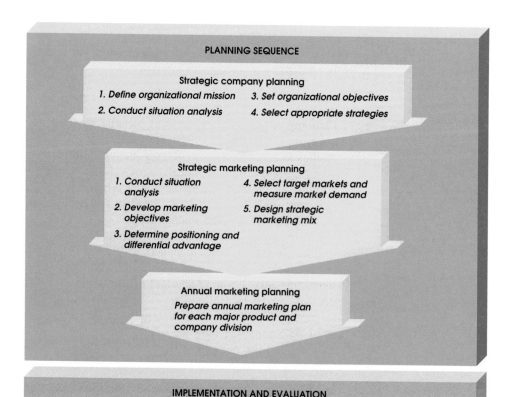

PLANNING SEQUENCE

Strategic company planning

1. Define organizational mission
2. Conduct situation analysis
3. Set organizational objectives
4. Select appropriate strategies

Strategic marketing planning

1. Conduct situation analysis
2. Develop marketing objectives
3. Determine positioning and differential advantage
4. Select target markets and measure market demand
5. Design strategic marketing mix

Annual marketing planning

Prepare annual marketing plan for each major product and company division

IMPLEMENTATION AND EVALUATION

tion analysis, we simply mean gathering and studying information pertaining to one or more specified aspects of an organization. We'll talk more about conducting a situation analysis in an upcoming section.

The third step in strategic company planning, *deciding on a set of objectives*, guides the organization in fulfilling its mission. Objectives also provide standards for evaluating an organization's performance.

By this point in its strategic planning, the organization has determined where it wants to go. The fourth step, *selecting appropriate strategies*, indicates how the firm is going to get there. **Organizational strategies** represent broad plans of action by which an organization intends to achieve its goals and fulfill its mission. Strategies are selected either for the entire company if it is small and has only a single product, or for each division if the company is large and has multiple products or units.

Do companies actually engage in strategic planning and then prepare a written plan? The results of one survey indicated that almost 70 percent of firms had strategic plans in place; among them, nearly 90 percent believed their strategic plans had been effective.[5] Interestingly, a larger proportion of younger firms (1 to 10 years old) than older firms had formal strategic plans.

Strategic Marketing Planning

After conducting strategic planning for the organization as a whole, management needs to lay plans for each major functional area, such as marketing or production. Of course, planning for each function should be guided by the organization-wide mission and objectives.

Strategic marketing planning is a five-step process:

1. Conduct a situation analysis.
2. Develop marketing objectives.
3. Determine positioning and differential advantage.
4. Select target markets and measure market demand.
5. Design a strategic marketing mix.

These five steps are shown in the middle of Figure 3-2, indicating how they relate to the four steps of strategic company planning. Each step is discussed below.

Situation Analysis

The first step in strategic marketing planning, *situation analysis*, involves analyzing where the company's marketing program has been, how it has been doing, and what it is likely to face in the years ahead. Doing this enables management to determine if it is necessary to revise the old plans or devise new ones to achieve the company's objectives.

Situation analysis normally covers external environmental forces and internal nonmarketing resources discussed in Chapter 2.[6] A situation analysis also considers the groups of consumers served by the company, the strategies used to satisfy them, and key measures of marketing performance.

As the basis for planning decisions, situation analysis is critical. But it can be costly, time-consuming, and frustrating. For example, it is usually difficult to extract timely, accurate information from the "mountains" of data compiled during a situation analysis. Moreover, some valuable information, such as sales or market-share figures for competitors, is often unavailable.

As part of a situation analysis, many organizations perform a **SWOT assessment**. In this activity, a firm identifies and evaluates its most significant *s*trengths, *w*eaknesses, *o*pportunities, and *t*hreats. To fulfill its mission, an organization needs to capitalize on its key strengths, overcome or alleviate its major weaknesses, avoid significant threats, and take advantage of the most promising opportunities.

We're referring to strengths and weaknesses in an organization's own capabilities. For example, a Sears' strength is its large size, which gives it—among other things—clout in dealing with suppliers. However, a weakness is its comparatively high operating expenses, which makes it difficult for Sears to compete on the basis of low prices.

Opportunities and threats often originate outside the organization. For example, an opportunity identified by Wal-Mart is the large number of metropolitan areas in which it has no stores. But a threat is the group of competitors (such as Kmart and Target) Wal-Mart encounters in these heavily populated areas.

http://www.wal-mart.com/

http://www.kmart.com/

http://www.targetstores.com/

Marketing Objectives

The next step in strategic marketing planning is to *determine marketing objectives*. Marketing goals should be closely related to company-wide goals and strategies. In fact, a *company strategy* often translates into a *marketing goal*. For example, to reach an organizational objective of a 20 percent return on investment next year, one organizational strategy might be to reduce marketing costs by 15 percent. This company strategy would become a marketing goal. In turn, converting all sales people from salaried compensation to a commission basis might be one of the marketing strategies adopted to achieve this marketing goal.

We already know that strategic planning involves matching an organization's resources with its market opportunities. With this in mind, each objective should be assigned a priority based on its urgency and potential impact on the marketing area and, in turn, the organization. Then resources should be allocated in line with these priorities.[7]

Positioning and Differential Advantage

The third step in strategic marketing planning actually involves two complementary decisions: *how to position a product in the marketplace* and *how to distinguish it from competitors*. A company needs to create an image for its product in the minds of consumers. Thus, **positioning** refers to a product's image in relation to directly competitive products as well as other products marketed by the same company.[8] For example, given rising health consciousness among many consumers, manufacturers of mayonnaise and similar products recognized the need to introduce products that would be perceived as more wholesome.[9] Hence, CPC International positioned its Hellmann's Dijonnaise, which combines no-fat mustard with some mayonnaise ingredients, but no egg yolks, as a healthful *and* tasty product. Positioning is discussed further in Chapter 9.

After the product is positioned, a viable differential advantage has to be identified. **Differential advantage** refers to any feature of an organization or brand perceived by customers to be desirable and different from those of the competition.[10] Nike's advantage revolves around its superior product design that combines the latest in technology and styling in its athletic footwear. Nordstrom, which has over 75 upscale retail stores in selected markets around the U.S., has built a powerful differential advantage combining very broad assortments of highly fashionable merchandise and peerless customer service.

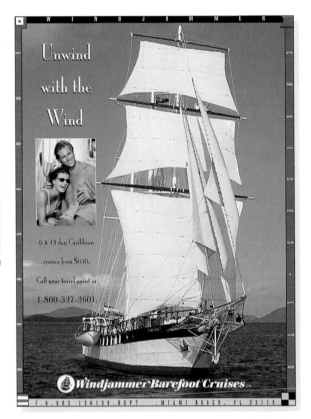

Besides striving for a differential advantage, a company has to avoid a **differential disadvantage** for its product. Consider U.S. automakers. During much of the 1970s and 1980s, their products were at a disadvantage to Japanese-produced cars with respect to price and perceived quality. Recently, U.S. automakers have worked feverishly to erase this differential disadvantage. Through better manufacturing processes, they have sought to reduce the prices and enhance the quality of American-made cars.[11]

The concepts of differential advantage and differential disadvantage apply to both goods and services and, in some areas such as retailing, to entire firms. One consultant believes that retailers can gain a differential advantage by developing one or more of four *est* dimensions—that is, the cheap*est* prices, the bigg*est* assortments, the hott*est* (most fashionable) merchandise, the easi*est* store to shop in. According to this observer, Nordstrom doesn't compete based on low prices but excels in the other three areas, making it the only retailer with three *est* advantages. Conversely, a firm risks a differential disadvantage if it is only average or "pretty good" on these four dimensions.[12]

Target Markets and Market Demand

Selecting target markets is the fourth step in marketing planning. A **market** consists of people or organizations with needs to satisfy, money to spend, and the willingness to spend it. For example, many people need transportation and are willing to pay for it. However, this large group is made up of a number of segments (that is, parts of markets) with various transportation needs. One segment may want low-cost, efficient transportation, for instance, while another may prefer luxury

YOU MAKE THE DECISION

WHICH MEAT HAS THE EDGE?

Each year in the U.S., every person consumes an average of almost 50 pounds of pork, a slightly smaller amount of chicken, and just under 65 pounds of beef. Is this good news for beef producers? Not really. Per capita consumption of beef has been declining for some time. In contrast, demand for pork has been growing steadily; the same can be said about chicken, although the rate of growth has slowed recently.

Clearly, beef producers face a marketing challenge. The pork industry was at a similar crossroads in the 1980s. Following extensive consumer research, pork producers decided to reposition their product as "the other white meat." The campaign successfully positioned pork closer to chicken, which has a healthful image in the minds of consumers, and further away from beef, which is perceived less favorably.

Coming up with a real differential advantage for beef is more difficult, however. They need to recognize that when purchasing meat, consumers are sensitive to prices but are also interested in other factors such as healthfulness and convenience in preparation.

What is—or could be—beef's differential advantage in relation to pork and chicken?

Sources: Rod Smith, "Producers Set Pork to Be 'First Meat' by 2000," *Feedstuffs*, June 19, 1995, pp. 1, 4; and Stephen Bennett, "Beef Fights Back," *Progressive Grocer*, April 1994, p. 131.

---

and privacy. That's why many airlines offer three somewhat different fares—coach, business, and first class. Market segmentation is discussed in Chapter 7.

Ordinarily it is impractical for a firm to satisfy all segments with different needs. Instead, a company targets its efforts on one or more of these segments. Thus a **target market** refers to a group of people or organizations at which a firm directs a marketing program.

Target markets must be selected on the basis of opportunities. And to analyze its opportunities, a firm must forecast demand (that is, sales) in its target markets. The results of demand forecasting will indicate whether the firm's targets are worth pursuing, or whether alternatives need to be identified. We'll consider demand forecasting in Chapter 7.

Marketing Mix

Next, management must design a **marketing mix**—the combination of a product, how it is distributed and promoted, and its price. Together, these four elements must satisfy the needs of the target market(s) and, at the same time, achieve the organization's marketing objectives. Let's consider the four elements and some of the concepts and strategies you'll learn about in later chapters:

- *Product.* Strategies are needed for managing existing products over time, adding new ones, and dropping failed products. Strategic decisions must also be made regarding branding, packaging, and other product features such as warranties.
- *Price.* Necessary strategies pertain to price flexibility, related items within a product line, terms of sale, and possible discounts. Also, pricing strategies for entering a market, especially with a new product, must be designed.
- *Distribution.* Here, strategies relate to the channel(s) by which ownership of products is transferred from producer to customer and, in many cases, the means by which goods are moved from where they are produced to where they are purchased by the final customer. In addition, strategies applicable to any middlemen, such as wholesalers and retailers, must be designed.

- *Promotion.* Strategies are needed to combine individual methods such as advertising, personal selling, and sales promotion into a coordinated campaign. In addition, promotional strategies must be adjusted as a product moves from the early stages to the later stages of its life. Strategic decisions must also be made regarding each individual method of promotion.

The four marketing-mix elements are interrelated; decisions in one area affect actions in another. To illustrate, design of a marketing mix is certainly affected by whether a firm chooses to compete on the basis of price *or* on one or more other elements. When a firm relies on price as its primary competitive tool, the other elements must be designed to support aggressive pricing. For example, the promotional campaign likely will be built around a theme of "low, low prices." In nonprice competition, however, product, distribution, and/or promotion strategies come to the forefront. For instance, the product must have features worthy of a higher price, and promotion must create a high-quality image for the product.

Each marketing-mix element contains countless alternatives. For instance, a producer may make and market one product or many, and they may be related or unrelated to each other. The product(s) may be distributed through wholesalers, to retailers without the benefit of wholesalers, or even directly to final customers. Ultimately, from the multitude of alternatives, management must select a combination of elements that will satisfy target markets and achieve organizational and marketing goals.

Annual Marketing Planning

Besides strategic planning for several years into the future, more specific, shorter-term planning is also vital. Thus strategic marketing planning in an organization leads to the preparation of an annual marketing plan, as shown in the bottom part of Figure 3-2. An **annual marketing plan** is the master blueprint for a year's marketing activity for a specified organizational division or major product. It is a written document.

A separate plan normally should be prepared for each major product and company division. Sometimes, depending on a company's circumstances, separate plans are developed for key brands and important target markets.[13] As the name

A COMMITMENT TO CUSTOMER SATISFACTION

ARE SMALL FIRMS AT A DISADVANTAGE IN SATISFYING CUSTOMERS?

Irrespective of its size, a company has to develop sound plans for satisfying customers and then has to implement them effectively. Skill and creativity are as important as size and resources. As a result, there's no guarantee of success or failure for either large or small firms.

Many small firms succeed, typically by avoiding head-to-head confrontations with large businesses and by devising creative plans for serving part of an entire market. Consider how two small, vastly different retailers have engaged in *strategic marketing planning* to attract shoppers and turn them into satisfied and loyal customers:

- Some years ago, Richard Ost started a tiny drugstore in a low-income, rundown section of Philadelphia. This wasn't his market of choice; rather, it was the only place a young pharmacist with few funds could open a drugstore. How could a "white boy from Northeast Philadelphia," his self-description, survive in a largely minority neighborhood? Any successful effort combines many ingredients. For example, Ost works long hours to serve customers personally and also oversee his employees' efforts. Perhaps most important, in analyzing his situation, he recognized that most residents of the neighborhood speak a foreign language. Thus he has programmed his computer to print labels for prescription containers as well as any accompanying instructions in the customer's preferred language. About 30 percent are written in Spanish, another 20 percent in Vietnamese. He also employs bilingual residents to assist customers who do not speak English.

- Jerome and Cathy Jenkins, in contrast, are African Americans striving to satisfy a predominant market of white business executives. With more and more men wearing colorful ties, Jerome decided there would be a strong demand for handmade ties. Cathy spent 10 months learning how to make ties. Friends and coworkers liked—and bought—the Jenkinses' first products. Encouraged, they joined with Jerome's brother Ken to open a retail outlet in a mall in downtown St. Louis. All they sell is handmade ties, but customers can choose from hundreds of different fabrics. The Jenkinses are also using computer technology to satisfy customers. According to Jerome, "We can create fabric from absolutely anything—designs, logos, family photos, absolutely anything."

Are these two firms successful? Ost has expanded from the initial pharmacy in 1982 to three today. The Jenkinses now have three stores and are considering a fourth. Both demonstrate the ability of small firms to engage in strategic planning, even if informally, and to devise clever ways of satisfying their customers and being successful.

To remain successful, how should Ost strengthen the marketing mix for his pharmacies? How about the Jenkinses?

Sources: Sean C. Spence, "Custom-Made Tie Retailer Opens in Columbia Mall," *Columbia* (Missouri) *Business Times*, July 22–Aug. 4, 1995, pp. 4, 7; and Thomas Petzinger, Jr., "Druggist's Simple Rx: Speak the Language of Your Customers," *The Wall Street Journal*, June 16, 1995, p. B1.

---

implies, an annual marketing plan usually covers 1 year. There are exceptions, however. Because of the seasonal nature of some products or markets, it is advisable to prepare plans for shorter time periods. For fashionable clothing, plans are made for each season, lasting just several months.

Purposes and Responsibilities

An annual marketing plan serves several purposes:

- It summarizes the marketing strategies and tactics that will be used to achieve specified objectives in the upcoming year. Thus it becomes the "how-to-do-it" document that guides executives and other employees involved in marketing.

- The plan also points to what needs to be done with respect to the other steps in the management process—namely, implementation and evaluation of the marketing program.
- Moreover, the plan outlines who is responsible for which activities, when they are to be carried out, and how much time and money can be spent.

The executive responsible for the division or product covered by the plan typically prepares it. Of course, all or part of the task may be delegated to subordinates.

Preparation of an annual marketing plan may begin 9 months or more before the start of the period covered by the plan. Early work includes necessary research and arranging other information sources. The bulk of the work occurs 1 to 3 months prior to the plan's starting date. The last steps are to have the plan reviewed and approved by upper management. Some revision may be necessary before final approval is granted. The final version of the plan, or relevant parts of it, should be shared with all employees who will be involved in implementing the agreed-upon strategies and tactics.

Recommended Contents

Annual marketing planning follows a sequence similar to strategic marketing planning. However, annual planning has a shorter time frame and is more specific—both with respect to the issues addressed and to the plans laid. Still, as shown in Table 3-1, the major sections in an annual plan are similar to the steps in strategic marketing planning.

In an annual marketing plan, more attention can be devoted to tactical details than is feasible in other levels of planning. As an example, strategic marketing

---

TABLE 3-1 Contents of an annual marketing plan

1. *Executive Summary.* In this one- or two-page section, the thrust of the plan is described and explained. It is intended for executives who desire an overview of the plan but need not be knowledgeable about the details.

2. *Situation Analysis.* Essentially, the marketing program for a major division of a company (called a strategic business unit) or product covered by the plan is examined within the context of pertinent past, present, and future conditions. Much of this section might be derived from the results of strategic marketing planning. Additional information of particular relevance to a 1-year planning period may be included in this section.

3. *Objectives.* The objectives in an annual plan are more specific than those produced by strategic marketing planning. However, annual objectives must help achieve organizational goals and strategic marketing goals.

4. *Strategies.* As in strategic marketing planning, the strategies in an annual plan should indicate which target markets are going to be satisfied through a combination of product, price, distribution, and promotion.

5. *Tactics.* Specific activities, sometimes called action plans, are devised for carrying out each major strategy included in the preceding section. For ease of understanding, strategies and tactics may be covered together. Tactics specifically answer the questions of *what, who*, and *how* for the company's marketing efforts.

6. *Financial Schedules.* This section normally includes two kinds of financial information: projected sales, expenses, and profits in what's called a pro forma financial statement; and the amounts of resources dedicated to different activities in one or more budgets.

7. *Timetable.* This section, often including a diagram, answers the question of *when* various marketing activities will be carried out during the upcoming year.

8. *Evaluation Procedures.* This section addresses the questions of *what*, *who*, *how*, and *when* connected with measuring performance against goals, both during and at the end of the year. The results of evaluations during the year may lead to adjustments in the plan's strategies and/or tactics or even the objectives to be achieved.

Assume you are the manager responsible for a line of handheld calculators used by executives and engineers. In the past year, your brand has fallen from second to third in terms of sales. You attribute the decline to an unfair comparative advertising campaign run by the new second-place firm. The firm used ads that pointed to alleged shortcomings in your calculators. Unexpectedly, you are presented with an opportunity to regain the upper hand when one of your sales people brings you a copy of that competitor's marketing plan for next year. The sales person found it on a chair following a seminar attended by representatives from a number of calculator makers. After studying this plan, you could adjust your plans to counter the other firm's strategies. Even though you didn't buy or steal the plan, is it ethical to read and use it?

planning might stress personal selling within the marketing mix. If so, the annual plan might recommend increased college recruiting as a source of additional sales people.

An annual marketing plan actually relates to all three steps of the management process, not just planning. That is, sections 5 through 7 deal with implementation and section 8 is concerned with evaluation.

To increase the likelihood of careful review, some firms limit annual marketing plans to a certain specified length, such as 20 pages. And you thought only instructors limited the length of written assignments!

Selected Planning Models

Over the past 20 to 25 years, a number of frameworks or tools—we'll call them *models*—have been designed to assist with strategic planning. Most of these models can be used with both strategic company planning *and* strategic marketing planning. In this section, therefore, we briefly discuss several planning models that have received ample attention in recent years. First, however, you need to be familiar with a form of organization, the strategic business unit, that pertains to these planning models.

Strategic Business Units

Most large and medium-sized companies—and even some smaller firms—consist of multiple units and produce numerous products. In such diversified firms, company-wide planning cannot serve as an effective guide for executives who oversee the organization's various divisions. The Philip Morris Company provides an example. The mission, objectives, and strategies in its tobacco division are—and must be—quite different from those in the Miller brewing or Kraft Foods divisions.

Consequently, for more effective planning and operations, a multibusiness or multiproduct organization should be divided according to its major markets or products. Each such entity is called a **strategic business unit (SBU)**. Each SBU may be a major division in an organization, a group of related products, or even a single major product or brand.

To be identified as an SBU, an entity should:

- Be a separately identifiable business.
- Have a distinct mission.

DIVIDING UP THE "PIE"

Possible SBUs for two giant companies and a non-profit organization are as follows:

- PepsiCo: Soft drinks, snack foods, and restaurants (and further subdivision of each of these areas is possible)

  http://www.pepsi.com/

- *The McGraw-Hill Companies, Inc.*: Educational and professional publishing, financial services, and information and media

  http://www.mcgraw-hill.com/

- *Your university or college*: Different schools (such as business and engineering) *or* different delivery systems (such as on-campus curricula and televised courses)

- Have its own competitors.
- Have its own executive group with profit responsibility.

The trick in setting up SBUs in an organization is to arrive at the *optimum* number. Too many can bog down top management in details associated with planning, operating, and reporting. Too few SBUs can result in each one covering too broad an area for managerial planning.

Let's now consider several well-known planning models.

*T*he General Electric Company markets a myriad of goods and services, including large steam turbines, financial services, broadcast and cable television, dishwashers, and—as shown in this ad—plastics. To organize its product mix and focus its business strategies, GE has established 12 strategic business units (SBUs): aircraft engines, appliances, capital services, electrical distribution/control, information services, lighting, medical systems, motors and industrial systems, the National Broadcasting Company, plastics, power systems, and transportation systems. Most large businesses rely on SBUs.

http://www.ge.com/

The Boston Consulting Group Matrix

Developed by a management consulting firm, the **Boston Consulting Group (BCG) matrix** dates back at least 25 years.[14] Using this model, an organization classifies each of its SBUs (and, sometimes, major products) according to two factors: its market share relative to competitors, and the growth rate of the industry in which the SBU operates. When the factors are divided simply into high and low categories, a 2×2 grid is created, as displayed in Figure 3-3.

In turn, the four quadrants in the grid represent distinct categories of SBUs or major products. The categories differ with respect not only to market share and industry growth rate but also to cash needs and appropriate strategies:

- *Stars.* High market shares and high industry growth rates typify SBUs in this category. However, an SBU that falls into this category poses a challenge for companies because it requires lots of cash to remain competitive in growing markets. Aggressive marketing strategies are imperative for stars to maintain or even build market share.

- *Cash cows.* These SBUs have high market shares and do business in mature industries (those with low growth rates). When an industry's growth diminishes, stars move into this category. Because most of their customers have been with them for some time and are still loyal, a cash cow's marketing costs are not high. Consequently, it generates more cash than can be reinvested profitably in its own operations. As a result, cash cows can be "milked" to support other SBUs that need more resources. Marketing strategies for cash cows seek to defend market share, largely by reinforcing customer loyalty.

- *Question marks* (sometimes called *problem children*). SBUs characterized by low market shares but high industry growth rates fit in this category. A question mark has not achieved a strong foothold in an expanding, but highly competitive, market. The question surrounding this type of SBU is whether it can gain adequate market share and be profitable. If management answers "no," then the SBU should be divested or liquidated. If management instead answers "yes," the firm must come up with the cash to build market share—more cash than the typical question mark generates from its own profits. Appropriate marketing strategies for question marks focus on creating an impact in the market by displaying a strong differential advantage and, thereby, building customer support.

- *Dogs.* These SBUs have low market shares and operate in industries with low growth rates. A company normally would be unwise to invest substantial funds

FIGURE 3-3

The Boston Consulting Group matrix.

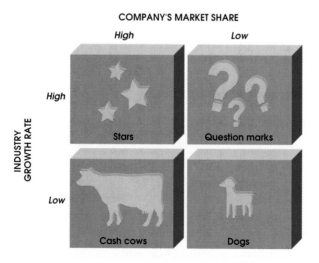

in SBUs in this category. Marketing strategies for dogs are intended to maximize any potential profits by minimizing expenditures *or* to promote a differential advantage to build market share. The company can instead say "Enough's enough!" and divest or liquidate a dog.

The portfolios of most organizations with numerous SBUs or major products include a mix of stars, cash cows, question marks, and dogs. Consider one company's situation. In the mid-1990s, Pepsi-Cola's flagship brands, Pepsi and Diet Pepsi, could be described as *cash cows*. A joint venture with Lipton produced a line of *stars*, Lipton bottled and canned iced teas. Pepsi's brand of sports drink, All Sport, was a *question mark* as it battled the well-entrenched Gatorade for a larger share of a growing market. Finally, Crystal could be labeled a *dog* because demand for clear colas was sluggish and Pepsi's brand, Crystal, had not gained many customers. Rather than abandoning Crystal, Pepsi sought to boost sales by repositioning it as a "citrus cola."[15]

In the financial arena, an investor needs a balanced portfolio with respect to risks and potential returns. Likewise, a company should seek a balanced portfolio of SBUs. Certainly, cash cows are indispensable. Stars and question marks are also integral to a balanced portfolio, because products in growing markets determine a firm's long-term performance. While dogs are undesirable, it's a rare company that doesn't have at least one.

One firm typically cannot affect the growth rate for an entire industry, however. (An exception might be the dominant firm in a fairly new, rapidly growing industry. A fairly recent example would be Rollerblade, Inc., in the in-line roller skating market.) If growth rate cannot be influenced, companies must turn to the other factor in the BCG matrix—market share. Hence, marketing strategies based on the BCG matrix tend to concentrate on building or maintaining market share, depending on which of the four SBU categories is involved. Various strategies require differing amounts of cash, which means that management must continually allocate the firm's limited resources (notably cash) to separate marketing endeavors.

The General Electric Business Screen

On the surface, the **General Electric (GE) business screen** appears to be very similar to the BCG matrix. This planning model, developed by GE with the assistance of the McKinsey consulting firm, also involves two factors and results in a grid.[16] But, as we shall see, the two models are different in significant respects.

Management can use the GE business screen to classify SBUs or major products based on two factors, market attractiveness and business position. Each factor is rated according to several criteria. *Market attractiveness* should be judged with respect to market growth rate (similar to the BCG matrix), market size, degree of difficulty in entering the market, number and types of competitors, technological requirements, and profit margins, among other criteria. *Business position* encompasses market share (as in the BCG matrix), SBU size, strength of differential advantage, research and development capabilities, production capacities, cost controls, and management expertise and depth, among others.

The criteria used to rate market attractiveness and business position are assigned different weights because some criteria are more important than others. Then each SBU is rated with respect to all criteria. Finally, overall ratings (usually numerical scores) for both factors are calculated for each SBU. Based on these ratings, each SBU is labeled as high, medium, or low with respect to (1) market attractiveness and (2) business position. For example, an SBU may be judged as having high market attractiveness but medium business position.

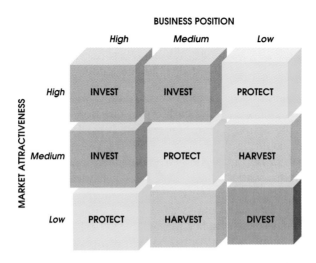

FIGURE 3-4
The General Electric business screen.

Following the ratings, an organization's SBUs are plotted on a 3 × 3 grid, as illustrated in Figure 3-4. The best location for an SBU is the upper left cell because it points to (1) the most attractive market opportunity and (2) the best business position to seize that opportunity. In contrast, the worst location is the lower right cell, for the opposite reasons. The nine cells have implications with respect to how resources are allocated and, in turn, what marketing strategies are suitable.

Every organization has to make decisions about how to use its limited resources most effectively. That's where these planning models can help—determining which SBUs should be stimulated for growth, which ones maintained in their present market position, and which ones eliminated. An SBU's evaluation as indicated by its location on the GE business screen suggests how it should be treated:

- *Invest strategy.* SBUs in the three cells in the upper left of the grid should receive ample resources. To strengthen and build these kinds of SBUs, bold, well-financed marketing efforts are needed.
- *Protect strategy.* Resources should be allocated selectively to SBUs along the diagonal running from the lower left to the upper right of the grid. This somewhat defensive approach helps an SBU maintain its present market position because it generates cash needed by other SBUs. For example, Kodak has spent large sums on marketing to protect its position in the color film industry.[17]
- *Harvest strategy.* Because they lack an attractive market and a strong business position, SBUs in the two cells just below the three-cell diagonal should not receive substantial new resources. Instead, expenditures should be curtailed to maximize any remaining profits. An alternative is to sell these SBUs.
- *Divest strategy.* SBUs in the lower right cell do not have much going for them. Hence, an SBU in this location should not receive any resources. Probably, the best approach is to eliminate it from the organization's portfolio by selling it or, failing that, shutting it down. In the face of entrenched competitors, small market share, and minimal profits, Monsanto Co. decided to divest its Dimension weedkiller less than 3 years after introducing the product.[18]

Firms typically employ more than one of these four strategies. To illustrate, after assessing its portfolio the Kraft Foods unit of the Philip Morris Company employed a *harvest* strategy by selling some businesses that had small profit margins and/or did not fit into its core activities. Divisions sold by Kraft have included specialty oils, food service, and baking (with such brands as Entenmann's and Oroweat). The chairman of this gigantic firm labeled the divested businesses "hip-

http://www.kodak.com/

http://www.monsanto.com/

popotamuses" rather than the preferred "greyhounds." Philip Morris is using the resources derived from the sales to support a *protect* strategy for key brands such as Maxwell House, Oscar Mayer, and Velveeta.[19]

Product-Market Growth Matrix

Most organizations' statements of mission and objectives focus on growth—that is, a desire to increase revenues and profits. In seeking growth, a company has to consider *both* its markets and its products. Then it has to decide whether to continue doing what it is now doing—only do it better—*or* establish new ventures. The **product-market growth matrix**, first proposed by Igor Ansoff, depicts these options.

Essentially, as shown in Figure 3-5, there are four product-market growth strategies:[20]

- *Market penetration.* A company tries to sell more of its present products to its present markets. Supporting tactics might include greater spending on advertising or personal selling. For example, the Wrigley gum company relies on this strategy, encouraging smokers to chew gum where smoking is prohibited.[21] Or a company tries to become a single source of supply by offering preferential treatment to customers who will concentrate all their purchases with it.
- *Market development.* A firm continues to sell its present products, but to a new market. For example, when the defense market softened, McDonnell Douglas devoted more resources to selling its helicopters in the commercial market.[22] Similarly, ski resort operators' efforts to attract families and foreigners represent market development.
- *Product development.* This strategy calls for a company to develop new products to sell to its existing markets. Some ski resorts have built dangerous, steep slopes in order to appeal to thrill-seeking "extreme" customers.[23] To better satisfy its clients (and undoubtedly to attract new customers as well), Holiday Inn Worldwide has multiple brands of hotels—"the upscale Crowne Plaza, the traditional Holiday Inn, the budget Holiday Inn Express, and the business-oriented Holiday Inn Select and Holiday Inn Suites & Rooms."[24]
- *Diversification.* A company develops new products to sell to new markets. This strategy is risky because it doesn't rely on either the company's successful products or its position in established markets. Sometimes it works, but sometimes it doesn't. As one (perhaps radical) example of diversification, the maker of the trendy Swatch timepieces decided to design and produce a car, the Swatchmobile![25]

As market conditions change over time, a company may shift product-market growth strategies. For example, when its present market is fully saturated, a company may have no choice other than to pursue new markets.

http://www.holiday-inn.com/

http://www.swatch-art.com/

FIGURE 3-5
Product-market growth matrix.

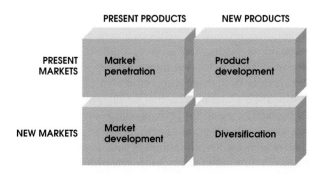

*Many companies, includ-
ing United Airlines, rely on
frequent-buyer programs,
such as Mileage Plus, as
one key means of achiev-
ing market penetration.*

http://www.ual.com/

Assessment of the Planning Models

Each of these planning models has been praised and criticized.[26] While each is somewhat distinctive, all share some common weaknesses and strengths.

The primary weakness is probably oversimplification. Each model bases its assessment of market opportunities and subsequent decisions on only two or three key factors. In this regard, the GE business screen, with its multiple criteria for assessing market attractiveness and business position, is an improvement over the Boston Consulting Group matrix.

Another weakness is the possibility of placing an SBU on a grid or choosing a strategy without relevant, reliable information. For example, whether market share is critical to a product's profitability is still debated. A third possible weakness is that the results from one of the models might be used to contradict or substitute for the critical business judgments made by line managers (such as a marketing vice president).

However, these models also possess noteworthy strengths. Most important is straightforward classification. That is, each model permits an organization to examine its entire portfolio of SBUs or major products in relation to criteria that influence business performance. A second strength is that the models can pinpoint attractive business opportunities and suggest ventures to avoid. Another strength of the models is that they encourage careful, consistent assessment of opportunities, allocation of resources, and formulation of strategies. Without planning models, these activities might be haphazard—for example, using one set of criteria this month and, with no good reason, another set next month.

The search for helpful planning aids is ongoing. For instance, in the mid-1990s, two consultants urged firms to develop their organizational strategies in terms of *value disciplines.*[27] According to this framework, a firm must increase the value offered to customers by cutting prices, improving products, or enhancing service. Doing so requires choosing—and effectively implementing—one of three value disciplines: operational excellence, product leadership, or customer intimacy. Dell Computer and Wal-Mart exemplify operational excellence, while Nike footwear and Acuvue disposable contact lenses illustrate product leadership. Customer intimacy emphasizes delivering precisely what specific customers really want and cannot find elsewhere. Cable & Wireless, a long-distance telephone carrier, avoids price competition with the industry giants by serving well small businesses that want a combination of services to meet their particular needs.

http://www.cwi.net/

Overall, we believe planning models can help management in allocating resources and also in developing sound business and marketing strategies. Of course, any planning model should supplement, rather than substitute for, managers' judgments and decisions.

A GLOBAL PERSPECTIVE

ARE THERE STRATEGIC LESSONS TO BE LEARNED FROM FOREIGN FIRMS?

More and more foreign firms are establishing operations—ranging from manufacturing plants to distribution networks to service facilities—in the U.S. Many have been hugely successful, others have faltered, and a few have failed. The experiences of two foreign companies provide valuable insights regarding effective and ineffective strategic planning:

- *Yamaha's product-market growth strategies.* One division of this Japanese enterprise achieved success by developing and then emphasizing its skill at transforming wood into musical instruments—first pianos and eventually guitars. Over time, it expanded into less related products such as furniture and skis as well as TVs and VCRs. Overall, its strategies were production-oriented rather than market-driven. Predictably, sales stagnated, and profits plunged. Recently, Yamaha has been seeking better tactics for its strategy of market penetration. Further, it is engaging in what is intended to be logical diversification. Yamaha is producing "chips" that create musical sounds and selling them to manufacturers of personal computers and video games. The firm is also developing high-tech products for the "upscale" end of the consumer market. One new item, a player piano priced from $8,000 to $30,000, relies on a built-in computer to record and play back performances.

http://www.yamaha.com/

- *Ikea's well-conceived strategic plans.* This Swedish firm hasn't suffered the problems experienced by Yamaha, at least not yet. Perhaps that's because Ikea has been so astute in situation analysis, particularly in judging consumer needs. Early on, Ikea saw that a large segment of the consumer market was willing to transport and assemble high-quality furniture in exchange for lower prices. Thus the 100 or so Ikea stores around the world, including a handful in the U.S., offer broad assortments of unassembled, well-designed Scandinavian furniture with comparatively low prices. These factors, combined with primarily suburban locations and wide-ranging services such as ample parking and day-care facilities, represent a powerful differential advantage for Ikea. This advantage has propelled the Swedish firm to the enviable position of the world's largest retailer of home furnishings.

Today, business competition knows no national boundaries. So, irrespective of the country in which competitors are headquartered or the specific location of the competition, business success requires comprehensive, yet clever, strategic planning.

Sources: Brenton R. Schlender, "The Perils of Losing Focus," *Fortune,* May 17, 1993, p. 100; "Furnishing the World," *The Economist,* Nov. 19, 1994, p. 79; and Richard Normann and Rafael Ramirez, "From Value Chain to Value Constellation: Designing Interactive Strategy," *Harvard Business Review,* July–August 1993, p. 66.

■ SUMMARY

The management process consists of planning, implementation, and evaluation. Planning is deciding now what we are going to do later, including when and how we are going to do it. Planning provides direction to an organization. Strategic planning is intended to match an organization's resources with its market opportunities over the long run.

In any organization, there should be three levels of planning: strategic company planning, strategic marketing planning, and annual marketing planning. In strategic company planning, management defines the organization's mission, assesses its operating environment, sets long-range goals, and formulates broad strategies to achieve the goals. This level of planning guides planning in different functional areas, including marketing.

Strategic marketing planning entails five steps: conduct a situation analysis, develop marketing objectives, determine positioning and differential advantage, select target markets and measure market demand, and design a marketing mix. Based on strategic marketing plans, an annual marketing plan lays out a year's marketing activities for each major product and division of an organization. An annual plan includes tactics as well as strategies. It is typically prepared by the executive responsible for the division or product.

Management can rely on one or more of the following models for assistance with strategic planning: the Boston Consulting Group matrix, the General Electric business screen, and Ansoff's product-market growth matrix. A planning model helps management see how best to allocate its resources and to select effective marketing strategies.

More about

*W*ith stores in only a dozen or so states, primarily on the West and East Coasts, Nordstrom has plenty of room for expansion. To date, it has been moving slowly into other areas, notably the Midwest. Further, with under 100 stores, the chain should be able to grow within its current markets.

Nordstrom's opportunities will be affected by various factors, including the following:

- According to *Consumer Reports*, consumers are shopping less at department stores than they did 5 years ago. The same readers survey showed that consumers are shopping more at other kinds of retailers, such as warehouse clubs and discount houses, and also through mail order.
- According to a survey of women sponsored by *Women's Wear Daily*, merchandise assortment (that is, the variety and selection of products) is the most common factor in choosing a favorite store. The next most common factors, all cited less than one-half as much as merchandise assortment, are price, store location, product quality, and brand names.

NORDSTROM

- Nordstrom has earned a sterling reputation for customer service. In the *Women's Wear Daily* survey, the retailer was rated the best store for sales personnel and service by more than three-quarters of the respondents. It's also top-rated with respect to store atmosphere.

Like any business, a department store needs to distinguish itself in some way. Most retailers seek a differential advantage through one or more of the following factors: low prices, high-quality merchandise, broad assortments, and extensive services. As it decides on both rate and direction of expansion, Nordstrom needs to consider whether the strategies and tactics that have served it so well in recent years need to be revised in any way.[28]

1. a. What comprises Nordstrom's differential advantage?
   b. Does this chain of department stores suffer from a differential disadvantage?
2. Which of the four strategies in the product-market growth matrix should Nordstrom emphasize in the future?

■ KEY TERMS AND CONCEPTS

Management (52)
Planning (52)
Strategic planning (52)
Strategic window (52)
Mission (53)
Objective (53)
Strategy (54)
Tactic (55)
Strategic company
 planning (56)

Situation analysis (56)
Organizational
 strategies (57)
Strategic marketing
 planning (57)
SWOT assessment (58)
Positioning (58)
Differential
 advantage (58)

Differential
 disadvantage (59)
Market (59)
Target market (60)
Marketing mix (60)
Annual marketing
 plan (61)
Strategic business
 unit (SBU) (64)

Boston Consulting Group
 (BCG) matrix (66)
General Electric (GE)
 business screen (67)
Product-market growth
 matrix (69)

■ QUESTIONS AND PROBLEMS

1. Should a small firm (either a manufacturer or a retailer) engage in formal strategic planning? Why or why not?

2. Every organization needs to define its mission. Using a customer-oriented approach (benefits provided or wants satisfied), answer the question "What business are we in?" for each of the following companies:
   a. Holiday Inn
   b. Adidas athletic shoes
   c. Apple computers
   d. Universal (movie) Studios
   e. Goodyear Tire and Rubber Co.

3. In the situation-analysis step of strategic marketing planning, what specific external environmental factors should be analyzed by a manufacturer of equipment used for backpacking in the wilderness?

4. Can a product have a differential advantage and a differential disadvantage at the same time?

5. Identify and explain the differential advantage or disadvantage for the primary product for one of the following organizations:
   a. Trans World Airlines

   b. Your university or college
   c. Victoria's Secret
   d. The United Way in your community
   e. Major-league baseball

6. For one of the five organizations listed immediately above, describe its target market(s).

7. a. What's the basic difference between the BCG matrix and the GE business screen?
   b. Which do you think is better, and why?

8. Use an example to explain the concept of a strategic business unit.

9. If you were the vice president of marketing for a large airline, which of the three planning models would you find most useful? Why?

10. "The European Union (EU), which seeks the economic unification of Europe, means absolute chaos for American firms trying to market to consumers in countries that belong to the EU. For a number of years, the situation will be so dynamic that U.S. executives should not waste their time on formal strategic planning related to European markets." Do you agree with this statement?

■ HANDS-ON MARKETING

1. Go to your school's library and obtain a copy of an annual report for a major corporation. Based on your examination of the year-end review, which of the following product-market growth strategies is being used by this company: market penetration, market development, product development, and/or diversification?

2. Talk with the owner or manager of a local firm about its marketing strategies. Based on the information you have obtained, determine the differential advantage or disadvantage for the firm's primary product. Then indicate how the advantage could be strengthened or how the disadvantage could be alleviated.

CHAPTER 4

Marketing Research and Information

Is
CBS
Gambling in Selecting Its Fall Schedule?

Employees of CBS television work the sidewalk outside Harrah's Casino Hotel in Las Vegas recruiting volunteers to come into their test center. The recruits, in groups of 25, are taken to an upstairs room in the casino where they watch the pilot episodes of new series being considered for the fall schedule. Their judgments, combined with those of others in similar groups, play a significant role in determining what shows appear on the network.

The TV networks present their prime-time schedules to potential advertisers in May of each year. Typically the pilot episodes of new shows are completed only a few weeks before the presentation date. As a result, consumer testing of the shows must be compressed into a short time period. Since the researchers want each show evaluated by several hundred people, a large pool of readily available judges is needed. Las Vegas, with 30 million visitors a year, provides the numbers. And with a median age of 45 years and household incomes averaging $45,000, Las Vegas visitors are viewed by CBS as fairly representative of TV audiences nationwide. In addition, vacationers have considerable schedule flexibility and are often in a mood to try something new, so recruiting volunteers is fairly easy.

Participants complete a questionnaire that includes demographic information and TV viewing behavior. Then they watch the show, and use a handheld device to indicate when they like or dislike something. The reactions of all the viewers are combined and converted into a second-by-second graph that executives can match with the show to identify segments, characters, and even lines that are well or poorly received. The testing procedure is better at identifying unpopular shows than it is at predicting hits. In fact, no show has tested poorly and then gone on to be successful.

CBS's competitors use more conventional testing procedures. NBC, for example, recruits consumers in several cities to watch pilots in their homes via cable. Then the viewers are interviewed for their reactions by phone. The executive in charge contends that the normal circumstances of watching the show at home produces a more accurate evaluation.[1]

What do you feel are the major benefits and limitations of the CBS approach to researching new shows?

http://www.cbs.com/

The efforts of CBS to evaluate new shows reflect one thing all organizations have in common—the need for information. And the creativity in the approach being used indicates that research is not easy. To develop effective strategy, all marketing managers need current, accurate information about the markets they are trying to reach, the macroenvironment affecting their particular industry, and the internal and external factors that influence their specific market. We're about to see where this information can be obtained and how to use it.

After studying this chapter, you should be able to explain:

CHAPTER GOALS

- What marketing research is, the need for it, and the variety of forms it takes.
- The systems that have been developed to increase the usefulness of data.
- The appropriate way to conduct a marketing research project.
- How to gather and use information about competitors.
- Who actually does marketing research.

The Marketing Research Function

A mass of data is available both from external sources and from within a firm. The challenge is how to transform the raw data into information and how to use the information effectively. To see how to do this, we will begin by briefly discussing why organizations need to do research. Then we will focus our attention on how research is performed and managed.

The Need for Marketing Research

Today many forces dictate that a firm must have access to timely information. Consider some of these factors and their relationship to information management:

- *Competitive pressure.* To be successful, companies must develop and market new products more quickly than ever before. This requires research to monitor customers' needs and to find out what current and potential competitors are doing.
- *Expanding markets.* Marketing activity is becoming increasingly complex and broader in scope as more firms operate in both domestic and foreign markets. Entering a foreign market requires information on business practices and customs.
- *Cost of a mistake.* Marketing is expensive. A failed marketing effort can cause severe—even fatal—damage to a firm. The adage "look before you leap" is particularly appropriate. Before undertaking a marketing program, a firm should analyze the market, the competition, and the prospective customers.
- *Growing customer expectations.* Despite their expectations, customers seldom volunteer to provide useful information to a firm. Researchers have suggested that only 1 in 10 dissatisfied customers complain. Firms need research to quickly identify problems and solve them before they result in lost business.

The 50 largest U.S. marketing research firms are paid over $5.5 *billion* a year by their clients from around the world for information to improve the quality of decision making.[2] Unaccounted for in this figure is the research done internally by firms and the hundreds of smaller marketing research companies. Obviously, research is an important part of marketing!

What Is Marketing Research?

Marketing research consists of all the activities that enable an organization to obtain the information it needs to make decisions about its environment, its marketing mix, and its present or potential customers. More specifically, **marketing**

research is the development, interpretation, and communication of decision-oriented information to be used in all phases of the marketing process. This definition has two important implications:

- Research plays a role in all three phases of the management process in marketing: planning, implementation, and evaluation.
- It recognizes the researcher's responsibility to go beyond collecting data to developing information that will be useful to managers.[3]

Scope of Marketing Research Activities

Depending on their needs and level of sophistication, marketing managers make use of four main sources of information.

One is regularly scheduled reports that are produced and sold by research firms. These are called *syndicated services* because they are developed with no particular client in mind, but are sold to anyone interested. An example is the National Total-Market Audit, produced by Audits & Surveys, Inc., a bimonthly national measure of total retail sales by brand. Subscribing to this service allows a marketer to regularly monitor retail sales of its own and competitors' products by type of outlet and geographic area.

The second source is a *marketing information system*, an activity internal to a firm that provides a continuous, scheduled, or on-demand flow of standardized reports. Marketing information systems are used by both managers and sales people. For example, a sales person sitting in a customer's office can use a laptop computer and a marketing information system to check on the availability of inventory. Other applications include tracking the sales performance of products and monitoring changing consumer tastes.

A *decision support system* is the third source. It is also internal, but it permits managers to interact directly with data through personal computers to answer specific questions. A manager, for example, might have a decision support system that given specific assumptions will estimate the impact of various levels of advertising on sales of a product.

The fourth source is a nonrecurring, proprietary *marketing research project*, conducted by a company's own staff or by an independent research firm, to answer a specific question. For example, Toro, a manufacturer of lawn mowers, might conduct a survey of retail dealers to identify the most common problems customers have with power mowers.

There are many syndicated services. They tend to be very specific to particular products or industries, so there is little we can say about them at this introductory level. Rather, we will concentrate our discussion on the other three sources.

http://www.surveys.com/

Marketing Information Systems

As computers became common business tools in the late 1950s and early 1960s, firms were able to collect, store, and manipulate larger amounts of data to aid marketing decision makers. Out of this capability developed the **marketing information system (MkIS)**—an ongoing, organized procedure to generate, analyze, disseminate, store, and retrieve information for use in making marketing decisions. Figure 4-1 illustrates the characteristics and operation of an MkIS. The ideal MkIS:

- Analyzes data using statistical analysis and mathematical models that represent the real world.
- Generates regular reports and recurring studies as needed.
- Integrates old and new data to provide information updates and identify trends.

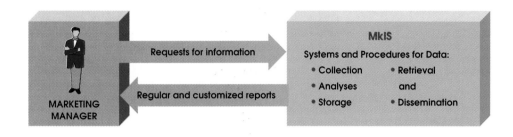

FIGURE 4-1

The structure of a marketing information system.

http://www.pg.com/

Designing a Marketing Information System

To build an MkIS, marketing managers must identify the information that will help them make better decisions. Working with researchers and systems analysts, managers then determine whether the data needed are available within the organization or must be procured, how the data should be organized, the form in which they should be reported, and the schedule according to which they will be delivered. For example, the manager at Procter & Gamble who is responsible for Tide wants to know the retail sales of all detergent brands by geographic area on a weekly basis. The same manager may want monthly reports on the prices that competitors are charging and how much advertising they are doing. Less frequently, possibly once a year, this manager needs to know about developments in the marketplace such as demographic changes that might affect Tide in the long term. In addition to these (and probably other) regular reports, the manager may periodically request special reports that can be compiled from existing data. For example, the Tide manager may want to see what share of the total market each detergent brand had by quarter over the last 5 years and a projection of how each is likely to perform over the next 3 years.

A well-designed MkIS can provide a continuous flow of this type of information for decision making. The storage and retrieval capability of an MkIS allows a wide variety of data to be collected and used as needed. With this capability, managers can continually monitor the performance of products, markets, sales people, and other marketing units.

An MkIS is of obvious value in a large company, where information is likely to get lost or distorted as it becomes widely dispersed. However, experience shows that even relatively simple information systems can upgrade management's decision making in small and medium-sized firms. How well an MkIS functions depends on three factors:

- The nature and quality of the data available.
- The ways in which the data are processed to provide usable information.
- The ability of the operators of the MkIS and the managers who use the output to work together.

Global Marketing Information Systems

As firms expand their operations beyond national borders, their needs for information also grow. Centrally managed international organizations must be informed about what is happening around the world. Thus, many companies are creating global marketing information systems. However, establishing worldwide agreement on the types and forms of information to maintain can be difficult. For example, Gillette, with two-thirds of its sales outside the U.S., must keep 30,000 technology-using employees in 76 countries integrated into a single system.[4]

Clearly, designing and operating a global MkIS can be more complex than developing one at the domestic level. It requires coordinating across all subsidiaries of a firm, recognizing differences in management styles and cultures, and an internal marketing effort to convince each unit of the value of timely, accurate information.

The features of an MkIS—a focus on preplanned, structured reports and centralized control over the information by computer specialists—resulted from the skills required to operate computers. Organizations were forced to depend on highly trained programmers working on large computers to produce the information requested by managers. However, personal computers with greatly enlarged capacity and user-friendly software have reduced that dependency and led to the development of decision support systems.

Decision Support Systems

A **decision support system (DSS)** is a computer-based procedure that allows a manager to interact with data and use various methods of analysis to integrate, analyze, and interpret information. Like an MkIS, the heart of a DSS is data—different types of data from a wide variety of sources. Typically, there are data describing customers, competitors, economic and social trends, and the organization's performance. Also like an MkIS, the DSS has methods for analyzing data. These methods range from simple procedures such as computing ratios or drawing graphs to sophisticated statistical techniques and mathematical models.

Where the MkIS and DSS differ is in the extent to which they permit managers to interact directly with the data. By combining personal computers and user-friendly software, the DSS allows managers to retrieve data, examine relationships, and even produce reports to meet their specific needs. This interactive capability makes it possible for managers to react to what they see in a set of data by asking questions and getting immediate answers. Figure 4-2 depicts the relationships in a DSS.

Consider this example. Midway through the year, a manager wants to compare actual sales of a product to what was forecast. Sitting down at her computer, she calls up the monthly forecasts and the actual sales figures. Discovering that sales fell slightly below the forecast in the most recent month, she commands the system to provide similar data for the company's other products. Finding that the other

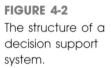

FIGURE 4-2

The structure of a decision support system.

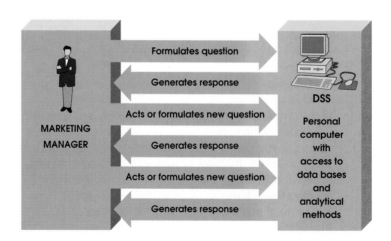

products are on target, she concludes that there may be a problem with the product in question. Next, she asks the system to break down the total sales figure by geographic areas and discovers that the poor sales results occurred in only two of seven regions.

Suspecting competitive activity, she then has the system retrieve and compare advertising levels and prices of her product and those of competitors in the markets where sales forecasts were achieved and where they weren't. Finding nothing out of the ordinary, she decides to examine distribution levels for the territories. Requesting data on the size and types of retail outlets over time, she finds that in the two regions where sales have slipped there has been a slow but steady decline in the type of small, independent retailers that account for a significant portion of the product's sales, and the effects are beginning to show up. Thus, her strategy is to investigate the use of alternative outlets for selling the product in these problem regions. Notice that, with an adequate DSS, this entire task was done in a short time by simply asking for information, analyzing it, and moving on to another question suggested by the analysis.

The DSS adds speed and flexibility to the MkIS by making the manager an active part of the research process. The increased use of desktop computers, user-friendly software, and the ability to link computer systems at different locations (networking) so several managers can work on the same problem have greatly enhanced the potential of DSS. However, these systems are costly to implement and maintain. As a result, the DSS may be limited to large organizations for the time being.

Databases

An MkIS or a DSS uses data from a variety of sources both within the organization and from outside suppliers. These data are organized, stored, and updated in a computer in what is called a **database.** Ordinarily a database will contain separate data modules on such topics as customers, competitors, industry trends, and environmental changes.

http://www.americanexpress.com/

Internally, data come from the sales force, marketing, manufacturing, and accounting. For example, American Express has 500 billion bits of data on how customers have used its 35 million charge cards to spend \$350 billion since 1991.[5] Externally, information is available from hundreds of suppliers. Companies such as A. C. Nielsen have developed computer systems to take the data captured from supermarket checkout systems to provide information on how well specific coupons work in various neighborhoods and which in-store displays are the most effective in generating sales. Once a database is created, the way an organization analyzes and combines the data in it determines its usefulness in planning and implementing strategy.

http://www.nielsen.com/

http://www.farmjournal.com/

One use of databases is to identify customers with specific interests. For example, the magazine *Farm Journal* has built a database consisting of its readers' family demographics, farm size, type of crops, and type of livestock. Using these data and sophisticated printing technology, each month the magazine is produced in as many as 8,000 different versions with tailored editorial and advertising content for different subscriber groups.[6]

Databases have allowed marketers to move from undifferentiated, mass marketing to much more narrowly defined markets. Some believe that through the management of databases, marketers will be able to reach the ultimate level of per-

A GLOBAL PERSPECTIVE

ARE DATABASES AN INVASION OF PRIVACY?

The European Union (EU), a political and economic alliance among the major countries of Western Europe, has demonstrated its concern about personal data stored in computers by proposing a regulatory policy for its members. These regulations will likely affect three areas:

* *Collection.* Consumers are often unaware that data collected by one firm are sold to others, or that information collected as research is used in direct-mail ad campaigns. One proposal requires that consumers be informed of all possible uses of personal data at the time they are being collected.
* *Use.* Proposals to restrict the use of personal data range from complete prohibition of some practices (such as firms exchanging lists of cus-

tomers) to requiring that the consent of the individual be obtained before data are used.
* *Data sharing.* Proposals range from the total elimination of the transfer of data between firms to restrictions on transferring data to firms outside the EU.

The implications of these regulations are significant for European marketers. First, they will increase the cost of collecting personal data. Second, restrictions on transferring data will make it more difficult or possibly even eliminate the use of information provided by third parties. For example, credit card companies routinely sell firms the names of likely prospects based on their past credit card purchases.

Source: Jim Besson, "Riding the Marketing Information Wave," *Harvard Business Review*, September–October 1993, pp. 150–160.

---

http://www.blockbuster.com/

sonalized marketing—targeting individuals. For example, Blockbuster has a database of its movie rentals to over 36 million households. Using a customer's prior selections, the firm prepares individualized direct-mail ads that recommend 10 similar movies.[7]

It would appear that the development and use of databases in marketing is a trend that will continue to grow. A recent national survey found that 56 percent of manufacturers and retailers are currently building databases, another 10 percent plan to do so, and 85 percent believe that databases will be essential in order to compete beyond the year 2000.[8]

Scanners and Single-Source Data

An important data source for databases is scanners, the electronic devices at retail checkouts that read the bar code on each item purchased. Scanners were originally intended to speed up checkout and reduce errors in supermarkets. By matching an item's unique code with price information stored in a computer, the scanner eliminated the need for clerks to memorize prices and reduced mistakes from hitting the wrong cash register key. However, retailers quickly discovered scanners could also produce information on purchases that could be used to improve decisions about how much of a product to keep in inventory and the appropriate amount of shelf space to allocate to each product.

A&P has gone a step further by adding the customer's identity to the purchases. Participants in the chain's "frequent shopper program" are given special discounts when they permit the cashier to run their membership card through a device at the checkout counter. This allows the store to combine data stored on the card about household demographics and life-style with the shopper's purchase behavior. A&P is then able to relate product choices to household characteristics.[9]

Knowing what people buy is even more valuable if you know what advertising they have been exposed to. Information Resources, Inc. (IRI), has created a database to provide this information. The firm has a sample of households for which it:

- Maintains a demographic profile.
- Monitors television viewing electronically.
- Records grocery purchases through a combination of identification numbers and scanners.

The result is that household demographics can be correlated to television advertising exposure and product purchases. The output is called **single-source data** because exposure to television advertising and product purchases can be traced to individual households, providing a single source for both types of data.

Marketing Research Projects

Before MkIS and DSS, much of what was called marketing research consisted of projects to answer specific managerial questions. Projects, some that are nonrecurring and others that are repeated periodically, are still an important part of marketing research. The tests CBS conducts on TV pilots, described at the beginning of the chapter, are examples. The results of a project may be used to make a particular decision. They could also become part of a database to be used in an MkIS or a DSS. Examples of marketing research projects are described briefly in Table 4-1. According to a recent study, the most common projects are studies of industry and market trends, and market-share analyses.[10]

Most marketing research projects follow the procedure outlined in Figure 4-3. Let's examine what goes into conducting a marketing research project.

Define the Objective

Researchers need a clear idea of what they are trying to learn—the objective of the project. Usually the objective is to solve a problem, but this is not always so. Often the objective is to better understand or *define* a problem or opportunity.

Sometimes it's simply to determine if there is a problem. To illustrate, a manufacturer of commercial air-conditioning equipment had been enjoying a steady

TABLE 4-1 Typical marketing research projects

Project	Objective
Concept test	To determine if a new-product idea is attractive to potential customers
Copy test	To determine if the intended message in an advertisement is being communicated effectively
Price responsiveness	To gauge the effect a price change would have on demand for a brand
Market-share analysis	To determine a firm's proportion of the total sales of a product
Segmentation studies	To identify distinct groups within the total market for a particular product
Customer satisfaction studies	To monitor how customers feel about an organization and its products

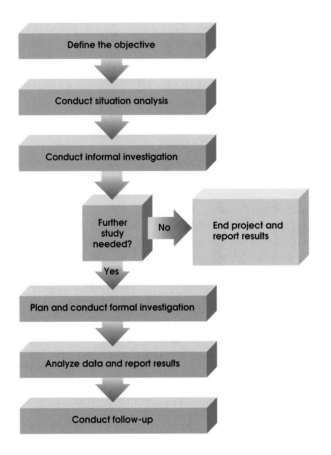

FIGURE 4-3
Marketing research procedure.

increase in sales volume over a period of years. Management decided to conduct a sales analysis. This research project uncovered the fact that, although the company's volume had been increasing, its share of the market had declined because the industry was growing even faster. In this instance, marketing research uncovered a problem that management did not know existed. After specifying the objective, the researcher is ready for the second step—the situation analysis.

Conduct a Situation Analysis

Next, the researchers try to get a "feel" for the situation surrounding the problem. They analyze the company, its market, its competition, and the industry in general. The **situation analysis** is a background investigation that helps in refining the research problem. It involves obtaining information about the company and its business environment by means of library research and extensive interviewing of company officials.

In the situation analysis, researchers also try to refine the problem definition and develop hypotheses for testing. A research **hypothesis** is a tentative supposition that if proven would suggest a possible solution to a problem. Some examples of testable hypotheses are:

- Sales of grocery items are significantly greater when they are placed on display racks outside their normal aisle positions.
- Many bank customers who use automatic teller machines for withdrawals do not know how to use them for deposits.

- The 30 percent of China's population that live in rural areas are either too poor or too hard to reach to be customers for imported products.
- Food taste preferences and eating habits are related to gender.[11]

The project then turns to generating data that can be used to test the correctness of the hypotheses.

Conduct an Informal Investigation

Having gotten a feel for the problem, the researchers are now ready to collect some preliminary data from the marketplace. This **informal investigation** consists of gathering readily available information from people inside and outside the company—middlemen, competitors, advertising agencies, and consumers.

The informal investigation is a critical step in a research project because it will determine whether further study is necessary. Decisions can frequently be made with information gathered in the informal investigation. For example, entrepreneurs considering China as a marketplace find it difficult to obtain useful market information. Even estimates of household per capita income vary widely. According to the Hong Kong manager of the J. Walter Thompson advertising agency, "The best way for anyone to judge [spending power] is to travel to [a city such as] Guangzhou and look at what people are buying and what they are wearing."[12] Such a trip might be enough to convince a manager that the market is ripe, additional research is needed, or that entry would be unwise at this time.

http://www.jwtworld.com/

Plan and Conduct a Formal Investigation

If the project warrants continued investigation, the researcher must determine what additional information is needed and how to gather it.

Select Sources of Information. Primary data, secondary data, or both can be used in an investigation. **Primary data** are the new data gathered specifically for the project at hand. When researchers at Marsh Supermarkets watched 1,600 shoppers move through the store, and discovered that 80 percent of the traffic was in 20 percent of the store—the produce, dairy, and meat sections—they were collecting primary data.[13] **Secondary data** are available data, already gathered for some other purpose. Household income figures taken from the U.S. Census of the Population, compiled by the federal government, are secondary data.

One of the biggest mistakes made in marketing research is to collect primary data before exhausting what can be learned from information available in secondary sources. Ordinarily, secondary information can be gathered much faster and at far less expense than primary data.

Sources of Secondary Data. Excellent sources of secondary information are readily available to marketing researchers.[14] One source is the many records and reports *inside* the firm itself. For example, the daily reports completed by sales people are used primarily to keep track of how they are spending their time. However, if they are examined over several months or years, they can provide a firm with important information on how the mix of customers is changing. Similarly, a contest with mail-in entries might be a good promotional tool. It also can be a source of information. Consumers who enter contests have indicated by their behavior that they are interested in particular products. Examining the geographic origins of these responses might indicate where the best potential markets are.

Outside the firm there are a number of excellent secondary data sources. The federal government is the largest provider of market information. Other sources

include trade and professional organizations, private research firms, universities, business publications, and, of course, any good library.

Researchers must be aware that there is risk associated with using secondary data. Because the user has no control over how, when, by whom, or why the data were collected, they may not meet the objectives of the research. For example, some projects are undertaken to prove a preconceived point. The results of this so-called advocacy research often get considerable publicity, but it may in fact be quite misleading. Thus researchers should check the source, motivation for the study, and definitions of key terms before relying on secondary data.

Sources of Primary Data. After exhausting all the available secondary sources considered pertinent, researchers may still lack sufficient data. If so, they must turn to primary sources and gather or purchase the information. In a company's research project, for instance, a researcher may interview the firm's sales people, middlemen, or customers to obtain the market information needed.

Select a Primary Data-Gathering Method. There are three widely used methods of gathering primary data: survey, observation, and experimentation. Because each method has strengths and weaknesses, the choice of which to use depends on the nature of the problem, but it will also be influenced by how much time and money are available for the project.

Survey Method. A **survey** consists of gathering data by interviewing people. Surveys may be conducted in person, by telephone, or by mail. The advantage of a survey is that information comes directly from the people you are interested in. In fact, it may be the only way to determine the opinions or buying plans of a group.

Surveys have several potential limitations:

- There are opportunities for error in the construction of the survey questionnaire and in the interviewing process.
- Surveys can be very expensive and time-consuming.
- Desired respondents sometimes refuse to participate, and those who do respond often cannot or will not give true answers.

As we will see below, careful design and execution of a survey can reduce the effects of these limitations.

Personal interviews are more flexible than phone or mail interviews because interviewers can probe more deeply if an answer is incomplete. Ordinarily, more information can be obtained by personal interview than by telephone or mail. They also have the advantage of being able to use various stimuli such as products, packages, and ads. Rising costs and other problems associated with door-to-door interviewing have prompted many market researchers to survey people in central locations, such as in shopping centers, airports, and parks. Because this technique was first used in shopping centers, it is generally called a *mall intercept* interview. However, there is growing concern about whether or not people interviewed in these settings are "typical" consumers.

Another popular face-to-face type of personal interview is the **focus group**. In a focus group, 4 to 10 people are led in a discussion by a moderator. General questions are often used to prompt participants into freely discussing the topic of interest. The strength of focus groups is found in the interaction of the participants. A comment by one person triggers thoughts and ideas in others, and the ensuing

*F*ocus groups are an important form of marketing research. A recent issue of Marketing News, *the biweekly newspaper of the American Marketing Association, included a directory of 225 companies specializing in this type of research. Besides providing the group meeting room, these companies offer services such as recruitment of participants; moderators to conduct the focus groups; a viewing room behind a one-way mirror so the client can observe the session without intruding; audio and video taping equipment; and a wide variety of equipment for presenting products, ads, and other discussion starters.*

Find out what hundreds of researchers already know...

Focus Suites is like no other facility you've ever tried.

- The expertise of our professional recruiters is unsurpassed in this industry.

- We have three separate, totally private 3-room suites.

- These extraordinary suites are available for the same cost or less than that of an ordinary facility.

Call today for a competitive bid on your next qualitative research project. Once you've tried us, you'll never be satisfied with an ordinary facility again.

The Right People... The Right Price... The Right Place

One Bala Plaza, Suite 622, 231 St. Asaphs Road, Bala Cynwyd, PA 19004 (215) 667-1110

interaction can produce valuable insights. For example, gender-related feelings about food (men associate meat with high status and masculinity) and taste (women snack more, prefer sweets, and are willing to experiment, while men lean toward substantial meals, salty snacks, and familiar flavors) were uncovered in focus groups.[15] The number of participants in focus groups are too few to permit researchers to make generalizations. Therefore, their use should be restricted to generating concepts and hypotheses that can be tested on large, representative samples of people.

In addition to their high cost and time-consuming nature, personal interviews also face the possible limitation of interviewer bias. An interviewer's appearance, style in asking questions, and body language can all influence a respondent's answers.

Telephone surveys can usually be conducted more rapidly than either personal or mail surveys. Since a few interviewers can make many calls from a central location, this method is easy to administer. Honda had its factory workers call 47,000 Accord buyers to interview them about their cars. This unusual survey had two objectives: to identify needed improvements in the car, and to let the employees hear firsthand what customers liked and disliked about the product.[16]

http://www.honda.com/

A telephone survey can also be timely. For instance, to determine the impact of a particular TV commercial, people can be contacted by phone within hours of the commercial's appearance, while their memories are still fresh. Telephone surveys have been used successfully with executives at work. When preceded by a letter introducing the study and a short call to make an appointment for the actual interview, these surveys can elicit a very high cooperation rate.

One limitation of telephone surveys is that the interview must be short or the respondent becomes impatient. Also, about 30 percent of households have unlisted numbers, have moved since the latest directory was printed, or have no telephone. To lower the cost of telephone interviewing and reduce the problems of unlisted numbers and outdated directories, some surveys are done with the aid of computers. To ensure that all telephone owners, even those with unlisted numbers, have an equal chance of being called, researchers use a method called *random digit dialing* in which computers randomly select and dial numbers.

A **mail survey** involves mailing a questionnaire to potential respondents, asking them to complete it, and having them return it by mail. Since interviewers are not used, this type of survey is not hampered by interviewer bias or problems connected with managing a team of interviewers. In addition, because there is no interviewer present, the respondent can remain anonymous. As a result, answers are more likely to be frank and honest.

A major problem with mail surveys is the compilation of an appropriate mailing list. In some cases lists are readily available. However, many studies require a sample for which there is no readily available mailing list. For example, if Ralston-Purina wants to survey a nationwide sample of pet owners, it might have a difficult time compiling a list. Fortunately, there are businesses, called list brokers, that develop and maintain mailing lists.

Another problem is the reliability of the information in the completed questionnaires. In a mail survey, researchers have no control over who actually completes the questionnaire or how carefully it is done.

One more problem is that a mail survey usually gets a low response rate, often less than 30 percent of those contacted. If the respondents have characteristics that differentiate them from nonrespondents on important dimensions of the survey, the results will be invalid. For example, in a community survey about interest in the local PBS television station, the people willing to take the time to respond are likely to be highly interested in public television and therefore not representative of the entire community. Techniques for improving mail response rates include prenotification by phone, offering a reward, and keeping the survey short and the questions simple.[17]

Observation Method. The **observation method** involves collecting data by observing the actions of a person. In observation research there is no direct interaction with the subjects being studied. For instance, an observation study by the Food Marketing Institute, a grocery industry trade association, found that although 77 percent of customers in supermarkets walk through the bakery, only 33 percent buy any baked goods.[18]

Information may be gathered by *personal observation* or *mechanical observation*. In one kind of personal observation, the researcher poses as a customer. This technique is used by retailers to get information about the performance of sales people or to determine what brands the sales people emphasize. Mechanical observation takes many forms. One, described earlier, is the scanners used in retail stores to record purchases. Other, more dramatic forms are eye cameras that measure

Casinos will soon be able to implant tiny electrodes in the poker chips used by gamblers. With sensors built into the gaming tables, it will be possible for a casino to monitor all bets and payoffs in real time. Thus, the electronic chips and sensors will do for the casinos what bar codes and scanners did for supermarkets—speed up the transactions and reduce errors. But also like scanners, the chips will make it possible to collect data, in this case on individual gamblers. Casinos will be able to do research and build databases. One use could be to determine across large samples of people how much reinforcement (winning) is necessary to keep people playing. Data could also be gathered on individuals. For example, a casino could collect and examine a person's betting patterns, or monitor how much individuals are winning or losing.

Is collecting information about the individual behavior of gamblers different from collecting grocery-buying information in the supermarket? Is it unethical for a casino to collect information in this way?

pupil dilation to record a person's response to a visual stimulus, such as an ad, and brain wave monitors to test whether reactions to an object—for example, a commercial—are primarily emotional or logical.

The observation method has several merits. It can provide highly accurate data about what consumers do in given situations. Usually consumers are unaware that they are being observed, so presumably they behave in their normal fashion. Thus the observational technique eliminates bias resulting from the interaction of the data gatherer and the persons observed. However, observation provides a very limited amount of information and, most important, it tells only *what* happens, but it cannot tell *why*. Observation cannot delve into motives, attitudes, or opinions. To illustrate, what might explain why many more shoppers visit supermarket bakery departments than actually make purchases in them? Interviews would be necessary to test your possible explanations.

Experimental Method. An **experiment** is a method of gathering primary data in which the researcher is able to observe the results of changing one variable in a situation while holding all other conditions constant. Experiments are conducted in laboratory settings or in the field. In marketing research, a "laboratory" is an environment over which the researcher has complete control during the experiment.

Consider this example. A small group of consumers is assembled and presented with a brief product description and proposed package for a new breakfast cereal. After they have examined the package, the people are asked whether they would buy the cereal, and their responses are recorded. Next, a similar group of consumers is brought together and presented with the identical package and product information, except that now a nutritional claim for the cereal is printed on the package. Members of this group are also asked if they would buy the product. The researcher had complete control over the test environment, and the only thing changed was the nutritional claim on the package. Therefore, any difference in buying intentions between the groups can be attributed to the claim.

Laboratory experiments can be used to test virtually any component of marketing strategy. However, recognize that the laboratory setting is not an actual purchase, so consumers' responses may be influenced by the situation. To overcome this problem, some experiments are conducted outside the controlled conditions of the lab, or in the field. A *field experiment* is similar to a laboratory experiment but is conducted under more realistic conditions. For example, the owner of a chain of retail stores might try a traffic-building promotional program in one or two

YOU MAKE THE DECISION

HOW FAR SHOULD RESEARCH BE ALLOWED TO GO?

A New Jersey marketing researcher has patented a watch that does much more than tell time. It is capable of monitoring everything that the person wearing it looks at on television or listens to on the radio, as well as what magazines he or she reads. The watch works by picking up impulses emitted by television and radio stations. Magazines would have miniature transmitters sewn into the binding.

The watch, called the Sellcheck, is still in the prototype stage. To actually place it in use, all broadcasters and publishers would have to agree on a common coding for the signals. But its introduction may not be far off. The vice president of research at Magazine Publishers of America, a trade association, says, "It, or something like it, will happen in the next five years."

How do you think consumers would respond to such a watch? Would you be willing to wear one?

Source: Terence P. Pare, "How to Find Out What They Want," *Fortune*, Autumn/Winter 1993, pp. 39–41.

*P*izza Hut first considered adding buffalo wings—chicken wings marinated in a spicy sauce—to its menu in 1994. But, was there sufficient demand for the product? How would consumers feel about buying chicken from a pizza place? What was the best flavor for the marinade? Some of these questions were addressed with marketing research, using product taste tests and test markets. Within a year buffalo wings developed into a fast-growing $400 million product, and Domino's and Little Caesar's quickly added them to their menus.

stores and then compare sales results with results in similar stores without the promotion. Certainly not everything in the stores can be controlled. However, if as far as the researchers can determine all other conditions in the stores remained similar, any differences in sales can be credited to the promotion.

A common experiment is test marketing. In **test marketing** the researcher duplicates real market conditions in a limited geographic area to measure consumers' responses to a strategy before committing to a major marketing effort. Test marketing is undertaken to forecast sales for a particular marketing mix or to compare the performance of different marketing mixes. For example, McDonald's test-marketed pizza in selected areas for over 2 years before deciding not to add it to their menu.

The advantage of test marketing over a survey is that it tells marketers how many people *actually buy* a product, instead of how many say they *intend to buy* it. However, there are several disadvantages. Test marketing is expensive; spending $500,000 to $1 million is not uncommon. It is time-consuming. Testing frequently lasts 9 to 12 months. Lever Bros. kept Lever 2000 deodorant soap in test for 2 years before going national. And another problem is the researcher's inability to control the situation. Tests are impossible to keep secret from competitors, who may intentionally disrupt the test by temporarily changing their marketing mixes. When Pepsi tested Mountain Dew Sport drink in Minneapolis, Quaker Oats, the maker of Gatorade, flooded the market with coupons and advertising.

Because of the inherent limitations of the kind of test marketing just described, researchers have tried to find faster, less expensive alternatives. One of these is the *simulated test market,* in which an assembled group of volunteers is shown ads for the product being tested as well as for other products. The group is then allowed to shop in a test store that resembles a small grocery store and includes the product being tested. Interviews are conducted immediately thereafter with buyers and nonbuyers of the tested product. In addition, follow-up interviews are conducted with the buyers after they have consumed the product. The entire set of data then goes into a statistical model that forecasts sales for the product.

The potential benefits of simulated test marketing include:

- Costs are lower than for a traditional test market.
- Results are produced in as little as 8 weeks.
- A simulated test can be kept secret.

The drawbacks are:

- Questionable accuracy for unique new products, because the forecasting models are based on the historical sales of similar products.
- Inability to predict the response of competitors or retailers.
- Inability to test changes in marketing variables such as packaging or distribution, due to the simulation's short duration.

Simulated test marketing has not replaced traditional test markets. In fact, the two methods are often used together, with the simulation results used to make marketing-mix modifications before beginning traditional test marketing.[19]

International marketers sometimes use a few countries as a test market for a continent or even the world. Colgate-Palmolive introduced Palmolive Optims shampoo and conditioner in the Philippines, Australia, Mexico, and Hong Kong. When sales proved satisfactory, distribution was expanded to large portions of Europe, Asia, Latin America, and Africa.

http://www.colgate.com/

Prepare Forms for Gathering Data. Whether interviewing or observing subjects, researchers use a questionnaire or form on which there are instructions and spaces to record observations and responses. It is not easy to design a data-gathering form that elicits precisely the information needed. Here are several fundamental considerations:

- *Question wording*. If a question is misunderstood, the data it produces are worthless. Questions should be written with the potential respondent in mind. Vocabulary, reading level, and familiarity with jargon all must be considered. A common wording error is to inadvertently include two questions in one. For example, the question "How would you evaluate the speed and efficiency of our service?" followed by a scale from good to bad is likely to cause problems. Some respondents may see the service as fast, which is good, but with too many mistakes, which is bad.
- *Response format*. Questions are designed for either check mark responses (such as yes–no, multiple choice, agree–disagree scales) or open-ended replies. Open-ended questions are often easier to write and frequently produce richer answers, but they require more effort from the respondent and therefore lower the level of cooperation. Open-ended questions are used most often in personal or telephone interviews, where the interviewer can probe for explanations and additional details.
- *Questionnaire layout*. The normal procedure is to begin with easier questions and move to the more difficult or complicated questions. To understand behavior, researchers must sometimes ask questions about possibly sensitive topics (for example, personal hygiene) or private matters (age, income). These questions are normally placed at the very end of a questionnaire.
- *Pretesting*. All questionnaires should be pretested on a group of respondents similar to the intended sample. Pretesting is designed to identify problems and make corrections and refinements prior to the actual study.

Complete books are available on questionnaire design. Extreme care and skill are needed to produce a questionnaire that maximizes the likelihood of getting a response while minimizing bias, misunderstanding, and respondent irritation.

Plan the Sample. It is unnecessary to survey or observe every person who could shed light on a research problem. It is sufficient to collect data from a sample if its reactions are *representative* of the entire group. We all frequently make

use of sampling. Often we base our opinion of a person on only one or two conversations. And we taste food before taking a larger quantity. The key in these personal issues and in marketing research is whether the sample provides accurate representation.

The fundamental idea underlying sampling is that a small number of items—a sample—if properly selected from a larger number of items—a universe—will have the same characteristics and in about the same proportion as the larger number. Obtaining reliable data with this method requires the right technique in selecting the sample.

Improper sampling is a source of error in many studies. One firm, for example, selected a sample of calls from all the calls made to its 800 number and used the information to make generalizations about its customers. Would you be comfortable saying these callers are representative of all the firm's customers or even all the dissatisfied ones? Though numerous sampling techniques are available, only by using a random sample can a researcher confidently make generalizations about a universe. A *random sample* is selected in such a way that every member of the universe has an equal chance of being included.

All other (nonrandom) samples are known as *convenience samples*. Convenience samples are quite common in marketing research, for two reasons. First, random samples are very difficult to get. Even though the researcher may *select* the subjects in a random fashion, there is no guarantee that they all will participate. Some will be unavailable and others will refuse to cooperate. As a result, researchers often resort to carefully designed convenience samples that reflect the characteristics of the universe as closely as possible. Second, not all research is done with the objective of generalizing to a universe. For example, to confirm the judgment of the advertising department, a researcher may be satisfied with the finding that a small group of respondents all take a similar message away from an ad.

A common question regarding sampling is: How large should a sample be? With random methods, a sample must be large enough to be truly representative of the universe. Thus the size will depend on the diversity of characteristics within the universe. All basic statistics books contain general formulas for calculating sample size. In the case of nonrandom samples, since the objective is not to make generalizations, researchers can select any size sample they and the managers using the data feel comfortable with.

Collect the Data. Collecting primary data by interviewing, observation, or both is often the weakest link in the research process. Even if the data-gathering procedure is designed with great care, the fruits of these labors may be lost if the data gatherers are inadequately trained or supervised.

Motivating data gatherers is difficult, because they frequently are part-time workers doing what is often a monotonous task. As a result, many problems may crop up at this point. For instance, poorly trained data gatherers may fail to establish rapport with respondents or may change the wording of questions. In extreme cases, there have even been instances where interviewers faked the responses and filled out the questionnaires themselves!

Analyze the Data and Present a Report

The value of research is determined by its results. And since data cannot speak for themselves, analysis and interpretation are key components of any project. Computers have made it possible for researchers to tabulate and process masses of data quickly and inexpensively. This tool can be abused, however. Managers have little use for reams of computer printouts. Researchers must be able to identify

*A*nswers given by respondents in marketing research surveys sometimes are filtered, disguised, or distorted. In an attempt to obtain untainted emotional responses, some researchers are attempting to directly measure brain waves. The procedure depicted here claims to bypass a person's perceptual defenses and gauge the amount of pleasure, arousal, and openness to messages generated by a visual stimulus. Critics suggest that such measurements are difficult, if not impossible, to obtain. They also question the artificial setting, which is based on lie detector technology.

pivotal relationships, spot trends, and find patterns—that's what transforms data into useful information.

The end product of the investigation is the researcher's conclusions and recommendations. Most projects require a written report, often accompanied by an oral presentation to management. Here communication skill becomes a factor. Not only must researchers be able to write and speak effectively, they must adopt the perspective of the manager in presenting research results.

Conduct a Follow-up

Researchers should follow up their studies to determine whether their results and recommendations are being used. Management may choose not to use a study's findings for several reasons. The problem that generated the research may have been misdefined, become less urgent, or even disappeared. Or the research may have been completed too late to be useful. Without a follow-up, the researcher has no way of knowing if the project was on target and met management's needs or if it fell short. As a result, an important source of information for improving research in the future would be ignored.

Competitive Intelligence

A research area that is only recently receiving widespread, serious attention is competitive intelligence. U.S. marketers have learned from their foreign counterparts that closely monitoring competitors can be extremely useful. Japanese firms in particular have made a science out of watching and learning from their rivals.

Though it sounds intriguing, **competitive intelligence** is simply the process of gathering and analyzing available public information about the activities and plans of competitors. The data used to study competitors come from a variety of internal and external sources. The most common are databases created and sold by research firms. The simplest of these are newspaper and magazine clipping services that monitor a large number of publications for articles on particular indus-

tries or companies. There are several thousand of these competitive database services available today.

Another source is government reports, produced and made available by U.S. and foreign government agencies. For example, the Japan Center for Information and Cultural Affairs provides government documents, statistics on Japan, and information on various Japanese trade groups. Along the same line, the European Union provides competitive and financial information on European business.

Employees, particularly sales people, are the primary internal source of competitive data. It has become a standard practice for firms to incorporate space for competitive information in the reporting forms used by sales people. Other employees, such as engineers, service personnel, and purchasing agents, can pick up and report helpful information if they are trained to be alert.

It is relatively common to use various observation techniques to collect competitive information. For example, representatives of consumer product manufacturers regularly shop retail stores to monitor competitors' prices and promotions. And it is not uncommon for a firm to buy a competitor's new product in order to examine and test it.

Clearly there is the potential for legal and ethical abuses in gathering competitive intelligence. Incidents of sifting through garbage, electronic eavesdropping, and hiring competitors' employees to learn their plans are not uncommon. Despite trade secret laws that make it illegal to acquire data through "improper means" such as theft, there are many unclear situations. Based on court opinions, attempts to get information when a competitor is taking reasonable care to conceal it from public exposure are unethical and may be illegal.

Many firms take elaborate precautions to protect the security of confidential information. Common techniques include limiting the circulation of sensitive documents, the use of paper shredders, and sensitizing employees to the importance of discretion. Of particular concern is the ease with which a thief can extract information from a careless sales person's or other employee's personal computer.[20]

Status of Marketing Research

Significant advances have been made in both quantitative and qualitative research methodology, and researchers are making effective use of the behavioral sciences, mathematics, and statistics. Still, many companies invest very little in determining market opportunities for their products. Several factors account for the less-than-universal acceptance of marketing research:

- *Predicting behavior is inexact.* Because of the many variables involved, marketing research often cannot predict future market behavior accurately. When dealing with consumer behavior, the researcher may be hard-pressed to determine present attitudes or motives (for reasons that will be explained in Chapter 5), much less what they will be next year.
- *Poor communications between researchers and managers.* The manager is frequently required to make quick decisions in the face of uncertainty, often with incomplete information. Researchers, on the other hand, are prone to approach problems in a cautious, scientific manner. This leads to disagreements about what research should be conducted, how long it should take, and the way in which the results should be presented.
- *A project orientation to research.* Many managers do not treat marketing research as a continuous process. Too often marketing research is viewed in a

fragmented, one-project-at-a-time manner. It is used only when management realizes that it has a marketing problem. The growth in the use of MkIS and DSS will likely improve this situation.

■ SUMMARY

Competitive pressure, expanding markets, the cost of making a mistake, and growing customer expectations all contribute to the need for marketing research. For a company to operate successfully today, management must develop a method for gathering and storing relevant data and converting it into usable information. Three tools used in research are the marketing information system, decision support systems, and the research project.

A marketing information system (MkIS) is an ongoing set of procedures designed to generate, analyze, disseminate, store, and retrieve information for use in making marketing decisions. An MkIS provides a manager with a regularly scheduled flow of information and reports. A decision support system (DSS) differs from an MkIS in that the manager, using a personal computer, can interact directly with data.

A marketing research project is undertaken to help resolve a specific marketing problem. The problem must first be clearly defined. Then a researcher conducts a situation analysis and an informal investigation. If a formal investigation is needed, the researcher decides which secondary and primary sources of information to use. Primary data are gathered using a survey, observation, or an experiment. The project is completed when data are analyzed and the results reported. Follow-up provides information for improving future research.

Researchers have recently developed a stronger interest in competitive intelligence, or finding out what competitors are currently doing and forecasting what they are likely to do in the future. Sales people are an important source of data for competitive intelligence.

Research is conducted internally by marketing research staff members and purchased externally from firms that specialize in doing research.

More about **CBS**

The popularity of a show determines how much a network can charge for advertising time surrounding it. Since today's TV viewer has so many options to choose from, the pressure to develop programming with high audience appeal is very intense. To help them make decisions, television executives use marketing research. The issue raised by this case is the quality of the research being done in Las Vegas by CBS. Let's consider some of the issues.

CBS is getting input from consumers about the shows. It is not relying on the opinions of a small group of executives. However, are these consumers—tourists visiting Las Vegas—representative of the television audience of America? One might argue that many television viewers are people who can't afford to go to Las Vegas. Another consideration is the type of person who selects Las Vegas as a tourism destination. Are they typical of U.S. residents? Finally, what type of person volunteers to participate in this or any research? According

to employees in the screening facility, some people schedule their Las Vegas trips to coincide with the testing to get a preview of upcoming shows.

The large number of people visiting Las Vegas makes recruiting participants for the research easier. And presumably part of the cost is absorbed by Harrah's Casino Hotel, since the testing is considered an added attraction that brings in prospective customers. However, are people on vacation, sitting in a room with a group of strangers, holding an electronic device, and recording their feelings by pushing buttons an accurate indication of what they would do at home under normal circumstances?

These are difficult questions, many of which involve trade-offs between the cost of the research, time, and precision. Marketing managers and researchers work together to make these choices and implement the research that will meet their needs.[21]

1. After reading this chapter, what, if any, additions or modifications would you propose to this effort to test new TV shows?

2. Respondents are allowed to participate "day after day" if they enjoy the process. What are the advantages and disadvantages of this policy?

■ KEY TERMS AND CONCEPTS

Marketing research (76)
Marketing information
    system (MkIS) (77)
Decision support system
    (DSS) (79)
Database (80)

Single-source data (82)
Situation analysis (83)
Hypothesis (83)
Informal
    investigation (84)
Primary data (84)

Secondary data (84)
Survey (85)
Personal interviews (85)
Focus group (85)
Telephone survey (86)
Mail survey (87)

Observation method (87)
Experiment (88)
Test marketing (89)
Competitive
    intelligence (92)

■ QUESTIONS AND PROBLEMS

1. Explain how a marketing information system differs from a decision support system.
2. Should the task of marketing research go beyond providing data to marketing managers?
3. Shortly after a patient used a credit card to pay a bill at a dentist's office, she received a telephone solicitation for dental insurance. This suggests that the credit card company is developing a database using the specific purchasing activity of cardholders and selling it. Does this raise an issue of invasion of privacy?
4. Evaluate surveys, observation, and experimentation as methods of gathering primary data in the following projects:
    a. A sporting goods retailer wants to determine college students' brand preferences for skis, tennis rackets, and golf clubs.
    b. A supermarket chain wants to determine shoppers' preferences for the physical layout of fixtures and traffic patterns, particularly around checkout counters.
    c. A manufacturer of conveyor belts wants to know who makes buying decisions for his product among present and prospective users.
5. Using the steps in the research process from the text, describe how you would go about investigating the feasibility of a copy shop adjacent to your campus.
6. Would it be appropriate to interview 200 students as they left their college football stadium about their feelings toward funding for athletics and then generalize the results to the student body? Why or why not?
7. If you were designing an academic program for the marketing researcher of the future, what areas of study would you include?

■ HANDS-ON MARKETING

1. Assume you work for a manufacturer of a liquid glass cleaner that competes with Windex and Glass Wax. Your manager wants to determine the amount of the product that can be sold throughout the country. To help the manager in this project, prepare a report that shows the following information for your home state and, if possible, your home city or county. Carefully identify the sources you use for this information.
    a. Number of households or families.
    b. Income or buying power per family or per household.
    c. Total retail sales in the most recent year for which you can find reliable data.
    d. Total annual sales of food stores, hardware stores, and drugstores.
    e. Total number of food stores.
2. Interview the manager of the bookstore that serves your school about the marketing information system it uses (keep in mind that it may be a very informal system).
    a. What are the data sources?
    b. How are the data collected?
    c. What reports are received and on what schedule?
    d. What problems arise with the MkIS?
    e. How could the MkIS be improved?
3. A group of wealthy business executives regularly spend time each winter at a popular ski resort—Aspen, Colorado; Sun Valley, Idaho; Snow Valley, Vermont; or Squaw Valley, California. The executives were intrigued with the possibility of forming a corporation to develop and operate a large ski resort in Utah. This would be a totally new venture and would be on U.S. Forest Service land. It would be a complete resort with facilities appealing to middle- and upper-income markets. What types of information might they want to have before deciding whether to go ahead with the venture? What sources of information would be used?

CASES FOR PART 1

APPLYING THE SOCIETAL MARKETING CONCEPT

Can an organization successfully implement the societal marketing concept? Ben & Jerry's ice cream is a company that has made a concern for the environment and a variety of social causes integral to the way it does business. Its mission has translated into actions such as developing Rainforest Crunch ice cream to help preserve the Brazilian rainforest, publishing a social performance evaluation right in the annual report, and implementing the company's credo: "Turning Values into Value."

In 1978, with the help of a $5 correspondence course in ice cream making from Pennsylvania State University, Ben Cohen and Jerry Greenfield invested $12,000 and opened a homemade ice cream parlor in a converted gas station in Burlington, Vermont. The next year they began delivering ice cream to grocery stores and restaurants. Another milestone was passed in 1985 when the company moved to a 43,000-square-foot facility in Waterbury, Vermont, where up to 400,000 gallons of ice cream could be produced each month. A second facility was opened in Springfield, Vermont, in 1988. Ben & Jerry's opened its own distribution center in Rockingham, Vermont, and a third manufacturing facility in St. Albans, Vermont. By 1994 the company employed 500 people and sales exceeded $150 million.

From the beginning, Ben & Jerry's operated more like a nonprofit company than a company concerned about profit. Ben Cohen described the business orientation as "caring capitalism." According to caring capitalism, money linked to social purpose can be an opportunity to do good. A basic tenet of caring capitalism is to connect with the customer. To do this Ben & Jerry's uses computer technology to build a customer database. The database is used to secure customer feedback on new products (over 100 prototypes are produced each year), and to involve its customers in the company's social projects.

The Ben and Jerry Foundation was established in 1985 after the company reached $10 million in sales. The company donates 7.5 percent of its pretax earnings to the foundation. The foundation makes awards to nonprofit and charitable organizations for projects that are "models for social change, projects infused with a spirit of generosity and hopefulness. . . ." In addition, Ben & Jerry's buys milk from Vermont dairy farmers for more than the market price because, in the owners' opinion, dairy farmers need the money more than the company needs profit.

In 1988, the following mission statement was adopted by the company:

Ben & Jerry's is dedicated to the creation and demonstration of a new corporate concept of linked prosperity. Our mission consists of three interrelated parts:

- *Product mission:* To make, distribute, and sell the finest quality, all-natural ice cream and related products in a wide variety of innovative flavors made from Vermont dairy products.

- *Social mission:* To operate the company in a way that actively recognizes the central role that business plays in the structure of society by initiating innovative ways to improve the quality of life of a broad community—local, national, and international.

- *Economic mission:* To operate the company on a sound financial basis of profitable growth, increasing value for our shareholders, and creating career opportunities and financial rewards for our employees.

In keeping with the social component of its mission statement, Rainforest Crunch ice cream was introduced in 1989 when Ben Cohen met anthropologist Jason Clay at a party after a Grateful Dead Rainforest Benefit concert. Cohen was looking for a distinctive nut to put into a new brittle ice cream. Clay mentioned he was involved in Cultural Survival Enterprises, a project attempting to preserve the rainforest by harvesting its fruits and nuts. Ben & Jerry's soon began purchasing nuts from a cooperative operated by forest people. To promote its involvement in saving the rainforest, the label of Rainforest Crunch contains the following message: "Money from these nuts will help Brazilian forest peoples start a nut shelling cooperative that they own and operate."

Peace Pops ice cream and frozen yogurt bars were developed in 1992. Peace Pops are packaged in wrappers and cartons made of recycled material. Each wrapper contains a message encouraging social involvement. The messages are written in vegetable- or water-based inks to symbolize the company's concern for the environment.

Ben & Jerry's customers are loyal, as indicated by an incident when the company entered the Boston market in 1983. Giant Häagen-Dazs threatened distributors with the loss of their business if they carried Ben & Jerry's ice cream, something no distributor could afford. Ben & Jerry's responded by taking out advertisements in *Rolling Stone*, asking readers to "help two Vermont hippies fight

the giant Pillsbury headquarters in Minneapolis." After receiving a large number of calls from outraged consumers, Häagen-Dazs backed off, allowing Ben & Jerry's to establish itself in the Boston market.

Other unconventional marketing activities have been used to reinforce customer loyalty. For example, in 1992 the company held daily circus performances where customers could taste new ice cream flavors. Plant tours provide a personal approach to building customer loyalty. Over 200,000 people a year visit the Waterbury ice cream plant.

Ben & Jerry's entered the Russian market in 1992. The company implemented its social mission from the start. As a goodwill gesture, it invested $500,000 in a plant in Russia to produce high-quality ice cream using mostly local ingredients. Because Russia lacks a developed wholesale-distribution system, expanding the market for its products required that the company invest in creating a new distribution system including purchasing trucks and training employees at stores that sell its ice cream. The extra costs of distribution are reflected in the price of its ice cream. However, Ben & Jerry's plans to keep the quality high in hopes that fickle Russian consumers will become loyal to its brand.

The phenomenal growth of Ben & Jerry's suggests that social responsibility and profit are compatible. However, in 1994 the company recorded its first loss, $1.9 million. At the 1995 shareholders' meeting, Cohen stated, "You know, people talk about how our social mission is affecting our profits negatively. But I want you to know that's a false dichotomy. Our social mission does not detract from our profits. Our social mission adds to our profits. This year is a test. But we will stay true to our roots, true to our soul, true to our dreams for the common good."

Critics charge that Ben & Jerry's mission of social responsibility is nothing more than a gimmick to appeal to the social conscience of gullible customers. For example, in 1993 La Soul, a minority-run supplier that employed recovering addicts, entered into an agreement to supply Ben & Jerry's with ingredients for its Low-Fat Apple Pie frozen yogurt. La Soul sold Ben & Jerry's $1.5 million in ingredients and received technical and financial support from the company. However, when sales of the flavor did not fulfill expectations, La Soul was dropped as a supplier leaving it $500,000 in debt. Understandably upset, Rev. James Carter of La Soul said, "Ben and Jerry's used us to sell ice cream. We've been discarded by a company that preaches caring capitalism." In fact, packages of Low-Fat Apple Pie frozen yogurt did describe the La Soul connection.

In 1993, the company admitted that some of its products contained artificial ingredients in spite of labels that listed all the ingredients as natural. Ben & Jerry's discovered the labeling error while responding to revised Food and Drug Administration (FDA) rules requiring companies to examine the precise ingredients of their products. However, FDA rules regulating the labeling of artificial ingredients had been in effect for several years. Furthermore, the company took advantage of an FDA rule allowing old packaging stock to be used before requiring new packaging with accurate labels.

In the case of Rainforest Crunch, at first the forest peoples cooperative was able to meet the demand for the nuts used in the ice cream. However, as the sales of the flavor grew, Ben & Jerry's ended up purchasing over 95 percent of the nuts from commercial suppliers, including the Matran family who has been alleged in the Brazilian press to have killed labor organizers. Ben & Jerry's removed "forest peoples" from the label of Rainforest Crunch in 1994 after some controversy about what was best for the people living in the rainforest.

In the summer of 1994, Ben & Jerry's initiated a search for a new CEO with the "Yo, I'm Your CEO" contest. The contest allowed anyone to apply by writing in 100 words or less why he or she would make the best CEO. The winner would receive the job and the runner-up got ice cream for life. Over 25,000 applications were submitted. On February 1, 1995, a press release announced Bob Holland as the winner. Attached to the press release was a poem Holland had written. What wasn't disclosed was the fact that the poem was written a month *after* he was selected. Also, a month *after* announcing the contest, Ben & Jerry's hired an executive search firm that found Holland. Company officials commented they didn't lie about the search firm; they just didn't mention it.

Given the low-growth forecasts for the U.S. ice cream market, it will be difficult for Ben & Jerry's to maintain its market share. However, financial results from 1995 indicate that earnings for the company are up over 1994. One thing is clear—in spite of recent criticism, the company doesn't intend to change its social mission and will continue to attempt to operate in a socially responsible fashion.

http://www.benjerry.com/

QUESTIONS

1. Why does Ben & Jerry's notion of "caring capitalism" attract so much attention?
2. What environmental forces are having an impact on the ice cream market? How likely are these forces to change the way Ben & Jerry's operates?
3. Would you describe any of Ben & Jerry's behavior as unethical?

Sources: "About Ben & Jerry's," Ben & Jerry's Public Relations Office; Neela Banerjee, "Ben & Jerry's Is Discovering That It's No Joke to Sell Ice Cream to Russians," *The Wall Street Journal*, Sept. 19, 1995, p. A18; Nick Gilbert, "1-800-22 Ethic," *Financial World*, Aug. 16, 1994, p. 20; "Ben & Jerry's: A Firm with a View," *Packaging Digest*, January 1993, p. 50; Murray Raphel, "What's the Scoop on Ben & Jerry's?" *Direct Marketing*, August 1994, p. 23; Gail Rosenbaum, "Different Drummer: Ben & Jerry's Preaches Peace, Profits and Ice Cream for Everyone," *Dairy Foods*, June 1992, p. 40; Hanna Rosin, "Here's the Scoop: Ben & Jerry's Progressive Image May Be Just So Much Hype," *Sacramento Bee*, Sept. 3, 1995, p. F1; and Andrew E. Serwer, "Ben & Jerry's: Corporate Ogre," *Fortune*, July 10, 1995, p. 30.

CASE 2   *Coke versus Pepsi*

COMPETING FOR AN ADVANTAGE

Coca-Cola and Pepsi-Cola are battling for supremacy of the global soft drink market. Consider the stakes: In the U.S. alone, the beverage market is valued at over $30 *billion* a year at the wholesale level.

Status Report

The creativity and effectiveness of each company's marketing strategy will ultimately determine the winner with respect to sales, profits, and customer loyalty. Currently, Coca-Cola leads on most counts. As of 1994, it held a 42 percent share of the U.S. soft drink market, compared to Pepsi's 32 percent. Coca-Cola's flagship brand, Coca-Cola Classic, grabbed 20 percent alone; the overall #3 brand, Diet Coke, added 9 percent. Pepsi-Cola's flagship brand, Pepsi, had an 18 percent share; its diet drink, Diet Pepsi, was the fifth leading seller with 6 percent.

The battle between Coca-Cola and Pepsi-Cola has spilled over into other beverage categories as well. In the ready-to-drink tea category, Pepsi-Cola's Lipton brand led with a 31 percent share, while Coca-Cola's Nestea brand is third with 21 percent. Competition is keen in the sports drink category as well. Coca-Cola's Powerade, with a 10 percent share, is in the #2 position behind Quaker Oats' Gatorade. Pepsi-Cola's All Sport is third with 5 percent. With its Minute-Maid, Hi-C, and Fruitopia brands, Coca-Cola leads in the juice category, with 25 percent of the market. In contrast, Pepsi's Ocean Spray juice drinks have just 5 percent.

To some extent, Coca-Cola's and Pepsi-Cola's brands appeal to different groups of consumers. For example, in terms of age and ethnicity, blacks aged 8 to 18 choose Coke brands over Pepsi brands by a margin of 35 to 28 percent. However, there are no differences in preferences among Hispanics in the same age group.

In some older age groups, there are more pronounced differences. Blacks aged 19 to 24 tend to consume more of Pepsi's brands (39 to 27 percent), while Hispanics in that age group consume more of Coke's brands (44 to 31 percent). Among people aged 35 to 49, Pepsi-Cola is favored over Coca-Cola by a wide margin—41 to 32 percent among blacks and 43 to 34 percent among Hispanics.

Distinctive Strategies and Styles

The two companies rely on somewhat different marketing strategies. As the market leader, Coca-Cola was rather slow in developing and bringing new products to market. In the early 1990s, however, the company began to introduce numerous products in most beverage categories. Among the recent introductions are Powerade sport drink and Fruitopia fruit drink. New products such as these allowed the company to capture 80 percent of the growth that occurred in the U.S. soft drink market in 1995. Coca-Cola's stepped-up new-products efforts upstaged Pepsi-Cola, which typically had been the innovator in this category.

Coca-Cola's management style and organization changed along with its approach to new products. Starting in 1990, efforts were made to hire marketing executives with good track records. The company also implemented cross-training of managers so it would be more difficult for cliques to form within the company.

Pepsi-Cola's marketing strategy has been based on taking risks, acting quickly, and innovating constantly. For example, it was the first major soft-drink company to compare its brands with those of competitors in ads. Pepsi-Cola also needs ample management talent. In 1993, with that in mind, the snacks and drinks divisions began to exchange personnel. The swaps were intended to help the company identify and seize new market opportunities.

The two companies have spent considerable amounts of money on marketing. In 1994, for instance, Coca-Cola spent $270 million on various forms of advertising, compared to Pepsi-Cola's $150 million. Expenditures on the mainstay Coca-Cola Classic and Pepsi brands were $85 million and $78 million, respectively.

Even such large marketing budgets can be used up quickly. Pepsi-Cola paid close to $1 million apiece for four 30-second commercials during the 1995 Super Bowl. The commercials were considered a great success as the name Pepsi was recalled by 53 percent of the respondents to a nationwide postgame survey. New forms of promotion are even more expensive. For example, Pepsi-Cola paid $68 million in 1995 for the right to attach its name to the new arena of the Denver Nuggets professional basketball team.

Counting on New Products

A critical part of both companies' strategies is new-product development. In 1994 Pepsi-Cola sought an edge when it introduced a mid-calorie soft drink, Pepsi XL. The brand is positioned as an innovative, fun drink. The target market is described as adventurous, outdoor types in their twenties. Pepsi XL was based on marketing research showing that numerous consumers switch between diet and regular soft drinks. Many consumers are calorie conscious but do not like the taste of diet colas. Thus Pepsi's marketing team thought a product with fewer calories could be a big hit.

Coca-Cola has matched Pepsi-Cola's flow of new products in the 1990s. For example, Fruitopia drinks were launched in 1994 with a marketing budget of $30 million. The brand achieved first-year sales of $60 million. Its success is based on providing customers with unusual flavors and a sense of fun. Within 1 year of its introduction, Fruitopia's distribution was expanded to seven countries.

Product development at both companies has not always gone smoothly. In fact, Coca-Cola had one of the biggest new-product foul-ups of all time. In spring 1985, the firm's senior vice president of marketing announced at a Coca-Cola bottlers' meeting that the formula for Coke was being changed. The intent of the change was to appeal to a younger target market. About $4 million was spent on marketing research between 1982 and 1985 to develop the new formula. The research included 200,000 blind taste tests. However, not all the taste tests used the same formula, and none of the participants was asked whether or not Coke's long-standing formula should be changed.

Almost immediately after the change, it was evident the new Coke formula was going to fail. That was easy to figure out when most consumers were ignoring the reformulated drink, choosing instead to buy up inventories of the original Coke! Other customers wrote or called Coca-Cola's headquarters demanding that the company bring back the old formula. On July 10, 1985, Coca-Cola announced the original formula would come back as Coca-Cola Classic. Now the "New Coke" has less than a 1 percent market share, while Coke Classic enjoys the largest portion of the soft drink market.

There's no guarantee that new products will succeed. Hence, it's not surprising that Pepsi-Cola has had its share of failures as well. The flops have included Pepsi Light in 1975, Pepsi Free in 1982, Pepsi AM in 1988, and Crystal Pepsi in 1992.

Searching for New Markets

Growth in soft drink consumption has slowed in the U.S., Western Europe, Mexico, and Japan. Consequently, the battle between Pepsi-Cola and Coca-Cola has shifted to emerging markets such as China, Russia, and India. Coca-Cola has been the more successful in these endeavors. The company has established bottling plants in China, Hungary, Russia, Thailand, and Vietnam. Currently, Coca-Cola bottles over one-half of the soft drinks outside the U.S. Foreign operations now contribute approximately 80 percent of the company's earnings.

Pepsi-Cola's global marketing strategy began in earnest in 1972 when the company entered the Soviet Union. Soon after, it expanded into other Eastern European countries. The efforts were not very successful, however, partly because they were based on barter. Pepsi-Cola's flavor concentrate was exchanged for such products as Romanian wine and Bulgarian forklifts. There was little demand for these products outside Eastern Europe. When communism collapsed in 1989, the company was left with

old, state-owned bottling plants and an image of being part of the past regimes.

Pepsi-Cola has again used direct comparisons, this time to compete with its larger rival in foreign markets. The strategy has had mixed results. In 1994, case sales of Pepsi jumped 13 percent in Guadalajara and Monterrey, Mexico, after 100,000 consumers compared Pepsi and Coca-Cola Classic in taste tests. However, Coca-Cola was able to thwart Pepsi-Cola in Argentina because that country prohibits comparison advertising.

In expanding into foreign countries, both companies have followed the marketing concept by offering products that meet consumer needs. Focus on "the global consumer" is epitomized by the introduction of Pepsi Max. A diet cola, Pepsi Max was introduced in Europe in 1993; it was placed on sale in China and Latin America a year later. Pepsi-Cola has high hopes for Pepsi Max because diet beverages account for only 4 percent of worldwide soft drink sales.

The product's flavor was formulated specifically for foreign tastes. Extensive marketing research was conducted before Pepsi Max was launched. The studies found that over 50 percent of the soft drink consumers in Britain, Germany, and Australia would like a low-sugar soft drink if it did not have a diet taste or image. Pepsi-Cola's scientists spent 2 years mixing and experimenting to find a formula that was favored by at least 40 percent of consumers in taste tests against Coca-Cola Classic.

Pepsi Max was positioned as a soft drink without sugar, but with maximum cola taste. After 1,000 interviews in Britain, the name Max on blue and red cans was found to effectively communicate this position. Pepsi-Cola distributed 3.5 million free cans of Max to stimulate trial of the product. A very high follow-up purchase rate, 80 percent, was achieved. Backed by an initial marketing budget of $40 million, Pepsi-Cola expects sales of Max to approach $1 billion within a few years.

Looking Ahead

Besides battling each other, both companies strive to stay one step ahead of smaller soft-drink companies. Risks must be taken, but—at the same time—disastrous failures that damage profits and image must be avoided. Prerequisites for success will be detecting changes in the environment and then developing and implementing marketing programs that satisfy consumers' shifting needs.

http://www.coca-cola.com/
http://www.pepsi.com/

QUESTIONS

1. What dimensions of their external and internal environments most affect Coca-Cola's and Pepsi-Cola's market opportunities and marketing strategies?

2. Based on the information in the case, apply the five-step process of strategic marketing planning to Pepsi XL.

3. Describe a research project that would determine how popular the taste of Pepsi XL is in comparison to Diet Pepsi.

Sources: Robert Frank, "Fruity Teas and Mystical Sodas Are Boring Consumers," *The Wall Street Journal*, Oct. 9, 1995, p. B1; Ernest Beck, "Where West Faced East, Colas Now War," *The Wall Street Journal*, Sept. 7, 1995, p. A9; Robert Frank, "Coca-Cola Is Shedding Its Once-Stodgy Image with Swift Expansion," The *Wall Street Journal*, Aug. 22, 1995, p. A1; Karen Benezra, "Diet Cola Daze," *BrandWeek*, Apr. 17, 1995, p. 32; "Beverage . . . By the Numbers," *BrandWeek*, Apr. 17, 1995, p. 48; Leah Rickard, "Remembering New Coke," *Advertising Age*, Apr. 17, 1995, p. C-16; Eleena de Lisser, "Pepsi to Spend Millions to Put Name on Arena," *The Wall Street Journal*, Mar. 3, 1995, p. B1; and Patricia Sellers, "Pepsi Opens a Second Front," *Fortune*, Aug. 8, 1994, pp. 70+.

PART TWO

Target Markets

So far you've learned that virtually all successful organizations are oriented toward satisfying their customers. You have also explored the environmental forces that affect marketing decision making. And you've seen how strategic planning is used to match an organization's resources with its market opportunities. We now move to an examination of customers—both individuals and organizations.

It stands to reason that an organization must determine who its potential customers are. Only after these customers are identified can the firm's management develop a marketing mix to satisfy their wants.

We will now investigate how an organization identifies its intended customers—its target markets. To do this, we begin with a description of the consumer market and consumer decision making in Chapter 5. Chapter 6 covers the business market and organizational buying behavior. Then, in Chapter 7, we introduce the concepts of market segmentation and target-market strategies.

Consumer Markets and Buying Behavior

Do Population Changes Suggest
AVON
Faces a Make-Over?

Avon was founded in 1886 when David McConnell hired a housewife to sell perfume door-to-door in Winchester, New Hampshire. For the next 65 years the company's marketing formula remained essentially the same: Hire housewives who want flexible hours and extra income to sell cosmetics to their neighbors. The concept was successful largely due to personal contact. With her regular visits to home-bound women, the "Avon Lady" made friends who developed into loyal customers. In the process, Avon's U.S. sales grew to $1.5 billion, much of it generated by 415,000 sales representatives.

However, times have changed. As the number of working women has increased, fewer potential customers can be found at home. In addition, with the average order at $20 or less, Avon reps find they have to work many hours to earn as much as they could at some other job.

With business stagnating, Avon has attempted several alternative marketing approaches. One was a program of offering products directly to customers through direct-mail ads and toll-free telephone numbers. The approach troubled the reps who disliked being bypassed, but Avon argued that it would attract new customers by appealing to people who preferred not to deal directly with an Avon representative. Despite considerable advertising support, the program was less successful than Avon executives had hoped. Because of its long reliance on personal selling, Avon found it had not developed a strong enough brand image to generate sales with ads alone.

Another approach was to create a multilevel personal selling structure. This is a common strategy of direct-sales firms in which representatives get a percentage of the sales of new reps they recruit and train. The move was intended to significantly increase the number of reps in the field. However, striving to increase their commissions, too many reps pushed their recruits to engage in high-pressure sales tactics. The result was a damaged reputation for Avon.

Still another strategy attempted was to add new products to the Avon line. Health care products, vitamins, lingerie, and clothing items have been offered by the reps and through direct-mail catalogs.[1]

How should Avon respond to changes that are taking place in the female population?

http://www.avon.com/

The total market may be divided into two broad segments, consumers and businesses. In this chapter we examine the consumer market, and in Chapter 6 we will discuss the business market. First, we will describe today's consumers, highlighting recent demographic changes that are influencing marketing. As Avon has discovered, these changes can have profound effects on performance. Then we will examine how consumers go about making purchase decisions, a process influenced by information sources, social environment, psychological forces, and situational factors.

After studying this chapter, you should be able to explain:

CHAPTER GOALS

- The factors that are commonly used by marketers to describe the consumer market.
- Important changes taking place within the consumer market.
- How consumers make purchase decisions.

The Consumer Market

Ultimate consumers buy goods and services for their own personal or household use. In the U.S., there are over 260 million consumers, living in 96 million households. They spend over $4.3 trillion a year on goods and services. The efforts of many marketers are focused on these (or more likely a subset of these) potential customers.

The composition of the consumer market is constantly changing. Consider that every hour the U.S. experiences 460 births, 250 deaths, and 100 new immigrants.[2] That means the mix of consumers is changing by over half a million people a month. Thus, the first challenge is to develop an understanding of what this market looks like and how it is changing. To develop an appreciation of this dynamic consumer market, we will examine its geographic distribution and several demographic dimensions.

Geographic Distribution

Marketing executives monitor current patterns and projected trends in the regional distribution of the population in order to plan their strategies. Figure 5-1 shows the projected changes in the population between 1980 and 2000. The biggest markets are in the East North Central, South Atlantic, and Middle Atlantic regions. These three regions together account for a little over half the nation's population. However, the greatest rate of population growth over the past four decades has occurred in the Southern and Western regions. By the year 2000 the three most populous states will be California, Texas, and Florida, in that order.

The Rural Population. The U.S. rural population declined steadily for many years, but this trend seems to have reversed. In the 1990s nearly four times as many Americans have taken up residence in rural areas as in the 1980s. Rural areas, although they contain only about one-fourth the total population, are now growing at nearly the same rate as cities. There are several explanations for this development. One is the growth in employment opportunities on the outer edges of large urban areas. People can take advantage of these jobs while still living in the country. Another factor is the growing number of retirees who are leaving the cities for rural areas with smaller communities and slower-paced life-styles.

Rather than view the increasing popularity of rural living as a temporary adjust-

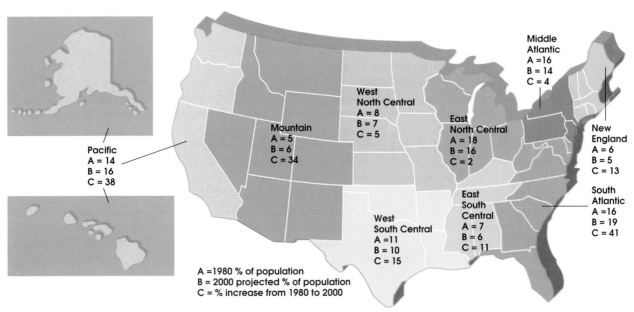

Middle
Atlantic
A =16
B = 14
C = 4

West
North Central
A = 8
B = 7
C = 5

East
North Central
A = 18
B = 16
C = 2

New
England
A = 6
B = 5
C = 13

Mountain
A = 5
B = 6
C = 34

Pacific
A = 14
B = 16
C = 38

East
South
Central
A = 7
B = 6
C = 11

South
Atlantic
A =16
B = 19
C = 41

West
South Central
A =11
B = 10
C = 15

A =1980 % of population
B = 2000 projected % of population
C = % increase from 1980 to 2000

FIGURE 5-1

Population distribution
in 1980, the projected
growth by 2000, and
the percentage
change in population
by regions.

*Source: Statistical Abstract of the
United States: 1995*, 115th ed.,
U.S. Bureau of the Census, Washington, DC, 1995, pp. 28, 34.

ment, some see it as a long-term, gradual deconcentration of the U.S. population. With advances in communication technology and the decline in industrial jobs, the need for people to concentrate in small areas is greatly diminished. As a result, the population may be slowly moving toward a country of smaller, more widely dispersed cities and towns. Certainly it is something to watch because such a change would have many implications. For example, it would be unfortunate for retailers with large stores and large mall operators who depend on masses of customers. On the other hand, this could be a good development for catalog retailers and merchants using the Internet to reach customers.[3]

The Urban Population. About 75 percent of the U.S. population live in large urban areas. Recognizing the importance of the urban population, the federal government established a three-part classification of metropolitan areas. Observing trends in these classifications provides a means of identifying growing and declining areas. The three categories are as follows:

- The **Metropolitan Statistical Area (MSA)** is the basic unit. An MSA has an urban population center of at least 50,000 and a total MSA population of at least 100,000. The boundaries of an MSA are drawn along county lines and may cross state borders. But the counties must be socially and economically integrated, and virtually all employment must be nonagricultural. There are about 325 MSAs. Of the 25 areas projected to grow at the fastest rate between now and 2005, only two (Orem, Utah, and Tacoma, Washington) are outside the South or Southwest.[4]

- A **Primary Metropolitan Statistical Area (PMSA)** is an MSA that has a population of at least 1 million. About 80 of the largest MSAs are categorized as PMSAs.

- A **Consolidated Metropolitan Statistical Area (CMSA)** is a giant urban center consisting of two or more adjacent PMSAs. The hub of each of the approximately 25 CMSAs is a very large city such as New York, Los Angeles, Chicago, or Philadelphia.

The Suburban Population.   As metropolitan areas have grown, their composition has also changed. The central cities are growing very slowly, and in some cases older, established parts of the cities are actually losing population. Much of the real growth is occurring in the suburbs of these cities. As families have moved to the suburbs, the economic, racial, and ethnic compositions of many cities (especially the core areas) are considerably different from their adjacent suburbs. For example, 60 percent of black households live in the central cities of large metro areas, but only 25 percent of black households reside in the suburbs. The changes in these areas have had several market implications.

First, some retailers have followed consumers from the cities to the suburbs. Since a great percentage of suburban people live in single-family residences, there is a vastly expanded market for lawn mowers, lawn furniture, home furnishings, and home repair products. Suburbanites are more likely to need two cars than city dwellers. They also are inclined to spend more leisure time at home, so there is a bigger market for home entertainment and recreation items.

Second, service organizations typically locate close to their markets. That's why personal service firms such as banks, fast-food establishments, florists, and travel agents open branches or start new ventures in the suburbs. In addition, many investment and insurance brokers, realtors, physicians and dentists, and other professional service firms have left the central cities. Some theaters, sports arenas, and other entertainment centers have closed their downtown sites and relocated in the suburbs.

A GLOBAL PERSPECTIVE

WILL TEENS BE THE ENTRÉE INTO GLOBAL MARKETING?

Advertising agencies such as DMB&B and marketing research firms such as Simmons Market Research Bureau are examining teen markets around the world to identify similarities and differences in consumer behavior. The reason is simple—huge numbers. There are about 30 million teenagers in the U.S., compared to 50 million in Europe; 57 million in Mexico, Brazil, and Argentina; and 42 million in Japan, Korea, Singapore, and Vietnam.

What they have found are some striking similarities. Linked by television that offers much of the same programming worldwide, increased international travel by young people, and global events such as the Olympics and soccer's World Cup, teens worldwide choose many of the same brands of clothing, electronic products, soft drinks, and fast food.

Participation sports are also uniting teens. Basketball continues to grow in popularity in Europe and South America, while soccer has increased in popularity in the U.S. Along with the sports come the athletes as product endorsers—a strategy particularly effective with teens.

But teens worldwide are not a single market yet. Ten years ago many European teens selected American brands to emulate their U.S. counterparts. Now, with greater economic unity in Europe, they have developed a stronger European identity and use more European brands.

Asian and European teens also dislike many American ads that are heavy on superlatives and brand comparisons. They prefer more subtle messages.

Sources: Shawn Tully, "Teens The Most Global Market of All," *Fortune*, May 16, 1994, pp. 90–97; and Cyndee Miller, "Teens Seen as the First Truly Global Consumers," *Marketing News*, Mar. 27, 1995, p. 9.

Third, the slow but steady migration of large retailers to the suburbs has created a void in the inner cities. Dissatisfied with the limited selection and higher prices of the remaining small independent stores, many inner-city residents make long shopping trips to the suburbs.

Consumer Demographics

Demographics are the vital statistics that describe a population. Popular demographic characteristics include age, gender, family life cycle, education, income, and ethnicity. They are important to marketers because they are closely related to the demand for many products. Changes in demographics signal the rise of new markets and the elimination of others. They help us anticipate the needs and wants of the population.

Age. Marketing executives need to be aware of how the population is changing with respect to age. For example, in the mid-1980s, for the first time in our history, the number of Americans aged 65 and over exceeded the number of teenagers. Looking ahead to the year 2000, there will be 275 million Americans, an increase of 26 million from 1990, and the average age of the population will continue to increase.

Table 5-1 will help you appreciate how the age distribution of the population changes over time. There are several things to notice about the data in the table. First, there are some quite dramatic swings in the population. For example, the number of people aged 45 to 54 will increase by 46 percent from 1990 to 2000. Changes in the age distribution are the result of several factors, including the quality of health care and nutrition. However, two key factors are the number of women who are of childbearing age at a specific point in time and the birth rate. The number of women of childbearing age is a function of the births that took place some years before, and it is therefore highly predictable. However, the birth rate is influenced by a wide variety of social and economic factors that are much less predictable.

A second point is that peaks and valleys in the population distribution move through time. For example, the 46 percent increase in 45-to-54-year-olds in 1990 to 2000 becomes a nearly identical increase in 55-to-64-year-olds in 2000 to 2010.

TABLE 5-1 Projected changes in the distribution of the U.S. population

	Percent change	
	1990–2000	**2000–2010**
Growth in the total population	7.1%	5.3%
Under 5 years old	−8.2	0.0
5–17 years old	7.0	−6.3
18–24 years old	−3.5	7.6
25–34 years old	−15.4	1.1
35–44 years old	15.9	−15.3
45–54 years old	46.0	16.1
55–64 years old	13.1	46.7
65–74 years old	−0.7	15.3
75 years old and above	26.2	10.1

Source: Adapted from James E. Person, Jr., ed., "Total Population by Age, Sex, and Race, 1995–2010," *Statistical Forecast of the United States*, Gale Research, Detroit, 1993, pp. 601–602.

Therefore, it is possible to track changes and, to the extent that behavior is related to age, anticipate what impacts they will have.

Gender.   At one time gender differences in marketing were quite distinct, but the lines are not as clear as they used to be. Two factors are particularly significant in this movement. One is the steady growth in working women and the other is the increasing overlap of male and female roles.

The number of women (married or single) working outside the home continues to increase. About three-fourths of women in their twenties and about one-half of women with children under 6 years old are working outside the home. By the year 2000 over 60 percent of women over 16 years old will be working outside the home. This is significant to marketers because the life-styles and buying behavior of women in the outside labor force are quite different from those of homemakers.

A challenge for marketers is to remember that women are now major purchasers of what were once male-dominated products such as insurance, mutual funds, cars, and business travel. In an interesting reversal, for the first time ever, women are now buying more athletic shoes than men.[5]

In another role shift, men are doing more grocery shopping. This is meaningful because it is a traditionally female role, and because the behavior of male and female grocery shoppers is so different. In the supermarket, men make more unplanned purchases, are less brand loyal, and less price conscious. They buy more beer, ice cream, and hot dogs, and less cottage cheese, yogurt, and salad dressing. These and other differences have implications for what products are offered, how they are advertised and displayed, and the selection of items to promote.[6]

Family Life Cycle.   **Family life-cycle stages**, the various forms families can take over time, are major determinants of behavior. A single-parent family (divorced, widowed, or never married) with dependent children faces social and economic problems quite different from those of a two-parent family. Young married couples with no children typically devote large shares of their income to clothing, autos, and recreation. When children start arriving, expenditure patterns shift as many young families buy and furnish a home. Families with teenagers find larger portions of the budget going for food, clothing, and educational needs.

Researchers have identified nine distinct life-cycle stages with different buying behavior:[7]

- *Bachelor stage*: young, single people
- *Young married*: couples with no children
- *Full nest I*: young married couples with children
- *Single parents*: young or middle-aged people with dependent children
- *Divorced and alone*: divorced without dependent children
- *Middle-aged married*: middle-aged married couples without children
- *Full nest II*: middle-aged married couples with dependent children
- *Empty nest*: older married couples with no children living with them
- *Older single*: single people still working or retired

Two rapidly growing groups that reflect our changing life-styles are singles and mingles—unmarried couples of the opposite sex living together. The Census Bureau reports that over 73 million adults are unmarried, nearly twice as many as in 1970. The number of singles households is also increasing at a much faster rate than family households. The impact that single people of either sex have on the market is demonstrated by such goods and services as apartments for singles, social

http://www.campbellsoups.com/

clubs for singles, and special tours, cruises, and eating places seeking the patronage of singles.

Singles in the 25-to-39 age bracket are especially attractive to marketers because they are such a large and affluent group. However, marketing to singles can be tricky. As Campbell Soup found out, even a good product can send the wrong message. When its Soup for One, a single-serving can of soup, didn't do well, a focus group explained why. Participants called it the "lonely soup." They liked the product but hated the name, because it reminded them that they would be eating alone.[8]

The number of mingles more than doubled between 1980 and 1993, reaching a total of 3.5 million couples. They still represent only a small part (3.5 percent) of all households. Nevertheless, the social and demographic phenomenon of mingles bears watching.[9]

Education and Income. Education has a significant impact on income. A high school diploma is worth about $600,000 in additional income over a lifetime, and a college degree is worth $1.5 million. For families where both spouses work (that is, over half the 54 million couples in the U.S.), these earnings figures can be doubled. About 80 percent of Americans over 25 have completed high school, and 20 percent have at least a bachelor's degree. Combine these observations with the fact that nearly 15 million Americans are enrolled in institutions of higher learning, an increase of 50 percent over just 20 years ago, and it suggests that the U.S. population is well educated and prosperous.

However, these figures don't represent the complete picture. In spite of the considerable increase in disposable income in the past 30 years, 37 million people (about 12 percent of the population) live below the government-defined poverty level. And the situation may get worse. It was recently reported that 90 million Americans over age 16 lack the basic skills necessary to hold a moderately demanding job.[10] Besides impacting earning potential, the skill deficiencies are also likely to affect these consumers' ability to perform such marketing-related tasks as reading package labels, understanding advertising messages, and following product directions.

Knowing what is happening to incomes is important because spending patterns are influenced by how much income people have. To illustrate the differences, the expenditure patterns of three income groups are compared in Table 5-2.

TABLE 5-2 Buying patterns by income group

Category	Income group		
	Lowest 20%	Middle 20%	Highest 20%
Average annual expenditures	**$13,464**	**$26,144**	**$57,597**
	Percent of total		
Housing, utilities, and furnishings	36	31	29
Transportation	14	18	16
Food	17	15	12
Clothing	6	6	6
Health care	8	6	4
Insurance and pensions	2	9	14
Other goods and services	17	15	19
Total expenditures	100	100	100

Source: Compiled from data in *Statistical Abstract of the United States: 1993*, 113th ed., U.S. Bureau of the Census, Washington, DC, 1993, pp. 454–455.

Here are some findings from Department of Labor studies of consumer spending:

- For all product categories, people in a given income bracket spend significantly more *total* dollars than those in lower brackets. However, the lower-income households devote a larger *percentage* of their total expenditures to some product categories, such as housing.
- In each successively higher-income group, the amount spent for food declines as a percentage of total expenditures.
- The percentage of total expenditures devoted to the total of housing, utilities, and home operation remains reasonably constant in the middle- and high-income brackets.
- The percentage of total expenditures for transportation, including the purchase of automobiles, tends to grow as incomes increase in low- and middle-income groups. The proportion levels off or drops a bit in higher-income brackets.
- In each successively higher-income group, a smaller percentage of total family expenditures goes for health care, but a higher percentage goes for insurance and pensions.

Ethnicity.   In many cities, the ethnic population is especially large. African Americans, Hispanics, and Asians constitute over 50 percent of the population in 25 of the nation's largest cities. These cities include Los Angeles, San Antonio, New Orleans, Miami, Atlanta, Baltimore, Washington, D.C., Detroit, and Chicago. During the 1990s, ethnic minorities will account for nearly 70 percent of total U.S. population growth.[11]

There are over 30 million African Americans with a combined buying power of more than $170 billion. According to estimates of the U.S. Census Bureau, the group will be 50 percent larger by the year 2025.

Another ethnic group that is well worth studying is made up of 20 million Hispanic people. This group is large and is increasing at a rapid rate. In fact, by the year 2000, Hispanics are expected to be the largest minority group in the U.S. Hispanics tend to be geographically concentrated in New York City, Miami, California, and the Southwest.

There are over 8 million Asians in the U.S., and the number is expected to grow to 17 million by 2010. As with other ethnic groups, Asians in the U.S. come from many different cultures and countries.

This broad overview of the consumer market should suggest to you its vibrancy and diversity. It also indicates that there are many ways to describe consumers. A challenge faced by marketers, which we will discuss in detail in Chapter 7, is how to most effectively describe particular markets. But first, let's continue our examination of consumers with a look at their decision making.

Consumer Decision Making

Why is consumer marketing difficult? The reason is simple: Consumers are complex and constantly changing. Not only is it difficult to anticipate what marketing program will work, but what worked yesterday may not work today. This is reflected in Avon's marketing efforts to women. There is still a strong market for cosmetics, but because of changes in their lives, women buy them differently today

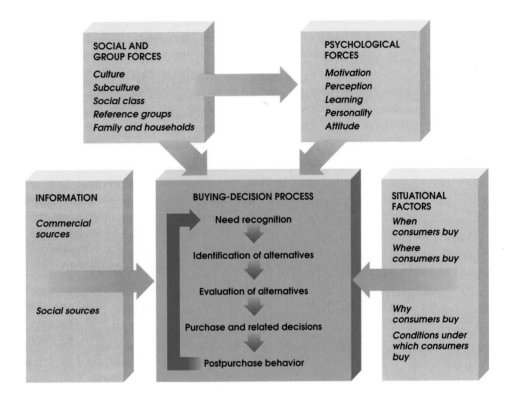

FIGURE 5-2

The consumer buying-decision process and the factors that influence it.

than they did in the past. Thus, a marketer like Avon must constantly improve its understanding of consumers and adapt its strategy.

Figure 5-2 brings all the dimensions of buying behavior together in a model that provides the structure for our discussion. The model features the buying-decision process and the four primary forces that influence each stage.

The Buying-Decision Process

To deal with the marketing environment and make purchases, consumers engage in a decision process. One way to look at that process is to view it as problem solving. When faced with a problem that can be resolved through a purchase ("I'm bored. How do I satisfy my need for entertainment?"), the consumer goes through a series of logical stages to arrive at a decision.

As shown in the center of Figure 5-2, the stages of the **buying-decision process** are:

1. *Need recognition.* The consumer is moved to action by a need.
2. *Identification of alternatives.* The consumer identifies alternative products and brands and collects information about them.
3. *Evaluation of alternatives.* The consumer weighs the pros and cons of the alternatives identified.
4. *Decision.* The consumer decides to buy or not to buy and makes other decisions related to the purchase.
5. *Postpurchase behavior.* The consumer seeks reassurance that the choice made was the correct one.

Though this model is a useful starting point for examining purchase decisions, the process is not always as straightforward as it may appear. Consider these possible variations:

- The consumer can withdraw at any stage prior to the actual purchase if the need diminishes or no satisfactory alternatives are available.
- The stages usually are different lengths and may overlap.
- The consumer is often involved in several different buying decisions simultaneously, and the outcome of one can affect the others.

A significant factor influencing how consumer decisions are made is the consumer's **level of involvement** or the amount of effort that is expended in satisfying a need. Some situations are *high* involvement. That is, when a need arises a consumer decides to actively collect and evaluate information about the purchase situation. These purchases entail all five stages of the buying-decision process.

Though it is risky to generalize since consumers are so different, involvement tends to be *greater* under any of the following conditions:

- The consumer lacks information about alternatives for satisfying the need.
- The consumer considers the amount of money involved to be large.
- The product has considerable social importance.
- The product is seen as having a potential for providing significant benefits.

Most buying decisions are for relatively low-priced products that have close, acceptable substitutes and therefore do not meet any of these conditions. These are *low*-involvement situations, in which the consumer either skips or moves very quickly through stages 2 and 3 of the decision process—identification of alternatives and evaluation of alternatives. Typical examples of low-involvement situations are the majority of purchases made in supermarkets, variety stores, and hardware stores. However, for a wealthy person the purchase of a country club membership could be a low-involvement experience, while for a person with a high need for social acceptance, purchasing toothpaste might be highly involving. Thus involvement must be viewed from the perspective of the consumer, not the product.

Impulse buying, or purchasing with little or no advance planning, is a form of low-involvement decision making. A shopper waiting in the checkout line at a grocery store who notices the headline "Plane Missing since 1939 Lands at LaGuardia" on an issue of *Weekly World News* and purchases a copy to satisfy his curiosity is engaging in impulse buying. Self-service, open-display retailing has conditioned shoppers to do more impulse buying. Consider, for example, how many of your purchases are unplanned (or impulsive). Because of the growth of this type of low-involvement purchasing, greater emphasis must be placed on promotional programs such as in-store videos demonstrating product benefits. Also, displays and packages must be made appealing, since they serve as silent sales people.

In the following discussion we examine the complete five-stage process that characterizes high-involvement buying decisions. However, keep in mind that the stages may have to be adjusted to fit the circumstances of a particular purchase situation.

Recognition of an Unsatisfied Need. Everyone has unsatisfied needs and wants that create discomfort. Some needs can be satisfied by acquiring and consuming goods and services. Thus, the process of deciding what to buy begins when a need that can be satisfied through consumption becomes strong enough to motivate a person. This need recognition may arise internally (for example, when you feel hungry). Or the need may be dormant until it is aroused by an external stimulus, such as an ad or the sight of a product. The decision process can also be triggered by the depletion of an existing product (your pen runs out of ink) or dissatisfaction with a product currently being used.

Becoming aware of a need, however, is not enough to generate a purchase. As consumers we have many needs and wants, but finite amounts of time and money. Thus there is competition among our needs.

Identification of Alternatives. Once a need has been recognized, the consumer must next identify the alternatives capable of satisfying the need. First, alternative products and then alternative brands are identified. Product and brand identification may range from a simple memory scan of previous experiences to an extensive external search.

The search for alternatives is influenced by:

- How much information the consumer already has from past experiences and other sources.
- The consumer's confidence in that information.
- The expected value of additional information or, put another way, what more information is worth in terms of the time and money to get it.

Evaluation of Alternatives. Once all the reasonable alternatives have been identified, the consumer must evaluate them before making a decision. The evaluation may involve a single criterion, or several criteria, against which each alternative is compared. For example, you might select a frozen dinner on price alone or on price, taste, and ease of preparation. When multiple criteria are involved, they typically do not carry equal weight. For example, preparation time might be more important than nutrition.

Because experience is often limited or dated and information from sources such as advertising or friends can be biased, evaluations can be factually incorrect. That is, a consumer may believe that the price of brand A is higher than that of brand B, when in fact the opposite is true. Marketers monitor consumers to determine what choice criteria they use, to identify any changes that may be taking place in their criteria, and to correct any damaging misperceptions.

Purchase and Related Decisions. After searching and evaluating, the consumer must decide whether to buy. Thus the first outcome is the decision to purchase or not to purchase the alternative evaluated as most desirable. If the decision is to buy, a series of related decisions must be made regarding features, where and when to make the actual transaction, how to take delivery or possession, the method of payment, and other issues. So the decision to make a purchase is really the beginning of an entirely new series of decisions that may be as time-consuming and difficult as the initial one.

Alert marketers recognize that the outcome of these additional decisions affects satisfaction, so they find ways to help consumers make them as efficiently as possible. For example, car dealers have speeded up loan approval, streamlined the process of tracking down a car that meets the buyer's exact specifications, and made delivery of the car a "miniceremony" to make the customer feel important.

Selecting a source from which to make a purchase is one of the buying decisions. Sources can be as varied as mail-order houses or manufacturers' outlets. The most common source is a retail store, and the reasons a consumer chooses to shop at a certain store are called **patronage buying motives**.

People want to feel comfortable when they shop. They want the assurance of being around people like themselves and in an environment that reflects their values. There are consumers, for example, who would feel uncomfortable shopping in an upscale store such as I. Magnin or Bergdorf-Goodman.

Patronage motives can range from something as simple as convenience when you want a soft drink, to something more complex, such as the atmosphere of a restaurant. Some common patronage motives are:

- Location convenience
- Service speed
- Merchandise accessibility
- Crowding
- Prices
- Merchandise assortment
- Services offered
- Store appearance
- Sales personnel
- Mix of other shoppers

Like the criteria consumers use to choose products and brands, their patronage motives will vary depending on the purchase situation. Successful retailers evaluate their customers carefully and design their stores accordingly. For example, some shoppers might be surprised to learn that such different women's wear stores as Victoria's Secret, Lerner New York, Lane Bryant, and Express all are part of The Limited Corp. A manufacturer, in turn, selects retailers with the patronage characteristics that complement its product and appeal to its market.

Postpurchase Behavior. What a consumer learns from going through the buying process has an influence on how he or she will behave the next time the same need arises. Furthermore, new opinions and beliefs have been formed and old ones have been revised. It's this change in the consumer that is indicated by an arrow in Figure 5-2 from the *postpurchase behavior* stage of the buying-decision process model back to the need-recognition stage.

Something else often occurs following a purchase. Have you ever gone through a careful decision process for a major purchase, selected what you thought was the best alternative, but then had doubts about your choice after the purchase? What you were experiencing is **postpurchase cognitive dissonance**—a state of anxiety brought on by the difficulty of choosing from among several alternatives. Unfortunately for marketers, dissonance is quite common; and if the anxiety is not relieved, the consumer may be unhappy with the chosen product even if it performs as expected!

Postpurchase cognitive dissonance occurs when each of the alternatives seriously considered by the consumer has both attractive and unattractive features. For example, in purchasing tires, the set selected may be the most expensive (unattractive), but they provide better traction on wet roads (attractive). The brand not chosen was recommended by a friend (attractive), but came with a very limited warranty (unattractive). After the purchase is made, the unattractive features of the product purchased grow in importance in the consumer's mind, as do the attractive features offered by the rejected alternatives. As a result, we begin to doubt the wisdom of the choice and experience anxiety over the decision. Dissonance typically increases: (1) the greater the importance of the purchase decision and (2) the greater the similarity between the item selected and item(s) rejected. Thus buying a house or car creates more dissonance than buying a candy bar.

AN ETHICAL DILEMMA?

Airlines regularly use a tactic called *overbooking* to cope with the often unpredictable behavior of consumers. That is, an airline will accept reservations for more seats than a plane has on any given flight. Flights are overbooked because in almost every case some number of people make reservations, but do not show up for the flight. So, to protect against unfilled seats and lost revenue, the airlines sell more seats than they have.

As you probably know, sometimes all the people holding reservations do show up, and there are not enough seats on the plane for everybody. As a result, some people must be "bumped"—that is, switched to a later flight. To entice some travelers to give up their reservations, the airlines often offer a totally or partially free ticket on a future flight.

Is the consumer behavior in this case—making a reservation and then failing to show up or cancel it—unethical? What about overbooking—selling something you don't have?

Consumers try to reduce their postpurchase anxieties. They avoid information (such as ads for the rejected products) that is likely to increase the dissonance. And they seek out information that supports their decision, such as reassurance from friends. Also, prior to the purchase, putting more effort into evaluating alternatives can increase a consumer's confidence and reduce dissonance. Sellers can reduce the likelihood of dissonance with reassuring messages in their advertising and personal selling, and with high-quality follow-up and postsale service programs.

With this background on the buying-decision process, we can examine what influences buying behavior. We'll begin with the sources and types of information used by consumers.

Information and Purchase Decisions

Purchase decisions require information. Until consumers know what products and brands are available, what features and benefits they offer, who sells them at what prices, and where they can be purchased, there won't be a decision process because there won't be any decisions to make.

As shown in Figure 5-2, there are two sources of buying information—the commercial environment and the social environment. The **commercial information environment** consists of all marketing organizations and individuals that attempt to communicate with consumers. It includes manufacturers, retailers, advertisers, and sales people whenever any of them are engaged in efforts to inform or persuade. The **social information environment** is comprised of family, friends, and acquaintances who directly or indirectly provide information about products. To appreciate the marketing significance of these social sources, consider how often your conversations with friends or family deal with purchases you are considering or have made.

Advertising is the most familiar type of commercial information. In the U.S., over $150 billion is spent every year on advertising of all types.[12] On average, the typical adult is exposed to about 300 ad messages a day, or almost 10,000 per month.[13] Commercial sources also include retail store clerks and telephone solicitors as well as consumers' physical involvement with products, such as trial product use and sampling.

The most common kind of *social information* is word-of-mouth communication—two or more people discussing a product. Other social sources include observing others using products and exposure to products in the homes of others. Recognizing the power of word-of-mouth communication, marketers try to stimulate it. For example, the "Friends and Families" long-distance telephone promotion by MCI offered discounts to subscribers who got several others to use the service as well.

When all the different types of information are considered, it becomes apparent that there is enormous competition for the consumer's attention. Consequently, the consumer's mind has to be marvelously efficient to sort and process this barrage of information. To better understand consumer behavior, we will begin by examining the social and group forces that influence the individual's psychological makeup and also play a role in specific buying decisions.

Social Influences

The ways in which we think, believe, and act are determined to a great extent by social forces. And our individual buying decisions—including the needs we experience, the alternatives we consider, and the way in which we evaluate them—are affected by the social forces that surround us. To reflect this dual impact, the arrows in Figure 5-2 extend from the social forces in two directions—to the psychological makeup of the individual and to the buying-decision process. Our description begins with culture, the force with the most *indirect* impact, and moves to the force with the most *direct* impact, the household.

Culture. **Culture** is a set of symbols and artifacts created by a society and handed down from generation to generation as determinants and regulators of human behavior. The symbols may be intangible (attitudes, beliefs, values, language) or tangible (tools, housing, products, works of art). They do not include instinctive acts. However, the way people perform instinctive biological acts such as eating is culturally influenced. Thus, everybody gets hungry, but what, when, and how people eat vary among cultures. For example, in the Ukraine, raw pig fat is considered a delicacy.

Cultures do change over time, as old patterns gradually give way to the new. During recent years in the U.S., cultural trends of far-reaching magnitude have occurred. Marketing executives must be alert to these changes so they can adjust their planning to be in step with, or even a little ahead of, the times. Some cultural trends affecting the buying behavior of U.S. consumers in recent years include the following:[14]

- *Time has become as valuable as money.* Americans feel overcommitted, with more obligations and demands on their time than they can fulfill. This has contributed to the growth in time-saving services (such as fast food) and labor-saving products (such as frozen entrées).
- *Two-income families are the norm.* When both adults in a household work outside the home, it affects not only the ability to buy but also the choice of products and the time in which to buy and consume them.
- *Gender roles are losing their identity.* This is reflected in educational opportunities, careers, clothing, and language.
- *Youthfulness is admired.* To be thought of as younger than your chronological age (once you're over 21!) is seen by most as a compliment. To remain healthy and free from disease, more Americans have made exercise a regular part of their lives. The growing opposition to smoking and alcohol consumption reflects this trend.

A marketer attempts to maximize the size of a market, while at the same time recognizing that it is not homogeneous. In its automatic teller machine (ATM) marketing effort, Citibank demonstrates concern for both of these factors. To maximize the size of the ATM market, Citibank belongs to programs that allow its customers to use the ATM machines of other banks and to make purchases at a variety of retail outlets using their ATM cards. At the same time, this ad indicates Citibank recognizes that in the ATM market subculture differences must be recognized and accommodated.

http://www.citibank.com/

Subcultures. In any society as heterogeneous as the one in the U.S., there are bound to be subcultures. **Subcultures** are groups in a culture that exhibit characteristic behavior patterns sufficient to distinguish them from other groups within the same culture. The behavior patterns that distinguish subcultures are based on factors such as race, nationality, religion, and urban-rural identification. Some of these were discussed earlier in the chapter in the context of demographic market forces.

A subculture takes on importance in marketing if it constitutes a significant part of the population and specific purchasing patterns can be traced to it. For example, increasing attention is being paid in the U.S. to behavioral influences stemming from racial and ethnic subcultures. Early immigrants came to America primarily from Europe. Now they come primarily from Asia and Latin America. West Coast cities have had large Chinese and Japanese populations for over a century. The new wave of Asian immigrants, however, includes people from Korea, Vietnam, and Thailand. These new subcultures bring with them different beliefs, customs, and languages that must be taken into consideration by firms attempting to sell to them.

Social Class. **Social class** is a ranking within a society determined by the members of the society. Social classes exist in virtually all societies, and people's buying behavior is often strongly influenced by the class to which they belong or to which they aspire.

Without making value judgments about whether one class is superior to or happier than another, sociologists have attempted to describe class structure in a meaningful way. One scheme useful to marketing managers is the five-class model developed by Coleman and Rainwater,[15] classifying people by education, occupation, and type of residential neighborhood.

Notice that income is not one of the classification factors. Social class is not an indication of spending capability; rather, it is an indication of preferences and life-style. For example, a young lawyer might make the same income as a middle-aged steel worker, but they probably have quite different family backgrounds, tastes, and aspirations.

In the summary of the five classes in U.S. society that follows, the population percentages are only approximations and may vary from one geographic area to another.

- The *upper class*, about 2 percent of the population, includes two groups: (1) socially prominent "old families," often with inherited wealth, and (2) newly rich corporate executives, owners of large businesses, and professionals. They live in exclusive neighborhoods and patronize fancy shops. They buy expensive goods and services, but they do not conspicuously display their wealth.
- The *upper-middle class*, about 12 percent of the population, is composed of moderately successful business and professional people and owners of medium-sized companies. They are well educated, have a strong desire for success, and push their children to do well. Their purchases are more conspicuous than those of the upper class. They live well, belong to private clubs, and support the arts and various social causes.
- The *lower-middle class*, about 32 percent of the population, consists of office workers, most sales people, teachers, technicians, and small business owners. As a group they are often referred to as white-collar workers. They strive for respectability and buy what is popular. Their homes are well cared for, and they save money to send their children to college. They are future-oriented, strive to move up to the higher social classes, have self-confidence, and are willing to take risks.
- The *upper-lower class*, about 38 percent of the population, is the blue-collar working class of production workers, semiskilled workers, and service personnel. These people are tied closely to family for economic and emotional support. Male-female roles are quite clearly defined. They live in smaller houses than the lower-middle class, drive larger cars, have more appliances, and watch bigger television sets. They buy American products, and stay close to home on vacations. Their orientation is short term, and they are very concerned about security.
- The *lower-lower class*, about 16 percent of the population, is composed of unskilled workers, the chronically unemployed, unassimilated immigrants, and people frequently on welfare. They are typically poorly educated, have low incomes, and live in substandard houses and neighborhoods. They tend not to have many opportunities; hence, they focus on the present. Often their purchases are not based on economic considerations. The public tends to differentiate within this class between the "working poor" and the "welfare poor."

Marketers recognize that there are substantial differences among classes with respect to buying behavior. Because of this diversity, different social classes are likely to respond differently to a seller's marketing program. Thus, it may be necessary to design marketing programs tailored to specific social classes.

Reference Groups. Each group in a society develops its own standards of behavior that then serve as guides, or frames of reference, for the members. Families and a circle of friends are such groups. Members share values and are expected to conform to the group's behavioral patterns. But a person does not have to be a member of a group to be influenced by it. There are groups we aspire to join (a campus honor society or club) and groups that we admire even though membership may be impossible (a professional athletic team). All of these are potential **reference groups**—groups of people who influence a person's attitudes, values, and behavior.

Studies have shown that personal advice in face-to-face groups is much more effective as a behavioral determinant than advertising. That is, in selecting products or changing brands, we are more likely to be influenced by word-of-mouth information from members of our reference groups than by ads or sales people. This is especially true when the information comes from someone we consider knowledgeable about the product and/or whom we trust.

Advertisers are relying on reference-group influence when they use celebrity spokespersons. Professional athletes, musicians, models, and actors can influence people who would like to be associated with them in some way—for example, Michael Jordan for Nike shoes and Elizabeth Hurley for Estée Lauder.

Reference-group influence in marketing is not limited to well-known personalities. Any group whose qualities a person admires can serve as a reference. For example, the physically fit, the socially conscious, and the professionally successful have all served as reference groups in advertising. The result of this process is reflected in advertising appeals using reference groups, such as Nike's "Just Do It" and Reebok's "Life Is Short, Play Hard" campaigns.

http://reebok.com/

Families and Households. A **family** is a group of two or more people related by blood, marriage, or adoption living together in a household. During their lives many people will belong to at least two families—the one into which they are born and the one they form at marriage. The birth family primarily determines core values and attitudes. The marriage family, in contrast, has a more direct influence on specific purchases. For example, family size is important in the purchase of a car.

A household is a broader concept that relates to a dwelling rather than a relationship. A **household** consists of a single person, a family, or any group of unrelated persons who occupy a housing unit. Thus an unmarried homeowner, college students sharing an off-campus apartment, and cohabiting couples are examples of households.

At one time marketers could safely assume that a household consisted of a married couple and their children. Not any more. More than 40 percent of American adults are single. Average household size in 1993 was 2.64 members, while average family size was 3.16 persons.[16] Both of these figures have been slowly declining for years. These long-term trends are due in large part to more single-parent families, childless married couples, and people living alone.

Sensitivity to household structure is important in designing marketing strategy. When research indicated that singles found mealtime particularly lonely, and often combined a meal with another activity such as reading or working to reduce the loneliness, marketers responded. Campbell's LeMenu is such a product, combining quality and convenience. Household structure also affects such dimensions as product size (How large should refrigerators be?) and the design of advertising (Who might be offended by the depiction of a "traditional" family in a TV ad?).

In addition to the impact household structure has on the purchase behavior of members, it is also interesting to consider the buying behavior of the household as a unit. Who does the buying for a household? Marketers should treat this question as four separate ones, because each may call for different strategies:

- Who influences the buying decision?
- Who makes the buying decision?
- Who makes the actual purchase?
- Who uses the product?

Different household members may assume these various roles, or one individual may play several roles in a particular purchase. In families, for many years the female household head did most of the day-to-day buying. However, as was described earlier, this behavior has changed as more women have entered the work force, and men and children have assumed greater household responsibility.

Psychological Factors

In discussing the psychological influences on consumer behavior, we will continue to use the model in Figure 5-2. One or more motives within a person activate goal-oriented behavior. One such behavior is perception; that is, the collection and processing of information. Other important psychological activities that play a role in buying decisions are learning, attitude formation, personality, and self-concept.

Motivation—The Starting Point.

To understand why consumers behave as they do, we must first ask why a person acts at all. The answer is, "Because he or she experiences a need." All behavior starts with a need. Security, social acceptance, and prestige are examples of needs. A need must be aroused or stimulated before it becomes a motive. Thus, a **motive** is a need sufficiently stimulated to move an individual to seek satisfaction.

We have many dormant needs that do not produce behavior because they are not sufficiently intense. Hunger strong enough to impel us to search for food and fear great enough to motivate a search for security are examples of aroused needs that become motives for behavior.

Identifying the motive(s) for behavior can range from simple to impossible. To illustrate, buying motives may be grouped on three different levels depending on consumers' awareness of them and their willingness to divulge them. At one level, buyers recognize, and are quite willing to talk about, their motives for buying most common, everyday products. At a second level, they are aware of their reasons for buying but will not admit them to others. Some people probably buy luxury cars to impress others. But when questioned about their motives, they may offer other reasons that they think will be more socially appropriate. The most difficult motives to uncover are those at the third level, where even the buyers cannot explain the factors motivating their buying actions. These are called unconscious or subconscious motives, and we will have more to say about them when we discuss personality.[17]

To further complicate our understanding, a purchase is often the result of multiple motives. Moreover, various motives may conflict with one another. In buying a new suit, a young man may want to (1) feel comfortable, (2) please his girlfriend, and (3) strive for economy. Accomplishing all three objectives in one purchase may be truly difficult! Finally, a particular motive may produce different behavior at different times.

Classification of Motives.

The broadest classification of motives is based on the source from which a need arises:

- Needs aroused from physiological states of tension (such as the need for sleep)
- Needs aroused from psychological states of tension (such as the needs for affection and self-respect)

A refinement of this concept was formulated by the psychologist Abraham Maslow. He identified a hierarchy of five need levels, arrayed in the order in which people seek to gratify them.[18] **Maslow's need hierarchy** is shown in Figure 5-3. Maslow recognized that a normal person is most likely to be working toward need satisfaction on several levels at the same time, and that rarely are all needs on a

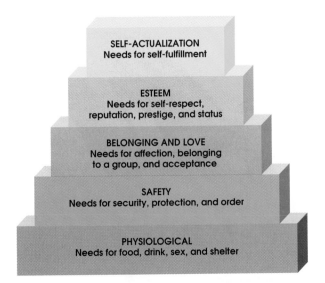

FIGURE 5-3 Maslow's hierarchy of needs.

given level fully satisfied. However, the hierarchy indicates that the majority of needs on a particular level must be reasonably well satisfied before a person is motivated at the next higher level.

With a greater understanding of motives, marketers are better prepared to design appealing products and stores. Much more needs to be done, however, to identify consumption-specific motives and to measure their strengths.

Perception. Since behavior can take many forms, a person gathers information from the environment to help in making a choice. **Perception** is the process of receiving, organizing, and assigning meaning to information or stimuli detected by our five senses. It is in this way that we interpret or give meaning to the world around us. Perception plays a major role in the stage of the buying-decision process where alternatives are identified.

What we perceive—the meaning we give something sensed—depends on the object and our experiences. In an instant the mind is capable of receiving information, comparing it to a huge store of images in memory, and providing an interpretation. Consumers make use of all five senses. Scents, for example, are powerful behavior triggers. Who can resist the aroma of popcorn in a theater or of fresh cookies in a supermarket bakery? As with all perception, memory plays a large part with aromas. A study of common odors that evoke pleasant childhood memories found that older consumers identified natural smells of horses, flowers, and hay. However, younger subjects associated pleasant recollections with the scent of Play-Doh and even jet fuel! Marketers are using this type of information to odorize products and shopping environments to create positive perceptions.[19]

Every day we come in contact with an enormous number of marketing stimuli. However, with the aid of **selective perception** techniques we are able to deal with the commercial environment.

- We pay attention by exception. That is, of all the marketing stimuli our senses are exposed to, only those with the power to capture and hold our attention have the potential of being perceived. This phenomenon is called *selective attention.*

*M*ilk has been hurt by accusations that farmers give cattle unnecessary or potentially harmful drugs, and the perception that milk is high in fat content (the actual figure is 3.5 percent). As a result, the industry has intensified its marketing effort to change consumers' perceptions of the product. The ads in the $36 million "Milk, What a Surprise" campaign initially contained only women, such as in the ad shown here, and were aimed at females ages 25 to 44. However, later ads featuring male personalities, such as pro-football player Steve Young and country music star Billy Ray Cyrus, suggest that the target has been broadened.

6.0, 6.0, 6.0, 6.0, 6.0! If I had to rate milk as an after-sports drink, it would definitely get the gold. Besides being a better source of potassium than the leading sports drink, it has more vitamins and minerals per ounce. And how do I like it? On ice, of course.

MILK
What a surprise!"

KRISTI YAMAGUCHI © 1995 NATIONAL FLUID MILK PROCESSOR PROMOTION BOARD

- As part of perception, new information is compared with a person's existing store of knowledge, or frame of reference. If an inconsistency is discovered, the new information will likely be distorted to conform to the established beliefs. Thus a snack-food "addict" may say, "All this talk about a balanced diet is just propaganda from the health food industry." This is *selective distortion*.
- We retain only part of what we have selectively perceived. For example, nearly 80 percent of Americans cannot remember a typical TV commercial 1 day after seeing it.[20] This is known as *selective retention*.

There are many communication implications in this selectivity process. For example, to grasp and hold attention, an ad must be involving enough to stimulate the consumer to seek more information. If the ad is too familiar, it will be ignored. On the other hand, if it is too complex, the ad will be judged not worth the time and effort to figure out. Thus, the goal is a mildly ambiguous first impression that heightens the consumer's interest.

Selective distortion tells us that marketers cannot assume that a message, even if it is factually correct, will necessarily be accepted as fact by consumers. In designing a message, the distance between the audience's current belief and the position proposed by the message must be considered. If the distance is large, a moderate claim may be more believable than a dramatic claim, and therefore more effective in moving consumers in the desired direction.

Even messages received undistorted are subject to selective retention. Consequently, ads are repeated many times. The hope is that numerous exposures will etch the message into the recipient's memory. This aim partially explains why a firm with very familiar products, such as Wrigley's, spends over $100 million a year on advertising.

A COMMITMENT TO CUSTOMER SATISFACTION

DECIDING THE COLORS OF THE PRODUCTS WE BUY

The Color Marketing Group is a 1,400-member association that meets twice a year to forecast the colors of new products. Colors for consumer products are selected at the spring meeting, and colors for business products are selected in fall. The group, which consists of color experts from the auto companies, paint and textile manufacturers, furniture and appliance makers, greeting cards, and other color-conscious industries, studies consumer trends and preferences to arrive at a set of coordinated colors they will all use in the upcoming year. These are crucial decisions because even a very good product may not be purchased if it does not blend into the consumer's decor. But coordination is not the whole story.

According to color analysts, colors communicate important meaning. See if you can match the following colors with what most consumers think they mean:

1. Primary red	A. Indicator of high status
2. Vivid pink	B. Natural tranquilizer
3. Yellow-based red	C. Instinctively preferred by men
4. Blue-based red	D. Instinctively preferred by women
5. Forest green	E. Calming
6. Yellow	F. Enhances excitement, fear, or anger
7. Deep sky blue	G. Encourages fantasizing
8. Pale blue	H. Increases anxiety and temper loss

Answers: 1–F; 2–E; 3–C; 4–D; 5–A; 6–H; 7–B; 8–G

Sources: Material supplied by the Color Marketing Group, Arlington, VA; and Carlton Wagner, "Color Cues," *Marketing Insights,* Spring 1990, pp. 42–46.

Learning. **Learning** involves changes in behavior resulting from observation and experience. It excludes behavior that is attributable to instinct such as breathing or temporary states such as hunger or fatigue. Interpreting and predicting consumer learning enhances our understanding of buying behavior, since learning plays a role at every stage of the buying-decision process.

No universally workable and acceptable learning theory has emerged. However, one with direct application to marketing strategy is stimulus-response theory.[21] According to **stimulus-response theory**, learning occurs as a person (1) responds to some stimulus by behaving in a particular way and (2) is rewarded for a correct response or penalized for an incorrect one. When the same correct response is repeated in reaction to the same stimulus, a behavior pattern, or learning, is established.

Once a habitual behavior pattern has been established, it replaces conscious, willful behavior. In terms of the purchase-decision process, this means that the consumer would go directly from the recognized need to the purchase, skipping the steps in between.

Marketers have "taught" consumers to respond to certain cues. For example:

- End-of-aisle displays in supermarkets suggest that the item is on sale.
- Sale signs in store windows suggest that bargains can be found inside.
- Large type in newspaper grocery ads suggests that the item is a particularly good bargain.

Learning is not a perfect predictor of behavior because a variety of other factors also influence a consumer. For example, a pattern of repeatedly purchasing the same brand may be disrupted by a person's desire for variety or novelty. Or a

temporary situation such as being short of money or pressed for time may produce behavior different than a learned response. Thus a learned response does not necessarily occur every time a stimulus appears.

Personality.   **Personality** is defined broadly as an individual's pattern of traits that influence behavioral responses. For example, we speak of people as being self-confident, domineering, introverted, flexible, and/or friendly, and as being influenced (but not controlled) by these personality traits in their responses to situations.

It is generally agreed that personality traits do influence consumers' perceptions and buying behavior. However, there is considerable disagreement as to the nature of this relationship—that is, *how* personality influences behavior. Many studies have been made of personality traits in relation to product and brand preferences in a wide variety of product categories, with mixed results. The findings generally have been too inconclusive to be of much practical value. Although we know, for example, that people's personalities often are reflected in the clothes they wear, the cars they drive (or whether they use a bike or motorcycle instead of a car), and the restaurants they eat in, we have not been successful in predicting behavior from particular personality traits. The reason is simple: Many things besides personality enter into the consumer buying-decision process.

The **psychoanalytic theory** of personality, formulated by Sigmund Freud at the turn of the century and later modified by his followers and critics, has had a tremendous impact on the study of human behavior. Freud contended that people have subconscious drives that cannot be satisfied in socially acceptable ways. As we learn that we cannot gratify these needs in a direct manner, we develop other, more subtle means of seeking satisfaction. This results in very complex reasons for some behavior.

One significant marketing implication is that a person's real motive(s) for buying a product or shopping at a certain store may be hidden. Sometimes even we ourselves do not understand why we feel or act as we do. Psychoanalytic theory has caused marketers to realize that they must appeal to buyers' dreams, hopes, and fears. Yet at the same time they must provide buyers with socially acceptable rationalizations for many purchases. Thus, we see ads emphasizing the practicality of $60,000 cars, the comfort of fur coats, and the permanence of diamond jewelry.

The Self-Concept.   Your **self-concept**, or *self-image*, is the way you see yourself. At the same time it is the picture you think others have of you. Psychologists distinguish between the *actual self-concept*—the way you see yourself—and the *ideal self-concept*—the way you want to be seen or would like to see yourself.

Studies of purchases show that people generally prefer brands and products that are compatible with their self-concept. However, there are mixed reports concerning the degree of influence of the actual and ideal self-concepts on brand and product preferences. Some researchers contend that consumption preferences correspond to a person's actual self-concept. Others hold that the ideal self-concept is dominant in consumers' choices.

Perhaps there is no consensus here because in real life we often switch back and forth between our actual and ideal self-concepts. A middle-aged man may buy some comfortable, but not fashionable, clothing to wear at home on a weekend, where he is reflecting his actual self-concept. But he may also buy some expensive, high-fashion clothing, envisioning himself as a young, active, upwardly mobile guy (ideal self-concept).

*S*aab developed a non-traditional campaign to attract and influence consumers with an independent, slightly rebellious self-concept. The impressionistic art and small photo of the actual car in this ad run counter to the conventional automobile format, but the nonconformist design is consistent with the appeal, "Find your own road."

http://www.saabusa.com/

Attitudes. An **attitude** is a learned predisposition to respond to an object or class of objects in a consistently favorable or unfavorable way.[22] In our buying-decision process model, attitudes play a major role in the evaluation of alternatives.

All attitudes have the following characteristics in common:

- Attitudes are *learned*. They are formed as a result of direct experiences with a product or an idea, indirect experiences (such as reading about a product in *Consumer Reports*), and interactions with social groups. For example, the opinions expressed by a friend about diet foods plus the consumer's favorable or unfavorable experience as a result of using diet foods will contribute to an attitude toward diet foods in general.
- Attitudes have an *object*. By definition, we can hold attitudes only toward something. The object can be general (professional sports) or specific (Chicago Cubs); it can be abstract (campus life) or concrete (the computer lab). In attempting to determine consumers' attitudes, the object of the attitude must be carefully defined. This is because a person might have a favorable attitude toward the general concept (exercise), but a negative attitude toward a specific dimension of the concept (jogging).
- Attitudes have *direction* and *intensity*. Our attitudes are either favorable or unfavorable toward the object. They cannot be neutral. In addition, they have a strength. For example, you may mildly like this text or you may like it very

much (we hope!). This factor is important for marketers, since both strongly held favorable and strongly held unfavorable attitudes are difficult to change.

- Finally, attitudes tend to be *stable* and *generalizable*. Once formed, attitudes usually endure, and the longer they are held, the more resistant to change they become. People also have a tendency to generalize attitudes. For instance, a person who likes the produce section in a particular supermarket has a tendency to form a favorable attitude toward the entire store.

A consumer's attitudes do not always predict purchase behavior. A person may hold very favorable attitudes toward a product but not buy it because of some inhibiting factor. Typical inhibitors are not having enough money or discovering that your preferred brand is not available when you want to buy it. Under such circumstances, purchase behavior may even contradict attitudes.

Changing strongly held attitudes can be difficult or impossible. When change is accomplished, it normally takes a long time and a lot of money. Consider how long it has taken to gain widespread acceptance of air bags in cars. They were initially ridiculed but now are frequently demanded by car buyers. When faced with unfavorable attitudes, and recognizing how difficult changing them will be, marketers frequently alter the product to conform to the attitudes.

Situational Influences

Often the situations in which we find ourselves play a large part in determining how we behave. Students, for example, act differently in a classroom than they do when they are in a stadium watching a football game. The same holds true of buying behavior. On spring break you might buy a souvenir that seems very strange when you get home. This is an example of **situational influence**, a temporary force associated with the immediate purchase environment that affects behavior.

Situational influences tend to be less significant when the consumer is very loyal to a brand and when the consumer is highly involved in the purchase. However, they often play a major role in buying decisions. The four categories of situational influences are related to when, where, and how consumers buy as well as the conditions under which they buy.

When Consumers Buy—The Time Dimension. Marketers should be able to answer at least three time-related questions about consumer buying:

- How is it influenced by the season, week, day, or hour?
- What impact do past and present events have on the purchase decision?
- How much time does the consumer have to make the purchase and consume the product?

The time of day influences the demand for some products. For example, because they associate it with breakfast, Americans drink 10 times as much orange juice as the Japanese. The time dimension of buying has implications for promotion scheduling. Promotional messages must reach consumers when they are in a decision-making frame of mind. It also influences pricing decisions, as when marketers adjust prices in an attempt to even out demand. For instance, supermarkets may offer double coupons on Tuesdays, usually a slow business day. If seasonal buying patterns exist, marketers can tailor their merchandise accordingly. In most parts of the U.S., the demand for bowling products peaks when the weather gets cold. However, in warm-weather areas, the reverse is true. The demand for bowling equipment peaks in the summer, when it is too hot for outdoor recreation. In

response, Kmart stores in the Phoenix area stock up on bowling products in the spring, while Kmarts in Detroit increase their stock in the fall.[23]

The second question concerns the impact of past or future events. For example, the length of time since you last went out to dinner at a nice restaurant may influence a decision on whether to go to a fancy restaurant tonight. Marketers need to know enough about the recent and planned behavior of consumers to anticipate the effects of these past and future events.

The growth and popularity of fast-food restaurants, quick-service oil-change outlets, and catalog retailers such as L.L. Bean and Lands' End are marketers' responses to the time pressure experienced by consumers. To help consumers conserve time, marketers are making large and small changes. For example, some photoprocessing operations return the developed prints by mail to eliminate the customers' second trip to pick up the pictures. To help customers locate specific products and therefore reduce shopping time, a number of supermarkets have computer-generated directories attached to their shopping carts.

Where Consumers Buy—The Physical and Social Surroundings. Physical surroundings are the features of a situation that are apparent to the senses, such as lighting, smells, weather, and sounds. Think of the importance of atmosphere in a restaurant or the sense of excitement and action created by the sights and sounds in a gambling casino. Music can be an important element in a store's strategy. In an experiment involving supermarket shoppers, the beat of background music apparently influenced behavior. Despite the fact that the shoppers reported paying little or no attention to the music, sales were 38 percent higher with slower background music than with faster music![24]

The social surroundings are the number, mix, and actions of other people at the purchase site. You probably would not go into a strange restaurant that has an empty parking lot at dinnertime. In a crowded store with other customers waiting, you will probably ask the clerk fewer questions and spend less time comparing products.

How Consumers Buy—The Terms of the Purchase. Terms and conditions of sale as well as the transaction-related activities that buyers are willing to perform affect consumer buying. For instance, for many years credit was extended only by retailers selling big-ticket items. However, today consumers can use credit cards at fast-food restaurants and grocery stores. Average credit card debt in the U.S. has increased to nearly $4,000 per household, and the amount of installment credit outstanding exceeds $1 trillion. It is anticipated that by the year 2000 there will be 1.3 *billion* credit cards in circulation.[25] Not only do consumers use credit for installment purchases (to buy things today with future income), but many now use credit for convenience. The ability to use American Express, VISA, MasterCard, or Discover Card to make a wide variety of purchases while not carrying cash is an attractive option to many consumers.

Marketers have also experimented with transferring functions or activities to consumers. What were once called "service stations" are now called "gas stations" because you pump your own gas and wash your own windshield. Consumers have shown a willingness to assemble products, sack their own groceries, and buy in case quantities—all in exchange for lower prices.

Conditions under Which Consumers Buy—States and Moods. Sometimes consumers are in a temporary state that influences their buying decisions. When

YOU MAKE THE DECISION

WILL SELF-SCANNING BENEFIT CONSUMERS AND RETAILERS?

Grocery retailers are testing a device that could improve one of the major bottlenecks in supermarkets, the checkout procedure. Consumers are provided with a handheld scanner that looks like a telephone receiver when they enter the store. The shopper scans each selected item as it is dropped in the shopping cart. Items can also be "unscanned" if the customer changes his or her mind. When the shopping is completed, the scanner prints a bill and the customer pays by swiping a credit card through the scanner.

The benefit of self-scanning is that it makes the checkout procedure quicker and less labor intensive. But there are some potential problems as well. The most obvious is intentional theft. However, when the device was tested in supermarkets in the Netherlands, theft in the stores actually declined. Other problems are mistakes by consumers, for example, forgetting to delete an item returned to the shelf, and the added effort required of the customer.

Will a product like this work in the U.S.?

Source: Tara Parker-Pope, "New Devices Add Up Bill, Measure Shoppers' Honesty," *The Wall Street Journal*, June 6, 1995, pp. B1+.

you are ill or rushed, you may be unwilling to wait in line or to take the time or care that a particular purchase deserves. Moods can also influence purchases. Feelings such as anger or excitement can result in purchases that otherwise would not have been made. In the exciting atmosphere of a rock concert, for example, you might pay more for a commemorative T-shirt than you would under normal circumstances. Sales people must be trained to recognize consumers' moods and adjust their presentations accordingly.

Marketers must also monitor long-term situational influences. The optimistic consumers of the 1980s were free-spending and apparently carefree. Household debt grew 50 percent faster than disposable income during the decade as the baby-boom generation acquired cars, homes, and household possessions. However, the recession that rocked the U.S. economy at the end of the 1980s produced many changes. It created more conservative buyers who saved more and purchased more carefully. One outcome of these changes was the disappearance of over 1,200 car dealerships in 1990.[26]

This chapter has dealt with the willingness to buy—part of our definition of marketing. We described the consumer market and examined the consumer's decision-making process. You should now appreciate just how difficult it is for marketers to identify needs and predict consumer buying behavior. In the next chapter we will examine the other category of buyers—the business market.

■ SUMMARY

The dynamic nature of the consumer market is reflected in its geographic distribution and its demographic characteristics. Geographically, the U.S. population is shifting toward the West and the South, and urban growth has slowed.

Demographics are the vital statistics that describe a population. They are useful to marketers

because they are related to behavior and they are relatively easy to gather. Demographics frequently used to describe consumers are age, gender, family life cycle, income, ethnicity, and other characteristics such as education, occupation, religion, and nationality.

The buying behavior of ultimate consumers can

be examined using a five-part model: the buying-decision process, information, social and group forces, psychological forces, and situational factors.

The buying-decision process is composed of five stages consumers go through in making purchases. Buying decisions are either high or low involvement. Low-involvement decisions include fewer stages, while high-involvement decisions consist of all five stages. The stages are need recognition, identification of alternatives, evaluation of alternatives, purchase and related decisions, and postpurchase behavior.

Information fuels the buying-decision process. Without it, there would be no decisions. There are two categories of information sources: commercial and social. Commercial sources include advertising, personal selling, selling by phone, and personal involvement with a product. Word of mouth, observation, and experience with a product owned by someone else are social sources.

Social and group forces are composed of culture, subculture, social class, reference groups, family, and households. Culture has the broadest and most general influence on buying behavior, while a person's household has the most immediate impact. Social and group forces have a direct impact on individual purchase decisions as well as a person's psychological makeup.

Psychological forces that impact buying decisions are motivation, perception, learning, personality, and attitude. All behavior is motivated by some aroused need. Perception is the way we interpret the world around us and is subject to three types of selectivity: attention, distortion, and retention.

Learning is a change in behavior as a result of experience. Stimulus-response learning involves drives, cues, responses, reinforcement, and punishment. Continued reinforcement leads to habitual buying and brand loyalty.

Personality is the sum of an individual's traits that influence behavioral responses. The Freudian psychoanalytic theory of personality has had a significant impact on marketing. It has caused marketers to realize that the true motives for behavior are often hidden. The self-concept is related to personality. Because purchasing and consumption are very expressive actions, they allow us to communicate to the world our actual and ideal self-concepts.

Attitudes are learned predispositions to respond to an object or class of objects in a consistent fashion. Besides being learned, all attitudes are directed toward an object, have direction and intensity, and tend to be stable and generalizable. Strongly held attitudes are difficult to change.

Situational influences deal with when, where, how, and why consumers buy, and the consumer's personal condition at the time of purchase. Situational influences are often so powerful that they can override all the other forces in the buying-decision process.

More about **AVON**

*N*one of the tactics described in the chapter opening have been particularly successful for Avon. What has worked is going overseas. By entering countries where a large portion of the women remain at home during the day and there is a significant desire to earn more income, the company has found increasing success. In Mexico, Argentina, China, Poland, Brazil, and a number of other countries, Avon now has more than three times as many representatives as it has in the U.S. And international sales now exceed U.S. sales by more than $1 billion.

Avon entered Mexico in 1958, and it is now the firm's biggest foreign market, accounting for more than 10 percent of total corporate sales. China, on the other hand, was introduced to Avon in 1990, and its growth has been much slower. A sales force of 25,000 produces about $15 million in sales, less than 4 percent of the Mexican total. Despite the slow start, Avon sees enormous potential as the Chinese economy grows and matures.

The examples go on and on. Sales in Brazil are over $300 million, and in Argentina they exceed $225 million. In both of these South American countries continued growth is expected. New markets are also being tapped. Avon has a growing presence in Eastern Europe, and recently entered India.

However, it is not all smooth sailing. In almost all these markets competition is growing. Mary Kay

Cosmetics is established in Taiwan, Mexico, and Argentina, and is moving into China and Poland. In addition, retailers like Wal-Mart, which offer similar cosmetics products at lower prices, are moving into these developing markets.[27]

1. How will the changes in the population affect Avon's future in the U.S.?
2. What market factors contribute to Avon's success in developing countries?

■ KEY TERMS AND CONCEPTS

Ultimate consumers (104)
Metropolitan Statistical Area (MSA) (105)
Primary Metropolitan Statistical Area (PMSA) (105)
Consolidated Metropolitan Statistical Area (CMSA) (106)
Demographics (107)
Family life-cycle stage (108)

Buying-decision process (111)
Level of involvement (112)
Impulse buying (112)
Patronage buying motives (114)
Postpurchase cognitive dissonance (114)
Commercial information environment (115)

Social information environment (115)
Culture (116)
Subculture (117)
Social class (117)
Reference groups (118)
Family (119)
Household (119)
Motive (120)
Maslow's need hierarchy (120)
Perception (121)

Selective perception (121)
Learning (123)
Stimulus-response theory (123)
Personality (124)
Psychoanalytic theory (124)
Self-concept (124)
Attitude (125)
Situational influences (126)

■ QUESTIONS AND PROBLEMS

1. Give two examples of goods or services whose market demand would be particularly affected by each of the following population factors:
   a. Regional distribution
   b. Urban-rural-suburban distribution
   c. Marital status
   d. Gender
   e. Age
2. List three population trends noted in this chapter (for instance, the over-65 segment is growing). Speculate on how each of the following types of retail stores might be affected by each of the trends:
   a. Supermarket
   b. Sporting goods store
   c. Drugstore
   d. Restaurant
3. When might the purchase of a color television be a low-involvement decision?
4. From a consumer behavior perspective, why is it incorrect to view the European Union or the countries of Asia as single markets?
5. Provide examples of a person and a group that could serve as reference groups in the choice of the following products:
   a. Shampoo
   b. Auto tune-up

   c. Office furniture
   d. Camera
6. What roles would you expect a husband, a wife, and their young child to play in the purchase of the following items?
   a. Nintendo
   b. Choice of a fast-food outlet for dinner
   c. Personal computer
   d. Lawn-care service
7. Does the psychoanalytic theory of personality have any practical application in the marketing of cars that have a top speed of 120 mph when the speed limit on most U.S. highways is 65 mph or less?
8. Explain how self-concept might come into play in the purchase of the following products:
   a. Eyeglasses
   b. Man's suit
   c. Eye shadow
   d. College education
9. Interview the manager of a store that sells big-ticket items (furniture, appliances, electronic equipment) about what methods, if any, the store uses to reinforce purchase decisions and to reduce the cognitive dissonance of its customers. What additional methods can you suggest?
10. What situational influences might affect a family's choice of a motel in a strange town while on vacation?

■ HANDS-ON MARKETING

1. From the most recent "Survey of Buying Power" (from *Sales & Marketing Management* magazine), record the available data for the county in which you live and one other county in your home state. Comment on how any differences you find may be useful to a fast-food franchisee looking for a location for a new outlet.

2. Have a friend describe a high-involvement purchase that he or she recently made. Show how each of the five stages described in the chapter is reflected in the description. Identify the primary social influences that played a part in the decision.

CHAPTER 6

Business Markets
and
Buying Behavior

After a Lengthy Grounding, Can
CESSNA
Single-Engine Planes Fly to New Heights?

Cessna is currently the world's sales leader in light and midsize business jets with over 60 percent of the market. It was also the leader in single-engine propeller planes until 1986 when the company stopped making them.

In 1977, when nearly 18,000 single-engine planes were sold, 9,000 of them were made by Cessna. But sales began to decline as first Cessna, then Beech, and finally Piper drastically cut back their production. By 1992 sales had dwindled to an industry total of 940 units. As a result, the average age of all single-engine planes in the U.S. is 28 years. The cause of the decline, the hoped-for recovery, and the marketing undertaken by Cessna make an interesting story.

A precedent-setting product-liability lawsuit against Piper in 1983 disrupted the single-engine airplane industry. Suits and settlements against all the producers increased each year after that. In 1989 manufacturers of airplanes approved by the Federal Aviation Administration (FAA) paid $210 million in damages and legal fees. Seeing no end in sight, the major firms ceased production either voluntarily or because of financial pressures.

In 1994 President Clinton signed into law the General Aviation Revitalization Act. This legislation limits a manufacturer's product liability for its planes to 18 years. That means the manufacturers bear no responsibility for nearly 70 percent of all the single-engine planes now flying. With the burden of liability lifted for these older planes, several of the former producers and some new entrants are getting into the business.

The primary markets for single-engine propeller planes are flight instructors and business users. Cessna plans to produce 2,000 planes a year. That decision is based in part on the results of a survey of all fixed-base operators, the businesses that provide services and fuel for small planes, and data from the FAA on the number and age of planes in operation.

The product designs—there are four Cessna single-engine models—are only slightly modified from 20 years ago. For example, fuel injection has replaced carburetors. With the industry essentially shut down during those years, there have been few major advances, and Cessna management is hesitant to tinker with success. The price for the basic model with instrument-flying capability is about $100,000. That is approximately equivalent to the mid-1970s price, taking inflation into consideration. The planes are distributed through the nearly 400 dealerships that double as flight training schools.

Promotion will include advertising in trade publications, but the primary effort will be direct mail. Over 50,000 student pilots register with the FAA each year for training to operate small planes. Since this list is a public record, Cessna has a readily available prospect list.[1]

How does this business market for single-engine planes differ from a consumer market?

http://www.cessna.com/

Whatever marketing strategies Cessna and the other light-plane makers adopt, one thing is clear. The primary target markets for these producers are individuals and organizations that will use the planes in conducting their businesses. The business market is big, rich, and widely diversified. It employs millions of workers in thousands of different jobs.

In many ways business markets are similar to the consumer markets we examined in Chapter 5, but there are also important differences. After studying this chapter, in addition to being able to describe how business markets differ from consumer markets, you should be able to explain:

CHAPTER GOALS

- The nature and scope of the business market.
- The components of the business market.
- The characteristics of business market demand.
- The determinants of business market demand.
- The buying motives, processes, and patterns in business markets.

Nature and Scope of the Business Market

The **business market** consists of all individuals and organizations that buy goods and services for one of the following purposes:

- *To make other goods and services.* Timex buys computer chips to make watches, and Henredon buys wood to make furniture.
- *To resell to other business users or to consumers.* Kroger's buys canned tuna fish to sell to consumers, and ReCellular, Inc., buys used cellular phones to refurbish and sell to cellular carriers.
- *To conduct the organization's operations.* The University of Vermont buys office supplies and electronic office equipment for use in the registrar's office, and the Mayo Clinic buys supplies to use in its surgical operating rooms.

Each buyer within the business market is termed a **business user**.

In the business market we deal with both consumer products and business products. **Business marketing**, then, is the marketing of goods and services to business users, as contrasted to ultimate consumers.

Because the business market is largely unknown to the average consumer, we are apt to underrate its significance. Actually, it is huge in terms of total sales volume and the number of firms involved. About 50 percent of all manufactured products are sold to the business market. In addition, about 80 percent of all farm products and virtually all mineral, forest, and sea products are business goods.[2] These are sold to firms for further processing.

The magnitude and complexity of the business market are also evident from the many transactions required to produce and market a product. Consider, for example, the business marketing transactions and total sales volume involved in getting leather workshoes to their actual users. First, cattle are sold through one or two middlemen before reaching a meatpacker. Then the hides are sold to a tanner, who in turn sells the leather to a shoe manufacturer. The shoe manufacturer may sell finished shoes to a wholesaler, who markets them to retail stores, or to employers that supply shoes for their workers. Each sale is a business marketing transaction.

In addition, the shoe manufacturer buys metal eyelets, laces, thread, glue, steel safety toe plates, heels and soles, and shoe polish. Consider something as simple as the shoelaces. Other industrial firms must first buy the raw cotton. Then they must spin, weave, dye, and cut the cotton so that it becomes shoestring material.

All the manufacturers involved have factories and offices with furniture, machinery, furnaces, lights, and maintenance equipment and supplies required to run them—and these also are business goods that have to be produced and marketed. In short, thousands of business products and business marketing activities come into play before almost any product—consumer good or business good—reaches its final destination.

The magnitude and complexity of the business market loom even larger when we consider all the business services involved throughout our workshoe example. Each firm engaged in any stage of the production process probably uses outside accounting and law firms. Several of the producers may use advertising agencies. And all the companies will use services of various financial institutions.

Every retail store and wholesaling establishment is a business user. Every bus company, airline, and railroad is part of this market. So is every hotel, restaurant, bank, insurance company, hospital, theater, and school. In fact, the total sales volume in the business market far surpasses total sales to consumers. This difference is due to the very many business marketing transactions that take place before a product is sold to its ultimate user.

Components of the Business Market

Traditionally, business markets were referred to as industrial markets. This caused many people to think the term referred only to manufacturing firms. But as you can see from what we just explained, the business market is a lot more than that. Certainly manufacturers constitute a major portion of the business market, but there are also six other components—agriculture, reseller, government, services, nonprofit, and international. Although they are often underrated or overlooked because of the heavy attention devoted to manufacturing, each is a significant part of the business market.

The Agriculture Market

The high level of income from the sale of agricultural products—over $190 billion in 1994—gives farmers, as a group, the purchasing power that makes them a highly attractive market. Moreover, world population forecasts and food shortages in many countries undoubtedly will keep pressure on farmers to increase their output. Companies hoping to sell to the farm market must analyze it carefully and be aware of significant trends. For example, both the proportion of farmers in the total population and the number of farms have been decreasing and probably will continue to decline. Counterbalancing this has been an increase in large corporate farms. Even the remaining "family farms" are expanding in order to survive. Farming is becoming more automated and mechanized. This means, of course, that capital investment in farming is increasing. **Agribusiness**—farming, food processing, and other large-scale farming-related businesses—is big business in every sense of the word.

Agriculture has become a modern industry. Like other business executives, farmers are looking for better ways to increase their productivity, cut their expenses, and manage their cash flows. Technology is an important part of the process. For example, an Illinois firm, Tri-R Innovations, has developed a sensor and remote steering system that guides a tractor between the rows in a field to avoid destroying any crops. And, as farms become fewer and larger, effectively marketing to them requires carefully designed strategies. For example, fertilizer producers such as International Mineral and Chemical Company have sales people that visit individual farms. There, working with the farmer, the sales rep analyzes the soil and crops to determine exactly what fertilizer mix is best for the particular farm. Based on the analysis, the manufacturer prepares the appropriate blend of ingredients as a special order.

The Reseller Market

Intermediaries in the American marketing system—approximately 500,000 whole-saling middlemen and 2.7 million retail establishments—constitute the **reseller market**. The basic activity of resellers—unlike any other business market seg-ment—is buying products from supplier organizations and reselling these items in essentially the same form to the resellers' customers. In economic terms, resellers create time, place, information, and possession utilities, rather than form utility.

Resellers also buy many goods and services for use in operating their busi-nesses—items such as office supplies, warehouses, materials-handling equipment, legal services, electrical services, and janitorial supplies. In these buying activi-ties, resellers are essentially no different from manufacturers, financial institutions, or any other segment of the business market.

It is their role as buyers for resale that differentiates resellers and attracts spe-cial marketing attention from their suppliers. To resell an item, you must please your customer. Usually it is more difficult to determine what will please an out-side customer than to find out what will satisfy someone within your own organi-zation. Consider an airline that decides to redesign the uniforms of its flight crews. Management can carefully study the conditions under which the uniforms will be worn and work closely with the people who will be wearing the uniforms to get their views. As a result, the airline should be able to select a design that will be both functional and acceptable. Contrast that with a retailer trying to anticipate what clothing fashions will be popular next spring. In both cases clothing is being purchased. However, the opportunity for interaction with the users and the greater interest by those likely to be affected by the purchase make buying for internal use less difficult and less risky than buying for resale.

http://foodcoop.com/kroger/

Buying for resale, especially in a large reseller's organization, can be a com-plex procedure. For a supermarket chain such as Kroger or Vons, buying is fre-quently done by a buying committee made up of experts on demand, supply, and prices. Department stores may retain resident buyers—independent buying agen-cies—located in New York or other major market centers to be in constant touch with the latest fashion developments.

The Government Market

The fantastically large **government market** includes over 86,000 federal, state, and local units that spend over $2.5 *trillion* a year buying for government institu-tions, such as schools, offices, hospitals, and military bases. Spending by the fed-eral government alone accounts for almost 25 percent of our gross national prod-uct. Spending at the state and local levels accounts for another 20 percent.

Government procurement processes are different from those in the private sec-tor of the business market. A unique feature of government buying is the competi-tive bidding system. Much government procurement, by law, must be done on a bid basis. That is, the government agency advertises for bids using a standard for-mat called a request for proposals (RFP) that states specifications for the intended purchase. Then it must accept the lowest bid that meets these specifications.

In other buying situations, the government may negotiate a purchase contract with an individual supplier. This marketing practice might be used, for instance,

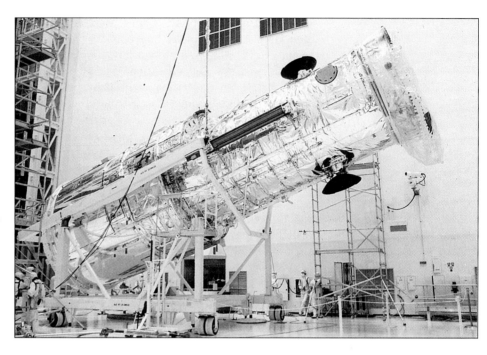

The Hubble Space Telescope, pictured here being prepared at the Kennedy Space Center, is an example of the government market. It cost NASA over $1.6 billion to build and launch the telescope into orbit. Then, when the mirrors in the telescope proved to be flawed, another $630 million was spent to conduct repairs in space. Many think the costs were worthwhile, because the telescope makes it possible for astronomers to view 97 percent of the known universe without the distortion caused by the earth's atmosphere.

http://www.nasa.gov/

http://www.zds.com/

when the Department of Defense wants someone to develop and build a new weapons system, and there are no comparable products on which to base bidding specifications.

A glance at an issue of the *Commerce Business Daily*, a U.S. government publication that lists business opportunities with the government, will give you some idea of the size of this market. The potential is sufficiently attractive that some firms concentrate almost exclusively on it. AM General Corporation, for example, developed the HUMMER, an all-terrain vehicle, in response to a Department of Defense RFP (request for proposals). The firm eventually expanded its marketing effort for the vehicle to other government agencies such as the Forest Service and business firms such as mining companies.

Despite the opportunities, many companies make no effort to sell to the government because they are intimidated by the red tape. There is no question that dealing with the government to any significant extent usually requires specialized marketing techniques and information. Some firms, such as Zenith Data Systems, have established special departments to deal with government markets. Also, there are information and guidelines available from agencies such as the General Services Administration and the Small Business Administration on the proper procedures for doing business with the government.

The Services Market

Currently, firms that produce services greatly outnumber firms that produce goods. That is, there are more service firms than the total of all manufacturers, mining companies, construction firms, and enterprises engaged in farming, forestry, and fishing. The **services market** includes all transportation carriers and public utilities, and the many financial, insurance, legal, and real estate firms. This market also includes organizations that produce and sell such diverse services as rental housing, recreation and entertainment, repairs, health care, personal care, and business services.

Service firms constitute a huge market that buys goods and other services. Hilton Hotels, for example, buy blankets and sheets from textile manufacturers. Hospitals in the U.S. and abroad buy supplies from Baxter Healthcare Company. The Chicago Cubs and other major-league teams buy their Louisville Slugger baseball bats from Hillerich and Bradsby. And all these service firms buy legal, accounting, and consulting advice from other service marketers.

The "Nonbusiness" Business Market

In recent years some long-overdue marketing attention has been given to the multi-billion-dollar market comprised of so-called nonbusiness or nonprofit organizations. The **nonbusiness market** includes such diverse institutions as churches, colleges and universities, museums, hospitals and other health care institutions, political parties, labor unions, and charitable organizations. Actually, each of these so-called nonbusiness organizations is a business enterprise. In the past, however, our society (and the institutions themselves) did not perceive a museum or a hospital as being a business. And many people today still feel uncomfortable thinking of their church, school, or political party as a business. Nevertheless, these organizations do virtually all the things that businesses do—offer a product, collect money, make investments, hire employees—except having profit as one of their goals. Therefore, they require professional management.

Nonprofit organizations also conduct marketing campaigns—albeit under a different name—in an effort to attract billions of dollars in contributions. In turn, they spend billions of dollars buying goods and services to run their operations.

The International Market

Exports by U.S. firms amount to over $640 billion, a figure that has increased steadily since the mid-1980s. The biggest recent growth in the **international market** has been in medical products, scientific instruments, environmental protection systems, and consumer goods.

Many small organizations are also heavily involved in the export market. These firms have benefited from improved communications with fax machines and 800 numbers, reduced language barriers as English becomes more common in global business, and help from the U.S. Commerce Department with trade fairs and "matchmaking" programs. By identifying niches where they have a quality or performance advantage, small U.S. firms have found foreign markets for such unexpected products as home aquariums, food blenders, wheelchairs, and auto wax.[3]

Another dimension of international business is foreign-based subsidiaries. Though these sales do not count as exports, they are a significant part of the operations of many firms. McDonald's had only a 6 percent increase in domestic sales in 1994, but foreign sales climbed by 20 percent and now account for half the firm's total volume. A significant number of U.S. firms receive over half their total revenue from overseas subsidiaries. Included are Exxon, IBM, Philip Morris, Procter & Gamble, and Coca-Cola.[4] Operating overseas has several benefits for U.S. firms:

- It gets them access to countries that participate in trade agreements that restrict imports from nonmembers. For example, a joint operation between Dow Chemical and Sumitomo in Japan to make high-performance plastics gives Dow greater access to the countries of the Pacific Rim than it would otherwise have.
- Manufacturing abroad allows firms to gain a better understanding of local markets and customers. Ford could have tried to export a windshield wiper to Europe that was designed for the U.S. market. Instead, through its German sub-

WHAT ARE THE MAJOR CHALLENGES OF DOING BUSINESS ABROAD?

The number of firms doing business on an international level is increasing. Particularly interesting is the number of small firms seeking out global opportunities. In 1992, only 11 percent of U.S. companies with less than 500 employees engaged in exporting. By 1994 that figure had grown to 20 percent.

While international markets may appear attractive to firms faced with intense competitive or regulatory pressure at home, there are many uncertainties and potential pitfalls for the unwary. Some common problems for smaller firms moving into the international arena are:

- *Volatile business climates.* Developing economies can be unstable, as the recent near collapse of the Mexican economy demonstrated. Small firms doing business in just one or two countries can be caught unprepared and experience significant unexpected losses.
- *Finding reliable business partners.* Most small firms must rely on overseas distributors to handle their products. Finding a partner in Brazil, China, or Poland that is capable and committed to handling an imported product can be difficult.

- *Achieving a product fit.* A product that is successful in its home country may not be attractive to customers abroad for any number of reasons. As a result, adjustments may be necessary. A U.S. car wax maker is packaging its product in smaller containers for the Mexican market to make it more affordable.
- *Obtaining financing.* Small firms often have difficulty obtaining financing to pay for manufacturing before any sales are made or to extend credit to customers. Lending institutions are uncomfortable with firms with few assets that are entirely dependent on one or a few products. These concerns are compounded when the firm moves into unknown, foreign markets.
- *Dealing with red tape.* Foreign governments often impose paperwork demands that are time-consuming and costly. Foreign customers may also expect importers to meet the International Organization for Standardization (ISO) guidelines. These quality standards for manufacturing, design, and servicing have been accepted by 91 countries. For a firm to achieve certification for its products is a lengthy and expensive process.

Sources: Amy Barrett, "It's a Small (Business) World," *Business Week*, Apr. 17, 1995, pp. 96–101; and Susan Enfield, "South of the Border Blues," *Sales & Marketing Management*, May 1995, pp. 79–84.

---

sidiary, Ford learned that it had to produce a specially designed wiper to accommodate the speeds on German autobahns (where there are no speed limits!).
- Foreign operations contribute to the volume of exports. Nearly 25 percent of all exports by U.S. firms are sales to affiliates located overseas.[5]

Characteristics of Business Market Demand

Four demand characteristics differentiate the business market from the consumer market: Demand is derived, demand tends to be inelastic, demand is widely fluctuating, and the market is well informed.

Demand Is Derived

The demand for a business product is derived from the demand for the consumer products in which that business product is used. Thus the demand for steel depends partially on consumer demand for automobiles and refrigerators, but it also depends on the demand for butter, baseball gloves, and CD players. This is because the tools, machines, and other equipment needed to make these items are made of steel. Consequently, as the demand for baseball gloves increases, Wilson Sporting Goods may buy more steel sewing machines or filing cabinets.

There are two significant marketing implications in the fact that business market demand is a derived demand. First, to estimate the demand for a product, a business marketer must be very familiar with how it is used. This is fairly easy for a company like Pratt & Whitney, a maker of jet engines. But what about the manufacturer of rubber O-rings (doughnut-shaped rings of all sizes that are used to seal connections)? Considerable research may be necessary to identify uses and users.

http://www.dupont.com/

http://www.nutrasweet.com/

Second, the producer of a business product may engage in marketing efforts to encourage the sale of its buyers' products. For example, Du Pont advertises to consumers, urging them when buying carpeting to ask specifically for products made with Du Pont's stain-resistant Stainmaster fiber. Similarly, the NutraSweet Company ran a consumer advertising campaign designed to build consumer loyalty for products sweetened with NutraSweet. The idea, of course, is that increases in consumer demand will, in turn, trigger increases in derived demand for these business products.

Demand Is Inelastic

Another characteristic of the business market is the demand elasticity of business products. Elasticity of demand refers to how responsive demand is to a change in the price of a product. (To review some economics, demand elasticity is explained early in Appendix A.)

The demand for many business products is relatively inelastic, which means that the demand for a product responds very little to changes in its price. There are two situations that contribute to inelasticity:

- If the cost of a part or material is a small portion of the total cost of a finished product. For example, if the price of buttons for men's jackets should suddenly rise or fall considerably, how much effect would it have on the price of jackets? Because the buttons are such a small part of the jacket, the price increase would not likely change the price of jackets. As a result, demand for jackets would remain the same, so there would be no appreciable change in the demand for buttons either.

   Even the cost of expensive capital equipment, such as a robot used in assembling automobiles, when spread over the thousands of units it helps produce, becomes a very small part of the final price of each one. As a result, when the price of the business product changes, there is very little change in the price of the related consumer products. Since there is no appreciable shift in the demand for the consumer goods, then—by virtue of the derived-demand feature—there is no change in the demand for the business product.

- If the part or material has no substitute. In 1994 and 1995 the cost of white bond paper increased over 50 percent because of a shortage of supply. Since paper is a major component of catalogs and magazines, producers of these products had no alternative but to buy it. The catalog and magazine publishers were unable to pass the increase along to their customers because it would have nearly doubled the price of their products. As a result, they were severely affected by the price change. The bond paper manufacturers, on the other hand, sold all they could produce at the higher price.

From a marketing point of view, there are three factors that can moderate the inelasticity of business demand. The factors that can create a situation in which the quantity demanded is affected by a change in price are:

- If the price change occurs in a single firm. An industry-wide cut in the price of steel belts used in tires will have little effect on the price of tires and there-

The steel industry has lost much of its packaging business to aluminum can makers. In an attempt to reverse this trend, the Steel Packaging Council is spending $12 million over five years on promotion to encourage more consumers to buy canned food and recycle more steel. Note, however, that this ad, like the others in the campaign, is not for steel cans but for a food item. Why? Because the Council recognizes that the demand for cans is totally derived from the demand for the beverages and food items contained in its cans.

http://www.steel.org/

The Cornish Hen came from a Canadian farm.
The peppers from the valleys of California.
And the mushrooms are from somewhere that's sure to surprise you.

Firm, velvety, delicate tasting mushrooms that come in a can might strike you as being a little, well, unexpected. But the fact is, today's modern steel can has proven to be one of the best ways to preserve the taste and nutrition that nature gives to over 1500 different foods. And when you use canned mushrooms to make Stuffed Cornish Hen Acadiana, you'll enjoy a meal that's truly unforgettable.
What's In A Can Will Surprise You.

STEEL PACKAGING COUNCIL, AMERICAN IRON AND STEEL INSTITUTE.

fore little effect on the demand for automobile tires. Consequently, it will cause minimal shift in the total demand for steel belts. The pricing policy of an individual firm, however, can substantially alter the demand for its products. If one supplier cuts the price of its steel belts significantly, the drop in price may draw a great deal of business away from competitors. Thus, in the short run, the demand curve faced by a single firm may be quite elastic. However, any advantage will likely be temporary, because competitors will almost certainly retaliate in some way to recapture their lost business.

- If we adopt a long-run time perspective. Much of our discussion thus far applies to short-term situations. Over the long run, the demand for a given business product is more elastic. If the price of cloth for women's suits rises, there probably will be no immediate change in the price of the finished garment. However, the increase in the cost of materials could very well be reflected in a rise in suit prices for next year. This rise could then influence the demand for suits, and thus for cloth, a year or more hence.
- If the cost of a specific business product is a significant portion of the cost of the finished good. We may generalize to this extent: The greater the cost of a business product as a percentage of the total price of the finished good, the greater the elasticity of demand for this business product.

Demand Is Widely Fluctuating

Although the demand for business goods does not change much in response to price changes, it does respond to other factors. In fact, market demand for most classes of business goods fluctuates considerably more than the demand for consumer products. The demand for installations—major plant equipment, factories, and so on—is especially subject to change. Substantial fluctuations also exist in the market for accessory equipment—office furniture and machinery, delivery trucks, and similar products. These fluctuations in the demand for finished goods tend to accentuate the swings in the demand for business raw materials and fabricating parts. We can see this very clearly when declines in demand in the construction and auto industries affect suppliers of lumber, steel, and other materials and parts.

A major reason for these fluctuations is that individual businesses are very concerned about having a shortage of inventory when consumer demand increases or being caught with excess inventory should consumer demand decline. Thus they tend to overreact to signals from the economy, building inventories when they see signs of growth in the economy and working inventories down when the signs suggest stagnation. When the actions of all the individual firms are combined, the effect on their suppliers is widely fluctuating demand. This is known as the *acceleration principle*. One exception to this generalization is found in agricultural products intended for processing. Because people have to eat, there is a reasonably consistent demand for animals intended for meat products, for fruits and vegetables that will be canned or frozen, and for grains and dairy products used in cereals and baked goods.

Fluctuations in the demand for business products can influence all aspects of a marketing program. In product planning, fluctuations in demand may stimulate a firm to diversify into other products to ease production and marketing problems. For example, IBM has moved from concentrating on large, mainframe computers to personal computers, software, microcomputer chips, and consulting. Distribution strategies may be affected. When demand declines, a manufacturer may discover that selling to some resellers is unprofitable, so they are dropped as customers. In its pricing, management may attempt to stem a decline in sales by cutting prices, hoping to attract customers away from competing firms. In a 10-year struggle with imported steel and alternative products such as aluminum and fiberglass, Bethlehem Steel has repeatedly reduced prices.

http://www.ibm.com/

http://www.bethsteel.com/

Buyers Are Well Informed

Typically, business buyers are better informed about what they are buying than ultimate consumers. They know more about the relative merits of alternative sources of supply and competitive products for three reasons. First, there are relatively few alternatives for a business buyer to consider. Consumers typically have many more brands and sellers from which to choose than do business buyers. Consider, for example, how many options you would have in purchasing a TV set. However, in most business situations a buyer has only a few firms that offer the particular combination of product features and service desired. Second, the responsibility of a buyer in an organization is ordinarily limited to a few products. Unlike a consumer who buys many different things, a purchasing agent's job is to be very knowledgeable about a narrowly defined set of products. Third, for most consumer purchases, an error is only a minor inconvenience. However, in business buying the cost of a mistake may be thousands of dollars or even the decision maker's job!

This need for information has a significant marketing implication. Sellers of business products place greater emphasis on personal selling than do firms that market consumer products. Business sales people must be carefully selected, properly trained, and adequately compensated. They must give effective sales presentations and furnish satisfactory service both before and after each sale is made. Sales executives are devoting increased effort to the assignment of sales people to key accounts to ensure that these reps are compatible with business buyers.

Determinants of Business Market Demand

To analyze a consumer market, a marketer would study the distribution of population and various demographics such as income, and then try to determine the consumers' buying motives and habits. Essentially the same type of analysis can be used by a firm selling to the business market. The factors affecting the market for business products are the number of potential business users and their purchasing power, buying motives, and buying habits. In the following discussion we'll identify several basic differences between consumer markets and business markets.

Number and Types of Business Users

Number of Buyers. The business market contains relatively few buying units compared to the consumer market. In the U.S. there are about 20 million business users, in contrast to about 260 million consumers divided among more than 95 million households. The business market seems even more limited in terms of most companies, because they sell to only a small segment of the total market. A firm that sells to U.S. manufacturers of light bulbs can cover 96 percent of the industry by contacting only 30 firms. Similarly, four firms produce 78 percent of lead pencils, and eight firms make 85 percent of household vacuum cleaners. Consequently, marketing executives need to pinpoint their market carefully by type of industry and geographic location. A firm that markets hard-rock mining equipment is not interested in the total business market, or even in all 30,000 firms engaged in all forms of mining and quarrying.

One very useful way of organizing information is the **Standard Industrial Classification (SIC) system**, which enables a company to identify relatively small segments of its business market.[6] In this federal-government designed system, all types of businesses in the U.S. are divided into 10 groups, with a range of two-digit code numbers assigned to each group as follows:

SIC range	Industry group
01 to 09	Agriculture, forestry, fishing
10 to 14	Mining
15 to 17	Contract construction
20 to 39	Manufacturing
40 to 49	Transportation and other public utilities
50 to 59	Wholesale and retail trade
60 to 67	Finance, insurance, and real estate
70 to 89	Services
90 to 97	Government—federal, state, local, and international
99	Others

A separate two-digit number is assigned to every major industry within each of the above groups. For example, within the manufacturing group (20 to 39), the food industry is 20 and the furniture industry is 25. Then three- and four-digit classification numbers are used to subdivide each of the major industries into smaller segments. Figure 6-1 illustrates the SIC codes for the dairy industry—a segment of the food-products category within the broad group of manufacturers.

MAJOR GROUPS: 2-DIGIT CODE		SUBGROUPS: 3-DIGIT CODE		INDUSTRIES: 4-DIGIT CODE	
20	Food	201	Meats	2021	Butter
21	Tobacco	202	Dairy products	2022	Cheese
23	Apparel	203	Canned fruit and vegetables	2023	Condensed and evaporated milk
25	Furniture	204	Grain mill products	2024	Ice cream and frozen desserts
26-39	Other manufacturing industries	205	Bakery products	2025	Fluid milk and cream
		206	Sugar and confectionary products		
		207	Fats and oils		
		208	Beverages		
		209	Miscellaneous food products		

FIGURE 6-1 Examples of SIC codes: dairy industry segment of food products.

The federal government publishes a considerable amount of market information for each four-digit industry classification. These data include the number of establishments, employment, and sales volume—all by geographic area. These valuable data are used by marketers to identify potential target industries, geographic markets, and patterns of growth and decline.

One limitation of data reported using SIC codes is that a multiproduct company is listed in only a single four-digit category. Thus, the diversity of a conglomerate such as Sara Lee, which produces bakery goods and hosiery, is hidden. Also, the government's nondisclosure rules prevent revealing information that will identify a given establishment. Consequently, four-digit detail is not available for an industry in a geographic location where this information would easily identify a particular company.

Size of Business Users. While the business market may be limited in the total number of buyers, it is large in purchasing power. A relatively small percentage of firms account for the greatest share of the value added to products by manufacturing. **Value added** is the dollar value of a firm's output minus the value of the inputs it purchased from other firms. If a manufacturer buys lumber for $40 and converts it into a table that it sells for $100, the value added by the manufacturer is $60.

Let's look at some examples from the latest available *Census of Manufactures*. Less than 2 percent of the firms—those with 500 or more employees—accounted for almost 50 percent of the total dollar value added by manufacturing and for almost 40 percent of the total employment in manufacturing. Firms with fewer than 100 employees accounted for 90 percent of all manufacturing establishments, but they produced only 23 percent of the value added by manufacturing.

The marketing significance of these facts is that buying power in many business markets is highly concentrated in a relatively few firms. That is, a high percentage of industry sales are accounted for by a very small number of firms. To illustrate, according to the *Census of Manufactures*, the U.S. has only:

- 65 thread mills
- 31 manufacturers of house slippers

- 26 producers of vegetable oil
- 17 cane sugar refineries

Therefore, sellers have the opportunity to deal directly with these business users. Middlemen are not as essential as in the consumer market.

Of course, these statements are broad generalizations covering the total business market. They do not take into account the variation in business concentration from one industry to another. In some industries—women's dresses, upholstered furniture, natural and processed cheese, and ready-mix concrete, for example—there are many producers and, therefore, a relatively low level of concentration. Nevertheless, even a so-called low-concentration industry represents far more concentration than anything in the consumer market.

Regional Concentration of Business Users.   There is substantial regional concentration in many major industries and among business users as a whole. A firm that sells products used in copper mining will find the bulk of its American market in Utah and Arizona. Hat manufacturers are located mostly in New England, and a large percentage of American-produced shoes come from New England and the Southeast.

The 8 states constituting the Middle Atlantic and East North Central census regions account for almost 40 percent of the total value added by manufacturing. Just 10 Standard Metropolitan Areas alone account for about 25 percent of the total U.S. value added by manufacturing.

Vertical and Horizontal Business Markets.   For effective marketing planning, a company should know whether the market for its products is vertical or horizontal. A **vertical business market** exists when a firm's product is usable by virtually all the firms in only one or two industries. For example, some precision instruments are intended only for the marine market, but every boatbuilder or shipbuilder is a potential customer. A **horizontal business market** is one in which the firm's product is usable by many industries. Business supplies, such as Pennzoil lubricating oils and greases, General Electric small motors, and Weyerhauser paper products, are examples of products with horizontal markets.

A company's marketing program ordinarily is influenced by whether its markets are vertical or horizontal. In a vertical market, a product can be tailor-made to meet the specific needs of one industry. However, the industry must buy enough to support this specialization. In addition, advertising and personal selling can be directed more effectively in vertical markets. In a horizontal market, a product is developed as an all-purpose item, to reach a larger market. However, because of the larger potential market, the product is likely to face more competition.

Buying Power of Business Users

Another determinant of business market demand is the purchasing power of business customers. This can be measured either by the expenditures of business users or by their sales volume. However, such information is not always available or is very difficult to estimate. In such cases purchasing power is estimated indirectly using an **activity indicator of buying power**—that is, some market factor related to sales and expenditures. Sometimes an activity indicator is a combined measure of purchasing power and the number of business users. Government agencies from the local to the federal level compile a wide range of useful statistics. Following are examples of activity indicators that give some idea of the purchasing power of business users.

Measures of Manufacturing Activity. Firms that sell to manufacturers might use as activity indicators the number of employees, the number of plants, or the dollar value added by manufacturing. One firm that sells work gloves determined the relative attractiveness of various geographic areas from the number of employees in manufacturing establishments within the areas. Another company which sold a product that controls stream pollution used two indicators to estimate potential demand: (1) the number of firms processing wood products (paper mills, plywood mills, and so forth) and (2) the manufacturing value added by these firms. These types of data are available in the *Census of Manufactures*, conducted and reported every 5 years. Yearly updates are available in the *Annual Survey of Manufactures*, a report based on a sample of 55,000 manufacturing firms.

Measures of Mining Activity. The number of mines operating, the volume of their output, and the dollar value of the product as it leaves the mine may all indicate the purchasing power of mining firms. These data are published every 5 years in the *Census of Mineral Industries*. This information is useful to any firm marketing business products related to extracting and processing everything from aluminum to zirconium.

Measures of Agricultural Activity. A company marketing agricultural products or equipment can estimate the buying power of its farm market by studying such indicators as cash farm income, acreage planted, or crop yields. A chemical producer that sells to a fertilizer manufacturer might study the same indices, because the demand for chemicals in this case derives from the demand for fertilizer. These data are in the *Census of Agriculture*.

Measures of Construction Activity. If a business is marketing building materials, such as lumber, brick, gypsum products, or builders' hardware, its market depends on construction activity. This can be gauged by the number and value of building permits issued. Another indicator is the number of construction starts by type of structure (single-family residence, apartment, or commercial). Local data are available from county and city records, while *Current Construction Reports*, published monthly by the U.S. Commerce Department, provides regional and national statistics.

Business Buying Behavior

Business buying behavior, like consumer buying behavior, is initiated when an aroused need (a motive) is recognized. This leads to goal-oriented activity designed to satisfy the need. Once again, marketers must try to determine what motivates the buyer, and then understand the buying process and buying patterns of business organizations in their markets.

The Importance of Business Buying

Business buying or purchasing, formerly a relatively minor function in most firms, is now an activity that top management is very much interested in. Once viewed as an isolated activity that focused primarily on searching out low prices, purchasing has become an important part of overall strategy for at least three reasons:

- Companies are making less and buying more. For example, Toyota buys $4.6 billion worth of parts from more than 440 U.S. suppliers for use in its production both in the U.S. and overseas. When outside suppliers become this significant, buying becomes a prime strategic issue.

- Firms are under intense quality and time pressures. To reduce costs and improve efficiency, firms no longer tolerate defective parts and supplies. Chrysler has 1,200 suppliers currently, but its goal is to reduce that number to 150 by the year 2000. One criterion in the selection process is quality. All Chrysler suppliers are annually rated on their product quality and ability to meet delivery schedules. In addition, Chrysler has implemented a real-time computer system that allows suppliers to check on the performance of their parts and supplies on a daily basis.[7]
- To get what they need, firms are concentrating their purchases with fewer suppliers and developing long-term "partnering" relationships. This level of involvement extends beyond a purchase to include such things as working together to develop new products and providing financial support.

Buying Motives of Business Users

Business **buying motives** are the needs that direct the purchasing behavior of business users. One view of buying motives is that business purchases are methodical and structured. Business buying motives, for the most part, are presumed to be practical and unemotional. Business buyers are assumed to be motivated to achieve the optimal combination of price, quality, and service in the products they buy. An alternative view is that business buyers are human, and their business decisions are certainly influenced by their attitudes, perceptions, and values. In fact, many sales people would maintain that business buyers seem to be motivated more toward personal goals than organizational goals, and the two are often in conflict.

The truth is actually somewhere in between. Business buyers have two goals—to further their company's position (in profits, in acceptance by society) and to protect or improve their position in their firms (self-interest). Sometimes these goals are mutually consistent. For example, the firm's highest priority may be to save money, and the buyer expects to be rewarded for negotiating a low price. Obviously the more consistent the goals are, the better for both the organization and the individual, and the easier it is to make buying decisions.

However, there are often significant areas where the buyer's goals do not coincide with those of the firm, as when the firm insists on dealing with the lowest-price supplier, but the buyer has developed a good relationship with another supplier and doesn't want to change. In these cases a seller must appeal to the buyer both on a rational "what's good for the firm" basis, and on a self-interest "what's

AN ETHICAL DILEMMA?

Recently a number of Honda of America executives pleaded guilty to charges that they accepted extravagant gifts in exchange for providing dealers with extra cars when demand was strong but supply was short. One manager admitted that over the years he had accepted from $2 million to $5 million in "gifts from friends" who also happened to be dealers. The gifts included a swimming pool for his home, Rolex watches, a helicopter tour of Hawaii, a Hong Kong shopping trip, and a pair of cowboy boots.

At what point does a "gift" become a bribe?

Source: Allison Lucas, "When Gift Giving Goes Too Far," *Sales & Marketing Management*, June 1995, p. 15.

in it for me" basis. Promotional appeals directed to the buyer's self-interest are particularly useful when two or more competing sellers are offering essentially the same products, prices, and postsale services.

Types of Buying Situations

In Chapter 5 we observed that consumer purchases can range from routine to complex buying decisions. In like manner the buying situations in business organizations vary widely in their complexity, number of people involved, and time required. Researchers in organizational buying behavior have identified three classes of business buying situations. The three **buy classes** are new-task buying, straight rebuy, and modified rebuy:

- **New-task buying.** This is the most difficult and complex buying situation because it is a first-time purchase of a major product. Typically more people are involved in new-task buying than in the other two situations because the risk is great. Information needs are high and the evaluation of alternatives is difficult because the decision makers have little experience with the product. Sellers have the challenge of discovering the buyer's needs and communicating the product's ability to provide satisfaction. A hospital's first-time purchase of laser surgical equipment and a company buying robots for a factory (or buying the factory itself) are new-task buying conditions.
- **Straight rebuy.** This is a routine, low-involvement purchase with minimal information needs and no great consideration of alternatives. The buyer's extensive experience with the seller has been satisfactory, so there is no incentive to search. An example is the repeat purchase of linens and towels by a hospital. These buying decisions are made in the purchasing department, usually from a predetermined list of acceptable suppliers. Suppliers who are not on this list may have difficulty getting in to make a sales presentation to the buyer.
- **Modified rebuy.** This buying situation is somewhere between the other two in terms of time and people involved, information needed, and alternatives considered. In selecting diagnostic equipment to test blood samples, a hospital would consider a small number of reputable suppliers and evaluate the new features added to the products since its last purchase.

Buying-Decision Process in Business

The buying-decision process in business markets is a sequence of five stages similar to the ones followed by consumers, as discussed in the preceding chapter. Not every purchase involves all five steps. Straight-rebuy purchases usually are low-involvement situations for the buyer, so they typically skip some stages. But a new-task purchase of an expensive good or service is likely to be a high-involvement, total-stage buying decision.

To illustrate the process, let's assume that Continental Baking Company, responding to increased concerns about nutrition, is considering using a fat substitute in some baked goods:

- *Need recognition.* Continental's marketing executives are sensitive to the concerns of many consumers about fat in their diets. The opportunity to produce high-quality, good-tasting baked goods without fat is very attractive, but finding the right substitute is the challenge.
- *Identification of alternatives.* The marketing staff draws up a list of product-performance specifications for the fat-free baked goods—attractive appearance,

*T*o have an effect, advertising must be noticed by the prospect. However, business-to-business print advertising is often accused of being dull and unimaginative. For example, interviews with over 10,000 managers by the ad testing firm Roper Starch International revealed that ads in consumer publications are considered much more attention-getting than ads in business publications. How does a business advertiser attract attention? Animals, children, and bright colors are often cited as effective devices, but do they contradict the image of a business advertiser? From the accompanying ad, it would appear that Ricoh isn't concerned. What do you think?

http://www.ricoh.com/

good taste, and reasonable cost. Then the purchasing department identifies the alternative brands and supply sources of fat substitutes that generally meet these specifications. Possibilities include Simplesse produced by NutraSweet/Kelco, Stella made by Staley, and a few others.

- *Evaluation of alternatives.* The production, research, and purchasing people jointly evaluate both the alternative products and sources of supply. They discover that some brands cannot withstand high temperatures, there are differences in how well they simulate the taste and texture of fat, and the approval from the Food and Drug Administration restricts the uses for others. The complete evaluation considers such factors as product performance and price as well as the suppliers' abilities to meet delivery schedules and provide consistent quality.
- *Purchase decision.* Based on the evaluation, the buyer decides on a specific brand and supplier. Next, the purchasing department negotiates the contract. Since large sums are involved, the contract will likely include many details. For example, the contract might go beyond price and delivery schedules to include the producer of the fat substitute providing marketing support for Continental's finished baked goods.
- *Postpurchase behavior.* Continental continues to evaluate the performances of the fat substitute and the selected supplier to ensure that both meet expectations. Future dealings with a supplier will depend on this performance evaluation and on how well the supplier handles any problems that may later arise involving its product.

Multiple Buying Influences—The Buying Center

One of the biggest challenges in business-to-business marketing is identifying the **buying center**, which consists of all the individuals or groups involved in the process of making a decision to purchase. This includes the individuals within and outside an organization that influence the buying decision as well as the person ultimately responsible for the decision.

Research suggests that the average size of a buying center ranges from three to five persons.[8] In other words, there are *multiple* buying influences, particularly in medium-sized and large firms. Even in small companies where the owner-managers make all major decisions, knowledgeable employees are usually consulted before certain purchases are made. The size and makeup of a buying center will vary depending on the product's cost, the complexity of the decision, and the stage of the buying process. The buying center for a straight rebuy of office supplies will be quite different from the center handling the purchase of a building or a fleet of trucks. Recognizing the existence of buying centers helps sellers appreciate that a successful sales effort seldom can be directed to a single individual.

A buying center includes the people who play any of the following **buying roles**:

- *Users*. The people who actually use the business product—perhaps a secretary, an executive, a production-line worker, or a truck driver.
- *Influencers*. The people who set the specifications and aspects of buying decisions because of their technical expertise, their organizational position, or even their political power in the firm.
- *Deciders*. The people who make the actual buying decision regarding the business product and the supplier. A purchasing agent may be the decider in a straight-rebuy situation. But someone in top management may make the decision regarding whether to buy an expensive computer system.
- *Gatekeepers*. The people who control the flow of purchasing information within the organization as well as between the firm and potential vendors. These people may be purchasing agents, secretaries, receptionists, or technical personnel.
- *Buyers*. The people who interact with the suppliers, arrange the terms of sale, and process the actual purchase orders. Typically this is the purchasing department's role. But again, if the purchase is an expensive, complex new buy, the buyer's role may be filled by someone in top management.

Several people in an organization may play the same role. For example, many people in an organization may use PCs for different purposes, but they need to be linked to a network for some shared activities. Or the same person may occupy more than one role. A secretary may be a user, an influencer, and a gatekeeper in the purchase of word processing equipment.

The variety of people contributing to any business buying decision, plus the differences among companies, present real challenges to sales people. As they try to determine "who's on first"—that is, determine who does what in a buying situation—sales reps often call on the wrong people. Even knowing who the decision makers are is not enough, because these people may be very difficult to reach and people move into and out of the buying center as the purchase proceeds through the decision process. This, in part, explains why a sales person typically has only a few major accounts.

Certainly the challenges presented in the business buying-decision process should suggest the importance of coordinating the selling activities of the business marketer with the buying needs of the purchasing organization.

Buying Patterns of Business Users

Buying behavior in the business market differs significantly from consumer behavior in several ways. These differences stem from the products, markets, and buyer-seller relationships in business markets.

Direct Purchase. In the consumer market, consumers rarely buy directly from the producer except in the case of services. In the business market, however, direct purchase by the business user from the producer is quite common even for goods. This is true especially when the order is large and the buyer needs much technical assistance. Computer memory-chip makers, such as Intel Corp. and Advanced Micro Devices, Inc., deal directly with personal computer manufacturers because the chip technology is changing so rapidly. From a seller's point of view, direct sale in the business market is reasonable, especially when there are relatively few potential buyers, they are big, or they are geographically concentrated.

http://www.intel.com/

http://www.amd.com/

Nature of the Relationship. Many business marketers take a broad view of exchanges. Rather than focus only on the immediate customer, they approach marketing as a value chain. That is, they consider the roles of suppliers, producers, distributors, and end users to see how each adds value to the final product. This perspective leads to a recognition of the importance of all the parties involved in successfully bringing a product to market and an emphasis on building and maintaining relationships.

Several traditional business practices tend to discourage relationship building.[9] For example, compensation plans for sales people that reward the volume of sales may result in customers' needs being overlooked. Likewise, the common accounting practice of treating each department in a firm as a cost center may cause managers to focus on cost minimization rather than customer service. And even the procedure of setting individual department performance goals may foster an environment of competition rather than cooperation.

Building and maintaining relationships may require changing the way business is done. For example, Apple Computer, which once relied exclusively on dealers, recognized that many of its larger customers needed specialized service. To satisfy this segment of the market and maintain strong ties to these key customers, the computer firm now has its own sales force calling directly on about 1,000 large accounts. However, many of the orders taken by the sales force are contracted out to dealers to ensure that they are protected.

http://www.apple.com/

Frequency of Purchase. In the business market, firms buy certain products very infrequently. Large installations are purchased only once in many years. Small parts and materials to be used in the manufacture of a product may be ordered on long-term contracts, so that a selling opportunity exists as seldom as once a year. Even standard operating supplies, such as office supplies or cleaning products, may be bought only once a month. Because of this buying pattern, a great burden is placed on the personal selling programs of business sellers. The sales force must call on potential customers often enough to keep them familiar with the company's products and to know when a customer is considering a purchase.

Size of Order. The average business order is considerably larger than its counterpart in the consumer market. This fact, coupled with the infrequency of purchase, spotlights the importance of each sale in the business market. Xerox agreed to pay Electric Data Systems, Inc. (EDS), $3.2 billion to supply all of its computer needs for 10 years.

Length of Negotiation Period. The period of negotiation in a business sale is usually much longer than in a consumer transaction. Some reasons for extended negotiations are:

- Several executives participate in the buying decision.
- The sale involves a large amount of money.
- The business product is made to order and considerable discussion is required to establish the specifications.

Reciprocity Arrangements. A highly controversial business buying practice is reciprocity: the policy of "I'll buy from you if you'll buy from me." Traditionally, reciprocity was common among firms marketing homogeneous basic business products (oil, steel, rubber, paper products, and chemicals).

There has been a significant decline, but not total elimination, of reciprocity. This decline has occurred for two reasons, one legal and the other economic. Both the Federal Trade Commission and the Antitrust Division of the Department of Justice have forbidden the practice of reciprocity in any *systematic* manner, particularly in large companies. A firm can buy from a customer, but it must be able to prove that it is not given any special privileges regarding price, quality, or service.

From an economic point of view, reciprocity may not make sense because the price, quality, or service offered by the seller may not be competitive. In addition, when a firm fails to pursue objectives that maximize profits, morale of both the sales force and the purchasing department may suffer.

Reciprocity is an area in which U.S. firms run into problems in doing business overseas. In many parts of the world, it is taken for granted that if I buy your product, you will buy mine.

Service Expctation. The user's desire for excellent service is a strong business buying motive that may determine buying patterns. Frequently a firm's only differentiating feature is its service, because the product itself is so standardized that it can be purchased from any number of companies. Consider the choice of suppliers to provide elevators for a major office building or hotel. The installation of the elevators is no more important than keeping them operating safely and efficiently. Consequently, in its marketing efforts, a firm such as Montgomery Elevator emphasizes its maintenance service as much as its products.

Sellers must be ready to furnish services both before and after the sale. For example, suppliers such as Kraft Foods conduct a careful analysis of a supermarket's customers and sales performance and then suggest a product assortment and layout for the store's dairy department. In the case of office copiers, manufacturers train the buyers' office staffs in the use of the equipment and, after the machines have been installed, offer other services, such as repairs by specially trained technicians.

Dependability of Supply. Another business buying pattern is the user's insistence on an adequate quantity of uniform-quality products. Variations in the *quality* of materials going into finished products can cause considerable trouble for manufacturers. They may be faced with costly disruptions in their production

A COMMITMENT TO CUSTOMER SATISFACTION

When a timing belt failed in its Perry, Georgia, processing plant, Frito-Lay faced the prospect of losing 25,000 pounds of potatoes. The plant manager contacted Motion Industries, a nearby industrial supplier, for a replacement part. Normally in such an emergency, delivery would take an hour. However, on this day all the roads into Perry were closed because of flooding from 10 inches of rain that had fallen in the previous 24 hours.

Rather than give up or wait until the flood receded, Motion rented a small plane, had the pilot fly over the Frito-Lay plant, and the needed part was dropped to the waiting maintenance manager on the ground.

If Motion lost money on this sale, was it a bad decision?

Source: Motion Industries, Inc., advertisement, *Purchasing*, July 13, 1995, p. 151.

processes if the imperfections exceed quality control limits. The emphasis on total quality management (TQM) has increased the significance of dependability. Now that it has been established that firms can operate with virtually zero defects, buyers expect a very high standard of performance.

Adequate *quantities* are as important as good quality. A work stoppage caused by an insufficient supply of materials is just as costly as one caused by inferior quality of materials. However, firms today refuse to buy in advance of their needs and tie up their resources in large inventories of supplies. This has led to just-in-time (JIT) delivery, in which suppliers are expected to provide sufficient quantities of a product just in time for the buyer's intended use.

Leasing. A growing tendency among firms in the business market is leasing business goods instead of buying them. In the past this practice was limited to large equipment, such as computers (IBM), packaging equipment (American Can Company), and heavy construction equipment. Presently, industrial firms are expanding leasing arrangements to include delivery trucks, automobiles used by sales people, machine tools, and other items that are generally less expensive than major installations.

Leasing has several merits for the lessor—the firm providing the equipment:

- Total net income—the income after charging off repairs and maintenance expenses—is often higher than it would be if the equipment were sold.
- The lessor's market may be expanded to include users who could not afford to buy the product, especially for large equipment.
- Leasing offers an effective method of getting users to try a new product. They may be more willing to rent a product than to buy it. If they are not satisfied, their expenditure is limited to a few monthly payments.

From the lessee's—or customer's—point of view, the benefits of leasing are:[10]

- Leasing allows users to retain their investment capital for other purposes.
- Firms can enter a new business with less capital outlay than would be necessary if they had to buy equipment.
- Leased products are usually repaired and maintained by lessors, eliminating one headache associated with ownership.
- Leasing is particularly attractive to firms that need equipment seasonally or sporadically, as in food canning or construction.

At this point you know what marketing is and how it fits into an organization's strategy. You also appreciate the importance of carefully defining and understanding consumer and business markets. With this background, we are now ready to explore the process of market segmentation and the selection of target markets.

■ SUMMARY

The business market consists of organizations that buy goods and services to produce other goods and services, to resell to other business users or consumers, or to conduct the organization's operations. It is an extremely large and complex market spanning a wide variety of business users that buy a broad array of business goods and services. Besides manufacturing, the business market includes the agriculture, reseller, government, services, nonprofit, and international components.

Business market demand generally is derived, inelastic, and widely fluctuating. Business buyers usually are well informed about what they are buying. Business market demand is analyzed by evaluating the number and kinds of business users and their buying power.

Business buying, or purchasing, has taken on greater strategic importance. Organizations are buying more and making less, under intense time and quality pressures, and developing long-term partnering relationships with suppliers. Business buying motives are focused on achieving a firm's objectives, but the business buyer's self-interest must also be considered.

The buying-decision process in business markets may involve as many as five stages: need recognition, identification of alternatives, evaluation of alternatives, purchase decision, and postpurchase behavior. The actual number of stages in a given purchase decision depends largely on the buying situation, whether new-task buy, straight rebuy, or modified rebuy.

The concept of a buying center reflects the multiple buying influences in business purchasing decisions. In a typical buying center are people playing the roles of users, influencers, deciders, gatekeepers, and buyers.

Buying patterns of business users often are quite different from patterns in the consumer market. In the business market, direct purchases (without middlemen) are more common, purchases are made less frequently, and orders are larger. The negotiation period usually is longer, and reciprocity arrangements are more common. The demand for service is greater, and the dependability of supply is more critical. Finally, leasing (rather than product ownership) is quite common in business marketing.

*More
about*

CESSNA

*T*he single-engine airplane market looks like a sure thing for Cessna, but there are some marketing issues to consider. First, it has been out of the market for over 10 years. Despite the pent-up demand and its outstanding reputation, Cessna cannot take the market for granted.

Second, this opportunity is attracting considerable attention. Foreign manufacturers such as Aerospatiale (from France) and Toyota are likely entrants. Domestic competition will come from the major players in the 1980s such as Piper, as well as new competitors such as Commander Aircraft.

Third, to avoid the cost (as much as $25 million) and the time (up to 3 years for certification by the Federal Aviation Administration) involved in designing a new plane, Cessna has chosen to go with slightly updated 20-year-old designs.

Finally, there is some question about whether the law limiting liability of plane manufacturers will hold up in court.[11]

1. What type of buying situation is the purchase of a single-engine propeller plane for most customers?
2. How would you describe the likely buying process used by most purchasers of this product?

■ KEY TERMS AND CONCEPTS

Business market (134)
Business users (134)
Business marketing (134)
Agribusiness (135)
Reseller market (136)
Government market (136)

Services market (137)
Nonbusiness market (138)
International market (138)
Standard Industrial Classification (SIC) system (143)
Value added (144)

Vertical business market (145)
Horizontal business market (145)
Activity indicator of buying power (145)
Buying motives (147)

Buy classes (148)
New-task buying (148)
Straight rebuy (148)
Modified rebuy (148)
Buying centers (150)
Buying roles (150)

■ QUESTIONS AND PROBLEMS

1. What are some marketing implications in the fact that the demand for business goods:
   a. Fluctuates widely.
   b. Is inelastic.
   c. Is derived.
2. What are the marketing implications for a seller in the fact that business customers are geographically concentrated and limited in number?
3. What differences would you expect to find between the marketing strategies of a company that sells to horizontal business markets and those of a company that sells to vertical business markets?
4. An American manufacturer has been selling word processors to a large oil company in Norway. In which of the three buy classes would you place this buyer-seller relationship? Is there any aspect of the relationship that is likely to fall into the straight-rebuy category?
5. Explain how the five stages in the buying-decision process might be applied in the following buying situations:
   a. New-task buying of a conveyor belt for a soft-drink bottling plant
   b. Straight rebuying of maintenance services for that conveyor belt
6. How would you go about determining who influences the buying decisions of business users?
7. NCR, IBM, Xerox, and other manufacturers of office equipment make a substantial proportion of their sales directly to business users. At the same time, wholesalers of office equipment are thriving. Are these two market situations inconsistent? Explain.

■ HANDS-ON MARKETING

1. Find an ad for a business good or service that is directed toward the business market and another ad for the same product that is directed toward consumers (such as an ad for leasing fleets of Chevrolets and an ad for Chevrolet aimed at consumers). Discuss the buying motives appealed to in the ads.
2. Interview a purchasing agent about buying a product that would qualify as a modified rebuy. Draw a diagram that shows the purchasing agent's perceptions of (a) the stages of the decision process; (b) who was in the buying center at each stage of the decision process; and (c) what role(s) each person played at each stage of the process. Comment on how this diagram might be useful to a sales person representing the product in question.

CHAPTER 7

Market Segmentation and Target-Market Strategies

Does
BLACK & DECKER's
View of the Market Hit the Nail on the Head?

Black & Decker is a well-known name in the power tool business. The company developed a reputation for making good quality electric drills, saws, and other tools. Its success, however, may have led to complacency that caused the firm to overlook the way the market for these products had evolved. That changed with the success of Japanese tool maker Makita and the continuing growth of the Sears Craftsman line.

In the early 1990s, Black & Decker management examined the tool market and concluded that it consisted of three segments—professionals, serious do-it-yourselfers, and household maintainers—each with quite different needs:

- Professionals are a business market. They are people who earn their living in the building trades. They demand durability and precision. Their tools have to hold up under continuous rough use, but they must also be sophisticated enough to do precise work.
- Do-it-yourselfers (DIYers) are a growing group. Their increasing numbers are reflected in the success of building supply retailers such as Builders Square and Home Depot. The sale of home improvement products amounts to over $75 billion a year and continued growth is projected. DIYers take on complicated projects so they need good tools, but most don't need professional-level durability.
- Household maintainers are the biggest group, but also the ones that spend the least on power tools. They do small projects around the house (hang pictures, repair faucets, assemble toys). They want the convenience power tools provide, but they only use them occasionally.

Though the Black & Decker line of tools could meet many of the needs of all three groups, it was not clearly positioned for any one. According to a B&D manager, "It's tough to sell a $130 cordless drill to professionals when the same brand name appears on a $30 drill. . . ."[1]

How will recognizing that the market is made up of groups with different needs affect Black & Decker's marketing strategy?

http://www.blackanddecker.com/

Black & Decker has divided the power tool market into several submarkets or segments, and designed different marketing mixes—products, distribution, pricing, and promotion—for each. In this chapter we will see why markets are segmented and how it is done. We will also consider the alternative target-market strategies a firm can choose from once a market has been segmented. After studying this chapter, you should be able to explain:

CHAPTER GOALS

- The related concepts of market segmentation and target markets.
- The process of market segmentation, including its benefits and conditions for use.
- Bases for segmenting consumer and business markets.
- Three target-market strategies: aggregation, single-segment strategy, and multiple-segment strategy.
- The most frequently used methods of forecasting the demand of market segments.

An Overview of Market Segments and Target Markets

In Chapter 2 we defined a market as people or organizations with (1) wants to satisfy, (2) money to spend, and (3) the willingness to spend it. However, within a total market there is always some diversity among the buyers. Not all consumers who wear pants want to wear jeans, and not everyone who buys golf clubs wants to pay the same price or purchase them from a golf-course pro shop. For some consumers the primary reason for taking a vacation cruise is rest and relaxation, but for others it is adventure and excitement. Among businesses, not all firms that use computers want the same amount of memory or speed, nor does every software buyer need the same amount of expert advice.

What we are seeing here is that within the same general market there are groups of customers—**market segments**—with different wants, buying preferences, or product-use behavior. In some markets these differences are relatively minor, and the benefits sought by consumers can be satisfied with a single marketing mix. In other markets, customers are unwilling to make the compromises necessitated by a single marketing mix. As a result, the segments must be targeted individually and alternative marketing mixes are required to reach them. Whether it is large or small, the specific group of customers (people or organizations) for whom the seller designs a particular marketing mix is a **target market**.

Before target markets can be selected, however, they must be identified and described. This process is called market segmentation.

Market Segmentation

The variation in customers' responses to a marketing mix can be traced to differences in buying habits, in ways in which the good or service is used, or in motives for buying. Customer-oriented marketers take these differences into consideration, but they usually cannot afford to tailor-make a different marketing mix for every customer. Consequently, most marketers operate between the extremes of one marketing mix for all and a different one for each customer. To do so involves **market segmentation**, a process of dividing the total market for a good or service into several smaller, internally homogeneous groups. The essence of segmentation is that the members of each group are similar with respect to the factors that influence demand. A major element in a company's success is the ability to segment its market effectively.

Benefits of Market Segmentation

Market segmentation is customer-oriented, and thus it is consistent with the marketing concept. In segmenting, we first identify the wants of customers within a submarket and then decide if it is practical to develop a marketing mix to satisfy those wants.

By tailoring marketing programs to individual market segments, management can do a better marketing job and make more efficient use of its marketing resources. A small firm with limited resources might compete very effectively in one or two small market segments. However, this same firm would be overwhelmed by the competition if it aimed for a major segment. For example, Estee Corp. has segmented the food market based on dietary restrictions. By producing items for diabetics—sugarless cookies, candy, salad dressings, jams, and desserts—the firm is able to meet the needs of a specific group while avoiding direct competition with giants in the food industry such as Kraft or General Foods. Advertising can also be more effective, because promotional messages—and the media chosen to present them—can be aimed toward a specific segment of the market. With a limited budget, Estee communicates with its target market by placing ads in specialty magazines for physicians and diabetics and doing direct-mail advertising to diabetics.

http://www.reyrey.com/

By developing strong positions in specialized market segments, medium-sized firms can grow rapidly. For example, the Oshkosh Truck Company in Wisconsin has become the world's largest producer of fire and rescue trucks for airports. And Reynolds & Reynolds Company, an Ohio firm, has most of the market for standard paper forms used by automobile dealers.

Even very large companies with the resources to engage in mass marketing supported by expensive national advertising campaigns are abandoning mass-market strategies. These companies embrace market segmentation as a more effective strategy to reach the fragments that once constituted a mass, homogeneous market in the U.S.

http://www.pg.com/

The marketing of bar soap illustrates these changing conditions nicely. At the turn of the century there were two major brands: Ivory, made by Procter & Gamble; and Lifebuoy, a Lever Bros. product. Today, in addition to Ivory, P&G offers Zest, Coast, Safeguard, Camay, Kirk's Castile, and Oil of Olay soaps. The Lever Bros. line has been extended to include Dove, Caress, Shield, Lux, and Lever 2000 as well as Lifebuoy. Other variations are different-size bars for sink and tub, colors to match bathroom decor, and liquid soap in pump dispensers. These developments reflect a market that has been segmented by skin type (dry versus oily), fragrance, the desire for convenience, and the primary benefit sought (such as cleaning dirty hands or body deodorizing). It is clear that all consumers use soap for cleansing, but they also expect other benefits from the soap they use. Hence many segments exist.

The Process of Market Segmentation

http://www.gatorade.com/

Markets are sometimes segmented intuitively; that is, a marketer relies on experience and judgment to decide what segments exist in a market and how much potential they offer. Others follow the lead of competitors or earlier market entrants. For example, Gatorade established the fact that the soft drink market includes a segment motivated by the desire to rapidly replenish body fluids. Following the success of Gatorade, many brands have been introduced that attempt to appeal to the same segment. Another alternative is to perform a structured analysis, often supported by some marketing research, in order to identify segments and measure their potential. This approach, even if done with a small budget, often produces insights and opportunities that would be overlooked otherwise.

The steps involved in segmenting a market in an organized fashion are:

1. *Identify the current and potential wants that exist within a market.* The marketer carefully examines the market to determine the specific needs being satisfied by current offerings, the needs current offerings fail to adequately satisfy, and the future needs that may not yet be recognized. This step may involve interviewing and/or observing consumers or firms to determine their behavior, levels of satisfaction, and frustrations.

   Within the market for wristwatches there is a common desire among customers to know the time, and all watches must accurately tell time. But there are customers who also want a watch to be a fashion accessory, a status symbol, an exercise timer, or an appointment reminder. There might be others who would like a watch to function as a computer, a voice recorder, a pulse monitor, a television receiver, or a telephone. Each of these wants represents a potential market segment within the wristwatch market.

2. *Identify the characteristics that distinguish among the segments.* The question is, What do prospects who share a particular want have in common that distinguishes them from other segments in the market with different wants? Among business firms it could be a physical feature (like size or location). Among consumers it might be an attitude or a behavior pattern. Tentative marketing mixes are devised for the various segments from the results of this step.

3. *Determine who has each want.* The final step is to estimate how much demand or potential sales each segment represents. These forecasts will determine which segments are worth pursuing.

A group that shares a want distinguishable from the rest of the market is a market segment. However, to be useful to marketers, a segmentation process must also meet some conditions:

- The bases for segmenting—that is, the characteristics used to describe what segments customers fall into—must be *measurable*, and data describing the characteristics must be *obtainable*. The age of customers is both measurable and obtainable. On the other hand, the "desire for ecologically compatible products" may be a factor useful in segmenting the market for mulching lawn mowers. But this characteristic is not easily measured, nor can the data be easily obtained.

- The market segment should be *accessible* through existing marketing institutions—middlemen, advertising media, company sales forces—with a minimum of cost and wasted effort. To reduce wasted coverage, some national magazines such as *Time* and *Sports Illustrated* and large metropolitan newspapers publish separate geographical editions. This allows an advertiser to run a magazine ad aimed at, say, a Southern segment of the market or a newspaper ad for particular suburbs, without having to pay for exposure in other, nontargeted areas.

- Each segment should be *large enough* to be profitable. Procter & Gamble found a segment of candy consumers that wants a low-calorie product. However, it is too small to justify the investment a line of confections would require.[2] In concept, management could treat each single customer as a separate segment.

http://www.timeinc.com/

Actually, this situation may be normal in some business markets, as when Boeing markets passenger airplanes to commercial airlines or when Citibank makes a loan to the government of Mexico or Argentina. It also occurs in selected consumer markets such as custom-designed homes. But in segmenting most consumer markets, a firm must not develop too broad an array of styles, colors, sizes, and prices, because the production and inventory costs would make it unprofitable.

Ultimate Consumers and Business Users— The First Cut

As we shall see, a company can segment its market in many different ways. And the bases for segmentation vary from one product to another. However, the first step is to divide a potential market into two broad categories: ultimate consumers and business users. This is what Black & Decker did in segmenting the power tool market.

The sole criterion for this first cut at segmenting a market is the customer's reason for buying. Recall from Chapter 5 that ultimate consumers buy goods or services for their own personal or household use and are satisfying strictly non-business wants. They constitute the consumer market. Business users, described in Chapter 6, are business, industrial, or institutional organizations that buy goods or services to use in their organizations, to resell, or to make other products. A manufacturer that buys chemicals to make fertilizer is a business user of these chemicals. Farmers who buy the fertilizer to use in commercial farming are business users of the fertilizer. And retailers who buy fertilizer to resell to consumers are also business users. (However, when homeowners buy fertilizer to use on their yards, they are ultimate consumers because they buy it for personal, nonbusiness use.) Supermarkets, art museums, and paper manufacturers that buy the service of a certified public accountant are business users of this service.

Segmenting a market into these two groups—consumers and businesses—is extremely significant from a marketing point of view because the two segments buy differently. Consequently, the composition of a seller's marketing mix will depend on whether it is directed toward the consumer market or the business market.

Segmenting Consumer Markets

Dividing a total market into ultimate consumers and business users results in segments that are still too broad and varied for most products. We need to identify some characteristics within each of these segments that will enable us to divide them further into more specific segments.

As shown in Table 7-1, there are a number of ways the consumer market can be segmented. The bases for segmentation include many of the characteristics used to describe the consumer market in Chapter 5, as well as some psychological and behavioral dimensions. We will discuss four bases for segmenting consumer markets:

- Geographic
- Demographic
- Psychographic
- Behavioral

TABLE 7-1 Segmentation bases for consumer markets

Segmentation basis	Typical market segments
Geographic:	
Region	New England, Middle Atlantic, and other census regions
City or MSA size	Under 25,000; 25,001–100,000; 100,001–500,000; 500,001–1,000,000; etc.
Urban-rural	Urban, suburban, rural
Climate	Hot, cold, sunny, rainy, cloudy
Demographic:	
Income	Under $10,000; $10,001–$25,000; $25,001–$35,000; $35,001–$50,000; over $50,000
Age	Under 6, 6–12, 13–19, 20–34, 35–49, 50–64, 65 and over
Gender	Male, female
Family life cycle	Young, single; young, married, no children; etc.
Social class	Upper class, upper middle, lower middle, upper lower, etc.
Education	Grade school only, high school graduate, college graduate
Occupation	Professional, manager, clerical, sales, student, homemaker, unemployed
Ethnic background	African, Asian, European, Hispanic, Middle Eastern, etc.
Psychographic:	
Personality	Ambitious, self-confident, aggressive, introverted, extroverted, sociable
Life-style	Activities (golf, travel); interests (politics, modern art); opinions (conservation, capitalism)
Values	Values and Life-Styles 2 (VALS2), List of Values (LOV)
Behavioral:	
Benefits desired	Examples vary widely depending on product: appliance—cost, quality, operating life; toothpaste—no cavities, plaque control, bright teeth, good taste, low price
Usage rate	Nonuser, light user, heavy user

Geographic Segmentation

Subdividing markets into segments based on location—the regions, counties, cities, and towns where people live and work—is **geographic segmentation**. The reason for this is simply that consumers' wants and product usage often are related to one or more of these subcategories. Geographic characteristics are also measurable and accessible—two of the conditions for effective segmentation. Let's consider how the geographic distribution of population may serve as a basis for segmentation.

Regional Population Distribution.   Many firms market their products in a limited number of geographic regions, or they may market nationally but prepare a separate marketing mix for each region. Supermarket chains such as Alpha Beta and Winn-Dixie concentrate their marketing efforts in specific geographic regions. Even supermarket giants such as Kroger and Safeway are unknown in some parts of the country. Campbell Soup Company has altered some of its soup and bean recipes to suit regional tastes, and General Foods uses different methods to promote Maxwell House coffee in different regions.

The regional distribution of population is important to marketers because people *within* a given region generally tend to share the same values, attitudes, and style preferences. However, significant differences do exist *among* regions because of differences in climate, social customs, and other factors. Thus bright, warm colors are preferred in Florida and the Southwest, while grays and cooler colors predominate in New England and the Midwest. People in the West are less formal than Easterners, and they spend more time outdoors. Consequently, in the Western region there is a large market for patio furniture, sports clothes, and outdoor recreation equipment.

Many organizations segment their markets on the basis of city size or population concentration; that is, they utilize an urban-suburban-rural distribution. Toys "R" Us, the largest chain of toy stores in the U.S., initially located stores only in metropolitan areas with populations exceeding 250,000 to ensure a sufficiently large customer base. In contrast, Wal-Mart's initial strategy was to locate only in towns of less than 35,000 people in order to minimize the amount of competition.

http://www.toysrus.com/

http://www.wal-mart.com/

A popular reference source used for geographic segmentation by marketers was mentioned as a secondary data source in Chapter 4. It is *Sales & Marketing Management* magazine's annual "Survey of Buying Power." This two-part report provides information on population, income, and spending behavior by state, county, major metropolitan area, television market, and newspaper market. With these data, a marketer can compare spending power and purchasing behavior across geographic areas.

http://www.claritas.com/

An example of how refined geographic segmentation can become is ZIP code (or geodemographic) clustering. This procedure was pioneered by the research firm, Claritas, with a system it calls PRIZM (short for Potential Rating Index for ZIP Markets). Using U.S. Census data on education, income, occupation, housing, ethnicity, urbanization, and other variables, Claritas grouped the 36,000 U.S. ZIP codes into 62 clusters or segments. Each cluster then was examined for similarities in life-styles and consumption behavior, and given descriptive names such as "kids and cul-de-sacs," "gray power," and "shotguns and pickups." Marketers use this information to identify ZIP codes for direct-mail promotions, to select locations for retail outlets, and to determine the best mix of products and brands to offer in a particular store.[3]

Demographic Segmentation

Demographics are the most common basis for segmenting consumer markets. They are frequently used because they are often strongly related to demand and are relatively easy to measure. Recall that several demographic variables were discussed in Chapter 5 when we described the consumer market. The most popular characteristics, used alone or in combination, for **demographic segmentation** are age, gender, family life-cycle stage, income, and education.

Age. Because our wants change as we go through life, population distribution by age is a useful basis for segmenting the market for many products. To illustrate the value of demographic segmentation, we will briefly examine some of the highlights and distinctive features of four age-based segments.

Youngsters. The 12-and-under age group affects expenditures in three ways. First, these children influence purchases made by their parents. A recent study estimates that children have an effect on about $130 billion in parental purchases a year.[4] Second, billions of dollars are spent on this group by their parents and grandparents. Third, these children buy goods and services for their own personal use.

Their total annual income from gifts, allowances, and odd jobs is estimated at $17 billion, and it is virtually all discretionary.[5]

Promotional programs are often geared to this market segment, but the media used to reach them is changing. The share of children watching Saturday morning TV shows has dipped 15 percent since 1986. To offset this decline, advertisers are broadening their media choices. For example, the number of special interest magazines for young people is increasing, making magazines a more popular place to advertise. Already on the market are children's versions of *Sports Illustrated* and *Field and Stream*. A 1995 survey found 73 magazines intended for children, compared to 16 in 1984.[6] Another medium is emerging for this computer-literate generation. Though their impact is difficult to measure, on-line computer services such as America Online and Prodigy are targeting children and appear to have significant potential.

Teenagers. Following a 15-year decline, the number of teenagers began growing in 1992, reaching 25 million in 1994. The number is projected to be 31 million by 2010. Many consumers in this age category have substantial incomes from part-time jobs and two income-earning parents, though one in four lives in a household headed by a single parent. Teenagers constitute a big market for videocassettes, apparel, cosmetics, stereos, records, and other personal luxury products. The teenage market is large and free-spending, and yet it has proved difficult for advertisers to reach. For example, few teens read a daily newspaper regularly. Yet marketers are attracted to this group because of its size and because its members have a considerable amount of money to spend, nearly $90 billion in 1995.[7]

http://www.hacienda.com/

One way to reach this market is through school. *Channel One*, a daily, ad-supported 12-minute TV news program is broadcast into over 12,000 high schools and middle schools across the U.S. *Channel One* gives schools satellite dishes and television sets in exchange for a guarantee that all the school's students will be exposed to the show.[8]

Middle Aged. The segment that will be ages 45 to 64 in the year 2000 will be an especially large and lucrative market. Many of these people are products of the post-World War II baby boom, and many were the social rebels of the late 1960s and early 1970s. As they move through middle age and approach retirement, they enter their highest earning years. Typically their personal situations, values, and life-styles are far different from those found among people of the same age in previous generations. Manufacturers are responding to these changes. Oldsmobile developed the Aurora, Toyota the Avalon, and Mercury the Mystique with more safety features, bigger engines, and greater interior space to appeal to this mature segment. Colgate, Crest, and other toothpaste makers that stressed cavity prevention to these people 20 years ago now are producing toothpastes to fight plaque—an adult dental problem.

Seniors. At the older end of the age spectrum are people over 65, a segment that is growing both in absolute numbers and as a percentage of the total population. This group's average household income ($17,000) is only about one-half as much as the average for all U.S. households. However, because they have fewer financial obligations, their per capita discretionary purchasing power of $5,633 is more than any other group. Manufacturers and retailers alike are beginning to recognize that people in this age group are logical prospects for small housing units, cruises and foreign tours, health products, and cosmetics developed especially for older people. Recognizing that grandparents purchase about 25 percent of all toys,

YOU MAKE THE DECISION

WHERE SHOULD YOU DRAW THE LINE ON AGE?

Demographic segmentation is sometimes undertaken using characteristics that are convenient or easily obtainable without sufficient regard to how logical or correct they are. Consider, for example, the notion of lumping all teenagers into one group and treating them as a market segment. All the numbers end in "teen," so there is a certain symmetry to combining them. However, it seems likely there are purchase situations in which 13- and 14-year-olds behave quite differently from 18- and 19-year-olds.

What are some marketing situations in which it would seem reasonable to treat all teenagers as a market segment, and some in which it would not?

---

http://www.faoschwartz.com/

F.A.O. Schwartz has added a "Grandma's Shop" to its largest stores to assist these gift buyers.[9]

Other Demographic Bases for Segmentation. The markets for certain consumer products are influenced by demographic factors that deserve special note. One is social class, a composite measure of several demographic characteristics that marketers have used for many years; the other is ethnic origin, a characteristic that is becoming increasingly popular as a basis for segmentation:

- Social class is a measure made up of a combination of demographic characteristics. The most commonly used indicator of social class includes level of education, type of occupation, and the type of neighborhood a person lives in. Because a person's social class—be it upper class or blue-collar working class—has a considerable influence on that person's choices in many product categories, companies frequently select one or two social classes as target markets and then develop a product and marketing mix to reach those segments.
- Ethnic origin is useful for segmenting the market for some products. There is a large market for Polish sausage in some Midwestern areas, and people of Mexican descent in the Southwest have product preferences that are quite different from those of, say, Asian American consumers living on the West Coast.

Segmenting markets based on ethnicity presents an interesting challenge. On the one hand, a company must understand an ethnic group's buying behavior and motivation. Studies by the Bureau of Labor Statistics and private research firms show that there are some distinct differences among races. For example, on the average, black and white Americans differ in income, level of education, and the likelihood of living in urban or rural areas. In addition, in some product categories, spending is distinctly different. Compared to whites, blacks as a group spend a greater portion of their income on meat, poultry, fish, sugar and other sweets, personal care products, laundry and cleaning products, and children's apparel, and less on entertainment, medical services, household furnishings, and alcoholic beverages.[10]

On the other hand, ethnic markets are not homogeneous units any more than any other population segment consisting of 20 or 30 million people. There is nearly as much diversity within every ethnic group as there is similarity. African American and Hispanic markets contain subgroups based on income, occupation, geographic location, and life-cycle stage. Thus, it would be a serious marketing error to be misled by aggregate figures and averages. For example, firms that make products for which skin color is a major choice determinant recognize this diversity.

WHERE HAVE THE CADILLAC BUYERS GONE?

For years Cadillac has relied on a market segment that is older, wealthy, male—and American. However, in recent years the brand hasn't been doing well. In 1994, 211,000 Cadillacs were sold in the U.S., down from 258,000 in 1990. By comparison, in the same year 157,000 Mercedes and BMWs were purchased in the U.S. Even more disturbing, only 4,825 Cadillacs were sold outside North America. What Cadillac is finding is that many buyers in its segment are opting for foreign luxury cars or sport-utility vehicles.

Most of Cadillac's problems are self-inflicted. By focusing on the domestic market, the GM division's response to weak sales was narrow and limited. The brand's reputation was damaged with the Allante, a two-seat roadster that failed to perform up to its $50,000 price tag, and the Cimarron, a compact whose size seemed to contradict the Cadillac image.

Now Cadillac is taking a broader view. If it is to prosper, many think the division has to adopt a global strategy. One step in that direction is the Catera, a German Opel that is sold in the U.S. under the Cadillac name. It combines luxury, sportiness, and less bulk than the traditional Cadillac. However, to be competitive in the luxury market, Cadillac has to sell many more cars, and that means entering world markets on a large scale. The "price" of global market entry is likely to include models that other luxury carmakers already offer—a four-wheel drive Cadillac and a sport-utility Cadillac. Just one of these would require an investment of $700 million. That's equivalent to $3,300 for every Cadillac sold in 1994.

Potential Cadillac buyers may be around, but the company must describe them differently than in the past. The challenge for Cadillac is to segment the luxury car market using a global perspective.

http://www.cadillac.com/

Sources: Gabriella Stern, "Cadillac Covets the Range Rover Crowd," *The Wall Street Journal*, Jan. 17, 1995, p. B1; and Jerry Flint, "A German Cadillac," *Forbes*, July 31, 1995, p. 60.

Prescriptives, a subsidiary of Estée Lauder cosmetic company, has a line of make-up foundations for black women with 115 different shades.[11]

Psychographic Segmentation

Demographic data are used to segment markets because these data are related to behavior and because they are relatively easy to gather. However, demographics are not in themselves the causes of behavior. Consumers don't buy windsurfing equipment because they are young. They buy it because they enjoy an active, outdoor life-style, and it so happens that such people are also typically younger. Thus, demographics often correlate with behavior, but they do not explain it.

Marketers often go beyond demographics attributes in an effort to better understand why consumers behave as they do. They engage in **psychographic segmentation**, which involves examining attributes related to how a person thinks, feels, and behaves. Using personality dimensions, life-style characteristics, and values, marketers are able to develop richer and more complete descriptions of segments.

Personality Characteristics. An individual's **personality** is usually described in terms of traits that influence behavior. Theoretically, they would seem to be a good basis for segmenting markets. Our experience tells us that compulsive people buy differently from cautious consumers, and quiet introverts do not buy the same things in the same way as gregarious, outgoing people.

However, personality characteristics pose problems that limit their usefulness in practical market segmentation. First, the presence and strength of these characteristics in the population are virtually impossible to measure. For example, how would you go about measuring the number of people in the U.S. who could be classified as aggressive? Another problem is associated with the accessibility condition of segmentation. There is no advertising medium that provides unique access to a particular personality type; that is, television reaches introverts as well as extroverts, aggressive people as well as timid people. So one of the major goals of segmentation, to avoid wasted marketing effort, is not likely to be accomplished using personality.

Nevertheless, firms often tailor their advertising messages to appeal to personality traits. Even though the importance of the personality dimension in a particular decision may be unmeasurable, the seller believes that it does play an influential role. Thus, in its ads, Saab suggests that you "peel off your inhibitions," and Toyota Supra is advertised as "pure excess."

Life-Style. **Life-style** relates to activities, interests, and opinions. Your life-style reflects how you spend your time and what your beliefs are on various social, economic, and political issues. It is a broad concept that overlaps what some consider to be personality characteristics.

People's life-styles undoubtedly affect what products they buy and what brands they prefer. Marketers are aware of this and often design their strategies based on life-style segments. For example, there are two equally large segments of Porsche buyers with quite different life-styles and reasons for buying the car. One group is driven by power and control. Called "top guns" at Porsche, they buy the car to be noticed. Another group, the "proud patrons," view a Porsche as a reward for hard work. To them, owning the car is an end it itself. They don't need the acknowledgment of others to derive satisfaction from a Porsche. Clearly, an ad that would appeal to the top guns could easily alienate the proud patrons.[12]

Although it is a valuable marketing tool, life-style segmentation has some of the same limitations as segmentation based on personality characteristics. It is difficult to accurately measure the size of life-style segments in a quantitative manner. Another problem is that a given life-style segment might not be accessible at a reasonable cost through a firm's usual distribution system or promotional program.

Values. According to psychologists, **values** are a reflection of our needs adjusted for the realities of the world in which we live. Research at the Survey Research Center at the University of Michigan has identified nine basic values that relate to purchase behavior.[13] The nine, which they call the List of Values (LOV), are:

- Self-respect
- Security
- Excitement
- Fun and enjoyment in life
- Having warm relationships

- Self-fulfillment
- Sense of belonging
- Sense of accomplishment
- Being well respected

While most people would view all these values as desirable, their relative importance differs among people. For example, people who highly value fun and enjoyment especially enjoy skiing, dancing, bicycling, and backpacking, while people who highly value warm relationships give gifts for no particular reason. Thus, the relative strength of values could be the basis for segmenting a market.

Behavioral Segmentation

Some marketers regularly attempt to segment their markets on the basis of product-related behavior—they utilize **behavioral segmentation**. In this section we briefly consider two of these: the benefits desired from a product and the rate at which the consumer uses the product.

Benefits Desired. From a customer-oriented perspective, the ideal method for segmenting a market is on the basis of customers' desired benefits. Certainly, using benefits to segment a market is consistent with the idea that a company should be marketing benefits and not simply the physical characteristics of a product. After all, a carpenter wants a smooth surface (benefit), not a Black & Decker electric sander (the product). However, in many cases benefits desired by customers do not meet the first condition of segmentation described above. That is, they are not easily measured because customers are unwilling or unable to reveal them. For example, what benefits do people derive from clothing that has the label on the outside? Conversely, why do others refuse to wear such clothing?

This Ramada campaign identifies specific features and benefits for well-defined market segments. It follows some very aggressive ads run in the early 1990s. As part of that campaign, guests were offered $5 in cash if they would say they had switched from Holiday Inn or any other chain to Ramada. And in 1993 the chain was sued by Hilton, Hyatt, and Marriott after it ran print ads that featured families who had the same last names as those used by competing chains and who were explaining why they preferred Ramada. Does the switch to a benefit-oriented approach suggest it is more effective?

http://www.ramadainn.com/

Performing benefit segmentation is a multistep process. First, the specific benefits consumers are seeking must be identified. This typically involves several research steps, beginning with the identification of all possible benefits related to a particular product or behavior through brainstorming, observing consumers, and listening to focus groups. Then, more focus groups are conducted to screen out unlikely or unrealistic benefits and to amplify and clarify the remaining possibilities. Finally, large-scale surveys are conducted to determine how important the benefits are and how many consumers seek each one.

http://www.mobil.com/

To illustrate, Mobil Corp. conducted a market segmentation study of gasoline buyers to determine how to design its gasoline stations. The study identified five primary segments. Contrary to conventional wisdom, only one, accounting for about 20 percent of the buyers, consisted of price shoppers. To attract the four more profitable nonprice segments, Mobil has begun offering things that appeal to them—nicer snack foods, quick service, a personal touch, privileges for regular customers, and cleaner facilities.[14]

Usage Rate.   Another basis for market segmentation is the rate at which people use or consume a product. A frequently used categorization of usage rates is nonusers, light users, medium users, and heavy users. Normally a company is most interested in the heavy users of its product because fewer than 50 percent of all users of a product typically account for 80 to 90 percent of the total purchases. For example, less than half of all coffee drinkers consume nearly 80 percent of all the coffee consumed. These heavy users are often referred to in an industry as the "heavy half" of the market. Many marketers aim their marketing efforts at retaining the consumers who make up the heavy half for their brand, and encouraging the heavy-half users of competitors' brands to switch.

Sometimes a marketer will select as a target market the nonuser or light user, intending to woo these customers into higher usage. Or light users may constitute an attractive niche for a seller simply because they are being ignored by firms that are targeting heavy users. Once the characteristics of these light users have been identified, management can go to them directly with an introductory low-price offer. Or a seller might get consumers to increase their usage rates by (1) describing new uses for a product (baking soda as a refrigerator deodorizer, chewing gum

AN ETHICAL DILEMMA?

In extensive marketing research among young adults, Everfresh Juice Company uncovered a segment that wants convenience and portability above all other features when it comes to drink containers. In response, the company produced the "Everflask," a juice container shaped like a whiskey flask. According to an Everfresh press release, "Consumers looking for a more convenient way to tote juice drinks in purses, lunch boxes and pockets will soon be able to 'ask for the flask.'"

A spokesperson for Mothers Against Drunk Driving (MADD) expressed her organization's outrage over the container. She pointed out "Packaging a juice drink in a liquor-type container encourages youth to emulate potentially risky health behavior. This is just inappropriate, unhealthy, and irresponsible."

Is meeting the legitimate needs of an identified market segment sufficient justification for producing a product?

Source: Neil D. Rosenberg, "MADD Outraged over Juice in Flask," *South Bend Tribune*, Feb. 2, 1995, p. A11.

as an alternative to cigarettes); (2) suggesting new times or places for use (soup as an after-school snack, air fresheners in school lockers); or (3) offering multiple-unit packaging (a 12-pack of soft drinks).

Segmenting Business Markets

Even though the number of buyers in a business market may be relatively few as compared to a consumer market, segmentation remains an important part of marketing. The reason is quite simple—a highly focused marketing effort directed at meeting the specific needs of a group of similar customers is both more efficient and more likely to be successful.

Table 7-2 lists a variety of segmentation bases used in business markets. As you can see, many of the bases are similar to some used for segmenting consumer markets. To get a feel for business market segmentation, let's look at some of the characteristics used to segment markets by (1) customer location, (2) customer type, and (3) transaction conditions.

Customer Location

Business markets are frequently segmented on a geographic basis. Some industries are geographically concentrated. For example, businesses that process natural resources locate close to the source to minimize shipping costs. Other industries are geographically concentrated simply because newer firms either spun off from or chose to locate near the industry pioneers. For example, several recreational vehicle manufacturers, including Skyline, Holiday Rambler, and Viking, are located in northern Indiana. A firm that sells to this industry would likely focus its efforts geographically.

Companies also segment international markets geographically. In considering developing countries, for example, a firm might consider the reliability of public utilities, the quality of the transportation system, and the sophistication of the distribution structure in deciding where to expand its operation.

TABLE 7-2 Segmentation bases for business markets

Segmentation basis	Typical market segments
Customer location:	
Region	Southeast Asia, Central America, Upper Midwest, Atlantic Seaboard
Locations	Single buying site, multiple buying sites
Customer type:	
Size	Sales volume, number of employees
Industry	SIC code
Organization structure	Centralized or decentralized; group or individual decision
Purchase criteria	Quality, price, durability, lead time
Type of use	Resale, component part, ornamental
Transaction conditions:	
Buying situation	Straight rebuy, modified rebuy, new buy
Usage rate	Nonuser, light user, heavy user
Purchasing procedure	Competitive bidding, lease, service contracts
Order size	Small, medium, large
Service requirements	Light, moderate, heavy

Customer Type

Size. Business customer size can be measured by such factors as sales volume, number of employees, number of production facilities, and number of sales offices. Many sellers divide their potential market into large and small accounts, using separate distribution channels to reach each segment. The seller's sales force may contact large-volume accounts directly, but to reach the smaller accounts, the seller may use a middleman or rely on telemarketing.

Industry. Any firm that sells to business customers in a variety of industries may want to segment its market on the basis of industry. For example, a company that sells small electric motors would have a broad potential market among many different industries. However, this firm will do better by segmenting its potential market by type of customer and then specializing in order to more completely meet the needs of organizations in a limited number of these segments. The SIC codes, described in Chapter 6, are particularly useful for this purpose because information published by the government and industry on such things as the number of firms, their size, and location is often organized according to this scheme.

Organization Structure. Firms approach buying in different ways. Some rely heavily on their purchasing departments to control information, reduce the number of options, and conduct negotiations. The selling effort to these companies would require a strong personal selling effort directed specifically at purchasing executives. It would also need excellent supporting materials if the product exceeded the technical expertise of the purchasing managers.

Other buyers opt for more continuous involvement in the purchase process by the people who will be affected by the purchase. They include many people in their decisions, hold meetings over a long period of time, and engage in a lot of paperwork. Government agencies are especially known for lengthy purchase decisions. For example, because of the extensive approval processes, obtaining an order to sell supplies to a prison often takes 2 or 3 years.[15] Selling to a market segment such as this requires many contacts, and would likely involve more people from the selling firm.

Purchase Criteria. All buyers want good quality, low prices, and on-time delivery. However, within a market there are groups for which one of these or some other purchase criterion is particularly significant. Consider the automotive business. General Motors buys over $90 *billion* in components, machinery, and equipment a year. In selecting suppliers GM has a formal process that takes into account a prospect's technical capabilities, defect rates, and delivery schedule among other criteria. However, in the opinion of many, price is the overriding factor in GM's purchase decisions.[16]

http://www.gm.com/

Transaction Conditions

The circumstances of the transaction can also be a basis for segmenting a market. Sellers may have to modify their marketing efforts to deal with different buying situations, order sizes, or service requirements.

Buying Situation. A new buy, as when United Airlines is faced with the decision of whether or not to buy Boeing 777 airplanes, is quite different from the straight rebuy when United decides to replenish its supply of the captain's wings it uses as souvenirs for child passengers. These buying situations, along with the modified rebuy, are sufficiently different that a business seller might well segment its market into these three buy-class categories. Or the seller could at least set up two segments by combining new buy and modified rebuy into one segment. Different marketing programs would be developed to reach each of these two or three segments.

Usage Rate.   Markets for most products can be divided among heavy users, light users, and nonusers (prospects). Heavy users appear to be the most attractive because of the volume they purchase, but they also generate the most competition. As an alternative to pursuing heavy users, some firms have found it profitable to avoid the competition by concentrating on light users.

Purchase Procedure.   Products can be leased, financed, or purchased outright. A price can be simply stated, negotiated, or submitted in a sealed bid. Consider how a bidding system affects a seller. Government agencies often buy on the basis of sealed bids; that is, each prospective seller submits a confidential bid in response to a detailed description of what the agency wants to buy. When the bids are opened, the agency is typically bound by law to accept the lowest bid unless it is clearly inappropriate. How is this different than a negotiated price? For one thing, the seller has only one chance to propose a price. Also, to compete in a sealed-bid market, it is important to have low costs. And good industry knowledge is essential in order to accurately predict what other firms will bid. These differences might cause a firm to treat the government as a distinct segment.

Segmentation identifies a firm's opportunities. The next step is to determine what would be necessary in the form of strategies to win the business of particular segments. A segment a firm chooses to pursue is called a *target market*.

Target-Market Strategies

Let's assume that a company has segmented the total market for its product. Now management is in a position to select one or more segments as its target markets. The company can follow one of three strategies—market aggregation, single-segment concentration, or multiple-segment targeting. To select a strategy, management must determine the desirability of each of the segments it has identified. Some guidelines that are helpful in making that evaluation are discussed next.

Guidelines in Selecting a Target Market

Four guidelines govern how to determine which segments should be chosen as target markets. First, target markets should be compatible with the organization's goals and image. For years many manufacturers resisted distributing their products through Kmart because of the chain's discount image. However, as Kmart achieved a high level of acceptability with consumers, image concerns seemed to disappear.

http://www.kmart.com/

http://www.3m.com/

A second guideline—consistent with our definition of strategic planning—is to match the market opportunity represented in the target markets with the company's resources. In examining new product opportunities, 3M considered many options but chose the do-it-yourself home-improvement market due to the marketing economies that could be achieved. The firm's name was already well known to consumers, and the products could be sold through many of the retail outlets already selling 3M products. Thus, entering this market was much less expensive than entering a market in which 3M was inexperienced.

Over the long run, a business must generate a profit to survive. This rather obvious statement translates into our third market-selection guideline. That is, an organization should seek markets that will generate sufficient sales volume at a low enough cost to result in a profit. Surprisingly, companies often have overlooked profit in their quest for high-volume markets. Their mistake is going after sales volume, not *profitable* sales volume. Seventh Generation, Inc., is a manufacturer of environmentally friendly household products. The firm found a market among hard-core environmentalists, but the segment was not large enough to sustain the business. To reach a larger segment that is environmentally conscious but also expects competitive prices and good quality, the firm carefully evaluated its line. The result is that half of its products have been replaced with items that are environmentally friendly and also less expensive or better quality than competing alternatives.[17]

Fourth, a company ordinarily should seek a market where there are the least and smallest competitors. A seller should not enter a market that is already saturated with competition unless it has some overriding differential advantage that will enable it to take customers from existing firms. Nobel Education Dynamics and Challenger are companies that operate chains of privately owned primary schools. The schools are designed to appeal to families that are dissatisfied with public schools but are unable to afford fancy private schools. The objective is to provide a solid education without frills. The differential advantage of these schools over traditional private schools is a lower price, while their private status gives them greater control over the students than exists in public schools.[18]

These are general guidelines. A seller still has to decide which specific segments to pursue and which strategy to follow. The three alternative strategies are detailed below.

Aggregation Strategy. By adopting a **market-aggregation strategy**—also known as a *mass-market strategy* or an *undifferentiated-market strategy*—a seller treats its total market as a single segment. An aggregate market's members are considered to be alike with respect to demand for the product. That is, customers are willing to make some compromises on less important dimensions in order to enjoy the primary benefit the product offers. In this situation, the total market is the firm's target. Therefore, management can develop a single marketing mix and reach most of the customers in the entire market. The company offers a single product for this mass audience; it designs one pricing structure and one distribution system for its product; and it uses a single promotional program aimed at the entire market. This is sometimes described as a "shotgun" approach (one program to reach a broad target).

When is an organization likely to adopt a market-aggregation strategy? In reality, the notion of an aggregate market is relatively uncommon. Even a commodity such as gasoline is provided at different octane levels, with or without ethanol, and with a variety of other additives. The total market for most types of products is too varied—too heterogeneous—to be considered a single, uniform entity. To speak of a market for vitamin pills, for example, is to ignore the existence of submarkets that differ significantly from one another. Because of these differences, One-A-Day vitamins are offered in a regular formula for adults, a special women's formula, and a children's formula called Flintstones.

Generally an aggregation strategy is selected after the firm has examined a market for segments and concluded that the majority of customers in the total market are likely to respond in very similar fashion to one marketing mix. This strategy would be appropriate for firms that are marketing an undifferentiated, staple product such as salt or sugar. In the eyes of many people, sugar is sugar, regardless of the brand, and all brands of table salt are pretty much alike.

The strength of a market aggregation strategy is in its cost minimization. It enables a company to produce, distribute, and promote its products very efficiently. Producing and marketing one product for the entire market means longer production runs at lower unit costs. Inventory costs are minimized when there is no (or a very limited) variety of colors and sizes of products. Warehousing and transportation are most efficient when one product is going to one market. Promotion costs are minimized when the same message is transmitted to all customers.

The strategy of market aggregation typically is accompanied by the strategy of product differentiation in a company's marketing program. **Product differentiation** occurs when, in the eyes of customers, one firm distinguishes its product from competitive brands offered to the same aggregate market. Through differentiation an organization creates the perception that its product is better than the competitors' brands, as when C&H Sugar advertises its product as "pure cane sugar from Hawaii." In addition to creating a preference among consumers for the seller's brand, successful product differentiation can also reduce price competition.

A seller differentiates its product either (1) by changing some appearance feature of the product—the package or color, for example—or (2) by using a promotional appeal that features a differentiating claim. For example, various brands of aspirin claim to be the most effective in relieving pain, although they all contain essentially the same ingredients.

Single-Segment Strategy. A **single-segment strategy**, also called a *concentration strategy*, involves selecting one segment from within the total market as the target market. One marketing mix is developed to reach this single segment. A company may want to concentrate on a single market segment rather than to take on many competitors in the broader market. For example, Harley-Davidson concentrates only on the super-heavyweight motorcycle market. It does not produce small street bikes or off-road bikes. In contrast, Honda competes in all segments of the motorcycle market. This strategy employs a "rifle" approach (a narrow program directed at a pinpointed target) in marketing activities.

When manufacturers of foreign automobiles first entered the U.S. market, they typically targeted a single segment. The Volkswagen Beetle was intended for the low-price, small-car market, and Mercedes-Benz targeted the high-income market. Today, of course, most of the established foreign car marketers have moved into a multisegment strategy. Only a few, such as Rolls-Royce and Ferrari, continue to concentrate on their original single segment.

A single-segment strategy enables a seller to penetrate one market in depth and to acquire a reputation as a specialist or an expert in this limited market. A company can initiate a single-segment strategy with limited resources. And as long as the single segment remains a small market, large competitors are likely to leave it alone. However, if the small market should show signs of becoming a large market, then the "big boys" may jump in. This is exactly what happened in the market for herbal teas. Starting in 1971, Celestial Seasonings, a then-small Colorado firm, specialized in this segment and practically owned the market for close to 10 years. But as herbal teas became more popular, this market segment began to attract major competitors such as the Lipton Tea Company.

The risk and limitation of a single-segment strategy is that the seller has "all its eggs in one basket." If the market potential of that single segment declines, the seller can suffer considerably. Also, a seller with a strong name and reputation in

http://www.gerber.com/

one segment may find it very difficult to expand into another segment. Sears, Roebuck, with an image as a retailer for the middle class, was not successful when it tried to move into the market for expensive furs and designer clothing. Gerber's, seen as a baby food company, was unable to market food in single-serving quantities to adults.

Multiple-Segment Strategy. Under a **multiple-segment strategy**, two or more different groups of potential customers are identified as target markets. A separate marketing mix is developed to reach each segment. For example, Sterling Winthrop, the maker of Bayer aspirin, has decided that all consumers may not want to treat pain in the same way, so the firm produces the Bayer Select line of five nonaspirin, symptom-specific pain relievers.

In a multiple-segment strategy, a seller frequently will develop a different version of the basic product for each segment. However, market segmentation can also be accomplished with no change in the product, but rather with separate distribution channels or promotional appeals, each tailored to a given market segment. Wrigley's, for example, targets smokers by promoting chewing gum as an alternative in situations where smoking is unwelcome. And Evian bottled water has broadened its market beyond athletes and fitness-oriented consumers to other groups including pregnant women and environmentalists.

A multiple-segment strategy normally results in a greater sales volume than a single-segment strategy. It also is useful for a company facing seasonal demand. Due to lower summer enrollments, many universities market their empty dormitory space to tourists—another market segment. A firm with excess production capacity may well seek additional market segments to absorb this capacity.

The sale of canned coffee in supermarkets has been declining while the market for specialty coffees has been expanding. Over the last 10 years, sales of gourmet coffee has grown at 9 percent a year to over $1 billion. Focusing on price has not helped the mass marketers reverse the trend. An alternative is to change the product to better meet the needs of the market. Folgers Singles is a blend of ground and freeze concentrated coffees that can be used in a microwave. It provides the consumer with added convenience and the manufacturer with a higher profit margin than gained from regular coffee sales.

Freshly brewed coffee for ten. For one.

Aroma-fresh pouch.

Contains ground roast coffee in its own filter.

Folgers' Coffee Singles
THE ULTIMATE ONE CUP COFFEE MACHINE.
Contains about 2/3 ground roast and 1/3 high quality freeze concentrated coffee. ©1993 The Procter & Gamble Company

Multiple segments can provide benefits to an organization, but the strategy has some drawbacks with respect to costs and market coverage. In the first place, marketing to multiple segments can be expensive in both the production and marketing of products. Even with today's advances in production technology, it obviously is less expensive to produce mass quantities of one model and one color than it is to produce a variety of models, colors, and sizes. And a multiple-segment strategy increases marketing expenses in several ways. Total inventory costs go up, because adequate inventories of each style, color, and the like, must be maintained. Advertising costs go up, because different ads may be required for each market segment. Distribution costs are likely to increase as efforts are made to make products available to various segments. Finally, general administrative expenses go up when management must plan and implement several different marketing programs.

One condition for useful segmentation is that the resulting segments be large enough to produce a profit. The potential of a segment is determined by forecasting how much it will buy. The process of forecasting demand is discussed next.

Forecasting Market Demand

Demand forecasting is estimating sales of a product during some defined future period. Forecasting is done to make various kinds of predictions. For example, a forecast can refer to an entire industry (such as apparel), to one firm's product line (Levi casual wear), or to an individual brand (Levi 501 jeans). Thus, for a forecast to be understood, it is important to make very clear what it describes.

Basic Forecasting Terms
In this section we'll define some terms so our discussion will be easier to follow.

Market Factor. A **market factor** is an item or element that (1) exists in a market, (2) is measurable, and (3) is related to the demand for a product in a known way. To illustrate, the "number of cars 3 years old and older" is a market factor related to the demand for replacement tires. It's a market factor because this statistic affects the number of replacement tires that can be sold.

In segmenting world markets geographically, McDonald's uses population, per capita income, and the number of people per store in the U.S. as market factors to forecast the number of stores a country can support.[19] The formula looks like this:

$$\frac{\text{Population of the country}}{\text{\# of people per McDonald's in U.S.}} \times \frac{\text{Per capita income of the country}}{\text{Per capita income of U.S.}} = \frac{\text{The number of stores the country can support}}{}$$

The formula, which produces a rough estimate that is adjusted for factors such as eating habits and competition, suggests the following:

Country	Market potential (no. of outlets)
China	784
Colombia	79
Pakistan	90
South Africa	190

Market Potential and Sales Potential. **Market potential** is the total sales volume that *all organizations* selling a product during a stated period of time in a specific market could expect to achieve under ideal conditions. **Sales potential** is the portion of market potential that a *specific company* could expect to achieve under ideal conditions. For example, market potential applies to all refrigerators, but sales potential refers only to a single brand of refrigerators (such as Whirlpool).

With either of these measures of potential, the market may encompass whatever group or area interests the forecaster. It could be the world, one country, or a smaller market defined by income or some other basis. For example, Whirlpool may consider the market potential for refrigerators in the Pacific states, or the sales potential for Whirlpool refrigerators in households with incomes of $25,000 to $50,000.

The term *potential* refers to a maximum level of sales assuming that (1) all marketing plans are sound and effectively implemented and (2) all prospective customers with the desire and ability to buy do so. Of course, few industries or companies achieve their full potential. Therefore, potential should not be the final outcome of demand forecasting. It is an intermediate step. We must move from *potential* sales to *probable* sales, which are estimated by preparing forecasts.

Market Share. A term used frequently in business as a performance measure, **market share** is the proportion of total sales of a product during a stated period in a specific market that is captured by a single firm. If Almega Corp. sold $210 million worth of turbine engines in 1996, and total industry sales of turbine engines that year were $7 billion, Almega's market share was 3 percent.

Market share can refer to entire industries (aircraft), segments of industries (single-engine business jets), or particular geographic areas (Pacific Rim), and can also apply to past, present, or future periods. For example, the steel industry, which has a 95 percent market share for canned food containers, is working to prevent a recurrence of the inroads in food packaging that were made by aluminum makers in the market for beverage cans.

Sales Forecast. A **sales forecast** is an estimate of probable sales for one company's brand of a product during a stated period in a specific market, assuming a defined marketing plan is used. Like measures of potential, a sales forecast can be expressed in dollars or product units. However, whereas market potential and sales potential are estimates based on general factors and market assumptions, a sales forecast is based on a specific marketing plan for the product.

A sales forecast is best prepared after market potential and sales potential have been estimated. Sales forecasts typically cover a 1-year period, although many

http://www.whirlpool.com/

*W*hen the sale of low-fat, low-cholesterol cookies grew 20 percent from 1989 to 1990, Nabisco responded. Rather than produce a low-fat version of an existing brand (and draw attention to the fat level in the original), Nabisco introduced SnackWell's. With a new brand in a developing product category, Nabisco was conservative in its forecast. However, the product was so successful that Nabisco ran into supply problems. You may recall that the company called attention to the shortage in its ads to further promote the product. All manufacturers would like to have such problems!

http://www.nabisco.com/

firms review and revise their forecasts quarterly or even monthly. Forecasts of less than a year may be desirable when activity in the firm's industry is so volatile that it is not feasible to look ahead an entire year. As a case in point, many retailers and producers in the fashion industry prepare forecasts for only one fashion season at a time. Hence, they prepare three or four forecasts a year.

Once a sales forecast has been prepared, it affects all departments in a company. The sales forecast is the basis for deciding how much to spend on various activities like advertising and personal selling. Planning the necessary amount of working capital, plant utilization, and warehousing facilities is based on anticipated sales. Scheduling production, hiring production workers, and purchasing raw materials also depend on the sales forecast.

Methods of Forecasting Sales

Here are some commonly used methods for predicting demand.

Market-Factor Analysis.   In many situations, future demand for a product is related to the behavior of certain market factors. When this is true, we can forecast future sales by studying the behavior of these market factors. Basically, **market-factor analysis** entails determining what these factors are and then measuring their relationship to sales activity.

Using market-factor analysis successfully requires (1) selecting the right market factors and (2) minimizing the number of market factors. The greater the number of factors, the greater the chance for erroneous estimates and the more difficult it is to determine how much each factor influences demand.

We can translate market-factor behavior into a demand forecast with the **direct-derivation method**. To illustrate, suppose that a producer of automobile tires wants to know the market potential for replacement tires in the U.S. in 1998. The primary market factor is the number and age of automobiles on the road. The first step is to estimate how many cars are prospects for new tires.

Assume that the producer's studies show (1) the average car is driven 10,000 miles per year and (2) the average driver gets 30,000 miles of use from a set of tires. This means that all cars that become 3 years old or multiples of 3 years old in 1998 can be considered to comprise the potential market for replacement tires during that year. From state and county auto license agencies as well as private organizations, the producer can obtain a reasonably accurate count of the number of cars that were sold in the U.S. in 1995 and therefore will be 3 years old in 1998. In addition, the producer can determine how many cars will become 6, 9, and 12 years old in 1998, and therefore would also be ready for another set of tires.

The number of cars in these age brackets multiplied by four (tires per car) should give the approximate market potential for replacement tires in 1998. Of course, we are dealing in averages. Not all drivers will get 30,000 miles from their tires, and not all cars will be driven 10,000 miles per year.

The direct-derivation method is simple, inexpensive, and requires little statistical analysis. Executives who are not statisticians can understand it and interpret its results. This method's main limitation is that it can be used only when it is possible to identify an easily measured market factor that affects the product's demand in a stable way.

Correlation analysis is a statistical refinement of the direct-derivation method. It is a measure of the association between potential sales of the product and the market factor affecting its sales. Detailed explanation of this statistical technique is beyond the scope of this text. However, in general, a correlation analysis measures, on a scale of 0 (no association) to 1 (perfect association), the variation between two data series. For example, the data series might be the number of dogs registered in Boulder, Colorado, each year from 1975 to 1995, and the sales of canned dog food in Boulder in the corresponding years.

Correlation analysis gives a more precise estimate of market demand than does direct derivation. That's because in direct derivation, the association is assumed to be 1.0 (that is, perfect). But rarely is there a perfect association between a market factor and the demand for a product. Correlation analysis therefore takes history into account in predicting the future. It also allows a researcher to include more than one market factor in the calculation.

Correlation analysis has two major limitations. For one thing, not all marketing executives understand it. For another, it can be used only when both of the following are available: (1) a sales history of the industry or firm consisting of at least 20 consecutive time periods, and (2) a corresponding history of the market factor being used to forecast demand. Last, correlation analysis depends on the assumptions, which can be quite unrealistic, that approximately the same relationship has existed between sales and the key market factor(s) during the entire period, and that this relationship will continue in the sales period being predicted.

Survey of Buyer Intentions.   A **survey of buyer intentions** involves asking a sample of current or potential customers how much of a particular product they would buy at a given price during a specified future period. Some firms maintain panels of consumers for use in such surveys. They also use their consumer panels as sounding boards for new-product ideas, prices, and other marketing decisions.

Selecting a representative sample of potential buyers can be a problem. For many consumer products, a large sample is needed because many groups with different buying patterns make up the market. Thus this method can be costly in terms of both money and time. This method has another serious limitation. Because it is one thing for consumers to *intend* to buy a product but quite another for them to *actually* buy it, surveys of buying intentions often show an inflated measure of market potential. Such surveys are probably most accurate in forecasting demand when (1) there are relatively few current or potential buyers, (2) the buyers are willing to express their buying intentions, and (3) their past records show a consistent relationship between their actual buying behavior and their stated intentions.

Test Marketing.   In **test marketing** to forecast demand, a firm markets a new product in a limited geographic area, measures sales, and then—from this sample—projects the product's sales over a larger area. Test marketing is used to determine whether there is sufficient demand for the new product. It also serves as a basis for evaluating new-product features and alternative marketing strategies. More details about test marketing, including its benefits and drawbacks, were presented in Chapter 4.

Past Sales and Trend Analysis.   A popular method of forecasting is based entirely on past sales. This technique is frequently used by small retailers whose main goal is to "beat last year's figures." In **past sales analysis**, the demand forecast is simply a flat percentage change applied to the volume achieved last year or to the average volume of the past few years.

This technique is simple and inexpensive. For a firm operating in a stable market, where its market share has remained constant for a period of years, past sales alone can be used to predict future volume. However, few companies operate in unchanging environments, making this method highly unreliable.

Trend analysis uses past sales data to calculate the rate of change in sales volume and uses it to forecast future sales. One type of trend analysis is a long-term projection of sales, usually computed with a statistical technique called regression. However, the statistical sophistication of long-term trend analysis does not offset the inherent weakness of basing future estimates only on past sales activity. A second type of trend analysis entails a short-term (several months) projection using a seasonal index of sales. Short-term trend analysis may be acceptable if a firm's sales follow a reliable seasonal pattern. For example, assume that the second quarter of the year historically produces sales about 50 percent higher than the first quarter. Hence, if sales reach 10,000 units in the first quarter, we can reasonably forecast sales of 15,000 units for the second quarter.

Sales-Force Composite. In sales forecasting, the **sales-force composite** consists of collecting from all sales people estimates of sales for their territories during the future period of interest. The total of all these estimates is the company's sales forecast.

A sales-force composite method can produce an accurate forecast if the firm has competent, well-informed sales people. Its strength is that it takes advantage of sales people's specialized knowledge of their own markets. Furthermore, it should make sales people more willing to accept their assigned sales quotas, since they participated in the process that produced the forecasts that serve as the basis for their quotas. A sales-force composite is most useful for firms selling to a market composed of a few large customers. Thus this method would be more applicable to sales of large electrical generators to energy utilities than to sales of small general-use motors to many thousands of firms.

This method also has limitations. A sales force may not have the time or the experience to do the research needed for sales forecasting, and managers must guard against sales people who overestimate or underestimate future sales, depending on circumstances. For instance, sales people are by nature optimistic and therefore may overestimate future possibilities. Or, if compensation is based on meeting sales quotas, sales people may underestimate future sales.[20]

Executive Judgment. Basically, **executive judgment** involves obtaining opinions from one or more executives regarding future sales. If these are informed opinions, based on valid measures such as market-factor analysis, then executive judgment can produce accurate forecasts. However, forecasting by executive opinion alone is risky, because such opinions are sometimes simply intuition or guesswork.

One specialized form of executive judgment is the **Delphi method**, named after the location of an oracle in ancient Greece. Developed by the Rand Corporation for use in environmental forecasting, this technique can also be applied in sales forecasting. It is especially applicable to products that are truly innovative or are significant technological breakthroughs.

The Delphi method begins with a group of knowledgeable individuals anonymously estimating future sales. Each person makes a prediction without knowing how others in the group have responded. These estimates are summarized, and the resulting average and range of forecasts are fed back to the participants. Now, knowing how the group responded, they are asked to make another prediction on the same issue. Participants may change or stick to their original estimates. This process of estimates and feedback is continued for several rounds. In some cases—

and usually in sales forecasting—the final round involves face-to-face discussions among the participants to produce a sales forecast consensus.

An advantage of the Delphi method is that it prevents one individual (for example, a top executive) from influencing others (a subordinate). And it permits each participant to consider the combined judgment of the group. If an individual's forecast is widely divergent from the group's average, the opportunity exists to justify or modify it in the next round. A potential disadvantage of the Delphi method—and of any executive judgment method—is that participants may lack the necessary information on which to base their judgments.

No method of sales forecasting is perfect. An executive's challenge is to choose an approach that is likely to produce the most accurate estimate of sales given the firm's particular circumstances. Since all techniques have limitations, companies should consider using more than one forecasting method when the marketing environment is volatile.

■ SUMMARY

A market consists of people or organizations with wants, money to spend, and the willingness to spend it. However, within most markets the buyers' needs are not identical. Therefore, a single marketing program for the entire market is unlikely to be successful. A sound marketing program starts with identifying the differences that exist within a market, a process called market segmentation, and deciding which segments will be pursued as target markets.

Most marketers adopt some form of market segmentation as a compromise between the extremes of a strategy that treats the market as an aggregate, undifferentiated whole, and a strategy that views each customer as a different market.

Market segmentation enables a company to make more efficient use of its marketing resources. Also, it allows a small company to compete effectively by concentrating on one or two segments. The apparent drawback of market segmentation is that it will result in higher production and marketing costs than a one-product, mass-market strategy. However, if the market is correctly segmented, the better fit with customers' needs will acually result in greater efficiency.

For segmentation to be effective (1) the bases for segmentation must be measurable with obtainable data, (2) the segments identified must be accessible through existing marketing institutions, and (3) the segments must be large enough to be potentially profitable.

The total market may be divided into two broad segments: ultimate consumers and business users. The four major bases used for further segmenting the consumer market are geographic, demographic, psychographic, and behavioral.

The business market may be segmented on the bases of (1) customer location, (2) customer type, and (3) transaction conditions. Normally, in either the consumer or business market, a seller will use a combination of two or more segmentation bases.

The three alternative strategies for selecting a target market are market aggregation, single segment, and multiple segment. Market-aggregation strategy involves using one marketing mix to reach a mass, undifferentiated market. With a single-segment strategy, a company still uses only one marketing mix, but it is directed at only one segment of the total market. A multiple-segment strategy entails selecting two or more segments and developing a separate marketing mix to reach each segment.

Forecasting involves estimating the demand of identified market segments. Management usually estimates the total sales that could be expected under ideal conditions for all firms comprising the industry—market potential—and for its particular product—sales potential. The final step in estimating demand is a sales forecast, indicating probable sales for the company's brand of a particular product in a future time period and with a specified marketing program. The forecast normally covers 1 year.

Specific methods used to forecast sales are market-factor analysis, survey of buyer intentions, test marketing, past sales and trend analysis, sales-force composite, and executive judgment. Management's challenge is to select the technique that is appropriate in a particular situation.

More about

BLACK & DECKER

To better meet the needs of the market, Black & Decker has reintroduced the DeWalt brand of professional caliber tools and the Quantum brand for the do-it-yourself (DIY) market.

DeWalt was a brand of durable radial-arm saws that Black & Decker acquired over 30 years ago but had largely ignored. Research showed that among professionals it still had a very positive image. After determining which tools professionals use most, B&D selected 30 of its drills, saws, and sanders for an expanded DeWalt line. The products were modified as needed (more power, longer cords, larger knobs, and switches that can be operated while wearing gloves), colored yellow to distinguish them from the black regular line, and placed on the market. DeWalt tools are priced 10 percent higher than Makita products to signal quality to the buyer.

Research indicated that Black & Decker tools are viewed as relatively unsophisticated by professional contractors. As a result, the B&D name does not appear on DeWalt products. To promote the brand, B&D put 26 DeWalt-logo emblazoned vans on the road to visit construction sites, auto races, rodeos, contractor events, and other places fre-quented by members of the target market in order to demonstrate the tools.

Because the DIY market is more diverse than professionals, B&D had to do more research. They talked to retailers and intensively studied consumers. The research included surveying power tool purchasers, observing DIYers in their workshops, and even accompanying them on tool shopping trips. The result was the Quantum line of tools, with several modifications suggested by consumers. For example, one innovation was a saw blade that stops in 2 seconds when it is shut off rather than the more typical 10 to 12 seconds. After examining several colors, green was selected because consumers associated it with quality and reliability.

The line is priced between $50 and $120, and sold through building supply retailers. In contrast to its image among professionals, research showed that DIYers respect B&D. To take advantage of this positive reputation, the Quantum product line also carries the B&D name. The introduction was supported by a $10 million advertising campaign.[21]

How can Black & Decker continue to take advantage of its segmentation and target-market strategies in the power tool business?

■ KEY TERMS AND CONCEPTS

Market segments (158)
Target market (158)
Market
   segmentation (158)
Geographic
   segmentation (162)
Demographic
   segmentation (163)
Psychographic
   segmentation (166)
Personality (166)
Life-style (167)

Values (167)
Behavioral
   segmentation (168)
Market-aggregation
   strategy (173)
Product
   differentiation (174)
Single-segment
   strategy (174)
Multiple-segment
   strategy (175)
Demand forecasting (176)

Market factor (176)
Market potential (176)
Sales potential (177)
Market share (177)
Sales forecast (177)
Market-factor
   analysis (178)
Direct-derivation
   method (178)
Correlation analysis (178)
Survey of buyer
   intentions (179)

Test marketing (179)
Past sales analysis (179)
Trend analysis (180)
Sales-force
   composite (180)
Executive
   judgment (180)
Delphi method (180)

■ QUESTIONS AND PROBLEMS

1. Give two examples of goods or services whose market demand would be particularly affected by each of the following population factors:
   a. Regional distribution
   b. Marital status
   c. Gender
   d. Age
   e. Urban-rural-suburban distribution

2. From the most recent "Survey of Buying Power" (from *Sales & Marketing Management* magazine), record the

available data for the county in which you live and another county with which you are familiar (maybe the one in which your school is located). Comment on how any differences you find may be useful to a fast-food franchisee looking for a location for a new outlet.

3. Using the psychographic bases discussed in this chapter, describe the segment likely to be the best market for:
   a. Ski resorts
   b. Good French wines
   c. Power hand tools
   d. Donations to United Way
   e. Outdoor barbecue grills

4. What users' benefits would you stress in advertising each of the following three products to each of these three markets?

Product	**Market**
a. Stereo tape player	a. Schoolteachers
b. Toothpaste	b. Retired people
c. 10-day Caribbean cruise	c. Working women

5. What demographic characteristics would you think are likely to describe heavy users of the following?

   a. Dog food
   b. Ready-to-eat cereal
   c. Videocassette recorders
   d. Pocket calculators

6. How would you segment the market for copying machines such as Xerox or Canon photocopiers?

7. How might the following organizations implement the strategy of market segmentation?
   a. Manufacturer of personal computers
   b. American Heart Association
   c. Universal Studios (Hollywood movies)
   d. Producer of CDs

8. What market factors might you use in estimating the market potential for each of the following products?
   a. Central home air-conditioning
   b. Electric milking machines
   c. First-class airline travel
   d. Sterling silver flatware

9. How would you determine (a) market potential and (b) a sales forecast for a textbook for an introductory marketing course?

■ HANDS-ON MARKETING

1. Interview three friends or acquaintances who all own athletic shoes but differ on some demographic dimension (for example, education or age). Using the criteria of demographics, psychological variables, and behavioral variables, describe in as much detail as possible the different market segment each represents.

2. Examine the annual reports (available in your library) of two consumer product marketers and two business product marketers to determine what target markets they are currently serving.

CASES FOR PART 2

DEFINING MARKET SEGMENTS

"Don't leave home without it." Since Karl Malden first uttered these words, the slogan has become one of the most memorable in advertising history. And consumers apparently accepted his advice. By 1994 American Express had over 35.4 million cardmembers (the company refers to its customers as members) worldwide who charged over $124 billion. But the news is not all good. American Express lost 2 million cardmembers between 1991 and 1993 as competition intensified in the credit card market.

American Express is composed of two divisions. The Travel Related Services division includes charge and credit cards, traveler's checks, and its travel agency. In 1994, this division contributed 72 percent of the company's revenues and 65 percent of its pretax earnings. The other division, American Express Financial Advisors, offers financial planning and investment services. This case focuses on the Travel Related Services division, and in particular the charge and credit cards.

Plastic cards used to make purchases come in a variety of forms:

- *Charge cards* require customers to pay the full balance every month. The American Express card is a charge card.
- *Credit cards* (e.g., VISA and MasterCard) provide a line of credit with a maximum amount that can be charged. If the entire outstanding balance is paid each month, no interest is incurred. However, if less than the full balance is paid, interest is charged on the remainder at an average annual rate of about 17 percent.
- *Debit cards* are extensions of a person's checking account. The amount of a purchase is automatically deducted from the checking account at the time of purchase.
- *ATM* (automatic teller machine) *cards* allow the cardholder to withdraw cash, inquire about an account balance, and make deposits in bank automatic teller machines. These cards may also be used as a debit card at gas stations, fast-food outlets, and supermarkets to make purchases.
- *Smart cards* may be the future of credit cards. They have an imbedded microchip that allows them to serve as ID, a credit card, a debit card, or an ATM card.

Although they compete for both merchants and card users, charge cards and credit cards generate revenue dif-

ferently. Charge card providers such as American Express earn income two ways. They charge merchants a fee for processing their credit sales, usually a small percentage of each sale, and they charge consumers an annual membership fee to have the card. Credit card providers such as VISA also charge merchants, but they frequently offer cards to consumers without an annual fee. Their major source of income is the interest consumers pay on any outstanding credit balance.

The American Express card was introduced in 1958, and today is one of the most recognizable brand names along with Coca-Cola and McDonald's. In spite of its name recognition, the company has lost market share to credit cards over the past 5 years. Two explanations have been offered. First, some merchants were upset about fees that were higher than those charged by VISA and MasterCard. Also hurting American Express were frequent promotional offers by VISA and MasterCard to waive their annual fees for consumers.

As the year 2000 approaches, American Express is changing its strategy to reach its potential. The success of its strategy depends on more effectively reaching three market segments: merchants, domestic cardholders, and international cardholders.

American Express's traditional target market has been business travelers and those who do business entertaining. The card has long been considered a "status card." The card is available in three different service levels:

- The Green Card has an annual fee of $55 and offers basic travel services. For example, if the card is lost or stolen, a replacement card is delivered within 24 hours from one of 1,700 travel service locations worldwide.
- The Gold Card carries a $75 annual fee and provides the cardmember with a 24-hour travel agent, free traveler's checks, and access to tickets for selected culture and sporting events—frequently in advance of public sale.
- Platinum cardmembers get the services that are available with the Green and Gold Cards plus "extra" services, such as calls reminding them of their mother's birthday. The annual fee of the Platinum Card is $300.

In addition to cards for individuals, American Express offers the Corporate Card that provides businesses a quarterly detailed statement of expenses by category and employee. It also covers lost or stolen luggage and $50,000 disability insurance when an airline ticket is purchased with the card.

In 1994, the American Express card was honored at 3.7 million businesses in 130 countries. Despite entering the market much later, VISA and MasterCard are accepted by 12 million outlets. Part of the reason why merchants adopted VISA and MasterCard is their lower merchant fees. American Express charges businesses an average of 3.2 percent per purchase. This compares to an average of 2 percent for VISA and MasterCard. American Express is trying to expand the number of merchants that accept its card by reducing the vendor fee to 2.8 percent. In addition, in 1992 American Express began expanding into nontraditional outlets such as Sears and Kmart, and established the goal of adding 200,000 new merchants a year to its distribution network.

In an effort to acquire more cardmembers, American Express is targeting other market segments including the less affluent. "We want people to feel they really can't conduct their business, travel, and personal lives without the American Express card," said Kenneth Chenault, president of American Express's U.S. Consumer Card group. However, some marketing experts question whether American Express can expand the number of cardmembers without pulling down its image.

New services and promotions are an integral part of American Express's marketing strategy. To gain a foothold in on-line services, American Express is offering electronic interactive services through America Online. ExpressNet allows cardmembers to review their American Express accounts, download statements into personal-finance software packages, and pay bills. In addition, users are able to make air, car rental, and hotel reservations. America Online serves a very specific but growing target market and provides more security than the Internet, the choice of VISA and MasterCard.

American Express has developed new cards in addition to using technology to expand its base of cardmembers. Not all of these cards have been successful. The Optima card, introduced in 1987, failed when generous credit approval standards caused American Express to incur large losses. The card utilized a different brand name and a blue color to differentiate it from the American Express card. More important, the Optima card was a credit, not a charge card. It allowed cardholders to pay the full balance or make extended payments at 16.75 percent, a slightly lower rate of interest than the rate charged by most bank credit cards.

American Express launched the Optima True Grace card in 1994 in response to consumer complaints that most credit cards do not permit a "grace period" for paying the bill before interest charges are accumulated. Interest on the True Grace Card does not start until 25 days after the close of the monthly billing cycle. The card is targeting current

American Express cardmembers as well as holders of other credit cards. At the end of the first year, there were 1.4 million cardholders of Optima True Grace, more than double the number the company expected.

American Express employs various promotion techniques to reach its target markets. The company uses cable television extensively to reach prospects with incomes of $50,000 or more as well as small business owners and managers. American Express became the official charge card of the National Basketball Association in 1995. The same year, the company agreed to waive its $55 annual fee for MCI telephone customers, and cobranded its Optima card with Hilton Hotels. The cobranded card has no annual fees for the customer and automatically enrolls the cardholder in Hilton's guest reward program.

Foreign countries represent a big growth market for charge and credit cards. American Express's traditional core customer, the business traveler, is emerging on a global level. American Express's 10.7 million cardmembers outside the United States accounted for $34 billion of its $124 billion in charges. However, this is only a small part of the worldwide market potential. In particular, the Asian credit card market has enormous promise. Over 50 million potential cardholders live in India, but only 2 million have credit cards. And China is virtually untapped, as only charge and debit cards are currently marketed there.

In Europe and Japan, American Express is well behind VISA and EuroCard, which is linked to MasterCard. EuroCard has 18.9 million customers in Europe and sales in 1994 totaled over $27 billion. One of the reasons for American Express's lack of success in Europe is its high merchant fees. American Express collects about 5 percent, whereas VISA takes only 1 percent of each purchase. Another reason for its slow growth is that in some countries American Express charges the customer a higher annual fee than the competition. For example, in Germany American Express charges an annual fee of $66 for the Green Card and $179 for a Gold Card, compared to $23 for a VISA card. As a result, American Express has only half the number of cardholders as the EuroCard in Germany. However, the company is trying to boost its market share through tie-in promotions. For example, the rental fee for a Mercedes MB 180C through Auto Europe is reduced if the transaction is made with an American Express card.

In Japan, American Express has about 740,000 cardmembers compared to the 14 million cardholders of Japan's JCB Co. bank consortium. American Express has decided to use a niche strategy in Japan by positioning the card as a status symbol. However, some of its strategies do not reflect a status appeal. For example, applications for an American Express card may be found in the back seat of Tokyo taxis. Also, by attempting to expand its merchant base in Japan, American Express may be losing its upscale image.

American Express's marketing effort extends beyond Europe and Japan to almost 30 countries, including Hong Kong, Spain, and Brazil. Rather than running the same advertisements that American Express has used in the U.S., advertising in foreign countries is adapted to local customers. For example, target markets in Indonesia and Thailand are more receptive to commercials that focus on being trendy and upwardly mobile. In Taiwan, advertising campaigns stress the credit card as a smarter way to pay for products. In Japan, advertisements depicting new ways of using a credit card (for example, Internet shopping) are more successful.

http://www.americanexpress.com/

QUESTIONS

1. How would you segment the market for charge and credit cards? For the American Express cards? The business (merchant) market?

2. How is American Express using consumer behavior concepts to position the American Express card? The Optima True Grace card?

Sources: Jon Berry, "Don't Leave Home without It, Wherever You Live," *Business Week*, Feb. 21, 1994, p. 76; "Finding the Core Customer," *BrandWeek*, Apr. 25, 1995, p. S15; Valerie Block, "Amex Checks in with New Coup: The Hilton Optima," *American Banker*, Sept. 13, 1995, p. 15; Lisa Fickenscher, "Amex Waiving Annual Fee for MCI Users," *American Banker*, May 5, 1995, p. 14; Jon Friedman, John Meehan, and David Greising, "Can Amex Win the Masses—And Keep Its Class?" *Business Week*, Oct. 9, 1989, p. 134; Linda Grant, "Why Warren Buffett's Betting Big on American Express," *Fortune*, Oct. 30, 1995, p. 70; Thomas Hoffman and Ellis Booker, "Amex Travels the 'Net," *Computerworld*, Feb. 27, 1995, p. 63; Robert Jennings, "American Express' Big Score: NBA Sponsorship," *American Banker*, May 12, 1995, p. 12; B. Bruce Knecht, "American Express to Try a Credit Card—Again," *The Wall Street Journal*, Sept. 6, 1994, p. B1; Jane L. Levere, "A German Bargain," *The New York Times*, Aug. 30, 1995, p. D16; Jill Smolowe, "Do You Still Know Me?" *Time*, Sept. 12, 1994, p. 60; and Fara Warner, "Booming Asia Lures Credit-Card Firms," *The Wall Street Journal*, Nov. 28, 1995, p. B3.

CASE 2 *The Gap*

ADAPTING TO CHANGING CONSUMER PREFERENCES

By all accounts The Gap is a marketing success story. The retail chain began by offering basic T-shirts and jeans that looked like designer clothes without the designer image or price. The Gap quickly grew into the most profitable specialty clothing store chain in America by positioning itself as offering "good style, good quality, good value." Its 800 stores do more than $3 billion in sales, and its divisions include GapKids, Banana Republic, and Old Navy stores.

The Gap's road to becoming a leader in specialty retailing was not without bumps. Donald Fisher started The Gap in 1969 out of frustration when a store refused to allow him to return a pair of Levi jeans that were too short. The first Gap store was located in San Francisco, and it stocked jeans in a wide range of sizes. The Gap soon expanded across the country, supported by a fixed 50 percent markup that Levi Strauss required of all retailers selling its jeans. However, in 1976 the Federal Trade Commission ruled that manufacturers such as Levi Strauss could not fix retail prices for their products. Jeans became a discounted product overnight. The Gap, which was totally dependent on jeans, had to find a new position.

After a futile attempt to position itself as a retailer of higher-margin clothing carrying its own brand, a back-to-basics merchandise strategy was found to have the greatest appeal among The Gap's customers. Gap stores stocked all-cotton apparel items in a deep assortment of colors. The Gap's strong ties to manufacturers, developed during its earlier efforts to sell its own store label, allowed the company to manage the quality of its products. Furthermore,

the company was able to control costs by designing its clothes in-house.

Expansion into children's clothing followed the success of Gap stores in the 1980s. GapKids stores feature simple, basic apparel items (for example, dresses and overalls) for newborns to young children.

The Gap acquired Banana Republic in 1983. Banana Republic grew rapidly as safari fashion became very popular with the release of movies such as the *Indiana Jones* series, *Out of Africa,* and *Romancing the Stone.* However, the safari image waned by 1988, necessitating a change in position for the 150-store chain. The position that produced the best financial results was as an upscale Gap with more adventurous fashions.

The Gap's merchandise assortment allowed it to become the "uniform of the middle class and middle aged." However, two core customer groups, teens and Generation Xers, began to turn away from The Gap's staple clothing items. Leo Burnett Co.'s semiannual "What is hot among kids" market research survey indicated that a negative image of The Gap began developing among teens as early as 1992. In that year, over 90 percent of teens surveyed labeled Gap clothes as "cool." This rating slipped to 83 percent by the summer of 1993, 75 percent by the winter of 1993, and 66 percent by the end of 1994. The loss of interest by these important market segments forced The Gap to appeal to new customers by becoming more fashion-oriented and launching new products and retail store concepts.

The Gap shifted its emphasis in merchandise away from unisex items to clothing that is gender-specific and fashion-oriented. The effort worked as the company's earnings increased by 23 percent from 1992 to 1993 despite a less favorable image among younger consumers. In addition, an effort was made to present a uniform picture of a Gap store by stocking all the styles available in all Gap stores, whereas smaller stores previously received only a narrow selection of inventory.

Another attempt to expand The Gap's customer base resulted in its entry into discount retailing in 1993. Forty-eight low-performing Gap stores were converted into Gap Warehouse discount stores. This decision represented a radical departure from The Gap's success formula that focused the company on being the leader of specialty clothing retailing. To prevent cannibalization of sales at Gap stores, Gap Warehouses sold separate lines of clothes that were similar to the Gap's basic products—jeans, khaki pants, and T-shirts—but carried everyday low prices. In addition, the material used in Gap Warehouse clothes was different from those stocked at Gap stores. Jeans received fewer stone-wash treatments, stitching was less detailed, and lighter-weight fabrics containing more polyester were used to control costs and keep retail prices low. Unlike The Gap that targets only adults, Gap Warehouses targeted adults and children.

The following year, The Gap launched a second entry into discount retailing to compete with mass merchants. Its Old Navy Clothing Co. stores carry specially designed apparel and accessories for consumers with incomes of $20,000 to $50,000. The Old Navy stores offer a wide selection of casual apparel items priced 20 to 25 percent below The Gap's clothing lines. Old Navy stores are positioned as one-stop clothing outlets with department store–style assortments of men's, women's, boys', girls', and babies' clothing. In addition, the stores stock The Gap's nonclothing products (for example, picture frames, address books, and decorative shopping bags).

The Gap introduced a line of bath and body products in a further attempt to serve new market segments. Gap Scents includes a line of soaps, lotions, shampoos, conditioners, shower gels, bath salts, and scented candles. The bath and body products are designed to target a market estimated to be worth $1 billion in 1994 and growing at 5 percent per year. In part, the development of Gap Scents was in response to the introduction of the Bath & Body Works chain by The Limited, The Gap's major competitor. The bath and body products are viewed by Gap management as the first step in making The Gap a life-style brand. If consumers begin to view The Gap as more than just a place for clothes, other product categories can be added.

Retailing also is undergoing radical changes. Consumers have become very selective in how they spend their time shopping. Since 1980, mall visits per month have been cut in half from 3 to 1.6. The number of stores visited per shopping trip has dropped from 7 to 3 over the same period of time. In addition, new technology is allowing retailers to control their costs as never before and devise new ways (for example, the Internet) to offer products to meet the needs of their customers. The face of specialty retailing will continue to be shaped in the 1990s as the Echo Boomer generation moves into its teens. These consumers switch brands easily and are comfortable with technology. One in three belongs to a minority group, compared to one in four in the general population. These teens have more purchasing power than previous generations and make many of their own purchase decisions, including clothes. The key to success for The Gap will be its ability to refine the position of its stores to meet the needs of their target markets while operating in an increasingly dynamic environment.

QUESTIONS

1. What social influences will have an effect on The Gap's future marketing strategy?
2. Was The Gap's entry into discount retailing with Gap Warehouse and Old Navy stores a mistake?
3. Given the changes taking place in retailing, what new products might The Gap offer?

As of publication, The Gap did not have a URL. As an alternative site, you can visit Armani Exchange at: http://www.armaniexchange.com/

Sources: Alice Cuneo, "Gap Floats Lower-Price Old Navy Stores," *Advertising Age,* July 25, 1994, p. 36; Christina Duff, "Bobby Short Wore Khakis'—Who's He and Who Cares?" *The Wall Street Journal,* Feb. 16, 1995, p. A1; Mary Kuntz, "Reinventing the Store: How Smart Retailers Are Changing the Way We Shop," *Business Week,* Nov. 27, 1995, p. 84; Russell Mitchell, "A Humbler Neighborhood for The Gap," *Business Week,* Aug. 16, 1993, p. 29; Russell Mitchell, "A Bit of a Rut at The Gap," *Business Week,* Nov. 30, 1992, p. 100; Russell Mitchell, "The Gap: Can the Nation's Hottest Retailer Stay on Top?" *Business Week,* Mar. 9, 1992, p. 58; Russell Mitchell, "The Gap Dolls Itself Up," *Business Week,* Mar. 21, 1994, p. 46; Elaine Underwood, "Gap Sets Scent Intro for November," *BrandWeek,* Aug. 22, 1994, p. 4; and Laura Zinn, "Teens, Here Comes the Biggest Wave Yet," *Business Week,* Apr. 11, 1994, p. 76.

PART THREE

Product

The planning, development, and management of the want-satisfying goods and services that are a company's products

In Part 2 we saw how markets are described and examined and how target markets are selected in keeping with the firm's marketing goals. The next step is to develop a marketing mix that will achieve these goals in the target markets. The marketing mix is a strategic combination of four elements: the organization's products, prices, distribution, and promotion. All these variables are closely interrelated.

In Part 3 the spotlight is on the first element of the marketing mix—the product. In Chapter 8 we define the term *product*, consider the importance of product planning and innovation, and discuss what needs to be done in developing new products. Chapter 9 deals mainly with product-mix strategies, management of the product life cycle, and a consideration of style and fashion. Chapter 10 discusses branding, packaging, and quality, among other features affecting a product's role in the marketing mix.

CHAPTER 8

Product Planning and Development

Should
GENERAL MOTORS
Electrify Its Product Mix?

eneral Motors—in fact, all automakers—seem to be schizophrenic about electric vehicles (EVs). Sometimes, they talk about progress in developing longer-lasting batteries or express enthusiasm about the sales prospects for electric-powered cars. More frequently, though, auto executives voice their opposition to state laws requiring the introduction of EVs or question whether this type of car can command a price that will allow manufacturers to cover their production and development costs.

Several years ago, General Motors (GM) announced its intention to develop its own brand of EV, the Impact. Since then, the project has sputtered. GM is not the only automaker working on an electric car; to differing degrees, most others also are. Facing some states' requirements to sell zero-emission cars by 1998, GM and the other automakers had to decide what to do regarding EVs.

At the development stage, the Impact was envisioned as having an aluminum skin, weighing no more than 2,200 pounds, and cruising at 55 miles per hour. The power would come from 32 10-volt lead-acid batteries. Fully charged, the Impact would have a driving range of at least 100 miles. Recharging would take about 6 hours on a normal 110-volt household outlet. Recharging time could drop to about 3 hours on a 220-volt outlet, but such outlets are uncommon in homes or public places.

For various reasons, GM wanted to introduce the Impact by the mid-1990s. To do so, the automaker needed to cut the time ordinarily required to design and produce a new car from 8 to 4 years. To accelerate the development process, GM formed a smaller, younger design team than normal and separated the team from the units that usually work on new cars. In addition, the company abandoned its normal practice of following a sequential process to design a car and instead assigned a variety of groups, including marketing and manufacturing, to work together on the project.

As an electric-powered car, the Impact has some inherent drawbacks. Perhaps most serious are the limited driving range and the need to recharge the batteries frequently. Further, it is fairly small and relatively expensive. The original estimates pegged the price at least $7,500—perhaps as much as $20,000—higher than a similar gasoline-powered car. Operating costs were gauged to be about twice those of a regular vehicle.

According to GM's original plan, the Impact would strengthen the company's position in the U.S. market. Further, the Impact would help rebuild GM's reputation for technological innovation. Because it relies on nonfossil fuels, the Impact also could position GM as more sensitive to environmental concerns. And last but not least, the new EV would help GM comply with a California law, which requires that by 1998 at least 2 percent of the new cars each automaker sells there be emission-free (that is, nonpolluting). The requirement rises to 10 percent in 2003. Similar laws have been enacted in New York and Massachusetts, with others expected. The automakers are trying to get the laws repealed, or at least relaxed.

Not waiting to see whether state requirements are retained, relaxed, or repealed, GM decided to introduce its EV in the fall of 1996. The two-seat EV1, essentially a renamed Impact, has a sticker price of $35,000. The introductory markets are Los Angeles, San Diego, Phoenix, and Tucson. GM chose to distribute the new EV1 through Saturn dealers in these areas.[1]

Did General Motors follow an appropriate process in developing the Impact electric vehicle?

http://www.gm.com/

Three factors stand out in the Impact case. First, even giant companies like General Motors need to develop new products. Second, managing the product component of a marketing mix is a difficult, complex task. And third, success with new products is not guaranteed, as numerous failures (ranging from the Merkur to the Yugo in the automotive field alone) indicate.

This chapter will provide you with insights regarding each of these important issues. Specifically, after studying this chapter, you should be able to explain:

CHAPTER GOALS

- The meaning of the word *product* in its fullest sense.
- What a "new" product is.
- The classification of consumer and business products.
- The relevance of these product classifications to marketing strategy.
- The importance of product innovation.
- The stages in the new-product development process.
- Criteria for adding a product to a company's line.
- Adoption and diffusion processes for new products.
- Organizational structures for product planning and development.

The Meaning of Product

In a *narrow* sense, a product is a set of basic attributes assembled in an identifiable form. Each product is identified by a commonly understood descriptive (or generic) name, such as steel, insurance, tennis rackets, or entertainment. Features such as brand name and postsale service that appeal to consumer motivation or buying patterns play no part in this narrow interpretation. According to this interpretation, an Apple and a Compaq would be the same good—a personal computer. And Disney World and Six Flags would be an identical service—an amusement park.

In marketing we need a broader definition of product to indicate that customers are not really buying a set of attributes, but rather benefits that satisfy their needs. Thus users don't want sandpaper; they really want a smooth surface. To develop a sufficiently broad definition, let's start with *product* as an umbrella term covering goods, services, places, persons, and ideas. Throughout this book, when we speak of products, we are using this broad connotation.

Thus a product that provides benefits can be something other than a tangible *good*. Red Roof Inn's product is a *service* that provides the benefit of a comfortable night's rest at a reasonable price. The Hawaii Visitors Bureau's product is a *place* that provides romance, sun and sand, relaxation, cross-cultural experiences, and other benefits. In a political campaign, the Democratic or Republican Party's product is a *person* (candidate) whom the party wants you to buy (vote for). The American Cancer Society is selling an *idea* and the benefits of not smoking. In Chapter 19 we discuss in more detail the marketing of intangible products such as services and ideas.

To further expand our definition, we treat each *brand* as a separate product. In this sense, Kodacolor film and Fujicolor film are different products. Squibb's aspirin and Bayer aspirin are also separate products, even though the only physical difference may be the brand name on the tablet. But the brand name suggests a product difference to the consumer, and this brings the concept of want-satisfaction into the definition. Going a step further, some consumers prefer one brand (Squibb's) and others favor a different brand (Bayer) of a similar product.

Any change in a feature (design, color, size, packaging), however minor, creates another product. Each such change provides the seller with an opportunity to use a new set of appeals to reach what essentially may be a new market. Pain relievers (Tylenol, Anacin) in capsule form are a different product from the same brand in tablet form, even though the chemical contents of the tablet and the capsule are identical. Seemingly minor product changes can be the key to success (or failure) in international markets. For example, to satisfy Japanese consumers, two modified versions of Oreo cookies were developed. One has less sugar in the cookie batter, the other omits the cream filling.[2]

We can broaden this interpretation still further. A Sony TV bought in a discount store on a cash-and-carry basis is a different product than the identical model purchased in a department store. In the department store, the customer may pay a higher price for the TV but buys it on credit, has it delivered free of charge, and receives other store services. Our concept of a product now includes the services that accompany it when purchased. A prime example is the warranty that assures a buyer of free replacement or repair of a defective product during a specified period of time.

We're now ready for a definition that is useful to marketers: As shown in Figure 8-1, a **product** is a set of tangible and intangible attributes, which may include packaging, color, price, quality, and brand, plus the seller's services and reputation. A product may be a good, service, place, person, or idea. In essence, then, customers are buying much more than a set of attributes when they buy a product. They are buying want-satisfaction in the form of the benefits they expect to receive from the product.

FIGURE 8-1

A product is much more than a set of physical attributes.

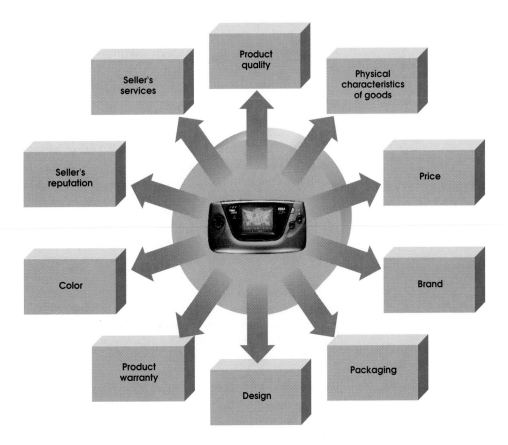

Classifications of Products

To design effective marketing programs, organizations need to know what kinds of products they are offering to potential customers. Thus it's helpful to separate *products* into homogeneous categories. First we will divide all products into two categories—consumer products and business products—that parallel our description of the market. Then we will subdivide each category still further.

Consumer and Business Products

Consumer products are intended for personal consumption by households. **Business products** are intended for resale, for use in producing other products, or for providing services in an organization. Thus the two types of products are distinguished based on *who will use them* and *how they will be used.*

The position of a product in its distribution channel has no bearing on its classification. Kellogg's cornflakes are categorized as consumer products, even if they are in the manufacturer's warehouses, in a freight line's trucks, or on retailers' shelves, *if ultimately they will be used in their present form by households.* However, Kellogg's cornflakes sold to restaurants and other institutions are categorized as business products no matter where they are in the distribution system.

Often it is not possible to place a product in only one class or the other. Seats on a United Airlines flight from Chicago to Phoenix may be considered a consumer product if purchased by students or a family going on vacation. But a seat on the same flight bought by a sales rep for business use is categorized as a business product. United Airlines, or any other company in a similar situation, recognizes that its product falls into both categories and therefore develops separate marketing programs for each market.

These distinctions may seem like "splitting hairs," but they are necessary for the strategic planning of marketing programs. Each major category of products ultimately goes to a distinctive type of market and thus requires different marketing methods.[3]

http://www.kelloggs.com/

http://www.ual.com/

Classification of Consumer Goods

For marketing purposes, distinguishing consumer goods from business goods is helpful but only a first step. The range of consumer goods is still too broad to be useful. Consequently, as shown in Table 8-1, they are further classified as convenience goods, shopping goods, specialty goods, and unsought goods. This classification is not based on intrinsic differences in the products themselves. Rather, it is based on how consumers go about buying a particular product. Depending on the buying behavior of different consumers, a single product—such as wine or dress slacks—can fall into more than one of the four categories.

Convenience Goods.   A tangible product that the consumer knows enough about before going out to buy it and then actually buys it with a minimum of effort is termed a **convenience good.** Normally the advantages resulting from shopping around to compare price and quality are not considered worth the required time and effort. A consumer is willing to accept any of several brands and thus will buy the one that is most accessible. For most buyers, convenience goods include many food items, inexpensive candy, drug sundries such as aspirin and toothpaste, and staple hardware items such as light bulbs and batteries.

TABLE 8-1 Categories of consumer goods: characteristics and marketing considerations

	Type of product*		
	Convenience	**Shopping**	**Specialty**
Examples:	Canned fruit	Furniture	Expensive suits
Characteristics:			
Time and effort devoted by consumer to shopping	Very little	Considerable	As much as necessary to find desired brand
Time spent planning the purchase	Very little	Considerable	Considerable
How soon want is satisfied after it arises	Immediately	Relatively long time	Relatively long time
Are price and quality compared?	No	Yes	No
Price	Usually low	Usually high	Usually high
Purchase frequency	Usually frequent	Infrequent	Infrequent
Marketing considerations:			
Length of channel	Long	Short	Short to very short
Retailer	Relatively unimportant	Important	Very important
Number of outlets	As many as possible	Few	Few; often only one in a market
Stock turnover	High	Lower	Lower
Gross margin	Low	High	High
Responsibility for advertising	Producer's	Joint responsibility	Joint responsibility
Point-of-purchase display	Very important	Less important	Less important
Brand or store name important	Brand name	Store name	Both
Packaging	Very important	Less important	Less important

*Unsought products are not included. See text explanation.

Convenience goods typically have a low unit price, are not bulky, and are not greatly affected by fad and fashion. They usually are purchased frequently, although this is not a necessary characteristic. Items such as Christmas tree lights or Mother's Day cards are convenience goods for most people, even though they may be bought only once a year.

Because a convenience good must be readily accessible when consumer demand arises, a manufacturer must be prepared to distribute it widely and rapidly. However, because most retail stores sell only a small volume of the total output of a convenience good (such as a particular brand of candy bar), it is not economical for the manufacturer to sell directly to all retail outlets. Instead the producer relies on wholesalers to sell the product to selected retailers.

Retailers usually carry several brands of the same type of convenience item, so they seldom promote any single brand. They are not interested in advertising convenience goods because many other stores carry the same brands (such as General Electric and Sylvania light bulbs). Thus any advertising by one retailer would help its competitors. As a result, much of the advertising burden is shifted to the manufacturer.

Shopping Goods. A tangible product for which consumers want to compare quality, price, and perhaps style in several stores before making a purchase is considered a **shopping good**. Examples of shopping goods—at least for most consumers—are fashionable apparel, furniture, major appliances, and automobiles. The process of searching and comparing continues as long as the customer believes that the potential benefits from a better purchase more than offset the additional time and effort spent shopping. A *better* purchase might be saving several hundred dollars on the purchase of a new car or finally finding a software package that prepares financial statements in the manner desired by the buyer.

With shopping goods, buying habits affect the distribution and promotion strategies of both manufacturers and middlemen (such as retail stores). Shopping-goods manufacturers require fewer retail outlets because consumers are willing to look around for what they want. To facilitate comparison shopping, manufacturers often try to place their products in stores located near other stores carrying competing items. Similarly, department stores and other retailers that carry primarily shopping goods like to be near each other.

Manufacturers usually work closely with retailers in marketing shopping goods. Since manufacturers use fewer retail outlets, they are more dependent on those they do select. Retail stores typically buy shopping goods in large quantities, and it's common for manufacturers to distribute directly to retailers. To buyers of a shopping good, the reputations of the stores carrying the product often are more important than the images of the manufacturers. For example, a consumer may be more loyal to a Circuit City store than to various brands of audio and video equipment, such as JVC and Sanyo.

Specialty Goods.   A tangible product for which consumers have a strong brand preference and are willing to expend substantial time and effort in locating the desired brand is called a **specialty good**. The consumer is willing to forgo more accessible substitutes to search for and purchase the desired brand. Examples of products usually categorized as specialty goods include expensive men's suits, stereo sound equipment, health foods, photographic equipment, and, for many people, new automobiles and certain home appliances. Various brands, such as Armani, Nikon, and BMW, have achieved specialty-good status in the minds of some consumers.

Since consumers *insist* on a particular brand and are willing to expend considerable effort to find it, manufacturers can use few retail outlets. Ordinarily the manufacturer deals directly with these retailers. The retailers are extremely important, particularly if the manufacturer uses only one in each area. And where the opportunity to handle the product is highly valued, the retailer may be quite willing to abide by the producer's policies regarding the amount of inventory that needs to be maintained, how the product should be advertised, or other marketing factors.

Because relatively few outlets are used *and* the product's brand name is important to buyers, both manufacturer and retailer advertise the product extensively. Often the manufacturer pays a portion of the retailer's advertising costs; and the name of the store carrying the specialty good frequently appears in the manufacturer's ads.

Unsought Goods.   There's one more, quite different category of goods. In fact, it's so unlike the other three categories that we have not included it in Table 8-1. Nevertheless, because some firms sell unsought goods, this category deserves brief discussion.

An **unsought good** is a new product that the consumer is not yet aware of *or* a product that the consumer is aware of but does not want right now. Most people are unaware of interactive movies, in which the audience determines to some degree the plot and outcome of the show by means of an electronic voting device attached to each seat.[4] For many consumers, video telephones are another unknown product. However, AT&T has invested substantial funds trying to remove its Video-Phone 2500, a telephone that can send moving pictures over phone lines, from the unsought category.

Currently unwanted products might include gravestones for those who have not lost a loved one and snow tires in the summer. An electric car, as discussed in the chapter-opening case, might be an unsought good for most people, either because they are unaware of it or do not want one after learning about it. As the name suggests, a firm faces a very difficult, perhaps impossible, advertising and personal selling job when trying to market unsought goods. The best approach may be to make consumers aware of the products so they will buy the advertised brand when the need arises.

Classification of Business Goods

As with consumer goods, the general category of *business goods* is too broad to use in developing a marketing program. Consequently, as shown in Table 8-2, we separate business goods into five categories: raw materials, fabricating materials and parts, installations, accessory equipment, and operating supplies. This classification is based on the product's broad *uses*. For example, a business good may be used in producing other products, in operating an organization, and in other ways we will discuss.

Raw Materials.   Business goods that become part of another tangible product prior to being processed in any way (except as necessary to assist in handling the product) are considered **raw materials**. Raw materials include:

- Goods found in their natural state, such as minerals, land, and products of the forests and the seas.
- Agricultural products, such as cotton, fruits, livestock, and animal products including eggs and raw milk.

Due to their distinctive attributes, these two groups of raw materials usually are marketed differently. For instance, the supply of raw materials in their natural state is limited, cannot be substantially increased, and often involves only a few large producers. Further, such products generally are of a commodity nature, must be carefully graded, and, consequently, are highly standardized. Consider coal as an example; it is extracted in great quantities and then is graded by hardness and sulfur content.

The characteristics of raw materials in their natural state affect how they are marketed. For example:

- Prices are normally set by supply and demand, approximating the conditions of perfect competition. As a result, individual producers have little or no control over the prevailing market price.
- Because of their great bulk, low unit value, and the long distances between producer and business user, transportation is an important consideration for natural raw materials.

TABLE 8-2 Categories of business goods: characteristics and marketing considerations

	Type of product				
	Raw materials	**Fabricating parts and materials**	**Installations**	**Accessory equipment**	**Operating supplies**
Examples:	Iron ore	Engine blocks	Blast furnaces	Storage racks	Paper clips
Characteristics:					
Unit price	Very low	Low	Very high	Medium	Low
Length of life	Very short	Depends on final product	Very long	Long	Short
Quantities purchased	Large	Large	Very small	Small	Small
Frequency of purchase	Frequent delivery; long-term purchase contract	Infrequent purchase, but frequent delivery	Very infrequent	Medium frequency	Frequent
Standardization of competitive products	Very much; grading is important	Very much	Very little; custom-made	Little	Much
Quantity of supply	Limited; supply can be increased slowly or not at all	Usually no problem	No problem	Usually no problem	Usually no problem
Marketing considerations:					
Nature of channel	Short; no middlemen	Short; middlemen only for small buyers	Short; no middlemen	Middlemen used	Middlemen used
Negotiation period	Hard to generalize	Medium	Long	Medium	Short
Price competition	Important	Important	Varies in importance	Not main factor	Important
Presale/postsale service	Not important	Important	Very important	Important	Very little
Promotional activity	Very little	Moderate	Sales people very important	Important	Not too important
Brand preference	None	Generally low	High	High	Low
Advance buying contract	Important; long-term contracts	Important; long-term contracts	Not usual	Not usual	Not usual

- Due to these same factors, natural raw materials frequently are marketed directly from producer to business user with a minimum of physical handling.
- There is very little branding or other product differentiation of this type of product. It is tough to distinguish one producer's coal from another producer's.

Agricultural products are supplied by small producers as well as larger corporate farms, typically located some distance from their markets. The supply is largely controllable by producers, but it cannot be increased or decreased rapidly. The product is perishable and is not produced at a uniform rate throughout the year. Most citrus fruits, for example, ripen in late winter and thus are readily available at that time of year and become less available in subsequent months. Standardization and grading are commonplace for agricultural products. Also, transportation costs are likely to be high relative to the product's unit value.

Many middlemen are needed to market agricultural products because producers are small and numerous and markets are distant. Transportation and warehousing greatly influence effectiveness *and* efficiency of distribution. Very little promotional activity is involved with agricultural products.

Fabricating Materials and Parts.   Business goods that become part of the finished product after having been processed to some extent fit into the category of fabricating materials and parts. The fact that they have been processed distinguishes them from raw materials. **Fabricating materials** undergo further processing; examples include pig iron going into steel, yarn being woven into cloth, and flour becoming part of bread. **Fabricating parts** are assembled with no further change in form; they include such products as zippers in clothing and semiconductor chips in computers.

Fabricating materials and parts are usually purchased in large quantities. Normally, buying decisions are based on the price and the service provided by the seller. To ensure an adequate, timely supply, a buyer may place an order a year or more in advance. Because consumers are concerned about price, service, and reliability of supply, most fabricating products are marketed directly from producer to user. Middlemen are used most often when the buyers are small in size and/or when buyers have small fill-in orders (after the large initial order) requiring rapid delivery.

Branding fabricating materials and parts is generally unimportant. However, some firms have successfully pulled their business goods out of obscurity by branding them. Talon zippers and the NutraSweet brand of sweeteners are examples.

Installations.   Manufactured products that are an organization's major, expensive, and long-lived equipment are termed **installations**. Examples are large generators in a dam, a factory building, diesel engines for a railroad, and blast furnaces for a steel mill. The characteristic of installations that differentiates them from other categories of business goods is that they directly affect the scale of operations in an organization producing goods or services. Adding 12 new Steelcase desks will not affect the scale of operations at American Airlines, but adding 12 Boeing 767 jet aircraft certainly will. Therefore, jet aircraft are categorized as installations, but desks normally are not.

The marketing of installations presents a real challenge, because each unit sold represents a large dollar amount. Often each unit is made to the buyer's detailed specifications. Also, much presale and postsale servicing is essential. For example, a large printing press requires installation, maintenance, and—inevitably—repair service. Sales are usually made directly from producer to business user; no middlemen are involved. Because installations are technical in nature, a high-caliber, well-trained sales force is needed to market installations. Because installations require careful, detailed explanation, promotion emphasizes personal selling.

Accessory Equipment.   Tangible products that have substantial value and are used in an organization's operations are called **accessory equipment**. This category of business goods neither becomes an actual part of a finished product nor has a significant impact on the organization's scale of operations. The life of accessory equipment is shorter than that of installations but longer than that of operating supplies. Some examples are point-of-sale terminals in a retail store, small power tools, forklift trucks, and office desks.

*S*ome products, including Talon zippers, are purchased by both business and consumer markets. For apparel manufacturers, zippers are a fabricating part in a piece of clothing. Most consumers presumably view a zipper as a convenience good, an item to be purchased as easily as possible. However, some consumers—perhaps those who sew their own clothes—may consider a Talon zipper to be a specialty good. They will expend extra effort to locate and buy Talon rather than another brand.

ONE OF THE FEW THINGS TALON DOESN'T MAKE A ZIPPER FOR.

Talon has hatched so many zippers that you'll find our name in more than two billion products. In fact, the consistent excellence and proven performance of our zippers have made the Talon name a symbol of quality. A reliable sign that tells you the rest of the product will be well-made, too. So be a smart shopper. Always look for and select the products that carry the Talon name. Of course, we don't make a zipper for an egg. But that's only because the manufacturer hasn't asked us for one.

The Talon® zipper says a lot about what it's in.

It is difficult to generalize about how accessory equipment should be marketed. For example, a manufacturer selling directly to a final customer is appropriate for some products in this category. This is true particularly when an order is for several units or when each unit is worth a lot of money. A manufacturer of forklift trucks may sell directly to customers because the price of a single unit is large enough to make this form of distribution profitable. Normally, however, manufacturers of accessory equipment use middlemen—for example, office-equipment distributors. The reasons: Typically, the market is geographically dispersed, there are many different types of potential users, and individual orders may be relatively small.

Operating Supplies. Business goods that are characterized by low dollar value per unit, a short life, and aid in an organization's operations without becoming part of the finished product are called **operating supplies**. Examples are lubricating oils, pencils and stationery, and heating fuel. Purchasers want to buy operating supplies with fairly little effort. Thus operating supplies are the convenience goods of the business sector.

As with the other categories of goods, the characteristics of operating supplies influence how they should be marketed. Because they are low in unit value and are bought by many different organizations, operating supplies—like consumer convenience goods—are distributed widely. Thus, the producing firm uses wholesaling middlemen extensively. Also, because competing products are quite standardized and there is little brand insistence, price competition is normally stiff.

Importance of Product Innovation

A business exists to satisfy customers while making a profit. Fundamentally, a company fulfills this dual purpose through its products. New-product planning and development are vital to an organization's success. This is particularly true now, given (1) rapid technological changes, which can make some products obsolete, and (2) the practice of many competitors to copy a successful product, which can neutralize an innovative product's advantage. Thus, as emphasized by a top executive at Pillsbury, "In the end, the company with the most new products wins."[5] Of course, these new products must be satisfying to customers and profitable for the firm.

Requirement for Growth

A guideline for management is "innovate or die." For many companies a substantial portion of this year's sales volume and net profit will come from products that did not exist 5 to 10 years ago. For example, in recent years, both Rubbermaid and Johnson & Johnson generated more than 25 percent of their sales from products that had been introduced during the preceding 5 years.[6]

http://www.rubbermaid.com/
http://www.jnj.com/

Because products, like people, go through a life cycle, new products are essential for sustaining a company's revenues and profits. Sales of a product grow and then, almost inevitably, decline; eventually, most products are replaced. The concept of the product life cycle is discussed in more detail in Chapter 9, but we mention it here because it has two significant implications for product innovation:

- Every company's present products eventually become outdated as their sales volume and market share are reduced by changing consumer desires and/or superior competing products. Once successful products that no longer exist or have been relegated to the lower shelves in supermarkets include White Cloud bathroom tissue, Lorna Doone cookies, Fab detergent, and Maypo cereal.[7]
- As a product ages, its profits generally decline. Introducing a new product at the right time can help maintain a firm's profits. In fact, companies that are leaders in terms of profitability and sales growth obtain 49 percent of their revenues from products introduced during the preceding 5 years. The corresponding figure for the least successful companies is 11 percent.[8]

Increased Selectivity

In recent years, prospective buyers have become more selective in their choices of products. Many consumers' disposable income was hurt by the recession of the early 1990s, and numerous firms' resources have been dissipated by organizational restructuring (sometimes referred to as *downsizing*). With reduced buying power, households and organizations have to be very careful in their purchases. Even consumers who escaped the negative effects of the recession are being selective in making additional purchases because they are already reasonably well fed, clothed, housed, transported, and equipped.

Another reason for more selective buying is that purchasers have to sort through an abundance (or, some would say, an excess) of similar products. Many new products are mere imitations of existing products and, as such, offer few if any added benefits. How many of the approximately 6,000 new toys or more than 1,500 new beverages, ranging from iced coffees to ultra-caffeine colas, that are introduced annually are really new?[9] This deluge of new products leads to "product indigestion" for consumers. The remedy is to develop *truly* new products—to *innovate*, not just *imitate*.

High Failure Rates

For many years, the "rule of thumb" has been that about 80 percent of new products fail. However, due to dissimilar definitions of *new product* and *failure*, the statistics often vary from one study to another. One company that tracks new-product introductions placed the rate of failure at even higher than 80 percent. According to another firm's annual survey, 72 percent of new products do not meet their primary business objectives. And finally, an examination of 11,000 new goods and services discovered that 56 percent are still on the market 5 years after being introduced. Of course, some of those products still on the market undoubtedly are on the brink of failure while others are hugely successful.[10]

Why do new products fail?[11] The most common problem is not being different than existing products. Consumers yawned at Pepsi A.M., which was intended for breakfast time, but was essentially the same as regular Pepsi. A new product is also likely to fail if it does not deliver on its promise. Beech Aircraft's Starship plane was supposed to perform like a jet at the price of a propeller plane. Instead, the finished product wound up performing like a propeller plane (indeed it was a turboprop) at the price of a jet![12] Further, a product is subject to failure if it is perceived as offering poor value in relation to its price. Priced at $4 to $7 apiece, the General Foods Culinova refrigerated dinners did not pass consumers' value test. Other factors that can undermine new products include poor positioning and lack of marketing support.

Considering how vital new products are to a company's growth, the large number of new-product introductions, and the high failure rates, product innovation deserves special attention. Firms that are inattentive to their new products may face financial ruin because of the high cost of product failure—often more than $10 million per occurrence in a large company. Organizations that effectively manage product innovation can expect to reap a variety of benefits—differential advantage, higher sales and profits, and a solid foundation for the future.

Development of New Products

It's often said that nothing happens until somebody sells something. This is not entirely true. First there must be something to sell—a good, service, person, place, or idea. And that "something" must be developed.

What Is a "New" Product?

Just what is a "new" product? Are the auto manufacturers' annual models new products? GM's proposed electric car? The Chevrolet Tahoe, which is sized between the Blazer and Suburban? Or, in other product categories, how about a clear cola such as Crystal Pepsi or a clear beerlike beverage such as Zima? How about a "flying" ballerina doll developed by Lewis Galoob Toys?[13] Or must a product be revolutionary, never before seen, before we can class it as *new*?

A COMMITMENT TO CUSTOMER SATISFACTION

HOW DO GREEN PRODUCTS WIN BOTH CUSTOMERS AND AWARDS?

More and more consumers are concerned about the quality of the natural environment. Many of them are interested in buying environmentally friendly products. So, in order to preserve the natural environment and/or satisfy a growing segment of consumers, companies are developing and introducing more "green products."

Some environmentally friendly products are winning awards as well as customers. Each year, the American Marketing Association bestows Edison Awards to the top green products. Several recent winners are worth examining:

- Nickel cadmium rechargeable batteries have been classified as health risks. Thus Rayovac developed Renewal rechargeables, which contain no mercury or cadmium. In addition, the Renewal is recyclable. The Renewal brand has stimulated sales growth in the previously stagnant category of rechargeable batteries.
- The U.S. Department of Agriculture invented Gridcore building panels, made of recycled materials such as corrugated cardboard and plastics. Gridcore Systems International has been granted the rights to manufacture and sell this product for use in furniture, exhibits, and stage sets. By using recycled materials, Gridcore saves trees and keeps waste out of landfills.
- 3M created an environmentally friendly version of steel-wool soap pads, made of recycled plastic bottles and biodegradable, phosphorous-free soap. Backed by advertising, 3M's Scotch-Brite Never Rust pads grabbed a 25 percent market share almost immediately.

Obviously, offer functional benefits to consumers, with respect to physical characteristics and target markets. However, they share similarities in terms of how they have achieved success in the marketplace:

- They offer functional benefits to consumers, with environmental benefits presented as another reason for buying the product.
- They deliver value.

Firms that strive for environmentally friendly products should consider these strategies.

What else could a manufacturer do to motivate more consumers to buy its line of environmentally friendly products?

Sources: Jacquelyn Ottman, "Edison Winners Show Smart Environmental Marketing," *Marketing News*, July 17, 1995, p. 16; and "Edison Environmental Awards," *Marketing News*, May 8, 1995, p. E9.

How new a product is affects how it should be marketed. There are numerous connotations of "new product," but we will focus our attention on three distinct categories of **new products**:

http://www.hp.com/

- Products that are *really innovative*—truly unique. A recent example is a security device that electronically compares the shape of a person's hand with the image of a hand encoded on an identification card.[14] Another example is a gadget developed by Hewlett-Packard Co. that permits viewers to participate in "interactive" TV programs. Still-to-be-developed products in this category would be a cancer cure and easily, inexpensively repaired automobiles. Any new product in this category satisfies a real need that is not being satisfied at the time it is introduced.
- Replacements that are *significantly different* from existing products in terms of form, function, and—most important—benefits provided. Johnson & Johnson's Acuvue disposable contact lenses and Sharp Corp.'s 3-inch thin TV that hangs on a wall like a picture are replacing some traditional models. Referring back

*E*gg•land's Best Inc. considers its eggs so new as to deserve a patent. According to the producer (not the hen, but the company), two Egg•land eggs contain 50 percent of the recommended intake of Vitamin E, compared to 6 percent for a pair of typical eggs. Whether consumers judge Egg•land's eggs to be really innovative, significantly different, or just imitative depends in large part on whether or not they want a large dose of Vitamin E in an egg.

to earlier examples, the electric car falls in this category. The Galoob firm hopes young girls perceive its flying doll to be significantly different—and better—than normal dolls.

- *Imitative* products that are new to a particular company but not new to the market. Usually, annual models of autos and new versions of cereals are appropriately placed in this category. In another situation, a firm may simply want to capture part of an existing market with a "me too" product. To maximize company-wide sales, makers of cold and cough remedies routinely introduce imitative products, some of which compete with a nearly identical product *from the same company*. That's the case with Dristan Sinus and CoAdvil, both put out by American Home Products.

Ultimately, of course, whether or not a product is new depends on how the intended market perceives it. If buyers consider it to be significantly different from competitive products in some relevant characteristic (such as appearance or performance), then it is indeed a new product. As in other situations, *perception is reality*!

New-Product Strategy

To achieve strong sales and healthy profits, every producer of business goods or consumer goods should have an explicit strategy with respect to developing and evaluating new products. This strategy should guide every step in the process of developing a new product.

A **new-product strategy** is a statement identifying the role a new product is expected to play in achieving corporate and marketing goals. For example, a new product might be designed to protect market share, meet a specific return-on-investment goal, or establish a position in a new market. Or a new product's role might be to maintain the company's reputation for innovation or social responsibility. The last outcome appeared to be a primary aim of McDonald's when it introduced the reduced-fat McLean Deluxe hamburger. While the McLean may have helped McDonald's rebut criticism about not being health conscious, it was a failure with respect to achieving sufficient sales.[15]

A new product's intended role also will influence the *type* of product to be developed. To illustrate:

Company goal		Product strategy		Recent examples
To defend market share.	$\rightarrow$	Introduce an addition to an existing product line or revise an existing product.	$\rightarrow$	Pizza Hut's "Big Foot" and "Stuffed Crust" pizzas.
To strengthen a reputation as an innovator.	$\rightarrow$	Introduce a *really* new product—not just an extension of an existing one.	$\rightarrow$	Palmtop computers introduced by Hewlett-Packard.

Only in recent years have many companies consciously identified new-product strategies. The process of developing new products has become more efficient *and* more effective for firms with strategies because they have a better idea of what they are trying to accomplish.

Stages in the Development Process

Guided by a company's new-product strategy, a new product is best developed through a series of six stages, as shown in Figure 8-2. Compared to unstructured development, the formal development of new products provides benefits such as improved teamwork, less rework, earlier failure detection, shorter development times, and—most important—higher success rates.[16]

At each stage, management must decide whether to proceed to the next stage, abandon the product, or seek additional information.[17] Here's a brief description of what should happen at each stage of the **new-product development process**:

1. *Generating new-product ideas.* New-product development starts with an idea. A system must be designed for stimulating new ideas within an organization and then reviewing them promptly. In one study, 80 percent of companies pointed to customers as their best source for new-product ideas.[18] A growing number of manufacturers are encouraging—in some cases, requiring—suppliers to propose innovations.[19]
2. *Screening ideas.* At this stage, new-product ideas are evaluated to determine which ones warrant further study.[20] Typically, a management team relies on its experience and judgment (rather than statistical data) to screen the pool of ideas.
3. *Business analysis.* A surviving idea is expanded into a concrete business proposal. During the stage of **business analysis**, management (a) identifies product features; (b) estimates market demand, competition, and the product's profitability; (c) establishes a program to develop the product; and (d) assigns responsibility for further study of the product's feasibility.
4. *Prototype development.* If the results of the business analysis are favorable, then a prototype (or trial model) of the product is developed. In the case of

FIGURE 8-2

Major stages in the new-product development process.

| Identify the strategic role of new products, then . . . | 1. Idea generation | 2. Screening of ideas | 3. Business analysis | 4. Prototype development | 5. Market tests | 6. Commercialization |

A GLOBAL PERSPECTIVE

HOW CAN NEW-PRODUCT IDEAS BE FOUND ON OTHER CONTINENTS?

Seeking added sales and perhaps a differential advantage, a growing legion of companies are scanning foreign markets for new-product ideas. Various products introduced fairly recently in the U.S.—including Whiskas cat food from Mars Inc., the Symphony chocolate bar from Hershey Foods, and Michelob Dry beer from Anheuser-Busch—originated in foreign markets.

Several factors prompt U.S. companies to look abroad for new-product ideas:

- Bored with mere imitations, consumers are willing to accept novel products.
- Truly innovative products, even potential breakthroughs, might be uncovered in foreign markets. At the extreme, Shaman Pharmaceuticals of South San Francisco is tapping the practical knowledge of "medicine men" (or shamans) in the rainforests of eastern Ecuador to identify tropical plants and trees that may contain curative compounds. This approach has helped the company develop several drugs.
- Marketing a foreign product in the firm's home country can be much cheaper than starting the development process from scratch. With that in mind, Prince, the sporting goods company, acquired the U.S. distribution rights for the Australian-made product Sports Action Machine

(SAM). The 9-foot tall, 400-pound SAM is a high-tech tennis ball machine that can fire 10 types of shots at 8 degrees of difficulty.

- An existing foreign product may be the best way of satisfying an ethnic market segment in the home country. For example, Colgate-Palmolive was confident the lighter texture and pleasing smell of its Fabuloso cleaner, developed abroad, would appeal to Hispanics in the U.S.

An established foreign product is not guaranteed success here. Following several guidelines can help:

- Concentrate on products that have achieved widespread success in foreign markets. Dry beers in Japan are a case in point. Still, they haven't been a big hit in the U.S.
- Don't just rely on the product's newness, but ensure it has a differential advantage.
- Stick to products that coincide with U.S. trends. A greater interest in healthful foods helped Kellogg's achieve success in the U.S. with Mueslix, a cereal combining grains, nuts, and fruits that was invented in Switzerland.

Sources: Frederick C. Klein, "New Aussie Giant Serves Up Aces; Our Man Is Bushed," *The Wall Street Journal*, May 26, 1995, p. B8; Thomas M. Burton, "Drug Company Looks to 'Witch Doctors' to Conjure Products," *The Wall Street Journal*, July 7, 1994, p. A1; Michael J. McCarthy, "More Companies Shop Abroad for New-Product Ideas," *The Wall Street Journal*, Mar. 14, 1990, pp. B1, B6; and Bob Hagerty, "Unilever Scours the Globe for Better Ideas," *The Wall Street Journal*, Apr. 25, 1990, p. A11.

---

services, the facilities and procedures necessary to produce and deliver the new product are designed and tested. That certainly is a necessary step in developing a new roller-coaster ride for an amusement park!

In the case of goods, a small quantity of the trial model is manufactured to designated specifications. Technical evaluations are carried out to determine whether it is practical to produce the product. A firm may be able to construct a prototype of a new type of cellular telephone, but be unable to manufacture the new product in large quantities or at a cost that is low enough to stimulate sales and still yield a profit. Further, lab tests are conducted to judge whether the proposed product will endure normal—even abnormal—usage. Apple Computer puts all new models of its PowerBooks through various durability tests that range from pouring a soft drink onto the computer to subjecting the screen to over 100 pounds of pressure.[21]

5. *Market tests.* Unlike the internal tests conducted during prototype development, **market tests** involve actual consumers. A new tangible product may be given

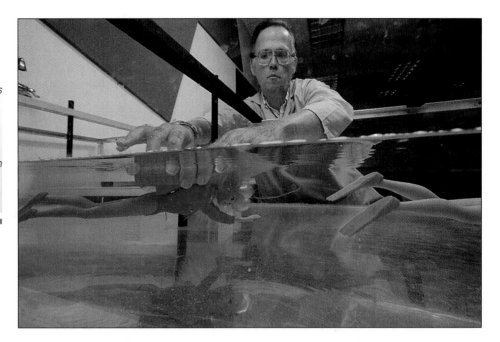

*V*irtually all products, even Barbie dolls, undergo various tests before (and also after) being introduced to the market. Some producers do the testing themselves; others outsource the testing to specialized firms. Here, a Barbie doll is being tested to determine its durability. Such tests can lead to safer and more reliable products.

to a sample of people for use in their households (in the case of a consumer good) or their organizations (a business good). Following the trial, users are asked to evaluate the product.

This stage in new-product development often entails test marketing, in which the product is placed on sale in a limited geographic area. Market tests often run for many months, even years. McDonald's typically tests potential products for years.[22]

Market-test findings, including sales and repeat purchases, are monitored by the company that developed the product and perhaps by competitors as well. The product's design and production plans may have to be adjusted as a result of test findings. Following market tests, management must make a final "go–no go" decision about introducing the product.

6. *Commercialization.* In this stage, full-scale production and marketing programs are planned and then implemented. Up to this point in development, management has virtually complete control over the product. However, once the product is "born" and made available for purchase, the external competitive environment becomes a major determinant of its destiny.

Note that the first two stages—idea generation and screening—are tied closely to the overall new-product strategy. This strategy can provide a focus for generating new-product ideas *and* a basis for evaluating them.

In the six-stage process, the first three stages are particularly critical because they deal with ideas and, as such, are the least expensive.[23] More important, many products fail because the idea or the timing is wrong—and the first three stages are intended to identify such situations. Each subsequent stage becomes more costly in terms of the dollars and human resources necessary to carry out the required tasks.

Trying to bring new products to market faster than their competitors, some companies skip stages in the development process. The most common omission is the fifth stage, market tests.[24] Without this stage, however, the company lacks the most telling reactions to the proposed product.

AN ETHICAL DILEMMA?

About 20 firms in the U.S. tell inventors they will help them refine their ideas for new products, prepare the necessary plans, develop prototypes, and line up business deals with manufacturers and other producers. Typically, an inventor pays the "matchmaker" an up-front fee of about $5,000. Thousands of people sign up with these invention-promotion firms annually.

Is it ethical for invention-promotion firms to charge substantial up-front fees?

Historically, the marketing of goods has received more attention than the marketing of services. Thus it is not surprising that the new-product development process is not as advanced in services fields as it is in goods industries.[25] Thus, service firms are almost starting with a clean slate as they devise a new-product development process that suits their distinctive circumstances.

Producer's Criteria for New Products

When should a company add a new product to its current assortment of products? Here are guidelines that some producers use in answering this question:

- There must be *adequate market demand*. Too often management begins with the wrong question, such as, "Can we use our present sales force?" or "Will the new item fit into our production system?" The necessary first question is, "Do enough people really want this product?" A product is destined to fail if it fills a need that doesn't exist or isn't important to consumers.[26]
- The product must *satisfy key financial criteria*. At least three questions should be asked: "Is adequate financing available?" "Will the new item reduce seasonal and cyclical fluctuations in the company's sales?" And most critical, "Can we make a sufficient profit with the product?"
- The product must be *compatible with environmental standards*. Key questions include "Does the production process avoid polluting the air or water?" "Will the finished product, including its packaging, be friendly to the environment?" And, "After being used, does the product have recycling potential?"
- The product must *fit into the company's present marketing structure*. The Bill Blass firm probably would find it practical to add designer sheets and towels to its product mix that features clothing, whereas the Sherwin Williams paint company would likely find it more difficult to add sheets and towels to its mix. Specific questions related to whether a new product will fit the company's marketing expertise and experience include "Can the existing sales force be used?" "Can the present channels of distribution be used?"

Besides these four issues, a proposed product must satisfy other criteria. For instance, it must be in keeping with the company's objectives and image. The product also must be compatible with the firm's production capabilities. And it must satisfy any pertinent legal requirements.

Middleman's Criteria for New Products

In considering whether to buy a new product for resale, middlemen such as retailers and wholesalers should apply all the preceding criteria except those related to production. In addition, a middleman should apply the following guidelines:

- The middleman must have *a good working relationship with the producer*. By distributing a new product, a middleman should stand to benefit from the producer's reputation, the possibility of getting the right to be the only company to sell the product in a given territory, and the promotional and financial help given by the producer.
- The producer and middleman must have *compatible distribution policies and practices*. Pertinent questions include "What kind of selling effort is required for the new product?" "How does the proposed product fit with the middleman's policies regarding repair service, alterations (for clothing), credit, and delivery?"
- As in the case of producers, the product must *satisfy key financial criteria*. At least two questions should be asked: "If adding a new product necessitates eliminating another product because of a shortage of shelf or storage space, will the result be a net gain in sales?" And, "Can we make a sufficient profit with the product?"

New-Product Adoption and Diffusion

The likelihood of achieving success with a new product, especially a really innovative product, is increased if management understands the adoption and diffusion processes for that product. Once again, we stress that organizations need to understand how prospective customers behave. The **adoption process** is the set of successive decisions an *individual person or organization* makes before accepting an innovation. **Diffusion** of a new product is the process by which an innovation spreads throughout a *social system* over time.[27]

By understanding these processes, an organization can gain insight into how a product is or is not accepted by prospective customers and which groups are likely to buy a product soon after it is introduced, later on, or never. This knowledge of buying behavior can be valuable in designing an effective marketing program.

Stages in Adoption Process

A prospective buyer goes through six **stages in the adoption process**—deciding whether to purchase something new:

Stage	Activity in that stage
Awareness	Individual is exposed to the innovation; becomes a prospect.
Interest	Prospect is interested enough to seek information.
Evaluation	Prospect judges the advantages and disadvantages of a product and compares it to alternatives.
Trial	Prospect adopts the innovation on a limited basis. A consumer tries a sample, if the product can be sampled.
Adoption	Prospect decides whether to use the innovation on a full-scale basis.
Confirmation	After adopting the innovation, prospect becomes a user who immediately seeks assurances that decision to purchase the product was correct.

Adopter Categories

Some people will adopt an innovation soon after it is introduced. Others will delay before accepting a new product, and still others may never adopt it. Research has identified five **innovation adopter categories**, based on the point in time when individuals adopt a given innovation. Nonadopters are excluded from this categorization. Characteristics of early and late adopters are summarized in Table 8-3. We should add that it's unlikely an individual will be in the same category (such as early adopter) for all products. It's possible a person may fall in one category for a specific product (like audio equipment) but go into another category for a much different product (like clothing).

Innovators. Representing about 3 percent of the market, **innovators** are venturesome consumers who are the first to adopt an innovation. In relation to later adopters, innovators are likely to be younger, have higher social status, and be in better financial shape. Innovators also tend to have broad social relationships involving various groups of people in more than one community. They are likely to rely more on nonpersonal sources of information, such as advertising, rather than on sales people or other personal sources.

Early Adopters. Comprising about 13 percent of the market, **early adopters** purchase a new product after innovators but sooner than other consumers. Unlike innovators, who have broad involvements *outside* a local community, early adopters tend to be involved socially *within* a local community. Early adopters are greatly respected in their social system; in fact, other people are interested in and influenced by their opinions. Thus the early-adopter category includes more opinion leaders than any other adopter group. Sales people are probably used more as information sources by early adopters than by any other category.

In the process of diffusion, a **change agent** is a person who seeks to accelerate the spread of a given innovation. In business, the person responsible for intro-

TABLE 8-3 Characteristics of early and late adopters of innovations

	Early adopters	Late adopters
Key characteristics:		
Venturesome	Innovators	
Respected	Early adopters	
Deliberate	Early majority	
Skeptical		Late majority
Tradition-bound		Laggards
Other characteristics:		
Age	Younger	Older
Education	Well educated	Less educated
Income	Higher	Lower
Social relationships: within or outside community	Innovators: outside Others: within	Totally local
Social status	Higher	Lower
Information sources	Wide variety; many media	Limited media exposure; limited reliance on outside media; reliance on local peer groups

ducing an innovative new product must be a change agent. Consider the electronic device that combines a microphone and transmitter to allow a parent to keep track of a child's whereabouts. Marketers of this device, with different brands such as Child Guardian and Beeper Kid, must be effective change agents, convincing consumers that it is worthwhile to spend $50 or more for this type of added safety.[28]

A change agent focuses the initial persuasive efforts, notably targeted advertising campaigns, on people who fit the demographic profile of early adopters. Other consumers respect—often request—the opinions of early adopters and eventually will emulate their behavior. Thus, if a firm can get early adopters to buy its innovative product and they are satisfied by it, then they will say good things about the new offering. This is called *word-of-mouth communication*. In turn, the broader market eventually will accept the product as well. Of course, unlike advertising that is controlled by the firm, word-of-mouth can be influenced through advertising but is still largely uncontrolled. And sometimes, it turns out to be unfavorable and harmful rather than favorable and helpful.[29]

Early Majority. The **early majority**, representing about 34 percent of the market, includes more deliberate consumers who accept an innovation just before the "average" adopter in a social system. This group is a bit above average in social and economic measures. Consumers in the early-majority group rely quite a bit on ads, sales people, and contact with early adopters.

Late Majority. The **late majority**, another 34 percent of the market, is a skeptical group of consumers who usually adopt an innovation to save money or in response to social pressure from their peers. They rely on members of the early and late majorities as sources of information. Advertising and personal selling are less effective with this group than is word-of-mouth communication.

Laggards. **Laggards** are consumers who are bound by tradition and, hence, are last to adopt an innovation. They comprise about 16 percent of the market. Laggards are suspicious of innovations and innovators; they wonder why anyone would pay a lot for a new kind of safety device, for example. By the time laggards adopt something new, it may already have been discarded by the innovators in favor of a newer concept. Laggards typically are older and usually are at the low end of the social and economic scales.

We are discussing only *adopters* of an innovation. For most innovations, there are many people who are *not* included in our percentages. They are **nonadopters**; they never adopt the innovation.

Characteristics Affecting Adoption Rate

Five characteristics affect the adoption rate for new products, especially truly innovative products:[30]

- *Relative advantage*: the degree to which an innovation is superior to currently available products. Relative advantage may be reflected in lower cost, greater safety, easier use, or some other relevant benefit. Safest Stripper, a paint and varnish remover introduced by 3M, has several advantages and thus scores high on this characteristic. The product contains no harmful chemicals, has no odor, and allows the user to refinish furniture indoors rather than having to work outdoors.

*A*ccording to 3M, which makes Safest Stripper paint and varnish remover, this product has a strong advantage over competing furniture-finish removers. But several other product characteristics also influence whether or not a consumer adopts a new product. To the extent it's easy and quick to use, Safest Stripper paint and varnish remover would score well in terms of compatibility and complexity. The product would not rate as highly with regard to trialability and observability because it would actually have to be used on a piece of furniture to judge its effectiveness.

- *Compatibility*: the degree to which an innovation coincides with the cultural values and experiences of prospective adopters. Since many consumers want to save time *and* satisfy their desires now rather than later, microwave popcorn certainly satisfies this characteristic.
- *Complexity*: the degree of difficulty in understanding or using an innovation. The more complex an innovation is, the more slowly it will be adopted—if it is adopted at all. Combined shampoo and conditioners certainly are simple to use, so adoption of them was not impeded by complexity. However, many forms of insurance and some consumer electronics products have problems with this characteristic.
- *Trialability*: the degree to which an innovation may be sampled on some limited basis. Setting aside the other characteristics, the greater the trialability, the faster will be the adoption rate. For instance, a central home air-conditioning system is likely to have a slower adoption rate than a new seed or fertilizer, which may be tried on a small plot of ground. In general, due to this characteristic, costly products will be adopted more slowly than will inexpensive products. Likewise, many services (such as insurance) are difficult to use on a trial basis, so they tend to be adopted rather slowly.
- *Observability*: the degree to which an innovation actually can be demonstrated to be effective. In general, the greater the observability, the faster the adoption rate. For example, a new weed killer that works on existing weeds probably

will be accepted sooner than a product that prevents weeds from sprouting. The reason? The latter product, even if highly effective, produces no dead weeds to show to prospective buyers!

A company would like an innovative product to satisfy all five characteristics discussed above. But few do. One-time cameras come close, however.[31] These cameras, which are usable for only one roll of film, come prepacked with film (reducing *complexity*), cost just $10 to $15 (contributing to *trialability*), and offer good value (representing *relative advantage*). They are widely distributed, which enhances *compatibility* with consumers' desire for convenient purchase—especially when we forget to bring our regular camera on a trip. The leading makers of one-time cameras, Kodak and Fuji, addressed *observability* by giving many of the cameras away in promotions so that consumers could use the product and see the results without bearing any risk or cost.

http://www.kodak.com/

http://www.fujifilm.co.jp/
index.html/

Organizing for Product Innovation

For new-product programs to be successful, they must be supported by a strong, long-term commitment from top management. This commitment must be maintained even when some new products fail. To implement this commitment to innovation effectively, new-product efforts must be soundly organized.

Types of Organization

There is no "one best" organizational structure for product planning and development. Many companies use more than one structure to manage these activities. Some widely used organizational structures for planning and developing new products are:

- **Product-planning committee.** Members include executives from major departments—marketing, production, finance, engineering, and research. In small firms, the president and/or another top-level executive often serve on the committee.
- **New-product department.** These units are small, consisting of five or fewer people. The department head typically reports to the company president. In a large firm, this may be the president of a division.
- **Venture team.** This small group, with representatives from engineering, production, finance, and marketing research, operates like a separate small business. Typically the team reports directly to top management.[32]
- **Product manager.** This individual is responsible for planning new products as well as managing established products. A large company may have many product managers who report to higher marketing executives.

Product innovation is too important an activity to handle in an unorganized, nonchalant fashion, figuring that somehow the job will get done. What's critical is to make sure that some person or group has the specific responsibility for new-product development—and is backed by top management.

As the new product is completed, responsibility for marketing it usually is shifted either to an existing department or to a new department established just for this new product. In some cases the team that developed the product may continue as the management nucleus of the new unit.

Integrating new products into departments that are already marketing established products carries two risks, however. First, executives who are involved with ongoing products may have a short-term outlook as they deal with day-to-day problems of existing products. Consequently, they may not recognize the long-term importance of new products and, as a result, neglect them. Second, managers of successful existing products often are reluctant to assume the risks inherent in marketing new products.

Shifting Arrangements

Beginning in the 1950s, many companies—Procter & Gamble, Pillsbury, and General Foods, to name a few—assigned the responsibility for planning new products as well as coordinating the marketing efforts for established ones to a product manager. Essentially, a *product manager*, sometimes called a *brand manager*, plans the complete marketing program for a brand or group of products. Specific tasks include setting marketing goals, preparing budgets, and drafting plans for advertising and personal selling activities. Developing new products along with improving established products may also be part of the job description.

The biggest drawback of this structure is that a company often saddles product managers with great responsibility but provides them with little authority. For instance, product managers are expected to develop the plan by which the sales force will market the product to wholesalers and retailers, but they have no real authority over the sales force. Their effectiveness depends largely on their ability to influence other executives to cooperate with their plans.

In the 1980s, many industries experienced slow growth in maturing markets, coupled with a trend toward strategic planning that stressed centralized managerial control. Because of these environmental forces, the product-manager structure was modified in some companies. For instance, Procter & Gamble added *category managers* who oversee the activities of a related group of product managers.[33]

Now, many firms are relying on team efforts—such as the product-planning committee or venture team discussed above—to develop new products.[34] Typically, these are *cross-functional* teams, consisting of representatives from not only market research and marketing but also product design, engineering, and manufacturing. One study in the chemical industry concluded that new-product development was more likely to be successful if carried out by a cross-functional team.[35] Further, Chrysler used cross-functional teams to reduce by 40 percent the time necessary to design and build its LH line of sedans.[36]

■ SUMMARY

The first commandment in marketing is "Know thy customer," and the second is "Know thy product." The relative number and success of a company's new products are a prime determinant of its sales, growth rate, and profits. A firm can best serve its customers by producing and marketing want-satisfying goods or services. The scarcity of some natural resources and a growing concern for our environment make social responsibility a crucial aspect of product innovation.

To manage its products effectively, a firm's marketers must understand the full meaning of *product*, which stresses that customers are buying want-satisfaction. Products can be classified into two basic categories—consumer products and business products. Each category is then subdivided, because a different marketing program is required for each distinct group of products.

There are many views as to what constitutes a *new* product. For marketing purposes, three cate-

gories of new products need to be recognized—innovative, significantly different, and imitative.

A clear statement of the firm's new-product strategy serves as a solid foundation for the six-stage development process for new products. At each stage, a firm needs to decide whether to proceed to the next stage or to halt the project. The early stages in this process are especially important. If a firm can make an early *and correct* decision to stop the development of a proposed product, a lot of money and labor can be saved.

In deciding whether or not to add a new product, a producer or middleman should consider whether there is adequate market demand for it. The product also should fit in with the firm's marketing, production, and financial resources.

Management needs to understand the adoption and diffusion processes for a new product. A prospective user goes through six stages in deciding whether

or not to adopt a new product. Adopters of an innovation can be divided into five categories, depending on how quickly they accept an innovation such as a new product. These categories are innovators, early adopters, early majority, late majority, and laggards. In addition, there usually is a group of nonadopters. Five characteristics of an innovation seem to influence its adoption rate: relative advantage, compatibility, complexity, trialability, and observability.

Successful product planning and development require long-term commitment and strong support from top management. Furthermore, new-product programs must be soundly organized. Most firms use one of four organizational structures for new-product development: product-planning committee, new-product department, venture team, or product manager. Recently, the trend has been away from product managers and toward team efforts for developing new products.

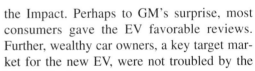

More about

GENERAL MOTORS

*I*f all went well, a successful electric vehicle (EV) could help the gigantic automaker boost revenues, gain market share, and strengthen its reputation with respect to both technological leadership and environmental protection. However, in some cases, new-product development takes a long time and encounters problems along the way. That's certainly been the case with the EV1 and its predecessor, the Impact.

In 1992, the Impact hit a big roadblock. GM announced it would not attempt to produce and market its own electric auto, but instead would enter into an alliance with Chrysler and Ford to design this product. Basically, after several years of poor performance, GM had to make various cutbacks in order to improve the company's financial condition. The Impact project was among the cutbacks not only because it required an estimated $1 billion in capital but also because the company became doubtful that it could sell enough Impacts to avoid a large loss.

Less than 2 years later, the alliance involving GM, Ford, and Chrysler disintegrated, largely because of disagreements over the composition of the electric battery. GM moved ahead with market tests, the fifth stage of new-product development. Consumers in selected cities around the U.S. were allowed to test-drive prototypes of

the Impact. Perhaps to GM's surprise, most consumers gave the EV favorable reviews. Further, wealthy car owners, a key target market for the new EV, were not troubled by the projected $25,000 price tag.

Still, the Impact and any other brands of EVs must overcome several major challenges. The driving range is still limited to only 70 to 80 miles before the lead-acid batteries require recharging. In addition, the high price will severely limit the target market.

GM hopes it can meet these challenges. Improved batteries, made of nickel metal-hydride, hold the promise of traveling 200 miles before recharging. The new battery is supposed to recharge to 60 percent of capacity in less than 15 minutes. Also, besides aiming the EV1 at wealthy individuals, GM sees potential in the fleet market, beginning not surprisingly with electric utilities.

GM believes the EV1's strongest appeal will be to environmentalists, auto enthusiasts, and consumers who like to buy innovative new products. The EV1 should benefit from its association with the Saturn model and Saturn dealers, both of which enjoy highly favorable reputations among car buyers.

GM is looking ahead to an electric-powered pickup truck. Meanwhile, Chrysler and Ford are working on

their own EVs—a minivan and a pickup truck, respectively. Eventually, all three automakers would like to recoup some of their massive investments in this new type of product by selling large numbers of EVs at a profit.[37]

1. a. How does the electric vehicle score with respect to the five characteristics affecting the rate at which innovations are adopted?

b. Based on the preceding assessment, how rapidly will the Impact (or another brand of EV) be adopted by consumers?

2. What should GM consider in deciding whether or not to continue its effort to produce and market the EV1?

■ KEY TERMS AND CONCEPTS

Product (193)
Consumer products (194)
Business products (194)
Convenience good (194)
Shopping good (196)
Specialty good (196)
Unsought good (197)
Raw materials (197)
Fabricating
    materials (199)

Fabricating parts (199)
Installations (199)
Accessory
    equipment (199)
Operating supplies (200)
New products (203)
New-product
    strategy (204)
New-product development
    process (205)

Adoption process (209)
Diffusion (209)
Stages in the adoption
    process (209)
Innovation adopter
    categories (210)
Innovators (210)
Early adopters (210)
Change agent (210)
Early majority (211)

Late majority (211)
Laggards (211)
Nonadopters (211)
Product-planning
    committee (213)
New-product
    department (213)
Venture team (213)
Product manager (213)

■ QUESTIONS AND PROBLEMS

1. In what respects are the products different in each of the following cases?
    a. A Whirlpool dishwasher sold at an appliance store and a similar dishwasher sold by Sears under its Kenmore brand name. Assume that Whirlpool makes both dishwashers.
    b. Sunbeam Mixmaster sold by a leading department store and the same model sold by a discount house.
    c. An airline ticket purchased through a travel agent and an identical ticket purchased directly from the airline.

2. a. Explain the various interpretations of the term *new product*.
    b. Give some examples, other than those cited in this chapter, of products in each of the three new-product categories.

3. "Because brand preferences are well established with regard to many items of women's clothing, these items—traditionally considered shopping goods—will move into the specialty-goods category. At the same time, however, other items of women's clothing can be found in supermarkets and variety stores, thus indicating that some items are convenience goods."
    a. Explain the reasoning in these statements.
    b. Do you agree that women's clothing is shifting away from the shopping-goods classification? Explain.

4. Compare the elements of a producer's marketing mix for a convenience good with those of the mix for a specialty good.

5. In which of the five categories of business goods should each of the following be included? And which products may belong in more than one category?
    a. Trucks
    b. Medical x-ray equipment
    c. Typing paper
    d. Copper wire
    e. Printing presses
    f. Nuts and bolts
    g. Paper clips
    h. Land

6. In developing new products, how can a firm make sure that it is being socially responsible with regard to scarce resources and our environment?

7. Assume that the following organizations are considering additions to their product lines. In each case, does the proposed product meet the criteria for adding a new product? Explain your decisions.
    a. McDonald's—salad bar
    b. Safeway—automobile tires
    c. Exxon—personal computers
    d. Banks—life insurance
    e. General Motors—outboard motors for boats

8. Several new products from foreign countries are described in the Global Perspective box. In your opinion, which ones will enjoy the greatest success in the U.S.? Explain your choices.

9. Describe the kinds of people who are most likely to be found in (a) the innovator category of adopters and (b) the late-majority category.

10. Why are many firms relying more on cross-functional teams and less on product managers for new-product development?

■ HANDS-ON MARKETING

1. Arrange a meeting with the manager of a large retail outlet in your community. Discuss two topics with the manager:

    a. What recently introduced product has been a failure or appears destined to fail?

    b. Did this product, in retrospect, satisfy the criteria for adding a new product? (Remember to consider not just the middleman's criteria but also applicable producer's criteria.)

2. Design (either in words or drawings) a new product that fits into one of the first two categories of new products—that is, a really innovative product or a significant replacement, not just an imitative product. Then evaluate how your proposed product rates with respect to the five characteristics of an innovation that influence the adoption rate.

Product-Mix
Strategies

Can
GENERAL MOTORS
Clarify Its Product Mix?

A company needs to develop exciting new products. That's what General Motors (GM) has done quite successfully with the Saturn and is working on with the new EV1 electric vehicle, as described in the Chapter 8 case. At the same time, however, a company must pay attention to its existing products. GM faces a mountain of challenges in doing this.

In the words of Ronald Zarrella, GM's top marketing executive, "We can't escape the fact that the way our vehicles have been targeted in the past, many are right on top of one another." GM has seven brands of motor vehicles: Chevrolet (with both cars and trucks), Pontiac, Saturn, Oldsmobile, Buick, Cadillac, and GMC (trucks only). Under these brands, there are about 75 different models, making it all but impossible to keep them distinct from one another.

Over the years, the Pontiac, Oldsmobile, and Buick lines have suffered from the greatest overlap. Despite subtle differences among them, all three were essentially in the midprice range and aimed at middle-aged car buyers. Likewise, any distinctions between Chevrolet and GMC trucks were hard to detect.

Further, Zarrella admitted that the automaker has not kept its products up to date compared to competing brands. The muddled and mundane brands go a long way toward explaining why more than one-third of car shoppers in 1994 did not even look at GM products. Thus GM faces the daunting task of both clarifying and revitalizing its overlapping product lines.

Zarrella's plan centers on aiming the seven lines at separate target markets, to the extent possible, and developing a distinctive, fresh image for each line. For example, although both Pontiac and Saturn will be targeted at young car buyers, Saturn will concentrate on consumers who lean toward import cars. Saturn will rely on a rational appeal, stressing such factors as dependability and friendly service, whereas Pontiac will have an emotional appeal, with its "sporty" image.

Zarrella has a vision for the other five lines as well: Cadillac will remain a luxury car targeted at affluent consumers who otherwise would buy a foreign brand such as Lexus or Mercedes. Buick, probably the biggest marketing challenge, will be presented to car buyers over age 50 as GM's "premium American car." Oldsmobile will be a "step-up" product, especially for Saturn buyers as they grow a little older but also for consumers who favor foreign brands such as Audi and Acura. Chevrolet will be GM's "mass-market" car and light-truck division, offering a wide variety of models. Finally, GMC will concentrate on trucks that are normally larger and more expensive than Chevrolet trucks.

To achieve the full benefits of clarifying its product lines, GM needs to do the same thing with its network of dealerships. Currently, the network comprises about 8,500 dealerships, carrying an average of 2.5 GM car and truck brands. However, there's little consistency with respect to which brands are offered by the same dealership. Further, there are too many dealerships of a particular brand in some large markets and too few in other smaller markets. GM's first step toward streamlining its distribution is to combine its Pontiac and GMC divisions, a move that was announced in early 1996.[1]

What has General Motors done right and wrong in trying to focus and differentiate its vehicle product lines?

http://www.gm.com/

A common thread concerning overlapping brands of motor vehicles permeates this case. That is, over time a company must make numerous decisions about its array of products. Whether the correct decisions are made—and made at the right time—greatly affects a company's degree of success, not just for a single year but for many years to come.

At any given time, a firm may be marketing some new products and some old ones, while others are being planned and developed. This chapter covers a number of strategic decisions pertaining to an organization's assortment of products. After studying this chapter, you should be able to explain:

CHAPTER GOALS

- The difference between product mix and product line.
- The major product-mix strategies:
  - Positioning
  - Alteration
  - Expansion
  - Contraction
- Trading up and trading down.
- Managing a product throughout a life cycle.
- Planned obsolescence.
- Style and fashion.
- The fashion-adoption process.

Product Mix and Product Line

Carma Labs Inc. sells only Carmex lip balm, and WD-40 Co. markets only WD-40 spray lubricant.[2] These examples notwithstanding, few firms rely on a single product; instead, most sell many products. A **product mix** is the set of all products offered for sale by a company. The structure of a product mix has both breadth and depth. Its **breadth** is measured by the number of product lines carried, its **depth** by the variety of sizes, colors, and models offered within each product line. A product-mix structure is illustrated in Figure 9-1.

A broad group of products, intended for essentially similar uses and having similar physical characteristics, constitutes a **product line**. Firms may delineate a product line in different ways. For the A. H. Robins Company, its various forms of Robitussin cough remedies (such as Pediatric and Maximum Strength syrups and cherry-flavored drops) represent a product line. However, for a large drugstore or supermarket, all brands of cough remedies—not just Robitussin products—comprise one of the store's many product lines.

FIGURE 9-1

Product mix—breadth and depth in a lawn and garden store.

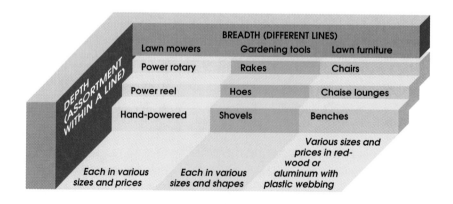

Product-Mix Strategies

http://budweiser.com/ab.html/

Anheuser-Busch Companies offered snack foods, family entertainment, baked goods, and about 20 brands of beer to consumers. Did this diverse assortment of products develop by accident? No—it reflected a planned strategy, as did the company's decision to dispose of the snack foods and baked goods divisions. To be successful in marketing, producers and middlemen need carefully planned strategies for managing their product mixes, as we'll see next.

Positioning the Product

Management's ability to bring attention to a product and to differentiate it in a favorable way from similar products goes a long way toward determining that product's revenues. Thus management needs to engage in **positioning**, which means developing the image that a product projects in relation to competitive products and to the firm's other products.

Regardless of which positioning strategy is used, the needs of the target market always must be considered. For example, Holiday Inns has developed three offerings to satisfy diverse target markets. Thus, the lodging firm now has Holiday Inn Express, Select, and Sunspree Resort properties in addition to its traditional hotels.[3] Likewise, to satisfy different consumers' desires regarding taste, Anheuser-Busch (A-B) has both regular and light beers at five different price levels. Ranging from highest to lowest prices, A-B sells Carlsberg, Michelob, Budweiser, Busch, and Natural in both regular and light versions. In addition, they appeal to other consumers with "dry" beer, malt liquor, and even nonalcoholic brews called O'Doul's and Busch NA.[4]

Marketing executives can choose from a variety of positioning strategies. Sometimes they decide to use more than one for a particular product. Here are several major positioning strategies.

Positioning in Relation to a Competitor.
For some products the best position is directly against the competition. This strategy is especially suitable for a firm that already has a solid differential advantage or is trying to solidify such an advantage. To fend off rival makers of microprocessors, Intel Corp. launched a campaign to convince buyers that its product is superior to competitors'. The company even paid computer makers to include the slogan, "Intel Inside," in their ads.[5] As the market leader, Coca-Cola introduces new products and executes its marketing strategies. At the same time, it keeps an eye on Pepsi-Cola, being sure to match any clever, effective marketing moves made by its primary competitor.

http://www.intel.com/

For other products, head-to-head positioning is exactly what *not* to do, especially when a competitor has a strong market position. In France, the La Cinq television network decided to compete directly against the well-established TF-1 network. La Cinq could not gain an advantage over TF-1, however, and this positioning error was a major reason for La Cinq's failure.[6]

One view is that underdogs should try to be the opposite of—or at least much different than—the market leader. For example, many years ago, Procter & Gamble achieved success by positioning Scope as the good-tasting alternative to Johnson & Johnson's more antiseptic-tasting mouthwash, Listerine. More recently, Southwest Airlines positioned itself effectively as the low-fare alternative to full-service airlines.[7]

*W*ith its "Intel Inside" branding strategy and related advertising program, Intel seeks to convince both manufacturers and buyers of personal computers that its microprocessor is superior to those of its competitors.

The right processor for all intelligent creatures.

Positioning in Relation to a Product Class or Attribute.   Sometimes a company's positioning strategy entails associating its product with (or distancing it from) a product class or attribute. Some companies try to place their products in a desirable class, such as "Made in the USA." In the words of one consultant, "There is a strong emotional appeal when you say, 'Made in the USA.'" Thus a small sportswear manufacturer, Boston Preparatory Co., is using this positioning strategy to seek an edge over larger competitors such as Calvin Klein and Tommy Hilfiger, which don't produce all of their products in the U.S.[8]

Other firms promote their wares as having an attractive attribute, such as "low energy consumption" or "environmentally friendly." This strategy is widely used now for food products. For example, Libby's, Campbell Soup, Kellogg's, and competing companies have introduced lines of foods with one common denominator—they contain no or very little salt. These items are positioned against products that are packed with the conventional amounts of salt. Sometimes what's in, rather than left out of, the product is emphasized. That's the case with Volvo, which constructed a steel frame around the passenger compartment of its brand of automobile.

http://www.car.volvo.se/

Positioning by Price and Quality.   Certain producers and retailers are known for their high-quality products and high prices. In the retailing field, Saks Fifth Avenue and Neiman Marcus are positioned at one end of the price-quality continuum. Discount stores such as Target and Kmart are at the other. We're not saying, however, that discounters ignore quality; rather, they stress low prices. Penney's tried—and for the most part succeeded in—repositioning its stores on the price-quality continuum by upgrading apparel lines and stressing designer names.[9]

As suggested in the chapter-opening case, positioning by price and quality is common in the automotive field. In recent years, "luxury" cars that accentuate quality and carry comparatively high prices have proliferated; consider entries such as Infiniti and Lexus. However, producers have struggled in differentiating their brand of luxury car from others with respect to important attributes such as performance, comfort, and safety. As a result, many consumers have become confused or uninterested.

In turn, some models have failed. One casualty was the Cadillac Allante, which was introduced specifically to regain sales lost to European-made prestige cars.

Product-Mix Expansion

Product-mix expansion is accomplished by increasing the depth within a particular line and/or the number of lines a firm offers to customers. Let's look at these options.

When a company adds a similar item to an existing product line with the same brand name, this is termed a **line extension**. For illustrations, pull the coupons insert out of your Sunday newspaper. You'll probably see examples such as Thomas' English muffins now offered in cranberry and oat bran versions as well as the original product; Ocean Spray announcing new flavors for its drinks; and Hidden Valley promoting its fat-free, as well as regular, salad dressings.

The line-extension strategy is also used by organizations in services fields. For example, universities now offer programs to appeal to prospective older students, and the Roman Catholic church broadened its line of religious services by adding Saturday and Sunday evening masses.

There are many reasons for line extensions. The main one is that the firm wants to appeal to more market segments by offering a wider range of choices for a particular product. Line extensions might be the most pronounced trend in marketing during this decade. As discussed in the box, "You Make the Decision," line extensions have become so common as to raise questions about their effectiveness.

YOU MAKE THE DECISION

HOW MANY PRODUCTS ARE TOO MANY?

In a typical year, more than 15,000 new (using the term loosely) products are placed in front of consumers who shop in supermarkets. Just in the category of pain relievers, there were more than 400 new entries over a 10-year period. New products keep coming out—sometimes as a steady stream, sometimes in a flood, but seldom at a trickle.

Does this flow of new offerings benefit consumers and retailers as well as the manufacturers of these products? A variety of evidence says "no." Many consumers cannot differentiate across the numerous alternatives—and get frustrated or angry in the process. Really, do you know the differences among the following remedies—Tylenol Flu, Tylenol Cold, Tylenol Sinus, and Tylenol Allergy Sinus, not to mention their different forms (tablets, caplets, gel caps, and the like)?

The basic problem may be that almost three-quarters of so-called new products are line extensions within an existing product category, in which the new entry represents a different form or promises an added benefit. Only about one-quarter of new products are a mix or line extension outside the company's current category, much less fresh brands or truly innovative products. In the opinion of a manager for McKesson Drug Co., which is a major distributor of over-the-counter remedies, "The amount of duplication is staggering."

The large number of new offerings also poses problems for retailers. Supermarkets, in particular, lack shelf space to add all or even most of the new products. According to a study conducted for the Food Marketing Institute, a trade association, the number of separate items (called stock-keeping units) carried by a supermarket can be reduced by 5 to 25 percent without reducing sales or causing consumers to think that the store offers a poor assortment of products.

How should a manufacturer decide how many separate items in a product line best serve the interests of consumers, retailers, and the firm itself?

Sources: The "1995 Innovation Survey," conducted by Group EFO Limited of Weston, CT; Joseph Weber, "Painkillers Are about to O.D.," *Business Week*, Apr. 11, 1994, pp. 54+; and Ira Teinowitz and Jennifer Lawrence, "Brand Proliferation Attacked," *Advertising Age*, May 10, 1993, pp. 1+.

Another way to expand the product mix, referred to as **mix extension**, is to add a new product line to the company's present assortment. Jell-O pudding pops and Bic disposable lighters, both successes, and Bic pantyhose and Adidas colognes, both failures, are examples of mix extension.

Johnson & Johnson's new products illustrate the distinction between mix extension and line extension. When J&J introduced a line of Acuvue disposable contact lenses, that's *mix* extension because it added another product to the company's product mix. In contrast, line extension adds more items within the same product line. When J&J adds new versions of Tylenol pain reliever, that's *line* extension.

Under a mix-extension strategy, the new line may be related or unrelated to current products. Furthermore, it may carry one of the company's existing brand names or may be given an entirely new name.

Typically, the new line is related to the existing product mix because the company wants to capitalize on its strengths and experience. Given the success of Reese's peanut butter cups, Hershey's thinks the brand says "peanut butter" to consumers, so it introduced a line of Reese's peanut butters. Hunt-Wesson holds the same view about its Swiss Miss brand and chocolate, so it developed Swiss Miss pudding and gelatin snacks. In both cases, the new lines carry one of the company's popular brands to benefit from consumers' familiarity with and good feelings toward that brand. We'll consider this approach in more detail when *brand equity* is discussed in the next chapter.

Alteration of Existing Products

Rather than developing a completely new product, management might do well to take a fresh look at the organization's existing products. Often, improving an established product, termed **product alteration**, can be more profitable and less risky than developing a completely new one. The substitution of NutraSweet for saccharin in diet soft drinks increased sales of those drinks.

Product alteration is not without risks, however. When Coca-Cola Co. modified the formula for its leading product and changed its name to New Coke, sales plunged. As a result, the old formula was brought back 3 months later under the Coca-Cola Classic name.

Redesigning the product itself can sustain its appeal or even initiate its renaissance. For example, the backup battery has generated excitement in the auto-battery industry. What's new—and presumably beneficial—about this redesigned product is that it has a built-in reserve power system for starting the engine when the main battery goes dead.[10] Disposable diapers have been redesigned to be less bulky and also in separate styles for girls and boys. For example, Kimberly-Clark markets two versions of Pull-Ups, which are disposable training pants for toddlers.

Alternatively, especially for consumer goods, the product itself is not changed but its packaging is altered. For example, Pillsbury developed a unifying background for the package of all its dessert mixes, a royal blue field with small white polka dots.[11] To gain a small differential advantage, some companies are offering their sliced and shredded cheeses in packages that reseal using zipperlike devices. Thus packages can be altered to enhance appearance or to improve the product's usability.

Product-Mix Contraction

Another strategy, **product-mix contraction**, is carried out either by eliminating an entire line or by simplifying the assortment within a line. Thinner and/or shorter product lines or mixes can weed out low-profit and unprofitable products. The intended result of product-mix contraction is higher profits from fewer products.

http://www.jnj.com/

http://www.hunt-wesson.com/

General Mills (Wheaties, Betty Crocker, Gold Medal flour) decided to concentrate on its food business and, consequently, sold its interest in Izod (the "alligator" apparel maker) and its lines of children's toys and games. In services fields, some travel agencies have shifted from selling all modes of travel to concentrate on specialized tours and trips to exotic places. And, to reduce their liability risks and insurance costs, many physicians have stopped offering obstetrical services.

During the 1990s, most companies have expanded—rather than contracted—their product mixes. Numerous line extensions document this trend. As firms find that they have an unmanageable number of products or that various items or lines are unprofitable, or both, product-mix pruning is likely. Many organizations will wind up with fewer product lines, and the remaining lines will be thinner and shorter. There are myriad examples of product-mix contraction, sometimes involving leading firms such as Procter & Gamble. Several years ago, the company dropped its line of orange juices by discontinuing its Citrus Hill brand. More recently, P&G abandoned its White Cloud brand of toilet tissue to place more emphasis on its top-selling Charmin brand.

http://www.pg.com/

Trading Up and Trading Down

The product strategies of trading up and trading down involve a change in product positioning *and* an expansion of the product line. **Trading up** means adding a higher-price product to a line to attract a broader market. Also, the seller intends that the new product's prestige will help the sale of its existing lower-price products.

Consider some examples of trading up. To its line of inexpensive sport watches, Swatch added an $80 Chrono stopwatch and other upgraded watches. And even pet-food manufacturers have traded up to "superpremium" lines, as illustrated by Kal Kan's Pedigree and Quaker Oats' King Kuts.

http://www.swatch-art.com/

Trading down means adding a lower-price product to a company's product line. The firm expects that people who cannot afford the original higher-price product or who see it as too expensive will buy the new lower-price one. The reason: The lower-price product carries some of the status and some of the other more substantive benefits (such as performance) of the higher-price item.

*O*n July 4, 1984, Jeremiah Tower opened Stars restaurant in San Francisco (left). Featuring "new American cooking," the restaurant became tremendously popular. The eating establishment's name had high levels of awareness. To capitalize on this awareness and to appeal to another segment of restaurant customers, Tower used a strategy of trading down. The new restaurant, named Stars Cafe (right), is located near its parent. It offers the same type of cuisine as Stars, but at lower prices in a more casual atmosphere.

http://www.marriott.com/

http://www.donnakaran.com/

The Marriott Corp. followed a trading-down strategy when it began building (1) Courtyard by Marriott hotels, targeted at the midprice market long dominated by chains such as Holiday Inn and Ramada Inn, and (2) Fairfield Inns, to compete in the economy-price market. Even some designers of highly fashionable women's clothing, such as Donna Karan and Bill Blass, are trading down by introducing lower-price lines.[12] The new lines are priced between $100 and $900 per item, typically less than one-half the price of their top lines.

Trading up and trading down are perilous strategies because the new products may confuse buyers, resulting in negligible net gain. It is equally undesirable if sales of the new item or line are generated at the expense of the established products. When *trading down*, the new offering may permanently hurt the firm's reputation and that of its established high-quality product. To reduce this possibility, new lower-price products may be given brand names unlike the established brands. That's why Givenchy and Christian Dior applied Life and Coordonnees labels, respectively, to their lower-price lines.

In *trading up*, on the other hand, the problem depends on whether the new product or line carries the established brand or is given a new name. If the same name is used, the firm must change its image enough so that new customers will accept the higher-price product. At the same time, the seller does not want to lose its present customers. The new offering may present a cloudy image, not attracting new customers but driving away existing customers. If a different brand name is used, the company must create awareness for it and then stimulate consumers to buy the new product.

The Product Life Cycle

As we saw in Chapter 8, a product's life cycle can have a direct bearing on a company's survival. The life cycle of a product consists of four stages: introduction, growth, maturity, and decline. The concept of product life *applies to a generic category of product* (microwave ovens and microprocessors, for example) and not to specific brands (Sharp and Intel, respectively). A **product life cycle** consists of the aggregate demand over an extended period of time for all brands comprising a generic product category.

A life cycle can be graphed by plotting aggregate sales volume for a generic product category over time, usually years. It is also worthwhile to accompany the sales volume curve with the corresponding profit curve for the product category, as shown in Figure 9-2. After all, a business is interested ultimately in profitability, not just sales.

The *shapes* of these two curves vary from one product category to another. Still, for most categories, the basic shapes and the relationship between the sales and the profit curves are as illustrated in Figure 9-2. In this typical life cycle, the profit curve for most new products is negative (signifying a loss) through much of the introductory stage. In the latter part of the growth stage, the profit curve starts to decline while sales volume is still rising. Profits decline because the companies in an industry usually must increase their advertising and selling efforts and/or cut their prices to sustain sales growth in the face of intensifying competition during the maturity stage.

Introducing a new product at the proper time will help maintain a company's desired level of profit. Striving to maintain its dominant position in the wet-shaving market, the Gillette Company faces that challenge often. A while back, a large French firm cut into Gillette's market share by introducing the highly successful

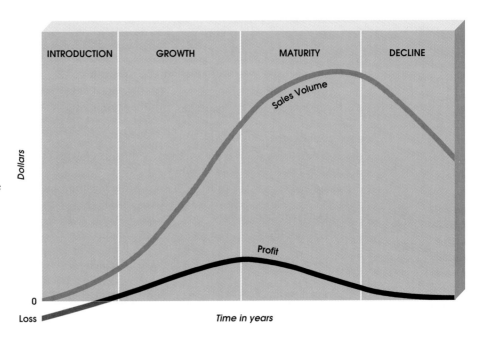

FIGURE 9-2

Typical life cycle of a product category.

During the introduction stage of a life cycle, a product category—and virtually all brands within it—is unprofitable. Total profits for the product category are healthy during the growth stage but then start to decline while a product's sales volume is still increasing.

Bic disposable razors. After considerable research and development, Gillette counterattacked with the new Sensor razor, featuring independently suspended blades. The strategy worked, as many consumers left the convenience of low-price disposable razors in favor of the better shaves provided by the higher-price Sensor razor. More recently, Gillette traded up again, introducing Sensor Excel with several enhancements over the first Sensor.[13]

If a new product lacks competition and is particularly appealing to consumers, a firm can charge a fairly high price and achieve strong profits. That's been the case with Sensor, so Gillette is reaping healthy profits from the wet-shaving market. Intel Corp. seeks a measure of control over prices by staying ahead of competition. To do so, it develops and introduces new generations of microprocessors only 2 or 3 years apart, even while demand is still growing for its current version.[14]

The product life-cycle concept has been criticized as lacking empirical support and being too general to be useful in specific cases.[15] Admittedly, the product life cycle is not perfect and it must be adapted to fit different circumstances. Nevertheless, it is both straightforward and powerful. A company's marketing success can be affected considerably by its ability to determine and adapt to the life cycles for each of its product categories.

Characteristics of Each Stage

Management must be able to recognize what part of the life cycle its product is in at any given time. The competitive environment and marketing strategies that should be used ordinarily depend on the particular life-cycle stage. Table 9-1 contains a synopsis of all four stages. Each stage is highlighted below.

Introduction. During the **introduction stage**, sometimes called the *pioneering stage*, a product is launched into the market in a full-scale marketing program. It has gone through product development, including idea screening, prototype, and market tests. The entire product may be new, such as a substitute for fat in prepared foods. Or it may be well known but have a significant novel feature that, in effect, creates a new-product category; the electric vehicle is an example.

TABLE 9-1 Characteristics and implications of different product life-cycle stages

	Stage			
	Introduction	**Growth**	**Maturity**	**Decline**
Characteristics				
Customers	Innovators	Mass market	Mass market	Loyal customers
Competition	Little if any	Increasing	Intense	Decreasing
Sales	Low levels, then rising	Rapid growth	Slow/no annual growth	Declining
Profits	None	Strong, then at a peak	Declining annually	Low/none
Marketing implications				
Overall strategy	Market development	Market penetration	Defensive positioning	Efficiency or exit
Costs	High per unit	Declining	Stable or increasing	Low
Product strategy	Undifferentiated	Improved items	Differentiated	Pruned line
Pricing strategy	Most likely high	Lower over time	Lowest	Increasing
Distribution strategy	Scattered	Intensive	Intensive	Selective
Promotion strategy	Category awareness	Brand preference	Brand loyalty	Reinforcement

Source: Adapted from material provided by Professor David Appel, University of Notre Dame.

For really new products, normally there is very little direct competition. However, if the product has tremendous promise, numerous companies may enter the industry early on. That has occurred in the multimedia-software field, where at least 1,000 firms are working to combine video, audio, and text on CD-ROM discs that entertain and/or educate consumers. Because the industry is in its infancy, product-development costs are high—typically over $300,000 per program—but demand is meager. As Bill Gates of Microsoft observed, "There are more people pursuing this opportunity than can be sustained."[16] Many firms have failed, and—according to Gates—others will follow.

Because consumers are unfamiliar with the innovative product or feature, a pioneering firm's promotional program is designed to stimulate demand for the entire product category rather than a single brand. Introduction is the most risky and expensive stage, because substantial dollars must be spent not only to develop the product but also to seek consumer acceptance of the offering. Many—perhaps most—new products are not accepted by a sufficient number of consumers and fail at this stage.

Growth. In the **growth stage**, or *market-acceptance stage*, sales and profits rise, frequently at a rapid rate. Competitors enter the market, often in large numbers if the profit outlook is particularly attractive. Mostly as a result of competition, profits start to decline near the end of the growth stage.

As part of firms' efforts to build sales and, in turn, market share, prices typically decline gradually during this stage. In high-tech fields, such as microprocessors, prices tend to fall sharply even as the industry is growing rapidly. According to George Fisher, Eastman Kodak's chairman, "The only thing that matters is if the exponential growth of your market is faster than the exponential decline of your prices."[17] Appropriate marketing strategies for this stage, as well as the other three, are summarized in Table 9-1.

Maturity. During the first part of the **maturity stage**, sales continue to increase, but at a decreasing rate. When sales level off, profits of both producers and middlemen decline. The primary reason: intense price competition.

Seeking to differentiate themselves, some firms extend their product lines with new models; others come up with a "new and improved" version of their primary brand. During this stage, the pressure is greatest on those brands that trail the #1 and #2 brands. During the latter part of this stage, marginal producers, those with high costs or no differential advantage, drop out of the market. They do so because they lack sufficient customers and/or profits.

Decline. For most products, a **decline stage**, as gauged by sales volume for the total category, is inevitable for one of the following reasons:

- A better or less expensive product is developed to fill the same need. Electronic microprocessors made possible many replacement products such as handheld calculators (which made slide rules obsolete) and video games (which may have pushed the category of board games such as Monopoly and Clue into their decline stage).
- The need for the product disappears, often because of another product development. For example, the broad appeal of frozen orange juice virtually eliminated the market for in-home mechanical or electrical fruit squeezers. (However, renewed interest in fresh foods has recently boosted sales of fruit squeezers.) Likewise, eight-track players were no longer needed once cassettes and compact discs supplanted eight-track tapes in the recorded music industry.
- People simply grow tired of a product (a clothing style, for instance), so it disappears from the market.

Seeing little opportunity for revitalized sales or profits, most competitors abandon the market during this stage. However, a few firms may be able to develop a small market niche and remain moderately successful in the decline stage. Some manufacturers of wood-burning stoves have been able to do this.

Length of Product Life Cycle

The total length of the life cycle—from the start of the introduction stage to the end of the decline stage—varies across product categories. It ranges from a few weeks or a short season (for a clothing fashion) to many decades (for autos or telephones). And it varies because of differences in the length of individual stages from one product category to the next. Furthermore, although Figure 9-2 suggests that all four life-cycle stages cover nearly equal periods of time, the stages in any given product's life cycle usually last for different periods.

Three variations on the typical life cycle are shown in Figure 9-3:

- In one, the product gains widespread consumer acceptance only after an extended introductory period (see part *a*). A case can be made that the videophone is following this path, since early models of this product were introduced, but attracted few customers, some years ago. The category of fat substitutes, which are used in making foods ranging from ice cream to salad dressings, appears to be languishing in the introduction stage of its life cycle.[18]
- In another variation, the entire life cycle begins and ends in a relatively short period of time (part *b*). This variation depicts the life cycle for a **fad**, a product or style that becomes immensely popular nearly overnight and then falls out of favor with consumers almost as quickly. Hula hoops and pet rocks are examples of past fads. Sheepskin footwear, called Uggs,[19] and piercing of body parts may be mid-1990s fads.

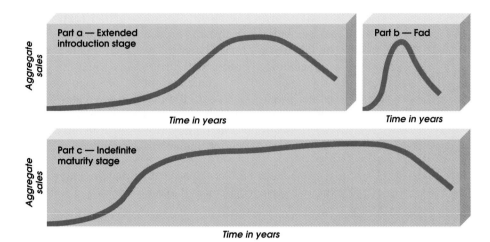

FIGURE 9-3
Product life-cycle variations.

- In a third variation, the product's mature stage lasts almost indefinitely (part *c*). This life cycle is illustrated by canned, carbonated soft drinks in the U.S. and also by the automobile with a gasoline-powered, internal-combustion engine. Other forms, such as electric- and solar-powered cars, have been proposed, but the automobile as we know it remains dominant.

Setting aside fads, which represent a special case, product life cycles are getting shorter generally. If competitors can quickly introduce a "me too" version of a popular product, it may move swiftly into the maturity stage. Or rapid changes in technology can make a product obsolete virtually overnight. Could this happen in the audio field as digital audio tapes are seen by some as a replacement for compact discs?

Moreover, a number of product categories do not make it through all four stages of the life cycle. Some fail in the introductory stage. That appeared to be the case in the 1980s with a product that plays videodiscs rather than videotapes. Now the product is appearing again, so perhaps it was just in a very extended introduction stage!

Also, since the life cycle refers to product categories rather than individual brands, not every brand proceeds through all four life-cycle stages. For instance, some brands fail early in the cycle. In the category of automobiles, that's what happened with brands such as Cord and LaSalle. Others are not introduced until the market is in the growth or maturity stage. The Saturn is a very successful example in the automotive field.

Life Cycle Is Related to a Market

When we say a product is in a specific stage of its life cycle, implicitly we are referring to a specific market. A product may be well accepted (growth or maturity stage) in some markets but still be striving for acceptance in other markets. At the time Ortho Pharmaceuticals introduced Retin-A as a treatment for acne, existing products already served this purpose. Thus the acne-treatment category probably was in the maturity stage. However, it was discovered that Retin-A might be effective in reducing facial wrinkles. (You'll have them someday!) In effect, it created a new product category. Hence, Retin-A fit into both the acne-treatment category that was in the maturity stage among teenagers and into the wrinkle-remover category that was in the introductory or perhaps early-growth stage among middle-age people.

In terms of geographic markets, a product may be in its maturity stage in one country and its introductory stage or perhaps even unknown in another country. For example, chilled coffee in cans and bottles is widely accepted in Japan—at least $4 *billion* in annual sales, in fact. Yet it is largely unknown in the U.S.—not yet $50 *million*. However, added growth is expected in North America, spurred in part by a new alliance between Pepsi-Cola and Starbucks Coffee to market chilled coffee-based beverages.[20] Nevertheless, Maxwell House and other companies are introducing new ready-to-drink coffee products (most sweet, flavored, and intended to be served chilled). Steel-belted radial tires were in their maturity stage in Western Europe well before they were introduced widely in the U.S. In contrast, so-called fast foods are a mature product category in America, but are less common in some other parts of the world.

Life-Cycle Management

To some degree, the collective actions of firms offering competing products in the same category affect the shape of the sales and profit curves over the course of a life cycle. Even single companies can have an impact. A giant firm may be able to shorten the introductory stage by broadening the distribution or increasing the promotional effort supporting the new product.

Generally, however, companies cannot substantially affect the sales and profit curves for a product category. Thus their task is to determine how best to achieve success within the life cycle for a category. For an individual firm, successful life-cycle management depends on (1) predicting the shape of the proposed product's cycle even before it is introduced and (2) successfully adapting marketing strategies at each stage of the life cycle.

Entry Strategies. A firm entering a new market must decide whether to plunge in during the introductory stage. Or it can wait and make its entry during the early part of the growth stage, after innovating companies have proven there is a viable market.

The strategy of entering during the introductory stage is prompted by the desire to build a dominant market position right away and thus lessen the interest of potential competitors and the effectiveness of actual competitors. This strategy worked for Sony with the Walkman, and Amana and Litton with microwave ovens. There is a benefit, called a pioneer advantage, to getting a head start in marketing a new type of product.[21] The hurdles may be insurmountable when you enter with a "me too" product and try to play catch-up.

However, delaying entry until the market is proven can sometimes pay off. Pioneering requires a large investment, and the risks are great—as demonstrated by the high failure rate among new products. Large companies with the marketing resources to overwhelm smaller innovating firms are most likely to be successful with a delayed-entry strategy. In one such case, Coca-Cola introduced Tab and then Diet Coke, and Pepsi-Cola introduced Diet Pepsi, and the two giants surpassed Royal Crown's Diet Rite Cola, an early pioneer.

Managing on the Rise. When sales are growing strongly and profits are robust in a product category, you might think marketing managers have little to do except tally up their anticipated bonuses. That's not the case. Decisions made during the growth stage influence (1) how many competitors enter the market and (2) how well the company's brand within a product category does both in the near and distant future.

During the growth stage of the life cycle, a company has to devise the right strategies for its brand(s) in that product category. Target markets have to be confirmed or, if necessary, adjusted. Product improvements must be formulated, prices assessed and perhaps revised, distribution expanded, and promotion enhanced.

http://www.nintendo.com/

Home video games were introduced in the 1970s, but the more captivating (perhaps addictive) Nintendo brand, in effect, created a new-product category in the 1980s. As the 1990s began, this product appeared to be in the growth stage of its life cycle. However, in the mid-1990s, video game sales stagnated. Nintendo developed a two-part strategy to boost sales: (1) use advanced technology to add more graphics, video, and sound to its game cartridges and (2) keep prices as low as possible, about $250 for its Ultra 64 game player. In contrast, Sega, a potent competitor, is concentrating less on cartridges and more on CD-ROM discs.[22]

http://www.sega.com/

Managing during Maturity. Common strategies to maintain or boost sales of a product during the maturity stage of its life cycle include not just line extension but also modifying the product, designing new promotion, and devising new uses for the product.[23] Such steps may lead to added purchases by present customers and/or may attract new customers.

To reach a new market, Time Inc. extended its *Sports Illustrated* line, introducing a new edition for kids. As sales in the North American cruise industry flattened out, some cruise lines modified their services by adding fitness programs and offering special theme cruises (sometimes in conjunction with a professional sports team).[24]

http://www.dupont.com/

The Du Pont Co. appears to be particularly adept at sustaining mature products, such as its Teflon protective coating and its Lycra fiber. Lycra is a brand of spandex, a fiber Du Pont invented in 1959. Even after the company's patent expired, demand for Lycra grew steadily. Du Pont's primary strategy to generate continuing interest in Lycra has been to develop improved versions of it. The product now is used in a variety of clothing, ranging from hosiery to women's fashions to bicycle shorts. Du Pont must sustain these efforts because Lycra is up against cheaper competing brands as well as the lingering effects of the recession in Europe, a market that has provided almost one-half the brand's sales.[25]

Surviving the Decline Stage. Perhaps it is in the decline stage that a company finds its greatest challenges in life-cycle management. For instance, the widespread use of video camcorders and the development of advanced microchips, both of which capture images without using film, may suggest the decline of photographic film as a product category. Eastman Kodak Co. is trying to prevent a decline while keeping pace with competitors in examining bold new products. With one such product, which Kodak calls Photo CD, consumers take pictures as they normally have. The big difference comes at the time of film processing, when the prints can be stored on a compact disc. Then they can be shown on a TV, if you have a videodisc player![26]

http://www.kodak.com/

When sales are declining, management has the following alternatives:

- Ensure that marketing and production programs are as efficient as possible.
- Prune unprofitable sizes and models. Frequently this tactic will *decrease* sales but *increase* profits.
- "Run out" the product; that is, cut all costs to the bare minimum to maximize profitability over the limited remaining life of the product.
- Best (and toughest) of all, improve the product in a functional sense, or revitalize it in some manner. Publishers of printed dictionaries may have done this.

*S*alt is certainly in the maturity stage of its life cycle. Given the persistent health concerns about excess salt in diets, it could be argued this product is in the decline stage. Facing this situation, Morton Inc. has identified new uses for its product. They include eradicating ketchup stains from carpet, removing rust from utensils such as scissors, and making pantyhose more resistant to runs by washing them in Morton Salt. And rather than letting consumers discover practical, new uses of salt on their own, Morton promotes them through advertising.

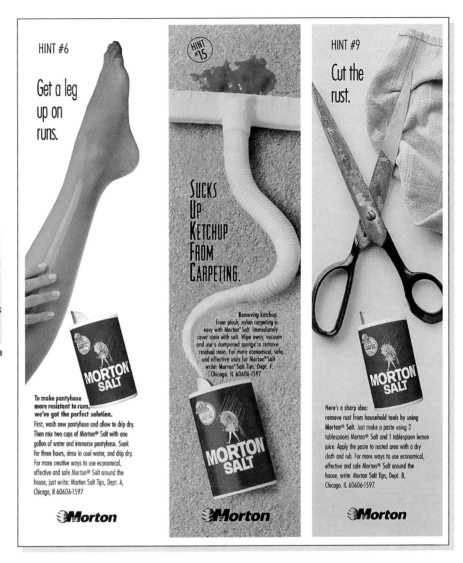

Other reference materials, including dictionaries on personal computers, seemed to have pushed the traditional dictionary into—or at least toward—decline. However, some publishers are working hard to maintain the appeal of the dictionary. Houghton Mifflin, for instance, added 16,000 new words to a recent edition and backed it with $2 million in promotion.[27]

If one of these alternatives doesn't work, management will have to consider **product abandonment**. The expense of carrying profitless products goes beyond what shows up on financial statements. For example, there is a very real cost to the managerial time and effort that is diverted to terminally ill products. Management often is reluctant to discard a product, however, partly because it becomes attached to the product over the years. Knowing when and how to abandon products successfully may be as important as knowing when and how to introduce new ones.

Either before or after abandoning a declining product, a company may redefine its mission to concentrate on a more promising venture. That's what Fluke Manufacturing did when its traditional test and measurement devices started to become obsolete because of computing technology. Thus it was no fluke that the

http://www.fluke.com/

company came up with the following mission statement: "To be the leader in compact professional electronic test tools."[28]

Planned Obsolescence and Fashion

American consumers seem to be constantly searching for "what's new" but not "*too* new." They want newness—new products, new styles, new colors. However, they want to be moved gently out of their habitual patterns, not shocked out of them. Consequently, many manufacturers use a product strategy of planned obsolescence. The intent of this strategy is to make an existing product out of date and thus to increase the market for replacement products. Consumers often satisfy their thirst for newness through fashion. And producers of fashions rely heavily on planned obsolescence, as we'll now see.

Nature of Planned Obsolescence

The term **planned obsolescence** is used to refer to either of two developments:

- **Technological obsolescence**. Significant technical improvements result in a more effective product. For instance, cassette tapes made phonograph records obsolete; now digital audio tapes threaten to make cassettes and compact discs obsolete. This type of obsolescence is generally considered to be socially and economically desirable, because the replacement product offers more benefits and/or a lower cost. Still, technological (or functional) obsolescence is sometimes criticized. For example, Intel has aggravated some producers of personal computers by bringing out new generations of microprocessors frequently, which reduces the salability of PCs that lack the latest technology.[29]
- **Style obsolescence**. Superficial characteristics of a product are altered so that the new model is easily differentiated from the previous model. Style obsolescence, sometimes called "psychological" or "fashion" obsolescence, is intended to make people feel out of date if they continue to use old models. Products subject to this type of obsolescence include clothing, furniture, and automobiles. Normally, when people criticize planned obsolescence, they mean style obsolescence.

In our discussion, when we speak of planned obsolescence, we will mean *only* style obsolescence, unless otherwise stated.

Nature of Style and Fashion

Although the words *style* and *fashion* are often used interchangeably, there is a clear distinction. A **style** is a distinctive manner of construction or presentation in any art, product, or endeavor (singing, playing, behaving). Thus we have styles in automobiles (sedans, station wagons), in bathing suits (one-piece, bikini), in furniture (early American, French provincial), and in dancing (waltz, "break").

A **fashion** is any style that is popularly accepted and purchased by successive groups of people over a reasonably long period of time. Not every style becomes a fashion. To be considered a fashion, or to be called "fashionable," a style must be accepted by many people. All styles listed in the preceding paragraph, except perhaps break dancing, qualify as fashions. All societies, ranging from contemporary primitive groups to medieval European societies, have fashions.

Fashion is rooted in sociological and psychological factors. Basically, most of us are conformists. At the same time, we yearn to look and act a *little* different from others. We probably are not in revolt against custom; we simply wish to be a bit distinctive but not be accused of having bad taste or disregarding norms. Fashion furnishes the opportunity for self-expression.

Fashion-Adoption Process

The fashion-adoption process reflects the concepts of (1) cultural, social-class, and reference-group influences on consumer buying behavior, as discussed in Chapter 5, and (2) the diffusion of innovation, as explained in Chapter 8. People usually try to imitate others at the same or the next higher socioeconomic level. One way of doing this is to purchase a product that is fashionable in the group you want to be like.

Thus the **fashion-adoption process** is a series of buying waves that arise as a particular style is popularly accepted in one group, then another group, and another, until it finally falls out of fashion. This movement, representing the introduction, rise, popular culmination, and decline of the market's acceptance of a style, is referred to as the **fashion cycle**. A case can be made that synthetic fibers such as polyester in clothing and the convertible model of automobile are two products that have run the full fashion cycle.

There are three theories of fashion adoption (see Figure 9-4):

- **Trickle-down**, where a given fashion cycle flows *downward* through several socioeconomic levels.
- **Trickle-across**, where the cycle moves *horizontally* and *simultaneously within* several socioeconomic levels.
- **Trickle-up**, where a style first becomes popular at lower socioeconomic levels and then flows *upward* to become popular among higher levels.

Traditionally, the *trickle-down* theory has been used to explain the fashion-adoption process. As an example, designers of women's apparel first introduce a style to opinion leaders in the upper socioeconomic groups. If they accept the style, it quickly appears in leading fashion stores. Soon the middle-income and then the

FIGURE 9-4
Fashion-adoption processes.

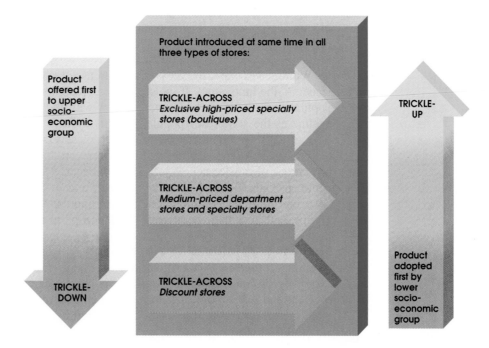

Product offered first to upper socio-economic group

TRICKLE-DOWN

Product introduced at same time in all three types of stores:

TRICKLE-ACROSS
Exclusive high-priced specialty stores (boutiques)

TRICKLE-ACROSS
Medium-priced department stores and specialty stores

TRICKLE-ACROSS
Discount stores

TRICKLE-UP

Product adopted first by lower socio-economic group

AN ETHICAL DILEMMA?

It's not uncommon for a dress style created by a noted designer to be copied by other clothing firms. Sometimes, in fact, "knockoffs" of new styles show up in department stores and discount houses *before* the original, high-price version reaches exclusive dress shops. This can happen if a competitor pays attention to public fashion shows that some (but a decreasing number of) designers still use to announce their fall fashion lines or otherwise obtains information about upcoming styles. Then the competing firm hurries through the production process, perhaps paying less attention to quality, and rushes the "knockoff" dresses into distribution channels.

Is it ethical or unethical for a firm to copy a style produced by a well-known designer and then to market this "knockoff"?

Sources: Teri Agins, "Fashion Knockoffs Hit Stores before Originals as Designers Seethe," *The Wall Street Journal*, Aug. 8, 1994, pp. A1, A4; and Phaedra Hise, "Taking Copycats to Task," *Inc.*, November 1993, p. 124.

lower-income markets want to emulate the leaders, and the style is mass marketed. As its popularity wanes, the style appears in bargain-price stores and finally is no longer considered fashionable.

Today the *trickle-across* theory best explains the adoption process for most fashions. It's true that there is some flow downward, and obviously there is an upward flow. But, by means of modern production, communication, and transportation, we can disseminate style information and products so rapidly that all social levels can be reached at about the same time. For example, within a few weeks of the beginning of the fall season, the same style of dress (but at different quality levels) appears (1) in small, exclusive dress shops appealing to the upper social class, (2) in large department stores aiming at the middle class, and (3) in discount houses and low-price women's ready-to-wear chain stores, where the target is the portion of the lower class that has some disposable income.

Most apparel manufacturers produce a wide *variety* of essentially one style. They also produce distinct *qualities* of the same basic style so as to appeal to different income groups.[30] When an entire cycle may last only one season, sellers cannot afford to wait for style acceptance to trickle down. They must introduce it to many social levels simultaneously.

Within each class, the dresses are purchased early in the season by the opinion leaders—the innovators. If the style is accepted, its sales curve rises as it becomes popular with the early adopters and then with the late adopters. Eventually, sales decline as the style loses popularity. This cycle is a horizontal movement, occurring virtually simultaneously within each of several socioeconomic levels.

The *trickle-up* process also explains some product-adoption processes. Consider how styles of music such as jazz and rap became popular. Also look at blue jeans, denim jackets, T-shirts, athletic footwear, and even pasta in the 1990s. They all have one thing in common: They were popular first with lower socioeconomic groups, and later their popularity "trickled up" to higher-income markets.

Marketing Considerations in Fashion

Accurate forecasting is critical to success in fashion merchandising. This is extremely difficult, however, because the forecaster must deal with complex sociological and psychological factors. Frequently a retailer or manufacturer operates largely on intuition and inspiration, tempered by considerable experience.

Accurate forecasting—indeed, effective marketing—has become increasingly difficult in women's fashions in recent years. The reason: Smaller numbers of female consumers are responding to annual style changes; many women are simply buying fewer clothes. Interestingly, some designers contributed to the problem, disrupting normal fashion cycles by telling women that "anything goes" with regard to clothing styles. With the industry in a serious slump in the mid-1990s, some producers of women's fashions were forced out of business. Other producers and many clothing retailers adjusted their product mixes to coincide with the marked trend toward more casual dress.[31]

When a firm's products are subject to the fashion cycle, management must know what stage the cycle is in at all times. Managers must decide at what point to get into the cycle and when to get out. Ordinarily a retailer cannot participate successfully in all stages of the fashion cycle at the same time. Thus a specialty apparel store—whose stocks are displayed in limited numbers without price tags—should get in at the start of a fashion trend. And a department store appealing to the middle-income market should plan to enter the cycle in time to mass-market the style as it is climbing to its peak of popularity. Fundamentally, retail executives must keep in mind the product's target market in deciding at which stage(s) of the life cycle its stores should offer fashionable apparel.

A GLOBAL PERSPECTIVE

DOES A WEAK DOLLAR CONVERT TO STRONG FASHION SALES?

In the U.S., as the first half of this decade ended, sales of expensive women's clothing were slumping and other categories of fashions were stagnant. More recently, however, sales for some fashion products have started to rise. In fact, the demand for some brands became so robust that rationing of limited inventories became necessary. What factors underlie the possible turnaround?

One reason is that some consumers have abandoned the simple, frugal life-style, along with its limited spending, they adopted in the early 1990s. As explained by the chairman of Bloomingdale's retail chain, "Women are asking themselves, 'What's wrong with spending money on myself? How many T-shirts do I need?' "

Another reason for the uptrend in fashion sales is the weak dollar. The president of Louis Vuitton North America Inc. offered this opinion, "The dollar differential is definitely contributing to sales. It's probably about half the equation."

A weak dollar certainly diminishes the buying power of U.S. residents when they travel elsewhere. However, when the dollar is weak compared to other nations' currencies, wealthy consumers from other countries find shopping in the U.S. affordable—and hence attractive. Their currency—whether it's the yen, mark, or krona—has quite a bit of buying power in the U.S.

Sales of luxury goods have risen the most along both coasts and in Hawaii. Consider the impact of one country's shoppers. More than 4 million Japanese visit the U.S. each year. Identical merchandise often carries much lower prices in America than in Japan. Thus it's not surprising that Japanese consumers spend about $2 billion in the U.S. annually.

To satisfy both American and foreign shoppers, companies that sell luxury goods are opening more outlets in the U.S., particularly in areas that cater to wealthy tourists. Further, some retailers that cater to foreign consumers are hiring sales people that speak at least one language besides English, most often Japanese or German.

Sources: Laura Bird, "Tired of T-Shirts and No-Name Watches, Shoppers Return to Tiffany and Chanel," *The Wall Street Journal*, Sept. 6, 1995, p. B1; and Lori Bongiorno, "Dollar Days for the Cartier Crowd," *Business Week*, Aug. 21, 1995, p. 53.

■ SUMMARY

Many strategic decisions must be made to manage a company's assortment of products effectively. To start, a firm must select strategies regarding its product mix. One decision is how to position the product relative to competing products and other products sold by the firm.

Another strategic decision is whether or how to expand the product mix by adding items to a line and/or introducing new lines. Altering the design, packaging, or other features of existing products is still another option among the strategies of selecting the best mix. The product mix also can be changed by eliminating an entire line or by simplifying the assortment within a line. Alternatively, management may elect to trade up or trade down relative to existing products.

Executives need to understand the concept of a product life cycle, which reflects the total sales volume for a generic product category. Each of the cycle's four stages—introduction, growth, maturity, and decline—has distinctive characteristics that have implications for marketing. Managing a product as it moves through its life cycle presents a number of challenges and opportunities. Eventually, a product category may lack adequate acceptance from consumers; at that point, all or most companies should abandon their versions of this product.

Planned obsolescence is a controversial product strategy, built around the concepts of style, fashion, and the fashion cycle. Fashion—essentially a sociological and psychological phenomenon—follows a reasonably predictable pattern. With advances in communications and production, the fashion-adoption process has moved away from the traditional trickle-down pattern. Today the process is better described as trickle-across. There also are examples of fashions trickling up. Managing a product, such as expensive apparel, through a fashion cycle may be even more challenging than adjusting another type of product's strategies during its life cycle.

More about

*A*utomobiles, as we know them, are definitely in the late maturity stage of their life cycle. Consequently, GM and other automakers face enormous challenges in gaining a differential advantage for each of their brands over the enormous number of competitors. GM is struggling to address that challenge.

For the most part, GM is positioning its various brands in relation to specified target markets. Buick, for instance, is aimed at car buyers over age 50. However, GM executives are also cognizant of competition as they have worked to refine the company's positioning strategies. Thus Cadillac is positioned against foreign brands of luxury cars, whereas Saturn competes directly with smaller, cheaper foreign brands.

In introducing Saturn in 1990, GM engaged in product-mix expansion. Even though it already had six lines of motor vehicles, it needed to create a smaller, reliable, economy-priced car that was perceived by consumers as "fresh" and, frankly, different than the typical GM product. This approach, combined with no-haggle pricing, has made Saturn a popular brand, although it is still not a profitable venture for the parent company.

GENERAL MOTORS

Now, GM is employing another strategy, product alteration, for the Cadillac brand. Because Cadillac's loyal customers are in their sixties and few if any young consumers aspire to own a Cadillac, GM is trying to revamp what once was the most prestigious automobile brand in the world. Overall, the Cadillac of the future, notably a new Catera model, will be smaller with a more rounded, understated appearance. The Fleetwood model, almost 3 feet longer than the Catera, disappears after the 1996 model year.

To differing degrees, all of GM's brands have been or are being modified. Still, GM has drawn criticism from some industry observers for not being even more aggressive in altering its products in order to update them and make them more appealing to increasingly value-oriented consumers. Competitors haven't been standing by idly. For example, Ford Motor Co. invested $3 billion to restyle its best-selling Taurus model. Introduced at the start of the 1996 model year, the updated Taurus features a new engine, transmission, interior, and exterior. Ford backed the restyled Taurus with a variety of lease deals and cash rebates, aimed at both Taurus owners and selected owners of comparable brands such as Honda Accord and Toyota Camry.

With seven brands and more than six dozen models, GM has had to consider an even more drastic measure, product-mix contraction. It might be better for the company as a whole to drop one or two brands in order to eliminate—or at least reduce—brand overlap. The recaptured resources could then be concentrated on the remaining brands. Buick and

even Cadillac have been mentioned as candidates for deletion.[32]

1. Should General Motors drop one or more of its brands, such as Buick or Cadillac, in order to strengthen its overall product assortment?
2. What else can GM do in order to manage its mix of seven brands of motor vehicles during the maturity stage of the life cycle?

■ KEY TERMS AND CONCEPTS

Product mix (220)	Product alteration (224)	Decline stage (229)	Style (234)
Breadth (220)	Product-mix	Fad (229)	Fashion (234)
Depth (220)	contraction (224)	Product	Fashion-adoption
Product line (220)	Trading up (225)	abandonment (233)	process (235)
Positioning (221)	Trading down (225)	Planned	Fashion cycle (235)
Product-mix	Product life cycle (226)	obsolescence (234)	Trickle-down theory (235)
expansion (223)	Introduction stage (227)	Technological	Trickle-across
Line extension (223)	Growth stage (228)	obsolescence (234)	theory (235)
Mix extension (224)	Maturity stage (229)	Style obsolescence (234)	Trickle-up theory (235)

■ QUESTIONS AND PROBLEMS

1. "It is inconsistent for management to follow concurrently the product-line strategies of *expanding* its product mix and *contracting* its product mix." Discuss.
2. "Trading up and trading down are product strategies closely related to the business cycle. Firms trade up during periods of prosperity and trade down during recessions." Do you agree? Why?
3. Name one category of goods and one category of services you believe are in the introductory stage of their life cycles. For each product, identify the market that considers your examples to be truly new.
4. What are two products that are in the decline stage of the life cycle? In each case, point out whether you think the decline is permanent. What recommendations do you have for rejuvenating the demand for either of these products?

5. How might a company's advertising strategies differ, depending on whether its brand of a product is in the introduction stage or the maturity stage of its life cycle?
6. What products, other than apparel and automobiles, stress fashion and style in marketing? Do styles exist among business products?
7. Is the trickle-across theory applicable to the fashion-adoption process in product lines other than women's apparel? Explain, using examples.
8. Planned obsolescence is criticized as a social and economic waste because we are urged to buy things we do not like and do not need. What is your opinion? If you object to planned obsolescence, what are your recommendations for correcting the situation?

■ HANDS-ON MARKETING

1. Select a product category in which you are interested. Go to the library and identify the national or state trade association for this product category. Then write to the association, requesting sales figures for this product over its history and other information that will allow you to plot the life cycle for this product. What stage of the life cycle is this product in? Explain.
2. Arrange a meeting with a supermarket manager or a

department manager in a supermarket. Discuss how the manager handles the challenge of line extensions. In which product category are line extensions most common? When new items are added to the line, how does the manager find space for the new entries—by giving more space to this category, dropping other items carrying this same brand, pruning other brands in this category, or some other means?

CHAPTER 10

Brands, Packaging, and Other Product Features

Does the
LEVI'S
Brand Fit More Than American Men?

*L*evi's is the dominant brand of denim jeans in the U.S., substantially ahead of competing brands Lee and Wrangler. However, American men are buying fewer pairs of jeans. And when they opt for jeans, many expect discounted prices. What's a company to do?

Facing this situation, Levi Strauss & Co. (LS) recognized that its primary assets are the enduring appeal of the Levi's brand and the basic product itself. The firm certainly faces a vastly different challenge than was faced by the company's founder, whose name, of course, was Levi Strauss. While selling canvas tents to the prospectors in the California gold rush more than 100 years ago, he found greater demand for durable pants. He satisfied the gold miners with pants made of cotton denim fabric. As the saying goes, "The rest is history."

Over the years, LS has tried to broaden its product line. Its move into fashionable clothing in the 1970s was a flop. In contrast, its introduction of the Dockers brand of cotton twill pants and related casual wear in the 1980s has been an enormous success. But the company's staple continues to be blue jeans. LS updates the basic product periodically. Compared to the mid-1980s, when most of Levi's pants were made from untreated denim, now they're stonewashed or treated in other ways.

Historically, the primary market for Levi's has been men in the U.S. However, this market does not have abundant growth potential. Thus LS has been paying a great deal of attention to other markets, namely foreign countries and American women.

In many locales around the world, the Levi's brand is widely recognized and evokes favorable images of American life. Because they are in great demand as a fashion item in many foreign countries, the Levi's brand can command high prices—sometimes two to three times higher than in the U.S. Already sold in dozens of countries around the globe, LS is continuing its international expansion. In late 1995, for example, the brand was introduced in India. Initial marketing efforts are focused on relatively affluent Indian consumers, who are likely to be familiar with the Levi's brand.

Since the early 1990s, LS has exerted substantial effort toward the female market in the U.S. A central element of the program is Personal Pair jeans, which are Levi's that are nearly custom-tailored for each woman. After a shopper's measurements are fed into a computer at the retail outlet, she receives a recommendation as to which of 400 different sizes are likely to fit well. The shopper tries on one or more pairs, and—assuming a good fit—places an order. The Personal Pair jeans arrive at the store or the customer's home several weeks later.

LS also launched an innovative TV advertising campaign to appeal to women. The animated "women in motion" ads showed that female consumers come in all sizes and shapes and that Levi's will fit every one of them. The attention LS has paid to American women is paying off.

Success in the future will depend on the ability of Levi Strauss & Co. to sustain its dominance in the men's jeans market in the U.S. Equally important will be the firm's efforts to build its Dockers brand and to satisfy foreign consumers as well as American women.[1]

How do you think Levi Strauss & Co. can protect and strengthen the Levi's brand name in the U.S. and in other countries?

http://www.levi.com/

241

As the Levi's case illustrates, a brand can be all-important for many products. Otherwise, how do you account for some consumers wanting Bayer aspirin and others preferring, or at least accepting, Walgreen's brand, when both are physically and chemically the identical product? Other consumers' choices are influenced not only by the brand but also by the package, design, or another product feature. Because these product features are important elements in a marketing program, we devote this chapter to them. After studying this chapter, you should be able to explain:

CHAPTER GOALS

- The nature and importance of brands.
- Characteristics of a good brand name.
- Branding strategies of producers and middlemen.
- Why and how a growing number of firms are building and using brand equity.
- The nature and importance of packaging and labeling.
- Major packaging strategies.
- The marketing implications of other product features—design, color, and product quality—that can satisfy consumers' wants.

Brands

The word *brand* is comprehensive; it encompasses other narrower terms. A **brand** is a name and/or mark intended to identify the product of one seller or group of sellers and differentiate the product from competing products.[2]

A **brand name** consists of words, letters, and/or numbers that can be *vocalized*. A **brand mark** is the part of the brand that appears in the form of a symbol, design, or distinctive color or lettering. A brand mark is recognized by sight but cannot be expressed when a person pronounces the brand name. Crest, Coors, and Gillette are brand names. Brand marks are the distinctively lined globe of AT&T and the horse and rider for Ralph Lauren's Polo brand. Green Giant (canned and frozen vegetable products) and Arm & Hammer (baking soda) are both brand names and brand marks.

A **trademark** is a brand that has been adopted by a seller and given legal protection. A trademark includes not just the brand mark, as many people believe, but also the brand name. The Lanham Act of 1946 permits firms to register trademarks with the federal government to protect them from use or misuse by other companies. The Trademark Law Revision Act, which took effect in 1989, is intended to strengthen the registration system to the benefit of U.S. firms.[3]

One method of classifying brands is on the basis of who owns them. Thus we have **producers' brands** and **middlemen's brands**, the latter being owned by retailers or wholesalers. Florsheim (shoes), Prozac (Eli Lilly & Company's antidepressant drug), Courtyard by Marriott (lodging), and ValuJet (discount airline) are producers' brands; Lucerne (Safeway), Craftsman (Sears), and Penncrest (J.C. Penney) are middlemen's brands.

The terms *national* and *private* have been used to describe producer and middleman brand ownership, respectively. However, marketing people prefer the *producer-middleman* terminology. To say that a brand of poultry feed marketed in three states by a small Birmingham, Alabama, manufacturer is a *national* brand, or that the brands of Wal-Mart and Sears are *private* brands, stretches the meaning of these two terms.

A GLOBAL PERSPECTIVE

WHO'S GOT THE BUD?

A company trying to establish a global brand may find another firm using the same brand in other countries. For example, Budweiser beer is marketed all over the world. However, Anheuser-Busch Companies (A-B), the St. Louis–based brewery, isn't the only company placing this brand on its beer. A century-old brewery in the Czech Republic, Budejovicky Budvar, sells a Budweiser brew not only in that country but also in other parts of Eastern Europe as well as Germany. The American brand is sold throughout most of the rest of the world. Further, the Czech brand is called "the beer of kings," and the American brand "the king of beers."

What's the problem? Essentially, both brewers lay claim to the Budweiser trademark. A-B began making Budweiser beer in the U.S. in 1876. Then in 1895, ethnic Czechs in a community called Budweis started a brewery to make and sell its own Budweiser beer. When the two enterprises began to expand into other countries, the dispute over the Budweiser trademark erupted.

Eventually, in 1939, the competing breweries agreed to divide up the world market with respect to where each concern could use the Budweiser brand.

The only area in which they go head-to-head is Great Britain, where the American brand outsells the Czech version by a 14-to-1 ratio.

Wanting to develop its version of Budweiser as a global brand, A-B has persisted in seeking an agreement with Budvar. In late 1995, A-B offered to pay the Czech brewery $200 million to gain the worldwide rights to the Budweiser name. The world's largest brewery also said it would agree to purchase 10 percent of the Czech Republic's finest hops (a key ingredient in beer) for at least 10 years.

Complicating the situation is the fact that the Czech brewery is owned by the government. As a result, Czech bureaucrats are trying to determine whether or not—or, more likely, when—to turn the brewery over to private interests. They would like to resolve that matter before entering into any agreement with A-B regarding the disputed trademark.

http://budweiser.com/ab.html/

Sources: Denise Smith Amos, "Peace Could Be Near in Bud War," *St. Louis Post-Dispatch*, Nov. 28, 1995, p. 7C; Robert L. Koenig, "Bud War," *St. Louis Post-Dispatch*, Oct. 22, 1995, p. 1A; "Another Round," *St. Louis Post-Dispatch*, Sept. 8, 1995, p. 3C; and Roger Thurow, "The King of Beers and Beer of Kings Are at Lagerheads," *The Wall Street Journal*, Apr. 3, 1992, p. A1.

Reasons for Branding

For consumers, brands make it easy to identify goods or services. They aid shoppers in moving quickly through a supermarket, discount house, or other retail store and in making purchase decisions. Brands also help assure consumers that they will get consistent quality when they reorder.

For sellers, brands can be promoted. They are easily recognized when displayed in a store or included in advertising. Branding reduces price comparisons. Because brands are another factor that needs to be considered in comparing different products, branding reduces the likelihood of purchase decisions based solely on price. The reputation of a brand also influences customer loyalty among buyers of services as well as business and consumer goods.[4] Finally, branding can differentiate commodities (Sunkist oranges, Morton salt, and Domino sugar, for example).

Brands rated the best in the U.S. and—for comparison purposes—in the United Kingdom and Argentina are shown in Table 10-1. There is little overlap across the top-10 lists; only Kodak and Mercedes-Benz are on all three. Also note that few services (Disney World, Disneyland, and UPS) cracked the U.S. list, just one service (Disney World) and one retailer (Marks & Spencer) are reflected in the U.K. rankings, and only goods comprise the Argentina list.

TABLE 10-1 The best brands—according to some surveys

Rank	In the U.S.	In the United Kingdom	In Argentina
1.	Kodak photographic film	Mercedes-Benz	Mercedes-Benz
2.	Disney World	BMW	Havana pastries
3.	Mercedes-Benz	Lego toys	La Senenisimo dairy products
4.	Disneyland	Fisher Price toys	Quilmes beer
5.	Hallmark greeting cards	Marks & Spencer stores	Peugeot automobiles
6.	Fisher Price toys	Disney World	JVC audio equipment
7.	Levi's jeans	Kellogg's Corn Flakes	Kodak photographic film
8.	United Parcel Service	Levi's jeans	Renault automobiles
9.	Arm & Hammer baking soda	Duracell batteries	Christian Dior apparel
10.	Reynolds Wrap aluminum foil	Kodak photographic film	Sony audio equipment

Note: What constitutes "best" was based on a survey of consumers in each of the three nations. In the U.S., for example, "Consumers were asked to rate brands on a scale of zero to 10, with 10 representing extraordinary quality and zero poor or unacceptable quality."

Sources: T. L. Stanley, "How They Rate," *Brandweek*, Apr. 3, 1995, pp. 45–48; and "As You Like It," *Marketing*, June 22, 1995. The ratings for Argentina were provided by Total Research Corporation, Princeton, NJ, the firm that conducts the annual EquiTrend surveys of perceived brand quality.

Not all brands are widely and favorably recognized by their target markets. And among those that are, many are unable to maintain a position of prominence. However, as a result of such activities as aggressive promotion and careful quality control, a few brands (Kodak cameras and Gillette razors) retain their leadership positions over a long time. Consequently, enormous amounts of money are spent to acquire companies that have dominant brands. RJR Company paid several *billion* dollars to acquire Nabisco, with its Oreo cookies and Ritz crackers. Various firms pursued Kraft Company (Velveeta cheese, Miracle Whip salad dressing, and other leading brands), with bids over $11 billion. Philip Morris eventually acquired Kraft.

Reasons for Not Branding

Two responsibilities come with brand ownership: (1) promoting the brand and (2) maintaining a consistent quality of output. Many firms do not brand their products because they are unable or unwilling to assume these responsibilities.

Some items remain unbranded because they cannot be physically differentiated from other firms' products. Clothespins, nails, and raw materials (coal, cotton, wheat) are examples of goods for which product differentiation, including branding, is generally unknown. The perishable nature of products such as fresh fruits and vegetables tends to discourage branding. However, well-known brands such as Dole pineapples and Chiquita bananas demonstrate that even agricultural products can be branded successfully.

Selecting a Good Brand Name

Some brand names are so good that they contribute to the success of products. For examples, consider DieHard batteries and the Roach Motel, which is a pest-eradication device, not a discount motel! It appears the top-ranked brands in Table 10-1 possess most of the desirable characteristics for a brand name. However, virtually none of these names suggests the product's benefits or uses—the first characteristic.

But it takes more than a clever brand name to ensure success in the marketplace. Witness People Express, the discount airline that failed despite the apt name. Other brand names are so poor that they are a factor in product failures. Occasionally products achieve success despite poor brand names—consider Exxon, which had no meaning when it was first introduced.

Choosing a name for a product may appear trivial, but it's not. Al Ries, a well-known consultant and author, has gone so far (perhaps too far) as to say, "The most important element in a marketing program—and the one over which marketing managers can exert the most control—is the naming of a product."[5]

The Challenge.   Nowadays, selecting a good brand name for a new product is especially challenging. The reason? We're running out of possibilities.[6] On the one hand, about 10,000 new products are launched annually; on the other hand, only 50,000 words comprise the standard desk-size dictionary. Further, many words either already adorn products (such as Pert Plus, Cascade, and Veryfine) or are unsuitable as brand names (such as obnoxious, hypocrite, and deceased).

One solution is to combine numbers with words and/or letters to form a brand name. Examples include Formula 409 (household cleaner), WD-40 (lubricant and protectant), and Lotus 1-2-3 (software).[7] Another possibility is to create a brand name that isn't part of the English language. Examples of so-called *morphenes* include Acura, Lexus, and Compaq.[8] The naming process isn't cheap, costing $25,000 and up for the name itself and then much more to promote the new brand.

Desirable Characteristics.   Various characteristics determine the desirability of a brand name for either a good or a service.[9] It's difficult to find a brand name that rates well on every attribute. Still, a brand name should have as many of the following five characteristics as possible:

- *Suggest something about the product, particularly its benefits and use.* Names connoting benefits include Beautyrest, Mr. Goodwrench, Minute Rice, and—perhaps best of all—DieHard. Product use is suggested by Dustbuster, Ticketron, and La-Z-Boy chairs.
- *Be easy to pronounce, spell, and remember.* Simple, short, one-syllable names such as Tide, Ban, Aim, and Surf are helpful. However, even some short names, such as NYNEX and Aetna, aren't easily pronounced by some consumers. Other brands that may not meet this criterion include Frusen-Glädjé (ice cream), Au Bon Pain (bakeries), and Asahi (beer).
- *Be distinctive.* Brands with names like National, Star, Ideal, United, Allied, or Standard fail on this point. Many services firms begin their brand names with adjectives connoting strength and then add a description of the business, creating brands such as Allied Van Lines and United Parcel Service. But are these really distinctive?
- *Be adaptable to additions to the product line.* A family name such as Kellogg, Lipton, or Ford may serve the purpose better than a highly distinctive name suggesting product benefits. When fast-food restaurants added breakfasts to their menus, McDonald's name fit better than Burger King or Pizza Hut. Likewise, names like Alaska Airlines and Southwest Airlines may inhibit geographic expansion more than a name such as United Airlines.
- *Be capable of registration and legal protection.* Brand names are covered under the Lanham Act, its 1989 revision, and other laws.

Protecting a Brand Name

A firm with a well-known, successful brand name needs to actively safeguard it. Otherwise, this valuable asset can be damaged—or even lost entirely—in either of two ways.

Product Counterfeiting. Some unscrupulous manufacturers engage in **product counterfeiting** by placing a highly regarded brand on their offering, disregarding the basic, yet critical fact that they do not own the rights to the brand. If you have ever been to Manhattan in New York, you probably have been offered "genuine" Rolex or Gucci watches for $10 to $20. Obviously, these are counterfeit products. Counterfeiting can be found in many product categories, including watches, leather goods, athletic footwear, and automobile replacement parts.[10] It's estimated that such "knockoffs" cost American companies more than $5 *billion* annually.[11]

It's unrealistic to think that counterfeiters can be eliminated entirely. However, companies are not powerless in combating knockoffs. First, they need to be on the lookout for counterfeit goods carrying one of their brands. Second, when imitations and their producers are identified, legal action should be taken against the violators. In particular, remedies can be sought under the Trademark Counterfeiting Act, a 1984 federal law. Convicted violators can be subject to stiff fines, jail sentences, seizure of counterfeit products, and freezing of their financial and business assets. Of course, combating counterfeiting can be time-consuming and costly. But firms cannot afford to ignore counterfeiting because this practice can "depreciate the value of a trademark owner's products."[12]

Generic Usage. Over a period of years, some brand names become so well accepted that they are commonly used instead of the generic names of the particular product categories.[13] Examples are listed in the margin. Originally these names were trademarks that could be used only by the owner.

What happened? Well, a brand name can become generic in two primary ways:

Generic terms that formerly were brand names

aspirin	nylon
brassiere	shredded
cellophane	wheat
escalator	thermos
harmonica	yo-yo
kerosene	zipper
linoleum	

- There is no simple generic name available, so the public uses the brand name as a generic name. This occurred with shredded wheat, nylon, and cellophane. The Formica Corporation wages an ongoing struggle, thus far successful, to retain the legal status of its Formica brand of decorative laminate.[14]
- As contradictory as it appears, sometimes a firm is too effective in promoting a brand name. Although not yet legally generic, names such as Levi's, Band-Aid, Scotch Tape, and Kleenex are on the borderline. These brand names have been promoted so heavily and so successfully that many people use them generically. To illustrate, which terms do you use in conversation—adhesive bandage or Band-Aid, facial tissue or Kleenex? We suspect the latter in both cases.

There are various means to prevent the generic use of a brand name:

- Use the brand name in conjunction with the company name—Polaroid Land camera, for example.
- Better yet, use the brand name together with the generic name—Dacron brand polyester, for instance.
- Right after the brand name, place the ® symbol (if your brand is a registered trademark) or ™ (if it is not registered).

http://www.rollerblade.ca/

- Call attention to and challenge improper use of your brand name. Rollerblade Inc. has gone so far as to sue competitors who use "rollerblade" as a generic word. Thus the maker of Rollerblades disdains a statement like "I broke my neck rollerblading" and prefers the term *in-line skating*.[15]

"But Mr. Carruthers, you said you needed forty Xeroxes."

Mr. Carruthers used our name incorrectly. That's why he got 40 Xerox copiers, when what he really wanted was 40 copies made on his Xerox copier.

He didn't know that Xerox, as a trademark of Xerox Corporation, should be followed by the descriptive word for the particular product, such as "Xerox duplicator" or "Xerox copier."

And should only be used as a noun when referring to the corporation itself.

If Mr. Carruthers had asked for 40 copies or 40 photocopies made on his Xerox copier, he would have gotten exactly what he wanted.

And if you use Xerox properly, you'll get exactly what you want, too.

P.S. You're welcome to make 40 copies or 40 photocopies of this ad. Preferably on your Xerox copier.

XEROX

Branding Strategies

Both producers and middlemen face strategic decisions regarding the branding of their goods or services.

Producers' Strategies

Producers must decide whether to brand their products and whether to sell any or all of their output under middlemen's brands.

Marketing Entire Output under Producer's Own Brands. Companies that rely strictly on their own brands usually are very large, well financed, and well managed. Polaroid, Maytag, and IBM, for example, have broad product lines, well-established distribution systems, and large shares of the market. It's particularly difficult for a new firm to employ this approach. Only a minority of manufacturers employ this strategy, and the number seems to be decreasing. A primary reason is that there are lots of opportunities to make products to which middlemen apply their own brands. The reasons why a producer relies strictly on its own brands were covered in the earlier section on the importance of branding to the seller.

Branding of Fabricating Parts and Materials. Some producers use a strategy of *branding fabricating parts and materials* (manufactured goods that become part of another product following subsequent manufacturing).[16] This strategy is

http://www.dupont.com/

used in marketing Dan River cottons, Acrilan fabrics, and many automotive parts such as spark plugs, batteries, and oil filters. Du Pont has consistently and successfully used this strategy, notably with its Lycra spandex fiber and Stainmaster stain repellant for carpets.

http://www.dolby.com/

With this strategy, the seller seeks to develop a market preference for its branded parts or materials. Dolby Labs seeks to create a market situation in which buyers insist that a stereo sound system include a Dolby noise-reduction component. Dolby Labs also wants to convince manufacturers that their stereo sound systems will sell better if they contain Dolby noise-reduction units.

This strategy is most likely to be effective when the particular type of fabricating parts or materials has two characteristics:

http://www.intel.com/

- The product is also a consumer good that is bought for replacement purposes—Champion spark plugs and Delco batteries, for example.
- The item is a key part of the finished product—a microprocessor within a personal computer, for instance. Intel Corp. developed the slogan "Intel Inside" to strengthen its product's position. The campaign was so successful that some computer makers, including IBM and Compaq, feared that the brand of personal computer would become less important than the brand of microprocessor contained in the machine. IBM, for one, quit using the "Intel Inside" slogan in its ads in order to place more emphasis on its own brand.[17]

Marketing under Middlemen's Brands.   A widespread strategy among manufacturers is to sell part or all of their output to middlemen for branding by these customers. Firms such as Borden, Keebler, and Reynolds Metals have their own well-known brands, and they also produce goods for branding by middlemen.

This approach allows a manufacturer to "hedge its bets." A company employing this strategy hopes its own brands will appeal to some loyal customers, while middlemen's brands are of interest to other, perhaps more cost-conscious shoppers.[18] Moreover, for a manufacturer, the output produced for middlemen's brands ordinarily represents additional sales. This strategy also helps a manufacturer fully utilize its plant capacity.

One drawback of this strategy is that the manufacturer may lose some customers for its own brands. Another drawback to marketing under middlemen's brands is that the producer's revenues depend on the strength of the middleman's marketing campaign for that brand. This problem grows as the proportion of a producer's output going to middlemen's brands increases.

A small proportion of manufacturers refuse to produce items for retailers' or wholesalers' brands. Gillette is one such company. The firm's top executive has said that manufacturing so-called private-label products would be "a sign of weakness." A company vice president was even more blunt, "If any manager did that, he should be shot by the shareholders."[19] This stubbornness will not eliminate competition from middlemen, however. Many middlemen want to market under their own brands. If one manufacturer refuses to sell to them, they simply go to another.

Middlemen's Strategies

The question of whether to brand must also be answered by middlemen.

Carry Only Producers' Brands.   Most retailers and wholesalers follow this policy. Why? They do not have the finances or other resources to promote a brand and maintain its quality.

Carry Both Producers' and Middlemen's Brands. Many large retailers and some large wholesalers stock popular producers' brands and also have their own brands. Sears, for instance, has used the slogan, "The brands you want at the store you trust." Sears offers an assortment of manufacturers' brands such as OshKosh and Michelin as well as its own brands such as Kenmore and Craftsman.[20]

Middlemen may find it advantageous to market their own brands, in place of or in addition to producers' brands, because it increases their control over their target markets. A retailer's brand can differentiate its products. If customers prefer a given retailer's brand, sometimes called a store brand, they can get it only from that retailer.

Prices on producers' brands sometimes are cut drastically when retail stores carrying these brands compete with each other. In recent years, price cutting has typified the marketing of clothing carrying the labels of designers such as Ralph Lauren and Liz Claiborne. A retailer might avoid at least some of this price competition by establishing its own appealing brands. As a result, some large retailers (Saks Fifth Avenue and Nordstrom, for example) have increased their stocks of upper-price apparel carrying the stores' brands. Some chains also have cut their stocks of clothing carrying designer brands.[21]

Furthermore, middlemen usually can sell their brands at prices below those of producers' brands and still earn higher gross margins. For example, in dry cereals, a store brand may provide up to twice as much gross profits as a producer's brand.[22] This is possible because middlemen often can acquire merchandise carrying their own brands at lower costs than similar merchandise carrying producers' brands. The costs may be lower because manufacturers have to pay to advertise and sell their own brands, but these costs are not included in the prices of products sold for branding by middlemen. Also, producers may offer good prices in this situation because they are anxious to get the extra business. In some cases, the costs may be lower because the quality of the products carrying middlemen's brands is lower than the quality of competing products bearing producers' brands.

Middlemen have to be careful in pricing their own brands. According to one study, if store brands of groceries are not priced at least 10 percent below producers' brands, many consumers will not buy them. However, if the store brand is more than 20 percent lower in price, some consumers become suspicious about quality. In contrast, another study concluded that other factors such as relative quality are more important than price level in determining the success of middlemen's brands versus producers' brands.[23]

Middlemen's brands have had their greatest impact in the marketing of consumer packaged goods, such as groceries and personal-care products. The Safeway supermarket chain has long relied on Lucerne and other brands it owns. Wal-Mart, the largest retailer in the U.S., is multiplying its store brands as well, with the Sam's American Choice label attached to colas, cookies, and other products. Loblaw's, the largest supermarket chain in Canada, has found great success with its President's Choice (PC) brand. In fact, Loblaw's has agreements with various American chains to distribute PC products in the U.S.[24]

In total, so-called private brands generate more than $30 *billion* in sales annually in the U.S. After years of gaining a larger share of supermarket sales, the growth of middlemen's brands leveled off in 1994. They still account for about 15 percent of total supermarket volume, with milk, fresh bread and rolls, and cheese at the top of the list.[25] In about 45 percent of the product categories stocked by supermarkets, the combined sales of private brands would place them among the three best-selling brands. In contrast to the leveling off in supermarkets,

Some retailers' brands of apparel

Nordstrom: Classiques Entier

Macy's: Charter Club, Austin Gray

Saks Fifth Avenue: The Works, SFA Collections

http://www.wal-mart.com/

http://www.weston.ca/loblaws/lcl.htm

middlemen's brands continue to expand their positions in drugstores and discount houses.[26]

All factors considered, neither producers' brands nor middlemen's brands have demonstrated a convincing competitive superiority over the other in the marketplace. Consequently, the "battle of the brands" shows every indication of remaining intense. In fact, over the last several years, some leading manufacturers, including Procter & Gamble and Philip Morris, have countered middlemen's brands by cutting prices on some of their well-known brands, including Pampers diapers, Tide detergent, and Marlboro cigarettes.[27]

Carry Generic Products. In the late 1970s, several supermarket chains introduced products sold under their generic names. **Generic products** are simply labeled according to the contents, such as pork and beans, peanut butter, cottage cheese, or paper towels. These unbranded products generally sell for at least 20 percent less than producers' brands and 10 to 20 percent less than middlemen's brands. They appeal to the most price-conscious consumers. Although they are the nutritional equivalent of branded products, generics may not have the color, size, and consistency of appearance of branded items.

Generic products captured a large enough share of total sales in some product categories to be a major factor in the battle of the brands. However, generics' market shares have leveled off and even declined in some categories. In fact, just between 1993 and 1994, total sales of generic products declined by 14 percent to $565 million, about one-fiftieth the sales of middlemen's brands.[28] As supermarkets have improved and promoted their own brands, a growing number of shoppers are choosing middlemen's brands as a compromise between generic products and producers' brands.

Strategies Common to Producers and Middlemen

Producers and middlemen alike must choose strategies with respect to branding their product mixes and branding for market saturation.

Branding within a Product Mix. At least three different strategies are used by firms that sell more than one product:

- *A separate name for each product.* This strategy is employed by Lever Brothers and Procter & Gamble. Because it follows this approach, most consumers are unaware of ConAgra, a food processor with about $25 billion in annual sales. But most consumers are familiar with its brands, such as Healthy Choice frozen dinners, Peter Pan peanut butter, and Armour lunch meat. Large beer makers are using this approach for new brands that are intended to convey a "microbrewery" image. Although the labels on the Icehouse and Red Dog brands refer to the Plank Road Brewery, they are actually made by Miller Brewing.[29]
- *The company name combined with a product name.* Examples include Johnson's Pledge and Johnson's Glo-Coat, and Kellogg's Rice Krispies and Kellogg's Corn Pops.
- *The company name alone.* Today few companies rely exclusively on this policy. However, it is followed for the most part by Heinz and Libby in the food field, as well as by Westinghouse and General Electric in various industries.

Using the company name for branding purposes, often termed **family branding**, makes it simpler and less expensive to introduce new, related products to a

*R*ed Devil, Inc. uses family branding to capitalize on the recognition and strength associated with the company name. Interestingly, while this ad stresses the Red Devil name, as well as the various areas of application (such as kitchen and bath), it assumes that readers know these products are caulking compounds and sealants, each tailored to a specific purpose.

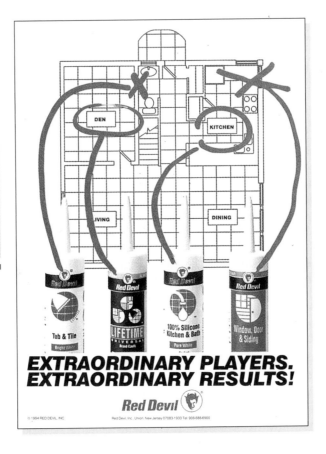

line.[30] Also, the prestige of a brand can be spread more easily if it appears on several products rather than on only one. Armor All Products took advantage of the smashing success of Armor All Protectant by adding other car-care products, such as Armor All Cleaner and Armor All Car Wax. The company name is best suited for marketing products that are related in quality, in use, or in some other manner.

Branding with the company name places a greater burden on the firm to maintain consistent quality among all products. One bad item can reflect unfavorably, even disastrously, on all other products carrying the same brand. For this reason, many companies prefer to let each individual product succeed or fail on its own—the first branding strategy in the list above.

Branding for Market Saturation. More and more frequently, firms are employing a **multiple-brand strategy** to increase their total sales in a market. They have more than one brand of essentially the same product, aimed either at the same target market or at distinct target markets. Suppose, for example, that a company has built one type of sales appeal around a given brand. To reach other segments of the market, the company may use other appeals with other brands. Two Procter & Gamble detergents, Tide and Dreft, illustrate this point. Some people feel that if Tide is strong enough to clean soiled work clothes, it should not be used on lingerie and other fine clothing. For these people P&G has Dreft, a detergent promoted as being more gentle than Tide.

http://www.pg.com/

Sometimes, multiple brands are necessary to penetrate separate target markets. For instance, Black & Decker (B&D) tools have strong appeal to do-it-yourselfers but not to professional tradespeople. Hence, B&D removed its company name from power tools aimed at tradespeople and switched to DeWalt, the name of a maker of high-quality stationary saws that was acquired by Black & Decker years ago.[31]

Building and Using Brand Equity

In the minds of many consumers, just having a brand name such as Sony, Kenmore, or Reebok adds value to a product. In particular, brands like these connote favorable attributes (such as quality or economy). What we're talking about is *brand equity*, one of the hottest topics in marketing during the 1990s. **Brand equity** is the value a brand adds to a product.[32]

If you're not convinced that a brand name by itself can have much value, consider the results of two studies. In one, the proportion of subjects choosing cornflakes cereal jumped from 47 percent when the brand was not known to 59 percent when the brand was identified as Kellogg's. In another study, conducted in 1993, when a sample of computer buyers was asked how much more or less they would pay for particular brands rather than the average computer brand, there was a range of $364. Consumers said they would pay $295 and $232 more for the IBM and Compaq brands, respectively. Other brands commanding a premium included Apple, Digital, and Dell. According to a 1995 update of this study, IBM still commands the largest premium, followed by Compaq, Hewlett-Packard, and Dell. It's evident that Kellogg's, IBM, Compaq, and many other brands have substantial equity.[33]

We tend to think of brand equity as a positive aspect of a product. Occasionally a brand will lack equity or even have negative equity. That is, it adds nothing or even detracts from the worth of a basic product to do what it's supposed to do. For example, in the 1993 study of personal computers, consumers indicated that a discount of $69 would be necessary for them to select the Packard Bell brand. Additional brands for which a discount would be expected, because of negative equity, include Zeos and NEC. In the services field, during the first half of the 1990s, Trans World Airlines suffered from financial problems and uneven customer service. Therefore, in the minds of many air travelers, the TWA brand had negative equity.

Building a brand's equity consists of developing a favorable, memorable, and consistent image—no easy task.[34] Product quality and advertising play vital roles in this endeavor. However, if substantial brand equity can be achieved, the organization that owns the brand can benefit in several ways:

- The brand itself can become a differential advantage, influencing consumers to buy a particular product. Examples include BMW, Häagen-Dazs, and Kenmore (Sears' brand of home appliances), to name several.
- Because it is expensive and time-consuming to build brand equity, it creates a barrier for companies that want to enter the market with a similar product.
- Brand equity can help a product survive changes in the operating environment, such as a business crisis or a shift in consumer tastes. Tylenol seemed to fare better than Perrier when both products faced crises involving their purity.

Brand equity is most often used to expand a product mix, especially to extend a product line.[35] Examples include Ocean Spray drinks in flavors other than the original cranberry, Wesson olive and canola oils, and Ann Taylor personal-care products.[36] Similarly, all or part of a strong brand name can be applied to a new product line. For instance, there are Courtyard by Marriott motels, Dole frozen desserts, and the Marquis by Waterford line of crystal ware.[37] The rationale for using an existing, strong brand name on a new item or line is that the brand's equity will convey a favorable impression of the product and increase the likelihood that consumers will at least try it.

If a brand has abundant equity, that does not necessarily mean it should be applied to other products. Procter & Gamble decided its hugely successful Crest name should be used on different kinds of toothpaste but not on other product categories such as mouthwash. In developing a spaghetti sauce, Campbell determined its popular brand name would not convey an Italian image, so it selected Prego as the name for its new sauce. Also, strong equity does not guarantee success for new items or lines using the well-regarded brands. Even with their famous brand names, Harley Davidson cigarettes, Levi's tailored men's clothing, Dunkin' Donuts cereal, and Swatch clothing did not pass the test of continuing consumer acceptance.

Trademark Licensing

Products with considerable brand equity have strong potential for **trademark licensing**, also called *brand licensing*. For example, Sunkist Growers licenses its popular Sunkist brand to numerous companies for their use on various items, including beverages and health products. Under this arrangement, the owner of a trademark grants permission (a license) to other firms to use its brand name and brand mark on their products. A licensee, which is the company that receives a license, ordinarily pays a royalty of about 5 to 10 percent of the wholesale price of each item bearing the licensed trademark. The royalty percentage varies depending on the amount of equity connected with the brand offered by a licensor, which is the company that owns it.

This branding strategy accounted for under $20 billion in retail sales in the early 1980s and now racks up over $75 *billion* in annual volume. Sales of licensed merchandise leveled off in the early 1990s—probably because of the sluggish economy—but are growing again. Toys featuring popular characters, such as the Mighty Morphin Power Rangers, account for about 12 percent of licensed sales volume. But the biggest category of licensed merchandise is apparel, with about one-third of licensed sales.[38]

Strategic decisions must be made by both the licensor and the licensee. Most fundamentally, Pierre Cardin (a licensor) must ask, "Should we allow other firms to use our designer label?" A manufacturer of eyeglass frames (a potential licensee) must ask, "Do we want to put out a line of high-fashion frames under the Pierre Cardin name?"

Owners of well-known brands are interested in licensing their trademarks for various reasons:

- *It can be very profitable.* There is little expense for the licensor. However, the licensor must set criteria for granting licenses and monitoring licensing arrangements to protect the reputation of its trademark.
- *There is a promotional benefit.* The licensor's name gets circulation far beyond the original trademarked item. Coppertone's decision to allow its brand name to be placed on various outdoor products such as casual footwear and umbrellas was explained as follows: "The more Coppertone's name appears on the right kind of products in appropriate categories, the more it will reinforce the brand's position in the market."[39]

YOU MAKE THE DECISION

WHO APPEARS MOST ON T-SHIRTS— THE RUGRATS OR BUZZ LIGHTYEAR?

Cartoon characters are highly visible in trademark licensing. The Walt Disney Co. alone has generated $15 *billion* in annual sales through licensing, most of it tied to animated films such as *Lion King*, *Pocahontas*, and—most recently—*Toy Story*. The giant entertainment enterprise has licensing agreements with about 600 firms in the U.S.

But Disney isn't the only player in licensing based on cartoon characters. The Teenage Mutant Ninja Turtles produced over $5 billion in licensed sales over an 8-year period. And likenesses of the disturbed Simpson family, from the popular TV show, have appeared on perhaps 100 different products.

Animated characters are widely used in trademark licensing because many are popular almost beyond belief. And they don't get divorced, get arrested, or engage in other embarrassing misdeeds! Of course,

their life span for licensing purposes can be very short, perhaps only several months.

Which cartoon characters will be the next hot properties in trademark licensing? The Rugrats from the children's show on cable TV? Buzz Lightyear, the spaceman, and Woody, the pull-string cowboy, from the hugely successful *Toy Story* film? The bugs that reside in the border town of Santo Bugito on a new TV production? Or Slick and Spin, the Incredible Crash Dummies?

For which cartoon character—one of the above or another one—should a toy company acquire a trademark license?

Sources: Pamela Davis-Diaz, "It's a Toy Story Stampede," *St. Petersburg Times*, Dec 7, 1995, p. 1E; Nanette Byrnes, "The Rugrats' Real Mom and Dad," *Business Week*, Oct. 16, 1995, pp. 143–144; Dale D. Buss, "Hot Names, Top Dollars," *Nation's Business*, August 1995, pp. 16–22; and Kevin Goldman, "Liked the Film? You Will Love the Lunch Box," *The Wall Street Journal*, June 20, 1995, p. B1.

Licensing also offers promise to potential licensees. Specific reasons for acquiring a trademark license are:

- *The likelihood of new-product success may be improved.* It's a lot easier for an unknown firm to get both middlemen and consumers to accept its product if it features a well-known trademark.
- *Marketing costs may be reduced.* One licensee explained that licensing is "a way of taking a name with brand recognition and applying it to your merchandise without having to do the advertising and brand building that is so expensive."[40] Any savings may offset the royalty fees paid to the licensor.

Packaging

Even after a product is developed and branded, strategies must still be devised for other product-related aspects of the marketing mix. One such product feature, and a critical one for some products, is **packaging**, which consists of all the activities of designing and producing the container or wrapper for a product.

Purposes and Importance of Packaging

Packaging is intended to serve several vital purposes:

- *Protect the product on its way to the consumer.* A package protects a product during shipment. Furthermore, it can prevent tampering with products, notably medications and food products, in the warehouse or the retail store. The design and size of a package can also help deter shoplifting. That's why small items, such as compact discs, come in larger than needed packages.

- *Provide protection after the product is purchased.* Compared with bulk (that is, unpackaged) items, packaged goods generally are more convenient, cleaner, and less susceptible to losses from evaporation, spilling, and spoilage. Also, "childproof" closures thwart children (and adults!) from opening containers of medications and other potentially harmful products.
- *Help gain acceptance of the product from middlemen.* A product must be packaged to meet the needs of wholesaling and retailing middlemen. For instance, a package's size and shape must be suitable for displaying and stacking the product in the store. An odd-shaped package might attract shoppers' attention, but if it doesn't stack well, the retailer is unlikely to purchase the product.
- *Help persuade consumers to buy the product.* Packaging can identify a product and thus may prevent substitution of competitive products. Packaging can also assist in getting a product noticed by consumers. Here's why that is important: "The average shopper spends 20 minutes in the store, viewing 20 products a second."[41] At the point of purchase—such as a supermarket aisle—the package can serve as a "silent sales person." In the case of middlemen's brands, which typically are not advertised heavily, packaging must serve as the means of communicating with shoppers. Furthermore, promotional copy on the package will last as long as the product is used in its packaged form.

Ultimately, a package may become a product's differential advantage, or at least a significant part of it. That was certainly true with Coca-Cola and its distinctive contour bottle. In the cases of convenience goods and operating supplies, most buyers consider one well-known brand about as good as another. Thus these types of products might be differentiated by a package feature—no-drip spout, reusable jar, or self-contained applicator (liquid shoe polish and glue, for example).

Historically, packaging was intended primarily to provide protection. Today, with its marketing significance fully recognized, packaging is a major factor in gaining distribution and customers. For instance, with shelf space at a premium, it's not easy for manufacturers to get their products displayed in retail outlets. If other marketing-mix elements are comparable, retailers are likely to purchase and display products having attractive, functional packaging. Therefore, full responsibility and authority for packaging should reside in a firm's marketing department.[42]

Packaging that works in the U.S. may not be successful in other parts of the world, notably Europe. In general, European consumers are accustomed to a more sophisticated package design than Americans. Compared to packages in the U.S., colors are more subtle and illustrations are more common on packages in Europe.

Packaging Strategies

When managing the packaging of a product, executives must make the following strategic decisions.

http://www.campbellsoups.com/

Packaging the Product Line. A company must decide whether to develop a family resemblance when packaging related products. **Family packaging** uses either highly similar packages for all products *or* packages with a common and clearly noticeable feature. Campbell Soup, for instance, uses virtually identical packaging on all its condensed soup products. When new products are added to a line, recognition and images associated with established products extend to the new ones. Family packaging makes sense when the products are of similar quality and have a similar use.

Multiple Packaging. For many years there has been a trend toward **multiple packaging**, the practice of placing several units of the same product in one container. Dehydrated soups, motor oil, beer, golf balls, building hardware, candy bars, towels, and countless other products are packaged in multiple units. Test after test has proved that multiple packaging increases total sales of a product.[43]

Changing the Package. When detected, a company needs to correct a poor feature in an existing package, of course. Unless a problem was spotted, firms stayed with a package design for almost 10 years. Now, for competitive reasons, packaging strategies and tactics are reviewed annually along with the rest of the marketing mix.[44]

Firms need to monitor—and consider—continuing developments, such as new packaging materials, uncommon shapes, innovative closures, and other new features (measured portions, metered flow). All are intended to provide benefits to middlemen and/or consumers and, as a result, are selling points for marketers.

A marketer may want to take advantage of new materials such as the aseptic container, made of laminations of paper, aluminum foil, and plastic. This airtight container, which keeps perishables fresh for 5 months without refrigeration, costs about one-half as much as cans and one-third as much as bottles. Already used for drink products, future applications of aseptic containers seem boundless.

To increase sales volume, many companies find it costs much less to redesign a package than to conduct an expensive advertising campaign. Snyder of Berlin, a company located in Pennsylvania, boosted sales of its brand of potato chips by 20 percent simply by adding an attention-grabbing hologram to the package.[45] And the Mariana Packing Co. in San José experienced a similar sales gain after it redesigned the bags containing its dried fruit products.[46]

Redesign of packaging is neither easy nor inexpensive, however. This task can cost from $20,000 for a simple, single product to $250,000 for a project that entails a product line and requires consumer research and testing. And these figures do not include the expense of promoting the new package design.[47]

*T*he American Plastics Council, the sponsor of this ad, promotes the use of plastics over other materials. The APC seeks an advantage for its product by describing how containers made of plastic address various criticisms of packaging. This ad deals, in particular, with the criticism that packaging depletes natural resources.

It's true. In the last 20 years, empty milk jugs have lost a lot of weight. In fact, plastics are helping lots of products and packaging slim

product with less packaging. • Even the plastic grocery bag uses 70 percent less plastic than it did in 1976. Big deal? You bet. Now it would

Would You Believe The Jug On The Right Is 45% Lighter?

down. That means using less energy and fewer raw materials to make them. Best of all, the milk jug on the right still holds the same amount of milk, delivering such benefits as shatter-resistance, a tamper-evident seal, a resealable cap and a convenient handle. • Soft drink bottles are slimmer too. That allows trucks to deliver more

take five trucks to deliver as many paper sacks as one truckload of plastic bags. Which also saves fuel. • To learn more, call the American Plastics Council at 1.800.777.9500 for a free booklet. • You'll find that, for a lightweight, the benefits of plastics are still pretty heavy.

American Plastics Council

PLASTICS MAKE IT POSSIBLE.
Visit us at http://www.plasticsresource.com

AN ETHICAL DILEMMA?

Facing rising costs of materials and ingredients, many manufacturers feel the need to increase prices. However, they fear consumer resistance. What can they do? Some producers turn to downsizing—reducing the amount of product in a package while maintaining the price.

For instance, several years ago, Kimberly-Clark shrank the number of disposable diapers in its packages by 10 percent but reduced the wholesale price only 7 percent. Kal Kan simply downsized a can of Pedigree Choice Cuts dog food from 14 to 13.25 ounces. The net result in both cases was a price increase that some consumers probably didn't notice.

Candy companies often adjust sizes based on the costs of ingredients, such as cocoa beans and sugar. Of course, downsizing is done quietly, but any increase in amount without a corresponding boost in price is promoted heavily.

Is downsizing ethical? Does your opinion depend on whether or not the company informs consumers about the reduced contents of the package?

Sources: Bernice Kanner, "Pinched Packages: Downsizing Comes to the Pantry," *St. Louis Post-Dispatch*, Mar. 26, 1995, p. E1; and John B. Hinge, "Critics Call Cuts in Package Size Deceptive Move," *The Wall Street Journal*, Feb. 5, 1991, p. B1.

Criticisms of Packaging

Packaging is in the public eye today, largely because of environmental issues. Specific concerns are:

- *Packaging is deceptive.* A common problem is that the package size conveys the impression of containing more than the actual contents. Government regulations plus greater integrity on the part of business firms regarding packaging have alleviated this concern to some extent.
- *Packaging is too expensive.* Even in seemingly simple packaging, such as for soft drinks, as much as one-half the production cost is for the container. Still, effective packaging reduces transportation costs and spoilage losses.
- *Packaging depletes natural resources.* This problem is magnified by firms that prefer larger-than-necessary containers. This criticism has been partially addressed through the use of recycled materials in packaging. A point in favor of packaging is that it minimizes spoilage, thereby reducing a different type of resource waste.
- *Some forms of plastic packaging and aerosol cans are health hazards.* Government regulations banned several suspect packaging materials, notably chlorofluorocarbons used as aerosol propellants. Just as important, a growing number of companies are switching from aerosol to pump dispensers.
- *Used and discarded packaging compounds the solid-waste problem.* Consumers' desire for convenience in the form of throwaway containers conflicts with their stated desire for a clean environment. This problem can be eased by using biodegradable materials in packaging.

Marketing executives are challenged to address these criticisms. At the same time, they must retain or even enhance the positive features of packaging, such as product protection, consumer convenience, and marketing support.

Labeling

Labeling, which is closely related to packaging, is another product feature that requires managerial attention. A **label** is the part of a product that carries information about the product and the seller. A label may be part of a package, or it may be a tag attached to the product. Obviously there is a close relationship among labeling, packaging, and branding.

Types of Labels
Labels fall into three primary kinds:

- A **brand label** is simply the brand alone applied to the product or package. Some oranges are stamped Sunkist or Blue Goose, and some clothes carry the brand label Sanforized.
- A **descriptive label** gives objective information about the product's use, construction, care, performance, and/or other pertinent features. On a descriptive label for a can of corn, there will be statements concerning the type of corn (golden sweet), style (creamed or in niblet kernels), can size, number of servings, other ingredients, and nutritional contents.
- A **grade label** identifies the product's judged quality with a letter, number, or word. Canned peaches are grade-labeled A, B, and C, and corn and wheat are grade-labeled 1 and 2.

Brand labeling is an acceptable form of labeling, but it does not supply sufficient information to a buyer. Descriptive labels provide more product information but not necessarily all that is needed or desired by a consumer in making a purchase decision.

Statutory Labeling Requirements
Labeling has received its share of criticism. Consumers have charged, for example, that labels contained incomplete or misleading information and there were a confusing number of sizes and shapes of packages for a given product. The public's complaints about false or deceptive labeling and packaging have led to a number of federal labeling laws.

The Food and Drug Act (1906) and its amendment, the Food, Drug, and Cosmetic Act (1938), provide explicit regulations for labeling drugs, foods, cosmetics, and therapeutic devices. Particularly noteworthy is the Fair Packaging and Labeling Act (1966). This law provides for (1) *mandatory* labeling requirements; (2) an opportunity for business to *voluntarily* adopt packaging standards that can limit the proliferation of the same product in different weights and measures; and (3) administrative agencies, notably the Food and Drug Administration and the Federal Trade Commission, with the *discretionary* power to set packaging regulations.

More recently, the Nutrition Labeling and Education Act (NLEA), which was passed in 1990 and enacted in 1994, established a set of **nutrition labeling** standards for processed foods.[48] The intent of this law is to ensure full disclosure of foods' nutritional contents. Labels must clearly state the amount of calories, fat, cholesterol, sodium, carbohydrates, and protein contained in the package's contents. In addition, the amounts must be stated as a percentage of a daily intake of 2,000 calories. Vitamin and mineral content also must be expressed as a percentage of the recommended daily allowance.

Under the NLEA, the Food and Drug Administration has issued standard definitions for key terms used in labeling, such as *light*, *lean*, and *good source*. To be labeled *light*, for example, a brand ordinarily has to contain one-half the fat or one-third fewer calories than standard products in this category. The NLEA allows firms to include on labels some health claims, such as fiber's value in preventing heart disease. And companies are permitted to list on labels endorsements of their products from health organizations such as the American Heart Association.

The nutrition-labeling changes mandated by the NLEA apply to about 200,000 packaged foods, including meat and poultry products. Obviously, these changes represented an enormous one-time expense to food manufacturers, with estimates ranging from $2 billion to $6 billion. Nevertheless, supporters argue that the new labeling requirements promote improved nutrition, thereby reducing health care costs. Of course, these savings will occur only if consumers read the labels and use the information in choosing foods.[49]

Finally, a 1992 amendment to the Fair Packaging and Labeling Act mandates metric labeling for selected products. Taking effect in 1994, this law requires that metric weights and measures be shown on labels along with traditional American weights and measures, such as inches, pounds, and pints. Rather than replacing the American system, as many companies feared, the metric information is supplementary.[50]

Other Want-Satisfying Features

A well-rounded program for product planning and development will include strategies and policies on several additional product attributes. Design, color, and quality are covered in this chapter. Two additional features, warranties and postsale service, are covered in Chapter 21 because they closely relate to the implementation of a company's marketing program.

Design and Color

One way to satisfy customers and gain a differential advantage is through **product design**, which refers to the arrangement of elements that collectively form a good or service. Good design can improve the marketability of a product by making it easier to operate, upgrading its quality, improving its appearance, and/or reducing manufacturing costs.

In fact, a distinctive design may be the only feature that significantly differentiates a product. Consider, as examples, two products marketed by Black & Decker Corp. One is a cordless drill/driver sold under the DeWalt brand, which was mentioned in the case related to Chapter 7. The product's design features a cushioned pistol grip, relatively light weight, and a powerful motor. The success of this drill/driver helped B&D reclaim its position of leadership in the market for professional power tools. In the consumer market, clever design is the main reason why B&D's SnakeLight has been such a sensational triumph. This product has a flexible body, allowing it to be wrapped around another object. As a result, the user has both hands free to perform the desired task. The SnakeLight's price is several times that of a traditional flashlight, which shows how creative design also can help a company improve its profit margins.[51]

For most consumer and business goods, ranging from furniture to electronic equipment, design has long been recognized as important. According to estimates, design accounts for only 2 percent of the total cost of producing and marketing a product. As a result, a design that's a hit with consumers can produce a giant return on investment for a firm.[52]

Today design is receiving even greater attention. According to an IBM executive, design has become "a strategic marketing tool." As evidence of this point, the results of one survey indicated that design budgets grew by at least 15 percent annually during the early 1990s.[53]

A growing number of firms have turned to low prices as a competitive tool. In turn, designers have been asked to rework some of their companies' products and lower the costs of making them as one way of maintaining profit margins.

Also, companies are being called upon to design products that are easily used by *all* consumers, including disabled individuals, the burgeoning number of senior citizens, and others needing special considerations. This approach is termed **universal design**. As one example, the Kohler Co. designed a bathtub with a door, eliminating the danger of having to climb into the tub. And home builders are featuring wider halls and doors in some models, in order to accommodate wheelchairs. Occasionally, products designed for the disabled or seniors are more appealing to other consumers than traditional designs. AT&T's Big Buttons telephone, for example, is a hit not just with the visually impaired but also with consumers who have small children and with those who like its playful styling.[54]

http://www.att.com/

Like design, **product color** often is the determining factor in a customer's acceptance or rejection of a product, whether it is a dress, a table, or an automobile. In fact, color is so important that the U.S. Supreme Court confirmed in early 1995 that the color of a product or its packaging can be registered as part of a trademark under the Lanham Act. Color by itself can qualify for trademark status when, according to the Court's ruling, it "identifies and distinguishes a particular brand, and thus indicates its source." The case under review involved greenish-gold dry-cleaning press pads manufactured by the Qualitex Company. Other distinctive colors that help to identify specific brands are Owens-Corning's pink insulation and Kodak's gold color-film boxes.[55]

As with other marketing-mix elements, a differential advantage might be gained by identifying the most pleasing color and in knowing when to change colors. In the mid-1990s, Ford Motor Co. calculated that green was *the* color for its Explorer model. Four of fifteen color choices for the 1996 Explorer were shades of green. Conversely, if a garment manufacturer or the person responsible for purchasing merchandise for a retail store guesses wrong on what will be the fashionable color in women's clothing, disaster may ensue.

http://www.ford.com/

Color can be extremely important for packaging as well as for the product itself. Color specialists say it's no coincidence that Nabisco, Marlboro, Coca-Cola, Campbell, and Budweiser are all top-selling brands. In each case, red is the primary color of their packaging or logo. Red may be appealing because it "evokes feelings of warmth, passion and sensuality." However, according to one color researcher, blue has overtaken red as the favorite color of American shoppers. Consider Pillsbury's and Snapple's blue logos, for instance.[56]

In the early 1990s, some firms in crowded industries sought an edge by eliminating color in their products. Pepsi introduced colorless Crystal Pepsi, trying to position it as healthier than caramel-colored colas; Coca-Cola countered with Tab Clear. In other categories, companies also brought out clear products, such as Palmolive Sensitive Skin liquid dishwashing detergent and Warner-Lambert's new version of Caladryl calamine lotion for treating poison ivy. Transparent products are intended to be associated with more favorable attributes such as "pure" and "mild." Of course, they may be perceived as little more than water. The popularity of such clear products has plummeted. The publisher of *New Product News* gave the verdict, "Clear is dead."[57]

Product Quality

There's no agreement on a definition of product quality, even though it is universally recognized as significant. One professional society defines **product quality** as the set of features and characteristics of a good or service that determine its ability to satisfy needs.[58] Despite what appears to be a straightforward definition, consumers frequently disagree on what constitutes quality in a product—whether it be a cut of meat or a performance by a rock musician. Personal tastes are deeply involved; what you like, another person may dislike. It is important to recognize, therefore, that quality—like beauty—is to a large extent "in the eyes of the beholder."

Besides personal tastes, individual expectations also affect judgments of quality. That is, a consumer brings certain expectations to a purchase situation. Sometimes you have high expectations, as with a movie about which you read rave reviews. Other times you have modest expectations, as with a course for next semester that is referred to as "not too boring." Your evaluation of a product's quality depends on whether the actual experience with the good or service exceeds, meets, or falls short of your expectations.

For some companies, *optimal* quality means that the product provides the consumer with an experience that meets, but does not exceed, expectations. The rationale is that there's no sense in incurring added costs to provide what amounts to *excessive* quality. Some firms that adopt this viewpoint supplement adequate product quality with superior customer service. According to one survey of personal-computer users, this approach can be effective in generating repeat customers.[59] Other businesses, however, strive to exceed consumers' expectations in order to produce high levels of customer satisfaction and, in turn, brand loyalty.

Since the mid-1980s, U.S. industry has paid more and more attention to product quality.[60] Frankly, there was substantial room for improved product quality in many fields. For instance, German and Japanese automakers were beating their

*A*ccording to a long-running advertising campaign, "Quality Is Job 1" at Ford Motor Company. In this particular ad, Ford stresses its safety features as a key aspect of quality. To help create a favorable impression, Ford compares its efforts to the caring nature of mothers. Other ads in this campaign have featured different aspects of quality, such as environmental protection.

http://www.ford.com/

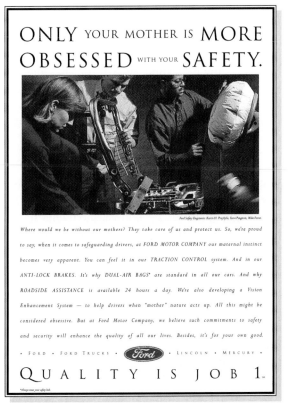

American competitors by turning out better performing, more reliable cars. Considering all goods, not just automobiles, American-made products rank third behind Japanese and German products with respect to consumer judgments of quality. After the U.S., there's a big drop to the next level of quality—which includes products from Great Britain, France, Canada, and Italy. According to this Bozell-Gallup study that focused on goods manufactured in 12 major exporting countries, products from Spain, China, Taiwan, Mexico, and finally Russia lag in terms of quality.[61] Product quality should be a primary consideration not only for manufacturers of goods but also for producers of services, as will be discussed in Chapter 19.

Because it is not easily duplicated, many organizations seek to build product quality to gain a differential *advantage*. In one survey of managers, quality was the most mentioned basis for a strong differential advantage.[62] At the least, an enterprise certainly needs to avoid a differential disadvantage related to product quality.

To seize an advantage or avert a disadvantage, a growing number of businesses, government agencies, and nonprofit entities have implemented **total quality management** (TQM) programs. TQM entails not just specific procedures, policies, and practices, but a philosophy that commits the organization to continuous quality improvement in all of its activities.

Another noteworthy quality-related development is called ISO 9000 (pronounced ICE-o nine thousand). **ISO 9000** is a set of related standards of quality management that have been adopted by about 60 countries, including the U.S. Companies that conform to ISO 9000 standards are awarded a certificate, which often puts them in a favorable position with large customers. Some critics say that the standards place too much emphasis on documenting what a producer is doing and pay too little attention to whether what's being done results in satisfactory products. As one skeptic observed, "You can certify a manufacturer that makes life jackets from concrete, as long as those jackets are made according to the documented procedures." Despite such criticism, many huge firms, such as Xerox, Philips Electronics, and Eastman Kodak, are requiring their key suppliers to earn ISO 9000 certification. Worldwide, tens of thousands of companies have earned ISO 9000 certification, with only a small fraction of them based in the U.S.[63]

■ SUMMARY

Effective product management involves developing and then monitoring the various features of a product—its brand, package, labeling, design, quality, warranty, and postsale service. A consumer's purchase decision may take into account not just the basic good or service but also the brand and perhaps one or more of the other want-satisfying product features.

A brand is a means of identifying and differentiating the products of an organization. Branding aids sellers in managing their promotional and pricing activities. The dual responsibilities of brand ownership are to promote the brand and to maintain a consistent level of quality. Selecting a good brand name—and there are relatively few really good ones—is difficult. Once a brand becomes well known, the owner may have to protect it from product counterfeiting and from becoming a generic term.

Manufacturers must decide whether to brand their products and/or sell under a middleman's brand. Middlemen must decide whether to carry producers' brands alone or to establish their own brands as well. In addition, middlemen must decide whether to carry generic products. Both producers and middlemen must set policies regarding branding groups of products and branding for market saturation.

A growing number of companies are recognizing that the brands they own are—or can be—among their most valuable assets. They are building brand equity—the added value that a brand brings to a product. Although it's difficult to build brand equity, doing so successfully can be the basis for expanding a product mix. Products with abundant brand equity also lend themselves to trademark licensing, a marketing arrangement that is growing in popularity.

Packaging is becoming increasingly important as sellers recognize the problems, as well as the marketing opportunities, associated with it. Companies must choose among strategies such as family packaging, multiple packaging, and changing the package. Labeling, a related activity, provides informa-

tion about the product and the seller. Many consumer criticisms of marketing target packaging and labeling. As a result, there are several federal laws regulating these activities.

Companies are now recognizing the marketing value of both product design and quality. Good design can improve the marketability of a product; it may be the only feature that differentiates a product. Projecting the appropriate quality image and then delivering the level of quality desired by customers are essential to marketing success. In many cases, firms need to enhance product quality to eliminate a differential disadvantage; in others, firms seek to build quality as a way of gaining a differential advantage.

More about LEVI'S

*L*evi Strauss's continuing move into foreign markets has been hugely successful. One odd indicator is the flood of counterfeit Levi's—something about "imitation is the sincerest form of flattery." A more meaningful indicator is that each year foreign markets account for a larger share of total LS sales. Likewise, LS is attracting more female customers. Over a 4-year period, sales of Levi's women's jeans increased by 400 percent. The Levi's brand is now challenging Lee for the top spot in the women's jeans market in the U.S.

For the past 10 years, LS has been working to duplicate its Levi's triumph with another brand of clothing, Dockers. The development of this line of cotton twill pants and related casual wear illustrates the company's global orientation. The name was borrowed from Levi's subsidiary in Argentina and applied to loose-fitting pants designed by its subsidiary in Japan. Positioned as distinct products, Levi's and Dockers are not supposed to compete with each other.

The Dockers line certainly has benefited from—and perhaps contributed to—the trend toward casual dress in formerly "white-collar" business settings. According to a 1994 survey, 90 percent of U.S. employees wear casual clothing to work at least occasionally. Such findings explain why an LS marketing specialist stated, "We don't even see it as a

trend anymore. We think it's a shift that's already taken place and will continue."

Besides advertising its merchandise to consumers, LS has been promoting casual work clothing in two added ways. It has distributed a newsletter to companies' human resource managers describing the rationale for casual dress in the workplace. Among other things, the newsletter presented casual wear as a no-cost benefit firms could provide to their employees. LS then provides interested companies with a kit that explains the nature of casual work clothing and offers guidelines on developing a reasonable dress policy.

In order to showcase the depth and breadth of assortment in its Dockers and Levi's brands, LS is establishing its own retail outlets. Around 200 stores will be opened in the U.S. over a 5-year period. (The company already operates almost 1,000 outlets in other countries.) Some of the stores will concentrate on Dockers' various lines, others will focus strictly on Levi's, and still others will clear out slow-moving or outdated merchandise at discounted prices.

As with Levi's jeans, LS is intent on extending the reach of the Dockers brand. The company almost waited too long to launch a line of wrinkle-resistant cotton twill pants. After falling far behind Farah and Haggar in this type of product, Levi Strauss finally entered the fray in late 1993. More recent additions include a Dockers Golf line and Dockers Authentics, a line of highly stylish casual wear aimed at male members of Generation X (that is, men in their twenties). Although the bulk of Dockers' $1 billion in annual sales comes from the U.S., international expansion is a priority for Dockers—just as with Levi's.[64]

1. How well do the Levi's and Dockers brands satisfy the criteria for a good brand name?
2. Do you agree with Levi Strauss's strategy of keeping the Dockers brand separate from the Levi's brand?

■ KEY TERMS AND CONCEPTS

Brand (242)
Brand name (242)
Brand mark (242)
Trademark (242)
Producer's brand (242)
Middleman's brand (242)
Product
  counterfeiting (246)

Generic products (250)
Family branding (250)
Multiple-brand
  strategy (251)
Brand equity (252)
Trademark licensing (253)
Packaging (254)
Family packaging (255)

Multiple packaging (256)
Label (257)
Brand label (258)
Descriptive label (258)
Grade label (258)
Nutrition labeling (258)
Product design (259)
Universal design (260)

Product color (260)
Product quality (260)
Total quality
  management (261)
ISO 9000 (261)

■ QUESTIONS AND PROBLEMS

1. Evaluate each of the following brand names in light of the characteristics of a good brand, indicating the strong and weak points of each name.
   a. Catviar (cat food)
   b. Kodak (cameras)
   c. Metropolitan (insurance)
   d. Hush Puppies (shoes)
   e. Federal Express (delivery service)
   f. Whirlpool (appliances)
2. Identify one brand that is on the verge of becoming generic.
   a. Why should a company protect the separate identity of its brand?
   b. What course of action should a company take to do so?
3. In which of the following cases should the company use its name as part of the product's brand name?
   a. A manufacturer of men's underwear introduces women's underwear.
   b. A manufacturer of hair-care products introduces a line of portable electric hair dryers.
   c. A chain of luxury hotels adds a chain of medium-price, all-suite hotels and another chain of lower-price, no-frills hotels.
4. A manufacturer of snow skis sold under a brand that has built up substantial equity acquires a company that markets ski boots carrying a brand that enjoys about the same amount of equity. What branding strategy should the acquiring organization adopt? Should all products

(skis and boots) now carry the ski brand? The boot brand? Is there some other alternative that you think would be better?
5. Why do some firms sell an identical product under more than one of their own brands?
6. Assume that a large department store chain proposed to the manufacturers of Maytag washing machines that Maytag supply the department store with machines carrying the store's brand. What factors should Maytag's management consider in making a decision? If the situation instead involved a supermarket chain and General Foods' Jell-O, to what extent should different factors be considered?
7. An American manufacturer plans to introduce its line of camping equipment (stoves, lanterns, ice chests) in several European Union countries. Should management select the same brand for all countries or use a different brand in each country? What factors should influence the decision? How should brand equity enter into the decision?
8. What changes would you recommend in the packaging of these products?
   a. Coke Classic
   b. Vidal Sassoon hair shampoo and conditioning rinse
   c. Potato chips
   d. Toothpaste
9. Give examples of products for which the careful use of color has increased sales. Can you cite examples to show that poor use of color may hurt a product's salability?

■ HANDS-ON MARKETING

1. Visit a large local supermarket and:
    a. Obtain the store manager's opinions regarding which products are excellently packaged and which are poorly packaged. Ask the manager for reasons.
    b. Walk around the store and compile your own list of excellent and poor packages. What factors did you use to judge quality of packaging?

2. Ask five students who are not taking this course to evaluate the following names for a proposed expensive perfume: Entice, Nitespark, At Risk, and Foreglow. For evaluation purposes, share with the students the characteristics of a good brand name. Also ask them to suggest a better name for the new perfume.

CASES FOR PART 3

DEVELOPING A PRODUCT MIX FOR A GROWING MARKET

Not all food products are created equal. For over 40 years, Estee has been the leading manufacturer of food products for people on medically restricted diets. Estee operates a 160,000-square-foot plant, and research and development laboratory in Parsippany, New Jersey. The company's success is due to a carefully designed, distinctive product-mix strategy that satisfies the needs of people with diabetes and other health conditions.

The market for medically related food products, also known as nutraceuticals, has grown at a phenomenal rate in recent years. Sales of reduced-sugar and reduced-sodium foods stood at $10 billion in 1990, and could be as high as $27 billion by the year 2000. The surge is projected to continue well into the twenty-first century as the U.S. population ages. The average life span of an American today is about 77 years. It is estimated that children born in the year 2000 will live an average of 92 to 96 years. When people reach the age of 50, more medical conditions, such as diabetes, cancer, and osteoporosis, occur. Estee is in a strong position to take advantage of these demographic changes.

According to Estee president Steve Silk, the mission of the company is to "... become the trusted nutritional friend of people over the age of 50. To narrow it a little, [our goal] is to provide superior tasting nutritionally correct foods for people on medically directed diets."

Two important aspects of Estee's product management are the development of new products and the elimination or repositioning of existing products that are not meeting company goals. Two-thirds of the company's sales are products such as sugarless cookies, wafers, and candies. Salad dressings, jams, and gelatin desserts comprise the other one-third of sales.

Estee has built its product-mix strategy around five factors: taste, packaging, marketing, affiliation with the American Diabetes Association (ADA), and the use of technology to develop new products.

Taste

The key element in the success of any food product is taste. Estee's products need to taste good without the benefit of sugar. The evolution of artificial sweeteners has helped the company improve the taste of its products. For example, Estee put NutraSweet in its candies soon after the U.S. Food and Drug Administration approved the artificial sweetener for use in food products. In addition, the company's research and development department improved the taste of its sugar-free cookies by altering the length of time they are baked.

Packaging

Estee's food products were packaged in the same way for over 20 years. The Nutritional Labeling and Education Act of 1990 forced the company to update the packaging and the nutritional claims made on its labels. The packaging change has helped the company present a more appealing image for its products and convey important product information to the target market.

Marketing

In 1990, the Estee Corporation brought in new talent to improve the effectiveness of its marketing efforts. One of the first moves was to shift from trying to be all things to all people to focusing on the company's core customers—diabetics. There are approximately 14 million diabetics in the U.S., and the number is growing at a rate of 10 percent per year.

In its quest to target—and satisfy—diabetics, Estee launched *Health*, a newsletter targeted toward people with diabetes. It provides information on such topics as labeling laws, new Estee products, and the American Diabetes Association. *Health* contains coupons to stimulate trial purchase of Estee products.

The newsletter also lists a toll-free 800 number to facilitate communication with the company.

Telephone calls to the company increased from under 100 to more than 2,300 per week after the first mailing of *Health*. Calls peaked eventually at 10,000 weekly. The enormous number of calls to the 800 number produced two particularly positive outcomes:

- Estee found that most diabetics are over 65 and have difficulty getting to the store. To better serve this target market, the firm initiated a mail-order business.
- The company used letters it received from customers to convince retailers that there was sufficient demand to justify stocking more of Estee's products.

Another component of Estee's marketing effort was the implementation of a category-management plan in the early 1990s. Sales data collected from individual retail stores were used to identify specific products that were either out of stock frequently or not selling. These data allowed the company to develop a three-tier system to define its product mix. Tier 1 consisted of the 67 top-selling items as determined by sales, profitability, and a balanced inventory of nutritional needs of customers. Tier 2 products contributed to sales volume, but were not considered high-priority items. Last, Tier 3 contained products that were not providing retailers with adequate profit margins.

Once all of the products in Estee's product mix were assigned to one of the three tiers, the company's sales force worked on increasing shelf displays for Tier 1 products. At the same time, the sales force reduced exposure for Tier 3 products, and in some cases pulled them off the shelf. Estee's product management plan resulted in the discontinuation of more than 100 items between 1993 and 1994, which left fewer than 100 different products in its mix. Furthermore, sales of Estee products increased 150 percent because of the more effective distribution and displays that resulted from the category-management plan.

American Diabetes Association

Estee entered into an exclusive alliance with the ADA in 1992. All of Estee's packages feature the ADA logo. Using pamphlets and videos, the company and the ADA work together to educate diabetics. Estee also sponsors ADA fundraising events, such as the Juvenile Diabetes Foundation Walk for the Cure.

Technology

Technology now allows some food products to be made that were not possible previously. A few examples follow:

- Using a food-formulation process it developed, Estee is the only manufacturer of a triple-flavor, triple-layer wafer.
- Esteem Calcium-Rich Drink Crystals was introduced in 1994 after Estee developed the technology that allowed a clean-tasting, highly soluble, fully utilizable calcium source to be put into food products. The company's first

nondiabetic product was developed to meet the needs of people who have osteoporosis, which is a softening of the bones that particularly afflicts older women. It is the twelfth leading cause of death in the U.S.
- Estee patented a technology in 1994 that provides for a gradual release of carbohydrates from food once it is ingested. The technology enabled Estee to reformulate some of its products, allowing diabetics better control of their blood sugar levels. In addition, the technology is being investigated for possible use in weight-control products.

Estee expects its sales to grow at a rate of 10 to 15 percent per year for the next 5 years. If the predicted growth occurs, sales will more than double to $100 million by the year 2000. New markets should fuel added growth. For example, Estee is beginning to explore the development of products for health-conscious eaters and "cosmetic" dieters. The future looks bright for Estee so long as the company is able to adjust its product mix to meet the needs of its customers.

QUESTIONS

1. What product-mix strategy is Estee using?
2. How is Estee's product line positioned? What other positioning possibilities are there?
3. Describe how Estee should use the six-step process for developing new products to create and launch a snack product for diabetics.
4. Is it wise for Estee to put the American Diabetes Association logo on its product labels?

Sources: Paul Rogers, "Pushing the Envelope," *SnackFood*, July 1, 1995, p. 32; "What It Takes to Do CM Right," *Progressive Grocer*, December 1994, p. 11; Lisa A. Tibbitts, "Estee Sorts Items Using Store-by-Store Data," *Supermarket News*, July 25, 1994, p. 6A; Gerry Khermouch, "Overseas Players Juice Move into Bottling Health," *BrandWeek*, Feb. 21, 1994, p. 16; and David Kiley, "Estee Takes a Wake-up Call," *Adweek*, Mar. 9, 1992, p. 24.

CASE 2   *Gatorade versus the Upstarts*

OUTRUNNING THE COMPETITION IN A MATURING MARKET

Few brands have come to define a product category to the extent that Gatorade does. The sports drink market was born in 1967 when a special beverage was developed for the University of Florida's football team, nicknamed the Gators. The drink was formulated to replace fluids in the body faster than water does. The intent was to give the Gators more late-game energy than the competition had. People began referring to the beverage as Gator-Aid.

Hence, when the decision was made to commercialize the drink, Gatorade was the logical choice for the brand name.

A Runaway Success Attracts Competition

By the time the Quaker Oats Co. acquired Gatorade in 1983, its annual sales volume had grown to $97 million. With the marketing muscle of Quaker, sales of Gatorade grew 20 percent per year for about 10 years. By 1994, sales had climbed to $1.2 billion. The brand enjoys around an 80 percent market share in a product category that has been growing at 6 to 10 percent per year.

Now Gatorade is distributed in 27 countries. Quaker's goal is to achieve $1 billion in overseas sales by the year 2000. To do so, the product will be marketed in more countries, especially in Latin America and Asia.

Gatorade's dominance in the fastest-growing product category of the beverage industry was bound to attract attention from potential competitors. Twenty new thirst-quenching products were introduced in 1992 alone, and nearly 50 competitors crowd the market. Every major soft drink manufacturer has introduced a brand that goes head-to-head with Gatorade. In addition, various supermarket chains have their own brands of thirst-quenching drinks. A sample of the competing offerings includes Shasta Cola's Body Works, A&W Brands' Everlast, Royal Crown's Enduro, and Dr. Pepper/Seven Up Company's Nautilus.

Being a new brand in a fast-growing market does not guarantee success, however. Effective product position is one of many prerequisites for success. Cool Down, a drink targeting upper-income women who exercise, failed because there was insufficient market potential in this particular niche. Even Quaker's own Freestyle, a fruity drink that targeted moderate exercisers among women, flopped.

The Giants Enter the Field

Two brands, Coca-Cola's PowerAde and PepsiCo's All Sport, are making the marketers of Gatorade sweat. Both brands were launched nationally in 1994 after 2 years in test markets.

PowerAde and All Sport were able to establish themselves despite being outspent three to one by Gatorade. Between 1993 and 1994, PowerAde doubled its market share to 10 percent, and All Sport more than tripled its share to over 5 percent. At the same time, Gatorade lost over 7 percentage points of market share. PowerAde and All Sport claim to have achieved as much as 20 percent market share in some geographic markets where all three brands are available.

Gatorade is positioned as the thirst-quenching drink that promotes rapid fluid absorption by the body. Its target market consists of serious athletes, typically young adult males and those who emulate them. By concentrating on this target market, Gatorade may have trouble in the future as the baby-boomer generation ages and probably reduces the frequency and vigor of its exercise. The marketers of Gatorade believe the product's customers will remain loyal as they age.

Mixing a Formula for Continued Growth

Gatorade's efforts to beat back the upstarts involve every element of the marketing mix:

Product.   All sports drinks are designed to replenish the fluids, minerals, and carbohydrates the body loses during exercise. These beverages contain electrolytes, such as potassium or sodium, and also may contain sweeteners. Gatorade is available in eight flavors and contains 110 milligrams of sodium per 8-ounce serving. Sodium causes the user to drink more and, thus, to rehydrate the body faster than water or other beverages.

Both All Sport and PowerAde consider taste to be the primary attribute that consumers use to select a sports drink. All Sport is available in four flavors and is carbonated to make it more drinkable. Targeting women as well as men, it has a sweeter taste than Gatorade. PowerAde distinguishes itself from Gatorade by having 33 percent more carbohydrates for added energy. It too comes in four flavors and has a sweeter taste than Gatorade. But, like Gatorade, it is aimed primarily at male athletes.

All three brands are available in both single-serving and large (32-ounce) plastic containers. Single-serving packages have a pop-up cap that allows the user to take a drink and then reseal the container. In addition, All Sport and PowerAde were launched with single-serving cans.

Pricing.   Besides the obvious appeal of a growing market, Pepsi and Coca-Cola were attracted to this product category because sports drinks are cheaper to make and command a higher price than soft drinks. Therefore, pricing plays a major role in Gatorade's attempt to maintain its position as the leading sports drink. The price of Gatorade has been discounted in markets where PowerAde and All Sport are marketed.

Price promotions are used frequently by the upstarts as well. In their efforts to gain a foothold, Coca-Cola and Pepsi offered retailers up to 50 percent discounts on cases of their respective brands of sports drinks.

Distribution.   In 1992 Quaker talked with Coca-Cola about using the giant company's distribution network. The negotiations fell through and Coca-Cola proceeded with the development of PowerAde. Now PowerAde and All Sport have a substantial advantage over Gatorade with respect to the brands' scope of distribution. Pepsi has about 1 million "sales points" (places where its products can be purchased) in its daily contact with 250,000 retailers. Coca-Cola has about 1.5 million sales points, 1 million of which are vending machines. Quaker lags well behind with only 200,000 sales points.

Quaker relies heavily on wholesalers, rather than on retailers, to help market Gatorade. All Sport and PowerAde are distributed through Pepsi's and Coca-Cola's bottling networks, respectively. These networks provide the two competing brands with the potential to be more broadly distributed than Gatorade. Ironically, Gatorade is distributed through Pepsi's distribution network in foreign countries, although Pepsi is a competitor in the U.S.

One-third of all sports drink sales are made in supermarkets, with the other two-thirds coming from convenience stores, vending machines, and fountain dispensers. Coca-Cola and Pepsi have a distinct advantage in fountain sales. The focus of Gatorade's current distribution plan is to expand its networks of convenience stores and vending machines. All three competitors see health clubs, workplaces, schools, and restaurants as potential distribution locations.

Promotion. Sponsorship of sporting events is the backbone of all three competitors' promotional strategies. Gatorade is the official sponsor of the National Football League's Punt, Pass, and Kick competition for 8-to-15-year-olds as well as the National Basketball Association's Hoop It Up three-on-three tournament. PowerAde was the official sponsor of the 1994 World Cup Soccer Championship and the 1992 and 1996 Olympics. All Sport sponsors collegiate basketball events.

In the face of aggressive competition from Coca-Cola and Pepsi, Quaker has doubled its promotional budget for Gatorade to $50 million per year. In 1992 Gatorade signed Michael Jordan to be its spokesperson and launched its "Be Like Mike" campaign. The affiliation with Michael Jordan included sponsorship of USA Basketball during the 1992 Olympics. The campaign included a different likeness of Jordan on the label of each flavor of Gatorade. When Jordan retired (temporarily) from professional basketball, Gatorade switched the thrust of its advertising to emphasize product benefits.

Both competing firms followed suit by recruiting famous athletes as spokespeople. All Sport signed up Shaquille O'Neal from basketball's Orlando Magic and Ken Griffey, Jr., from baseball's Seattle Mariners. PowerAde secured the endorsements of Steve Young and Jerry Rice, both of the San Francisco 49ers football team.

The Competition Continues

At times, the competition among the three brands has grown testy. One such instance involved the protection of trade secrets. In 1994 Quaker management hired a Pepsi executive, Don Uzzi, to head the Gatorade division. When Quaker raided Pepsi a second time, recruiting William Redmond to manage Gatorade's field operations, Pepsi sued to protect its trade secrets. According to Pepsi, Redmond knew all about the strategic plan for All Sport. Pepsi

obtained a judgment prohibiting Redmond from being involved with any Gatorade planning for his first 6 months on the Quaker payroll.

Continued leadership of the sports drink market requires Gatorade to take the initiative rather than wait and then react to competitors' moves. Sustained growth depends on product innovations, not "me-too" products. Therefore, Gatorade must continue to focus on research and development to meet the ever-changing needs of the sports drink consumer.

Gatorade can prevail. After all, Gatorade defeated Coca-Cola and Pepsi at this same game once before. In 1985 Coca-Cola launched a sports drink called Max, only to withdraw it 2 years later when it failed to achieve sales objectives. Similarly, in 1990 Pepsi conducted an unsuccessful test market of Mountain Dew Sport.

QUESTIONS

1. What are the strengths and weaknesses of the Gatorade brand name?
2. What positioning strategy should Gatorade use to maintain its position of leadership in the sports drink market?
3. What changes in the product itself or its packaging would help Gatorade compete effectively against All Sport and PowerAde?

http://www.gatorade.com/

Sources: Patricia Sellers, "Can Coke and Pepsi Make Quaker Sweat?" *Fortune*, July 10, 1995, p. 20; "Beverage . . . By the Numbers," *BrandWeek*, Apr. 17, 1995, p. 48; Greg Burns and Maria Mallory, "Gatorade Is Starting to Pant," *Business Week*, Apr. 18, 1994, p. 98; Terry Lefton, "Big League Players Learn Grass Roots Can Be a Hit," *BrandWeek*, Dec. 13, 1993, p. 22; Marcy Magiera, "Gatorade Gains as Cola Giants Muscle In," *Advertising Age*, Nov. 8, 1993, p. 16; Richard Gibson, "Coca-Cola and PepsiCo Are Preparing to Give Gatorade a Run for Its Money," *The Wall Street Journal*, Sept. 29, 1992, p. B1; Jagannath Dubashi, "Quaker Oats: The Gatorade Effect Wears Off," *Financial World*, July 7, 1992, p. 12; "The Thirst of Champions," *Economist*, June 6, 1992, p. 83; and "Gatorade Is Cornerstone to Quaker's Growth," *Advertising Age*, May 18, 1992, p. 12.

PART FOUR

Price

The development of a pricing structure and its use as part of the marketing mix

We are in the process of developing a marketing mix to reach our target markets and achieve our marketing goals. Having completed product planning, we turn now to pricing, where we face two tasks. First, we must determine the base price for a product that is consistent with our pricing objectives; this endeavor is covered in Chapter 11. Second, we must decide on strategies (such as discounts and value pricing) to employ in modifying and applying the base price; these strategies are discussed in Chapter 12.

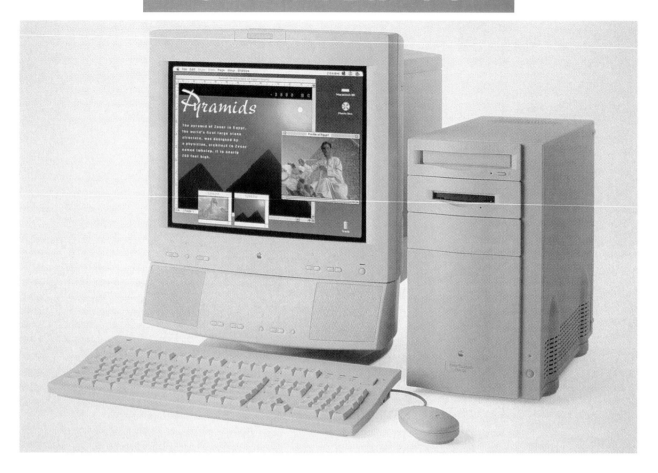

Price
Determination

Have Pricing Problems
Taken a Bite out of
APPLE?

For many years, Apple Computer Inc. followed a simple marketing formula: Offer technologically advanced, user-friendly personal computers, disdain price competition, and promote the products creatively, building an image as "the hippest box in the business." The formula worked very well, making Apple one of the 100 largest industrial firms in the U.S.

In recent years, however, consumers' attitudes and needs regarding personal computers (PCs) shifted, and the roster of competitors has grown stronger. Many observers have criticized Apple for not revising its marketing formula quickly enough. The company's approach to pricing has come under particular scrutiny.

Apple's share of the PC market started to erode in 1993, dropping from a high approaching 10 percent to less than 8 percent. A loss of 2 percentage points in a growing industry with over $100 *billion* in annual sales represents over $2 billion in lost revenues.

Apple's own decisions contributed to its apparent decay. For instance, it resisted price cuts in order to preserve profit margins. Unfortunately, that meant selling fewer machines. Furthermore, the firm's top executive at the time disdained licensing, which means allowing other manufacturers to produce "clones"—similar, but lower-price versions of selected Apple PCs. Apple's stance discouraged software firms from developing new programs that use the company's Macintosh operating system. Instead many shifted their efforts toward creating software for Windows, a competing—and hugely successful—operating system produced by Microsoft Corp. Not surprisingly, Apple's resistance to licensing has been labeled one of the greatest blunders of the PC era.

Michael Spindler, Apple's chief executive then, realized the company needed more market share to remain a serious contender. Thus a new marketing formula was devised: Present the market with two alternatives—the renowned Apple brand at competitive prices as well as "clones" at still lower prices. This approach was intended to draw added customers, especially in the burgeoning home market, as well as entice software firms to develop programs using the Macintosh operating system.

In 1994, Apple launched a new line of Power Macintosh PCs. In mid-1995, prices of the basic Power Macs were competitive with other brands, perhaps slightly less than IBM and Hewlett-Packard but still above Packard Bell and AST. Apple believes a reputation for high quality and the enduring appeal of its brand allow it to have higher prices than newer brands that emphasize low prices. In one interview, Spindler went so far as to call Packard Bell "an el cheapo packeteer."

The plan went awry, however, when Apple executives seriously underestimated demand. The company could not produce enough of the new product because of a shortage of essential components. Unable to produce a sufficient number of the Power Macs, the company realized it could not lower prices and further stimulate demand. As a result, Apple did not recapture market share even with a popular new-product line.

When Apple cannot fill an order, the damage is greater than it would be for another computer manufacturer. Power Macs contain microprocessors and an operating system that are unique to the Apple brand. Thus an unsatisfied consumer is forced to buy another brand, most of which contain "Wintel"—the Windows operating system from Microsoft and microprocessors from Intel. A consumer who switches and learns how to operate a different type of PC may be unwilling to return to an Apple product at a later date.[1]

What advice would you give Apple Computer Inc. regarding the pricing of its products?

http://www.apple.com/

"How much should we charge for our personal computers?" "How does price fit into our marketing mix?" Apple Computer Inc. faces these questions constantly. These kinds of questions are asked any time an organization introduces a new product or considers changing the price on an existing one.

In this chapter we cover the role of price in the marketing mix—what price is, how it can be used, and how it is set relative to such factors as product costs, market demand, and competitors' prices. After studying this chapter, you should be able to explain:

CHAPTER GOALS
- The meaning of price.
- The significance of price in our economy, in a consumer's mind, and to an individual firm.
- The concept of value and how it relates to price.
- Major pricing objectives.
- Key factors influencing price.
- The types of costs incurred in producing and marketing a product.
- Approaches to determining prices, including cost-plus pricing, marginal analysis, and setting prices in relation only to other prices in the market.
- Break-even analysis.

In this chapter we will discuss major methods used to determine a price. Before being concerned with actual price determination, however, executives—and you—should understand the meaning and importance of price.

Meaning of Price

Some pricing difficulties occur because of confusion about the meaning of *price*, even though the concept is easy to define in familiar terms. Simply, **price** is the amount of money and/or other items with utility needed to acquire a product. Recall that *utility* is an attribute with the potential to satisfy wants.

Thus price may involve more than money. To illustrate, the price of a rare Mickey Mantle baseball card may be (1) $500; (2) the rookie cards for 10 players, including Barry Bonds and Cal Ripken; or (3) some combination of dollars and baseball cards. Exchanging goods and/or services for other products is termed **barter**. Because our economy is not geared to a slow, ponderous barter system, we typically state price in monetary terms and use money as our medium of exchange.

Practical problems arise when we try to state simply the price of a product. Suppose you paid $325 for a desk, but your instructor paid only $175 for one of similar size. At first glance, it looks as if the instructor taught the student a lesson! But consider this: Your desk—which has a beautiful finish—was delivered to your apartment, and you had a year to pay for it. The instructor, a do-it-yourself buff, bought a partially assembled desk with no finish on it. It had to be assembled and then stained and varnished. The seller provided neither delivery nor credit. Now who paid the higher price? The answer is not as easy as it first appeared.

This example indicates that the definition depends on determining exactly what is being sold. A seller usually is pricing a combination of (1) the specific good or service that is the object of the transaction, (2) several supplementary services (such as a warranty), and (3) in a very real sense, the want-satisfying benefits provided by the product. Sometimes it is difficult even to define the price of the predominant good or service itself. On one model of automobile, a stated price may include radio, power steering, and power brakes. For another model of the same brand,

PRICE IS WHAT YOU PAY FOR WHAT YOU GET

Here are prices under various names:

- Tuition → Education
- Interest → Use of money
- Rent → Use of living quarters or a piece of equipment for a period of time
- Fare → Taxi ride or airline flight
- Fee → Services of a physician or lawyer
- Retainer → Lawyer's or consultant's services over a period of time
- Toll → Long-distance phone call or travel on some highways

- Salary → Services of an executive or other white-collar worker
- Wage → Services of a blue-collar worker
- Commission → Sales person's services
- Dues → Membership in a union or a club

And in socially undesirable situations, there are prices called blackmail, ransom, and bribery.

Source: Suggested in part by John T. Mentzer and David J. Schwartz, *Marketing Today*, 4th ed., Harcourt Brace Jovanovich, San Diego, 1985, p. 599.

these three items may be priced separately. So, to know the real price of a product, you need to look at the identifiable components that make up that product.

Importance of Price

Price is significant in our economy, in the consumer's mind, and in an individual firm. Let's consider each situation.

In the Economy

A product's price influences wages, rent, interest, and profits. Price is a basic regulator of the economic system because it influences the allocation of the factors of production: labor, land, capital, and entrepreneurship. High wages attract labor, high interest rates attract capital, and so on. As an allocator of resources, price determines what will be produced (supply) and who will get the goods and services produced (demand).

Criticism of the American system of reasonably free enterprise and, in turn, public demand for added restraints on the system are often triggered by negative reactions to prices or pricing policies. To reduce the risk of government intervention, businesses need to establish prices in a manner and at a level that consumers and government officials consider socially responsible.

In the Consumer's Mind

At the retail level, a small segment of shoppers is interested primarily in low prices, and another segment of about the same size is indifferent regarding price in making purchases.[2] The majority of consumers are somewhat sensitive to price but are also concerned with other factors, such as brand image, store location, service, quality, and value. According to a major study of sales data for 18 product categories in a chain of 83 supermarkets, consumers' relative interest in price varies across demographic groups. Consumers with one or more of the following attributes are likely to be price sensitive: low income level; small house; large family; and member of a minority group.[3]

Another consideration is that some consumers' perceptions of product quality vary directly with price.[4] Typically, the higher the price, the better the quality is

What do you think are the quality and price levels of the Giorgio line of beauty products? Giorgio positions its brand as top quality, and reinforces this image with limited distribution and relatively high prices. Nevertheless, to attract new buyers and to reward loyal customers, Giorgio occasionally provides a "gift" in conjunction with a major purchase, $35 in this case. This type of incentive is viewed as more compatible with its image than reduced prices would be.

perceived to be. Haven't you been concerned about product quality—such as when you are looking at ads for compact disc players—if the price is unexpectedly low? Or, at the other extreme, have you selected a restaurant for a special dinner because you heard it was fairly high priced so you thought it would be very nice? Consumers' perceptions of quality may be influenced not just by price but also by such factors as store reputation and advertising.

Price is also important as a component of value. During the 1990s, more and more prospective buyers, both in consumer and business markets, have been demanding better value in the goods and services they purchase. **Value** is the ratio of perceived benefits to price and any other incurred costs. Examples of *other incurred costs* include time associated with shopping for the product, time and gasoline used traveling to the place of purchase, and time and perhaps aggravation assembling the product.

When we say a product has ample value, we don't necessarily mean it is inexpensive or has a very low price. Rather, good value indicates that a particular product has the kinds and amounts of potential benefits—such as quality, image, and purchase convenience—consumers expect at a particular price level.

Many businesses are responding to consumers' calls for more value by devising new products. Holiday Inn Express, Fairfield Inn, and Hampton Inn, all relatively new entries in the lodging field, stress value. They do this through some combination of maintaining essential elements (nice, clean rooms); adding a new element or two (for example, a breakfast buffet at Holiday Inn Express);

dropping other elements (room service, bellhops, and perhaps swimming pools) to cut costs; and/or lowering prices.[5]

Other businesses are striving for better value with existing products. Asea Brown Boveri, a manufacturer of power transformers and other large, expensive equipment, has worked hard to enhance product quality *and* pare production costs. With lower costs, the urge to increase prices in order to maintain profits is lessened. Another avenue to enhanced value is to give customers more at the same price. California Pizza Kitchen has used that approach by providing larger portions and holding the line on prices.[6]

http://www.cpk.com/

Attention to value was certainly heightened by the recession of the early 1990s. However, the increased emphasis on value probably reflects a more fundamental shift in consumer attitudes. In the opinion of Jack Welch, chairman of General Electric, we are now in the "value decade." According to a private investor who serves on several corporate boards, "The management challenge of the 1990s is to reduce costs—and increase the perceived value of the product."[7] Consumers' greater interest in the ratio of benefits to price has created a new approach to pricing, not surprisingly called "value pricing," which we will discuss in Chapter 12.

In the Individual Firm

A product's price is a major determinant of the market demand for it. Price affects a firm's competitive position and its market share. As a result, price has a considerable bearing on a company's revenues and net profits. Through prices, money comes into an organization.

Some businesses use higher prices to convey an image of superior quality. This method makes sense only to consumers who consider quality important. It's most likely to work well in the case of services and certain goods for which consumers have difficulty judging quality on an objective basis. To be highly effective in signaling superior quality, the high price should be combined with other conspicuous elements of the marketing mix, such as a compelling advertising message and an appealing package design.[8]

Prices are important to a company most of the time—but not always. Several factors can limit how much effect pricing has on a company's marketing program. Differentiated product features, a favorite brand, high quality, convenience, or some combination of these and other factors may be more important to consumers than price. As we saw in Chapter 10, one object of branding is to *decrease* the effect of price on the demand for a product. Thus we need to put the role of pricing in a company's marketing program in its proper perspective: It is only one of four marketing-mix elements that must be skillfully combined—and then adapted over time—to achieve business success.

Pricing Objectives

Every marketing activity—including pricing—should be directed toward a goal. Thus management should decide on its pricing objective before determining the price itself.[9] Yet, as logical as this may sound, few firms consciously establish a pricing objective.

To be useful, the pricing objective management selects must be compatible with the overall goals set by the firm and the goals for its marketing program. Let's assume that a *company's goal* is to increase return on investment from its present level of 15 percent to 20 percent within 3 years. It follows that the primary *pricing goal* during this period should be to achieve some stated percentage return on investment. It would be questionable, in this case, to adopt a primary pricing goal of maintaining the company's market share or of stabilizing prices.

We will discuss the following **pricing objectives**:

- Profit-oriented:
  - To achieve a target return
  - To maximize profit
- Sales-oriented:
  - To increase sales volume
  - To maintain or increase market share
- Status quo-oriented:
  - To stabilize prices
  - To meet competition

Recognize that all these objectives can be sought—and hopefully attained—not just through pricing but also through other marketing activities such as product design and distribution channels. And all these objectives are ultimately aimed at satisfactory performance over the long run. For a business, that requires ample profits.

Profit-Oriented Goals

Profit goals may be set for the short or long term. A company may select one of two profit-oriented goals for its pricing policy.

Achieve a Target Return. A firm may price its product to *achieve a target return*—a specified percentage return on its *sales* or on its *investment*. Many retailers and wholesalers use a target return *on sales* as a pricing objective for short periods such as a year or a fashion season. They add an amount to the cost of the product, called a *markup*, to cover anticipated operating expenses *and* provide a desired profit for the period. Safeway or Kroger's, for example, may price to earn a net profit of 1 percent on a store's sales. A chain of men's clothing stores may have a target profit of 6 percent of sales, and price its products accordingly. (Markup and other operating ratios are discussed fully in Appendix A following this chapter.)

Achieving a target return *on investment* is measured in relation to a firm's net worth (its assets minus its liabilities). This pricing goal is often selected by the leading firm in an industry. Target-return pricing is used by industry leaders such as Du Pont, Alcoa, and Exxon because they can set their pricing goals more independently of competition than smaller firms in the industry. The leaders may price so that they earn a net profit that is 15 or 20 percent of the firm's net worth.

Maximize Profits. The pricing objective of making as much money as possible is probably followed more than any other goal. The trouble with this goal is that to some people, *profit maximization* has an ugly connotation, suggesting profiteering, high prices, and monopoly.

In both economic theory and business practice, however, there is nothing wrong with profit maximization. Theoretically, if profits become high in an industry because supply is short in relation to demand, new capital will be attracted to increase production capacity. This will increase supply and eventually reduce profits. In the marketplace it is difficult to find many situations where profiteering has existed over an extended period of time. Substitute products are available, pur-

AN ETHICAL DILEMMA?

Earlier this decade, Johnson & Johnson (J&J) introduced a drug that can prevent the recurrence of colon cancer after surgery. The drug's generic name is levamisole; J&J's brand of the drug is Ergamisol. J&J priced Ergamisol at a level that equates to almost $1,500 for a year's supply. An older version of the same drug used for treating sheep for worms costs about $15 for a year's supply. J&J said the high price for Ergamisol was necessary so that the company could recover the enormous costs of developing it. Critics, including a cancer expert at the Mayo Clinic, dismissed J&J's defense and instead said that finding a new use for an old drug doesn't justify a huge price increase.

Is it ethical to charge a seemingly high price for a product that could be a life-or-death necessity?

http://www.jnj.com/

Sources: Ruth Shalit, "Bitter Pills: The End of Drug Research?" *The New Republic*, Dec. 13, 1993, pp. 19+; and Marilyn Chase, "Doctor Assails J&J Price Tag on Cancer Drug," *The Wall Street Journal*, May 20, 1992, p. B1.

---

chases are postponable, and competition can increase to keep prices at a reasonable level.

Where prices are unduly high and entry into the field is severely limited, public outrage may balance the scales. Such was the case with AZT, a drug that prolongs the lives of AIDS patients. At first, Burroughs Wellcome Co. set AZT's price equivalent to about $8,000 for a 1-year supply per patient. Following outcries from AIDS patients and their supporters, the company cut the price of AZT by 20 percent. If market conditions and public opinion do not bring about reasonable prices, government may intervene.[10]

A profit-maximization goal is likely to be far more beneficial to a company if it is pursued over the *long term*. To do this, however, firms may have to accept modest profits or even losses over the short term. For example, a company entering a new geographic market or introducing a new product frequently does best by initially setting low prices to build a large clientele. Repeat purchases from this large group of customers may allow the firm to maximize its profits over the long term.

The goal should be to maximize profits on *total output* rather than on each single product. In fact, a company may maximize total profit by setting low, relatively unprofitable prices on some products in order to stimulate sales of others. In its advertising on televised athletic events, the Gillette Company frequently promotes razors at very low prices. The firm hopes that once customers acquire Gillette razors, they will become loyal customers for Gillette blades, which generate healthy profits for the company.

Sales-Oriented Goals

In some companies, management's pricing is focused on sales volume. The pricing goal may be to increase sales volume or to maintain or increase the firm's market share.

Increase Sales Volume. This pricing goal of *increasing sales volume* is typically adopted to achieve rapid growth or to discourage other firms from entering a market. The goal is usually stated as a percentage increase in sales volume over some period, say, 1 year or 3 years. Management may seek higher sales volume by discounting or by some other aggressive pricing strategy. Drug Emporium, a chain of over 200 drugstores in 25 states, appears to have adopted this objective.

*T*he major online computing services—America
Online, CompuServe, and
Prodigy—battle for sales
and, in turn, market share.
To gain new customers,
these firms give their product away—on a trial basis.
Here, America Online offers
a free 10-hour trial. In
another promotion, recipients of the promotional
mailer could earn added
free time by sending an
enclosed "free trial" kit to a
friend. The online services
expect to gain paying
customers once the free
time is used up.

http://www.aol.com/

Very low prices, "deep discounts" in the terms of the trade, are its primary means of boosting sales volume. Drug Emporium tries to buy merchandise that carries special discounts. Thus its customers cannot count on the most popular brands always being in stock; however, they can be pleasantly surprised by different bargains from one week to the next.[11]

Occasionally companies are willing to incur a loss *in the short run* to expand sales volume or meet sales objectives. Clothing stores run end-of-season sales, and auto dealers offer rebates and below-market loan rates on new cars. Many vacation spots, such as golf courses and resorts, reduce prices during off-seasons to increase sales volume.

Maintain or Increase Market Share. In some companies, both large and small, the pricing objective is to *maintain or increase market share*. Why is market share protected or pursued so vigorously? In growing fields, such as computers and other technology-based products, companies want large shares in order to gain added clout with vendors, drive down production costs, and/or project a dominant appearance to consumers. In the chapter-opening case, Apple Computer certainly exhibited this drive for market share.

Most industries today are not growing much, if at all, *and* have excess production capacity. Many firms need added sales to utilize their production capacity more fully and, in turn, gain economies of scale and better profits. Since the size of the "pie" isn't growing in most cases, businesses that need added volume have to grab a bigger "slice of the pie"—that is, greater market share. The U.S. auto and airline industries illustrate these situations.

Other firms are intent on maintaining their market shares. Several years ago, for instance, the Japanese yen rose considerably in relation to the American dollar. Japanese products—autos, for example—became more expensive in American dollars and their makers faced the prospect of losing market share. To maintain their shares, Toyota, Nissan, and Honda accepted smaller profit margins and reduced their costs so that they could lower their selling prices in the U.S.

Status Quo Goals

Two closely related goals—*stabilizing prices* and *meeting competition*—are the least aggressive of all pricing goals. They are intended simply to maintain the firm's current situation—that is, the status quo. With either of these goals, a firm seeks to avoid price competition.

Price stabilization often is the goal in industries where (1) the product is highly standardized (such as steel or bulk chemicals) *and* (2) one large firm, such as Phelps Dodge in the copper industry, historically has acted as a leader in setting prices. Smaller firms in these industries tend to "follow the leader" when setting their prices. What is the reason for such pricing behavior? A price cut by any one firm is likely to be matched by all other firms in order to remain competitive; therefore, no individual firm gains, but all may suffer smaller profits. Conversely, a price boost is unlikely to be matched. But the price-boosting firm faces a differential disadvantage, because other elements of a standardized product such as gasoline are perceived to be fairly similar.

Even in industries where there are no price leaders, countless firms deliberately price their products to meet the prevailing market price. This pricing policy gives management an easy means of avoiding difficult pricing decisions.

Firms that adopt status quo pricing goals to avoid price competition are not necessarily passive in their marketing. Quite the contrary! Typically these companies compete aggressively using other marketing-mix elements—product, distribution, and especially promotion. This approach, called *nonprice competition*, will be discussed in Chapter 12.

Factors Influencing Price Determination

Knowing the objective of its pricing, a company can move to the heart of price management: determining the base price of a product. **Base price**, or *list price*, refers to the price of one unit of the product at its point of production or resale. This price does not reflect discounts, freight charges, or any other modifications such as leader pricing and value pricing, all of which will be discussed in the next chapter.

The same procedure is followed in pricing both new and established products. Pricing an established product usually is less difficult than pricing a new product, however, because the exact price or a narrow range of prices may be dictated by the market.[12] Other factors, besides objectives, that influence price determination are discussed next.

Estimated Demand

In pricing, a company must estimate the total demand for the product. This is easier to do for an established product than for a new one. The steps in estimating demand are (1) determine whether there is a price the market expects and (2) estimate what the sales volume might be at different prices.

The **expected price** of a product is the price at which customers consciously or unconsciously value it—what they think the product is worth. Expected price usually is expressed as a *range* of prices rather than as a specific amount. Thus the expected price might be "between $250 and $300" or, for another product, "not over $20."

A producer must also consider a middleman's reaction to price. Middlemen are more likely to promote a product if they approve its price. Sometimes they don't. For instance, retailers—notably Wal-Mart—complained when Rubbermaid Inc. tried to raise prices in 1995. The manufacturer thought it needed to, after the cost

http://www.rubbermaid.com/

A GLOBAL PERSPECTIVE

IS PRICING THE SAME IN ARGENTINA AND ZAMBIA AS IN THE UNITED STATES?

As noted in a U.S. government publication, "Setting the right price for your product can be the key to success or failure in the international marketplace." However, price setting becomes more complex when the firm's goods and services are aimed at foreign markets.

Let's take a look at four factors that are distinctive to pricing in international settings:

• *Fluctuating exchange rates.* Different currencies around the world exchange at various rates, which fluctuate daily. Fluctuating exchange rates require marketers to monitor their prices in foreign markets and, in turn, to adjust them frequently.

• *Price controls.* Following severe inflation or a change in the ruling government, price controls are sometimes instituted in a nation. That happened fairly recently in Brazil, Argentina, and Mexico. Price controls either freeze prices at existing levels or place ceilings on prices for products such as essentials. A U.S. firm can try to anticipate price controls (by detecting severe inflation, for example) and adjust prices upward prior to controls being instituted. After prices are controlled, a company might introduce a modified product that is not covered by the price controls.

• *Price differences across countries.* For various reasons, exchange rates and price controls among them, a product may carry vastly dissimilar prices from one country to another. A drug may cost several times more in Germany than in Italy, for example. The formation of the European Union and the passage of the North American

Free Trade Agreement are major steps toward creation of multicountry markets. More and more distributors and consumers expect to receive the lowest prices available in this larger market, either Western Europe or North America. Thus, in many situations, a company has to determine the appropriate base price for a group of countries rather than a single country.

• *Antidumping laws.* Such statutes are intended to prevent foreign companies from pricing their products so low as to harm domestic producers of similar products. For example, country A's antidumping law would stipulate that a firm from country B cannot set the price of its product sold in country A below either the presumed cost to produce it or its price in country B. Antidumping laws appear to be spreading around the globe.

Other factors, such as costs and competitors' present and potential prices, must be taken into account when a company sets prices for foreign markets. Moreover, a firm should consider its pricing objectives prior to establishing prices for products sold in different markets around the world. For example, low prices may be used to establish a foothold in a country that a firm believes has long-term potential. Pricing for foreign markets presents challenges *and opportunities* because of such factors as fluctuating exchange rates and price controls.

Sources: Hermann Simon, "Pricing Problems in a Global Setting," *Marketing News*, Oct. 9, 1995, pp. 4, 8; and James K. Weekly, "Pricing in Foreign Markets: Pitfalls and Opportunities," *Industrial Marketing Management*, May 1992, pp. 173–179. The opening quotation is drawn from "Prices, Quotations, and Terms of Sale Are Key to Successful Exporting," *Business America*, Oct. 4, 1993, p. 12.

of resin (a major ingredient in its various plastic housewares and toys) more than doubled. However, rather than antagonize retailers, Rubbermaid settled for smaller increases, which hurt the company's profits.[13]

It's possible to set a price too low. If the price is much lower than what the market expects, sales may be lost. For example, it probably would be a mistake for L'Oreal, a well-known cosmetics maker, to put a $1.49 price tag on its lipstick or to price its imported perfume at $3.49 an ounce. In all likelihood, shoppers would be suspicious about product quality, or their self-concept would not let them buy such low-priced products.

http://www.lorealcosmetics.com/

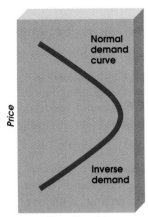

FIGURE 11-1
Inverse demand.

After raising a product's price, some organizations have experienced a considerable increase in sales. When this occurs, it indicates that customers infer better quality from the higher prices. This situation is called **inverse demand**—the higher the price, the greater the unit sales. Inverse demand usually exists only within a given price range and only at low price levels. At some point (see Figure 11-1), inverse demand ends and the usual-shaped curve is evident. That is, demand declines as prices rise.

How do sellers determine expected prices? They may submit products to experienced retailers or wholesalers to gauge the selling price the market will accept for a particular item. Or they may go to customers. A business goods manufacturer, for instance, might get price estimates by showing models or blueprints to engineers working for prospective customers. Another alternative is to ask a sample of consumers what they would expect to pay for the product, or which item in a list of alternatives with known prices is most similar to the test product. Using such methods, a seller can determine a reasonable range of prices.

It is extremely helpful to estimate what the sales volume will be at several different prices. By doing this, the seller is, in effect, determining the demand curve for the product. Moreover, the seller is gauging *price elasticity of demand*, which refers to the responsiveness of quantity demanded to price changes. (Price elasticity of demand is covered in more detail in Appendix A following this chapter.)

Sellers can choose from several methods to estimate sales at various prices. Recall some of the demand-forecasting methods discussed in Chapter 7—survey of buyer intentions, test marketing, executive judgment, and sales-force composite, for example. These methods can be used in this situation as well.[14]

Competitive Reactions

Competition greatly influences base price. A new product is distinctive only until competition arrives, which is inevitable. The threat of potential competition is greatest when the field is easy to enter *and* profit prospects are encouraging. Competition can come from these sources:

- *Directly similar products*: Nike versus Adidas or Reebok running shoes.
- *Available substitutes*: DHL airfreight versus Consolidated Freightways truck shipping or Union Pacific rail freight.
- *Unrelated products seeking the same consumer dollar*: Videocassette recorder (VCR) versus a bicycle or a weekend excursion.

In the cases of similar and substitute products, a competitor may adjust its prices. In turn, other firms have to decide what price adjustments, if any, are necessary to retain their customers.

Other Marketing-Mix Elements

A product's base price is influenced considerably by the other ingredients in the marketing mix.

Product. We've already observed that a product's price is affected by whether it is a new item or an established one. Over the course of a life cycle, price changes are necessary to keep the product competitive. A product's price is also influenced by whether (1) it may be leased as well as purchased outright, (2) it may be returned by the customer to the seller for a refund or exchange, and (3) a trade-in is involved.

The end use of the product must also be considered. For instance, there is little price competition among manufacturers of packaging materials or producers of

industrial gases, so their price structure is stable. These business products are only an incidental part of the final article, so customers will buy the least expensive product consistent with the required quality.

Distribution Channels. The channels and types of middlemen selected will influence a producer's pricing. A firm selling both through wholesalers and directly to retailers often sets a different factory price for these two classes of customers. The price to wholesalers is lower because they perform services that the producer would have to perform—such as providing storage, granting credit to retailers, and selling to small retailers.

Promotion. The extent to which the product is promoted by the producer or middlemen and the methods used are added considerations in pricing. If major promotional responsibility is placed on retailers, they ordinarily will be charged a lower price for a product than if the producer advertises it heavily. Even when a producer promotes heavily, it may want retailers to use local advertising to tie in with national advertising. Such a decision must be reflected in the producer's price to retailers.

Cost of a Product

http://www.tcg.com/

Pricing of a product also should consider its cost. A product's total unit cost is made up of several types of costs, each reacting differently to changes in the quantity produced. In many industries, especially those based on leading-edge technologies such as microprocessors and optic fibers, a product's costs are viewed—and treated—in much different ways than they were just a decade or so ago. For instance, without an additional charge, Teleport Communications installs more optic fibers than a customer requests. Why? As technology surely advances, the customer will want more capacity. The company installs it now because the cost of extra fibers is far less than the cost of labor to do the job in the future. Several software producers give away hundreds of thousands of copies of their product when it is introduced in order to gain favorable word-of-mouth publicity and, in turn, sales of related software and future upgrades of this product.[15]

The cost concepts in the box, "Various Kinds of Costs" (p. 286), are fundamental to our discussion of pricing. These concepts and their interrelationships are illustrated in Table 11-1 and Figure 11-2. The interrelationship among the various *average costs per unit* from the table is displayed graphically in the figure. It may be explained briefly as follows:

- The **average fixed cost curve** declines as output increases, because the total of the fixed costs is spread over an increasing number of units.
- The **average variable cost curve** usually is U-shaped. It starts high because average variable costs for the first few units of output are high. Variable costs per unit then decline as the company realizes efficiencies in production. Eventually the average variable cost curve reaches its lowest point, reflecting optimum output with respect to variable costs (not total costs). In Figure 11-2 this point is at three units of output. Beyond that point the average variable cost rises, reflecting the increase in unit variable costs caused by overcrowded facilities and other inefficiencies. If the variable costs per unit were constant, then the average variable cost curve would be a horizontal line at the level of the constant unit variable cost.
- The **average total cost curve** is the sum of the first two curves—average fixed cost and average variable cost. It starts high, reflecting the fact that total *fixed*

TABLE 11-1 An example of costs for an individual firm

Total fixed costs do not change in the short run, despite increases in quantity produced. Variable costs are the costs of inputs—materials and labor, for example. Total variable costs increase as production quantity rises. Total cost is the sum of all fixed and variable costs. The other measures in the table are simply methods of looking at costs per unit; they always involve dividing a cost by the number of units produced.

(1) Quantity produced	(2) Total fixed costs	(3) Total variable costs	(4) Total costs (2) + (3)	(5) Marginal cost per unit	(6) Average fixed cost (2) ÷ (1)	(7) Average variable cost (3) ÷ (1)	(8) Average total cost (4) ÷ (1)
0	$256	$ 0	$256		Infinity	Infinity	Infinity
1	256	84	340	$ 84	$256.00	$84	$340.00
2	256	112	368	28	128.00	56	184.00
3	256	144	400	32	85.33	48	133.33
4	256	224	480	80	64.00	56	120.00
5	256	400	656	176	51.20	80	131.20

costs are spread over so few units of output. As output increases, the average total cost curve declines because unit fixed cost and unit variable cost are decreasing. Eventually the point of lowest total cost per unit is reached (four units of output in the figure). Beyond that optimum point, diminishing returns set in and average total cost rises.

- The **marginal cost curve** has a more pronounced U-shape than the other curves in Figure 11-2. The marginal cost curve slopes downward until the second unit of output, at which point the marginal costs start to increase.

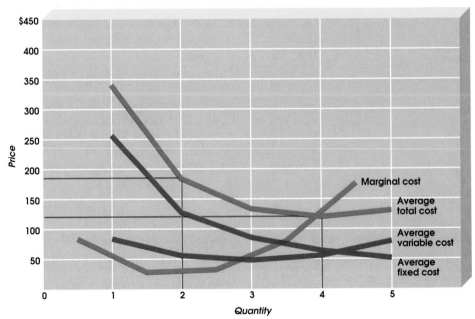

FIGURE 11-2 Unit cost curves for an individual firm.

This figure is based on data in Table 11-1. Here we see how *unit* costs change as quantity increases. Using cost-plus pricing, two units of output would be priced at $184 each, whereas four units would sell for $120 each.

VARIOUS KINDS OF COSTS

- A **fixed cost**, such as rent, executive salaries, or property tax, remains constant regardless of how many items are produced. Such a cost continues even if production stops completely. It is called a fixed cost because it is difficult to change in the short run (but not in the long run).
- **Total fixed cost** is the sum of all fixed costs.
- **Average fixed cost** is the total fixed cost divided by the number of units produced.
- A **variable cost**, such as labor or materials, is directly related to production. Variable costs can be controlled in the short run simply by changing the level of production. When production stops, for example, all variable production costs become zero.
- **Total variable cost** is the sum of all variable costs. The more units produced, the higher is this cost.
- **Average variable cost** is the total variable cost divided by the number of units produced. Average variable cost is usually high for the first few units produced. And it decreases as production increases because of such things as quantity discounts on materials and more efficient use of labor. Beyond some optimum output, it increases because of such factors as crowding of production facilities and overtime pay.
- **Total cost** is the sum of total fixed cost and total variable cost for a specific quantity produced.
- **Average total cost** is total cost divided by number of units produced.
- **Marginal cost** is the cost of producing and selling one more unit. Usually the marginal cost of the last unit is the same as that unit's variable cost.

Note the relationship between the average total cost curve and the marginal cost curve. The average total cost curve slopes downward *as long as the marginal cost is less than the average total cost*. Even though marginal cost increases after the second unit, the average total cost curve continues to slope downward until the fourth unit. This occurs because marginal cost—even when going up—is still less than average total cost.

The two curves—marginal cost and average total cost—intersect at the lowest point of the average total cost curve. Beyond that point (the fourth unit in the example), the cost of producing and selling the next unit is higher than the average cost of all units. The data in Table 11-1 show that producing the fifth unit reduces the average fixed cost by $12.80 (from $64 to $51.20), but causes the average variable cost to increase by $24. From then on, therefore, the average total cost rises. This occurs because the average variable cost is increasing faster than the average fixed cost is decreasing.

Cost-Plus Pricing

We are now at the point in price determination to talk about setting a *specific* selling price. Most companies establish their prices using one of the following methods:

- Prices are based on *total cost plus a desired profit*.
- Prices are based on *marginal analysis*—a consideration of both market demand and supply.
- Prices are based only on *competitive market conditions*.

According to a survey that examined what approaches are used to price new products, 9 percent of companies "guesstimate" what the base price for a new product should be, while 37 percent match what competitors charge for similar offerings. One-half the responding firms charge what the market will bear, if conditions allow. The most common approach, used by 52 percent of the companies, is to choose a price that is intended to cover costs and provide a fair profit.[16] (Because the total is more than 100 percent, it's evident that most firms use more than one approach.)

Let's first discuss the most popular method, **cost-plus pricing**, which means setting the price of one unit of a product equal to the total cost of the unit plus the desired profit on the unit. Suppose that King's Kastles, a contractor, figures the labor and materials required to build and sell 10 condominiums will cost $750,000, and other expenses (office rent, depreciation on equipment, management salaries, and so on) will be $150,000. The contractor wants to earn a profit of 10 percent on the total cost of $900,000. This makes cost plus desired profit $990,000. So, using the cost-plus method, each of the 10 condos is priced at $99,000.

While it is an easily applied method, cost-plus pricing has limitations. One is that it does not recognize various types of costs or the fact that these costs are affected differently by changes in level of output. In our housing example, suppose that King's Kastles built and sold only eight condos at the cost-plus price of $99,000 each. As shown in Table 11-2, total sales would then be $792,000. Labor and materials chargeable to the eight condos would total $600,000 ($75,000 per house). Since the contractor would still incur the full $150,000 in overhead expenses, the total cost would be $750,000. This would leave a profit of $42,000, or $5,250 per condominium instead of the anticipated $9,000. On a percentage basis, profit would be only 5.6 percent of total cost rather than the desired 10 percent.

A second limitation of this pricing approach is that market demand is ignored. That is, cost-plus pricing assumes that cost determines the value of a product, or what customers are willing to pay for it. But what if the same number of units could be sold at a higher price? Using cost-plus pricing, the seller would forgo some revenues. Conversely, if fewer units are produced, each would have to sell for a higher price to cover all costs and show a profit. But if business is slack and output must be cut, it's not wise to raise the unit price. Another limitation of this method is that it doesn't recognize that total unit cost changes as output expands

TABLE 11-2 King's Kastles: an example of cost-plus pricing

Actual results often differ from planned outcomes because various types of costs react differently to changes in output.

King's Kastles' costs, selling price, and profit	Number of condominiums built and sold by King's Kastles	
	Planned = 10	**Actual = 8**
Labor and materials costs ($75,000 per condo)	$750,000	$600,000
Overhead (fixed) costs	150,000	150,000
Total costs	$900,000	$750,000
Total sales at $99,000 per condo	990,000	792,000
Profit: Total	$ 90,000	$ 42,000
Per condo	$9,000	$5,250
As percent of cost	10%	5.6%

or contracts. However, a more sophisticated approach to cost-plus pricing can consider such changes.

Prices Based on Marginal Costs Only

Another approach to cost-plus pricing is to set *prices based on marginal costs only*, not total costs. Refer again to the cost schedules shown in Table 11-1 and Figure 11-2, and assume that a firm is operating at an output level of three units. Under marginal cost pricing, this firm could accept an order for one more unit at $80 or above, instead of the total unit cost of $120. The revenue from a unit sold at $80 would cover its variable costs. However, if the firm can sell for a price above $80—say, $85 or $90—the balance contributes to the payment of fixed costs.

Not all orders can be priced to cover only variable costs. Marginal cost pricing may be feasible, however, if management wants to keep its labor force employed during a slack season. It may also be used when one product is expected to attract business for another. Thus a department store may price meals in its café at a level that covers only the marginal costs. The reasoning is that this café will bring shoppers to the store, where they will buy other, more profitable products.

Pricing by Middlemen

At first glance, cost-plus pricing appears to be widely used by retailing and wholesaling middlemen. A retailer, for example, pays a given amount to buy products and have them delivered to the store. Then the merchant adds an amount, called a markup, to the acquisition cost. This markup is estimated to be sufficient to cover the store's expenses and provide a reasonable profit. Thus a building materials outlet may buy a power drill for $30 including freight, and price the item at $50. The $50 price reflects a markup of 40 percent based on the selling price, or 66 percent based on the merchandise cost. Of course, in setting prices, middlemen also should take into account the expectations of their customers.

Various types of retailers require different percentage markups because of the nature of the products handled and the services offered. A self-service supermarket has lower costs and thus can have a lower average markup than a full-service delicatessen. Figure 11-3 shows examples of markup pricing by middlemen. (Markups are discussed in more detail in Appendix A.)

Is cost-plus pricing really used by middlemen? For the following reasons, it's safe to say that cost-plus pricing is *not* used widely by middlemen:

- Most retail prices are merely offers. If customers accept the offer, the price is fine. If they reject it, the price usually will be changed quickly, or the product may even be withdrawn from the market. Prices thus are always on trial.
- Many retailers don't use the same markup on all the products they carry. A supermarket will have a markup of 6 to 8 percent on sugar and soap products, 15 to 18 percent on canned fruit and vegetables, and 25 to 30 percent on fresh meats and produce. These different markups for distinctive products reflect competitive considerations and other aspects of market demand.
- A middleman usually doesn't actually set a base price but only adds a percentage to the price already set by the producer. The producer's price is set to allow each middleman to add a reasonable markup and still sell at a competitive retail price.

The key price is set by the producer, with an eye on the final market. Thus what seems to be cost-plus pricing by middlemen is usually market-influenced pricing.

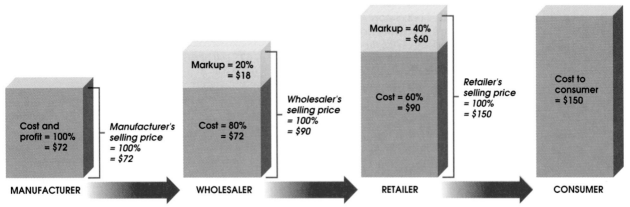

FIGURE 11-3 Examples of markup pricing by retailers and wholesalers.

Evaluation of Cost-Plus Pricing

Since a firm should be market-oriented and cater to consumers' wants, why are we considering cost-plus pricing? Simply, cost-plus pricing must be understood because it is referred to often in business. Further, it is used by numerous firms because it is straightforward and easy to explain.[17]

The traditional perspective has been that costs should be a determinant of prices, but not the only one. Costs are a floor for a company's prices. If goods are priced below this floor for a long time, the firm will be forced out of business.

In recent years, inflation has diminished and firms have had great difficulty raising prices. As a result, a new perspective is that price should determine costs. That is, a firm may not have much flexibility in setting its price so costs must be reduced if profits are to be realized. If this perspective is accepted, production processes must be reengineered to squeeze out costs wherever possible.[18] The appropriate conclusion is that used by itself, cost-plus pricing is a weak and unrealistic method because it ignores market conditions, notably demand and competition.

Break-Even Analysis

One way to consider both market demand and costs in price determination is using **break-even analysis** to calculate break-even points. A **break-even point** is that quantity of output at which total revenue equals total costs, *assuming a certain selling price*. There is a different break-even point for every selling price. Sales exceeding the break-even point result in a profit on each additional unit. The higher sales are above the break-even point, the higher will be the total and unit profits. Sales below the break-even point result in a loss to the seller.

Determining the Break-Even Point

The method of determining a break-even point is illustrated in Table 11-3 and Figure 11-4. In our example, Futon Factory's fixed costs are $25,000, and variable costs are constant at $30 per unit. In our earlier example (Table 11-1 and Figure 11-2), we assumed that unit variable costs are *not* constant but fluctuate. To simplify our break-even analysis, we now assume that variable costs *are* constant.

TABLE 11-3 Futon Factory: computation of break-even point

At each of several prices, we wish to find out how many units must be sold to cover all costs. At a unit price of $100, the sale of each unit contributes $70 to cover overhead expenses. The Futon Factory must sell about 357 units to cover its $25,000 in fixed costs. See Figure 11-4 for a depiction of the data in this table.

(1) Unit price	(2) Unit variable costs	(3) Contribution to overhead (1) − (2)	(4) Overhead (total fixed costs)	(5) Break-even point (rounded) (4) ÷ (3)
$ 60	$30	$ 30	$25,000	833 units
80	30	50	$25,000	500 units
100	30	70	$25,000	357 units
150	30	120	$25,000	208 units

The total cost of producing one unit is $25,030—Futon Factory obviously needs more volume to absorb its fixed costs! For 400 units, the total cost is $37,000 ($30 multiplied by 400, plus $25,000). In Figure 11-4 the selling price is $80 a unit and variable costs of $30 per unit are incurred in producing each unit. Consequently, any revenue over $30 contributes to covering fixed costs (sometimes termed *overhead*). When the price is $80, that would be $50 per unit. At a price of $80, the break-even point is 500 units, because a $50 per-unit contribution will just cover overhead of $25,000.

FIGURE 11-4 Break-even chart for Futon Factory with an $80 selling price.

Here the break-even point is reached when the company sells 500 units. Fixed costs, regardless of quantity produced and sold, are $25,000. The variable cost per unit is $30. If this company sells 500 units, total costs are $40,000 (variable cost of 500 × $30, or $15,000, plus fixed costs of $25,000). At a selling price of $80, the sale of 500 units will yield $40,000 revenue, and costs and revenue will equal each other. At the same price, the sale of each unit above 500 will yield a profit.

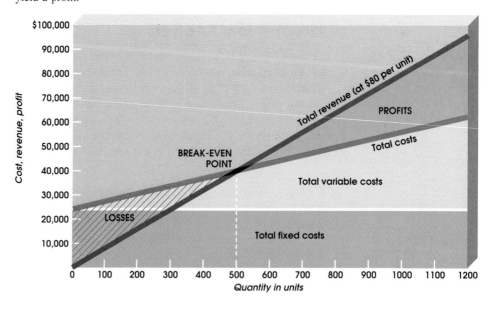

Stated another way, variable costs for 500 units are $15,000 and fixed costs are $25,000, for a total cost of $40,000. This amount equals the revenue from 500 units sold at $80 each. So, at an $80 selling price, the break-even volume is 500 units. Figure 11-4 shows a break-even point for an $80 price. However, it is highly desirable to calculate break-even points for several different selling prices.

The break-even point may be found with this formula:

$$\text{Break-even point in units} = \frac{\text{total fixed costs}}{\text{unit contribution to overhead}}$$

Because unit contribution to overhead equals selling price less the average variable cost, the working formula becomes:

$$\text{Break-even point in units} = \frac{\text{total fixed costs}}{\text{selling price} - \text{average variable cost}}$$

Evaluation of Break-Even Analysis

Two basic assumptions underlie break-even analysis: (1) Total fixed costs are constant. (2) Variable costs remain constant per unit of output. Actually, fixed costs may change (although usually not in the short term) and average variable costs normally fluctuate. Therefore, break-even analysis cannot be used conclusively in most companies.

Another drawback of break-even analysis is that it cannot tell us whether or not we *can* actually sell the break-even amount. Table 11-3, for example, shows what revenue will be at the different prices *if* the given number of units can be sold at these prices. The amount the market will buy at a given price could be below the break-even point. If that happens, the firm will not break even—it will show a loss.

Despite these limitations, management should not dismiss break-even analysis as a pricing tool. Even in its simplest form, break-even analysis is helpful because in the short run many firms experience reasonably stable cost and demand structures.[19]

Prices Based on Marginal Analysis

Another pricing method, marginal analysis, also takes account of both demand and costs to determine the best price for profit maximization. Firms with other pricing goals might use *prices based on marginal analysis* to compare prices determined by different means.

Determining the Price

To use marginal analysis, the price setter must understand the concepts of average and marginal revenue as well as average and marginal cost. **Marginal revenue** is the income derived from the sale of the last unit. **Average revenue** is the unit price at a given level of unit sales; it is calculated by dividing total revenue by the number of units sold.

Referring to the hypothetical demand schedule in Table 11-4, we see that Limos for Lease can sell one unit (that is, lease one limousine for a 2-hour period on a weekend night) at $80. To attract a second customer and thereby lease two limos on the same night, it must reduce its price to $72 for each unit. Thus the company receives an additional $64 (marginal revenue) by selling a second unit. After the fourth unit, total revenue declines each time the unit price is lowered in order to sell an additional unit. Hence, there is a negative marginal revenue.

TABLE 11-4 Limos for Lease: demand schedule for an individual firm

At each market price a certain quantity of the product—in this example, a 2-hour rental of a limousine on a weekend night—will be demanded. Marginal revenue is simply the amount of additional money gained by selling one more unit. Limos for Lease gains no additional marginal revenue after it has rented its fourth limo at a price of $53.

Units sold (limos leased)	Unit price (average revenue)	Total revenue	Marginal revenue
1	$80	$ 80	
			$64
2	72	144	
			45
3	63	189	
			23
4	53	212	
			−2
5	42	210	
			−6
6	34	204	

Marginal analysis is illustrated in Figure 11-5. We assume that a company—a services firm like Limos for Lease or a manufacturer—will continue to produce and sell its product as long as revenue from the last unit sold exceeds the cost of producing this last unit. That is, output continues to increase as long as marginal revenue exceeds marginal cost. At the point where they meet, production theoretically should cease. Ordinarily a company will not want to sell a unit at a price less than its out-of-pocket (variable) costs of producing it. The optimum volume of output is the quantity level at which *marginal cost equals marginal revenue*, or quantity Q in Figure 11-5*a*.

Thus the unit price is determined by locating the point on the average revenue curve that represents an output of quantity Q—the level at which marginal cost equals marginal revenue. Remember that average revenue represents the unit price. Referring to Figure 11-5*b*, in which the average revenue curve has been added, the unit price at which to sell quantity Q is represented by point C—that is, price B.

The average total cost curve has been added in Figure 11-5*c*. It shows that for output quantity Q, the average unit cost is represented by point D—that is, unit cost A. Thus, with a price of B and an average unit cost of A, the company enjoys a unit profit given by B minus A in the figure. Total profit is quantity Q times the unit profit.

FIGURE 11-5 Price setting and profit maximization through marginal analysis.

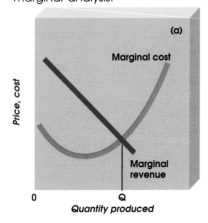

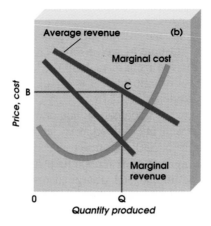

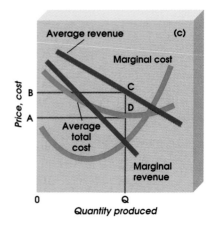

Evaluation of Marginal Analysis Pricing

Marginal analysis has been used sparsely as a basis for price setting. According to businesspeople, it can be a help in studying past price movements. However, many managers think marginal analysis cannot serve as a practical basis for setting prices unless accurate, reliable data can be obtained for plotting the curves.

On the brighter side, management's knowledge of costs and demand is improving. Computerized databases are bringing more complete and detailed information to management's attention all the time. And experienced management in many firms can do a fairly accurate job of estimating marginal and average costs and revenues.

Prices Set in Relation to Market Alone

Cost-plus pricing is one extreme among pricing methods. At the other extreme is *prices set in relation to the market alone*. The seller's price may be set right at the market price to meet the competition, or it may be set above or below the market price.

Pricing to Meet Competition

Pricing to meet competition is simple to carry out. In a situation with multiple suppliers, a firm should ascertain what the prevailing market price is and, after allowing for customary markups for middlemen, arrive at its own selling price. To illustrate, a manufacturer of women's shoes knows that retailers want to sell the shoes for $70 a pair and have an average markup of 40 percent of their selling price. Consequently, after allowing $28 for the retailer's markup, the producer's price is $42. This manufacturer then has to decide whether $42 is enough to cover costs and provide a reasonable profit. Sometimes a producer faces a real squeeze if its costs are rising but the market price is holding firm.

One situation in which management might price a product right at the market level is when competition is keen and the firm's product is not differentiated significantly from competing products.[20] To some extent, this pricing method reflects the market conditions of **perfect competition**. That is, product differentiation is absent, buyers and sellers are well informed, and the seller has no discernible control over the selling price. Most producers of agricultural products and small firms marketing well-known, standardized products use this pricing method.

The sharp drop in revenue occurring when the price is raised above the prevailing market level indicates that the individual seller faces a **kinked demand** (see Figure 11-6). The prevailing price is at A. Adjusting this price is not beneficial to the seller.

- Above the prevailing price, demand for the product drops sharply, as indicated by the fairly flat average revenue curve beyond point P. Above price A, demand is highly elastic and, as a result, total revenue declines.
- Below price A, demand for the product increases very little, as shown by the steeply sloping average revenue curve and the negative marginal revenue curve below point P. Demand is highly inelastic and, as a result, total revenue still declines.

In the case of kinked demand, total revenue decreases each time the price is adjusted from the prevailing price, A in Figure 11-6. The prevailing price is well established. Consequently, when a single firm reduces its price, its unit sales will not increase very much—certainly not enough to offset the loss in average revenue.

FIGURE 11-6

Kinked demand curve.

This type of curve faces firms selling well-known, standardized products as well as individual firms in an oligopolistic market structure. The kink occurs at the point representing the prevailing price, A. At prices above A, demand declines rapidly. A price set below A results in very little increase in volume, so revenue is lost; that is, marginal revenue is negative.

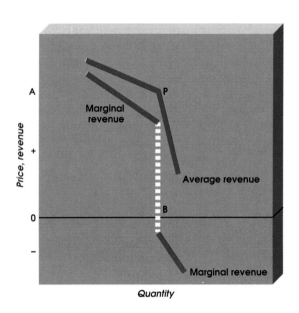

So far in our discussion of pricing to meet competition, we have observed market situations that involve *many* sellers. Oddly enough, this same pricing method is often used when the market is dominated by a *few* firms, each marketing similar products. This type of market structure, called an **oligopoly**, exists in such industries as copper, aluminum, soft drinks, breakfast cereals, auto tires, and even among barber shops and grocery stores in a small community. When the demand curve is kinked, as in Figure 11-6, oligopolists should simply set prices at a competitive level and leave them there. Typically they do.

Pricing below Competition

A variation of market-based pricing is to set a price *below* the level of your main competitors. **Pricing below competition** is done by discount retailers, such as Wal-Mart, Target, and Drug Emporium, which stress low markup, high volume, and few customer services (including sales people). They price heavily advertised, well-known brands 10 to 30 percent below the suggested list price, which is nor-

YOU MAKE THE DECISION

CAN YOU DEAL WITH A KINKED DEMAND CURVE?

Intense price competition has characterized the airline industry in the U.S. since it was deregulated. Attempting to increase the number of passengers, an airline such as United cuts its price on a heavily traveled route, New York to Los Angeles, for example. However, competitors on this route, such as American, Delta, and Trans World Airlines, usually match

that lower fare immediately. As a result, there is no significant shift in the market share held by each airline on that route. But another result is that the market price settles—at least temporarily—at the lower level. Unless the number of passengers increases substantially, the profits of all airlines flying this route and matching the cut-rate prices are likely to suffer.

What marketing strategies might an airline use to avoid having to match a competitor's price cut?

mally charged by full-service retailers. Even full-service retailers may price below the competitive level by eliminating specific services. Some gas stations offer a discount to customers who pay with cash instead of a credit card.

The risk in pricing below competition is that consumers begin to view the product (or an entire retail store) as an undifferentiated commodity, such as coal and bulk salt, with the entire focus on price differences. If that happens, and some would say it already has in fields such as personal computers, then consumers choose the brand with the lowest price. In turn, competing firms are likely to wind up in a price war that diminishes or eliminates profits. One observer asked a question that applies to any industry in which firms rely on price as a way to gain an edge over competitors: "How can restaurant chains ever expect to charge top dollar again after relentlessly pushing value [low] prices?"[21]

Pricing above Competition

Producers or retailers sometimes set their prices *above* the prevailing market level. Usually, **pricing above competition** works only when the product is distinctive or when the seller has acquired prestige in its field. Most communities have an elite clothing boutique and a prestigious jewelry store where prices are noticeably above the level set by other stores with seemingly similar products. However, a gas station that has a strong advantage based on a superior location (perhaps the only such station for many miles on an interstate highway) may also be able to use above-market pricing.

Above-market pricing often is employed by manufacturers of prestige brands of high-cost goods such as autos (Ferrari, Mercedes), crystal (Waterford), leather products (Gucci, Fendi), and watches (Breguet, Rolex). Patek Philippe, a Swiss firm, makes only about 15,000 watches per year, but they are priced in the range of $5,000 to $400,000—per watch! Above-market pricing also is used for business goods. Sometimes it can be effective for relatively low-cost goods. Premier Industrial, for example, prices its fasteners and tubing at least 10 percent higher—and occasionally much higher—than competing products. Premier, an industrial

*A*re these hair-care enterprises pricing below, above, or at the level of competition? Although it's difficult to tell from their store fronts, Supercuts tries to keep its prices below competitors'. To make a profit despite its small margins, Supercuts tries to control its expenses and serve a large volume of customers. In contrast, Vidal Sassoon's prices tend to be above competitors'. As a result, customers expect to receive not only high-quality hair care but also some pampering.

distributor, can do this because—unlike competitors—it accepts small orders and ships an order within 24 hours.[22]

Some services firms also price above their competitors. In the hotel industry, the Ritz Carlton and Fairmont chains have used this approach successfully. Flying only between New York and Los Angeles, MGM Grand Air decided to price above—far above—competition, charging $2,000 for a round-trip flight. Its jets had niceties such as swivel-and-tilt seats that cost $8,000 apiece and 35 video monitors that allowed passengers to choose from among three movies. However, very few travelers were willing to pay this steep tab, and the airline ceased to operate in early 1995.[23]

In the "thrifty 1990s," compared to the "free-spending 1980s," many businesses are having difficulty with above-market prices. Donna Karan, Giorgio Armani, and other designers of clothing that is definitely priced above market (such as $2,000 for a suit) have faced some consumer resistance. So most of them have introduced separate lines carrying brands such as DKNY and lower prices (but still not inexpensive at about $600 per suit!). Armani opened A/X stores to sell basic clothes at above-market prices. However, the venture faltered as many shoppers found it easy to pass up jeans priced above $65 and T-shirts that cost upwards of $25.[24]

http://www.donnakaran.com/
http://www.armaniexchange.com/

The basic pricing methods covered in this chapter (cost-plus and marginal analysis, for instance) are equally applicable in the marketing of goods *and* services by businesses. Pricing of services by companies and nonprofit organizations will receive still more attention in Chapter 19.

■ SUMMARY

In our economy, price influences the allocation of resources. In individual companies, price is one significant factor in achieving marketing success. And in many purchase situations, price can be of great importance to consumers. However, it is difficult to define price. A general definition is: Price is the amount of money and/or other items with utility needed to acquire a product.

Before setting a product's base price, management should identify its pricing objective. Major pricing objectives are to (1) earn a target return on investment or on net sales, (2) maximize profits, (3) increase sales, (4) hold or gain a target market share, (5) stabilize prices, and (6) meet competition's prices.

Besides the firm's pricing objective, other key factors that influence price setting are: (1) demand for the product, (2) competitive reactions, (3) strategies planned for other marketing-mix elements, and (4) cost of the product. The concept of elasticity refers to the effect that unit-price changes have on the number of units sold and on total revenue.

Three major methods used to determine the base price are cost-plus pricing, marginal analysis, and setting the price in relation only to the market. For cost-plus pricing to be effective, a seller must consider several types of costs and their reactions to changes in the quantity produced. A producer usually sets a price to cover total cost. In some cases, however, the best policy may be to set a price that covers marginal cost only. The main weakness in cost-plus pricing is that it completely ignores market demand. To partially offset this weakness, a company may use breakeven analysis as a tool in price setting.

In actual business situations, price setting is influenced by market conditions. Hence, marginal analysis, which takes into account both demand and costs to determine a suitable price for the product, is a useful price-determination method. Price and output level are set at the point where marginal cost equals marginal revenue. The effectiveness of marginal analysis in setting prices depends on obtaining reliable cost data.

For many products, price setting is relatively easy because management simply sets the price at the level of competition. Pricing at prevailing market levels makes sense for firms selling well-known, standardized products and sometimes for individual firms in an oligopoly. Two variations of market-level pricing are to price below or above the levels of primary competitors.

More about

The Windows 95 operating system from Microsoft Corp. basically erased any edge Apple Computer Inc. had with respect to ease of use. Apple's own errors damaged its market share. Some observers wonder whether the company can continue to operate on its own. The advisability of Apple merging with IBM or Sun Microsystems has even been suggested.

To put the luster back on its products, to bolster its financial fortunes, and to assure its future viability, Apple must strengthen its marketing formula. Perhaps more than anything, the computer maker needs added market share. A sound approach to pricing is a key to gaining share.

Apple faces challenges in all four major segments of the PC market. In the home segment, it has gained share but not as much as Packard Bell, which became the top-selling brand. Despite the new line of Power Macs, Apple has been losing ground in both the education and corporate segments. The company has made gains in the government segment, but the potential in this area is much smaller than in the home and corporate segments.

Here are some options Apple is now using or considering for the future:

- Price at or below competing products to attract more household buyers. Of course, the success of this strategy depends on accurate forecasts of demand and, in turn, a reliable, sufficient supply of products. As with any option, this strategy has risks, notably that intense price competition could harm the company's profits.
- Offer leading-edge PCs with advanced graphics and/or multimedia capabilities to sophisticated computer users, especially in the corporate segment. If these products are superior to competing

APPLE

brands, they should be able to command higher prices.
- License its basic design and operating system to other manufacturers so they can produce and market lower-price clones of Apple PCs. If successful, this technique would result in more widespread usage of Apple-style machines, which could entice more software developers to create new programs for use on PCs that rely on the Apple, rather than Windows, operating system. There's little disagreement that more and better software attracts additional customers. The risk of this approach is that the clones are immensely successful, causing sales of Apple's own brand to decline sharply.

Apple requires more share to be taken seriously not only by software developers but also by large corporations and government agencies that want to build large networks of compatible PCs. Apple executives have admitted the company needs to double its market share to about 20 percent

In early 1996, Apple's board of directors concluded that decisive action was called for. Hence, they brought in a new chief executive, Gilbert Amelio, to replace Michael Spindler. Within weeks, Amelio announced (1) a price cut of around 10 percent on Macintosh Performa computers and (2) a licensing agreement that allows Motorola to build Apple-style PCs. Apple's quest for added market share and profits continues.[25]

1. Which pricing objective(s) does it appear Apple is pursuing?
2. Which of the options discussed above, or other marketing and pricing strategies, should Apple use in the future?

■ KEY TERMS AND CONCEPTS

Price (274)	Average variable cost	Average variable	Average revenue (291)
Barter (274)	curve (284)	cost (286)	Pricing to meet
Value (276)	Average total cost	Total cost (286)	competition (293)
Pricing objectives (278)	curve (284)	Average total cost (286)	Perfect competition (293)
Base price (list price) (281)	Marginal cost curve (285)	Marginal cost (286)	Kinked demand (293)
Expected price (281)	Fixed cost (286)	Cost-plus pricing (287)	Oligopoly (294)
Inverse demand (283)	Total fixed cost (286)	Break-even	Pricing below
Average fixed cost	Average fixed cost (286)	analysis (289)	competition (294)
curve (284)	Variable cost (286)	Break-even point (289)	Pricing above
	Total variable cost (286)	Marginal revenue (291)	competition (295)

■ QUESTIONS AND PROBLEMS

1. a. Explain how a firm's pricing objective may influence the promotional program for a product.
   b. Which of the six pricing goals involves the largest, most aggressive promotional campaign?
2. What marketing conditions might logically lead a company to set "meeting competition" as a pricing objective?
3. What is your expected price for each of the following articles? How did you arrive at your estimate in each instance?
   a. A new type of cola beverage that holds its carbonation long after it has been opened; packaged in 12-ounce (355-milliliter) and 2-liter bottles.
   b. A nuclear-powered 23-inch table-model television set, guaranteed to run for 10 years without replacement of the original power-generating component; requires no battery or electric wires.
   c. An automatic garage-door opener for residential housing.
4. Name three products, including at least one service, for which you think an inverse demand exists. For each product, within which price range does this inverse demand exist?
5. In Figure 11-2, what is the significance of the point where the marginal cost curve intersects the average total cost curve? Explain why the average total cost curve is declining to the left of the intersection point and rising beyond it. Explain how the marginal cost curve can be rising while the average total cost curve is still declining.
6. What are the merits and limitations of the cost-plus method of setting a base price?
7. In a break-even chart, is the total *fixed* cost line always horizontal? Is the total *variable* cost line always straight? Explain.
8. Referring to Table 11-3 and Figure 11-4, what would be Futon Factory's break-even points at prices of $50 and $90, if variable costs are $40 per unit and fixed costs remain at $25,000?
9. A small manufacturer sold ballpoint pens to retailers at $8.40 per dozen. The manufacturing cost was 50 cents for each pen. Expenses, including all selling and administrative costs except advertising, were $19,200. How many dozen must the manufacturer sell to cover these expenses and pay for an advertising campaign costing $6,000?
10. In Figure 11-5, why would the firm normally stop producing at quantity Q? Why is the price set at B rather than at D or A?

■ HANDS-ON MARKETING

1. Select 10 items that college students purchase frequently at a supermarket. Be specific in describing the items (for example, a six-pack of Diet Coke). Conduct separate interviews with five of your fellow students, asking them to indicate the price of each item at the supermarket closest to campus. Compare the students' answers with the actual prices charged by that supermarket. How many of the 50 answers were within 5 percent of the actual price? Within 10 percent? Do these results, admittedly from a small and nonrepresentative sample, suggest that consumers are knowledgeable and concerned about grocery prices?

2. Identify one store in your community that generally prices *below* the levels of most other firms and one that prices *above* prevailing market levels. Arrange an interview with the manager of each store. Ask both managers to explain the rationale and procedures associated with their pricing approaches. Also ask the manager of the store with below-market prices how profits are achieved with such low prices. Ask the manager of the store with above-market prices how customers are attracted and satisfied with such high prices.

Marketing Math

Marketing involves people—customers, middlemen, and producers. Much of the business activity of these people is quantified in some manner. Consequently, knowledge of certain concepts in economics, accounting, and finance is essential for decision making in many areas of marketing. With that in mind, this appendix presents an overview—or, for many of you, a review—of (1) price elasticity of demand, (2) the operating statement, (3) markups, and (4) analytical ratios.

Price Elasticity of Demand

Price elasticity of demand refers to the responsiveness of quantity demanded to price changes. Specifically, it gauges the effect that a change in the price of a product has on amount sold and on total revenue. (Total revenue—that is, total sales in dollars—equals the unit price times the number of units sold.)

We say demand is **elastic** when (1) reducing the unit price causes an increase in total revenue *or* (2) raising the unit price causes a decrease in total revenue. In the first case, the lower price results in a boost in quantity sold that more than offsets the price cut—hence, the increase in total revenue. In the second case, the higher price results in a large drop in quantity sold that more than counters the potential gain from the price rise—hence, the decrease in total revenue.

These elastic demand situations are illustrated in Figure A-1. We start with a situation where, at $5 a sandwich, the Campus Sandwich Company sells 100 units and the total revenue (TR) equals $500. When the firm lowers the price to $4, the quantity sold increases to 150 and total revenue also goes up—to $600. When the

FIGURE A-1
Elastic demand.

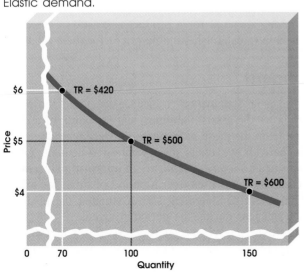

FIGURE A-2
Inelastic demand.

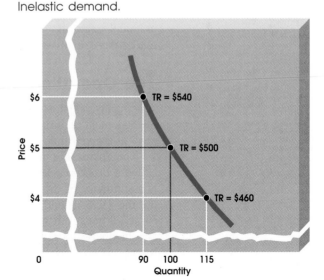

299

price is boosted to $6, however, the quantity sold drops off so much (to 70 sandwiches) that total revenue also declines (to $420). Thus demand is *elastic* when the price change (either up or down) and total revenue change move in the *opposite* direction.

Demand is **inelastic** when (1) a price cut causes total revenue to decline *or* (2) a price rise results in an increase in total revenue. In each of these situations, the changes in unit price more than offset the relatively small changes in quantities sold. That is, when the price is cut, the increase in quantity sold is not enough to offset the price cut, so total revenue goes down. And when the unit price is raised, it more than counters the decline in quantity sold, so total revenue goes up. Simply, demand is *inelastic* when the price change and the resulting change in total revenue go in the *same* direction.

Inelastic demand situations are illustrated in Figure A-2. Again we start with a unit price of $5, Paperbacks and More sells 100 units, and total revenue is $500. When the store lowers the unit price to $4, the quantity of books sold increases to 115. But this is not enough to offset the price cut, so total revenue declines to $460. When the unit price is raised to $6, the quantity sold falls off to 90. But the price increase more than offsets the drop in quantity sold, so total revenue goes up to $540.

In general, the demand for necessities (salt, sugar, cigarettes, gasoline, telephone service, gas and electric service) tends to be inelastic. If the price of gasoline goes up or down, say 10 or 15 cents a gallon, the total number of gallons sold does not change very much. Simply, consumers need gasoline for their car. Conversely, the demand for products purchased with discretionary income (luxury items, large appliances, furniture, autos) typically is much more elastic. That is why the demand for new electronics products often soars as prices decline in the early stages of the life cycle.

Moreover, the demand for individual *brands* is more elastic than is the demand for the broader *product* category. If consumers encounter an unsatisfactory price on an individual brand, they ordinarily can purchase an alternative brand. However, if they are displeased with the prices in an entire product category, they may not be able to find an alternative type of product to meet their needs. Thus the demand for Continental Airlines or Hertz rental cars is far more elastic (price-sensitive) than is the demand for air travel or rental cars in general.

Price elasticity of demand is not just a theoretical concept in economics. It has practical value. By gauging whether demand for a product is elastic or inelastic, marketing executives are better able to establish suitable prices for their products.

The Operating Statement

A company prepares two main financial statements—a balance sheet and an operating statement. A **balance sheet** shows the assets, liabilities, and net worth of a company at a given time—for example, at the close of business on December 31, 1996.

The focus of our attention here, however, is the operating statement. Often called a *profit-and-loss statement* or an *income statement*, an **operating statement** is a summary of the firm's income and expenses over a period of time, for example the 1996 calendar year. The operating statement shows whether the business earned a net profit or suffered a net loss during the period covered.

An operating statement can cover any period of time. To fulfill income tax requirements, virtually all firms prepare a statement covering operations during a calendar year or another 12-month period called a fiscal year. It is also common for businesses to prepare monthly, quarterly, and/or semiannual operating statements.

Table A-1 is an operating statement for a hypothetical firm, the Alpha-Zeta Company, which could be either a wholesaler or a retailer. The major difference between the operating statement of a middleman and that of a manufacturer is the cost-of-goods-sold section. A manufacturer shows the cost of goods *manufactured*, whereas the middleman's statement shows net *purchases*.

The essence of business is very simple. A company buys or makes a product and then (hopefully) sells it for more than it cost. From the sales revenue, the seller intends to cover the cost of the merchandise and the expenses of the business and have something left over, which is called **net profit**. These relationships form the basic structure of an operating statement:

- Sales minus cost of goods sold equals gross margin.
- Gross margin minus expenses equals net profit.

TABLE A-1 Example of an operating statement for a wholesaler or a retailer

The Alpha-Zeta Company
Operating Statement for Year Ending December 31, 1996

Gross sales		$87,000	
Less: Sales returns and allowances	$ 5,500		
Cash discounts allowed	1,500	7,000	
Net sales			$80,000
Cost of goods sold:			
Beginning inventory, January 1 (at cost)		$18,000	
Gross purchases	$49,300		
Less: Cash discounts taken on purchases	900		
Net purchases	$48,400		
Plus: Freight in	1,600		
Net purchases (at delivered cost)		50,000	
Cost of goods available for sale		$68,000	
Less: Ending inventory, December 31 (at cost)		20,000	
Cost of goods sold			48,000
Gross margin			$32,000
Expenses			
Sales-force salaries and commissions		$11,000	
Advertising		2,400	
Office supplies		250	
Taxes (except income tax)		125	
Telephone and fax		250	
Delivery expenses		175	
Rent		800	
Heat, light, and power		300	
Depreciation		100	
Insurance		150	
Interest		150	
Bad debts		300	
Administrative salaries		7,500	
Office salaries		3,500	
Miscellaneous expenses		200	
Total expenses			27,200
Net profit before taxes			$ 4,800

An example based on the Alpha-Zeta Company in Table A-1 follows:

	Sales	$80,000
less	Cost of goods sold	48,000
equals	Gross margin	32,000
less	Expenses	27,200
equals	Net profit	$ 4,800

Now let's look at the primary components in an operating statement.

Sales

The first line in an operating statement records **gross sales**—the total amount sold by an organization, stated in dollars. From this figure the Alpha-Zeta Company (hereafter, A-Z) deducts sales returns and sales allowances. A-Z also deducts discounts granted to employees when they purchase merchandise or services.

In virtually every firm at some time during an operating period, customers want to return or exchange merchandise. In a **sales return**, the customer is refunded the full purchase price in cash or credit. In a **sales allowance**, the customer keeps the merchandise but is given a reduction from the selling price because of some dissatisfaction. The income from the sale of returned merchandise is included in a company's gross sales, so returns and allowances must be deducted to calculate net sales.

Net Sales

The most important figure in the sales section of the statement is **net sales**, which represents the net amount of sales revenue, out of which the company will pay for the products and all its expenses. The net sales figure is also the one on which many operating ratios are based. It is designated as 100 percent (of itself), and the other items are then expressed as a percentage of net sales.

Cost of Goods Sold

As we work toward determining A-Z's net profit, we deduct from net sales the cost of the merchandise. To calculate the **cost of goods sold** in a retail or wholesale operation, we start with the value of any merchandise on hand at the beginning of the period. To this we add the net cost of what is purchased during the period. From this total we deduct the value of whatever remains unsold at the end of the period.

In Table A-1 the firm started with an inventory worth $18,000, and during the course of the year, it purchased goods that cost $50,000. Thus A-Z had a total of $68,000 worth of goods available for sale. If all were sold, the cost of goods sold would have been $68,000. At the end of the year, however, there was still $20,000 worth of merchandise on hand. Thus, during the year, A-Z sold goods that cost $48,000.

We just spoke of merchandise *valued at* a certain figure or *worth* a stated amount. Actually, the problem of inventory valuation is complicated and sometimes controversial. The rule of thumb is to value inventories at what they cost or their current market value, whichever is lower. The application of this rule in the real world may be difficult. Assume that a store buys six beach balls at $5 each and the following week buys six more at $6 each. The company places all 12, jumbled, in a basket display for sale. Then one is sold, but there is no marking to indicate whether its cost was $5 or $6. Thus the inventory value of the remaining 11 balls may be $60 or $61. If we multiply this situation by thousands of purchases and sales, we begin to see the depth of the problem.

A figure deserving some comment is the **net cost of delivered purchases**. A company starts with its gross purchases at billed cost. Then it must deduct any purchases that were returned or any purchase allowances received. The company should also deduct any cash discounts taken for payment of the bill within a specified period of time. Deducting purchase returns, allowances, and discounts gives the net cost of purchases. Freight charges paid by the buyer (called **freight in**) are added to net purchases to determine the net cost of *delivered* purchases.

In a manufacturing concern, the cost-of-goods-sold section has a slightly different form. Instead of determining the cost of goods *purchased*, the firm determines the cost of goods *manufactured*, as in Table A-2. Cost of goods manufactured ($50,000) is added to the beginning inventory ($18,000) to ascertain the total goods available for sale ($68,000). Then, after the ending inventory of finished goods has been deducted ($20,000), the result is the cost of goods sold ($48,000).

To find the cost of goods *manufactured*, a company starts with the value of goods partially completed (beginning inventory of goods in process—$24,000). To this beginning inventory figure is added the cost of raw materials, direct labor, and factory overhead expenses incurred during the period ($48,000). The resulting figure is the total goods in process during the period ($72,000). By deducting the value of goods still in process at the end of the period ($22,000), management finds the cost of goods manufactured during that span of time ($50,000).

Gross Margin

Gross margin is determined by subtracting cost of goods sold from net sales. Gross margin, sometimes called *gross profit*, is a key figure in the entire marketing program. When we say that a certain store has a *margin* of 30 percent, we are referring to the gross margin.

TABLE A-2 Cost-of-goods-sold section of an operating statement for a manufacturer

Beginning inventory of finished goods (at cost)			$18,000
Cost of goods manufactured:			
Beginning inventory, goods in process		$24,000	
Plus: Raw materials	$20,000		
Direct labor	15,000		
Overhead	13,000	48,000	
Total goods in process		$72,000	
Less: Ending inventory, goods in process		22,000	
Cost of goods manufactured			50,000
Cost of goods available for sale			$68,000
Less: Ending inventory, finished goods (at cost)			20,000
Costs of goods sold			$48,000

Expenses

Operating expenses are deducted from gross margin to determine net profit. The operating expense section includes marketing, administrative, and miscellaneous expenses. It does not, of course, include the cost of goods purchased or manufactured, since these costs have already been deducted.

Net Profit

Net profit is the difference between gross margin and total expenses. Obviously, a negative net profit is a loss. Our example does not include taxes, which would reduce the net profit figure.

Markups

Many retailers and wholesalers use markup percentages to determine the selling price of an article. Normally the selling price must exceed the cost of the merchandise by an amount sufficient to cover operating expenses and still leave the desired profit. The difference between the selling price of an item and its cost is the **markup**, sometimes referred to as the *mark-on*.

Typically, markups are expressed in percentages rather than dollars. A markup may be expressed as a percentage of either the cost or the selling price. Therefore, we must first determine which will be the *base* for the markup. That is, when we speak of a 40 percent markup, do we mean 40 percent of the *cost* or 40 percent of the *selling price*?

To determine the markup percentage when it is based on *cost*, we use the following formula:

$$\text{Markup } \% = \frac{\text{dollar markup}}{\text{cost}}$$

When the markup is based on *selling price*, the formula to use is:

$$\text{Markup } \% = \frac{\text{dollar markup}}{\text{selling price}}$$

All interested parties must know which base is being used in a given situation. Otherwise there can be considerable misunderstanding. To illustrate, suppose that Allan Aaron runs a clothing store and claims he needs a 50 percent markup to make a small net profit. Blanche Brister, who runs a competitive store, says she needs only a 33⅓ percent markup and that Aaron must be either inefficient or a big profiteer.

Actually, both merchants are using identical markups, but they are using different bases. Each seller buys hats at $6 apiece and sets the selling price at $9. This is a markup of $3 per hat. Aaron is expressing his markup as a percentage of cost—hence the 50 percent figure ($3 ÷ $6 = 0.5, or 50 percent). Brister is basing her markup on the selling price ($3 ÷ $9 = 0.333, or 33⅓ percent).

It would be a mistake for Aaron to try to get by on Brister's 33⅓ percent markup, as long as Aaron uses cost as his base. If Aaron used the 33⅓ percent markup, but *based it on cost*, the markup would be only $2. And the selling price would be only $8. This $2 markup, averaged over the entire hat department, would not enable Aaron to cover his usual expenses and make a profit. *It is conventional to state markup percentages as a percentage of selling price.*

Markup Based on Selling Price

The following diagram shows the relationships among selling price, cost, and markup. It can be used to calculate these figures regardless of whether the markup is stated in percentages or dollars, and whether the percentages are based on selling price or cost:

		Dollars	**Percentage**
	Selling price		
less	Cost	—	—
equals	Markup		

As an example, suppose a merchant buys an article for $90 and knows the markup based on selling price must be 40 percent. What is the selling price? By filling in the known information in the diagram, we obtain:

		Dollars	**Percentage**
	Selling price		100
less	Cost	90	—
equals	Markup		40

The percentage representing cost must then be 60 percent. Thus the $90 cost is 60 percent of the selling price. The selling price is then $150. That is, $90 equals 60 percent of the selling price. Then $90 is divided by 0.6 (or 60 percent) to get the selling price of $150.

A common situation facing merchants is to have competition set a ceiling on selling prices. Or possibly the sellers must buy an item to fit into one of their price lines. Then they want to know the maximum amount they can pay for an item and still get their normal markup. Assume that the selling price of an article is set at $60—set by competition or by a $59.95 price line. The retailer's normal markup is 35 percent. What is the most the retailer should pay for this article? Again let's fill in what we know in the diagram:

		Dollars	**Percentage**
	Selling price	60	100
less	Cost	—	
equals	Markup		35

The dollar markup is $21 (35 percent of $60). So by simple subtraction we find that the maximum cost the merchant will want to pay is $39.

Series of Markups

Markups are figured on the selling price at *each level of business* in a channel of distribution. A manufacturer applies a markup to determine its selling price. The manufacturer's selling price then becomes the wholesaler's cost. The wholesaler must determine its own selling price by applying its usual markup percentage based on its—the wholesaler's—selling price. The same procedure is carried out by the retailer, using the wholesaler's selling price as its—the retailer's—cost.

The following calculations illustrate this point:

Producer's cost $ 7
Producer's selling price $10   } Producer's markup = $3, or 30%

Wholesaler's cost $10
Wholesaler's selling price $12   } Wholesaler's markup = $2, or 16⅔%

Retailer's cost $12
Retailer's selling price $20   } Retailer's markup = $8, or 40%

Markup Based on Cost

If a firm customarily deals in markups based on cost—and sometimes this is done among wholesalers—the same diagrammatic approach may be employed. The only change is that cost will equal 100 percent. The selling price will be 100 percent plus the markup based on cost. As an example, a firm bought an article for $70 and wants a 20 percent markup based on cost. The markup in dollars is $14 (20 percent of $70). The selling price is $84 ($70 plus $14):

		Dollars	Percentage
	Selling price	84	120
less	Cost	70	100
equals	Markup	14	20

The relationship between markups on cost and markups on selling price is important. For instance, if a product costs $6 and sells for $10, there is a $4 markup. This is a 40 percent markup based on selling price, but a 66⅔ percent markup based on cost. The following may be helpful in understanding these relationships and in converting from one base to another:

If selling price = 100%   If cost = 100%

$10 = 100%   { 60% ⟶ Cost = $6.00   ⟵ 100% } $10 = 166⅔%
             { 40% ⟶ Markup = $4.00 ⟵ 66⅔% }

The relationships between the two bases are stated in the following formulas:

$$\% \text{ markup on selling price} = \frac{\% \text{ markup on cost}}{100\% + \% \text{ markup on cost}}$$

$$\% \text{ markup on cost} = \frac{\% \text{ markup on selling price}}{100\% - \% \text{ markup on selling price}}$$

To illustrate the use of these formulas, let's say that a retailer has a markup of 25 percent on *cost*. This retailer wants to know what the corresponding figure is, based on selling price. In the first formula we get:

$$\frac{25\%}{100\% + 25\%} = \frac{25\%}{125\%} = 0.2, \text{ or } 20\%$$

A markup of 33⅓ percent based on *selling price* converts to 50 percent based on cost, according to the second formula:

$$\frac{33\frac{1}{3}\%}{100\% - 33\frac{1}{3}\%} = \frac{33\frac{1}{3}\%}{66\frac{2}{3}\%} = 0.5, \text{ or } 50\%$$

The markup is closely related to gross margin. Recall that gross margin is equal to net sales minus cost of goods sold. Looking below gross margin on an operating statement, we find that gross margin equals operating expenses plus net profit.

Normally the initial markup in a company, department, or product line must be set a little higher than the overall gross margin desired for the selling unit. The reason? Some reductions will be incurred before all the articles are sold. Due to one factor or another, certain items will not sell at the original price. They will have to be marked down—reduced in price from the original level. Some pilferage, damage, and other shortages also typically occur.

Analytical Ratios

From a study of the operating statement, management can develop several ratios to evaluate the results of its marketing program. In most cases net sales is used as the base (100 percent). In fact, unless specifically mentioned to the contrary, all ratios reflecting gross margin, net profit, or any operating expense are stated as a percentage of net sales.

Gross Margin Percentage
The ratio of gross margin to net sales is termed simply **gross margin percentage**. In Table A-1 the gross margin percentage for A-Z is $32,000 ÷ $80,000, or 40 percent.

Net Profit Percentage
The ratio called **net profit percentage** is determined by dividing net profit by net sales. For A-Z this ratio is $4,800 ÷ $80,000, or 6 percent. This percentage may be calculated either before or after taxes are deducted, but the result should be labeled to show which it is.

Operating Expense Ratio
When total operating expenses are divided by net sales, the result is the **operating expense ratio**. Using the figures in Table A-1, this ratio for A-Z is $27,200 ÷ $80,000, or 34 percent. In similar fashion we may determine the expense ratio for any given cost. Thus we note in the table that rent expense was 1 percent, advertising 3 percent, and sales-force salaries and commissions 13.75 percent.

Stockturn Rate
Management often measures the efficiency of its marketing operations by means of the **stockturn rate**. This figure represents the number of times an amount equal to the average size of the firm's inventory is *turned over*, or sold, during the period under study. The rate is calculated on either a cost or a selling-price basis. Both the numerator and the denominator of the fraction must be expressed in the same terms, either cost or selling price.

On a *cost* basis, the formula for stockturn rate is:

$$\text{Stockturn rate} = \frac{\text{cost of goods sold}}{\text{average inventory at cost}}$$

The average inventory can be determined by adding beginning and ending inventories and dividing the result by 2. In Table A-1 the average inventory is ($18,000 + $20,000) ÷ 2 = $19,000. The stockturn rate then is $48,000 ÷ $19,000 = 2.53. Because inventories usually are abnormally low at the first of the year in anticipation of taking physical inventory, this average may not be representative. Consequently, some companies find their average inventory by adding the book inventories at the beginning of each month and then dividing this sum by 12.

Now let's assume inventory is recorded on a *selling-price* basis, as is done in most large retail organizations. Then the stockturn rate equals net sales divided by average inventory at selling price. Sometimes the stockturn rate is computed by dividing the number of *units* sold by the average inventory expressed in *units*.

Wholesale and retail trade associations in many types of businesses publish figures showing the average stockturn rate for their members. A firm with a low rate of stockturn is not generating sufficient sales volume or is carrying too much inventory. In either case, it is likely to be spending too much on storage and inventory. The company runs a higher risk of obsolescence or spoilage.

If the stockturn rate gets too high, the company's average inventory may be too low. Often a firm in this situation is using hand-to-mouth buying (that is, buying small quantities and selling all or most of them before replenishing inventory). In addition to incurring high handling and billing costs, the company is likely to be out of stock on some items.

Markdown Percentage

Sometimes retailers are unable to sell products at the originally stated prices. When this occurs, they often reduce these prices to move the products. A **markdown** is a reduction from the original selling price. The size of an individual markdown is expressed as a percentage of the original selling price. To illustrate, a retailer purchases a hat for $6 and marks it up 40 percent to sell for $10. The hat does not sell at that price, so it is marked down to $8. Now the seller may advertise a price cut of 20 percent (which is $2 ÷ $10).

Management frequently finds it helpful to determine the markdown percentage. Then the size and number of markdowns and the reasons for them can be analyzed. Retailers, particularly, analyze markdowns.

Markdown percentage is calculated by dividing total dollar markdowns by total net sales during a given period. Two important points should be noted. First, the markdown percentage is determined in this fashion whether the markdown items were sold or are still in the store. Second, the percentage is calculated with respect to total net sales, and not only in connection with sales of marked-down articles. As an example, assume that a retailer buys 10 sports hats at $6 each and prices them to sell at $10. Five hats are sold at $10. The other five are marked down to $8, and three are sold at the lower price. Total sales are $74 and total markdowns are $10. The retailer has a markdown ratio of $10 ÷ $74, or 13.5 percent.

Markdowns do not appear on the profit-and-loss statement because they occur *before* an article is sold. The first item on an operating statement is gross sales. That figure reflects the actual selling price, which may be the selling price after a markdown has been taken.

Return on Investment

A commonly used measure of managerial performance and of the operating success of a company is its rate of return on investment. We use both the balance sheet and the operating statement as sources of information. The formula for calculating **return on investment** (ROI) is as follows:

$$\text{ROI} = \frac{\text{net profit}}{\text{sales}} \times \frac{\text{sales}}{\text{investment}}$$

Two questions may come to mind. What do we mean by "investment"? Why do we need two fractions? It would seem that the sales component in each fraction would cancel out, leaving net profit divided by investment as the meaningful ratio.

To answer the first query, consider a firm whose operating statement shows annual sales of $1,000,000 and a net profit of $50,000. At the end of the year, the balance sheet reports:

Assets	$600,000	Liabilities		$200,000
		Capital stock	$300,000	
		Retained earnings	100,000	400,000
	$600,000			$600,000

The ROI figure is obviously affected by which figure we use. But is the investment $400,000 or $600,000? The answer depends on whether we are talking to the stockholders or to the company executives. Stockholders are more interested in the return on what they have invested—in this case $400,000. The ROI calculation then is:

$$\text{ROI} = \frac{\text{net profit } \$50,000}{\text{sales } \$1,000,000} \times \frac{\text{sales } \$1,000,000}{\text{investment } \$400,000} = 12\tfrac{1}{2}\%$$

Management, on the other hand, is more concerned with total investment, as represented by total assets ($600,000). This is the amount that the executives must manage, regardless of whether the assets were acquired by stockholders' investment, retained earnings, or loans from outside sources. Within this context the ROI computation becomes:

$$\text{ROI} = \frac{\text{net profit } \$50,000}{\text{sales } \$1,000,000} \times \frac{\text{sales } \$1,000,000}{\text{investment } \$600,000} = 8\tfrac{1}{3}\%$$

Regarding the second question, we use two fractions because we are dealing with two separate elements—the rate of profit on sales and the rate of capital turnover. Management really should determine each rate separately and then multiply the two. The rate of profit on sales is influenced by marketing considerations—notably, sales volume, price, product mix, and advertising effort. Capital turnover is a financial consideration that is not involved directly with costs or profits—only with sales volume and assets managed.

To illustrate, say our company's profits doubled with the same sales volume and investment because of an excellent marketing program this year. In effect, we doubled our profit rate with the same capital turnover:

$$\text{ROI} = \underbrace{\frac{\text{net profit } \$100,000}{\text{sales } \$1,000,000}}_{10\%} \times \underbrace{\frac{\text{sales } \$1,000,000}{\text{investment } \$600,000}}_{1\frac{2}{3}} = 16\frac{2}{3}\%$$

$$= 16\frac{2}{3}\%$$

As expected, this 16⅔ percent is twice the ROI calculated above.

Now assume that we earned our original profit of $50,000 but did it with an investment of only $500,000. We cut the size of our average inventory, and we closed some branch offices. By increasing our capital turnover from 1.67 to 2, we raised the ROI from 8⅓ percent to 10 percent, even though sales volume and profits were unchanged:

$$\text{ROI} = \underbrace{\frac{\$50,000}{\$1,000,000}}_{5\%} \times \underbrace{\frac{\$1,000,000}{\$500,000}}_{2} = 10\%$$

$$= 10\%$$

Now let's say we increased our sales volume—we doubled it—but did not increase our profit ($50,000) or original investment ($600,000). The cost-profit squeeze has brought us "profitless prosperity." The following results occur:

$$\text{ROI} = \underbrace{\frac{\$50,000}{\$2,000,000}}_{2\frac{1}{2}\%} \times \underbrace{\frac{\$2,000,000}{\$600,000}}_{3\frac{1}{3}} = 8\frac{1}{3}\%$$

$$= 8\frac{1}{3}\%$$

The profit rate was cut in half, but this was offset by a doubling of the capital turnover rate. The result was that the ROI was unchanged.

■ QUESTIONS AND PROBLEMS

1. Construct an operating statement from the following data and compute the gross margin percentage:

Purchases at billed cost	$15,000
Net sales	30,000
Sales returns and allowances	200
Cash discounts given	300
Cash discounts earned	100
Rent	1,500
Salaries	6,000
Opening inventory at cost	10,000
Advertising	600
Other expenses	2,000
Closing inventory at cost	7,500

2. Prepare a retail operating statement from the following information and compute the markdown percentage:

Rent	$ 9,000
Closing inventory at cost	28,000
Sales returns	6,500
Cash discounts allowed	2,000
Salaries	34,000
Markdowns	4,000
Other operating expenses	15,000
Opening inventory at cost	35,000
Gross sales	232,500
Advertising	5,500
Freight in	3,500
Gross margin as percentage of sales	35

3. What percentage markups *on cost* correspond to the following percentages of markup on selling price?
   a. 20 percent
   b. 37½ percent
   c. 50 percent
   d. 66⅔ percent

4. What percentage markups *on selling price* correspond to the following percentages of markup on cost?
   a. 20 percent
   b. 33⅓ percent
   c. 50 percent
   d. 300 percent

5. A hardware store bought a gross (12 dozen) of hammers, paying $602.40 for the total order. The retailer estimated operating expenses for this product to be 35 percent of sales, and wanted a net profit of 5 percent of sales. The retailer expected no markdowns. What retail selling price should be set for each hammer?

6. Competition in a line of sporting goods limits the selling price on a certain item to $25. If the store owner feels a markup of 35 percent is needed to cover expenses and return a reasonable profit, what is the most the owner can pay for this item?

7. A retailer with annual net sales of $2 million maintains a markup of 66⅔ percent based on cost. Expenses average 35 percent. What are the retailer's gross margin and net profit in dollars?

8. A company has a stockturn rate of five times a year, a sales volume of $600,000, and a gross margin of 25 percent. What is the average inventory at cost?

9. A store has an average inventory of $30,000 at retail and a stockturn rate of five times a year. If the company maintains a markup of 50 percent based on cost, what are the annual sales volume and cost of goods sold?

10. From the following data, compute the gross margin percentage and the operating expense ratio:

    Stockturn rate = 9
    Average inventory at selling price = $45,000
    Net profit = $20,000
    Cost of goods sold = $350,000

11. A ski shop sold 50 pairs of skis at $90 a pair, after taking a 10 percent markdown. All the skis were originally purchased at the same price and had been marked up 60 percent on cost. What was the gross margin on the 50 pairs of skis?

12. A women's clothing store bought 200 suits at $90 each. The suits were marked up 40 percent. Eighty were sold at that price. The remaining suits were each marked down 20 percent from the original selling price, and all were sold. Compute the sales volume and markdown percentage.

13. An appliance retailer sold 60 portable cassette players at $40 each after taking markdowns equal to 20 percent of the actual selling price. Originally all the cassette players had been purchased at the same price and were marked up 50 percent on cost. What was the gross margin percentage earned in this situation?

14. An appliance manufacturer produced a line of small appliances advertised to sell at $30. The manufacturer planned for wholesalers to receive a 20 percent markup, and retailers a 33⅓ percent markup. Total manufacturing costs were $12 per unit. What did retailers pay for the product? What were the manufacturer's selling price and percentage markup?

15. A housewares manufacturer produces an article at a full cost of $4.80. It is sold through a manufacturers' agent directly to large retailers. The agent receives a 20 percent commission on sales, the retailers earn a margin of 30 percent, and the manufacturer plans a net profit of 10 percent on the selling price. What is the retail price of this article?

16. A building materials manufacturer sold a quantity of a product to a wholesaler for $350, and the wholesaler in turn sold it to a lumberyard. The wholesaler's normal markup was 15 percent, and the retailer usually priced the item to include a 30 percent markup. What is the selling price to consumers?

17. From the following data, calculate the return on investment, based on a definition of *investment* that is useful for evaluating managerial performance:

Net sales	$800,000
Gross margin	280,000
Total assets	200,000
Cost of goods sold	520,000
Liabilities	40,000
Average inventory	75,000
Retained earnings	60,000
Operating expenses	240,000
Markup	35%

CHAPTER 12

Pricing
Strategies

Could
BOEING's
Prices Be in a Nosedive?

How things change! For many years, the Boeing Company was able to raise prices of each new model of jetliner (707, 727, and so on) and get close to its asking price in making a sale to an airline. But no more. To sell 55 of its 737s to Scandinavian Airlines Systems (SAS) in 1995, for example, Boeing had to reduce its list price from above $30 million to about $20 million each. And, in order to secure a late-1995 order from Singapore Airlines, Boeing had to agree to repurchase the planes up to 10 years from now at a predetermined price.

Founded in 1916 by William Boeing and Conrad Westervelt, the company grew largely by selling military aircraft to the U.S. government. You may have heard of the B-17 and B-29 bombers, both Boeing products. Eventually, the firm's focus shifted to commercial aircraft. Its first passenger jet, the 707, was introduced in 1958; its latest, the 777, in 1995.

Boeing is one of the biggest companies in the U.S. and consistently ranks as the country's largest exporter. However, even giants struggle occasionally. Boeing's revenues and profits fell 14 percent and 31 percent, respectively, from 1993 to 1994. The firm rebounded in 1995; by July, it wrote up more new-plane orders than it had for all of 1994. Nevertheless, it's unlikely that Boeing will ever be able to avoid price competition and ring up such healthy profits as it did for much of the preceding three decades.

What happened? Most fundamentally, airline economics changed following deregulation of the industry some years ago. For years, competition has prevented airlines from increasing their fares and revenues enough to keep up with escalating costs—including the prices of new planes. Specifically, in constant dollars, revenue per seat (a common measure in the airline industry) has dropped by one-half since 1960, but cost per seat has soared by almost one-half during the same period.

In response, airlines complained about manufacturers' price increases. More significantly, many postponed new purchases and instead refurbished their old, but still serviceable jetliners. For example, rather than buying new Boeing planes costing more than $20 million apiece, Northwest Airlines opted to refurbish 40 of its DC-9s for about $5 million apiece.

For numerous reasons, competition among manufacturers of commercial jetliners has intensified. Boeing is still the dominant firm in the commercial jetliner industry, having produced the majority of jetliners since the inception of jet air travel. However, there are several aggressive European manufacturers, most notably Airbus Industrie that is backed by the governments of four countries—France, Germany, Great Britain, and Spain. Further, McDonnell Douglas Corp. is a persistent U.S.-based competitor.

McDonnell's Douglas Aircraft Co. has struggled even more than Boeing in recent years. When its market share dropped from more than 20 percent to about 10 percent during the first half of this decade, Douglas turned to price as a competitive weapon. Although Douglas lost the big SAS order to Boeing, later in 1995 it won an order from ValuJet for up to 100 of the new MD-95 jetliners. To secure the large order necessary to launch the new product, McDonnell reportedly reduced the price per plane from close to $40 million to about $20 million. However, the fatal crash of a ValuJet flight in 1996 may jeopardize this order.

Orders for new jetliners have surged, undoubtedly in large part because of the manufacturers' price cuts. In fact, given the length of time it takes to produce a large commercial jetliner, Boeing has a backlog of orders representing several years of work.[1]

Was it wise for Boeing to lower its prices?

http://www.boeing.com/

Fundamentally, in managing the price element in a company's marketing mix, management first must decide on its pricing goal and then set the base price for a good or service. The final task, as shown in Figure 12-1, is to design pricing strategies that are compatible with the rest of the marketing mix. Many strategic questions related to price must be answered—not just by Boeing as in the preceding case, but by all firms. These questions include: Will our company compete primarily on the basis of price, or on other factors? What kind of discount schedule should be adopted? Will we occasionally absorb freight costs? Are our approaches to pricing ethical and legal?

In this chapter we primarily discuss ways in which a firm adjusts a product's base price to coincide with its overall marketing program. After studying this chapter, you should be able to explain:

CHAPTER GOALS

- Price competition, notably value pricing, and nonprice competition.
- Pricing strategies for entering a market, notably market skimming and market penetration.
- Price discounts and allowances.
- Geographic pricing strategies.
- Special pricing situations, notably one-price and flexible-price approaches, leader pricing, everyday low pricing and high-low pricing, and reactive and proactive changes.
- Legal issues associated with pricing.

We will use the term *strategy* frequently in this chapter, so let's review its meaning. A **strategy** is a broad plan of action by which an organization intends to reach its goal. To illustrate, a company may adopt a strategy of expanding product lines that enjoy substantial brand equity. Another strategy would be to offer quantity discounts to achieve the goal of a 10 percent increase in sales this year.

Price versus Nonprice Competition

In developing a marketing program, management has to decide whether to compete primarily on the basis of price or the nonprice elements of the marketing mix. This choice obviously affects other parts of the firm's marketing program.

FIGURE 12-1

The price-determination process.

The first two steps were discussed in Chapter 11. The third step is the subject of this chapter.

SELECT PRICING OBJECTIVE

SELECT METHOD OF DETERMINING THE BASE PRICE:

| Cost-plus pricing | Price based on both demand and costs | Price set in relation to market alone |

DESIGN APPROPRIATE STRATEGIES:

Price vs. nonprice competition

Skimming vs. penetration

Discounts and allowances

Freight payments

One price vs. flexible price

Psychological pricing

Leader pricing

Everyday low vs. high-low pricing

Resale price maintenance

Price Competition

A company engages in **price competition** by regularly offering products priced as low as possible and accompanied by a minimum of services. Consumer electronics, computers, and air travel are just several of the myriad industries characterized by rigorous price competition at the present time. In the retail sector, discount houses, such as Target and Dollar General, compete largely on the basis of price.

Price competition has been spreading to other parts of the world as well. For example, price reductions are becoming more common throughout Europe. This switch in competitive strategy was due to the elimination of various trade barriers and, for a while, the continent's economic woes. Price competition is even emerging in Japan, as described in the Global Perspective box.

In Chapter 11 we discussed how more and more consumers are seeking better value in their purchases. In response, many companies in diverse industries are using what's called **value pricing**. This form of price competition aims to improve a product's value—that is, the ratio of its benefits to its price and related costs. To implement value pricing, a firm typically: (1) offers products with lower prices but the same, or perhaps added, benefits; and (2) at the same time seeks ways to slash expenses so profits do not suffer.

Value also can be improved by introducing a much better product with a somewhat higher price than competing entries. Goodyear's Aquatred radial tire, Gillette's Sensor razor, and Intel's Pentium microprocessor chip all illustrate this approach.[2] Despite these notable examples, this approach is not that common today.

During the 1990s, value pricing has become a pivotal marketing trend in fields as diverse as air travel, groceries, personal computers, and fast food. Consider an

A GLOBAL PERSPECTIVE

HAS PRICE COMPETITION FINALLY COME TO JAPAN?

For centuries, nonprice competition has been the prevailing business practice in Japan. Historically, the price of a product—say a Bridgestone bicycle—was identical at all retail outlets.

Recently, there have been signs that price competition may be dawning in Japan, especially in the retail sector. Discounting, called *price destruction* by the Japanese press, can be found in some department stores and specialty retail outlets. One pacesetter has been Isao Nakauchi, head of the gigantic Daiei retail firm, which among other things has more than 350 department stores. In his words, "My purpose is to deregulate everything so that Japanese prices are closer to the rest of the world."

Factors related to both demand and supply explain the start of price competition in Japan. First, in tough economic times, Japanese consumers desired—even demanded—relief from high prices.

Second, given how strong the yen is compared to other currencies, Japanese manufacturers found it difficult to boost exports. Some decided they needed to sell more in their homeland, which led to selective price cuts. Third, a few foreign companies gained distribution for their products in Japan. In some cases, domestic producers had to react to the newcomers' lower prices.

What's ahead? Price competition will not be the norm in Japan for many years, if ever. Some large manufacturers, such as electronics manufacturer Matsushita and cosmetics maker Shiseido, are trying to maintain firm controls over their prices. However, at least at the retail level, there's likely to be a gradual increase in price competition in Japan. As Nakauchi explained, "People have changed their way of buying."

Sources: James Sterngold, "Elusive Price Cuts Intrigue Japan," *The New York Times*, Nov. 9, 1994, pp. C1, D9; Edith Terry, "Japan: Where the Prices Are *Insane!*" *Fortune*, Oct. 31, 1994, p. 21; Yumiko Ono, "Japanese Retailer Shows Low Prices Suit Salarymen Fine," *The Wall Street Journal*, Feb. 14, 1994, p. A8; and Kathleen Morris, "Adam Smith in Tokyo," *Financial World*, Jan. 4, 1994, pp. 22–24.

example. Earlier this decade, Taco Bell trimmed prices on some of its mainstays such as tacos and burritos and introduced cheaper snack-size items (since dropped). Equally important, the fast-food chain attacked its cost structure, particularly labor costs. Its employees now "assemble" tacos and other items from meats and vegetables cooked, sliced, and otherwise prepared by outside suppliers and delivered to the outlets.[3] The giant of fast foods, McDonald's, responded with Extra Value Meals. Besides conveying added value, these combinations of menu items are intended to encourage customers to spend a little more on each purchase.[4]

http://www.mcdonalds.com/

Value pricing certainly emphasizes the price element of the marketing mix. But that's not enough. The chairman of Compaq, the computer maker, stated it in this way: "If all you have to offer is price, I don't think it's a successful long-term strategy in the value decade."[5] Consequently, value pricing depends on creatively combining all elements of the marketing mix in order to maximize benefits in relation to price and other costs. With a value-pricing strategy, products often have to be redesigned to expand benefits and/or shave costs. Relationships among channel members and customers have to be strengthened to generate repeat sales. Steps toward this end include frequent-buyer programs, toll-free customer service lines, and hassle-free warranties. And advertising has to be revamped to provide more facts and fewer emotional appeals.

Nonprice Competition

In **nonprice competition**, sellers maintain stable prices and attempt to improve their market positions by emphasizing other aspects of their marketing programs. Of course, competitors' prices still must be taken into consideration, and price changes will occur over time. Nevertheless, in nonprice competition, the emphasis is on something other than price.

Using terms familiar in economic theory, we can differentiate price and nonprice competition. In *price* competition, sellers attempt to move up or down their individual demand curves by changing prices. In *nonprice* competition, sellers attempt to shift their demand curves to the right by means of product differentiation, promotional activities, or some other technique. In Figure 12-2, the demand

FIGURE 12-2

Shift in demand curve for skis.

Nonprice competition can shift the demand curve for a product. A company selling skis in the European market used a promotional program to sell more skis at the same price, thereby shifting DD to D'D'. Volume increased from 35,000 to 55,000 units at $350 (point X to point Y). Besides advertising, what other devices might this firm use to shift its demand curve?

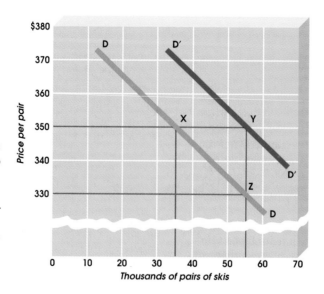

curve faced by the producer of a given model of skis is DD. At a price of $350, the producer can sell 35,000 pairs a year in the European market. On the basis of price competition alone, sales can be increased to 55,000 if the producer is willing to reduce the price to $330. The demand curve is still DD.

However, the producer is interested in boosting sales without any decrease in selling price. Consequently, the firm embarks on a fresh promotional program—a form of nonprice competition. Suppose that enough new customers are persuaded to buy at the original $350 price that unit sales increase to 55,000 pairs a year. In effect, the firm's entire demand curve has been shifted to position D'D'.

With price competition, many consumers will buy a brand only as long as it has the lowest price. There is little customer loyalty when price is the only feature differentiating products from each other. As one consultant advised retailers, "Long-term price competition can take a devastating toll on profits."[6]

With nonprice competition, however, a seller keeps some advantage when a competitor decides to undersell. Thus, many firms stress nonprice competition—and others would like to rely on it rather than price competition. Wanting to be masters of their own destinies, companies believe they have more control in nonprice competition.

The best approach in nonprice competition is to build strong—if possible, unassailable—brand equity for the firm's products. Two methods of accomplishing this are to develop distinctive, hopefully unique, products and to create a novel, appealing promotional program. In addition, some firms emphasize the variety and quality of the supplementary services they offer to customers.[7]

Market-Entry Strategies

In preparing to enter the market with a new product, management must decide whether to adopt a skimming or a penetration pricing strategy.

Market-Skimming Pricing

Setting a relatively high initial price for a new product is referred to as **market-skimming pricing**. Ordinarily the price is high in relation to the target market's range of expected prices. That is, the price is set at the highest possible level that the most interested consumers will pay for the new product.

Market-skimming pricing has several purposes. Since it should provide healthy profit margins, it is intended primarily to recover research and development costs as quickly as possible. Lofty prices can be used to connote high quality. Market-skimming pricing is likely to curtail demand to levels that do not outstrip the firm's production capacities. Finally, it provides the firm with flexibility, because it is much easier to lower an initial price that meets with consumer resistance than it is to raise an initial price that has proven to be too low to cover costs. Even though the price may be lowered gradually, the high initial prices associated with market skimming are subject to criticism from consumers and government officials.

Market-skimming pricing is suitable under the following conditions:

- The new product has distinctive features strongly desired by consumers.
- Demand is fairly inelastic, most likely the case in the early stages of a product's life cycle. Under this condition, lower prices are unlikely to produce greater total revenues.

*A*ccording to its manufacturer, the EV Warrior is "the first mass-produced street-legal electric vehicle of any type in the modern era." It can be pedaled like a regular bicycle, or the rider can rely on the built-in electric power for going up hills. The suggested retail price for the EV Warrior ranges from $1,399 (Model EVS) to $1,899 (Model EVX). Because of its innovativeness and the presumably limited market for this type of vehicle, The Electric Bicycle Company evidently used a market-skimming pricing strategy.

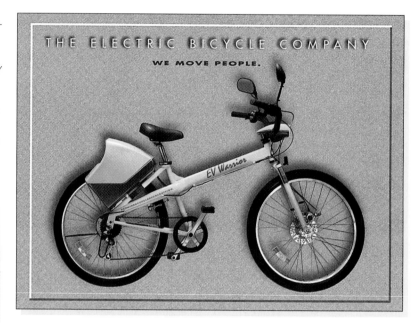

THE ELECTRIC BICYCLE COMPANY
WE MOVE PEOPLE.

http://www.evwarrior.com/

http://www.lorealcosmetics.com/

- The new product is protected from competition through one or more entry barriers such as a patent.

Market skimming is used for various products, notably in pricing new technological goods such as cellular telephones and high-definition TVs. In a much different industry, L'Oreal uses market-skimming pricing for innovative cosmetics such as Niosôme, a wrinkle-fighting facial cream.[8]

Market-Penetration Pricing

In **market-penetration pricing**, a relatively low initial price is established for a new product. The price is low in relation to the target market's range of expected prices. The primary aim of this strategy is to penetrate the mass market immediately and, in so doing, generate substantial sales volume and a large market share. At the same time, it is intended to discourage other firms from introducing competing products.

Market-penetration pricing makes the most sense under the following conditions:

- A large mass market exists for the product.
- Demand is highly elastic, typically in the later stages of the life cycle for a product category.
- Substantial reductions in unit costs can be achieved through large-scale operations. In other words, economies of scale are possible.
- Fierce competition already exists in the market for this product or can be expected soon after the product is introduced.

http://www.datastorm.com/

Datastorm, a software company located in Columbia, Missouri, used market-penetration pricing with Procomm Plus, which connects computers with networks and electronic bulletin boards through a modem. Penetration pricing has been effective, producing an 85 percent market share among customers with IBM computers. Another software company, Computer Associates, used the ultimate in pen-

http://www.cai.com/

etration pricing—it chose to give away the first million copies of its Simply Money accounting program! General Magic recently did likewise with a new piece of software, Magic Cap for Windows. Both firms decided on this radical strategy for similar reasons, primarily to create favorable word of mouth to motivate later buyers and to stimulate purchases of upgrades and complementary software by the beneficiaries of the giveaways.[9]

Discounts and Allowances

Discounts and allowances result in a deduction from the base (or list) price. The deduction may be in the form of a reduced price or some other concession, such as free merchandise or advertising allowances. Discounts and allowances are common in business dealings.

Quantity Discounts

Quantity discounts are deductions from a seller's list price intended to encourage customers to buy in larger amounts or to buy most of what they need from the seller offering the deduction. Discounts are based on the size of the purchase, either in dollars or in units.

A **noncumulative discount** is based on the size of an *individual order* of one or more products. A retailer may sell golf balls at $2 each or at three for $5. A manufacturer or wholesaler may set up a quantity discount schedule such as the following, used by a manufacturer of industrial adhesives:

Boxes purchased in single order	Percent discount from list price
1–5	None
6–12	2.0
13–25	3.5
Over 25	5.0

Noncumulative quantity discounts are intended to encourage large orders. Many expenses, such as billing, order filling, and salaries of sales people, are about the same whether the seller receives an order totaling $10 or one totaling $500. Consequently, selling expense as a percentage of sales decreases as orders grow in size. With a noncumulative discount, a seller shares such savings with a purchaser of large quantities.

A **cumulative discount** is based on the total volume purchased *over a specified period*. This type of discount is advantageous to a seller because it ties customers closely to that firm. The more total business a buyer gives a seller, the greater the discount.

Cumulative discounts can be found in many industries. Airline frequent-flyer and hotel frequent-guest programs are one example. In a much different field, Monsanto Co. offered a form of cumulative discount in order to gain more purchases of Posilac, a drug that stimulates milk production in cows. To qualify for the discount, farmers had to agree to purchase the drug for at least 6 months.[10] Cumulative discounts also are common in selling perishable products. These discounts encourage customers to buy fresh supplies frequently, so that the buyer's merchandise will not become stale.

Quantity discounts can help a producer achieve real economies in production as well as in selling. On the one hand, large orders (motivated by a noncumulative discount) can result in lower production and transportation costs. On the other hand, frequent orders from a single customer (motivated by a cumulative discount) can enable the producer to make much more effective use of production capacity. Thus the producer might benefit even though individual orders are small and do not generate savings in marketing costs.

Trade Discounts

Trade discounts, sometimes called *functional discounts*, are reductions from the list price offered to buyers in payment for marketing functions the buyers will perform. Storing, promoting, and selling the product are examples of these functions. A manufacturer may quote a retail price of $400 with trade discounts of 40 percent and 10 percent. The retailer pays the wholesaler $240 ($400 less 40 percent), and the wholesaler pays the manufacturer $216 ($240 less 10 percent). The wholesaler is given the 40 and 10 percent discounts. The wholesaler is expected to keep the 10 percent to cover costs of wholesaling functions and pass on the 40 percent discount to retailers. Sometimes, however, wholesalers keep more than the 10 percent—and it's not illegal for them to do so.

Note that the 40 and 10 percent discounts do not constitute a total discount of 50 percent off list price. They are not additive because the second discount (in this case, 10 percent) is computed on the amount remaining after the preceding discount (40 percent) has been deducted.

Cash Discounts

A **cash discount** is a deduction granted to buyers for paying their bills within a specified time. The discount is computed on the net amount due after first deducting trade and quantity discounts from the base price. Every cash discount includes three elements, as indicated in Figure 12-3:

- The percentage discount.
- The period during which the discount may be taken.
- The time when the bill becomes overdue.

FIGURE 12-3
Parts of a cash discount.

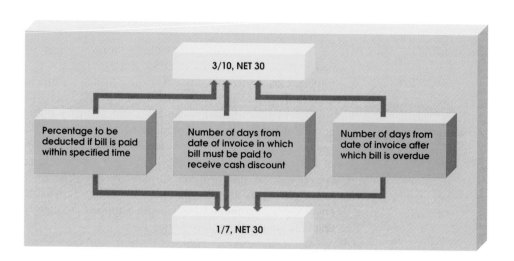

Let's say a buyer owes $360 after other discounts have been granted and is offered terms of 2/10, n/30 on an invoice dated October 8. This means the buyer may deduct a discount of 2 percent ($7.20) if the bill is paid within 10 days of the invoice date—by October 18. Otherwise the entire (net) bill of $360 must be paid in 30 days—by November 7.

There are almost as many different cash discounts as there are industries. For example, in women's fashions, large discounts and short payment periods have been common; thus a cash discount of 5/5, n/15 would not be surprising. Such differences persist not so much for business reasons but because of tradition in various industries.

Most buyers are eager to pay bills in time to earn cash discounts. The discount in a 2/10, n/30 situation may not seem like very much. But this 2 percent is earned just for paying 20 days in advance of the date the entire bill is due. If buyers fail to take the cash discount in a 2/10, n/30 situation, they are, in effect, borrowing money at a 36 percent annual rate of interest. Here's how we arrived at that rate: In a 360-day business year, there are 18 periods of 20 days. Paying 2 percent for one of these 20-day periods is equivalent to paying 36 percent for an entire year.

Other Discounts and Allowances

A manufacturer of goods such as air conditioners or toys purchased on a seasonal basis may consider granting a **seasonal discount**. This discount of, say, 5, 10, or 20 percent is given to a customer who places an order during the slack season. Off-season orders enable manufacturers to better use their production facilities and/or avoid inventory-carrying costs. Many services firms also offer seasonal discounts. For example, Club Med and other vacation resorts lower their prices during the off-season.

http://www.clubmed.com/

Forward dating is a variation on both seasonal and cash discounts. A manufacturer of fishing tackle might seek and fill orders from wholesalers and retailers during the winter months. But the bills would be dated April 1, with terms of 2/10, n/30 offered as of that date. Orders filled in December and January help to maintain production during the slack season for more efficient operation. The forward-dated bills allow wholesale or retail buyers to pay their bills after the season has started and they have generated some revenue from the products delivered earlier.

A **promotional allowance** is a price reduction granted by a seller as payment for promotional services performed by buyers. To illustrate, a producer of builders' hardware gives a certain quantity of free goods to dealers who prominently display its line. Or a clothing manufacturer pays one-half the cost of a retailer's ad featuring its product.

The Robinson-Patman Act and Price Discrimination

The discounts and allowances discussed here may result in various prices for different customers. Such price differentials represent **price discrimination**. In certain situations price discrimination is prohibited by the Robinson-Patman Act, one of the most important federal laws affecting a company's marketing program. (Any federal law regulating pricing is applicable only in cases where there is *interstate* trade. However, many states have pricing statutes that cover sales *within* the state—that is, *intrastate* trade.)

Main Provisions of the Act. The **Robinson-Patman Act**, passed in 1936, was intended to curb price discrimination by large retailers. It was written in very general terms, so over the years it has also become applicable to manufacturers.

Not all price differentials are illegal under the act. Price discrimination is unlawful only when the effect *may be* to substantially injure competition. In other words, a price difference is allowed if it does not substantially reduce competition. This law does *not* apply to sales to ultimate household consumers, because presumably they are not in business competition with each other.

Defenses and Exceptions.   Price discrimination is legal in response to changing conditions that affect the marketability of products. For instance, differentials are allowed in cases of seasonal obsolescence (for products such as Christmas decorations), physical deterioration (fruits and vegetables), and going-out-of-business sales. Competitive considerations also are relevant. As one example, retailers accused pharmaceutical companies of illegal discrimination, claiming the prices hospitals and health maintenance organizations (HMOs) pay are often only a small fraction of what retail pharmacies must pay for identical products. The manufacturers said the differentials are necessary—and legal—because hospitals and HMOs choose other firms' products if they are not given significant price concessions.[11] That is, typically a price differential is allowable if it is needed to meet competitors' prices.

Price differentials also are permissible if they do not exceed differences in the cost of manufacture, sale, or delivery of the product (see Figure 12-4). Cost differences may result from (1) variations in the quantity sold or (2) various methods of sale or delivery of the product. Thus, if selling a large quantity of a product directly to Safeway is more efficient than selling a small quantity through wholesalers to a neighborhood grocery store, the producer can legally offer Safeway a lower price per unit of the product. Such differentials are allowable even though there is a reasonable probability of injuring competition.

Under the Robinson-Patman Act, a buyer is as guilty as the seller if the buyer *knowingly* induces or receives an unlawful price differential. This provision is intended to restrain large buyers from demanding discriminatory prices. From a practical standpoint, however, it has been difficult to prove that the buyer *knowingly* received an unlawful price differential.

Various types of promotional services and materials are lawful *only* if they are offered to all competing customers on proportionally equal terms. For example, assume that a large chain receives promotional support valued at $15,000 when it purchases $750,000 of goods from a manufacturer. Another retailer should not expect the same dollar amount of support on a much smaller—say, $40,000—order. However, the second retailer is entitled to the same percentage amount of support as given to the large chain—2 percent in this case. The $40,000 order should yield promotional services and materials valued at $800. Despite the straightforward math, disputes frequently arise over what is meant by "proportionally equal terms." This concept and its legal implications are examined further in Chapter 16, in connection with a firm's promotional program.

Quantity discounts result in different prices to various customers. Consequently, these discriminatory prices could be illegal under the Robinson-Patman Act if it is shown that they injure competition. To justify price differentials stemming from its quantity discount schedule, a firm must rely on the cost defense provided in the act. In a nutshell, quantity discounts are legal if the resulting price differentials do not exceed differences in the cost of manufacturing, selling, or delivering the product.

FIGURE 12-4

The Robinson-Patman Act.

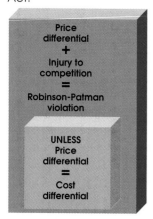

Price differential + Injury to competition = Robinson-Patman violation

UNLESS Price differential = Cost differential

Trade discounts are not addressed in the Robinson-Patman Act or in its predecessor, the Clayton Act. However, court cases many years ago established that separate discounts could be given to distinct classes of buyers. That is, one discount could be granted to wholesalers and another to retailers, as long as all buyers within a given group were offered the same discount.

Geographic Pricing Strategies

In pricing, a seller must consider the costs of shipping goods to the buyer. These costs grow in importance as freight becomes a larger part of total variable costs. Pricing policies may be established whereby the buyer pays all the freight expense, the seller bears the entire cost, or the seller and buyer share this expense. The strategy chosen can influence the geographic limits of a firm's market, locations of its production facilities, sources of its raw materials, and its competitive strength in various geographic markets.

Point-of-Production Pricing

In a widely used geographic pricing strategy, the seller quotes the selling price at the point of production, and the buyer selects the mode of transportation and pays all freight costs. Usually referred to as **FOB factory pricing** (or *FOB mill pricing*), this strategy is the only one of the four discussed in this section in which the seller does not pay any of the freight costs. The seller pays only for loading the shipment aboard the freight carrier—hence the term *FOB*, which stands for *free on board*.

Under FOB factory pricing, the seller nets the same amount on each sale of similar quantities. The delivered price to the buyer varies according to the freight costs. In purchasing goods from a manufacturer in Columbia, Missouri, differences in freight costs surely will provide a customer in St. Louis with a lower delivered price than a customer in Pittsburgh.

The Federal Trade Commission has considered FOB factory pricing to be legal. However, this pricing strategy has serious marketing and financial implications. In effect, FOB factory pricing makes a given seller more attractive to nearby customers and much less attractive to distant customers. The reason? Since the customers bear the freight costs, they prefer to deal with suppliers located close to them, rather than far away. Thus the firm in Pittsburgh mentioned in the preceding paragraph probably would seek suppliers in Pennsylvania or nearby Ohio and West Virginia as alternatives to the supplier in Missouri. Of course, this assumes that alternative suppliers are comparable with respect to other important factors, such as product quality.

Uniform Delivered Pricing

Under **uniform delivered pricing**, the same delivered price is quoted to all buyers regardless of their locations. This strategy is sometimes referred to as *postage stamp pricing* because of its similarity to the pricing of first-class mail service. Using our same example, if the Missouri manufacturer adopted uniform delivered pricing, the delivered cost of goods would be the same for the businesses in Pittsburgh and St. Louis—and elsewhere across the country.

Uniform delivered pricing is typically used where freight costs are a small part of the seller's total costs. This strategy is also used by many retailers who believe "free" delivery is an additional service that strengthens their market position.

With a uniform delivered price, the net revenue to the seller varies depending on the freight cost involved in each sale. In effect, buyers located near the seller's factory pay some of the costs of shipping to more distant locations. Critics of FOB factory pricing usually favor a uniform delivered price. They maintain that the freight cost should not be charged separately to customers any more than other single marketing or production expenses.

Zone-Delivered Pricing

Zone-delivered pricing divides a seller's market into a limited number of broad geographic zones and then sets a uniform delivered price for each zone. The freight charge built into the delivered price is an average of the charges to all points within a zone. An Eastern firm that quotes a price and then says "Slightly higher west of the Rockies" is using a two-zone pricing system. Zone-delivered pricing is similar to the system used in pricing package-delivery services (such as offered by UPS).

When using this pricing strategy, a seller must walk a tightrope to avoid charges of illegal price discrimination. The zones must be drawn so that all buyers who compete for a particular market are in the same zone. This condition is almost impossible to meet in dense population areas, such as the East and Midwest.

Freight-Absorption Pricing

To penetrate distant markets, a seller may be willing to absorb part of the freight cost. Thus, under **freight-absorption pricing**, a manufacturer will quote to the customer a delivered price equal to its factory price *plus* the freight costs that would be charged by a competitive seller located near that customer. In our continuing example, let's assume the manufacturing firm in Missouri agreed to freight absorption. Then the customer in Pittsburgh would not be charged full freight costs, but only the costs that would be charged by a competing supplier located close to the customer—say, in Youngstown, Ohio.

A freight-absorption strategy is adopted to offset competitive disadvantages of FOB factory pricing. With an FOB factory price, a firm is at a price disadvantage when trying to sell to buyers located in markets near competitors' plants. The reason? Since buyers pay the freight costs under FOB factory pricing, these charges will grow as the distance between supplier and customer increases. A nearby supplier has an advantage over more distant suppliers—at least with respect to freight costs. Because of the differences in freight costs, freight absorption erases any price advantage.

A seller can continue to expand its geographic market as long as its net revenue after freight absorption is larger than its marginal costs for units sold. If a manufacturer's costs of producing, selling, and shipping one more unit—that is, its marginal cost—is $75, then freight-absorption pricing makes sense so long as the revenue received by the manufacturer exceeds $75. The firm's revenue would consist of the selling price of the product plus any freight costs charged to the buyer.

Freight absorption is particularly useful to a firm that has (1) excess capacity, (2) high fixed costs, and (3) low variable costs per unit of product. In these cases, management must constantly seek ways to cover fixed costs. Freight-absorption pricing is one means of generating additional sales volume to do that.

Freight absorption is legal if it is used independently and not in collusion with other firms. Also, it must be used only to meet competition. In fact, if it is practiced properly, freight absorption can strengthen competition by breaking down geographic monopolies.

Special Pricing Strategies and Situations

To be effective in setting initial prices, evaluating existing prices, and adjusting them as necessary, a firm needs to be aware of a variety of special pricing strategies and situations.[12]

One-Price and Flexible-Price Strategies

Early in its pricing deliberations, management should decide whether to adopt a one-price or a flexible-price strategy. Under a **one-price strategy**, a seller charges the *same* price to all similar customers who buy identical quantities of a product. Under a **flexible-price strategy** (also called a *variable-price strategy*), similar customers may pay *different* prices when buying identical quantities of a product. Although you may think otherwise, this practice is normally legal.

In the U.S., the one-price strategy is more common than the variable-price strategy. Most retailers, for example, follow a one-price policy. This strategy shifts the focus from price to other factors, such as product quality. A one-price strategy can build customer confidence in a seller—whether at the manufacturing, wholesaling, or retailing level—because the buyer does not have to worry that other customers paid lower prices. Thus, with a one-price strategy, weak bargainers need not think they are at a disadvantage.

A flexible-price strategy abounds in buying situations involving trade-ins. With flexible pricing, buyer-seller bargaining often determines the final price.[13] Both factors, trade-ins and bargaining, are common in automobile retailing. Thus, even though window-sticker prices may suggest a one-price policy, variable pricing has been the norm in selling cars.

Flexible pricing is also used in many other fields.[14] Several airlines, Continental and TWA for example, have used aggressive flexible pricing to enter new markets and to increase their market shares on existing routes. (However, this strategy hasn't produced consistent profits for these two enterprises.) Their new business

YOU MAKE THE DECISION

SHOULD A FIRM ELIMINATE ALL OF ITS PRICING FLEXIBILITY?

In the Ethical Dilemma box in Chapter 11, the pricing of one drug, Ergamisol, was discussed. Now let's look at the pricing of another drug, Lotensin, used to treat high blood pressure. Ciba-Geigy Corp., the maker of Lotensin, has assured customers of a constant price on this drug for the rest of their lives.

Here's how this strategy is carried out: Any patient prescribed Lotensin during the first year following the drug's introduction could enroll in the constant-price program. (The enrollment period was subsequently extended through 1997.) Once enrolled, Ciba-Geigy promises to reimburse patients for any

difference between Lotensin's initial price and higher prices on subsequent purchases—if prices rise. Because retail prices can vary, the drug maker has a maximum refund per prescription. Recognizing that 28 million Americans have problems with blood pressure, Ciba-Geigy believes this pricing strategy will take customers away from other brands of high-blood-pressure medicine.

Under what conditions is Ciba-Geigy's novel pricing strategy likely to be effective?

http://www.ciba.com/

Sources: "Combination ACEI/Diuretic Offers Widest Dose Flexibility and Lifetime Price Guarantee," *PR Newswire*, May 23, 1994; and J. D. Solomon, "Drug Maker Guarantees Cost," *USA Today*, July 24, 1991, p. 2B.

comes from two sources—passengers now flying on other airlines and passengers who would not fly at higher prices. Especially in the second group, demand for air travel is highly elastic. The trick is to keep apart the segment of pleasure travelers (in which demand tends to be elastic) and the segment of business travelers (in which demand is typically inelastic). Airlines separate these segments by placing restrictions on lower-price tickets—requiring advance purchase and a Saturday night stay in the destination city, for example.

http://www.saturncars.com/

Pricing strategies change over time. For instance, during the 1990s, a growing number of auto dealers have switched to—or experimented with—a one-price strategy. In launching the Saturn model, General Motors stressed a one-price policy so as to minimize haggling over prices between the consumer and the sales person. The number of auto dealers that have curtailed bargaining over price is growing, but it is still only about 10 percent of all dealerships. The majority of dealers using a one-price strategy believe it has a positive impact on sales growth *and* on profits. Perhaps surprisingly, consumer reactions to set prices is mixed. In fact, just over one-half of car shoppers say they like to negotiate price.[15]

A **single-price strategy** is an extreme variation of the one-price strategy. Not only are all customers charged the same price, but all items sold by the firm carry a single price! This approach originated many decades ago. A shoe chain, for instance, priced its entire inventory at $6.66 per pair. And more than 30 years ago, Motel 6 (where they "leave the light on" for you) initially priced all rooms at $6 a night for single occupancy.

In the early 1990s, chains such as Everything's $1.00 and Dollar Bill$ grew rapidly by offering frugal shoppers a variety of merchandise ranging from grocery items to cosmetics at a single price of $1. Other chains, such as One Price Clothing Stores and Simply 6, attracted customers with assorted clothing at a single price. Single-price stores typically purchase discontinued products as well as production overruns from a variety of sources at a small fraction of their original costs. This merchandise is often outdated and/or shoddy. Now it appears that consumers are no longer infatuated with stores using a single-price strategy In fact, two chains of "dollar stores" have filed for bankruptcy. Low prices cannot sell unappealing merchandise for long.[16]

Price Lining

Price lining involves selecting a limited number of prices at which a business will sell related products. It is used extensively by retailers of apparel. The Athletic Store, for instance, sells several styles of shoes at $39.88 a pair, another group at $59.95, and a third assortment at $79.99.

For the consumer, the main benefit of price lining is that it simplifies buying decisions. For the retailer, price lining helps in planning purchases. The buyer for The Athletic Store can go to market looking for shoes that can be sold at one of its three price points.

Rising costs can put a real squeeze on price lines. That's because a company hesitates to change its price line every time its costs go up. But if costs rise and prices are not increased accordingly, profit margins shrink and the retailer may be forced to seek products with lower costs.

Odd Pricing

Earlier, we briefly discussed pricing strategies that might be called *psychological* pricing: pricing above competitive levels, raising an unsuitably low price to increase sales, and price lining. All these strategies are intended to convey desirable images about products.

Odd pricing, another psychological strategy, is commonly used in retailing. **Odd pricing** sets prices at uneven (or odd) amounts, such as 49 cents or $19.95, rather than at even amounts. Autos are priced at $13,995 rather than $14,000, and houses sell for $119,500 instead of $120,000. Odd pricing is often avoided in prestige stores or on higher-priced items. Expensive men's suits, for example, are priced at $750, not $749.95.

The rationale for odd pricing is that it suggests lower prices and, as a result, yields greater sales than even pricing. According to this reasoning, a price of 98 cents will bring in greater revenue than a $1 price for the same product. Research has indicated that odd pricing can be an effective strategy for a firm that emphasizes low prices.[17]

Leader Pricing and Unfair-Practices Acts

Many firms, primarily retailers, temporarily cut prices on a few items to attract customers. This strategy is called **leader pricing**. The items on which prices are cut are termed **leaders**; if the leader is priced below the store's cost, it's a **loss leader**.

Leaders should be well-known, heavily advertised products that are purchased frequently. The idea is that customers will come to the store to buy the advertised leaders and while there will buy other, regularly priced merchandise. The net result, the firm hopes, will be increased total sales volume and net profit.

More than 20 states have **unfair-practices acts**, sometimes called *unfair-sales acts*, to regulate leader pricing. Typically, these laws prohibit a retailer or wholesaler from selling an item below invoice cost *plus*, depending on the particular state, either a markup of several percent or the firm's cost of doing business.[18]

In a recent, widely publicized test of this type of law, three Arkansas drugstores charged that Wal-Mart's pharmacies sold some prescription drugs below cost in order to drive small competitors out of business. The giant discounter admitted it sold some products below cost but did so to provide value to customers rather than to destroy competitors. Originally, a court ruled for the drugstores, concluding that Wal-Mart did in fact engage in predatory pricing. Ultimately, the Arkansas Supreme Court overturned the decision. The court stated, "Drugstores are far from destroyed. There is simply enhanced competition in the area."[19]

According to their supporters, these laws eliminate price cutting intended to drive other products or companies out of business. However, such laws permit firms to use leaders—if their price is *above* the stipulated minimum.

According to critics, unfair-practices acts reduce retailers' freedom to set prices. Going a step further, the purpose of a business is to make a profit on the *total* enterprise, not necessarily on each transaction. Thus unfair-practices acts limit retailers' ability to determine how best to generate profits. Also, the minimum prices stipulated by these laws may result in higher prices, which hurts consumers' pocketbooks. In some states these laws have been declared unconstitutional.

Everyday Low Pricing and High-Low Pricing

Everyday low pricing (EDLP) is "the hottest retailing pricing trend," according to one source.[20] It may be hot, but it's not really new. Basically, **everyday low pricing** involves consistently low prices and few if any temporary price reductions. This strategy is featured by some large discounters such as Wal-Mart and by warehouse clubs such as Price/Costco. Most supermarkets using EDLP are not "pure" in that they actually offer temporary price reductions on a rather frequent basis.[21] In these situations, it could be said that EDLP is as much a promotional theme as it is a pricing strategy.

As the headline underscores, Wal-Mart is one of the leading practitioners of everyday low pricing. In fact, the ad stresses "every day" next to the Twinkle Bear's price. Still, even though it uses everyday low pricing, this ad also shows that Wal-Mart occasionally reduces its prices. With a slogan of "Better every day low prices!" Wal-Mart clearly competes on the basis of price.

http://www.wal-mart.com/

http://www.azstarnet.com/dillards/

For a company that intends to engage in price competition, the alternative to EDLP is **high-low pricing**, which entails offering relatively low prices on some products and higher prices on others. This strategy combines frequent price reductions and aggressive promotion to convey an image of very low prices. Many supermarkets and department stores rely on this approach. Some consumer advocates have criticized the use of high-low pricing, asserting that it misleads shoppers. The concern is that most transactions are made at reduced prices, which means that the so-called low prices are normal rather than real bargains.[22]

Which is better—EDLP or high-low pricing? Let's consider one specific case and a broader study. Unlike other department store chains, Dillard's has emphasized EDLP since the mid-1980s. It worked for a while, but recently Dillard's profits dipped even though sales continued to grow.[23] A controlled experiment that compared the effects of the two pricing strategies on 26 product categories in a chain of 86 grocery stores is more conclusive. EDLP increased sales somewhat, whereas high-low pricing resulted in slightly lower volume. More important, though, profits fell 18 percent with EDLP but jumped almost as much with high-low pricing.[24]

Earlier this decade, the arena for EDLP expanded. A manufacturer typically offers retailers a variety of discounts and allowances to stock and promote its brands. In addition, it often provides short-term "special deals" involving larger

http://www.pg.com/

deductions and perhaps even free merchandise. Recently, Procter & Gamble (P&G) eliminated most special deals on about one-half its products, ranging from Jif peanut butter to Oxydol detergent, replacing the deals with consistently lower prices. There were two reasons for the shift: First, consistent selling prices should even out supermarket orders, which would improve production efficiency. Second, if retail prices become more stable, consumers might be less price-oriented and more loyal to P&G's well-known brands of products.

Supermarkets said EDLP hurt their profits because special discounts and allowances were less available to them. However, because P&G has a great deal of power in its distribution channels (a topic covered in the next chapter), the giant manufacturer has been able to stick with EDLP. Because there's no clear "winner" between these approaches, one projection is that some manufacturers of products distributed through supermarkets will emphasize EDLP, others will rely on high-low pricing, and still others will turn to hybrid approaches.[25]

Resale Price Maintenance

Some manufacturers want to control the prices at which middlemen resell their products; this is termed **resale price maintenance**. Manufacturers seek to do this to protect the brand's image. Publicly, they state that their control of prices—and avoidance of discounted prices—provides middlemen with ample profit margins. In turn, middlemen should be able to give consumers expert sales help and other services when they buy the manufacturers' products from middlemen. Critics, however, claim that control over prices leads to inflated prices and excessive profits.

One way in which producers can gain a bit of control, and perhaps provide guidance to retailers, is with a **suggested list price**. This price is set by a manufacturer at a level that provides retailers with their normal markups. To illustrate, a producer sells to, say, a hardware store a certain product for $6 a unit. It recommends a retail price of $10, which would furnish the store with its normal markup of 40 percent of selling price. This is only a *suggested* retail price. Retailers have the right to sell the product for less or more than the suggested price.

Other manufacturers try even harder to control their products' retail prices. Such effort is worthwhile only for a producer selling to relatively few retailers that want very much to carry the product. A manufacturer may even threaten to stop shipment of products to retailers that price products substantially below suggested list prices.

Is aggressive action to control retail prices legal? From about 1930 to 1975, a set of state and federal laws permitted manufacturers to set minimum retail prices for their products. The state laws became known as *fair-trade laws*.[26] However, such price controls were prohibited by the federal Consumer Goods Pricing Act of 1975. Thus a producer no longer can set resale prices, impose them on resellers, and have such actions supported by law.

Nevertheless, the ruckus over resale price maintenance has continued for two reasons. First, according to critics, the federal government ignored companies' illegal efforts to control prices throughout the 1980s. The tide may have turned recently, as the Federal Trade Commission (FTC) appears committed to investigating charges of illegal pricing.[27] Second, ordinarily a manufacturer trying to control its prices comes into conflict with retailers desiring to use low prices as a competitive weapon.

Friction over resale price maintenance has been common in the athletic shoes industry. For example, Reebok established a policy prohibiting retailers from pricing its premier shoes below "suggested" levels and from discounting other lines

http://reebok.com/

by more than 10 percent. Stores not complying with the policy risked having their supply of Reebok products cut off. Other makers of athletic shoes have similar policies. The FTC charged Reebok with violating antitrust laws by trying to set the retail prices for its shoes. While admitting no guilt, Reebok agreed to abandon its controversial policy and pay a total of $9.5 million to the 50 states that initiated the action against the company.[28]

Reactive and Proactive Changes

After an initial price is set, a number of situations may prompt a firm to change its price. As costs increase, for instance, management may decide that raising price is preferable to maintaining price and either cutting quality or promoting the product aggressively. According to a pricing consultant, "Small companies are more reluctant to raise prices than their large counterparts."[29] Obviously, it's wise to raise prices gradually and with little fanfare.

Temporary price cuts may be used to sell excess inventory or to introduce a new product. Also, if a company's market share is declining because of strong competition, its executives may react initially by reducing price. Small firms' price cuts typically are not matched by large competitors, unless they significantly diminish the larger firm's sales. Decreasing price makes the most sense when enough new customers are attracted to offset the smaller profit margin per sale.[30] Nevertheless, for many products, a better long-term alternative to a price reduction is improving the overall marketing program.

Any firm can safely assume that its competitors will change their prices—sooner or later. Consequently, every firm should have guidelines on how it will react. If a competitor *boosts* price, a short delay in reacting probably will not be perilous. However, if a competing firm *reduces* price, a prompt response normally is required to avoid losing customers.

In the absence of collusion, occasional price reductions occur even in an oligopoly with relatively few firms, because the actions of all sellers cannot be controlled. Every so often some firm will cut its price, especially if sales are flat.

AN ETHICAL DILEMMA?

Many retailers use electronic systems in which a checkout clerk scans bar codes on products to automatically ring up prices. Now, as described in the "You Make the Decision" box in Chapter 5, some stores are considering similar "self-scanning" systems that allow shoppers to check out on their own.

Both systems have the potential for ethical problems, but let's focus here on store-controlled (as contrasted with self-scanning) electronic systems. One government official said some stores have an error rate as high as 15 percent. According to a survey in California, overcharges outnumber undercharges by a ratio of 1.5 to 1. A similar study in Michigan revealed a 4-to-1 ratio in the stores' favor. Retailers say any

mispricing is due to human error, specifically clerks failing to put price reductions into the scanning system's computer. Some consumers and their advocates charge retailers put price *increases* into the system before price *decreases*. That means the store is in an advantageous position compared to consumers when price changes are made.

Have retail chains acted unethically with their electronic checkout scanning systems?

Sources: Tara Parker-Pope, "New Devices Add Up Bill, Measure Shoppers' Honesty," *The Wall Street Journal*, June 6, 1995, p. B1; and Catherine Yang, "Maybe They Should Call Them 'Scammers,'" *Business Week*, Jan. 16, 1995, pp. 32–33.

The level of price competition can be vigorous. Consider the long-distance telecommunications industry, for instance. In a single year, the three leading firms promoted discount plans under the labels of True Savings, Friends and Family Connections, and Sprint Sense.[31] It's difficult to differentiate a commodity such as telecommunications, so price competition is likely to continue.

From a seller's standpoint, the big disadvantage in price cutting is that competitors will retaliate—and not let up. A **price war** may begin when one firm decreases its price in an effort to increase its sales volume and/or market share. The battle is on if other firms retaliate, reducing price on their competing products. Additional price decreases by the original price cutter and/or its competitors are likely to follow until one of the firms decides it can endure no further damage to its profits. Most businesses would like to avoid price wars.

Always part of business, price wars seem to be epidemic in the 1990s, breaking out in numerous fields ranging from cigarettes to air travel. Back-and-forth price cuts along with improved features have characterized the personal computer (PC) field for a number of years. With Packard Bell using low prices to become the volume leader in PCs for the home market, other firms such as Compaq and even IBM had to cut prices. As a result of the ongoing price war, there are now two tiers in the PC field: technological innovations carrying high prices, and fairly standard "commodities" with low, and declining, prices.[32]

Price wars can be harmful to a firm, especially one that is financially weaker. One article listed the damages as follows: "Customer loyalty? Dead. Profits? Imploding. Planning? Up in smoke."[33] After extended price wars, some companies in industries as different as groceries and personal computers have gone out of business.

In the short term, consumers benefit from price wars through sharply lower prices. But over the longer term, the net effects on consumers are not clear-cut. Ultimately, a smaller number of competing firms might translate to fewer product choices and/or higher prices for consumers.[34]

■ SUMMARY

After deciding on pricing goals and setting the base (or list) price, marketers must establish pricing strategies that are compatible with the rest of the marketing mix. A basic decision facing management is whether to engage primarily in price or nonprice competition. Price competition establishes price as the primary, perhaps the sole, basis for attracting and retaining customers. A growing number of businesses are adopting value pricing to improve the ratio of benefits to price and, in turn, win customers from competitors. In nonprice competition, sellers maintain stable prices and seek a differential advantage through other aspects of their marketing mixes. Common methods of nonprice competition include offering distinctive and appealing products, promotion, and/or customer services.

When a firm is launching a new product, it must choose a market-skimming or a market-penetration pricing strategy. Market skimming uses a relatively high initial price, market penetration a low one.

Strategies also must be devised for discounts and allowances—deductions from the list price. Management has the option of offering quantity discounts, trade discounts, cash discounts, and/or other types of deductions. Decisions on discounts and allowances must conform to the Robinson-Patman Act, a federal law regulating price discrimination.

Freight costs must be considered in pricing. A producer can require the buyer to pay all freight costs (FOB factory pricing), or a producer can absorb all freight costs (uniform delivered pricing). Alternatively, the two parties can share the freight costs (freight absorption).

Management also should decide whether to charge the same price to all similar buyers of identical quantities of a product (a one-price strategy) or to set different prices (a flexible-price strategy). Many organizations, especially retailers, use at least some of the following special strategies: price lining—selecting a limited number of prices at which to sell related products; odd pricing—setting prices at uneven (or odd) amounts; and leader pricing—temporarily cutting prices on a few items to attract customers. Some forms of leader pricing are illegal in a number of states. A company must also choose between everyday low pricing and high-low pricing, which puts noticeably low prices on selected products while having higher prices on all others.

Many manufacturers are concerned about resale price maintenance, which means controlling the prices at which middlemen resell products. Some approaches to resale price maintenance are more effective than others; moreover, some methods may be illegal.

Market opportunities and/or competitive forces may motivate companies to initiate price changes or, in other situations, to react to other firms' price changes. A series of successive price cuts by competing firms creates a price war, which can harm the profits of all participating companies.

More about

A ccording to Frank Shrontz, retiring chairman of the Boeing Company, commercial airlines "will increasingly demand airplanes that are flexible, efficient and cheaper to own and operate." If his projection is accurate, Boeing faces challenges—and, of course, opportunities—in both pricing and manufacturing its products.

To maintain its dominant position in the commercial jetliner industry, Boeing intends to "deliver more value to our customers than anyone else can," says Ron Woodard, president of the company's Commercial Airline Group. According to Woodard, that entails developing superior products. With that in mind, Boeing offers six versions of the 737 jetliner. They are similar in terms of flight-crew rating requirements. But each differs with respect to range, speed, and seating capacity (from 100 to 189 people).

To deliver value, Boeing also needs competitive prices. For decades, the firm based its prices on its production costs. Recently, Boeing has had to become more attuned to market conditions. In fact, to an increasing degree, prices for its jetliners reflect what airlines are willing to pay for new aircraft.

With relatively few competitors, the commercial jetliner industry is an oligopoly. As such, the dominant firm—Boeing in this case—exerts a large influence on prices. Thus, for many years, Boeing was able to increase prices in order to cover its high production costs. Eventually, the airlines would not or could not accept further increases. Now, according to some observers

BOEING

such as a top executive with Airbus, Boeing is the leader in *reducing* prices for jetliners.

To maintain or even reduce its prices, Boeing has had to slash its production and operating costs. Its manufacturing processes, which were designed prior to the advent of computers, have been reengineered and streamlined. The intent is not only to pare expenses but also to improve quality and reduce the time required to build a plane from the 1992 norm of 18 months to 6 months.

Any successful organization needs new products that satisfy changing customer needs. Consequently, Boeing is considering three all-new airplanes, as contrasted with improved versions of existing models. One is a "super jumbo" jetliner that could seat up to 800 passengers. This project is "on hold" because of lack of interest from airlines. A second possibility is a supersonic transport (SST) that would fly up to 1,600 miles per hour. Boeing actually built an SST prototype more than 25 years ago, but abandoned the project when the federal government would not subsidize it. The third, and most practical, is a jetliner with a seating capacity of 100 that would be designed with Asian markets in mind.[35]

1. Which pricing strategies described in Chapter 12 are being used by Boeing?
2. When introducing new products, should Boeing rely on market-skimming or market-penetration pricing?

■ KEY TERMS AND CONCEPTS

Strategy (314)
Price competition (315)
Value pricing (315)
Nonprice
   competition (316)
Market-skimming
   pricing (317)
Market-penetration
   pricing (318)
Quantity discount (319)
Noncumulative
   discount (319)
Cumulative discount (319)

Trade (functional)
   discount (320)
Cash discount (320)
Seasonal discount (321)
Forward dating (321)
Promotional
   allowance (321)
Price
   discrimination (321)
Robinson-Patman
   Act (321)
FOB factory (mill)
   pricing (323)

Uniform delivered
   pricing (323)
Zone-delivered
   pricing (324)
Freight-absorption
   pricing (324)
One-price strategy (325)
Flexible-price (variable-
   price) strategy (325)
Single-price
   strategy (326)
Price lining (326)
Odd pricing (327)

Leader pricing (327)
Leaders (327)
Loss leader (327)
Unfair-practices (unfair-
   sales) acts (327)
Everyday low
   pricing (327)
High-low pricing (328)
Resale price
   maintenance (329)
Suggested list price (329)
Price war (331)

■ QUESTIONS AND PROBLEMS

1. For each of the following products, should the seller adopt a market-skimming or a market-penetration pricing strategy? Support your decision in each instance.
   a. High-fashion dresses styled and manufactured by Yves St. Laurent
   b. An exterior house paint that wears twice as long as any competitive brand
   c. A cigarette that is *totally* free of tar and nicotine
   d. A tablet that converts a gallon of water into a gallon of automotive fuel
2. As economic unification is being attained and trade barriers are being removed throughout the multination European Union (EU), numerous companies are deliberating how best to achieve sales and profits in all or part of this huge market. Name two U.S. brands that well might adopt a market-skimming pricing strategy in the EU, and two others that should use a market-penetration strategy.
3. Carefully distinguish between cumulative and noncumulative quantity discounts. Which type of quantity discount has the greater economic and social justification? Why?
4. A manufacturer of appliances quotes a list price of $800 per unit for a certain model of refrigerator and grants trade discounts of 35, 20, and 5 percent. What is the

manufacturer's selling price? Who might get these various discounts?

5. The Craig Charles Company (CCC) sells to all its customers at the same published price. One of its sales managers discerns that Jamaican Enterprises is offering to sell to one of CCC's customers, Rocky Mountain Sports, at a lower price. CCC then cuts its price to Rocky Mountain Sports but maintains the original price for all other customers. Is CCC's price cut a violation of the Robinson-Patman Act?
6. "An FOB point-of-production price system is the only geographic price system that is fair to buyers." Discuss.
7. An Eastern firm wants to compete in Western markets, where it is at a significant disadvantage with respect to freight costs. What pricing alternatives can it adopt to overcome the freight differential?
8. Under what conditions is a company likely to use a variable-price strategy? Can you name firms that employ this strategy other than when a trade-in is involved?
9. On the basis of the topics covered in this chapter, establish a set of price strategies for the manufacturer of a new glass cleaner that is sold through a middleman to supermarkets. The manufacturer sells the cleaner at $15 for a case of a dozen 16-ounce bottles.

■ HANDS-ON MARKETING

1. Talk to the owner or a top executive of a firm in your community regarding whether this company emphasizes price or nonprice competition and the reasons for following this course. Also ask whether its approach is similar to or dissimilar from the normal approach used by competitors to market the primary product sold by this firm.
2. Conduct a follow-up to see what's happening with Procter & Gamble's everyday low pricing (EDLP). Do this by interviewing the manager of a large supermarket in

your community. Ask the manager if P&G is using EDLP in its dealing with this chain and, if so, whether this supermarket chain likes or dislikes EDLP and what, if anything, the chain has done in response to P&G's EDLP. If the manager says P&G is not using EDLP, inquire why. If the manager is not familiar with P&G's EDLP, ask whether you can talk in person or by telephone with one of the chain's buyers who purchase packaged goods from P&G.

CASES FOR PART 4

MAINTAINING PRICE LEADERSHIP

The airline industry is flying high once again. In the past several years, more than a dozen new airlines have taken off. As many as 10 more are awaiting government approval. The new entrants have one thing in common—they hope to duplicate the success of Southwest Airlines by imitating its strategy of modest fares backed by tightly controlled costs.

Success from a Simple Strategy

Southwest started service in 1971, with four planes that served three Texas cities—Dallas, Houston, and San Antonio. When it outgrew the in-state market, the airline expanded into interstate service in 1978. By 1995, Southwest had spread its wings far enough to be the nation's sixth largest airline, as measured by number of passengers carried, and the eighth largest, based on revenues. The airline has 19,000 employees and ranks first in market share in more than one-half the largest city-pair markets. Southwest has the distinction of being the only airline to return a profit every year over the past 20 years. Further, it has averaged a 12 percent annual return on investment since it first lifted off.

How has Southwest achieved such phenomenal success in the face of stiff competition? Basically, Southwest offers no-frills service at low fares on relatively short flights. Additional benefits the airline provides include simple scheduling, ticketless travel, and point-to-point service.

The core of Southwest's marketing strategy is the short-haul domestic route. An average trip of 394 miles that lasts about an hour allows the airline to be at or near the top in periodic measures of on-time performance. Southwest serves airports that are readily accessible, rather than large, crowded international airports.

The Necessity of Low Costs

In order to offer low prices and earn healthy profits, Southwest Airlines works especially hard to control its costs. It emphasizes rapid turnaround times, about 15 minutes, which is a sharp contrast to the industry average of 45 minutes. Rapid turnaround allows Southwest's planes to be in the air an average of 11 hours per day, as compared to 8 hours for other airlines.

By using only a single type of aircraft, the Boeing 737, the carrier has reduced employee training costs and spare-parts inventories. Further, the company does *not* provide any of the following typical airline services: assigned seating, in-flight meals, a first-class section, or interairline luggage transfers.

Southwest has been able to maintain its price leadership position by focusing on lower costs measured by available-seat-miles (ASMs). The company has a sizable advantage over much larger airlines. Southwest's ASM was 7.1 cents in 1994; in contrast, American, Delta, Northwest, TWA, United, and USAir all had ASMs of more than 12 cents.

Maintaining the Advantage

Southwest has taken four steps to protect against competitive inroads to its ASM advantage:

- The airline continues to hone its strategy of building passenger traffic in short-haul markets. Southwest accomplishes this by reducing fares to provide passengers the opportunity to make more trips and by adding planes to facilitate customer scheduling of the additional trips. Between 1990 and 1995, the airline more than doubled its fleet to include 226 airplanes. The acquisition of Morris Air Corp. in 1994 alone upped Southwest's capacity by 29 percent.

- Southwest has added a limited number of longer flights. To a point, longer trips allow the airline to cut its ASM—in some cases, to just over 4 cents. However, eventually incremental costs begin to escalate as Southwest is forced to offer more costly benefits, such as in-flight meals and more leg room, demanded by passengers on longer flights. "What we are talking about is flying a longer haul as an adjunct or add-on to our basic market niche," said Herb Kelleher, Southwest's chairman and CEO. The carrier sees long-haul routes growing to no more than 10 percent of its business in the future.

- Southwest continually looks for ways to reduce costs while improving customer service at the same time. Thus the airline introduced ticketless travel in 1995. In less than a year, 30 percent of its passengers were flying ticketless, saving the company $25 million. Furthermore, to strengthen customer loyalty, Southwest passengers are able to use the Internet to check flight information and to buy tickets.

- Southwest enjoys a mutually beneficial working relationship with its employees. On average, Southwest's pilots fly more hours per month than do pilots for other major carriers. In 1995, the company and its pilots' association reached an agreement that froze pilots' salaries through 1999. In exchange, the pilots can earn (1) bonuses tied to company profitability and (2) annual options to buy stock from a pool of 1.4 million shares.

Another key ingredient in Southwest's employee relations plan is maintaining a high level of morale. For starters, the airline exerts great effort to recruit employees who fit the company's culture. Finding the right employee, however, takes longer now than ever before. The company uses a process called target selection to identify the qualities of good Southwest employees. For example, 35 of its top pilots were interviewed to identify the characteristics they had in common. Potential new pilots are screened against the most important characteristics to make sure they will fit Southwest's culture. As a result, instead of interviewing 20 people to fill a position as was done in the past, the company now interviews as many as 50.

To maintain morale, Southwest pays its employees salaries comparable to industry norms. Humor (such as flight attendants' sometimes funny comments) is encouraged to create a fun, friendly work environment that pays off in good customer service. High employee morale means low employee turnover, which in turn helps maintain low costs. Counting retirements, Southwest's turnover is around 7 percent per year—about one-half the industry average.

Expansion Plans and Reactions

Low-fare airlines compete on routes that account for approximately 40 percent of the passenger traffic in the United States. Southwest selects new markets where there are too few flights and high fares. When it enters a market, fares drop by as much as 70 percent. This action often triggers a price war, which in turn increases passenger traffic in the new market.

Before starting service to a new city, Southwest launches a comprehensive public relations program that emphasizes community relations, special events, and direct marketing. The intent is to build awareness of Southwest Airlines and to make it a part of the community even before service starts to the city. As an example, Southwest used a baseball theme when it entered Baltimore in 1993 because the city was the site of the All-Star game that year.

Although other airlines have implemented a marketing strategy emphasizing low prices and modest services, few have achieved enduring success. ValuJet, Western Pacific, and Kiwi International Airlines have copied Southwest's approach. For example, ValuJet passengers use a ticketless system, no meals or assigned seats are offered, and only short hauls are flown. Western Pacific's flight attendants wear khaki pants and tennis shoes, and entertain passengers with games, jokes, and giveaways. Also unique to

Western Pacific is its flying billboards. The airline sells the fuselages of its planes to other companies for advertising space.

Some large, established airlines also have decided to supplement their regular air service with low-fare, no-frills, low-cost service. Delta Airlines announced late in 1995 that it would launch a low-fare, short-haul airline. Armed with concessions from its pilots' union that included lower pay, more flight hours, and more efficient work rules, the airline has a goal of pruning its average-seat-mile (ASM) cost to be competitive with Southwest.

Established airlines that have initiated a head-to-head showdown with Southwest have met with mixed success. Continental Airlines abandoned its Continental Lite entry when it could not finance its half-price fare sale long enough to gain a foothold in the market. To counter Continental Lite, Southwest dropped its fares still further and replaced its slogan, which was "Just Plane Smart." The new slogan, "*The* Low Fare Airline," leaves little doubt that Southwest knows passengers want low fares.

Some major airlines have not pursued the low-cost strategy. Alaska Airlines has positioned itself as maintaining varied services while cutting its fares. Alaska Airline's marketing campaign aimed at the value-oriented customer uses the slogan, "For the same price [as other low-fare airlines], you just get more!"

United and Southwest in a Dogfight

Nowhere is the battle between Southwest and a competitor fiercer than in the skies over the lucrative California market. United Airlines started its United Shuttle in October 1994. The airline distinguished itself from Southwest by offering a first-class section, assigned seats, and a frequent-flier program—all for the same low fare that Southwest charged. United also expected to benefit from strong brand equity in California. It also sought to capitalize on its hub in San Francisco, a key pair city not only for destinations within California but for various other West Coast cities.

Southwest, which enjoys a 50 percent market share in California, responded with more flights and fare cuts on both the short- and long-haul routes that were served by United. Because of the fare wars, United predicted that its Shuttle would not show a profit until at least 1997. Despite this pessimistic profit projection, United Shuttle's flight schedule grew in 6 months from 184 to 342 flights per day within California. Southwest's scheduled flights in this market rose less, from 433 to 465 daily.

The likelihood of United Shuttle's staying aloft depends on its ability to reach its goal of an ASM cost of 7.4 cents. The question is whether United's pockets are deep enough to cover its losses until this cost reduction is achieved. United Shuttle took away about 10 percent of Southwest's passengers within the first year of their dogfight.

Flying into the Future

Although the airline has scaled back its market expansion plans, Southwest thinks it can expand capacity about 15 to 20 percent annually. However, in the tumultuous world of low-fare airline competition, Southwest is highly distinctive in the way it plans for the future. Kelleher, the CEO, said Southwest does not prepare strategic plans in the traditional sense. He added, "We don't even do one-year plans. When we bump up against some benchmark that requires us to make a major decision, we review our strategic definition of the airline and decide whether we should depart from it."

http://www.iflyswa.com/

QUESTIONS

1. What pricing strategies does Southwest Airlines employ to compete against other airlines?
2. What types of costs must Southwest and other airlines control to remain competitive?

3. What can Southwest do to fend off the competition posed by new airlines that imitate its low-price strategy?

Sources: Carl Quintanilla, "Delta Takes Aim at Small Rivals, but USAir May Be in Crossfire," *The Wall Street Journal,* Dec. 12, 1995, p. B4; Scott McCartney, "Airline Industry's Top-Ranked Woman Keeps Southwest's Small-Fry Spirit Alive," *The Wall Street Journal,* Nov. 30, 1995, p. B1; Bryan Gruley and Scott McCartney, "Flock of New Low-Fare Carriers Means Savings for Consumers, U.S. Study Says," *The Wall Street Journal,* Nov. 2, 1995, p. A4; David Barboza, "Imitation of Southwest by Several No-Frills Airlines May Be the Highest Form of Flattery," *The New York Times,* Oct. 5, 1995, p. C5; Anthony Velocci, "More City Pairs Await Southwest," *Aviation Week & Space Technology,* Aug. 7, 1995, p. 40; Scott McCartney, "Southwest Airlines May Be Heading into Calmer Skies," *The Wall Street Journal,* July 17, 1995, p. B4; Susan Chandler, "Not Bad, for a Dumb Idea," *Business Week,* Feb. 20, 1995, p. 40; Wendy Zellner et al., "Go-Go Goliaths," *Business Week,* Feb. 13, 1995, pp. 64+; Wendy Zellner, Eric Schine, and Susan Chandler, "Dogfight over California," *Business Week,* Aug. 15, 1994, p. 32; Jennifer Lawrence, "Integrated Mix Makes Expansion Fly," *Advertising Age,* Nov. 8, 1993, p. S10; and Bridget O'Brian, "Southwest Airlines Is a Rare Air Carrier: It Still Makes Money," *The Wall Street Journal,* Oct. 26, 1992, p. A1.

CASE 2 Home Depot

IMPLEMENTING A PRICING STRATEGY

How do you build a business from the ground up? Some answers (and at least a couple of questions) can be found in the fairly brief history of Home Depot. The Atlanta-based company established its first two stores in 1978. Within a few years, Home Depot had become the leader in an industry that sells home-improvement products to consumers and building supplies to contractors and other businesses. Home Depot now dominates this industry that generates over $100 billion in annual sales.

A Humble Start but Not for Long

Home Depot had a most inauspicious beginning. Bernard Marcus and Arthur Blank started the company soon after losing their jobs with a fast-growing chain of home-improvement stores in Southern California. They were unable to finance construction of a prototype Home Depot store so they leased a building that previously housed a discount store. They stocked the first store with 18,000 items ranging from paint to plumbing supplies.

On opening day, Marcus and Blank gave their children 700 $1 bills and stationed them at the store entrance. Their assignment was to hand the $1 bills to departing customers as a way of saying thank you. However, before the end of the day, the children had to move into the parking lot and give people money to come into the store. Although sales were slow at first, favorable comments about Home Depot began to spread fairly soon. Two more stores were opened in 1980. There are now more than 350 Home Depots in the U.S. and Canada.

The firm is one of the strongest financial performers in the entire country. In fact, Home Depot averaged 36 percent sales growth and 44 percent profit improvement annually between 1990 and 1994. The chain expects to have 800 outlets by 1998. Home Depot is exploring the possibility of entering Mexico and South America. By the year 2000, Home Depot expects to have $25 billion in sales, which would represent an estimated 13 percent of the home-improvement and building-supplies market.

Ingredients for Success

What is Home Depot's secret? The company faces the same challenges as any other business: selecting the right target market, maintaining an inventory of products that prospective and repeat customers desire, identifying cost-effective store sites, and planning an offensive strategy to beat the competition. Home Depot found that a blend of low prices, excellent customer service, and a large assortment of products differentiated it from the other 500 firms in the industry. Thus the typical Home Depot store is 130,000 square feet, has 150 employees, averages $40 million in annual sales, and stocks about 35,000 items. Competitors' stores typically are smaller and stock far fewer items.

Home Depot stresses that its prices are below those of competing outlets. Its massive size provides enormous buying power, allowing the firm to extract relatively low prices from suppliers. For example, power tools and accessories are often sold at 10 percent below what most competitors pay for the same products. To survive, smaller firms in this industry have to avoid a price war with Home Depot. The survivors focus instead on offering ample service, employing knowledgeable sales people, reducing inventory costs, and reacting quickly to changes in local markets.

Home Depot uses small, local suppliers where possible. According to Blank, "We definitely want local suppliers. They understand local building codes and frequently offer products that are unique to those areas. That is one of the reasons we have five merchandising regions now in the U.S.—two in the western part of the country, two in the southern part of the country, and one in the northeast." Home Depot's size also helps the chain acquire some products that are sold only in its stores.

A key factor in Home Depot's well-regarded service is its 300,000 employees. According to Blank, "Competitors can copy our fixtures and the way we set up our merchandise. They can copy our vendors and our pricing. But what they can't copy is what goes on between the ears of the employees—their commitment to taking care of the customer no matter what." Employee compensation at Home Depot is higher than compensation paid by competitors. In addition, every full-time employee has an equity interest under the company's stock ownership plan.

To stay in touch with shoppers, Marcus and Blank—who are the firm's chief executive officer and president, respectively—still work occasionally on the store sales floor. Home Depot also requires the outside members of its board of directors to visit 12 stores every quarter to further strengthen the connection with the company's employees.

Speaking about the company's formula for success, Blank said, "When a customer leaves the store, he or she feels a bond with the store. Something happened in that store beyond buying a product. They found somebody in that store who really cared about their problem, or their project, or their dream list. It wasn't just someone sticking a product in their hand and sending them on their way. That's what really creates the bond with the customer."

Expanding in Waves

Home Depot's rapid expansion follows from a carefully orchestrated plan. The company enters new markets in waves. Three or four stores are opened around the perimeter of a city in the first wave. Each store is located to serve about 100,000 households with a median income of at least $45,000. The second wave begins as soon as the initial stores' combined sales total $50 million. The city is "filled in" with additional stores over a 3- to 5-year period. Recently, some stores have been opened in areas with fewer than 100,000 households.

Home Depot may close a store and open two stores in its place under either of two conditions:

- If the store surpasses $400 per square foot in sales, indicating the store is too crowded.

- If the growth rate in sales lags behind the inflation rate, indicating the outlet is not performing up to expectations.

Building for the Future

To maintain its leadership role in the home-improvement and building-supplies market requires continual adaptation. According to Blank, "The whole focus of the company is to take today's standards and accept them for what they are but say we have to improve upon them for the future. Maintaining what we do today is just not going to cut it. . . . We spend 80 to 90 percent of our time focusing on the issues and problems, what the competition is doing, what our customers are looking for, what they are not finding in our stores, what stores are having problems."

While expanding the number of Home Depots, the firm is also experimenting with a new type of outlet, named CrossRoads. Targeted toward rural do-it-yourselfers, the first such store opened in Quincy, Illinois, in 1995. The prototype Crossroads store consists of a 115,000 square-foot store and an adjoining 100,000 square-foot lumberyard.

A warehouse-style outlet, CrossRoads not only stocks Home Depot's usual assortment of products but also includes other departments such as work clothing, pet and animal supplies, and agricultural equipment. The store also carries a full range of major appliances to meet the needs of people building or remodeling their home. CrossRoads is designed as a one-stop shopping experience. The new chain's target market consists of owners of "ranchettes" having 10 to 20 acres with some horses, a small herd of livestock, and/or a few acres of a cash crop.

http:www.homedepot.com/

QUESTIONS

1. What factors (including demand, competition, costs, and other marketing-mix elements) are likely to influence Home Depot's pricing in the future?

2. How can firms that sell home-improvement products to consumers and building supplies to contractors and other businesses use nonprice competition to achieve a differential advantage?

Sources: Theodore Roth, "Home Depot Standing at the CrossRoads," *Columbia* (Missouri) *Daily Tribune,* Aug. 28, 1995, p. 1B; Wendy Zellner et al., "Go-Go Goliaths," *Business Week,* Feb. 13, 1995, pp. 64+; William Darrow, "Home Depot and the Home Center Industry: Competitive Strategies and Mobility Barriers," *Mid-Atlantic Journal of Business,* December 1994, pp. 227+; William Schober, "1994 Giants: Poised for Aggressive Growth," *Building Supply Home Centers,* February 1994, p. 40; Graham Button, "Keeping in Touch," *Forbes,* Nov. 22, 1993, p. 72; John Johnson, "Battling Back against the Giants," *Industrial Distribution,* May 1993, p. 54; "Blank Fills Out the Niche for Home Depot Growth," *Advertising Age,* Feb. 1, 1993, p. S5; Jim Cory, "When Home Depot Comes to Town," *Chilton's Hardware Age,* July 1992, p. 81; and Roger Thompson, "There's No Place Like Home Depot," *Nation's Business,* February 1992, p. 30.

PART FIVE

Distribution

The arrangements necessary to transfer ownership of a product and transport the product from where it is produced to where it is finally consumed

We are in the process of developing a marketing program to satisfy the firm's target markets and achieve the goals established in strategic marketing planning. So far, we have considered the product and price elements in the marketing mix. Now we turn our attention to the distribution system—the means for getting the product to the market.

The distribution part of the marketing mix encompasses several broad topics: (1) strategies for selecting and operating distribution channels; (2) the retail market and the major retailing institutions used in distribution; and (3) the wholesale market, the major wholesaling institutions used in distribution, and the primary arrangements for physically distributing materials and supplies to production facilities and then moving finished products to target markets. These topics are covered in Chapters 13, 14, and 15, respectively.

CHAPTER 13

Channels
of
Distribution

Are New Channels Pumping Up or Puncturing GOODYEAR's Sales?

Earlier this decade, Goodyear Tire and Rubber Co. had a serious problem. The way in which the manufacturer distributed its lines of tires was not in tune with the desires of much of the tire-buying market. Even Goodyear's chairman admitted, "Too many people were telling us that it was not convenient for them to purchase Goodyear products, because there wasn't an outlet where they preferred to shop."

More and more consumers wanted to buy tires at outlets that stock multiple brands at discount prices or at big warehouse clubs that carry fewer brands but offer steeper discounts. In contrast, Goodyear sold its tires only through its company-owned stores and independent dealers that featured the company's products. The company also had other problems, such as too few new products. Over a 4-year period, Goodyear lost three valuable percentage points of market share for automobile replacement tires. Michelin of France and Bridgestone of Japan gained at the U.S. tiremaker's expense.

In addition, independent dealers depending on Goodyear products were not faring well. Consumers wanted to shop a full range of prices at a tire dealer, but Goodyear was slow to respond to the market's desires. Consequently, Goodyear's dealers lost sales to competitors. Belatedly, the company provided dealers with cheaper All-American Decathlon and Concorde lines of tires.

Eventually, Goodyear took a bold step to reach more consumers—the company arranged to sell seven of its tire lines through Sears. The Goodyear brands supplied to Sears included the popular Arriva, Eagle GT, and Wrangler HT. The agreement was a logical step for Goodyear, since Sears sells more tires than any other retailer.

At the same time, Goodyear tried to strengthen other elements of its marketing mix. New tires were launched at a faster pace. The leading introduction has been the Aquatred, which is supposed to provide superior traction on wet roads. The tiremaker also boosted its advertising budget, to better promote its growing number of tire lines.

Early financial results following the sweeping changes in Goodyear's distribution arrangements were promising. In particular, market share was regained. Encouraged, the company continued to expand its distribution by reaching agreements with Wal-Mart and Discount Tire to sell its tires. In 1995, Goodyear was selected to be the exclusive tire supplier to over 800 Penske Auto Centers located in Kmart stores nationwide.

Still, the path followed by Goodyear has been bumpy in places. Many of its long-standing dealers were angered or alienated—or both—when the manufacturer expanded its distribution channels to include Sears and other outlets. Some are still upset that they lost their exclusive rights to the well-known Goodyear brands. Others believe they have been hurt by added price competition. As explained by one independent dealer, "To be competitive [with Sears], we have had to lower our margins and spend more money to promote the products, so we are making less money on Goodyear."[1]

All factors considered, was it wise for Goodyear to expand its distribution by selling through Sears, warehouse clubs, and discount outlets?

http://www.goodyear.com/

Even before a product is ready for market, management should determine what methods and routes will be used to get it there. This means establishing strategies for the product's distribution channels and physical distribution. Then, as illustrated by Goodyear's situation, distribution activities and relationships need to be monitored and adjusted over time.

Distribution is garnering more attention. Consider, for instance, the title of one news report, "Improved Distribution, Not Better Production, Is Key Goal in Mergers." During the mid-1990s, distribution considerations were important as Walt Disney and Capital Cities/ABC merged and Eli Lilly acquired PCS Health Systems.[2]

Managing a distribution channel often begins with a producer. Therefore, we will discuss channels largely from the vantage point of a producer. As you will see, however, the problems and opportunities that middlemen face in managing their channels are similar to those faced by producers. After studying this chapter, you should be able to explain:

CHAPTER GOALS

- The nature and importance of middlemen.
- What a distribution channel is.
- The sequence of decisions involved in designing a channel.
- The major channels for goods and services.
- Vertical marketing systems.
- How to choose specific channels and middlemen.
- Intensity of distribution.
- The nature of conflicts and control within distribution channels.
- Legal considerations in channels.

Middlemen and Distribution Channels

Ownership of a product has to be transferred somehow from the individual or organization that makes it to the consumer who needs and buys it. Goods also must be physically transported from where they are produced to where they are needed. Services ordinarily cannot be shipped but rather are produced and consumed in the same place (as we'll discuss in Chapter 19).

Distribution's role within a marketing mix is getting the product to its target market. The most important activity in getting a product to market is arranging for its sale and the transfer of title from producer to final customer. Other common activities (or functions) are promoting the product, storing it, and assuming some of the financial risk during the distribution process.

A producer can carry out these functions in exchange for an order—and, hopefully, payment—from a customer. Or producer and consumer can share these activities. Typically, however, firms called middlemen perform some of these activities on behalf of the producer or the consumer.

A **middleman** is a business firm that renders services related *directly* to the sale and/or purchase of a product as it flows from producer to consumer. (Note that in business, *middleman* is a traditional, gender-neutral term.) A middleman either owns the product at some point or actively aids in the transfer of ownership. Often, but not always, a middleman takes physical possession of the product.

Middlemen are commonly classified on the basis of whether or not they take title to the products being distributed. **Merchant middlemen** actually take title to the products they help to market. The two groups of merchant middlemen are wholesalers and retailers. **Agent middlemen** never actually own the products, but they do arrange the transfer of title. Real estate brokers, manufacturers' agents, and travel agents are examples of agent middlemen.

How Important Are Middlemen?

Some critics say prices are high because there are too many middlemen performing unnecessary or redundant functions. Especially during a recession, some manufacturers draw this conclusion and seek to cut costs by eliminating wholesaling middlemen.[3] While middlemen can be eliminated from channels, lower costs may not always be achieved. The outcome is not predictable because of a basic axiom of marketing: *You can eliminate middlemen, but you cannot eliminate essential distribution activities that they perform.* These activities—such as creating assortments and storing products—can be shifted from one party to another in an effort to improve efficiency. However, someone has to perform the various activities—if not a middleman, then the producer or the final customer.[4]

Middlemen may be able to carry out distribution activities better or more cheaply than either producers or consumers. Moreover, it is usually not practical for a producer to deal directly with ultimate consumers. Think for a moment how inconvenient your life would be if there were no retail middlemen—no supermarkets, gas stations, or ticket sales outlets, for instance.

Middlemen serve as purchasing agents for their customers. Conversely, they act as sales specialists for their suppliers. Consider the sales role performed by Lotus Light Enterprises, a distributor that represents about 400 companies and their 7,500 different teas, herbal products, and related items. According to a Lotus Light manager, "Our most important service is providing a forum for our customers' products. We show their products to retailers and exhibit them at trade shows."[5] As illustrated in Figure 13-1, middlemen also provide financial services for both suppliers and customers. And their storage services, capability to divide large shipments into smaller ones for resale, and market knowledge benefit suppliers and customers alike.

What Is a Distribution Channel?

A **distribution channel** consists of the set of people and firms involved in the transfer of title to a product as the product moves from producer to ultimate consumer or business user. A channel of distribution always includes both the producer and the final customer for the product in its present form as well as any middlemen such as retailers and wholesalers.

FIGURE 13-1

Typical activities of a middleman.

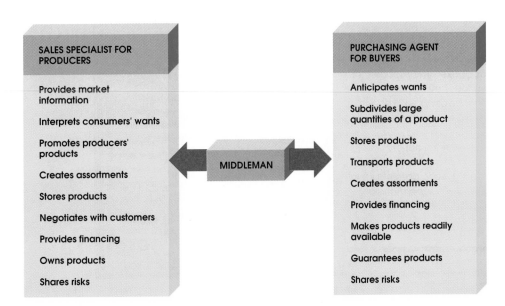

The channel for a product extends only to the last person or organization that buys it without making any significant change in its form. When its form is altered and another product emerges, a new channel is started. When lumber is milled and then made into furniture, two separate channels are involved. The channel for the *lumber* might be lumber mill → broker → furniture manufacturer. The channel for the *finished furniture* might be furniture manufacturer → retail furniture store → consumer.

Besides producer, middlemen, and final customer, other institutions aid the distribution process. Among these *intermediaries* are banks, insurance companies, storage firms, and transportation companies. However, because they do not take title to the products and are not actively involved in purchase or sales activities, these intermediaries are not formally included in the distribution channel.

This chapter focuses on the flow (or transfer) of *ownership* for a product, while part of Chapter 15 examines the *physical* flow of goods. These flows are distinct; consequently, different institutions may carry them out. For example, a contractor might order roofing shingles from a local distributor of building materials. To minimize freight and handling costs, the product might be shipped directly—that is, shingles manufacturer → contractor. But the channel for title (and ownership) would be manufacturer → distributor → contractor.

Designing Distribution Channels

Similar firms often have dissimilar channels of distribution. For instance, large sellers of auto insurance use different channels. To reach prospective customers, Aetna uses independent agents who typically sell several brands of insurance. In

http://www.aetna.com/

*S*napple beverages are distributed through different channels than carbonated soft drinks. Typically, soft drink companies manufacture and sell a syrup to bottlers, who add water and carbonation, and then bottle or can the product. In contrast, Snapple Beverage Corporation works with copackers to produce the various beverages. The finished Snapple product is sold to independent distributors, who sell to various retail outlets. To boost Snapple sales, distributors strive to obtain special displays in supermarkets and other high-volume outlets.

http://www.snapple.com/

contrast, State Farm markets through agents who sell only its brand of insurance products. Some years ago, Allstate sales people had offices located in Sears stores. Now that Allstate is no longer owned by Sears, the firm uses an approach similar to State Farm.

A company wants a distribution channel that not only meets customers' needs but also provides an edge on competition. Some firms gain a differential advantage with their channels. Caterpillar uses construction-equipment dealers that provide customers with many valued services, ranging from advice about equipment financing to rapid fulfillment of orders for repair parts. Northwestern Mutual Life seeks a competitive edge by supplying its agents with what it intends to be the best training in the insurance field. To market a right-hand-drive Saturn in Japan, General Motors decided to use the same approach that worked in the U.S., namely establishing dealerships that sell various Saturn models but no other brands of automobiles.[6]

To design channels that satisfy customers and outdo competition, an organized approach is required.[7] As shown in Figure 13-2, we suggest a sequence of four decisions:

1. *Specifying the role of distribution.* A channel strategy should be designed within the context of the entire marketing mix. First, the firm's marketing objectives are reviewed. Next, the roles assigned to product, price, and promotion are specified. Each element may have a distinct role, or two elements may share an assignment. For example, a manufacturer of pressure gauges may use both middlemen and direct-mail advertising to convince prospective customers that it is committed to servicing the product following the sale.

2. *Selecting the type of channel.* Once distribution's role in the overall marketing program has been agreed on, the most suitable type of channel for the company's

FIGURE 13-2

Sequence of decisions to design a distribution channel.

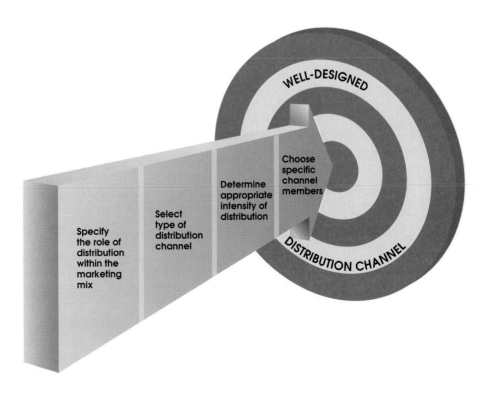

Specify the role of distribution within the marketing mix

Select type of distribution channel

Determine appropriate intensity of distribution

Choose specific channel members

WELL-DESIGNED

DISTRIBUTION CHANNEL

product must be determined. At this point in the sequence, a firm needs to decide whether middlemen will be used in its channel and, if so, which types of middlemen.[8]

To illustrate the wide array of institutions available, as well as the difficulty of channel selection, consider a manufacturer of compact disc (CD) players. If the firm decides to use middlemen, it must choose among many different types. At the retail level, the range of institutions includes specialty audio-video outlets, department stores, discount houses, and mail-order firms.

3. *Determining intensity of distribution.* The next decision relates to intensity of distribution—that is, the number of middlemen used at the wholesale and retail levels in a particular territory. As we will see later, the target market's buying behavior and the product's nature have a direct bearing on this decision. Because of the desires of prospective customers, Goodyear found it necessary to intensify its distribution and, as a result, added new channels.

4. *Choosing specific channel members.* The last decision is selecting specific firms to distribute the product. For each type of institution, there are usually numerous specific companies from which to choose.

Assume that the manufacturer of CD players prefers two types of middlemen: department stores and specialty outlets. If the CD players will be sold in Chicago, the producer must decide which department stores—Marshall Field and/or Montgomery Ward & Co.—will be asked to distribute its product line. Also, one or more consumer electronics chains—from a group including United Audio Centers and Circuit City—might be selected. Similar decisions must be made for each territory in the firm's market.

When selecting specific firms to be part of a channel, a producer should consider whether the middleman sells to the customers that the manufacturer wants to reach and whether the middleman's product mix, pricing structure, promotion, and customer service are all compatible with the manufacturer's needs. A producer should also assess the market, the product, its own company, and the middlemen.

In this design sequence, the first decision relates to broad marketing strategy, the second and third to channel strategies, and the last to specific tactics. In the next two major sections, we cover in more detail these channel strategies. First we will look at the major channels traditionally used by producers and at two special channels. Then factors that most influence a company's choice of channels can be discussed. After that, we will consider how many middlemen should be used by a firm.

Selecting the Type of Channel

Firms may rely on existing channels, or they may devise new channels to better serve current customers and to reach new prospects. For instance, besides selling through various types of retailers, Levi Strauss & Co. has started opening its own stores featuring, of course, Levi apparel. In contrast, a small company named New Pig (that's the real name) decided not to use conventional middlemen such as supermarkets and hardware stores to sell a new dust cloth with special dirt-attracting properties. Instead, to reach a primarily female target market, this enterprising firm distributes its product through beauty salons.[9]

Most distribution channels include middlemen, but some do not. A channel consisting only of producer and final customer, with no middlemen providing assistance, is called **direct distribution**. ServiceMaster uses a direct approach to sell

http://www.levi.com/

http://www.iflyswa.com/

its building cleaning services to both residential and commercial customers. Southwest Airlines derives about one-half of its sales from direct distribution. Under this arrangement, individuals use a free 800 telephone number to book a seat on a Southwest flight or, in some airports, they can do it themselves through a computer terminal.[10]

In contrast, a channel of producer, final customer, and at least one level of middlemen represents **indirect distribution**. TWA, Delta, and most other airlines depend heavily on an indirect approach, involving travel agents, to market air travel services to consumers. One level of middlemen—retailers but no wholesaling middlemen, for example—or multiple levels may participate in an indirect channel. (For consumer goods, sometimes a channel in which wholesalers are bypassed but retailers are used is termed *direct*, rather than indirect, distribution.) With indirect distribution a producer must determine the type(s) of middlemen that will best serve its needs. The range of options at the wholesale and retail levels will be described in the next two chapters.

Major Channels of Distribution

Diverse distribution channels exist today. The most common channels for consumer goods, business goods, and services are described next and summarized in Figure 13-3.

Distribution of Consumer Goods. Five channels are widely used in marketing tangible products to ultimate consumers:

- *Producer → consumer*. The shortest, simplest distribution channel for consumer goods involves no middlemen. The producer may sell from door to door or by mail. For instance, Southwestern Company uses college students to market its books on a house-to-house basis. Some personal computer makers, such as Dell and Gateway, sell directly to final users.[11]
- *Producer → retailer → consumer*. Many large retailers buy directly from manufacturers and agricultural producers. To the chagrin of various wholesaling middlemen, Wal-Mart has increased its direct dealings with producers.
- *Producer → wholesaler → retailer → consumer*. If there is a traditional channel for consumer goods, this is it. Small retailers and manufacturers by the thousands find this channel the only economically feasible choice.
- *Producer → agent → retailer → consumer*. Instead of using wholesalers, many producers prefer to rely on agent middlemen to reach the retail market, especially *large-scale* retailers. For example, Clorox uses agent middlemen (such as PMI-Eisenhart, a food broker) to reach retailers (such as Dillon's and Schnucks, both large grocery chains), which in turn sell Clorox's cleaning products to consumers.
- *Producer → agent → wholesaler → retailer → consumer*. To reach *small* retailers, producers often use agent middlemen, who in turn call on wholesalers that sell to large retail chains and/or small retail stores. Working as an agent on behalf of various grocery-products manufacturers, PMI-Eisenhart sells to some wholesalers (such as Supervalu) that distribute a wide range of products to retailers (such as Dierberg's, a supermarket chain in the St. Louis area). In turn, Dierberg's offers its assortment of products to final consumers.

Distribution of Business Goods. A variety of channels is available to reach organizations that incorporate the products into their manufacturing process or

FIGURE 13-3
Major marketing channels for different categories of products.

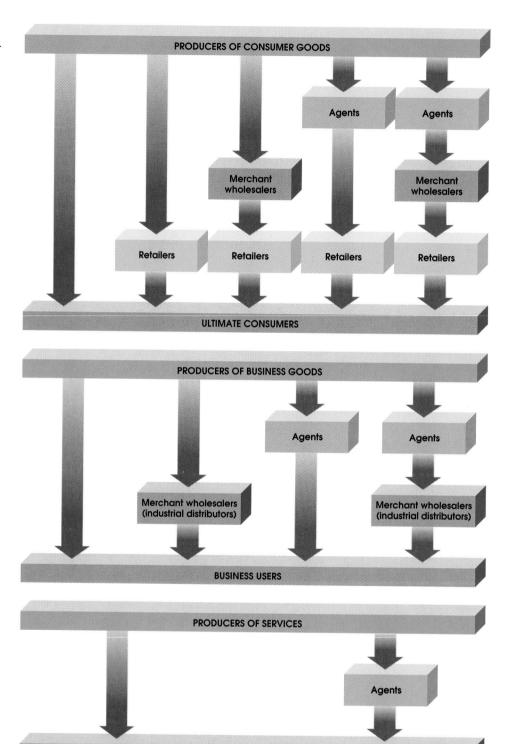

use them in their operations.[12] In the distribution of business goods, the terms *industrial distributor* and *merchant wholesaler* are synonymous. The four common channels for business goods are:

- *Producer → user*. This direct channel accounts for a greater *dollar* volume of business products than any other distribution structure. Large installations, such as jet engines, air-conditioning systems, and elevators (all of which are made by divisions of United Technologies), are usually sold directly to users.
- *Producer → industrial distributor → user.* Producers of operating supplies and small accessory equipment frequently use industrial distributors to reach their markets. Manufacturers of building materials and air-conditioning equipment are two examples of industries that make heavy use of industrial distributors.
- *Producer → agent → user*. Firms without their own sales departments find this a desirable channel. Also, a company that wants to introduce a new product or enter a new market may prefer to use agents rather than its own sales force.
- *Producer → agent → industrial distributor → user*. This channel is similar to the preceding one. It is used when, for some reason, it is not feasible to sell through agents directly to the business user. For example, the order size may be too small to justify direct selling. Or decentralized inventory may be needed to supply users rapidly, in which case the storage services of an industrial distributor are required.

Distribution of Services. The intangible nature of services creates special distribution requirements. There are only two common channels for services:[13]

- *Producer → consumer*. Because a service is intangible, the production process and/or sales activity often require personal contact between producer and customer. Thus a direct channel is used. Direct distribution is typical for many professional services, such as health care and legal advice, and personal services, such as haircutting and weight-loss counseling. However, other services, including travel and insurance, may also rely on direct distribution.
- *Producer → agent → consumer*. While direct distribution often is necessary for a service to be performed, producer-customer contact may not be required for distribution activities. Agents frequently assist a services producer with transfer of ownership (the sales task). Many services, notably travel, lodging, advertising media, entertainment, and insurance, are sold through agents. However, various advances in computing and communications technologies make it easier for customers to deal directly with service providers, thereby threatening the role of agents. This is particularly true in the travel industry where buyers can use the telephone or on-line services like CompuServe to book their own plane and hotel reservations.[14]

http://www.compuserve.com/

Multiple Distribution Channels

Many, perhaps most, producers are not content with only a single distribution channel. Instead, for reasons such as reaching two or more target markets or avoiding total dependence on a single arrangement, they employ **multiple distribution channels**. For example, Sherwin-Williams paints and Goodyear tires are distributed through wholesalers, independent retailers, large retail chains, and the manufacturers' own stores. (Similarly, many companies establish multiple *supply* channels to ensure that they have products when needed.)

Use of multiple channels occurs in several distinct situations.[15] A manufacturer is likely to use multiple channels to reach *different types of markets* when selling:

*P*izzeria Uno's restaurants, featuring "original Chicago style deep dish pizza," have been quite successful. In fact, some customers prefer this brand of pizza so much that they want to prepare it at home. As a result, the company developed a line of products for sale in grocery stores, notably supermarkets. Now, Pizzeria Uno reaches consumers through multiple distribution channels centered on its restaurants and also grocery stores.

- The same product (for example, sporting goods or computers) to both consumer and business markets.[16]
- Unrelated products (margarine and paint; rubber products and plastics).

Multiple channels are also used to reach different segments within a single market when:

- Size of the buyers varies greatly. An airline may sell directly to travel departments in large corporations, but rely on travel agents to reach small businesses and ultimate consumers.
- Geographic concentration differs across parts of the market. A manufacturer of industrial machinery may use its own sales force to sell directly to customers that are located close together, but may employ agents in sparsely populated markets.

A significant trend involves selling the *same brand to a single market* through channels that compete with each other; this is sometimes called *dual distribution*. Many independent insurance agents are concerned (even angry) because insurance companies are arranging for banks to sell their products.[17] Producers may open their own stores, thereby creating dual distribution, when they are not satisfied with the market coverage provided by existing retail outlets. Or they may establish their own stores primarily as testing grounds for new products and marketing techniques.

Although multiple distribution channels provide benefits to the producer, they can aggravate middlemen—as Goodyear found out. For example, many owners of franchised Carvel Ice Cream Bakery Stores rebelled when faced with multiple channels. The franchisees (who are middlemen) claimed their marketing efforts were undermined and sales and profits reduced when the producer decided to sell its ice cream in supermarkets as well as in franchised stores.[18]

Sometimes it is possible to arrange multiple channels in such a way that a firm's middlemen do not get upset. One approach, which is difficult to achieve, is to

develop separate marketing strategies for each different channel. For example, the Scotts Company sells some of its lawn-care products to large discount chains but reserves other products only for smaller stores.[19]

Vertical Marketing Systems

Historically, distribution channels stressed the independence of individual channel members. That is, a producer used various middlemen to achieve its distribution objectives. However, the producer typically was not concerned with middlemen's needs. Conversely, wholesalers and retailers were more interested in maintaining their freedom than in coordinating their activities with a producer. These priorities of conventional distribution channels provided an opportunity for a new type of channel.

During the past three decades, the vertical marketing system has become *the* dominant form of distribution channel. A **vertical marketing system (VMS)** is a tightly coordinated distribution channel designed specifically to improve operating efficiency and marketing effectiveness. A VMS illustrates the concept of function shifting that was discussed earlier in this chapter. In a VMS no marketing function is sacred to a particular level or firm in the channel. Instead, each function is performed at the most advantageous position in the channel.

The high degree of coordination or control characterizing a VMS is achieved through one of three means: common ownership of successive levels of a channel; contracts between channel members; or the market power of one or more members. Table 13-1 shows these three distinct forms of vertical marketing systems.

In a **corporate vertical marketing system**, a firm at one level of a channel owns the firms at the next level or owns the entire channel. Sherwin-Williams and Goodyear, for example, own retail outlets. Also, a growing number of apparel makers are opening retail stores to feature their brands of clothing.

Middlemen may also engage in this type of vertical integration. For example, many grocery chains, including Kroger's, own food-processing facilities, such as dairies, which supply their stores. And various large retailers, including Sears, own all or part of manufacturing facilities that supply their stores with many products.

TABLE 13-1 Types of vertical marketing systems

Type of system	Control maintained by	Examples
Corporate	Ownership	Singer (sewing machines), Goodyear (tires), Tandy Corp. (electronics)
Contractual:		
Wholesaler-sponsored voluntary chain	Contract	Western Auto stores, IGA stores
Retailer-owned cooperative	Stock ownership by retailers	True Value hardware stores
Franchise systems:	Contract	
Manufacturer-sponsored retailers		Ford, Chrysler, and other auto dealers
Manufacturer-sponsored wholesalers		Coca-Cola and other soft drink bottlers
Marketers of services		Wendy's, Midas Muffler, Holiday Inn, National car rentals
Administered	Economic power	Hartman luggage, General Electric, Kraft dairy products

In a **contractual vertical marketing system**, independent producers, wholesalers, and retailers operate under contracts specifying how they will try to improve the effectiveness and efficiency of their distribution. Three kinds of contractual systems have developed: wholesaler-sponsored voluntary chains (for example, Supervalu grocery stores); retailer-owned cooperatives (True Value hardware stores); and franchise systems (Domino's pizza and Midas automotive maintenance and repairs). All will be discussed in Chapter 14.

An **administered vertical marketing system** coordinates distribution activities through (1) the market and/or economic power of one channel member or (2) the willing cooperation of channel members. Sometimes the brand equity possessed by a manufacturer's product is strong enough to gain the voluntary cooperation of retailers in matters such as inventory levels, advertising, and store display. This situation is illustrated by Corning in ovenware, Rolex in watches, and Kraft in food products. It's important to note, however, that retailers—especially giant ones such as Wal-Mart—are more likely to dominate channel relationships now than in prior years. To satisfy Wal-Mart, Procter & Gamble has established an office in Bentonville, Arkansas, in the same town as the largest retailer's headquarters.[20]

http://www.wal-mart.com/

In the distant past, competition in distribution usually involved two different conventional channels. For instance, two producer → retailer → consumer channels tended to compete with each other. More recently, competition pitted a conventional channel against some form of VMS. Thus a traditional producer → retailer → consumer channel, such as Van Heusen shirts sold through various department stores, battled an administered VMS for business, such as cooperative merchandising efforts between Arrow and a specific chain of department stores.

Increasingly, the most common competitive battles are between different forms of vertical marketing systems. For example, a corporate system (the stores owned by Goodyear) competes with a contractual system (Firestone's franchised dealers). Considering the potential benefits of vertical marketing systems with respect to both marketing effectiveness and operating efficiencies, they should continue to grow in number and importance.

Factors Affecting Choice of Channels

If a firm is customer-oriented (and it better be if it hopes to prosper), its channels are determined by consumer buying patterns. The nature of the market should be the key factor in management's choice of channels. Other considerations are the product, the middlemen, and the company itself.

Market Considerations. A logical starting point is to consider the target market—its needs, structure, and buying behavior:

- *Type of market.* Because ultimate consumers behave differently than business users, they are reached through different distribution channels. One analyst explained the situation in the personal computer field: "There's a large corporate market and a large home market and they shop in different places." Because of these distinct buying patterns, numerous traditional computer dealers have been able to prosper despite the onslaught of other distribution means such as mail order, "superstores" (such as Incredible Universe), and various retailers (ranging from Dillard's to Sam's Club).[21] Retailers, by definition, serve ultimate consumers, so they are not in channels for business goods.
- *Number of potential customers.* A manufacturer with few potential customers (firms or industries) may use its own sales force to sell directly to ultimate con-

http://www.boeing.com/

http://reebok.com/

sumers or business users. Boeing uses this approach in selling its jet aircraft. For a large number of customers, the manufacturer would likely use middlemen. Reebok relies on numerous middlemen, notably retailers, to reach the large number of consumers in the market for athletic footwear. A firm using middlemen does not need as large a sales force as a company selling directly to final consumers.

- *Geographic concentration of the market.* When most of a firm's prospective customers are concentrated in a few geographic areas, direct sale is practical. This is the situation in the textile and garment manufacturing industries. When customers are geographically dispersed, direct sale is likely to be impractical because of high travel costs. Sellers may establish sales branches in densely populated markets and use middlemen in less concentrated markets. Some small American manufacturers are turning to specialized middlemen, called *trade intermediaries*, to crack foreign markets. Manufacturers sell their goods to trade intermediaries at lower-than-normal wholesale prices in exchange for the intermediaries' ability to secure distribution in markets around the globe.[22]
- *Order size.* When either order size or total volume of business is large, direct distribution is economical. Thus a food-products manufacturer would sell directly to large supermarket chains. The same manufacturer, however, would use wholesalers to reach small grocery stores, whose orders are usually too small to justify direct sale.[23]

Product Considerations.   While there are numerous product-related factors to consider, we will highlight three:

- *Unit value.* The price attached to each unit of a product affects the amount of funds available for distribution. For example, a company can afford to use its own employee to sell a nuclear-reactor part that costs more than $10,000. But it would not make sense for a company sales person to call on a household or a business firm to sell a $2 ballpoint pen. Consequently, products with low unit values usually are distributed through one or more levels of middlemen. There are exceptions, however. For instance, if order size is large because the customer buys many units of a product at the same time from the company, then a direct channel may be economically feasible.
- *Perishability.* Some goods, including many agricultural products, physically deteriorate fairly quickly. Other goods, such as clothing, perish in a fashion sense. As will be discussed further in Chapter 19, services are perishable because of their intangible nature. Perishable products require direct or very short channels.
- *Technical nature of a product.* A *business* product that is highly technical is often distributed directly to business users. The producer's sales force must provide considerable presale and postsale service; wholesalers normally cannot do this. *Consumer* products of a technical nature provide a real distribution challenge. Ordinarily, because of other factors discussed in this section, producers cannot sell directly to the consumer. As much as possible, they try to sell directly to retailers, but even then product servicing often poses problems.

Middlemen Considerations.   Here we begin to see that a company may not be able to arrange exactly the channels it desires:

- *Services provided by middlemen.* Each producer should select middlemen offering those marketing services that the producer either is unable to provide or cannot economically perform. For instance, independent agents have the capa-

bility to explain the technical aspects of competing products from different insurance companies to prospective buyers. Firms from other countries seeking to penetrate business markets in the U.S. commonly utilize industrial distributors. This is because they furnish needed capabilities such as market coverage, sales contacts, and storage of inventories.[24]

• *Availability of desired middlemen.* The middlemen preferred by a producer may not be available. They may carry competing products and, as a result, not want to add another line. Famous Amos Chocolate Chip Cookie Corp. faced this challenge. The company was unable to get its product on the shelves of a sufficient number of supermarket chains. Hence, Famous Amos has boosted sales by relying on alternative middlemen—warehouse clubs, vending machines, and even Burger King restaurants.[25]

• *Producer's and middleman's policies.* When middlemen are unwilling to join a channel because they consider a producer's policies to be unacceptable, the producer has fewer channel options. Some retailers or wholesalers, for example, will carry a producer's line only if they receive assurance that no competing middlemen will carry the line in the same territory. Recently, a growing number of small manufacturers have become very frustrated with the demands for lower prices and other concessions that are placed on them by giant retailers such as Wal-Mart and Home Depot. Thus makers of various products ranging

*I*t's not always easy for manufacturers to find suitable distributors. To do so, they may resort to advertising in trade publications. In this case, Protectoseal, which is a manufacturer of products for storing and handling flammables, is seeking a limited number of distributors which "welcome a close factory-distributor partnership."

from children's clothing to garden products have decided—very reluctantly—to not do business with these retailers.[26]

Company Considerations. Before choosing a distribution channel for a product, a company should consider its own situation:

- *Desire for channel control.* Some producers establish direct channels because they want to control their product's distribution, even though a direct channel may be more costly than an indirect channel. By controlling the channel, producers can achieve more aggressive promotion and can better control both the

A GLOBAL PERSPECTIVE

CAN AMERICAN COMPANIES PENETRATE THE JAPANESE DISTRIBUTION SYSTEM?

Sensing an enormous opportunity, many U.S. companies have been trying to distribute their products in Japan. Good luck! Some firms have found the challenge to be insurmountable, while others persist. Even the "Big Three" American automakers have had great difficulty establishing effective distribution arrangements in Japan.

Manufacturers in Japan tend to dominate the channels for distributing their products. Further, compared to the U.S. and Western European countries, wholesalers and retailers are numerous—some would say innumerable—in Japan. Thus, ownership of goods typically passes through several wholesaling middlemen before reaching retailers in Japan. Then, at the retail level, there are about 1 million "papa-mama" stores, as the Japanese call them. The number of such stores is declining, but they still account for a large proportion of retail sales—perhaps 50 percent—compared to only several percent in the U.S. In addition, many government regulations protect traditional distribution channels and deter change.

Changing consumer needs and government attitudes are beginning to modify the complex and, according to many observers, inefficient Japanese distribution system. To build distribution channels and gain success in Japan, some enterprising U.S. businesses have used such strategies as the following:

- *Finding a product niche in a traditional channel.* Despite their comparatively large size, some of the trading companies that have dominated distribution in Japan for many years do not have

complete product lines. If so, they may be receptive to importing a foreign product.
- *Using nontraditional channels.* General Electric tripled the sales of its large refrigerators in Japan by bypassing its normal distributor, Toshiba Corp., and dealing directly with Kojima Co., a chain of electronics superstores.
- *Forming joint ventures.* This distribution arrangement is jointly owned by a Japanese firm and a foreign company. A joint venture between Nestlé and a domestic wholesaler captured 75 percent of the instant-coffee market in Japan.

What's on the horizon for Japanese distribution? Apparently, traditional wholesalers and retailers will lose ground to new distribution approaches. For example, after several years of negotiation, Toys "R" Us opened its first stores in Japan; to date, they are immensely successful. In a broader sense, discount houses, large shopping centers, home-shopping channels on TV, and catalog retailing are finding favor with Japanese consumers who want to save money and/or time. Sounds a lot like the U.S., doesn't it?

Sources: The description of Japanese distribution is based on Toshiaki Taga and Yukihiko Uehara, "Some Characteristics of Business Practices in Japan," *Journal of Marketing Channels*, Vol. 3, No. 3, 1994, pp. 71–89; and Yoshihiro Tajima, "Japan's Markets and Distribution System," *Journal of Marketing Channels*, Vol. 3, No. 3, 1994, pp. 3–16. (The entire Vol. 3, No. 3 issue of *Journal of Marketing Channels* examines distribution channels in Japan.) The entry strategies are drawn from James D. Goodnow and Rustan Kosenko, "Strategies for Successful Penetration of the Japanese Market or How to Beat Japan at Its Own Game," *The Journal of Business and Industrial Marketing*, Winter 1992, pp. 41–49. The GE example is drawn from Norihiko Shirouzu, "Flouting 'Rules' Sells GE Fridges in Japan," *The Wall Street Journal*, Oct. 31, 1995, pp. B1, B2.

http://www.ibm.com/

freshness of merchandise stocks and their products' retail prices. In mid-1992, IBM started experimenting with mail-order sales of its personal computers. In bypassing middlemen, IBM hoped to enhance service to final customers and improve customer satisfaction ratings for its PCs. This particular channel did not work for IBM, although it has for other PC marketers such as Dell and Gateway.[27]

- *Services provided by seller.* Some producers make decisions about their channels based on the distribution functions desired (and occasionally demanded) by middlemen. For instance, numerous retail chains will not stock a product unless it is presold through heavy advertising by the producer.
- *Ability of management.* The marketing experience and managerial capabilities of a producer influence decisions about which channel to use. Many companies lacking marketing know-how turn the distribution job over to middlemen.
- *Financial resources.* A business with adequate finances can establish its own sales force, grant credit to its customers, and/or warehouse its own products. A financially weak firm uses middlemen to provide these services.[28]

In a few cases, virtually all factors point to a particular length and type of channel. However, there often is not a single "best" channel. In most cases the guiding factors send mixed signals. If a company with an unproven product having low profit potential cannot place its product with middlemen, it may have no other option but to try to distribute the product directly to its target market.

Determining Intensity of Distribution

At this point in designing a channel, a firm knows what role has been assigned to distribution within the marketing mix, and which types of middlemen will be used (assuming indirect distribution is appropriate). Next the company must decide on the **intensity of distribution**—that is, how many middlemen will be used at the wholesale and retail levels in a particular territory.

There are many degrees of intensity. As shown in Figure 13-4, we will consider the three major categories—ranging from *intensive* to *selective* to *exclusive*. Distribution intensity ordinarily is thought to be a single decision. However, if the channel has more than one level of middlemen (wholesaler and retailer, for example) or the firm is using multiple channels, the appropriate intensity must be selected for each level and channel.

Different degrees of intensity may be appropriate at successive levels of distribution. A manufacturer can often achieve intensive retail coverage with selective, rather than intensive, wholesale distribution. Or selective intensity at the retail level may be gained through exclusive intensity at the wholesale level. Of course, the wholesaling firm(s) will determine which retail outlets actually receive the

FIGURE 13-4

The intensity-of-distribution continuum.

INTENSIVE	SELECTIVE	EXCLUSIVE
Distribution through every reasonable outlet in a market	Distribution through multiple, but not all, reasonable outlets in a market	Distribution through a single wholesaling middleman and/or retailer in a market

product. Despite this lack of control, a producer should plan the levels of intensity needed at both the wholesale and retail levels.

Intensive Distribution

Under **intensive distribution**, a producer sells its product through every available outlet in a market where a consumer might reasonably look for it. Ultimate consumers demand immediate satisfaction from convenience goods and will not defer purchases to find a particular brand. Thus intensive distribution is often used by manufacturers of this category of product. Ice cream makers, such as Carvel and Häagen-Dazs, eventually decided they needed intensive, rather than more selective, distribution. As a result, they started to sell through supermarkets in addition to their franchised outlets.

Retailers often control whether a strategy of intensive distribution actually can be implemented. For example, a new manufacturer of toothpaste or a small producer of potato chips may want distribution in all supermarkets, but these retailers may limit their assortments to four fast-selling brands.

Except when they want to promote low prices, retailers are reluctant to pay to advertise a product that is sold by competitors. Therefore, intensive distribution places much—perhaps most—of the advertising and promotion burden on the producer. Many producers offer cooperative advertising, in which they reimburse middlemen for part of the cost of ads featuring the producer's product.

Selective Distribution

In **selective distribution**, a producer sells its product through multiple, but not all possible, wholesalers and retailers in a market where a consumer might reasonably look for it. Selective distribution is appropriate for consumer shopping goods, such as various types of clothing and appliances, and for business accessory equipment, such as office equipment and handheld tools. As described in the chapter-opening case, deciding its tires needed broader distribution, Goodyear moved from a rather selective approach toward intensive distribution by adding Sears stores as additional sales outlets.

In contrast, a company may shift to a selective distribution strategy after some experience with intensive distribution. The decision to change usually hinges on the high cost of intensive distribution or the unsatisfactory performance of middlemen. Certain middlemen perennially order in small, unprofitable amounts; others may be poor credit risks. Eliminating such marginal middlemen may reduce the number of outlets *but* increase a company's sales volume. Many companies have found this to be the case simply because they were able to do a more thorough selling job with a smaller number of accounts.

A firm may move toward more selective distribution to enhance the image of its products, strengthen customer service, improve quality control, and/or maintain some influence over its prices. For instance, Step 2, a manufacturer of large, plastic toys, decided not to distribute through discount stores in order to protect its image and profit margins.[29] Of course, whether or not Step 2's efforts to control its prices at the retail level are fruitful is open to question.

Exclusive Distribution

Under **exclusive distribution**, the supplier agrees to sell its product only to a single wholesaling middleman and/or retailer in a given market. At the wholesale level, such an arrangement is normally termed an exclusive *distributorship*; at the retail level, an exclusive *dealership*. A manufacturer may prohibit a middleman that holds an exclusive distributorship or dealership from handling a directly competing product line.

Producers often adopt an exclusive distribution strategy when it is essential that the retailer carry a large inventory. Thus exclusive dealerships are frequently used in marketing consumer specialty products such as expensive suits. This strategy is also desirable when the dealer or distributor must furnish installation and repair service. For this reason, manufacturers of farm machinery and large construction equipment grant exclusive distributorships.

Exclusive distribution helps a manufacturer control the last level of middleman before the final customer. A middleman with exclusive rights is usually willing to promote the product aggressively. Why? Interested customers will have to purchase the product from this middleman because no other outlets in the area carry the same brand. However, a producer suffers if its exclusive middlemen in various markets do not serve customers well. Essentially a manufacturer has "all its eggs in one basket."

An exclusive dealer or distributor has the opportunity to reap all the benefits of the producer's marketing activities in a particular area. However, under exclusive distribution, a middleman may become too dependent on the manufacturer. If the manufacturer fails, the middleman also fails (at least for that product). Another risk is that once sales volume has been built up in a market, the producer may add other dealers or, worse yet, drop all dealers and establish its own sales force.

Conflict and Control in Channels

Distribution should be—and occasionally is—characterized by goals shared by suppliers and customers and by cooperative actions. But conflicts as well as struggles for control are fairly common. To manage distribution channels effectively requires an understanding of both conflict and control, including techniques to (1) decrease conflict, or at least its negative effects, and (2) increase a firm's control within a channel.

Channel conflict exists when one channel member perceives another channel member to be acting in a way that prevents the first member from achieving its distribution objectives. Firms in one channel often compete vigorously with firms in other channels; this represents horizontal conflict. Even within the same channel, firms disagree about operating practices and try to gain control over other members' actions; this illustrates vertical conflict.

Horizontal Conflict

Horizontal conflict occurs among firms on the same level of distribution. The personal computer field provides an excellent example. Virtually all PCs used to be sold through conventional computer stores. Now PCs can be purchased through many other means—at office-supply outlets, department stores, warehouse clubs, consumer-electronics retailers, and gigantic new computer "superstores" such as Comp USA and CompuAdd, and of course by mail order.[30]

http://www.compusa.com/

Basically, horizontal conflict is a form of business competition. It may occur among:

- *Middlemen of the same type*: Maryvale Hardware (an independent retailer) versus Fred's Friendly Hardware (another independent retailer), for example.

- *Different types of middlemen on the same level*: Fred's Friendly Hardware (an independent retailer) versus Dunn Edwards Paint (a store within a large chain) versus Kmart (a single department in a store within a giant chain).

The main source of horizontal conflict is **scrambled merchandising**, in which middlemen diversify by adding product lines not traditionally carried by their type of business. Supermarkets, for instance, expanded beyond groceries by adding health and beauty aids, small appliances, records, snack bars, and various services. Retailers that originally sold these product lines became irritated both at supermarkets for diversifying and at producers for using multiple distribution channels. Banks selling insurance, mutual funds, and trust services is another example of scrambled merchandising in the previously tradition-bound world of financial services.

Scrambled merchandising and the resulting horizontal competition may stem from consumers, middlemen, or producers. Many *consumers* prefer convenient, one-stop shopping, so stores broaden their assortments to satisfy this desire. *Middlemen* constantly strive for higher gross margins and more customer traffic, so they increase the number of lines they carry. Perhaps with that in mind, a supermarket chain in Germany began to sell Mexican-made Volkswagen Beetles in its stores, much to the chagrin of regular VW dealers.[31] *Producers* seek to expand their market coverage and reduce unit production costs (through economies of scale), so they add new outlets. Such diversification intensifies horizontal conflict.

Vertical Conflict

Perhaps the most severe conflicts in distribution involve firms at different levels of the same channel. **Vertical conflict** typically occurs between producer and wholesaler *or* producer and retailer.

http://www.deere.com/

Producer versus Wholesaler. A producer and a wholesaler may disagree about aspects of their relationship. For instance, Deere & Co. has argued with its distributors about whether they must restrict their sales efforts to the Deere brand or can sell other brands of farm equipment as well. When profit margins are squeezed because of intense price competition, producer-wholesaler friction is probable. That occurred in the beer industry earlier this decade, straining relationships between brewers such as Coors and Miller and their distributors.[32]

Why do conflicts arise? Basically, manufacturers and wholesalers have differing points of view. On the one hand, manufacturers think that wholesalers neither promote products aggressively nor hold sufficient inventories. And they contend that wholesalers' services cost too much. On the other hand, wholesalers believe that producers either expect too much (such as requiring an extensive inventory of the product) or do not understand the wholesaler's primary obligation to customers.

Channel conflict sometimes stems from a manufacturer's attempts to bypass wholesalers and deal directly with retailers or consumers. Direct sales occur because either producers or customers are dissatisfied with wholesalers' services or market conditions invite or require this approach. Battles about direct sales are more common in channels for consumer, rather than business, goods.

To bypass wholesalers, a producer has two alternatives:

- *Sell directly to consumers*. Producers may employ door-to-door or mail-order selling. They may also establish their own distribution centers in various areas or even their own retail stores in major markets. Clothing makers, such as Van

Heusen and Harve Benard, own and operate numerous factory outlets (more on this type of store in the next chapter).[33] Typically, producers use this approach as a supplementary, rather than sole, form of distribution.

- *Sell directly to retailers.* Under certain market and product conditions, selling directly to retailers is feasible and advisable. An ideal retail market for this option consists of retailers that buy large quantities of a limited line of products. Luxottica Group of Italy, which makes more eyeglass frames than any other company, eliminated most of its wholesale distributors. According to the firm, doing so not only boosted its profit margins but also improved service to its customers, mainly optical shops in Italy, the U.S., and other countries.[34]

Direct distribution—a short channel—places a financial and managerial burden on the producer. The manufacturer must operate its own sales force and handle physical distribution of its products. Further, a direct-selling manufacturer also faces competition from its former wholesalers, which no doubt will begin distributing competitive products.

Wholesalers, too, can improve their competitive position. Their options include:

- *Improve internal management.* Many wholesalers have modernized their operations. Functional, single-story warehouses have been built outside congested downtown areas, and mechanized materials-handling equipment has been installed. Computers have improved order processing, inventory control, and billing.
- *Provide management assistance to retailers.* Wholesalers have realized that improving retailers' operations benefits all parties. Wholesalers help meet certain retailers' needs, such as store layout, merchandise selection, promotion, and inventory control.
- *Form a voluntary chain.* In this form of vertical marketing system, a wholesaler contractually agrees to furnish management services and volume buying power to a group of retailers. In turn, the retailers promise to buy all, or almost all, their merchandise from the wholesaler. Examples of wholesaler-sponsored voluntary chains include IGA (grocery field) and Western Auto (automotive and related products).
- *Develop middlemen's brands.* Some large wholesalers have successfully established their own brands. Supervalu has developed its Flavorite brand for groceries and Chateau for personal-care products. A voluntary chain of retailers provides a built-in market for the wholesaler's brands.

http://www.igainc.com/

Producer versus Retailer.   As illustrated by the chapter-opening case, another struggle for channel control occurs between manufacturers and retailers. Conflict between these channel members—in fact, between any two parties—is likely to intensify during tough economic times. Conflict is also bound to occur when producers compete with retailers by selling from house to house or through producer-owned stores. A number of apparel makers—including Levi, Polo, and Liz Claiborne—have opened retail outlets. In doing so they have aggravated department stores and specialty retailers that also carry their brands.[35]

Producer and retailer may also disagree about terms of sale or conditions of the relationship between the two parties. In recent years large retail chains, particularly department stores and discount houses, have demanded not only lower prices but also more service from suppliers. Sometimes, producers find it costly and, in some cases, nearly impossible to comply with the retailers' new policies.

The policies cover the gamut, including automatic deductions in place of returning damaged merchandise, larger contributions to advertising and other promotion expenses, and even the quality of hangers on which apparel is hung (so that the retailer doesn't have to pay for hangers and rehang the merchandise when it is received at the store).[36]

Conflict also has occurred as some large retailers, especially in the grocery field, have demanded a so-called **slotting allowance** to place a manufacturer's product on store shelves. In some cases, companies with new products are required to pay a fee of $100 to over $1,000 per store for each version of the product. Manufacturers with popular brands typically do not have to pay these fees. Further, some small producers cannot afford them. Manufacturers criticize slotting allowances, claiming they stifle the introduction of new products, particularly those developed by small companies. Supermarkets contend they must find a way to recoup the costs of reviewing the flood of new products, stocking some of them, and removing failures.[37]

Both producers and retailers have methods to gain more control. Manufacturers can:

- *Build strong consumer brand loyalty.* Creative and aggressive promotion is a key in creating such loyalty.
- *Establish one or more forms of vertical marketing system.* Procter & Gamble uses the administered type of VMS, dedicating special teams to work with key customers, such as Wal-Mart and Target.
- *Refuse to sell to uncooperative retailers.* This tactic may not be defensible from a legal standpoint.
- *Arrange alternative retailers.* Squeezed by large retail chains, some producers are building their distribution strategy around smaller specialty stores. Although risky, a number of apparel makers, such as Dion-Jones Ltd. and Christine Albers Inc., have taken this course of action.[38]

Effective marketing weapons are also available to retailers. They can:

- *Develop store loyalty among consumers.* Skillful advertising and strong store brands are means of creating loyal customers.
- *Improve computerized information systems.* Information is power. Knowing what sells and how fast it sells is useful in negotiating with suppliers.
- *Form a retailer cooperative.* In this type of vertical marketing system, a group of retailers (usually fairly small ones) bands together to establish and operate

AN ETHICAL DILEMMA?

In exchange for shelf space in their stores, some supermarket chains require manufacturers to pay slotting allowances (as discussed in a nearby section of this chapter). Part or all of the revenues a chain receives from this policy might be passed on to consumers in the form of lower prices. Or the chain could retain these revenues to cover added labor costs associated with shelving new products and/or to boost profits. Assume that you are a supermarket-chain vice president who is responsible for establishing policies regarding relationships with suppliers.

Is it ethical for your chain to demand slotting allowances from manufacturers?

a wholesale warehouse. The primary intent is to gain lower merchandise costs through volume buying power. Examples of retailer cooperatives include True Value hardware stores and Certified Grocers.

Who Controls Channels?

Every firm would like to regulate the behavior of the other companies in its distribution channel. When a channel member is able to do this, it has **channel control**. In many situations, including distribution channels, power is a prerequisite for control. **Channel power** is the ability to influence or determine the behavior of another channel member. There are various sources of power in distribution channels. They include expertise (for example, possessing vital technical knowledge about the product or valuable information about customers), rewards (providing financial benefits to cooperative channel members), and sanctions (removing uncooperative firms from the channel). Not surprisingly, the types of power used to influence distributors have a strong effect on their levels of satisfaction.[39]

Traditionally, manufacturers have been viewed as controlling channels—that is, making the decisions regarding types and number of outlets, participation of

YOU MAKE THE DECISION

HOW DID BLACK PEARLS PERFUME LOSE THE SCENT OF MONEY?

Only weeks before the new Black Pearls perfume was scheduled to be introduced in September 1995, the launch was canceled. What happened? Basically, Unilever Group's Elizabeth Arden division, which developed the Black Pearls fragrance, lost a bet that it could change its business arrangements with upscale department stores that distribute fairly expensive perfumes.

Black Pearls was to be the fourth fragrance promoted by actress Elizabeth Taylor. Earlier she was associated with Passion, White Diamonds, and Fragrant Jewels. All had been sold first through Macy's, Bloomingdale's, and other upscale retailers that are part of chains such as Dayton Hudson Corp. The relative prestige of the stores that sell a particular perfume brand affects sales.

In early summer 1995, the perfume maker announced that the amount of money given to stores to help cover salaries of retail employees who sell the Arden brand was being cut from 5 to 3 percent of sales. In turn, upscale department store chains refused to carry the new perfume.

Arden thought that Black Pearls, with Elizabeth Taylor as its spokeswoman, would have enough appeal to allow it to dictate new terms to retailers. The

perfume maker, however, overlooked the fact that it is just third among cosmetics brands carried by department stores. Thus it did not have abundant power in its channels.

Pulling the plug on Black Pearls cost Arden as much as $15 million for product-development and other marketing costs that already had been incurred. Arden's reputation probably was hurt as well. Not coincidentally, Arden's president announced her resignation right after halting the introduction.

Black Pearls was relaunched in 1996 after Elizabeth Arden mended its relationship with the Federated and May chains. The perfume maker agreed to provide the chains with the usual 5 percent of sales to offset some retail selling expenses. Penney's and Sears were not included in Arden's relaunch plans.

Who was hurt most by the canceled launch of Black Pearls—upscale department stores, Penney's and Sears, Elizabeth Arden, Elizabeth Taylor, or consumers?

http://www.unilever.com/

Sources: Teri Agins, "Liz's Perfume Gets Star Role in Prime Time," *The Wall Street Journal*, Feb. 5, 1996, pp. B1, B5; Teri Agins, "Arden Cancels Fall Launch of Liz Taylor's Fragrance," *The Wall Street Journal*, Aug. 30, 1995, p. B1; Teri Agins, "Elizabeth Taylor's Glamorous New Scent Will Get a Less Than Glamorous Launch," *The Wall Street Journal*, Aug. 17, 1995, pp. B1, B5; and Julie L. Belcove, "New Doors for Black Pearls," *WWD (Women's Wear Daily)*, Aug. 11, 1995, p. 6.

individual middlemen, and business practices to be followed by a channel. But with the enormous size and strong customer loyalty that some middlemen—particularly retailers—now possess, this is a one-sided, outdated point of view.

Middlemen now control many channels. Certainly the names Safeway, Ward's, and Nordstrom mean more to consumers than the names of many producers' brands sold in these stores. Large retailers are challenging manufacturers for channel control, just as many manufacturers seized control from wholesalers years ago. As one article explained, "Powerful chains—May and Dillard in particular—drive hard bargains with vendors, requiring them to pay a bigger share of advertising and promotional expenses."[40] Even small retailers can be influential in local markets because their reputations may be stronger than their suppliers' prestige.

Manufacturers contend they should assume the leader's role in a channel because they create the new products and need greater sales volume to benefit from economies of scale. Conversely, retailers also stake a claim for leadership, because they are closest to ultimate consumers and, as a result, are best able to know consumers' wants and to design and oversee channels to satisfy them. Various factors have contributed to retailers' growing ability to control channels. Perhaps most notably, many retailers have implemented electronic scanning devices, which has given them access to more accurate, timely information about sales trends of individual products than producers have.[41]

A Channel Viewed as a Partnership

Sometimes, members see a channel as a fragmented collection of independent, competing firms.[42] This is a myopic viewpoint. Instead, suppliers and middlemen should think of channels as partnerships aimed at satisfying end users' needs rather than as something they "command and control." The head of Sutter Home Winery attributes his firm's long-term success to arranging good distributors and working cooperatively with them: "I have always felt it was a real partnership."[43]

http://www.sutterhome.com/

Partnerships within distribution channels can entail a variety of cooperative activities which are most effective when they benefit both parties. A supplier may be asked to get involved in a customer's new-product development efforts. An

*T*he Tennant Co. of Minneapolis, Minnesota, manufactures sweepers and scrubbers for large building floors and parking lots. Stiff competition requires that it produce top-quality products. To do so, Tennant decided to prune its roster of suppliers and to work very closely with the remaining suppliers. Representatives of large suppliers are even invited to serve on Tennant's new-product development teams.

increasingly common occurrence is for a firm to provide a supplier with forecasts of the company's sales and/or information about existing inventory levels so the supplier can better schedule its production and fill the customer's orders in a timely fashion. For example, Bailey Controls, which makes control systems for large manufacturing plants, provides this information to one of its suppliers, Future Electronics, through an electronic data interchange system. Bailey has an even closer partnership with another supplier, Arrow Electronics, which actually has a warehouse at Bailey's factory.[44]

Developing and sustaining these partnerships require more than frequent conversations between a sales person and a purchasing agent. Typically, a supplier's top executives also meet with their counterparts in customer organizations. For example, the Baxter hospital supply firm uses the information about the customer's mission and strategies that comes out in such meetings to develop means to better serve that customer and to cut costs. The company also has discovered (happily) that strong partnerships with customers yield a differential advantage over competitors.[45]

There are other potential benefits of partnering. Lower inventory and operating costs, improved quality of products and service, and more rapid filling of orders are all possible, but by no means assured. There are risks as well. A close working relationship often requires sharing sensitive information, which may be misused by the other party; worse yet, it may wind up in a competitor's hands. Because firms entering into a partnership often reduce the number of other suppliers or customers with which they do business, they may have fewer options to turn to if the relationship doesn't work out.[46]

A COMMITMENT TO CUSTOMER SATISFACTION

HOW DOES STEINWAY KEEP ITS RELATIONSHIPS WITH DEALERS IN TUNE?

In recent years, several piano manufacturers have gone out of business, succumbing to sagging demand in the industry. In contrast, Steinway & Sons is more successful than the company has ever been during its almost 150 years making pianos. How can that be?

Unlike the failed firms, Steinway & Sons had the financial resources to survive the economic downturn. As the economy improved, demand rebounded. Moreover, the company never compromises its adherence to top quality. Steinway holds over 100 patents and has resisted mass production. A vice president said the Steinway approach is "to build to a standard and not to a price."

Besides being master craftspeople, Steinway & Sons are virtuoso marketers. In particular, they pay great attention to strengthening—and satisfying—their network of dealers. The company developed a dealer-support program called "The Working Partnership." The program covers various marketing activities that affect sales and profits for the dealers and, in turn, for Steinway & Sons. For example, a dealer who wants to launch a special promotion can select from more than 20 plans prepared by Steinway. Each plan includes sample advertising and even examples of invitations that can be sent to prospective customers.

Steinway & Sons also recognizes its top dealers annually. Steinway even arranged for Van Cliburn, the famed pianist, to present the awards in 1995. The awards recognize not just sales but other contributing factors such as customer service, sales training, and product knowledge. To help maintain harmony in the dealer network, the annual award winners also are given the opportunity to provide advice to the company's top management.

What else can Steinway & Sons do to sustain strong relationships with its dealers?

http://www.g2g.com/steinway/

Sources: Megan Winzeler, "Steinway Strikes a Chord," *Sales & Marketing Management*, August 1995, p. 16; and "Steinway Dealers Meet Van Cliburn," *The Music Trades*, March 1995, p. 184.

To increase coordination and facilitate partnerships within channels, many large firms have pared the number of suppliers with which they do business. Some observers suggest, however, that the resulting "preferred vendor" lists are a means for sizable customers to dominate relatively small suppliers. As implied, channel partners are not necessarily equals. Still, given the potential sales volume that comes with being a preferred vendor, most suppliers are willing to meet the demands of powerful customers.[47]

Many channel partnerships really are part of a broader, significant trend called *relationship marketing* (which will be discussed further in Chapter 22). In the context of distribution channels, relationship marketing refers to a concerted effort by a company not only to work closely with customers to better understand and satisfy their needs but also to develop long-term, mutually beneficial relationships with them. Conversely, customers can seek to engage in relationship marketing with their suppliers.[48]

Legal Considerations in Managing Channels

Attempts to control distribution are subject to legal constraints. We will now discuss legal aspects of four control methods sometimes employed by suppliers (usually manufacturers). Each method is limited by the Clayton Antitrust Act, Sherman Antitrust Act, or Federal Trade Commission Act. None of the four methods is illegal by itself. Distribution control becomes unlawful when it is judged to (1) substantially lessen competition, (2) create a monopoly, or (3) restrain trade.

Exclusive Dealing

A manufacturer that prohibits its dealers from carrying products of its competitors is engaged in **exclusive dealing**. If a manufacturer stipulates that any store carrying its Perfecto Gas Grill not carry competing brands of outdoor barbecue grills, this is exclusive dealing. Such an arrangement is likely to be *illegal* when:

- The manufacturer's sales volume is a substantial portion of total volume in a given market. Competitors are thus excluded from a major part of the market.
- The contract is between a large manufacturer and a much smaller middleman, the supplier's power is considered inherently coercive, and is thus in restraint of trade.

However, some court decisions have held that exclusive dealing is *permissible* when:

- Equivalent products are available in a market or the manufacturer's competitors have access to equivalent dealers. In these cases exclusive dealing may be legal if competition is not lessened to any large degree.
- A manufacturer is entering a market, or its total market share is so small as to be negligible. An exclusive-dealing agreement may actually strengthen the producer's competitive position if the middlemen decide to back the product with a strong marketing effort.

Tying Contracts

When a supplier sells a product to a middleman only under the condition that the middleman also buy another (possibly unwanted) product from the supplier, the two companies have entered into a **tying contract**. If Paramount Products requires middlemen to buy unpopular, old models of cassette players in order to be able to buy popular, new models of compact disc players, that's a tying contract.

A manufacturer pushes for a tying agreement in several situations. When there are shortages of a popular product, a supplier may see an opportunity to unload other, less desired products. When a supplier relies on exclusive dealers or distributors (in appliances, for example), it may want them to carry a full line of its products. Or when a company grants a franchise (as in fast foods), it may see the franchisees as captive buyers of all the equipment and supplies needed to operate the business. Both Domino's and Little Caesar franchisees have claimed that a tying contract results in their paying excessive prices for dough and other supplies. According to the franchisees, their franchise rights are tied to a requirement that they purchase only from the parent company or approved vendors.[49]

In general, tying contracts are considered to violate antitrust laws. There are exceptions, however. Tying contracts may be *legal* when:

- A new company is trying to enter a market.
- An exclusive dealer or distributor is required to carry the manufacturer's full product line, but is not prohibited from carrying competing products.

Refusal to Deal

To select—and perhaps control—its channels, a producer may refuse to sell to certain middlemen. This practice is called **refusal to deal**. A 1919 court case established that manufacturers can select the middlemen to whom they will sell, so long as there is no intent to create a monopoly. Independent service companies charged Eastman Kodak Co. with trying to monopolize the business of repairing its brand of photocopiers. In late 1995, a federal jury agreed, deciding that Kodak illegally refused to sell parts for its photocopiers and related equipment to independent service companies. Under the verdict, the 11 companies will receive more than $70 million in damages from Kodak.[50]

A manufacturer's decision to end or diminish a relationship with a wholesaler or retailer may not be legal. Generally it is *illegal* to drop or withhold products from a middleman for (1) carrying competitors' products, (2) resisting a tying contract, or (3) setting prices lower than desired by the manufacturer. Several years ago, the New York attorney general charged that Stride Rite Corp. held back Keds shoes from retailers that did not abide by the manufacturer's "suggested" retail prices. Eventually, Stride Rite agreed to pay over $7 million to resolve the claim.[51]

http://www.kodak.com/

Exclusive-Territory Policy

Under an **exclusive-territory policy**, a producer requires each middleman to sell *only* to customers located within an assigned territory. In several court cases, exclusive (also called *closed*) sales territories were ruled unlawful because they lessened competition and restrained trade. The courts sought to encourage competition among middlemen handling the *same* brand.

Exclusive territories may be *permitted* when:

- A company is small or is a newcomer in the market.
- A producer establishes a corporate vertical marketing system and retains ownership of the product until it reaches the final buyer.
- A producer uses independent middlemen to distribute the product under consignment, in which a middleman does not pay the supplier until after the merchandise is sold.

As you can see, these conditions certainly are subject to interpretation. Thus it is not uncommon for conflicts to be settled by the courts.

■ SUMMARY

The role of distribution is getting a product to its target market. A distribution channel carries out this assignment with middlemen performing some tasks. A middleman is a business firm that renders services directly related to the purchase and/or sale of a product as it flows from producer to consumer. Middlemen can be eliminated from a channel, but someone still has to carry out their essential functions.

A distribution channel is the set of people and firms involved in the flow of title to a product as it moves from producer to ultimate consumer or business user. A channel includes producer, final customer, and any middlemen that participate in the process.

Designing a channel of distribution for a product occurs through a sequence of four decisions: (1) delineating the role of distribution within the marketing mix; (2) selecting the proper type of distribution channel; (3) determining the appropriate intensity of distribution; and (4) choosing specific channel members.

A variety of channels are used to distribute consumer goods, business goods, and services. Firms often employ multiple channels to achieve broad market coverage, although this strategy can alienate some middlemen. Because of deficiencies in conventional channels, vertical marketing systems have become widespread in distribution. There are three forms of vertical marketing systems: corporate, contractual, and administered.

Numerous factors need to be considered in selecting a distribution channel. The primary consideration is the nature of the target market. Others relate to the product, the middlemen, and the company itself.

Distribution intensity refers to the number of middlemen a producer uses at the wholesale and retail levels in a particular territory. It ranges from intensive to selective to exclusive.

Firms that distribute goods and services sometimes clash. There are two types of conflict: horizontal (between firms at the same level of distribution) and vertical (between firms at different levels of the same channel). Scrambled merchandising is a prime cause of horizontal conflict. Vertical conflict typically pits producer against wholesaler or retailer. Manufacturers' attempts to bypass middlemen are a prime cause of vertical conflict.

Channel members frequently strive for some control over one another. Depending on the circumstances, either producers or middlemen can achieve the dominant position in a channel. The firms comprising a particular channel are served best if they all view their channel as a partnership requiring coordination of distribution activities. Partnerships in channels are part of a significant trend called relationship marketing.

Attempts to control distribution may be subject to legal constraints. In fact, some practices—such as exclusive dealing and tying contracts—may be ruled illegal.

More about

GOODYEAR

*G*oodyear executives have expressed their satisfaction with the results obtained by selling some of the firm's brands of tires through Sears and discount outlets. But other industry observers say the tiremaker shouldn't be too pleased. According to *Modern Tire Dealer*, Goodyear gained just a single percentage point of market share in the 3 years following the change in distribution strategy.

One thing is clear. Many long-standing Goodyear dealers have been displeased by the tiremaker's added distribution intensity. Given that most of Goodyear's sales still come through independent dealers, it's certainly not in the company's best long-term interests to

have an adversarial relationship with these distributors. To appease the dealers, Goodyear has been making a number of moves such as the following:

- Some tires, including the popular Aquatred II, are sold only through the 3,000 independent dealers— and not through Sears, Wal-Mart, and Discount Tire.
- Dealers that buy greater quantities qualify for larger discounts, thereby improving their profit margins.
- To give consumers reasons to visit the dealers' stores, the tiremaker is introducing new products more frequently. Applying market segmentation, the

new tires have various designs to match the diverse driving patterns of different groups of consumers. At the extreme, Goodyear has developed a set of sports car tires in which each of the four tires is slightly different.

Despite these initiatives, several distributors in California filed suit, claiming that Goodyear's added distribution intensity was a breach of contract and hurt their profit margins. Less dramatic, but maybe more significant, a number of dealers are stocking brands of tires that compete—directly or indirectly—with Goodyear tires. Some have added the well-known Michelin and Bridgestone brands, but more have augmented their product mixes with less-well-known but lower-priced brands. Evidently, Goodyear has not satisfied all of its independent dealers.[52]

1. Should Goodyear retain its strategy of multiple channels of distribution, including its arrangements with Sears and discount outlets?
2. a. If not, what should Goodyear do to strengthen its distribution?
   b. If so, what else should Goodyear do to retain and satisfy its independent dealers?

■ KEY TERMS AND CONCEPTS

Middleman (342)
Merchant
  middleman (342)
Agent middleman (342)
Distribution
  channel (343)
Direct distribution (346)
Indirect distribution (347)
Multiple distribution
  channels (349)

Vertical marketing system
  (VMS) (351)
Corporate vertical
  marketing system (351)
Contractual vertical
  marketing
  system (352)
Administered vertical
  marketing
  system (352)

Intensity of
  distribution (356)
Intensive distribution (357)
Selective distribution (357)
Exclusive
  distribution (357)
Channel conflict (358)
Horizontal conflict (358)
Scrambled
  merchandising (359)

Vertical conflict (359)
Slotting allowance (361)
Channel control (362)
Channel power (362)
Exclusive dealing (365)
Tying contract (365)
Refusal to deal (366)
Exclusive-territory
  policy (366)

■ QUESTIONS AND PROBLEMS

1. Which of the following institutions are middlemen? Explain.
   a. Avon sales person
   b. Electrical wholesaler
   c. Real estate broker
   d. Railroad
   e. Advertising agency
   f. Grocery store
   g. Stockbroker
   h. Bank
2. Which of the channels illustrated in Figure 13-3 is most apt to be used for each of the following products? Defend your choice in each case.
   a. Fire insurance
   b. Single-family residences
   c. Farm hay balers
   d. Washing machines
   e. Hair spray
   f. An ocean cruise
3. "The great majority of business sales are made directly from producer to business user." Explain why this occurs, first in terms of the nature of the market, and then in terms of the product.
4. "You can eliminate middlemen, but you cannot eliminate essential distribution activities." Discuss how this statement is supported or refuted by vertical marketing systems.
5. A small manufacturer of fishing lures is faced with the problem of selecting its channel of distribution. What reasonable alternatives does it have? Consider particularly the nature of its product and the nature of its market.
6. Is a policy of intensive distribution consistent with consumer buying habits for convenience goods? For shopping goods? Is intensive distribution normally used in the marketing of any type of business goods?
7. From a producer's viewpoint, what are the competitive advantages of exclusive distribution?
8. A manufacturer of a well-known brand of men's clothing has been selling directly to one dealer in a Southern city for many years. For some time the market has been large enough to support two retailers very profitably. Yet the present dealer objects strongly when the manufacturer suggests adding another outlet. What alternatives does the manufacturer have in this situation? What course of action would you recommend?
9. "Manufacturers should always strive to select the lowest-cost channel of distribution." Do you agree? Should they always try to use the middlemen with the lowest operating costs? Why or why not?
10. What advice regarding distribution channels would you give to a small American company that makes stylish women's clothing and desires to distribute the product line in Japan?

■ HANDS-ON MARKETING

1. Arrange an interview with either the owner or a top-level manager of a small manufacturing firm. Inquire about (a) what distribution channel(s) the company uses for its primary product, (b) what factors were the greatest influences in arriving at the channel(s), and (c) whether the company would prefer some other channel(s).

2. Visit with either a supermarket manager or a buyer for a supermarket chain to learn more about slotting allowances and any other charges they levy on manufacturers. Inquire whether such charges have led to channel conflict and how the supermarket chain is handling this type of situation. Also ask whether any grocery-products manufacturers refuse to pay slotting allowances and whether the chain ever waives the fees.

CHAPTER 14

Retailing

Can
PENNEY's
Earn More Than Pennies with Fashionable Values?

After a 15-year effort to reposition its stores, the J.C. Penney Co. is now refining its "value equation," while also seeking to update its facilities and diversify its management. At the same time, Penney's is implementing a strategy for expanding into foreign markets.

For decades, J.C. Penney Co. had been the second largest chain of department stores, behind Sears. Then in the early 1980s, top management devised new marketing strategies that would allow Penney's not only to step out of Sears' shadow but also to attract more customers and build both sales and profits in the future. Basically, Penney's decided to trade up, focusing on female consumers with higher incomes than its traditional customers. To attract these customers, the chain chose to abandon so-called hard goods (notably large appliances), giving up about $1.8 billion in annual sales, in order to concentrate on soft goods (notably apparel).

Branding strategies were at the core of Penney's repositioning plan. Its merchandise buyers set out to arrange for leading manufacturers' brands in Penney's stores. The endeavors were fruitful, corralling such brands as Levi's and OshKosh B'Gosh. The emphasis on "name" brands continues. For instance, Penney's is the only chain to distribute Ivana Trump's new line of perfumes and related products. An equally important strategy was to develop and promote Penney's own brands. These efforts have been a rousing success, and have resulted in a stable of prominent brands, including Worthington career apparel, Hunt Club sportswear, Arizona jeans, and Stafford men's suits. Penney's places its own brands only on merchandise that meets stringent quality standards. Its "store" brands now account for at least one-half of the company's sales volume.

Penney's almost went too far with its trading up.

During the recession of the early 1990s, shoppers balked at the chain's higher prices. Top management, led by James Oesterreicher (now the company's CEO), refined its overall strategy to emphasize value. Besides trimming prices, Penney's strove to further enhance the quality of its merchandise, particularly its own brands. According to the head of merchandising, "Today's consumer is . . . thinking more about quality and fashion, combined with her demand for competitive pricing. That's the equation for value."

To underscore its commitment to value, Penney's started a new "Value Right" program in 1995. The intent of the program is to show that its store brands have "the right fashion . . . the right quality . . . the right price." Hangtags were placed on about 100 products, telling shoppers that if they buy that item and later find a similar item offering better value, they can return the original item to Penney's for a refund.

Penney's certainly has a full business agenda. On top of that, most retailers—including Penney's—were put to a special test during the mid-1990s. Collectively consumers were burdened with high levels of debt and so were reluctant to spend any more than absolutely necessary. Further, there was an excess of retail stores. This combination of factors provoked intense price competition among retailers. Like many other large chains, Penney's financial performance suffered. For example, its 1995 sales of $20.5 billion were essentially the same as the preceding year; sales volume in stores open at least 1 year slipped 1 percent; and the chain's profits fell 21 percent. The challenge never ends for Penney's![1]

How effectively has the J.C. Penney Co. combined product and pricing strategies to reposition the chain for added growth and profits?

http://www.jcpenney.com/

Distributing consumer products begins with the producer and ends with the ultimate consumer. Between the two there is usually at least one middleman—a retailer. The many types of retailing institutions and their marketing activities are the subjects of this chapter.

You have abundant experience with retailing—as a consumer. And perhaps you also have worked in retailing. This chapter builds on that experience and provides insights about retail markets, different types of retailers, and key strategies and trends in retailing. After studying this chapter, you should be able to explain:

CHAPTER GOALS

- The nature of retailing.
- What a retailer is.
- Types of retailers classified by form of ownership.
- Types of retailers classified by marketing strategies.
- Forms of nonstore retailing.
- Trends in retailing.

Nature and Importance of Retailing

For every successful giant retailer like Penney's, thousands of tiny retailers serve consumers in very small areas. Despite their differences, all have two common features: They link producers and ultimate consumers, and they perform valuable services for both. In all likelihood, all these firms are retailers, but not all of their activities may qualify as retailing. Let's see how that can be.

Retailing and Retailers

If a Winn-Dixie supermarket sells floor wax to a gift shop operator to polish the shop's floor, is this a retail sale? When a Chevron gas station advertises tires for sale at the "wholesale price," is this retailing? Can a wholesaler or manufacturer engage in retailing? When a service such as Aamco transmission repair is sold to an ultimate consumer, is this retailing? Obviously, we need to define some terms, particularly *retailing* and *retailer*, to answer these questions and to avoid misunderstandings later.

Retailing (or *retail trade*) consists of the sale, and all activities directly related to the sale, of goods and services to ultimate consumers for personal, nonbusiness use. While most retailing occurs through retail stores, it may be done by any institution. Avon selling cosmetics door to door and Tupperware selling plastic containers at lunchtime meetings at a factory are engaging in retailing, as is a farmer selling vegetables at a roadside stand.

Any firm—manufacturer, wholesaler, or retailer—that sells something to ultimate consumers for their nonbusiness use is making a retail sale. This is true regardless of *how* the product is sold (in person or by telephone, mail, or vending machine) or *where* it is sold (in a store or at the consumer's home). However, a firm engaged *primarily* in retailing is called a **retailer**. In this chapter we will concentrate on retailers rather than on other types of businesses that make only occasional retail sales.

Most people associate the term *retailer* with the sale of goods rather than with services. In fact, the U.S. *Census of Retail Trade* concentrates on goods, whereas a separate *Census of Service Industries* covers the wholesaling and retailing of services. While this chapter focuses primarily on retailers of *goods*, much of what is said—particularly regarding marketing strategies—also applies to retailers of *services*.

Economic Justification for Retailing

As discussed in Chapter 13, all middlemen basically serve as purchasing agents for their customers and as sales specialists for their suppliers. To carry out these roles, retailers perform many activities, including anticipating customers' wants, developing assortments of products, acquiring market information, and financing.

It is relatively easy to become a retailer. No large investment in production equipment is required, merchandise can often be purchased on credit, and store space can be leased with no "down payment." This ease of entry into the retail business results in fierce competition and better values for customers.

To enter retailing is easy; to fail is even easier! To survive in retailing, a firm must do a satisfactory job in its primary role—catering to consumers. Stanley Marcus, the former chairman of Neiman Marcus, described a successful retailer as "a merchant who sells goods that won't come back to customers who will."[2] Of course, a retail firm also must fulfill its other role—serving producers and wholesalers. This dual role is both the justification for retailing and the key to success in retailing.

http://www.neimanmarcus.com/

Size of the Retail Market

Retail sales in 1994 totaled more than $2.2 *trillion*, as shown in Figure 14-1. The increase in total sales volume has been tremendous—fivefold from the early 1970s to the mid-1990s. Even adjusting for the rise in prices, total retail sales and per capita retail sales have gone up considerably.

There are about 2.7 million retail stores in the U.S. The jump in number of stores between 1982 and 1992 (the year of the most recent retail census) coincided with a growing population and rising consumer incomes.

FIGURE 14-1 Total retail trade in the United States.

Sales volume has increased steadily over the past 20-plus years. In contrast, note that the number of retail stores rose substantially between 1982 and 1992 after a period of relative stability in the preceding 10 years.

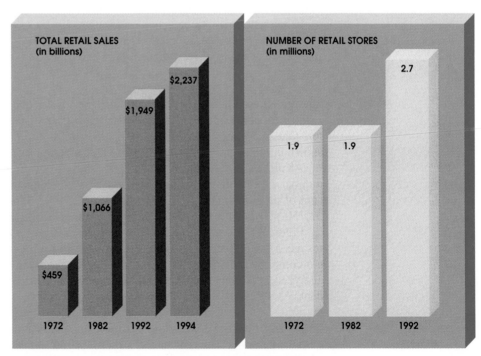

Note: The number of retail stores has not been reported more recently than 1992.
Sources: Statistical Abstract of the United States: 1995, 115th ed., U.S. Bureau of the Census, Washington, D.C., 1995, p. 782; *1992 Census of Retail Trade,* Nonemployer Statistics Series—Summary, U.S. Bureau of the Census, Washington, D.C., 1995, p. 3; and corresponding censuses from prior years.

Operating Expenses and Profits

Total operating expenses for retailers average 28 percent of retail sales. In comparison, wholesaling expenses run about 11 percent of *wholesale* sales or 8 percent of *retail* sales.[3] Thus, roughly speaking, retailing costs are about 2½ times the costs of wholesaling when both are stated as a percentage of the sales of the specific type of middleman.

Higher retailing costs are generally related to the expense of dealing directly with ultimate consumers—answering their questions, showing them different products, and so on. Compared to wholesale customers, ultimate consumers typically expect more convenient locations with nicer decor, both of which drive up retailers' costs. Also, compared to wholesalers, retailers typically have lower total sales and lower rates of merchandise turnover, and buy smaller quantities of merchandise so their overhead costs are spread over a smaller base of operations. Furthermore, retail sales people often cannot be used efficiently because customers do not come into stores at a steady rate.

Retailers' costs and profits vary depending on their type of operation and major product line. Assorted kinds of retailers earn wide-ranging gross margins—the difference between net sales and cost of goods sold. For instance, gross margins for auto dealers and gasoline service stations are in the vicinity of 15 percent, whereas margins for retailers of clothing, shoes, and jewelry are around 40 percent. However, healthy gross margins do not necessarily translate into the highest levels of net profits. Some retailers with small gross margins are able to serve customers well with low operating expenses, thereby winding up with substantial profit margins. Conversely, other retailers have large gross margins but incur heavy operating expenses, resulting in meager profits.

Just as retail firms' gross margins range widely, so do their net profits. Supermarkets typically earn a profit of less than 1 percent of sales, compared to as much as 10 percent for some specialized retailers. In general, retailers' net profits average about 3 percent of sales. This modest figure may surprise people who suspect that retailers make enormous profits.

Store Size

Most retail establishments are very small. In the last available census year, about 11 percent of stores operating the full year had annual sales below $100,000 (which is less than $275 per day, if a store is open every day of the year). Not surprisingly, as shown in Figure 14-2, less than 1 percent of all retail sales were made by these stores.

At the same time there is a high degree of concentration in retailing. A small number of establishments account for a large share of retail trade. Only 25 percent of all stores had an annual sales volume over $1 million (which is just under $2,750 per day), but they accounted for about 81 percent of total retail sales.

Figure 14-2 does not tell the full story of large-scale retailing because it represents a tabulation of individual *store* sales and not *company* sales volume. A single company may own many stores, as in the case of chains. When retail sales are analyzed by companies, the high degree of concentration becomes even more evident. As shown in Table 14-1, the combined sales of the 10 largest retailers make up almost 14 percent of total retail trade.

Stores of different sizes face distinct challenges and opportunities. Buying, promotion, personnel relations, and expense control are influenced significantly by whether a store's sales volume is large or small. Size of a retail business creates certain advantages and disadvantages, several of which are described in Table

FIGURE 14-2 Distribution of stores and retail sales by size of store.

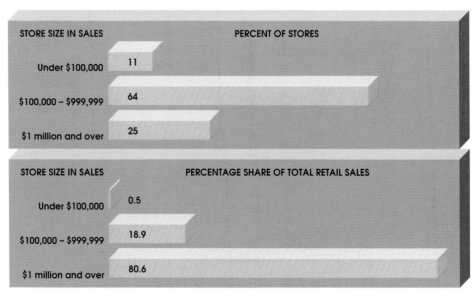

14-2. Considering these factors, large stores ordinarily—but not always—have a competitive advantage over small stores.

Small retailers face a variety of difficulties, and many fail. According to a study of retail businesses with one or two outlets and total sales under $2 million, one in five are losing money. Among those making at least some money, one in four reported pretax income under $10,000.[4]

TABLE 14-1 Worldwide sales of 10 largest retailers based in the United States

Retailer	1995 sales (billions)	1995 net profit as percent of sales	Percent change in sales, 1991–1995
1. Wal-Mart Stores	$ 93.6	2.9	+113
2. Sears, Roebuck	34.9	5.2	+ 8
3. Kmart	34.4	(1.7)*	+ 17
4. Kroger	23.9	1.3	+ 12
5. Dayton Hudson	23.5	1.3	+ 46
6. J.C. Penney	21.4	3.9	+ 29
7. American Stores	18.3	1.7	− 12
8. PriceCostco	18.2	.7	+ 52
9. Safeway	16.4	2.0	+ 9
10. Home Depot	15.5	4.7	+201
Total sales volume	$300.1		
Average for top 10 firms		2.2	+ 48

*Kmart reported a loss of $571 million in 1995.

Sources: Company annual reports and Distribution Research Program, The University of Oklahoma.

TABLE 14-2 Competitive positions of large and small retail stores

Selected bases for evaluation	Who has the advantage?
Division of labor and specialization of management	Large-scale retailers—their biggest advantage.
Flexibility of operations—merchandise selection, services offered, store design, reflection of owner's personality	Small retailers—their biggest advantage.
Buying power	Large retailers buy in bigger quantities and thus get lower costs.
Access to desirable merchandise	Large retailers promise suppliers access to large numbers of customers, whereas a single small retailer may be viewed as insignificant.
Development and promotion of retailer's own brand	Large retailers.
Efficient use of advertising, especially in citywide media	Large retailers' markets match better with media circulation.
Ability to provide top-quality personal service	Small retailers, if owners pay personal attention to customers and also to selecting and supervising sales staff.
Opportunity to experiment with new products and selling methods	Large retailers can better afford the risks.
Financial strength	Large retailers have resources to gain some of the advantages noted above (such as private brands and experimentation).
Public image	Small retailers enjoy public support and sympathy. However, this public often votes with its wallet by shopping at big stores.

How do small retailers succeed? They understand their target market very well. Then, in seeking to satisfy their consumers, they need to differentiate themselves from large retailers.[5] Here are two possible avenues not just to survival but to success:

- Many consumers seek benefits that small stores often provide better than large stores. For instance, some people seek high levels of shopping convenience. Small outlets located near residential areas offer such convenience. Other consumers desire abundant personal service. A small store's highly motivated owner-manager and well-supervised sales staff may surpass a large store on this important shopping dimension.
- Numerous small retailers have formed or joined contractual vertical marketing systems. These entities—called retailer cooperatives, voluntary chains, or franchise systems—give members some of the advantages of large stores, such as specialized management, buying power, and a well-known name.

Physical Facilities

Later in this chapter we will classify retailers according to their product assortments, price strategies, and promotional methods. Here, we'll look at **physical facilities**, which represent the distribution element of a retailer's marketing mix.

Some firms engage in *nonstore* retailing—by selling through catalogs or door to door, for example—but many more firms rely on retail *stores*. Firms that operate retail stores must consider three aspects of physical facilities:

- *Location.* It is frequently stated that there are three keys to success in retailing: location, location, and location! Although overstated, this axiom does suggest the importance that retailers attach to location. Thus a store's site should be the first decision made about facilities. Considerations such as surrounding population, traffic, and cost determine where a store should be located.
- *Design.* This factor refers to a store's appearance, both exterior and interior.
- *Layout.* The amount of space allocated to various product lines, specific locations of products, and a floor plan of display tables and racks comprise the store's layout.

As might be expected, retail locations tend to follow the population. Consequently, the bulk of retail sales occur in urban, rather than rural, areas. And suburban shopping areas have become more and more popular, while many downtown areas have declined.

Shopping centers have become the predominant type of retail location in most suburban areas. A **shopping center** consists of a planned grouping of retail stores that lease space in a structure that is typically owned by a single organization and that can accommodate multiple tenants. Shopping centers can be classified by size and market served:

- *Convenience center.* Usually consists of 5 to 10 outlets, such as a dry cleaner, branch bank, convenience grocery store, and video rental store.
- *Neighborhood center.* Has 11 to 25 tenants, including a large supermarket and perhaps a drugstore.
- *Community center.* Includes 26 to 50 stores and features a discount house and/or major specialty store (such as Circuit City or Marshall's). In addition, it may also include a supermarket or a warehouse club (such as Sam's Club or PriceCostco). Given its composition of stores, a community center draws shoppers from a larger area than does a neighborhood center.
- *Regional center.* Anchored by one or more department stores and complemented by as many as 200 smaller retail outlets; typically an enclosed, climate-controlled mall. Many regional shopping centers are gigantic. The biggest, Mall of America in suburban Minneapolis, opened in 1992. In an enclosed mall, it combines several hundred retailers with a theme park, miniature golf course, two lakes, and more than a dozen movie theaters—all adjacent to 17,000 free parking spaces. (Is that all there is?) Surprising many skeptics, this "megamall" is quite successful in terms of drawing shoppers (around 40 million a year), which is generating satisfactory sales for most retailers with stores there.[6]

In the 1960s and 1970s, regional shopping centers became the hub of shopping and social activities in many communities. In the 1980s, however, construction of new regional malls slowed considerably as the market became saturated. Eventually many shoppers grew too time-conscious to spend much time shopping or socializing at a huge mall. The average amount of time consumers spent in malls dropped from 12 to 4 hours per month between 1980 and 1990. And a mid-1990s survey revealed that more than one-third of shoppers planned to shop at malls less frequently than in the past.[7]

*T*o boost traffic at large shopping centers, developers are striving for a distinctive ambiance and are adding various types of entertainment. Competing with other diversions, the Forum Shops in Las Vegas have recreated a Roman street. This mall, housing 70 upscale retailers adjacent to the Caesars Palace casino, has a painted-sky ceiling that changes color over the course of a day. Other features include gladiator battles nightly and robotic statues that "come alive" hourly.

Some observers are pessimistic about the future of regional centers. One forecast suggests that perhaps one-sixth of the 1,800 large malls will fail over the next several years. A consultant stated simply, "Regional malls clearly have a life cycle, and a lot of them are in their last throes." With such forecasts, it's not surprising that relatively few regional centers are being built in the 1990s. But many existing enclosed malls are being renovated and modernized to be more appealing to shoppers. Often, more amusements and entertainments are taking center stage in today's malls.[8]

A relatively new type of shopping center is providing stiff competition for regional malls—in fact, for many types of locations. A *power center* has several popular limited-line stores (such as Circuit City, Home Depot, and Toys "R" Us), but not a traditional department store anchor. The strong appeal—and surging growth—of power centers lies in the fact that the anchors typically stress value.[9]

The growth of suburban shopping, especially in regional malls, led to decreased retail sales in many urban downtown areas. Some cities have worked to revitalize their downtown shopping districts. Historical buildings or neighborhoods are often converted to shopping areas—for example, Ghirardelli Square (formerly a chocolate factory) in San Francisco. Enclosed shopping centers featuring distinctive designs—for instance, Water Tower Place in Chicago—are successful in a number of downtown areas. However, other downtown shopping centers—for example, Underground Atlanta, The Conservatory in Minneapolis, and the Pavilion in San Jose—have failed to attract or retain sufficient shoppers. Some retailers, such as Montgomery Ward, Target, and even Toys "R" Us, are moving back downtown into nonmall locations.[10]

Classification of Retailers

To understand how retailers serve both suppliers and customers, we will classify retailers on two bases:

1. Form of ownership
2. Marketing strategies

Any retail store can be classified according to both bases, as illustrated by the following comparison of Sears and a neighborhood paint store:

| Sample stores | Classification bases | |
	Form of ownership	Marketing strategies
Sears	Corporate chain	Department store with broad, relatively deep assortments, moderate prices, and levels of personal service that vary across departments.
Neighborhood paint store	Independent	Limited-line store that has narrow, relatively deep assortments, avoids price competition, and provides extensive personal service.

Retailers Classified by Form of Ownership

The major forms of ownership in retailing are corporate chain, independent, and contractual vertical marketing system (VMS). The VMS category includes several types of organizations: wholesaler-sponsored voluntary chains, retailer-owned cooperatives, and franchise systems.

Corporate Chains

A **corporate chain** is an organization of two or more centrally owned and managed stores that generally handle the same lines of products. Three factors differentiate a chain from an independent store and the contractual form of VMS:

- Technically, two or more stores constitute a chain. Many small merchants that open several stores in shopping centers and newly populated areas do not think of themselves as chains, however. Consequently, it might be more meaningful to consider a larger number of stores as a reasonable minimum when categorizing a retailer as a chain. In fact, the U.S. Bureau of the Census considers 11 stores to be the minimum size for a chain.
- A corporate chain has central ownership; as we'll see soon, a contractual VMS does not.
- Due to centralized management, individual units in a chain typically have little autonomy. Strategic decisions are made at headquarters, and operations typically are standardized for all the units in a chain. Although a major factor in the success of chains, standardization is a mixed blessing because it often translates into inflexibility. And that means a chain sometimes cannot adjust rapidly to local market conditions.

Corporate chains continue to increase their share of total retail trade. Between 1980 and 1994, the proportion of retail sales made by chains with 11 or more stores rose from 37 percent to 40 percent. In the same period, chains grabbed a larger share of sales in all major areas of retail trade except variety stores and eating places.[11]

Chains are more common in some kinds of retailing than in others. Chains dominate the department store business, accounting for 99 percent of retail sales. But chains are not very significant among auto and home supply stores or eating places, generating just 36 percent and 24 percent of sales, respectively.[12] Essentially, chains are large-scale retailing institutions. As such, they possess the comparative strengths and weaknesses outlined in Table 14-2.

Independent Stores

An **independent retailer** is a company with a single store that is not affiliated with a contractual vertical marketing system. Most retailers are independents, and most independents are quite small. Of course, an independent department store or supermarket can have $10 million or more in annual sales, so it may have more economic power than small chains consisting of a few stores. Still, independents usually have the characteristics of small retailers presented in Table 14-2.

Independent retailers typically are viewed as having higher prices than chain stores. However, because of differences in merchandise and services, it is difficult to compare the prices of chains and independents directly. For instance, chains often have their own private brands that are not sold by independents. Also, independents and chain stores frequently provide customers with different levels—and perhaps quality—of services. Many customers are willing to pay extra for services they consider valuable, such as credit, delivery, alterations, installation, a liberal return policy, and friendly, knowledgeable personal service.

Contractual Vertical Marketing Systems

In a **contractual vertical marketing system**, independently owned firms join together under a contract specifying how they will operate. The three types of contractual VMS are discussed below.

Retailer Cooperatives and Voluntary Chains. The main difference between these two types of systems is who organizes them. A **retailer cooperative** is formed by a group of small retailers that agree to establish and operate a wholesale warehouse. In contrast, a **voluntary chain** is sponsored by a wholesaler that enters into a contract with interested retailers.

Historically these two forms of contractual VMS have been organized for defensive reasons—to enable independent retailers to compete effectively with large, strong chains. They do this by providing their retail members with volume buying power and management assistance in store layout, employee and management training programs, promotion, accounting, and inventory control systems.

Retailer cooperatives are declining, but still have strong representatives in groceries (Certified Grocers) and hardware (True Value). Voluntary chains are prevalent in the grocery field (IGA, Supervalu). They are also found in hardware (Ace) and auto supplies (Western Auto) stores.

Franchise Systems. **Franchising** involves a continuing relationship in which a parent company provides the right to use its trademark and management assistance in return for payments from the owner of the individual business unit. The parent company is called a *franchisor*, whereas the owner of the unit is called a *franchisee*. The combination of franchisor and franchisees is called a *franchise system*. This type of contractual VMS is growing steadily, generating at least $800 *billion* in annual sales and accounting for over one-third of all retail sales in the U.S.[13]

There are two kinds of franchising:

- **Product and trade name franchising.** Historically the dominant kind, product and trade name franchising is prevalent in the automobile (Ford, Honda) and petroleum (Chevron, Texaco) industries. It is a distribution agreement under which a supplier (the franchisor) authorizes a dealer (the franchisee) to sell a product line, using the parent company's trade name for promotional purposes. The franchisee agrees to buy from the franchisor and also to abide by specified policies. The focus in product and trade name franchising is on *what is sold*.

- **Business format franchising.** Much of franchising's growth and publicity over the past three decades has involved the business format kind (used by firms such as Kentucky Fried Chicken, Midas, and H & R Block). This kind of franchising covers an entire method (or format) for operating a business. A successful retail business sells the right to operate the same business in another geographic area. The franchisee expects to receive from the parent company a proven method of operating a business; in return, the franchisor receives from each business owner payments and also conformance to policies and standards. The focus here is on *how the business is run*.

MAIL BOXES ETC.®

*M*ost of the recent growth in franchising has involved business-format franchises offering services to consumer and/or business markets. Many franchises have become very well known; others are working toward that level of recognition.

In business format franchising, the franchisor may be a manufacturer that provides franchisees with merchandise. More often, this is not the case. For example, Little Professor Book Centers, Inc., does not sell books to its franchised stores; rather, the stores buy their inventory from wholesalers. The franchisor is supposed to provide management assistance, especially marketing expertise, to franchisees.

Selling franchises can be attractive to a successful retail business that wants to expand. Among the advantages:

- Rapid expansion is expedited, because franchisees provide capital when they purchase franchises.
- Because they have an investment at risk, franchisees typically are highly motivated to work hard and adhere to the parent company's proven format.

Buying a franchise can offer protection to an independent store that faces stiff competition from chains or to a prospective new retail store. Among the benefits:

- Franchisees can use the parent company's well-known trade name, which should help attract customers.
- Various forms of management assistance are provided to franchisees prior to as well as after opening the store, including site-selection and store-layout guidance, technical and management training, promotional programs, and inventory control systems.

Franchising is not without problems. Some franchises are based on poor products or unsound business practices and consequently fail. Further, a number of franchisees criticize franchisors for practices such as the following: enticing prospective franchisees by projecting unrealistically high revenues or unrealistically low operating costs; not providing franchisees with the promised and necessary levels of business support; locating too many of the company's outlets in the same market; or unjustifiably terminating or not renewing the franchise agreement. Conversely, franchisors have their own complaints, notably that some franchisees deviate from the system's policies and practices. Battles between franchisors and franchisees in courtrooms are increasingly common. As in most business fields, if self-regulation is ineffective, added regulation at the federal and state levels is likely.[14]

Despite some challenges, continued growth in franchising is expected. For one thing, a number of franchisors are seeking stronger partnerships with their franchisees.

YOU MAKE THE DECISION

WOULD YOU BUY A RETAIL FRANCHISE?

Many products reach consumer markets through franchised retail outlets. Consider these examples:

Product category	Sample franchises
Fast food and other prepared food	McDonald's, Domino's, Subway, Arby's
Automotive repairs	Midas, Car-X, Jiffy Lube
Clothing	T-Shirts Plus, Just Pants, Fashions under $10
Hair care	Fantastic Sam's, Supercuts
Groceries and other food products	7-Eleven, Rocky Mountain Chocolate Factory
Education programs	Sylvan Learning Center, Arthur Murray School of Dance
Home decorating products	Wallpapers to Go, Decorating Den, Stained Glass Overlay

The cost of buying a franchise varies greatly. As the samples from the retail food field at the top of the next column illustrate, some are inexpensive and others are steep.

Sources: Jeffrey A. Tannenbaum, "Franchisers Want to Tone Down Their Industry's Hype," *The Wall Street Journal*, Mar. 11, 1996, p. B2; Jeffrey A. Tannenbaum, "Brice Offers Its Frozen-Yogurt Franchisees a Sweet Deal," *The Wall Street Journal*, Nov. 9, 1995, p. B2; and Jeffrey A. Tannenbaum, "Mail Boxes Etc. Delivers Profits but Not to Everyone," *The Wall Street Journal*, Oct. 13, 1993, p. B2. Estimated costs provided by Jeff Kolton, Frandata Corp., Washington, D.C.

Brand name	Type of business	Approximate up-front franchise fee	Approximate total start-up costs
Subway	Sandwich shop	$10,000	$100,000
Mr. Rooter	Sewer and drain cleaning	$17,500	$60,000
Rainbow International	Carpet dyeing and cleaning	$15,000	$40,000
Hardee's	Fast-food restaurant	$15,000	$1.2 million

Most, but not all, franchise systems are successful. For example, some I Can't Believe It's Yogurt and TCBY frozen yogurt outlets have struggled. The demand for their product is seasonal, plus they face harsh competition from various food purveyors, including other brands of frozen yogurt shops. And some owners of Mail Boxes Etc. franchises have charged that the parent company exaggerates the financial prospects for this business. A growing number of people involved with franchising believe the industry needs less hype about "Get rich quick" opportunities and a greater focus on the realities of franchising, which is a viable form of business ownership that typically demands hard work from franchisors.

If you were going to open a retail business, would you do it as an independent or would you purchase a franchise?

http://alphagraphics.com/

AlphaGraphics, a franchisor of print shops, heeded a request from its franchisees and restructured the financial arrangement between the parties. Similarly, the franchisor of Taco John's restaurants revamped the working agreements with its franchisees.[15]

http://www.berlitz.com/

http://www.dnb.com/

Many small retailers will continue to use franchising defensively—to achieve a viable competitive position against corporate chains. Ambitious, successful retailers and service firms, such as Berlitz in language training and Dun & Bradstreet in financial services, are employing it as an offensive tool—for rapid expansion. Numerous products, especially services, lend themselves to franchising. Among the projected growth areas for franchising are energy-conservation companies, collection agencies, and learning-skills centers.[16]

Prospective business owners will continue to buy franchises because of the two key attributes—a degree of independence and a variety of management assistance. In fact, many people with little or no business experience have purchased franchises for this reason. A growing share—perhaps more than 30 percent—of franchise buyers are people who were employed previously by large corporations. New franchisees include laid-off production and office employees as well as numerous managers and executives who were victims of corporate restructuring. Such new entrants view franchising as a way of determining their own financial destiny.[17]

Retailers Classified by Marketing Strategies

Whatever its form of ownership, a retailer must develop marketing-mix strategies to succeed in its chosen target markets. In retailing, the marketing mix emphasizes product assortment, price, location, promotion, and customer services. This last element consists of services designed to aid in the sale of a product. They include credit, delivery, gift wrapping, product installation, merchandise returns, store hours, parking, and—very important—personal service.

We will now describe the major types of retail stores, paying particular attention to three elements of their marketing mixes:

- Breadth and depth of product assortment.
- Price level.
- Amount of customer services.

Table 14-3 classifies retail stores on the basis of these three elements.

Some types of retail stores, such as category-killer stores (described in detail later in the chapter), are fairly new and growing rapidly. Others, such as variety stores, are diminishing in importance. Still others, particularly department stores, are under competitive pressure to modify some strategies. We will see that certain

TABLE 14-3 Retail stores classified by key marketing strategies

Type of store	Breadth and depth of assortment	Price level	Amount of customer services
Department store	Very broad, deep	Avoids price competition	Wide array
Discount house	Broad, shallow	Emphasizes low prices	Relatively few
Limited-line store	Narrow, deep	Traditional types avoid price competition; newer kinds emphasize low prices	Vary by type
Specialty store	Very narrow, deep	Avoids price competition	At least standard; extensive in some
Off-price retailer	Narrow, deep	Emphasizes low prices	Few
Category-killer store	Narrow, very deep	Emphasizes low prices	Few to moderate
Supermarket	Broad, deep	Some emphasize low prices; others avoid price disadvantages	Few
Convenience store	Narrow, shallow	High prices	Few
Warehouse club	Very broad, very shallow	Emphasizes very low prices	Few (open only to members)

retailers are similar to others because new or modified institutions have filled the "strategic gaps" that once separated different types of retail institutions.

Department Stores

Long a mainstay of retailing in the U.S., a **department store** is a large-scale retailing institution that has a very broad and deep product assortment, tries not to compete on the basis of price, and provides a wide array of customer services. Familiar department store names include Filene's, Dillard's, Foley's, Dayton Hudson, Rich's, May Company, Marshall Field, Sears, J.C. Penney, and Montgomery Ward.

Traditional department stores offer a greater variety of merchandise *and* customer services than any other type of retail store. They feature both "soft goods"—such as apparel, sheets, towels, and bedding—and "hard goods"—including furniture, appliances, and consumer electronics. Department stores also attract and satisfy consumers by offering many customer services, such as alterations, various credit plans, and bridal registry. The combination of distinctive, appealing merchandise and numerous customer services is supposed to allow the stores to maintain the manufacturers' suggested retail prices. That is, department stores strive to charge "full" or "nondiscounted" prices.

Department stores face serious challenges.[18] Because of their prime (that is, busy but expensive) locations and abundant customer services, their operating expenses are considerably higher than most other retailers. Many producers' brands that used to be available exclusively through department stores are now widely distributed and are often available at discounted prices in other outlets. And the quality of personal service, especially knowledgeable sales help, has deteriorated in many department stores.

Intense horizontal competition also tests department stores. Other types of retail institutions—such as discount houses and "off-price" retailers—are aggressively trying to lure shoppers away from department stores by offering lower prices. To varying degrees, retail chains such as Kmart, Wal-Mart, Circuit City, and Home Depot vie with traditional department stores. The convenience of catalogs represents still another form of competition.[19]

Because of competitive pressures and marketing deficiencies, some department store chains have had to seek temporary bankruptcy protection or have gone out of business entirely. This list includes previously revered names such as Macy's, Federated Department Stores, Bonwit Teller, and Garfinckel's. Overall, department stores' share of total retail trade dropped about 5 percentage points from the early 1980s to the early 1990s. In the last several years, however, strategic changes have helped department stores stabilize their collective position in the retail sector.[20]

Striving for an advantage, many department stores have modified their target markets and/or elements of their marketing mixes. Some department store chains, for example, have dropped several lines of hard goods, including major appliances and sporting goods. Instead, they are placing greater emphasis on clothing, jewelry, cosmetics, and other product lines that appeal to more upscale shoppers. The chapter-opening case recounts Penney's efforts in this regard. Few department store chains can equal Sears' success with respect to revising and strengthening marketing strategies. To attract more female shoppers, Sears has revamped its assortment of merchandise and remodeled many of its stores, among other changes. Advertising has promoted "the softer side of Sears." After a sizable loss in 1992, Sears' retail operations recorded steadily increasing profits the next 3 years.[21]

Most department stores are also trying to be more price-competitive. They do not need to match the lower prices of rivals that lack extensive assortments and a variety of customer services. Many shoppers will pay a small premium to enjoy

the "extras" offered by chains such as Rich's, May Company, Carson Pirie Scott, and even Sears, J.C. Penney, and Montgomery Ward. However, it's essential that department stores provide good value. Computer-based inventory-control systems help stores stock the right types and amounts of merchandise to satisfy customers and, at the same time, avoid the costs of excess inventories.

Discount Houses

Discount retailing involves comparatively low prices as a major selling point combined with reduced costs of doing business. Several institutions, including off-price retailers and warehouse clubs, which will be discussed shortly, rely on discount retailing as their main marketing strategy.

The prime example of discount retailing is the **discount house**, a large-scale retailing institution that has a broad, shallow product assortment, low prices, and few customer services. A discount house normally carries a broad assortment of soft goods (particularly apparel) and hard goods (including popular brands of appliances and home furnishings) and advertises them heavily. Wal-Mart, Kmart, and Target are the largest discount-house chains. Discount houses have had a major impact on retailing, prompting many retailers to lower their prices.

Some discount chains have been trading up. For example, Kmart has tried to evolve from a no-frills discounter to a retailer of value-priced, top-quality merchandise, much of which carries well-known brand names. Toward that end, Kmart committed $3.5 billion to renovate many of its more than 2,000 stores. Kmart's efforts have been hugely unsuccessful for many reasons, including poor merchandise selection, inadequate distribution networks, and a diversion of resources to other company-owned chains such as Sports Authority and Office-Max.[22] Target, a division of Dayton Hudson Corp., has been more successful in its efforts to trade up. The slogan, "Basics Plus Fashion," underscores Target's emphasis not only on staple merchandise but also on more stylish soft goods. As much as possible, Target gives top billing to its own brands rather than those of manufacturers.[23]

Such upgrading brings discount houses into competition with department stores and some other types of retailers. This strategic change may result in better gross margins, but it usually brings higher expenses. Recognizing that, Wal-Mart has stayed true to its basic approach—selling consumables (paper products and over-the-counter drugs, for example) and hard goods at sharply discounted prices. To keep prices down and still earn satisfactory profits, the largest retailer negotiates hard (some say mercilessly) with suppliers to obtain low merchandise costs and also pares operating expenses wherever possible.[24]

Wal-Mart and, to a lesser extent, Kmart, are also committing more and more resources to a much expanded discount house, called a **supercenter**. Basically, it is a combined discount house and complete grocery store. Wal-Mart's more than 300 supercenters are different than discount houses in several noteworthy ways: larger size, wider aisles, more attractive decor, broader assortment of merchandise, and added customer services, including new technological devices such as shopping carts with video screens. Demonstrating its commitment to this format, Wal-Mart's plan in the mid-1990s was to open more new supercenters than new regular discount houses.[25]

Limited-Line Stores

Much of the "action" in retailing in recent years has been in **limited-line stores**. This type of institution has a narrow but deep product assortment and customer services that vary from store to store. Traditionally, limited-line stores selling

products such as clothing, baked goods, and furniture strove for full, or nondiscounted, prices. As we'll discuss below, however, new types of limited-line retailers have gained a foothold by emphasizing low prices.

Breadth of assortment varies somewhat across limited-line stores. A store may choose to concentrate on:

- Several related product lines (shoes, sportswear, and accessories).
- A single product line (shoes).
- Part of one product line (athletic footwear).

We identify limited-line stores by the name of the primary product line—furniture store, hardware store, or clothing store, for example. Some retailers such as grocery stores and drugstores that used to be limited-line stores now carry much broader assortments because of scrambled merchandising, a strategy we described in the preceding chapter.

Specialty Stores. A very narrow and deep product assortment, often concentrating on a specialized product line (baked goods) or even part of a specialized product line (cinnamon rolls), is offered to consumers by a **specialty store**. Examples of specialty stores are donut shops, furriers, athletic footwear stores, meat markets, and dress shops. (Specialty *stores* should not be confused with specialty *goods*. In a sense, specialty stores are misnamed, because they may carry any of the categories of consumer goods that were discussed in Chapter 8, not just specialty goods.)

Most specialty stores strive to maintain manufacturers' suggested prices, although they may offer their own store brands at lower prices. Typically, they provide at least standard customer services. Some specialty retailers, however, emphasize extensive customer services, particularly knowledgeable and friendly sales help.

The largest specialty retailer is The Limited, Inc., which features a variety of clothing chains, virtually all aimed at different segments of female shoppers. The Limited's array of stores includes Victoria's Secret, Lerner New York, Express, Structure, Abercrombie & Fitch, Bath & Body Works (which sells toiletries), and—of course—its signature Limited Stores. After remarkable growth during the 1980s, the corporation has found the going much tougher in recent years. Besides facing stiff competition, some divisions have not done well in selecting appealing merchandise for their particular target markets.[26]

The prosperity of specialty stores depends on their ability to attract and then satisfy consumers who especially want deep assortments and extensive, top-quality services. Successful specialty store chains include Bed, Bath & Beyond, which concentrates on sheets, towels, and related products; Bombay, which sells furniture and other decorating items with a British Victorian theme; and Noodle Kidoodle, which features educational toys that stimulate creativity and thinking.[27] Sunglass Hut International is the epitome of a specialty retailer. The firm stuffs 1,000 different pairs of sunglasses into its tiny outlets (typically, kiosks of about 300 square feet). The combination of broad assortment, low prices, and 1,600 convenient locations has allowed Sunglass Hut to ring up annual sales exceeding $250 million.[28]

Some forecasts for specialty stores, especially those selling clothing, are grim. Specialty retailers in malls face a twofold challenge—the specialty format no longer appeals to many consumers, and malls are experiencing reduced shopper traffic. According to a 1995 report by Management Horizons, a consulting firm,

"No sector of retailing is at greater risk over the next five years." To survive and prosper, specialty stores must offer merchandise that satisfies smaller demographic segments in specific local markets.[29]

Off-Price Retailers. When some discount houses decided to trade up during the 1980s, **off-price retailers** positioned themselves below discount houses with lower prices on selected product lines. This type of institution features a narrow, deep product assortment, low prices, and few customer services. Off-price retailers are most common in the areas of apparel and footwear. Store names such as Marshall's, Ross Dress for Less, and Payless ShoeSource are known to consumers in many locales.

Off-price retailers concentrate on well-known producers' brands. They often buy manufacturers' excess output, inventory remaining at the end of a fashion season, or irregular merchandise at lower-than-normal wholesale costs. In turn, their prices are much lower than prices for regular, in-season merchandise sold in other stores. Customers are attracted by the low prices and fairly current fashions.

Factory outlets are a special type of off-price retailer. They usually sell a single company's merchandise. Many popular brands, such as Esprit, Calvin Klein, Corning, L.L. Bean, Paul Revere, Royal Doulton, and Dansk, can be found in factory outlets. Factory outlets used to stock mainly clearance items or imperfect products (called *seconds*). Now they are more likely to feature the same merchandise that can be found on other retailers' shelves—typically at lower prices than are charged by other retailers. Some manufacturers, including Phillips-Van Heusen Corp., even produce some apparel specifically for their outlet stores.

Factory outlets have been growing rapidly, now ringing up more than $13 billion in annual sales. This type of retail institution gives manufacturers another channel for their products—one over which they have complete control. Consumers appreciate the lower prices typically found in factory outlets. According to one survey, 87 percent of factory-outlet customers considered the savings worth any added travel time.[30] Not everyone is pleased by the growth of factory outlets, however. Most notably, other retailers do not like their suppliers competing directly with them. To avoid aggravating retailers that distribute the same products, factory-outlet centers are often—but not always—located some distance from major malls and downtown shopping areas.[31]

Like most types of retail institutions, many off-price chains and factory-outlet centers have been confronting serious challenges. For example, the T.J. Maxx chain, which is owned by TJX Cos., has been struggling to improve its paltry profit margins. In contrast, both Marshall's, acquired by TJX in 1995, and Payless ShoeSource, recently spun off by May Department Stores to become a separate firm, have suffered from flat sales. Basically, during the mid-1990s, most retailers' clothing sales were stagnant. Further, off-price retailers face stiffer price competition not only from discount houses but also from department stores. In like manner, the growing numbers of retailers that are located in regional shopping centers and stress value pricing are giving some shoppers second thoughts about whether the trip to a factory-outlet center is worthwhile.[32]

Category-Killer Stores. A phenomenon of the 1980s, a **category-killer store** has a narrow but very deep assortment, low prices, and few to moderate customer services. As the name suggests, they are designed to destroy all competition in a specific product category.[33] Successful category killers include Ikea in home furnishings, Circuit City in consumer electronics, Home Depot in building

supplies, and Toys "R" Us. Other product areas with category killers are office supplies, housewares, recorded music, and sporting goods.

A category killer concentrates on a single product line or several closely related lines. What distinguishes a category killer is the combination of many different sizes, models, styles, and colors of the products *and* low prices. For example, either a Borders or a Barnes & Noble bookstore ordinarily exceeds 30,000 square feet, about 10 times the size of the typical mall bookstore, and carries over 100,000 titles. Incredible Universe outlets are even bigger—about 185,000 square feet. They feature 85,000 items spanning consumer electronics, computing, and home appliances as well as a rotunda stage for entertainment and product demonstrations. Part of Tandy Corp., which also owns Radio Shack stores, Incredible Universe is not yet profitable. Therefore, the ability of these stores to attract sufficient customers and make money is still unproven.[34]

http://www.tandy.com/

Category-killer stores are taking sales and customers away from long-standing retailers, including discount houses and department stores. Sustained growth is forecast for this type of retail store. The format is being tried with other products, such as used cars. CarMax, a division of Circuit City Stores Inc., already is shooting for 50 dealerships by the turn of the century. Each dealer maintains an inventory of around 1,000 not-too-used cars and trucks. Shoppers use touch-screen computers to sort through the alternatives before test-driving vehicles of interest to them. To help make shoppers feel comfortable, CarMax employs a one-price ("no haggle") strategy. The new chain's first four stores averaged more than $70 million in sales during 1995. Not surprisingly, competitors, such as AutoNation, already are starting up. And traditional new-car dealers, which derive a substantial portion of their profits from used cars, are contemplating how they should react to this new competitive threat.[35]

http://www.circuitcity.com/

Supermarkets

As with *discount*, the word *supermarket* can be used to describe a method of retailing *and* a type of institution. As a method, **supermarket retailing** features several related product lines, a high degree of self-service, largely centralized checkout, and competitive prices. Supermarket retailing is used to sell various kinds of merchandise, including building materials, office products, and—of course—groceries.

As a term, *supermarket* usually refers to an institution in the grocery retailing field. In this context a **supermarket** is a retail institution that has a moderately broad, moderately deep product assortment spanning groceries and some nonfood lines, and offers relatively few customer services. Most supermarkets emphasize price. Some use price *offensively*, featuring low prices to attract customers. Others use price *defensively*, relying on leader pricing to avoid a price disadvantage. Having very thin gross margins, supermarkets need high levels of inventory turnover to achieve satisfactory returns on invested capital.

Stores using the supermarket *method* of retailing now dominate grocery retailing. As these stores added more products and more selling space, some were called *superstores* and *combination stores*. Like the new *supercenters* discussed in the section on discount houses, superstores and combination stores are much expanded versions of supermarkets.

For many years the supermarket has been under siege from competitors. A grocery shopper can choose among not only many brands of supermarkets (Publix, Safeway, Albertson's, and Vons, to name several) but also various types of institutions (warehouse stores, meat and fish markets, convenience stores, and now

supercenters). Supermarkets reacted to competitive pressures in either of two ways: Some cut costs and stressed low prices, offering more private brands and generic products and few customer services. Others expanded their store size and assortments, adding more nonfood lines (especially products found in drugstores) and groceries attuned to a particular market area (foods that appeal to a specific ethnic group, for example). They also added various service departments, including video rentals, restaurants, delicatessens, financial institutions, and pharmacies.[36]

Convenience Stores

To satisfy increasing consumer demand for convenience, particularly in suburban areas, the **convenience store** emerged several decades ago. This retailing institution concentrates on convenience groceries and nonfoods, typically has higher prices than other grocery stores, and offers few customer services. Gasoline, fast foods, and selected services (such as car washes and automated teller machines) can also be found in many convenience stores.

The name *convenience store* reflects its appeal and explains how its higher prices are justified. Convenience stores are typically located near residential areas and are open extended hours; in fact, some never close. Examples of convenience store chains are 7-Eleven (originally open from 7 a.m. to 11 p.m. but now open 24 hours daily in most locations), Stop N Go, and Convenient Food Mart.

Convenience stores compete to some extent with both supermarkets and fast-food restaurants. Furthermore, in the 1980s petroleum companies modified many of their service stations by phasing out auto repairs and adding a convenience groceries section. For example, Arco has AM/PM Mini Marts and both Shell Oil and Texaco have Food Marts.

During the mid-1990s, convenience stores were in the doldrums. Real sales growth is projected to be under 2 percent annually through the year 2000. As a result, convenience store chains are adjusting their marketing strategies. Circle K, for example, has revamped the basic layout of its stores, creating miniature departments. In addition, the chain has experimented with branded gasoline and take-out food stores located adjacent to its convenience stores.[37]

Warehouse Clubs

Another institution that has mushroomed since the mid-1980s is the **warehouse club**, sometimes called a *wholesale club*. A combined retailing and wholesaling institution, it has very broad but very shallow product assortments, extremely low prices, and few customer services. Warehouse clubs are open only to members who pay an annual fee of about $25. Their target markets are small businesses (some purchasing merchandise for resale) and select groups of employees (government workers and school personnel, for example), as well as members of credit unions.

A warehouse club carries about the same breadth of assortment as a large discount house but in much less depth. For each item, the club stocks only one or two brands and a !imited number of sizes and models. It is housed in a warehouse-type building with tall metal racks that display merchandise at ground level and store it at higher levels. Prices for household consumers typically are about 5 percent higher than prices offered to business members. Customers ordinarily must pay cash and handle their own merchandise—even heavy, bulky items.

This format, which originated in Europe many years ago, was first applied successfully in the U.S. in the mid-1970s by the Price Club. From the mid-1980s until the early 1990s, in particular, the growth of warehouse clubs was impressive. Then

The owner of a small independent bookstore runs short of "best-sellers" during the peak Christmas season. Obtaining more inventory from the store's normal supplier, a wholesaler in another city, takes several days. In the meanwhile, thousands of dollars of sales would be lost. A warehouse club about 5 miles from the bookstore carries a limited selection of books; in fact, they are priced at about the bookstore's wholesale cost. By buying best-sellers at the warehouse club, substituting new price stickers for the warehouse club's stickers, and getting the books on the store's shelves within a couple of hours rather than several days, the independent bookstore builds sales during this critical selling period and satisfies its customers.

Considering that customers do not know the bookstore acquired some of its best-sellers from a warehouse club and then resold them, is this ethical business behavior on the part of the bookstore owner?

---

this type of institution encountered problems because of the economic recession combined with intense horizontal competition among warehouse clubs, supermarkets, and discount houses. In addition, as they moved beyond the regions in which they started, warehouse clubs competed with each other to an increasing degree. In 1993, several competing firms (including Kmart's Pace Membership Warehouses) failed, and two of the three largest warehouse club organizations merged, forming PriceCostco. Now the two leading groups of warehouse clubs are Sam's Club (owned by Wal-Mart) and PriceCostco. Together they register about 85 percent of the sales of this type of institution.[38]

http://www.pricecostco.com/

http://www.samsclub.com/

Warehouse clubs have some limitations. Some shoppers want a broader assortment of products and smaller quantities or packages. As with other retailing institutions, modifications and refinements are under way. Greater emphasis is being placed on business customers, rather than individuals and households purchasing for their own consumption. To do so, Sam's redesigned its newsletter for business customers, stressing useful information about various industries. The Wal-Mart division also established a sales force to solicit business from larger organizations. In contrast, PriceCostco has added perishable foods (fresh meat, produce, baked goods) and more specialty departments (pharmacy, optical shop). It also mailed out booklets of discount coupons to boost purchases by members and to attract new members.[39]

Nonstore Retailing

A large majority—perhaps 90 percent—of retail transactions are made in stores. However, a growing volume of sales is taking place away from stores. Retailing activities resulting in transactions that occur away from a retail store are called **nonstore retailing**.

It is "guesstimated" that sales volume through nonstore retailing is in the range of $200 billion to $250 billion annually.[40] Based on this figure, nonstore sales account for just over 10 percent of total retail trade.

We will consider four types of nonstore retailing: direct selling, telemarketing, automatic vending, and direct marketing. (Rather than worrying about the confus-

ing names, focus on the features and competition across the four types.) Each type may be used not just by retailers but by other types of organizations as well.

Direct Selling

In the context of retailing, **direct selling** is defined as personal contact between a sales person and a consumer away from a retail store. This type of retailing has also been called *in-home selling* but, as we shall see, the changing roles of women have made this term less accurate.[41] Annual volume of direct selling in the U.S. was about $16.5 billion in 1994. These sales were rung up by more than 6 million independent direct sales people. According to one survey, during a 12-month period, 57 percent of consumers bought a product from a company using direct selling; in comparison, 69 percent made a catalog purchase during the same period.[42]

There are many well-known direct-selling companies, including Avon, Mary Kay, Tupperware, Electrolux (vacuums), Amway, Shaklee (vitamins and food supplements), West Bend (cookware), and World Book. Diverse products are sold through direct selling. This channel is particularly well suited for products that require extensive demonstration (cosmetics, household cleaning products).

The two kinds of direct selling are door to door and party plan. Sometimes *door-to-door selling* involves "cold canvasing," meaning no advance selection of prospects. More often, initial contact occurs through a mailed-in coupon, by telephone, or by a friend, neighbor, or coworker.

Under *party-plan selling*, an individual invites some friends to a party. These guests understand that a sales person—say, for a cosmetics or a housewares company—will make a sales presentation. The sales rep has a larger prospective market and more favorable selling conditions than if these people were approached individually door to door. And the guests get to shop in a friendly, social atmosphere. However, it is increasingly difficult to entice women with crowded schedules to attend sales parties. Consequently, Tupperware has lost both reps and sales in the U.S. (although its international operations have done well).[43]

http://www.tupperware.com/

With so many women—more than one-half—now working outside the home, direct-selling firms have had to find new ways of making contact with prospective customers. For instance, many reps call on employees in the workplace or give sales parties at lunchtime in offices. As you might suspect, some employers take a dim view of such selling in the workplace. To reach new customers and win back former clients, Avon began mailing catalogs to selected homes. To avoid alienating its sales force, Avon will pay reps a commission on any catalog orders placed by customers in their areas. The first-year sales results from this new approach were disappointing, however. Mary Kay Corp., another large direct-selling firm, also has been experimenting with this approach.[44]

Direct selling has drawbacks. Sales commissions run as high as 40 to 50 percent of the retail price; of course, they are paid only when a sale is made. Recruiting, training, motivating, and retaining good sales people—most of whom are part-timers—are difficult tasks. Moreover, some sales people use "high-pressure" tactics or are fraudulent. To minimize this problem, nearly all states have "cooling off" laws that permit consumers to nullify a party-plan or door-to-door sale for several days after the transaction.

Direct selling also offers significant benefits. Consumers have the opportunity to buy at home or at another convenient nonstore location. For the seller, direct selling offers the boldest method of trying to persuade ultimate consumers to make

a purchase. The seller takes products to the shopper's home or workplace and even demonstrates them for the consumer.

Like other forms of nonstore retailing, direct selling is utilized in all countries. It's particularly widespread in Japan. In fact, Japan accounts for about 45 percent of the worldwide volume of direct selling, the U.S. almost 25 percent, and all other countries the rest.[45]

Telemarketing

Sometimes called *telephone selling*, **telemarketing** refers to a sales person initiating contact with a shopper and closing a sale over the telephone. Telemarketing may entail cold canvasing from the phone directory. Or it may rely on prospects who have requested information from the company or whose demographics match those of the company's target market.

Many products that can be bought without being seen are sold over the telephone. Examples are pest-control services, magazine subscriptions, credit cards, and athletic club memberships. Our best "guesstimate" of the annual volume of telemarketing in the retail sector is around $50 billion.[46]

Telemarketing sales have been increasing—and should continue to—for several reasons. Fundamentally, some people appreciate the convenience of making a purchase by phone. The introduction of outgoing WATS lines about 25 years ago made telemarketing to distant locations more cost-effective. Costs have also been reduced by computers that can automatically dial a telephone number, even deliver a taped message and record information the buyer gives to complete the sale. Using bilingual sales reps, some large companies are using telemarketing to generate purchases by immigrant and ethnic consumers in the U.S.[47]

Telemarketing is not problem-free. Working conditions of telephone sales reps, especially those that work for large telemarketing firms, is one serious issue. Often encountering hostile people on the other end of the line and experiencing many more rejections than closed sales, few of this type of sales person last very long. It's not uncommon for annual turnover to average 100 percent.[48]

Telemarketing's reputation has been damaged by the incessant and/or unethical sales practices of certain practitioners. Some firms call at almost any hour of the day or night. This tactic is criticized as violating consumers' right to privacy (and uninterrupted meals). Because of such problems, the Federal Communications Commission recently ruled that telemarketing firms must maintain—and abide by—lists of consumers who do not want to be called. The new rules ban calls before 8 a.m. and after 9 p.m. In addition, some telemarketing involves outright fraud—attempts to obtain a person's credit card number for illegal use, to cite one example. To protect consumers, the Federal Trade Commission adopted a rule requiring telemarketers to inform consumers that the intent of the call is to sell them a product, which must be identified. In addition, the rule allows federal and state officials to seek stiff fines against fraudulent operators.[49]

Automatic Vending

The sale of products through a machine with no personal contact between buyer and seller is called **automatic vending**. The appeal of automatic vending is convenient purchase. Products sold by automatic vending are usually well-known, presold brands with a high rate of turnover. The large majority of automatic vending sales comes from the "4 C's": cold drinks, coffee, candy, and cigarettes. It is

estimated that vending rings up about $25 billion in annual sales, which represents more than 1 percent of all retail trade.[50]

Vending machines can expand a firm's market by reaching customers where and when they cannot come to a store. Thus vending equipment is found almost everywhere, particularly in schools, workplaces, and public facilities. Automatic vending has high operating costs because of the need to replenish inventories frequently. The machines also require maintenance and repairs.

The outlook for automatic vending is uncertain. The difficulties just mentioned may hinder future growth. Further, some entrepreneurs may avoid the vending-machine business because of a rising number of scams. However, vending innovations give reason for some optimism. Some machines now sell a "debit card" that can be used to make vending purchases. When this card is inserted into a vending machine, the amount of the purchase is deducted from the credit balance. Also, there is a continuing flow of new products for vending machines, including freshly squeezed orange juice, microwaved pizzas, heatable diet dinners, cappuccino, and even French fries. New technology allows operators to monitor vending machines from a distance, thereby reducing the number (and lost revenues) of out-of-stock or out-of-order machines. Of course, all of these technological advances are costly.[51]

Direct Marketing

There is no consensus on the exact nature of direct marketing. In effect, it comprises all types of nonstore retailing other than direct selling, telemarketing, and automatic vending. In the context of retailing, we define **direct marketing** as using advertising to contact consumers who, in turn, purchase products without visiting a retail store. (Be careful to distinguish among the terms direct *marketing*, direct *selling*, and direct *distribution*!)

Direct marketers contact consumers through one or more of the following media: radio, TV, newspapers, magazines, catalogs, mailings (direct mail), and now by the Internet. Consumers order by telephone, mail, or computer. Direct marketing is big business: Currently it accounts for perhaps $130 billion to $140 billion in annual retail sales![52]

http://www.spiegel.com/

http://www.sharperimage.com

Some companies started out in nonstore retailing and later established massive chains of retail stores; Sears and Ward's are prime examples. Other firms concentrated exclusively on direct marketing for many years; Spiegel typifies this group. More and more companies that have relied solely or predominantly on direct marketing are opening stores now to expand their marketing efforts; The Sharper Image is a good example. Direct marketers can be classified as either general-merchandise firms, which offer a wide variety of product lines, or specialty firms, which carry only one or two lines such as books or fresh fruit.

Under the broad definition, the many forms of direct marketing include:

- *Direct mail,* in which firms mail to consumers letters, brochures, and even product samples, and ask them to purchase by mail or telephone. This form of direct marketing is best for selling a variety of services, such as credit cards and athletic club memberships, and well-known goods, such as magazines, recorded music, and even fruitcakes. The 100-year-old Collin Street Bakery, located in Corsicana, Texas, generates 95 percent of its business by mail. Each year, it ships about 1.5 million fruitcakes to 400,000 customers.[53]
- *Catalog retailing*, in which companies mail catalogs to consumers or make them available at retail stores. After expanding at an annual rate of 10 percent

*T*o an increasing extent, firms that engage in catalog retailing—ranging from Sears to J. Crew—are relying on specialized catalogs rather than bigger, broad-assortment catalogs. Here, L.L. Bean emphasizes outdoor clothing and gear for springtime. Other Bean catalogs are much more specialized, such as a catalog featuring rugs, lamps, and other furnishings for the home or vacation cottage. Another Bean catalog, 72 pages long, focuses strictly on products related to fly fishing—not just apparel, but even Aqua Stealth wading shoes and, of course, artificial flies.

http://www.llbean.com/

http://www.qvc.com/

during the 1980s, catalog retailing has been growing at one-half that rate—perhaps less—during this decade. This slump has hurt giant retailers (such as Penney's and Ward's) and established catalog retailers (such as Spiegel, L.L. Bean, and J. Crew). Many smaller catalog firms have failed. In 1993, Sears terminated its giant catalog because the "Big Book" was losing money on more than $3 billion in annual sales. Now, belatedly according to critics, Sears is distributing a number of specialized catalogs in niches ranging from auto accessories to apparel for large women.[54]

- *Televised shopping*, in which various categories of products are promoted on dedicated TV channels and through *infomercials*, which are TV commercials that run for 30 minutes or even longer on an entertainment channel. The leading shopping channels, QVC and the Home Shopping Network, sell jewelry, consumer electronics, home decor, and other products at relatively low prices. Infomercials have been used to sell a variety of items, including cutlery, sprays to color and disguise thinning hair, and home-based businesses. Televised shopping grew dramatically during the 1980s, but has slowed down in recent years.[55]

- *Online retailing*, in which consumers use their computers to shop for products and make purchases, primarily through commercial online services (such as America Online and Prodigy) and the World Wide Web, the graphic part of the Internet. Online retailing is in its infancy, generating a meager total of about $125 million in sales during 1995. Thus far, most vendors have not come up with the right marketing mix. For example, assortments are very limited, discounts are rare, and the graphic "storefronts" too often are not particularly attractive or entertaining. Also, the expense of establishing an appealing, functional Web site is considerable, ranging from $300,000 to $3 million or more.

A GLOBAL PERSPECTIVE

HOW FAR WILL RETAILERS GO TO FIND THE LAND OF OPPORTUNITY?

With stiff competition and skittish consumers, times are tough for many retailers in the U.S. Because of or despite these challenges, many American retail firms are expanding around the globe. Some examples: Toys "R" Us has cracked the code for gaining access to the Japanese market; Wal-Mart's early international efforts range from Mexico City to Hong Kong; and Foot Locker plans to have 1,000 stores in Europe.

It's not just American *stores* that are found in foreign markets. *Nonstore* retailers are also looking abroad for new customers. Lands' End now reaches almost that far with its catalog operations. Avon, a direct-selling firm, is deriving a growing share of its revenues from emerging markets such as Brazil, China, and Poland. In many foreign countries, most women are still at home, there are few formidable retail chains as competitors, and the prospective earnings are attractive to potential sales reps.

The attraction of foreign markets varies from one area to the next. Some countries have a growing middle class, with ample purchasing power. Consumers in many nations desire American brands. In a number of countries, the local currency is strong in relation to the U.S. dollar, making American merchandise affordable.

International expansion has its own problems and pitfalls. Typically, there's less economic strength or stability. An economic downturn, as occurred in Mexico, can force American retailers to postpone or even cancel further development. Shopping behavior is often very different in foreign countries, with consumers buying in much smaller quantities and from more vendors. Catalog companies struggle to locate good mailing lists in South America, Asia, and Africa. Also consider that a riot nearly resulted when an enormous number of shoppers showed up at the opening of a Disney Company store in Hong Kong. Of course, any retailer would like that "problem"!

Will more U.S. retailers venture into other countries? Perhaps not as many as might be expected. A 1993 survey by Ernst & Young revealed that only 23 percent of the 250 largest U.S. retailers had foreign operations, *and* another 2 percent anticipated such expansion. The other 75 percent said they were content to remain in the U.S.

Sources: Edith Hill Updike, "Japan Is Dialing 1 800 BUYAMERICA," *Business Week*, June 12, 1995, pp. 61, 64; Carla Rapoport, "Retailers Go Global," *Fortune*, Feb. 20, 1995, pp. 102+; Veronica Byrd, "The Avon Lady of the Amazon," *Business Week*, Oct. 24, 1994, pp. 93–94; and Stephanie M. Shern, "Going Global," *Chain Store Age Executive*, February 1994, pp. 38–39.

However, as vendors gain online experience, it is expected that the effectiveness of Web sites should improve as the costs decline. Further, it is estimated that as many as 30 million potential buyers will be online within the next several years, most of them computer proficient and many of them with substantial buying power. For these reasons, the prospects for online retailing are bright, with predicted sales of around $5 billion by the beginning of the new century.[56]

Direct marketing has drawbacks. Consumers must place orders without seeing or touching the actual merchandise (although they may see a picture of it). To offset this, direct marketers must offer liberal return policies. Furthermore, catalogs and, to some extent, direct-mail pieces are costly and must be prepared long before they are issued. Price changes and new products can be announced only through supplementary catalogs or brochures. This type of nonstore retailing has also been criticized as an invasion of personal privacy, especially when customer lists are sold by direct-marketing firms.

Like other types of nonstore retailing, however, direct marketing provides shopping convenience. Direct marketers enjoy low operating expenses because they do not have the overhead of retail stores. As with the other forms of nonstore retailing, the desire of many consumers for more shopping convenience points to future growth for direct marketing. However, firms in direct mail, catalog retailing, and/or televised shopping must surmount stiff competition and rising costs to achieve steady growth.

Institutional Change in Retailing

As consumers change, so do forms of retailing. Executives would like to anticipate major changes before they occur. To some extent this is possible, as many evolutionary changes in retailing have followed a cyclical pattern called the **wheel of retailing**.[57] This theory states that a new type of retailer often enters the market as a low-cost, low-price store. Other retailers as well as investors do not take the new type seriously. However, consumers respond favorably to the low prices and shop at the new institution. Over time this store takes business away from other retailers that initially ignored it and retained their old strategies.

Eventually, according to the wheel of retailing, the successful new institution trades up to attract a broader market, achieve higher margins, and gain more status. Trading up improves the quality of products sold and adds customer services. Sooner or later, high costs and, ultimately, high prices (as perceived by its target markets) make the institution vulnerable to new retail types. The next innovator enters as a low-cost, low-price form of retailing, and the evolutionary process continues.

There are numerous examples of the wheel of retailing. To mention a few, chain stores grew at the expense of independents during the 1920s, particularly in the grocery field. In the 1950s discount houses placed tremendous pressure on department stores, which had become staid, stagnant institutions. The 1980s saw the expansion of warehouse clubs and off-price retailers, which have forced many institutions—supermarkets, specialty stores, and department stores—to modify their marketing strategies.

Now, discount houses may be starting to trade up. Venture Stores, after many years of struggling to compete effectively with larger discount chains, no longer wants to be called a discount store. Venture is repositioning itself as a "family value department store" and upgrading its merchandise assortment and store appearance. Even more significant, Wal-Mart is placing a growing number of new stores in upscale metropolitan locations, far from its middle-class rural roots. To appeal to higher-income consumers, these stores feature more expensive merchandise, including computers and jewelry as well as stylish apparel.[58]

What will be the retailing innovations of the next 10 years? Given the surge in Internet usage, perhaps various kinds of online retailing? Some other form of nonstore retailing? Or a new type of low-cost, low-price store such as supercenters, or giant specialty retailers that dwarf even category killers?

Retail firms must identify and respond to significant trends that affect retailing by developing—and, as necessary, modifying—their need-satisfying marketing strategies. According to one retailing expert, stores that prosper in the future will (1) provide consumers with a distinctive bundle of benefits, (2) stress value, not just low prices, (3) save their customers time and energy, and (4) make shopping fun. Of course, as the saying goes, that's "easier said than done."[59]

■ SUMMARY

Retailing is the sale of goods and services to ultimate consumers for personal, nonbusiness use. Any institution (such as a manufacturer) may engage in retailing, but a firm engaged primarily in retailing is called a retailer.

Retailers serve as purchasing agents for consumers and as sales specialists for producers and wholesaling middlemen. They perform many specific activities, such as anticipating customers' wants, developing product assortments, and financing.

There are about 2.7 million retail stores in the U.S.; collectively they generated about $2.2 trillion in sales during 1994. Retailers' operating expenses run about 28 percent of retail sales. Their profits are usually a very small fraction of sales, generally about 3 percent.

Most retail firms are small—either single stores or several stores under common ownership. However, chains account for 40 percent of retail sales. Small retailers can survive—and even prosper—if they remain flexible and pay careful attention to personally serving customers' needs.

Besides product, price, promotion, and customer services, retailers also must make strategic decisions regarding physical facilities. Specific decisions concern location, design, and layout of the store. Downtown shopping areas declined as suburban shopping centers grew. Now regional shopping centers are feeling competitive pressures from many sources, including new power centers.

Retailers can be classified by (1) form of ownership, including corporate chain, independent store, and various kinds of contractual vertical marketing systems (notably franchising), and (2) key marketing strategies. Also, types of retailers, distinguished according to product assortment, price levels, and customer service levels, include department stores, discount houses, limited-line stores (notably specialty stores, off-price retailers, and category-killer stores), supermarkets, convenience stores, and warehouse clubs. Mature institutions such as department stores, discount houses, and supermarkets face strong challenges from new competitors, particularly chains of category-killer stores in various product categories.

Although the large majority of retail sales are made in stores, 10 percent or more occur away from stores. And this proportion is growing steadily. Four major forms of nonstore retailing are direct selling, telemarketing, automatic vending, and direct marketing. Each type has advantages as well as drawbacks.

Changes in retail institutions can frequently be explained by a theory called the wheel of retailing. To succeed, retailers need to identify significant trends and ensure that they develop marketing strategies to satisfy consumers.

More about

PENNEY's

*T*he J.C. Penney Co. has more than 1,200 stores, representing over 100 million square feet of retail space. The chain's annual sales have surpassed $20 billion. A key to future sales growth, according to CEO James Oesterreicher, is "to have the customer think of J.C. Penney first for every category of merchandise we compete in." Already, the company has achieved the #1 position in such diverse categories as jeans, window coverings, and diamonds!

Besides continually monitoring its product and pricing strategies, and revising them as necessary, Penney's top executives realize that they need to pay attention to store locations as well. With that in mind, activities are under way to upgrade its stores in the U.S. and to set up various kinds of operations in foreign markets.

Over the years, Penney's has spent at least $100 million annually to renovate existing stores. The efforts were accelerated in 1995, when the retailer announced a 3-year program to remodel at least 500 stores at a cost of over $600 million. In the words of a VP, one purpose of the renovations is "to present a more consistent Penney's store throughout any particular market." The interiors will be opened up to allow shoppers to see various departments and more merchandise displays. Following customers' suggestions, store aisles will be widened and lighting improved. Penney's also intends to open new stores selectively.

At the same time, the company is looking at foreign opportunities in Japan, Portugal, Mexico, the United Arab Emirates, Singapore, China, and other nations. Penney's is using various approaches, depending on market conditions. For example, in countries where competition is not too severe, real estate is affordable, and the regulatory environment is reasonable, Penney's plans to own and operate stores itself. That's the case in Mexico. Its two new stores in Monterrey, for example, replicate a Penney's store in the U.S. in order to appeal to Mexican consumers who have shopped at the company's stores in Texas. Much of the stores' merchandise is the same as in the U.S., although the prices in Mexico are about 10 to 15 percent higher. The stores' assortment includes some brands, such as Colours by Alexander Julian and Jantzen sportswear, that are not available to Penney's in the U.S. Facing an unhealthy economic climate in Mexico, Penney's has postponed further expansion in that country.

In other markets, the company will license local retailers to open separate J.C. Penney Collection stores, featuring its brands of soft goods, or small shops in other stores, focusing on specific Penney's lines, such as Hunt Club apparel. In markets with strong consumer demand but imposing barriers to opening stores, Penney's will use catalogs to generate sales and will arrange for third parties to take orders, acquire the goods from Penney's in the U.S., and distribute the merchandise to customers.[60]

1. Will Penney's emphasis on leading brands and upgraded stores allow its stores in major malls to compete effectively with new types of retailers such as category killers?
2. At a time when it faces stiff competition in the U.S., is it wise for Penney's to expand into foreign markets?

■ KEY TERMS AND CONCEPTS

Retailing (retail trade) (372)
Retailer (372)
Physical facilities (376)
Shopping center (377)
Corporate chain (379)
Independent retailer (380)
Contractual vertical marketing system (380)

Retailer cooperative (380)
Voluntary chain (380)
Franchising (380)
Product and trade name franchising (380)
Business format franchising (381)
Department store (384)
Discount retailing (385)
Discount house (385)

Supercenter (385)
Limited-line store (385)
Specialty store (386)
Off-price retailer (387)
Category-killer store (387)
Supermarket retailing (388)
Supermarket (388)
Convenience store (389)

Warehouse club (wholesale club) (389)
Nonstore retailing (390)
Direct selling (391)
Telemarketing (392)
Automatic vending (392)
Direct marketing (393)
Wheel of retailing (396)

■ QUESTIONS AND PROBLEMS

1. In each of the following situations, is the seller a *retailer* and is the transaction a *retail sale*?
   a. Avon representative selling cosmetics door to door.
   b. Independent contractor selling lawn-care services door to door.
   c. Farmer selling produce door to door.
   d. Farmer selling produce at a roadside stand.
   e. Sporting goods store selling uniforms to a professional baseball team.
2. What recommendations would you offer to a department store chain for reducing retailing costs? What would you recommend to discount houses in this regard?
3. Support or refute the following statements, using facts and statistics where appropriate:
   a. "Retailing is typically small-scale business."
   b. "There is a high degree of concentration in retailing today; the giants control the field."

4. The ease of entry into retailing undoubtedly contributes to the high failure rate among retailers, which—in the view of some—creates economic waste. Should entry into retailing be restricted? If so, how could this be done?
5. Do you agree that there are three keys to success in retailing—location, location, and location? How do you reconcile this with the fact that there is so much price competition in retailing at the present time?
6. What can department stores do to strengthen their competitive positions?
7. "The supermarket, with its operating expense ratio of 20 percent, is the most efficient institution in retailing today." Do you agree with this statement? In what ways might supermarkets further reduce their expenses?
8. "Door-to-door selling is the most efficient form of retailing because it eliminates wholesalers and retail stores." Discuss.

9. According to the wheel of retailing, what new retail institutions might we see in the future?
10. Of the types of retail stores discussed in the chapter, which ones do you think have been or would be most successful in foreign countries? Which ones have been or would be unsuccessful in other countries? Explain your answers.

■ HANDS-ON MARKETING

1. Arrange an interview with a small retailer. Discuss with this merchant the general competitive positions of small and large retailers, as covered in this chapter. Which, if any, of these points does the small retailer disagree with, and why? Also ask what courses of action this merchant takes to achieve or maintain a viable competitive position. Interview a second small retailer, ask the same questions, and compare your answers.

2. Write to the headquarters of two retail franchise systems with which you are familiar and request information provided to prospective purchasers of a franchise. (Local units of the franchise systems should be able to supply you with the headquarters' mailing addresses.) Once you have received the information, evaluate whether you would like to own either of these franchises. What criteria did you use in making this evaluation?

CHAPTER 15

Wholesaling and Physical Distribution

Does
SUPERVALU
Have an Advantage in Grocery Distribution?

With annual sales exceeding $17 *billion*, Supervalu Inc. is the second largest grocery distributor in the U.S. Despite its massive size, the firm concluded that significant trends in the industry required "a new business vision." Supervalu's vision for the future, labeled "Advantage," includes several major changes in how it does business.

About three-quarters of the revenues of Supervalu, which is headquartered just outside Minneapolis, are derived from wholesaling activities. It operates a wholesaler-sponsored voluntary chain that is the primary supplier of merchandise and management services to more than 4,100 independent grocery stores in 48 states. The remaining revenues come from about 300 retail outlets that are owned and run by the company.

According to Michael Wright, Supervalu's chairman, Advantage's goals include lower cost of goods, more efficient distribution, added market share, and new business opportunities. The Advantage program has three main elements: (1) Providing more support to its primary customers; (2) enhancing relationships with suppliers and retailers in its channels; and (3) restructuring the physical flow of goods. Wright stressed that Advantage should strengthen its customers, which in turn would benefit Supervalu.

One way in which Supervalu serves independent grocery stores is to offer them middlemen's brands, also called private-label merchandise. Grocery retailers—especially independent stores—depend on middlemen's brands to remove them from direct price competition with large discounters and to provide them with better profit margins. Supervalu has a variety of brands, including Flav-o-rite, Chateau, and Homebest, in some product categories. Recently, the wholesaler developed a "premium" brand to compete with well-known producers' brands such as Green Giant and Kellogg's. The Preferred Selection brand will cover 150 items, ranging from salsa to cereal, that are priced 5 to 10 percent lower than competing producers' brands. Supervalu's multiple brands give grocery stores a chance to distinguish themselves by stocking a line of private-label products that are not available at competing stores, some of which might be supplied by Supervalu.

A key element of Advantage has been the restructuring of Supervalu's distribution. Previously the company was divided into 25 operating divisions. The new arrangement consolidates previously dispersed activities into seven marketing regions and four regional centers for better distribution of the firm's goods. The new marketing structure is intended primarily to enhance services provided to Supervalu's customers, whereas the revamped distribution structure is aimed mainly at reducing expenses and, in turn, wholesale prices. Supervalu expects improved profits as well.

A Merrill Lynch financial analyst was unimpressed with Advantage, saying it consisted of "standard restructuring practices" that are common in many large corporations during the 1990s. Another analyst expressed concern that the program's financial benefits "are long-range and not very certain." Supervalu's Wright agreed that the costs are short term and the potential benefits are more long term. A third analyst was more impressed with the wholesaler's plans, stressing that even large distributors need as much "economic power" as possible to be secure in their channels.[1]

Does the Advantage program assure Supervalu Inc. of maintaining a position of leadership in grocery wholesaling?

Although consumers shop regularly at the stores of retailers, they rarely see the establishments of wholesaling middlemen. Also, beyond noticing transportation carriers such as trucks and trains, consumers have little exposure to how products actually are moved from the point of production to the point of final sale. As a result, wholesaling and physical distribution are often misunderstood—and occasionally criticized—by consumers.

Nevertheless, wholesaling middlemen can be essential members of a distribution channel, and physical distribution is an integral aspect of marketing most goods. Therefore, it's critical that you understand the nature and managerial issues of both wholesaling and physical distribution. This chapter will provide you with insight into how wholesale markets, wholesaling institutions, and physical distribution activities relate to marketing. After studying this chapter, you should be able to explain:

CHAPTER GOALS

- The nature and economic justification of wholesaling and the role of wholesaling middlemen.
- Differences across three categories of wholesaling middlemen.
- Major types of merchant wholesalers, agent wholesaling middlemen, and manufacturers' sales facilities, and the services they render.
- What physical distribution is.
- The systems approach to physical distribution.
- How physical distribution can strengthen a marketing program and reduce marketing costs.
- The five subsystems within physical distribution: inventory location and warehousing, materials handling, inventory control, order processing, and transportation.

Nature and Importance of Wholesaling

Wholesaling and retailing enable what is produced to be purchased for consumption. We already know retailing involves sales to ultimate consumers for their personal use. Now we'll see what the role of wholesaling is in the marketing system.

Wholesaling and Wholesaling Middlemen

Wholesaling (or *wholesale trade*) is the sale, and all activities directly related to the sale, of goods and services to businesses and other organizations for (1) resale, (2) use in producing other goods or services, or (3) operating an organization. When a business firm sells shirts and blouses to a clothing store that intends to resell them to final consumers, this is wholesaling. When a mill sells flour to a large bakery for making bread and pastries, this is also a wholesale transaction. And when a firm sells uniforms to some organization for its employees to wear in carrying out their duties, this is wholesaling as well.

Sales made by one producer to another are wholesale transactions, and the selling producer is engaged in wholesaling. Likewise, a discount house is involved in wholesaling when it sells calculators and office supplies to a business firm. Thus wholesaling includes sales by any firm to any customer *except* an ultimate consumer who is buying for personal, nonbusiness use. From this perspective, all sales are either wholesale or retail transactions—distinguished only by the purchaser's intended use of the good or service.

In this chapter we will focus on firms engaged *primarily* in wholesaling. This type of company is called a **wholesaling middleman**. We will not be concerned with retailers involved in occasional wholesale transactions. And we will not focus on manufacturers and farmers because they are engaged primarily in production rather than wholesaling. Keep in mind, then, that *wholesaling* is a business *activity* that can be carried out by various types of firms, whereas a *wholesaling middleman* is a business *institution* that concentrates on wholesaling.

Economic Justification for Wholesaling

Most manufacturing firms are small and specialized. They don't have the capital to maintain a sales force to contact the many retailers or final users that are (or could be) their customers. Even for manufacturers with sufficient capital, some of their products or lines generate such a small volume of sales that it would not be cost-effective to establish a sales force to sell them.

At the other end of the distribution channel, most retailers and final users buy in small quantities and have only a limited knowledge of the market and sources of supply. Thus there is often a gap between the seller (producer) and the buyer (retailer or final user).

A wholesaling middleman can fill this gap by providing services of value to manufacturers and/or retailers. For example, a wholesaling middleman can pool the orders of many retailers and/or final users, thereby creating a market for the small producer. At the same time, a wholesaling middleman selects various items from among many alternatives to form its product mix, thereby acting as a buying service for small retailers and final users. Essentially, as we will see at several points in this chapter, the activities of a wholesaling middleman create time, place, and/or possession utility.

Consider a couple of examples of how wholesaling middlemen serve producers and retailers. Although the beer industry is dominated by several large breweries, wholesale distributors are still vital because they handle small but important tasks such as securing added shelf space and arranging local promotions for the brewer's brands. In the office supplies field, where large discounters such as Staples are grabbing market share, wholesalers need to serve the discounters and also cater to the needs of independent dealers that are fighting for survival. A wholesaler does this by supplying a very broad assortment of products to the independents, and distinctive services (such as special-order catalogs) to the discounters.[2]

From a broad point of view, wholesaling brings to the total distribution system the economies of skill, scale, and transactions:

http://www.staples.com/

- Wholesaling *skills* are efficiently concentrated in a relatively few hands. This saves the duplication of effort that would occur if many producers had to perform wholesaling functions themselves. For example, one wholesaler's warehouse in Memphis, Tennessee, saves many manufacturers from having to build their own warehouses to provide speedy service to customers in this area.
- Economies of *scale* result from the specialization of wholesaling middlemen performing functions that might otherwise require several small departments run by producing firms. Wholesalers typically can perform wholesaling functions more efficiently than can most manufacturers.
- *Transaction* economies come into play when retailers and/or wholesaling middlemen are introduced between producers and their customers. Let's assume that four manufacturers want to sell to six retailers. As shown in Figure 15-1, *without* a middleman, there are 24 transactions; *with* one wholesaling middleman, the number of transactions is cut to 10. Four transactions occur when all

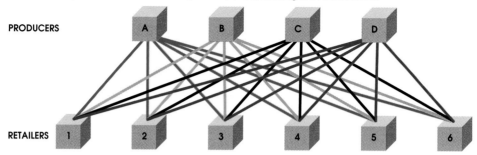

Four producers each sell directly to six retailers, resulting in 24 transactions:

PRODUCERS

RETAILERS

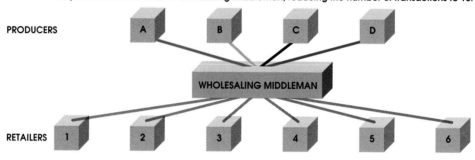

Four producers use the same wholesaling middleman, reducing the number of transactions to 10:

PRODUCERS

WHOLESALING MIDDLEMAN

RETAILERS

FIGURE 15-1
The economy of transactions in wholesaling.

the producers sell to the middleman, and another six occur when the middle-man sells to all the retailers.

Size of the Wholesale Market

The total annual sales volume of wholesaling middlemen was more than $3.2 *trillion* in 1992 (the year of the last published national census of wholesale trade). As shown in Table 15-1, this level of sales represents an increase of 62 percent over 1982 and 366 percent over 1972. Even if the effects of inflation are taken into account, these figures still reflect a major increase in wholesale trade.

You might be surprised to see in Table 15-1 that total wholesale trade exceeds total retail trade by a wide margin. How can this be, especially considering that a product's retail price is higher than its wholesale price? We can find an explanation by considering the customers of wholesaling middlemen. Fully two-thirds of the sales of wholesaling middlemen are made to organizations *other than* retailers.[3] For example, some products sold to nonretailers are *business* goods (such as large printing presses or iron ore) that, by definition, are never sold at retail. Others may be *consumer* goods (such as groceries or toys) that are sold more than once at the wholesale level, with all such transactions counted as part of total wholesale trade. Thus total wholesale trade is greater than total retail trade because wholesale trade includes sales of business goods and successive sales of consumer goods at the wholesale level.

At last count 495,000 wholesaling middlemen conducted business in the U.S. According to Table 15-1, the number of such establishments rose substantially—by one-third, in fact—from the early 1970s to the early 1990s. These statistics document that wholesaling middlemen are appearing in more and more distribution channels.

TABLE 15-1 Total wholesale trade versus total retail trade in the United States

Total wholesale sales increased 62 percent between 1982 and 1992. Compare these figures with the growth in retail sales over the same period.

Year	Number of wholesaling middlemen	Wholesale sales (billions)	Retail sales (billions)
1992	495,000	$3,239	$1,949
1982	416,000	1,998	1,066
1972	370,000	695	459

Sources: *1992 Census of Wholesale Trade*, Geographic Area Series—U.S., U.S. Bureau of the Census, Washington, D.C., 1995, p. US-9; *1992 Census of Retail Trade*, Nonemployer Statistics Series—Summary, U.S. Bureau of the Census, Washington, D.C., 1994, p. 3; and corresponding censuses from prior years.

Profile of Wholesaling Middlemen

A producer or retailer considering the use of wholesaling middlemen must know what options are available, whom these middlemen serve, and how they operate.

Major Categories. Wholesaling middlemen vary greatly in products carried, markets served, and methods of operation. We will discuss about 10 different types of wholesaling middlemen. Nevertheless, all fit into three categories developed by the U.S. Bureau of the Census (see Figure 15-2). Brief descriptions of the categories follow, with more details presented later in the chapter:

- **Merchant wholesaler**: an independently owned firm that engages primarily in wholesaling and takes title to (that is, owns) products being distributed. Sometimes these firms are referred to simply as *wholesalers*, *jobbers*, or *industrial distributors*.[4] Merchant wholesalers form the largest segment of wholesaling firms when measured by either number of establishments or sales volume.
- **Agent wholesaling middleman**: an independent firm that engages primarily in wholesaling by actively negotiating the sale or purchase of products on behalf

FIGURE 15-2
Types of wholesaling institutions.

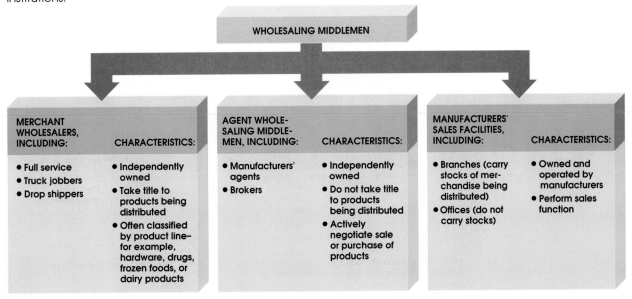

of other firms but that does *not* take title to (that is, does not own) products being distributed.

- **Manufacturer's sales facility**: an establishment that engages primarily in wholesaling and is owned and operated by a manufacturer but is physically separated from manufacturing plants.[5] Manufacturers' sales facilities are common in fields ranging from major appliances to plumbing equipment to electrical supplies. The two major types are similar except in one important respect. A **manufacturer's sales branch** carries an inventory of the product being sold, but a **manufacturer's sales office** does not.

Wholesaling middlemen are not part of every distribution channel, of course. According to one survey, 32 percent of business goods manufacturers rely on merchant wholesalers. Another 42 percent use agent wholesaling middlemen, and the remaining 26 percent distribute their products directly (perhaps using sales branches or offices) to final customers.[6]

The statistics in Figure 15-3 indicate that merchant wholesalers account for the majority of sales made through wholesaling middlemen. During the 1960s and 1970s, merchant wholesalers continually increased their share of wholesale trade, while the other two categories declined. In recent years, however, the shares of wholesale trade captured by the three categories of wholesaling middlemen have stabilized.[7]

Operating Expenses and Profits.   Total operating expenses for wholesaling middlemen average about 11 percent of *wholesale* sales; operating expenses for retailers run about 28 percent of *retail* sales. Therefore, generally speaking, the expenses of wholesaling middlemen take about 8 percent of the ultimate consumer's dollar.[8]

Operating expenses vary widely across the several categories of wholesaling middlemen:

- Merchant wholesalers have the highest average operating expenses, at 14 percent of sales. However, the range is wide. For example, operating expenses for wholesalers of a complete assortment of grocery products typically are below 10 percent of sales, compared with as much as 30 percent for office-equipment wholesalers.

FIGURE 15-3

Share of wholesale trade, by category of institution.

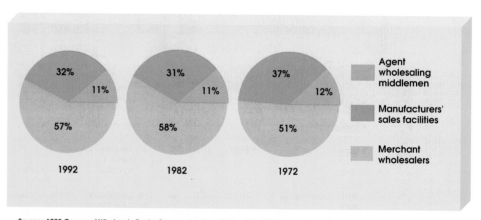

Source: *1992 Census of Wholesale Trade*, Geographic Area Series–U.S., U.S. Bureau of the Census, Washington, D.C., 1995, p. US–9; and corresponding censuses from prior years.

- Agent wholesaling middlemen have fairly low costs, around 4.5 percent of sales, largely because they do not have to carry inventories.
- The two types of manufacturers' sales facilities generally have much different cost structures. Sales offices' operating expenses are about 4 percent of sales; sales branches' expenses are around 11 percent, because of the costs incurred in storing merchandise.

These costs need to be interpreted carefully. We should not conclude that agent wholesaling middlemen are highly efficient and merchant wholesalers inefficient because of the disparity in their expenses. The differences in costs are partially traceable to differences in the services they provide. Also, because of factors such as perishability, value in relation to bulk, and special storage requirements, there are tremendous variations in the expenses connected with wholesaling various products. For example, jewelry has much higher value in relation to bulk than furniture, so this factor would suggest lower storage costs for jewelry as a percentage of value. However, any savings on this factor might be offset by added expenses of providing ample security for jewelry in inventory.

Net operating profit expressed as a percent of net sales is rather modest for wholesaling middlemen and is considerably lower than net profit for retailers (except for large grocery stores). Generally, wholesaling profits range from 1.5 to 4 percent of sales.

Merchant Wholesalers

Wholesaling middlemen that take title to products—that is, merchant wholesalers—are common in the marketing of both consumer goods and business goods. We'll examine several types next.

Full-Service Wholesalers

An independent merchant middleman that performs a full range of wholesaling functions is a **full-service wholesaler**. This type of middleman may handle consumer and/or business products that may be manufactured or nonmanufactured (such as grown or extracted), and are imported, exported, or made and sold domestically.

The forms of assistance offered by full-service wholesalers are summarized in Table 15-2. The Fleming Companies, Supervalu's primary competitor, exemplifies how a full-service wholesaler operates. As the largest wholesaler of groceries and related products, Fleming helps independent grocery stores remain viable by providing them with the business tools that grocery chains have. Fleming offers more than 100 different services to its customers. These services include demographic studies, development of marketing plans for grocery stores, advertising support, and shelf space allocation guidelines.[9]

http://www.amana.com/

Individual manufacturers in various industries have begun to distribute their products directly, thereby eliminating wholesalers in their channels. Amana Refrigeration, a maker of home appliances, decided to end its relationships with merchant wholesalers and deal directly with appliance retailers. Obviously, this action displeased—and perhaps devastated—many wholesalers that had carried the Amana line. At least one, Cooper Distributing of Newark, New Jersey, took the manufacturer to court, claiming the termination lacked "good cause" and thus was illegal.[10]

TABLE 15-2 Full-service wholesalers' typical services to customers and to producers

Service	Description
Buying	Act as purchasing agent for customers.
Creating assortments	Buy from many suppliers to develop an inventory that matches customers' needs.
Subdividing	Buy in large quantities (such as a truckload) and then resell in smaller quantities (such as a dozen).
Selling	Provide a sales force for producers to reach small retailers and other businesses, at a lower cost than producers would incur by having their own sales forces.
Transportation	Make quick, frequent deliveries to customers, reducing customers' risks and investment in inventory.
Warehousing	Store products in facilities that are nearer customers' locations than are manufacturing plants.
Financing	Grant credit to customers, reducing their capital requirements. Aid producers by ordering and paying for products before purchase by customers.
Risk taking	Reduce a producer's risk by taking title to products.
Market information	Supply information to customers about new products and producers' special offers and to producer-suppliers about customers' needs and competitors' activities.
Management assistance	Assist customers, especially small retailers, in areas such as inventory control, allocation of shelf space, and financial management.

To remain an integral part of distribution channels, it's better for wholesalers to serve than to sue. To remain competitive, many distributors have expanded their services. Some assist manufacturers with warranty claims, while others offer training for customers' employees. As a specific example, Sales Systems Ltd. built its own product-testing labs so it can help customers with quality control. This distributor of industrial fasteners, located in Portsmouth, Virginia, also does some limited assembly of spare-parts kits.[11]

Partnerships between wholesalers and either producers or customers are increasingly common. Ordinarily, these arrangements represent the administered type of vertical marketing system (discussed in the two preceding chapters). To cite one example, Safety Equipment Co. formed a partnership with a major customer, Tampa Electric Co. To become the utility's sole supplier of safety items, the Tampa-based distributor agreed to provide special services, such as a customized catalog, and to meet stringent performance standards, such as guaranteed next-day delivery of orders.[12]

To maintain their competitiveness and boost profits, merchant wholesalers are also striving to improve their own operations. Two common avenues are enhanced quality and advanced technology. For instance, the Wallace Co., a distributor to the oil and chemical industries in Houston, is providing added training to its employees to improve its customer service. In 3 years, the company's record of on-time deliveries improved from 75 percent to 92 percent.[13]

Full-service wholesalers comprise the majority of merchant wholesaling middlemen. They have held their own in competitive struggles with other forms of indirect distribution, including manufacturers' sales facilities and agent middlemen. While full-service wholesalers have gained in some industries, they have lost ground in others.

The total number of merchant wholesalers may decline because of increasing mergers and acquisitions. Even large wholesalers are feeling the urge to merge. For example, two of the four largest grocery wholesalers, Fleming Companies and Scrivner Inc., joined together in 1994, after the other two, Supervalu and Wetterau,

CAN WHOLESALERS SUCCEED WITH THEIR OWN RETAIL OUTLETS?

In many industries, manufacturers occasionally bypass wholesalers and distribute their goods directly to final customers. To meet this threat, wholesalers need to fortify their competitive positions.

One action some wholesalers take to be more competitive—and to boost sales and profits—is to establish retail outlets. Does this strategy produce the desired results? Supervalu, the subject of the opening case, has expanded its retail grocery operations but has retreated from general-merchandise retailing. Let's consider what happened when Supervalu's primary competitor and a vastly different company followed this path.

For years, the Fleming Companies Inc. resisted the temptation to move into retailing. However, the wholesaler saw that large supermarket chains, such as Albertson's and A & P, increasingly were dealing directly with manufacturers. Further, sales of independent grocery stores, which represent Fleming's primary target market, have been flat—perhaps even declining. According to one source, "For wholesalers like Fleming, operating their own stores is becoming a matter of survival."

Fleming's inevitable move into retailing was expedited when it acquired Scrivner Inc., another large wholesaler. Scrivner operated a variety of successful chains, including Jubilee Foods and Market Basket in New York State and Rainbow in Minneapolis. It's too early to tell whether Fleming's move into retailing will produce solid financial results.

Earlier this decade, Intelligent Electronics Inc. (IE) was well established as a wholesaler of well-known brands of personal computers and related accessories. IE grew and profited by serving independent stores that were authorized dealers for various brands of PCs. Then IE moved into retailing by acquiring BizMart, a chain of office-supply outlets. IE saw BizMart as a means by which it could sell PCs—as well as office supplies—directly to final customers.

BizMart turned out to be a disaster for IE, consuming more than $15 million. As IE learned, the prerequisites for success are different in retailing than in wholesaling. BizMart suffered from poor locations, weak advertising, and intense competition from other computer sellers (including some IE customers) and the booming office-supply outlets. Within 2 years, IE sold BizMart and returned to wholesaling.

To solidify their positions in distribution channels, is it wise for wholesalers to establish retail outlets?

Sources: Kathryn Jones, "A Move along the Food Chain," *The New York Times*, July 2, 1994, pp. 1, 26; and Leslie Scism, "Intelligent Electronics, Wiser Now, Returns to a Profit," *The Wall Street Journal*, July 15, 1993, p. B4.

---

merged 2 years earlier.[14] A growing number of distributors believe they need to be bigger to maintain their competitive edge. Smaller wholesalers will have to decide whether they intend to acquire, be acquired, or somehow insulate themselves from this trend—perhaps by serving small market niches.

Other Merchant Wholesalers

Two types of merchant wholesalers with distinctive operations also warrant brief description:

- **Truck jobbers**, also called *truck distributors*, carry a selected line of perishable products and deliver them by truck to retail stores. Truck jobbers are common in the food-products field. Each jobber carries nationally advertised brands of fast-moving, perishable or semiperishable goods, such as candies, dairy products, potato chips, or tobacco products. Truck jobbers furnish fresh products so frequently that retailers can buy perishable goods in small amounts to minimize the risk of loss. But truck jobbers are saddled with high operating

A GLOBAL PERSPECTIVE

WHY DO GRAY MARKETS GIVE PRODUCERS AND MIDDLEMEN GRAY HAIR?

Occasionally items are sold through distribution channels that are not authorized by the manufacturer. This practice, typically called *gray marketing* or sometimes *export diversion*, accounts for about $10 billion in sales annually in the U.S. It usually involves products made in one country and destined for sale in another country.

Cameras, computer disk drives or entire PCs, perfumes, cars, and liquor are among the diverse products sold through gray markets. Ordinarily, gray marketing arises when a product with a well-known brand name carries different prices under different circumstances. For example, a product's wholesale price may vary depending on the country to which it is sold or the quantity purchased.

Gray marketing takes many forms. Usually, a wholesaling middleman, such as an import or export agent, purchases a product made in one country and agrees to distribute it in a second country, but instead diverts the product to a third country (often the U.S.). Because the product typically is sold at a discount in a reputable outlet, not on the "black market" or from the trunks of cars, it isn't apparent that normal distribution has not been used.

So what's wrong with gray marketing? After spending time and money to promote the product, authorized distributors lose sales to the gray market. Manufacturers then have to placate their authorized distributors. Gray marketing also disrupts a producer's distribution and pricing strategies. Moreover, when consumers buy products through the gray market, they may wind up without warranties or service contracts.

Still, some parties (but definitely not authorized distributors) see benefits in gray marketing. Unauthorized distributors are able to sell products they normally cannot acquire. To sell excess output, some manufacturers allow gray marketing. Consumers pay lower prices for popular products and may also find them at more outlets.

Some manufacturers have concluded that it's too difficult and costly to fight gray marketing. But other producers try to minimize it by revising price schedules and distribution policies and taking unauthorized distributors to court. Some are even claiming their innovative products or at least their distinctive packages are creations, like music, and are seeking protection under copyright laws. Gray marketing represents one more challenge for both producers and wholesaling middlemen.

Sources: Amy Borrus, "Exports That Aren't Going Anywhere," *Business Week*, Dec. 4, 1995, pp. 121, 124; Faye Rice, "Closeout Sale on Gray Goods," *Fortune*, Apr. 3, 1995, p. 17; and Robert E. Weigand, "Parallel Import Channels—Options for Preserving Territorial Integrity," *Columbia Journal of World Business*, Spring 1991, pp. 53–60.

costs, caused primarily by the small order size and inefficient use of their trucks (for example, only during parts of the day).

- **Drop shippers**, also known as *desk jobbers*, sell merchandise for delivery directly from the producer to the customer. Drop shippers do not physically handle the product. They are common in only a few product categories, including coal, lumber, and building materials, that are typically sold in very large quantities and that have high freight costs in relation to their unit value.

Agent Wholesaling Middlemen

As distinguished from merchant wholesalers, agent wholesaling middlemen (1) do *not* take title to products and (2) typically perform fewer services. As shown in Table 15-3, product characteristics and market conditions determine whether a distribution channel should include agent or merchant wholesaling middlemen. For their assistance, agent middlemen receive a commission intended to cover their

TABLE 15-3 Factors suggesting which type of wholesaling middlemen should be used in a channel

Factors	Favoring agent wholesaling middlemen	Favoring merchant wholesalers
Nature of product	Nonstandard, perhaps made to order	Standard
Technicality of product	Simple	Complex
Product's gross margin	Small	Relatively large
Number of customers	Few	Many
Concentration of customers	Concentrated geographically and in a few industries	Dispersed geographically and in many industries
Frequency of ordering	Relatively infrequently	Frequently
Time between order and receipt of shipment	Customer satisfied with relatively long lead time	Customer requires or desires shorter lead time

Source: Adapted from Donald M. Jackson and Michael F. d'Amico, "Products and Markets Served by Distributors and Agents," *Industrial Marketing Management*, February 1989, pp. 27–33.

expenses and to provide a profit. Commission rates vary greatly, ranging from about 3 to 10 percent, depending mainly on the nature of the product and the services performed.

Agent wholesaling middlemen lost more than one-fourth of their share of wholesale trade between 1967 and 1977. In the case of agricultural products, agent middlemen were replaced by merchant wholesalers or by direct sales to food-processing companies and grocery stores. Likewise, for manufactured goods, agent middlemen were supplanted by merchant wholesalers or direct distribution. Since then, agents have fought back. In fact, their share of total wholesale trade has been constant at 11 percent since 1977.[15]

For the foreseeable future, even if the number of merchant wholesalers does drop as is projected, agent wholesaling middlemen probably will not gain ground. Instead, merchant middlemen—smaller in number but larger in size—may grab a larger share of total wholesale trade away from agent wholesaling middlemen and manufacturers' sales facilities.

On the basis of sales volume, the most significant types of agent wholesaling middlemen are manufacturers' agents, brokers, and commission merchants. These three types as well as several special types of agent wholesaling middlemen are described next.

Manufacturers' Agents

An independent agent wholesaling middleman that sells part or all of a manufacturer's product mix in an assigned geographic territory is a **manufacturers' agent**, or *manufacturers' representative*. Agents are not employees of the manufacturers; they are independent business firms. Still, they have little or no control over prices and terms of sale, which are established by the manufacturers they represent.

Because a manufacturers' agent sells in a limited territory, each producer uses multiple agents to fully cover its total market. Manufacturers' reps have year-round relationships with the companies (often called principals) they represent. Each agent usually serves several noncompeting manufacturers of related products. For example, a manufacturers' agent may specialize in toys and carry an assortment of noncompeting lines in board games, dolls, learning materials, and outdoor play equipment.

Manufacturers' agents are used extensively in distributing many types of consumer and business goods, ranging from sporting goods to heating and air-conditioning vents and ductwork. Their main service to manufacturers is selling. Because a manufacturers' agent does not carry nearly as many lines as a full-service wholesaler, an agent can be expected to provide knowledgeable, aggressive selling.

Manufacturers' agents are most helpful to:

- A small firm that has a limited number of products and no sales force.
- A business that wants to add a new, possibly unrelated line to its existing product mix, but its present sales force either is not experienced in the new line or lacks familiarity with the new market. In this situation, a company's own sales force and its agents may cover the same geographic market, but for different product lines.
- A firm that wants to enter a new market that is not yet sufficiently developed to warrant the use of its own sales force.

When a manufacturer finds it is not feasible to have its own sales force, a manufacturers' agent is often practical. An agent can be cost-effective because its major expenses (travel and lodging) are spread over a number of manufacturers' lines. Also, producers pay agents a commission, which is a percentage of sales volume, so agents are paid only for what they actually sell.

There are limitations to what manufacturers' agents do. Agents usually do not carry an inventory of merchandise, do not install machinery and equipment, and typically are not equipped to furnish customers with repair service. However, to remain viable, manufacturers' reps are adding new marketing services. Some assist their principals in developing new products, while others offer telemarketing and direct-mail programs.[16]

Some manufacturers' agents operate on a commission as low as 2 percent of net sales; others earn as much as 20 percent. Depending on how difficult the product is to sell and whether it is stocked by the agent, operating expenses of reps can vary greatly. However, they average about 6 percent of sales.[17]

Brokers

A **broker** is an independent agent wholesaling middleman that brings buyers and sellers together and provides market information to one party or the other. It furnishes information about many topics, including prices, products, and general market conditions. In recent years, manufacturers' agents and brokers have become more similar with respect to attributes and services. Typically, they do not physically handle the products being distributed.

Most brokers work for sellers, although some represent buyers. Brokers have no authority to set prices. They simply negotiate a sale and leave it up to the seller to accept or reject the buyer's offer.

Brokers are used in selling real estate and securities, but they are most prevalent in the food field. For example, a seafood broker handles the output from a salmon cannery, which operates only about 3 months each year. The canner employs a broker to find buyers among retail stores, wholesalers, and other institutions such as government agencies.

Brokers receive relatively small commissions, normally less than 5 percent of sales. They provide limited services and, as a result, incur fairly low expenses—about 3 percent of sales.[18]

AN ETHICAL DILEMMA?

Through gray marketing, products wind up being distributed outside a manufacturer's authorized distribution channels. For example, an exporter may establish a relationship with a European manufacturer to distribute its line of stereo equipment in South America (but not in the U.S.). However, without the manufacturer's knowledge, the exporter diverts a large shipment for sale in the U.S. Assume that you're the stereo-equipment buyer for a chain of discount houses. The exporter contacts you about purchasing some stereos at prices substantially below the normal wholesale price.

Would it be ethical to buy these stereos for resale in your stores? Would your view depend on whether you knew for sure that the stereos were indeed gray market goods?

Other Agent Wholesaling Middlemen

Four additional types of agent wholesaling middlemen account for smaller shares of wholesale trade than manufacturers' reps and brokers. Nevertheless, they are very important for certain products and in specific markets. These middlemen are:

- **Commission merchants**, common in the marketing of many agricultural products, set prices and terms of sale, sell the product, and perhaps physically handle it. (Despite the word *merchant*, a commission merchant is an *agent* middleman that normally does not take title to the products being handled and sold.)
- **Auction companies** help assembled buyers and sellers complete their transactions. They provide (1) auctioneers who do the selling and (2) physical facilities for displaying the sellers' products. Although they make up only about 1 percent of total wholesale trade, auction companies are extremely important in the wholesaling of used cars and certain agricultural products (such as tobacco, livestock, and fruit).
- **Selling agents** essentially substitute for a marketing department by marketing a manufacturer's entire output. Although selling agents transact only about 1 percent of wholesale trade, they play a key role in distributing textile products and coal and, to a lesser extent, apparel, food, lumber, and metal products.
- **Import-export agents** bring together sellers and buyers from different countries. Export agents work in the country in which the product is made; import agents are based in the country where the product will be sold.

Nature and Importance of Physical Distribution

After a company establishes its channels of distribution, it must arrange for the physical distribution of its products through these channels. **Physical distribution**, which we use synonymously with *logistics*, consists of all the activities concerned with moving the right amount of the right products to the right place at the right time. As described in one article, "Virtually the entire economy depends on the arcane and complex science of logistics to get billions of parts and supplies into U.S. manufacturing plants on time and to distribute finished products efficiently to consumers."[19]

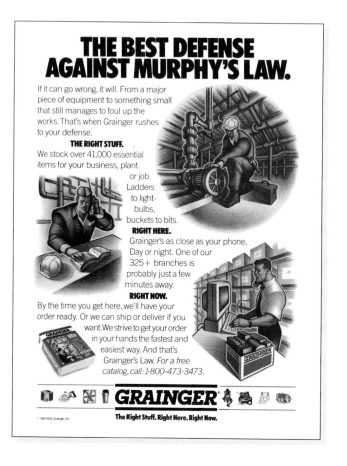

In its full scope, physical distribution for manufacturers includes the flow of *raw materials* from their sources of supply to the production line *and* the movement of *finished goods* from the end of the production line to the final users' locations. Middlemen manage the flows of goods *onto* their shelves as well as *from* their shelves to customers' homes, stores, or other places of business.

The activities comprising physical distribution are:

- Inventory location and warehousing
- Materials handling
- Inventory control
- Order processing
- Transportation

A decision regarding any one of these activities affects all the others. Location of a warehouse influences the selection of transportation methods and carriers; the choice of a carrier influences the optimum size of shipments.

Increasing Attention to Physical Distribution

A business faces a problem (or maybe it's an opportunity) when it has a warehouse full of patio furniture in Atlanta but unsatisfied customers in New Orleans, or too many ski parkas in Phoenix and too few in Missoula. These examples underscore that the appropriate assortment of products must be in the right place at the right time to maximize the opportunity for profitable sales. Compaq Computer admits to losing as much as $1 billion in sales during 1994 because it did *not* have its products available where they could be sold. A top executive of the computer maker said, "We've changed the way we develop products, manufacture, market, and advertise. The one piece of the puzzle we haven't addressed is logistics."[20]

Through the years, management has made progress in reducing production costs and also some marketing expenses. Physical distribution may be the last marketing area with substantial opportunities for cost cutting. And the potential savings are great. For certain products, such as furniture and building materials, physical distribution represents the largest operating expense. For other products, as much as one-half the wholesale cost is incurred in transportation and warehousing. Profits are small for many businesses engaged in distribution, so any savings are appreciated. A supermarket, for instance, typically earns a net profit of 1 percent of sales. Thus every $1 a supermarket saves in physical distribution costs has the same effect on profit as a $100 increase in sales!

Effective physical distribution also can be the basis by which a firm gains and sustains a differential advantage. On-time delivery, which requires effective physical distribution, can provide an edge. With that in mind, Caterpillar is able to deliver replacement parts within 72 hours for 99.7 percent of all orders.[21]

http://www.caterpillar.com/

Opportunities to better satisfy customers, cut costs, and/or gain a competitive edge expanded greatly in 1980. During that year, two new federal laws (the Motor Carrier Act and the Staggers Act) completed the deregulation of marketing activities related to *interstate* transportation.[22] Previously, pricing by railroads, airlines, and trucking companies had been subject to restrictive regulations. By the beginning of 1995, *intrastate* trucking was basically deregulated as well.

Since deregulation, transportation firms have been able to decide which rates (prices) and levels of service would best satisfy their target markets. For example, Landair Transport Inc. promises on-time deliveries and, in fact, 99 percent of shipments arrive within 15 minutes of the scheduled time. Toward this end, Landair has equipped its trucks with satellite-tracking devices (see the nearby Commitment

*M*ost trucking companies use two-way wireless communications. From this large "nerve center" at Schneider National's headquarters, about 450 employees keep track of all 10,000 of the company's trucks. This system has improved Schneider's performance in several ways, notably cutting internal costs by nearly one-quarter and boosting on-time deliveries from under 90 percent to almost 99 percent.

http://www.schneiderlogistics.com/

box).[23] From another perspective, companies that ship goods are now better able to shop around for rates and service levels that best meet their needs.

Systems Approach to Physical Distribution

We have occasionally alluded to marketing as a *total system* of business activities rather than a series of fragmented operations. Nowhere is this clearer than in physical distribution. But it has not always been this way. Traditionally, physical distribution activities were fragmented.

In many firms, physical distribution is still uncoordinated. If you ask, "Who's in charge of physical distribution?" too often the answer is "No one." Responsibility for it is delegated to various units that often have conflicting, perhaps opposite, goals. The production department, for instance, is interested primarily in long production runs to minimize unit manufacturing costs, even though the result may be high inventory costs. In contrast, the finance department wants a minimum of funds to be tied up in inventories. At the same time, the sales department wants to have a wide assortment of products available at locations near customers.

Uncoordinated conditions like these make it impossible to achieve a flow of products that satisfies the firm's goals. To alleviate this problem, a number of firms are establishing separate departments responsible for all physical distribution activ-

A COMMITMENT TO CUSTOMER SATISFACTION

IT'S 10 P.M., DO YOU KNOW WHERE YOUR SHIPMENT IS?

In years past, trucking companies and other freight carriers were not able to keep good track of their equipment (trucks, railcars). As one manager admitted, "We didn't know where trucks were, in Florida or Tennessee." As a result, carriers could not inform customers about the status of their shipments. Or at least they could not do so with much reliability.

All that's changed. Most transportation firms can pinpoint the location of their equipment; in fact, many monitor shipments on a real-time basis. Schneider National, based in Green Bay, Wisconsin, started this movement in 1988. Today Schneider knows within 100 feet where all of its 10,000 trucks are at any time.

How is this done? Schneider and some other carriers have equipped their trucks with satellite-tracking devices and on-board computers. This system permits two-way communication between truck and company office. Tracking systems are also used by railroads and other modes of transportation.

A carrier's real-time monitoring should satisfy customers because they can know not only the pre-

cise location of a shipment but also its expected arrival time. A carrier benefits too. For instance, a tracking system helps a trucking company reroute rigs to avoid bad weather or other delays and direct them to the proper gate at the customer's facility, both of which increase the efficiency of expensive transportation equipment. On-board computers also are used to track how long drivers are on the road, which is limited by federal laws, and how fast they drive, which affects fuel costs.

In the future, shipments on various modes of transportation will be tracked even more closely. New technology will enable monitoring not just location but also security, temperature, and other relevant conditions.

Why are carriers or their customers willing to bear the costs associated with real-time monitoring of shipments?

Sources: Warren Cohen, "Taking to the Highway," *U.S. News & World Report*, Sept. 18, 1995, pp. 84–87; Ronald Henkoff, "Delivering the Goods," *Fortune*, Nov. 28, 1994, pp. 64+; and Rick Tetzeli, "Cargo That Phones Home," *Fortune*, Nov. 15, 1993, p. 143.

ities. Even when this occurs in large firms, physical distribution usually is separated from the marketing department. This separation causes problems when a company is trying to formulate coordinated marketing strategies, including physical distribution. Under a **systems approach to physical distribution**, individual physical distribution activities are brought together in a unified way.

To implement a systems approach, some companies are contracting out, or outsourcing, their physical distribution function. It's more and more common for logistics companies to manage firms' distribution processes under a multiyear contract. Caliber Logistics, for example, operates a warehouse for a unit of Hewlett-Packard that produces computer printers. Besides handling the storage function, Caliber Logistics employees deliver needed parts and materials to the nearby H-P manufacturing plant. To date, H-P is pleased with the arrangement, probably because its costs in this area have gone down 10 percent. Going a couple steps further, Ryder System Inc. oversees the entire physical distribution for GM's Saturn division, from suppliers' shipments to deliveries of new cars to dealer showrooms.[24]

The growth of **contract logistics** reflects a broader trend in the U.S. whereby firms are outsourcing various business tasks ranging from payroll to public relations. By the start of the next century, contract logistics could be a $50 billion business annually, three times its size in 1994. Manufacturers probably will outsource as much as 30 percent of their physical distribution activities, up from about 12 percent in the mid-1990s.

The Total Cost Concept

As part of a systems approach to physical distribution, executives should apply the **total cost concept**. That is, a company should determine the set of activities that produces the best relationship between costs and profit for the *entire* physical distribution system. This approach is superior to focusing strictly on the separate costs of individual distribution activities.

http://www.ryder.com/

*S*ome companies are dedicated to providing a complete set of physical distribution activities, called contract logistics, to various organizations. Caliber Logistics, formerly Roadway Logistics Systems, promises customers "heightened customer satisfaction, faster production, and improved logistics methods." Caliber furnishes physical distribution activities—such as warehousing, finished-goods distribution, and integrated shipment management—and broader services—such as business process reengineering.

http://www.calibersys.com/

MISSION STATEMENT
To Design, Develop, & Apply
Logistics Solutions
That Improve
Our Customers'
Competitive Positions
Worldwide.

caliber
logistics

Too often, a company attempts to minimize the cost of only one aspect of physical distribution—transportation, for example. Management might be upset by the high cost of air freight. But the higher costs of air freight may be more than offset by savings from (1) lower inventory costs, (2) less insurance and interest expense, (3) lower crating costs, and (4) fewer lost sales because of out-of-stock conditions. The point is *not* that air freight is the best mode of transportation. Which mode is best varies with the situation. The key point is that physical distribution should be viewed as a *total* process, with all of the related costs being analyzed.

Strategic Use of Physical Distribution

The strategic use of physical distribution may enable a company to strengthen its competitive position by providing more customer satisfaction and/or by reducing operating costs. The management of physical distribution can also affect a firm's marketing mix—particularly product planning, pricing, and distribution channels. Each opportunity is described below.

Improve Customer Service. A well-run logistics system can improve the service a firm provides its customers—whether they are middlemen or ultimate users. For an example of an extensive distribution network established with this goal in mind, see Figure 15-4. Furthermore, the level of customer service directly affects demand. This is true especially in marketing undifferentiated products (such as chemicals and most building materials) where effective service may be a company's only differential advantage. For example, Hillenbrand Industries Inc. is

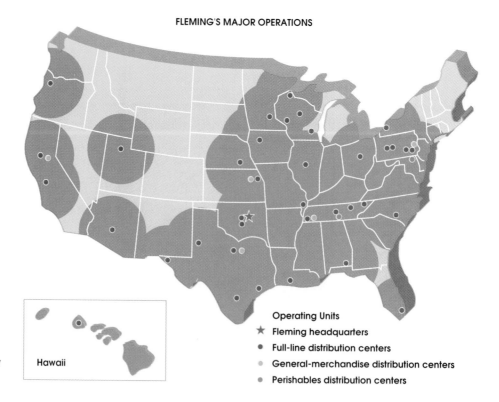

FIGURE 15-4

Fleming Companies' distribution network.

Fleming's distribution centers provide it with better control over product supply and quality.

set up to deliver any one of 300 casket models to its funeral-home customers, ordinarily within 48 hours.[25]

To ensure reliable customer service, management should set standards of performance for each subsystem of physical distribution. These standards should be quantitatively measurable. Some hypothetical examples:

- Electronics manufacturer: Make delivery within 5 days after receiving an order, with no more than 20 percent of the shipments by air.
- Sporting goods wholesaler: Fill 99.5 percent of orders accurately, without increasing the size of the order-fulfillment staff.
- Industrial distributor: Fulfill at least 85 percent of orders received from inventory on hand, but maintain a stockturn of 30 days.

Reduce Distribution Costs.   Many avenues to cost reductions may be opened by effective physical distribution management. For example, eliminating unneeded warehouses will lower costs. Inventories—and their attendant carrying costs and capital investment—may be reduced by consolidating stocks at fewer locations.

http://www.nsc.com/

When National Semiconductor applied the total cost concept, it committed to a major investment, building a distribution center in Singapore. All computer chips assembled in East Asia are shipped to this facility, where they are sorted and sent by air freight to customers around the world. The chip maker contracted with Federal Express to manage this distribution process. Over a 2-year period, distribution costs shrank from 2.6 percent to 1.9 percent of sales. On a sales base of a couple *billion* dollars, that's a considerable savings.[26]

Create Time and Place Utilities.   Storage, which is part of warehousing, creates *time utility*. Storage is essential to correct imbalances in the timing of production and consumption. An imbalance can occur when there is *year-round consumption* but only *seasonal production*, as in the case of agricultural products. For instance, time utility is created and value is added when bananas are picked green and allowed to ripen in storage. And skillful use of warehousing allows a producer to store a seasonal surplus so that it can be marketed long after the harvest has ended. In other instances warehousing helps adjust *year-round production* to *seasonal consumption*. A manufacturer may produce lawn mowers on a year-round basis; during the fall and winter, the mowers are stored for sale in the spring and summer.

Transportation adds value to products by creating *place utility*. A fine suit hanging on a manufacturer's rack in New York City has less value than an identical suit displayed in a retailer's store in Baltimore. Transporting the suit from New York to Baltimore creates place utility and adds value to it.

Stabilize Prices.   Careful management of warehousing and transportation can help stabilize prices for an individual firm or for an entire industry. If a market is temporarily glutted with a product, sellers can store it until supply and demand conditions are better balanced. Such use of warehousing facilities is common in the marketing of agricultural products and other seasonally produced goods.

The judicious movement of products from one market to another may enable a seller to (1) avoid a market with depressed prices or (2) take advantage of a market that has a shorter supply and higher prices. If demand for heating oil is stronger in Akron, Ohio, than in Des Moines, Iowa, a producer should be able to achieve greater revenues by shifting some shipments from Des Moines to Akron.

Influence Channel Decisions.   Decisions regarding inventory management have a direct bearing on a producer's selection of channels and the location of middlemen. Logistical considerations may become paramount, for example, when a company decides to decentralize its inventory. In this case management must determine (1) how many sites to establish and (2) whether to use wholesalers, the company's own warehouses, or public warehouses. One producer may select merchant wholesalers that perform storage and other warehousing services. Another may prefer to use a combination of (1) manufacturers' agents to provide aggressive selling and (2) public warehouses to distribute the products ordered.

Control Shipping Costs.   Managers with shipping responsibilities need to ensure that their companies enjoy the fastest routes *and* the lowest rates for whatever methods of transportation they deem to use. The pricing of transportation services is one of the most complicated parts of American business. The rate, or tariff, schedule is the carrier's price list. Typically it is complex. To cite one example, shipping rates vary for many different types of goods, depending on many factors including not only distance to the destination but also the bulk and weight of the products. Therefore, being able to interpret a tariff schedule properly is a money-saving skill for a manager with shipping responsibilities.

Tasks in Physical Distribution Management

Physical distribution refers to the actual physical flow of products. In contrast, **physical distribution management** is the development and operation of processes resulting in the effective and efficient physical flow of products.

To improve their physical distribution management, some firms are forming logistics alliances. Under such an arrangement, a manufacturer and one or more firms conducting specialized physical distribution activities work cooperatively. They jointly plan and implement the physical flows that will get the right goods to the right places in the right amounts at the right time. This type of alliance extends beyond normal business cooperation in several ways, including the ongoing nature of the relationship. Sears Business Systems has formed a logistics alliance with Itel Distribution Systems, and Procter & Gamble and Wal-Mart have done likewise.[27]

Irrespective of whether a firm is part of a logistics alliance or handles this function on its own, an effective physical distribution system is built around five interdependent subsystems: inventory location and warehousing, materials handling, inventory control, order processing, and transportation. Each must be carefully coordinated with the others.

Inventory Location and Warehousing

The name of the game in physical distribution is inventory management. One important consideration is *warehousing*, which embraces a range of functions, such as assembling, dividing (bulk-breaking), and storing products and preparing them for reshipping. Management must also consider the size, location, and transporting of inventories. These four areas are interrelated. The number and locations of inventory sites, for example, influence inventory size and transportation methods. These interrelationships are often quite complex.

Distribution Centers.   An effective inventory-location strategy may involve the establishment of one or more **distribution centers**. Such facilities are

http://www.gm.com/

planned around markets rather than transportation requirements. The idea is to develop under one roof an efficient, fully integrated system for the flow of products—taking orders, filling them, and preparing them for delivery to customers.

Distribution centers have been established by many well-known firms. The Limited, for example, uses its center in Columbus, Ohio, as the hub of its physical distribution system. In 1994, General Motors established a new distribution center in Orlando, Florida, with an inventory of about 1,500 new Cadillacs. The intent was to boost sales by reducing delivery times. According to GM's research, about 10 percent of serious prospects don't buy a Cadillac because it's not available right away. With the new distribution center, carss arrive at any Cadillac dealership in Florida within 1 day of an order. This arrangement increases delivery costs; however, it reduces inventory of new cars a dealer must carry at its facility, thereby paring inventory costs.[28]

Distribution centers can cut costs by reducing the number of warehouses, pruning excessive inventories, and eliminating out-of-stock conditions. Considering that companies are in business to sell goods, not to store or ship them, warehousing and delivery times must be cut to a minimum. Distribution centers can help in this regard as well.

Types of Warehouses.   Any producer, wholesaler, or retailer has the option of operating its own private warehouse or using the services of a public warehouse. A **private warehouse** is more likely to be an advantage if (1) a company moves a large volume of products through a warehouse, (2) there is very little, if any, seasonal fluctuation in this flow, and (3) the goods have special handling or storage requirements.

A **public warehouse** offers storage and handling facilities to individuals or companies. Public warehousing costs are a variable expense. Customers pay only for the space they use, and only when they use it. Public warehouses can also provide office and product display space, and accept and fill orders for sellers. Furthermore, warehouse receipts covering products stored in certain types of public warehouses may be used as collateral for bank loans.

Materials Handling

Selecting the proper equipment to physically handle products, including the warehouse building itself, is the *materials handling* subsystem of physical distribution management. Equipment that is well matched to the task can minimize losses from breakage, spoilage, and theft. Efficient equipment can reduce handling costs as well as time required for handling.

Modern warehouses are huge one-story structures located in outlying areas where land is less expensive and loading platforms are easily accessed by trucks and trains. Conveyor belts, forklift trucks, and other mechanized equipment are used to move merchandise. In some warehouses the order fillers are even outfitted with in-line skates!

Containerization is a cargo-handling system that has become standard practice in physical distribution. Shipments of products are enclosed in large metal or wood containers. The containers are then transported unopened from the time they leave the shipper's facilities (such as a manufacturer's plant) until they reach their destination (such as a wholesaler's warehouse). Containerization minimizes physical handling, thereby reducing damage, lessening the risk of theft, and allowing for more efficient transportation.

Inventory Control

Controlling the size and composition of inventories, which represent a sizable investment for most companies, is essential to any physical distribution system. The goal of *inventory control* is to fill the orders placed by customers promptly, completely, and accurately while minimizing both the investment and fluctuations in inventories.

Customer-Service Requirements.   Inventory size is determined by balancing costs and desired levels of customer service. Different customers have varying needs regarding order fulfillment. Some individuals or organizations expect the order to be completely filled almost immediately if they are to be satisfied. Others are less demanding and will accept an occasional out-of-stock item or a slight delay in receiving an order. Management must identify and respond to differences in expected levels of customer service.

When a company knows its customers' expectations regarding order fulfillment, it then must decide what percentage of orders it intends to fill promptly from inventory on hand. Out-of-stock conditions result in lost sales, loss of goodwill, even loss of customers. Yet to be able to fill 100 percent of orders promptly may require an excessively large and costly inventory.

Economic Order Quantity.   Management must establish the optimal quantity for reorder when it is time to replenish inventory stocks. The **economic order quantity (EOQ)** is the volume at which the sum of inventory-carrying costs and order-processing costs are at a minimum. Typically, as order size increases, (1) inventory-carrying cost goes up (because the average inventory is larger) and (2) order-processing cost declines (because there are fewer orders).

In Figure 15-5, point EOQ represents the order quantity having the lowest total cost. Actually, the order quantity that a firm considers best (or optimal) often is larger than the EOQ. That's because management must try to balance the sometimes conflicting goals of low inventory costs and responsive customer service. For various reasons, such as gaining a differential advantage, a firm may place a

FIGURE 15-5
Economic order
quantity.

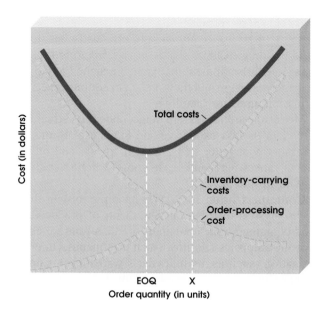

higher priority on customer service than on inventory costs. To completely fill orders in a timely manner may well call for a larger order quantity than the EOQ—for example, quantity X in Figure 15-5.

Just-in-Time. First widely used in Japan, **just-in-time (JIT)** is the integration of inventory control, purchasing, and production scheduling. Applying JIT, a firm buys in small quantities that arrive *just in time* for production and then it produces in quantities *just in time* for sale. When effectively implemented, the just-in-time concept has many benefits. By purchasing in small quantities and maintaining low inventory levels of parts and finished goods, a company can achieve dramatic cost savings because fewer items are damaged, stolen, or otherwise become unusable. Production and delivery schedules can be shortened and made more flexible and reliable. The Japanese found that quality improves with JIT purchasing. When order quantities are small and deliveries frequent, a company can quickly spot and correct a quality problem in the products received.[29]

The JIT concept was adopted slowly in the U.S., largely due to long-standing business practices. Unlike Japan, channel relations in the U.S. historically were adversarial, with each party negotiating forcefully to gain an advantage. Also, many American firms felt more secure with a large inventory of parts and supplies. Thus JIT represented a radical change for companies in the U.S.

Eventually, the JIT philosophy was adopted in the American auto industry and then was implemented by other leading firms, such as IBM, Xerox, Apple, Black & Decker, and General Electric. Often, the results were quite positive. Xerox eliminated 4,700 suppliers in 1 year, and Black & Decker cut more than 50 percent of its suppliers in 2 years.[30] An organization that relies on JIT tends to use fewer suppliers because a high level of coordination is needed. JIT puts pressure on a supplier to meet a manufacturer's needs in a very timely fashion. In some instances, it has created friction between vendor and customer.

An updated version of JIT, labeled *JIT II*, stresses closer working relationships between manufacturers and suppliers. Under JIT II, a company provides a supplier with sales forecasts and other useful information, some of which may be confidential. In turn, a supplier often places one of its employees at the customer's plant to handle all or part of the purchasing function. To satisfy the manufacturer's needs, such as low costs, the supplier's employee may even place orders with competing suppliers. As with any business practice, there are potential problems with JIT II, such as sharing of confidential data. Hence, some companies are applying JIT or JIT II, while many others are not convinced the improvements in customer service are sufficient to justify the additional costs.[31]

Channel members—even entire channels—that employ JIT (or JIT II) effectively can gain a differential advantage. Firms or channels that ignore it risk a differential disadvantage.[32]

Market-Response Systems. JIT's focus tends to be on production and the relationship between a producer and its suppliers. There's a parallel trend, however, involving producers or middlemen of finished goods and their customers. Several labels, such as *quick response*, have been used to describe this counterpart to JIT; we prefer **market-response systems**. The central idea is that a purchase by a final customer, one who intends to consume the product, should activate a process to produce and deliver a replacement item. In this way, a product is pulled through a channel based on demand rather than being pushed through based on short-term price reduction or other inducements, which often result in excess inventories.

The intent of a market-response system is similar to that of JIT, namely to have just the right amount of goods in stock to satisfy demand and then to replenish exhausted stocks rapidly. By minimizing the quantity of inventory that languishes in middlemen's warehouses, a market-response system can shrink the funds channel members have tied up in inventory and also reduce their operating expenses. Consumer prices may also drop—or at least not rise as much.

The grocery industry's version of a market-response system has been labeled *efficient consumer response (ECR)*. There's abundant enthusiasm about ECR within this industry, although it's still in the early stages of implementation. However, projected savings from ECR are $30 billion a year.[33]

Of course, what makes a market-response system feasible are advances in computer technology. A key element of such a system is linking a middleman and its supplier by computer. These computer-based arrangements affect order processing as well as inventory control. We'll discuss them jointly in the following section.

Order Processing

Still another part of the physical distribution system is a set of procedures for receiving, handling, and filling orders. This *order processing* subsystem should include provisions for billing, granting credit, preparing invoices, and collecting past-due accounts. Consumer ill will results if a company makes mistakes or is slow in filling orders. In addition, inefficient order processing can lead to unnecessarily large inventories. That's why more and more firms have turned to computers to execute most of their order-processing activities. At the same time, some suppliers are even providing customers with computer technology to use in placing orders.

There have been various computer-based advances in order processing, with names such as *electronic data interchange (EDI)* and *automatic replenishment*. Under EDI, orders, invoices, and perhaps other business information as well are transmitted by computer rather than by mail. As such, EDI speeds up the process and literally reduces the associated paperwork. For Bergen Brunswig, a drug wholesaler, EDI handles 99 percent of the orders received from customers and 95 percent of the orders placed with suppliers.[34] Under automatic replenishment, a retail store's computer knows when a product has been sold and, in turn, notifies the supplier's computer that a replacement item is needed.

http://www.bergenbrunswig.com/

The efforts of VF Corp. illustrate the requirements and benefits of working closely with customers to bring about improvements in inventory control and order processing. The apparel maker, based in Wyomissing, Pennsylvania, is using computer technology to track what is selling at the retail level and then to rapidly replenish store shelves with its brands, including Lee and Wrangler jeans and Vanity Fair women's underwear. Various retailers, including Penney's and Wal-Mart, have agreed to allow VF's computers to be linked to their computers. Each night a store's computer sends to VF's computer precise information about which of the manufacturer's products were sold that day. Then VF ships replacement items, either from existing inventory or as soon as they are produced. The replacements can be on the store shelf as soon as 2 days later.

Like other manufacturers and retailers, VF has found that automatic replenishment works better with staple items, like basic jeans, rather than trendy merchandise, like swimwear. Still, the benefits of automatic replenishment to both parties are considerable, ranging from the supplier achieving a tighter bond with customers to the middleman facing fewer out-of-stock situations.[35]

Transportation

A major function of the physical distribution system in many companies is *transportation*—shipping products to customers. Management must decide on both the mode of transportation and the particular carriers. In this discussion we will focus on *intercity* shipments.

Major Modes. Railroads, trucks, pipelines, water vessels, and airplanes are the leading modes of transportation. In Table 15-4 these five methods are compared on the basis of criteria likely to be used by physical distribution managers in selecting a mode of transportation. Of course, the comparisons in the table are generalizations. The ratings of alternative modes of transportation can vary from one manager to the next, even within the same buying center in an organization.[36]

The relative use of each of the five major modes, along with trends in use, are shown in Table 15-5. Note that the table does not cover *intracity* freight traffic or ocean coastal traffic between U.S. ports. Virtually all intracity shipping is done by motor truck. As indicated in the table, the use of trucks has expanded greatly over the past 40 years. On all measures, however, railroads are by far the major intercity freight carrier. Even as their relative position slipped between 1950 and 1970, the absolute amount of railroad freight increased considerably. The railroads' position has stabilized since 1980; in fact, they are now experiencing a resurgence.[37]

Intermodal Transportation. Using two or more modes of transportation to move freight is termed **intermodal transportation**. The intent of this approach is to seize the advantages of multiple forms of transportation. Over a recent 10-year period, intermodal traffic jumped 60 percent.[38]

TABLE 15-4 Comparison of transportation methods

Selection criteria	Transportation method				
	Rail	**Water**	**Highway**	**Pipeline**	**Air**
Speed (door-to-door time)	Medium	Slowest	Fast	Slow	Fastest
Cost of transportation	Medium	Lowest	High	Low	Highest
Reliability in meeting delivery schedules	Medium	Poor	Good	Excellent	Good
Variety of products carried	Widest	Widest	Medium	Very limited	Somewhat limited
Number of geographic locations served	Very many	Limited	Unlimited	Very limited	Many
Most suitable products	Long hauls of carload quantities of bulky products, when freight costs are high in relation to product's value	Bulky, low-value non-perishables	Short hauls of high-value goods	Oil, natural gas, slurried products	High-value perishables, where speed of delivery is all-important

TABLE 15-5 Distribution of intercity freight traffic in the United States based on ton miles

Specific mode	Percent of total		
	1994	**1970**	**1950**
Railroads	39	40	56
Trucks	28	21	16
Oil pipelines	18	22	12
Water vessels	15	17	15
Air	*	*	*
Total	100	100	100

*Less than 1 percent of total.

Notes: A *ton mile* refers to one ton of freight being transported one mile. The 1950 column does not total to 100 percent due to rounding.

Source: *Railroad Facts*, 1995 edition, Association of American Railroads, Washington, D.C., 1995, p. 32.

So-called **piggyback service** involves carrying truck trailers on railroad flatcars. For example, a shipment of auto glass is loaded on J. B. Hunt Transport trucks at the Libbey-Owens-Ford plant near Toledo, Ohio. The truck trailers are placed on a Santa Fe Pacific train in Chicago for a trip to Los Angeles. There, Hunt trucks take the auto glass to its destination in Fontana, California. This form of intermodal transportation provides (1) more flexibility than railroads alone can offer, (2) lower freight costs than trucks alone, and (3) less handling of goods.[39]

Another form of intermodal transportation combines ships or barges with either railroads or trucks, or both. One version of *fishyback service* transports loaded trailers on barges or ships. The trailers may be carried piggyback fashion by railroad to the dock, where they are transferred to the ship. Then, at the other end of the water trip, the trailers are loaded back onto trains for completion of the haul. In an alternative use of the fishyback service, merchandise is trucked directly to ports, where the trailer vans are loaded on barges. At the end of the water journey, the vans are trucked to the receiving station.

Currently, the transportation industry is looking at new types of intermodal equipment. One alternative is a truck trailer that is easily converted to a railcar by attaching railroad wheels![40]

Freight Forwarders.   A specialized marketing institution serving firms that ship in less-than-full-load quantities is called a **freight forwarder**. Its main function is to consolidate less-than-carload or less-than-truckload shipments from several shippers into full-load quantities. The freight forwarder picks up the merchandise at the shipper's place of business and arranges for delivery at the buyer's door. A small shipper benefits from the speed and minimum handling associated with large shipments. A freight forwarder also provides the small shipper with traffic management services, such as selecting the best transportation methods and routes.

Package-Delivery Firms.   A major development of the past 30 years has been the formation of companies that deliver small shipments of packages and high-priority mail. The movement toward just-in-time purchasing certainly has contributed to the continuing growth of package-delivery companies.

You surely are familiar with such package-delivery firms as United Parcel Service (UPS), Federal Express (FedEx), and Airborne Freight. All these firms com-

http://www.ups.com/
http://www.fedex.com/
http://www.airborne-express.com/

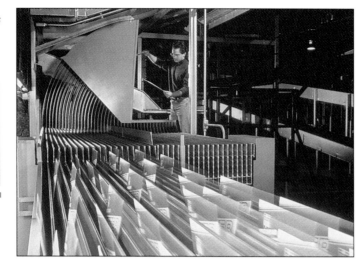

*U*nited Parcel Service ships about 12 million packages daily! At this particular facility, UPS's "all-points international air hub" in Louisville, Kentucky, around 700,000 packages are sorted and routed daily. Whenever possible, automation is substituted for manual labor.

http://www.ups.com/

http://www.usps.com/

pete vigorously not only among themselves but also with the U.S. Postal Service. The competition is particularly intense in the overnight-delivery market, where FedEx and UPS go head-to-head. Each giant tries to surpass the other with respect to delivery times, technology that helps customers prepare and then track their shipments, and—of course—low prices.[41]

In many respects, these companies offer the same services as freight forwarders. However, whereas the typical forwarder does not have its own transportation equipment, package-delivery firms do. Companies such as UPS and FedEx are essentially combined cargo airlines and trucking companies. Furthermore, package-delivery firms, in effect, use intermodal transportation. Consider FedEx, for example. A package is picked up by truck, shipped intercity or overseas by plane, and delivered locally by truck.

■ SUMMARY

Wholesaling consists of the sale, and all activities directly related to the sale, of goods and services for resale, use in producing other goods or services, or operating an organization. Firms engaged primarily in wholesaling, called wholesaling middlemen, provide economies of skill, scale, and transactions to other firms involved in distribution.

Three categories of wholesaling middlemen are merchant wholesalers, agent wholesaling middlemen, and manufacturers' sales facilities. The first two are independent firms; the third is owned by a manufacturer. Merchant wholesalers take title to products being distributed; agent wholesaling middlemen do not. In recent years, the shares of total wholesale trade captured by the three categories have stabilized.

Merchant wholesalers, which account for the majority of wholesale trade, include both full-service and limited-service wholesalers. Of the three major categories of wholesaling middlemen, mer-

chant wholesalers offer the widest range of services and thus incur the highest operating expenses.

Agent wholesaling middlemen lost ground to merchant wholesalers during the 1960s and 1970s. The main types of agent middlemen are manufacturers' agents and brokers. Because they perform more limited services, agent middlemen's expenses tend to be lower than merchant wholesalers'.

Physical distribution is the flow of products from supply sources to the firm and then from the firm to its customers. The goal of physical distribution is to move the right amount of the right products to the right place at the right time. Physical distribution costs are a substantial part of total operating costs in many firms. Moreover, physical distribution is probably the only remaining source of possible cost reductions in many companies.

Although physical distribution activities are still fragmented operationally and organizationally in

many firms, they should be treated as a system. The total cost concept should be applied to physical distribution—that is, the focus should be on the cost of physical distribution in its entirety, rather than on the costs of individual elements. However, management should strive *not* for the lowest total cost of physical distribution, but for the best balance between customer service and total cost. Effective management of physical distribution can help a company gain an advantage over competitors through better customer service and/or lower operating costs. To improve their physical distribution, some firms are turning to contract logistics.

The operation of a physical distribution system requires management's attention and decision making in five areas: (1) inventory location and warehousing, (2) materials handling, (3) inventory control, (4) order processing, and (5) transportation. They should not be treated as individual activities but as interrelated components within a physical distribution system. Effective management of these five subsystems requires an understanding of distribution centers, economic order quantity, just-in-time processes, market-response systems, and intermodal transportation.

More about

SUPERVALU

*A*s large as it is, Supervalu believes it must continue to grow in order to gain more economic power. The Advantage program is intended to help in that regard. At the same time, Supervalu is expanding on two other fronts—retailing and international.

Like its larger competitor, Fleming Companies, Supervalu is increasing the number of retail stores it owns and operates. For example, more Save-A-Lot stores, which feature private-brand groceries at discount prices, are being opened. Expansion of Supervalu's Shop-'n-Save and Laneco chains is also expected.

Increasingly, giant supermarket chains are bypassing wholesalers and dealing directly with manufacturers. Supervalu believes a larger retail presence will protect the company against any erosion in its wholesale business. Further, gross margins in retailing are typically twice those in wholesaling.

A major question is whether Supervalu's retail operations help or hurt its customers. One concern is that Supervalu's own retail stores could be given better treatment than other customers. Supervalu management says that more retail volume should give the wholesale operation greater economies of scale. In turn, this would result in lower prices for customers.

On the international front, Supervalu intends to become a major wholesale exporter, particularly to countries along the Pacific Rim. Supervalu International's early efforts have focused on Japan, where consumers are frustrated by the high prices of groceries. Added price competition and more large supermarkets are changing the face of grocery retailing in Japan. As a result, Japanese grocery stores need to secure better wholesale prices. Supervalu intends to satisfy this need.

The high costs of agriculture and production in Japan provide a major opportunity for Supervalu. Food products produced in the U.S. and shipped to Japan can be sold by a local supermarket under its own brand at lower prices than comparable items produced in that country. To seize this opportunity, Supervalu has to gain access to the complex Japanese distribution system.

Supervalu International, based in Tacoma, Washington, generates over $100 million in annual sales. Compared to the parent company's domestic revenues of more than $16 billion, the export division is tiny. But it has been growing rapidly, 20 percent per year, and has ambitious plans.[42]

1. Can Supervalu continue to increase the number of company-owned retail stores without jeopardizing its relationships with the independent grocery stores that are its customers?
2. Which avenue of expansion—domestic retailing or international wholesaling—holds the most promise for Supervalu?

■ KEY TERMS AND CONCEPTS

Wholesaling (402)
Wholesaling
    middleman (402)
Merchant
    wholesaler (405)
Agent wholesaling
    middleman (405)
Manufacturer's sales
    facility (406)
Manufacturer's sales
    branch (406)
Manufacturer's sales
    office (406)

Full-service
    wholesaler (407)
Truck jobber (409)
Drop shipper (410)
Manufacturers'
    agent (411)
Broker (412)
Commission
    merchant (413)
Auction company (413)
Selling agent (413)

Import-export
    agents (413)
Physical distribution
    (logistics) (413)
Systems approach to
    physical
    distribution (417)
Contract logistics (417)
Total cost concept (417)
Physical distribution
    management (420)
Distribution center (420)
Private warehouse (421)

Public warehouse (421)
Containerization (421)
Economic order
    quantity (EOQ) (422)
Just-in-time (JIT) (422)
Market-response
    systems (423)
Intermodal
    transportation (425)
Piggyback service (425)
Freight forwarder (426)

■ QUESTIONS AND PROBLEMS

1. Which of the following are wholesaling transactions?
   a. Color Tile sells wallpaper to an apartment building contractor and also to the contractor's wife for her home.
   b. General Electric sells motors to Whirlpool for its washing machines.
   c. A shrimp "farmer" sells shrimp to a local restaurant.
   d. A family orders carpet from a friend, who is a home-decorating consultant, at 50 percent off the suggested retail price. The carpet is delivered directly to the home.

2. As shown in Figure 15-3, agent wholesaling middlemen and manufacturers' sales facilities have lost part of their share of wholesale trade to merchant wholesalers since the early 1970s. How do you explain this shift?

3. Why is it that manufacturers' agents often can penetrate a market faster and at a lower cost than a manufacturer's sales force?

4. Which type of wholesaling middleman, if any, is most likely to be used by each of the following firms? Explain your choice in each instance.
   a. A small manufacturer of a liquid glass cleaner to be sold through supermarkets.
   b. A small canner in Vermont packing a high-quality, unbranded fruit product.
   c. A small-tools manufacturing firm that has its own sales force selling to the business market and now wants to add backyard barbecue equipment to its product mix.
   d. A North Carolina textile mill producing unbranded towels, sheets, pillowcases, and blankets.

5. Looking to the future, which types of wholesaling middlemen do you think will increase in importance, and which ones will decline? Explain.

6. "The goal of a modern physical distribution system in a firm should be to operate at the lowest possible *total* costs." Do you agree?

7. Name some products for which you think the cost of physical distribution constitutes at least one-half the total price of the goods at the wholesale level. Can you suggest ways of decreasing the physical distribution cost of these products?

8. "A manufacturer follows an inventory-location strategy of concentration rather than dispersion. This company's inventory size will be smaller, but its transportation and warehousing expenses will be larger than if its inventory were dispersed." Do you agree? Explain.

9. "The use of public warehouse facilities makes it possible for manufacturers to bypass wholesalers in their channels of distribution." Explain.

10. For each of the following products, determine the best transportation method for shipping them to a distribution center in the community where your school is located. In each case the buyer (not the seller) will pay all freight charges, and, unless specifically noted, time is not important. The distribution center has a rail siding and a loading/unloading dock for trucks.
   a. Disposable diapers from Wisconsin. Total shipment weight is 112,000 pounds.
   b. A replacement memory card for your computer, which is now inoperative. Weight of shipment is 1.5 pounds, and you need this card in a hurry.
   c. Blank payroll checks for your company. (There is a sufficient number of checks on hand for the next two weekly paydays.) Shipment weight is 100 pounds.
   d. Ice cream from St. Louis. Total shipment weight is 42,000 pounds.

■ HANDS-ON MARKETING

1. Interview the owner or a manager at a firm that is a type of merchant wholesaler (such as a full-service wholesaler). Ask the owner or manager to describe the firm's activities, its differential advantage or disadvantage at the present time, and the company's prospects for the future. Conduct a similar interview with the owner or a manager at a firm that is a type of agent wholesaling middleman (such as a broker). How do you explain any discrepancies between the interview results and the content of this chapter (other than saying that the chapter must be wrong)?

2. A manufacturer of precision lenses used in medical and hospital equipment wants to ship a 5-pound box of these lenses from your college town to a laboratory in Stockholm, Sweden. The lab wants delivery in 5 days or less. The manufacturer wants to use a package-delivery service but is undecided as to which shipper to choose. Compile and compare the types of services provided and prices charged by Federal Express, United Parcel Service, and one other package-delivery firm.

Just as creative, sound marketing decisions can help a business succeed, one or more poor marketing decisions can spell disaster for an organization. Such is the case with Kmart Corp., the second largest retailer in the U.S. In the late 1980s, the company decided to refurbish many of its existing Kmart stores while at the same time diversifying into other types of retail formats. This strategy has not worked well for Kmart. In fact, the giant firm has been plagued by rumors of bankruptcy.

The Beginning

Kmart Corp. is the descendant of an organization founded in 1899 in Detroit by Sebastian S. Kresge. The first S. S. Kresge stores represented a new type of retailing that featured low-price merchandise sold for cash in relatively small buildings with sparse furnishings. Kresge grew over the next five decades to become one of several successful "variety store" chains.

Eventually, Kresge was challenged by new forms of competition. By the late 1950s, it became clear that a new type of store emphasizing discount prices was emerging. The company's management responded by launching Kmart in 1962. This new chain of stores, called discount houses at the time, offered a much wider selection of merchandise than Kresge stores but was similar to Kresge operations in other respects.

Kmart was positioned as a conveniently located, one-stop-shopping store where consumers could buy a wide variety of quality merchandise at discount (or below-the-market) prices. Kmart stores occupied about 75,000 square feet of space, provided plenty of free parking, and were located by themselves in high-traffic suburban areas.

Kmart and other discounters, such as Wal-Mart and Target, prospered by serving different markets. Target focused on somewhat more "upscale" consumers with higher income levels and offered more stylish soft goods prone to occasional "sale" prices. Wal-Mart served consumers in small, rural towns and sold its merchandise at deeply discounted prices on an everyday basis. Compared to the competing chains, Kmart focused more on the professional middle class rather than on blue-collar workers from lower socioeconomic groups.

Although Kmart experienced occasional problems, sales and profits grew for several decades. Wal-Mart and

Target succeeded as well. Not all discount-house chains were so fortunate, however. W. T. Grant, Ames, and E. J. Korvette eventually went bankrupt or were reorganized.

Changing the Marketing Strategy

Kmart's basic marketing strategy changed with the appointment of Joseph Antonini as chairman and chief executive officer in October 1987. At that time, Kmart was the largest discount retailer in the U.S. It had nearly twice as many stores (2,223 to 1,198) and more sales ($25 billion to $16 billion) than Wal-Mart. Nevertheless, Kmart faced many problems. Some Kmarts were old, with broken light fixtures, cramped shelves, and cheap displays.

Kmart Corp. made three strategic changes in an effort to maintain the growth and improve the profitability of the company. The first was a 5-year, $3.5 billion renovation program designed to make all Kmart stores more appealing and "customer-friendly."

Key components of the renovation plan were:

- *Better presentation of merchandise.* The traditional Kmart layout by product category was supplemented or sometimes replaced by a new "shop concept." Departments, such as hardware, paint, and electrical, were merged into a single do-it-yourself department. The intent of each shop, or combined department, was to present a group of complementary goods so that shoppers would buy several related items rather than just a single product.
- *The addition of well-known brands in both soft and hard goods.* The merchandising executives at Kmart thought that consumers would generalize their feelings about the quality of so-called name brands to Kmart's own brands.
- *Improved technology.* The goal was to track inventory better and to facilitate the ordering of merchandise. Point-of-purchase scanners provided a record of every sale and transmitted sales data to corporate headquarters by satellite technology. This system enabled Kmart to respond more quickly to what's new, what's in demand, and what's creating repeat customers.
- *Reduced prices.* Seeking to maintain its reputation for low prices, Kmart cut several thousand prices. The focus of the new strategy was on providing consumers good value by offering quality products at low prices.
- *Image enhancement.* One step in this direction was to sign up celebrities to endorse Kmart products. For

*Based on an earlier version prepared by Professor James W. Camerius of Northern Michigan University.

example, Martha Stewart was hired as the chain's "lifestyle spokesperson and consultant."

- *Adoption of a new promotion theme and corporate logo.* The goal was to strengthen Kmart's identity in the minds of consumers. "The quality you need, the price you want" became Kmart's theme as it moved into the 1990s. The new logo consisted of a big red "K" with the word "mart" written in white script inside it. The logo was later changed by adding the word "Today's" across the corner of the K.
- *Modernized interior and exterior appearance.* Aisles were widened and brighter lighting was installed. New counters and garment racks gave the stores a more modern look and held more merchandise.

Kmart's second major strategic change was to seek more growth by acquiring specialty retail chains. In 1984, Kmart bought Builders Square, a chain of home-improvement centers, and Waldenbooks' 900 stores. Kmart's buying spree continued, with purchases of Makro Inc. in 1988 and PACE Membership Warehouse, Inc., in 1989. Both firms operated membership warehouse clubs that sold fresh and frozen groceries, apparel, and durable goods at low prices.

As a third strategic change, Kmart began opening Super Kmart stores in 1991. These supercenters, 150,000 square feet in size, are expected to gross between $40 million and $50 million in annual sales, compared to a typical Kmart store with 100,000 square feet and $20 million in annual sales. Super Kmarts are open 24 hours a day.

Despite Kmart's commitment to growth, Wal-Mart surpassed Kmart as the largest discount retailer in the U.S. in 1990. Still, early on, Kmart's three strategies produced promising results. For example, as a group, larger (over 110,000 square feet), renovated Kmarts reported 17 percent higher sales and 12 percent more customers than smaller Kmarts that had not been changed. By the beginning of 1993, Kmart Corporation operated over 4,400 retail stores. About one-half were traditional Kmarts, and the rest were different formats—primarily various kinds of limited-line stores.

The Downfall

Faced with increasingly intense competition, particularly from Wal-Mart, Kmart's three-part strategy soon began to unravel. Part of the reason for Kmart's decline was the difference in marketing strategies between the two discounters. For example, Wal-Mart invested in distribution centers around which its stores were located. These actions not only improved customer satisfaction but also helped the company lower its costs to 15.8 percent of sales, the lowest ratio in the industry. Further, in contrast to Kmart, Wal-Mart committed a tremendous amount of resources to develop a company-wide computer system linking cash registers to headquarters. This system, which was superior to

Kmart's, allowed the larger retailer to quickly restock items in individual stores.

Meanwhile, Kmart focused on image enhancement and diversification. Despite a heavy investment in a computer inventory system, Kmart customers often encountered empty shelves or incorrect prices at the cash register. (In fact, the problem of charging incorrect prices led to a 1994 lawsuit, in which the Riverside County district attorney alleged that 72 Kmarts in California were overcharging customers.) In addition, Kmart lacked tight cost controls, resulting in a cost-to-sales ratio of 22.2 percent. The expansion into specialty retailing also meant higher operating costs. Kmart's specialty chains contributed 30 percent of sales, but only 15 percent of operating profit in 1992. Furthermore, the investment required to open Super Kmarts and expand the specialty chains detracted from the efforts to renovate traditional Kmarts.

Seeking to Rebound

In 1993, it was apparent to Kmart's management that the strategies implemented in the late 1980s were not working. Thus, in a 13-month period beginning in November 1993, Kmart sold its PACE warehouses to Wal-Mart, announced the gradual closure of 800 Kmart stores, and disposed of its OfficeMax and Sports Authority specialty chains. Then, in March 1995, Joseph Antonini was forced out as Kmart's top executive. He was replaced by Floyd Hall, the former head of the rival Target chain.

Kmart's new management team encountered critical problems, including:

- Dissatisfied customers who rated Wal-Mart and Target better than Kmart with respect to service, quality, and value. In addition, 49 percent of shoppers surveyed indicated they would drive past a Kmart to get to a Wal-Mart. And apparently they often did, because a typical Wal-Mart customer averaged 32 visits per year to Wal-Mart stores, compared to 15 visits to Kmart for a Kmart customer.
- A less affluent, aging target market relative to Wal-Mart customers. The average Kmart customer is over 55, has no children at home, and earns less than $20,000 per year. Typical Wal-Mart customers are under 44, have children at home, and earn less than $40,000. According to industry analysts, for Kmart to be competitive again, it must pull entire families into its stores and convince them to spend more money than they intended.
- A product mix burdened with numerous low-margin items that, to make matters even worse, often had to be marked down because of competitors' promotional sales. This predicament reduced Kmart's profit margins and also damaged its already shaky image.
- A shortage of cash, which caused a lowering of Kmart's debt rating to just above "junk bond" status.

The poor rating meant the company incurred higher interest costs when it borrowed money.
- Vendors who were worried about Kmart's ability to pay for its purchases. Some vendors shortened the time Kmart had to pay from 90 to 30 days, putting additional pressure on the company's cash flows.

Kmart's strategy to improve its situation hinges on its ability to appeal to a younger, middle-class customer and change the assortment of products in its stores. With this in mind, Kmart is investing added resources in inventory control systems to assure that customers are able to get the merchandise they want, when they want it. Additional efforts also are aimed at improving customer service. For example, each Kmart store has a TLC ("Think Like a Customer") team that is charged with coordinating new customer-oriented ideas. Such ideas include allowing Kmart sales associates to substitute a similar product at the same discounted price if the store runs out of a sale item.

Kmart is also testing various alternatives with respect to store layout and product selection. The Pantry, a section located near store entrances, offers low-margin items such as paper towels, pet food, and certain grocery items. The intent of The Pantry is to utilize Kmart's well-located stores to draw in customers for low-margin products in hopes they will buy more profitable ones while they are in the store.

QUESTIONS

1. a. Which feature(s) of a Super Kmart have the potential to be this type of store's differential advantage?
   b. Its differential disadvantage?
2. Given the continuing growth of some kinds of limited-line stores, do you agree with Kmart's decision to sell off its specialty retail operations such as OfficeMax and Sports Authority?
3. As Kmart seeks different ways of attracting customers, should it expand into one or more types of nonstore retailing?

http://www.kmart.com/

Sources: Robert Brener, "Kmart Fights Yuletide Blues, but Stronger Sales Needed," *The Wall Street Journal,* Dec. 22, 1995, p. B4; Bill Vlasic and Keith Naughton, "Kmart: Who's in Charge Here?" *Business Week,* Dec. 4, 1995, p. 104; Mary Kuntz et al., "Reinventing the Store," *Business Week,* Nov. 27, 1995, p. 84; "Kmart Executive Says Openings, Closings Are Planned for 1996," *The Wall Street Journal,* Oct. 31, 1995, p. A15; Kevin Goldman, "Campbell Mithun Shows Its Stuff in a Kmart Makeover Campaign," *The Wall Street Journal,* Aug. 3, 1995, p. B7; Gerry Khermouch, "Target Hits Bullseye," *BrandWeek,* June 5, 1995, p. 22; Christina Duff and Bob Ortega, "How Wal-Mart Outdid a Once-Touted Kmart in Discount Store Race," *The Wall Street Journal,* Mar. 24, 1995, p. A1; Christine Duff, John Dorfman, and Joann Lublin, "Kmart's Embattled CEO Resigns Post under Pressure from Key Shareholders," *The Wall Street Journal,* Mar. 22, 1995, p. A3; and Barbara Solomon, "Ringing Up Sales," *American Management Association,* February 1995, p. 38.

CASE 2 *Federal Express*

SEEKING AN ADVANTAGE IN A MATURING INDUSTRY

"FedEx It!" These words are synonymous with the overnight delivery of letters and packages. However, Federal Express (FedEx) is now locked in a fierce battle with United Parcel Service (UPS), DHL Worldwide Express (DHL), and the United States Postal Service (USPS) for leadership of the overnight delivery business in the U.S. The challenge facing FedEx is how to establish a lasting differential advantage in this highly competitive, maturing distribution industry.

Payoff from a Term Paper

As an undergraduate student at Yale, Frederick Smith wrote a paper that criticized existing package-shipping services and proposed a different system. For his efforts, Smith received a grade of C. Undeterred, Smith developed a new overnight delivery service in 1973 and named it Federal Express.

Overnight delivery is a specialized physical-distribution service that ships packages from one location to another by the next day. Customers can either drop off a shipment at the delivery firm's facility or have it picked up for a slightly higher fee.

FedEx sputtered following its start. Individuals and organizations were either not aware of or not interested in the overnight delivery of letters and packages. In large part because of extensive advertising by FedEx, potential customers came to recognize the service's benefits. Demand soared, and the company became profitable within several years of starting up. By 1983, FedEx surpassed $1 *billion* in annual revenues. FedEx has since grown to annual sales exceeding $8 *billion.*

The overnight delivery business rings up sales of over $18 billion yearly. Global overnight shipments totaled 1.1 billion packages in 1994, with 61 million packages sent from the U.S. to other countries. Letters and documents, including lengthy legal briefs and drafts of ads, are the obvious—but not the only—items delivered by FedEx and its competitors. Overnight delivery is used for many other products, ranging from repair parts to computer components to live animals. Common to all these items is that speed of delivery is essential. Most overnight delivery companies guarantee delivery by a specific time; if deadlines are not met, they provide full refunds on request.

FedEx and UPS are integrated carriers. They own their fleets of planes and delivery trucks, and pilots and drivers are company employees. Integration provides each company with maximum control over its operations.

Like some commercial airlines, overnight delivery firms use a hub-and-spoke system. That is, packages go from the shipper's location to a sorting hub. FedEx's hubs are located in Memphis, Tennessee; Oakland, California; and Newark, New Jersey. At the hubs, packages are sorted and sent on to their final destinations.

The Major Players

The three competitors have attempted to gain market share by excelling in different characteristics of the basic service:

- FedEx emphasizes speed and dependability, backed by an annual promotional budget of about $40 million. The company claims that 99.5 percent of its deliveries are made by the customer's deadline. FedEx accounts for approximately 44 percent of the next-day shipments and 30 percent of the overnight shipments from the U.S. to other countries.
- Most of UPS's business is ground delivery of shipments by means of trucks. The company is more than twice the size of FedEx, with 1994 revenues of over $19 billion and an annual promotion budget of about $60 million. UPS entered the overnight delivery business in 1985 and is a formidable competitor for FedEx. The giant firm, which serves most countries of the world, acquired the coveted official sponsorship of the 1996 Olympics. UPS commands 27 percent of domestic overnight shipments and over 10 percent of overseas shipments.
- DHL, the oldest competitor in the express shipping business, is positioned as *the* choice for overseas shipments. In 1994, the company delivered 95 million packages, with about 75 percent going from the U.S. to other countries. Overall, DHL makes about 2 percent of domestic shipments and 13.5 percent of foreign shipments.
- The U.S. Postal Service, an agency of the federal government, is trying to operate like a large (in fact, a very large) business. The USPS provides overnight delivery, called Express Mail, at a basic rate comparable to its competitors. It also offers delivery of packages weighing up to 2 pounds in 2 or 3 days. This service, called Priority Mail, has a $3 price.

There are niche players in this industry as well. For example, Airborne Express "cherry picks" high-volume, business-to-business accounts. The firm has been very successful in its selected niche and represents 17 percent of domestic shipments, but less than 5 percent of overseas shipments.

Bases for Competition

Because the primary benefit of overnight delivery to the customer is speed, the three main business competitors have attempted to upstage each other on this one dimension. According to Peter Fredo, vice president of advertising for UPS, "It's no longer an issue of overnight, but rather what time of day." For different prices, FedEx guarantees delivery by various times of the day, the earliest being 8:30 a.m. UPS's *Early AM* service now guarantees overnight delivery by 8 a.m.

The competition has extended to same-day delivery. DHL has been offering this service, both domestically and internationally, since the start of the 1990s. On the same day in April 1995, both UPS and FedEx announced that they were matching DHL by offering same-day service.

All the emphasis on speed has made differentiation among companies difficult. Thus other dimensions have been explored as ways to gain a differential advantage.

Technology that enhances customer service is one such dimension. According to Robert Miller, vice president of FedEx, "Technology has become the key basis for differentiation. . . . It cuts across all parts of the company's operations, including aircraft that can land in severe weather, sophisticated customer service operations and package-tracking software."

FedEx established a home page on the World Wide Web in 1995. DHL also appeared on the Internet in 1995, displaying destination information and various DHL telephone numbers that customers may need.

One key technological advance is shipping software:

- DHL introduced software in 1995 that allows customers to determine where their shipments are at any time of the day.
- FedEx's Power Ship software, which also debuted in 1995, allows customers to request a pickup, print shipping labels, and track deliveries from a personal computer. The software has been distributed to over 11 million customers.
- In addition to its "800 PICK UPS" telephone line, UPS customers can use CompuServe or Prodigy to place orders or obtain information about the status of shipments. In addition, in 1995 UPS introduced MaxiCode, which is a machine-read label that is attached to packages. The label stores shipping information that helps expedite delivery. UPS is building a new hub on the outskirts of Chicago with machines that can read MaxiCodes.

Cost Cutting and Price Competition

Recently, the primary players in the overnight delivery business have emphasized cost cutting and, in turn, lower prices. DHL launched a 4-year, $1.25 billion project to improve its computer technology, communications, and handling facilities. UPS has spent $120 million to build new sorting hubs in Dallas, Texas; Rockford, Illinois; and Columbia, South Carolina. FedEx is investing $1.8 billion to switch to used Airbus Industrie planes from more costly Boeing 727s. FedEx also uses interactive video training to teach its employees the 700 identification codes needed to sort packages at its hubs and help service agents provide

customers with consistent information. The training videos have improved customer satisfaction rates, cut employee training time, and saved FedEx more than $3 million in training costs per year.

All these cost-cutting efforts, together with competitive pressures, have driven down prices. UPS has even introduced "distance-based pricing." Under this plan, prices are not flat rates but, rather, are based on the distance between the points of origination and destination. As a result of price competition, the industry's profit margin in the domestic market has shrunk to about 8 percent, compared to 12 percent in 1990.

Added Market Opportunities

The large overnight delivery firms continue to compete aggressively with respect to speed, technology, customer service, and price. At the same time, they are looking for market segments with untapped potential. FedEx, for instance, is actively pursuing more small accounts, which currently represent about one-third of its total business. The company's Value Plan uses price incentives for volume as a way of rewarding repeat purchases while discouraging switching to competitors. DHL also targets low-volume customers, but only in very specific geographic markets. UPS uses price structures based on volume and geography for business-to-business shipments.

Each of the three primary competitors also has a logistics unit that contracts with mail-order companies to handle their shipping needs. FedEx has agreements with L.L. Bean, Sharper Image, and Neiman Marcus. Competition for these large accounts is intense. UPS grabbed the account of Gateway 2000, which sells computers by mail order, away from FedEx. Retaliating, FedEx lured Williams-Sonoma away from UPS. "Our industry has become central to how companies do business, and they are putting within our hands increasingly larger parts of their businesses," said FedEx's Miller.

International markets represent the biggest potential for the overnight delivery business. According to FedEx's Miller, "Without development of an international network, you can't be a player." FedEx entered the European market in 1984. However, FedEx encountered numerous problems. To begin with, the company found it difficult to secure the necessary approvals to operate from foreign governments. The company kept all its forms and brochures in English, which failed to recognize language barriers in foreign markets and the potential of gaining an "ugly American" image. Its 5 p.m. deadline for package pickups across Europe did not consider the fact that firms in some countries work much later than this time. For example, in Spain, employees work to at least 8 p.m. Between 1985 and 1992, FedEx lost as much as $3 billion on its European operations. Its fortunes in Europe have improved since then, however.

FedEx has had a smoother path in Asia. FedEx received permission to use Asian routes purchased from

Tiger International (Flying Tigers). From its hub in Subic Bay in the Philippines, FedEx is serving Malaysia; Singapore; Taipei, Taiwan; Seoul, South Korea; and Tokyo and Osaka, Japan. FedEx has been successful in Asia despite cultural differences that work against overnight delivery in this part of the world. "Asians like to put letters in someone's hands to pass it off," said John Flick, international public relations manager for UPS.

UPS's business in Asia should increase after it completes its hub in Taiwan in 1998. However, its European operations have an accumulated loss of $1 billion since the 1980s. And DHL, although a strong international competitor, lacks capital to build facilities that match FedEx and UPS in foreign countries.

Future Prospects

The demand for overnight delivery service is projected to grow in the near future. However, there are some threats to the long-run performance of the industry. Although technology has allowed overnight delivery firms to provide faster and faster service, other technological advances represent a serious threat. For example, it is estimated that more than 30 percent of the letters sent by overnight delivery could be transmitted by facsimile machine or electronic mail (e-mail).

Other threats, or at least challenges, include those customers who become less interested in overnight delivery and more receptive to 2- or 3-day delivery at lower prices. In addition, demand has changed from documents to goods, as companies use express delivery companies for just-in-time inventory systems.

One of the biggest threats facing companies in the overnight delivery market is how to balance costs, while at the same time offering a full range of services. In an industry where fast is expected, the key to success is to make fast, faster. Is it possible for a package that's shipped today to be delivered yesterday?

http://www.fedex.com/

QUESTIONS

1. What can FedEx do to develop a differential advantage that cannot be quickly copied by its competitors?
2. What opportunities in specialized physical distribution services could FedEx pursue?

Sources: Lisa Colman, "Overnight Isn't Fast Enough," *BrandWeek*, July 31, 1995, p. 26; Emory Thomas, Jr., "Federal Express Is Set to Expand in Asian Market," *The Wall Street Journal*, July 24, 1995, p. A2; Alan Salomon, "Delivering a Market Battle," *Advertising Age*, July 17, 1995, p. I18; David Greising, "Watch Out for Flying Packages," *Business Week*, Nov. 14, 1994, p. 40; Robert Frank, "Federal Express Grapples with Changes in U.S. Market," *The Wall Street Journal*, July 5, 1994, p. B3; William Wilson, "Video Training and Testing Supports Customer Service Goals," *Personnel Journal*, June 1994, p. 47; Laurie M. Grossman, "Federal Express, UPS Face Off on Computers," *The Wall Street Journal*, Sept. 17, 1993, p. B1; and "All Strung Up," *The Economist*, Apr. 17, 1993, p. 70.

PART SIX

Promotion

Designing and managing the marketing-mix element to inform, persuade, and remind current and potential customers

We have examined product, price, and distribution—three of the four marketing-mix elements used by an organization to reach its target markets and achieve its marketing goals. To complete the marketing mix, we now turn our attention to promotion.

Chapter 16 provides an overview of promotion, including the various types of promotion, its use as a form of communication, management issues of promotion including the promotion mix, budget, and campaign concept, and the regulation of promotion. Chapter 17 looks at the personal selling process and sales-force management. Advertising, sales promotion, public relations, and publicity are the subjects of Chapter 18.

CHAPTER 16

The Promotional Program

Has
ALEVE
Given the Rest of the Analgesic Market a Headache?

In January 1994 the Food and Drug Administration approved a milder version of a prescription analgesic (pain reliever) called Naprosyn for sale without a prescription, or what is called "over the counter" (OTC). Naprosyn as a prescription drug had annual sales of $400 million, mostly to arthritis sufferers. So the potential for the OTC version, called Aleve, appeared to be very good.

In a joint venture, Aleve is manufactured by Syntex Laboratories and marketed by Procter & Gamble. So it has the marketing know-how and the resources of a premier packaged goods firm behind it. However, the situation in 1994 was not all rosy. The OTC pain-reliever market was already quite crowded. First there was aspirin, led by brands such as Bayer and Anacin. Then there were newer products such as Advil, Tylenol, and Nuprin. And there were many lower-priced private brands that, when combined, ranked second in total analgesic sales. Also, the FDA gave Syntex and P&G exclusive rights to manufacture and market the product for just 3 years from the approval date. After that, other firms could introduce generic versions. So the challenge was clear: Quickly establish a strong position for Aleve as an OTC pain reliever that would withstand not only the competition of existing brands but the threat of lower-priced imitations a few years down the road.

To accomplish this goal, P&G put together a potent distribution plan and promotion campaign. The promotion budget for the introduction was set at $100 million. It consisted of:

- $60 million in print and TV ads.
- $40 million in advertising to health professionals, personal selling to the retail trade and influentials (such as medical personnel and pharmacists), consumer education, sampling, and couponing.

Efforts to secure distribution for Aleve were highly successful. Before the launch, it was stocked by over 90 percent of the stores that carry pain relievers.

In formulating the promotional campaign, P&G commissioned some consumer research on pain. The study found that 75 percent of adults suffer pain, such as backache, muscular pain, arthritis, menstrual pain, dental pain, and headache, at least once every 3 months. P&G also discovered the majority of respondents felt that improved skill at describing their pain would be helpful in deciding what to do about it and in selecting an appropriate pain reliever. These findings led to the development of the consumer booklet called *Pain Talk*, which was distributed free to consumers. In addition to information about pain, the booklet includes a series of questions that enable people to understand their pain better.

Aleve's differential advantage is that one dose lasts 8 to 12 hours. Ads carry the tag line "All day strong, all day long." It comes in a childproof, easy-open container. In a move that is not characteristic of P&G, but one that reflects the intense competition in this market, the ads for Aleve make direct comparisons with other pain relievers. Though the ads target several audiences, including sports-related aches and pains, normal headaches, and other common pain, a major potential market is arthritis sufferers, many of whom are familiar with the prescription version.[1]

How important is promotion to the success of a new brand like Aleve?

http://www.pg.com/

439

Like all marketers, Procter & Gamble was faced with deciding how much and what types of promotion to undertake on behalf of its product, Aleve. These decisions are complicated by the fact that there are many forms of promotion and no two marketing situations are exactly alike. This chapter will help you understand how promotion decisions like these are made by describing what promotion is and how it fits into a firm's total marketing program. After studying this chapter, you should be able to explain:

CHAPTER GOALS

- The components of promotion and how they differ.
- The role promotion plays in an organization and in the economy.
- How the process of communicating relates to effective promotion.
- The concept and design of the promotional mix.
- The promotional campaign.
- Alternative promotional budgeting methods.
- The major types of promotion regulation.

Nature of Promotion

Promotion, in whatever form it takes, is an attempt to influence. More specifically, **promotion** is the element in an organization's marketing mix that serves to inform, persuade, and remind the market of a product and/or the organization selling it, in hopes of influencing the recipients' feelings, beliefs, or behavior.

Promotional Methods

There are five forms of promotion: personal selling, advertising, sales promotion, public relations, and publicity. Each has distinct features that determine in what situations it will be most effective:

- **Personal selling** is the direct presentation of a product to a prospective customer by a representative of the organization selling it. Personal selling takes place face-to-face or over the phone, and it may be directed to a middleman or a final consumer. We list it first because, across all businesses, more money is spent on personal selling than on any other form of promotion.
- **Advertising** is impersonal communication that the sponsor has paid for and in which the sponsor is clearly identified. The most familiar forms of ads are found in the broadcast (TV and radio) and print (newspapers and magazines) media. However, there are many other advertising vehicles, from direct mail to billboards and, more recently, the Internet.
- **Sales promotion** is demand-stimulating activity designed to supplement advertising and facilitate personal selling. It is paid for by the sponsor and frequently involves a temporary incentive to encourage a sale or purchase. Many sales promotions are directed at consumers. The majority, however, are designed to encourage the company's sales force or other members of its distribution channel to sell its products more aggressively. When sales promotion is directed to the members of the distribution channel, it is called *trade promotion*. Included in sales promotion are a wide spectrum of activities, such as event sponsorships, contests, trade shows, in-store displays, rebates, samples, premiums, discounts, and coupons.
- **Public relations** encompasses a wide variety of communication efforts to contribute to generally favorable attitudes and opinions toward an organization and its products. Unlike most advertising and personal selling, it does not include a specific sales message. The targets may be customers, stockholders, a government agency, or a special-interest group. Public relations can take many

Since the idea was introduced in 1936, Oscar Mayer Wienermobiles have traveled the highways of America promoting the company's products. The latest version is a 27-foot-long, 10-foot-high "hot dog hot rod" built on a General Motors chassis. There are actually six identical Wienermobiles that tour the country and attend national events such as the Super Bowl and Mardi Gras. The vehicles are driven by 12 recent college graduates (selected from 800 applicants) who spend a year as hot dog ambassadors of goodwill.

forms, including newsletters, annual reports, lobbying, and support of charitable or civic events. The Goodyear blimps and the Oscar Mayer Wienermobiles are familiar examples of public relations devices.

- **Publicity** is a special form of public relations that involves news stories about an organization or its products. Like advertising, it involves an impersonal message that reaches a mass audience through the media. But several things distinguish publicity from advertising: It is not paid for, the organization that is the subject of the publicity has little or no control over it, and it appears as news and therefore has greater credibility than advertising. Organizations seek good publicity and frequently provide the material for it in the form of news releases, press conferences, and photographs. When a picture of a company's CEO appears on the cover of a major business publication and is accompanied by a flattering article in the magazine, it is often attributable to the efforts of the firm's public relations department. There also is, of course, bad publicity, which organizations try to avoid or deflect.

The Communication Process and Promotion

Communication is the verbal or nonverbal transmission of information between someone wanting to express an idea and someone else expected or expecting to get that idea. Because promotion is a form of communication, much can be learned about structuring effective promotion by examining the communication process.

Fundamentally, communication requires only four elements: a message, a source of the message, a communication channel, and a receiver. In practice, however, important additional components come into play:

- The information that the sending source wants to share must first be *encoded* into a transmittable form. In marketing this means translating an idea ("You can trust Maytag to produce quality products") into words ("The lonely repairman"), pictures, or a combination of the two.
- Once the message has been transmitted through some communication channel, the symbols must be *decoded*, or given meaning, by the receiver. The received message may be what the sender intended ("Maytag appliances are reliable") or something else that is possibly less desirable ("Maytag exaggerates the quality of its appliances"), depending on the recipient's frame of reference.

http://www.maytag.com/

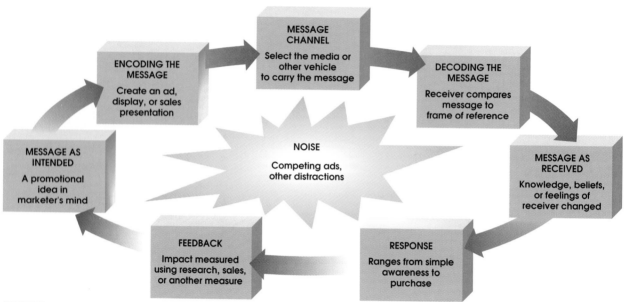

FIGURE 16-1
The communication process in promotion.

- If the message has been transmitted successfully, there is some change in the receiver's knowledge, beliefs, or feelings. As a result of this change, the receiver formulates a *response*. The response could be nonverbal (a smile while watching a humorous Maytag ad), verbal (suggesting to a friend that Maytag stresses reliability), or behavioral (visiting an appliance store to examine a Maytag product).
- The response serves as *feedback*, telling the sender whether the message was received and how it was perceived by the recipient. Through feedback the sender can learn what a communication accomplished. Then a new message can be formulated and the process begun again.
- All stages of the process can be affected by *noise*—that is, any external factor that interferes with successful communication. (All other ads, but particularly those for competing appliance brands, are noise for Maytag.)

Figure 16-1 illustrates these components of a communication process, and relates them to promotion activities.

What does the communication process tell us about promotion? First, the act of encoding reminds us that messages can take many forms. Messages can be physical (a sample, a premium) or symbolic (verbal, visual), and there are a myriad of options within each of these categories. For example, the form of a verbal message can be factual, humorous, or even threatening.

Second, the number of channels or methods of transmitting a message are limited only by the imagination and creativity of the sender. Most promotional messages are transmitted by familiar channels such as the voice of a sales person, the airwaves of radio, the mail, the side of a bus, or the lead-in to a feature in a movie theater. Each channel has its own characteristics in terms of audience reach, flexibility, permanence, credibility, and cost. In selecting a channel, a marketer must have clearly defined objectives and a familiarity with the features of the many alternatives. For example, how would you promote a medical product that permits easier breathing for people with allergies, sinus congestion, or snoring problems if you were constrained by a very limited budget? The marketers of Breathe Right, a product that expands nasal passages and comes in the form of a butterfly-shaped bandage

A dramatic presentation is necessary when the audience decoding and interpreting the message is uninterested or poorly informed.

that is placed across the bridge of the nose, sent a case to every team in the National Football League. When the product began showing up on television screens and in newspaper photos, curious consumers began asking questions and demand took off.

Third, how the message is decoded or interpreted depends on its form (encoding and transmission) and the capability and interest of the recipient. In designing and sending messages, marketers must be sensitive to the audience. What is their vocabulary and level of verbal sophistication? What other messages have they received? What experiences have they had? What will get and hold their attention?

Finally, every promotion should have a measurable objective. The response and feedback provided by the recipients can be used to determine if the objective is accomplished. Feedback may be collected in many forms—changes in sales, recall of advertising messages, more favorable attitudes, increased awareness of a product or an organization—depending on the objective of the promotion. For some promotional activities the objective may be modest, for example, an increase in the audience's awareness of a brand. For others, such as a direct-mail solicitation, the objective would be a particular level of sales. Without objectives, there is no way of evaluating the effectiveness of a message.

The Purposes of Promotion

One of the attributes of a free-market system is the right to use communication as a tool of influence. In our socioeconomic system, that freedom is reflected in the promotional efforts by businesses to influence the feelings, beliefs, and behavior of prospective customers. Let's examine how promotion works from an economic perspective and from a marketing perspective.

Promotion and Imperfect Competition
The American marketplace operates under conditions of imperfect competition, characterized by product differentiation, emotional buying behavior, and incomplete market information. A company uses promotion to provide more information

YOU MAKE THE DECISION

HOW POWERFUL IS COMMUNICATION?

Combine a half-truth with a suspicious audience willing to believe the worst, and some interesting and amusing communication can occur. Opponents of standardization in the European Union (EU) and tabloid newspapers eager to increase sales have distorted some proposals and regulations that have come out of the EU headquarters. The objective is to make the EU's standardization efforts look poorly thought out if not preposterous. Many Europeans, willing to believe the worst, have accepted the messages as facts. Some examples:

- Chocolates would be made with blood as an ingredient.
- All taxi cabs in the EU would be painted white.
- Certain maggots would be banned as fishing bait because they suffer when put on a hook.
- Fishing boats would be required to carry 200 condoms.
- Curved cucumbers would be banned.
- Valentine cards would be banned as a form of sexual harassment.
- Pizzas would have to be 11 inches in diameter.
- Square gin bottles would be outlawed.
- Stale bread could not be fed to British swans.

How can a skillful communicator influence perceptions?

Source: Dana Milbank, "Will Unified Europe Put Mules in Diapers and Ban Mini-Pizza?" *The Wall Street Journal*, June 22, 1995, pp. B1+.

for the decision maker's buying-decision process, to assist in differentiating its product, and to persuade potential buyers.

In economic terms, the purpose of promotion is to change the *location* and *shape* of the demand (revenue) curve for a company's product. (See Figure 16-2 and recall the discussion of nonprice competition in Chapter 12.) Through promotion a company strives to increase its product's sales volume at any given price (Figure 16-2a); that is, the firm seeks to shift its demand curve to the right. Simply stated, promotion is intended to make a product more attractive to prospective buyers.

A firm also hopes that promotion will affect the demand elasticity for its product (Figure 16-2b). Recall from Appendix A that elasticity is the responsiveness of demand to a change in price. The intent is to make the demand more *inelastic* when price increases, and more *elastic* when price decreases. In other words, management wants promotion to increase the attractiveness of a product so the quantity demanded will decline very little if price goes up (inelastic demand), and sales will increase considerably if price goes down (elastic demand).

Promotion and Marketing

Promotion serves three essential roles—it informs, persuades, and reminds prospective customers about a company and its products. The relative importance of these roles varies according to the circumstances faced by a firm.

The most useful product or brand will be a failure if no one knows it is available! Because distribution channels are often long, a product may pass through many hands between a producer and consumers. Therefore, a producer must *inform* middlemen as well as the ultimate consumers or business users about the product. Wholesalers, in turn, must inform retailers, and retailers must inform consumers. As the number of potential customers grows and the geographic dimensions of a market expand, the problems and cost of informing the market increase.

Franklin Sports Industries sells over $100 million a year of all types of sporting goods. Achieving that level of success in a market dominated by names such as Wilson and Spalding required a unique promotion strategy to create awareness of its brand name. Franklin developed a high-quality batting glove with its name in large letters across the back. Dozens of the gloves were given to professional and college baseball teams. Before long, nearly every batter who appeared on TV or in a sports

FIGURE 16-2

The goal of promotion is to change the pattern of demand for a product.

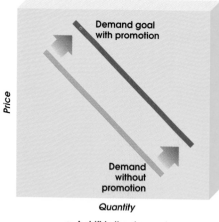

a. A shift in the demand curve to the right.

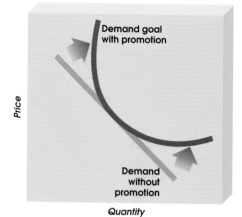

b. Changing the shape (or elasticity) of the demand curve.

magazine prominently displayed the Franklin name. The exposure gave Franklin credibility with sporting goods stores, which then began stocking its gloves and other products. Thus, a major purpose of promotion is to disseminate information—to let potential customers know about a product's existence, availability, and price.

Another purpose of promotion is *persuasion*. The intense competition among different industries, as well as among different firms in the same industry, puts tremendous pressure on the promotional programs of sellers. In our economy of abundance, even a product designed to satisfy a basic physiological need requires strong persuasive promotion, since consumers have many alternatives to choose from. Campbell Soup Company has been selling soup for over 120 years and has annual soup sales of over $1.8 billion. Studies show that virtually every U.S. household has some Campbell's soup in the pantry. Yet the firm spends over $60 million a year advertising soup because of strong competition from existing brands and new products targeted at the same market.[2] In the case of a luxury product, for which sales depend on the ability to convince consumers that the product's benefits exceed those of other luxuries, persuasion is even more important.

Consumers also must be *reminded* about a product's availability and its potential to satisfy. Sellers bombard the marketplace with thousands of messages every day in the hope of attracting new consumers and establishing markets for new products. Given the intense competition for consumers' attention, even an established firm must constantly remind people about its brand to retain a place in their minds. It is unlikely that a day goes by, for example, in which you don't see some form of promotion (an ad, in-store display, counter sign, billboard, or imprinted T-shirt) for Coca-Cola. In fact, the company spends over $95 million a year on advertising for Coca-Cola Classic *alone*. Thus, much of a firm's promotion may be intended simply to offset competitors' marketing activity by keeping its brand in front of the market.[3]

Promotion and Strategic Marketing Planning

A company's personal selling, advertising, and other promotional activities should form a coordinated promotional program within its total marketing plan. These activities are fragmented in many firms, with potentially damaging consequences.

http://www.campbellsoups.com/

http://www.coca-cola.com/

*C*oupons are now available in store aisles from dispensers with blinking red lights. Compared to free-standing inserts in a newspaper (the traditional method for distributing coupons) in-store dispensers don't require the consumer to remember to bring the coupon to the store. Though the redemption rate is much higher than for other methods of couponing, at only 16 percent it is surprisingly low. Apparently, many consumers who take coupons from dispensers decide not to buy the products or forget to turn them in at the checkout.

For example, advertising directors and sales-force managers may come into conflict over resources. But this wouldn't happen if the elements comprising promotion were a coordinated part of a firm's overall strategic marketing plan.

To be effective, promotional activities must also be coordinated with product planning, pricing, and distribution, the other marketing-mix elements. Promotion is influenced, for instance, by how distinctive a product is and whether its price is above or below the competition. A manufacturer or middleman must also consider its promotional interdependence with other firms in the distribution channel. For example, Chrysler recognizes that its success is closely tied to the performance of its dealers. Therefore, in addition to advertising its automobiles directly to consumers, Chrysler trains the dealers' sales people in how to show effectively a car and conduct a test-drive, and offers cash incentives to dealers with high customer-satisfaction scores.

http://www.chrysler.com/

Promotion should also contribute to a firm's overall strategic plan. Bausch & Lomb has achieved success with contact lenses by concentrating much of its promotional efforts on educating physicians. However, with the growing popularity of disposable lenses, the distribution of contacts has shifted from doctors' offices to optical retailers. To maintain its position as market leader, Bausch & Lomb found it necessary to shift its promotional efforts from physicians to lens wearers. In particular, it concentrates on teenagers with ads on MTV, free trial offers in teen magazines, and book covers and gym bags distributed in high schools.

A GLOBAL PERSPECTIVE

CAN STANDARDIZED COMMUNICATION BE PART OF A GLOBAL MARKETING STRATEGY?

There has been considerable discussion about how much a firm engaged in international markets can or should standardize its strategy. Of particular interest is the area of communications. If a firm used the same brand name and advertising worldwide, it could achieve a consistent worldwide image, reduce its costs, and simplify its decision making. However, cultural differences and idiosyncrasies of language make standardization in communications more difficult than, say, in manufacturing or accounting. For example, imagine how American consumers would respond to the brand names Pocari Sweat (a sports drink), Plopp Chocolates, or Choco Sand (a cream-filled cookie) if they were marketed in the U.S. Despite the possible problems, some firms standardize both their brand and advertising (Coca-Cola), some standardize the brand but vary the advertising (Volvo), some alter the brand names, but maintain common advertising themes (Procter & Gamble), and some make no attempt at standardization.

To investigate the extent that brand and advertising standardization are linked, two researchers examined 78 Canadian firms with international sales. They found a high degree of brand standardization (78 percent), but relatively little advertising standardization (18 percent). Of the firms that engaged in some standardization, only 17 percent standardized both their brand and advertising.

These results suggest that the decision to standardize is multidimensional. The nature of the product, the culture and language of the target market, and even the presence of a competitor with a similar name may make standardization inappropriate. For example, when it attempted to enter Eastern Europe, Budweiser found that an established local brand of beer with the same name already existed. Thus, to suggest that all firms should standardize their global communications strategy would be an oversimplification.

Source: Dennis M. Sandler and David Shani, "Brand Globally but Advertise Locally?" *Journal of Product & Brand Management*, No. 2, 1993, pp. 59–71.

Determining the Promotional Mix

A **promotional mix** is an organization's combination of personal selling, advertising, sales promotion, public relations, and publicity. An effective promotional mix is a critical part of virtually all marketing strategies. Product differentiation, market segmentation, trading up and trading down, and branding all require effective promotion. Designing an effective promotional mix involves a number of strategic decisions, as we shall now see.

Factors Influencing the Promotional Mix

These four factors should be taken into account when determining the promotional mix: (1) the target market, (2) the nature of the product, (3) the stage in the product's life cycle, and (4) the amount of money available for promotion.

Target Market. As in most areas of marketing, decisions on the promotional mix will be greatly influenced by the audience or target market. At least four variables affect the choice of a promotional method for a particular market:

- *Readiness to buy*. A target market can be in any one of six stages of buying readiness. These stages—awareness, knowledge, liking, preference, conviction, and purchase—are called the **hierarchy of effects** because they represent stages a buyer goes through in moving toward a purchase and each defines a possible goal or effect of promotion.

  At the *awareness* stage the seller's task is to let the buyers know that the product or brand exists. Here the objective is to build familiarity with the product and the brand name. Benetton has used what has become known as "shock advertising" to attract attention. A controversial series of print ads depicted various forms of human suffering including a dying AIDS victim, refugees jumping overboard from a ship, and a pool of blood from a war casualty. More recent Benetton ads, one showing an arm tattooed "HIV positive," have been banned in Germany.[4] These particular ads have attracted attention, but some observers feel they have overstepped the boundary of good taste.

  Knowledge goes beyond awareness to learning about a product's features. Enterprise Rent-A-Car uses as its symbol an automobile wrapped up as a package to signal that the company delivers the car to the renter's home. In a market with several well-established brands, Enterprise had to find a way to quickly and easily inform consumers how its service is unique.

  Liking refers to how the market feels about the product or brand. Promotion can be used to move a knowledgeable audience from being indifferent to liking a brand. A common technique is to associate the item with an attractive symbol or person. No Fear apparel company uses endorsements from over 200 athletes to communicate its message of taking on and overcoming the fear that accompanies all worthwhile tasks.[5]

  Creating *preference* involves distinguishing among brands such that the market prefers yours. It is not uncommon to like several brands of the same product, but the customer can't make a decision until one brand is preferred over the alternatives. Ads that make direct comparisons with the competition are intended to create a preference. In the competition for long-distance customers, MCI compares its price to AT&T's, while AT&T compares its service reputation to that of MCI.

  Conviction entails the actual decision or commitment to purchase. A student may prefer the IBM PC over a clone, but not yet be convinced to buy a

http://www.benetton.com/

http://www.mci.com/
http://www.att.com/

computer. The promotion objective here is to increase the strength of the buyer's need. Trying a product and experiencing the benefits that come from using it are very effective in strengthening the conviction to own it. Radio Shack encourages consumers to visit its stores and try its computers, and auto dealers invite consumers to test-drive new cars.

Purchase can be delayed or postponed indefinitely, even for customers who are convinced they should buy a product. The inhibitor might be a situational factor such as not having enough money at the moment, or a natural resistance to change. Action may be triggered through a promotional price discount or the offer of additional incentives. Microsoft's Windows 95 software package hit the market amidst unprecedented publicity and strong consumer demand. Yet some computer stores used it as an incentive, giving it away to consumers who purchased a PC.

- *Geographic scope of the market.* Personal selling may be adequate in a small local market, but as the market broadens geographically, greater emphasis is usually placed on advertising. The exception would be a firm that sells to concentrated pockets of customers scattered around the country. For example, the market for certain plastics is heaviest in Ohio and Michigan, because these plastics are used by component suppliers to the auto industry. In this case, emphasis on personal selling may be feasible.

- *Type of customer.* Promotional strategy depends in part on what level of the distribution channel the organization hopes to influence. Final consumers and middlemen sometimes buy the same product, but they require different promotion. To illustrate, 3M Company sells its computer diskettes to final consumers through computer and office supply stores. Promotion to dealers includes sharing the cost of yellow pages ads and advertising in specialized business magazines such as *Office Products Dealer*. Different ads aimed at final consumers are run in magazines such as *Personal Computing*, *Fortune*, and *Business Week*. In many situations middlemen may strongly affect a manufacturer's promotional strategy. Large retail chains may refuse to stock a product unless the manufacturer agrees to provide adequate promotional support.

    Another consideration is the variety among the target markets for a product. A market with only one type of customer will call for a different promotional mix than a market with many target markets. A firm selling large power saws used exclusively by lumber manufacturers may rely only on personal selling. In contrast, a company selling portable handsaws to consumers and to construction firms will probably include an ample portion of advertising in its mix. Personal selling would be prohibitively expensive in reaching the firm's many customers.

- *Concentration of the market.* The total number of prospective buyers is another consideration. The fewer potential buyers there are, regardless of where they are located, the more effective personal selling is, compared with advertising. For example, there are only 31 manufacturers of household vacuum cleaners in the U.S., and 8 of those produce 85 percent of all the machines. Clearly, for a firm selling a component part for vacuum cleaners, personal selling would be the best way to reach this market.

Nature of the Product. Several product attributes influence promotional strategy. The most important are:

- *Unit value.* A product with low unit value is usually relatively uncomplicated, involves little risk for the buyer, and must appeal to a mass market to survive. As a result, advertising would be the primary promotional tool. In contrast, high-unit-value products often are complex and expensive. These features suggest the need for personal selling. BMW dealers are being encouraged to have sales people get out of the showroom and call on prospects. By increasing the personal selling effort through techniques such as delivering cars to potential customers for test drives, BMW hopes to stimulate declining U.S. sales.

- *Degree of customization.* If a product must be adapted to the individual customer's needs, personal selling is necessary. Thus, you would expect to find an emphasis on personal selling for something like home remodeling or an expensive suit of clothing. However, the benefits of most standardized products can be effectively communicated in advertising. Although this principle holds true for many products, it is being challenged by firms implementing what is known as *mass customization.* Advances in production techniques and information management have made it possible to customize some products for large markets. Recall the case introducing Chapter 10. Levi Strauss produces individual, custom-fit jeans for women. A customer's measurements are taken in a retail store, transmitted by computer to a Levi factory, and a custom-fit pair of jeans is produced and sent to the store.

- *Presale and postsale service.* Products that must be demonstrated, for which there are trade-ins, or that require frequent servicing to keep them in good working order lend themselves to personal selling. Typical examples are riding lawn mowers, power boats, and personal computers.

Stage in the Product Life Cycle.   Promotion strategies are influenced by a product's life-cycle stage. When a new product is introduced, prospective buyers must be informed about its existence and its benefits, and middlemen must be convinced to carry it. Thus both advertising (to consumers) and personal selling (to middlemen) are critical in a product's introductory stage. At introduction a new product also may be something of a novelty, offering excellent opportunities for publicity. Later, if a product becomes successful, competition intensifies and more emphasis is placed on persuasive advertising. Table 16-1 shows how promotional strategies change as a product moves through its life cycle.

http://www.levi.com/

*S*ome nontraditional "media" are being used to gain access to hard-to-reach consumers. In this example, sponsors provide backboards, rims, and nets on school playgrounds in exchange for placing the donor-company's logo on the board along with a motivational message. So far, over 1,500 backboards have been placed in major metro areas. How does this type of exposure benefit the sponsor?

TABLE 16-1 Promotional strategies for different product life-cycle stages

Market situation	Promotional strategy
Introduction Stage	
Customers are not aware of the product's features, nor do they understand how it will benefit them.	Inform and educate potential customers that the product exists, how it might be used, and what want-satisfying benefits it provides.
	In this stage, a seller must stimulate primary demand—the demand for a type of product—as contrasted with selective demand—the demand for a particular brand. For example, producers had to sell consumers on the value of compact discs in general before they considered it feasible to promote a particular brand.
	Normally, heavy emphasis must be placed on personal selling. Exhibits at trade shows are also used extensively in the promotional mix. A trade show gives a new product broad exposure to many middlemen. Manufacturers also rely heavily on personal selling to attract middlemen to handle a new product.
Growth Stage	
Customers are aware of the product's benefits. The product is selling well, and middlemen want to handle it.	Stimulate selective (brand) demand as competition grows. Increase emphasis on advertising. Middlemen share more of the total promotional effort.
Maturity Stage	
Competition intensifies and sales level off.	Advertising is used more to persuade rather than only to provide information. Intense competition forces sellers to devote larger sums to advertising and thus contributes to the declining profits experienced in this stage.
Decline Stage	
Sales and profits are declining. New and better products are coming into the market.	All promotional efforts are cut back substantially. The focus moves to reminding remaining customers.

Funds Available.   Regardless of what may be the most desirable promotional mix, the amount of money available for promotion is the ultimate determinant of the mix. A business with ample funds can make more effective use of advertising than a firm with limited financial resources. Small or financially weak companies are likely to rely on personal selling, dealer displays, or joint manufacturer-retailer promotions. For example, Earth's Best, a manufacturer of organic baby food that sells at a price 50 percent higher than major brands like Gerber's, is a small firm with a limited promotional budget. To stretch its budget as far as possible, Earth's Best uses a highly targeted newsletter to maintain contact with interested consumers, reduced-price coupons to gain trial, and an 800 phone number consumers can use to ask questions and find out which retailers carry the brand.[6]

Lack of money may limit the options a firm has for its promotional effort. For example, television advertising can carry a particular promotional message to far

http://www.earthsbest.com/

http://www.gerber.com/

more people and at a lower cost per person than most other media. Yet a firm may have to rely on less expensive media, such as yellow pages advertising, because it lacks the funds to take advantage of television's efficiency.

Choosing a Push or a Pull Strategy

As we have seen, producers aim their promotional mix at both middlemen and end users. A promotion program aimed primarily at middlemen is called a **push strategy**, and a promotion program directed primarily at end users is called a **pull strategy**. Figure 16-3 contrasts these two strategies.

Using a push strategy means a channel member directs its promotion primarily at the middlemen that are the next link forward in the distribution channel. The product is "pushed" through the channel. Take the case of a hardware producer that sells its tools and replacement parts to household consumers through wholesalers and retailers such as Ace and True Value. The producer will promote heavily to wholesalers, which then also use a push strategy to retailers. In turn, the retailers promote to consumers. A push strategy usually involves a lot of personal selling and sales promotion, including contests for sales people and displays at trade shows. This promotional strategy is appropriate for many manufacturers of business products, as well as for various consumer goods.

With a pull strategy, promotion is directed at end users—usually ultimate consumers. The intention is to motivate them to ask retailers for the product. The retailers, in turn, will request the product from wholesalers, and wholesalers will order it from the producer. In effect, promotion to consumers is designed to "pull" the product through the channel. This strategy relies on heavy advertising and sales promotion such as premiums, samples, or in-store demonstrations.

Retailers have little incentive to provide shelf space for minor variations of existing brands unless they are confident the products will sell. So manufacturers of consumer packaged goods often use a pull strategy to get new products stocked on supermarket shelves. For example, to introduce Aleve, P&G supplemented its sales effort to retailers by spending $60 million on consumer advertising. At this spending level, retailers had some assurance that the brand would sell.

FIGURE 16-3
Push and pull promotional strategies.

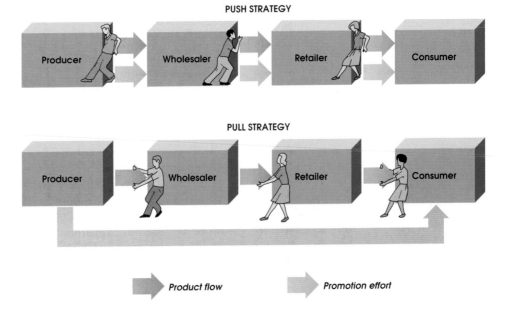

The Campaign Concept

Having examined the factors that influence the promotional mix, we turn our attention to a promotional campaign. In planning the promotional program for an organization, management should think in terms of the campaign concept. A **campaign** is a coordinated series of promotional efforts built around a defined theme and designed to reach an agreed-upon goal in a specified period of time. In effect, a campaign is an exercise in strategic planning.

http://www.ibm.com/

Although the term "campaign" is probably thought of most often in connection with the advertising component of promotion, it should embrace the entire promotional program. In developing a campaign, a company coordinates its advertising, personal selling, sales promotion, public relations, and publicity to accomplish an objective. For example, in the early 1990s, IBM's promotional efforts had become highly fragmented. The company was using over 80 advertising agencies around the world, and its ads were sending mixed messages. To rectify the problem, the 80 agencies were replaced by one; all packaging, brochures, and trade show booths were standardized to present a unified image; and IBM sports sponsorships were consolidated in a few big events in order to better showcase its technology. Promotion at IBM is now built around the theme of being a technology innovator that is accessible and responsive.[7]

A company may conduct many types of promotional campaigns, and even run some concurrently. Depending on objectives and available funds, a firm may have local, regional, national, and international campaigns all running at the same time. Moreover, a firm may have one campaign aimed at consumers, and another at wholesalers and retailers.

http://www.ppg.com/

A promotional campaign begins with an objective. When PPG Industries acquired Olympic Stain and Lucite, it set out to make these paint brands category leaders in the $14 billion coatings market.[8] Next, the buying motives of the target market are examined to determine the best selling appeal. To be successful, the promotion campaign must offer ways customers can solve their problems, satisfy their desires, or reach their goals. PPG focused on do-it-yourselfers with TV advertising. By expanding the Lucite and Olympic product lines, and providing simplified instructions for specific painting projects, the company got the market's attention and showed how the brands would meet consumers' needs.

A campaign revolves around a theme or central idea. A *campaign theme* is simply the promotional appeals dressed up in a distinctive, attention-getting form. The theme for Lucite is "Lucite's right," presented with a paint splash symbol. It expresses the product's benefits—the right paint for the job.

With the theme established, each of the promotion-mix components is carefully coordinated in a strategy that is called **integrated marketing communications**. This means that:

- The advertising program consists of a series of related, well-timed, carefully placed ads that reinforce personal selling and sales promotional efforts.
- The personal selling effort is coordinated with the advertising program. The sales people must be fully informed about the advertising part of the campaign—the theme, media used, and schedule for the appearance of ads. The sales force should be prepared to explain and demonstrate the product benefits stressed in the ads. The sales people also should transmit the promotional message to middlemen so they can take part in the campaign.
- The sales promotional devices, such as point-of-purchase display materials, are coordinated with other aspects of the campaign. New display materials must

be prepared for each campaign. They should reflect the ads and appeals used in the current campaign to maximize the campaign's impact at the point of sale.

- Publicity and public relations efforts are scheduled to coincide with the other mix components and to emphasize the same theme.

The last step in a campaign is to evaluate the results. The outcome is compared with the objective to determine if the promotional effort was successful. Unfortunately, in evaluating promotion it is impossible to precisely separate the effects caused by a campaign from what would have occurred without it. As a result, it is impossible to determine exactly the value of a campaign. However, by comparing the cost of a campaign with the results, a firm can decide if the campaign was generally a success or a failure and identify ways of improving future efforts. In the case of PPG Industries, Olympic Stain has become the number-one exterior stain in the U.S., and Lucite is ahead of its forecasted performance.[9]

The Promotional Budget

Establishing promotional budgets is extremely challenging because management lacks reliable standards for determining how much to spend altogether on advertising or personal selling, and how much of the total budget to allocate to each promotional-mix element. A firm may have the alternative of adding five sales people or increasing its trade show budget by $200,000 a year, but it cannot determine precisely what increase in sales or profits to expect from either expenditure. As a result, rather than one generally accepted approach, there are four common **promotional budgeting methods**: percentage of sales, all available funds, following the competition, and budgeting by task or objective. These methods are frequently discussed in connection with the advertising budget, but they may be applied to any promotional activity as well as to determine the total promotional budget.

Percentage of Sales

The promotional budget may be related in some way to company income, as a percentage of either past or anticipated sales. A common approach for determining the sales base is to compute an average between the previous year's actual sales and expected sales for the coming year. Some businesses prefer to budget a fixed amount of money per unit of past or expected future sales. Manufacturers of products with a high unit value and a low rate of turnover (automobiles or appliances, for example) frequently use the unit method.

Because the percentage-of-sales method is simple to calculate, it is probably the most widely used budgeting method. Moreover, it sets the cost of promotion in relation to sales income, making it a variable rather than a fixed expense.

There are two important limitations of basing promotional expenditures on past sales. First, management is effectively making promotion a *result* of sales when, in fact, it is a *cause* of sales. Second, using the percentage of past sales method reduces promotional expenditures when sales are declining—just when promotion usually is most needed.

All Available Funds

A new company or a firm introducing a new product frequently plows all available funds into its promotional program. The objective is to build sales and market share as rapidly as possible during those early, critical years. After a time, management generally finds it necessary to invest in other things, such as new

SHOULD PROMOTION BE TREATED AS AN EXPENSE OR AN INVESTMENT?

Promotional activities generally are budgeted as current operating expenses, implying that their benefits are used up immediately. Through the years, however, several economists and executives have proposed that advertising (and presumably other promotional efforts) be treated as capital investment. Their reason is that the benefits and returns on these expenditures are like investments, often not immediately evident, instead accruing over several years. For example, a company like Holiday Inn may build awareness and familiarity with a consumer for years through its advertising before it actually realizes a sale.

Would it affect management's thinking to treat promotion as an expense for accounting purposes, but as an investment for marketing purposes?

equipment or expanded production capacity, so the method of setting the promotional budget is changed.

Follow Competition

A weak method of determining the promotional budget, but one that is used occasionally, is to match the promotional expenditures of competitors or to spend in proportion to market share. Sometimes only one competitor is followed. In other cases, if management has access to industry average expenditures on promotion through a trade association, these become company benchmarks.

There are at least two problems with this approach. First, a firm's competitors may be just as much in the dark regarding how to set a promotional budget. Second, a company's promotional goals may be quite different from its competitors' because of differences in strategic marketing planning.

Task or Objective

The best approach for establishing the promotional budget is to determine the tasks or objectives the promotional program must accomplish and then decide what they will cost. The task method forces management to realistically define the goals of its promotional program.

This is often called the *buildup method* because of the way the budget is constructed. For example, a company may elect to enter a new geographic market. Management determines this venture will require 10 additional sales people. Compensation and expenses of these people will cost a total of $520,000 per year. Salary for an additional sales supervisor and expenses for an extra office and administrative needs will cost $70,000. Thus in the personal selling part of the promotional mix, an extra $590,000 must be budgeted. Similar estimates can be made for the anticipated costs of advertising, sales promotion, and other promotional tools. The promotional budget is built up by adding up the costs of the individual promotional tasks needed to reach the goal of entering a new territory.

Regulation of Promotional Activities

Because a primary objective of promotion is to sell something through persuasion, the potential for abuse always exists. As a result, some firms must be discouraged or prevented from intentional or unintentional misrepresentation. In addition, some consumers, because they lack particular knowledge or skills, need protection from being misled. Thus, there is a need for regulation to discourage the occurrence of abuses and to correct those that do occur.

Regulations have been established by the federal government and most state and local governments in response to public demand. In addition, many individual business firms have established voluntary guidelines for their promotional activities.

Federal Regulation

Federal regulation of promotional activities applies to firms engaged in *interstate* commerce. It is authorized by three major pieces of legislation: the Federal Trade Commission Act and the Robinson-Patman Act, both administered by the Federal Trade Commission (FTC), and the Lanham Trademark Act.

The measure that has the broadest influence on promotional messages is the **Federal Trade Commission Act**. The act prohibits unfair methods of competition. And, according to FTC and federal court decisions, clearly one area of unfair competition is false, misleading, or deceptive advertising.[10]

Under the original Federal Trade Commission Act, false or misleading advertising had to injure a competitor before a violation could be charged. This loophole led to the enactment of the **Wheeler-Lea Amendment** to the FTC Act in 1938. This amendment considerably strengthened the original act by specifying that an unfair competitive act violates the law if it injures the *public*, regardless of the effect it may have on a competitor.

The FTC has plenty of clout—particularly in cases of possibly false or deceptive advertising. For example, the commission may require a company to *substantiate* its advertising claims by submitting test results or other supporting research. Furthermore, this supporting information may be made public even if it could embarrass the company. If the FTC determines advertising is deceptive, it requests that the advertiser sign a *consent decree*, which amounts to an agreement to stop making the deceptive claim. Another FTC regulatory tool is the *cease-and-desist order*. If an ad or a claim is deemed deceptive, and the advertiser refuses to sign a consent decree, the FTC may compel a firm to remove it from circulation. A cease-and-desist order may be appealed to the FTC and fought in federal court, during which time the advertising is allowed to continue.

The FTC also has the authority to order *restitution* to compensate consumers for damages resulting from a false ad. However, because of the severe damage it could do to a company, the FTC has seldom resorted to requiring restitution.

Probably the FTC's most potent remedy is *corrective advertising*. A consent decree or a cease-and-desist order may force a firm to stop running a deceptive ad, but that does not rectify the incorrect impressions already made by the ad. Corrective advertising, paid for by the offending firm, and with the content and schedule approved by the FTC, is intended to correct misinformation resulting from the allegedly false ads. Among the products for which corrective ads have been run are Hawaiian Punch, Profile Bread, STP motor oil additive, Listerine mouthwash, and Ocean Spray cranberry juice. For example, to counteract a long-running claim, Listerine was required to include messages in $10 million worth of advertising that it did not cure colds or lessen their seriousness. Since corrective ads have proven to be only marginally successful in eliminating false impressions, their use has been curtailed. However, they remain an option and may serve to deter advertisers who might be tempted to use misleading claims.

The **Robinson-Patman Act**, which is best known for outlawing price discrimination, has two sections relating to promotional allowances offered to wholesalers and retailers. These sections state that a seller must offer promotional services or payments for them, on a *proportionally equal* basis to all competing wholesalers or retailers. Thus, if a manufacturer wants to furnish in-store demonstrators, advertising support, or any other type of promotional assistance, it must make it available proportionally to all firms competing in the resale of the product. "Proportionally equal" has sometimes been hard to define. Generally the courts have accepted the amount of the product purchased as a basis for allocation. Say, for example, that Martin's, a regional supermarket chain, buys $150,000 worth of merchandise per year from a grocery wholesaler, and Hank's, a neighborhood grocery store, purchases $15,000 worth from the same wholesale firm. The wholesaler may legally offer Martin's promotional allowances valued at 10 times those offered to Hank's.

The 1946 **Lanham Trademark Act** made false claims about one's own products illegal. It was broadened in 1988 by the **Trademark Law Revision Act** to encompass comparisons made in promotional activity. Under this law, a firm can seek damages if a competitor in its advertising or promotions makes false comparisons. For example, if a firm compared the price of its lesser-quality product to the price of a competitor's superior-quality product without disclosing the quality differences, it would be engaging in a false comparison. In a precedent-setting case, Jartran was required to pay U-Haul $40 million for misleading comparisons of the rental fees and sizes of their trucks.

Several other federal agencies are involved in the regulation of promotion. The Federal Communications Commission (FCC) licenses radio and television stations. Its mandate, to ensure that public interest is considered, combined with its authority to remove or deny the renewal of licenses, gives the FCC considerable power over the content of advertising. In addition, the FCC oversees the telephone industry, giving it jurisdiction over telemarketing.

The Food and Drug Administration (FDA) is responsible for the regulation of labeling, packaging, branding, ingredient listing, and advertising of packaged food and drug products. The FDA is responsible for warning labels that appear in food and drug ads, and it has established legal definitions for terms such as "natural," "light," and "low fat" when they are used in advertising and promotion. The U.S. Postal Service regulates advertising done through the mail. Of particular concern is the use of the mail to commit fraud or distribute obscene material. The Postal Service also oversees sales promotions such as premiums, contests, coupons, and samples that are sent through the mail.

State and Local Regulation

Legislation at the state level is intended to regulate promotional activities in *intrastate* commerce. Most of these state statutes are patterned after a model developed by *Printers' Ink* magazine in 1911 to establish truth in advertising. Today 44 states have **Printers' Ink statutes** to punish "untrue, deceptive, or misleading" advertising. Several states have also established separate state agencies to handle consumer protection, and some states' attorneys general have taken a very proactive stance in regulating promotional activity.

A general type of local legislation that affects personal selling is the so-called **Green River ordinance** (so-named because Green River, Wyoming, was one of the first towns to enact such a law). Green River ordinances restrict sales people who represent firms located outside the affected city and who sell door to door or call on business establishments. To operate in a community with a Green River ordinance, a sales person is typically required to register locally and purchase a license. Supposedly passed to protect local citizens from fraudulent operators, the measures also serve to insulate local businesses from outside competition.

AN ETHICAL DILEMMA?

Promotions for planned communities—complete towns constructed by developers with strict design, layout, and appearance restrictions—often emphasize neighborliness even before the first street is paved. With themes like a sense of community and the friendliness of small-town living, the promotional programs use people's fear of crime and social isolation common in big cities to attract home buyers. Critics of the appeals argue that a sense of community cannot be "manufactured." It comes from the efforts of residents, and it requires a flexibility and spontaneity not found in planned developments.

Is it ethical to portray a product in terms of what it *might become* rather than what it *actually is*? In the case of planned communities, is it ethical to show ads portraying neighborhood parties, holiday parades, and children on school playgrounds when all that exists is undeveloped land?

Source: Fara Warner, "Ads Show Idyllic Villages, but Buyers Should Beware," *The Wall Street Journal*, May 10, 1995, p. B1.

Regulation by Private Organizations

Numerous private organizations exert considerable control over the promotional practices of business. For example, the Council of Better Business Bureaus and several advertising trade associations joined forces to create a self-regulation process. The result is an agency called the National Advertising Division (NAD), which investigates complaints of false and misleading advertising brought by competitors, consumers, and local Better Business Bureaus. If NAD finds an ad unsatisfactory, it will negotiate with the advertiser to discontinue or modify the ad. In a recent year the NAD conducted 87 investigations. In about 35 percent of the cases the ad claims were substantiated and the complaints were rejected. Though NAD cannot force compliance or sanction an advertiser in any way, in nearly all the remaining cases the ads were changed or dropped.[11]

The media also serve a regulatory role. Virtually all publications and broadcasters have established standards for acceptable advertising. Some standards affect an entire industry; for example, hard liquor ads are banned by broadcasters. Others deal with the specifics of how a product can be advertised. For example, in ads directed at children, the three major networks have specified that the words "just" and "only" cannot be used in reference to price. Standards in the print media tend to vary by the size and type of publication. Some are quite strict. For example, *Good Housekeeping* and *Parent* magazines test products to substantiate the claims before ads are accepted. Finally, some trade associations have established codes of ethics that include standards for sales-force behavior and advertising activity.

■ SUMMARY

Promotion, the fourth component of a company's total marketing mix, is essential in modern marketing. The three primary methods of promotion are personal selling, advertising, and sales promotion. Other forms include public relations and publicity.

Promotion is communication. Fundamentally, the communication process consists of a source sending a message through a channel to a receiver. The success of communication depends on how well the message is encoded, how easily and clearly it can be decoded, and whether any noise interferes with its transmission. Feedback, the response created by a message, is a measure of how effective a communication has been.

The purposes of promotion are to inform, persuade, and remind customers. In economic terms, that means changing a firm's demand curve—either shifting it to the right or changing its shape to make demand inelastic when prices increase and elastic when prices decrease.

Promotion must be integrated into a firm's strategic planning because effective execution requires that all elements of the marketing mix—product, price, distribution, and promotion—be coordinated. When deciding on the promotional mix (the combination of advertising, personal selling, and other promotional tools), management should consider (1) the nature of the market, including the type of customer, the prospect's readiness to buy, and the geographic scope of the market; (2) the nature of the product, including unit value, the degree of customization required, and the amount of presale and postsale service; (3) the stage of the product's life cycle; and (4) the funds available for promotion.

A basic decision is how much promotional effort should be focused on middlemen and how much should be directed to end users. The options are a push strategy, which involves concentrating promotional effort on the next link forward in the distribution channel, and a pull strategy, in which promotion is focused primarily on the final buyer.

A promotional campaign is a coordinated series of efforts built around a defined theme and designed to reach a predetermined goal. The key to a successful promotional campaign is to carefully plan and coordinate advertising, sales promotion, personal selling, public relations, and publicity.

Because the effects of promotion are unpredictable, it is difficult to set a dollar figure for the total promotional budget. The most common method is to set the budget as a percentage of past or anticipated sales. Other methods include using all available funds and following the competition. The best approach is to set the budget by establishing the promotional objectives and then estimating how much it will cost to achieve them.

In response to the desire to protect consumers and curb abuses, there are a number of federal laws and agencies regulating promotion. Promotional practices also are regulated by state and local legislation, by private organizations, and by industry.

More about

ALEVE

The analgesic market in the mid-1990s exceeded $2.5 billion. Aleve's goal was to capture $200 million in sales its first year. Because the market is mature, it was assumed that most of the sales would have to come at the expense of existing brands.

However, the competition was not willing to watch quietly as its market share was eroded by this newcomer. Virtually all brands retaliated to the introduction of Aleve. For example:

- Johnson & Johnson got FDA approval for a version of Tylenol called Extended Relief that also lasts 8 to 12 hours, and launched it with a $40 million ad campaign. In addition J&J joined with the Arthritis Foundation to launch a pain-relief brand under that nonprofit group's name.
- Sterling Winthrop, the maker of Bayer aspirin, increased its ad spending by $20 million and began focusing on aspirin as a means of preventing heart attacks.

- American Home Products Corporation, parent of the maker of Advil, sued P&G on the grounds that the ad claims for Aleve are unsubstantiated. AHP's position is that the 8- to 12-hour dosage claim made by Aleve refers to how frequently the product can be safely taken, not to how long it is effective.
- Upjohn Co., maker of Motrin IB, and Bristol-Meyers Squibb, maker of Nuprin, also significantly increased their advertising.

The effect of this activity by Procter & Gamble and its competitors was to increase the total demand for analgesics. As for Aleve, only 3 months after its introduction, it had achieved a 6.5 percent share of the market, making it the #3 brand.[12]

1. Following the market's response to the flurry of activity that surrounded the launch of Aleve, are more new analgesics likely to be introduced?
2. What role will promotion play in the future of the brands in this market?

■ KEY TERMS AND CONCEPTS

Promotion (440)
Personal selling (440)
Advertising (440)
Sales promotion (440)
Public relations (440)
Publicity (441)
Communication (441)
Promotional mix (447)

Hierarchy of effects (447)
Push strategy (451)
Pull strategy (451)
Campaign (452)
Integrated marketing
   communications (452)
Promotional budgeting
   methods (453)

Federal Trade
   Commission Act (455)
Wheeler-Lea
   Amendment (455)
Robinson-Patman Act (455)
Lanham Trademark
   Act (456)

Trademark Law Revision
   Act (456)
Printers' Ink statutes (456)
Green River
   ordinance (456)

■ QUESTIONS AND PROBLEMS

1. Relate the components of the communication process model to the following situations:
   a. A college student trying to convince her father to buy her a used car.
   b. A sales person presenting a car to a college student.
2. Explain how the nature of the market affects the promotional mix for the following products:
   a. Contact lenses
   b. Golf balls
   c. Plywood
   d. Take-out fried chicken
   e. Compact discs
   f. Mainframe computers
3. Describe how classifying consumer goods as convenience, shopping, or specialty goods helps determine the best promotional mix.
4. Evaluate each of the following products with respect to the criteria for advertisability. Assume that sufficient funds are available.
   a. Automobile tires
   b. Revlon cosmetics
   c. Light bulbs
   d. 10-minute automobile oil changes
   e. College education
   f. Luggage

5. Explain why personal selling would or would not likely be the main ingredient in the promotional mix for each of the following products:
   a. Checking accounts
   b. Home swimming pools
   c. Liquid laundry detergent
   d. Large order of McDonald's french fries
6. Explain whether retailer promotional efforts should be stressed in the promotional mix for the following:
   a. Levi's 501 jeans
   b. Sunkist oranges
   c. Women's cosmetics
   d. Bank credit cards
7. Select three current promotional campaigns and identify the central idea—the theme—being communicated.
8. Assume you are marketing a liquid that removes creosote (and the danger of fire) from chimneys in home fireplaces. Briefly describe the roles you would assign to advertising, personal selling, sales promotion, and publicity in your promotional campaign.
9. Do you think we need additional legislation to regulate advertising? To regulate personal selling? If so, explain what you would recommend.

■ HANDS-ON MARKETING

1. An ad should have a particular objective that should be apparent to a careful observer. For each of the following promotional objectives, find an example of a print ad:
   a. Primarily designed to inform.
   b. Primarily designed to persuade.
   c. Primarily designed to remind.
2. A promotional campaign is a coordinated series of promotional efforts built around a single theme and de-signed to reach a predetermined goal. A campaign often includes advertising, sales promotion, personal selling, public relations, and publicity. For an important event at your school (such as a homecoming, recruiting new students, a fund-raising effort), describe the promotional tools used in the campaign and evaluate their appropriateness based on the criteria in the chapter for designing a promotional mix.

CHAPTER 17

Personal Selling and Sales Management

Can
AGCO
Continue to Reap What It Has Sown?

AGCO Corporation, a manufacturer of farm equipment, was founded in 1990 when the CEO, Robert Ratliff, put together a team to buy Deutz-Allis, a tractor producer. By 1995, the firm had sales of $2.1 billion and profits of $129 million. Even at that, AGCO has less than 10 percent of the North American market (it also does business in Europe, Asia, and Africa). Still, the firm's growth rate has surprised virtually everyone because the farm-equipment market has been in the doldrums for several years.

Much of AGCO's success can be attributed to its extensive product line, its sales force, and its dealer network. To develop its product line, the firm has bought out well-known brands such as White, Hesston, and Massey-Ferguson. Equally important, AGCO has purchased the dealer contracts of these acquired brands. As a result, the firm not only gets established brand names, it gets dealers familiar with them. In this way, AGCO has developed a dealer network of over 7,000 outlets, 3,000 of them in North America.

Volume bonuses based on their total AGCO sales encourage dealers to carry several of AGCO's many products and brands. In addition, there are trips to resorts for dealers who meet their quotas on each AGCO product they sell.

But the dealers do not operate on their own. Other manufacturers have reputations for loading dealers with products that don't sell. To the contrary, AGCO has provided incentives to its sales force to make certain that doesn't happen.

AGCO compensation for sales reps is 50 percent salary and 50 percent commission. However, the commissions are paid only when the *dealer* makes a sale. As a result, the sales force is totally focused on the success of the dealers. They help the dealers analyze the local market, forecast sales, and develop marketing strategies.

For example, sales people use their experience to help dealers (each serves about 25) make decisions on the allocation of their promotional budgets. In addition, sales people are required to conduct two training sessions per year, per brand in their territories. Since it is common for 10 brands to be sold in a territory, a typical AGCO sales person conducts 20 dealer training programs a year.

Another important part of AGCO's personal selling effort is its telephone-based dealer service operation. Dealers can call with technical questions about a product, a request for a replacement part, or even to find the nearest dealer with a product a customer wants. The traditional system forced a dealer to spend a day or two tracking down a sales person when there was a problem or question. This dedicated telemarketing system, staffed by well-trained people and supported by a computerized information system, gives dealers quick answers. In addition, it frees up the sales people to spend their time selling products.[1]

How else can Robert Ratliff utilize AGCO's sales force to continue the company's remarkable growth?

The importance of personal selling in most organizations can seldom be under-stated. The emphasis placed on selling by Agco and the success it has produced certainly supports this position. Agco's innovations in sales-force management and telemarketing have established a new standard in its industry and left the competition scrambling to catch up.

After studying this chapter, you should be able to explain:

CHAPTER GOALS

- The role that personal selling plays in our economy and in an organization's marketing program.
- The variety of personal selling jobs.
- The changing patterns of personal selling.
- The personal selling process.
- The major tasks in staffing and operating a sales force.
- Key issues in evaluating a sales person's performance.

Nature of Personal Selling

The goal of all marketing efforts is to increase profitable sales by offering want-satisfaction to consumers over the long run. **Personal selling**, the personal communication of information to persuade somebody to buy something, is by far the major promotional method used to reach this goal. To illustrate, the number of people employed in advertising is about 500 *thousand*. In personal selling, the number is close to 13 *million*. In many companies, personal selling is the largest single operating expense, often equaling 8 to 15 percent of sales. In contrast, advertising costs average 1 to 3 percent of sales.

In Chapter 16 we discussed four factors that influence an organization's promotional mix—the market, the product, the product's life-cycle stage, and the money available for promotion. Referring to those four factors, personal selling is likely to carry the bulk of the promotional load when:

- The market is concentrated geographically, in a few industries, or in a few large customers.
- The product has a high unit value, is quite technical in nature, or requires a demonstration.
- The product must be fitted to an individual customer's need, as in the case of securities or insurance.
- The sale involves a trade-in.
- The product is in the introductory stage of its life cycle.
- The organization does not have enough money to sustain an adequate advertising campaign.

Merits of Personal Selling

Personal selling is the individual, *personal* communication of information, in contrast to the mass, *impersonal* communication of advertising, sales promotion, and other promotional tools. This means that personal selling is *more flexible* than these other tools. Sales people can tailor their presentations to fit the needs and behavior of individual customers. They can see their customers' reactions to a particular sales approach and make adjustments on the spot.

Also, personal selling usually can be *focused* on individuals or firms that are known to be prospective customers, thus minimizing wasted effort. In contrast, advertising messages are often wasted on people who in no way are real prospects.

Another advantage of personal selling is that its goal is to actually *make a sale*. Advertising usually has a less ambitious goal. It is often designed to attract

attention, provide information, and arouse desire, but seldom does it stimulate buying action or complete the transfer of title from seller to buyer.

On the other hand, a full-fledged personal selling effort is *costly*. Even though personal selling can minimize wasted effort, the cost of developing and operating a sales force is high. Another disadvantage is that a company may find it difficult to attract the *quality of people* needed to do the job. At the retail level, many firms have abandoned their sales forces and shifted to self-service selling for this very reason.

Scope of Personal Selling

Most of us recognize that some personal selling is involved when a student buys a Honda motorcycle or an Ann Taylor store sells a dress to a woman who works in an advertising agency. But you should recognize that some personal selling is also involved when (1) Citicorp recruits a graduating senior who majored in finance or, conversely, a student tries to convince Citicorp to hire her; (2) a minister talks to a group of students to encourage them to attend church services; (3) a lawyer tries to convince a jury that her client is innocent; or even (4) a boy persuades his mother to give him some chocolate chip cookies. The point is that a form of personal selling occurs in nearly every human interaction.

In business situations, there are two kinds of personal selling, as shown in Figure 17-1. One is where the customers come to the sales people. Called **inside selling**, it primarily involves retail store sales. In this kind of selling, we also include the sales people at catalog retailers such as Lands' End or L.L. Bean, who take telephone orders. By far, most sales people in the U.S. fall into this first category.

In the other kind of personal selling, known as **outside sales**, sales people go to the customer. They make contact by mail, telephone, or field selling. In these last cases, sales people sell in person at a customer's place of business or home.

Most outside sales forces usually represent producers or wholesaling middlemen, selling to business users and not to household consumers. However, in our definition of an outside sales force, we also include (1) producers who sell directly

FIGURE 17-1
Scope of personal selling.

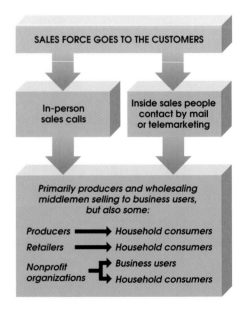

*T*ower Records' Web site (http://towerrecords.com) is a good example of what is happening in on-line retailing. Visitors to the site can take a 360-degree visual tour of any of the 170 different Tower Records stores from Hong Kong to Sacramento. The system allows a shopper to select from over 10,000 albums with delivery in as little as one day. Eventually it will be possible to locate a particular album with only a few words of the lyrics or even a description of the album cover—all from the comfort of home. Will systems like this replace retail sales people?

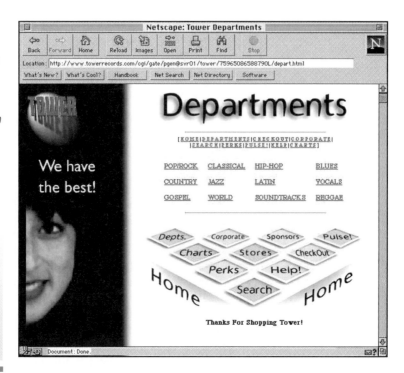

to household consumers—for example, insurance companies such as State Farm or Northwestern Mutual and in-home sellers such as Avon Products; (2) representatives of retail organizations who go to consumers' homes to demonstrate a product, give advice, or provide an estimate, such as sales people for some furniture stores and home heating and air-conditioning retailers; and (3) representatives of nonprofit organizations—for example, charity fund raisers, religious missionaries, and workers for political candidates.

Today some companies have a sales force that goes to the customers, but not in person. Instead, these reps are "going to the customers" by means of the telephone, computers, and facsimile (fax) machines. In effect, some outside selling is becoming electronic, and the term **telemarketing** describes such communications systems. Many firms have used telephone selling for decades, and some sales reps regularly contact customers by mail or phone. What is different about telemarketing is the new telecommunications equipment used in "going to the customer." In addition, firms use telemarketing in a sales-support function, as was described in the chapter-opening case.

Nature of Sales Jobs

The sales job of today is quite different from the stereotype of the past. The images of high pressure, false friendship, and glibness are largely outdated. Even the stereotype of the sales *man* is much less evident as more and more women enter professional selling.

The Professional Sales Person.   A new type of sales rep has emerged—the professional sales person. Today these reps are managers of a market area—their territories. They engage in a total selling job identifying prospects, servicing their customers, building goodwill, selling their products, and training their customers' sales people. Today's reps act as a mirror of the market by relaying market information back to the firm. They organize much of their own time and effort. They

YOU MAKE THE DECISION

ARE THERE REASONABLE OPPORTUNITIES FOR WOMEN IN SALES?

Business-to-business selling was generally considered a male occupation because of the long and often unusual hours and the amount of travel. The situation appears to be changing, but parity for women is still in the future. For example, a nationwide study of women in sales found that they make up only 26 percent of the business-to-business sales forces compared to 46 percent of the work force as a whole. The pay gap is also significant. According to the Census Bureau, men in sales earn 42 percent more than women. And more than five times as many men as women earn more than $50,000 a year in sales. However, when these figures are adjusted for age, experience, and length of time on the job, the gap diminishes significantly. Also, the pay for women in sales is rising much faster than for men.

Sales offers an excellent opportunity for advancement because results are easily measured. However, women are sometimes discouraged from seeking sales positions by such things as hiring criteria that emphasize team sports participation in school, the small number of women who have achieved sales management positions, and traditional stereotypes. For example, firms that have had an all-male sales force are often concerned about how their customers will react to a female sales person.

Women have been most successful in consumer product fields such as health care, food, and beverages. They have been less successful in commodity industries such as steel, paper, and chemicals.

Should a firm with a predominantly male sales force make an extra effort to hire females?

Sources: Sue Shellenbarger, "Sales Offers Women Fairer Pay, but Bias Lingers," *The Wall Street Journal*, Jan. 24, 1995, p. B1; and Timothy D. Schellhardt, "Labor Letter," *The Wall Street Journal*, Mar. 29, 1995, p. A1.

often take part in recruiting new sales people, sales planning in their territories, and other managerial activities.

Whose sales forces best reflect this professionalism? *Sales & Marketing Management* magazine conducts an annual survey among sales executives and customers to identify America's best sales forces. The criteria used are:

- *Accuracy*: Do the sales people take care of details?
- *Availability*: Are the sales people responsive to customers' requests?
- *Credibility*: Do customers view the sales people as important resources?
- *Partnership*: Are the sales people sought out for advice?
- *Trust*: Are customers confident that the sales people will keep their word?
- *Discovery*: Do the sales people offer ideas that improve customers' businesses?

Results for 1995 are presented in Table 17-1.

TABLE 17-1 America's best sales forces in 1995

Company	Industry
Mutual Life Insurance Company of New York (MONY)	Insurance and investments
Union Pacific Railroad	Transportation
Carnival Cruise Lines	Travel and leisure
Contract Wallcoverings, Inc.	Commercial wallcovering
Ecolab—Institutional Div.	Cleaning products

In some cases the winning sales organization is only one unit of the company's entire sales force. As a result, the groups represented here range in size from 9 sales people to over 2,000.

Source: Geoffrey Brewer, Andy Cohen, Ginger Trumfio, Allison Lucas, Weld F. Royal, and Mick Zangari, "1995 Best Sales Force Awards," *Sales & Marketing Management*, October 1995, pp. 52–63.

Wide Variety of Sales Jobs. The types of sales jobs and the activities involved in them cover a wide range. Consider the job of a Coca-Cola driver–sales person who calls routinely on a group of retail stores. That job is in another world from the IBM rep who sells a computer system for managing reservations to Delta Airlines. Similarly, a sales rep for Avon Products selling door to door in Japan or China has a job only remotely related to that of a Cessna airplane rep who sells executive-type aircraft to Dow Chemical and other large firms in the U.S.

The *types of sales jobs* differ in terms of the creative selling skills required, from the simple to the complex. The classification that follows is adapted from one developed years ago by Robert McMurry, a noted industrial psychologist:

1. *Driver–sales person.* In this job the sales person primarily delivers the product—for example, soft drinks or fuel oil. The selling responsibilities are secondary, though most of these sales people are authorized and even encouraged to look for opportunities to increase sales to existing accounts.
2. *Inside order taker.* This is a position in which the sales person takes orders and assists customers at the seller's place of business—for example, a retail clerk on the sales floor at a J.C. Penney store or a telephone representative at a catalog retailer such as Eddie Bauer or L.L. Bean. Most customers have already decided to buy, and the sales person's job is to serve them efficiently.
3. *Outside order taker.* In this position the sales person goes to the customer in the field and requests an order. An example is an Agco sales person calling on a farm-equipment dealer, or a sales rep for a radio station selling advertising time to local businesses. The majority of these sales are repeat orders to established customers, although these sales people seek new business and occasionally do introduce new products to customers.
4. *Missionary sales person.* This type of sales job is intended to build goodwill, perform promotional activities, and provide information and other services for existing or potential customers. This sales person is not expected to solicit an order. An example of this job is a missionary sales rep for Seagram's distillery or a detail sales person for a pharmaceutical firm such as Merck or Lilly.
5. *Sales engineer.* In this position the major emphasis is on the sales person's ability to explain the product to a prospective customer, and also to adapt the product to the customer's particular needs. The products involved here typically are complex, technically sophisticated items. A sales engineer usually provides technical support, and works with another sales rep who calls regularly on a given account.
6. *Creative sales person—an order getter.* This involves the creative selling of goods and services, but also social causes and ideas (including campaigns such as "Say no to drugs" and "Stop smoking"). This category contains the most complex, difficult selling jobs—especially the creative selling of services, because you can't see, touch, taste, or smell them. Customers often are not aware of their need for a seller's product. Or they may not realize how that product can satisfy their wants better than the product they are now using. Creative selling often involves designing a system to fit the needs of a particular customer. For example, to make a sale, AT&T will design a communications system for a hospital, or Otis elevator will develop a vertical lift system especially for a new office building.

In summary, the above six types of sales jobs fall into three groups: order taker (categories 1, 2, and 3), sales-support personnel (categories 4 and 5), and order getter (category 6). One organization may have several different types of sales jobs.

IBM, for instance, has sales people in all of the above categories except driver–sales person.

The Cost of Personal Selling.   Selling is expensive. The average cost of a sales call by an order getter is $513, and over 50 percent of sales people responding to a survey of Fortune 1000 companies say it takes from three to six calls to make a sale to a new customer. Sales people spend on average $2,045 per month on travel and $600 per month on entertainment.[2] Thus, considered solely from a cost point of view, the sales function needs to be efficiently managed.

The Uniqueness of Sales Jobs.   The features that differentiate sales jobs from other jobs are:

- The sales force is largely responsible for *implementing a firm's marketing strategies*. Moreover, it's the sales reps who generate the revenues that are managed by the financial people and used by the production people.
- Sales people are typically the most visible *representatives of their company* to customers and to society in general. Many sales jobs require the rep to socialize with customers who frequently are upper-level executives in their companies. Opinions of the firm and its products are formed on the basis of impressions made by sales people in their work and in outside activities. The public ordinarily does not judge a company by its factory or office workers.
- Sales reps operate with *little or no direct supervision*. For success in selling, a sales rep must work hard physically and mentally, be creative and persistent, and show considerable initiative. This all requires a high degree of motivation.
- Sales jobs frequently *involve considerable traveling* and time away from home. Many companies have reduced sales travel time by redesigning sales territories, routing sales trips better, and relying more on telemarketing. Nevertheless, being in the field, sales people deal with a seemingly endless stream of customers who may seem determined not to buy their products. These stresses, coupled with long hours and traveling, require a mental toughness and physical stamina rarely demanded in other jobs. Personal selling is hard work!

Changing Patterns in Personal Selling

Traditionally, personal selling was a face-to-face, one-on-one situation between a sales person and a prospective buyer. This situation existed both in retail sales involving ultimate consumers and also in business-to-business transactions. In recent years, however, some very different selling patterns have emerged. These new patterns reflect a growing purchasing expertise among consumers and business buyers, which, in turn, has fostered a growing professionalism in personal selling. Let's discuss four of these patterns.

Selling Centers

To match the expertise of the buying center, especially in business markets, a growing number of firms on the selling side have adopted the organizational concept of a selling center. A **selling center** is a group of people representing a sales department as well as other functional areas in a firm such as finance, production, and research and development (R&D) brought together to meet the needs of a particular customer. This is sometimes called a *sales team* or *team selling*.

Team selling is expensive, and is therefore usually restricted to accounts that have a potential for high sales volume and profit. Procter & Gamble, for example,

http://www.pg.com/

http://www.att.com/

has selling teams assigned to large retailers such as Wal-Mart. When AT&T sells to a large multinational firm such as Nestlé's, then AT&T will send a separate selling team to deal with each of Nestlé's major divisions.

Most sales teams are ad hoc groups, assembled to deal with a particular opportunity. Except for the sales person, the team members have other responsibilities in the firm. This creates several managerial issues. For example, who directs a team—the most senior person involved, the sales person who organizes the team, or the most experienced member? What happens when the buying center decides it prefers working with a senior manager on the team or the technical expert who "speaks their language" rather than the sales person? Also, how should team members be evaluated and compensated? Despite these challenges, the increasing complexity of sales has made team selling increasingly popular.

Systems Selling

The concept of **systems selling** means selling a total package of related goods and services—a system—to solve a customer's problem. The idea is that the system will satisfy the buyer's needs more effectively than selling individual products separately. Xerox, for example, originally sold individual products, using a separate sales force for each major product line. Today, using a systems-selling approach, Xerox studies a customer's office information and operating problems. Then Xerox provides a total automated system of machines and accompanying services to solve that customer's office problems.

http://www.xerox.com/

Global Sales Teams

As companies expanded their operations to far-flung corners of the globe, they expected their suppliers to do the same. Having products readily available, understanding local conditions, and providing quick service became essential to maintaining global customers. So, many firms established sales offices or distribution centers in foreign locations near important customers. Now, to service their largest and most profitable global customers, sellers are forming global sales teams. A **global sales team** is responsible for all of its company's sales to an account anywhere in the world. For example, AMP Inc., a $3.5 billion supplier of connection systems, uses a global sales team to serve the needs of IBM worldwide. The team manager is located close to the customer's headquarters, and the team members are prepared to deal with issues and opportunities wherever they may occur.

http://www.amp.com/

Relationship Selling

Developing a mutually beneficial relationship with selected customers over time is **relationship selling**. It may be an extension of team selling, or it may be developed by individual sales reps in their dealings with customers. In relationship selling, a seller discontinues the usual practice of concentrating on maximizing the number and size of individual transactions. Instead, the seller attempts to develop a deeper, longer-lasting relationship built on trust with key customers—usually larger accounts.

Unfortunately, often there is not much trust found in buyer-seller relationships, either in retailer-consumer selling or in business-to-business selling. In fact, in some circles selling is viewed as adversarial, with one side winning and the other side losing. For example, a buyer may try to squeeze the last penny out of the seller in price negotiations, even with the knowledge that the agreed-on price may make it difficult for the seller to perform adequately.

How do sellers build trust? First and foremost, there must be a customer orientation. The seller must place the customers' needs and interests on a par with its own. From that will follow a shared vision of success, an expanded time horizon that looks beyond the immediate sale, and a perspective that the parties to a transaction are partners not adversaries.

Many large companies—Procter & Gamble, Hyatt Hotels, RJR Nabisco, Kraft General Goods, and ABB (Asea Brown Boveri, a Swiss-based manufacturer of industrial equipment), to name just a few—have realigned their sales forces to engage in relationship selling.

Telemarketing

Earlier we described telemarketing as the innovative use of telecommunications equipment and systems as part of the "going to the customer" category of personal selling. Under certain conditions, telemarketing is attractive to both buyers and sellers. Buyers placing routine reorders or new orders for standardized products by telephone or computer use less of their time than in-person sales calls. Many sellers find that it increases selling efficiency. Sellers face the high costs of keeping sales people on the road; selling by telemarketing reduces that expense. Also, routine selling by telemarketing allows the field sales force to devote more time to creative selling, major account selling, and other more profitable selling activities.

Here are examples of selling activities that lend themselves nicely to a telemarketing program:

http://www.baxter.com/

- Seeking leads to new accounts and identifying potentially good customers that sales reps can follow up with in-person calls.
- Processing orders for standardized products. Some customers of Baxter International (hospital supplies) have prepared their computers to communicate directly with Baxter's computers to determine shipping dates and to place orders.
- Dealing with small-order customers, especially where the seller would lose money if field sales calls were used.
- Improving relations with middlemen. As the opening case describes, Agco uses telemarketing to answer dealers' questions about inventory management,

*E*stimates of sales generated through telemarketing are about $400 billion a year, and predictions are for continued rapid growth. However, there are concerns about telemarketing, especially efforts directed to households. Quality may be deteriorating as marketers seek greater speed and lower costs through automatic dialing, recorded messages, and inadequately trained personnel.

service, and replacement parts. This gives the dealers a single source for assistance, saving them time and effort.

• Improving communications with middlemen in foreign countries and competing better against manufacturers in those countries. In Europe, for example, the auto, chemical, steel, and shipbuilding industries have developed electronic communication systems involving manufacturers, suppliers, and even customs and shipping agents.

The Personal Selling Process

The **personal selling process** is a logical sequence of four steps that a sales person takes in dealing with a prospective buyer. See Figure 17-2. This process leads, hopefully, to some desired customer action and ends with a follow-up to ensure customer satisfaction. The desired action usually is to get the customer to buy a good or a service. However, the same four-step process may be used equally well in other marketing situations. For example, RJR Nabisco persuades Safeway to give Oreo cookies a good shelf location in a special promotion program; or Northwestern University persuades alumni to contribute to a special fund-raising effort; or BMW wants its dealers to do some local advertising of their automobiles.

http://www.nabisco.com/

http://www.bmwusa.com/

Prospecting

The first step in the personal selling process is really two related steps. *Prospecting* consists of identifying possible customers and then qualifying them—that is, determining whether they have the necessary potential to buy. They are combined as a single step because they are typically done at the same time.

Identifying Prospective Customers. A rep may start the identification process by drawing up a profile of the ideal prospect. Analyzing the firm's data base of past and current customers can help determine characteristics of an ideal prospect. From this profile a seller can start a list of potential customers.

Many sources can be used to build a list of prospects. The rep's sales manager may prepare a list; current customers may suggest new leads; trade associations and industry directories can be good sources; the customer lists of related but noncompeting businesses can be purchased; and leads can come from people mailing in a coupon or phoning an 800 number stated in an ad.

A little thought often will suggest logical prospects. Homestead House (furniture store) and US West (telephone company) find prospects in lists of building permits issued. Insurance companies (Northwestern Mutual or Prudential), real

FIGURE 17-2
The personal selling process.

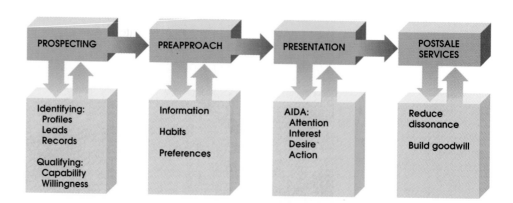

estate firms (Re/Max, Century 21), and even local diaper services use marriage and birth announcements in newspapers as sources.

Qualifying Prospects. After identifying prospective customers, a seller should *qualify* them—that is, determine whether they have the necessary willingness, purchasing power, and authority to buy. To determine willingness to buy, a seller can seek information about any changes in the prospect's situation. For example, a business firm or a household consumer may have had a recent problem with an insurance provider. In this case there may be an opportunity for a sales person from a competing insurer to get that prospect's business.

http://www.dnb.com/

To determine a prospect's financial ability to pay, a seller can refer to credit-rating services such as Dun & Bradstreet. For household consumers or small businesses in an area, a seller can get credit information from a local credit bureau. Identifying who has the authority to buy in a business or a household can be difficult, as we saw back in Chapters 5 and 6. In a business, the buying authority may rest with a committee or an executive in a distant location. Besides determining the buying authority, a seller also should identify the one or more persons who influence the buying decision. A purchasing agent may have buying authority, but what he or she buys may depend on the recommendation of an office secretary, a factory engineer, or a vice president.

Preapproach to Individual Prospects

Before calling on prospects, sales people should conduct a *preapproach*—learning all they can about the persons or companies to whom they hope to sell. This might include finding out what products the prospects have used in the past, what they are now using, and their reactions to these products. In business-to-business selling, a sales person or selling team should find out how buying decisions are made in the customer's organization. (Remember, in Chapter 6 we discussed the various roles played in the buying-decision process in business firms.) A sales rep can target the right people if he or she knows who is the gatekeeper, who influences and/or makes the buying decision, and who actually makes the purchase.

Finding out something about the prospect's personal life—interests, activities, and habits—as well as gathering some insights into the preferred business practices of the prospect can be useful. Sales people should try to get all the information they can, so that they will be able to tailor their presentations to individual buyers.

Presenting the Sales Message

With the appropriate preapproach information, a sales person can design a sales presentation that will attract the prospect's *attention*. The sales person will then try to hold the prospect's *interest* while building a *desire* for the product and, when the time is right, attempt to stimulate *action* by closing the sale. This approach, called **AIDA** (an acronym formed by the first letters of *A*ttention, *I*nterest, *D*esire, and *A*ction), is used by many organizations.

Attract Attention—the Approach. The first task in a sales presentation is to attract the prospect's attention and to generate curiosity. In cases where the prospect is aware of a need and is seeking a solution, simply stating the seller's company and product may be enough. However, more creativity often is required.

For instance, if the sales person was referred to the prospect by a customer, the right approach might be to start out by mentioning this common acquaintance. Or a sales person might suggest the product benefits by making some startling statement. One sales training consultant suggests greeting a prospect with the question, "If I can cut your selling costs in half, and at the same time double your sales volume, are you interested?"

Hold Interest and Arouse Desire.   After attracting the prospect's attention, the challenge for the sales rep is to hold it and stimulate a desire for the product with a sales presentation. There is no universal format here, but, when it is practical, a product demonstration is invaluable. However, a sales person has to be careful not to overdo a demonstration. Recently a car sales person in Des Moines was sued after he convinced a customer to climb into the trunk of a Chrysler Concorde to experience its spaciousness. He then slammed the trunk lid shut and bounced the car a few times (apparently to demonstrate its smooth ride)! Not surprisingly, the prospect did not buy the car.[3] Whatever format is followed in the presentation, the sales person must always show how the product will benefit the prospect.

Some companies train their sales people to use a canned sales talk—a memorized presentation designed to cover all points determined by management to be important. All of the firm's reps give the same presentation, verbatim or with minor changes. Companies engaging in telephone selling or door-to-door selling (Encyclopedia Britannica, for example) use canned sales talks. Although many people consider this a poor practice, canned talks have time and again proved to be effective. Nevertheless, they are used less and less today, because companies believe that flexible presentations can be more personal and tailored for individual customers' needs.

Meet Objections and Close the Sale.   After explaining the product and its benefits, a sales person should try to close the sale—that is, obtain the customer's agreement to buy. (This is the final A in AIDA—achieving the desired action.)

As part of the presentation, the sales person may periodically venture a trial close to test the prospect's willingness to buy. By posing some "either-or" questions that presume the prospect has decided to buy, a sales person can bring the presentation to a head. For example, "Would you prefer that the installation be done immediately or would it be better to have it done next week?" or "Do you plan to charge this or pay cash?"

The trial close is important because it gives the sales person an indication of how near the prospect is to a decision. Sometimes sales are lost simply because the rep fails to ask for the order.

The trial close also tends to uncover the buyer's objections. A sales person should encourage buyers to state their objections. Then the sales person has an opportunity to meet the objections and bring out additional product benefits or reemphasize previously stated points. The toughest objections to answer are those that are unspoken. A sales person must identify and resolve the real objections before a sale can be closed.

Postsale Services

An effective selling job does not end when the order is written up. The final stage of a selling process is a series of postsale activities that can build customer goodwill and lay the groundwork for future business. Even if it is not his or her direct responsibility, an alert sales person will follow up sales to ensure that no problems occur in delivery, financing, installation, employee training, and other areas that are important to customer satisfaction.

Postsale service reduces the customer's postpurchase cognitive dissonance—the anxiety that usually occurs after a person makes a buying decision (discussed

CAN U.S. FIRMS SUCCESSFULLY IGNORE THE CONVENTIONAL WISDOM ON HOW TO SELL IN CHINA?

China, with over a billion consumers, is the biggest potential market in the world and it remains largely untapped. Despite the small amount of large-scale free-enterprise marketing done in China, there are several generally accepted notions about how marketing can and cannot be done there. For example, it is generally believed that only the wealthiest Chinese consumers can afford foreign products, so it is suggested that market potential estimates are highly exaggerated. Another belief is that the weak Chinese transportation infrastructure prevents the widespread distribution needed by mass marketers. There is also the belief that the Chinese government will not let a foreign firm capture a significant share of any market.

Procter & Gamble may be proving these and other "conventional wisdoms" incorrect with marketing techniques new to China and innovative personal selling. For example, using a promotional technique that was introduced in the U.S. in the 1950s, Procter pays washing machine manufacturers to include a box of its detergent with every new machine sold.

One of P&G's major strategies is to blitz a market with representatives of all types. To make that possible, the firm has become a major employer of top university graduates for its sales force. In addition, when entering a new geographic area P&G hires thousands of housewives and retirees to pass out samples in their neighborhoods. P&G's objective is to have every retailer carry its brands. However, China is filled with small retailers and street vendors. So the 200-plus cities with 200,000 or more residents are canvassed by uniformed P&G representatives who make sales pitches to every retailer no matter what their size.

What's the result? P&G has become the largest daily-use consumer product company in China. Its sales of $450 million exceed those of all other domestic and foreign competitors. However, the company sees this as only a fraction of the potential that is yet to be tapped. Even more important, after several years of investing in manufacturing capability and marketing, P&G's China operation is now profitable.

Sources: Joseph Kahn, "P&G Viewed China as a National Market and Is Conquering It," *The Wall Street Journal*, Sept. 12, 1995, pp. A1+; and Craig S. Smith, "Doublemint in China: Distribution Isn't Double the Fun," *The Wall Street Journal*, Dec. 5, 1995, pp. B1+.

---

in Chapter 5). In this final stage of the selling process, a sales person can minimize the customer's dissonance by (1) summarizing the product's benefits after the purchase, (2) repeating why the product is better than alternatives not chosen, (3) describing how satisfied other buyers have been with the product, and (4) emphasizing how satisfied the customer will be with the product.

Strategic Sales-Force Management

Managing the personal selling function is a matter of applying the three-stage management process (planning, implementation, and evaluation) to a sales force and its activities. Sales executives begin by setting sales goals and planning sales-force activities. This involves forecasting sales, preparing sales budgets, establishing sales territories, and setting sales quotas. Then a sales force must be organized, staffed, and operated to implement the strategic plans and reach the goals that were set. The final stage involves evaluating the performance of individual sales people as well as appraising the total sales performance.

Effective sales-force management starts with a qualified sales manager. Finding the right person for this job is not easy. In many organizations the common practice when a sales management position becomes available is to reward the most productive sales person with a promotion. The assumption is that as a manager, an effective sales person will be able to impart the necessary wisdom to make others equally successful.

However, the qualities that lead to effective sales management are often diametrically opposed to the attributes of a successful sales person. Probably the biggest difference in the positions is that sales people tend to be self-motivated and self-reliant. They often work independently, receiving all the credit or blame for their successes or failures. In contrast, sales managers must work through and depend on others, and must be prepared to give recognition rather than receive it. Herein lies the dilemma. It is an unusual person who can be a successful sales manager without previous selling experience. To be effective, a sales manager must understand customers, appreciate the role of the sales person, and have the respect of the sales force. These attributes can only be acquired by spending time in sales.

The resolution may come in not using the sales management position as a reward for outstanding sales performance. Rather, the criteria for sales management should be respectable sales performance coupled with the necessary attributes of management.

Staffing and Operating a Sales Force

Since most sales executives spend the bulk of their time in staffing and operating their sales forces, we will discuss these activities in some detail. Figure 17-3 shows what's involved.

Recruitment and Selection

Selecting personnel is the most important management activity in any organization. This is true whether the organization is a business, an athletic team, or a college faculty. Consequently, the key to success in managing a sales force is selecting the right people. No matter what the caliber of sales management, if a sales force is distinctly inferior to that of a competitor's, the competitor will win.

Sales-force selection involves three tasks:

1. Determine the type of people needed by preparing a written job description.
2. Recruit an adequate number of applicants.
3. Select the most qualified persons from among the applicants.

Determining Hiring Specifications.   The first step is to establish the proper hiring specifications, just as if the company were purchasing equipment or supplies rather than labor. To establish these specifications, management must first know what the particular sales job entails. This calls for a detailed job analysis and a written job description. This written description will later be invaluable in training, compensation, and supervision.

Determining the qualifications needed to fill the job is the most difficult part of the selection function. Because sales jobs differ significantly, researchers have virtually abandoned the search for a general set of attributes that explain selling success. Even within a particular firm where the sales job is reasonably well

FIGURE 17-3
Staffing and operating
a sales force.

defined, it is difficult to determine the characteristics that make a good sales person. As one approach, some companies have analyzed the personal histories of their existing sales representatives in an effort to determine the traits common to successful (and unsuccessful) performers. Even when a firm feels that it knows what the important attributes are, we cannot measure to what degree each quality should be present. Nor do we know to what extent an abundance of one can offset the lack of another.

Recruiting Applicants.   A planned system for recruiting a sufficient number of applicants is the next step in selection. A good recruiting system:

- Operates continuously, not only when sales-force vacancies occur.
- Is systematic in reaching all appropriate sources of applicants.
- Provides a flow of more qualified applicants than is needed.

To identify recruits, large organizations often use placement services on college campuses or professional employment agencies. Smaller firms that need fewer new sales people may place classified ads in trade publications and daily newspapers. Many firms solicit recommendations from company employees, customers, or suppliers.

Matching Applicants with Hiring Specifications.   Sales managers use a variety of techniques to determine which applicants possess the desired qualifications, including application forms, interviews, references, credit reports, psychological tests, aptitude tests, and physical examinations. Virtually all companies ask candidates to fill out application forms. In addition to providing basic screening information, the application indicates areas that should be explored in an interview.

No sales person should be hired without at least one personal interview. And it is usually desirable to have several interviews conducted by different people in different physical settings. Pooling the opinions of a number of people increases the likelihood of discovering any undesirable characteristics and reduces the effects of one interviewer's possible bias. An interview helps an employer to determine (1) the applicant's degree of interest in the job, (2) the match between the requirements of the job and the applicant's skills, and (3) the applicant's motivation to work hard.

The individuals involved in the selection process need to be aware of the laws against discrimination to avoid inadvertent violations. For example, it is illegal to ask on an application or in an interview a person's age or marital status. Testing for intelligence, attributes, or personality, though legal under the proper conditions, is somewhat controversial. Some companies avoid testing for fear that they will be accused of discrimination. However, employment tests are legitimate selection tools as long as the attributes measured can be shown to predict job performance.

Assimilating New Sales People

After sales people are hired, management should integrate them into the company family. Often this step is overlooked entirely. Potential sales people are carefully selected and are wined and dined to recruit them into the firm. Then, as soon as they are hired, the honeymoon is over, and they are left to shift for themselves. However, since selling by its nature involves a considerable amount of rejection by prospects, the new sales person needs support in order to avoid becoming discouraged. A wise sales manager will recognize that the new people must be made comfortable with the details of the job, their fellow workers, and their status in the firm if they are to be successful.

AN ETHICAL DILEMMA?

Qualified sales people are hard to find, especially experienced sales people who are familiar with a recruiter's industry. One way to get such people is to aggressively recruit them from a competitor's sales force. Not only do these reps know the business, they might also bring along some of their customers. Competitors object strongly to this "pirating," as they call it. They have spent much money training these reps, and they now benefit from the reps' sales productivity. The recruiting companies believe that taking sales people from competitors is no different than taking customers. That's called competition.

Is it ethical for a sales manager to directly approach a competitor's sales rep with a job offer?

Training a Sales Force

Virtually all companies put new and inexperienced sales people through an orientation and sales training program, often lasting weeks or months. On average, it costs a company over $6,000 to train a newly hired sales person.[4] But even experienced sales people need continual training to improve their selling skills, learn about new products, and improve their time- and territory-management practices. W. W. Grainger, a company that sells motors, safety equipment, and other products used to maintain buildings and factories, puts new sales people through a 6- to 8-week orientation course. In addition, the entire sales force gets 20 to 30 days of training on selling skills and product knowledge each year. Grainger has tripled its sales—from $1 billion to $3 billion—in 11 years, and management attributes much of its success to this continual training.[5]

http://www.grainger.com/

Motivating a Sales Force

Sales people, especially outside sales forces, require a high degree of motivation. Think back to our earlier discussion about the nature of a sales job—the pressures of role ambiguity and role conflict, for example. Also consider how a sales job is different from most other jobs. Sales people often work independently, without supervision and guidance from management. Outside sales people work most of the time away from the support and comfort of home office surroundings.

Consequently, management faces a challenge in motivating sales people. One key is to determine what motivates the sales reps—is it a need for money, status, control, accomplishment, or something else? People differ in what motivates them, and the motivations change over a person's life. A young sales person is more likely to be motivated by money, while an older sales person may be more interested in recognition.

Sales executives can draw from a wide assortment of specific motivational tools. Financial incentives—compensation plans, expense accounts, fringe benefits— serve as basic motivators, but they don't always push people to exceptional performance. Nonfinancial rewards—job enrichment, praise from management, recognition and honor awards (pin, trophy, certificate)—may stimulate some reps. Sales meetings and sales contests are often-used alternatives. Many firms provide cruises, resort trips, and other travel incentives as rewards to top-performing sales reps.

Compensating a Sales Force

Financial rewards are still by far the most widely used tool for motivating sales people. Consequently, designing and administering an effective sales compensation plan is a big part of a sales manager's job. Financial rewards may be direct

*I*suzu does more than run eye-catching ads to promote its products. To motivate its 600 dealers, the company offers an unusual five-month travel and merchandise incentive program. First, the top 100 dealers, based on four months' sales, are selected for a holiday trip to a fancy resort. Then these 100 dealers earn bonus points for their sales in the fifth month. The bonus points are converted to spending accounts for a one-day "use it or lose it" shopping spree at an upscale mall near the resort. In 1994 the 100 dealers spent $1.2 million at Fashion Island, a Newport Beach mall. Each year the promotion has been used, Isuzu has set sales records. Are the records the result of the incentive, the ads, or something else?

http://www.isuzu.com/

monetary payments (salary, commission) or indirect monetary compensation (paid vacations, pensions, insurance plans).

Establishing a compensation system calls for decisions concerning the level of compensation as well as the method of compensation. The *level* refers to the total dollar income that a sales person earns over a period of time. Level is influenced by the type of person required for the job and the competitive rate of pay for similar positions. The *method* is the system or plan by which the sales person will reach the intended level.

The three widely used **methods of sales-force compensation** are straight salary, straight commission, and a combination plan. A *salary* is a fixed payment for a period of time during which the sales person is working. A *salary-only plan* (called a straight salary) provides security and stability of earnings for a sales rep. This plan gives management control over a rep's efforts, and the reps are likely to spend time on nonselling activities that cater to the customer's best interests. The main drawback of a straight salary is that it does not offer an incentive for sales people to increase their sales volume. Also, a straight salary is a fixed cost for the firm, unrelated to sales volume or gross margin.

Straight-salary plans typically are used when:

- Compensating new sales people or missionary sales people.
- Opening new territories.
- Selling a technical product with a lengthy period of negotiation.

A *commission* is a payment tied to a specific unit of accomplishment. Thus a rep may be paid 5 percent of every dollar of sales or 8 percent on each dollar of gross margin. A *straight-commission plan* (commission only) tends to have just the opposite merits and limitations of a straight salary. A straight commission provides considerable incentive for sales people to sell, and it is a variable cost related directly to a rep's sales volume or gross margin. On the other hand, it is difficult to control straight-commission people. And it is especially difficult to get them to perform tasks for which no commission is paid.

Straight-commission plans may work well when:

- Great incentive is needed to generate sales.
- Very little nonselling work is required, such as setting up displays in retail stores.
- The company is financially weak and must relate its compensation expenses directly to sales or gross margins.
- The company is unable to supervise the sales force when they are outside the company's offices.

A heavy emphasis on commissions can cause employees to lose sight of the importance of the customer. Sears, Roebuck, for example, abandoned the commission plan in its auto centers after California officials alleged that the sales reps were recommending unnecessary auto repairs. The reps were doing this to meet quotas and boost their commissions.

The ideal *combination compensation plan* has the best features of both the straight-salary and the straight-commission plans, with as few of their drawbacks as possible. To reach this ideal, a combination plan must be tailored to a particular firm, product, market, and type of selling. Today about three-quarters of the firms in the U.S. use some kind of a combination plan.

Supervising a Sales Force

Supervising a sales force is difficult because sales people often work independently and where they cannot be continually observed. And yet supervision serves both as a means of ongoing training and as a device to ensure that company policies are being carried out.

An issue that management must resolve is how closely to supervise. If too close, it can create a role conflict for the sales person. One of the attractions of selling is the freedom it affords sales people to develop creative solutions to customers' problems. Close supervision can stifle that sense of independence. Conversely, too little supervision can contribute to role ambiguity. Sales people who are not closely supervised may lack an understanding of the expectations of their supervisors and companies. They may not know, for example, how much time to spend servicing existing accounts and how much developing new business.

The most effective supervisory method is personal observation in the field. Typically, at least half a sales manager's time is spent traveling with sales people. Other supervisory tools are reports, correspondence, and sales meetings.

Evaluating a Sales Person's Performance

Managing a sales force includes evaluating the performance of sales people. Sales executives must know what the sales force is doing in order to reward them or make constructive proposals for improvement. By establishing performance standards and studying sales people's activities, management can develop new training programs to upgrade the sales force's efforts. And, of course, performance evaluation should be the basis for compensation decisions and other rewards.

Performance evaluation can also help sales people identify opportunities for improving their efforts. Employees with poor sales records know they are doing something wrong. However, they may not know what the problem is if they lack objective standards by which to measure their performance.

Both quantitative and qualitative factors should be used as bases for performance evaluation. **Quantitative bases** generally have the advantage of being specific and objective. **Qualitative bases**, although often reflecting broader dimensions of behavior, are limited by the subjective judgment of the evaluators. For either type of appraisal, management faces the difficult task of setting standards against which a rep's performance can be measured.

Quantitative Bases

Sales performance should be evaluated in terms of *inputs* (efforts) and *outputs* (results). Together, inputs such as number of sales calls per day or customer service activity, and outputs such as sales volume or gross margin, provide a measure of selling effectiveness.

Useful quantitative input measures include:

- Call rate—number of calls per day or week.
- Direct selling expenses—total dollars or a percent of sales.
- Nonselling activities—promotion displays set up, training sessions held with distributors or dealers.

Some quantitative output measures useful as evaluation criteria are:

- Sales volume by product, customer group, and territory.
- Sales volume as a percent of quota or territory potential.
- Gross margin by product line, customer group, and territory.
- Orders—number and average dollar amount.
- Closing rate—number of orders divided by number of calls.
- Accounts—percent of existing accounts sold and number of new accounts opened.

http://www.ibm.com/

An increasing number of firms, among them IBM and Hallmark, are using customer satisfaction as a performance indicator. In fact, a recent survey of over 200 companies found 26 percent using customer satisfaction as a component in their sales-force evaluation processes.[6]

Satisfaction is measured a number of different ways, from detailed questionnaires that customers complete to counting the number of complaints received from customers. Assessing satisfaction reflects a recognition by companies that there is more to selling than making a sale. Firms have discovered that finding a new customer is much more difficult and expensive than keeping an existing one. As a result, they have shifted their emphasis from a single-minded focus on sales volume to satisfaction. This allows a sales person to nurture a small account with considerable potential rather than always go for the big order. And it discourages sales people from engaging in detrimental actions such as loading up customers with unneeded inventory in order to meet a sales quota.

Qualitative Bases

In some respects, performance evaluation would be much easier if it could be based only on quantitative criteria. The standards would be absolute, and the positive and negative deviations from the standard could be measured precisely.

Quantitative measures would also minimize the subjectivity and personal bias of the evaluators. However, many qualitative factors must be considered because they influence a sales person's performance. Some commonly used factors are:

- Knowledge of products, company policies, and competitors.
- Time management and preparation for sales calls.
- Customer relations.
- Personal appearance.
- Personality and attitude—cooperation, creativity, resourcefulness.

A successful evaluation program will appraise a sales person's performance on all the factors that can be related to performance. Otherwise management may be misled. A high daily call rate may look good, but it tells us nothing about how many orders are being written up. A high closing rate may be camouflaging a low average order size or a high sales volume on low-profit items.

■ SUMMARY

Personal selling is the main promotional method used in American business—whether measured by number of people employed, by total expenditures, or by expenses as a percentage of sales. The total field of personal selling comprises two broad categories. One covers selling activities where the customers come to the sales people—primarily retail store or retail catalog selling. The other includes all selling situations where the sales people go to the customer—primarily outside sales forces.

The sales job today is not what it used to be. A new type of sales rep—a professional sales person—has been developing over the past few decades. But this new breed of sales rep still faces problems of role ambiguity and role conflict. Sales jobs today range from order takers through support sales people (missionary sellers, sales engineers) to order getters (creative sellers). Sales positions differ from other jobs in several respects. Some changing patterns in personal selling have emerged in recent years—patterns such as selling centers (team selling), systems selling, global sales teams, relationship selling, and telemarketing.

The personal selling process consists of four steps, starting with prospecting for potential buyers and then preapproaching each prospect. The third step is the sales presentation, which includes attracting attention, arousing buyer interest and desire, meeting objections, and then hopefully closing the sale. Finally, postsale activities involve follow-up services to ensure customer satisfaction and reduce dissonance regarding the purchase.

The sales management process involves planning, implementing, and evaluating sales-force activities within the guidelines set by the company's strategic marketing plan. The tasks of staffing and operating a sales force present managerial challenges in several areas. The key to successful sales-force management is to do a good job in selecting sales people. Then plans must be made to assimilate these new people into the company and to train them. Management must set up programs to motivate, compensate, and supervise a sales force. The final stage in sales-force management is to evaluate the performance of the individual sales people.

More about   **AGCO**

*E*veryone at AGCO has selling responsibility, not just the sales force. That includes Robert Ratliff, the CEO. He spends more than half his time at conventions, company meetings, and dealer conclaves to learn what his customers and retailers are thinking and saying.

Annually, in each of the company's 12 sales regions, Ratliff holds four open meetings for dealers. He and other top executives listen to all the problems and complaints (as well as the compliments) the dealers have. They either offer solutions on the spot or promise to investigate. As a result of one of these meetings, the firm instituted a no-fault guarantee to ensure that a faulty product will be repaired immediately or replaced.

Ratliff also conducts 2½-day sessions with elected panels of dealers twice a year. The meetings produce a list of the top-10 dealer problems for AGCO to address. A few months later, a written response of what the company is doing about them is sent to the dealers.[7]

1. How important are sales people to AGCO's success?
2. How is AGCO creating relationships with farm-equipment dealers?

■ KEY TERMS AND CONCEPTS

Personal selling (462)
Inside selling (463)
Outside sales (463)
Telemarketing (464)

Selling center (467)
Systems selling (468)
Global sales teams (468)
Relationship selling (468)

Personal selling
  process (470)
AIDA (471)
Methods of sales-force
  compensation (477)

Quantitative evaluation
  bases (479)
Qualitative evaluation
  bases (479)

■ QUESTIONS AND PROBLEMS

1. The cost of a full-page, four-color advertisement in one issue of *Sports Illustrated* magazine is much more than the cost of employing two sales people for a full year. A sales-force executive is urging her company to eliminate a few of these ads and, instead, to hire more sales people. This executive believes for the same cost a single good sales person working for an entire year can sell more than one ad in an issue of *Sports Illustrated*. How would you respond?

2. Would systems selling make more sense for a soft drink bottler or a plumbing supplies distributor? Why?

3. Refer to the classification of sales jobs from driver–sales person to creative seller and answer the following questions:
   a. In which types of jobs are sales people most likely to be free from close supervision?
   b. Which types are likely to be the highest paid?
   c. For which types of jobs is the highest degree of motivation necessary?

4. What are some sources you might use to acquire a list of prospects for the following products?
   a. Bank accounts for new area residents
   b. Dental X-ray equipment

   c. Laptop computers
   d. Contributors to the United Way
   e. Baby furniture and clothes

5. If you were preparing a sales presentation for the following products, what information about a prospect would you seek as part of your preparation?
   a. Two-bedroom condominium
   b. New automobile
   c. Carpeting for a home redecorating project

6. What sources should be used for recruiting sales applicants in each of the following firms? Explain your choice in each case.
   a. A Marriott Hotel that wants companies to use the hotel for conventions
   b. IBM, for sales of mainframe (large) computers

7. Compare the merits of straight-salary and straight-commission plans of sales compensation. What are two types of sales jobs in which each plan might be desirable?

8. How might a firm determine whether a sales person is using high-pressure selling tactics that might injure customer satisfaction?

9. How can a sales manager evaluate the performance of sales people in getting new business?

■ HANDS-ON MARKETING

1. Review your activities of the past few days and identify those in which:
   a. You did some personal selling.
   b. People tried to sell something to you.
   Select one situation in each category where you thought the selling was particularly effective, and explain why.

2. Interview three students from your school who recently have gone through the job-interviewing process conducted by companies using your school's placement office. Use the personal selling process described in the chapter to evaluate the students' sales efforts. Prepare a report covering your findings.

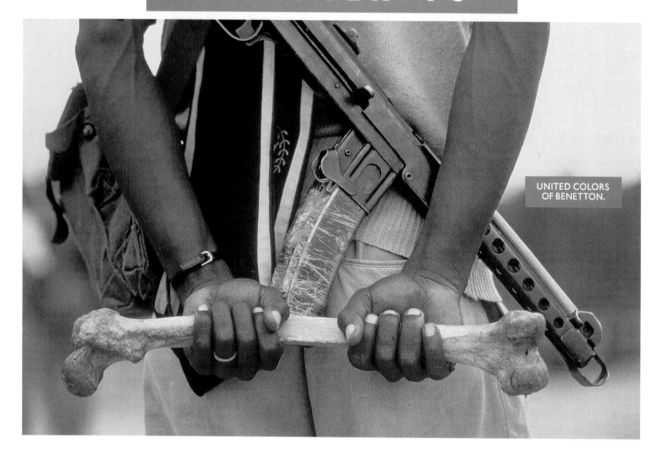

UNITED COLORS
OF BENETTON.

Advertising, Sales Promotion, and Public Relations

Is There a Limit to How Far
BENETTON
Advertising Can Go?

Benetton created a retailing revolution in the 1980s with its distinctive, casual clothing at affordable prices. And it grew rapidly through a franchising system in which the retail operator provides the capital for the store. By 1994 the company, still operated by the Italian family that started it, had grown into an international retailing colossus with 7,000 stores and sales of $1.7 billion. In recent years, however, sales have flattened and profits have declined.

Benetton is experiencing a number of problems, some of which have been around for a while. For example, the number of stores in the U.S. has declined from 500 in the late 1980s to around 150 now. The firm also has been criticized for permitting stores to locate too close together, shipping goods late, and—probably the worst accusation that can be made about a fashion merchandiser—not keeping its merchandise up to date. Benetton produces two seasonal collections a year. In contrast, competitors such as The Gap and Zara (in Spain) change their styles every 4 to 6 weeks. As a result, Benetton franchisees complain that their merchandise looks tired and stale.

However, Benetton's biggest problem may be its advertising. The company spends just 4 percent of sales on advertising worldwide annually. That's about $80 million—much less than any other leading clothes retailer.

But it's not the amount of advertising that upsets the franchisees and stirs up controversy; it's the recent themes. The company has relied exclusively on shock images dealing with social issues such as racism, AIDS, and war. For example, some of the ads are photos of:

- The blood-soaked uniform of a dead Bosnian soldier.
- A man dying of AIDS.
- A white child wearing angel's wings alongside a black child with devil's horns.
- Refugees jumping over the side of a freighter into the ocean.

They include only the slightest mention of the company, but no pictures of the company's merchandise.

The ads, Benetton contends, are to further the consideration and discussion of important social issues, while also creating brand awareness. Critics say the ads are exploitative, in bad taste, and have nothing to do with a commercial venture. Some newspapers, including *The Los Angeles Times* and several in France, rejected the ad showing the dead soldier's clothing. They described it as excessively violent and an ad for terrorism. In Germany, a coalition of Benetton retailers have successfully sued the company, claiming that the controversial ads destroyed their businesses. Similar suits have been filed in France.

Recently Benetton toned down its ads. In the company's first ever television advertising in the U.S. and in print ads in Europe, more traditional models in the firm's clothes are featured. In the process, the retailer has attempted a modest repositioning. According to company executives, the ads appearing in *Vogue* and *The New York Times* as well as on cable stations in Chicago and Washington, D.C., are aimed at a slightly older audience.[1]

What should be the objective of Benetton's advertising, and how should the firm go about accomplishing its objective?

http://www.benetton.com/

Advertising, sales promotion, and public relations are the mass-communication tools available to marketers. As its name suggests, mass communication uses the same message for everyone in an audience. The mass communicator trades off the advantage of personal selling, the opportunity to tailor a message to each prospect, for the advantage of reaching many people at a lower cost per person.

The term *mass* communications does not imply indiscriminate efforts to reach large audiences. Marketers are constantly seeking refinements that will allow them to present their messages to more specifically defined target audiences.

This chapter examines nonpersonal, mass-communication promotional tools—advertising, sales promotion, and public relations. After studying this chapter, you should be able to explain:

CHAPTER GOALS

- The nature and scope of advertising.
- Characteristics of the major types of advertising.
- How advertising campaigns are developed and advertising media are selected.
- The alternative ways firms organize their advertising efforts.
- What sales promotion is and how it is managed.
- The role of public relations and publicity in the promotional mix.

Nature and Scope of Advertising

All advertisements have four features:

- A verbal and/or visual message.
- A sponsor who is identified.
- Delivery through one or more media.
- Payment by the sponsor to the media carrying the message.

Advertising, then, consists of all the activities involved in presenting to an audience a nonpersonal, sponsor-identified, paid-for message about a product or organization.

Advertising in one form or another is used by most organizations. The significance of advertising is indicated by the amount of money spent on it. In 1994, total U.S. advertising expenditures were over $150 billion, nearly three times the amount spent in 1980. Table 18-1 shows the relative importance of the major advertising media over the past 25 years. Throughout this period newspapers have been the most widely used medium, based on total advertising dollars spent. Newspapers' share has declined, however, as the proportion spent for television and direct-mail advertising has increased.

Advertising as a Percentage of Sales

http://www.pg.com/

The amounts spent on advertising can seem daunting. For example, Procter & Gamble spent over $60 million on advertising just to introduce the pain reliever Aleve. And as this chapter's opening case described, Benetton's expenditure of $80 million per year is low in its product category. Table 18-2 shows the 10 companies with the largest dollar expenditures for advertising in the U.S. Not surprisingly, these are companies with which we are all familiar. However, to gauge advertising spending, we should measure it against some benchmark rather than simply look at the totals. For example, advertising expenses frequently are expressed as a percentage of a company's sales. Similar figures, except by industry rather than firm, are presented in Table 18-3. Notice how much variation exists across industries.

TABLE 18-1 Advertising expenditures in the United States, by medium

Advertising expenditures declined in 1991, the first decrease in half a century, but began increasing again in 1992. In 1994, newspapers maintained a slight (less than 1 percent) first-place position among media, but television is a close second and direct mail is growing rapidly.

Medium	1994 dollars spent (in billions)	1994 (%)	1990 (%)	1980 (%)	1970 (%)
Newspapers	34	23	25	28	29
Television	34	23	22	21	18
Direct mail	30	20	18	14	14
Radio	11	7	7	7	7
Yellow pages	10	7	7	–	–
Magazines	8	5	5	6	7
Business papers	3	2	2	3	4
Outdoor	1	1	1	1	1
Miscellaneous*	19	13	12	20	20
Total percentage		100	100	100	100
Total dollars (in billions)	$150		$128	$55	$20

*Before 1988 this category included yellow pages. Also includes transportation advertising, weekly newspapers, regional farm publications, and point-of-purchase advertising.

Sources: Robert J. Cohen, "More Gains Foreseen for '95 Ad Spending," *Advertising Age*, May 8, 1995, p. 36; 1980 figures from *Advertising Age*, Mar. 22, 1982, p. 66. Others adapted from *Advertising Age*, Nov. 17, 1975, p. 40.

Industry averages can, however, be misleading. How much an individual firm spends on advertising is influenced by its resources and objectives more than by what other firms in the industry are doing. Coca-Cola spends an amount equal to about 4 percent of its sales on advertising, while Royal Crown's ad budget is nearly 40 percent of its sales. Despite this proportional difference, Coca-Cola spends about $9 on advertising for every dollar spent by Royal Crown.

http://www.coca-cola.com/

Advertising Cost versus Personal Selling Cost

While there are no accurate figures for the cost of personal selling, we do know it far surpasses advertising expenditures. Only a few manufacturing industries, such as drugs, toiletries, cleaning products, tobacco, and beverages, spend more on

TABLE 18-2 Top-10 national advertisers in 1994, based on total expenditures in the United States

Company	*Advertising expenditures* Dollars (in millions)	As percent of U.S. sales
1. Procter & Gamble	2,690	13.8
2. Philip Morris	2,413	5.4
3. General Motors	1,929	1.8
4. Ford	1,186	1.2
5. Sears, Roebuck	1,134	2.1
6. AT&T	1,103	NA
7. PepsiCo	1,098	6.0
8. Chrysler	972	NA
9. Disney	935	NA
10. Johnson & Johnson	934	11.7

Source: "100 Leading National Advertisers," *Advertising Age*, Sept. 27, 1995, p. 16. Percent of sales figures computed from several sources.

TABLE 18-3 Advertising as a percent of sales for selected industries

Industry (SIC code)	Advertising as a percent of sales
Games and toys (3944)	18.1
Cleaning and polishing products (2842)	17.3
Motion pictures (7812)	12.7
Watches and clocks (3873)	8.5
Perfumes and cosmetics (2844)	8.2
Apparel (2300)	5.4
Soft drinks (2086)	3.0
Farm machinery (3523)	1.0

Source: "1995 Advertising to Sales Ratios for the 200 Largest Ad Spending Industries," *Advertising Age*, Aug. 14, 1995, p. 26.

advertising than on personal selling. Advertising runs 1 to 3 percent of net sales in many firms, whereas the expenses of recruiting and operating a sales force are typically 8 to 15 percent of sales.

At the wholesale level, advertising costs are very low. Personal selling expenses for wholesalers, however, may run 10 to 15 times more than their expenditures for advertising. Even among many retailers, including some with self-service operations, the total cost of their customer-contact employees is substantially higher than what they spend on advertising.

Types of Advertising

Advertising can be classified according to (1) the target audience, either consumers or businesses; (2) what is being advertised, a product versus an institution; and (3) the objective sought, the stimulation of primary or selective demand. To fully appreciate the scope and types of advertising, it is essential to understand these three classifications.

http://www.moneymag.com/

Consumer and Business-to-Business Advertising. An ad is directed at either consumers or businesses; thus it is either **consumer advertising** or **business-to-business advertising**. Retailers by definition sell only to consumers; therefore, they are the only organizations that are not faced with this choice. The publisher of *Money* magazine, for example, must decide what portion of its advertising budget will be used to attract businesses to advertise in the magazine, and what portion will go toward selling magazines.

Product and Institutional Advertising. All advertising may be classified as product or institutional. **Product advertising** focuses on a particular product or brand. It is subdivided into direct-action and indirect-action product advertising.

- *Direct-action* advertising seeks a quick response. For instance, a magazine ad containing a coupon or an 800 number may urge the reader to send or call immediately for a free sample, or a supermarket ad in a local newspaper stresses this week's specials.
- *Indirect-action* advertising is designed to stimulate demand over a longer period of time. It is intended to inform or remind consumers that the product exists and to point out its benefits. Dave Thomas, appearing in ads as a spokesperson for Wendy's, is an example. Most network television advertising is indirect action, whereas much local television advertising is direct action.

http://www.wendys.com/

http://www.ford.com/

Institutional advertising presents information about the advertiser's business or tries to create a favorable attitude—build goodwill—toward the organization. In contrast to product advertising, institutional advertising is not intended to sell a specific product. Its objective is to create a particular image for a company. Ford, for example, has spent millions over the years communicating its corporate philosophy with the "Quality Is Job 1" campaign.

Primary-Demand and Selective-Demand Advertising. **Primary-demand advertising** is designed to stimulate demand for a generic category of a product such as coffee, oranges, or garments made from cotton. In contrast, **selective-demand advertising** is intended to stimulate demand for individual brands such as Folgers coffee, Sunkist oranges, and Liz Claiborne sportswear.

Primary-demand advertising is used in either of two situations. The first is when the product is in the introductory stage of its life cycle. This is called *pioneering advertising*. The objective of pioneering advertising is to inform, not to persuade, the target market. Recall from Chapter 5 that a consumer must first be made aware of a product before becoming interested in or desiring it. In recent years pioneering ads have been run for digital compact cassettes, videophones, and virtual-reality projectors.

The other use of primary-demand advertising occurs throughout the product life cycle and therefore is considered *demand-sustaining advertising*. It is usually done by trade associations trying to stimulate or sustain demand for their industry's product. Thus, the National Fluid Milk Processor Promotion Board encourages us to consume more milk with its campaign depicting celebrities with milk "mustaches."

Selective-demand advertising is essentially competitive advertising. It pits one brand against the rest of the market. This type of advertising is employed when a product is beyond the introductory life-cycle stage and is competing for market share with several other brands. Selective-demand advertising emphasizes a brand's special features and benefits—its differential advantage.

Selective-demand advertising that makes reference to one or more competitors is called comparative advertising. In **comparative advertising** the advertiser either directly—by naming a rival brand—or indirectly, through inference, points out differences between the competing brands. Recently AT&T and MCI both have used comparative ads in their competition for the long-distance telephone market, and Aleve, Tylenol, and Advil ads have all included direct comparisons. Comparative advertising is encouraged by the Federal Trade Commission as a means of stimulating competition and disseminating useful information to consumers.

Developing an Advertising Campaign

An **advertising campaign** consists of all the tasks involved in transforming a theme into a coordinated advertising program to accomplish a specific goal for a product or brand. For example, you probably can recall the messages offered up by Little Caesars toga-clad "Pizza Pizza" man and Coca-Cola's polar bears even if you've grown tired of the messengers.

An advertising campaign is planned within the framework of the overall strategic marketing program and the promotional campaign. Before designing an advertising campaign, management must:

- Know who the target audience is.
- Establish the overall promotional goals.

- Set the total promotional budget.
- Determine the overall promotional theme.

With these tasks completed, the firm can begin formulating an advertising campaign. The steps in developing a campaign are defining objectives, establishing a budget, creating a message, selecting media, and evaluating effectiveness.

Defining Objectives

The purpose of advertising is to sell something—a good, service, idea, person, or place—either now or later. This goal is reached by setting specific objectives that can be expressed in individual ads that are incorporated into an advertising campaign. Typical objectives are:

- *Support personal selling.* Advertising may be used to acquaint prospects with the seller's company and products, easing the way for the sales force.
- *Improve dealer relations.* Wholesalers and retailers like to see a manufacturer support its products with advertising.
- *Introduce a new product.* Consumers need to be informed even about line extensions that make use of familiar brand names.
- *Expand the use of a product.* Advertising may be used to lengthen the season for a product (as Lipton did for iced tea); increase the frequency of replacement (as Fram did for oil filters); or increase the variety of product uses (as Arm & Hammer did for baking soda).
- *Counteract substitution.* Advertising reinforces the decisions of existing customers and reduces the likelihood that they will switch to alternative brands.

Establishing a Budget

Once a promotional budget has been established (discussed in Chapter 16), it must be allocated among the various activities comprising the overall promotional program. In the case of a particular brand, a firm may wish to have several ads, as well as sales promotion and public relations activities, directed at different target audiences all at the same time. To introduce the redesigned 1996 Taurus, Ford undertook a $100 million promotional campaign. It included direct mail to owners of rival makes, gifts for selected consumers for test-driving the car, network television advertising, national and local newspaper ads, and parties in Ford dealerships when the car was unveiled. Since all these efforts must be paid for from the promotional budget, the potential value of each must be weighed and allocations made accordingly.

One method that firms use to extend their budgets is cooperative advertising. **Cooperative advertising** is a joint effort by two or more firms intended to benefit each of the participants. There are two types of cooperative ads—vertical and horizontal. *Vertical cooperative advertising* involves firms on different levels of distribution. For example, a manufacturer and a retailer share the cost of the retailer's advertising of that manufacturer's product. Frequently the manufacturer prepares the actual ad, leaving space for the retailer's name and address. Then the manufacturer and retailer share the media cost of placing the ad. Many retail ads in newspapers involve co-op funds.[2] Cooperative ads are also common on radio, and they appear quite frequently on local television.

Another type of vertical cooperation is an *advertising allowance*, or cash discount offered by a manufacturer to a retailer, to encourage the retailer to advertise or prominently display a product. The difference between cooperative advertising and an advertising allowance is that with co-op advertising the manufacturer has control over how the money is actually spent.

Cooperative arrangements benefit retailers by providing them with extra funds for promotion. Manufacturers also benefit because cooperative advertising provides them with local identification for their products. In addition, a manufacturer's ad dollars go further because rates charged by local media (such as a daily newspaper) are typically lower for ads placed by local firms than for ads placed by national advertisers.

Horizontal cooperative advertising is joint advertising in which two or more firms on the same level of distribution, such as a group of retailers, share the costs. For example, all the stores in a suburban shopping center may run a joint newspaper ad. The principal benefit is that by pooling their funds, the stores achieve greater exposure than if they advertised individually.

Creating a Message

Whatever the objective of an advertising campaign, the individual ads must accomplish two things: get and hold the *attention* of the intended audience, and *influence* that audience in the desired way. Attention can be achieved in many ways. (Recall our discussion of perception in Chapter 5.) Television makes possible special effects, as for example the changing face shapes in the Gillette Sensor ad and the Energizer bunny. Radio can use listeners' imaginations to create mental images that would be impossible to actually produce. Surprising, shocking, amusing, and arousing curiosity are all common techniques to gain attention. Thus a print ad might be mostly white space, or a billboard might show the product in an unusual setting.

http://www.energizer.com/

If the ad succeeds in getting the audience's attention, the advertiser has a few seconds to communicate a message intended to influence beliefs and/or behavior. The message has two elements, the appeal and the execution. The *appeal* in an ad is the reason or justification for believing or behaving. It is the benefit that the individual will receive as a result of accepting the message.

Some advertisers mistakenly focus their appeal on product features or attributes. They either confuse attributes with benefits, or assume that if they present the product's attributes, the audience will infer the correct benefits. Telling consumers that a breakfast cereal contains fiber (an attribute) is much less meaningful than telling them that because it contains fiber, consuming it reduces the likelihood of colon cancer (the benefit).

Execution is combining in a convincing, compatible way the feature or device that gets attention with the appeal. An appeal can be executed in different ways. Consider the ways you could communicate the benefits of a luxury automobile—presenting performance statistics, obtaining the endorsements of respected authorities, collecting testimonials from satisfied owners, or describing the meticulous manufacturing process are all possibilities. Rather than any of these, Mercedes introduced its $40,000 E-class model with photos of deceased celebrities (Bing Crosby, Errol Flynn, Marlene Dietrich, and others) at the height of their fame with their luxury cars. Accompanied by the caption, "All born too soon," this execution attracts attention and implies that people able to select any alternative would find the E-class desirable.

http://www.mercedes-net.com/

Selecting Media

In describing the steps in developing an advertising campaign, we have discussed creating an advertising message before describing the selection of **advertising media** in which to place the ad. In reality these decisions are made simultaneously. Both the message and the choice of media are determined by the appeal and the target audience.

A GLOBAL PERSPECTIVE

WHY ARE MANY U.S. ADS INEFFECTIVE IN JAPAN?

Despite the volume of trade, travel, and communication between the U.S. and Japan, advertising that works in one country is often ineffective in the other. Recently two senior Japanese advertising executives commented on how U.S. and Japanese advertisements differ:

• In the U.S., the product is usually the focus of an ad. In Japan, the company that makes or sells the product is emphasized.
• Japanese advertising seeks a strong, short-term impact. U.S. ads attempt to create a consistent, long-term effect.
• In the U.S., unknown individuals "off the street" are frequently used to endorse products, while the Japanese rely almost exclusively on celebrity endorsers.
• In Japan, ad appeals are frequently changed, while in the U.S., advertisers select appeals with the intent of using them for a long time.
• U.S. ad messages are direct and specific. In Japan ads tend to be subtle, with a greater tendency toward suggestion than clear statements.
• Japanese ads tend to make use of fewer words than U.S. ads.

The principal reason for the differences is the fact that Western cultures tend to focus on the individual, while the Japanese emphasize the person as part of a community or family. Since the buyer and seller feel they share similar attitudes and values, there is a high degree of trust in Japanese society. As a result, it would be considered disrespectful to question the quality of a respected company's products. Conversely, it would be unnecessary and inappropriate for a seller to make the type of superlative claims that are common in U.S. ads.

Sources: Hideo Ishikawa, "Exploring Differences in Japan, U.S. Culture," *Advertising Age*, Sept. 18, 1995, p. I8; and Jack Russell, "'Challenge of Change' Visits Japan," *Advertising Age*, Sept. 18, 1995, p. I8.

Advertisers need to make decisions at each of three successive levels to determine which specific advertising medium to use:

1. Which type of medium will be used—newspaper, television, radio, magazine, or direct mail? What about the less prominent media of billboards, the Internet, and yellow pages?
2. Which category of the selected medium will be used? Television has network and cable; magazines include general-interest (*Newsweek*, *People*) and special-interest (*Popular Mechanics*, *Runner's World*) categories; and there are national as well as local newspapers.
3. Which specific media vehicles will be used? An advertiser that decides first on radio and then on local stations must determine which stations to use in each city.

Here are some general factors that will influence media choice:

• *Objectives of the ad*. The purpose of a particular ad and the goals of the entire campaign influence which media to use. For example, if the campaign goal is to generate appointments for sales people, the company may rely on direct mail. If an advertiser wants to induce quick action, newspaper or radio may be the medium to use.
• *Audience coverage*. The audience reached by the medium should match the geographic area in which the product is distributed. Furthermore, the selected medium should reach the desired types of prospects with a minimum of wasted coverage. Wasted coverage occurs when an ad reaches people who are not

prospects for the product. Many media—even national and other large-market media—can be targeted at small, specialized market segments. For example, *Time* magazine publishes regional editions with different ads in the East, Midwest, and West. Large metropolitan newspapers publish suburban editions as well as regional editions within the city.

- *Requirements of the message.* The medium should fit the message. For example, magazines provide high-quality visual reproductions that attract attention along with printed messages that can be carefully read and evaluated. As a result, consumers prefer magazines as a source for food products ads.[3]

- *Time and location of the buying decision.* If the objective is to stimulate a purchase, the medium should reach prospective customers when and where they are about to make their buying decisions. Research by the Radio Advertising Bureau shows that radio scores the highest in immediacy of exposure. Over 50 percent of adults were last exposed to radio within 1 hour of making their largest purchase of the day. This factor highlights one of the strengths of point-of-purchase advertising, for example, on shopping carts and in the aisles of supermarkets, which reach consumers at the actual time of purchase.

- *Media cost.* The cost of each medium should be considered in relation to the amount of funds available to pay for it and its reach or circulation. For example, the cost of network television exceeds the available funds of many advertisers. To compare various media, advertisers use a measure called **cost per thousand (CPM)**, which is the cost of reaching a thousand people, one time each, with a particular ad.

Beyond these general factors, management must evaluate the advertising characteristics of each medium it is considering. We have carefully chosen the term *characteristics* instead of advantages and disadvantages because a medium that works well for one product is not necessarily the best choice for another product. To illustrate, a characteristic of radio is that it makes its impressions through sound and imagination. The roar of a crowd, the rumbling of thunder, or screeching tires can be used to create mental images quickly and easily. But radio will not do the job for products that benefit from color photography. Let's examine the characteristics of the major media.

Newspapers.   As an advertising medium, newspapers are flexible and timely. Ads can be inserted or canceled on very short notice and can vary in size from small classifieds to multiple pages. Pages can be added or dropped, so the space in newspapers is not limited in the way that time is constrained on TV and radio. Newspapers can be used to reach an entire city or, where regional editions are offered, selected areas. Cost per person reached is relatively low.

On the other hand, the life of newspapers is very short. They are discarded soon after being read. They are viewed as providing fairly complete coverage of a local market. However, in many large cities, circulation of daily newspapers has decreased. Also, because newspapers don't offer much format variety, it is difficult to design ads that stand out.

Television.   Television combines motion, sound, and special visual effects. Products can be demonstrated as well as described on TV. It offers wide geographic coverage, and flexibility in when the message can be presented. However, television is a relatively expensive medium. It costs around $400,000 to create and produce a 30-second network television commercial. As a result, fewer ads are being made, and they are being kept on the air longer. Air time is also expensive. For example, Table 18-4 shows how the cost of an ad in prime time has increased over the years. Because TV ads lack permanence, they must be seen and understood immediately. As a result, TV does not lend itself to complicated messages.

Cable is changing television as an advertising medium. Over 50 percent of American homes have cable, with an average of 20 broadcast stations per household, and these numbers will only increase in the future. The result is more fragmented markets and specialized broadcasting, making it difficult to reach a mass market. On the positive side, the specialized programming on cable channels such as MTV, CNBC, and ESPN offers an advertiser a more homogeneous group of viewers at a lower price (because the audience is smaller) than broadcast networks.

Advertisers are also taking television to attractive target audiences—young professionals, teenagers, working women—who have become less accessible through traditional media. To reach them, firms such as Whittle Communications and CNN are using what is called place-based television. By putting TVs in classrooms, waiting rooms, supermarkets, airports, health clubs, and other places where there are "captive audiences," they provide advertisers with otherwise unavailable viewers.

http://www.hacienda.com/
http://www.cnn.com/

Direct Mail. Direct mail is the most personal and selective of all media. A division of Walt Disney Corp. that sells time-share vacations at Disney resorts has created a data base that includes information on over 300,000 prospects. Using extensive data on their customers' demographics and past purchase behavior, Disney has developed a description of a typical time-share purchaser. The description is used to select prospects who are sent direct-mail packages and are contacted by sales representatives.[4]

Highly specialized direct-mail lists can also be purchased (among the thousands available are lists of air traffic controllers, wig dealers, college professors, pregnant women, and disc jockeys), but they can be expensive. Printing and postage fees make the cost of direct mail per person reached quite high compared with other media. However, because direct mail goes only to the people the advertiser wishes to contact, there is almost no wasted coverage.

Reaching the prospect does not, however, ensure that the message is received. Direct mail is pure advertising. It is not accompanied by editorial matter (unless the advertiser provides it). Therefore, a direct-mail ad must attract its own readers. This is critical when you consider that the average American home receives more than 10 direct-mail pieces a week and that the recipient of a direct-mail ad decides in 4 seconds whether to discard or open it.

TABLE 18-4 The cost of prime time advertising on network television

Year	Program	Type of ad	Cost
1970	*Bewitched*	60 seconds	$ 5,200
	Best of Everything	60 seconds	4,000
1972	*Bonanza*	30 seconds	26,000
	Peyton Place	30 seconds	27,500
1980	*M*A*S*H*	30 seconds	150,000
	Dallas	30 seconds	145,000
1992	*Murphy Brown*	30 seconds	310,000
	Roseanne	30 seconds	290,000
1995	*Seinfeld*	30 seconds	490,000
	Home Improvement	30 seconds	475,000

Sources: "50 Years of TV Advertising: The Buying and Selling," *Advertising Age*, Spring 1995, p. 29; and Joe Mandese, "Seinfeld Is NBC's $1M/minute-man," *Advertising Age*, Sept. 18, 1995, pp. 1+.

AN ETHICAL DILEMMA?

Holders of First Omni Bank credit cards received a direct-mail promotion that included a check for $4 and a description of the Pet Care Savings Club. The promotional piece begins, "The enclosed bank check is real and is yours to cash right now. It is just the first of many rebate checks you will be receiving—when you cash in on the many benefits of the Pet Care Savings Club." It goes on to explain that the recipient has been selected to receive a 30-day complimentary trial membership in the club. This is followed by an enumeration of the club's benefits, including unspecified cash amounts for veterinary visits, grooming care, and pet food.

In fine print on the back of the check (above the endorsement space) is the following statement:

My signature authorizes you to enroll me as a member in the Pet Care Savings Club. My

complete Pet Care Savings Club Membership Kit will be sent to me promptly by return mail. I understand there is a 30 day free trial period during which time I may cancel my membership by calling 1-800-388-7387. Unless I notify you that I do not wish to continue my membership beyond this trial period, I authorize you to bill the $49.95 annual membership fee, and all subsequent renewals at the then-current annual membership fee, to my First Omni Bank credit card account. I will be personally notified prior to renewal with the option to discontinue my membership at that time. This check cannot be used as payment towards your First Omni Bank account balance.

Is it ethical to make a "free" offer that commits a consumer to charges unless the seller is notified?

Radio. Over the past decade, radio has enjoyed a rebirth as an advertising and cultural medium. When interest in television soared after World War II, radio audiences (especially for national network radio) declined so dramatically that some people predicted radio's demise. However, since 1980 over 1,200 new radio stations (75 percent of them FM) have gone on the air. Radio is a low-CPM medium because of its broad reach. Nearly 80 percent of Americans listen to a radio daily. With programming ranging from all-talk to rock-and-roll to country music, certain target markets can be pinpointed quite effectively.

Radio makes only an audio impression, relying entirely on the listener's ability to retain information heard and not seen. Also, audience attention is often at a low level, because radio is frequently used as background for working, studying (Is your radio on now?), or some other activity.

http://www.yellowpages.com/

Yellow Pages. The yellow pages—a printed directory of local business names and phone numbers organized by type of product—has been around since the late 1800s. Today there are over 6,400 annual yellow pages directories in the U.S., and total yellow pages advertising revenue exceeds both radio and magazines. The yellow pages are a source of information with which most consumers are familiar. And they are used by consumers at or very near the buying decision. On the negative side, yellow page ads are difficult to differentiate, and an advertiser's message is surrounded by the messages of competitors.

Magazines. Magazines are the medium to use when high-quality printing and color are desired in an ad. Magazines can reach a national market at a relatively low cost per reader. In recent years, the rapid increase in special-interest magazines and regional editions of general-interest magazines has made it possible for advertisers to reach a selected audience with a minimum of wasted circulation. Magazines are usually read in a leisurely fashion, in contrast to the haste in which

*S*chools are strapped for money, but they want to provide families with monthly lunch menus. Advertisers want to reach students, but traditional media are declining in effectiveness. The solution? Sponsored lunch menus. What you see here is the cover panel of a 14-page, brightly colored, 1-month menu calendar. The calendar and some nutritional tips take up four pages, with the remainder made up of ads and coupons for goods and services that range from frozen foods to home videos. The Louisville, Kentucky, school district claims it saves about $200,000 a month by using the sponsored menus. What do you think of this medium?

other print media are read. This feature is especially valuable to the advertiser with a lengthy or complicated message. Magazines have a relatively long life, anywhere from a week to a month, and a high pass-along readership.

With less flexible production schedules than newspapers, magazines require ads to be submitted several weeks before publication. In addition, because they are published weekly or monthly, it is more difficult to use topical messages. Magazines are often read at times or in places—on planes or in doctors' offices, for instance—far removed from where a buying impulse can be acted on.

Outdoor Advertising. Spending on outdoor advertising remains fairly constant, at just over $1 billion a year. Low cost per exposure is its chief advantage, though the total cost of a national billboard campaign can be quite high. Because of the mobile nature of our society, outdoor ads reach a large percentage of the population. For example, a billboard on Route 80 in New Jersey has the potential of being seen by 45,000 people a day. But because it is seen by people "on the go," billboard advertising is appropriate only for brief messages. The rule of thumb is six words or less.

Billboards can provide intense market coverage within an area. However, unless the advertised product is a widely used good or service, considerable wasted circulation will occur, since many of the passersby will not be prospects. Finally, the landscape-defacing criticism of outdoor advertising may be a consideration for some advertisers.

Interactive Media. The fastest developing interactive medium is the Internet, which consumers access using personal computers. As noted in Chapter 2, the Internet began as an electronic network for information sharing by scientists. But with the emergence of an Internet subsystem known as the World Wide Web, millions of organizations and individuals now have direct access to one another through computers. The opportunity this has created has not been lost on marketers who can use it to communicate advertising messages. This medium is interactive because the recipient has to take the initiative to tap into the sender's message. Once the interaction has begun, the recipient can request additional information and even buy a product.

The Internet is particularly popular with companies selling products that involve extensive decision making. For example, a consumer interested in buying a car might begin by using the Internet on a personal computer to find out which companies make minivans. From there, the consumer could move on to information about performance, safety features, technical specifications, and prices of specific makes. The next step might be a page that identifies dealers in the area, their respective inventories, and financing alternatives.[5]

Media decision makers abroad are faced with different conditions that require local knowledge. For example, the move toward greater democracy has created new media options in some Eastern European countries, where private radio and television stations now can run up to four times as much advertising as was permitted on state-owned stations. On the other hand, print media in most of the world cannot offer the special editions and narrowly targeted audiences available in highly developed countries.

Evaluating the Advertising Effort

In managing its advertising program, a company should carefully evaluate the effectiveness of previous ads and use the results to improve the quality of future ads. Top executives want proof that advertising is worthwhile. They want to know whether dollars spent on advertising are producing as many sales as could be reaped from the same dollars spent on other marketing activities.

Difficulty of Evaluation.   It is hard to measure the sales effectiveness of advertising. By the very nature of the marketing mix, all elements—including advertising—are so intertwined that it is nearly impossible to measure the effect of any one by itself. Factors that contribute to the difficulty of measuring the sales impact of advertising are:

- *Different objectives*. Though all advertising is ultimately intended to increase sales, individual ads may not be aimed at producing immediate results. Some ads simply announce new store hours or service policies. Other ads build goodwill or contribute to a company's image.
- *Effects over time*. Even an ad designed to have an immediate sales impact may produce results weeks or months after it appears. An ad may plant in the consumer's mind a seed that doesn't blossom into a sale for several weeks.
- *Measurement problems*. Consumers cannot usually say when or if a specific ad influenced their behavior, let alone if it caused them to buy. Human motivation is too complicated to be explained by a single factor.

In spite of these problems, advertisers try to measure advertising effectiveness because they must—and some knowledge is better than none. An ad's effectiveness may be tested before it is presented to the target audience, while it is being presented, or after it has completed its run.

Methods Used to Measure Effectiveness.   Ad effectiveness can be measured directly and indirectly. **Direct tests**, which measure or predict the sales volume attributable to an ad or a campaign, can only be used with a few types of ads. Tabulating the number of redemptions of a reduced-price coupon incorporated in an ad will indicate its effectiveness. Coupons frequently are coded so they can also be traced to the publications from which they came. Another direct test that is used to predict sales measures the number of inquiries received from an ad that offers additional information to prospects who call or write in.

Most other measures are **indirect tests** of effectiveness, or measures of something other than actual behavior. One of the most frequently used measures is advertising recall. Recall tests are based on the premise that an ad can have an effect only if it is perceived and remembered. Three common recall tests are:

- *Recognition*—showing people an ad and asking if they have seen it before.
- *Aided recall*—asking people if they can recall seeing any ads for a particular brand.
- *Unaided recall*—asking people if they can remember seeing any ads within an identified product category.

Refinements are constantly being made in advertising testing. Developments in areas such as laboratory test markets and computer simulations hold promise for the future. However, the complexity of decision making, combined with the multitude of influences on the buyer, will continue to make measuring the effectiveness of advertising a difficult task.

Organizing for Advertising

There are three ways a firm can manage its advertising:

- Develop an internal advertising department.
- Use an outside advertising agency.
- Use a combination of an internal department and an outside advertising agency.

Regardless of which alternative is selected, generally the same specialized skills are necessary to do the advertising job. Creative people are needed to prepare the copy, generate audio and/or video material, and design the formats. Media experts are required to select the appropriate media, buy the time or space, and arrange for the scheduled appearance of the ads. And managerial skills are essential to plan and administer the entire advertising program.

Internal Departments

All these advertising tasks, some of them, or just overall direction can be performed by an internal department. A company whose advertising is a substantial part of its marketing mix will usually have its own advertising department. Large retailers, for example, have their own advertising departments, and many do not use advertising agencies at all. If a company has adopted the marketing concept, the advertising department head will report to the organization's top marketing executive.

Advertising Agencies

Many companies, especially producers, use advertising agencies to carry out some or all of their advertising activities. An **advertising agency** is an independent company that provides specialized advertising services and may also offer more general marketing assistance.

Advertising agencies plan and execute entire advertising campaigns. They employ more advertising specialists than their clients do, because they spread the cost over many accounts. A client company can benefit from an agency's experience gained from other products and clients. Many large agencies have expanded the services they offer to include sales promotion, public relations, and even broader marketing assistance. As a result, they are frequently called upon to assist in strategic planning, new-product development, package design, and selecting product names.

Inside Department and Outside Agency

Many firms have their own advertising department and also use an advertising agency. The internal advertising department acts as a liaison with the agency, giving the company greater control over this major expenditure. The advertising department approves the agency's plans and ads, is responsible for preparing and administering the advertising budget, and coordinates advertising with personal selling. It may also handle direct marketing, dealer displays, and other promotional activities if they are not handled by the agency.

Sales Promotion

Sales promotion is one of the most loosely used terms in the marketing vocabulary. We define **sales promotion** as demand-stimulating devices designed to supplement advertising and facilitate personal selling. Examples of sales promotion devices are coupons, premiums, in-store displays, trade shows, samples, in-store demonstrations, and contests.

Sales promotions are conducted by producers and middlemen. The target for producers' sales promotions may be middlemen, end users—households or business users—or the producers' own sales forces. Middlemen direct sales promotion at their sales people or prospects further down the channel of distribution.

Nature and Scope of Sales Promotion

Sales promotion is distinct from advertising or personal selling, but these three forms of promotion are often used together in a coordinated fashion. For example, prospective customers may be generated from people who enter a contest to win a copier at the Canon exhibit at an office equipment trade show. These prospects might be sent some direct-mail advertising and then be contacted by a sales person.

There are two categories of sales promotion: *trade promotions*, directed to the members of the distribution channel, and *consumer promotions*, aimed at

*I*nteractive store displays, like the one pictured here, provide advertising at the point of purchase. The displays ask consumers questions, either on a screen or by voice, and use their answers to guide them to the correct product. Thus far, interactive media have been most popular with products that are somewhat technical such as swimming pool chemicals and over-the-counter medications, as shown here. Because consumers often enter the store aware of their need but not knowing which product is ideal, point-of-purchase advertising can be very effective.

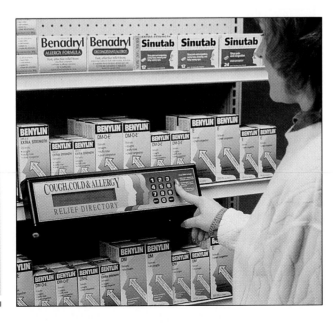

consumers. It may surprise you to learn that manufacturers as a group spend about twice as much on trade promotion as they do on advertising, and an amount about equal to their advertising on consumer promotions.[6]

The magnitude of sales promotion activities is mind-boggling. Though no statistics are available on total expenditures, the billings of the top-150 sales promotion agencies amount to nearly $900 million. However, that is only a small part of the total. For example, in the first half of 1995, AT&T alone gave consumers over $100 million in cash, travel credits, and merchandise incentives for switching long-distance carriers from MCI to AT&T.[7] Millions of people attend trade shows each year, and billions of dollars are spent on point-of-purchase displays in retail stores. And the number of contests and the dollar value of their prizes more than doubled from the mid-1980s to 1990.

http://www.att.com/

Sales promotion as a proportion of all promotion grew rapidly in the early 1990s. Several factors in the marketing environment contribute to the popularity of sales promotion:

- *Short-term results.* Sales promotions such as couponing and trade allowances produce quicker, more measurable sales results. However, critics of this strategy argue that these immediate benefits come at the expense of building brand equity. They believe that an overemphasis on sales promotion may undermine a brand's future.
- *Competitive pressure.* If competitors are offering buyers price reductions, contests, or other incentives, a firm may feel forced to retaliate with its own sales promotions.
- *Buyers' expectations.* Once they are offered purchase incentives, consumers and channel members get used to them and soon begin expecting them.
- *Low quality of retail selling.* Many retailers use inadequately trained sales clerks or have switched to self-service. For these outlets, sales promotion devices such as product displays and samples often are the only effective promotional tools available at the point of purchase.

Sales promotion should be included in a company's promotion plans, along with advertising and personal selling. This means setting sales promotion objectives and strategies, determining a sales promotion budget, and selecting appropriate sales promotion techniques.

One problem management faces is that many sales promotion techniques are short-run, tactical actions. Coupons, premiums, and contests, for example, are designed to produce immediate (but short-lived) responses. As a result, they tend to be used as stopgap measures to reverse unexpected sales declines rather than as integrated parts of a marketing program.

Determining Objectives and Strategies.   Three broad objectives of sales promotion were suggested when the term was defined in Chapter 16:

- Stimulating business user or household demand for a product.
- Improving the marketing performance of middlemen and sales people.
- Supplementing advertising and facilitating personal selling.

A single sales promotion technique may accomplish one or two—but probably not all—of these objectives.

Determining Budgets.   The sales promotion budget should be established as a specific part of the budget for the total promotional mix. If sales promotion is included in an advertising or public relations budget, it may be overlooked or poorly integrated with the other components of promotion. Setting a separate budget for sales promotion forces a company to recognize and manage it.

Within the concept of developing an integrated promotion strategy, the amount budgeted for sales promotion should be determined by the task or objective method. This forces management to consider specific objectives and the sales promotion techniques that will be used to accomplish them.

Directing the Sales Promotion Effort.   Many marketers plan and implement their sales promotion efforts internally. Others rely on specialized agencies. Sales promotion agencies fall into two primary categories. The first category is called *promotional service agencies*. They specialize in executing sales promotion programs such as sampling and couponing. The other type of organization, called a *promotional marketing agency*, provides management advice and strategic planning of sales promotion as well as execution of the resulting program. As the use of sales promotion has increased, more organizations have sought out promotional marketing agencies for guidance. Rather than treat sales promotion as a periodic, single-shot sales stimulator, more firms are now integrating it into a planned strategy with long-term goals.

Selecting the Appropriate Techniques.   A key step in sales promotion management is deciding which devices will help the organization reach its promotional goals. Factors that influence the choice of promotional devices include:

- *Nature of the target audience.* Is the target group loyal to a competing brand? If so, a high-value coupon may be necessary to disrupt customers' purchase patterns. Is the product bought on impulse? If so, an eye-catching point-of-sale display may be enough to generate sales.
- *Nature of the product.* Does the product lend itself to sampling, demonstration, or multiple-item purchases?
- *Cost of the device.* Sampling to a large market may be prohibitively expensive.
- *Current economic conditions.* Coupons, premiums, and rebates are good options during periods of recession or inflation, when consumers are particularly price conscious.

Common sales promotion techniques are shown in Table 18-5, where they are divided into three categories based on the target audience: business users or households, middlemen, and producers' sales forces. To illustrate the significance of sales promotion, several of these techniques are described below.

Sampling.   Sampling is the only sure way of getting a product in the hands of potential customers. And if behavior is any indication, many firms consider this important. In a survey on promotional practices, 77 percent of packaged goods marketers reported using sampling in their promotional mixes.[8]

Sampling is not a new technique. A New Jersey promotions firm has been assembling samples of relevant products and distributing them to new mothers for over 45 years. However, in order to get the product in the right hands, creativity has increased. For example, S. C. Johnson, the maker of Off! insect repellent, placed samples of its product in a million new Sunbeam barbecue grills. And snack food makers have joined with Blockbuster to give video renters samples of new products.

http://www.blockbuster.com/

The cost of sampling per person reached is much higher than advertising. However, the conversion rate (the proportion of people exposed who buy the product) is typically around 10 percent for sampling, which is considerably better than advertising.

TABLE 18-5 Major sales promotion devices, grouped by target audience

Business users or households	Middlemen and their sales forces	Producers' own sales forces
Coupons	Trade shows and exhibitions	Sales contests
Cash rebates	Point-of-purchase displays	Sales training manuals
Premiums (gifts)	Free goods	Sales meetings
Free samples	Advertising allowances	Packets with promotional materials
Contests and sweepstakes	Contests for sales people	
Point-of-purchase displays	Training middlemen's sales forces	
Product demonstrations	Product demonstrations	Demonstration model of product
Trade shows and exhibitions		
Advertising specialties	Advertising specialties	

Couponing. Coupons are the most frequently used form of consumer sales promotion by manufacturers. And consumers like them. In a recent study, 95 percent of the consumers surveyed had used coupons during the previous 30 days.[9] That's not surprising, because the volume of couponing is staggering. Over 300 *billion* coupons are distributed a year, and more than 6 billion (less than 2 percent!) are redeemed by consumers.[10] Couponing has experienced steady growth—over 1,200 percent during the last 20 years—with particularly dramatic increases in the early 1990s. However, it seems to have leveled off recently. Many marketers, including major firms such as General Mills, Procter & Gamble, Kraft, and Ralston Purina, believe that consumers have reached the saturation point with coupons. As a result, they are cutting back on the number of coupons and shifting the promotional dollars to either more advertising or lower prices.[11]

The most common methods of distributing coupons are as free-standing inserts (FSI) in newspapers, by direct mail, and packaged with other products. However, an increasing number of coupons are being distributed in retail stores. One technique is to offer coupons in a dispenser attached to the retail shelf where a product is displayed. The rationale is that consumers, at the point of purchase, may be influenced to select a particular brand if a coupon is readily available. Not surprisingly, these coupons have a redemption rate nine times higher than coupons included in newspapers. Another method growing in popularity is to electronically dispense coupons at the checkout counter based on what a consumer has purchased. Thus, when a shopper buys a particular brand of a product, a coupon might be issued for a competing alternative. This approach is designed to encourage brand switching on the consumer's next shopping trip.

Couponing has increased in other parts of the world, but the methods of distribution are different from those in the U.S. Over 80 percent of coupons in the U.S. are FSIs. In Canada, coupons are most often included as a part of ads. Spanish and Italian marketers place coupons in or on packages. And in several European countries, coupons are distributed door to door.[12]

Results from retailers show that coupons can produce a quick boost in sales. And a recent study suggests that just seeing a coupon can affect sales of a product. The researchers found that shoppers who did not use coupons proved to be more likely to buy a brand immediately after a coupon appeared for it. They surmised that some consumers who see a coupon, even if they don't actually use it, pick up the message it conveys.[13]

Critics of coupons point out that they are expensive. The major breakfast cereal companies issue 100 coupons a year for every person in America, but only about 2 per person are redeemed. That results in a cost of $1.22 per redeemed coupon. Another problem is that they may undermine brand loyalty. Coupons teach consumers to seek out the best bargains rather than consistently select a particular brand.[14]

Sponsorships and Event Marketing. Corporate sponsorship of events has become a major promotional activity. Worldwide expenditures exceed $11 billion, with nearly $5 billion of the total spent in North America. About 60 percent of the sponsorships are for sports events. The remainder includes concerts and entertainment tours, festivals and fairs, the arts, and causes.[15]

Sponsorship is typically viewed as a long-range image-building activity, but it can also have an effect on sales. In a survey of auto-racing fans, 48 percent said they would almost always purchase a NASCAR sponsor's product over a competitor's, and 42 percent switched brands when a product became a NASCAR sponsor.[16]

http://www.ppg.com/

Sponsorship activity can be extensive. For instance, Pittsburgh Paint and Glass, the world's largest manufacturer of auto paints, is the primary sponsor of 17 Indy-style car races. On a more modest level, Michelin sponsored the diaper-changing area at a Virginia air show.

The principal difficulty with justifying sponsorship expenditures is measuring their effectiveness. Since sales are usually not the primary objective, the value of a sponsorship is frequently determined by the amount of publicity it generates for the sponsor (and comparison of that to the cost of an equivalent amount of advertising), or a survey of attendees before and after an event to determine awareness and brand preference.

Trade Shows. Associations in industries as diverse as computers, sporting goods, food, and broadcasting sponsor trade shows. There are nearly 5,000 trade shows a year in Canada and the U.S. alone. About half restrict attendance to business

*C*orporate sponsorship is growing in popularity because it is a highly targeted and relatively inexpensive form of promotion. For example, Air Canada is paying $14 million over 20 years to have its name on the new stadium in Toronto (shown here). Other recent stadium sponsorship agreements are the Pepsi Center in Denver, 3Com Park in San Francisco, and Trans World Dome in St. Louis. For about $1 million a year, the cost of two or three 30-second ads on prime-time network television, a stadium sponsor can have its name in front of every visitor as well as the audiences viewing televised events from the stadium.

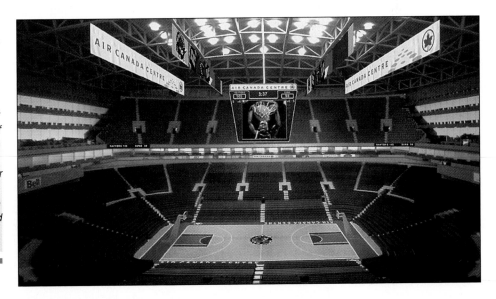

http://www.aircanada.ca/

representatives, while the remainder allow consumers to attend. In a typical year, trade shows host about 1.3 million exhibitors and attract 85 million visitors.[17]

The attraction of a trade show is efficiency. In one place and in a compressed amount of time, trade shows allow buyers and sellers to see and interact with many of their counterparts. They also tend to attract decision makers. In a recent survey of trade show attendees, 26 percent made a purchase at the show, and 51 percent asked that a sales representative be sent to their company.[18]

On the other hand, trade shows are expensive for exhibitors. In addition to the cost of the booth and the living expenses of the company representatives during the show, transporting equipment and display material is costly. As a result, firms are selective about the trade shows they attend, often requiring the sponsors to provide demographic profiles of the attendees.

The trade show industry grew by over 70 percent during the 1980s, and is projected to grow another 35 percent by the year 2000.[19] Much of the growth is expected to come from offshoots of existing broad-based events. Like advertising, trade shows are seeking out narrower market segments and offering more specialized topics.

Product Placements. For many years firms have paid fees to have their products used as props in movies, and the practice is growing. On TV shows, paid placements must be disclosed to the audience, so networks generally disapprove of their use. You may have noticed product placements in the James Bond movie *Goldeneye* (IBM computers, BMW, Perrier, and Omega), or the TV shows *Baywatch* (Hawaiian Tropic suntan products) and *Seinfeld* (TV Guide, Snapple, Mars candy bars, Junior Mints). But if you're like most viewers, these props simply added to the realism of the shows, and that is the strength of a product placement. It connects the product with the show's characters in a noncommercial way, creating a positive association for the audience.[20]

Public Relations

Public relations is a management tool designed to favorably influence attitudes toward an organization, its products, and its policies. It is an often overlooked form of promotion. In most organizations this promotional tool is typically a stepchild, relegated far behind personal selling, advertising, and sales promotion. There are several reasons for management's lack of attention to public relations:

- *Organizational structure.* In most companies, public relations is not the responsibility of the marketing department. If there is an organized effort, it is usually handled by a small public relations department that reports directly to top management.
- *Inadequate definitions.* The term public relations is used loosely by both businesses and the public. There are no generally accepted definitions of the term. As a result, what actually constitutes an organized public relations effort often is not clearly defined.
- *Unrecognized benefits.* Only recently have many organizations come to appreciate the value of good public relations. As the cost of promotion has gone up, firms are realizing that positive exposure through the media or as a result of community involvement can produce a high return on the investment of time and effort.

Nature and Scope of Public Relations

Public relations activities typically are designed to build or maintain a favorable image for an organization with its various publics—customers, prospects, stockholders, employees, labor unions, the local community, and the government. We're aware that this description is quite similar to our definition of institutional advertising. However, unlike advertising, public relations need not use the media to communicate its message.

Good public relations can be achieved in many ways. Some examples are supporting charitable projects (by supplying volunteer labor or other resources), participating in community service events, sponsoring nonprofessional athletic teams, funding the arts, producing an employee or customer newsletter, and disseminating information through exhibits, displays, and tours. Major firms such as Exxon and Johnson & Johnson sponsor shows on public television (PBS) as part of their public relations effort.

http://www.jnj.com/

Publicity as a Form of Public Relations

Publicity is any communication about an organization, its products, or policies through the media that is *not* paid for by the organization. Publicity usually takes the form of a news story appearing in the media or an endorsement provided by an individual, either informally or in a speech or interview. This is good publicity.

There is also, of course, bad publicity—a negative story about a firm or its product appearing in the media. In a society that is increasingly sensitive about the environment and in which news media are quick to report mistakes, organizations tend to focus on this negative dimension of publicity. As a result, managers are so concerned with avoiding bad publicity that they overlook the potential of good publicity.

There are three means for gaining good publicity:

- *Prepare a story (called a* news release) *and circulate it to the media.* The intention is for the selected newspapers, television stations, or other media to report the information as news.
- *Personal communication with a group.* A press conference will draw media representatives if they feel the subject or speaker has news value. Company tours and speeches to civic or professional groups are other forms of individual-to-group communications.
- *One-on-one personal communication, often called* lobbying. Companies lobby legislators or other powerful people in an attempt to influence their opinions, and subsequently their decisions.

Publicity can help to accomplish any communication objective. It can be used to announce new products, publicize new policies, recognize employees, describe research breakthroughs, or report financial performance. But to receive coverage, the message, person, group, or event being publicized must be viewed by the media as newsworthy. This is what distinguishes publicity from advertising—publicity is not "forced" on the audience. This is also the source of its primary benefit. The credibility of publicity typically is much higher than advertising. If we tell you our product is great, you may well be skeptical. But if an independent, objective third party says on the evening news that our product is great, you are more likely to believe it.

Other benefits of publicity are:

- *Lower cost than advertising or personal selling.* Publicity usually costs less because there are no media space or time costs for conveying the message and no sales people to support.
- *Increased readership.* Many consumers are conditioned to ignore advertising or at least pay it scant attention. Publicity is presented as editorial material or news, so it gets greater readership.

- *More information*. Because it is presented as editorial material, publicity can contain greater detail than the usual ad. More information and persuasive content can be included in the message.
- *Timeliness*. A company can put out a news release very quickly when some unexpected event occurs.

Of course, publicity also has limitations:

- *Loss of control over the message*. An organization has no guarantee that a news release will appear in the media. In addition, there is no way to control how much or what portion of a publicity release the media will print or broadcast. First Chicago Bank restructured several of its consumer accounts and added a $3 service charge for some transactions if they are done by a teller rather than an automatic teller machine. To get the message out, the bank held a press conference. According to First Chicago, the resulting news stories presented the changes in a negative way and confused customers. The result was an uproar among customers and a flurry of activity by competitors hoping to capture accounts from First Chicago.[21]
- *Limited exposure*. The media will typically use publicity material to fill space when there is a lack of other news and only use it once. If the target audience misses the message when it is presented, there is no second or third chance.
- *Publicity is not free*. Even though there are no media time and space costs, there are expenses in staffing a publicity department and in preparing and disseminating news releases.

Recognizing the value of publicity, some organizations have special units to generate news releases. For example, Reebok operates the Aerobic Information Bureau to link the firm with consumer interests through news releases about health research and performance-aiding opportunities.

■ SUMMARY

Advertising, sales promotion, and public relations are the nonpersonal, mass-communications components of a company's promotional mix. Advertising can be directed to consumers or businesses, and focuses on products or institutions. Direct-action product ads call for immediate action, while indirect-action product ads are intended to stimulate demand over a longer time period. Product ads are also classified according to whether they are intended to stimulate primary or selective demand. Primary-demand ads are designed to introduce a new product, to stimulate demand for a generic product, or to sustain demand for an industry's products. Selective-demand ads, which include competitive and comparative advertising, are intended to increase the demand for a particular brand.

In vertical cooperative advertising, manufacturers and their retail dealers share the cost of advertising the manufacturer's product at the local level.

Horizontal cooperative advertising involves joint sponsorship of ads by firms operating at the same level of distribution.

Total advertising expenditures are large, but the average cost of advertising in a firm is typically 1 to 3 percent of sales. This is considerably less than the average cost of personal selling. Most advertising dollars are spent on newspapers. Television and direct mail are close behind. Other frequently used advertising media are radio, magazines, yellow pages, and outdoor displays.

An advertising campaign should be part of a total promotional program. The steps in designing a campaign include defining specific objectives, establishing a budget, creating a message, selecting media, and evaluating the advertising effort. Objectives can range from creating awareness of a brand to generating sales. Vertical and horizontal cooperative arrangements can have a significant impact on advertising budgets. The advertising message—consisting of the appeal and the execution of the ad—is influenced by the target audience and the media used to deliver the message.

A major task in developing a campaign is to select the advertising media—the general type, the particular category, and the specific vehicle. The choice should be based on the characteristics of the medium, which determine how effectively it conveys the message, and its ability to reach the target audience.

A difficult task in advertising management is evaluating the effectiveness of the advertising effort—both the entire campaign and individual ads. Except for sales results tests, commonly used techniques measure only recall of an ad. To operate an advertising program, a firm may rely on its own advertising department, an advertising agency, or a combination of the two.

Sales promotion consists of demand-stimulating devices designed to supplement advertising and facilitate personal selling. The amount of sales promotion increased considerably in the early 1990s, as management sought measurable, short-term sales results.

Sales promotion should receive the same strategic attention that a company gives to advertising and personal selling, including setting objectives and establishing a budget. Sales promotion can be directed toward final consumers, middlemen, or a company's own employees. To implement its strategic plans, management can choose from a variety of sales promotion devices. Some of the most common are samples, coupons, sponsorships, and trade shows. Like advertising, sales promotion performance should be evaluated.

Public relations is a management tool designed to favorably influence attitudes toward an organization, its products, and its policies. It is a frequently overlooked form of promotion. Publicity, a part of public relations, is any communication about an organization, its products, or policies through the media that is *not* paid for by the organization. Typically these two activities are handled in a department separate from the marketing department in a firm. Nevertheless, the management process of planning, implementation, and evaluation should be applied to their performance in the same way it is applied to advertising, sales promotion, and personal selling.

More about

BENETTON

When it comes to advertising, Benetton is not quite as independent as it used to be. The management now attempts to gain the support of its retailers by involving them before it develops a controversial campaign.

However, Benetton's excursion into controversy is apparently not over. In the last few years, the firm acquired several sporting goods lines including Prince tennis rackets, Rollerblade in-line skates, Nordica ski boots, and Kastle skis. These were combined with some sportswear brands under the name Benetton SportSystem. The firm then launched a $27 million print ad campaign that appears in such magazines as *Tennis*, *Skiing*, and *Racket*. The ads include Jesus being crucified by Roman soldiers, German Olympians during the Hitler era giving the Nazi salute, and a boat overloaded with Cuban refugees.

The firm has diversified in other directions as well. Recently Benetton became the major owner of

Euromercato, an Italian superstore chain, and GS-Autogrill, a chain of roadside restaurants and supermarkets. These moves have increased the concerns of the sportswear franchisees, who fear that the clothing portion of the business will get even less attention from Benetton management.[22]

1. Benetton ads have generated enormous publicity for the company:
   a. Does that justify the techniques used?
   b. Do the firm's franchisees have a right to complain about the ads Benetton chooses to run?
2. Advertising has been the primary promotional tool for the Benetton sportswear business. Is that likely to be the case for the sporting goods product lines, the superstore chain, and the roadside restaurant and supermarket chain?

■ KEY TERMS AND CONCEPTS

Advertising (484)
Consumer advertising (486)
Business-to-business
    advertising (486)
Product advertising (486)
Institutional
    advertising (487)

Primary-demand
    advertising (487)
Selective-demand
    advertising (487)
Comparative
    advertising (487)

Advertising
    campaign (487)
Cooperative
    advertising (488)
Advertising media (489)
Cost per thousand
    (CPM) (491)

Direct tests (495)
Indirect tests (496)
Advertising
    agency (496)
Sales promotion (497)
Public relations (502)
Publicity (503)

■ QUESTIONS AND PROBLEMS

1. How do you account for the variation in advertising expenditures as a percentage of sales among the different companies in Table 18-2?
2. Select a general type of advertising medium for each of the following products and explain your choice.
   a. Wooden pallets
   b. Hanes pantyhose
   c. Tax-preparation service
   d. Mortuary
   e. Toys for young children
   f. Plastic clothespins
3. Many grocery product and candy manufacturers earmark a good portion of their advertising budgets for use in magazines. In contrast, department stores use newspapers more than local radio stations as an advertising medium. Are these media choices wise for these industries and firms? Explain.
4. Why is it worthwhile to pretest advertisements before they appear in the media? How could a test market be used to pretest an ad? (You may want to refresh your memory with a review of test marketing in Chapter 4.)
5. What procedures can a firm use to determine how many sales dollars resulted from a direct-mail ad? How would you determine whether any sales were cannibalized from the future?
6. Is sales promotion effective for selling expensive consumer products such as houses, automobiles, or cruise trips? How about expensive business products?
7. What advantage would sampling offer over advertising for a new brand of sunscreen lotion?
8. Explain how sales promotion might be used to offset weak personal selling in retail stores.
9. Bring to class an article from a daily newspaper that appears to be the result of a firm's publicity efforts. Summarize the points made in the article that may benefit the firm. Could advertising create the same benefits?

■ HANDS-ON MARKETING

1. Common appeals or benefits and examples of product categories in which they are frequently used include:

   • Physical well-being (food, nonprescription drugs)
   • Social acceptance (cosmetics, health and beauty aids)
   • Material success (automobiles, investments)
   • Recognition and status (clothing, jewelry)
   • Sensory pleasure (movies, candy)
   • Time savings (prepared foods, convenience stores)

   • Peace of mind (insurance, tires)

   Find print ads that make use of five of these appeals.
2. Visit a supermarket, drugstore, or hardware store, and make a list of all the sales promotion tools that you observe. Describe how each one relates to the sales promotion objectives described in the chapter. Which do you feel are particularly effective, and why?

CASES FOR PART 6

CASE 1 PowerBar

ADJUSTING A PROMOTION STRATEGY

A heightened sensitivity to health and fitness issues is reflected in the behavior of many consumers. For example, 61 percent of Americans say they read nutritional labels before buying a packaged food item for the first time, and over 50 percent claim to engage in some form of regular exercise. These consumers make up a market that means increased sales for some existing products and the development of new products. For example, sales of physical fitness equipment and athletic clothing have steadily increased. Likewise, dietary supplements and vitamins are growing in popularity. And in the food industry, products are being reformulated to reduce or eliminate undesirable ingredients such as sodium and fat.

A New Product Category

An interesting new product category that has developed to meet the needs of health- and fitness-conscious consumers is energy bars. They may look a little like candy bars, but that's where the similarity ends. Energy bars are low in fat, highly nutritious, and easily digested. They also contain an abundance of calories. Among the brands are PowerBar, Gator-Bar (made by Quaker Oats), and VO2 Max, a Mars, Inc., product. The energy bar category is forecast to grow 20 percent a year and reach $200 million in sales by the year 2000.

The Development of PowerBar

PowerBar, the product of Powerfoods, Inc., defined the energy bar category. It was developed by a world-ranked marathoner, Brian Maxwell. The stimulus for PowerBar grew out of Maxwell's frustration with tiring during long training sessions and races. Nothing available on the market seemed to provide him with the energy boost to solve the problem, so he took it upon himself to create a product that would satisfy his needs and, he hoped, other athletes' needs as well.

It took 3 years, hundreds of experimental batches, and dozens of tests to find a formulation that produced the combination of energy and taste Maxwell was seeking. The first flavor, malt-nut and chocolate, was introduced to the public in 1986 when the American cycling team ate them during the Tour de France. Maxwell was confident he was onto something when during the following year he sold 55,000 PowerBars by mail order from the basement of his home. Later that year Maxwell began distributing Power-Bars through retail bicycle shops.

Within 1 year almost all American world-class cyclists and triathletes were consuming PowerBars to boost their energy levels. In 1988, when PowerBar became the official energy bar of the U.S. Olympic cycling team, manufacturing was expanded and a berry-flavored version was introduced. Distribution was also broadened to include health clubs, gyms, and sporting goods stores.

In 1991, PowerBar recorded its first international sales, and by the end of the year the product was available in 26 countries. In the U.S., distribution continued to expand to include supermarkets and convenience stores. Apple-cinnamon flavor was introduced in 1993, and the next year a new production facility in Boise, Idaho, came on line, pushing annual production to over 40 million bars. By 1995, banana and mocha PowerBars had been introduced, and the company reported over $30 million in sales, 9 percent from outside the U.S.

The Anatomy of a PowerBar

Understanding how PowerBars work requires a brief nutrition lesson. Carbohydrates supply most of the energy during the early stages of physical activity. During a longer period of sustained effort, after the body has used up the available supply of carbohydrates, additional energy is produced by burning fat. However, this process is less efficient and the exerciser experiences a noticeable decrease in energy. A PowerBar contains 42 grams of maltodextrin, a complex carbohydrate that, when consumed shortly before intense physical activity, replenishes the body's primary energy sources as they are consumed.

Another important ingredient is oat bran, a soluble fiber. When a PowerBar and water interact in the stomach, the oat bran contributes to the formation of a kind of "gel." This gel is highly digestible. Equally important, it eliminates the sloshing of food in the stomach that an athlete would find uncomfortable. A PowerBar also includes 100 percent of the recommended daily amounts of vitamins C, E, and B, as well as minerals such as iron, zinc, calcium, potassium, and magnesium that can be depleted during exercise.

Although originally designed for athletes, PowerBar and other energy bars can be eaten as dietary supplements or stored as emergency food by hikers and campers. A mylar wrapper on PowerBars gives them a 6-month shelf life. The addition of more flavors has expanded the variety and increased the use of the product.

Marketing Strategies

PowerBars' current promotion mix is split approximately 80 percent for event sponsorship and 20 percent for media advertising. According to Maxwell, the emphasis on sponsorship is particularly important because it allows the firm to "educate athletes at our booths and with our products and meet the needs of athletes on a one-on-one basis." To that end, Powerfoods sponsors more than 4,000 events a year, including the PowerBar International Women's Challenge bicycle race. "We try to be part of the editorial (by educating athletes about nutrition) as well as advertising, and event sponsorship is perfect for that," commented Maxwell. Media advertising is primarily placed in fitness magazines. Endorsements are a key component of the Powerfoods advertising strategy. Endorsers include golfers Tom Lehman and Michelle McGann, tennis players Mark Woodforde and Todd Woodbridge, and mountain biker Henrik Djernis.

The various brands of energy bars approach the market in different ways. Among the competitors are:

- PowerBar. Positioned as athletic energy food, it claims to provide "Fuel for Optimum Performance." Its retail price is about $.70 per ounce.
- Tiger Sport. Made by Weider Nutrition, this product is described as "The Ultimate Performance Bar," and is also targeted at athletes. It is advertised in *Running World, Shape,* and *Backpacker,* and is priced at $.52 per ounce.
- Nutrablast. Made in Sacramento, it has adopted a broader positioning as an energy bar rather than a sports performance bar. It targets the "urban triathlete," someone who is balancing work, family, and self. The product sells for about $.70 per ounce.
- GatorBar. A product of Quaker Oats, this brand is an attempt to leverage the equity of the Gatorade brand. It is priced at about $.76 per ounce.
- VO2 Max. This brand takes its name from the maximum amount of oxygen absorbed by the lungs. A product of the Mars, Inc., candy company, it has an athletic positioning.
- EdgeBar. A product of N-ER-G Products of Richmond, California, it claims to be "Nutritional Energy Food." It is priced at about $.75 per ounce.
- ATP Tour. Made by Proline International and priced at about $.66 per ounce, it is positioned as a "Nutritional Snack for People on the Go."

The marketing clout of larger firms has been felt by Powerfoods, Inc. For example, Quaker Oats, the maker of Gatorade, outbid PowerBar for the sponsorship of the Ironman Triathlon and the publicity it generates among amateur athletes.

The Future

In the short time since the birth of energy bars, makers have expanded the target market from athletes to all consumers looking for a quick, nutritious snack. "People are leading a more stressed-out, busy lifestyle," said Shelley Thode, president of Nutrablast. "The bottom line is they need more energy." More recently the product category appears to be more sensitive to taste. For example, ads for MLO's Performance Bar claim it is "A High Protein Energy Bar That Tastes Like a Candy Bar!" The notion is that fitness-inclined snackers might substitute a good-tasting energy bar for a candy bar. In response, some candy brands—notably Mars' Snickers and Nestlé's Baby Ruth—have been repositioned as energy boosters.

It appears that PowerBar has identified a need and a product to satisfy it. However, as the number of suppliers grows and competition intensifies, one strategy is to further expand the target market. But, in the process of attracting a larger customer base, the category runs the risk of losing its uniqueness. A challenge for PowerBar's promotion effort will be to communicate its identity in an effective and efficient manner.

http://www.powerbar.com/

QUESTIONS

1. Is Powerfoods, Inc.'s promotion strategy, stressing sponsorship of athletic events and endorsements by professional athletes, a good one? Are there other sponsorships PowerBar should consider?
2. How should Powerfoods go about setting the promotion budget for PowerBar?
3. What are some appropriate promotional objectives for PowerBar?
4. What should be Powerfoods' campaign theme for PowerBar as the market expands and competition increases?

Sources: Pam Weisz, "The Candy Bar of the '90s?" *BrandWeek,* May 29, 1995, p. 21; Advertisement, "New PowerBar Flavor Can Mean Big Profits for Grocery Retailers," *Progressive Grocer,* July 1995, p. 11; Brian Maxwell, "The Marketing 100," *Advertising Age,* June 26, 1995, p. S-24; Andy Freeberg, "A Marathon Man with Marketing Power," *Business Week,* Nov. 7, 1994, p. 56; and *PowerBar News* 1994.

REMAINING DOMINANT IN THE SALTY SNACK MARKET

Frito-Lay has won the war, or at least the most recent battle. Using a combination of product introductions, strong distribution channels, price discounts, massive promotional expenditures, and responses to competitive moves, the company vanquished the likes of Borden, Inc., and Anheuser-Busch to remain atop the snack food market. Now the future appears bright as no major global competitor seems prepared to challenge Frito-Lay's dominance.

The Strategy

Though "salty snacks" may not sound substantial, each market share point represents about $75 million in sales. Frito-Lay controls over 50 percent of the $2 billion potato chip market, 72 percent of the over $1 billion tortilla chip segment, and over 13 percent of the $450 million (and growing) pretzel market. Just how did Frito-Lay come to control one-half of this $15 billion U.S. salty snack market? The company's growth strategy stresses value, variety, and visibility. The company's products must offer reasonable *value* because salty snacks represent a want rather than a need. *Variety* of product offerings is a key ingredient that keeps consumers from becoming bored. *Visibility* results from being accessible in retail outlets and promoted in various media, and translates into impulse purchases.

The Battle

Frito-Lay's main rival, Borden, made a full-scale commitment to challenge for the number 1 spot in the salty snack market in the 1980s. Borden's strategy, which stressed the acquisition of several regional brands, worked well initially as the company built its salty snack business to $1 billion in sales and a 12 percent market share. Although Borden's salty snack business was less than a third the size of Frito-Lay's, it was more than twice the size of any other competitor.

Everything changed in 1988 when Anheuser-Busch (A-B) decided to move its Eagle Snacks from a niche player to a widely distributed brand. To gain visibility, A-B began paying supermarkets up to $500 a linear foot for shelf space. This touched off a price war that Frito-Lay refused to lose. Backed by a large war chest, Frito-Lay matched every program A-B and Borden implemented with devastating results. By 1992, A-B had spent $15 million to $20 million on television advertising and offered deep price discounts, but gained only a modest 4 percent market share. Borden too spent heavily on advertising and discounts, only to see its market share drop to less than 4 percent.

In 1994, continued price competition and ever higher slotting allowances convinced Borden to sell off the re-

gional snack companies it had acquired. The next year A-B sold its snack business after failing to generate a profit in the previous 15 years. The price war waged by the major brands also negated an advantage usually held by private-label competitors. The war resulted in over 25 percent of all salty snack purchases being made with cents-off deals. Thus, national brands were often available at the same prices as private brands.

Secrets of Success

How did Frito-Lay establish such dominance? The answers can be found in its marketing operations.

The majority of salty snack sales are made by mom-and-pop grocery stores, convenience stores, and vending machines. Only about 25 percent of the sales are through supermarkets. Frito-Lay has achieved distribution leadership in all of these channels by building a national network of 42 plants, 12,800 delivery people, over 900 tractor trailers, and timely information. Inventories are managed through sales information fed back to headquarters by delivery personnel using handheld computers.

New products also are important to Frito-Lay's success, and reflect a customer focus. Capitalizing on a renewed taste for pretzels, the company introduced Rold Gold pretzels in 1993. Backed by promotion expenditures of $5 million featuring actor Jason Alexander of *Seinfeld*, the brand soon grabbed 13.5 percent of the pretzel market. Also in 1993, the company spent $100 million to roll out Doritos Tortilla Thins. This included $50 million to redesign Doritos with round corners so they would be easier to eat and result in fewer broken chips at the bottom of the bag. These changes were not made because the brand's sales were slumping. To the contrary, the brand's dollar sales were up 6 percent, and volume and market share was up as well.

"We're responding to what people tell us they want. . . . We aren't trying to correct a problem, but to accelerate the growth of our biggest brand. . . . We're trying to make it harder for other companies to compete against us," said Roger Bedusco, Frito-Lay's vice president of tortilla chip marketing. The expenditures were justified in light of projected sales for the brand of $450 million in the first year.

Frito-Lay's size gives it a huge advantage in an industry where trade promotions are a way of life. For example, during the 1993 holiday season, 65 percent of Eagle's and 63 percent of Frito-Lay's potato chip volume were sold at a discount. Frito-Lay is one of the few companies that can afford the up to $40,000 a foot annual fee that some retail chains charge for shelf space. In addition, the company can match or outspend the competition on other promotions. In

1993, Frito-Lay spent $60 million on advertising its brands, when A-B spent less than $2 million on Eagle.

Price promotion remains an integral part of the Frito-Lay strategy because it works. For example, the firm found that lowering the price of its large bags by 40 cents during special promotions can increase sales and profits by as much as 10 percent. Frito has also offered new package sizes to generate additional sales. When a 25-cent bag was introduced, many of Frito's smallest retail customers were able to increase their sales fourfold.

Frito-Lay has remained in the chips by investing heavily in event sponsorships as well as traditional advertising, and trade and price promotions. In 1993, the Lay's brand was successfully promoted on ABC's Monday Night Football with its "Betcha can't eat just one" challenge. The company's Fritos brand sponsored Billy Ray Cyrus's concert tour in 1993, which provoked an unusual response and excellent publicity. Life-size cutouts of the singer were stolen from stores by his fans. A Kmart in Missouri "lost" 200 in a day before deciding to raffle them off. Frito-Lay also sponsored the 1995 Tostitos Fiesta Bowl, the college football championship game between the University of Nebraska and the University of Florida. Every time a coach or player was interviewed, it was against a backdrop embossed with the Tostitos brand name.

Next Conquest

Having conquered the U.S. salty snack market, Frito-Lay is now turning its attention toward the $17 billion non-U.S. snack market. Americans eat about 20 pounds of salty snacks per year, eight times the world average. The company is implementing everything from new packaging and advertising campaigns to overhauling manufacturing techniques and stressing higher quality standards as part of its strategy to increase the amount of snacks foreign consumers eat.

Frito-Lay is spending more than $50 million on the overseas advertising of its brands which includes a more uniform Lay's logo. Satisfying different tastes remains the biggest challenge for the company. Salt and vinegar potato chips are favored in Europe, whereas fish flavors are preferred in Asia. The company even adapted its Cheetos brand to suit Chinese tastes. The popular bright orange corn puffs covered in cheese were not selling in China because the Chinese do not like cheese. So Frito-Lay removed the cheese and more than 100 million bags were sold. So successful was the "cheese-less" Cheetos that the company is building a new $30 million plant in China and introducing a seafood flavor Cheetos.

Will Frito-Lay continue to dominate the U.S. salty snack market and gain control of the global market? Only time will tell. The key to its long-run success will be the development of new products, and a corresponding execution of an effective marketing strategy that meets the needs of its target markets.

http://www.fritolay.com/

QUESTIONS

1. What promotional mix should Frito-Lay implement in the U.S. now that it has defeated Borden and Anheuser-Busch? What promotional mix should it implement in overseas markets?
2. Can Frito-Lay discontinue the use of price discounts to sell its products?

Sources: Robert Frank, "Potato Chips to Go Global—or So Pepsi Bets," *The Wall Street Journal,* Nov. 30, 1995, p. B1; Robert Frank, "Frito-Lay Devours Snack-Food Business," *The Wall Street Journal,* Oct. 27, 1995, p. B1; Karen Benezra, "Brock Party," *BrandWeek,* Mar. 27, 1995, p. 25; Glenn Collins, "Pepsico Pushes a Star Performer," *The New York Times,* Nov. 3, 1994, p. D1; Jennifer Lawrence, "Frito-Lay Crunches Past Salted Snack Foes," *Advertising Age,* Sept. 28, 1994, p. 32; Richard Gibson, "Frito-Lay Soars as Eagle Snacks Eyes Ways to Lift Market Share," *The Wall Street Journal,* Mar. 1, 1994, p. B7; Karen Benezra, "Frito-Lay Dominates, While Others Pick Up Loose Chips," *BrandWeek,* Feb. 7, 1994, p. 31; Betsy Spethmann, "Sponsors Sing a Profitable Tune in Concert with Event Promos," *BrandWeek,* Jan. 24, 1994, p. 20; and Bill Saporito, "Why the Price Wars Never End," *Fortune,* Mar. 23, 1992, p. 68.

PART SEVEN

Marketing in Special Fields

Marketing programs for marketers of services in for-profit and nonprofit organizations, and for firms marketing across national borders

Two areas of marketing deserve our special attention: the marketing of services, in contrast to goods, which is addressed in Chapter 19, and the marketing of goods and services across national boundaries, which is the focus of Chapter 20.

The discussion of services marketers includes both profit-seeking companies and institutions in which the goal is something other than profit. For example, a not-for-profit organization may have educational, cultural, or charitable objectives. For-profit and nonprofit organizations are discussed in the same chapter because most nonprofit organizations market services rather than goods. Thus, they are a special type of services marketers.

The unique features of services and international trade—plus their importance in our society and economy—make these two chapters essential in your study of marketing.

CHAPTER 19

Services Marketing by For-Profit and Nonprofit Organizations

Can
ENTERPRISE
Stay in the Auto Rental Fast Lane?

Enterprise Rent-A-Car began as an auto-leasing business in 1957. The company's founder, Jack Taylor, was a new-car sales person who realized that leasing offered advantages to certain customers. With the financial support of the dealership he worked for, Taylor began a leasing business that, by the early 1960s, had evolved into a car-rental business. Starting with 17 cars at one location in St. Louis, the business has grown to 232,000 cars in over 2,000 locations. Continuing its rapid growth, Enterprise was recognized in 1994 by *Auto Rental News* as the largest auto-rental organization in the U.S., surpassing such better-known firms as Hertz, Avis, and Budget.

Like all good marketers, Enterprise began by segmenting the potential market and selecting a particular target. In examining the rental market, Taylor noted that the established firms specialized in renting cars at airports to business and leisure travelers. Rather than go head-to-head with the likes of Hertz and Avis, he looked for other user segments. What he found were consumers and businesses that temporarily need rental cars because their vehicles have been damaged or stolen. However, serving this market requires a strategy that is quite different than the one used by the traditional car-rental firms.

The first issue is price. Insurers are responsible for an insured motorist's economic losses from being without a car. And consumers with a car in the garage for repairs can be in a pinch for transportation. But unlike business travelers, price is a key consideration for both of these segments. So Enterprise has to find ways to keep its costs down. One tactic is to keep its rental cars for up to 18 months before selling them. In comparison, the other major rental companies turn their cars over in about 6 months. Another significant factor is the cost of retail locations. Firms pursuing the leisure and business air travelers have expensive downtown and airport locations. Enterprise selects suburban store-front and shopping-strip locations that are less expensive. The re-sulting lower costs allow Enterprise to offer rental rates as much as 30 percent below other firms.

Promotion is another difference. Hertz and Avis do a lot of expensive television and other mass-media advertising. Enterprise recognizes that the insurance and repair replacement markets are largely controlled by two groups. One is auto insurance adjusters, who approve payments for their clients' rental cars. The other is auto-body shop operators, who are frequently asked for rental recommendations by customers. So, in addition to a small amount of advertising, Enterprise managers develop close ties with these businesses in their local areas. They have found that where the customer has little time to shop for the product and is concerned with the condition of his or her own car, reputation and referrals are key success ingredients.

A problem Enterprise has to overcome is the dispersion of its customers. Airplane travelers arrive and depart from a single place, so deciding where to locate an auto-rental business serving this market is simple. But the insurance and repair market is not concentrated. Consumers needing a car can be anywhere in a city. Enterprise has taken this apparent problem and turned it into a positive, differentiating service by locating branch offices near where people live and work. It also brings the rental car to the customer by providing customer pickup service. This presents a special employee scheduling challenge for Enterprise managers because, like all services, the demand for auto rental is somewhat unpredictable.

To motivate employees, nearly everyone at Enterprise has his or her compensation tied to profits. The company also stresses promotion from within. Though a college graduate may start out vacuuming cars, within 2 years the person is expected to be managing a rental location and shortly after that, overseeing several offices.[1]

What element of its marketing strategy will be most important in Enterprise's future growth?

Enterprise is marketing a service—auto rental. Most auto-rental companies have long understood the importance of marketing, and they generally have done a good marketing job. Consider the worldwide success of Hertz, and the way Avis has effectively positioned itself as the "We try harder!" underdog. Unfortunately, such skillful marketing does not exist in all services industries. In many service firms, marketing is a new or little known—and in some cases, little respected—business activity. As we approach the year 2000, however, it is increasingly evident that service organizations must become more marketing-oriented to survive.

After studying this chapter, you should be able to explain:

CHAPTER GOALS

- What services are and what they are not.
- The importance of services in our economy.
- The evolution of attitudes toward services marketing.
- The characteristics of services, and the marketing implications of these characteristics.
- The extended concept of customers in nonprofit services marketing.
- Planning a marketing mix for services marketing.
- The future of services marketing.

Nature and Importance of Services

The U.S. has moved beyond the economic stage where goods production is the main activity to the point where it has become the world's first services economy. About half of all consumer expenditures are for services. Projections to the year 2000 indicate that services will attract an even larger share of consumer spending. Services have also had an impact on employment. More than three-fourths of the nonfarm labor force is employed in service industries, and over two-thirds of the nation's gross national product is accounted for by services. The U.S. Department of Labor predicts that over 21 million new jobs will be created between 1986 and 2000, with about 90 percent of them in service industries.

A drawback of the services boom is that the prices of most services have been going up considerably faster than the prices of most goods. You are aware of this if you have had your car or TV set repaired, or paid a medical bill recently.

When we say that services account for close to one-half of consumer expenditures, we still grossly understate the economic importance of services. These figures do not include the vast amounts spent for business services. By all indications, spending for business services has increased even more rapidly than spending for consumer services. The market for business services has boomed as business has become increasingly complex, specialized, and competitive. As a consequence, management has been forced to call in experts to provide services in research, taxation, advertising, labor relations, and a host of other areas.

The Nonprofit Sector

Another service sector consists of nonprofit organizations. Churches, charities, schools, and many other organizations generate billions of dollars and have the potential to affect millions of people. As we will see, these organizations engage in a considerable amount of marketing.

If nonprofits do an ineffective marketing job, the costs are high. Empty beds in hospitals and empty classrooms constitute a waste of resources a society can ill afford. There are additional social and economic costs of ineffective nonprofit marketing. If the death rate from smoking rises because the American Cancer Society and similar organizations cannot persuade people that smoking is harmful, we all lose. When antilitter organizations fail to convince people to control their solid-waste disposal, society suffers. Thus, marketing by nonprofit organizations should be treated as a serious undertaking with important consequences.

Definition of Services

What constitutes a service? The term is difficult to define because, invariably, services are marketed in conjunction with goods. All services require supporting goods (you need an airplane to provide air transportation service), and goods require supporting services (to sell even a shirt or a can of beans calls at least for a cashier's service). Furthermore, a company may sell a combination of goods and services. Thus, along with repair service for your car, you might buy spark plugs or an oil filter. Therefore, it may be helpful to think of every product as a mix of goods and services located on a continuum ranging from mostly goods to mostly services, as shown in Figure 19-1.

For purposes of a definition, it is useful to separate services into two classes. In the first are services that are the main *purpose or object* of a transaction. Suppose you rent a car from Enterprise. The company makes a car available (tangible good) to provide the rental service. But you are buying the use of the car, not the car itself. In the second class are services that *support or facilitate* the sale of a good or another service. Thus, when you buy a compact disc player, you may want technical information (a service) from a sales person and the opportunity to pay with a credit card (another service). These are often called supplementary services.

Considering these distinctions, we define **services** as identifiable, intangible activities that are the main object of a transaction designed to provide want-satisfaction to customers. This definition excludes supplementary services that support the sale of goods or other services.

Scope of Services

The wide range of services marketed by profit-seeking firms is reflected in the following classification by industry:

- *Housing:* Rentals of hotels, motels, apartments, houses, and farms.
- *Household operations:* Utilities, house repairs, repairs of equipment in the house, landscaping, and household cleaning.
- *Recreation and entertainment:* Theaters, spectator sports, amusement parks, rental and repair of equipment used to participate in recreation and entertainment activities.
- *Personal care:* Laundry, dry cleaning, beauty care.
- *Medical and other health care:* All medical services, dental, nursing, hospitalization, optometry, and other health care.

FIGURE 19-1
A goods-services continuum.

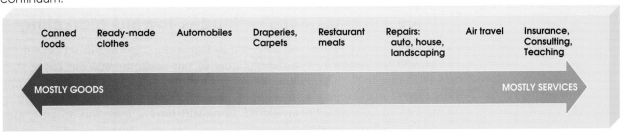

| Canned foods | Ready-made clothes | Automobiles | Draperies, Carpets | Restaurant meals | Repairs: auto, house, landscaping | Air travel | Insurance, Consulting, Teaching |

MOSTLY GOODS   MOSTLY SERVICES

- *Private education:* Vocational schools, nursery schools, some continuing education programs.
- *Business and other professional services:* Legal, accounting, and management consulting.
- *Insurance, banking, and other financial services:* Personal and business insurance, credit and loan service, and investment counseling.
- *Transportation:* Freight and passenger service on common carriers, automobile repairs and rentals, and express package delivery.
- *Communications:* Telephone, fax, computer, and copying services.

These groups are not separated into business and consumer services as we did with goods because most of these services are purchased by both market groups.

The scope of services is expanded considerably when we add nonprofit organizations. There are thousands of organizations where profit is not an operational goal. Together they engage in a wide range of activities:

- *Educational:* Private grade schools, high schools, colleges, universities.
- *Cultural:* Museums, zoos, symphony orchestras, opera and theater groups.
- *Religious:* Churches, synagogues, temples, mosques.
- *Charitable and philanthropic:* Welfare groups (Salvation Army, United Way, Red Cross), research foundations, fund-raising groups.
- *Social cause:* Organizations dealing with family planning, civil rights, stopping smoking, preventing heart disease, environmental concerns, those for or against abortion, or for or against nuclear energy.
- *Professional and trade:* Labor unions, certification groups, and associations (American Marketing Association, American Management Association).
- *Social:* Fraternal organizations, civic clubs.
- *Health care:* Hospitals, nursing homes, health research organizations (American Cancer Society, American Heart Association), HMOs (health maintenance organizations).
- *Political:* Political parties, individual politicians.

You may note some overlap in the preceding two lists. For example, private education appears on both lists, because some educational institutions are profit-seeking, while others are nonprofit. Also, most museums and hospitals are nonprofit, but some are profit-seeking.

Finally, the scope of services is broadened considerably if we include government services, which cut across several of the categories in these lists. For example, the U.S. National Park Service competes with private forms of outdoor recreation. And many government organizations are heavily involved in marketing. For example, the U.S. Postal Service has adopted a customer-oriented design that will be used for all new or renovated post offices. The layout resembles a convenience store and incorporates many features of fast-food restaurants.[2]

http://www.usps.gov/

Service Organizations' Attitudes toward Marketing

The growth in services has not been due to marketing expertise in services firms. The growth has resulted from the maturing of our economy and our rising standard of living. It is interesting to trace the changes in service organizations' attitudes toward marketing. These changes have occurred in many firms only during the past 15 to 20 years. Other service firms still have a long way to go toward realizing a marketing orientation.

In Prior Years

Traditionally, service industries—both for-profit and nonprofit—have not been marketing-oriented. They have lagged behind sellers of goods in accepting the marketing concept and in adopting marketing techniques.

We can identify some reasons for this situation. In many industries—particularly professional services—the sellers think of themselves only as producers or creators, and not as marketers, of the service. Proud of their abilities to conduct an audit, diagnose an illness, or give legal advice, they do not consider themselves businesspeople.[3]

Top management in many service firms has not understood (1) what marketing is, or (2) how it contributes to a company's success. Many service firms have lacked an executive whose sole responsibility is marketing—the counterpart of the vice president of marketing in a firm that produces goods.

Most nonprofit organizations were not at all comfortable with the idea of marketing. To them, marketing meant advertising or personal selling; they didn't understand the concept of a total marketing program. The basic problem was that most nonprofit groups did not think of themselves as running a business. As a result, they did not employ many business techniques, including marketing.

Perhaps the choice of terms is important. The governing body in a church, for instance, is unlikely to object to "informational notices" in newspapers or in the yellow pages regarding church activities, but might be uncomfortable calling the same thing "advertising." When church members go to foreign lands to bring new members into the fold, the churches don't call this activity "personal selling." It is "missionary work."

In defense of firms in certain service industries, however, it's clear that external influences contributed to the neglect of marketing. Up until the 1980s, several large service industries were heavily regulated by federal and state governments or professional associations. Banking and all major forms of interstate transportation services, for example, were severely restricted in marketing practices such as pricing, distribution, market expansion, and product introduction. In the fields of law, accounting, and health care, various state laws and professional association regulations prevented and, to varying degrees, still prevent their members from engaging in advertising, price competition, and other marketing activities.

Today's Changing Scene

In recent years, marketing in services industries—both for-profit and nonprofit—has changed considerably. Consumer protests, new laws, and court decisions have removed many of the governmental and professional association restrictions on marketing in some services industries. These changes, along with increased competition, have generated a growing awareness of marketing challenges and opportunities in services industries in general. Over the years the success of such companies as Marriott, Club Med, Avis, and Federal Express has been due in large part to their marketing orientation.

Nonprofit organizations have been slower than their profit-seeking counterparts in employing modern management techniques. But changing economic conditions have made nonprofits realize they must do a better job managing and marketing their operations. Nonprofits have suffered reductions in federal aid, tax law changes that discourage gift giving, and a slowdown in corporate contributions. At the same time, competition for funds is coming from a new generation of social causes such as AIDS, Alzheimer's disease, child abuse, and drunk driving. As the president of the Easter Seal Society said, "Commitment [to a given cause] isn't enough any more. You also have to have professionalism, or you're going to go out of business."[4] Consequently, many nonprofit institutions have begun to adopt modern business techniques, including marketing with a customer orientation.

Some government agencies are also recognizing the benefits of adopting a marketing orientation. Interesting examples are the auto licensing and registration departments in many states. They have employed innovations such as vending-type machines for obtaining license plates and mobile units to serve locations where there are large groups of customers. As a result, they have lowered costs, increased revenue, and produced happier customers.[5]

Developing a Strategic Marketing Program

Fundamentally, services are marketed in the same way as goods. And marketing in nonprofit and government service organizations is basically the same as in profit-seeking firms. Whether its focus is goods or services, for-profit or not-for-profit, the organization should first select and analyze its target markets. Then the company should design a coordinated marketing mix—the goods or services, the price structure, the distribution system, and the promotional activities—around a differential advantage.

In practice, however, there are four *services characteristics*—**intangibility**, **inseparability**, **heterogeneity**, and **perishability**—that differentiate services from goods. These distinctive characteristics create special marketing challenges and opportunities that lead to strategies and tactics different than those used in the marketing of goods.

Characteristics of Services

Intangibility. Because services are intangible, it is impossible for customers to sample—taste, feel, see, hear, or smell—a service before they buy it. Consequently, a company's promotional program must be explicit about the benefits to be derived from the service, rather than emphasizing the service itself. Four promotional strategies that may be used to suggest service benefits and reduce the effect of intangibility are:[6]

http://www.carnivalcruise.com/

- *Visualization.* For example, Carnival Cruise Lines depicts the benefits of its cruises with ads that show people dancing, dining, playing deck games, and visiting exotic places.

http://www.qantas.com/
http://www.prudential.com/
http://www.gmgoodwrench.com/

- *Association.* The intent is to connect the service with a tangible good, person, object, or place. The Australian airline, Qantas, uses a cuddly koala in its advertising to project a warm, friendly image. Prudential Insurance suggests stability and security with its Rock of Gibraltar. General Motors uses Mr. Goodwrench to build confidence in its auto-repair service.

http://www.americanexpress.com/

- *Physical representation.* American Express uses color—gold or platinum—for its credit card services to symbolize wealth and prestige. Enterprise shows its rental cars wrapped as a package in its TV ads to emphasize its unique delivery feature.

http://www.nwa.com/

- *Documentation.* Northwest and other airlines cite facts and figures in their ads to support claims of dependability, performance, care for passengers, and safety.

Inseparability. Services typically cannot be separated from the creator-seller of the service. Moreover, many services are created, dispensed, and consumed simultaneously. For example, dentists create and dispense almost all their services

A COMMITMENT TO CUSTOMER SATISFACTION

WOULD A JOB GUARANTEE MAKE IT EASIER TO SELECT A COLLEGE?

Services are very difficult to evaluate in advance of consumption because of the intangibility characteristic. As a result, a consumer must base a prepurchase judgment on some tangible feature of the service firm or provider. In the case of a college, that might be the appearance of the campus or the description of the courses. One school has taken a more dramatic step to reduce the intangibility factor.

St. John Fisher College in Rochester, New York, is offering a refund of up to $5,000 to students who, with a good faith effort, are unable to find a job within 6 months of graduation.

This strategy goes beyond suggesting benefits to reduce the effects of intangibility. How could the school use documentation of previous students to accomplish a similar goal?

Source: Chad Rubel, "Some Colleges Guarantee Their Students Will Succeed at Work," *Marketing News*, Oct. 9, 1995, pp. 1+.

---

at the same time, *and* they require the presence of the consumer for the services to be performed. The same is true of beauticians and most teachers.

A service's inseparability means that services providers are involved concurrently in the production and the marketing efforts. And the customers receive and consume the services at the production site—in the firm's "factory," so to speak. Consequently, customers' opinions regarding a service frequently are formed through contacts with the production-marketing personnel and impressions of the physical surroundings in the "factory."

From a marketing standpoint, inseparability limits distribution. It frequently means that direct sale is the only possible channel of distribution, and an individual seller's services cannot be sold in very many markets. This characteristic limits the scale of operation in a services firm. One person can teach only so many students in a day or treat only so many medical patients.

As an exception to the inseparability feature, some services may be sold by a person who is representing the creator-seller. A travel agent, insurance broker, or rental agent, for instance, may represent, promote, and sell services that will be provided at a later time by the institutions producing them.

Heterogeneity. It is impossible for a service industry, or even an individual seller of services, to standardize output. Each "unit" of the service is somewhat different from every other "unit" of the same service because of the "human factor" in production and delivery. Delta Air Lines, for example, does not give the same quality of service on each flight. All performances of the Boston Pops Orchestra, or all haircuts you get, are not of equal quality.

An added complication is that it is often difficult to judge the quality of a service, such as when you visit a physician, or get advice from a minister or rabbi. (Of course, we can say the same thing about some goods we purchase.) It is particularly difficult to forecast quality in advance of buying some services. You pay to see the Chicago Cubs play without knowing whether it will be an exciting or a dull baseball game.

To offset heterogeneity, service companies should pay special attention to the product-planning and implementation stages of their marketing programs. From the beginning, management must do all it can to ensure consistency of quality and to maintain high levels of quality control. Service quality will be given special attention later in this chapter.

Perishability. Services are highly perishable because they cannot be stored. Unused rental cars, empty seats in a stadium, and idle house painters all represent business that is lost forever. Furthermore, the market for many services fluctuates considerably by season, by day of the week, and by hour of the day. Many ski lifts sit idle all summer, whereas golf courses in some areas go unused in the winter. The ridership of city buses fluctuates greatly during the day.

There are exceptions to this generalization regarding the perishability and storage of services. In health and life insurance, for example, the service is purchased by a person or a company. Then it is held by the insurance company (the seller) until needed by the buyer or the beneficiary. This holding constitutes a type of storage.

The combination of perishability and fluctuating demand poses promotion, product-planning, scheduling, and pricing challenges to services executives. Some organizations have developed new uses for idle capacity during off-seasons. During the summer, ski resorts operate their ski lifts for hikers and sightseers. Advertising and creative pricing are also used to stimulate demand during slack periods. Marriott Hotels offer lower prices and family packages on weekends. AT&T charges lower rates for long-distance calls during nights and weekends.

http://www.marriott.com/
http://www.att.com/

The Service Customer. For-profit business executives define their market as present and potential customers. They then direct their marketing toward this one market.

In contrast, nonprofit organizations must aim at two markets. One is the **donor market**—the contributors of money, labor, or materials to the organization. The

This ad is part of an image-building campaign. When the savings and loan scandal became public, the accounting profession was criticized for failing to uncover the problems before they reached crisis proportions. Several large accounting firms became the targets of highly publicized negligence lawsuits. To offset the negative publicity, the American Institute of Certified Public Accountants undertook a $3 million ad campaign. Critics of the campaign feel the money will be wasted. They would prefer an internal focus, communicating and enforcing the profession's ethical standards. How do image-building ads relate to service intangibility?

http://www.aicpa.org/

SOME SMALL COMPANIES TRY TO DESIGN A RETIREMENT PLAN WITHOUT A CPA. SOME SMALL COMPANIES HAVE BEEN OUT IN THE SUN TOO LONG.

You wouldn't go swimming alone in some tropical lagoon without knowing what is below the surface. Why then would you go plunging into the unfamiliar waters of retirement planning without a trusted guide beside you? A CPA can look beneath the numbers. Tell you the tax consequences of one pension plan over another. Show you the best ways to diversify your funds. Guide you through the pros and cons of investment options and suggest which might be best suited to you and your employees. You see numbers. We see opportunities.

CPA

THE CPA. NEVER UNDERESTIMATE THE VALUE.

other is the **client market**—the recipients of money or services from the organization. This recipient market is much like the customer market for a for-profit business. However, nonprofit institutions—such as churches, hospitals, or universities—don't refer to their clients as customers. Instead, they call them parishioners, patients, or students. Because a nonprofit organization must deal with two different markets, it must develop two different marketing programs—one directed at its donors, the other aimed at its clients.

Selecting Target Markets

Selecting target markets is essentially the same, whether a firm is marketing a good or a service. From Chapters 5 through 7, we know that services marketers need to understand the components of population and income—the demographic factors—and how they affect the market for a service. Marketers also must try to determine their customers' buying behavior—their buying motives and patterns. The psychological determinants of buying behavior—motivation, perceptions, attitudes, personality—become more important when marketing services rather than goods. This is because we cannot touch, smell, or taste the service offered. Also, the sociological factors of social-class structure and reference groups are significant determinants of buying behavior in services markets.

In the course of selecting target markets, the concept of market segmentation has been adopted by many services marketers. We find apartment complexes for students and others for the over-55 crowd. Some car-repair shops target owners of foreign cars. Limited-service motel chains (Motel 6, Days Inn) cater to the economy-minded segment. Hotels providing only suites (Embassy Suites, Residence Inns) seek to attract families and business travelers who prefer a "home away from home."

Segmentation strategies are especially useful for nonprofit marketers. Remember, they have two quite separate markets to analyze—donors and clients. Each of these two markets usually needs to be further segmented in some detail. A broad (nonsegmented) appeal to the donor market is likely to produce poor results. Trying to be all things to all people in the client market may mean being "nothing to nobody" and going broke in the process.

Many nonprofit organizations segment their client markets, although they probably do not consider it market segmentation. For instance, country clubs develop different programs for golfers, tennis players, swimmers, and card players. Symphony orchestras design special programs for children or arrange bus transportation and matinee performances for senior citizens.

Product Planning

The planning and development of goods has its counterpart in the marketing of services—by either a profit-seeking or nonprofit organization. The nonprofit institution, however, requires one product-planning program for its donor market and one for its client market. The intangibility, high perishability, and inability to store services present significant product-planning challenges in services marketing. In terms of product planning, a marketer of services must make strategic decisions regarding:

- What services it will offer.
- What service-mix strategies it will adopt.
- What features, such as branding and warranty, the services will have.
- How it will manage service quality.

Services Offering.   New services are just as important to a service company as new goods are to a goods-producing firm. Many service firms have become successful by identifying a previously unrecognized or unsatisfied consumer want. Consider the health care producers that have entered the newly recognized market niche of limited-service nursing and hospital care. These firms provide a lower-cost alternative for patients who no longer need all the equipment and services of a traditional hospital, but who still need some therapy or other care before going home.

Like goods marketers, service firms seek ways to differentiate their offerings. This is particularly important for services because of the intangibility characteristic. In the absence of physical differences, competing services may appear very similar to the customer. One option is to expand the product, preferably by adding noticeable, attractive physical features. For example, British Airways installed showers in its arrival and departure lounges in Heathrow Airport.[7] However, an added feature should be one that cannot be easily duplicated by competitors or it will be neutralized. In the case of Heathrow showers, American Airlines and United Airlines quickly followed the lead of British Airways. The net effect is none of the airlines has an advantage but all have increased costs.

http://www.british-airways.com/

In most nonprofit organizations the "product" offered to *clients* typically is a service (education, health care, religion, culture), a person (in politics), a cause (stop smoking or don't do drugs), or a cash grant (research foundation). Some nonprofits offer goods such as food and clothing to clients, but these goods are incidental to the main services provided by the organization.

The key to selecting the services to offer is for an organization to decide (1) what "business" it is in and (2) what client markets it wants to reach. If a church views its mission only as providing religious services, its assortment will be limited. If this church views its mission broadly—as providing fellowship, spirituality, and personal development—it will offer more services to more markets. The church may then offer family counseling services, day-care services, religious education courses, and social activities for single people.

Planning the services offering to the *donor* market is more difficult. An organization asks people to donate their money or time to a cause. The money or time is the price that contributors pay in order to make the organization's services available. But what are they getting for this price? What are the contributors buying with their donations? Donors receive an assortment of benefits that include:

- Feeling good about themselves or relieving their guilt.
- Supporting their favorite organizations.
- Receiving a tax deduction.
- Contributing to their status in reference groups.
- Supporting their religious beliefs.

Product-Mix Strategies.   Several of the product-mix strategies discussed in Chapter 9 can be employed by services marketers. Consider the strategy of *expanding the line.* BayBanks, Inc., of Boston offers the traditional checking and savings accounts, but it has also added credit cards, debit cards, electronic bill paying, and securities transactions to its package of financial services.[8]

http://www.baybank.com/

In the nonprofit field, symphony orchestras expand their line by offering children's concerts and pop concerts for teenagers and college students. Universities have added adult night classes, TV programs, and concentrated between-semester courses.

*W*ith 2.4 million weddings a year, the bridal market is a $32 billion business. Much of the total is made up of services. Typical purchases include a facility for a reception, music, catering, and a honeymoon trip. Now Disney, one of America's best service marketers, offers a complete matrimonial package through a department called Fairytale Weddings. There are several options, but one of the most popular is the "Cinderella." The bride arrives at the wedding site in a glass coach, drawn by six white horses. A fairy godmother and stepsisters attend the reception, and dessert is served in a white chocolate slipper.

http://www.disney.com/

http://www.visa.com/

Carnival Cruise Lines *contracted its services mix* by selling a casino hotel in the Bahamas—part of a series of moves designed to get the cruise ship company out of the resort business. Because of the high cost of malpractice insurance, some physicians have contracted their product mix by discontinuing the practice of obstetrics.

In response to mounting criticism from their graduates and business firms, collegiate business schools have been *altering their services offering*. Changes in the national accreditation rules for business schools are leading to changes in what they teach and how they teach it.

Managing the life cycle of a service is another strategy. Recognizing that the credit card industry is in the maturity stage, VISA sought ways to maintain its growth. The answer was new uses—new markets—rather than issuing cards to more people. For starters, VISA targeted dentists, physicians, supermarkets, theaters, and even fast-food outlets, trying to get them to encourage their customers to pay with a VISA card. Likewise, amusement parks such as Knott's Berry Farm in California, Six Flags, and Great America have avoided the sales-decline stage of the life cycle by periodically adding new attractions.

Product Features. The emphasis in product planning is different for services than for goods. For example, packaging is nonexistent in services marketing. However, other features—branding and quality management, for example—present greater challenges for services industries.

Branding of services is a problem because maintaining consistent quality, a responsibility of brand ownership, is difficult. Also, the intangibility characteristic means a brand cannot be physically attached to the service itself.

A services marketer's goal should be to create an effective brand image. The strategy to reach this goal is to develop a total theme that includes more than just a good brand name. To implement this strategy, the following tactics frequently are employed:[9]

- Use a *tangible object* to communicate the brand image. The blanket of Nationwide Insurance, Merrill Lynch's bull, and the good hands of Allstate symbolize what these firms stand for.
- Develop a *memorable slogan* to accompany the brand. "Your true choice" by AT&T and "You'll love the way we fly" by Delta Air Lines are descriptive and easily remembered.
- Use a *distinctive color scheme* on all tangible aspects of the service. Avis's red or Hertz's black and gold office decor, counters, uniforms, and shuttle vans are highly recognizable.

Nonprofit organizations have been slow to adopt branding and color. The little that has been done suggests that these features provide effective marketing support. For many years, colleges have used nicknames (a form of brand name) primarily for their athletic teams, but also to identify their students and alumni. Most universities have school colors—another feature that helps increase the market's recognition of the school. Among health research organizations, the Lung Association has registered as a trademark its double-barred Christmas Seal cross. Likewise, the trademarks of the Girl Scouts, Boy Scouts, YMCA, and Salvation Army are readily recognized by many people.

Management of Service Quality. In Chapter 10, we noted the elusiveness of product quality. Service quality is particularly difficult to define, measure, control, and communicate. Yet in services marketing, the quality of the service is critical to a firm's success. Two airlines each fly a Boeing 747 for the same fare; two auto-repair shops each use factory-authorized parts and charge the same price; and two banks each handle the same U.S. currency at identical interest rates. Assuming similar times and locations, quality of service is the only factor that differentiates what is offered by these firms.

However difficult it may be to define **service quality,** management must understand two things: First, *quality is defined by the customer, not by the producer-seller.* Your hairstylist may be delighted with the job done on your hair. But if you think your hair looks terrible, then the service quality was poor. Second, service

AN ETHICAL DILEMMA?

McNeil Consumer Products, a division of Johnson & Johnson, reached an agreement with the Arthritis Foundation. In exchange for placing the foundation's trademarked name on the company's pain relievers, McNeil has committed to providing $1 million a year to the foundation's research on arthritis. Other nonprofit organizations have endorsed particular brands. For example, Crest toothpaste has prominently displayed the American Dental Association's endorsement for years. And for a while the American Heart Association placed its seal of approval on selected products. However, in those cases, the nonprofit organizations received nothing in return for their endorsements.

To further their objectives, should nonprofit organizations endorse products in return for financial support?

Source: Susan Gaines, "A Marriage of Convenience," *Business Ethics,* November/December 1994, p. 10.

quality that does not meet customer *expectations* can result in lost sales from present customers and a failure to attract new customers.

Consequently, management must (1) determine the expectation level of its target market and (2) strive to maintain consistent service quality at or above that level. Expectations are based on information from personal and commercial sources, promises made by the service provider, and experience with the particular service as well as other similar services. To determine customers' expectations, a service provider must do some research. Gathering data on the target market's past behavior, existing perceptions and beliefs, and exposure to information can provide the basis for estimating expectations.

With the desired level of performance set, the next challenge is standardizing service performance—that is, maintaining consistency in service output. Service performance typically varies even within the same organization. This is true in such diverse fields as opera, legal services, landscaping, baseball, hospital care, and marketing courses. The reason is simple: services are most often performed by people and their behavior is very difficult to standardize.

As part of managing service quality, an organization should design and operate an ongoing quality-improvement program that will monitor the level and consistency of service quality. A related, but also hard, task is to evaluate service quality by measuring customer satisfaction—that is, customers' perceptions of the quality of an organization's services.

In the 1980s some U.S. services firms followed the lead of goods-producing companies and adopted a concept that has long been used in Japan—*total quality management (TQM)*. Results so far have been mixed. In the services field, Federal Express, for example, has made TQM work, while Florida Power & Light has cut back on its TQM program. For TQM to work effectively, a company must be patient and look for results over the long run—traits not found in abundance in American business.[10]

http://www.unitedway.org/

To standardize the quality of their local operations, some nonprofit organizations are copying the operating structures used by commercial franchise systems. For example, Camp Fire Girls and Boys and United Way provide local units with managerial expertise, performance evaluation, marketing guidance, and purchasing services in exchange for a fee. This provides the local unit with policies to achieve consistency in all its operations, a high level of managerial expertise, and valuable operating economies.[11]

Pricing Structure

In services marketing there is a great need for managerial skill in pricing. Because services are perishable, they cannot be stored, and demand for them often fluctuates considerably. Each of these features has significant pricing implications. To further complicate pricing, customers often have a "do-it-yourself" alternative, as in auto or home repairs. As we discussed in Chapters 11 and 12, there are two tasks in designing a *pricing structure*: determine the base price and select strategies to adjust the base price.

Price Determination in For-Profit Firms. At least two of the three major pricing methods discussed in Chapter 11 are used by services marketers—cost-plus and prices based on the market alone. Electric power and telephone companies, for example, use a cost basis to set prices that will generate a predetermined rate of return on investment. Painters, plumbers, and electricians frequently price their services on a cost-plus basis. Airlines, on the other hand, tend to meet

Being customer-oriented also makes good business sense. When insurance companies announced they would pay for only 24 hours of post-birth hospital care, St. Joseph Medical Center was among several hospitals that began a "Mother's Day" program, offering new mothers an additional 24 hours of room and board at no extra cost. The hospital's administrator points out that the offer is a health, not a promotional, issue. However, as this ad indicates, it permits the hospital to position itself as a particularly concerned maternity care provider.

competitors' prices, especially on routes served by two or more airlines, even if those prices result in a financial loss.

The characteristics of services (perishability, for example) suggest that the elasticity of demand for a service should influence its price. Interestingly enough, sellers often do recognize inelastic demand upward. For example, prices are raised significantly for the final concert of a popular musical group or a championship sporting event. But they fail to act in an opposite fashion when faced with an elastic demand—even though a lower price would increase unit sales, total revenue, utilization of facilities, and probably net profit.

Price Determination by Nonprofits. Pricing in nonprofit organizations is different from pricing in a for-profit firm. In the first place, pricing becomes less important when profit making is not a goal. Also, a nonprofit organization is faced with special forms of pricing in the donor market and in the client market.

In the donor market, nonprofit organizations do not set the price—the amount of the donation. That price is set by contributors when they decide how much they are willing to pay (donate) for the benefits they expect to receive. However, a price is often suggested—for example, donate 1 day's pay or volunteer for 1 day a month. And the suggested price is often translated into a client benefit (for example, the amount of food or clothing $100 will provide in an underdeveloped country) to provide the donor with a basis for valuing the contribution.

In the client market, some nonprofit organizations face the same pricing situation, and can use the same methods, as profit-seeking firms. Museums and opera companies, for example, must decide on admission prices; fraternal organizations must set a dues schedule; and colleges must determine how much to charge for tuition. But most nonprofit organizations cannot use the same pricing methods employed by business firms. The nonprofit organizations know that they cannot cover their costs with prices charged to clients. The gap between anticipated revenues and costs must be made up by contributions. As yet, there simply are no real guidelines for nonprofit pricing.

Also, some nonprofit groups tend to believe there are no client-pricing considerations, because there is no monetary charge to the client. Actually, the goods or services received by clients rarely are free—that is, without a price of some kind. The client almost always pays a price—in the form of travel and waiting time and, perhaps, embarrassment or humiliation—that a money-paying client would not have to pay. Poor children who have to wear donated, second-hand clothing certainly are paying a price if their classmates ridicule those clothes.

Pricing Strategies. Several of the pricing strategies we discussed in Chapter 12 are applicable in services marketing—in both profit-seeking and nonprofit organizations. *Discount strategies,* for example, are widely used in marketing services. A season pass for the Metropolitan Opera or the Los Angeles Symphony Orchestra costs less per performance than tickets purchased for individual performances. Daily rates charged by Hertz or Avis are lower if you rent a car for a week or a month at a time. These are forms of a quantity discount.

A *flexible-price* strategy is used by many service organizations. Museums and movie theaters offer lower prices for children and senior citizens. In some cities, bus transportation costs less during off-peak hours. The University of Colorado charges a higher tuition in its business and engineering colleges than in arts and sciences. On the other hand, the University of Notre Dame and many other universities typically follow a *one-price* strategy. That is, all students pay the same tuition for a full load of course work.

Price competition among service providers varies by industry. Where it has become more common, the use of price competition seems to evolve through three stages:

1. Price is rarely mentioned as organizations attempt to compete on other dimensions. For example, a health maintenance organization (HMO) will run an ad explaining its services, but not dwelling much on price.
2. The seller uses a segmentation strategy and targets a given market at a specific price. A law firm, for example, will prominently advertise its low prices for divorce proceedings or the preparation of a will.
3. Out-and-out price competition occurs as firms stress comparative prices in their advertising. The airlines and long-distance phone companies have engaged extensively in advertising that compares their prices with those of competitors.

Price competition is particularly intense in service industries where the products are viewed as highly interchangeable, such as fast food. Interestingly, in areas where the products should be fairly easy to differentiate, such as professional services, price competition seems to be increasing.

Distribution System

Designing a distribution system in a services organization (whether it be for-profit or nonprofit) involves two tasks. One is to select the channels of distribution, and the other is to provide physical facilities for the distribution of the services.[12]

Channels of Distribution. The channel for most services is short and quite simple because of the inseparability characteristic. That is, a service usually cannot be separated from its producer. It is created, sold, and consumed simultaneously. Barbers give haircuts; dentists fix teeth; the United Way solicits donations and dispenses relief services; and your favorite radio station entertains you. The channel of distribution for all these service examples is from producer directly to consumer; no middlemen are involved.

The only other frequently used channel includes one agent middleman. For example, an agent or broker often is used when marketing securities, travel arrangements, or housing rentals. To generate increased contributions, a political party or a university may employ an outside fund-raising organization. Theaters or athletic teams may sell tickets through independent ticket agencies such as Ticket Master.

http://www.ticketmaster.com/

Short channels usually means more control on the part of the seller. With direct distribution or only a single middleman, it would seem that service marketers should be able to reduce the heterogeneity or variance in the service from one transaction to another. However, since the service provider is also creating the service, a single firm may operate many of these short channels. For example, McDonald's has over 14,000 outlets in 79 countries, all producing and distributing the product. Thus, the control problems are in the number of channels to be managed, not their length.

http://www.mcdonalds.com/

Distribution Facilities. A good location is essential when a service is distributed directly from producer to consumer, especially today because consumers are so convenience-oriented. Some services marketers have broadened their distribution base by extending their locations, thus offsetting to some extent the limitations imposed by the inseparability factor. For some years now, automated teller machines have provided some banking services at locations away from the bank. American Express and insurance companies have broadened their services distribution by setting up vending machines in airports. And as was described in the opening case, Enterprise delivers rental cars.

Nonprofit organizations try to provide arrangements to make donor contributions easy and convenient. Besides cash and checks, charities use payroll deductions, installment plans, and credit cards. If you are contributing used goods, the Disabled American Veterans may collect them at your residence.

Location is also critical when dealing with nonprofits' client markets. Universities set up branch campuses; they also offer correspondence courses. The Salvation Army locates its stores in low-income neighborhoods. Big-city museums arrange for portable exhibits to be taken to small towns.

The physical surroundings—the atmosphere—in the distribution of a service influence considerably a prospective customer's perception of that service and its creator-producer. Because services are intangible, prospects look to the service facility itself and the people working there to form a prepurchase evaluation. Understanding this situation, Premier Bancorp in New Orleans has replaced institutional furnishings and steel security gratings in its lobby with comfortable furniture, easily accessible employees, and an atmosphere that resembles a retail store more than a bank.[13]

Promotional Program

Several types of promotion are used extensively in services marketing—in both profit-seeking and nonprofit organizations. In fact, promotion is the one part of the marketing mix with which services marketers are most familiar and adept. Unfortunately, many services firms, especially nonprofit organizations, believe that promotion and marketing are the same thing.

Personal Selling.   Because of the inseparability characteristic, personal selling plays a role in the promotional programs of most service firms. Face-to-face contact between buyer and seller is required in order to make a transaction. Thus, it is important that a service employee be skilled at customer relations as well as capable of producing a quality service.

Personal selling is frequently employed by nonprofit organizations in soliciting donations. A door-to-door campaign may be used, and potentially large donors may be approached by fund raisers (sales people). At Christmastime, Salvation Army volunteers—dressed as Santa Claus—collect donations in downtown areas and shopping malls. Many nonprofit organizations also use personal selling to reach their clients. For centuries, religious missionaries recruited new members by personal contact—personal selling. Colleges send admissions officers, alumni, and current students to talk to high school students, their parents, and their counselors. All of these personal representatives may not be called sales people, but that is exactly what they are.

Whether they realize it or not, any employee of a service firm who comes in contact with a customer is, in effect, part of that firm's sales force. In addition to a regular sales force, customer-contact personnel might include airline-counter attendants, law-office receptionists, package delivery people, bank tellers, ticket takers, and ushers at ballparks or theaters.

We use the term **service encounter** to describe a customer's interaction with any service employee or with any tangible element such as a service's physical surroundings (bank, ballpark, medical office). Customers form opinions of a company and its service on the basis of service encounters. Consequently, management must prepare its contact personnel and physical surroundings for these encounters. This preparation, in effect, involves managing a sales force—including recruiting, training, and supervision. Many service organizations, especially the nonprofits, do not think in these terms and, as a result, have not developed the managerial skills to perform these tasks effectively.

Advertising.   For years, advertising has been used extensively in many service fields—transportation, recreation, and insurance, for example. What is new is the use of advertising by professional-services firms, including legal, accounting, and medical services. Previously, professional associations in these fields prohibited advertising on the grounds that it was unethical. These associations still try to limit and control advertising. However, several courts and regulatory agencies have ruled that prohibiting a professional firm from advertising is restraint of trade and thus a violation of antitrust laws. At the same time, some states have laws that regulate TV advertising by lawyers, and others are considering similar legislation.

Nonprofit organizations use advertising extensively to reach their donor markets. Mass media (newspapers, television, radio) frequently are used in annual fund-raising drives. Direct mail can be especially effective in reaching particular donor-market segments, such as cash contributors, religious or ethnic groups, or college alumni.

Forming an alliance with a for-profit organization can be another valuable source of promotion for nonprofits. Called *cause marketing,* it involves developing a relationship that generates sales for the firm and publicity (along with a

WHAT CHALLENGES ARE FACED BY ADVERTISERS IN CHINA?

Advertising as it is known in the Western world has been permitted in China only since about 1980. Despite its relative youth, it is an important service industry in that country. The agencies that produce and place ads and the media that carry them currently generate $4 billion in revenue, and the figure is expected to grow to over $20 billion by the year 2000.

As it has everywhere, the ad industry in China is experiencing growing pains. The difference is that China's problems are greatly condensed in time because the country is joining a world in which commercial communication is very sophisticated.

One problem is exaggerated claims. Chinese consumers have seen ads for toothpaste purported to cure cancer, a soap that will eliminate wrinkled skin, and a pill that is supposed to cure hepatitis in minutes. These and similar claims have spawned a comprehensive set of ad regulations that, among other things, ban unscientific or superstitious claims in food, beverage, cosmetic, and pharmaceutical advertising. Thus far the regulations have been interpreted quite strictly, resulting in the banning of the Duracell bunny (because the ads make comparative claims), Budweiser's "King of Beers" slogan (since it can't be substantiated), and most mass-media cigarette advertising (determined to be an unhealthy product). In fact, in 1995, 100 of the 1,500 television ads examined under the legislation were deemed inappropriate.

Operating procedures in the industry are also still developing. For example, the media regularly discriminate against foreign ad agencies. Foreign firms are commonly charged four to five times more than locals for television advertising time and magazine space, they frequently are required to pay in advance, and their scheduled ads are often removed for special programs or articles. To date, the Chinese government has not shown any interest in controlling the discrimination.

With a population of 1.2 billion people and consumer spending expected to be nearly $750 billion early in the next century, China is viewed as a market with outstanding potential. However, the Chinese are having some difficulty coming to grips with commercial communication. As a result, advertisers and advertising agencies that want to do business in China are likely to experience a variety of frustrations for quite some time, because advertising as it is known in most of the world is still in its infancy.

Sources: Dexter Roberts, "Winding Up for the Big Pitch," *Business Week,* Oct. 23, 1995, p. 52; "New Chinese Advertising Laws Affect Foreign Multinationals," Information Access Company, Newsletter Database, Vol. 6, No. 4, June 1, 1995; and Sally D. Goll, "Chinese Officials Attempt to Ban False Ad Claims," *The Wall Street Journal,* Feb. 28, 1995, pp. B1+.

---

http://www.pmedia.com/Avon/

donation) for the nonprofit organization. Recent examples include Avon's Breast Cancer Awareness Crusade in conjunction with the National Cancer Institute and the YWCA, and Dollar Rent A Car's support of Special Olympics International.[14]

http://www.ivy.tec.in.us/

Nonprofit groups also can communicate with client markets through advertising. To offset declining enrollments, colleges and universities run ads. For example, Ivy Tech State College in Indiana with 22 campuses developed a multimedia campaign to demonstrate how its graduates become valuable employees.[15] And a growing number of churches advertise aggressively in print media and on radio and TV to increase their membership and attendance.[16]

Other Promotional Methods.   Various forms of sales promotion are frequently used by services marketers. Laundry and dry-cleaning firms, opticians, and auto-repair shops include reduced-price offers in coupon books mailed periodically to local households. Travel agents, ski resorts, and landscaping services have displays

http://www.redcross.org/

at sports shows or home shows. These displays show the beneficial results of using the service. The United Way, Red Cross, and other charitable organizations frequently have booths in shopping malls.

Many service firms, especially in the recreation and entertainment fields, benefit considerably from free publicity. Sports coverage by newspapers, radio, and television provides publicity, as do newspaper reviews of movies, plays, and concerts. Travel sections in newspapers help sell transportation, housing, and other services related to the travel industry.

The Future of Services Marketing

Until recently, many services industries enjoyed growth, supported by government and professional-association regulation, the absence of significant foreign competition, and a strong economy. But the service environment is changing, bringing with it a focus on increasing productivity and measuring customer-satisfying performance.

The Changing Services Environment

Several factors have stimulated intense competition in many services industries in recent years:

- Increased foreign competition in several fields—the Japanese in banking, the Germans and English in retailing, and several countries in air transportation.
- Reduced government regulation in some industries—airlines, trucking, and banking, for example.
- Court decisions approving advertising in the medical, legal, and other professions.
- Increases in the supply of some service providers—physicians, dentists, and lawyers, for example—bringing competition to previously protected fields.
- Technology that has dramatically changed some service industries and created others—facsimile machines have diminished the need for overnight delivery of documents, and video tape players have produced the video-rental store. Technological advances have also brought automation (banks' automatic teller machines, for example) and other industrial features to formerly manual-labor services industries.

The impact of these developments is dramatic. Chains and franchise systems are replacing the small-scale, independent service firm and professional in many fields. Examples include health care (Kaiser and Humana); auto repairs and maintenance (Midas Muffler and Jiffy Lube); optical (Pearle and Lenscrafters); and real estate brokerage (Re/Max and Century 21).

Need for Increased Productivity

The changing services environment has exposed the inefficiency and poor management in many services industries and clearly demonstrates the need for restructuring.[17] This inefficiency—and the resultant need to increase productivity—is probably the biggest opportunity facing services industries today.

Not long ago, attempts to increase services productivity were focused on a manufacturing-based approach. For example, Burger King and McDonald's adopted assembly-line techniques and increased their output per worker. The most widely adopted technology was some form of computer-based information system that increased the efficiency of operations. And for several years this manufacturing-based model for increasing service productivity was successful.

However, the basic premise of the manufacturing model is that machines and technology are the primary keys to increased productivity; that the people who deliver the services are less important. But this premise simply no longer works in the competitive services environment of the 1990s. Instead, a model is needed that puts customer-contact workers first, and then designs the business operations around these people.[18]

Performance Measurement

Profit-seeking service firms can evaluate their performance by using quantitative measures such as profitability, market share, or return on investment, and then compare these figures with industry averages and trends. For most nonprofit organizations, however, there are no similar measures. Consequently, measuring marketing performance in nonprofits is a real managerial challenge. At present, this task is very difficult, if not impossible.

Nonprofit organizations can quantify the contributions they receive, but the result reflects only their fund-raising abilities. It does not measure the services rendered to their clients. How do you quantitatively evaluate the performance of, say, the Red Cross? Perhaps by the number of people the organization houses and feeds after a hurricane or some other natural disaster? Or by the number of people trained in first aid and life-saving techniques? Churches, museums, and YMCAs can count their attendance, but how do they measure the services and benefits they provide their clients?

The analysis and management of customer complaints is an evaluation tool that can be used by both nonprofit and profit-seeking organizations. The complaint-management process involves keeping track of (1) customer complaints, (2) how they are resolved by company employees, and (3) whether the complaint handling was satisfactory enough so that the complaining customer ends up as a returning customer. Hampton Inns, a hotel chain, effectively uses this complaint-management process to:

- Determine where to concentrate their customer-satisfaction attention.
- Compare the profitability of various complaint-handling activities.
- Demonstrate to customer-contact employees the importance of complaint management and superior customer service.[19]

Prospects for Growth

Services will continue to take an increasing share of the consumer dollar, just as they have done over the past 40 years. This forecast seems reasonable even for periods of economic decline. History shows that the demand for services is less sensitive to economic fluctuations than the demand for goods. The demand for commercial services should also continue to expand as business becomes more complex and as management further recognizes its need for specialized support services. In professional services especially, the use of marketing programs is expected to increase considerably during the coming decade. This expansion will occur as physicians, lawyers, and other professionals come to understand the economic benefits they can derive from an effective marketing program.[20]

The significance of nonprofit marketing will increase as the people in these organizations understand what marketing is and what it can do for them. As we noted earlier in this chapter, nonprofit firms typically have a limited concept of marketing, even though they attempt some aspects without calling it marketing. The marketing activities they do perform (usually promotion) are not well coordinated, and the people in charge of them usually have other duties and titles. In a university, for example, personal selling may be managed by the director of admissions, fund raising coordinated by a director of development, and advertising done through an office of public information. For a more effective marketing job, most nonprofits need a more formal, recognizable marketing structure.

■ SUMMARY

The scope of services marketing is enormous. About half of what we spend goes for services, and more than 75 percent of nonfarm jobs are in services industries. The nonprofit field includes thousands of organizations spanning educational, cultural, religious, charitable, social, health care, and political activities. Marketing in nonprofit organizations is included in this chapter because most of these organizations market services rather than goods.

The growth in services has not been matched by service management's understanding or acceptance of the marketing concept. Many service organizations have been slow to adopt marketing techniques that, in goods marketing, have brought satisfaction to consumers and profits to producers. In nonprofit organizations, especially, many people do not understand what marketing is and what it can do for them.

Most product offerings are a mix of tangible goods and intangible services, somewhere between mostly goods and mostly services. To distinguish between goods and services, we define services as separately identifiable, intangible activities that are the main object of a transaction designed to provide want-satisfaction.

Services are intangible, usually inseparable from the seller, heterogeneous, highly perishable, and widely fluctuating in demand. These characteristics that differentiate services from goods have several marketing implications.

Most nonprofit organizations must deal with two markets: donors, the contributors to the organization; and clients, the recipients of the organization's money or services. Consequently, a nonprofit organization must develop two separate marketing programs: one to attract resources from donors and one to provide services to clients.

Developing a program for marketing services is much the same as for goods, but takes into account the characteristics of services. Management first identifies its target market, especially using market segmentation strategies, and then designs a marketing mix around a differential advantage to provide want-satisfaction for the market.

In the product-planning stage, services firms use various product-mix strategies, and they should try to brand their services. Consistently maintaining a level of quality that the customer expects is critical to a company's success. Service firms must determine base prices and select appropriate pricing strategies. Pricing in nonprofit organizations often is quite different from pricing in profit-seeking businesses.

Channels of distribution are quite simple in services marketing, and middlemen are not often used. The main physical distribution challenge is to locate the services organization where it can most effectively serve its markets. Regarding promotion, services firms use personal selling and advertising extensively—and often aggressively and quite effectively. These organizations are recognizing the importance of service encounters and customer-contact personnel.

The changing services environment in the 1990s has exposed the inefficiency in services industries and demonstrates the need to restructure the operations in many firms to increase productivity. The growth in both for-profit and nonprofit services organizations is expected to continue.

More about

ENTERPRISE RENT-A-CAR

Vhat does Enterprise Rent-A-Car have in common with better-known car-rental companies such as Hertz and Avis? Since they all rent cars for short time periods, they may seem to be nearly identical. However, the fact is they are more different than they are alike.

Enterprise provides slightly older cars, from non-airport locations, at lower prices. The company relies more on personal selling and referrals by influentials than on mass-media advertising to customers. It focuses on a different need (emergency rentals), and overcomes the dispersion of its customers by providing delivery and pickup services.

This positioning has worked very well for Enterprise. The firm has made a profit every month for over 20 years. But, can this segment sustain Enterprise's growth as competitors move in, or must the company look elsewhere?

Enterprise may find it necessary to develop niche markets. One such opportunity is a by-product of changes in leisure-travel behavior. More consumers are taking frequent, brief vacations within a few hundred miles of home. For many of these short trips, renting an economical, reasonably new car rather than traveling by some other means or putting miles on their own cars may be an attractive option.

Other possibilities are rental cars for visiting relatives and college students home for the holidays.

Enterprise must also continue to search for ways to keep its expenses down without reducing the quality of its service. One area of concern is the tangible element of its product. Rental cars are subject to a high rate of abuse. For instance, a Texas renter placed a 450-pound prize calf in an Enterprise sedan to protect it during a rain storm! Also, because renters are unfamiliar with the cars and are often driving in strange environments, rental cars are involved in accidents more frequently than privately owned autos.[21]

1. Like all service firms, Enterprise must adapt to the characteristics of intangibility, inseparability, perishability, and heterogeneity.
   a. What elements of Enterprise's marketing strategy reflect a sensitivity to these characteristics?
   b. What else could Enterprise do to adapt to these characteristics of services?
2. How would Enterprise have to change its marketing effort if it decides to pursue other auto-rental markets?

■ KEY TERMS AND CONCEPTS

Services (515)
Intangibility (518)
Inseparability (518)

Heterogeneity (518)
Perishability (518)

Donor market
 (contributors) (520)
Client market
 (recipients) (521)

Service quality (524)
Service encounter (529)

■ QUESTIONS AND PROBLEMS

1. What are some marketing implications of the fact that services possess the characteristic of intangibility?
2. Services are highly perishable and are often subject to fluctuations in demand. In marketing an amusement park, how can a company offset these factors?
3. Cite some examples of large services firms that seem to be customer-oriented, and describe what these firms have done to create this impression.
4. Identify the various segments of the donor market for your school.
5. Present a brief analysis of the market for each of the following service firms. Make use of the components of a market discussed in Chapters 5 through 7.

   a. Hospital in your city
   b. Hotel near a large airport
   c. Indoor tennis club
6. What are some ways in which each of the following service firms might expand its product mix?
   a. Certified public accountant (CPA)
   b. Hairstyling salon
   c. Bank
7. A financial consultant for a private university suggested a change in the school's pricing methods. He recommended that the school discontinue its present one-price policy, under which all full-time students pay the same tuition. Instead, he recommended that the tuition vary by

departments within the university. Thus, students majoring in high-cost fields of study, such as engineering or a laboratory science, would pay higher tuition than students in lower-cost fields, such as English or history. Should the school adopt this recommendation?

8. Explain how the concept of the marketing mix (product, price, distribution, promotion) is applicable to the marketing of the following social causes:
   a. The use of returnable bottles, instead of the throw-away type
   b. The prevention of heart ailments
   c. A campaign against smoking
   d. Obeying the speed limit

9. How would you measure the marketing performance of each of the following?
   a. A church
   b. Your school
   c. The Republican Party
   d. A group in favor of gun control

■ HANDS-ON MARKETING

1. Grade the marketing performance of a sample of profit-seeking services firms in your college community by asking 10 of your friends to rate each of them on a scale of 10 (excellent performer) to 1 (very poor performer). Compute an average "performance score" for each firm. Based on your survey, identify those that are doing a good marketing job and those that are not. In your report, explain briefly the reasons that contribute to the ratings of the two best and two worst performers.

2. Interview a sample of foreign students on your campus and prepare a report summarizing five major differences and five major similarities between the colleges in their home countries and your school. Include such topics as classroom atmosphere, evaluation of students, student-professor relations, campus political activities, and campus social life. What explains these similarities and differences?

CHAPTER 20

International Marketing

Can
TOYS "R" US
Continue to Play the Growth Game?

The retailing formula for Toys "R" Us was developed by Charles Lazarus and introduced in 1957. It consists of a narrow but very deep merchandise assortment and discount prices made possible by dealing directly with manufacturers. Toys "R" Us (TRU) was so successful that it became the prototype for the classification of retailers called category killers. Using the same formula, two similar chains—Kids "R" Us and Babies "R" Us—have been developed by Lazarus.

The success of TRU did not go unnoticed by competitors. Discount chains like Kmart, Wal-Mart, and Target (a division of Dayton-Hudson) expanded their toy offerings. However, more significant than their product assortment is the strategy of these competitors to treat toys as low-margin traffic builders. That is, they use low prices on toys to attract customers who also buy other things. As a result, they often have lower toy prices than TRU.

In the late 1970s, TRU management observed that the competitive environment in many countries was similar to what it had originally encountered in the U.S.: Toys were sold at high markups by small specialty stores or departments in large stores. In addition, demand seemed to depend only on the presence of children, and parents and grandparents who want to give them gifts. Thus, it set out to duplicate its domestic success in other countries.

TRU's first international foray was into Canada in 1984. The move was met with skepticism from observers who felt that retailing is culture-bound, and that transferring a successful format from one country to another would be difficult if not impossible. Recognizing the challenge, TRU made adjustments. According to a senior executive: "In every country we enter, we try to think globally and act locally."

In Canada, TRU installed strong local managers with the authority to adapt the operation to the market's tastes and preferences. To keep costs down and permit low prices, inventory was carefully managed through an efficient distribution system and sophisticated point-of-sale data-gathering technology that permitted the firm to respond quickly to sales trends. Finally, TRU engaged in aggressive promotion of the stores. The Canadian operation proved successful, and the procedure that was utilized became a prototype for expansion into England, Taiwan, Singapore, Hong Kong, Australia, and Germany.

By 1995 TRU had a total of over 900 stores (600 in the U.S.), sales of $8.7 billion, and 22 percent of the toy market. It is the eighth largest discount retailer in the U.S.

With the domestic market virtually saturated, TRU is emphasizing international expansion. For example, in 1994 it opened more stores outside the U.S. than inside, and it now has operations in more than 20 countries. With nearly 200 stores in Western Europe, TRU has achieved a critical mass that led to the establishment of several distribution centers located throughout Western Europe. The firm anticipates more growth in Western Europe, and Eastern Europe is viewed as an enormous untapped opportunity.

TRU is using franchising to expand into certain parts of the world. Its first franchised store is in Dubai. Franchising permits rapid growth with minimal risk for TRU, making it an attractive way to enter politically unstable areas such as the Middle East, Pakistan, and Bangladesh. With its record of success and plans for growth, some think TRU will become the first truly international retailer.[1]

What challenges will Toys "R" Us face as it continues its international expansion?

http://www.toysrus.com/

537

A firm interested in international marketing is faced with many decisions. The most basic is the choice of the level of operations, from simply exporting goods to investing in manufacturing or distribution abroad as Toys "R" Us has done. Then there are marketing-mix decisions, such as what to call the product and how best to inform the market about its existence. These and many more decisions must be made for a business that will operate in cultural, economic, and legal systems that are likely to be quite different from those in its home country. Given this complexity we need to examine international marketing in some detail.

After studying this chapter, you should be able to explain:

CHAPTER GOALS

- The importance of international marketing to firms and countries.
- The impact of the macroenvironmental factors of culture, economics, and political/legal forces on international marketing.
- Alternative organizational structures for operating in foreign markets.
- Strategic considerations in formulating international marketing programs.
- The role of trade balances in international marketing.

The Attraction of International Marketing

International marketing takes place when an organization markets its products in two or more countries. The fundamentals of marketing apply internationally in the same way they apply domestically. Whether an Ohio firm sells in Toledo, Taiwan, or Timbuktu, its marketing program should be built around an appealing product that is properly priced, promoted, and distributed to a market that has been carefully selected.

International markets are vital to many companies. Several large U.S. firms earn more than half their aftertax profits from overseas marketing and production operations. IBM and Boeing Company regularly get about half their annual sales revenues from outside the U.S. You probably recognize Sony, Benetton, Bic, Gucci, Heineken, Toyota, and Adidas as foreign firms. But what about Lipton, Lever Bros., Columbia Pictures, Shell Oil, A&P, and Burger King? Did you know that these firms are also owned by non–U.S. companies?

To get an idea of how significant international trade is, consider that France, Canada, and the United Kingdom each export an amount equal to 25 percent of what they produce a year, and that Germany exports about $400 billion in products annually. And in countries you might not expect, exporting is also very significant. For example, Brazil's exports amount to $35 billion, and South Korea's are over $60 billion a year.

A firm moves beyond domestic markets into international trade for several reasons:

- *Potential demand in foreign markets.* There is a strong demand for a wide variety of consumer products all over the world. McDonald's exemplifies this as well as any firm. It has over 4,700 stores in 73 countries outside the U.S.[2] And within the developing as well as the developed nations of the world, there is a demand for business products such as machine tools, construction equipment, and computers.
- *Saturation of domestic markets.* Firms—even those with no previous international experience—look to foreign markets. As described in the opening case, Toys "R" Us found foreign markets highly attractive, in part because of strong competitors such as Kmart and Wal-Mart.

*M*any U.S. firms seeking export markets in Asia have bypassed Japan, choosing China and Southeast Asia instead. Firms have been discouraged by Japan's trade restrictions and multi-layered distribution system that add costs. However, recent inroads suggest a change may be occurring. For example, Japanese consumers have become more price conscious and discount retailers are growing rapidly. And U.S.-made personal computers, software, and cellular phones are showing gains. The GAP, Inc.'s new 8,000-square-foot store in the heart of Tokyo, pictured here, is one of the most recent signs of growing U.S. interest in Japan.

- *Comparative advantage.* Some countries possess unique natural or human resources that give them an edge when it comes to producing particular products. This factor, for example, explains South Africa's dominance in diamonds, and the ability of developing countries in Asia with low wage rates to compete successfully in products assembled by hand.
- *Technological advantage.* In one country a particular industry, often encouraged by government and spurred by the efforts of a few firms, develops a technological advantage over the rest of the world. For example, the U.S. dominated the computer industry for many years because of technology developed by companies such as IBM and Hewlett-Packard.

Organization Structures for International Markets

In deciding to market in a foreign country, management must select an appropriate organizational structure. There is a range of methods for operating in foreign markets (see Table 20-1), representing successively greater international involvement.

Exporting

The simplest way to operate in foreign markets is by exporting, either directly to foreign importers or through import-export middlemen. Because it is the easiest way to get into international markets, exporting is popular with small firms. In international markets, just as in domestic markets, there are both merchant and agent middlemen.

An **export merchant** is a middleman operating in the manufacturer's country that buys goods and exports them. Very little risk or investment is involved. Also, minimal time and effort are required on the part of the exporting producer. However, the exporter has little or no control over merchant middlemen.

TABLE 20-1 The range of structures for operating in foreign markets

Exporting directly or through import-export middlemen	Company sales branches	Licensing foreign producers	Contract manufacturing by foreign producers	Joint ventures and strategic alliances	Wholly owned subsidiaries	Multinational corporations
Low involvement abroad						High involvement abroad

An **export agent** may be located in either the manufacturer's country or in the destination country. The agent negotiates the sale of the product and may provide additional services such as arranging for international financing, shipping, and insurance on behalf of the manufacturer, but does not own the goods. Greater risk is involved, because the manufacturer retains title to the goods. Because they typically deal with a number of manufacturers, both types of middlemen generally are not aggressive marketers, nor do they generate a large sales volume.

To counteract some of these deficiencies, management can export through its own **company sales branches** located in foreign markets. Operating a sales branch enables a company to (1) promote its products more aggressively, (2) tailor its distribution network to the product, and (3) control its sales effort more completely. Several brewers, including Dutch-based Heineken, Stroh's of the U.S., and Bass in Britain, use company branches to market nonalcoholic beverages in Saudi Arabia.[3] Branch offices are used rather than export agents because the marketing task demands special attention. Alcoholic beverages are illegal in Saudi Arabia, so the marketing effort for products made by beer companies are required to meet numerous regulations. It's unlikely that an export agent would provide the necessary care.

With an international sales branch, management now has the task of managing a sales force. The difficulty is that these sales people are either employees sent from the home country who are unfamiliar with the local market, or foreign nationals who are unfamiliar with the product and the company's marketing practices.

Contracting

Contracting involves a legal relationship that allows a firm to enter a foreign market indirectly, quickly establish a market presence, and experience a limited amount of risk. One form of contracting is a licensing arrangement. **Licensing** means granting to another producer—for a fee or royalty payment—the right to use one's production process, patents, trademarks, or other assets. For example, in Japan, the Suntory brewery is licensed by Anheuser-Busch to produce Budweiser beer, while in England, Budweiser is brewed under license by the Watney brewery. Producers run the risk of encouraging future competition by licensing. A licensee may learn all it can from the producer and then proceed independently when the licensing agreement expires.

Franchising has allowed many U.S. service retailers, such as McDonald's, KFC, and Toys "R" Us, to expand overseas rapidly and with minimal risk. Franchising combines a proven operating formula with local knowledge and entrepreneurial initiative.

In **contract manufacturing**, a marketer, such as Sears, Roebuck, contracts with a foreign producer to supply products that Sears then markets in the producer's country. For example, rather than import U.S.–made tools and hardware for its department stores in Mexico, Brazil, and Spain, Sears contracts with local manufacturers to supply many of these products.

Contracting offers companies flexibility with minimal investment. It allows a producer to enter a market that might otherwise be closed to it because of exchange restrictions, import quotas, or prohibitive tariffs.

Direct Investment

Another alternative is **direct investment**—a company can build or acquire production or distribution facilities in a foreign country. Table 20-2 shows the amount of foreign investment made by the firms in five major countries in 1994. Note that these are not sales figures, nor do they include products exported from these countries. They are limited to investments in facilities and equipment outside a firm's home country during a single year.

The magnitude of foreign investments is a direct reflection of the strength of a country's economy in comparison to the rest of the world. For example, in 1990 with a booming economy, Japan led the world in foreign investment with $48 billion, and the U.S. was fourth with $26 billion. However, the situation was reversed by 1994 when the Japanese economy slumped and U.S. productivity and competitiveness picked up.[4] Direct investment can take the form of a joint venture or a wholly owned foreign subsidiary.

http://www.acer.com/

A **joint venture** is a partnership arrangement in which the foreign operation is owned in part by the domestic company and in part by a foreign company. Acer, a Taiwanese personal computer maker, is quickly gaining access to new markets through joint ventures. The firm already has 5 percent of the world PC market, but it plans to become truly global by entering into 21 joint ventures around the world by the year 2000.[5] Acer provides the products, and the local partner offers familiarity with market and marketing expertise. Ford Motor Co. has formed a joint venture with Mahindra & Mahindra Ltd. of India to initially assemble Ford Escorts and eventually manufacture Ford Fiestas in India. In this situation, Ford provides the design expertise and the Indian firm operates the assembly and production facilities.[6]

http://www.ford.com/

When the controlling interest (more than 50 percent) is owned by foreign nationals, the domestic firm has no real control over the marketing or production activities. However, a joint venture may be the only structure, other than licensing, through which a firm is legally permitted to enter some foreign markets. Joint ventures are frequently undertaken on a country-by-country basis. For example, in less than a year, Royal Crown Cola entered Mexico, Argentina, Syria, Portugal, Australia, and Indonesia on the basis of joint ventures.[7]

Some major corporations have created a hybrid version of a joint venture called a strategic alliance. A **strategic alliance** is a formal, long-term agreement between

TABLE 20-2 Direct foreign investment by major industrial countries in 1994

Country	Direct investment abroad ($ billions)
United States	46
United Kingdom	25
France	23
Germany	21
Japan	18

Source: G. Pascal Zachery, "U.S. Companies Again Hold Wide Lead over Rivals in Direct Investing Abroad," *The Wall Street Journal*, Dec. 6, 1995, pp. A2+.

http://www.british-airways.com/
http://www.usair.com/

firms to combine their capabilities and resources to accomplish global objectives without joint ownership. For example, British Airways and USAir have formed a strategic alliance. For the time being, they are integrating their flight schedules, ticketing, prices, catering, and advertising. The arrangement gives British Airways access to U.S. cities and allows USAir to offer its customers convenient routes to over 70 countries.[8]

http://www.philips.com/

Wholly owned subsidiaries in foreign markets are foreign-based assembly or manufacturing facilities. They are commonly used by companies that have evolved to an advanced stage of international business. Philips Electronics, a Dutch firm that is the world's largest maker of picture tubes for televisions and computer monitors, has a factory in Ohio to supply the U.S. market.

http://www.vw.com/

With a wholly owned foreign subsidiary, a company has maximum control over its marketing program and production operations. To ensure that the product is made and presented in the same way around the world, the company makes use of subsidiaries rather than licensees. For example, Volkswagen produces its all-time most successful model, the Beetle, in Mexico and Brazil. Interestingly, the cars are being exported to Germany where they are finding a receptive market.[9] A wholly owned subsidiary requires a substantial investment of money, labor, and managerial attention.

Multinational Corporation

This leads us to the highest level of international involvement—one reached by very few companies as yet. It is the truly global enterprise—the **multinational corporation**—in which both the foreign and the domestic operations are integrated and are not separately identified. A regional sales office in Atlanta is basically the same as one in Paris. Business opportunities abroad are viewed in the same way as those in the home country. That is, domestic opportunities are no longer automatically considered to be more attractive. From a strategic point of view, a true multinational firm does not view itself as an American firm (General Motors), or a Swiss firm (Nestlé), or a Dutch firm (Shell Oil) that also has plants and markets in other countries. In a truly worldwide enterprise, strategic marketing planning is done on a global basis.

http://www.hersheys.com/

Even though we have described these operating methods as distinct, it is not uncommon for a firm to use more than one of them at the same time. To illustrate, Hershey exports candy to Canada, is involved in a joint venture with the largest candy company in Scandinavia, and has a wholly owned subsidiary in Germany, Gubor, a boxed-chocolate company.[10]

Strategic Planning for International Marketing

Firms that have been very successful in domestic marketing have no assurance whatsoever that their success will be duplicated in foreign markets. Satisfactory performance overseas is based on (1) understanding the environment of a foreign market; and (2) gauging which domestic management practices and marketing-mix elements should be transferred directly to foreign markets, which ones modified, and which ones not used at all.

The term **global marketing** describes a strategy in which essentially the same marketing program is employed around the world. The firm probably most often associated with a globalized strategy is Coca-Cola, which derives over 10 percent of its sales from international markets.[11] However, despite selling the same products and using common promotional themes all over the world, even Coca-Cola adapts its strategy to local markets. For example, in India, Coca-Cola acquired two local brands, Thums Up, a cola, and Limca, a lime-flavored drink. Rather than replace them with its own brands, Coca-Cola continued to market the two drinks because they have strong customer loyalty.

Analysis of the Environment

Throughout the world, market demand is determined by the number of people, the ability to buy, and buying behavior. Also, human wants and needs have a universal similarity. People need food, clothing, and shelter. They seek a better quality of life in terms of lighter workloads, more leisure time, and social recognition and acceptance. But at about this point, the similarities in foreign and domestic markets seem to end, and the differences in culture, the economic environment, and political and legal forces must be considered.

Social and Cultural Forces.   Culture is a set of shared values passed down from generation to generation in a society. These values determine what is socially acceptable behavior. Some of the many cultural elements that can influence a company's marketing program are described below.

Family.   In some countries the family is an extremely close-knit unit, whereas in others the family members act more independently. The family situations in each country may require a distinctive type of promotion, and perhaps even different types of products.

Social Customs and Behavior.   Customary behavior is often hard to understand. In taking medicine, for example, English and Dutch consumers prefer white pills, the French like purple, and all three dislike red, which is the most popular color in the U.S. In other instances, preferences are quite easily explained. Such is the case with the grocery shopping behavior of Mexican consumers. Wal-Mart is disappointed with the performance of its stores in Mexico. Though consumers will buy general merchandise in the Wal-Mart stores, they don't buy groceries there. The reasons are simple. Many don't have cars and most have small refrigerators, so they don't buy food in advance of their needs. In addition, many Mexicans are accustomed to buying fresh food from specialty shops and outdoor markets, so they find packaged items in the store unappealing.[12]

Education.   The educational level in a country affects the literacy rate, which in turn influences advertising, branding, and labeling. The brand mark may become the dominant marketing strategy feature if potential customers cannot read and must recognize the article by the picture on the label.

Language Differences.   Language differences also pose problems in international marketing. In fact, language is offered as one of the primary explanations for the high failure rate of mergers between companies from different countries.[13]

In marketing strategy, a literal translation of advertising copy or a brand name may result in ridicule of a product, or even enmity toward it. Clairol introduced a curling iron in Germany called the Mist Stick only to discover that mist is a German slang word for manure. Some words even have different meanings in countries that claim to speak the same language. Mars, the U.S. candy maker, introduced its Snickers candy bar in England under the name Marathon, because snickers sounds too much like knickers, the British term for women's underpants.[14]

YOU MAKE THE DECISION

WHAT SHOULD BE DONE TO PREPARE INTERNATIONAL MARKETERS FOR ASSIGNMENTS ABROAD?

Behavior can be interpreted differently depending on where in the world it occurs. Consider these examples that could cause problems for an uninformed marketer.

Body Language

- Standing with your hands on your hips is a gesture of defiance in Indonesia.
- Carrying on a conversation with your hands in your pockets makes a poor impression in France, Belgium, Finland, and Sweden.
- When you shake your head from side to side, that means "yes" in Bulgaria and Sri Lanka.
- Crossing your legs to expose the sole of your shoe is unacceptable in Muslim countries.

Physical Contact

- Patting a child on the head is a grave offense in Thailand or Singapore, since the head is revered as the location of the soul.
- In an Oriental culture, touching another person is considered an invasion of privacy, while in Southern European and Arabic countries it is a sign of warmth and friendship.

Promptness

- Being on time is a sign of respect in Japan. In Sweden, guests are expected to show up before the appointed time.

- In Latin countries and the Middle East, your host or business associate would be surprised (and probably not prepared) if you arrived at the appointed hour.

Eating

- In China, burping and discreetly picking your teeth at the table are acceptable.
- Refusing a cup of coffee in Saudi Arabia insults the host.
- It is rude to leave anything on your plate when eating in Norway, Switzerland, or France.
- In Egypt, it is rude not to leave something.
- Tipping for service is seen as an insult in China and Japan.

Gifts

- Flowers are always acceptable, but white flowers are reserved for funerals in France, as are purple flowers in Brazil.
- Gifts in business dealings may be viewed as bribes in Hong Kong, but in Japan they are almost obligatory.

Is providing lists such as this adequate, or should firms engaged in international business provide more formal preparation for employees?

Source: Judith Florman, "Mind Your Manners," *Life Today*, September 1993, pp. 35–37.

Economic Environment. In international marketing a firm must closely examine the economic conditions in a particular country. A nation's infrastructure and stage of economic development are key economic factors that affect the attractiveness of a market and suggest what might be an appropriate marketing strategy.

Infrastructure. A country's ability to provide transportation, communications, and energy is its **infrastructure**. Depending on the product and the method of marketing, an international marketer will need certain levels of infrastructure development. For example, a consumer goods manufacturer selling a low-priced product requires a transportation system that will permit widespread distribution. How about communications? Some firms would find it impossible to do business without the availability of newspapers in which to advertise or telephones with which to contact other businesses.

There is a danger in assuming that systems a marketer takes for granted domestically will be available elsewhere. The international marketer must recognize what infrastructure is needed and what is available. For example, in the U.S. there are 50 phones for every 100 people, while in the former East Germany there are about 1.5 phones for every 100 people.[15]

Level of Economic Development. The level of economic development in a country is a general indication of the types of products that are likely to be in demand. The most common criterion for assessing development is gross national product (GNP), a measure of the value of all goods and services produced in a country during a year.

Among the world's approximately 150 nations, about 80 are categorized as *less developed countries* because they have a GNP of less than $1,700 per capita. These countries lack most or all resources for growth and often rely heavily on foreign aid. They frequently have unstable governments and overpopulation problems. Countries in this category include Ethiopia, Somalia, Sudan, Afghanistan, Burma, Haiti, and Bangladesh. Most of these less developed countries are not attractive markets for most consumer goods or for highly technical products. However, they should not be totally ignored. Less developed countries are very eager to acquire technology that will, for example, allow them to increase agricultural output.

In the next level are countries that have an average GNP between $1,700 and $5,500. This group of about 35 nations, including Chile, Malaysia, and Mexico, are described as *newly industrialized countries*. They combine an eager work force, low wages, and reasonably stable governments to produce high rates of economic growth. They typically export manufactured goods and import technology and consumer goods. These are highly attractive markets for firms that have a technological advantage.

Finally, there are the *highly industrialized countries*, which have an average per capita GNP over $5,500. About 35 nations fall into this category, including the U.S., Canada, Japan, Germany, France, and England. They have well-developed infrastructures, high levels of education and literacy, stable governments, constantly advancing technology, and well-trained work forces. These countries are heavily involved in exporting a wide variety of goods. Although these are the wealthiest countries, they are also the ones in which a foreign firm is likely to face the stiffest competition.

Note that a classification like this can be useful, but its simplicity may make it misleading. For example, Saudi Arabia, because of its oil revenues and small population, is in the same group as Switzerland, Japan, and the U.S. However, Saudi Arabia's level of economic development is quite different. Thus, when analyzing ability to buy in a given foreign market, management must also examine such indicators as the (1) distribution of income, (2) rate of growth of buying power, and (3) extent of available financing.

Competition. Sometimes overlooked by firms considering international opportunities are the strength and resilience of the native competition. The new entrant must have a differential advantage sufficiently strong to overcome the loyalty built up by established brands and the nationalism that may motivate buyers to support local producers.

International marketers can also expect local competitors to design strategies to protect their businesses. Toys "R" Us, for example, accused a Japanese firm, Akachan Honpo Company, of violating Japan's Large-Scale Retail Stores Law. The regulation, which is designed to protect small stores, requires large retailers to shut

A country's potential as a market and a source of competition can change rapidly. Korea is a case in point. Not long ago, it was mainly known for low-quality soft goods. Today it is the world's fifth-largest auto manufacturer and a leading producer of high-tech goods. Led by conglomerates such as Hyundai, Daewoo, and Samsung, Korean industry is focused on becoming a major economic force. Already Korea has the highest number of Ph.D.s per capita in the world, and it has moved ahead of Sweden, Australia, and the Netherlands in economic strength.

down for 20 days a year and close daily by 8 p.m. Akachan Honpo has 70 stores that sell directly to consumers but stay open more days and later hours than the law permits. Its defense? By charging its customers an annual membership fee, the store claims it is a wholesale business and therefore exempt from the law.[16]

Political and Legal Forces. The principal political concerns of international marketers are the stability of governments and their attitudes toward free trade. Obviously, an unstable government adds to the risk of doing business in a country. For example, the frequent coups in several central African countries make them less attractive places to do business than Southeast Asia. The other political concern is the risk of **expropriation**, or having an investment in a country taken by the host government. Large-scale expropriation has become relatively uncommon because it has such a long-term negative effect on any future foreign investments. The last major occurrences were in the oil-producing countries in the Persian Gulf during the 1970s.

Trade Barriers. The major legal forces affecting international marketers are barriers created by governments to restrict trade and protect domestic industries. Examples include the following:

- **Tariff**—a tax imposed on a product entering a country. Tariffs are used to protect domestic producers and/or raise revenue. To illustrate, South Korea has a combination of tariffs and taxes that double the price of a car imported from the U.S.[17]
- **Import quota**—a limit on the amount of a particular product that can be brought into a country. Like tariffs, quotas are intended to protect local industry. For example, agreements between the U.S. and Mexico are phasing out quotas on U.S. corn sales to Mexico, and Mexican sales of peanuts, oranges, and sugar to the U.S.

- **Local-content law**—a regulation specifying the proportion of a finished product's components and labor that must be provided by the importing country. For example, to be sold in Taiwan, Japanese cars must be at least partially assembled there. To comply with a local-content law, a firm may import most of a product's parts, buy some locally, and have the final product assembled locally. These laws are used to provide jobs and protect domestic businesses.
- **Boycott**—a refusal to buy products from a particular company or country. Boycotts, also called embargoes, are used by a government to punish another country for what are perceived to be unfair importation rules.

Trade Agreements. Trade agreements reduce trade barriers by giving preferential treatment to firms in the member countries. However, they may also result in member countries establishing barriers to trade with the rest of the world. Thus they have implications for all marketers. By examining several major trade agreements, we can form an impression of the role they play in international marketing:

- **The General Agreement on Tariffs and Trade (GATT)**. This organization was created in 1948 to develop fair-trade practices among its members. Today over 120 countries participate in periodic negotiations on issues such as tariff reductions, import restrictions, local-content rules, and subsidization of industry by government.

  Recent GATT negotiations resulted in a 40 percent decrease in tariffs around the world, significant reductions in the subsidies countries provide for their firms engaged in exporting, and the extension of trading rules beyond just goods to include investments and services.[18] In addition, GATT provides a forum for airing trade disputes between countries, but it does not guarantee that solutions to disagreements will be found. Though many barriers remain and progress is slow, GATT makes international trade easier and signals an increasing global commitment to free trade.
- **The European Union (EU)**. This political and economic alliance evolved from the Treaty of Rome in 1957 that brought together France, Italy, Belgium, West Germany (now the combined East and West Germanys), Luxembourg, and the Netherlands. It was originally called the European Common Market and later the European Community. It is now known as the European Union or EU. Over the years membership has grown to include Denmark, Great Britain, Greece, Spain, Ireland, Portugal, Austria, Sweden, and Finland (see Figure 20-1).[19]

  The EU's overriding objective is to liberalize trade among its members. More specifically, the goal is a single market for its members that would permit the free movement of goods, services, people, and capital. In addition, the members would be governed by the same set of rules for transporting goods, regulating business, and protecting the environment.

  The timetable for accomplishing this dramatic plan was the end of 1992. While much progress had been made by then, many issues were unresolved. For example, something as seemingly simple as allowing citizens of the member countries to travel freely across borders has been difficult to implement. The original goal was to eliminate all border checks on goods and individuals by 1990. But by 1995 only half the members had implemented the agreement. The others, concerned about drug traffickers and criminals, maintained their controls.[20] Other large stumbling blocks to free trade are a common currency and a shared central bank. Despite delays and setbacks, it is clear that greater liberalization of trade in Europe is inevitable.

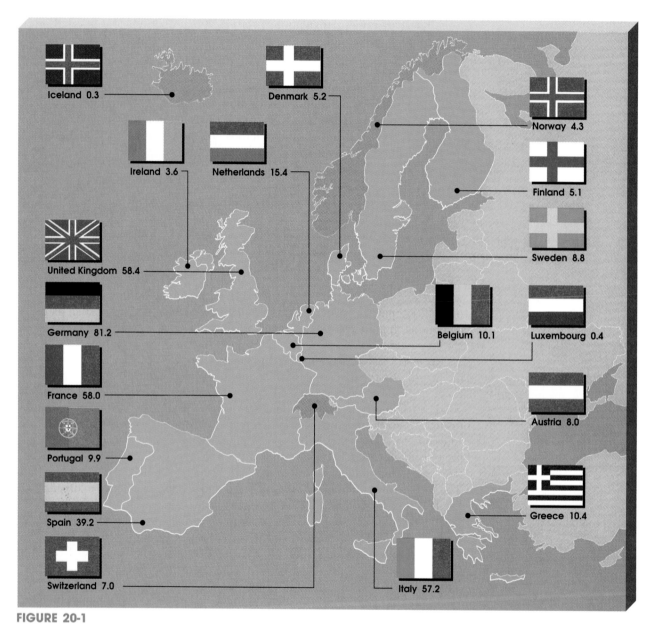

FIGURE 20-1

The European Union countries (green) and the European Economic Area countries (pink) in 1995 (with population figures in millions).

The prospect of a market of 370 million consumers with the same regulations for advertising, packaging, and distribution is very attractive. To illustrate, because of national border restrictions and administrative delays, a truck traveling from London to Milan under the old system could be expected to average only about 12 miles per hour. Without the delays, the duration of the trip would be reduced by at least 50 percent.[21]

Several European countries, notably Switzerland, Norway, and Iceland, object to certain aspects of the EU agreement and have chosen not to join. To improve their economic options and increase their negotiating strength, these three nations created an economic treaty called the *European Economic Area (EEA)*. One of their objectives is to gain as much trading access to the EU as possible short of full membership.

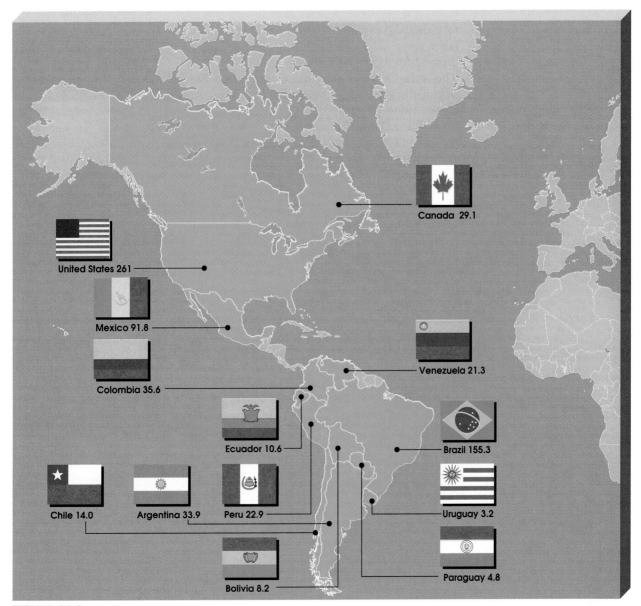

FIGURE 20-2
The Americas (with population figures in millions).

The EU almost surely will continue to expand as several Central and Eastern European countries first become associate members (having the same trading privileges) and then full members (with a say in policy making). These countries, which now consume very small amounts of Western goods, are seen as primary growth markets.

- **The North American Free Trade Agreement (NAFTA)**. The U.S. and Canada forged a pact in 1989 to eliminate tariffs between the two countries over a 10-year period. The agreement was expanded in 1994 to include Mexico, creating a North American free-trade zone. It will likely add a number of other Western Hemisphere countries soon. (See Figure 20-2.)

Canada is already the U.S.'s largest trading partner, and Mexico is third (behind Japan). As a result, NAFTA, which is being phased in, is unlikely to produce a dramatic increase in trade. Most analysts expect to see some manufacturing and assembly jobs move from the U.S. to Mexico as firms seek lower labor costs. This, in turn, will raise incomes in Mexico and create greater demand for U.S. and Canadian goods.

- **The Asia-Pacific Economic Cooperation forum (APEC).** Eighteen Pacific Rim nations participate in this trade pact—Australia, Brunei, Canada, Chile, China, Hong Kong, Indonesia, Japan, Malaysia, Mexico, New Zealand, Papua New Guinea, the Philippines, Singapore, South Korea, Taiwan, Thailand, and the U.S. Their representatives met for the first time in 1992. The objective of the members, which account for 45 percent of the world's international trade, is to create a free-trade zone in the Pacific. South Asia and the Asian side of the Pacific Rim are shown in Figure 20-3. Not surprisingly, given the number of participants in APEC, progress is slow. The current goal is to have the major trade barriers substantially eliminated by 2020.[22]

- **The Association of Southeast Asian Nations (ASEAN).** This pact was established in 1967 as a free-trade zone joining Brunei, Indonesia, Malaysia, the Philippines, Singapore, and Thailand. The ASEAN nations have a combined population of 330 million and a gross domestic product of over $400 billion. The U.S. has exports exceeding $30 billion to ASEAN and imports of nearly $45 billion. The rapid growth in these nations has led analysts to predict that by the year 2000 their imports from the U.S. could triple.[23]

- Other trade agreements are in existence or are being developed. The *Mercursor*, or Common Market of the South, involves Argentina, Brazil, Paraguay, and Uruguay. It permits 90 percent of the trade among these countries to occur tariff-free. A similar agreement, called the *Andean Pact*, has reduced trade barriers among Venezuela, Colombia, Ecuador, Peru, and Bolivia. Seven South Asian nations—India, Pakistan, Bhutan, Bangladesh, the Maldives, Nepal, and Sri Lanka—have formed the *South Asian Association for Regional Cooperation (SAARC)*. With a population of over a billion people, these countries acting in concert have the potential to become a global force. However, traditional rivalries and political problems have thus far hindered the implementation of an effective free-trade arrangement.

What do regional trade agreements mean for the rest of the world? While they may eventually eliminate *internal* trade barriers, trade agreements create fears that *external* barriers may restrict entry of products from outside the member countries. Recognizing these concerns, some coalitions are undertaking efforts to build good relations with nonmember countries. For example, in 1995, the U.S. and the EU established an accord called the New Transatlantic Agenda that commits them to working toward establishing common product standards, agreement on standards for television programming, and many other trade-related issues.[24]

It is too soon to measure the impact of trade agreements. However, the growth of regional economic trading blocs is a significant development that will create both opportunities and challenges for international marketers.

These accords should not cause us to overlook other areas of the world. An unknown at this time is the potential in Eastern Europe, Russia, and the rest of the former Soviet Union. It is impossible to predict how successful these countries will be in moving toward capitalism, or how long it will take. However, the potential of the Commonwealth of Independent States (CIS), headed by Russia, and other countries such as Poland and Hungary, is enormous.

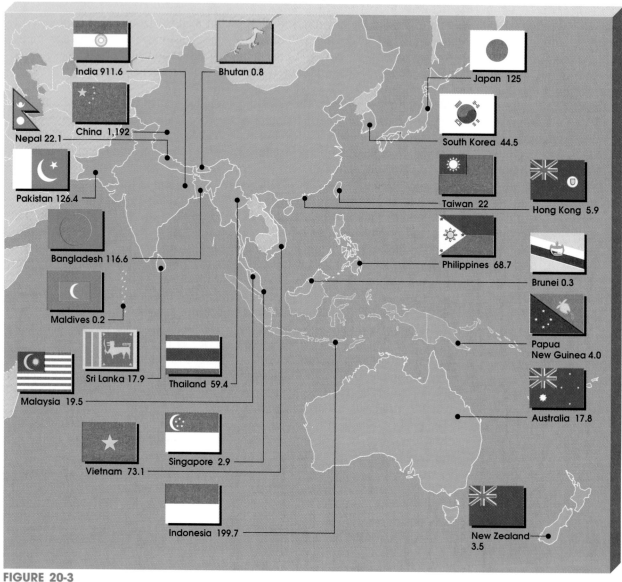

FIGURE 20-3
The Asian side of the Pacific Rim (with population figures in millions).

Looking ahead to the year 2000 and thereafter, perhaps the area with the greatest international marketing potential is China, with its *1.2 billion* consumers. Already we have seen glimpses of these possibilities. Foreign cosmetic sales in China, unheard of a few years ago, are soaring. Kentucky Fried Chicken opened the largest store in its chain on the square across from Chairman Mao's mausoleum in Beijing. China also has significant potential as an exporter. By 1990, the country was a major exporter of clothing. And China is using American and European investments in a quest to become a significant international exporter of automobiles, semiconductors, and telecommunications equipment.[25]

http://
www.kentuckyfriedchicken.com/

Designing the Marketing Mix

Having examined the environment of a foreign market, the manager is prepared to design a marketing mix that will effectively meet customers' needs and accomplish the organization's objectives. As the following discussion suggests, domestic practices have to be modified or entirely replaced in international marketing.

Marketing Research. The scarcity of reliable statistical data may be the single biggest problem in many foreign markets. Typically, the quality of the data is related directly to a country's level of economic development. However, the nature of the data varies widely. For example, most nations (including England, Japan, France, Spain, and Italy) do not ask about income in their national censuses.

Another problem is a lack of uniformity among countries in how they define measures such as unemployment and the cost of living. As a result, comparisons across countries are often unreliable. In some parts of the world, figures on population and production may be only crude estimates. In less developed countries, studies on such things as buying habits or media coverage are even less likely. It is only in the 1990s that China has been able to report television audience figures, even in the largest urban areas.

Another challenge arises when collecting data directly from customers and prospects. In the design of a research project, the lack of reliable lists makes it very difficult even to select a representative sample. Telephone surveys, for example, are likely to be invalid if telephone service is not available to virtually the entire population of a country. Even conducting a focus group can be very difficult. For example, in Saudia Arabia gatherings of four or more people are banned except for family and religious meetings, and in Spain there is a "courtesy effect" in which participants try not to be negative.[26]

The quality of data also depends on the willingness of people to respond accurately when researchers pose questions about attitudes or buying habits. Gathering useful data is very difficult in societies where opinion polls are relatively uncommon, strangers are viewed with suspicion, government is not trusted, or individuals feel that purchase choices and opinions are a private matter.

A GLOBAL PERSPECTIVE

WHERE WILL THE GROWTH IN WORLD TRADE OCCUR?

The U.S. Department of Commerce has identified 10 markets that it predicts will account for 75 percent of the growth in world trade over the next 10 to 15 years. The predictions are based on population, physical size, recent growth, and regional political power. The Commerce Department further predicts that by 2010 the imports of these countries will exceed Japan and the EU combined.

The markets and their projected change from 1994 are:

Market	Imports in 1994 (billions)	Projected imports in 2010 (billions)
China	$116	$577
South Korea	102	236
Mexico	61	119
Indonesia	32	97
India	27	79
Brazil	36	69
Turkey	23	67
South Africa	23	38
Argentina	22	28
Poland	21	18

Sources: "Finding the Next Japan," *Sales & Marketing Management*, August 1995, p. 83; and *International Financial Statistics*, International Monetary Fund, March 1996, pp. 67, 69.

Product Planning. A critical question in product planning concerns the extent to which a company can market the same product in several different countries. *Product extension* describes the situation in which a standard product is sold in two or more countries. For example, Gillette sells the same razor blades worldwide, and Levi Strauss also has been successful in marketing its 501 brand of jeans in many countries. The benefits of standardization can be significant. If Ford is able to design cars that can be sold around the world, it estimates that its $8 billion annual product-development budget can be reduced *by billions*.[27]

We can make a few broad generalizations regarding product extensions. The best bet for standardization is in the area of durable business goods. In such industries as aircraft, computers, and tractors, the worldwide market (at least among industrialized nations) is quite uniform. For example, the Boeing Company is selling its two-engine 777 airliner to both Singapore Airlines and United Airlines.

Somewhere in the middle of our standardization spectrum, we can place consumer durable goods such as cameras, watches, pocket calculators, small appliances, and television sets. The most difficult goods to standardize globally are food and drink products and wearing apparel. (Here Coca-Cola and Levi Strauss are exceptions.) This difficulty can be traced to national tastes and habits. For example, U.S. consumers eat four times as much dry cereal per capita as the French.[28] Even with national markets such as the U.S., we often find strong regional differences in food and clothing preferences.

A second option is *product adaptation*, modifying a product that sells successfully in one market to suit the unique needs or requirements of other markets. Procter & Gamble modified its Max Factor line of cosmetics with brighter colors for Latin Americans, and its Vidal Sassoon shampoo with more conditioners for the Asian market.[29] After Cheetos snacks tested poorly with Chinese consumers, PepsiCo tested 600 flavors before selecting two it felt would appeal to Chinese tastes.[30]

The third alternative product strategy is *invention*, the development of an entirely new product for a foreign market. For example, Maybelline developed a high-humidity face makeup formula for the Asian Pacific market.

Marketers must study carefully the cultural and economic environment of any market—foreign or domestic—before planning products for that particular market. In Europe, for example, large refrigerators are popular in the north because consumers prefer to shop once a week. In contrast, Southern Europeans enjoy shopping at open-air markets daily and therefore opt for small refrigerators. The British, on the other hand, consume large quantities of frozen foods so they demand considerable freezer space.[31]

Branding and labeling are other considerations in foreign marketing. As suggested earlier, the brand mark may be the only part of the label that consumers in some countries can recognize.

Most firms would prefer to use the same brand name in domestic and foreign markets, since it provides greater overall familiarity and recognition and can also produce some economies in promotion. However, names are often culture-bound. For example, the name of a fragrance that was considered sensual, mysterious, and romantic in London and Düsseldorf was considered cold, aloof, and lonely in Mexico City and Munich.

Marketers must also be alert to shifting tastes. In Europe during the 1970s and 1980s, there was a definite preference for European brands. However, in the mid-1990s, many U.S. brands developed a special appeal. For example, sales were up for Jeeps, advertised as "The American Legend," Goodyear tires with images of

Campbell Soup Company has extended its brand around the world by adapting its products to local tastes. For example, in Asia, where corn-based soups are popular, Campbell has introduced four varieties: Corn with Chicken, Corn with Ham, Corn with Mushrooms, and Golden Corn. In Australia, Campbell's Cream of Pumpkin soup became a top seller in less than a year. Mexico, where 9 billion servings of soup are consumed a year, is also an attractive market. Two of the most popular brands are Crema de Flor de Calabaza and Crema de Chile Poblano.

http://www.campbellsoups.com/

the Indianapolis 500 race, and Budweiser beer at premium prices. Some attribute the popularity to greater exposure of U.S. films and TV shows in Europe.[32] Another possibility is the perception that the quality of U.S. products is improving.[33]

Pricing.   In earlier chapters, we recognized that determining the base price and formulating pricing strategies are complex tasks, frequently involving trial-and-error decision making. These tasks become even more complex in international marketing. An exporter faces variables such as currency conversion, differences in what is included in price quotations, and often a lack of control over middlemen's pricing.

Cost-plus pricing is relatively common in export marketing. Because of additional physical distribution expenses, tariffs, and other export costs, foreign prices usually are considerably higher than domestic prices for the same product. For example, the Jeep Cherokee costs about $12,000 more in Japan than in the U.S.[34] At the retail level, price bargaining is quite prevalent in many foreign markets—especially in Asia, Africa, and South America—and must be taken into consideration in setting the initial price.

Sometimes companies engage in **dumping**—selling products in foreign markets at prices below those charged for the same goods in their home markets. The price may be lowered to meet foreign competition or to dispose of outmoded products. There have been frequent charges that Japanese auto and electronics firms have engaged in dumping in the U.S. to increase sales and build their market shares. Dumping, which frequently involves selling goods below cost, is viewed as an unfair business practice by most governments, and generally results in threats of tariffs or establishment of quotas.

An issue of growing concern is the differential charged for an identical brand in different countries.[35] Differentials of 30 to 150 percent are not uncommon. A French consumer can cross the border into Germany and buy a Volkswagen Jetta for one-third less than it costs in France.

Price differences result from the strength of demand, the complexity of the distribution structures in various countries, and differences in tax systems. With the easy flow of information across borders and increased travel by consumers, price differentials add considerable complexity to the job of middlemen, especially retailers, doing business in several countries. They also encourage arbitrage—the purchase and sale of a product in different markets to benefit from the unequal prices.

Prices may be quoted in the seller's currency or in the currency of the foreign buyer. Here we encounter problems of foreign exchange and conversion of currencies. As a general rule, a firm engaged in foreign trade—whether it is exporting or importing—prefers to have the price quoted in its own national currency. Risks from fluctuations in foreign exchange then are shifted to the other party in the transaction.

An alternative to currency-based pricing is **countertrade** or *barter*. Rather than buy goods with cash, some countries arrange to trade domestically made products for imported goods. PepsiCo, for example, has traded soft drinks to Poland for wooden chairs that are used in its U.S. Pizza Hut stores.[36] Two reasons for countertrade are:

http://www.pepsi.com/

- *Lack of hard currency.* Less developed countries may not have enough "hard" currency (the money of countries viewed in world markets as reasonably stable) to buy needed capital goods. So they trade their less sophisticated products for equipment and technology. A Canadian firm selling steel in Indonesia was compensated in palm oil, coffee, timber, and rattan furniture.
- *Inadequate marketing structure.* Some countries do not have a marketing structure that encourages or permits international trade. Without global distribution systems, adequate promotion, or the ability to provide service, they cannot sell their domestic goods overseas. To overcome this problem, these countries may require foreign firms that import products into the country to accept local goods in total or partial payment. Both China and Romania require that importers accept countertrade.

Agreements between manufacturers and middlemen in the same industry are tolerated to a far greater extent in many foreign countries than in the U.S. They are allowed even when the avowed purpose of the combination is to restrain trade and reduce competition. Recognizing this, Congress passed the Webb-Pomerene Act in 1918. This law allows American firms to join this type of trade combination in a foreign country without being charged with violation of American antitrust laws.

The best known of these international marketing combinations is the cartel. A **cartel** is a group of companies that produce similar products and act collectively to restrain competition in manufacturing and marketing. Cartels exist to varying degrees in steel, aluminum, fertilizers, petroleum products, rayon, and sulfur.[37] Probably the world's best-known cartel is OPEC, the Organization of Petroleum Exporting Countries, which has tried—with varying degrees of success—to control the price of crude oil.

Distribution Systems. Studying the environment in a foreign market helps in understanding the distribution system, since marketing institutions, such as various types of retailers, result from their environment. For example, one-stop shopping is still unknown in most parts of the world. In many countries, people buy in small units, sometimes literally on a meal-to-meal basis. Also, they buy in small specialty stores. In contrast to the U.S. where shopping is often viewed as a chore, in many places it is a major part of social life.

In Western European countries, some of the traditional shopping patterns are changing, however. Astute retailers capitalize on environmental change by introducing innovations that anticipate trends in the environment. Several European retailers have done a good job of innovating. Within a few years, they have moved from the stage of small, specialized stores to a variety of retailing concepts as advanced as any in the world. For example, in mass retailing, the *hypermarché* in France and the *Verbrauchermarkt* in Germany are huge self-service superstores operating very profitably and at much lower gross margins than similar American stores.

Middlemen and Channels of Distribution. International middlemen were introduced earlier in this chapter in connection with organizational structures for international marketing. Foreign middlemen representing importers and operating within foreign countries are, in general, less aggressive and perform fewer marketing services than their counterparts selling domestically produced products. The foreign marketing situation, however, usually argues against bypassing these middlemen. Often the demand is too small to warrant establishing a sales office or branch in the foreign country. Also, in many countries, knowledge of the market may be more important than knowledge of the product, even for high-technology products. And sometimes government controls preclude the use of a firm's sales organization abroad. Thus, middlemen in foreign countries ordinarily are a part of the channel structure.

Physical Distribution. Various aspects of physical distribution in foreign marketing are quite different from anything found on the domestic scene. Generally, physical distribution expenses account for a much larger share of the final selling price in foreign markets than in domestic markets. Problems caused by humidity, pilferage, handling, and inadequate marking must be considered in international shipments. Requirements regarding commercial shipping, insurance, and government documents complicate foreign shipping. As noted earlier, one of the primary benefits of economic alliances like the EU is the efficiency they bring to physical distribution. With the free movement of goods across European borders, distribution time and expense will be drastically reduced.

Bribery in International Distribution. Bribes, kickbacks, and sometimes even extortion payments are facts of life in international distribution. Bribery is so rooted in many cultures that it is described with special slang words. It's called *mordida* (small bite) in Latin America. The French call it *pot de vin* (jug of wine). In Italy there is *la bustarella* (the little envelope), left on a bureaucrat's desk to cut the red tape. South Koreans use *ttuk kab* (rice cake expenses).

Revelations about the amount of bribery led Congress to pass the Foreign Corrupt Practices Act in 1977. The act prohibits a U.S. company, its subsidiaries, or representatives from making payments to high-ranking foreign government officers and political parties. The law, however, does not exclude small, facilitating payments to foreign government clerks who are not policy makers since these are a way of life in many parts of the world.

What complicates this situation is the fact that bribery is not a sharply defined activity. Sometimes the lines are blurred between a bribe, a gift to show appreciation, a reasonable commission for services rendered, and a finder's fee to open a distribution channel. For example, businesses in South Korea make contributions

to government officials to mark major holidays. According to South Korean executives, the payments are not made to obtain favors. Rather, they serve to protect a firm from punitive treatment by government bureaucrats.[38] Realistically, in some foreign markets a seller must pay a fee or commission to an agent to get in touch with prospective buyers. Without paying such fees, there is simply no effective access to those markets.

Advertising. Rather than discuss promotion in its entirety, we limit our discussion to standardizing advertising messages as illustrative of the strategic problems in international promotion. Recognize, however, that there are issues related to other aspects of advertising, personal selling, and sales promotion that international marketers must deal with. For example, Avon is selling its products door to door from Argentina to Vietnam, and adapting its techniques to each country's culture.[39]

Because advertisers must capture and hold attention, they make use of a variety of communication devices such as humor, contrast, and surprise. The difficulty in international advertising is that what works in one culture might take on quite a different meaning in another. For example, a major controversy was generated by a Toyota ad in Italy that presented a lighthearted contrast between the Italian government's image as corrupt and the value and reliability of a Toyota Carina.[40]

This, as well as many other advertising failures by international marketers, raises the question of how much advertising can be standardized in international markets.[41] In the past, little thought was given to standardization, and separate programs (copy, appeals, and media) were tailored for each country, or even for regions within a country. For example, as recently as 1988, Parker Pens was advertised around the world using over 30 different themes.

While complete uniformity is not typical, today there is much support for the idea of commonality in international ad campaigns. Many companies use basically the same appeals, theme, copy, and layout in all or much of their international advertising—particularly in Western European countries. Unilever successfully uses the same appeal for Dove bar soap—contains "one-quarter cleansing cream"—in Australia, France, Germany, Italy, and the U.S.[42] Similarly, Toys "R" Us only slightly modifies television ads developed in the U.S. for use in Germany and Japan.

Standardization of advertising is spurred by the increase in international communications and entertainment. Many TV broadcasts reach audiences all over the world through satellite and cable networks. Many American and European magazines and newspapers circulate across national borders. In addition, vacation and business travel from one country to another is quite common.

AN ETHICAL DILEMMA?

In most countries in the Middle East, it is generally not possible for a foreign marketer to sell directly to a branch of the government or to local private firms. Invariably, sales are made through local agents who have personal contacts (often family members) in the buying organizations. To make sales under these conditions, some foreign firms pay these agents commissions well beyond what is reasonable for the tasks they perform.

If your firm wished to expand into international markets, would you consider it ethical to make such payments to agents?

A second factor contributing to the standardization of advertising is production costs. Producing quality advertising is very expensive, so the opportunity to achieve savings by repeating the same ideas or executions in various parts of the world is attractive. Unilever uses the same advertising appeal for its Impulse Body Spray (combination deodorant and fragrance) in over 40 countries. Other brands adopting global appeals are Gillette for its Sensor razor, Procter & Gamble's Pert Plus/Wash and Go shampoo, Snuggles fabric softener, and Nescafé coffee. However, in each of these cases the advertiser customizes the execution of the appeal to fit the local markets.[43]

Perhaps the issue comes down to this point: The goal of advertising is the same in any country, namely to communicate information and persuasive appeals effectively. For some products, the appeals are sufficiently universal and the markets are sufficiently homogeneous to permit the use of very similar advertising in several countries. It is only the media strategy and the details of a message that must be fine-tuned to each country's cultural, economic, and political environment. However, care must be taken to recognize differences in national identity and characteristics that may require specialized advertising in a particular country.

International Trade Balances

What are the prospects for international marketing? At the macro level, high levels of exports are very important to the health of a nation's economy. To appreciate this relationship, we need to examine the concepts of balance of payments and balance of trade, and we will use the U.S. as an example.

A country's **balance of payments** is an accounting record of all of its transactions with all the other nations of the world. The major categories of expenditures and income in a country's balance of payments are military and foreign aid, investments abroad, profits returned on foreign investments, tourism, and its trade balance. These terms are self-explanatory except for a country's **trade balance**, which is the difference between what it exports and what it imports. When exports exceed imports, the balance is positive and the country is said to have a trade *surplus*. When imports exceed exports, the balance is negative and the country has a trade *deficit*.

By definition, a country's balance of payments must balance. That is, the outflow of wealth must equal the inflow. So, for example, if the foreign tourism expenditures of a country's citizens (outflow) exceed the expenditures of tourists visiting the country (inflow), the difference must be made up by one of the other balance-of-payment categories. What happens if there is not enough surplus in the other categories to offset a deficit? Then the country must borrow to make up the difference, and that is where the problem lies. As a country's debt grows, it is faced with pressure to raise taxes and lower government spending.

Historically, the U.S. has had large expenditures in four areas that significantly affect the balance of payments: (1) military forces stationed overseas, (2) foreign aid, (3) oil imports, and (4) American tourist travel abroad. To offset these expenditures and maintain equilibrium in the U.S. balance of payments, American businesses had to generate a substantial trade surplus. That is, exports of goods and services had to greatly exceed imports. Up to about 1970 this was not a problem, because the U.S. generally had a positive balance of trade. Then the balance declined to the point where it was not sufficient to offset the expenditures abroad.

Through most of the 1980s, the U.S. ran a huge negative (unfavorable) balance of trade. It improved in the late 1980s and early 1990s, with a low of $29 billion in 1991, but it remained negative. Since then, it has steadily increased, amounting to $106 billion in 1994.[44] Large trade deficits have a direct negative effect on jobs, investment, and growth.

Several factors affect a country's balance of trade. In the case of the U.S., the most significant are:

- *Consumer preferences*. U.S. consumers have come to know and buy many imported products.
- *Technology*. The "technology gap" between the U.S. and other major industrial countries is narrowing or has disappeared entirely, so the U.S. does not enjoy the same technology advantage that it once did.
- *Trade barriers*. Many countries have established barriers that severely limit, or entirely prohibit, the importation of products that might compete with their domestic output.
- *Subsidized industries*. Some foreign countries aid their export trade more than the U.S. These subsidies often enable the producers to sell their products in foreign markets at prices lower than the prices of domestic producers.
- *Tax structure*. Some countries derive substantial revenue from indirect taxes, such as a value-added tax, which are often rebated when products are exported. As a result, companies in these countries have an added incentive to seek markets abroad.
- *Relative marketing capabilities*. Firms worldwide have narrowed the gap between their marketing skills and those of the more developed nations.

The foreign trade situation in the U.S. has changed from a bright spot to a problem. Imports probably will remain high because of the factors described above. Consequently, the U.S. must continue to expand its exports by:

- Offsetting higher labor costs with improved productivity.
- Adapting marketing efforts to foreign cultures.
- Investing in the future by taking a longer-range view than currently is typical among most U.S. firms.

■ SUMMARY

Many companies in the U.S. and abroad derive a substantial share of their total sales and profits from their foreign marketing operations. Firms engage in international marketing because of demand abroad and the saturation of domestic markets, and because they have either a comparative or a technological advantage.

In terms of organizational structure, the simplest way to operate in a foreign market is to export through middlemen specializing in foreign trade. Another method is to export through company sales branches located in foreign countries. More involved approaches include contracting, engaging in a joint venture, or forming a wholly owned sub-

sidiary. The most fully developed organizational structure for international marketing is the multinational corporation.

As in domestic marketing, international marketers must adapt to the macroenvironment. Differences in the social and cultural environment are reflected in family values, customs, education, and language. Critical economic conditions include the infrastructure in a market and a country's stage of economic development. Political and legal forces unique to international marketing are trade barriers and international trade agreements. Economic alliances in Europe (EU), North America (NAFTA), Asia (ASEAN), and elsewhere in the world have implications for marketers in both member and non-member nations.

To develop an international marketing program, a basic issue is how global or standardized the marketing can be. In some cases each of the marketing-mix elements requires modification or adaptation. This is made more difficult by the fact that marketing research is quite primitive in many parts of the world.

International trade contributes to the growth of a nation's economy. For the U.S., trade surpluses are needed to offset deficits in other balance-of-payment categories. In recent years, the U.S. balance of trade has been adversely affected by consumers' preferences for imported products, entry barriers, and other policies of foreign governments, as well as the growing technological and marketing capabilities of other countries.

More about

TOYS "R" US

*B*esides its overall strategy of larger stores and lower prices than the competition, Toys "R" Us (TRU) has successfully employed some tactics globally; for example, the chain sells two nontoy items, disposable diapers and infant formula, at deep discounts. These products attract young parents who discover the other merchandise and become regular customers.

However, circumstances in some parts of the world forced TRU to adjust its strategy. Japan proved to be a particularly difficult challenge. There was strong local opposition from retailers that feared the chain would put them out of business. Another obstacle was the distribution system. The many layers of middlemen common in Japan contribute to the high prices for consumer goods. To duplicate the formula that made it successful elsewhere, TRU wanted to deal directly with manufacturers to reduce costs. However, many Japanese toy makers were not eager to sell directly to TRU because doing so would upset their existing distributors and retailers. With persistence and compromise (for example, TRU agreed to close its stores every day by 8 p.m. and shut down for a 30-day vacation each year, as is the custom of many Japanese retailers), a store was opened in 1991. The chain now has over 30 stores in Japan.

Another strategy used in TRU's international marketing is to enter into joint ventures with local partners who are familiar with the business methods of the target country. It also allows international managers considerably more freedom than their U.S. counterparts in adapting stores to local customs and tastes. For example, each store carries a large inventory of locally produced items, such as traditional board games in Malaysia and porcelain dolls in Japan. And some old standbys are adapted to make them more familiar. For example, in the Hong Kong version of Monopoly,

Boardwalk and Park Place are replaced by the local suburbs of Sheko and Repulse Bay.

Toy retailing in the U.S. possesses some unique features that may have implications for TRU's continued international growth. First, there is the product mix. Video games have become a major factor, but rapid technological changes quickly render popular products obsolete. Second, it is a business of fads, most of which are unpredictable. For example, the Mighty Morphin Power Rangers were a megahit toy, but there is no telling what or when the next hit will be. Finally, as toys become more sophisticated, self-service selling becomes less acceptable.

To decrease its dependence on particular products and to offset the price competition of general merchandise discounters, TRU is revising its domestic retail strategy. The goal is to move away from operating like a toy supermarket with merchandise stacked to the ceiling toward a more fun, exciting place to shop. The repositioned stores include interactive displays, licensed departments, and shops-within-a-shop. Among the boutiques in operation or under development are a Warner Bros. shop with licensed characters on apparel, lunch boxes, pillows, and stationery; a Learning Center with computer hardware and software, CD-ROM selections, and other learning aids; a plush toy shop with stuffed animals and dolls; and a Lego shop with life-sized models and a play table.

Despite its success, TRU, like all businesses, has to adapt and innovate. The challenge is to make the correct move at the right time.[45]

1. What role will environmental factors play in the continued international growth of Toys "R" Us?
2. In what components of its marketing program can Toys "R" Us use a global strategy and in what components is a local strategy called for?

■ KEY TERMS AND CONCEPTS

International
  marketing (538)
Export merchant (539)
Export agent (540)
Company sales
  branch (540)
Contracting (540)
Licensing (540)
Franchising (540)
Contract
  manufacturing (540)
Direct investment (541)

Joint venture (541)
Strategic alliance (541)
Wholly owned
  subsidiary (542)
Multinational
  corporation (542)
Global marketing (542)
Infrastructure (544)
Expropriation (546)
Tariff (546)
Import quota (546)
Local-content law (547)

Boycott (547)
General Agreement on
  Tariffs and Trade
  (GATT) (547)
European Union
  (EU) (547)
North American Free
  Trade Agreement
  (NAFTA) (549)
Asia-Pacific Economic
  Cooperation forum
  (APEC) (550)

Association of Southeast
  Asian Nations
  (ASEAN) (550)
Dumping (554)
Countertrade or
  barter (555)
Cartel (555)
Balance of
  payments (558)
Trade balance (558)

■ QUESTIONS AND PROBLEMS

1. A U.S. luggage manufacturing company with annual sales of $120 million has decided to market its products in Western Europe. Describe the alternative organizational structures this company should consider.

2. Interview some foreign students on your campus to determine how their native buying habits differ from yours. Consider such factors as when, where, and how people in their country buy. What roles do various family members play in buying decisions?

3. Many countries have a low literacy rate. In what ways might a company adjust its marketing program to overcome this problem?

4. If an American company uses foreign middlemen, it must usually stand ready to supply them with financial, technical, and promotional help. If this is the case, why is it not customary to bypass these middlemen and deal directly with the ultimate foreign buyers?

5. To become more competitive in world markets, U.S. manufacturers must continue improving product quality. Locate a recent article from a business publication that describes the efforts of a U.S. firm to improve quality and summarize it for the class.

6. Examine the ads in a foreign magazine in your college or city library. Particularly note the ads for American products, and compare these with the ads for the same products in American magazines. In what respect do the foreign ads differ from the domestic ads? Are there significant similarities?

7. "Prices of American products are always higher in foreign countries than at home because of the additional risks, expenses of physical distribution, and extra middlemen involved." Discuss.

8. What should a country such as the U.S. do to reduce its trade deficits?

■ HANDS-ON MARKETING

1. Report on export marketing activities of companies in the state where your school is located. Consider such topics as the following: What products are exported? How many jobs are created by export marketing? What is the dollar value of exports? How does this figure compare with the value of foreign-made goods imported into the state?

2. Select one product—manufactured or nonmanufactured—for export, and choose the country to which you would like to export it. Examine the macroenvironmental factors described in the chapter and prepare an analysis of the market for this product in the selected country. Be sure to include the sources of information you use.

CASES FOR PART 7

CASE 1   *AT&T versus MCI versus SPRINT*

BIG THREE COMPETITION IN LONG-DISTANCE CALLING

The telephone industry, until 1984 monopolized by "Ma Bell" (AT&T), has become known for the intensity of its competition. The Telecommunications Act of 1996 intensifies competition even more. The act removes government barriers in local and long-distance calling, cable TV, broadcasting, and wireless services. It impacts an industry that currently accounts for over $76 billion in long-distance telephone service and is predicted to grow to $1 trillion in annual revenue by the year 2000. To understand how the telecommunications industry got to this point and the marketing strategies that are available to long-distance service providers requires a brief history lesson.

The Competitive Marketplace

For decades, telephone service in the U.S. was a regulated monopoly. AT&T provided everything needed to complete a telephone call: telephone equipment, transmission lines, switching stations, and repair services. However, that began to change in the late 1960s:

- In 1968, the Federal Communications Commission (FCC) for the first time ruled that non-AT&T equipment, the Carterfone (a device that connected two-way radios to the telephone network), could be attached to the Bell system.
- Microwave Communications Inc. (MCI) became AT&T's first long-distance competitor when it won approval from the FCC in 1972 to transmit calls between Chicago and St. Louis.
- AT&T's first local competitor, Teleport, was licensed by the FCC in 1984. In that same year, AT&T settled a federal antitrust suit and spun off 22 local telephone companies into 7 "Baby Bells," Nynex, Bell Atlantic, Ameritech, US West, Bell South, SBC (Southwestern Bell), and PacTel. AT&T kept its more profitable long-distance service and research and development operation, Bell Labs. The "Baby Bells" were allowed to operate only regional telephone service.

Ever since MCI paved the way that led to the breakup of AT&T, the two companies have been intense competitors. A third major player, Sprint, soon entered the long-distance market. Ten years after the breakup, AT&T is still the market leader with 60 percent of the total; MCI follows with 20 percent and Sprint has 10 percent. Other smaller competitors are #4 Worldcom with just under 5 percent and

even smaller Frontier Corp. The market has been growing at between 6 and 10 percent a year since the breakup of AT&T.

Flexing Marketing Muscle

From the outset, MCI positioned itself as a less expensive alternative to AT&T. Indeed, price was an obvious way for MCI and Sprint to gain market share. Although price wars are good for consumers in that they lower long-distance rates and speed the advancement of services such as customized billing and calling card plans, they impact the profitability of the companies. Profitability also is affected by annual marketing budgets, over $2.6 billion in the case of AT&T and $1.2 billion for MCI, that escalate as competitors try to protect market share and attract new customers.

In long-distance calling, price discounts have taken the form of different calling plans. MCI's "Friends & Family" plan, launched in the early 1990s, has been very successful in building its market share. The plan provides savings of up to 20 percent when a customer calls people who are part of a designated "calling circle." Sprint and AT&T countered with plans of their own. AT&T's "True Rewards" program gives customers who make at least $25 per month in calls a point per dollar redeemable for AT&T minutes, cash, or frequent-flier miles on Delta, United, and US Air. Each point is worth about 20 seconds, 5 cents cash, or 5 frequent-flier miles. MCI offers 5-miles-per-$1 of long-distance calls on American, Northwest, or Southwest Airlines. Sprint's plan, "The Most," provides 10 points for each dollar of calls. Five thousand points are redeemable for two free movie tickets at a United Artists cinema or a free hour of Sprint calling. For 100,000 points, the customer receives two free three-night cruises aboard the Royal Caribbean Cruise Line from Miami to the Bahamas. By 1994, the Big Three long-distance companies were marketing 30 different calling plans.

Rebates are another common form of price discount. In 1995, AT&T used rebates up to $200 to entice former customers to return. MCI followed AT&T's lead with a counteroffer of travel credits. Consumers began snapping up the offers, known as becoming "spinners" or "rate-surfers." The industry practice of churning customers has become a significant problem. "Checks (payments to get customers to switch long-distance carriers) have hurt the marketplace, teaching people to shop around for the best buy, while breeding increasingly disloyal feelings," said Wally

Meyer, vice president of marketing and sales for Sprint. Furthermore, an analyst noted, "The constant advertising and promotions have had a lot to do with that (that is, encouraging switching), but so do other efforts like telemarketing and direct mail." The cost of AT&T's consumer giveaways for the first half of 1995 reached $100 million.

Despite the amount of marketing effort expended by the Big Three over the past decade, fully 67 percent of U.S. households do not belong to a calling plan. The companies are now looking for other ways, besides price, to differentiate themselves and sign up these nonplan customers. One way has been to add features to their long-distance services. For example, all three companies allow the caller to leave a message for people who do not have answering machines. The caller can specify when the message, transmitted in the caller's voice, is to be delivered. Alternatively, the computer will call every 20 minutes for the first hour and once every hour for up to 5 hours. Depending on the company, the caller can delay the message for up to 7 days.

They all also offer some version of a prepaid calling card. AT&T's Prepaid Card costs 60 cents per minute and tells the caller how many minutes remain on the card, with a 60-second warning before the card runs out. Sprint's Long-Distance Greetings card is sold through Hallmark card shops in Atlanta, Chicago, Kansas City, Los Angeles, and New York. MCI's PhoneCash is available in various denominations (for example, $10, $20, and $50).

Revising the Strategies

AT&T and MCI are trying to stop the price wars by reducing their discounts. MCI's new "Friends & Family" customers receive a 10 percent discount if their monthly bills are at least $9.50, rather than a 25 percent discount at the $10 level under the original plan. AT&T's "True Reach Savings" matched the move by MCI. Sprint's "Sprint Sense" is aimed at simplifying a confusing marketplace. Off-peak calls cost a flat 10 cents per minute and peak calls cost 22 cents per minute.

Another way the Big Three are raising prices is by bundling services sold to customers. Sprint is packaging cable programming with its long-distance service. AT&T offers discounts for cellular service and satellite TV. MCI is pushing low-price Internet access. However, years of discounting have left more than 16 percent of customers prone to switching.

A part of the 1996 Telecommunications Act allows the Big Three to compete with the regional Bells for local telephone customers. AT&T has already applied for authorization to provide local telephone service in all 50 states. AT&T intends to offer one-stop shopping, all under its name and billable to its Universal Card. AT&T's strategy is to build brand loyalty in advance of the Bells's entrances into the long-distance market. However, the Bells have a major weapon, the access charge, to counter this competitive threat. The access charge represents up to 50 percent of

a long-distance call and is paid by customers of the Big Three to the regional Bells to connect their calls. In addition, the same law allows the Bells to offer long-distance services, which may make AT&T vulnerable. The reason is that AT&T has the largest number of consumers, and they are the most likely to become the Bells's long-distance customers. For example, 60 percent of all long-distance calls made within Ameritech's territory end within its five-state region.

Future Developments

AT&T announced, in 1995, that it planned to focus on telecommunications and would restructure into three separate companies: AT&T (long-distance communications, wireless, and credit cards), NCR (computer division), and Lucent (communications equipment). Also, AT&T is seeking alliances to market its AT&T World Partners program in an effort to strengthen its global presence. According to a corporate identity consultant, "AT&T has done a good job in securing the position of the great enabler that links people together. They're looking at a more narrowly defined communications market. In fact, all long-distance companies are going to be more than long distance. It's time for everyone to start repositioning themselves in this converging marketplace." AT&T Chairman Robert E. Allen pledged, "We intend to be the premier deliverer of a whole range of services: local, long-distance, wireless, entertainment."

Acquisitions have been a major part of the Big Three's strategies to strengthen their competitive positions. AT&T acquired McCaw Cellular in 1994. Sprint bought cellular provider, Centrel, in 1993, and expanded its global connection by selling 20 percent of Sprint to Deutsche Telekom and France Telecom. British Telecom purchased 20 percent of MCI in 1993, giving MCI a foothold in foreign markets that has eluded AT&T. Furthermore, in 1996, MCI announced agreements with News Corp. to offer satellite TV service and a broad partnership with Microsoft to develop Internet services.

The first merger of two regional Bell companies, SBC and PacTel, was announced in 1996. Nynex and Bell Atlantic also entered into merger discussions that same year. These mergers are predicted to lead to further consolidation of the telecommunications industry. "There's probably going to be only four to six global gangs emerge over the next five years as all of this sorts out," commented Gerald Taylor, president of MCI. In fact, SBC already has a global presence through its partial ownership of Telefonos de Mexico. However, future expansion by the Bells into global long-distance service will be slowed by outdated networks (only 71 percent of the Bells's networks connect to digital switches, compared to 100 percent for the Big Three). In addition, the brand awareness, technology, and marketing skills that the Big Three honed through fierce competition over the past decade will not be easy for the Bells to duplicate. Only one thing is certain, the way we communicate in the future will be shaped largely by the marketing strategies of the winner of the continuing telephone war.

http://www.att.com/
http://www.mci.com/
http://www.sprint.com/

QUESTIONS

1. What are the differential advantages of AT&T, MCI, and Sprint in the U.S.? In other countries?
2. What characteristics of services should AT&T, MCI, and Sprint take into account when designing their marketing strategies to compete against each other and the "Baby Bells" for long-distance customers? For local telephone customers?

Sources: Catherine Arnst and Michael Mandel, "The Coming Telescramble," *Business Week*, Apr. 8, 1996, p. 64; Catherine Arnst, "The

Giants Aren't Sleeping," *Business Week*, Apr. 8, 1996, p. 70; Peter Elstrom, "Think Local—and Invade," *Business Week*, Apr. 8, 1996, p. 69; Leslie Cauley, "Cellular-Phone Spinoff Marked Start of Slide Leading to PacTel Deal," *The Wall Street Journal*, Apr. 2, 1996, p. A1; John Keller and Gautam Naik, "SBC-PacTel Merger Is Likely to Ring In an Era of Alliances among Baby Bells," *The Wall Street Journal*, Apr. 2, 1996, p. B1; Pat Sloan, "Post-Breakup AT&T Stays $1B Advertiser," *Advertising Age*, Sept. 25, 1995, p. 1; Kim Cleland, "Calling Up a Trio of New Savings Plans," *Advertising Age*, Sept. 4, 1995, p. 3; Gautam Naik, "Phone Price Wars May Be Far from Over," *The Wall Street Journal*, Aug. 21, 1995, p. A2; Gautam Naik, "AT&T Seems to Call Truce in Price Wars," *The Wall Street Journal*, Aug. 18, 1995, p. A3; Kate Fitzgerald, "AT&T, MCI Ringing Up Bigger Cash Lures," *Advertising Age*, May 8, 1995, p. 6; John Keller, "MCI and Sprint Unveil Deep Discounts, New Services in Fresh Fight with AT&T," *The Wall Street Journal*, Jan. 6, 1995, p. A3; John Keller, "AT&T Starts Making Inroads against MCI," *The Wall Street Journal*, Dec. 14, 1994, p. A4; Terry Lefton, "Truth Hurts AT&T's Rivals," *BrandWeek*, Oct. 17, 1994, p. 128; Kerry Hannon "Long-Distance Lures," *U.S. News & World Report*, Feb. 21, 1994, p. 71; Bart Ziegler and Mark Lewyn, "Who's Afraid of AT&T?" *Business Week*, June 14, 1993, p. 32; and John Keller, "AT&T, MCI, Sprint Raise the Intensity of Their Endless War," *The Wall Street Journal*, Oct. 20, 1992, p. A1.

CASE 2   *Walt Disney Co.*

INTERNATIONAL EXPANSION OF AN ENTERTAINMENT COMPANY

It's a small world after all. It's a small world after all. It's a small world after all. It's a small, small world.

So goes the song of a popular attraction at Disney's theme parks, and it might describe the attitude at the Walt Disney Co. In a little more than a decade, the firm has grown from two U.S.–based theme parks and a movie studio to an international entertainment concern that includes professional sports franchises, additional theme parks in Japan and France, cable and network television, real estate holdings, publishing, retail stores, and theater productions. The force behind Disney's transition is Michael Eisner who, with Frank Wells, took charge in 1984. Just one measure of their impact is the international presence of the company. Prior to 1984, only 9 percent of Disney's revenue came from international operations. Today, over 23 percent of sales are overseas.

From Theme Parks to Entertainment Company

When Eisner arrived at Disney, he found it heavily dependent on the cyclical theme park business for nearly 80 percent of its operating profits. Movie production focused on animation and low-budget films that earned a G rating. The company also had dabbled in the resort business, but never fully reached its potential. Eisner determined that long-term success required diversification of the company's operations and expansion into fast-growing international markets. With a vision of building a global entertainment company, he embarked on a series of acquisitions and ventures that would transform Disney into the entertainment powerhouse it is today. The financial results of these efforts are clear. Every year since Eisner arrived, profit margins and return on equity increased annually by 20 percent or more.

The first step in diversifying was to reduce the company's dependence on theme parks for revenue. Beginning in 1984, a concentrated effort was made to increase the proportion of revenue generated by filmed entertainment. The release of several popular animated films, *The Little Mermaid, Beauty and the Beast, Aladdin,* and *Pocahontas,* together with several successes from Disney's Miramax unit (for example, *Pulp Fiction*) and television production (for example, *The Golden Girls* and *Home Improvement*), increased the proportion of film revenues from 1 percent of total revenues in 1984 to 43 percent in 1994. A major contributor in this transition was *The Lion King*, the second-biggest-grossing film ever, with $740 million in box office sales worldwide. Adding $1 billion in *Lion King* merchandise sales made for a tidy return on the $50 million it took to make the film. Home video release of popular Disney classics such as *Cinderella, Sleeping Beauty,* and *Snow White* (which sold 36 million copies worldwide) also contributed significantly to the success of the film component of the company.

Diversification continued when Disney moved into professional sports with The Mighty Ducks National Hockey League franchise. The team name came from the popular 1992 Disney movie, which grossed over $50 million. The link between professional sports and filmmaking points to the synergy that Disney strives to achieve in its operations as an endless number of cross-promotional opportunities abound between sports and films. In 1996, Disney continued its expansion into professional sports by acquiring a share of the California Angels major-league baseball team.

Everything was working like a fine-tuned engine. However, the sudden death of Wells in a helicopter crash in April 1994 led to some internal confusion and the defections of several experienced Disney executives. In 1994, Jeffrey Katzenberg, chairman of Walt Disney Motion Pictures Group, was passed over for Wells's former position, so he left Disney to start DreamWorks with Steven Spielberg and David Geffen. Eisner moved quickly to plug the hole by replacing Katzenberg with Joe Roth, former studio chief at 20th Century-Fox. One of the tasks facing Roth is to broaden the audience for Disney films. To accomplish this, Roth plans to make fewer, but better, movies with big stars rather than rely on animated films as Katzenberg did. "We're going to strengthen our brand, and we're going to leverage it," said Roth.

A giant leap forward in Disney's effort to become the leading international entertainment company occurred on July 31, 1995. That was the day Disney bid $19 billion to purchase Capital Cities/ABC Inc. Although Disney has had shows on television for decades (for example, *Disney's Wonderful World of Color*) and owns the cable Disney Channel, the purchase of ABC provides the company with more variety in its programming and enhances its ability to attract a wider audience. The two companies combined created the world's largest entertainment conglomerate and positioned Disney to become the dominant player in the world of entertainment.

Other developments include the addition of a cruise line, the renovation of Epcot Center, an expansion of the over 380 Disney Store chain, and the creation of The Disney Institute. Disney purchased an island in the Bahamas and launched Disney Family Cruises by commissioning two $350-million cruise ships. "It's a logical extension of the leisure time entertainment business that we're in," remarked Thomas Elrod, president of marketing and entertainment at Walt Disney Attractions. The need to update Epcot Center was reflected in its performance. Disney was forced to offer discounts and other promotions to hold annual attendance at 10 million visitors. A Denmark pavilion was added and other attractions have or will be refurbished. For example, General Motors is opening a new World of Motion pavilion.

Disney's retail stores offer a large potential for merchandising its famous characters and movies. The stores carry Disney-related gifts, animation art, apparel, books, and audio and video tapes. The global presence of Disney is reflected in the fact that the store with the highest sales revenue is located on the Champs Elysees in Paris.

One of Disney's newest ideas is The Disney Institute. This "fantasy vacation" is designed to make a person's dreams come true. The concept is similar to fantasy baseball camps, where customers play ball and mingle with the "greats" from various teams, such as the Yankees. At The Disney Institute the customer trains to be a gourmet chef or sing in an opera.

Euro Disney

Disney's theme parks have been a core part of its business since Disneyland opened in California in 1955. Disney World in Orlando, Florida, opened in 1971, followed by a theme park in Tokyo in 1982. Disney's latest attempt to bridge an ocean was the 1992 opening of a $4 billion park 20 miles east of Paris.

Euro Disneyland represented a major move by Disney to be a complete entertainment stop for some 11 million annual visitors. The company made several mistakes in developing Disney World and the Tokyo park. For example, Disney decided to accept royalties rather than invest in resort hotels around the park in Tokyo. With Disney World, the company failed to control hotel development and owns only a small fraction of the rooms. In both cases, Disney lost control and a valuable source of revenue. To avoid a recurrence, in designing and building Euro Disneyland, Disney owns 5,200 hotel rooms in six hotels and the Davy Crockett Cabin Camp, a campground.

But problems still emerged. The local reaction to the presence of Euro Disneyland was not very auspicious. The park was characterized as "a cultural Chernobyl" by French intellectuals. To make matters worse, important cultural differences were overlooked by Disney. For example, the French drink wine with meals, but the park had a rule against serving wine. Despite such problems, 3.6 million visitors walked through the gates of Euro Disney in the first 100 days. However, a combination of a cold French winter and an economic recession in Europe resulted in a quick drop in attendance and a $900 million loss at the end of the first year. By early 1994, the park's losses totaled nearly $2 billion, and questions surfaced about its viability.

"We built too big a park, too nice a park, and too expensive a park. . . . Then we didn't market it well. If we had built fewer hotel rooms at moderate prices, they would have filled up. But we built 5,200 rooms, all expensive," recalls Richard Nanala, head of Disney Stores. Eisner suggested that Euro Disney might have to close unless costs were slashed and revenues increased. Creditor banks were induced to forgive 18 months of interest (about $300 million) and postpone for 3 years principal installments on $3.1 billion in debt. In exchange, the Walt Disney Co. eliminated royalties and management fees for at least 5 years and sold 10 percent of Euro Disney to Prince al-Waleed of Saudi Arabia. To raise revenue, ticket prices were cut by 22 percent; 10 new attractions, such as Space Mountain, were added; and hotel rates were cut. The park also changed its name to Disneyland Paris.

As a result of these changes, park attendance jumped 21 percent from 8.8 million visitors in 1994 to 10.7 million visitors in 1995. Higher attendance meant hotel occupancy rates increased from 55 to 60 percent over the same time period. The financial result of these changes was Euro Disney's first annual profit ($23 million) in 1995. The park is now the #1 tourist attraction in France, accounting for more visitors than such notable landmarks as the Louvre and Eiffel Tower.

The Future

In spite of the problems with Euro Disney, the company has considered building other theme parks. In 1992, Disney proposed a "Disney Sea" theme park as part of a $3 billion "Port Disney" Entertainment Center in Long Beach, California. However, the idea had to be abandoned after regulatory and environmental concerns were raised. In 1994, the company unveiled plans to build a $750 million theme park 35 miles from Washington, D.C., near the Manassas Civil War battlefield. "Disney's America" was to be based on U.S. history. However, the plan ran into opposition at the outset from people concerned about the commercialization of the historic Virginia countryside and the portrayal of American history through robotics, so it was postponed until an undisclosed future date.

Disney continues to search for opportunities that are consistent with its domestic and international expansion plans. What Disney does next will be part business analysis and part imagination. Whatever that proves to be, one thing is certain, the Walt Disney Co. is favorably positioned to be the leader in global entertainment well into the next century.

http://www2.disney.com/

QUESTIONS

1. What other opportunities should Disney pursue to complete its transition into a global entertainment company?
2. Should Disney continue its diversification strategy? If so, why? If not, what strategy should it implement?
3. What factors should Disney consider when deciding whether a theme park should be built in a particular country?

Sources: Thomas Kamm, "Euro Disney Posts First Annual Profit, Stock Slides 14%," *The Wall Street Journal*, Nov. 16, 1995, p. A17; Ronald Grover and Michael Oneal, "Disney: Room for Two Lion Kings?" *Business Week*, Aug. 28, 1995, p. 28; "After a Wild Ride, Disneyland Paris Finally Makes Profit," *St. Louis Post-Dispatch*, July 30, 1995, p. 5E; Brian Coleman, "Euro Disney Posts Its First Profit $35.5 Million for Its Third Quarter," *The Wall Street Journal*, July 26, 1995, p. A9; Martha T. Moore, "Disney Magic at Work in Europe," *USA Today*, July 26, 1995, p. 3B; Marianne Wilson, "Disney's One-Two Punch," *Chain Store Age Executive*, July 1995, p. 92; Thomas R. King, "Joe Roth Reshapes Disney with Stars in Live Action," *The Wall Street Journal*, June 30, 1995, p. B1; John Huey, "Eisner Explains Everything," *Fortune*, Apr. 17, 1995, p. 45; Jeffery D. Zbar, "Spreading the Disney World," *Advertising Age*, Apr. 17, 1995, p. 26; Thomas Donlan, "An Empty Vision," *Barron's*, Aug. 1, 1994, p. 51; Vincent Schodolski, "Of Mice and Marketing," *Chicago Tribune*, Apr. 24, 1994, p. 6; Thomas King, "Disney Plans to Perk Up an Enervated Epcot," *The Wall Street Journal*, Mar. 14, 1994, p. B1; Jolie Solomon, "Mickey's Trip to Trouble," *Newsweek*, Feb. 14, 1994, p. 34; Lisa Gubernick, "Mickey n'est pas fini," *Forbes*, Feb. 14, 1994, p. 42; John P. Cortez, "Sports Teams Help Two Giants Score in Cross-Marketing," *Advertising Age*, Mar. 15, 1993, p. 31; Peter Gumbel and David Jefferson, "Disney Continues Drive to Expand World-Wide," *The Wall Street Journal*, Nov. 20, 1992, p. B4; and David Lawday, "'Ow-Dee to Frere Mickey," *U.S. News & World Report*, Apr. 13, 1992, p. 18.

PART EIGHT

Managing the Marketing Effort

Implementing a company's marketing program, evaluating its performance, appraising the role of marketing in our society today, and considering what it may be tomorrow

Up to this point, we have dealt separately with how a firm selects its target markets and then develops and manages the four elements of its marketing mix for those markets. Now we bring those separate areas together as we present an overview of an organization's *total* marketing program.

We will apply the basic management process to a company's marketing program. Recall that the strategic planning stage was introduced in Chapter 3. We will discuss the implementation and evaluation stages of the management process in Chapter 21. Then, in the final chapter, we will appraise the current position of marketing in the American socioeconomic system and consider where marketing is headed.

Marketing Implementation and Evaluation

How Did
TACO BELL
Become as Hot as a Jalapeño Pepper?

Taco Bell, a division of PepsiCo, dominates the Mexican-style restaurant market like few other companies dominate their areas of business. Total sales of all such restaurants are in the vicinity of $10 *billion,* and Taco Bell rings up about one-half that annual volume. Further, within the fast-food category, Taco Bell commands a market share of around 80 percent. Still, outlets serving Mexican food capture only about 5 percent of total restaurant sales, so there's room for substantial growth.

How has Taco Bell become so successful? The obvious answer is creative, effective marketing plans, and that's certainly true. However, a less obvious—but equally important—answer relates to the chain's implementation of its plans.

Although Taco Bell was founded in 1962 in Downey, California, and then was acquired by PepsiCo in 1978, the chain's rapid rise really began in 1988 when value became its focus. Basically, Taco Bell cut its prices and emphasized three tiers of menu items—59, 79, and 99 cents. Other leading fast-food competitors, including McDonald's and Burger King, have since adopted their own forms of value pricing.

For Taco Bell's value pricing to be successful, the firm needed to lower its costs and add space to accommodate more customers. Thus Taco Bell revamped how its plans were implemented. According to a senior vice president of the firm, "We've changed the way we think about ourselves, moving from a company that prepares food to one that feeds hungry people." Taco Bell launched a "K minus" program, in which the K referred to kitchen. Basically, most of the labor-intensive food preparation—such as cooking beef, shredding cheese, and slicing vegetables—was moved out of the restaurants and delegated to outside firms. With this switch, the restaurants could concentrate on final assembly and customer service. Further, the kitchens in Taco Bell restaurants were reduced in size so that more customer seating could be added. The savings from "outsourcing" most of the food preparation reduced Taco Bell's costs, which helped the chain earn profits while offering value pricing.

Taco Bell's strongest appeal has been to young cost-conscious males (typically 18 to 35 years of age) and to children. To reach a third market segment, more health-conscious, older men as well as women, the company decided to introduce Border Lights in early 1995. These are low-fat (or at least *lower*-fat) versions of many popular items on its menu.

The Border Lights plan required skillful implementation. To generate customer satisfaction and repeat sales, the low-fat items had to be as tasty as the regular items, and the level of quality had to be maintained over time. Further, Taco Bell decided that to have a resounding impact on the market, an entire menu of Border Lights (not just a couple of low-fat items) was necessary. To do this, the chain had to come up with lower-fat versions of three-quarters of the items on its menu; the regular items were retained as well. Taco Bell's top management has high hopes for its restaurant chain (seeking $20 billion in annual sales by the year 2000) and particularly for Border Lights (which are supposed to be 25 percent of total sales by 2000).[1]

Has Taco Bell backed its marketing plans with effective implementation?

The Taco Bell case illustrates not just clever strategic plans but also effective implementation of strategies and tactics and ongoing evaluation of results. In Chapter 3 we defined the management process in marketing as planning, implementing, and evaluating marketing in an organization. This process is illustrated in Figure 21-1, which is identical to Figure 3-1. Most of this book has dealt with **planning** a marketing program. For example, we discussed how to select target markets and how to design a strategic program to deliver want-satisfaction to those markets.

Now in this chapter we discuss the implementation and evaluation of a marketing program. **Implementation** is the operational stage during which an organization attempts to carry out its strategic plan. At the end of an operating period (or even during the period) management should conduct an **evaluation** of the organization's performance. This stage involves determining how well the organization is achieving the goals set in its strategic planning and then, as necessary, preparing new or modified plans.

After studying this chapter, you should be able to explain:

CHAPTER GOALS

- The role of implementation in the management process.
- Organizational structures used to implement marketing programs.
- Warranties and postsale service as means of assuring customer satisfaction.
- The role of a marketing audit in evaluating a marketing program.
- The meaning of misdirected marketing effort.
- The steps comprising the evaluation process in marketing.
- Sales volume analysis.
- Marketing cost analysis.
- How findings from sales and cost analyses can be used by managers.

Implementation in Marketing Management

There should be a close relationship among planning, implementation, and evaluation. Without strategic planning, a company's operational activities—its implementation tactics—can go off in any direction, like an unguided missile. In the early 1980s, there was tremendous interest in strategic planning, sparked by management consulting firms. Then disenchantment set in, as many companies came to realize that strategic *planning* alone was not enough to ensure success. These plans had to be *effectively implemented.*[2] As one marketing executive said, "Too often those hot-shot planners could not sell a pair of shoes to a guy who is standing barefooted on a very hot sidewalk with a $50 bill in his hand."

FIGURE 21-1 The management process in marketing.

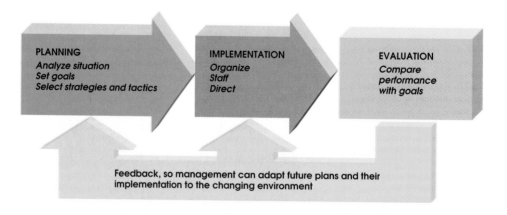

PLANNING
Analyze situation
Set goals
Select strategies and tactics

IMPLEMENTATION
Organize
Staff
Direct

EVALUATION
Compare performance with goals

Feedback, so management can adapt future plans and their implementation to the changing environment

Good planning cannot overcome poor implementation. But effective implementation often can overcome poor planning. Fortunately, in the 1990s considerably more attention is being devoted to implementing a company's strategies. Several years ago, for example, Chrysler spent $30 million to reeducate over 100,000 employees in its dealerships. This training program supported the introduction of the Chrysler Concorde, Dodge Intrepid, and Eagle Vision—the first completely new Chrysler cars since the early 1980s. Chrysler was concerned that dealers who had sold its earlier line of cars didn't know how to sell the sophisticated new cars to young, discerning customers.[3]

http://www.chrysler.com/

Implementation comprises three activities:

- *Organizing the marketing effort.* Once a company has developed its strategic marketing plan, an early activity is to organize the people who will implement it. The relationship between marketing and the other functional divisions of the firm must be defined. Then, within the marketing department, management must design an organization that will implement both strategies and tactics.
- *Staffing the organization.* For plans to produce the intended results, an organization needs skilled, dedicated employees to carry them out well. Thus selection of people is all-important—no matter what organization is being staffed. A college football coach's success depends greatly on his ability to recruit the right players. A political party's success depends on its ability to select the candidate who will attract the most votes. And a sales manager's success depends in great measure on the sales people whom the manager selects. In most marketing organizations, the sales force plays a vital role in implementing a company's plans. Consequently, in Chapter 17 we discussed a process for selecting sales people.
- *Directing the execution of marketing plans.* In this third phase of implementation, revenues are generated by carrying out the firm's strategies and tactics. To do so, management needs to direct the work of the people who have been selected and organized as the company's marketing team. Success in this phase depends to a large extent on four important aspects of managing employees—delegation, coordination, motivation, and communication.

*S*iemens, a giant German firm that operates in industries ranging from electronics to transportation, promotes its emphasis on "precision thinking." Siemens conducts a variety of training programs to build a highly skilled work force. Siemens has also restructured, shifting from a traditional, rigid hierarchy to a more entrepreneurial, flexible organization that will help the company succeed in the face of increasingly intense competition.

http://www.siemens.com/

1847. That was then.

Werner Siemens opens his first factory, a small shop to manufacture the world's most advanced telegraph.

1996. This is now.

All across America, more than 80 Siemens manufacturing and assembly plants are turning out an astonishing variety of high-tech electronic and electrical products with quality American industry can count on. Over 20,000 Siemens U.S. employees have manufacturing jobs in these plants, and are helping to build products in a wide range of fields, including energy, communications, automotive, medical and automation technology. In fact, 14% of Siemens' $8.0 billion annual sales are derived from exports from these factories to the rest of the world. **Siemens. Precision Thinking.**

Detailed discussion of staffing and directing an organization is beyond the scope of this marketing text. In-depth coverage of these topics can be found in basic management books. However, it is appropriate in this text to consider how organizational structures are used to implement marketing programs.

Organizing for Implementation

Organizational structures are receiving increasing attention in companies—both American and foreign—as management recognizes that yesterday's arrangements may hinder operations in today's dynamic environment. Now satisfying customers profitably requires talking with—and listening to—customers. Teamwork across business functions such as marketing and production is also essential. Traditional organizational structures, however, isolate different business functions and have many managerial layers between customers and decision makers. Recognizing these contradictions, AT&T, Xerox, Siemens (the huge German electronics concern), and Motorola's Government Electronics Group are among many firms that have made significant organizational changes in recent years.[4]

In a very real sense, traditional vertical structures are being replaced by horizontal organizations.[5] Several specific trends are noteworthy:

- *Fewer organizational levels.* The intent is to facilitate communication among executives who develop strategic plans, the employees who have continuing contact with the market, and the firm's customers.
- *Cross-functional teams.* By having personnel from various departments work on a project, not only are barriers among functions broken down but the best combination of expertise and experience can be focused on the assignment.
- *Employee empowerment.* Granting more authority to middle-level executives in decentralized locations can stimulate innovation and generate faster responses to market shifts.

http://www.modicon.com/

Revising an organizational structure is challenging, because doing so requires that employees give up long-standing, comfortable arrangements. But the results often justify the effort. Modicon Inc., a manufacturer of automation-control equipment, used to consider product development strictly as an engineering task. Now the process is carried out by a 15-person team representing marketing, manufacturing, and finance in addition to engineering. Under the new arrangement, the time required to develop six software packages was cut by two-thirds. Changes such as that made by Modicon demonstrate that many firms are seeking better structures and illustrate some of the more common revisions. Undoubtedly, other new organizational structures will emerge in response to changing environments.[6]

Company-Wide Organization

In Chapter 1 we stated that one of the three components of the marketing concept is to coordinate all marketing activities. In firms that are production-oriented or sales-oriented, typically we find fragmented marketing activities. The sales force is separate from advertising, and sales training may be under the human resources department.

In a marketing-oriented enterprise, all marketing activities are coordinated under one executive, who usually is at the vice presidential level. This executive reports directly to the president and is on an equal organizational footing with top executives in finance, production, and other major functions, as shown in Figure 21-2.

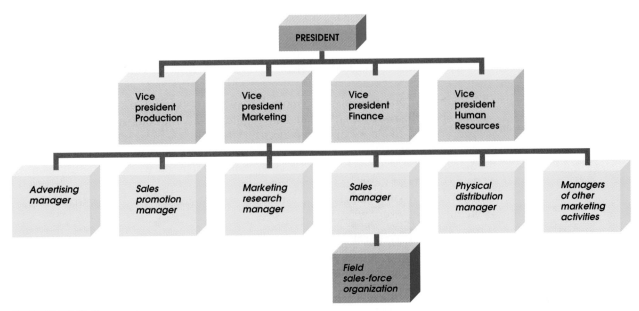

FIGURE 21-2 Company organization embracing the marketing concept.

Another aspect of organizational coordination is to establish effective working relationships between marketing and each of the other major functional areas. Marketing can help production, for example, by providing accurate sales forecasts. Production can return the favor with desired quality products precisely when needed to fill customers' orders. Marketing and finance people can work together to establish pricing and credit policies.[7] Cross-functional teams, as described earlier, can break down organizational barriers, improve coordination across functional areas, and expedite work on major processes such as product development.

Organization within the Marketing Department

Within the marketing department—especially in medium-sized or large firms—the sales force frequently is specialized in some organizational fashion. This is done to effectively implement the company's strategic marketing plan. Most often, the sales force is organized in one of three forms of specialization: geographic territory, product line, or customer type. Sometimes a hybrid form is created by combining the best features of two standard forms.

Geographic Specialization. Perhaps the most widely used method of specializing selling activities is on the basis of **geographic specialization.** Each sales person is assigned a specific geographic area—called a territory—in which to sell. Several sales people representing contiguous territories are placed under a territorial sales executive, who reports directly to the general sales manager. These territorial executives usually are called district or regional sales managers, as shown in Figure 21-3A (see p. 575).

A geographic organization usually ensures better implementation of sales strategies in each local market and better control over the sales force. Customers can be serviced quickly and effectively, and local sales reps can respond better to competitors' actions in a given territory. As its major drawback, a geographic organization does not provide the product expertise or other specialized knowledge that some customers may want. To address that problem, the professional imaging division of Eastman Kodak Company switched from a geographic alignment of its

http://www.kodak.com/

sales force to one that also takes into account sales people's expertise and customer needs. Rather than calling on all kinds of customers in a territory, say Atlanta, a Kodak rep now works with certain types of customers, say commercial color labs or professional resellers, in a somewhat larger geographic area.[8]

Product Specialization. Another basis for organizing a sales force is **product specialization**, as illustrated in Figure 21-3B. A company such as a meat packer may divide all of its products into two lines—meat products and fertilizers. One group of sales reps sells only the line of meats, while another group sells the fertilizer line. Each group reports to its own product sales manager who, in turn, reports to the general sales manager.

This type of organization is especially well suited for companies that are marketing:

- Complex technical products—a manufacturer of several electronic products.
- Unrelated or dissimilar products—a company marketing luggage, folding tables and chairs, and toy building blocks.
- Thousands of items—a hardware wholesaler.

The main advantage of a product-specialized sales organization is the attention each product line can get from the sales force. A drawback is that more than one sales rep from the same company may call on the same customer. This duplication not only is costly but also may irritate and confuse customers.

Customer Specialization. In recent years, many companies have divided their sales departments on the basis of **customer specialization**. Customers may be grouped by type of industry or channel of distribution. An oil company may divide its markets by industries, such as railroads, auto manufacturers, and farm-equipment producers, as shown in Figure 21-3C. A firm that specializes its sales operations by channel of distribution may have one sales force selling to wholesalers and another dealing directly with large retailers.

As more companies fully implement the marketing concept, the customer-specialization type of organization is likely to increase. Certainly the basis of customer specialization is consistent with the customer-oriented philosophy that underlies the marketing concept. That is, the organizational emphasis is on customers and markets rather than on products.

A variation of customer specialization is the **major-accounts organization**. Many companies are adopting this structure as a better way to deal with large, important customers. A major-accounts organization usually involves team selling—a concept introduced in Chapter 17. A selling team, consisting perhaps of a sales rep, a sales engineer, a financial executive, and a manufacturing person, will negotiate with a buying team from the customer's organization. Procter & Gamble, for example, has established a series of selling teams, each specializing in a broad product category (cleaning products, food products) to better service key accounts such as Wal-Mart.

Postsale Follow-Through

It is shortsighted to think that marketing ends when a sale is made. In line with the marketing concept, a firm should be committed to ensuring that customers are fully satisfied. If that is accomplished, it's likely that organizational objectives

FIGURE 21-3 Major forms of sales organization.

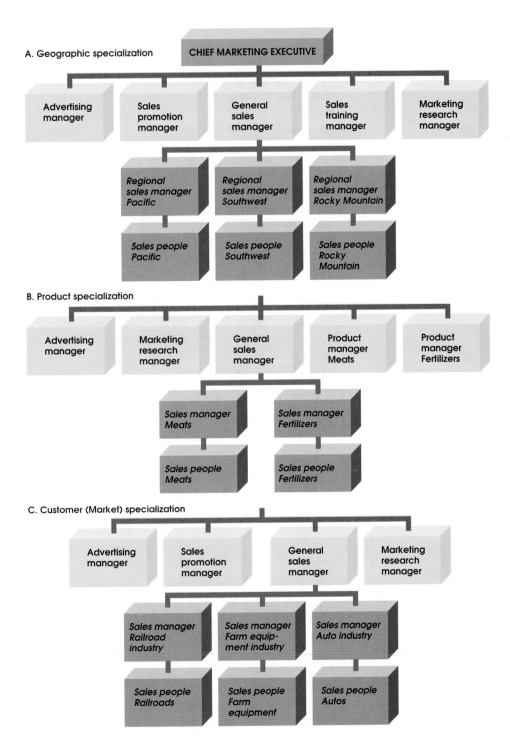

A. Geographic specialization

CHIEF MARKETING EXECUTIVE

- Advertising manager
- Sales promotion manager
- General sales manager
  - Regional sales manager Pacific
    - Sales people Pacific
  - Regional sales manager Southwest
    - Sales people Southwest
  - Regional sales manager Rocky Mountain
    - Sales people Rocky Mountain
- Sales training manager
- Marketing research manager

B. Product specialization

- Advertising manager
- Marketing research manager
- General sales manager
  - Sales manager Meats
    - Sales people Meats
  - Sales manager Fertilizers
    - Sales people Fertilizers
- Product manager Meats
- Product manager Fertilizers

C. Customer (Market) specialization

- Advertising manager
- Sales promotion manager
- General sales manager
  - Sales manager Railroad industry
    - Sales people Railroads
  - Sales manager Farm equipment industry
    - Sales people Farm equipment
  - Sales manager Auto industry
    - Sales people Autos
- Marketing research manager

(including desired levels of profits) will be achieved *and* that loyal customers will be created, thereby contributing to the future vitality of the company.

Two elements of a marketing program are implemented largely after a sale is made. Customer satisfaction—as well as future revenues—require that a company provide its customers with suitable warranties and competent postsale service. Thus we should consider important aspects of each of these marketing activities.

Warranties

The purpose of a **warranty,** which we use interchangeably with *guarantee,* is to assure buyers they will be compensated if the product does not perform up to reasonable expectations. Years ago, courts seemed to recognize only an **express warranty**—one stated in written or spoken words. Usually this form of reassurance was quite limited in its coverage and seemed mainly to protect the seller from buyers' claims. As a result, the following caution was appropriate: "Caveat emptor," which means "Let the buyer beware."

But times change! Consumer complaints led to a governmental campaign to protect the consumer in many areas, including product warranties. Courts and government agencies have broadened the scope of warranty coverage by recognizing **implied warranty.** This means a warranty was *intended,* although not actually stated, by the seller. Furthermore, producers are being held responsible, even when the sales contract is between the retailer and the consumer. Now the caution is: "Caveat venditor," or "Let the seller beware."

Passage of the Consumer Product Safety Act (1972) reflected the changed attitude regarding product liability and injurious products. This federal legislation created the Consumer Product Safety Commission (CPSC), which has the authority to establish mandatory safety standards for many consumer products not covered by separate laws or other agencies. The CPSC can publish information regarding injurious products—naming brands and producers. It can ban the distribution of these products without a court hearing. And top management of offending companies may face criminal—not just civil—charges.

During the past two decades, many producers were held liable for product-caused injury. In many cases, firms were liable even if they were not negligent in production. The term *product liability* became common in business, and numerous lawsuits ensued. **Product liability** is a legal action asserting that an illness, accident, or death resulted from the named product because it was harmful, faulty, or inadequately labeled. Basically, liability results from one or more of three problems: a flaw in the product design, a defect in production, or a deficiency in warning the customer about proper use and potentially harmful misuse of the product.[9]

Over the past 10 years, product-liability claims have involved entire product categories, including asbestos insulation and breast implants, as well as specific brands of toys, tampons, pharmaceuticals, birth-control devices, tires, and chain saws, among others. Claims have also been filed against firms offering services such as auto repairs and weight-loss programs. For example, Nutri/System Inc. was sued by a group of consumers who alleged that their gallbladders were damaged as a result of the company's weight-loss services.

In many product-liability cases, juries have granted very large settlements to the plaintiffs. The largest such award in 1995 was for $350 million. In this case, Turbomeca S.A. was found liable because an engine in a helicopter made by this French firm failed during flight, resulting in a fatal crash. Overall, though, juries are making smaller awards to successful plaintiffs. In 1995, the average award in state courts was about one-half the average of 2 years earlier.[10]

The wave of product-liability claims has dissipated. An explanation might be found in safer products, more extensive warning labels, and/or less optimism about a settlement large enough to justify the effort of a lawsuit. Still, thousands of claims are filed every year. Product liability remains an issue of great consequence to companies because of the financial risk as well as the adverse publicity connected with consumers' damage claims.[11]

Congress and the courts continue to wrestle with the controversial issue of product liability. It has proven to be difficult to write a law that is considered fair by groups on both sides of the issue. Yet everybody recognizes the need for legislation to bring some clarity and uniformity out of the confusion created by the variations in state laws, court decisions, and financial settlements. And product-liability problems are likely to increase for companies marketing in Western Europe. European laws now provide compensation to consumers in cases of demonstrated bodily injury or property damage from products—even when there has been no negligence on the part of the seller.

Producers have responded to legislation and consumer complaints by broadening and simplifying their warranties. Manufacturers are also using expanded labels on their goods to tell consumers not to misuse the product and to inform them of almost every conceivable danger associated with using it. Such **warning labels** may go so far as to state: "Do not drive with sun shield in place. Remove from windshield before starting ignition." Or for another product: "Do not use ladder in front of unlocked doors." And, believe it or not, on a handheld hair dryer: "Never use while sleeping." Producers are hopeful such blatant and seemingly obvious warnings will protect them against claims that they did not properly inform consumers about the product's use, misuse, and potential dangers.[12]

Besides such protective measures, some companies are making their warranties more satisfying to customers. Simple, straightforward guarantees, such as "Absolutely, positively overnight" and "No questions asked," are increasingly common. Xerox Corp. instituted a guarantee under which the customer, not the company, decides whether a poorly functioning product should be replaced with a new model.[13]

http://www.xerox.com/

It is standard practice to offer a full refund of the purchase price to a dissatisfied buyer. Various manufacturers, retailers, and especially services firms also offer displeased patrons other forms of appeasement. For example, Delta Dental Plan of Massachusetts has sent a $50 check to any of its policyholders who gets transferred from employee to employee when seeking an answer to an insurance question.[14]

http://www.wal-mart.com/
http://www.goodyear.com/

Many sellers are using their warranties as promotional devices to stimulate purchases by reducing consumers' risks. Wal-Mart's simple guarantee, "Satisfaction Guaranteed," is convincing in that regard. In early 1996, Goodyear gained an edge over its competitors by placing a limited lifetime tread warranty on its Infinitred tires, the first such warranty in the industry.[15] Finally, it's worth stressing that effective handling of consumers' complaints related to warranties can be a significant factor in strengthening a company's marketing program.

Postsale Service

Many companies have to provide **postsale service,** notably repairs, to fulfill the terms of their warranties. Other firms offer postsale services such as maintenance and repairs to gain a differential advantage over competitors, or at least to fully satisfy their customers. With more complex products and increasingly demanding and vocal consumers, postsale service has become essential. A constant consumer gripe is that manufacturers and retailers do *not* provide adequate repair service for the products they sell.

Some businesses use postsale services to augment their revenues. Companies such as Otis and Montgomery, both of which sell elevators, rely on their service contracts for a substantial portion of their sales and profits. To process customers' requests for repairs, Otis established a center that handles over 1 million calls a year, ranging from a broken escalator to people trapped in an elevator.[16]

A manufacturer can shift the main burden for postsale service to middlemen, compensate them for their efforts, and possibly even train their service people. This approach is evident in the automobile and personal computer industries. Or a manufacturer can establish regional factory service centers, staff them with well-trained company employees, and strive to make product servicing a separate profit-generating activity. This approach is found in the appliance industry.

Recently, some manufacturers of costly computers, office equipment, and medical diagnostic equipment have developed "smart" products. With built-in sensors and microcomputers, such products can diagnose themselves and/or allow a technician to conduct a diagnosis from a distance by means of either wired or wireless telecommunications. This innovation expedites repairs and, by so doing, cuts aggravating "down time" for valuable products. Further, labor costs associated with repairs may be reduced, thereby improving the manufacturer's profit margins on service contracts.[17]

Some manufacturers consider the postsale service market so lucrative they want to keep it to themselves. To do so, they might limit availability of replacement parts. As discussed in Chapter 13, in a 1995 court decision, Eastman Kodak was found guilty of refusing to supply independent service companies with replacement parts for its photocopiers and related equipment.[18]

Consumers become frustrated if they cannot voice their complaints and get their postsale service problems solved.[19] As described in the Commitment to Customer Satisfaction box (see p. 580), marketing-oriented responsive producers have established toll-free telephone lines to their customer service departments. Postsale service, like other elements of the marketing mix, can be either a differential advantage or a disadvantage for an organization. Thus it certainly should be on the list of matters managers need to heed constantly.

Evaluating Marketing Performance

Soon after a firm's plans have been set in operation, the process of evaluation should begin. Without evaluation, management cannot tell whether a plan is working and what factors are contributing to its success or failure. Evaluation log-

CAN THE CUSTOMER BE RIGHT SOMETIMES?

In many countries—particularly those that are converting from command to free-market economies—friendly, competent customer service is not the norm. Typically, it's the exception. Consider just a couple of examples: When German telephone customers complained about overcharges, the Deutsche Telekom AG firm constantly denied responsibility. In Russia, clerks in state-owned stores literally turned their backs on shoppers who wanted to examine merchandise in a display case and to customers who had a question about a product they had purchased.

Why the neglect of customers? The most obvious reason is lack of either competition or financial incentive. These factors describe some firms, such as Telekom in Germany, holding monopolies in free-market economies. These same factors characterized most state-owned enterprises in command economies. Commercial airlines in the former Soviet Union typically would not even guarantee a return flight when a customer purchased a ticket.

But customer service is spreading around the world, albeit slowly, because of increased competition and more demanding customers who, through travel or media, have learned about better service. Thus, when an angry customer complained about a problem with an account at a Russian bank, the teller politely discussed the situation with the irritated patron. She applied skills learned at a training program. The teller commented, "In Soviet times, we wouldn't have paid attention to the customer." Even in China, some progress is evident. Trying to instill politeness in state workers after so many years of communism is not easy. One of the first steps was to prohibit workers in airports, hospitals, stores, and other state-owned enterprises from using common phrases that show disdain for shoppers. Among the 50 banned phrases: "Ask someone else" and "Don't you see I'm busy? What's the hurry?"

Sources: Gabriela Teodorescu, "Service with a Smile . . . in Russia?" *The Wall Street Journal*, Aug. 16, 1995, p. A6; "China Begs of Its Workers: 'Manners, Please,'" *The Wall Street Journal*, Aug. 16, 1995, p. A6; and Greg Steinmetz, "Customer-Service Era Is Reaching Germany Late, Hurting Business," *The Wall Street Journal*, June 1, 1995, pp. A1, A6.

ically follows planning and implementation. Planning sets forth what *should* be done. Evaluation shows what *really was* done. A circular relationship exists, as illustrated in Figure 21-4. Plans are made, they are put into action, the results of those actions are evaluated, and new plans are prepared on the basis of this evaluation.

Previously we discussed evaluation as it relates to individual parts of a marketing program—the product-planning process, the performance of the sales force, and the effectiveness of the advertising program, for instance. Now let's look at the evaluation of the *total marketing effort*.

FIGURE 21-4 The circular relationship among management tasks.

The Marketing Audit

A marketing audit is an essential element in a total evaluation program. An audit implies a review and evaluation of some activity. Thus a **marketing audit** is a comprehensive review and evaluation of the marketing function in an organization—its philosophy, environment, goals, strategies, organizational structure, human and financial resources, and performance.[20]

It's true that a marketing audit involves evaluation. But it's more than that. As suggested by Figure 21-4, the results of any evaluation—including a marketing audit—represent vital input to an organization's planning. In advocating the value of marketing audits in the banking industry, one writer stressed, "Simply stated, a [strategic] marketing plan should only be written after the completion of an intensive, objective marketing audit."[21]

A COMMITMENT TO CUSTOMER SATISFACTION

ARE 1-800 LINES WORTH THE COST?

Every organization wants compliments about its offerings and operations. A growing number of companies welcome—even invite—bad news and dumb questions from customers. To accept compliments, complaints, and queries, most large firms have installed 1-800 numbers that can be dialed at no charge to the caller. An early-1990s study found that over two-thirds of manufacturers offer a toll-free number.

What caused the rush to 1-800 numbers? Basically, they can increase the likelihood of satisfying a customer. Most callers are seeking information. Pillsbury's representatives respond to questions ranging from "Can I add chocolate chips to the brownie mix?" to "What's wrong with your flour?"

Equally important, a toll-free inbound line can reduce the possibility that a dissatisfied customer stays that way. A person with a complaint can air the problem and get a response from the company's representative. Oftentimes, the disgruntled customer also gets a coupon for a reduced price or even a free product. According to one study, a caller whose complaint is not handled satisfactorily tells around ten people about the poor treatment provided by the company, whereas a customer who is satisfied by the call tells an average of five people.

A 1-800 number can be expensive. Pillsbury, for example, spends several million dollars yearly so that about a dozen reps can handle an average of 2,000 calls daily. Some firms (but not Pillsbury) have abandoned their 1-800 numbers, but most consider the results well worth the expense. As the head of a research agency explained, "It's just about keeping the customers you've got."

What's ahead? It's likely that many companies will establish websites on the Internet to serve basically the same purposes as a 1-800 number. This arrangement may allow customers to interact with each other. What's unknown is whether websites will replace or supplement firms' 1-800 numbers.

For what kinds of companies are 1-800 numbers worthwhile?

Sources: Carl Quintanilla and Richard Gibson, "'Do Call Us': More Companies Install 1-800 Phone Lines," *The Wall Street Journal,* Apr. 20, 1994, pp. B1, B4; and Richard Gibson, "Pillsbury's Telephones Ring with Peeves, Praise," *The Wall Street Journal,* Apr. 20, 1994, pp. B1, B4.

A complete marketing audit is an extensive and difficult project. That's why it is conducted infrequently—perhaps every several years. However, a company should not delay a marketing audit until a major crisis arises.

The rewards of a marketing audit can justify the effort. Management can identify problem areas in marketing. By reviewing its strategies, the firm is likely to keep abreast of its changing marketing environment. Successes can also be analyzed, so the company can capitalize on its strong points. The audit can spot lack of coordination in the marketing program, outdated strategies, or unrealistic goals. Furthermore, an audit should anticipate future situations. It is intended for "prognosis as well as diagnosis. . . . It is the practice of preventive as well as curative marketing medicine."[22]

Misdirected Marketing Effort

One of the benefits of evaluation is that it helps correct **misdirected** (or misplaced) **marketing effort.**

The 80–20 Principle.   In most firms, a large proportion of the total orders, customers, territories, or products accounts for only a small share of total sales or profit. Conversely, a small proportion produces a large share of sales or profit. This relationship has been characterized as the **80–20 principle.** That is, the large majority (say, 80 percent) of the orders, customers, territories, or products contribute only a small fraction (say, 20 percent) of sales or profit. On the other hand, relatively few of these selling units account for the large majority of the volume or profit. We use the 80–20 figure simply to highlight the misplacement of marketing effort. In reality, of course, the percentage split varies from one situation to another.

The basic reason for the 80–20 split is that almost every marketing program includes some misdirected effort. Marketing efforts and costs are proportional to the *numbers* of territories, customers, or products, rather than to their actual sales volume or profit. For example, approximately the same order-filling, billing, and delivery expenses are involved whether a $500 suit or a $25 necktie is sold in a May Company department store. Or a manufacturer such as Xerox may assign one sales person to each territory. Yet usually there are differences in the actual sales volume and profit among the territories. In each example the marketing effort (cost) is not in line with the actual return.

Reasons for Misdirected Effort. Frequently, executives cannot uncover their misdirected effort because they lack sufficient information. The **iceberg principle** is an analogy that illustrates this situation. Only a small tip of an iceberg is visible above the surface of the water, and the huge submerged part represents the hidden danger. The figures representing total sales or total costs on an operating statement are like the visible tip of an iceberg. The detailed figures representing sales, costs, and other performance measures for each territory or product correspond to the dangerous submerged part.

Total sales or cost figures are too general to be useful in evaluation; in fact, they often are misleading. A company may show satisfactory overall sales and profit figures. But when these totals are subdivided by pertinent factors such as geographic territories, individual products, or various time periods, serious weaknesses often are discovered. A manufacturer of audio equipment showed an overall increase of 12 percent in sales and 9 percent in net profit on one product line in 1 year. But management wasn't satisfied with this "tip of the iceberg." In analyzing the figures more closely, the executives found that the sales change within territories ranged from an increase of 19 percent to a decrease of 3 percent. Profit increased as much as 14 percent in some territories, but was down 20 percent in one.

A more basic cause of misplaced marketing effort is that executives must make decisions based on inadequate knowledge of the exact nature of marketing costs. In other words, management often lacks knowledge of (1) the disproportionate spread of marketing effort, (2) reliable standards for determining what should be spent on marketing, and (3) what results should be expected from these expenditures.

As an illustration, a company may spend $250,000 more on advertising this year than last year. But management ordinarily cannot state what the resulting increase in sales volume or profit should be. Nor do the executives know what would have happened if they had spent the same amount on (1) new-product development, (2) management training seminars for middlemen, or (3) some other aspect of the marketing program.

The Evaluation Process

The evaluation process—whether a complete marketing audit or only an appraisal of individual components of the marketing program—involves three steps:

1. Find out *what* happened. Get the facts, compare actual results with goals and budgets to determine where they differ.
2. Find out *why* it happened. Determine what specific factors in the marketing program accounted for the results.
3. Decide *what to do* about it. Plan the next period's program so as to improve on unsatisfactory performance and capitalize on the aspects that were done well.

To evaluate a total marketing program, we need to analyze results. To do this, two tools are available—sales volume analysis and marketing cost analysis. We'll discuss both of these tools using the Great Midwest Company ("the other GM")—a firm that markets office furniture. This company's fourteen-state market is divided into four sales districts, each with seven or eight sales people and a district sales manager. The company sells to office equipment wholesalers and directly to large business users. GM's product mix is divided into four groups—desks, chairs, filing equipment, and office accessories (wastebaskets and desk sets, for example). Some of these products are manufactured by GM and some are purchased from other firms.

Sales Volume Analysis

A **sales volume analysis** is a detailed study of the Net Sales section of a company's profit and loss statement (operating statement). Management should analyze its sales volume in total and by relevant subdivisions such as geographic territories and product lines. These sales figures should be compared with company goals and industry performance.

We start with an analysis of Great Midwest's total sales volume, as shown in Table 21-1. Annual sales doubled from $18 million to $36 million during the 10-year period ending with 1996. Furthermore, sales increased each year, with the exception of 1993. In most years, planned sales goals were met or surpassed. Thus far in our analysis, the company's situation is encouraging.

A study of total sales volume alone is usually insufficient and may even be misleading. Remember the analogy of an iceberg! To learn what is going on in the "submerged" parts of the market, we need to analyze sales volume by other relevant dimensions—sales territories, for example.

Table 21-2 is a summary of the planned sales goals and actual sales results in Great Midwest's four sales districts. A key measurement is the *performance percentage* for each district—that is, actual sales divided by sales goal. A performance percentage of 100 means that the district did exactly what was expected. From the table we see that the Great Lakes and Heartland districts did just a little better than was expected. The Delta district passed its goal by a wide margin. But the High Plains district was quite a disappointment.

So far in our evaluation, we know a little about *what* happened in GM's districts. Now management has to figure out *why* it happened and *what should be done* about it. These are the difficult steps in evaluation. GM's executives need to determine why the High Plains district did so poorly. The fault may lie in some aspect of the marketing program, or competition may be especially strong in that district. They also should find out the reasons for the Delta district's success, and whether this information can be used in the other regions.

This brief examination of two aspects of sales volume analysis shows how this evaluation tool may be used. However, for a more useful evaluation, GM's executives should go much further. They should analyze their sales volume by indi-

TABLE 21-1 Annual sales volume of Great Midwest Company, industry volume, and company's share in 14-state market

Year	Company volume (in millions of dollars)	Industry volume in company's market (in millions of dollars)	Company's percentage share of market
1996	36.0	900	4.0
1995	34.7	825	4.2
1994	33.1	765	4.3
1993	30.4	660	4.6
1992	31.7	705	4.5
1991	28.0	600	4.7
1990	24.5	510	4.8
1989	22.5	465	4.8
1988	21.8	450	4.8
1987	18.0	360	5.0

TABLE 21-2 District sales volume in Great Midwest Company, 1996

District	Sales goals (in millions of dollars)	Actual sales (in millions of dollars)	Performance percentage (actual ÷ goal)	Dollar variation (in millions)
Delta	$10.8	$12.5	116	+1.7
Great Lakes	9.0	9.6	107	+ .6
Heartland	7.6	7.7	101	+ .1
High Plains	8.6	6.2	72	−2.4
Total	$36.0	$36.0		

vidual territories within districts and by product lines. Then they should carry their territorial analysis further by examining volume by product line and customer group *within* each territory. For instance, even though the Delta district did well overall, the iceberg notion may apply here. The fine *total* performance in this district may be covering up weaknesses in an individual product line or territory.

Market-Share Analysis

Comparing a company's sales results with its goal is a useful evaluation, but it does not indicate how the company is doing relative to its competitors. We need a **market-share analysis** to compare the company's sales with the industry's sales. We should analyze the company's share of the market in total, as well as by product line and market segment.

Probably the major obstacle encountered in market-share analysis is in obtaining industry sales information in total and in sufficient detail. Trade associations and government agencies are possible sources for industry sales volume statistics in many fields.

Great Midwest Company is a good example of the value of market-share analysis. Recall from Table 21-1 that GM's total sales doubled over a 10-year period, with annual increases in nine of those years. But, during this span, the annual sales for all competing firms in this geographic area increased from $360 million to $900 million (a 150 percent increase). Thus the company's market share actually *declined* from 5 to 4 percent. Although GM's annual sales increased 100 percent, its market share declined 20 percent.

The next step is to determine *why* Great Midwest's market position declined. The number of possible causes is quite large—and this is what makes management's task so difficult. A weakness in almost any aspect of GM's product line, distribution system, pricing structure, or promotional program may have contributed to the loss of market share. Or the culprit might have been competition. There may be new competitors in the market that were attracted by the rapid growth rates. Or competitors' marketing programs may be more effective than Great Midwest's.

Marketing Cost Analysis

An analysis of sales volume is helpful in evaluating and controlling a company's marketing effort. A volume analysis, however, does not tell us anything about the *profitability* of this effort. Management needs to conduct a marketing cost analysis to determine the relative profitability of its territories, product lines, or other marketing units. A **marketing cost analysis** is a detailed study of the Operating Expenses section of a company's profit and loss statement. As part of this analysis, management may establish budgetary goals, and then study the variations between budgeted costs and actual expenses.

Types of Marketing Cost Analysis
A company's marketing costs may be analyzed:

- As they appear in its ledger accounts and profit and loss statement.
- After they are grouped into activity classifications.
- After these activity costs have been allocated to territories, products, or other marketing units.

Analysis of Ledger Expenses. The simplest and least expensive marketing cost analysis is a study of the *object of expenditure* costs as they appear in the firm's profit and loss statement. These figures come from the company's account-

AN ETHICAL DILEMMA?

The *Discipline of Market Leaders* was published in early 1995. The book's basic premise to business executives is that a company should not try to do everything well, but should strive to have the best price, best product, or best solution in a particular market. Shortly after being released, the book moved onto the prestigious best-seller list compiled by *The New York Times.* By landing *Discipline* on the best-seller list, Michael Treacy and Fred Wiersema, the consultants who wrote the book, not only could earn added royalties but also could command higher fees for speaking engagements. CSC Index, the firm where the authors worked, could benefit from added consulting business.

One investigation suggests that *Discipline* became a best-seller as a result of a scheme to boost sales at bookstores that the *Times* monitors in order to assemble its best-seller list. Reportedly, CSC staff members placed bulk orders at numerous book retailers. To prevent the *Times* from detecting a large order from a single organization, which would be disregarded in compiling the best-seller list, the books allegedly were charged to various CSC employees and shipped to many locations around the U.S.

Would attempting to inflate sales in order to seize a spot on a best-seller list be ethical or unethical behavior by a book's authors?

Sources: Willy Stern, "Did Dirty Tricks Create a Best-Seller?" *Business Week,* Aug. 7, 1995, pp. 22–25; and Michael Treacy and Fred Wiersema, "How Market Leaders Keep Their Edge," *Fortune,* Feb. 6, 1995, pp. 88–90, 94, 96, 98.

ing ledger records. The simplified operating statement for the Great Midwest Company on the left side of Table 21-3 is the model we shall use in this discussion.

The procedure is to analyze each cost item (salaries and media space, for example) in detail. We can compare this period's total with the totals for similar periods in the past, and observe the trends. In addition, we can compare actual costs with budgeted expense goals. We should also compute each expense as a percentage of net sales. Then, we should compare these expense ratios with industry figures, which are often available through trade associations.

Analysis of Activity Costs. Total costs should be allocated among the various marketing activities, such as advertising or warehousing, for more effective control. Management then can analyze the cost of each of these activities.

The procedure here is first to identify the major activities, and then to allocate each ledger expense among those activities. As indicated in the expense distribution sheet on the right-hand side of Table 21-3, we have decided on five activity cost groups in our Great Midwest example. Some items, such as the cost of media space, can be apportioned entirely to one activity (advertising). For other expenses, the cost must be spread among several activities. So management must decide on some reasonable basis for allocation among these activities. For example, property taxes may be allocated according to the proportion of total floor space occupied by each activity. Thus the warehouse accounts for 46 percent of the total area (square feet) of floor space in the firm, so the warehousing and shipping activity is charged with $60,000 (46 percent) of the property taxes.

An analysis of the costs of the marketing activities gives executives more information than they can get from an analysis of ledger accounts alone. Also, an analysis of activity expenses in total provides a starting point for management to analyze costs by territories, products, or other marketing units.

Analysis of Activity Costs by Product or Market. The third and most beneficial type of marketing cost analysis is a study of the costs and profitability of specific components of a product assortment or total market. This type of analysis breaks out a product assortment by lines or individual items or divides up a market by territories, customer groups, or order sizes.

TABLE 21-3 Profit and loss statement and distribution of natural expenses to activity cost groups, Great Midwest Company, 1996

Profit and loss statement (in $000)			Expense distribution sheet (in $000)				
			Activity (functional) cost groups				
Net sales		$36,000					
Cost of goods sold		23,400	Personal selling	Advertising	Warehousing and shipping	Order processing	Marketing administration
Gross margin		12,600					
Operating expenses:							
Salaries and commissions	$2,710	→	$1,200	$ 240	$ 420	$280	$ 570
Travel and entertainment	1,440	→	1,040				400
Media space	1,480	→		1,480			
Supplies	440	→	60	35	240	70	35
Property taxes	130	→	16	5	60	30	19
Freight out	3,500	→			3,500		
Total expenses		9,700	$2,316	$1,760	$4,220	$380	$1,024
Net profit		$2,900					

By combining a sales volume analysis with a marketing cost study, a researcher can prepare a complete operating statement for each product or market component. These individual statements can then be analyzed to determine how they affect the total marketing program. Cost analysis by product or market enables management to pinpoint trouble spots much more effectively than does an analysis of either ledger-account expenses or activity costs.

The procedure for a cost analysis by product or market is similar to that used to analyze activity costs. The total of each activity cost (the right-hand part of Table 21-3) is allocated on some basis to each product or market segment being studied. Let's walk through an example of a cost analysis, by sales districts, for the Great Midwest Company, as shown in Tables 21-4 and 21-5.

First, for each of the five GM activities, we select an allocation basis for distributing the cost of that activity among the four districts. These bases are shown in the top part of Table 21-4. Then we determine the number of allocation "units" that make up each activity cost, and we find the cost per unit. This completes the allocation scheme, which tells us how to allocate costs to the four districts:

- Personal selling expenses pose no problem because they are direct expenses, chargeable to the district in which they are incurred.
- Advertising costs are allocated on the basis of the number of pages of advertising run in each district. GM purchased the equivalent of 88 pages of advertising during the year, at an average cost of $20,000 per page ($1,760,000 ÷ 88).
- Warehousing and shipping expenses are allocated on the basis of the number of orders shipped. Since 10,550 orders were shipped during the year at a total activity cost of $4,220,000, the cost per order is $400.
- Order-processing expenses are allocated according to the number of invoice lines typed during the year. Since there were 126,667 lines, then the cost per line is $3.
- Marketing administration—a totally indirect expense—is divided equally among the four districts, with each district being allocated $256,000.

TABLE 21-4 Allocation of activity costs to sales districts, Great Midwest Company, 1996

Activity		Personal selling	Advertising	Warehousing and shipping	Order processing	Marketing administration
			Allocation Basis			
Allocation basis		Direct expense to each district	Number of pages of advertising	Number of orders shipped	Number of invoice lines	Equally among districts
Total activity cost		$2,316,000	$1,760,000	$4,220,000	$380,000	$1,024,000
Number of allocation units			88 pages	10,550 orders	126,667 lines	4 districts
Cost per allocation unit			$20,000	$400	$3	$256,000
			Allocation of Costs			
Delta district <	units	—	27 pages	3,300 orders	46,000 lines	—
	cost	$650,000	$540,000	$1,320,000	$138,000	$256,000
Great Lakes district <	units	—	19 pages	2,850 orders	33,000 lines	—
	cost	$606,000	$380,000	$1,140,000	$99,000	$256,000
Heartland district <	units	—	22 pages	2,300 orders	26,667 lines	—
	cost	$540,000	$440,000	$920,000	$80,000	$256,000
High Plains district <	units	—	20 pages	2,100 orders	21,000 lines	—
	cost	$520,000	$400,000	$840,000	$63,000	$256,000

The final step is to calculate the amount of each activity cost to be allocated to each district. The results are shown in the bottom part of Table 21-4. We see that $650,000 of personal selling expenses were charged directly to the Delta district and $606,000 to the Great Lakes district, for example. Regarding advertising, the equivalent of 27 pages of advertising was run in Delta, so that district is charged with $540,000 (27 pages × $20,000 per page). Similar calculations provide advertising activity cost allocations of $380,000 to Great Lakes; $440,000 to Heartland; and $400,000 to High Plains.

Regarding warehousing and shipping expenses, 3,300 orders were shipped to customers in the Delta district, at a unit allocation cost of $400 per order, for a total allocated cost of $1,320,000. Warehousing and shipping charges are allocated to the other three districts as indicated in Table 21-4.

To allocate order-processing expenses, management determined that 46,000 invoice lines went to customers in the Delta district. At $3 per line (the cost per allocation unit), Delta is charged with $138,000. Each district is charged with $256,000 for marketing administration expenses.

After the activity costs have been allocated among the four districts, we can prepare a profit and loss statement for each district. These statements are shown in Table 21-5. Sales volume for each district is determined from the sales volume analysis (Table 21-2). Cost of goods sold and gross margin for each district are obtained by assuming that the company's gross margin of 35 percent ($12,600,000 ÷ $36,000,000) was maintained in each district.

Table 21-5 subdivides Great Midwest's total results into profit and loss statements for each of the company's four districts. For example, we note that the Delta district's net profit was 11.8 percent of sales ($1,471,000 ÷ $12,500,000). In sharp contrast, High Plains did rather poorly, earning a net profit of only 1.5 percent of net sales ($91,000 ÷ $6,200,000).

At this point in our performance evaluation, we have completed the *what happened* stage. The next stage is to determine *why* the results are as depicted in Table 21-5. As mentioned earlier, it is difficult to answer this question. In the High Plains district, for example, the sales force obtained only about two-thirds as many orders as in the Delta (2,100 versus 3,300). Was this because of poor selling, poor sales training, more severe competition in the High Plains district, or some other reason among a multitude of possibilities?

TABLE 21-5 Profit and loss statements for sales districts (in $000), Great Midwest Company, 1996

	Total	Delta	Great Lakes	Heartland	High Plains
Net sales	$36,000	$12,500	$9,600	$7,700	$6,200
Cost of goods sold	23,400	8,125	6,240	5,005	4,030
Gross margin	12,600	4,375	3,360	2,695	2,170
Operating expenses:					
Personal selling	2,316	650	606	540	520
Advertising	1,760	540	380	440	400
Warehousing and shipping	4,220	1,320	1,140	920	840
Order processing, billing	380	138	99	80	63
Marketing administration	1,024	256	256	256	256
Total expenses	9,700	2,904	2,481	2,236	2,079
Net profit (in dollars)	$ 2,900	$ 1,471	$ 879	$ 459	$ 91
Net profit (as percentage of sales)	8.1%	11.8%	9.2%	6.0%	1.5%

After a performance evaluation has determined why district results came out as they did, management can move to the third stage in its evaluation process. That final stage is, *what should management do about the situation?* This stage will be discussed briefly after we have reviewed two major problem areas in marketing cost analysis.

Problems in Cost Analysis

Marketing cost analysis can be expensive in time, money, and labor. In particular, the task of allocating costs is often quite difficult.

Allocating Costs. The problem of allocating costs becomes evident when total activity costs must be apportioned among individual territories, products, or other marketing units. Operating costs can be divided into direct and indirect expenses. **Direct costs,** also called *separable expenses,* are incurred totally in connection with one market segment or one unit of the sales organization. Thus salary and travel expenses of the sales representative in the Delta district are direct expenses for that territory. The cost of newspaper space to advertise the company's line of desks is a direct cost of marketing that product. Allocating direct expenses is easy. They can be charged entirely to the marketing unit that incurred them.

The allocation difficulty arises in connection with **indirect costs,** also called *common costs* or *overhead.* These expenses are incurred jointly for more than one marketing unit. Therefore, they cannot be charged totally to one market segment.

Within the category of indirect costs, some expenses are *variable* and others are *fixed.* (These two types of costs were introduced in Chapter 11.) Order filling and shipping, for example, are largely variable. They would *decrease* if some territories or products were eliminated. They would *increase* if new products or territories were added. On the other hand, marketing administrative expenses are more fixed. The cost of the chief marketing executive's staff and office would remain about the same, whether or not the number of territories or product lines was changed.

Any method selected for allocating indirect expenses has obvious weaknesses that can distort the results and mislead management. Two commonly used allocation methods are to divide these costs (1) equally among the marketing units being studied (territories, for instance) or (2) in proportion to the sales volume in each marketing unit. But each method gives a different result for the total costs for each marketing unit.

Full Cost versus Contribution Margin. In a marketing cost analysis, two means of allocating indirect expenses are (1) the contribution-margin (also called contribution-to-overhead) method and (2) the full-cost method. A controversy exists regarding which of these two approaches is better for managerial control purposes.

In the **contribution-margin approach,** only direct expenses are allocated to each marketing unit being analyzed. These costs presumably would be eliminated if that marketing unit were eliminated. When direct expenses are deducted from the gross margin of the marketing unit, the remainder is the amount which that unit is contributing to cover total indirect expenses (or overhead).

In the **full-cost approach,** all expenses—direct and indirect—are allocated among the marketing units under study. By allocating *all* costs, management can determine the net profit of each territory, product, or other marketing unit.

For any specific marketing unit, these two methods can be summarized as follows:

Contribution margin	Full cost
Sales $	Sales $
less	*less*
Cost of goods sold	Cost of goods sold
equals	*equals*
Gross margin	Gross margin
less	*less*
Direct expenses	Direct expenses
equals	*less*
Contribution margin (the amount available to cover indirect expenses plus a profit)	Indirect expenses
	equals
	Net profit

Proponents of the *full-cost* approach contend that a marketing cost study is intended to determine the net profitability of the units being studied. They believe that the contribution-margin method does not fulfill this purpose and may be misleading. A given territory or product may be showing a contribution to overhead. Yet, after indirect costs are allocated, this product or territory may actually have a net loss. In effect, say the full-cost proponents, the contribution-margin approach is the iceberg notion in action. That is, the visible tip (the contribution margin) looks good, while the submerged part may be hiding a net loss.

Contribution-margin supporters contend that it is not possible to accurately allocate indirect costs among product or market segments. Furthermore, items such as administrative costs are not all related to any *one* territory or product. Therefore, the marketing units should not bear any of these costs. Advocates of the contribution-margin approach also say that a full-cost analysis may show that a product or territory has a net loss, but this unit may be contributing something to overhead. Some executives might recommend that the losing product or territory be eliminated. But they are overlooking the fact that the unit's contribution to overhead would then have to be borne by other units. With the contribution-margin approach, there would be no question about keeping this unit as long as there is no better alternative.

Use of Findings from Volume and Cost Analyses

So far we have been dealing with the first two stages of marketing performance evaluation—finding out *what happened* and *why it happened*. Now we're ready to see some examples of how management might use the results from a combined sales volume analysis and marketing cost analysis.

Territories

Knowing the net profit (or contribution to overhead) of territories in relation to their potential gives management several possibilities for action. It may decide to adjust (expand or contract) territories to bring them into line with current sales potential. Or, if territorial problems stem from weaknesses in the distribution system, changes in channels of distribution may be needed. Firms that use manufacturers' agents may find it advisable to establish their own sales forces in growing markets, for instance. If intense competition is the cause of unprofitable volume in some districts, modifications in the promotional program may be necessary.

Of course, a losing territory might be abandoned completely. An abandoned region may have been contributing something to overhead, however, even though a net loss was shown. Management must recognize that this contribution must now be carried by the remaining territories.

Global Telecommunication Solutions, Inc. (GTS) sells prepaid long-distance telephone cards. Rather than using a calling card, a consumer can purchase a prepaid card that carries a predetermined amount of long-distance calling time. To market its card, GTS has entered into agreements, both in the U.S. and in Canada, with various products (as shown here) and organizations (such as major-league baseball and Sesame Street). GTS must compile and analyze sales and cost data to determine which agreements are worth continuing and which should be ended.

Products

When the profitability of each product or group of products is known, unprofitable models, sizes, or colors can be eliminated. Sales people's compensation plans may be altered to encourage the sale of high-margin items. Channels of distribution may be changed. Instead of selling all of its products directly to business users, for instance, a machine-tools manufacturer shifted to industrial distributors for standard products of low unit value. The company thereby improved the profitability of these products.

Management may decide to discontinue a losing product. But it should not do so without first considering the effect this decision will have on other items sold by the company. Often a low-volume or unprofitable product must be carried simply to round out the product assortment. Supermarkets, for example, carry salt and sugar even though these are profitless for a store. Customers expect a grocery store to carry those items. If they are not available at one store, that seller will lose business, because shoppers will go to other stores that do carry a full complement of grocery products.

Customer Classes and Order Sizes

By combining a sales volume analysis with a cost study, executives can determine the profitability of each group of customers. If one market segment is unprofitable or generates too little profit, then changes may be required in the pricing structure when selling to these customers. Or perhaps customers that have been sold to directly by a producer's sales force should be turned over to wholesaling middlemen. A manufacturer of air conditioners made just such a move when it found that direct sales to individual building contractors were not profitable.

A difficulty plaguing many firms today is the **small-order problem.** Many orders are below the break-even point. Revenue from each of these orders is actually less than allocated expenses. This problem occurs because several costs, such as billing or direct selling, are essentially the same whether the order amounts to $10 or $10,000. Management's immediate reaction may be that no order below the break-even point should be accepted. Or small-volume accounts should be dropped from the customer list. Such decisions may be harmful, however. Some of those small-order customers may, over time, grow into large, profitable accounts.

Management should first determine *why* certain accounts are small-order problems and then figure out how to correct the situation. Proper handling can often turn a losing account into a satisfactory one. For example, a small-order handling charge, which customers would willingly pay, might change the profit picture entirely.

■ SUMMARY

The management process in marketing is the planning, implementation, and evaluation of the marketing effort in an organization. Implementation is the stage in which an organization attempts to carry out its strategic planning. Strategic planning is virtually useless if it is not implemented effectively.

Implementation includes three activities—organizing, staffing, and directing. In organizing, the company should first coordinate all marketing activities into one department whose top executive reports directly to the president. Then, within the marketing department, the company may utilize some form of organizational specialization based on geographic territories, products, or customer types.

Two elements of a marketing program, warranties and postsale service, are implemented largely after a sale is made. Warranties require considerable management attention these days because of consumer complaints and governmental regulations. Product liability is an issue of great consequence to companies because of the financial risk associated with consumers' claims of injuries caused by the firms' products.

Many companies provide postsale service, mainly repairs, to fulfill the terms of their warranties and/or to augment their revenues. To promote customer satisfaction, a number of firms are improving their methods of inviting and responding to consumer complaints.

The evaluation stage in the management process involves measuring performance results against predetermined goals. Evaluation enables management to determine the effectiveness of its implementation and to plan corrective action where necessary. A marketing audit is a key element in a total marketing evaluation program. Most companies are victims of at least some misdirected marketing effort. That is, the 80–20 and iceberg principles are at work in most firms because marketing costs are expended in relation to the number of marketing units (territories, products, customers), rather than to their profit potential. Too many companies do not know how much they should spend for marketing activities, or what results they should get from these expenditures.

Two tools for identifying misdirected marketing efforts are a sales volume analysis and a marketing cost analysis. One problem in marketing cost analysis is allocating costs—especially indirect costs—to the marketing units. Given detailed analyses, management can study sales volume and marketing costs by territories, product lines, customer classes, and/or order sizes. The findings from these analyses can be helpful in shaping decisions regarding a company's marketing program.

More about

TACO BELL

To attain $20 billion in sales by the year 2000, Taco Bell's top management obviously needs to expand the chain in various ways. Presently, there are more than 4,500 Taco Bell restaurants—about 70 percent owned by the company and the remainder owned and operated by franchisees. The company also has over 10,000 additional "points of access" (or POAs) where Taco Bell food can be obtained. These POAs range from areas in convenience stores to school lunch programs to kiosks in airports. More restaurants are planned, but even greater growth is anticipated in the nontraditional POAs, such as kiosks on college campuses and small units in food courts in large shopping malls.

Given its rapid growth and different approach to doing business (notably, outsourcing most of the food preparation), Taco Bell decided to revise the organizational structure for managing its operations. Previously, a field supervisor would oversee and control a group of about six Taco Bell restaurants. Under the new plan, the individual restaurants were given more opportunity to manage themselves. In turn, field supervisors were converted to market managers, who provide advice and support to about 20 restaurants.

In addition, considering the rapid growth of the nontraditional POAs, another position was added to the organizational structure. Each of the new restaurant general managers (RGMs) oversees a "portfolio" of Taco Bell operations, particularly POAs but typically also some regular restaurants. The exact mix in an RGM's portfolio depends on the types and number of POAs and regular units in a particular market.

To improve efficiency and assure customer satisfaction in the future, Taco Bell plans to involve its customers in the service function. With this in mind, the chain has tried out a system that allows patrons to place their own orders using a computer terminal in the restaurant. This setup could reduce labor costs and reduce the time a customer must wait before receiving a meal. And any wait can be made less noticeable because entertainment and promotions can also be shown on the computer screens.

After customers consume their meals, Taco Bell wants to hear from them—especially in the case of a dissatisfying experience. To invite consumers to share their compliments or complaints, Taco Bell posts in its restaurants the toll-free telephone number for its customer service department. Satisfied customers are vital to the success of any firm, but especially to Taco Bell, which wants to increase its sales by 300 percent in less than a decade.[23]

1. Will Taco Bell's revamped organization, emphasizing market managers and restaurant general managers, be able to supervise Taco Bell units closely enough to maintain customer satisfaction and low costs?
2. With its new menu items, such as Border Lights, and its broad collection of regular and nontraditional units, how should Taco Bell go about evaluating its marketing performance?

■ KEY TERMS AND CONCEPTS

Planning (570)	Major-accounts organization (574)	Misdirected (misplaced) marketing effort (580)	Marketing cost analysis (584)
Implementation (570)	Warranty (576)	80–20 principle (580)	Direct costs (588)
Evaluation (570)	Express warranty (576)	Iceberg principle (581)	Indirect costs (588)
Geographic specialization (573)	Implied warranty (576)	Sales volume analysis (582)	Contribution-margin approach (588)
Product specialization (574)	Product liability (576)	Market-share analysis (583)	Full-cost approach (588)
Customer specialization (574)	Warning label (577)		Small-order problem (590)
	Postsale service (577)		
	Marketing audit (579)		

■ QUESTIONS AND PROBLEMS

1. "Good implementation in an organization can overcome poor planning, but good planning cannot overcome poor implementation." Explain, using examples from business periodicals, such as *Business Week* and *The Wall Street Journal*.
2. Give some examples of companies that are likely to organize their sales force by product groups.
3. A manufacturer of small aircraft designed for executive transportation, Cessna for example, has decided to implement the concept of a selling center. Who should be on this company's selling teams? What problems might this manufacturer encounter when it uses team selling?
4. Explain the relationship between a warranty on small electric appliances and the manufacturer's distribution system for these products.
5. a. Should the primary role of postsale service be to assure customer satisfaction or to generate added revenues for the firm?
   b. Would the way in which postsale service is carried out vary depending on its primary role within the firm?
6. A sales volume analysis by territories indicates that the sales of a manufacturer of roofing materials have increased 12 percent a year for the past 3 years in the territory comprising South Carolina, Georgia, and Florida. Does this indicate conclusively that the company's sales volume performance is satisfactory in that territory?
7. A manufacturer found that one product accounted for 35 to 45 percent of the company's total sales in all but 2 of the 18 territories. In each of those two territories, this product accounted for only 14 percent of the company's volume. What factors might account for the relatively low sales of this article in the two districts?
8. What effects may a sales volume analysis by product have on training, supervising, and compensating the sales force?
9. "Firms should discontinue selling losing products." Discuss.
10. Should a company stop selling to an unprofitable customer? Why or why not? If not, then what steps might the company take to make the account a profitable one?

■ HANDS-ON MARKETING

1. Interview a sales executive (a) in a manufacturing company and (b) in either a securities brokerage or a real estate brokerage firm to find out how they motivate their sales forces. As part of your report, give your evaluation of each motivational program.

2. Interview a marketing executive to find out how the total marketing performance is evaluated in his or her company. As part of your report, include your appraisal of this company's evaluation program.

CHAPTER 22

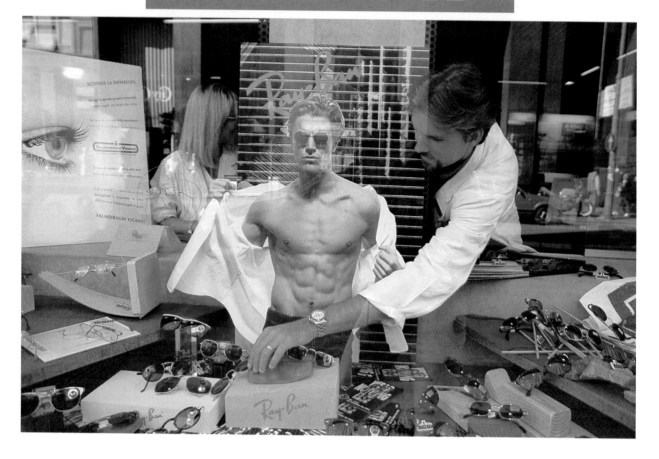

Marketing:
Appraisal
and
Prospects

Was BAUSCH & LOMB's *Vision Distorted?*

Following 12 consecutive years of rapid growth in sales and profits, Bausch & Lomb's 1994 sales increased only slightly and profits declined by nearly $90 million. What lay behind these developments and led to the resignation of the CEO raises interesting questions about Bausch & Lomb's marketing practices and the management style that allowed them to occur.

Bausch & Lomb (B&L) is a manufacturer of optical products (Ray-Ban and Outlook sunglasses, Optima contact lenses), oral-care products (Interplak), and hearing aids (Miracle Ear). From its beginning, B&L had a history of capitalizing on opportunities. The company's first product, developed in the mid-1880s, was a molded, hard-rubber eyeglass frame that cost less than the metal alternative. Its next major success was the development of Ray-Ban nonglare sunglasses for pilots. Over the years they became an international fashion statement. As a result, Ray-Ban now controls 40 percent of the world market for premium-priced sunglasses.

In 1971, B&L obtained the exclusive U.S. rights to produce a soft contact lens developed in Czechoslovakia. The company established a reputation with eye doctors, opticians, and consumers as the industry leader in contact lenses, and soon controlled nearly one-fourth of the worldwide market. However, in the 1980s disposable contact lenses were introduced by Johnson & Johnson, and price competition among lens makers increased.

As part of its early 1980s growth strategy, B&L began setting high sales and earnings goals for all division managers. In addition, incentive pay for managers was heavily weighted to encourage sales. High goals and performance incentives are not unusual in business. However, B&L has been accused of maintaining the pressure despite circumstances that called for adjustments, and then either condoning or ignoring questionable tactics to reach the goals.

By 1993 managers were engaging in some practices that raised eyebrows when they were uncovered. For example:

- The Hong Kong division booked sales that were apparently fictitious since the glasses were never paid for and auditors later found them in a warehouse.
- To meet sales goals, division heads regularly offered large discounts just before the end of a month or quarter. Buyers soon figured out that by delaying their orders they could negotiate lower prices. As a result, it was not uncommon for the B&L distribution centers to ship 70 percent of a month's sales during the last 3 days of the month.
- Optima contact lenses, sold since the 1970s for $70, were repackaged under the brand names Seequence 2 and Medalist and sold as "frequent replacement" lenses to compete with Johnson & Johnson's disposable contacts. These newer brands were priced as low as $7.50.
- Unordered goods were shipped to accounts without authorization and recorded as sales.
- Some distributors were forced to take a 2 years' supply of Optima lenses under the threat of losing B&L as a source of supply.
- B&L encouraged gray marketing by overstocking distributors. For example, to offset intense competition and high import duties in some Asian countries, B&L's Hong Kong division sold Ray-Ban glasses to distributors at 10 to 30 percent below U.S. and European prices. These distributors, in turn, would sell the product to wholesalers in Europe.[1]

Are activities such as these inappropriate or are they to be expected in the business world?

For the most part, we have approached marketing from the viewpoint of the firm, addressing the challenges facing an individual producer or middleman in managing its marketing activity to achieve its goals. Bausch & Lomb presents an interesting illustration of the way goals influence the means used to achieve them, and how that might create problems for an organization.

In this final chapter, we examine the societal dimensions of marketing that were touched on briefly in Chapters 1 and 2. Our discussion begins by identifying the major criticisms of marketing and responses to these criticisms. Then we take a look at the role of ethics in marketing.

Your introduction to marketing concludes with a look into the future. We will highlight some developments and the ways they are changing the practice of marketing.

After studying this chapter, you should be able to explain:

CHAPTER GOALS

- A societal perspective for evaluating marketing performance.
- The major criticisms of marketing.
- Consumer, government, and business responses to consumer discontent.
- Consumerism and its effect on marketing.
- The ethical responsibilities of marketers.
- Trends influencing future marketing activity.
- Some strategic adjustments necessary to cope with change.

Evaluating Marketing

Before we can begin to appraise marketing, we have to agree on a basis for evaluating performance—what the objective of marketing should be. In our discussion of the marketing concept, we said that an organization's objective is to determine consumers' wants and satisfy them. Thus, from the point of view of the *individual organization*, if the firm's target market is satisfied and the organization's objectives are being met, then the marketing effort can be judged successful.

This standard makes no distinction between organizations whose behavior is detrimental to society and those whose activities are socially acceptable. It ignores ethics and good citizenship. Firms that pollute the environment or stimulate unwholesome demand could qualify as good marketers right along with firms that behave responsibly. Therefore, we must take a broader, *societal view* that incorporates the best interests of others as well as the desires of a particular target market and the objectives of the marketer to satisfy that market.

Marketing must balance the wants of consumers, the objectives of the organization, *and* the welfare of society. There is evidence all around us of the essential nature of these three criteria. If a product does not *meet consumers' needs*, the consumers will not buy it and it will be forced from the market. Clear products—gasoline, soap, beer, soft drinks—have largely disappeared because they offered only novelty, a benefit that quickly fades.[2] The largest failure in recent marketing history, estimated to have cost RJR Nabisco $300 million, was Premier, a smokeless cigarette. This product was intended to be the answer to society's criticism of smoking, but neither critics nor smokers found it satisfactory.[3]

Likewise, if a firm behaves in a fashion viewed as *detrimental to society*, government will intervene, as it did when there were accusations that Archer-Daniels-Midland, a giant food and agricultural products company, was colluding with competitors to fix prices. And some products are discontinued because they fail to *achieve the organization's objectives.* Following accusations of declining attendance and inadequate civic support, a number of major-league sports franchises have moved to new cities where they expect to generate higher profits. For example, the Los Angeles Rams football team moved to St. Louis and the Quebec Nordiques hockey team is now the Colorado Avalanche.

Criticisms of Marketing

Criticisms of marketing center on action or inaction that relates to the balance among the wants of customers, the well-being of society, and organizational objectives. These criticisms of marketing can be categorized as follows:

- *Exploitation.* Marketers are sometimes accused of taking unfair advantage of consumers or situations. For example, it is not uncommon to hear reports of price gouging following hurricanes and floods. Another form of exploitation is misleading prospects with false or incomplete information. The chief executive of an herbal medicine firm said, "We're learning to use the thesaurus" in describing his firm's effort to claim as much as possible for its products without violating government regulations on advertising.[4] These behaviors may meet the organization's goal of sales and profits, but they may be detrimental to consumers, society, or both.

- *Inefficiency.* Some critics feel that marketers use more resources than are necessary to accomplish their objectives. Ford is said to have spent $3 billion redesigning the Ford Taurus, already one of the most successful automobile models in history. There are also accusations about unnecessary distribution functions, and excessive numbers of brands in many product categories. These kinds of practices result in higher costs to organizations, higher prices to consumers, and, some say, a waste of society's resources.

- *Stimulating unwholesome demand.* Some marketers have been criticized for promoting the purchase of products viewed as unhealthy or dangerous. Cigarette makers have been accused of encouraging young people to smoke. And, because of their widespread misuse, many people believe that the marketing of inexpensive handguns is socially unacceptable.

- *Illegal behavior.* Laws are passed to protect individuals, organizations, and society in general. Marketers are expected to abide by these laws, even when violating a law may benefit consumers or an organization. Collusion between would-be competitors, for instance, may meet the needs of the organizations involved. It might even result in lower prices for consumers than price competition, because the colluding firms could more accurately forecast demand and significantly reduce their promotion expenditures. However, it is detrimental to competitors of the colluding firms. Therefore, since the behavior is unfair to others in society, it is unacceptable.

Another way of looking at the criticisms of marketing is through the components of the marketing mix—product, price, distribution, and promotion. Some specific examples are described below, but keep in mind that these are not general abuses. They are allegations, often with some merit, but they do not reflect typical business practice.

Product. Criticisms of products generally center on how well they meet buyers' expectations. Critics charge that some products are of inadequate quality to withstand normal use, or are unsafe. Other examples include packages that appear to contain more of a product than they actually do; labels that provide insufficient or misleading information; and products advertised as "new" that appear to offer only trivial changes. Critics also argue that style obsolescence, particularly in clothing, encourages consumers to discard products before they are worn out, and that there is an unnecessary proliferation of brands in many food and household product categories such as breakfast cereal, cosmetics, and pet food. As a result, buyers are confused and production capacity is wasted.

Price. Everyone would like to pay less for products, but most buyers are satisfied with what they consider a fair exchange. Complaints about prices usually arise from the perception that the seller is making an excessive profit, or that the buyer has been misled about prices because of hidden charges or complicated terms of sale. A recent accusation is that some supermarkets advertise reduced prices but don't program the reductions into their checkout scanners. As a result, consumers who aren't alert get charged the original price. Critics feel that price competition has been largely replaced by nonprice competition in the form of unnecessary product features that add more to the cost than to the value of a product.

Distribution. Of the four marketing-mix variables, the least understood and appreciated by consumers is distribution. In part, this is due to the fact that consumers are aware that there is no change in the appearance of a product between the time it leaves the factory and when they buy it from a retailer. Yet the price of the product, as it flows through the channel of distribution, may double. Channels are sometimes seen as having too many levels of middlemen, and channel members are accused of performing needless or repetitive functions. Some manufacturers pressure channel members to carry their less attractive products in order to get their more attractive ones. As a result, the channel members have higher capital and inventory costs, which are passed along to customers.

Promotion. The most frequent accusations against marketing focus on promotion—especially personal selling and advertising. Most of the complaints about personal selling are aimed at the retail level and the allegedly poor quality of retail service.

Criticisms of advertising fall into two categories—social and economic. From a social viewpoint, advertising is charged with overemphasizing material standards of living and underemphasizing cultural and moral values. The counterargument is that advertising does not create society's values, it reflects them. A product cannot be successful unless it satisfies the needs of the market. Granted some of those needs may be distasteful to certain segments of the population, but that doesn't make satisfying them inappropriate.

The economic criticisms center on the effect of advertising on prices and competition. The price argument goes like this. Advertising, particularly persuasive as opposed to informative ads, merely shifts demand from one brand to another. As a result, it only adds to the individual firms' marketing costs without increasing aggregate demand. Since the advertising must be paid for, the price of the product goes up. There is a counterargument that advertising results in lower prices because it is an efficient method of reaching many people at a low cost per person. The mass market generated by the advertising results in economies of scale in purchasing, manufacturing, and distribution. These economies result in lower costs that more than offset the advertising expense, and the firm is able to charge lower prices than would be possible without the ads.

The other economic criticism of advertising is made from the perspective of competitive impact. It suggests that large firms differentiate their products through advertising. That is, through extensive advertising, they create the impression in consumers' minds that their brands are better than the brands of less-well-known rivals. In this way they create barriers to market entry for new or smaller firms. The result is an industry with a small number of firms, which leads to higher prices and higher profits. The counterargument to this position is that advertising informs consumers about a product. If consumers find the information persuasive, they will try the product and return for more if they are satisfied. If they are not satisfied, no amount of advertising will bring them back. The fact that larger firms advertise more than smaller firms simply indicates that their products are valued by consumers.

Advertising is also accused of manipulating impressionable people, especially children; making statements that are false, deceptive, or in bad taste; making exaggerated claims for products; and overusing fear and sexual appeals. Critics also argue that there is simply too much advertising and that ad placement is often offensive. For example, many people resent "captive advertising" that is presented on cable TV in places like schools, doctors' waiting rooms, and airports.

Right or wrong, marketers must take all allegations seriously because they reflect the perceptions of many people. We'll see next how marketers and society can deal with the allegations and the perceptions.

Understanding the Criticisms

To evaluate the charges against marketing, we must understand what actually is being criticized. Is the object of the complaint ultimately the U.S. economic system? An entire industry? A particular firm? If the criticism applies to a firm, is the marketing department or some other department the culprit?

Our free-enterprise system encourages competition, and government regulatory bodies for many years have judged competition by the number of competitors in an industry. Thus when we complain about the number of toothpaste or cereal brands on the market, we are really criticizing the system.

Within a particular firm, a faulty product may result from production, not marketing problems. Clearly, a failure in manufacturing does not make consumers' complaints less valid. The point is that marketing is not to blame for every business mistake.

AN ETHICAL DILEMMA?

Industry-sponsored promotions are appearing all over public schools. Posters and lesson plans provided by firms offer information on everything from nutrition to study habits. Channel One gives schools video equipment with the requirement that students watch a 10-minute news show each day that is interspersed with 2 minutes of commercial messages. School buses are adorned with corporate logos on their sides. Fast-food companies give the schools coupons to use as rewards for students' good performance. With schools strapped for cash, some see these promotions as a source of much needed revenues. Others find it inappropriate for ads and other forms of promotion to appear in an educational setting.

Is it unethical for a firm to offer a school an incentive to distribute its promotional materials?

Source: Betsy Wagner, "Our Class Is Brought to You Today by . . . ," *U.S. News & World Report*, Apr. 24, 1995, p. 63.

We also need to consider the sources of criticism. Some critics are well intentioned and well informed. They point out real weaknesses or errors needing correction, such as deceptive packaging, misleading advertising, and irresponsible pricing. But some critics are simply ill informed. They do not understand the utilities provided by distribution functions or are not aware of the costs of producing and selling a product. As a result, though their criticisms may have popular appeal, they cannot withstand careful scrutiny.

There are other types of critics whose views do not reflect the sentiments of society. To serve their own interests, they vociferously criticize behavior they find objectionable. Some of the protests against the use of advertising by health professionals and lawyers is an example. We must examine criticism carefully to separate the legitimate from the erroneous and self-serving.

Operating in a socially undesirable manner is unacceptable. Fortunately, this kind of behavior is only a small part of all the marketing that occurs, although it is widely publicized. More common, and more disturbing, are the situations that are not clear-cut. These are debatable issues such as full disclosure in advertising (What is the meaning of "full"?); planned obsolescence (How long should a product last?); and the cost of marketing (How much should it cost to develop, distribute, and promote a product?).

Responses to Criticisms of Marketing

Efforts to address the problems that exist in or result from marketing activity have come from consumers, the government, and business organizations. In the following paragraphs we discuss some of these responses to marketing problems.

Consumer Responses

A consumer acting alone is unlikely to have much effect on a firm or an industry. However, a group of consumers acting in unison can have an impact. This is known as **consumerism**, a protest against and the attempts to remedy perceived injustices in the relationships between businesses and consumers. Many consumers believe that, in a transaction, a business has much more power than the consumer. Consumerism is an expression of this opinion and an effort to obtain a more equal balance of power between buyers and sellers.

Scope of Consumerism. Consumerism covers three broad areas:

- *Discontent with direct buyer-seller relationships.* This is the original and still the main focus of consumerism. Efforts to remove potentially hazardous toys from the market is an example.
- *Discontent with nonprofit organizations and governmental agencies.* Consumerism extends to all exchange relationships. The performance of organizations such as schools (quality of education, performance of students on standardized tests, number of class days per year); hospitals (medical care costs, malpractice); and public utilities (rate increases, eliminating service to people unable to pay their bills) has been scrutinized and subjected to organized and spirited consumer protests.
- *Discontent of those indirectly affected by the behavior of participants in an exchange.* Transactions can sometimes have a negative impact on others. For example, farmers buy insecticides and pesticides from chemical companies.

However, runoffs containing these products are said to pollute water supplies, rivers, and lakes. Thus an exchange has created a problem for a third party or group.

Consumer Actions. Consumer reactions to marketing problems have ranged from complaints registered with offending organizations to boycotts (refusing to buy a particular product or to shop at a certain store). Consumer groups have recognized their potential power and have become more active politically. They organize mass letter-writing campaigns to editors, legislators, and business executives. And they support consumer-oriented political candidates, conduct petition drives, and gain media attention through sit-ins and picketing.

In recent years, organizations at both the local and national levels have brought greater attention to consumer protection. Some of these organizations are multi-issue groups (Common Cause, National Consumers' League) and others are special-interest groups (American Association of Retired Persons, Mothers Against Drunk Driving). Some organizations deal primarily with buyer-seller exchange relationships (Consumers Union), while others support broader causes with exchange implications (Sierra Club, Audubon Society).

Consumerism in the Future. Cultural conditions seem to have moved us away from brief periods of heightened consumerism to a more constant level of concern. Consumers today are generally more sensitive to social and environmental issues. Along with sources of dissatisfaction already described, the plight of the poor, waste disposal, urbanization, and the treatment of animals in medical and cosmetic research are other social and environmental causes receiving attention.

In addition, more people are willing and able to take an active role in consumerism. Compared to earlier generations, young people are better educated, more articulate, and more inclined to speak out. People of all ages are generally less intimidated by large organizations and less willing to accept the status quo. Responding to this increased public sensitivity, many politicians are also demonstrating greater concern for societal issues.

Since problems remain, consumerism in the remainder of the decade will focus on some of the same areas as in the past. For example, fair treatment for disadvantaged consumers and personal safety will be major concerns. In addition, waste management, efficient utilization of resources, and the preservation of natural beauty are environmental issues that will likely draw continued attention.

Government Responses

At the federal level there are many laws designed to protect consumers. One set asserts the "right to safety," including auto safety, toy safety, and the purity and integrity of virtually every product on the market. Federal legislation also supports consumers' "right to be informed." These regulations deal with such issues as labeling requirements, nutritional content of food, disclosure of the interest rate on credit purchases, and advertising messages.

Several federal regulatory agencies are empowered to protect consumers. Among the most significant are the Food and Drug Administration, Federal Trade Commission, Environmental Protection Agency, and Consumer Product Safety Commission. For example, Campbell Soup Co. changed its advertising after the Federal Trade Commission charged that Campbell ads linking the low-cholesterol, low-fat content of its soups with a reduced risk of heart disease misled consumers because they did not include a warning about the soups' high sodium content.[5]

http://www.campbellsoups.com/

In state legislatures there has been considerable interest in consumer-support laws. Most states and large cities regulate door-to-door selling (as discussed in Chapter 14). Furthermore, the attorney general's offices in most states have become much more active in consumer protection. In the past they focused on obviously fraudulent behavior such as get-rich-quick schemes and soliciting for nonexistent charities. Recently, however, many have broadened their scope and quickened their pace. For example, the offices in several states cooperated in uncovering and pursuing situations in which Sears' auto-center service personnel were systematically recommending unneeded repairs to customers' cars.

There are also proactive efforts by government agencies to discourage the consumption of products deemed unsafe or unwholesome. One example is the warning labels on cigarettes and alcoholic beverages. In another instance, the Minnesota Department of Public Health conducted a television and radio antismoking advertising campaign aimed at women. Governments in over 20 countries operate ecology-labeling programs that permit products meeting certain standards to carry a particular designation.[6]

It is difficult to judge the effectiveness of government effort, since it depends on one's perspective. From the point of view of many consumer advocates, the government is too slow to act, and too many issues are ignored or overlooked. Alternatively, those who believe that competition provides sufficient regulation would prefer fewer laws and view government activity as interference.

In evaluating consumer protection, we need to recognize that there are trade-offs. For example, there are costs involved in providing more information, designing and manufacturing products to eliminate all hazards, and keeping the environment clean. These costs ultimately must be paid for by consumers and, therefore, must be weighed against the expected benefits. Often these are difficult comparisons; some, for instance, involve costs incurred now for benefits not realized until some time in the future or accruing to only a few people.

In an effort to open its market of 900 million consumers to foreign firms, India has reduced its import duties on many goods. However, equally severe barriers remain. For example, Indian consumers who see Western products as a threat to their culture have staged violent protests against Pepsi and KFC. Another problem is the unethical pirating of brand names. In this photo, the Indian government drew attention to its opposition to the practice by having an elephant destroy pirated Mickey Mouse toys.

Business Responses

An increasing number of businesses are making substantive responses to consumer problems. Here are a few examples:

http://www.att.com/

- *Better communications with consumers.* Many firms have responded positively to the desire of consumers to be heard. No-charge 800 phone numbers have become an integral part of customer service because they are easy to use and allow consumers to speak directly to a representative of the firm. AT&T has two toll-free 800 directories, one for consumers and one for businesses, with over 180,000 listings.
- *More and better information for consumers.* Companies such as Goodyear Tire and Rubber, American Express, Coca-Cola, Oscar Mayer Foods, and Gulf Oil all work with the federal government's Consumer Information Center to publish and distribute noncommercial educational pamphlets. On topics such as personal financial planning, credit rights, and how to approach a company with a complaint, the pamphlets must meet government standards for accuracy, objectivity, and completeness. Also, warranty and instructional information is constantly improving. Guarantees and warranties are being made simpler and easier to read. Manufacturers' instruction manuals on the assembly, use, and care of their products are more detailed and accurate.
- *More carefully prepared advertising.* Concerns about false and misleading claims as well as ads that might be offensive to some group or simply in poor taste have caused firms to review advertising content very carefully. But the system is not perfect. Some consumers, for example, are distressed by mass-media ads for personal-care products and undergarments, ads that are directed to young children, and ads that rely on sexually oriented themes.

The fact that there are marketing "problems" indicates some marketers are engaging in inappropriate behavior. Thus we should go beyond responses by consumers, government, and business to examine how the problems can be prevented. This brings us to a discussion of ethics and social responsibility.

Ethics and Marketing

Ethics are standards of moral conduct. To act in an ethical fashion is to conform to an accepted standard of moral behavior. Undoubtedly, virtually all people prefer to act ethically. It is easy to be ethical when no hardship is involved—when a person is winning and life is going well. The test comes when things are not going well—when pressures build. These pressures arise in all walks of life, and marketing is no exception.

Marketing executives face the challenge of balancing their own best interests (recognition, pay, and promotion) with the best interests of their organizations, consumers, and society into a workable guide for their daily activities. In any situation they must be able to distinguish what is ethical from what is unethical and act accordingly, regardless of the possible consequences. However, as you have seen in the Ethical Dilemma boxes presented throughout this book and the Bausch & Lomb chapter-opening case, what constitutes acceptable behavior is often far from straightforward.

Setting Ethical Guidelines

Many organizations have formal codes of ethics that identify specific acts (bribery, accepting gifts) as unethical and describe the standards employees are expected to live up to. Over 90 percent of the 1,000 largest U.S. companies have ethics codes,[7] as do many smaller businesses. These guidelines lessen the chance that an employee will knowingly or unknowingly violate a company's standards. In addition, ethics codes strengthen a company's hand in dealing with customers or prospects who encourage unethical behavior. For young or inexperienced executives, these codes can be valuable guides, helping them resist the pressure to compromise personal ethics in order to move up in the firm.

http://www.arthurandersen.com/

However, every decision cannot be taken out of the hands of the manager. Furthermore, determining what is right and what is wrong can be extremely difficult. It is not realistic for an organization to construct a two-column list of all possible practices, one headed "ethical" and the other "unethical." Rather, a marketer must be able to evaluate a situation and formulate a response. Arthur Andersen and Co. has developed an ethical reasoning model that can be taught to current and future managers.[8] The model expands the traditional cost-benefit analysis to include all the individuals and groups affected, not just the decision maker's organization, to help clarify the ethical dimensions of a decision. The procedure consists of:

1. Identifying the decision options and the likely consequences of each.
2. Identifying all individuals and organizations that will be positively or negatively affected by the consequences of each option.
3. Estimating the negative impact (costs) and positive impact (benefits) of each option from the point of view of the affected party, taking into consideration each one's particular interests and needs.
4. Ranking the costs and the benefits of each option and making a decision.

This approach is an attempt to be systematic and logical in ethical decisions. It will work only if the decision maker can be objective and impartial, and if there are sufficient time and motivation to do the required analysis. However, ethical situations are frequently charged with emotion and decisions must be made quickly. Thus, an alternative approach that attempts to personalize the situation may be more practical. When faced with an ethical problem, honest answers to the following questions should indicate which route to follow:

- Would I do this to a friend?
- Would I be willing to have this done to me?
- Would I be embarrassed if this action were publicized nationally?

Pragmatic Reasons for Behaving Ethically

Marketing executives should practice ethical behavior because it is morally correct. While this is simple and beautiful in concept, it is not sufficient motivation for everyone. So let's consider four pragmatic reasons for ethical behavior:

- *To reverse declining public confidence in marketing.* Periodically we hear about misleading package labels, false claims in ads, phony list prices, and infringements of well-established trademarks. Though such practices are limited to only a small proportion of marketing, they damage the reputations of all marketers. To reverse this situation, business leaders must demonstrate convincingly that they are aware of their ethical responsibilities and will fulfill them. Companies must set high ethical standards and enforce them. Moreover, it is in management's interest to be concerned with the well-being of consumers, since they are the lifeblood of a business.
- *To avoid increases in government regulation.* Our economic freedoms sometimes have a high price, just as our political freedoms do. Business apathy, resistance, or token response to unethical behavior simply increases the prob-

ability of more government regulation. Indeed, most governmental limitations on marketing are the result of management's failure to live up to its ethical responsibilities at one time or other. Moreover, once some form of government control has been introduced, it is rarely removed.

- *To retain the power granted by society.* Marketing executives wield a great deal of social power as they influence markets and speak out on economic issues. However, there is responsibility tied to that power. If marketers do not use their power in a socially acceptable manner, that power will be lost in the long run.
- *To protect the image of the organization.* Buyers often form an impression of an entire organization based on their contact with one person. More often than not, that person represents the marketing function. You may base your opinion of a retail store on the behavior of a single sales clerk. As Procter & Gamble put it in an annual report: "When a Procter & Gamble sales person walks into a customer's place of business . . . that sales person not only represents Procter & Gamble, but in a very real sense, that person is Procter & Gamble."

http://www.pg.com/

Socially Responsible Behavior

Ethical behavior goes beyond avoiding wrongdoing. The ethical marketer recognizes that the position he or she holds in society carries with it certain obligations. Thus, **social responsibility** involves improving the well-being of society. Besides obeying the law and meeting the normal and reasonable expectations of the public, socially responsible organizations and individuals lead the way in setting the standards of business and community performance. For example, Dollar General Stores, a general merchandise chain targeted at households with incomes of $25,000 or less, is experimenting with a store placed in a Nashville housing project. The firm is learning what will work in a setting avoided by most retailers, and community members are gaining pride and self-respect as the store's employees.[9]

Ethics and the Consumer

Acting ethically is not a one-way street. Consumers also have a responsibility to behave ethically. Business firms are increasingly experiencing unethical consumer behavior. Shoplifting, fraudulent coupon redemption, vandalism, fraudulent check cashing, and other consumer abuses have become major costs for organizations. Although determining exactly how much consumer fraud occurs is virtually impossible, reliable estimates are disheartening:[10]

- Recent figures for shoplifting place the amount at $5 billion to $25 billion per year and increasing. The five largest U.S. retailers alone lose about $2 billion annually to shrinkage (errors, employee theft, and shoplifting), with shoplifting accounting for the largest portion.
- More than 500 million bad checks are written each year.
- Credit card fraud amounts to over $1 billion per year.
- The cost to the retailing and banking industries of check-related fraud is $10 billion per year.

Of course, the high incidence of unethical consumer behavior does not excuse inappropriate business practices. These examples simply illustrate how widespread unethical behavior has become. What the facts make abundantly clear is the need for a system-wide exploration of ways to reduce this problem in business, among consumers, and within all other social institutions.

Prospects for the Future

Let's move now from looking at how marketers can and should behave to a description of what lies ahead for marketing. More specifically, in order to be more effective and efficient, what do marketers need to know and what do they need to do?

Consider, for example, the high failure rate of new products. In the grocery category alone, 20,000 new products are introduced every year. The firms that produce these products have high hopes for them. But the unhappy truth is that most fail. What explains the failures? Part of the problem is an inability to accurately anticipate the future. Although the future cannot be predicted with certainty, it need not be a complete mystery. Managers are responsible for monitoring what is happening in the marketplace, identifying opportunities, and responding with want-satisfying products. In what follows, we have tried to give you a flavor of that process by describing market trends and noting some of the likely marketing responses to them.

Marketplace Trends

Successful marketers are those who anticipate trends and respond to them in a want-satisfying way, while also achieving the organization's financial objectives. The question is, how are trends spotted? One approach is to track the changes in the environment, in business behavior, and, of course, in the ultimate consumers. Examples of each are described below.

The Environment.
There are changes taking place in the environment all the time. However, some developments are particularly significant because they impact our lives so dramatically. One of these is the convergence of personal computers and the Internet, a combination that potentially will revolutionize the way we send and receive information.

For this technology to have its effect, individuals had to become comfortable using computers. This has largely been accomplished through the widespread availability of computers on the job, in schools, and more recently in homes. In a recent survey of adult Americans, 72 percent said they are comfortable with computer technology.[11] The next step was to provide widespread interaction between computer users, no matter their location or equipment. The Internet has made that possible. Though it has been in existence for over 25 years, the Internet's personal and commercial potential has only recently begun to be explored.

The two most dramatic features of the Internet are electronic mail and the World Wide Web. Subscribers to an on-line service can transmit electronic messages (e-mail) across the street or across the globe. And the World Wide Web, a system of networks on the Internet, has created a vast electronic library and marketplace.

The Web has enormous commercial potential. Experiments are under way with chains such as Winn-Dixie and Vons to see how effectively consumers can use the system to buy products that normally would require a trip to a supermarket or drugstore. Its graphics capability permits pictures and video to be sent anywhere in the world. Through its intricate links, it allows buyers and sellers to find one another. Virtual malls are being created that will permit consumers to visually visit stores and make purchases in front of their computers.

The number of people using this technology is growing rapidly. In late 1995 it was estimated that 37 million people in the U.S. and Canada had access to the Internet.[12] To communicate with these potential customers, the number of businesses setting up Web sites is expanding geometrically. It seems no one wants to be left out of this developing medium.

Business Behavior. Marketers also try to monitor what other businesses are doing. New products and business ventures reflect the best thinking of the managers who introduce them. Much can be learned from their successes and failures. To illustrate, let's consider what some of the hot areas of business development are.

Certainly one is related to the Internet described above. Producing the hardware and software, as well as providing the services users will need, is a booming industry. There are also products being developed for the Web. For example, Paul Allen, Microsoft's cofounder, has created Starwave Corp. It is a commercial service on the Web that charges subscribers for up-to-the-minute information on spectator sports, entertainment, outdoor recreation, parenting, and more.

Other growth industries are legalized gambling, midscale restaurants (between fast food and formal dining), home health care, family entertainment centers, microbreweries, educational toys, and adventure tourism. What other opportunities are businesses acting on? Among the areas growing in popularity are golf, holistic approaches to fitness, aromatherapy, virtual reality, and videoconferencing.[13] By examining developments such as these and investigating their commercial aspects, marketers identify new ideas and refine their thinking.

Demographic Changes. The size and makeup of the U.S. population are changing. The Census Bureau is predicting a population of 276 million by the year 2000, and 325 million by 2020.[14] In addition to its size, the composition of the population is changing. By the year 2000, one-third of all U.S. children will be from minority groups. Not surprisingly, the population is also getting older. In 1950 only 10 percent of the population was over age 65; by 2030 that proportion will double as senior citizens become the fastest-growing age group.

Households are also changing. By 2000 only about 50 percent of households will be married couples. Single-parent households will increase by 50 percent, nonfamily households will more than double, and more people than ever will be living alone. In addition, the proportion of women who work outside the home will continue to increase.

http://www.starwave.com/

This is an actual screen from a promotional service available on the Internet. Subscribers to the service scan ads on their home computers and print the coupons they want to use. Marketers are able to specify the demographics and geographic locations of targeted consumers, so the package received by a particular household is customized. When a coupon is printed, it includes a unique household ID code. Then, when the coupon is redeemed, it can be traced to the user. Marketers using the service are provided with demographic, life-style, and product preference data on the individual households that receive, print, and redeem a coupon. The resulting data base is used to design and direct the firm's promotional program.

What do these demographic changes tell us? First, the changing composition of the population will force marketers who have become comfortable targeting baby boomers to make adjustments. The next generation, born between the mid-1960s and mid-1970s, is entering the mainstream of life as consumers who are very different than their predecessors. They are the first generation of latchkey children, dual-career households, and a parental divorce rate of 50 percent. They are experienced buyers, having been involved at an earlier age in household decision making and purchasing than any previous generation. And they have had more exposure to advertising, particularly on television, than the groups that have gone before them. Some observers feel that this translates into a generation of more sophisticated and cynical consumers who will require marketers to rethink products and appeals to be successful.

Time will become even more valuable as we approach the end of the century. Smaller households, single-parent families, the proportion of two-wage-earner households, and the high proportion of working women all mean fewer people to perform normal household chores. The resulting time pressure on households will result in a growing demand for things like day care for children and elderly parents, greater convenience in shopping, and electronic purchasing.

New marketing opportunities will emerge. For example, the aging population creates the need for products modified to accommodate the physical limitations of the elderly (labels and instructions in large print, easy-to-open containers, equipment and vehicles to aid mobility), as well as expanded marketing opportunities in such areas as travel and tourism and health and medical care.

Greater ethnic diversity will result from increases in the Hispanic, Asian American, and African American populations. These groups are large enough to attract the attention of marketers, but they present interesting challenges. When, for example, do their similarities suggest that they should be treated as a single segment? Campbell Soup's Casera brand of beans failed to meet the firm's expectations because it was targeted at a broad spectrum of Hispanics. What Campbell failed to recognize is the considerable diversity in food preferences across various Hispanic groups.[15]

Dramatic developments are taking place in other parts of the world as well.[16] The world population is expected to increase to 6.2 billion by 2000, and expand by another 2 billion by 2025. The fastest-growing areas are Africa, Latin America, and South Asia. One interesting trend is the rapid expansion of urban areas in developing countries. By the year 2000, 17 of the 20 largest urban areas in the world will be in developing countries! The only other cities in the top 20 will be Tokyo, New York, and Los Angeles. The world's largest cities will be Mexico City and São Paulo.

Of course, more people does not necessarily translate into potential markets. Africa, for example, is expected to continue having very low or negative rates of per capita economic growth. Many Latin American countries have large foreign debts. Since debt is reduced by internal economic growth and a positive balance of trade, these countries try to limit imports. Thus, marketers will have to examine developments closely to determine where opportunities exist.

Strategic Issues

The one certainty that marketers can count on is that change is inevitable. A common response to change is simply to react as it occurs. However, realizing that change is a constant, marketers should initiate strategic proactive efforts to improve performance. Several are described in this section.

Instilling a Market-Driven Orientation. Describing the marketing concept and implementing it in an organization are two different things. The concept—combining a customer orientation with coordinated marketing and the organization's goals—certainly has intuitive appeal, yet many organizations seem unable to practice it consistently. Despite having been taught in business schools for over 50 years, its effective implementation seems to be the exception rather than the rule. Practicing the marketing concept requires at least the following:[17]

- *Give the customer priority*. The marketing concept focuses on the customer's needs. However, when faced with the choice of putting the customer first or meeting their own needs, employees often find it difficult to give the customer priority. Instilling this orientation requires top-management commitment. Lip service is not sufficient. Employees must see management put the customer first. If employees see imperfect products leave the factory or ads with exaggerated claims, they can only conclude that management doesn't respect its customers.

- *Displays of customer orientation must be rewarded*. Employees must be empowered to make decisions that recognize the importance of customers and be publicly rewarded for those decisions.

- *Organizations must remain in contact with the market*. This means having detailed, accurate market knowledge. Buyers are becoming less and less willing to compromise to satisfy their desires. Marketers must develop more marketing programs for smaller markets. Good information and decision-support systems are needed in making these decisions. In consumer marketing this means conducting research on a continuous basis. In business-to-business marketing it may mean creating new structures. We'll have more to say about this below.

- *A firm needs to be best at something*. A sustainable differential advantage must be established. Every successful firm matches its capabilities with its customers' needs better than the competition. That uniqueness may be in market knowledge, low-cost manufacturing, product development, distribution, or some other dimension. Who, for example, would think that Nike could produce a line of shoes that would fail? It did. A line of casual shoes never made a dent in the market. Being skilled at producing and marketing athletic shoes did not automatically transfer to another product, even a closely related one. Nike's differential advantage is in sports and fitness products. That is what it does well and where its advantage exists.

- *All exchange partners, not just customers, must be satisfied*. Exchange partners of an organization include its customers, suppliers, middlemen, owners, regulators, and anyone else it interacts with. If suppliers, for example, consider their exchanges with an organization unsatisfactory, they will not do everything in their power to ensure that the final customers' needs will be met. The same is true of employees. Essential to satisfying final customers are strong, positive relationships among all the parties who contribute to bringing a product to market.

http://www.nike.com/

Adopting a Global Orientation. To be successful in the future, marketers must adopt a global orientation toward markets, products, and marketing activity. In the past most firms could be successful by focusing on the domestic market and outperforming local rivals. However, that has changed. Now firms, both large and small, are going where the markets are the most attractive. For example, consumers in Kuala Lumpur buy American products at Makro, a Dutch-owned retail chain. Other retailers are rapidly expanding around the world. Carrefour, a French firm, operates a huge store in Shanghai, Kmart has more than a dozen stores in Eastern Europe, and Wal-Mart has joint ventures in Hong Kong and China.[18]

Small firms that once viewed selling in international markets as too complicated or unprofitable are also finding ways to compete. A recent survey estimates that nearly 25 percent of small businesses (those with fewer than 500 employees) exported products in 1995. Small businesses accounted for over half of all manufactured goods exported from the U.S. Producers of such diverse products as industrial drill bits, horse feed, car soap, scooters for the disabled, and oil spill cleanup equipment have found markets abroad.[19]

Organizations must also think globally when it comes to products. U.S. firms have learned manufacturing techniques from foreign competitors that get products to market quicker and with a higher quality level. But there are important lessons to be learned in marketing as well. One area is product development.

Historically, U.S. firms have maintained their departmental structure when developing products. In the case of automobiles, for example, the design department might come up with an idea for a new engine. The idea would then go to engineering, which might decide the idea was too difficult or costly and bounce it back. The idea would either die or be revised for reconsideration. This process, multiplied many times, would take an enormous amount of time and would lead to many unsatisfactory compromises.

An alternative is a product-development team headed by a leader with real power. The team consists of representatives from all departments—engineering, design, purchasing, finance, marketing, and manufacturing—who are responsible to the team leader. In this system, if the team decides the car needs a new engine, each representative carries the proposal back to his or her department and makes certain the job gets done. This team approach is used by Japanese automakers. It was

http://www.chrysler.com/

adopted by Chrysler to develop its LH line of midsize cars (Eagle Vision, Dodge Intrepid, and Chrysler Concorde) and resulted in significant time and cost savings.

In designing products, from ingredients to packaging, labeling, and branding, firms should consider global implications. If a possibility exists for expanding internationally, the time to build compatibility into the product is at the beginning. For example, major soap and detergent makers once thought that standardized fragrances were impossible because preferences varied so much from country to country. However, they now assemble data on fragrance preferences from around the world in search of transnational similarities in tastes. Avon conducted a simi-

http://www.avon.com/

lar search in selecting the name for Far Away, a fragrance that is sold in 10 countries. By thinking globally, a firm can avoid problems such as having to change the ingredients, brand name, packaging material, or label information in order to enter foreign markets.

Emphasizing Quality and Value. In the 1970s many U.S. industries recognized that the quality of their products was significantly below the quality of competitors' products from other countries. To correct the problem, they adopted a variety of quality-instilling techniques. One of the most popular was developed by two American consultants, W. Edwards Deming and Joseph Juran, and has been practiced by the Japanese since the 1950s. Called **total quality management (TQM)**, it is the application of quality principles to all endeavors of an organization, not just manufacturing. It is a business philosophy that stresses a teamwork approach that involves every employee of a company.

A GLOBAL PERSPECTIVE

NAFTA, TAFTA, AND FTAA—ALPHABET SOUP OR THE FUTURE OF TRADE IN THE WESTERN HEMISPHERE?

The North American Free Trade Agreement (known as NAFTA) linking the U.S., Canada, and Mexico went into effect in January 1994. The most important feature of the agreement calls for the elimination of tariffs and import quotas over a period of 15 years. (A preexisting agreement between Canada and the U.S. to reduce trade barriers in 10 years went into effect in 1989.) Supporters promised dramatic short-term benefits, and critics predicted only gloom and doom. In fact, none of the forecasts have come true. The phasing-in of the agreement along with the unexpected 40 percent devaluation of the peso in December 1994 dampened its immediate effects. So, it remains unclear if or how NAFTA will ultimately benefit or harm its participants.

Despite the uncertainty surrounding NAFTA, the foreign ministers of the European Union (EU) countries are working with the U.S. on TAFTA, the Trans Atlantic Free Trade Agreement. Although trade between the U.S. and the EU countries is relatively free of barriers already, there are a number of differences in standards an agreement might address. For example, the wall sockets in Europe differ from those in the U.S., so electric plugs and appliances are not interchangeable, and the required automobile safety features differ, so cars must be designed differently for domestic and export markets. Thus, the short-term

objectives of TAFTA are more modest than those of NAFTA; however, the ultimate goal is to make trade across the Atlantic easier and more efficient.

And then there's FTAA, the Free Trade Area of the Americas. The 34 countries in the Western Hemisphere with democratically elected governments are meeting with the goal of having an agreement by 2005 that will remove or reduce the barriers to trade. If an agreement is worked out, it will encompass a $12 trillion market with over 800 million consumers.

What are the implications of these developments for the marketers of the future? It seems clear that the movement toward reduced trade barriers is unstoppable. Lower barriers means that foreign trade and investment opportunities will certainly grow. However, it also means that firms will face intensified competition as foreign products increasingly invade their local markets. Maybe most important, the marketing executive of the future who only understands his or her own domestic market, a task viewed as daunting just a few years ago, will be hopelessly unprepared to deal with the challenges of the next century.

Sources: Thomas F. McLarty III, "Hemispheric Free Trade Is Still a National Priority," *The Wall Street Journal*, May 26, 1995, p. A11; Susan Enfield, "South of the Border Blues," *Sales & Marketing Management*, May 1995, pp. 79–84; Bob Davis, "Two Years Later, the Promises Used to Sell NAFTA Haven't Come True, but Its Foes Were Wrong, Too," *The Wall Street Journal*, Oct. 26, 1995, pp. 124+; and Kyle Pope and Robert S. Greenberger, "Europe Seeks Trade Pact with U.S. Similar to NAFTA," *The Wall Street Journal*, Nov. 27, 1995, p. A16.

Advocates of TQM believe it is as important to satisfy "internal customers" as it is to satisfy final users. So, for example, marketing managers are viewed as customers of the marketing research staff. TQM also involves changes in the way things are done, from manufacturing processes to record keeping.

Quality improvement may require a reexamination of the way business is evaluated. For example, it takes time to improve quality, but U.S. managers and investors have been conditioned to reward short-term results. Also, quality is more easily achieved when management and labor have a cooperative working relationship, but in many American businesses the atmosphere is more adversarial than cooperative. For U.S. firms to be competitive into the next century, the focus on quality must continue.

Creating value is the process of translating customer benefits into a product. To avoid risk and pursue short-term results, some firms focus on trivial adjustments. They make superficial changes and call the product "new," spend inordinate amounts of time figuring out how much they can exaggerate in their ads without violating the law, or change the package simply to draw attention to the product. **Value marketing**, on the other hand, means making significant improvements in a product to provide the customer with real benefits.

Improving the value customers receive from a product is often difficult. It requires an intimate understanding of customers' needs, creative thinking that frequently goes beyond the traditional ideas in an industry, and a willingness to take risks. For example, following a year of record earnings, United Parcel Service (UPS) undertook a major overhaul of its operations described by a senior vice president as "one of the three or four defining moments for this company." In order to keep its prices down and speed up package delivery, UPS is making sweeping changes. The changes involve transferring its phone centers to an outside supplier, giving delivery personnel more authority, and redesigning the tracking system for lost packages.[20]

http://www.ups.com/

Developing Environmental Sensitivity. Quality applies to more than making products that work better or longer. A broader issue is the general quality of everyday life and the way we treat the environment. In the past a seller's commitment to a single issue (for example, using recycled materials or making a product biodegradable) was enough to get customers' attention.

In the future we are likely to see a more careful evaluation of the value of product features that seem to add more to style than substance. One area in which this is evident is a heightened interest in the physical environment. The dissipation of the atmosphere's ozone layer, the disappearance of rainforests, increases in acid rain, and the "greenhouse effect" have all become international concerns. Other environmental issues of growing significance are waste disposal and landfills, air and water pollution, and biodegradability.

Green marketing is any marketing activity of a firm that is intended to create a positive impact or lessen the negative impact of a product on the environment in order to capitalize on consumers' concerns about environmental issues. Green marketing efforts range from simply altering advertising claims to the development of entirely new products.

Most firms have moved beyond viewing green marketing as looking for an exploitable or advertisable feature to making significant operational changes. The next step is to make environmental concerns an integral part of the business system. This will require a new way of thinking about consumption. One example is to make products so that the materials, components, and packages can be used longer and reused either in part or whole, a process called **reconsumption**.[21] There are several forms of reconsumption:

- Containers can be designed so they can be refilled.
- Preventive maintenance programs can be planned and implemented so products last longer.
- Components can be designed to permit removal and repair so an entire product isn't discarded because of a single part's failure.
- Products can be designed to have an alternative use when the primary function is completed.

http://www.baxter.com/

Making reconsumption work depends on the development of manufacturing and marketing methods that make it profitable. Baxter International, a medical products manufacturer, works closely with its hospital customers to reduce pollution and increase recycling. Baxter has found that this is good business. Its initiatives in areas such as reducing unnecessary packaging, improving the disposal of infectious waste, and recycling equipment recently saved the $9 billion company $48 million in one year.[22]

An environmental orientation requires that basic concepts be rethought. For example, manufacturers have focused for years on ways to assemble things efficiently. Now the focus must switch to development of technologies for separating materials. For example, the makers of telephone directories are now able to deink old directory pages so they can be used in making new directories.[23]

Marketing functions will also have to be redesigned. Channels of distribution, for example, will have to flow both ways. In order for reconsumption to occur, packages, products, and parts will have to be returned to the seller. Methods must be constructed to collect used or consumed goods as efficiently as new goods are now distributed. To meet the needs of customers and gain their cooperation, these collection systems will have to be as easy to understand and operate as our existing one-way distribution methods.

Ultimately, businesses and entire industries will be built around recycling. For example, a Georgia firm called Global Green is making uniforms and costumes for Disney employees out of plastic thread made from recycled soft drink bottles.[24]

Clearly, value and quality in many forms are critical to customer satisfaction and therefore must have a high priority with management. The challenge for managers will be to identify or develop systems that can be successfully implemented and sustained within the American business culture.

Dealing with Market Fragmentation.　There was a time when a packaged-goods manufacturer could develop a quality product, advertise it nationally to households using the national media, stock retailers' shelves, and have a reasonable chance of success. But the situation has changed. The availability of data has allowed marketers to identify smaller and smaller market segments—to engage in **market fragmentation**.

Firms can build elaborate descriptions of markets using scanner data that produce detailed purchase behavior on a store-by-store basis; Census Bureau data that provide demographic information down to the city block; and a variety of other sources such as warranty registration cards, contest entries, and rebate requests. With this information, they are able to design products and assortments tailored specifically to small customer groups.

http://www.mcdonalds.com/　Evidence of this fragmentation is everywhere. McDonald's, the king of hamburgers, not only has expanded its variety of burgers but also has test-marketed fish-and-chips, fried chicken, pizza, and carry-out groceries. From 1947 to 1984 Procter & Gamble had only one Tide. Today there are five versions, including Liquid Tide and Tide with Bleach. Consider the case of Kraft and cream cheese. In a 30-store experiment, Kraft matched the profiles of shoppers who buy various flavors of cream cheese (plain, diet, strawberry-flavored) with a demographic description of consumers living in the area of each supermarket. Then the inventory in each store was adjusted to emphasize the flavors most likely to be desired. The result was an increase in profit over the previous year of nearly 150 percent.[25]

As competitors pinpoint small segments, a firm can no longer expect large numbers of consumers to compromise their needs and wants and buy standardized products. Rather, it must tailor goods and services to meet the needs of small market segments. Called **niche marketing**, this strategy significantly complicates the marketer's job. One version of a product is replaced by several. Different ads must be produced and new media found to reach different consumers. Retailers must choose among many product variations, not all of which can be stocked. The added variety complicates inventory management, distribution, and personal selling.

Fragmented markets and the resulting proliferation of products and brands have led to adjustments in promotional spending. Let's see how that has happened. First, for products that have small target markets, mass media are impractical. Given a niche brand's potential sales, mass media result in a considerable amount of wasted coverage and are therefore too expensive. So marketers shift their budgets to more highly focused promotion vehicles, such as specialized cable networks, direct mail, and coupons.

In an age of fragmented markets, advertisers are searching for new ways to reach busy, highly mobile consumers. Among the alternatives that have been developed are:

- TV broadcasts featuring commercials and interspersed with news and entertainment anywhere consumers gather—airports and workout facilities, for example.
- Shopping carts with screens that present video commercials.
- Ads on the stall doors in public rest rooms.
- Magazines with highly targeted advertising distributed only in selected locations such as physicians' waiting rooms.
- TV monitors that show ads on gasoline pumps while people fill up their cars.

Coincidentally, the power of retailers is increasing. Retailers simply cannot stock all the brands and variations of products that are being produced for niche markets. And because fewer products command a mass market, the retailer has more discretion over which ones to stock. As a result, manufacturers are compelled to provide more trade promotions in the form of discounts, point-of-sale material, slotting allowances, and cooperative advertising funds in order to get products onto store shelves. The net effect of fragmented markets is a shift in promotional spending from mass-media advertising to consumer and trade promotions.

*C*ompaq Computer Corp. and Fisher-Price, the toy maker, have teamed up to create a line of computer toys for children ages 3 to 7. The toys require some computer attachments such as oversize keyboards and steering wheel-like controls designed for small hands. The firms plan to release a stream of adventure and learning software packages to keep youngsters amused. If this product line is successful, look for similarly highly targeted offerings for such groups as senior citizens and teenagers.

http://www.compaq.com/

Market fragmentation is simply a refinement of segmentation. Marketers have known about segments within markets for many years. As we discussed in Chapter 4, techniques have been developed using demographic, behavioral, and geographic data to enable marketers to better target their efforts. What has changed as our society has become more complex and diversified are the number and size of market segments.

Where will this lead? There are already indications that the next level of sophistication involves marketing to each customer individually. This development is discussed in the next section.

Building Relationships.   In Chapter 18 we described how the shift of promotional funds away from advertising to various sales promotion tools had the effect of exchanging consumer loyalty for short-term sales. However, recent figures indicate that the decline in advertising has stopped. This is a positive sign for those who believe that advertising helps establish a long-term relationship between consumers and a brand.

However, relationship building has gone far beyond advertising. **Relationship marketing** is an ongoing interaction between a buyer and a seller in which the seller continuously improves its understanding of the buyer's needs, and the buyer becomes increasingly loyal to the seller because its needs are being so well satisfied.

Relationship marketing depends on the ability to amass large amounts of data about individual customers and to draw conclusions from those data about needs and preferences. You may recall from Chapter 4 that these masses of data are called *databases*. They are constructed by capturing individual purchasing behavior, asking customers questions, recording complaints and inquiries, and collecting information from public records. Using the information, the marketer creates a product customized to each individual buyer. When this is done for a number of buyers, it is called **mass customization**.[26]

YOU MAKE THE DECISION

ARE MARKETERS VIOLATING THE PRIVACY OF CONSUMERS?

A consumer survey by Yankelovich Partners found that 90 percent of consumers believe that laws are needed to protect consumers' privacy. In the same study, 66 percent considered the sale of a mailing list without the permission of those whose names are on the list a serious privacy violation.

Consumers using their computers and on-line services to make purchases may be inadvertently giving the shopping service large amounts of personal and life-style data. For example, a grocery shopping service could track a household's alcohol consumption, medication usage, and even religious preference by its purchasing behavior.

Marketers' objectives are not sinister. They simply desire information to more efficiently target their prospects and customize their messages. However, consumers believe they have the right to make inquiries, purchase products, and interact with business without having personal information collected and used.

How can these differing views be reconciled?

Sources: Cyndee Miller, "Concern Raised over Privacy on Infohighway," *Marketing News,* Jan. 2, 1995, pp. 1+; and Chad Rubel, "Marketing Briefs," *Marketing News,* Nov. 20, 1995, p. 10.

http://www.individual.com/

The operation of Individual, Inc., a firm that collects and distributes published articles on specific topics to clients, illustrates mass customization. The typical approach for a firm such as Individual is to assemble articles on "hot" topics, produce a catalog listing the topics, and let prospective clients search the catalog and order what they desire. This hit-or-miss strategy forces the customers to sort through a variety of options, and probably make some compromises in terms of exactly what they want. An alternative, which Individual uses, is to define with a customer as carefully as possible exactly what its information needs are. Articles on the topic are then collected from over 400 publications and continuously transmitted to the client. Regularly, over a period of several weeks, the client is asked to rate every article on a scale from "very relevant" to "not relevant." This information is fed into a computer which uses it to refine the customer's choices. In the first week, a typical customer finds about 40 to 60 percent of the articles are on target. However, by the fourth or fifth week, 80 to 90 percent of the articles being sent are useful.

Successful relationship marketing has several components:

- A firm first decides which customers and prospects it wants to build a relationship with, since some are more attractive than others.
- A system is developed for collecting and managing the information about each customer.
- Instead of complete products, a firm needs to develop components or processes that can be assembled in different ways to meet customers' individual needs. For example, a hotel can put together many combinations of alternative methods for making a reservation, the various check-in procedures, the numerous on-site facilities and services, and different payment methods to suit the needs of individual customers.
- Sales people need to be transformed into customer managers who focus on improving the relationship with customers through information.

Pressured by the desire for short-term results, marketers have often emphasized immediate sales over the development of relationships. However, as in the examples above, the situation appears to be changing. Firms have discovered it costs several times more to get a new customer than to retain an existing one. So in both consumer and business-to-business marketing, there has been an increased recognition of the value of relationship building and customer retention. The question is, Will it spread throughout all businesses?

■ SUMMARY

In addition to the financial analysis of marketing performance that was discussed in Chapter 21, a firm's marketing performance should also be appraised from a broad, societal perspective. Thus, evaluation of an organization's marketing efforts must consider how well the organization satisfies the wants of its target customers, meets its own needs, and serves the best interests of society.

Some marketers have been criticized for being exploitative and inefficient, for committing illegal acts, and for stimulating unwholesome demand. The allegations of wrongdoing apply to all four market-

ing-mix elements, but are most frequent in the area of promotion. Many criticisms of marketing are valid. However, the offensive behavior is confined to a small minority of all marketers, and some of the criticism is based on issues that are more complicated than they first appear.

Efforts to address marketing abuses have come from consumers, government, and business. Organized consumer actions are called consumerism. Consumer responses to marketing problems have included protests, political activism, and support of special-interest groups. Conditions that provide an impetus for widespread consumerism—sensitivity to social and environmental concerns, and the willingness to become actively involved—are present today.

Government at the federal, state, and local levels passes and enforces consumer-protection legislation. Businesses have responded to criticism by improving communications, providing more and better information, upgrading products, and producing more sensitive advertising.

Ethical behavior is the best remedy for the charges against marketing. Many organizations have established codes of conduct to help employees behave ethically. However, it is not possible to have a rule for every situation. Managers can use a form of cost-benefit analysis to evaluate the ethics of alternatives. Another method of judging the ethics of a particular act is to personalize the situation.

Besides being morally correct, ethical behavior by organizations can restore public confidence, avoid government regulation, retain the power granted by society, and protect the image of the organization.

Consumers also have a responsibility to act ethically. The volume of credit card misuse, check fraud, coupon misredemption, and shoplifting suggests that a system-wide exploration of ways to reduce unethical behavior is needed.

Trends can be identified by monitoring the environment, other businesses, and changes in the population. An important environmental development is the Internet.

Marketers will react to these and other changes, but they will also have to make some basic strategic adjustments to compete in the twenty-first century. Among the needed adjustments are instilling a market-driven orientation, adopting a global orientation, emphasizing quality and value, developing environmental sensitivity, dealing with fragmented markets, and building customer relationships.

More about

BAUSCH & LOMB

*M*any of the accusations against Bausch & Lomb (B&L) have been denied by the management. Others are attributed to bad decisions by some misguided managers. Whatever the explanation, the situation characterizes a common challenge. Managers are expected to produce short-term results and at the same time behave responsibly, looking out for the long-term best interests of the company, its customers, and society.

B&L has made several changes in the way it does business:

- Standards now exist for the amount of inventory a distributor can be asked to take.
- Incentive pay for managers includes more long-term goals, and short-term earnings have been deemphasized.
- B&L is attempting to reduce the gray marketing problem by centrally tracking the distribution of its products. Now a distributor cannot improve its performance by selling products to wholesalers or retailers in another distributor's territory.

The questionable practices at B&L may have been only a combination of reactions to competitive conditions and loose management control. Daniel Gill, who was CEO at the time, said, "Unfortunately, when you have operations scattered throughout the world, people do things they shouldn't, but I don't think there is a larger problem."

It is also possible that these events occurred because B&L executives thought top management considered the accomplishment of financial goals more important than ethical behavior. Warren Bennis, a well-known business author, has said a CEO "may believe he's telling them not to get into trouble, but if all the verbal and nonverbal signs sent out focus on making the numbers, he's giving them a license to do unethical things." In either case, situations such as the one that occurred at B&L should sensitize current and future marketers to the pressures that managers face.[27]

1. How did the behavior at Bausch & Lomb measure up on the three dimensions of the societal view of the marketing concept?
2. What options should a manager have when he or she believes the organization's performance goals are unreasonable?
3. What can B&L do to restore its reputation with middlemen and consumers?

■ KEY TERMS AND CONCEPTS

Consumerism (600)

Ethics (603)

Social
    responsibility (605)

Total quality
    management
    (TQM) (610)

Value marketing (612)

Green marketing (612)

Reconsumption (612)

Market
    fragmentation (613)

Niche marketing (613)

Relationship
    marketing (615)

Mass customization (615)

■ QUESTIONS AND PROBLEMS

1. Can all criticisms of marketing be dismissed on the basis of critics who are poorly informed or acting in their own interest?

2. What indicates that middlemen make reasonable profits?

3. Some people believe there are too many fast-food outlets in their communities. Is there a method for reducing the number of these outlets that will meet the needs of all parties affected?

4. React to the following criticisms of advertising:
   a. It costs too much.
   b. It is in bad taste.
   c. It is false and deceptive.
   d. It creates monopolies.

5. What proposals do you have for regulating advertising to reduce the occurrence of false or misleading claims?

6. What specific recommendations do you have for reducing the cost of advertising?

7. What are the social and economic justifications for "paternalistic" laws such as seat belt regulations and health warnings on cigarette packages and alcoholic-beverage containers?

8. How would you respond to the argument that coupon misredemption is just another cost of doing business?

9. What might prevent organizations from adopting the strategic changes described in the chapter as necessary to compete effectively in the future?

10. Could a marketer combine green marketing with the notions of market fragmentation and niche marketing?

■ HANDS-ON MARKETING

1. Examine the following items:
   a. A snack-food package
   b. An owner's manual for a power tool
   c. An apartment lease
   d. A credit card application
   What information does each contain that would be helpful to a consumer in making a purchase decision? How clearly is the information presented? What additional information would be useful?

2. Ask the managers of three firms in the same industry:
   a. What foreseeable developments will have the greatest impact on marketing in your industry over the next 5 years?
   b. How do you think the industry should respond to these developments?

CASES FOR PART 8

Sears, Roebuck & Company

MAINTAINING MOMENTUM AFTER A SUCCESSFUL REPOSITIONING

The luster has returned to an American icon—Sears, Roebuck & Company. In the early 1990s, Sears activated a marketing strategy that was designed to reposition the nation's third-largest retailer. The repositioning has been an overwhelming success. Since posting a loss of nearly $3 billion in 1992, Sears has lifted operating profits to $1 billion in 1995. And the firm's profits are expected to continue to grow through the turn of the century. Not surprisingly, Sears' success is attributed to its ability to specify its target market and then meet the needs of this group of shoppers.

Earlier Repositioning Attempts

For over a century, Sears' target market was "middle America." The chain's customers were mostly male and interested in hard goods (for example, appliances, hardware, and automotive products). Sears tried to grow in the early 1980s by embarking on a strategy of diversification. The retailer moved away from its core retail business by acquiring companies, such as Dean Witter financial services and Coldwell Banker real estate, and by launching new enterprises, such as the Discover Card in 1985.

The diversification strategy boosted sales to over $50 billion by the late 1980s. However, the retail division was struggling. Too many of Sears' large department stores, which accounted for nearly 60 percent of the firm's sales, were located in geographic areas that were stagnant or growing very little.

Further, Sears faced eroding customer loyalty and tough competition—which were not unrelated factors. Discount retailers, such as Wal-Mart and Kmart, grabbed market share by undercutting Sears' prices. Specialty-store chains, such as The Limited, Circuit City, and Toys "R" Us, struck at the core of Sears' customer base. J.C. Penney and Montgomery Ward repositioned themselves by offering fashion-oriented assortments that reflected the changing needs of consumers. In contrast, Sears' traditional assortment, with a noticeable lack of fashion-oriented merchandise, generated a lukewarm response from shoppers.

Sears developed a new strategy that focused on refurbishing the chain's stores; adding well-known producers' brands such as Sony, Levi's, OshKosh B'Gosh, and General Electric; emphasizing value through everyday low prices (EDLP); and offering better service. According to Sears, busy shoppers benefit from EDLP because they do not have to shop all over looking for reduced prices. However, quite soon after EDLP was introduced, too many consumers concluded that Sears' new prices were the same as, or even higher than, competitors'.

A Repositioning Clicks

Finally, in late 1992, under the direction of then Sears chairman Edward Brennan and current chairman Arthur Martinez, a plan was prepared to overhaul and redefine the fundamental nature of Sears. The overhaul contained three major elements:

*   Selling its financial services units, including Dean Witter, Coldwell Banker, and Allstate Insurance. Sears divested itself of these units in order to focus on its core business of retailing.
*   Closing its immense, but unprofitable catalog division. The division generated over $3 billion in annual sales but had not earned a profit since the mid-1980s.
*   Remaking over 800 Sears stores into a focused chain of moderately priced department stores located in large, climate-controlled shopping malls. The company closed more than 100 stores located in inner-city, non-mall locations and reduced Sears' work force by 15 percent to about 50,000 employees.

The revitalization of Sears' retail stores was the key to the new strategy's success. The company knew it could not reduce costs enough to match Wal-Mart's and Kmart's low prices, while still earning a profit. There also was some question as to whether Sears could upgrade its merchandise and enhance its image sufficiently to compete against upscale department stores such as Nordstrom and Lord & Taylor. The face-lift of the Sears stores included modernized decor, softer lighting, fancier displays, wider aisles, and presentation of goods in ways that mimicked more expensive department stores.

In addition, Sears stepped up its efforts to attract more women to its stores. Women shop and buy more than men. Women have represented about 70 percent of department store sales, compared to 50 percent of Sears' sales. Furthermore, the majority of women work outside the home and spend a considerable amount of their clothing budget on business apparel. Sears decided to target working women between the ages of 35 and 64 who have annual household incomes of $15,000 to $45,000 and shop at malls regularly.

Sears' product mix was revised to reflect its focus on women. Beauty products, apparel, and home fashions (bedding, housewares, and decorating items) were given more space in Sears' stores. In particular, the retailer set a goal of building apparel to 40 percent of store sales, up from 27 percent in 1992.

The marketing budget also was modified to reflect retailing as Sears' core business. Specifically, advertising stressed building the equity of the Sears brand and promoting selected product lines.

Gaining Momentum and Moving On

Sears launched its repositioning effort with a $40 million "softer side of Sears" advertising campaign. Rather quickly, more and more women could be found in the firm's department stores. The repositioning effort was highly effective.

To sustain its success, Sears has five priorities:

- Focus on core businesses where Sears has the capacity to win and grow.
- Position Sears as an even more attractive place to shop.
- Tailor the assortments of individual stores to satisfy the needs of local consumers.
- To accelerate cost and productivity improvements throughout the company.
- Create a new culture and set of values to lead Sears into the future.

Sears added 3.4 million square feet of apparel space in 1994 to provide shoppers with popular national brands that complement the chain's own brands. The intent is to position Sears' stores as having a flair for fashion and providing good value. Although consumers are spending less on apparel than they did in the 1980s, they still demand fashionable merchandise.

As another step in luring middle-income women to Sears' stores, the company created its own cosmetics brand. The 600-item Circle of Beauty line of makeup, skin-care products, and fragrances was introduced in September 1995. The packaging color is an elegant, dark green, and the package does not mention the Sears name. Circle of Beauty costs much less than brands such as Chanel. A lipstick retails for about $8.50, compared with $20 for Chanel. Recognizing the growing number of Hispanic customers, Sears' cosmetics brochures are printed in Spanish as well as English. The chain's research found that customers were intimidated by department stores that keep cosmetics behind glass, but that they still wanted help in choosing the right product. Thus, Sears allows shoppers to test Circle of Beauty products while sales associates wait to answer questions. The campaign increased the sales of soft goods (including apparel), though sales of such products still only represent a third of store sales.

By the end of 1995, 50 percent of Sears' 800 department stores had been remodeled. As explained by Allan Stewart, president of Sears' retail store operations, "Our target customer has less time than ever before to shop. Our stores must be more than merely pleasant in appearance—they must be customer-friendly and easy to navigate."

By divesting its Discover Card operations, Coldwell Banker, and 20 percent of both Allstate and Dean Witter, Sears was able to pare its debt costs by $200 million a year. These savings, coupled with an increase in marketing productivity, have helped Sears keep its prices lower than those of competitors such as J.C. Penney.

Responding to the declining number of shoppers that visit malls and a corresponding slowdown in mall construction, Sears began to open a number of free-standing stores in community centers and in small towns. Locations away from malls are designed to attract customers who do not shop at Sears. These stores are expected to add $4 billion in sales by the year 2000.

Moving beyond Department Stores

Besides department stores, by 1995 the company had opened a total of over 80 Sears Hardware stores featuring tools, hardware, and garden items and Sears Homelife stores emphasizing furniture and mattresses. In addition, over 300 Sears dealer stores (appliances, electronics, and home and garden gear) have been opened since 1992. By the turn of the century, the giant retailer plans to have 500 Sears Hardware stores, 250 Homelife stores (which will carry all of Sears' furniture and mattresses by 1997), and 800 Sears dealer stores.

Sears also is seeking to rejuvenate its auto-service operations. In 1995, Sears entered into a joint venture to open at least 450 Jiffy Lube quick-oil-change shops in its auto-service centers. This joint effort is expected to help the department store chain erase the tarnished image it received in 1992 when regulators in several states claimed Sears' employees systematically recommended unnecessary auto repairs. In addition, this alliance is supposed to sustain sales of the auto-service centers, which account for about 10 percent of Sears' store revenues.

Sears discontinued its "Big Book" catalog in 1993. Since then, the firm has established joint ventures with six small companies to mail fourteen specialty catalogs featuring merchandise, such as leather jackets, auto accessories, and large women's clothes. Sears and its partners mailed 150 million catalogs in 1995. Sears brings the strength of its database of 24 million credit-card customers to these joint ventures. This represents a low-cost, low-risk method of operating in the fast-growing catalog business.

The print and broadcast advertising campaign promoting "the softer side of Sears" had a positive impact on the firm's target market. This theme has been followed by a "many sides of Sears" campaign backed by a $50 million budget. Men, women, grandparents, kids, and couples are incorporated into the new ads to illustrate the diversity of customers that Sears serves—and hopefully satisfies. During the 1995 Christmas season, the company modified its memorable jingle to "the merry side of Sears."

What about the Future?

The growth in Sears' sales from the 1994 to 1995 Christmas seasons was the greatest of any large retailer. Sears attributed this performance to the marketing strategies put in place during the preceding 3 years.

However, problems still exist. Although more than 70 percent of purchases at Sears are now made by women, the department stores still have an image as a place to buy tools and car batteries. Furthermore, Sears' own research indicates that many shoppers view its women's corporate wear and better dress clothing as lacking quality and style.

Can Sears continue its winning ways? As with virtually all firms, the path to continued success will be uphill. Competition remains stiff. In addition, new technological developments such as the Internet present challenges as well as opportunities for Sears.

http://www.yellowpages.ca/sears/index.htm

QUESTIONS

1. Do Sears' strategies take into account the major trends related to population changes discussed in Chapter 22? If not, what strategic changes would you recommend?

2. What is Sears' differential advantage over other department stores such as J.C. Penney and discount stores such as Wal-Mart?

Sources: Robert Berner, "Sears's Softer Side Paid Off in Hard Cash This Christmas," *The Wall Street Journal*, Dec. 29, 1995, p. B4; Patricia Sellers, "Sears: In with the New . . . ," *Fortune*, Oct. 16, 1995, pp. 96+; Susan Chandler, "Drill Bits, Paint Thinner, Eyeliner," *Business Week*, Sept. 25, 1995, p. 83; Genevieve Buck, "Deft Quickstep, Fast Turnaround Propel Martinez," *Chicago Tribune*, Aug. 6, 1995, p. C1; Susan Chandler, "Where Sears Wants America to Shop Now," *Business Week*, June 12, 1995, p. 39; Gregory A. Patterson, "Sears Rolls Out Stand-Alone Outlets in Move to Boost Presence Outside Malls," *The Wall Street Journal*, May 25, 1995, p. A5; Gregory A. Patterson, "Sears Picks Jiffy Lube to Oil Auto-Service Operations," *The Wall Street Journal*, Mar. 23, 1995, p. B4; Susan Chandler, "Strategies for the New Mail Order," *Business Week*, Dec. 19, 1994, p. 82; Kate Fitzgerald, "The Latest Side of Sears," *Advertising Age*, May 2, 1994, p. 1; Robert England, "Penney-Wise?" *Financial World*, Apr. 26, 1994, p. 36; Sears, Roebuck and Co. 1994 Annual Report, p. 9; and Bob Garfield, "Sears' Soft Sell Works—in Ads," *Advertising Age*, Sept. 20, 1993, p. 1.

CASE 2　*Nike versus Reebok*

INTENSE COMPETITION FEATURING MICHAEL VERSUS SHAQ—AND MUCH MORE

Since the first running shoe was invented over 100 years ago, the athletic footwear market in the U.S. has grown to over $7 billion in annual sales. About 300 million pairs of athletic footwear, or "sneakers," are sold worldwide each year. An average pair lasts about 6 months.

A market of this size that combines fashion, utility, fitness, glamour, and personalities is sure to attract stiff marketing competition. And it certainly has. Indeed, competition for market share has become so fierce that some notable names are in danger of being eliminated from the market. The well-known manufacturers of sneakers—Nike, Reebok, L. A. Gear, Fila, New Balance, Adidas, and others—are seeking marketing programs that will allow them not to just survive but to grow and be profitable into the next century.

Insights from the Past

An understanding of the sneakers market requires a careful look at the past 30 years. In the 1960s, function was the main attribute that consumers considered when purchasing a pair of sneakers. Converse's Chuck Taylor All Stars and Keds were the dominant brands. In addition, a few manufacturers (for example, Adidas) marketed specialized shoes for track and court-related sports.

Market conditions changed dramatically in the 1970s when the adult health and physical-fitness movement began. Suddenly, a large market, composed of people in their twenties and thirties, developed for jogging and running shoes. In addition, "wannabes" (people who weren't actually involved in jogging and running but wanted to convey a sporting image) began to wear sneakers as a fashion statement. The switch from function to fashion started a race that upstarts and well-known manufacturers alike wanted to win.

A Sporting Goods Manufacturers survey in the late 1980s indicated that over 90 percent of the U.S. population owned at least one pair of athletic shoes, and over 70 percent buy a new pair each year. Furthermore, the survey identified four definable market segments:

- Pragmatists, who want economy, comfort, and durability (30 percent).
- Performance-conscious young males, who desire reliable performance when involved in athletic competition (30 percent).
- Appearance-conscious consumers, who are interested in style, color, and wardrobe coordination (25 percent).
- Fashion leaders, who want to be trendsetters by being the first to buy a particular style (15 percent).

How different competitors have approached this changing market provides some insight into what marketing strategies they might use in the future.

Just Doing It

In 1964, Phil Knight and his former track coach at the University of Oregon, Bill Bowerman, launched Blue Ribbon Sports. The objective of Blue Ribbon Sports was to unseat Adidas as the market leader for running shoes. Knight's initial strategy was to bring the Tiger brand of Japanese-made running shoes to the U.S. Later, believing they could design a better shoe for the competitive runner, Knight and Bowerman formed Nike. The company name was taken from Greek mythology in which Nike is the goddess of victory.

Nike started with a product-oriented philosophy and focused initially on running shoes. The company thought that well-designed, performance-enhancing shoes would create their own market—or would "sell themselves." Early marketing efforts consisted of Knight persuading several of the top American distance runners to try the new shoes. The hope was that this reference group would influence the purchase decisions of a much larger group of consumers.

Nike's sales grew rapidly, reaching $14 million by 1976. During the next 5 years, sales and profits grew at an astonishing rate of 75 percent per year. The growth over this period was primarily fueled by sneakers becoming a fashion item. By the early 1980s, 80 percent of so-called athletic footwear were purchased for nonathletic purposes.

Everything seemed to be going Nike's way. Then, two events (actually missteps by Nike) in the 1980s changed the competitive landscape in the sneakers industry:

- Assuming that the market for running shoes would stop growing soon, Nike extended its product line to include casual shoes. The new shoes were very functional, but ignored fashion—and, as a result, failed.
- Equally bad, Nike completely overlooked the aerobics boom. When the company finally did produce a shoe for aerobics, it was highly functional but unattractive.

These missteps resulted in a decline in Nike's market share from 50 percent in 1980 to 22 percent by 1986. To reverse the trend, Nike had to become more marketing-oriented. Its revamped strategy recognized consumer desires for appearance, style, and image, as well as functional performance. As Knight said, "We've come around to saying that Nike is a marketing-oriented company. . . . The design elements and functional characteristics of the product itself are just part of the overall marketing process."

The invention of "air technology" was the result of Nike's new marketing orientation. In 1979, Nike introduced a shoe with an air sac in the heel. By the time Air Jordans were introduced in 1988, 50 models with air sacs produced sales of over $40 million. Air Jordans focused on the basketball shoe category, which accounts for 25 percent of the total sales of athletic footwear. Air Jordans combined performance, style, and a highly successful advertising campaign.

Nike's advertising also reflected an understanding of consumer motivations for purchasing an athletic shoe. The "Just Do It" campaign appealed to every person's desire to improve regardless of his or her athletic abilities. Featuring Bo Jackson, a multisport star at the time, the "Bo Knows" campaign combined humor and the desire for exceptional performance. The "Just Do It" campaign was relaunched in 1995 to illustrate the variety of Nike's product line.

In the 1990s, Nike expanded its product line into the high-growth hiking footwear market. Its Outdoor Division produced over $200 million in sales in 1994 and is expected to generate $500 million in sales by 1998. In addition, Nike is pushing its way into soccer and other international sports, as most of the growth in the $13.5 billion global athletic footwear market is coming from emerging markets. Nike is striving to build sales in such key markets as China, Germany, Mexico, and Japan. To ensure consistent quality, Nike has acquired equity interests in many of its worldwide partners.

A key to Nike's profitability is its inventory control system, called Futures. To obtain guaranteed delivery times and discounts up to 10 percent, retailers must place up to 80 percent of their orders at least 6 months in advance of delivery dates. The Futures system allows Nike to plan production in a way that maximizes efficiency.

Having sports stars endorse its products remains a significant part of Nike's promotional strategy. Many of its endorsers, including Michael Jordan and Ken Griffey, Jr., are almost omnipresent on TV screens. In addition, Nike has reached agreements with many professional and collegiate teams to brandish the Nike "swoosh" and wear the company's footwear. Numerous coaches, such as Duke University's basketball coach, Mike Krzyzewiski, are under contract to Nike.

Another way by which Nike promotes its brand and products is through sponsorship of the Nike Tour, the secondary circuit for members of the Professional Golfers Association. This sponsorship secured instant credibility for Nike in the sizable golf shoe market.

Nike's current marketing strategy seems to be working well. The company has over 23 percent of the world market (including the U.S.) compared to 20 percent for Reebok and 10 percent for Adidas, a German company. In the U.S., Nike holds a commanding 37 percent share, which is 17 percentage points more than Reebok.

A Shaq Attack

Reebok is an offshoot of a British company, J. W. Foster and Sons, a manufacturer of high-quality athletic shoes in England for over 80 years. Paul Fireman, an outdoor equipment distributor, noticed Reebok shoes at an international sportswear trade show and signed an agreement to become the company's U.S. licensee. The first products Reebok introduced in the U.S. were running shoes. However, because this market was dominated by Nike, Fireman had to look for other opportunities to gain a foothold in the U.S.

Fireman found the niche he was looking for in a style of women's shoes that was color coordinated with athletic clothing and could be worn during an aerobics workout. The shoe was successfully promoted directly to aerobics instructors. By the end of 1983, sales had reached $13 million. In 1986, with shoes that combined comfort and fashionable appearance, Reebok raced past Nike into the leading position in the athletic footwear market in the U.S.

The company began expanding its product line into basketball shoes, tennis shoes, and children's sneakers (Weeboks). Basketball shoes are particularly important in three ways: The market is growing, the shoes are worn for casual as well as athletic purposes, and basketball players—perhaps more than any other athletes—are celebrities who influence teenagers' shoe-buying decisions.

In 1989, Reebok introduced The Pump. Although Nike was first to launch an inflatable shoe, The Pump combined the convenience of having an inflation device in the tongue of the shoe with the psychological value of the pump being visible. The Pump was successful. Nevertheless, in that same year, Nike recovered from its earlier mistakes to reclaim the top position in the U.S. athletic footwear market.

In 1993, to counter Nike's surge, Reebok signed Shaquille O'Neal to a 5-year, $15 million contract. Reebok thought that having "The Shaq" as an endorser would enhance its brand's combined performance and fashion image. The Shaq Attack sneaker seemed tailor-made for teens, but sales were disappointing. Consumers wanted black shoes that were priced under $100, but the Shaq Attack was white and came with a $130 price tag. As a result of misreading consumer sentiment, sales of the Reebok basketball shoe fell 20 percent during the first half of 1993. Now, Reebok's share of the $1.75 billion basketball shoe market is about 15 percent, compared to Nike's 50 percent.

Reebok shifted its strategy to challenge Nike in the high-performance shoe market. The company introduced dozens of new shoes, including The Instapump (a modified version of The Pump), and shoes for the rapidly growing hiking footwear shoe market. The Instapump is expected to claim 10 percent of the firm's sales within 3 years. With this new strategy, Fireman boldly predicted that Reebok would reclaim the leading position in this industry.

Recognizing that its "UBU" and "Physics behind Physique" campaigns failed, Reebok is intent on developing an effective, enduring promotional theme. The company's "Planet Reebok" theme, first used in 1994, seems to symbolize diversity of needs and wants regarding footwear, the desirability of individualism, and Reebok's global scope.

Despite the new strategy and endorsers such as O'Neal and Dallas Cowboys running back Emmitt Smith, Reebok shoes continued to lose favor with teenage boys. This market segment accounts for 20 percent of the U.S. athletic shoe market. Furthermore, profitability suffered as operating expenses rose from 24 percent of sales in 1991 to over 32 percent in 1995. Big shareholders eventually had enough and called for the ouster of Fireman. Although Fireman beat back the challenge, problems persisted. Because of factors such as internal conflicts, 50 percent of Reebok's design staff as well as several marketing and product-development managers left the company.

The turmoil even caused O'Neal to reconsider his endorsement agreement. However, management changes instituted in late 1995 and the introduction of a new psychedelic Shaqnosis shoe led to a happier O'Neal. Another development is seen as at least as important in improving Reebok's performance. Vishex, a honeycomb-celled air bladder, was scheduled for a fall 1996 launch. Other noteworthy steps by Reebok include developing shoes exclusively for the Foot Locker retail chain, introducing shoes in the more acceptable $80 to $100 price range, securing the designation as the "official shoe" of the 1996 Summer Olympics, and developing more lines of athletic and casual apparel.

At the same time, Reebok is trying to improve profits by reducing production costs. This is being done by shifting manufacturing to lower-wage countries in Asia, such as China, Indonesia, and Thailand. A pair of sneakers that retails for $70 costs about $20 to manufacture. However, other operating expenses leave the company's profit at about $6 per pair.

Reebok's 1995 sales results were not particularly strong. However, there were several bright spots—such as sales of Reebok athletic footwear in international markets, Rockport casual shoes, and Greg Norman golf shoes. In 1996, Reebok sold its Avia subsidiary in order to concentrate on its core brands of shoes, notably Reebok, Greg Norman, and Rockport.

The Also Rans

Several smaller players in the sneakers industry are trying to maintain their respective niches and avoid getting squeezed out of the competition. Fila, an Italian company, vaulted from seventh to third place in the U.S. sneakers market in 1995. The 70-year-old manufacturer of shoes and apparel increased its athletic shoe sales from $84 million to $500 million by targeting inner-city youths with its boldly designed sneakers. Fila's endorsers include young basketball standouts Grant Hill and Jerry Stackhouse.

Once dominant in the running shoe segment of the athletic footwear market, Adidas is showing signs that it might be able to regain some of the market share it lost in the early 1980s. Adidas's worldwide sales reached $2.3 billion in 1995, but only 18 percent was from the U.S. market. To increase its market share in the U.S., the firm increased its marketing budget. The move produced results, boosting Adidas's market share to 10 percent.

Another "niche player," New Balance, had worldwide sales of $310 million in 1994. The company operates four of the five remaining factories in the U.S. that cut and stitch athletic shoes. To take advantage of growing consumer interest in a product's country of origin, New Balance advertises that its products are "made in the USA." Having production facilities in the U.S. has other advantages as well. Although American workers earn between $10 and $12 per hour compared to $1 per day for workers in China, New Balance offers its retailers the ability to adjust their orders weekly. In contrast, other manufacturers that rely on overseas production require 6 months' lead time. Furthermore, New Balance offers five different widths, giving it an advantage over competing firms.

New Balance doesn't pursue paid endorsements and spends a relatively small amount on promotion ($6 million yearly, compared to over $200 million for Nike). Considering that 60 million Americans have wide feet, the company expects to sell 4 million pairs by 1996. Bill Clinton, one American with wide feet, wears New Balance running shoes.

Although L. A. Gear had a significant impact on the sneakers industry, its future is uncertain. In 1985, Robert Greenberg introduced the "Southern California lifestyle look" to sneakers for girls between the ages of 9 and 17. These shoes, which were decorated with sequins, fringes, and rhinestones and with pictures of surfers, palm trees, and beaches, achieved over $220 million in sales by 1988. To reach its target market and reinforce its positioning strategy, L. A. Gear sold its shoes primarily through department stores and women's shoe stores.

After sales reached $900 million in 1990, L. A. Gear began to experience trouble. The firm's product line included over 400 styles. When the growth in the sneakers market slowed, L. A. Gear faced large inventory costs. A new management team returned the company to profitability through such steps as reducing the product line to about 150 styles. However, whereas L. A. Gear was once in a neck-and-neck battle with Nike and Reebok for industry leadership, it now lags far behind them with respect to sales and profits.

Future Challenges

Demographic changes have led to a surge in sales of hiking footwear (which doubles as casual wear for some people) and of expensive, high-tech, neoprene-and-velcro sandals. The sports sandal market alone reached $240 million in 1995. These trends have footwear manufacturers scrambling to launch their own versions of these products.

Nike's and Reebok's efforts regarding hiking footwear and sandals have sputtered thus far. Still, one financial analyst commented, "The big marketing guns may well triumph in the end, though. . . . The folks at Nike and Reebok are savvy people who know their customers. . . . In many cases they've hired away people from rugged outdoor companies to help chart their courses."

http://www.nike.com/
http://reebok.com/

QUESTIONS

1. What demographic and social and cultural trends in the U.S. and globally, including those discussed in Chapter 22, should manufacturers of athletic footwear recognize as they design their future marketing strategies?
2. Is it wise for a sneakers company to center its marketing strategy on a brand image built around endorsements by well-known athletes?
3. Which product-market strategy or strategies, as discussed in Chapter 3, would you suggest that Nike pursue in order to maintain its leadership of the sneakers market?
4. What product-mix strategy should Reebok implement to challenge Nike?

Sources: Geoffrey Smith, "Reebok Is Tripping over Its Own Laces," *Business Week*, Feb. 26, 1996, p. 62; "Reebok's Sale of Avia Will Result in Charge for Fourth Quarter," *The Wall Street Journal*, Jan. 18, 1996, p. B9; Joseph Pereira, "It's Official: Reebok Is Outrun by Nike in High-End Event," *The Wall Street Journal*, Oct. 18, 1995; "Nike's Strike," *The Economist*, Sept. 30, 1995, p. 78; Jeff Jensen, "Nike's Hard-Driving Methods Hit Nerve," *Advertising Age*, Sept. 18, 1995, p. 4; David Fischer, "Global Hopscotch," *U.S. News & World Report*, June 5, 1995, p. 43; "Shoe Playoff: Reebok's Shaq Up against Nike's Jordan," *St. Louis Post-Dispatch*, May 9, 1995, p. 6C; Eric Hollreiser, "Nike Veers to Women, Away from Sport-Specific Ads," *BrandWeek*, Feb. 13, 1995, p. 9; Dagmar Mussy, "Adidas Strides on Its Own Path," *Advertising Age*, Feb. 13, 1995, p. 6; Jeff Jensen, "Reebok Slowly Hones Sports Savvy Image," *Advertising Age*, Feb. 13, 1995, p. 6; Dori Yang, Michael Oneal, Charles Hoots, and Robert Neff, "Can Nike Just Do It?" *Business Week*, Apr. 18, 1994, p. 86; Joseph Pereira, "Sports Sandals, Boots Step on Sneaker Sales," *The Wall Street Journal*, Apr. 14, 1994, p. B1; Eric Randall, "Nike Makes Strides to Regain Footing," *USA Today*, Mar. 17, 1994, p. 3B; and Geoffrey Smith and Mark Maremont, "Can Reebok Regain Its Balance?" *Business Week*, Dec. 20, 1993, p. 108.

Careers in Marketing

After college, then what? For most people it means a job. But your goal should be more than just finding employment. Your first full-time job after graduation should serve as a springboard to a successful career. To provide yourself with every opportunity, you should begin your preparation as early as possible in college, and launch your actual job search at least one term, and preferably 9 months, before graduation.

To get you thinking about your postgraduation ambitions and upcoming job search, this appendix first discusses choosing a career. Then a variety of career opportunities in marketing are described. Finally, guidelines on obtaining a postgraduation job are presented in a section that is relevant to all students regardless of major.

Choosing a Career

One of the most significant decisions you will ever make is choosing a career. This career decision will influence your future happiness, self-fulfillment, and well-being. Yet, unfortunately, career decisions often seem to be based on insufficient information, analysis, and evaluation of alternatives.

Early in the career-decision process, everyone should spend some time in introspection. Introspection is the process of looking into yourself and honestly assessing what you want and what you have to offer. Let's look briefly at what this involves.

What Do You Want?

Perhaps this question would be better worded if we asked, "What is important to you in life?" To answer this broad question, you must answer several more specific ones, such as the following:

- Do you want your career to be the main event in your life? Or do you see a career only as the means of financing leisure-time activities?
- How important are money and other financial rewards?
- How important are the social surroundings, climate, and other aspects of the environment in which you live?
- Would you prefer to work for a large company or a small organization?
- Would you prefer living and working in a small town or in an urban area?
- Are you willing to relocate to another part of the country? How often would you be willing to move?
- How important is the social prestige of your career?
- Do you prefer work that is evenly paced or occasionally hectic? How do you deal with the pressure of deadlines?
- Do you need tangible signs of results on a job to feel fulfilled?
- Do you prefer to work alone or as part of a team?

Another way to approach the question of what you want from a career is to identify—in writing—your goals in life. List both your intermediate-term goals (3 to 5 years from now) and your long-term goals (10 years or more).

Still another approach is to simply describe yourself in some detail. By writing a description of your personality, likes and dislikes, and hopes and fears, you may be able to identify various careers that would (or would not) fit your self-image.

What Can You Offer?

Next you need to identify in some detail your strong and weak points. Why would anyone want to hire you? What skills have you developed? What experience—work, education, extracurricular activities—do you have that might be attractive to prospective employers?

An important consideration is your work experience. Employers are less concerned with where you have worked than they are with the initiative you demonstrate in finding a job and your performance on the job. To gain some exposure to what goes on in business, consider a job with a temporary help agency. Manpower Inc., for example, employs 100,000 people in the summer. Another option is a summer internship. Many students make an extra effort to find an internship in the summer before their last year of college. Firms often use these positions to groom future employees. Burlington Industries assigns mentors to all its interns, and each is given two formal evaluations during the summer.

Since the attributes sought by business aren't acquired overnight, you should start developing them early in your college program. However, keep in mind that prospective employers are much more interested in what a person *accomplished* in various roles than how many different titles he or she had. So be selective, and do a few things well.

What Are the Marketing Jobs?

In Chapter 1 we noted that about one-quarter to one-third of all civilian jobs are in the field of marketing. These jobs cover a wide variety of activities and a great range of qualifications and aptitudes. For instance, jobs in personal selling call for a set of qualifications that are different from those in marketing research. A person who is likely to be successful in advertising may not be a good prospect in physical distribution. Consequently, the aptitudes and skills of different individuals make them candidates for different types of marketing jobs.

In this section we shall briefly describe the major jobs in marketing, grouping them by title or activity. The types of positions that are most often available to graduating students are summarized in Table B-1.

Personal Selling

Sales jobs are by far the most numerous of all the jobs in marketing. Personal selling spans a broad array of activities, organizations, and titles. Consider the following people: a driver-sales person for Coca-Cola, a sales clerk in a department store, a sales engineer providing technical assistance in sales of hydraulic valves, a representative for Boeing selling a fleet of airplanes, and a pharmaceutical representative visiting physicians and pharmacists to introduce new drugs. All these people are engaged in personal selling, but each sales job is different from the others.

TABLE B-1 Eight entry-level marketing jobs for college graduates

Job title	Comments
Sales representative	Responsible for selling the organization's goods or services to customers. Customers may be ultimate consumers, middlemen, or other organizations.
Sales (or marketing) support person	Assists sales manager and staff in implementing programs, such as trade shows and dealer or sales-force incentive programs. Marketing support position involves broader responsibility, including assisting in product development and distribution.
Customer service representative	Assists customers after the sale, often by handling complaints and requests for information or service. Common in the business-goods sector.
Retail management executive trainee	Position is common in department store chains. After training, usually moves through rotating assignment in buying and management of selling department. Ultimately, person focuses on either buying or store management.
Assistant store manager	Position is common in chains that have small specialty stores in shopping centers. Assists in overseeing day-to-day activities of the store, especially staffing and display. In effect, is a trainee position.
Assistant media buyer	Common starting position in an advertising agency. Assists buyer in purchasing advertising space and time for firms that are the agency's clients. Another entry-level position, working for either an agency or an advertiser, is junior copywriter.
Research trainee	Found in various large organizations and in marketing research firms. After or during training, assists with one or more phases of the research process, such as data collection, data analysis, or report preparation.
Assistant (or assistant to) product manager	Assists in planning and, especially, implementing marketing program for a specific brand or product line. Most commonly found in large companies that sell consumer goods or services.

Sales jobs of one sort or another are available in virtually every locality. This means that you can pretty well pick the area where you would like to live, and still get involved in personal selling.

There are opportunities to earn a very high income in personal selling. This is especially true when the compensation plan is straight commission, or is a combination of salary plus a significant incentive element.

A sales job is the most common entry-level position in marketing. Furthermore, as illustrated in Figure B-1, a sales job is a widely used stepping stone to a management position. There is no better way to learn about a company's products or its customers!

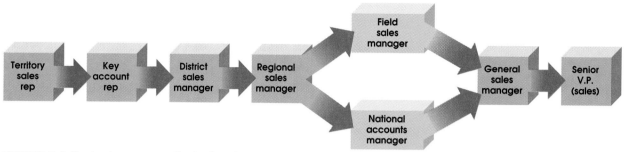

FIGURE B-1 Typical career path starting in personal selling.

Many companies recruit people for sales jobs with the intention of promoting some of these people into management positions. Personal selling and sales management jobs are also a good route to the top in a firm because it is relatively easy to measure a person's performance and productivity in selling.

A sales job is different from other jobs in several significant ways that will be discussed in Chapter 17. Sales people represent their company to customers and to the public in general. The public ordinarily does not judge a firm by its factory or office personnel. Also, outside sales people (those who go to the customers) operate with very little or no direct personal supervision. They must have considerable creativity, persistence, and self-motivation. Furthermore, sales jobs often involve traveling and require much time away from home and family. Among white-collar jobs, personal selling generally rates low in social status and prestige.

All in all, selling is hard work, but the potential rewards are immense. Certainly no other job contributes as much to the success of an organization. Remember—nothing happens until somebody sells something!

Store Management

Retailing is second only to personal selling in terms of number of job opportunities for new college graduates. The two primary areas of opportunity in department store, specialty, and discount chains are in merchandising or buying (described in the next section) and store management.

Store managers have a great deal of responsibility and authority. A store manager's authority related to acquiring merchandise (the buying function) varies greatly from one firm to the next. However, once the merchandise arrives in the store, the manager has the responsibility and authority for displaying, selling, and controlling the inventory. Store managers in most companies, either directly or indirectly through department heads, oversee personal selling, promotion, credit, personnel management, and store security.

The entry-level position for store management is typically assistant department manager, department manager, or assistant store manager, depending on the size of the store. The performance of a store or department manager is directly measurable in terms of sales or profits. Therefore, speed of advancement into higher positions is determined primarily by the quality and quantity of results produced by the manager.

Buying and Purchasing

Most medium-size and larger organizations employ people who specialize in buying, as opposed to selling, goods and services. In one type of position, people select and acquire merchandise for resale. In another type of position, people purchase goods and services not for resale but for use in a manufacturing process or in operating an organization.

Every retail organization needs people to buy merchandise for resale. Frequently the route to the top in retailing is through the buying (also called merchandising) division of the business. Large retailers have many positions for buyers and assistant buyers. Each merchandise department normally has a buyer. Consequently, you often have a chance to work with particular products that interest you.

There are also centralized buying offices that buy for several different stores or chains. These resident buying offices are usually in New York City and a few other large cities.

A purchasing agent is the business market counterpart of the retail store buyer. Virtually all firms in the business market have purchasing departments. People in these departments buy raw materials and supplies for the production, office, and sales departments in their firms.

Retail buyers and purchasing agents need many of the same skills. They must be able to analyze markets, determine merchandise needs, and negotiate with sellers. It is also necessary to have some knowledge of credit, finance, and physical distribution.

Advertising

Opportunities in advertising can be found in many different jobs in various organizations. The three primary areas of opportunity are:

- Advertisers, including manufacturers, retailers, and service firms. Many of these organizations prepare and place their own ads. In some of these firms the advertising department is a large one.
- Various media (including newspapers, radio and TV stations, and magazines) that carry ads.
- Advertising agencies that specialize in creating and producing individual ads and entire promotion campaigns.

Jobs in advertising encompass a number of aptitudes and interests—artistic, creative, managerial, research, and sales. The advertising field holds real opportunity for the artistic or creative person. Agencies and advertising departments need copywriters, artists, photographers, layout designers, printing experts, and others to create and produce ads.

Account executive is a key position in advertising agencies. People in this position are the liaisons between the agency and its clients (the advertisers). Account executives coordinate the agency's efforts with the clients' marketing programs.

Another group of advertising jobs involves the placement of ads. On the advertisers' side, this entails allocating the advertising budget by planning an advertising schedule and selecting the media. On the media side, every TV and radio network and station, all newspapers and magazines, and every other advertising outlet employ sales people. Advertisers and agencies also often need people who can conduct buyer-behavior studies and other marketing research.

Sales Promotion

The main function of sales promotion is to tie together the activities in personal selling and advertising. Effective sales promotion requires imagination and creativity, coupled with a sound foundation in marketing fundamentals.

One aspect of sales promotion is the design and creation of retailers' in-store displays and window displays. Another aspect deals with trade shows and other company exhibits. Sales promotion activities also include the development and management of premium giveaways, contests, product sampling, and other types of promotion.

Marketing Research

Marketing research jobs cover a broad range of activities that will be outlined in Chapter 4. People are hired for marketing research jobs by manufacturers, retailers, services marketers, government agencies, and other organizations. There are also a large number of specialized marketing research companies. Generally, however, there are fewer jobs in marketing research than in personal selling or in retailing.

Marketing researchers are problem solvers. They collect and analyze masses of information. Thus they need an aptitude for precise, analytical work. Some quantitative skills are needed, particularly an understanding of statistics.

Product/Brand Management

In Chapter 8 we discuss briefly the position of product manager in connection with the organizational structure for new-product planning and development. Product managers (sometimes called brand managers) are responsible for planning and directing the entire marketing program for a given product or group of products.

Early on, product managers make decisions about packaging, labeling, and other aspects of the product itself. Product managers are also responsible for the marketing research necessary to identify the market. They plan advertising, personal selling, and sales promotional programs for their products. Product managers are concerned with pricing, physical distribution, and legal issues of the product.

In many respects, being a product manager is like running your own business. Product managers must have good analytical skills to keep abreast of what competitors are doing and what is happening in the market. They also need to be tactful and persuasive to gain the cooperation of functional areas such as manufacturing and sales.

Physical Distribution

Many jobs exist in the field of physical distribution, and the prospects are even brighter as we look ahead to the year 2000 and beyond. More and more firms are expected to adopt the systems approach in physical distribution (described in Chapter 15) to control the huge expenses involved in materials movement and warehousing.

Manufacturers, retailers, and all other goods-handling firms have jobs that involve two stages of physical distribution. First the product must be moved to the firm for processing or resale. Then the finished products must be distributed to the markets. These physical distribution tasks involve jobs in transportation management, warehousing, and inventory control. In addition, many transportation carriers and warehousing firms also provide a variety of jobs that may interest you.

Public Relations

The public relations department is a valuable connection between an organization and its various publics. The department must deal with, or go through, the news media to reach these publics. Public relations people must be especially good in communications. In fact, these people often have college degrees in communications or journalism, rather than in marketing.

In essence, the job of public relations is to project the desired company image. More specifically, public relations people are responsible for telling the public about the company—its products, community activities, social programs, environmental improvement activities, labor policies, and views regarding controversial issues. Public relations specialists are particularly important—and very visible—when a company responds to adverse publicity. Such publicity may come from a governmental investigation or a charge of unethical practices or unsafe products, as when Johnson & Johnson dealt with the Tylenol tampering and Wal-Mart responded to charges of selling goods made with child labor.

Whether disseminating favorable publicity or responding to adverse publicity, the company's position must be stated in a clear, understandable, and—above all—believable fashion.

Consumer Affairs and Protection

The broad area of consumer affairs and protection encompasses several activities that provide job and career opportunities. Many of these jobs are an outgrowth of the consumer movement to be discussed in Chapter 22. Many companies have a consumer affairs department to handle consumer complaints. Several federal and state agencies keep watch on business firms and provide information and assistance to consumers. Grocery products manufacturers and gas and electric companies regularly hire college graduates to aid consumers in product use. Government and private product-testing agencies hire people to test products for safety, durability, and other features.

Other Career Areas

In this short appendix it is not possible to list all the careers that stem from marketing. We have, however, covered the major areas. You may get additional career ideas from the next section, which deals with organizations that provide these opportunities.

Where Are the Marketing Jobs?

In this section we briefly describe the types of companies and other organizations that provide jobs in marketing. This section also includes comments on jobs in international marketing and a comparison of job opportunities in large versus small organizations.

Types of Organizations

Literally millions of organizations provide jobs and career opportunities in marketing. The organizations can be grouped into the following categories.

Manufacturing.   Most manufacturing firms provide career opportunities in all the activities discussed in the previous section. In their promotional mix, some manufacturers stress personal selling while others rely more on advertising. Even small companies offer job opportunities in most of the categories we have mentioned.

Because most manufacturers make products that are used by other businesses, their names are not familiar to the general public. Unfortunately, many college graduates overlook some of these potentially excellent employers just because they don't recognize their corporate names. Starting salaries are often higher in manufacturing firms than in retailing and the other organizations described next.

Retailing. Retailing firms provide more marketing jobs by far than does any other organizational category, but most of these jobs are not intended for college graduates. Careers in retailing are not well understood by college students, who may equate retailing with clerking in a department store or filling shelves in a supermarket. Students often perceive that retail pay is low and that retail work-hours include a lot of evenings and weekends.

Actually a career in retailing offers many attractive features for college graduates. There are opportunities for very rapid advancement for those who display real ability. Performance results, such as sales and profits, are quickly and highly visible. If you can produce, management will generally note this fact in a hurry.

While the starting pay in many (but not all) stores is lower than in manufacturing, the compensation in higher-level retailing jobs typically is excellent. There are good retailing jobs in virtually every geographic area. Also, large retail chains (such as the May Company and Wal-Mart) generally have excellent management-training programs for newly hired college graduates.

Perhaps the main attractions in retailing are less tangible. Retailing can be an exciting field. You are constantly involved with people—customers, suppliers, and other workers. And there are challenges in merchandise buying, especially finding out what will sell well—what customers really want.

It is easier to start a career in retailing than in many other fields. In large stores there are jobs involving personnel management, accounting controls, and store operations (receiving, credit, and customer service departments). However, the lifeblood of retailing is the buying and selling of merchandise or services. Thus the more numerous and better-paying positions are in merchandising and store management. A typical career path is presented in Figure B-2. Note that after several years of experience in both areas, a retail manager often decides to concentrate on merchandising or store management.

Wholesaling. Career opportunities in wholesaling generally are less well understood and appreciated than those in retailing or manufacturing. Wholesaling firms typically do not recruit on college campuses, and they generally have a low profile among students.

Yet opportunities are there. Wholesalers of consumer products and industrial distributors provide many jobs in buying, personal selling, marketing research,

FIGURE B-2 Typical career path in a department store chain.

and physical distribution. Manufacturers' agents, brokers, and the other agent middlemen discussed in Chapter 15 also offer jobs and careers. Wholesaling middlemen are increasing in numbers and in sales volume, and their future is promising.

Services Marketing. The broad array of service industries that will be discussed in Chapter 19 provides a bonanza of job and career opportunities in marketing. Many of these fields are expected to experience rapid growth during the 1990s. The travel, hospitality, education, finance, entertainment, health care, communications, and professional services fields are prime examples. Recognizing the importance of marketing, many of these industries and the organizations within them are now adding marketing-related personnel. Most of these firms really are retailers of services. Consequently, many of the statements we made earlier about retailing careers are relevant here.

Other Business Areas. Besides the general types of organizations just described, more specialized business firms hire college graduates for marketing-related positions. Entry-level opportunities can be found with communications media (such as TV stations), advertising agencies, franchise systems, participation and spectator sports organizations, public utilities, and transportation firms (such as truck lines).

Nonprofit Organizations. As will be described in Chapter 19, nonprofit organizations are realizing that marketing is the key to their success. Consequently, it is likely that jobs and careers in many nonprofit organizations will open up in large numbers. Consider the wide variety of nonprofit organizations—hospitals, museums, educational institutions, religious organizations, foundations, charities, and political parties, among others. Given this diversity, you can expect to find a wide range of marketing-related positions in nonprofit organizations.

Government. Countless federal and state government organizations hire people for marketing positions. Here we include the major cabinet departments—agriculture, defense, human services, and the others. We also include all the regulatory agencies. Government organizations employ people in purchasing, marketing research, public relations, physical distribution, consumer affairs and protection, and even advertising and sales promotion. Sometimes students tend to overlook the many marketing career opportunities in government.

Careers in International Marketing

Students who like to travel and experience different cultures may want to work at least part of the time in foreign countries. They may be interested in careers in international marketing, and they may even major in international business in college. Typically, however, companies do not hire college graduates and immediately assign them to jobs in international marketing. People are normally hired for entry-level positions in the domestic divisions of a company's operations. Then, after some years of experience with the firm, an employee may have an opportunity to move into the firm's international divisions. If you have international aspirations, begin looking for companies that have or are developing international markets. You would also be wise to study a second language and take advantage of opportunities to learn about other cultures.

Large versus Small Companies

Should you go to work for a large company or a small firm? Or should you go into business for yourself upon graduation? For over a decade now, more and more students have been saying that they want to work for a small company. They feel that there is more freedom of action, more rapid advancement, and less restraint on their life-styles in smaller firms.

Perhaps so. And certainly no one should discourage you from a career in small business. *But*, we typically recommend to students (who ask for advice) that they start their careers in a big company. Then, after a few years, they can move into a smaller firm. There are three reasons for this recommendation:

- A large firm is more likely to have a good training program in your chosen field of activity. Many students have little or no practical marketing experience. The fine training programs provided by numerous large manufacturers, retailers, and major services marketers can be critical in launching a career.
- You can learn something about how a big company operates. After all, when you go into a smaller firm, large companies will be your competitors. So the more you know about them, the better able you will be to compete with them.
- After working for awhile for a big company, you may change your mind and decide to stay with the larger firm after all. On the other hand, let's say that you want to go to a small company after you have worked a few years at a big firm. At that point it will be relatively easy to move from a large company to a smaller one. If you start in a small firm, however, and later want to move into big business, it is not so easy to move.

We have discussed various career fields and types of organizations that hire people in these fields. Now let's take a brief look at how you should go about getting a job with one of these organizations.

How Do You Search for a Job?

This book and your entire course are designed to teach you the fundamentals involved in developing and managing a marketing program. These fundamentals are applicable regardless of whether you are marketing a good, service, idea, person, or place.

Now let's see whether we can apply these fundamentals to a program designed to market a person—*you!* We shall discuss a marketing approach that you can use to get a job and to start a career. Though we are focusing on a marketing career, this same approach can be used in seeking jobs and careers in any field.

Identify and Analyze the Market

The first step in building a marketing program is to identify and analyze the market. In this case the market consists of prospective employers. Right now you don't know exactly who comprises that target market. So you must research several possible markets and then eventually narrow down your choice. In effect, we are talking about "choosing a career." Much of what we discussed in the first section of this appendix is applicable here.

You should initially get as much information as you can regarding various career opportunities in marketing. For information sources you might start with one or two professors whom you know reasonably well. Then turn to the placement office in your school, or wherever postgraduation jobs are listed. Many companies prepare recruiting brochures for students that describe the company and explain its career opportunities.

Newspapers and business journals are another good information source. *The Wall Street Journal* and the business sections of large-city newspapers can be useful. Periodicals such as *Business Week*, *Marketing News*, *Advertising Age*, and trade publications in many individual industries are helpful. Sometimes, looking carefully through *Moody's Manual of Investments*, Standard and Poor's *Register*, or even a series of company annual reports can give you ideas about firms you might like to work for. You should exchange information with other students who are also in the job market. Use course assignments such as term projects and papers to investigate various industries and firms.

In summary, learn all you can about a broad cross-section of firms and industries. Then, from this information search, zero in on one or two industries and a few companies that are your leading choices. You will now be ready to develop the marketing mix that will be effective in marketing yourself to your target markets.

Product

In this case the "product" you are planning and developing is yourself and your services. You want to make yourself as attractive as possible to your market—that is, prospective employers.

Start your product planning by listing in some detail your strong and weak points. These will lead into another list—your qualifications and achievements. This introspection is something we discussed in the first section of this appendix in connection with choosing a career.

When you are considering your qualifications, it may help to group them into broad categories such as these:

- Education—schools attended, degree earned, grade-point average, major, favorite subjects.
- Work experience—part-time and full-time responsibilities.
- Honors and awards.
- Extracurricular activities and accomplishments—offices, memberships, committees, volunteer activities.
- Hobbies.

Later we will discuss the presentation of your qualifications in a personal data sheet.

An important aspect of product planning is product differentiation. How can you differentiate yourself from all the other college grads? What have you done that is different, unusual, or exceptional? This doesn't have to be earthshaking—just something that shows a trait such as initiative, imagination, or perseverance.

Another part of product planning is packaging. When you go for an interview, be sure that the external package looks attractive. People do judge you by your appearance, just as you judge products by the way they look. This means paying attention to what you wear and how you are groomed. A good impression starts with prospective employers' first meetings with you.

Price

"What salary do you expect?" "How much do you think we should pay you?" These are two of the questions a prospective employer might ask in a job interview. If you have not done some thinking in advance regarding the price you want for your services, these questions may throw you.

As part of your marketing program, find out what the market price is for people entering your field. Talk with placement officers, career counselors, professors, and other students who are in the job market. From these sources you should get a pretty good idea of starting salaries in entry-level positions. Use this information to decide *before* the interview on a range of salaries for yourself. Remember that income can be stated in several different ways. For example, there may be a base salary, the possibility of a bonus, and fringe benefits such as the use of a company-supplied car.

Distribution Channel

There are only a few major channels you are likely to use in marketing yourself to prospective employers. The simplest channel is your placement office, assuming that there is one on your campus. Most colleges, through their placement offices, host and assist companies that send job recruiters to do on-campus interviewing.

Another channel is help-wanted ads in business journals, trade journals, and newspapers. Perhaps the most difficult, but often the most rewarding, channel is going directly to firms in which you are especially interested—knock on doors or write letters seeking a job interview. Many employers look favorably on people who display this kind of initiative in their job search.

Promotion

Other than planning and developing an excellent product, the most important ingredient in your marketing mix is a good promotion (or communications) program. Your promotion will consist primarily of written communications (a form of advertising) and interviewing (a form of personal selling).

To stand out from the crowd and be noticed, job applicants have tried everything from singing telegrams to skywriting. One enterprising student rented the sides of an 18-wheeler. Soon after his name, phone number, and plea for a job began cruising the nation's highways, he received several hundred calls.

Most applicants use more conventional approaches. Frequently your first contact with a prospective employer is a cover letter in which you state briefly why you are writing to that company and what you have to offer. You enclose a personal résumé, and you request an appointment for an interview.

Cover Letter. In the opening paragraph of your cover letter, you should indicate why you want to work for the firm. Mention a couple of key points regarding the firm—points you learned from your research. In the second paragraph, you can present a few highlights of your own experience or personality that make you an attractive prospect. In the third paragraph, state that you are enclosing your résumé, and request an appointment for an interview, even suggest some dates and a time when you will telephone to arrange the meeting.

Résumé. A résumé (also called a curriculum vita or personal data sheet) is really a brief history of yourself. Personal computers and word processing packages make it possible to design a distinctive and very professional-appearing résumé. You can start with biographical information such as your name, address, and phone number. Then divide your résumé into sections, including education, work experience, and activities that were described in the product section.

You will need some references—people who know you well and can speak to your personal attributes or professional capabilities. Family friends, former employers or supervisors, and college instructors are typically used. To save space, one approach is simply to state at the end of the résumé, "References furnished upon request." An alternative is to list your references by name (along with their titles, addresses, and phone numbers) at the bottom of your résumé or on a separate sheet. The thinking behind this approach is that you should make it as easy as possible for a prospective employer to check your references. Of course, you should obtain permission before you use a person as a reference.

It is difficult to overstate the value of a persuasive cover letter and a distinctive résumé. They are critically important elements in your job search. They certainly are two of the most important ads you will ever write.

Interview.   Rarely is anyone hired without one or more interviews. In some cases, as when recruiters visit your campus, the interview is your initial contact with the firm. In other situations the interviews come as a result of your letter of introduction and résumé.

The interview is an exercise in personal selling—in this case, you are selling yourself. People are often uncomfortable and uptight in interviews, especially their first few, so don't be surprised or disappointed if you are. One way to reduce your anxiety and increase the likelihood of impressing the interviewer is to prepare yourself to answer tough questions that may be asked:

- Why should we hire you?
- What are your distinctive strengths?
- Do you have any weaknesses, and how do you plan to overcome them?
- What challenges have you successfully overcome?
- What kind of job do you expect to have in 5 years?

Your performance in an interview often determines whether or not you get the job. So be on your toes—be honest in your answers, and try to look more relaxed and confident than you may feel!

After interviews with a company have been completed, it is worthwhile to write a letter to each of the interviewers. Thank them for the opportunity to learn about their company and, if appropriate, restate your interest in the job.

Evaluating Job Offers.   You are likely to receive multiple job offers *if*:

- The economy is fairly healthy.
- You have at least an acceptable academic record.
- You conduct an aggressive job search.
- You develop a persuasive cover letter and professional résumé.
- You perform well in job interviews.

You should evaluate the suitability of a single job offer or compare multiple job offers against a set of criteria that are important to you. The criteria you select and the importance you place on them require some careful thought. Below are examples of criteria you might consider.

- Will you be happy in your work? It is no accident that we frequently hear about "Blue Monday" (the weekend of freedom is finished and I have to go back to work) and "TGIF" (Thank God It's Friday). Many people in society are not happy with their jobs. Normally, half or more of your waking hours will be spent at work, commuting to and from work, or doing job-related work at home. So you should look for a job and career that you will enjoy.

- Does the career fit your self-image? Are the job and career in line with your goals, dreams, and aspirations? Will they satisfy you? Will you be proud to tell people about your job? Will your spouse (and someday your teenage children) be proud of you in that career?
- What demands or pressures are associated with the career? Some people thrive on pressure. They constantly seek new challenges in their work. Other people look for a more tranquil work experience. They do not want a job with constant demands and deadlines to meet.
- Do the financial factors meet your needs? How does the starting salary compare with those of other jobs? Consider what the job is likely to pay after you have been there 3 to 5 years. Some engineering jobs, for example, have high starting salaries, but soon hit a salary ceiling. In contrast, some marketing jobs have lower starting salaries but no upper limits.
- Are there opportunities for promotion? You should evaluate the promotion patterns in a job or in a firm. Try to find out how long it normally takes to reach a given executive level. Study the backgrounds of presidents of a number of large companies in the industry. Did they come up through engineering, the legal department, sales or marketing, accounting, or some other area?
- Are the travel considerations suitable? Some jobs involve a considerable amount of travel whether you are an entry-level worker or an executive. Other jobs are strictly in-house, with no travel at all.
- Is there job or career "transportability"? Are there similar jobs in many other geographic areas? If both you and your spouse are career-oriented, what will happen to you if your spouse is transferred to another city? One nice thing about careers such as teaching, retailing, nursing, and personal selling is that generally these jobs exist in considerable numbers in many different locations.
- What is the supply-and-demand situation in this field? Determine generally how many job openings currently exist in a given field, as compared with the supply of qualified applicants. At the same time, study the future prospects regarding this supply-and-demand condition. Determine whether a present shortage or overcrowding of workers in a field is a temporary situation or is likely to exist for several years.

Where Is There More Information?

We encourage you to keep in mind the questions and guidelines presented in this appendix as you take this course and progress through your academic program. To provide you with additional advice and guidance, several excellent reference sources are listed below. It's not too early to start thinking about—and planning—your search for a postgraduation job!

- Richard Nelson Bolles, *The 1996 What Color Is Your Parachute? A Practical Manual for Jobhunters and Career Changers*, Ten Speed Press, Berkeley, CA, 1996.
- Joyce Lain Kennedy, *Hook Up, Get Hired: The Internet Job Search Revolution*, John Wiley & Sons, New York, 1995.
- Martin Yate, *Résumés That Knock 'Em Dead*, Adams Publishing, Holbrook, MA, 1995.

CHAPTER 1

1. John Riha, "Reinventing the Legend," *World Traveler*, February 1995, pp. 36–41.
2. John J. Fialka, "Parents Love, Coaches Hate a 'Safer' Baseball," *The Wall Street Journal*, May 24, 1994, p. B1.
3. N. J. (Dusty) Rodes, "Pittsburgh Launches Huge Marketing Initiative," *Marketing News*, Jan. 30, 1995, p. 3.
4. Robert J. Keith, "The Marketing Revolution," *Journal of Marketing*, January 1960, p. 37.
5. Geraldine E. Williams, "High Performance Marketing: An Interview with Nike's Phil Knight," *Harvard Business Review*, July–August 1992, p. 92.
6. "Meet the New Consumer," *Fortune*, Autumn/Winter 1993, pp. 7–8.
7. Sonya S. Hamilton, "You Don't Say?" *Sales & Marketing Management*, October 1994, pp. 111–112.
8. Richard Gibson, "Frito-Lay Soars as Eagle Snacks Eye Ways to Lift Market Share," *The Wall Street Journal*, Mar. 1, 1994, p. B7.
9. Robert Johnson, "In the Chips," *The Wall Street Journal*, Mar. 22, 1991, p. B1.
10. Chuck Hawkins, "Will Home Depot Be 'The Wal-Mart of the '90s'?" *Business Week*, Mar. 19, 1990, pp. 124–125.
11. Cyndee Miller, "Churches Turn to Research for Help in Saving New Souls," *Marketing News*, Apr. 11, 1994, p. 1.
12. Shelby D. Hunt and Robert M. Morgan, "Relationship Marketing in the Era of Network Competition," *Marketing Management*, Vol. 3, No. 1, 1994, pp. 18–28.
13. Stan Rapp and Thomas L. Collins, "The New Marketing: Sell and Socialize," *The New York Times*, Feb. 20, 1994, p. 11.
14. Frederick E. Webster, Jr., "Defining the New Marketing Concept," *Marketing Management*, Vol. 2, No. 4, 1993, pp. 22–31.
15. For more insights into this concept, see Frederick E. Webster, Jr., "Executing the New Marketing Concept," *Marketing Management*, Vol. 3, No. 1, 1994, pp. 8–16.
16. For a complete discussion of ethics in marketing, see Gene R. Laczniak and Patrick E. Murphy, *Ethical Marketing Decisions: The Higher Road*, Allyn & Bacon, New York, 1993.
17. Allison Lucas, "When Gift Giving Goes Too Far," *Sales & Marketing Management*, June 1995, p. 15.
18. W. Mathews, "Codes of Ethics: Organizational Behavior and Misbehavior," in William C. Frederick, ed., *Research in Corporate Social Performance and Policy*, JAI Press, Greenwich, CT, 1987, pp. 107–130.
19. Kenneth Labich, "The New Crisis in Business Ethics," *Fortune*, Apr. 20, 1992, pp. 167+.
20. Laczniak and Murphy, op. cit., p. 202.
21. Labich, loc. cit.
22. D. Kirk Davidson, "High Stakes Cause Ethical Problems," *Marketing News*, May 22, 1995, p. 8.
23. Stuart Elliott, "Loneliness in a Long-Running Pitch," *The New York Times*, May 5, 1992, pp. D1+. For an overview of quality issues, see David Greising, "Making Quality Pay," *Business Week*, Aug. 8, 1994, pp. 54–59.
24. Shawn Tully, "The Value Sell at $115 Million," *Fortune*, Autumn/Winter 1993, p. 86.
25. Richard J. Schonberger, "Is Strategy Strategic? Impact of Total Quality Management on Strategy," *Academy of Management Executive*, August 1992, pp. 80–87.
26. C. Carl Pegels, *Total Quality Management*, Boyd & Fraser Publishing, Danvers, MA, 1995, pp. 137–141.
27. Joseph B. White, "Value Pricing Is Hot as Shrewd Customers Seek Low-Cost Quality," *The Wall Street Journal*, Mar. 12, 1991, p. A1.
28. Amy Barrett, "It's a Small (Business) World," *Business Week*, Apr. 17, 1995, pp. 96–101.
29. Bhushan Bahree, "World's Trade Growth Outpaces Gains in Output," *The Wall Street Journal*, Nov. 17, 1995, p. A6.
30. Riha, loc. cit.

CHAPTER 2

1. Richard Gibson, "McDonald's Resolves to Improve Service, Acknowledging a 'Lousy' Track Record," *The Wall Street Journal*, Dec. 28, 1995, p. A3; Richard Gibson, "At McDonald's, New Recipes for Buns, Eggs," *The Wall Street Journal*, June 13, 1995, p. B1; Andrew E. Serwer, "McDonald's Conquers the World," *Fortune*, Oct. 17, 1994, pp. 103–104; and Patricia Sellers, "Look Who's Learned about Value," *Fortune*, Oct. 18, 1993, pp. 75, 78.
2. For a study of how senior executives in one industry scan their operating environments, see Ethel Auster and Chun Wei Choo, "How Senior Managers Acquire and Use Information in Environmental Scanning," *Information Processing and Management*, September–October 1994, pp. 607–618.
3. Ram Subramanian, Nirmala Fernandes, and Earl Harper, "Environmental Scanning in U.S. Companies: Their Nature and Their Relationship to Performance," *Management International Review*, Vol. 33, No. 3, 1993, pp. 271–286.
4. Some of the statistics and examples in this paragraph and the following one are drawn from Charles D. Schewe and Geoffrey E. Meredith, "Digging Deep to Delight the Mature Adult Consumer," *Marketing Management*, Winter 1994, p. 22. Others come from Stanley Kranczer, "Outlook for U.S. Population Growth," *Statistical Bulletin* (Metropolitan Life Insurance Co.), October 1994, pp. 18+.
5. Kranczer, loc. cit.
6. Gary L. Berman, "The Hispanic Market: Getting Down to Cases," *Sales & Marketing Management*, October 1991, p. 66.
7. Laura Zinn, "Run to the Supermarket and Pick Me Up Some Cactus," *Business Week*, June 20, 1994, pp. 70–71.
8. "The Future of Households," *American Demographics*, January 1995, p. 15.
9. "Seizing the Dark Day," *Business Week*, Jan. 13, 1992, p. 26.
10. Christopher Farrell and Zachary Schiller, "Stuck!" *Business Week*, Nov. 15, 1993, pp. 146–148+. For an essay that describes price deflation in retailing and recommends strategies for coping with deflation, see Walter K. Levy, "Beware, the Pricing Genie Is out of the Bottle," *Retailing Issues Letter*, November 1994, pp. 1–4.
11. Joseph Pereira, "Toys 'R' Us Grows Up, Finds Life Isn't All Fun, Games,"

The Wall Street Journal, Mar. 20, 1995, p. B6.

12. Laura Litvan, "Going 'Green' in the '90s," *Nation's Business*, February 1995, p. 31.

13. C. Mitchell Adrian and Michael D. Richard, "An Examination of Purchase Behavior versus Purchase Attitudes for Environmentally Friendly and Recycled Consumer Goods," *Southern Business Review*, Spring 1995, pp. 1–15.

14. Kevin Goldman, "'Green' Campaigns Don't Always Pay Off, Survey Finds," *The Wall Street Journal*, Apr. 11, 1994, p. B8.

15. Ibid.

16. Peter Stisser, "A Deeper Shade of Green," *American Demographics*, March 1994, p. 28.

17. Ibid., p. 29.

18. Cyndee Miller, "Study Dispels '80s Stereotypes of Women," *Marketing News*, May 22, 1995, p. 3.

19. Teri Agins, "Many Women Lose Interest in Clothes, to Retailers' Dismay," *The Wall Street Journal*, Feb. 28, 1995, p. A1.

20. Maria Mallory, Dan McGraw, and Jill Jordan Sieder, "Women on a Fast Track," *U.S. News & World Report*, Nov. 6, 1995, pp. 60+; and Miller, loc. cit.

21. Diane Crispell, "The New World of Men," *American Demographics*, January 1992, pp. 38–43.

22. Eugene H. Fram, "Stress and Strategic Opportunity," *Marketing Management*, Vol. 2, No. 1, 1993, pp. 59–64.

23. Jeanne Whalen, "Taco Bell Cuts the Fat, Aims for Hefty Sales," *Advertising Age*, Feb. 13, 1995, p. 36.

24. Viveca Novak and Joseph Pereira, "Reebok and FTC Settle Price-Fixing Charges," *The Wall Street Journal*, May 5, 1995, p. B1.

25. Stratford Sherman, "Will the Information Superhighway Be the Death of Retailing?" *Fortune*, Apr. 18, 1994, p. 99.

26. Paul M. Eng, "Big Business on the Net? Not Yet," *Business Week*, June 26, 1995, p. 100.

27. Cyndee Miller, "Marketers Find It's Hip to Be on the Internet," *Marketing News*, Feb. 27, 1995, p. 2. Also see Michael H. Martin, "Why the Web Is Still a No-Shop Zone," *Fortune*, Feb. 5, 1996, pp. 127–128.

28. Gary McWilliams, "At Compaq, a Desktop Crystal Ball," *Business Week*, Mar. 20, 1995, pp. 96–97.

29. Gibson, "At McDonald's, New Recipes for Buns, Eggs," loc. cit.; Serwer, loc. cit.; Sellers, loc. cit.; additional material from Jeanne Whalen, "McDonald's Shaking Marketing, Agencies," *Advertising Age*, Sept. 19, 1994, p. 4.

CHAPTER 3

1. Barbara Solomon, "Ringing Up Sales," *Management Review*, February 1995, pp. 38+; "Which Stores Are Best?" *Consumer Reports*, November 1994, pp. 719–721; and Michael Marlow, "Nordstrom Is Ranked King of Customer Service," *Women's Wear Daily*, Oct. 26, 1994, p. 12.

2. Many writers and executives use the terms *control* and *evaluation* synonymously. We distinguish between them. To speak of control as only one part of the management process is too restrictive. Rather than being an isolated managerial function, control permeates virtually all other organizational activities. For example, management *controls* its operations through the goals and strategies it selects. Also, the type of organizational structure used in the marketing department determines the degree of *control* over marketing operations.

3. Derek F. Abell, "Strategic Windows," *Journal of Marketing*, July 1978, pp. 21–26.

4. David Kirkpatrick, "As the Internet Sizzles, Online Services Battle for Stakes," *Fortune*, May 1, 1995, pp. 86–87.

5. *Pulse of the Middle Market—1990*, BDO Seidman, New York, 1990, pp. 12–13.

6. A technique for assessing a firm in relation to other firms in an industry is presented in Emilio Cvitkovic, "Profiling Your Competitors," *Planning Review*, May–June 1989, pp. 28–30.

7. Malcolm H. B. McDonald, "Ten Barriers to Marketing Planning," *The Journal of Business and Industrial Marketing*, Winter 1992, p. 15.

8. Edward DiMingo, "The Fine Art of Positioning," *The Journal of Business Strategy*, March/April 1988, pp. 34–38.

9. Suein L. Hwang, "Its Big Brands Long Taunted as Fatty, CPC Tries a More 'Wholesome' Approach," *The Wall Street Journal*, Apr. 20, 1992, pp. B1, B4.

10. Differential advantage in the context of services industries is examined in Sundar G. Bharadwaj, P. Rajan Varadarajan, and John Fahy, "Sustainable Competitive Advantage in Service Industries: A Conceptual Model and Research Proposition," *Journal of Marketing*, October 1993, pp. 83–99. An excellent earlier article stressing that strategy should focus on customer needs, not just on beating competition, is Kenichi Ohmae, "Getting Back to Strategy," *Harvard Business Review*, November–December 1988, pp. 149–156.

11. To learn about a new theory that goes beyond the concept of differential advantage to consider a firm's resources, especially market orientation, see Shelby D. Hunt and Robert M. Morgan, "The Comparative Advantage Theory of Competition," *Journal of Marketing*, April 1995, pp. 1–15.

12. Norman H. McMillan, "EST Retailing: How to Stay out of the Black Hole," *International Trends in Retailing*, Winter 1993, pp. 60–75.

13. An excellent source of information on how various companies prepare their marketing plans is Howard Sutton, *The Marketing Plan*, The Conference Board, New York, 1990.

14. *The Experience Curve Reviewed: IV. The Growth Share Matrix of the Product Portfolio*, Boston Consulting Group, Boston, 1973.

15. Laura Zinn, "Does Pepsi Have Too Many Products?" *Business Week*, Feb. 14, 1994, pp. 64+; and "Pepsi Sees Citrus Appeal in Its Crystal," *Advertising Age*, July 18, 1994, p. 12.

16. Discussed in Derek F. Abell and John S. Hammond, *Strategic Marketing Planning*, Prentice-Hall, Englewood Cliffs, NJ, 1979.

17. Keith H. Hammonds, "25 Executives to Watch: Kay Whitmore," *The 1990 Business Week 1000*, p. 145.

18. Robert Steyer, "Monsanto Drops Product," *St. Louis Post-Dispatch*, Jan. 17, 1994, p. 11BP.

19. Steven Lipin and Yumiko Ono, "Philip Morris's Bakery Unit Is for Sale; Asking Price Is Put at About $1 Billion," *The Wall Street Journal*, July 17, 1995, p. A3.

20. First proposed by H. Igor Ansoff, "Strategies for Diversification," *Harvard Business Review*, September–October 1957, pp. 113–124. For an updated discussion, see H. Igor Ansoff, *The New Corporate Strategy*, John Wiley & Sons, New York, 1988, pp. 82–85. In the more recent discussion, Ansoff substituted the term *mission* for *market* in the matrix. We still prefer—and thus retain—the original term.

21. Brett Pulley, "Wrigley Is Thriving, Despite the Recession, in a Resilient Business," *The Wall Street Journal*, May 29, 1991, pp. A1, A8.

22. Adam Goodman, "McDonnell Puts Spin on Commercial Helicopters," *St. Louis Post-Dispatch*, Sept. 2, 1991, p. 4BP.

23. Sandra Dallas and Gary McWilliams, "Going to Extremes—To Lure the Hot Dogs Back," *Business Week*, Mar. 13, 1995, p. 100.

24. David Greising, "Major Reservations," *Business Week*, Sept. 26, 1994, p. 66.

25. Kevin Helliker, "Can Wristwatch Whiz Switch Swatch Cachet to an Automobile?" *The Wall Street Journal*, Mar. 4, 1994, p. A1.

26. Improvements worth considering are suggested in the following articles: R. A. Proctor and J. S. Hassard, "Towards a New Model for Product Portfolio Analysis," *Management Decision*, Vol. 28, No. 3, 1990, pp. 14–17; and Rick Brown, "Making the Product Portfolio a Basis for Action," *Long Range Planning*, February 1991, pp. 102–110.

27. Michael Treacy and Fred Wiersema, "How Market Leaders Keep Their Edge," *Fortune*, Feb. 6, 1995, pp. 88–90, 94, 96, 98; their ideas are fully described in Michael Treacy and Fred Wiersema, *The Discipline of Market Leaders*, Addison-Wesley Inc., Boston, 1995.

28. Solomon, loc. cit.; "Which Stores Are Best?" loc. cit.; Marlow, loc. cit.; additional material from Debra Grill, "Playing Favorites," *Women's Wear Daily*, October 1994, p. 22.

CHAPTER 4

1. Elizabeth Jensen, "CBS Tests Out Its Pilots at a Las Vegas Lab," *The Wall Street Journal*, May 23, 1995, p. B1.

2. Jack Honomichl, "The Honomichl 50," *Marketing News*, June 5, 1995, pp. H1–H43.

3. The American Marketing Association defines marketing research as follows: "Marketing research is the function which links the consumer, customer, and public to the marketer through information—information used to identify and define marketing opportunities and problems; generate, refine, and evaluate marketing actions; monitor marketing performance; and improve understanding of marketing as a process. Marketing research specifies the information required to address these issues; designs the methods for collecting information; manages and implements the data collection process; analyzes the results; and communicates the findings and their implications." Peter D. Bennett, ed., *Dictionary of Marketing Terms*, 2d ed., American Marketing Association, Chicago, 1995, pp. 169–170. Although comprehensive (and a good illustration of what happens when a committee writes a definition), we found this definition too cumbersome. Therefore, we have opted for our more concise version.

4. Edward Cone, "All the Right Moves," *INFORMATIONWEEK*, Dec. 26, 1994, pp. 35–42.

5. Laurie Hays, "Using Computers to Divine Who Might Buy a Gas Grill," *The Wall Street Journal*, Aug. 8, 1994, p. B1.

6. Jim Bessen, "Riding the Marketing Information Wave," *Harvard Business Review*, September–October 1993, pp. 150–160.

7. Jonathan Berry, John Verity, Kathleen Kerwin, and Gail DeGeorge, "Database Marketing," *Business Week*, Sept. 5, 1994, pp. 56–62.

8. Berry et al., loc. cit.

9. Bessen, loc. cit.

10. Thomas C. Kinnear and Ann R. Root, eds., *1994 Survey of Marketing Research*, American Marketing Association, Chicago, 1995, p. 48.

11. In fact all these hypotheses were part of research projects. If you would like to learn more about them and the results, see Michael J. McCarthy, "James Bond Hits the Supermarket: Stores Snoop on Shoppers' Habits to Boost Sales," *The Wall Street Journal*, Aug. 25, 1993, p. B1; William M. Bulkeley, "Marketers Mine Their Corporate Databases," *The Wall Street Journal*, June 14, 1993, p. B6; Laurence Zuckerman, "Buying Power," *The Wall Street Journal*, Dec. 10, 1993, p. R15; and Diane Goldner, "What Men and Women Really Want to Eat," *The New York Times*, Mar. 2, 1994, p. C1.

12. Laurence Zuckerman, "Buying Power," *The Wall Street Journal*, Dec. 10, 1993, p. R15.

13. McCarthy, loc. cit.

14. For an excellent reference list of major secondary sources of business information, see James Woy, ed., *Encyclopedia of Business Information Sources 1995–96,* 10th ed., Gale Research, Detroit, 1994.

15. Diane Goldner, "What Men and Women Really Want to Eat," *The New York Times*, Mar. 2, 1994, p. C1.

16. Terence P. Pare, "How to Find Out What They Want," *Fortune*, Autumn/Winter 1993, pp. 39–41.

17. Bill Farrell and Tom Elken, "Adjust Five Variables for Better Mail Surveys," *Marketing News*, Aug. 29, 1994, p. 20. If you are interested in the variety of response-rate factors that have been studied, see A. J. Faria and John R. Dickinson, "Mail Survey Response, Speed, and Cost," *Industrial Marketing Management*, February 1992, pp. 51–60.

18. McCarthy, loc. cit.

19. To learn which cities are most frequently used as test markets and the reasons they are chosen, see Judith Waldrop, "All-American Markets," *American Demographics*, January 1992, pp. 24–30. A useful comparison of various test marketing techniques is found in Leslie Brennan, "Meeting the Test," *Sales & Marketing Management*, March 1990, pp. 57–65.

20. Milo Geyelin, "Why Many Businesses Can't Keep Their Secrets," *The Wall Street Journal*, Nov. 20, 1995, pp. B1+.

21. Jensen, loc. cit.

CHAPTER 5

1. Veronica Byrd and Wendy Zellner, "The Avon Lady of the Amazon," *Business Week*, Oct. 24, 1994, pp. 93–94; and Suein L. Hwang, "Updating Avon Means Respecting History without Repeating It," *The Wall Street Journal*, Apr. 4, 1994, pp. A1+.

2. "U.S. Population Changes per Hour," Population Reference Bureau, Inc., 1992.

3. Kenneth M. Johnson and Calvin L. Beale, "The Rural Rebound Revisited," *American Demographics*, July 1995, pp. 46–54.

4. Diane Crispell, "The Hottest Metros," *American Demographics*, April 1995, pp. 4–6.

5. Joseph Pereira, "Women Jump ahead of Men in Purchases of Athletic Shoes," *The Wall Street Journal*, May 26, 1995, p. B1.

6. Suein L. Hwang, "From Choices to Checkouts, the Genders Behave Very Differently in Supermarkets," *The Wall Street Journal*, Mar. 22, 1994, pp. B1+.

7. Several family life-cycle models have been developed in marketing, most notably William Wells and George Gubar, "Life Cycle Concepts in Marketing Research," *Journal of Marketing Research*, November 1966, pp. 355–363; Patrick E. Murphy and William A. Staples, "A Modernized Family Life Cycle," *Journal of Consumer Research*, June 1979, pp. 12–22; and Mary C. Gilly and Ben M. Enis, "Recycling the Family Life Cycle: A Proposal for Redefinition," in Andrew A. Mitchell, ed., *Advances in Consumer Research*, Association for Consumer Research, Ann Arbor, MI, 1982. The models are compared and suggestions are made for how they can be modified to better represent households in Charles M. Schaninger and William D. Danko, "A Conceptual and Empirical Comparison of Alternative Household Life Cycle Models," *Journal of Consumer Research*, March 1993, pp. 580–594.

8. Jon Berry, "Forever Single," *Adweek's Marketing Week*, Oct. 15, 1990, pp. 20–24.

9. *Statistical Abstract of the United States: 1994*, 114 ed., U.S. Bureau of the Census, Washington, DC, 1994, p. 56.

10. Paul Gray, "Adding Up the Under-Skilled," *Time*, Sept. 20, 1993, p. 75.

11. Leah Rickard and Jeanne Whalen, "Retail Trails Ethnic Changes," *Advertising Age*, May 1, 1995, pp. 1+.

12. R. Craig Endicott, "Advertising Fact Book," *Advertising Age*, Jan. 6, 1992, p. S-11.

13. Michael McCarthy, "Mind Probe," *The Wall Street Journal*, Mar. 22, 1991, p. B2.

14. A good source of cultural trends is *American Demographics* magazine. See, for example, Thomas E. Miller, "New Markets for Information," *American Demographics*, April 1995, pp. 46–54.

15. For an update on the Coleman and Rainwater classification, see Richard P. Coleman, "Continuing Significance of Social Class to Marketing," *Journal of Consumer Research*, December 1983, pp. 265–280.

16. *Statistical Abstract*, op. cit., pp. 58, 61.

17. There are some researchers who believe that consumers have hidden or subconscious motives for many activities, from skiing to wearing a necktie. For a compilation of observations about motivation derived from psychoanalytic techniques, see Ernest Dichter, *The Handbook of Consumer Motivation*, McGraw-Hill, New York, 1964.

18. A. H. Maslow, *Motivation and Personality*, Harper & Row, New York, 1954, pp. 80–106.

19. For more on the effects of scent on buyer behavior, see Barbara Carlton, "Thank Carl Klumpp for the Sweet Smell of Right Guard," *The Wall Street Journal*, May 11, 1995, pp. A1+; and Kyle Pope, "Technology Improves on the Nose as Scientists Try to Mimic Smells," *The Wall Street Journal*, Mar. 1, 1995, pp. B1+.

20. McCarthy, loc. cit.

21. A more complete discussion of learning theories as they apply to marketing can be found in books on consumer behavior. See William L. Wilkie, *Consumer Behavior*, 3d ed., John Wiley & Sons, New York, 1994.

22. This classic definition is from Gordon W. Allport, "Attitudes," in C. A. Murchinson, ed., *A Handbook of Social Psychology*, Clark University Press, Worcester, MA, 1935, pp. 798–844.

23. Joe Schwartz, "Climate-Controlled Customers," *American Demographics*, March 1992, pp. 24–32.

24. Ronald E. Millman, "Using Background Music to Affect the Behavior of Supermarket Shoppers," *Journal of Marketing*, Summer 1982, pp. 86–91.

25. *Statistical Abstract of the United States*: 1993, 113th ed., U.S. Bureau of the Census, Washington, DC, 1993, pp. 510, 521–522.

26. Eva Pomice and Dana Hawkins, "The New Fear of Buying," *U.S. News & World Report*, Mar. 4, 1991, pp. 44–45.

27. Byrd and Zellner, loc. cit.; Hwang, loc. cit.; and Avon 1994 Annual Report.

CHAPTER 6

1. Howard Banks, "Cleared for Takeoff," *Forbes*, Sept. 12, 1994, pp. 116–122; *Textron Annual Report*, 1994, p. 13; Barbara Carton, "Cessna Says It Will Make More Small Planes," *The Wall Street Journal*, Mar. 14, 1995, p. B1; Andy Zipser, "Into the Wild Blue Yonder," *Barron's*, Aug. 15, 1994, p. 14; David Frum, "Crash," *Forbes*, Nov. 8, 1993, p. 62; and Joe Mullich, "Database Gold Mine Lifts Cessna's Return to the Air," *Business Marketing*, April 1995, pp. 1+.

2. The statistics on the business market cited in this chapter come from Bureau of the Census publications. A particularly useful source is the *Statistical Abstract of the United States*, an annual publication that summarizes a myriad of facts.

3. Amy Barrett, "It's a Small (Business) World," *Business Week*, Apr. 17, 1995, pp. 96–101.

4. Brian Zajac, "Weak Dollar, Strong Results," *Forbes*, July 17, 1995, p. 274.

5. Therese Eiben, "U.S. Exporters on a Global Roll," *Fortune*, June 29, 1992, pp. 94–95.

6. For a description of the Standard Industrial Classification system and a complete listing of all SIC numbers and classifications, see *Standard Industrial Classification Manual*, U.S. Government Printing Office, Washington, DC, 1972, and also the *1987 Supplement*. Also see "SIC: The System Explained," *Sales & Marketing Management*, Apr. 22, 1985, pp. 52–53.

7. "Chrysler Pushes Quality Down the Supply Chain," *Purchasing*, July 13, 1995, pp. 125–128.

8. Robert D. McWilliams, Earl Naumann, and Stan Scott, "Determining Buying Center Size," *Industrial Marketing Management*, February 1992, pp. 43–49.

9. Dean Tjosvold, Lindsay Meredith, and R. Michael Wellwood, "Implementing Relationship Marketing," *Journal of Business & Industrial Marketing*, No. 4, 1993, pp. 5–17.

10. Julie Candler, "Leasing's Link to Efficiency," *Nation's Business*, May 1995, pp. 30–34.

11. Banks, loc. cit.; *Textron Annual Report*, loc. cit.; Carton, loc. cit.; Zipser, loc. cit.; Frum, loc. cit.; and Mullich, loc. cit.

CHAPTER 7

1. Norton Paley, "Back from the Dead," *Sales & Marketing Management*, July 1995, pp. 30–31; Suzanne Oliver, "New Personality," *Forbes*, Aug. 15, 1994, p. 114; and Susan Caminiti, "A Star Is Born," *Fortune*, Autumn/Winter 1993, pp. 44–47.

2. Gabriella Stern, "Attempt to Cut Candy Calories Sours for P&G," *The Wall Street Journal*, Aug. 25, 1995, pp. B1+.

3. Christina Del Valle and Jon Berry, "They Know Where You Live—And

How You Buy," *Business Week*, Feb. 7, 1994, p. 89.

4. Bernice Kanner, "Marketers Discover That Youth Is a Fountain of Sales," *St. Louis Post-Dispatch*, Apr. 9, 1995, p. 3E.

5. Ibid.

6. Ibid.

7. T. L. Stanley, "Get Ready for Gen Y," *Brandweek*, May 15, 1995, pp. 36–37.

8. Jeff Jensen, "A New Read on How to Reach Boys," *Advertising Age*, Aug. 23, 1993, pp. S-10+.

9. For more information on elderly consumers, see Charles D. Schewe and Geoffrey E. Meredity, "Digging Deep to Delight the Mature Adult Consumer," *Marketing Management*, Winter 1994, pp. 21-36.

10. Melissa Campanelli, "The African-American Market: Community, Growth, and Change," *Sales & Marketing Management*, May 1991, pp. 75–81.

11. Peter Kerr, "Cosmetic Makers Read the Census," *The New York Times*, Aug. 29, 1991, pp. C1+.

12. Alex Taylor III, "Porsche Slices Up Its Buyers," *Fortune*, Jan. 16, 1995, p. 24.

13. Lynn R. Kahle, Sharon E. Beatty, and Pamela Homer, "Alternative Measurement Approaches to Consumer Values: The List of Values (LOV) and Values and Lifestyles (VAL)," *Journal of Consumer Research*, December 1986, pp. 405–409.

14. Allanna Sullivan, "Mobil Bets Drivers Pick Cappuccino over Low Prices," *The Wall Street Journal*, Jan. 30, 1995, pp. B1+.

15. Kevin Helliker, "Expanding Prison Population Captivates Marketers," *The Wall Street Journal*, Jan. 9, 1995, p. B1.

16. David C. Smith "Inside GM Purchasing, Part II," *Ward's Auto World*, May 1995, p. 69.

17. Laura M. Litvan, "Going 'Green' in the '90s," *Nation's Business*, February 1995, pp. 30–32.

18. Lisa Gubernick, "Midmarket Schools," *Forbes*, July 31, 1995, pp. 46–48.

19. Andrew E. Serwer, "McDonald's Conquers the World," *Fortune*, Oct. 17, 1994, pp. 103–116.

20. For more information on the role of sales people in forecasting, see William Keenan, Jr., "Numbers Racket," *Sales & Marketing Management*, May 1995, pp. 64–76.

21. Paley, loc. cit.; Oliver, loc. cit.; and Caminiti, loc. cit.

CHAPTER 8

1. Based on "California, Arizona to Get First Crack at GM's Electric Car," *Columbia* (Missouri) *Daily Tribune*, Jan. 7, 1996, p. 7A; Donald W. Nauss, "Pulling the Plug: Auto Makers Hope to Thwart Electrical Car Mandate," *St. Louis Post-Dispatch*, Mar. 26, 1995, p. 5E; David Woodruff, "Shocker at GM: People Like the Impact," *Business Week*, Jan. 23, 1995, p. 47; David Woodruff, "GM: All Charged Up over the Electric Car," *Business Week*, Oct. 21, 1991, pp. 106, 108; and Therese R. Welter, "GM Makes an Impact," *Industry Week*, Jan. 21, 1991, pp. 40–41.

2. Yumiko Ono, "Some Kids Won't Eat the Middle of an Oreo," *The Wall Street Journal*, Nov. 20, 1991, p. B1.

3. For a different classification scheme that provides strategic guidelines for management by relating products and prices, along with an excellent bibliography on product classification, see Patrick E. Murphy and Ben M. Enis, "Classifying Products Strategically," *Journal of Marketing*, July 1986, pp. 24–42. Also see Ernest F. Cooke, "The Relationship between a Product Classification System and Marketing Strategy," *Journal of Midwest Marketing*, Spring 1987, pp. 230–240.

4. Jeffrey A. Trachtenberg, "Interactive Movies: Hot Medium or Smell-O-Vision, Part Three?" *The Wall Street Journal*, Jan. 16, 1995, p. B1.

5. Kathleen Deveny, "Failure of Its Oven Lovin' Cookie Dough Shows Pillsbury Pitfall of New Products," *The Wall Street Journal*, June 17, 1993, p. B1.

6. Joseph Weber, "A Big Company That Works," *Business Week*, May 4, 1992, pp. 124–127+; and Zachary Schiller, "At Rubbermaid, Little Things Mean a Lot," *Business Week*, Nov. 11, 1991, p. 126. For a description of 3M's many successes and some recent problems related to product innovation, see Thomas A. Stewart, "3M Fights Back," *Fortune*, Feb. 5, 1996, pp. 94–99.

7. Stuart Elliott, "The Famous Brands on Death Row," *The New York Times*, Nov. 7, 1993, p. 1F.

8. According to Thomas P. Hustad, editor of the *Journal of Product Innovation Management*, as quoted in Christopher Power, "Flops," *Business Week*, Aug. 16, 1993, p. 82.

9. Marshall Sella, "Will a Flying Doll . . . Fly?" *The New York Times Magazine*, Dec. 25, 1994, p. 22; and Laurie M. Grossman, "New 'Quick Hit' Product Plan Is Risky for Coke," *The Wall Street Journal*, Nov. 22, 1993, p. B1.

10. Respectively, Marketing Intelligence, Inc., as cited in Deveny, loc. cit.; the "1995 Innovation Survey," conducted by Group EFO Limited of Weston, CT; and Kuczmarski & Associates, as described in Power, op. cit., pp. 76–77.

11. The reasons for failure are drawn from the "1995 Innovation Survey," loc. cit.

12. Alan Farnham, "It's a Bird! It's a Plane! It's a Flop!" *Fortune*, May 2, 1994, pp. 108–110.

13. Sella, op. cit., pp. 20–25+.

14. Eugene Carlson, "Some Forms of Identification Can't Be Handily Faked," *The Wall Street Journal*, Sept. 14, 1993, p. B2.

15. Richard Gibson, "Too Skinny a Burger Is a Mighty Hard Sell, McDonald's Learns," *The Wall Street Journal*, Apr. 15, 1993, pp. A1, A6.

16. These benefits and a "stage gate system" for new-product development are described in Robert G. Cooper and Elko J. Kleinschmidt, "Stage Gate Systems for New Product Success," *Marketing Management*, Vol. 1, No. 4, 1993, pp. 20–29. For an approach to improve the management of multiple new-product development projects, see Steven C. Wheelwright and Kim B. Clark, "Creating Project Plans to Focus Product Development," *Harvard Business Review*, March–April 1992, pp. 70-82.

17. For a report on the criteria used in making "go–no go" decisions in the product-development process, see Ilkka A. Ronkainen, "Criteria Changes across Product Development Stages," *Industrial Marketing Management*, August 1985, pp. 171–178.

18. "Study: Launching New Products Is Worth the Risk," *Marketing News*, Jan. 20, 1992, p. 2.

19. Neal Templin and Jeff Cole, "Manufacturers Use Suppliers to Help Them Develop New Products," *The Wall Street Journal*, Dec. 19, 1994, pp. A1, A6.

20. For more on the first two stages, termed *opportunity identification*, see Linda Rochford, "Generating and Screening New Product Ideas," *Industrial Marketing Management*, November 1991, pp. 287–296.

21. Faye Rice, "Secrets of Product Testing," *Fortune*, Nov. 29, 1994, pp. 166–171.

22. Gibson, op. cit., p. A6.
23. Cooper and Kleinschmidt, op. cit., pp. 22–23.
24. "Study: Launching New Products Is Worth the Risk," loc. cit. For a discussion of automakers' efforts to dramatically reduce the time required to develop new models, see Valerie Reitman and Robert L. Simison, "Japanese Car Makers Speed Up Car Making," *The Wall Street Journal*, Dec. 29, 1995, pp. B1, B13.
25. Howard Schlossberg, "Services Development Lags Behind New Products," *Marketing News*, Nov. 6, 1989, p. 2.
26. "No Yen for Chocolate Salsa? You've Got Company," *St. Louis Post-Dispatch*, Dec. 20, 1994, p. 5C.
27. For foundations of diffusion theory and a review of landmark studies on diffusion of innovation, see Everett M. Rogers, *Diffusion of Innovations*, 3d ed., Free Press, New York, 1983.
28. Susan Chira, "High-Tech Safety: Will Parents Buy It?" *The New York Times*, Feb. 17, 1994, p. C1.
29. Denise Smith Amos, "Are You an 'Influential'? Advertisers Want You," *St. Louis Post-Dispatch*, Aug. 6, 1995, pp. E1, E9.
30. Rogers, loc. cit.
31. Joan E. Rigdon, "For Cardboard Cameras, Sales Picture Enlarges and Seems Brighter Than Ever," *The Wall Street Journal*, Feb. 11, 1992, p. B1.
32. See Frank G. Bingham and Charles J. Quigley, Jr., "Venture Team Application to New Product Development," *Journal of Business and Industrial Marketing*, Winter–Spring 1989, pp. 49–59.
33. For more on P&G's preparation for product planning and development in the 1990s, see Alecia Swasy, "In a Fast-Paced World, Procter & Gamble Sets Its Store in Old Values," *The Wall Street Journal*, Sept. 21, 1989, pp. A1, A18; and Jolie Solomon and Carol Hymowitz, "P&G Makes Changes in the Way It Develops and Sells Its Products," *The Wall Street Journal*, Aug. 11, 1987, pp. 1, 12.
34. Various arrangements are discussed in Eric M. Olson, Orville C. Walker, Jr., and Robert W. Ruekert, "Organizing for Effective New Product Development: The Moderating Role of Product Innovativeness," *Journal of Marketing*, January 1995, pp. 48–62.
35. Cooper and Kleinschmidt, op. cit., p. 23.
36. Power, op. cit., p. 80.
37. "California, Arizona to Get First Crack at GM's Electric Cars," loc. cit.; Woodruff, "Shocker at GM . . . ," loc. cit.; Woodruff, "GM: All Charged Up . . . ," loc. cit.; Welter, loc. cit.; additional material from Matthew L. Wald, "G.M. and Ovonic to Make Batteries for Electric Cars," *The New York Times*, Dec. 3, 1994, p. 40.

CHAPTER 9

1. "GM Merges Pontiac and GMC Units," *St. Louis Post-Dispatch*, Feb. 21, 1996, p. 7C; Gabriella Stern, "GM Takes Step to Overhaul Its Auto Dealership System," *The Wall Street Journal*, June 26, 1995, p. A3; and Gabriella Stern, "GM's New Marketing Chief Seeks Clarity amid Muddle of Overlapping Car Lines," *The Wall Street Journal*, May 1, 1995, p. A3.
2. David Kiley, "Going It Alone: One-Brand Companies," *Adweek's Marketing Week*, Nov. 26, 1990, pp. 20–22.
3. Based on a Holiday Inns, Inc., ad in *USA Today*, Apr. 12, 1995, p. 12A.
4. Richard Gibson and Marj Charlier, "Fresher Bud Image Requires Light Touch," *The Wall Street Journal*, Nov. 25, 1994, p. B1; and Robert Manor, "Turning On the Tap," *St. Louis Post-Dispatch*, Apr. 7, 1991, pp. F1, F8.
5. Russell Mitchell, "Intel Isn't Taking This Lying Down," *Business Week*, Sept. 30, 1991, pp. 32-33.
6. Barbara Rudolph, "The Clock Strikes Five," *Time* (Australian edition), Apr. 13, 1992, p. 60.
7. For more on this approach, see Jack Trout and Al Ries, "*Don't* Follow the Leader," *Sales & Marketing Management*, February 1994, pp. 25–26; and William Keenan, Jr., "Drawing the Line," *Sales & Marketing Management*, August 1993, pp. 32–36.
8. Kevin Goldman, "More Made-in-the-USA Claims Show Up," *The Wall Street Journal*, Jan. 15, 1993, p. B5.
9. Holly Haber, "Penney's New CEO Outlines Agenda for Improving Market Share," *Daily News Record*, Jan. 26, 1995, p. 7; and Wendy Zellner, "Penney's Rediscovers Its Calling," *Business Week*, Apr. 5, 1993, pp. 51–52.
10. Carlee R. Scott, "Car Batteries Go for New Gadget to Charge Sales," *The Wall Street Journal*, Mar. 1, 1990, p. B1.
11. Laura Bird, "Romancing the Package," *Adweek's Marketing Week*, Jan. 21, 1991, pp. 10–11, 14.
12. The information about designer clothing in this paragraph and the following one is drawn from Bianca Riemer and Laura Zinn, "Haute Couture That's Not So Haute," *Business Week*, Apr. 22, 1991, p. 108.
13. Laurie Freeman, "Sensor Still Helping Gillette Fend Off Razor Challenges," *Advertising Age*, Sept. 28, 1994, p. 20; and Lawrence Ingrassia, "Gillette Holds Its Edge by Endlessly Searching for a Better Shave," *The Wall Street Journal*, Dec. 10, 1992, pp. A1, A6.
14. Robert D. Hof, "Intel: Far Beyond the Pentium," *Business Week*, Feb. 20, 1995, pp. 88–90.
15. The criticisms are summarized in Geoffrey L. Gordon, Roger J. Calantone, and C. Anthony di Benedetto, "Mature Markets and Revitalization Strategies: An American Fable," *Business Horizons*, May–June 1991, pp. 39–50. Alternative life cycles are proposed in Edward D. Popper and Bruce D. Buskirk, "Technology Life Cycles in Industrial Markets," *Industrial Marketing Management*, February 1992, pp. 23–31; and C. Merle Crawford, "Business Took the Wrong Life Cycle from Biology," *The Journal of Product & Brand Management*, Winter 1992, pp. 51–57.
16. Don Clark, "Multimedia's Hype Hides Virtual Reality: An Industry Shakeout," *The Wall Street Journal*, Mar. 1, 1995, pp. A1, A6.
17. Neil Gross and Peter Coy, "The Technology Paradox," *Business Week*, Mar. 6, 1995, p. 77.
18. Jennifer Lawrence, "Whatever Happened to OLESTRA?" *Advertising Age*, May 2, 1994, pp. 16–18.
19. Elizabeth Snead, "Trendy Feet Say 'Ah' to All-Season Uggs," *USA Today*, June 21, 1995, p. 1D.
20. William Turcsik, "Study Projects Growth to Slow for Ready-to-Drink Iced Tea," *Supermarket News*, Apr. 24, 1995, p. 108; and Sarah McRitchie, "Savour the Flavour," *Dairy Industries International*, November 1993, p. 43.
21. Gerard J. Tellis and Peter N. Golder, "Pioneer Advantage: Marketing Logic or Marketing Legend," *USC Business*, Fall/Winter 1995, pp. 49–53.
22. Jim Carlton, "Nintendo, Gambling with Its Technology, Faces a Crucial Delay," *The Wall Street Journal*, May 5, 1995, pp. A1, A4.
23. Ten distinct strategies are described in Joel R. Evans and Gregg Lombardo,

"Marketing Strategies for Mature Brands," *Journal of Product & Brand Management*, Vol. 2, No. 1, 1993, pp. 5–19. For a discussion of four strategies—recapture, redesign, refocus, and recast—that are particularly applicable to *business* products, see Paul C. N. Michell, Peter Quinn, and Edward Percival, "Marketing Strategies for Mature Industrial Products," *Industrial Marketing Management*, August 1991, pp. 201–206. The approach used by Pillsbury to manage its refrigerated dough products is summarized in Michael J. Paxton, "Managing Mature Markets," *The Journal of Product & Brand Management*, Vol. 1, No. 4, 1992, pp. 41–45.

24. For a case study that reports how a nonfood consumer packaged-goods company sought to win market share from an entrenched competitor, see D. K. (Skip) Smith and William Weber, "Winning Share from a Dominant Competitor in a Slow-Growth Consumer Market," *Journal of Product & Brand Management*, Vol. 2, No. 4, 1993, pp. 20–32. For a study examining business products, see Jorge Vasconcellos, "Key Success Factors in Marketing Mature Products," *Industrial Marketing Management*, November 1991, pp. 263–278.

25. Ronald Fink and Alexandra Ourusoff, "Stretched Too Thin?" *Financial World*, Mar. 1, 1994, p. 30; and Monica Roman, "How Du Pont Keeps 'Em Coming Back for More," *Business Week*, Aug. 20, 1990, p. 68.

26. John W. Verity, "Does Film Have a Future?" *Business Week*, Nov. 15, 1993, p. 33; and Joan E. Rigdon, "Kodak Tries to Prepare for Filmless Era without Inviting Demise of Core Business," *The Wall Street Journal*, Apr. 18, 1991, p. B1.

27. Meg Cox, "Ad Blitz Turns Dictionary into Best Seller," *The Wall Street Journal*, Oct. 23, 1992, p. A9A.

28. Bill Saporito, "How to Revive a Fading Firm," *Fortune*, Mar. 22, 1993, p. 80.

29. Hof, loc. cit.

30. For an example, see Riemer and Zinn, loc. cit.

31. Teri Agins, "Many Women Lose Interest in Clothes, to Retailers' Dismay," *The Wall Street Journal*, Feb. 28, 1995, pp. A1, A8.

32. Stern, "GM Takes Step . . . ," loc. cit.; Stern, "GM's New Marketing Chief

. . . ," loc. cit.; Kathleen Kerwin, "A Caddy That's Not for Daddy," *Business Week*, Dec. 18, 1995, pp. 87–88; Oscar Suris, "The Engine Driving the Taurus: Its Marketing," *The Wall Street Journal*, Sept. 11, 1995, pp. B1, B6; "Why Buyers, Dealers Like Saturn Concept," *USA Today*, Aug. 28, 1995, p. 4B; Gabriella Stern, "As Old Cadillac Buyers Age, the GM Division Fights to Halt Slippage," *The Wall Street Journal*, Aug. 24, 1995, pp. A1, A9; and Gabriella Stern, "Buick Confronts Its Fuddy-Duddy Image," *The Wall Street Journal*, June 19, 1995, pp. B1, B4.

CHAPTER 10

1. "Levi's for Women," *Advertising Age*, Sept. 26, 1995, p. S-35; "Levi's to Join Lee in Entering Indian Jeans Market," *Daily News Record*, Apr. 25, 1995, p. 4; Faye Rice, "One Writer's Hunt for the Perfect Jeans," *Fortune*, Apr. 17, 1995, p. 30; Mark Henricks, "Levi Strauss Searches Its Soul," *Apparel Industry Magazine*, January 1995, pp. 30+; and Richard W. Bruner, "Levi's Hungry to Crack Down on Fakes in Hungary," *Daily News Record*, Dec. 29, 1994, p. 5.

2. Adapted from Peter D. Bennett, ed., *Dictionary of Marketing Terms*, American Marketing Association, Chicago, 1988, p. 18.

3. For a description of recent changes in trademark law and court decisions on trademarks as well as their marketing implications, see Dorothy Cohen, "Trademark Strategy Revisited," *Journal of Marketing*, July 1991, pp. 46–59.

4. Fred Selnes, "An Examination of the Effect of Product Performance on Brand Reputation, Satisfaction and Loyalty," *Journal of Product & Brand Management*, Vol. 2, No. 4, 1993, pp. 45–60; and David Shipley and Paul Howard, "Brand-Naming Industrial Products," *Industrial Marketing Management*, February 1993, pp. 59–66.

5. Al Ries, "What's in a Name?" *Sales & Marketing Management*, October 1995, p. 36. This article also discusses eight attributes of a desirable brand name.

6. Material in this paragraph and the following one are drawn from Suein L. Hwang, "Picking Pithy Names Is Getting Trickier as Trademark Applications Proliferate," *The Wall Street Journal*, Jan. 14, 1992, p. B1.

7. For a thorough discussion of such brand

names, see Teresa Pavia and Janeen A. Costa, "The Winning Number: Consumer Perceptions of Alpha-Numeric Brand Names," *Journal of Marketing*, July 1993, pp. 85–98.

8. For more on creating so-called *morphenes*, see Casey McCabe, "What's in a Name?" *Adweek's Marketing Week*, Apr. 16, 1990, p. 22.

9. See also Kim Robertson, "Strategically Desirable Brand Name Characteristics," *The Journal of Product & Brand Management*, Summer 1992, pp. 62–72. For a good discussion of the special opportunities and challenges associated with the branding of services, see Vicki Clift, "Name Service Firms for the Long Haul," *Marketing News*, Dec. 6, 1993, p. 10; and Leonard L. Berry, Edwin F. Lefkowith, and Terry Clark, "In Services, What's in a Name?" *Harvard Business Review*, September–October 1988, pp. 28–30. Some of the examples in this section are drawn from this last source.

10. Russell E. Brooks and Gila E. Gellman, "Combating Counterfeiting," *Marketing Management*, Vol. 2, No. 3, 1993, pp. 49–51.

11. Catherine Yang, "Out! Out! Damned Knockoffs," *Business Week*, Sept. 11, 1995, p. 6.

12. Brooks and Gellman, loc. cit.

13. An excellent summary of this challenge and a list of safeguards are contained in Maxine S. Lans, "On Your Mark: Get Set or It May Go," *Marketing News*, Sept. 26, 1994, p. 12.

14. Jack Alexander, "What's in a Name? Too Much, Said the FTC," *Sales & Marketing Management*, January 1989, pp. 75, 78.

15. Carrie Goerne, "Rollerblade Reminds Everyone That Its Success Is Not Generic," *Marketing News*, Mar. 2, 1992, p. 1.

16. For an excellent discussion of the nature and benefits of this strategy, see Donald G. Norris, "Ingredient Branding: A Strategy Option with Multiple Beneficiaries," *Journal of Consumer Marketing*, Summer 1992, pp. 19–31.

17. Bradley Johnson, "IBM, Compaq Tire of 'Intel Inside' Track," *Advertising Age*, Sept. 19, 1994, p. 52.

18. Gabriella Stern, "Big Companies Add Private-Label Lines That Vie with Their Premium Brands," *The Wall Street Journal*, May 21, 1993, p. B1.

19. Patricia Sellers, "Brands: It's Thrive or Die," *Fortune*, Aug. 23, 1993, p. 53.

20. Peter H. Farquhar, "Strategic Challenges for Branding," *Marketing Management*, Vol. 3, No. 2, 1994, p. 12.

21. Teri Agins, "Big Stores Put Own Labels on Best Clothes," *The Wall Street Journal*, Sept. 26, 1994, p. B1.

22. Greg Burns, "A Froot Loop by Any Other Name," *Business Week*, June 26, 1995, p. 72.

23. The study was conducted by Professor Raj Sethuraman of the University of Iowa, and reported in Richard Gibson, "Store-Brand Pricing Has to Be Just Right," *The Wall Street Journal*, Feb. 14, 1992, p. B1. The second study was summarized in Stephen J. Hoch, "Private Label a Threat? Don't Believe It," *Advertising Age*, May 24, 1993, p. 19.

24. Clyde H. Farnsworth, "Quality: High. Price: Low. Big Ad Budget? Never," *The New York Times*, Feb. 6, 1994, p. F10.

25. The statistics and examples to this point in the paragraph are drawn from Emily DeNitto, "Back into Focus," *Brandweek*, May 29, 1995, pp. 22–26.

26. Heather Pauly and Adam Levy, "Brand Names Singing Blues," *St. Louis Post-Dispatch*, Aug. 26, 1993, p. 7C.

27. Gabriella Stern, "As National Brands Chop Prices, Stores Scramble to Defend Private-Label Goods," *The Wall Street Journal*, Aug. 23, 1993, p. B1.

28. DeNitto, op. cit., p. 25.

29. Suein L. Hwang, "Philip Morris Makes Dave's—But Sh! Don't Tell," *The Wall Street Journal*, Mar. 2, 1995, p. B1.

30. There are potential disadvantages as well as advantages to introducing new products under the family brand. For more on this, see Barbara Loken and Deborah Roedder John, "Diluting Brand Beliefs: When Do Brand Extensions Have a Negative Impact?" *Journal of Marketing*, July 1993, pp. 71–84.

31. Norton Paley, "Back from the Dead," *Sales & Marketing Management*, July 1995, pp. 30+.

32. This definition is drawn from the comprehensive examination of brand equity in Peter H. Farquhar, "Managing Brand Equity," *Journal of Advertising Research*, August/September 1990, pp. RC-7–RC-12. For more on brand equity, see the first book devoted entirely to this important topic: David A. Aaker, *Managing Brand Equity: Capitalizing on the Value of a Brand Name*, The Free Press, New York, 1991.

33. The Kellogg's example was described by Farquhar, "Managing Brand Equity," op. cit., p. RC-7. The 1993 study of personal computers was summarized in Kyle Pope, "Computers: They're No Commodity," *The Wall Street Journal*, Oct. 15, 1993, p. B1; the 1995 update was described in Jim Carlton, "Marketing Plays a Bigger Role in Distributing PCs," *The Wall Street Journal*, Oct. 16, 1995, p. B4.

34. Farquhar, "Managing Brand Equity," op. cit., pp. RC-8–RC-10.

35. For a discussion of the potential advantages and disadvantages of using brand equity in this way, see David Aaker, "Brand Extensions: The Good, the Bad, and the Ugly," *Sloan Management Review*, Summer 1990, pp. 47–56.

36. The efforts of Ann Taylor, The Gap, and Victoria's Secret to capitalize on their strong brand equity by introducing fragrances and bath products are described in Pam Weisz, "'Trying to Move from the Wardrobe to the Bathroom," *Brandweek*, Apr. 24, 1995, pp. 36, 38.

37. For more on the rationale for the Marquis by Waterford line as well as a new Embassy line of dinnerware also introduced by Waterford Wedgwood PLC, see Judith Valente, "A New Brand Restores Sparkle to Waterford," *The Wall Street Journal*, Nov. 10, 1994, p. B1.

38. Statistics in this paragraph come from "The Licensing Letter," as reported in Dale D. Buss, "Hot Names, Top Dollars," *Nation's Business*, August 1995, p. 18; and "Selling with License: Making Big Money with Other People's Ideas," *St. Louis Post-Dispatch*, June 7, 1992, p. 5E.

39. "Coppertone Gives More Products a Place in the Sun," *Sales & Marketing Management*, May 1990, p. 40.

40. Buss, op. cit., p. 17.

41. Eliot Schreiber, "Retail Trends Shorten Life of Package Design," *Marketing News*, Dec. 5, 1994, p. 7.

42. For recommendations on managing the packaging aspect of a company's marketing mix, see Richard T. Hise and James U. McNeal, "Effective Packaging Management," *Business Horizons*, January–February 1988, pp. 47–51.

43. For further discussion of package-design strategies that can boost sales and profit, see Sue Bassin, "Innovative Packaging Strategies," *Journal of Business Strategy*, January–February 1988, pp. 38–42.

44. Schreiber, loc. cit.

45. Alison L. Sprout, "New Packaging That's Thriftier! Niftier! And Cooks Your Food!" *Fortune*, Sept. 5, 1994, p. 109.

46. Roberta Maynard, "What a Difference a Package Makes," *Nation's Business*, February 1994, p. 8.

47. Laura Bird, "Romancing the Package," *Adweek's Marketing Week*, Jan. 21, 1991, p. 10.

48. Information about the National Labeling and Education Act is drawn from Chris Baum, "NLEA Compels Food Packagers to Redesign," *Packaging*, May 1994, p. 21; Pam Black, "Dietary Info That's Easier to Digest," *Business Week*, Mar. 21, 1994, p. 119; and John Sinisi, "New Rules Exact a Heavy Price as Labels Are Recast," *Brandweek*, Dec. 7, 1992, p. 3.

49. For a study that examines the impact of the NLEA on consumers' processing of nutrition information, see Christine Moorman, "A Quasi-Experiment to Assess the Consumer and Informational Determinants of Nutrition Information Processing Activities: The Case of the Nutrition Labeling and Education Act," Working Paper, University of Wisconsin–Madison, October 1995.

50. Laura M. Litvan, "Sizing Up Metric Labeling Rules," *Nation's Business*, November 1994, p. 62.

51. Joseph Weber, "A Better Grip on Hawking Tools," *Business Week*, June 5, 1995, p. 99.

52. Brian Dumaine, "Design That Sells and Sells and . . . ," *Fortune*, Mar. 11, 1991, pp. 86 and 88, respectively.

53. Bruce Nussbaum, "Is In-House Design on the Way Out?" *Business Week*, Sept. 25, 1995, p. 130.

54. "Business Bulletin," *The Wall Street Journal*, Feb. 23, 1995, p. A1; and Bruce Nussbaum, "What Works for One Works for All," *Business Week*, Apr. 20, 1992, pp. 112–113. For a description of a related notion, termed *user-centered design*, see Artemis March, "Usability: The New Dimension," *Harvard Business Review*, September–October 1994, pp. 144–149.

55. Nancy Arnott, "Shades of Distinction," *Sales & Marketing Management*, June 1995, p. 20; Paul M. Barrett, "Color in the Court: Can Tints Be Trademarked?" *The Wall Street Journal*, Jan. 5, 1995, p. B1; and Junda Woo, "Rulings Clash over Colors in Trademarks," *The Wall Street Journal*, Feb. 25, 1993, p. B1.

56. Meera Somasundaram, "Red Packages Lure Shoppers Like Capes Flourished at Bulls," *The Wall Street Journal*, Sept. 18, 1995, p. A13B.

57. Kathleen Deveny, "Anatomy of a Fad: How Clear Products Were Hot and Then Suddenly Were Not," *The Wall Street Journal*, Mar. 15, 1994, p. B1.

58. Ross Johnson and William O. Winchell, *Marketing and Quality Control*, American Society for Quality Control, Milwaukee, 1989, p. 2.

59. Scott McCartney, "Middling Quality as a Marketing Plus? Survey Finds a Link," *The Wall Street Journal*, May 16, 1994, p. B6.

60. For a list of reasons why product quality is so important and for a discussion of the marketing function's role in quality management, see Neil A. Morgan and Nigel F. Pierce, "Market Led Quality," *Industrial Marketing Management*, May 1992, pp. 111–118.

61. "Japan's Rising Tide," *Advertising Age*, May 29, 1995, p. 3; and "Who Makes the Best Products?" *Business Week*, Mar. 14, 1994, p. 8.

62. D. A. Aaker, "Managing Assets and Skills: The Key to a Sustainable Competitive Advantage," *California Management Review*, Winter 1989, pp. 91–106.

63. Ronald Henkoff, "The Hot New Seal of Quality," *Fortune*, June 28, 1993, pp. 116–118, 120.

64. Henricks, loc. cit.; Kevin Whitelaw, "Gobbling Up the Gen-X Market," *U.S. News & World Report*, Oct. 9, 1995, p. 68; Jane Weaver, "Dress Down with *GQ*," *Inside Media*, July 12, 1995, p. 15; Cyndee Miller, "A Casual Affair," *Marketing News*, Mar. 13, 1995, p. 1; and Thembi Mhlambiso, "Dockers Fetes Its Five Years," *Daily News Record*, Jan. 7, 1992, p. 11.

CHAPTER 11

1. Jim Carlton, "What's Eating Apple? Computer Maker Hits Some Serious Snags," *The Wall Street Journal*, Sept. 21, 1995, p. A1; Jim Carlton, "Apple Is Facing Widespread Shortages of Its Products," *The Wall Street Journal*, Aug. 11, 1995, p. B8; David Kirkpatrick, "No Longer Cool: Apple's Internet Inaccessibility Is a Troubling Turn," *Fortune*, Aug. 7, 1995, p. 30; Jim Carlton, "Apple Reduces Prices on Line of Power Macs," *The Wall Street Journal*, Aug. 7, 1995, p. B1; and Charles McCoy, "Apple Chief Shows Still Waters Can Run Deep—and Angry," *The Wall Street Journal*, July 14, 1995, p. A3.

2. Survey conducted for *Progressive Grocer* magazine, as reported in Albert D. Bates, "Pricing for Profit," *Retailing Issues Newsletter*, September 1990, pp. 1–2. This newsletter is published by Arthur Andersen & Co. in conjunction with the Center for Retailing Studies at Texas A&M University.

3. Stephen J. Hoch, Byung-Do Kim, Alan L. Montgomery, and Peter E. Rossi, "Determinants of Store-Level Price Elasticity," *Journal of Marketing Research*, February 1995, p. 28.

4. For an in-depth discussion of this topic, along with excellent bibliographies, see David J. Curry and Peter C. Riesz, "Prices and Price/Quality Relationships: A Longitudinal Analysis," *Journal of Marketing*, January 1988, pp. 36–51; Valarie A. Zeithaml, "Consumer Perceptions of Price, Quality, and Value: A Means-End Model and Synthesis of Evidence," *Journal of Marketing*, July 1988, pp. 2–22.

5. Pauline Yoshihashi, "Limited-Service Chains Offer Enough to Thrive," *The Wall Street Journal*, July 27, 1992, p. B1.

6. Rahul Jacob, "Beyond Quality and Value," *Fortune* (special issue), Autumn/Winter 1993, pp. 8, 10.

7. Jack Welch was quoted in Stratford Sherman, "How to Prosper in the Value Decade," *Fortune*, Nov. 30, 1992, p. 91; the other quotation is drawn from Christopher Farrell and Zachary Schiller, "Stuck!" *Business Week*, Nov. 15, 1993, p. 148.

8. Frank Alpert, Beth Wilson, and Michael T. Elliott, "Price Signaling: Does It Ever Work?" *Journal of Product & Brand Management*, Vol. 2, No. 1, 1993, pp. 29–41.

9. For a list of 21 pricing objectives and a discussion of objectives as part of a strategic pricing program for industrial firms, see Michael H. Morris and Roger J. Calantone, "Four Components of Effective Pricing," *Industrial Marketing Management*, November 1990, pp. 321–329.

10. Richard A. Spinello, "Ethics, Pricing and the Pharmaceutical Industry," *Journal of Business Ethics*, August 1992, pp. 617+; and Marilyn Chase, "Burroughs Wellcome Cuts Price of AZT under Pressure from AIDS Activists," *The Wall Street Journal*, Sept. 19, 1989, p. A3.

11. "Deep Discounters Prove Tenacious," *Chain Drug Review*, July 3, 1995, p. 102.

12. For a discussion of new-product pricing, taking into account the product's perceived benefits and entry time, see Eunsang Yoon, "Pricing Imitative New Products," *Industrial Marketing Management*, May 1991, pp. 115–125.

13. Zachary Schiller, "The Revolving Door at Rubbermaid," *Business Week*, Sept. 18, 1995, pp. 80–83.

14. For a report on how this is done in the business market, see Michael H. Morris and Mary L. Joyce, "How Marketers Evaluate Price Sensitivity," *Industrial Marketing Management*, May 1988, pp. 169–176.

15. Neil Gross and Peter Coy, "The Technology Paradox," *Business Week*, Mar. 6, 1995, pp. 76–81, 84.

16. "Pricing Gets Easier (Sort Of)," *Inc.*, November 1993, p. 124.

17. Morris and Calantone, op. cit., p. 323.

18. Farrell and Schiller, op. cit., pp. 146, 148.

19. For an approach to break-even analysis that includes semifixed costs and is of more practical value in situations typically faced by marketing executives, see Thomas L. Powers, "Breakeven Analysis with Semifixed Costs," *Industrial Marketing Management*, February 1987, pp. 35–41.

20. G. Dean Kortge and Patrick A. Okonkwo, "Perceived Value Approach to Pricing," *Industrial Marketing Management*, May 1993, p. 134.

21. Dan Koeppel, "Fast Food's New Reality," *Adweek's Marketing Week*, Mar. 30, 1992, pp. 22–23.

22. Margaret Studer, "Switzerland's Luxury-Watch Industry Continues to Defy Economic Downturn," *The Wall Street Journal*, Aug. 10, 1992, p. A5B; and Thomas T. Nagle, "Managing Price Competition," *Marketing Management*, Vol. 2, No. 1, 1993, p. 41.

23. "Scheduled Luxury Air Service Ends," *Travel Weekly*, Jan. 9, 1995, p. 8; and Doug Carroll, "MGM Upgrades Its Fleet in Grand Style," *USA Today*, Apr. 25, 1990, p. 2B.

24. John Rossant, "Will A/X Get the Ax?" *Business Week*, May 30, 1994, p. 48; and Susan Caminiti, "The Pretty Payoff

in Cheap Chic," *Fortune*, Feb. 24, 1992, pp. 71, 73.

25. Carlton, "What's Eating . . . ," loc. cit.; Carlton, "Apple Reduces Prices . . . ," loc. cit.; Julie Schmit, "Motorola Will Use Apple Technology," *USA Today*, Feb. 20, 1996, p. 3B; "Apple Cuts Prices," *Columbia* (Missouri) *Daily Tribune*, Feb. 6, 1996, p. 6B; Kathy Rebello, "Apple's Assault," *Business Week*, June 12, 1995, pp. 98–99; and Jim Carlton, "Master of Cheap Clones May Hold Key to Fate of Apple Computers," *The Wall Street Journal*, Apr. 14, 1995, p. A1.

CHAPTER 12

1. Jeff Cole, "Boeing Is Victor in Battle for Singapore Air Order," *The Wall Street Journal*, Nov. 15, 1995, p. A3; William Flannery and Kathleen Best, "Airline Order Boosts MD-95," *St. Louis Post-Dispatch*, Oct. 20, 1995, pp. 1A, 14A; Alex Taylor III, "Boeing: Sleepy in Seattle," *Fortune*, Aug. 7, 1995, pp. 92+; Jeff Cole, "Boeing Is Expected to Win $1.6 Billion Order for Planes," *The Wall Street Journal*, July 25, 1995, pp. A2, A5; and Jeff Cole, "Boeing Is Offering Cuts in Prices of New Jets, Rattling the Industry," *The Wall Street Journal*, Apr. 24, 1995, pp. A1, A8.

2. Christopher Farrell and Zachary Schiller, "Stuck!" *Business Week*, Nov. 15, 1993, p. 150.

3. Eleena de Lisser, "Taco Bell, Low-Price King, Will Offer Low-Fat Line," *The Wall Street Journal*, Feb. 6, 1995, p. B1; and Bill Saporito, "Why the Price Wars Never End," *Fortune*, Mar. 23, 1992, pp. 68+.

4. Patricia Sellers, "Look Who Learned about Value," *Fortune*, Oct. 18, 1993, p. 75.

5. Stratford Sherman, "How to Prosper in the Value Decade," *Fortune*, Nov. 30, 1992, p. 98. For more on this topic, see Christopher Power, "Value Marketing," *Business Week*, Nov. 11, 1991, pp. 132+.

6. Albert D. Bates, "Pricing for Profit," *Retailing Issues Newsletter*, September 1990, p. 1.

7. For three recommended forms of non-price competition for retailers, see Bates, op. cit., p. 4.

8. William Echikson, "Aiming at High and Low Markets," *Fortune*, Mar. 22, 1993, p. 89.

9. The Datastorm example comes from Gene Koprowski, "The Price Is Right," *Marketing Tools*, September 1995, p. 56; the Computer Associates scenario from Neil Gross and Peter Coy, "The Technology Paradox," *Business Week*, Mar. 6, 1995, pp. 76–77; and the General Magic example from "General Magic Plans Giveaway to Boost Sales," *The Wall Street Journal*, Sept. 14, 1995, p. B1.

10. Robert Steyer, "Monsanto Offers Discounts to Dairy Farmers," *St. Louis Post-Dispatch*, Oct. 22, 1995, p. 1E.

11. Joseph Weber, "Can a 1,245% Markup on Drugs Really Be Legal?" *Business Week*, Nov. 1, 1993, p. 34.

12. For further discussion of pricing strategies and policies, see Gerard J. Tellis, "Beyond the Many Faces of Price: An Integration of Pricing Strategies," *Journal of Marketing*, October 1986, pp. 146–160.

13. For an in-depth discussion of flexible pricing including a theoretical model and managerial implications, see Kenneth R. Evans and Richard F. Beltramini, "A Theoretical Model of Consumer Negotiated Pricing: An Orientation Perspective," *Journal of Marketing*, April 1987, pp. 58–73.

14. For a report on the managerial, legal, and ethical aspects of flexible pricing in business markets, see Michael H. Morris, "Separate Prices as a Marketing Tool," *Industrial Marketing Management*, May 1987, pp. 79–86.

15. James Bennet, "Buying without Haggling as Cars Get Fixed Prices," *The New York Times*, Feb. 1, 1994, pp. A1, A12; and "Car Buyers Like Single Price," *St. Louis Post-Dispatch*, Sept. 1, 1992, p. 6B.

16. Louise Lee, "Dollar Stores, Once the Rage, Are Now Failing," *The Wall Street Journal*, Nov. 25, 1994, p. B1.

17. Robert M. Schindler and Lori S. Warren, "Effects of Odd Pricing on Price Recall," *Journal of Business*, June 1989, pp. 165–177; Robert Blattberg and Kenneth Wisniewski, "How Retail Price Promotions Work: Empirical Results," Marketing Working Paper No. 42, University of Chicago, 1987.

18. For a study of the effects of unfair-sales laws on price levels and competition between small stores and large grocery warehouses, see Willard F. Mueller and Thomas W. Paterson, "Effectiveness of State Sales-below-Cost Laws: Evidence from the Grocery Trade," *Journal of Retailing*, Summer 1986, pp. 166–185.

19. "Wal-Mart Wins Suit over Low-Price Strategy," *St. Louis Post-Dispatch*, Jan. 10, 1995, p. 7C; and Bob Ortega, "Wal-Mart Loses a Case on Pricing," *The Wall Street Journal*, Oct. 13, 1993, p. A3.

20. Koprowski, op. cit., p. 61.

21. Stephen J. Hoch, Xavier Drèze, and Mary E. Purk, "EDLP, Hi-Lo, and Margin Arithmetic," *Journal of Marketing*, October 1994, pp. 16–27.

22. Patrick J. Kaufmann, N. Craig Smith, and Gwendolyn K. Ortmeyer, "Deception in Retailer High-Low Pricing: A 'Rule of Reason' Approach," *Journal of Retailing*, Summer 1994, pp. 15+.

23. Stephanie Anderson Forest, "Dillard's Has a Dilly of a Headache," *Business Week*, Oct. 3, 1994, pp. 85–86.

24. Hoch et al., loc. cit.

25. John Bissell, "EDLP Reconsidered: What Marketers Are Saying Now," *Brandweek*, June 21, 1993, p. 11.

26. For a discussion of the legal status of resale price maintenance, plus some steps that manufacturers can take to avoid legal problems when establishing resale price maintenance programs, see Mary Jane Sheffet and Debra L. Scammon, "Resale Price Maintenance: Is It Safe to Suggest Retail Prices?" *Journal of Marketing*, Fall 1985, pp. 82–91.

27. Viveca Novak and Joseph Pereira, "Reebok and FTC Settle Price-Fixing Charges," *The Wall Street Journal*, May 5, 1995, p. B1; and Paul M. Barrett, "FTC's Hard Line on Price Fixing May Foster Discounts," *The Wall Street Journal*, Jan. 11, 1991, p. B1.

28. Barrett, loc. cit.; and Gary Strauss, "Athletic-Shoe Makers Pressure Retailers on Prices," *USA Today*, Dec. 10, 1992, p. 4B.

29. Michael Selz, "Small Firms Use Variety of Ploys to Raise Prices," *The Wall Street Journal*, June 17, 1993, p. B1.

30. Thomas T. Nagle, "Managing Price Competition," *Marketing Management*, Vol. 2, No. 1, 1993, p. 45.

31. John J. Keller, "MCI and Sprint Unveil Deep Discounts, New Services in Fresh Fight with AT&T," *The Wall Street Journal*, Jan. 6, 1995, p. A3.

32. Jim Carlton, "Price War Puts Powerful PCs Closer to Home," *The Wall Street Journal*, Apr. 3, 1995, p. B1; Andrew Kupfer, "Who's Winning the PC Price Wars," *Fortune*, Sept. 21, 1992, pp. 80–82; and Kathy Rebello, "They're Slashing as Fast as They Can," *Business Week*, Feb. 7, 1992, p. 40.

33. Andrew E. Serwer, "How to Escape a Price War," *Fortune*, June 13, 1994, pp. 82+.

34. John R. Wilke, "PC Giants' Price War Hurts Tiny Makers," *The Wall Street Journal*, Nov. 2, 1992, p. B1; and Katia Hetter, "Grocery Rivals Plunge Houston into a Price War," *The Wall Street Journal*, Aug. 20, 1992, p. B1.

35. Taylor, loc. cit.; and Cole, "Boeing Is Offering Cuts . . . ," loc. cit. Additional material drawn from "Boeing Strengthens Market Position in 1995," *PR Newswire*, July 31, 1995; and "Boeing Chairman Sees Changing Marketplace," *PR Newswire*, Mar. 7, 1995.

CHAPTER 13

1. Raju Narisetti, "Penske Auto Center Gives Goodyear Exclusive Tire Pact," *The Wall Street Journal*, Oct. 10, 1995, p. B9; Raju Narisetti, "Goodyear Plans to Offer Tire Models Available Only for Independent Dealers," *The Wall Street Journal*, Jan. 23, 1995, p. A5; and Myron Magnet, "The Marvels of High Margins," *Fortune*, May 2, 1994, pp. 73–74.

2. Bernard Wysocki, Jr., "Improved Distribution, Not Better Production, Is Key Goal in Mergers," *The Wall Street Journal*, Aug. 29, 1995, pp. A1, A2.

3. Michael Selz, "Independent Sales Reps Are Squeezed by the Recession," *The Wall Street Journal*, Dec. 27, 1991, p. B2.

4. The concept of shifting activities, the possibility of manufacturers shifting some functions away from their firms, and the opportunity for small wholesalers to perform added functions to maintain their economic viability are all discussed in Ronald D. Michman, "Managing Structural Changes in Marketing Channels," *The Journal of Business and Industrial Marketing*, Summer/Fall 1990, pp. 5–14.

5. Julie Candler, "How to Choose a Distributor," *Nation's Business*, August 1993, p. 46.

6. Gabriella Stern and Nichole M. Christian, "GM Plans to Sell Saturn Line in Japan in Network of Stand-Alone Dealerships," *The Wall Street Journal*, June 2, 1995, p. A4; and Allan J. Magrath, "Differentiating Yourself via Distribution," *Sales & Marketing Management*, March 1991, pp. 50, 56, 57.

7. An alternative approach, which emphasizes market analysis, is presented in Allan J. Magrath and Kenneth G. Hardy, "Six Steps to Distribution Network Design," *Business Horizons*, January–February 1991, pp. 48–52.

8. For more on selecting channels for international markets, especially the decision of whether to use middlemen, see Saul Klein, "Selection of International Marketing Channels," *Journal of Global Marketing*, Vol. 4, 1991, pp. 21–37.

9. The two examples are drawn from "Levi's Plans Own Stores," *Marketing News*, Jan. 30, 1995, p. 1; and "Unconventional Channels," *Sales & Marketing Management*, October 1988, p. 38.

10. Bridget O'Brian, "Southwest Airlines Fares Well Minus Some Reservations," *The Wall Street Journal*, Aug. 3, 1994, p. B4.

11. Peter Burrows, "The Computer Is in the Mail (Really)," *Business Week*, Jan. 23, 1995, pp. 76–77; and Paul M. Eng, "The PC Is Not in the Mail," *Business Week*, July 11, 1994, p. 42.

12. An excellent discussion of distribution channels for business goods and services is found in Michael D. Hutt and Thomas W. Speh, *Business Marketing Management*, 5th ed., The Dryden Press, Ft. Worth, Tex., 1995, pp. 372–408.

13. For an instructive discussion of this topic, see Donald H. Light, "A Guide for New Distribution Channel Strategies for Service Firms," *The Journal of Business Strategy*, Summer 1986, pp. 56–64.

14. O'Brian, loc. cit.; and Zachary Schiller, "Making the Middleman an Endangered Species," *Business Week*, June 6, 1994, pp. 114–115.

15. Rowland T. Moriarty and Ursula Moran, "Managing Hybrid Marketing Systems," *Harvard Business Review*, November–December 1990, pp. 146–155.

16. For extensive discussion of this approach to serving distinct markets, see John A. Quelch, "Why Not Exploit Dual Marketing?" *Business Horizons*, January–February 1987, pp. 52–60.

17. John R. Wilke and Leslie Scism, "Insurance Agents Fight an Intrusion by Banks, but Other Perils Loom," *The Wall Street Journal*, Aug. 8, 1995, pp. A1, A5.

18. Jeffrey A. Tannenbaum, "Carvel Strategy Frosts Many Franchisees," *The Wall Street Journal*, Dec. 20, 1994, pp. B1, B2.

19. The Scotts example comes from Valerie Reitman, "Manufacturers Start to Spurn Big Discounters," *The Wall Street Journal*, Nov. 30, 1993, p. B1. For further discussion of the advantages and disadvantages of multiple channels as well as ways to minimize conflict resulting from multiple channels, see Martin Everett, "When There's More Than One Route to the Customer," *Sales & Marketing Management*, August 1990, pp. 48–50+.

20. Allison Lucas, "Can You Sell to Wal-Mart?" *Sales & Marketing Management*, August 1995, p. 14.

21. Kyle Pope, "Forecasts Aside, Dealers of PCs Thrive Again," *The Wall Street Journal*, Feb. 1, 1994, pp. B1, B3.

22. Michael Selz, "More Small Firms Are Turning to Trade Intermediaries," *The Wall Street Journal*, Feb. 2, 1993, p. B2.

23. For more on the idea that market considerations should determine a channel structure, see Louis W. Stern and Frederick D. Sturdivant, "Customer-Driven Distribution Systems," *Harvard Business Review*, July–August 1987, pp. 34–41.

24. Bert Rosenbloom and Trina L. Larsen, "How Foreign Firms View Their U.S. Distributors," *Industrial Marketing Management*, May 1992, pp. 93–101.

25. "Putting the Aim Back into Famous Amos," *Sales & Marketing Management*, June 1992, p. 31.

26. Reitman, op. cit., pp. B1, B2; and Christina Duff, "Nation's Retailers Ask Vendors to Help Share Expenses," *The Wall Street Journal*, Aug. 4, 1993, p. B4.

27. Burrows, op. cit., p. 76; and Paul B. Carroll, "IBM Will Test Selling Its PCs by Mail Order," *The Wall Street Journal*, Apr. 29, 1992, p. B5.

28. Candler, op. cit., pp. 45–46, provides a good overview of the services that a distributor can provide to small manufacturers and, in turn, various factors that should be considered in selecting a distributor.

29. Reitman, op. cit., pp. B1, B2.

30. Burrows, op. cit., pp. 76–77; and Lois Therrien, "Whatever Happened to the Corner Computer Store?" *Business Week*, May 20, 1991, pp. 131+. A behind-the-scenes look at what happens when a customer orders a PC from Dell Computer is contained in Stephanie Losee, "Mr. Cozzette Buys a Computer," *Fortune*, Apr. 18, 1994, pp. 113–116.

31. Cacilie Rohwedder and Brandon Michener, "Mexican-Made VW Beetles Are Selling Like Wurst at German Supermarkets," *The Wall Street Journal*, Oct. 25, 1995, p. A17.

32. Marj Charlier, "Coors Looks to Local Distributors for National Growth," *The Wall Street Journal*, June 28, 1993, p. B6.

33. Teri Agins, "Apparel Makers Are Refashioning Their Operations," *The Wall Street Journal*, Jan. 13, 1994, p. B4.

34. Bill Saporito, "Cutting Out the Middleman," *Fortune*, Apr. 6, 1992, p. 96.

35. "Levi's Plans Own Stores," *Marketing News*, Jan. 30, 1995, p. 1. For details about the start of this trend and the resulting conflicts, see Teri Agins, "Clothing Makers Don Retailers' Garb," *The Wall Street Journal*, July 13, 1989, p. B1.

36. Christina Duff, "Big Stores' Outlandish Demands Alienate Small Suppliers," *The Wall Street Journal*, Oct. 27, 1995, pp. B1, B5; and Christina Duff, "Nation's Retailers Ask Vendors to Help Share Expenses," *The Wall Street Journal*, Aug. 4, 1993, p. B4.

37. "Business Bulletin," *The Wall Street Journal*, May 11, 1995, p. A1; and Richard Gibson, "Supermarkets Demand Food Firms' Payments Just to Get on the Shelf," *The Wall Street Journal*, Nov. 1, 1988, pp. 1, 14.

38. Duff, "Big Stores' Outlandish Demands Alienate Small Suppliers," op. cit., p. B5.

39. James E. Zemanek, Jr., and James W. Hardin, "How the Industrial Salesperson's Use of Power Can Affect Distributor Satisfaction: An Empirical Examination," *Journal of Marketing Channels*, Vol. 3, No. 1, 1993, pp. 23–45.

40. Agins, loc. cit.

41. The emerging dominance of gigantic retailers and their dictates to manufacturers are described in Zachary Schiller and Wendy Zellner, "Clout!" *Business Week*, Dec. 21, 1992, pp. 66–69+. Customer market power in relation to channel control is covered in Gul Butaney and Lawrence H. Wortzel, "Distributor Power versus Manufacturer Power: The Customer Role," *Journal of Marketing*, January 1988, pp. 52–63.

42. For a model showing a range of channel relationships, see John T. Gardner, W. Benoy Joseph, and Sharon Thach, "Modeling the Continuum of Relationship Styles between Distributors and Suppliers," *Journal of Marketing Channels*, Vol. 2, No. 4, 1993, pp. 1+.

43. Allan J. Magrath, "The Hidden Clout of Middlemen," *The Journal of Business Strategy*, March/April 1990, p. 41. The Sutter example comes from Candler, op. cit., p. 45. For further ideas on how to build a good producer-middleman relationship, see James A. Narus and James C. Anderson, "Distributor Contributions to Partnership with Manufacturers," *Business Horizons*, September–October 1987, pp. 34–42.

44. Neal Templin and Jeff Cole, "Manufacturers Use Suppliers to Help Them Develop New Products," *The Wall Street Journal*, Dec. 19, 1994, p. A1; and Myron Magnet, "The New Golden Rule of Business," *Fortune*, Feb. 21, 1994, pp. 60–64.

45. B. G. Yovovich, "Partnering at Its Best," *Business Marketing*, March 1992, pp. 36–37.

46. Magnet, "The New Golden Rule of Business," loc. cit.

47. Agins, loc. cit.

48. John R. Nevin, "Relationship Marketing and Distribution Channels: Exploring Fundamental Issues," *Journal of Marketing Channels*, Vol. 23, No. 4, 1995, pp. 327–334.

49. Jeffrey A. Tannenbaum, "Franchisees Balk at High Prices for Supplies from Franchisers," *The Wall Street Journal*, July 5, 1995, pp. B1, B2.

50. Wendy Bounds, "Jury Finds Kodak Monopolized Markets in Services and Parts for Its Machines," *The Wall Street Journal*, Sept. 19, 1995, p. A4.

51. Joseph Pereira, "Stride Rite Agrees to Settle Charges It Tried to Force Pricing by Retailers," *The Wall Street Journal*, Sept. 28, 1993, p. B5.

52. Magnet, "The Marvels of High Margins," loc. cit.; and Zachary Schiller, "And Fix That Flat Before You Go, Stanley," *Business Week*, Jan. 16, 1995, p. 35.

CHAPTER 14

1. Louise Lee, "Penney Moves to Restore Shiny Image," *The Wall Street Journal*, Mar. 25, 1996, p. B4; Laura Bird, "Christmas Wasn't Merry for Many Stores, and New Year Outlook Is Little Happier," *The Wall Street Journal*, Jan. 5, 1996, p. B1; David Moin, "Penney's to Use Refunds to Tout Its Brands' Value," *WWD (Women's Wear Daily)*, July 13, 1995, p. 2; "Penney's Getting a Deal on Ivana Trump Scent," *WWD*, June 7, 1995, p. 23; "J.C. Penney Reaping the Rewards of Soft Lines Transition," *Discount Store News*, May 15, 1995, p. 45; and Holly Haber, "Penney's New CEO Outlines Agenda for Improving Market Share," *Daily News Record*, Jan. 26, 1995, p. 7.

2. As quoted in Lou Grabowsky, "Globalization: Reshaping the Retail Marketplace," *Retailing Issues Letter*, November 1989, p. 4.

3. *1987 Census of Retail Trade*, Subject Series, U.S. Bureau of the Census, Washington, D.C., 1991, p. 2-9; and *1992 Census of Wholesale Trade*, Geographic Area Series—U.S., U.S. Bureau of the Census, Washington, D.C., 1995, p. US-9. The 8 percent figure was calculated by multiplying the 11 percent representing wholesale operating expenses by 72 percent, the remainder after the 28 percent representing retailing operating expenses is subtracted from the 100 percent representing retail sales (or the consumer's dollar).

4. Stanley N. Logan, "The Small Store—A Struggle to Survive," *Retailing Issues Letter*, January 1995, p. 2.

5. Ibid., pp. 1–6. This essay outlines five ways in which small stores can learn what their customers want and also describes several means of differentiation.

6. For a status report on the Mall of America, see Sally Apgar, "That's Entertainment!" *St. Louis Post-Dispatch*, Aug. 24, 1995, p. 5C. For more facts and figures about the Mall of America, see Dan Koeppel, "The Mall's Last Hurrah," *Adweek's Marketing Week*, June 22, 1992, pp. 20–24.

7. The survey results are described in Kenneth Labich, "What It Will Take to Keep People Hanging Out at the Mall," *Fortune*, May 29, 1995, pp. 102–106. The statistics about average shopping times are contained in Jonathan R. Laing, "The New Ghost Towns," *Barron's*, Mar. 16, 1992, p. 8. Both articles present an analysis of large shopping centers.

8. The pessimistic forecasts and the quotation come from Labich, op. cit., p. 103. Mall renovations are described in Mitchell Pacelle, "Malls Add Fun and Games to Attract Shoppers," *The Wall Street Journal*, Jan. 23, 1996, p. B1; and Gregory A. Patterson, "Malls Draw Shoppers with Ferris Wheels and Carousels," *The Wall Street Journal*, June 22, 1994, p. B1.

9. Ellen Neuborne, "Stores Siphon Shoppers from Regional Malls," *USA Today*, June 13, 1995, p. 1B.

10. Gregory A. Patterson, "All Decked Out, Stores Head Downtown," *The Wall Street Journal*, Feb. 15, 1994, pp. B1, B7; and Laurie M. Grossman, "Developed to Reinvigorate Downtowns, Many Urban Malls Are Disappointments," *The Wall Street Journal*, Nov. 16, 1992, p. B1.

11. *Statistical Abstract of the United States: 1995*, 115th ed., U.S. Bureau of the Census, Washington, D.C., 1995, p. 783.

12. Ibid.

13. Andrew E. Serwer, "Trouble in Franchise Nation," *Fortune*, Mar. 6, 1995, p. 116.; and Meg Whittemore, "New Directions in Franchising," *Nation's Business*, January 1995, p. 48.

14. Jeffrey A. Tannenbaum, "Chain Links," *The Wall Street Journal*, May 22, 1995, p. R18; and Michele Galen and Laurel Touby, "Franchise Fracas," *Business Week*, Mar. 22, 1993, pp. 68–70+. The quotation is from Serwer, loc. cit.

15. Serwer, loc. cit.

16. Growth areas for franchising are suggested in Whittemore, loc. cit. The move of successful companies into franchising is mentioned in Jeffrey A. Tannenbaum, "Big Companies Bearing Famous Names Turn to Franchising to Get Even Bigger," *The Wall Street Journal*, Oct. 18, 1995, p. B1. Factors contributing to franchising's continued growth are outlined in Bruce J. Walker, "Retail Franchising in the 1990s," *Retailing Issues Letter*, January 1991, pp. 1–4.

17. Serwer, op. cit., p. 116.

18. David Rachman and Keith J. Fabes, "The Decline of the Traditional American Department Store," *Journal of Marketing Channels*, Vol. 1, No. 3, 1992, pp. 39+.

19. Babette Morgan, "Department Stores Have Some Advantages in Defending Turf," *St. Louis Post-Dispatch*, Jan. 17, 1994, p. 12BP.

20. Gregory A. Patterson, "Department Stores, Seemingly Outmoded, Are Perking Up Again," *The Wall Street Journal*, Jan. 4, 1994, pp. A1, A4; Gretchen Morgenson, "Back to Basics," *Forbes*, May 10, 1993, pp. 56, 58; and Stephanie Strom, "Department Stores' Fate," *The New York Times*, Feb. 3, 1992, p. A1.

21. Robert Berner, "Sears's Softer Side Paid Off in Hard Cash This Christmas," *The Wall Street Journal*, Dec. 29, 1995, p. B4.

22. Patricia Sellers, "Kmart Is Down for the Count," *Fortune*, Jan. 15, 1996, pp. 102–103; and Christina Duff and Bob Ortega, "How Wal-Mart Outdid a Once-Touted Kmart in Discount-Store Race," *The Wall Street Journal*, Mar. 24, 1995, pp. A1, A4.

23. Gerry Khermouch, "Target Hits Bullseye," *Brandweek*, June 5, 1995, pp. 22+; and Susan Chandler, "'Speed Is Life' at Dayton Hudson," *Business Week*, Mar. 27, 1995, pp. 84, 86.

24. Bill Saporito, "And the Winner Is Still . . . Wal-Mart," *Fortune*, May 2, 1994, pp. 62–65, 68, 70.

25. Saporito, op. cit., pp. 64–65; Louise Lee and Kevin Helliker, "Humbled Wal-Mart Plans More Stores," *The Wall Street Journal*, Feb. 23, 1996, pp. B1, B4; and Babette Morgan, "Discount Distress," *St. Louis Post-Dispatch*, Aug. 6, 1995, p. E1.

26. Susan Caminiti, "Can The Limited Fix Itself?" *Fortune*, Oct. 17, 1994, pp. 161–162+.

27. Kevin Thomson, "Oodles of Opportunity," *Sales & Marketing Management*, August 1995, pp. 20, 22; and Stuart Mieher, "Stores Offering Stylish Products Fare Very Well," *The Wall Street Journal*, Dec. 15, 1992, p. B1.

28. Mary Kuntz, "Reinventing the Store," *Business Week*, Nov. 27, 1995, p. 89.

29. Fred Faust, "Retail Chains Want Back in Fashion," *St. Louis Post-Dispatch*, Jan. 21, 1996, pp. 1D, 8D.

30. The annual sales figure is from Stephanie Anderson Forest, "I Can Get It for You Retail," *Business Week*, Sept. 18, 1995, pp. 84–88; the survey results were reported in Caity Olson, "Outlet Stores Win Satisfied Consumers," *Advertising Age*, July 11, 1994, p. 33.

31. Kevin Helliker, "Thriving Factory Outlets Anger Retailers as Store Suppliers Turn into Competitors," *The Wall Street Journal*, Oct. 7, 1991, p. B1.

32. Jerri Stroud, "May Co. Will Spin Off Payless Shoe Chain," *St. Louis Post-Dispatch*, Jan. 18, 1996, pp. 1C, 5C; Geoffrey Smith, "Can TJX Turn Off-Price On?" *Business Week*, Oct. 30, 1995, p. 44; and Forest, loc. cit.

33. Sometimes category killers are referred to as *superstores*. Using this term in this context can create confusion, however, because it is also applied to very large supermarkets.

34. For more about two chains of category-killer stores, see Mary Kuntz, "Reinventing the Store," *Business Week*, Nov. 27, 1995, pp. 84–89, 92, 96; and Babette Morgan, "Borders Enters Big Bookstore Competition Here," *St. Louis Post-Dispatch*, Mar. 20, 1995, p. 3BP.

35. Kathleen Kerwin, "Used-Car Fever," *Business Week*, Jan. 22, 1996, pp. 34–35; and Mike McKesson, "Superstore Excels at Selling Used Cars," *South Bend Tribune*, Jan. 4, 1996, p. D1.

36. For less-than-optimistic forecasts about supermarkets *and* department stores as well as some prescriptions for both types of institutions, see Richard A. Rauch, "Retailing's Dinosaurs: Department Stores and Supermarkets," *Business Horizons*, September–October 1991, pp. 21–25.

37. Louise Lee, "Circle K Pushes for a New Look at Convenience Stores," *The Wall Street Journal*, Nov. 6, 1995, p. B4.

38. Wendy Zellner, "Why Sam's Wants Businesses to Join the Club," *Business Week*, June 27, 1994, pp. 48, 53; and Bob Ortega, "Warehouse-Club War Leaves Few Standing and They Are Bruised," *The Wall Street Journal*, Nov. 18, 1993, pp. A1, A6.

39. Louise Lee, "Warehouse Clubs Embrace Marketing to Fill the Aisles," *The Wall Street Journal*, Nov. 17, 1995, p. B4; and Zellner, loc. cit.

40. This estimate (perhaps better labeled a "guesstimate") of the total annual volume of nonstore retailing represents a sum of the estimates for the four types that are discussed in subsequent sections.

41. The implications for the direct-selling field of the changing roles of women and other socioeconomic trends are discussed in Vic Sussman, "Return of the Pink Cadillac," *U.S. News & World Report*, Sept. 17, 1990, pp. 71, 74. For seven articles covering various aspects of direct selling, see the *Journal of Marketing Channels*, Vol. 2, No. 2, 1992.

42. The sales estimate and number of sales people were both contained in a 1995 Fact Sheet distributed by the Direct Selling Association, Washington, D.C. The purchase incidences are from Robert A. Peterson, Gerald Albaum, and Nancy M. Ridgway, "Consumers Who Buy from Direct Sales Companies," *Journal of Retailing*, Summer 1989, p. 275.

43. Laurie M. Grossman, "Families Have Changed but Tupperware Keeps Holding Its Parties," *The Wall Street Journal*, July 21, 1992, p. A1.

44. Suein L. Hwang, "Updating Avon Means Respecting History without Repeating It," *The Wall Street Journal*, Apr. 4, 1994, pp. A1, A4; and Jeffrey A. Trachtenberg, "Catalogs Help Avon Get a Foot in the Door," *The Wall Street Journal*, Feb. 28, 1992, p. B1.

45. The worldwide sales figures, which do not include China, are drawn from a December 1995 Fact Sheet distributed by the Worldwide Federation of Direct Selling Associations, Washington, D.C.

46. Based on figures contained in *Economic Impact: U.S. Direct Marketing Today*, Direct Marketing Association, Inc., New York, 1995, pp. 28, 32. The estimated sales refer only to direct orders, not to subsequent sales that were based on leads and store traffic generated by telemarketing.

47. Nanette Byrnes, "Dialing for *Dinero*," *Business Week*, July 10, 1995, p. 108.

48. Dana Milbank, "Telephone Sales Reps Do Unrewarding Jobs That Few Can Abide," *The Wall Street Journal*, Sept. 23, 1993, pp. A1, A8.

49. "FTC Adopts Rules to Combat Fraud in Telemarketing," *The Wall Street Journal*, Aug. 17, 1995, p. A10; and Mary Lu Carnevale, "FCC Adopts Rules to Curb Telemarketing," *The Wall Street Journal*, Sept. 18, 1992, p. B1.

50. The estimate for annual sales is based on "Coke Machine Modems Send Distress Signals," *Marketing News*, Oct. 9, 1995, p. 20; and Timothy L. O'Brien, "Vending Scams Are on the Rise, Officials Warn," *The Wall Street Journal*, July 1, 1994, p. B1.

51. "Coke Machine Modems. . . ," loc. cit.; O'Brien, loc. cit.; Sana Siwolop, "Vending-Machine Technology Pushes Electronic Frontier," *The New York Times*, July 17, 1994, p. F7; Trish Hall, "Vending Machines, the Next Generation in Dining," *The New York Times*, Sept. 9, 1992, pp. C1, C6; and Cyndee Miller, "Vending Industry Cooks Up New Meals in Machines," *Marketing News*, Oct. 28, 1991, p. 1.

52. Based on figures contained in *Economic Impact: U.S. Direct Marketing Today*, loc. cit. The estimated sales refer only to direct orders, not to subsequent sales that were based on leads and store traffic generated by telemarketing. Although we considered it separately, telemarketing is sometimes included under the umbrella of direct marketing. Another term often associated with direct marketing, *mail order*, actually refers to the way an order is placed and/or delivered, whereas the types we describe focus on the way contact is made with consumers.

53. Stephanie Anderson Forest, "The World Is Their Fruitcake," *Business Week*, Dec. 25, 1995, p. 48.

54. Sears' problems and prospects with catalogs are summarized in Susan Chandler, "Strategies for the New Mail Order," *Business Week*, Dec. 19, 1994, pp. 82+. The trials and tribulations of various firms engaged in catalog retailing are covered in Cyndee Miller, "It Was the Worst of Times," *Marketing News*, Mar. 15, 1993, p. 1.

55. Ted Duncombe, "TV Sales Pitchers See Long Game," *St. Louis Post-Dispatch*, July 26, 1995, p. 8C; and Mark Robichaux, "TV Shopping Losing Its Shine for Retailers," *The Wall Street Journal*, Nov. 22, 1994, pp. B1, B6.

56. The sales figures and forecasts as well as the challenges and opportunities for online retailing are drawn from Michael H. Martin, "Why the Web Is Still a No-Shop Zone," *Fortune*, Feb. 5, 1996, pp. 127–128; and Joan E. Rigdon, "Blame Retailers for Web's Slow Start as a Mall," *The Wall Street Journal*, Aug. 16, 1995, pp. B1, B6. The cost of developing a Web site was contained in "Business Bulletin," *The Wall Street Journal*, Jan. 25, 1996, p. A1.

57. The wheel of retailing was first described in M. P. McNair, "Significant Trends and Developments in the Postwar Period," in A. B. Smith, ed., *Competitive Distribution in a Free, High-Level Economy and Its Implications for the University*, The University of Pittsburgh Press, Pittsburgh, 1958, pp. 17–18.

58. Louise Lee, "Discounter Wal-Mart Is Catering to Affluent to Maintain Growth," *The Wall Street Journal*, Feb. 7, 1996, pp. A1, A6; and Fred Faust, "Goodbye Discount, Hello 'Family Value,'" *St. Louis Post-Dispatch*, Dec. 3, 1995, pp. 1E, 8E.

59. Leonard L. Berry, "Stores with a Future," *Retailing Issues Letter*, March 1995, pp. 1–4. Also see Kuntz, op. cit., pp. 84+; and Meg Whittemore, "Retailing Looks to a New Century," *Nation's Business*, December 1994, pp. 18–24.

60. Lee, loc. cit.; "J.C. Penney Reaping the Rewards of Soft Lines Transition," loc. cit.; Haber, loc. cit.; Holly Haber, "Penney's Sees Earnings Growing in Double Digits through 2000," *WWD*, Aug. 25, 1995, p. 2; and Bob Ortega, "Penney Pushes Abroad in Unusually Big Way as It Pursues Growth," *The Wall Street Journal*, Feb. 1, 1994, pp. A1, A7.

CHAPTER 15

1. Steve Weinstein, "The Reinvention of Supervalu," *Progressive Grocer*, January 1996, pp. 26+; Russell Redman, "Supervalu Widens Premium Line," *Supermarket News*, Apr. 24, 1995, p. 102; "Supervalu to Realign Logistics, Marketing," *Supermarket News*, Mar. 20, 1995, p. 1; "Having It Both Ways," *Supermarket Business*, January 1995, p. 57; Elliot Zwiebach, "Supervalu to Pare Staff, Sell Off About 30 Stores," *Supermarket News*, Dec. 12, 1994, p. 1; Steve Weinstein, "The Cost-Cutting Program," *Progressive Grocer*, December 1994, p. 30; "Supervalu Embarks on 'New Vision,'" *Supermarket News*, Sept. 26, 1994, p. 1; and David Orgel, "Supervalu Thinks Big," *Supermarket News*, May 23, 1994, p. 1.

2. Richard A. Melcher, "Cut Out the Middleman? Never," *Business Week*, Jan. 10, 1994, p. 96; and Marj Charlier, "Existing Distributors Are Being Squeezed by Brewers, Retailers," *The Wall Street Journal*, Nov. 22, 1993, pp. A1, A6.

3. *1987 Census of Wholesale Trade*, Subject Series—Miscellaneous Subjects, U.S. Bureau of the Census, Washington, D.C., 1990, p. 4-3.

4. The term *merchant wholesaler*, or *wholesaler*, is sometimes used synonymously with *wholesaling middleman*. This is not accurate, however. *Wholesaling middleman* is the all-inclusive term, covering the three major categories of firms engaged in wholesale trade, whereas *wholesaler* is more restrictive, applying to only one category, namely, merchant wholesaling middlemen.

5. Because manufacturers' sales facilities are owned by manufacturers rather than being truly independent, they could be viewed as a *direct* distribution channel, rather than as distinct middlemen used in indirect distribution. Although this view has merit, we treat manufacturers' sales facilities as a category of middlemen because the Census Bureau does and also because they are separate from manufacturing firms by location, if not by ownership.

6. Donald M. Jackson and Michael F. d'Amico, "Products and Markets

Served by Distributors and Agents," *Industrial Marketing Management*, February 1989, p. 28.

7. *1977 Census of Wholesale Trade*, Geographic Area Series—U.S., U.S. Bureau of the Census, Washington, D.C., 1980, p. US-9; and *1967 Census of Wholesale Trade*, Geographic Area Series—U.S., U.S. Bureau of the Census, Washington, D.C., 1970, p. US-9. For a comprehensive historical analysis of wholesaling, see Robert F. Lusch, Deborah Zizzo, and James M. Kenderine, *Foundations of Wholesaling: A Strategic and Financial Chart Book*, Distribution Research Program, University of Oklahoma, Norman, 1996.

8. Average operating expenses in this paragraph and the following one are based on the *1992 Census of Wholesale Trade*, Geographic Area Series—U.S., U.S. Bureau of the Census, Washington, D.C., 1995, p. US-9; and the *1987 Census of Retail Trade*, Subject Series, U.S. Bureau of the Census, Washington, D.C., 1991, p. 2-9. The 8 percent figure was calculated by multiplying the 11 percent representing wholesale operating expenses by 72 percent, the remainder after the 28 percent representing retail operating expenses is subtracted from the 100 percent representing retail sales (or the consumer's dollar).

9. For more about this leading wholesaler's strategies, see Kathryn Jones, "A Move along the Food Chain," *The New York Times*, July 2, 1994, pp. 1, 26.

10. Jeffrey A. Tannenbaum, "Cold War: Amana Refrigeration Fights Tiny Distributor," *The Wall Street Journal*, Feb. 26, 1992, p. B2.

11. Michael Selz, "Firms Innovate to Get It for You Wholesale," *The Wall Street Journal*, July 23, 1993, pp. B1, B2. For recommendations on how wholesalers can compete effectively with chains of category-killer stores and warehouse clubs that tend to buy directly from manufacturers, see Robert F. Lusch and Deborah Zizzo, *Competing for Customers*, Distribution Research and Education Foundation, Washington, D.C., 1995, pp. 80–108.

12. Selz, op. cit., p. B1.

13. Joseph Weber, "The Practice of Making Perfect," *Business Week*, Jan. 14, 1991, p. 86.

14. Early signs of this trend were reported in Joseph Weber, "Mom and Pop Move Out of Wholesaling," *Business Week*, Jan. 9, 1989, p. 91. The two mergers were described in Jones, loc. cit.; and

Jerri Stroud, "Wetterau Makes a Logical Match," *St. Louis Post-Dispatch*, June 15, 1992, pp. 6BP, 7BP. For an in-depth profile of Supervalu, Inc., and nine other high-performing wholesalers plus financial and operating statistics summaries for 291 U.S. and Canadian wholesalers, see Lusch, Zizzo, and Kenderine, loc. cit.

15. *1977 Census of Wholesale Trade*, loc. cit.; and *1967 Census of Wholesale Trade*, loc. cit.

16. Melissa Campanelli, "Agents of Change," *Sales & Marketing Management*, February 1995, pp. 71–75.

17. *1992 Census of Wholesale Trade*, loc. cit.

18. Ibid.

19. Jon Bigness, "In Today's Economy, There Is Big Money to Be Made in Logistics," *The Wall Street Journal*, Sept. 6, 1995, pp. A1, A9.

20. Ronald Henkoff, "Delivering the Goods," *Fortune*, Nov. 28, 1994, p. 64.

21. Anil Kumar and Graham Sharman, "We Love Your Product, but Where Is It?" *Business Edge*, October 1992, p. 21. For a discussion of how firms can achieve a differential advantage through superior physical distribution, see Donald W. Bowersox, John T. Mentzer, and Thomas W. Speh, "Logistics Leverage," *Journal of Business Strategies*, Spring 1995, pp. 36–49.

22. For more details about transportation deregulation, see Lewis M. Schneider, "New Era in Transportation Strategy," *Harvard Business Review*, March–April 1985, pp. 118–126.

23. Bruce G. Posner, "Growth Strategies," *Inc.*, December 1989, p. 125.

24. This paragraph and the next one are based in part on Bigness, loc. cit., and Henkoff, op. cit., pp. 64–66, 70, 74, 76, 78.

25. Tom Murray, "Just-in-Time Isn't Just for Show—It Sells," *Sales & Marketing Management*, May 1990, p. 64.

26. Henkoff, op. cit., pp. 66, 70, 74.

27. For more details on this type of business arrangement, see Donald J. Bowersox, "The Strategic Benefits of Logistics Alliances," *Harvard Business Review*, July–August 1990, pp. 36–45.

28. Gabriella Stern, "Cadillac Will Test Distribution Method to Cut Delivery Time and Dealer Stock," *The Wall Street Journal*, Aug. 16, 1994, p. A5.

29. For further discussion of JIT, see Marvin W. Tucker and David A. Davis, "Key Ingredients for Successful Imple-

mentation of Just-in-Time: A System for All Business Sizes," *Business Horizons*, May–June 1993, pp. 59–65; and Gary L. Frazier, Robert E. Spekman, and Charles R. O'Neal, "Just-in-Time Exchange Relationships in Industrial Markets," *Journal of Marketing*, October 1988, pp. 52–67.

30. The Xerox and Black & Decker results are described by Earnest C. Raia, "Journey to World Class (JIT in USA)," *Purchasing*, Sept. 24, 1987, p. 48.

31. Fred R. Bleakley, "Some Companies Let Suppliers Work on Site and Even Place Orders," *The Wall Street Journal*, Jan. 13, 1995, pp. A1, A6.

32. Implications of JIT for channels are discussed in Steve McDaniel, Joseph G. Ormsby, and Alicia B. Gresham, "The Effect of JIT on Distributors," *Industrial Marketing Management*, May 1992, pp. 145–149.

33. Jerri Stroud, "Big Savings Seen in Food Handling," *St. Louis Post-Dispatch*, Dec. 11, 1994, pp. E1, E8.

34. Robert F. Lusch, Deborah Zizzo, and James M. Kenderine, "Strategic Renewal in Distribution," *Marketing Management*, Vol. 2, No. 2, 1993, p. 24.

35. Joseph Weber, "Just Get It to the Stores on Time," *Business Week*, Mar. 6, 1995, pp. 66–67.

36. For research results indicating that perceptions of different modes vary across members of a buying center, see James H. Martin, James M. Daley, and Henry B. Burdg, "Buying Influences and Perceptions of Transportation Services," *Industrial Marketing Management*, November 1988, pp. 305–314.

37. David Hage, "On the Right Track," *U.S. News & World Report*, Mar. 21, 1994, pp. 46+.

38. Ibid.

39. Joseph Weber, Seth Payne, Kevin Kelly, and Stephanie A. Forest, "The Great Train Turnaround," *Business Week*, Nov. 2, 1992, pp. 56–57; and Sally Solo, "Every Problem Is an Opportunity," *Fortune*, Nov. 16, 1992, p. 93.

40. Lore Croghan, "Wabash National: It's a Truck, It's a Train, It's . . . RoadRailer?" *Financial World*, Feb. 21, 1995, p. 14.

41. Robert Frank, "Efficient UPS Tries to Increase Efficiency," *The Wall Street Journal*, May 24, 1995, pp. B1, B4; and Marc Rice, "Competition Fierce in Complex Business of Delivering Packages," *Marketing News*, May 22, 1995, p. 5.

42. Steve Wilhelm, "Food Wholesaler Supervalu Leads Way into Japan Market,"

Puget Sound Business Journal, July 28, 1995, p. 12; Elliot Zwiebach, "Super-valu Starts Store Restructuring," *Supermarket News*, Jan. 16, 1995, p. 1; and Matthew Schifrin, "Middleman's Dilemma," *Forbes*, May 23, 1994, p. 67.

CHAPTER 16

1. Kathi Gannon, "OTC Naproxen Sodium Set to Shake OTC Analgesics," *Drug Topics*, Feb. 7, 1994, p. 34; Iris Rosendahl, "Breaking the Pain," *Drug Topics*, July 11, 1994, p. 94; Laura Bird, "P&G's New Analgesic Promises Pain for Over-the-Counter Rivals," *The Wall Street Journal*, June 16, 1994, p. B9; and Emily DeNitto, "P&G Analgesics Headache," *Advertising Age*, Jan. 17, 1994, pp. 3+.
2. Data from Information Resources, Inc., reported in Betsy Spethmann, "Returning to Core Business," *Superbrands, 1995*, Oct. 17, 1994, pp. 100–104.
3. Gerry Khermouch, "Competition Spurs Growth," *Superbrands, 1995*, Oct. 17, 1994, pp. 69–73.
4. Bruce Horovitz, "Benetton Ads Banned in Germany," *USA Today*, July 7–9, 1995, p. 1A.
5. Jeff Jensen, "Jim Hancock: No Fear," *Advertising Age*, June 26, 1995, p. S-28.
6. Mark Pawlosky, "Health Food for Babies Is Slow to Grow," *The Wall Street Journal*, June 14, 1995, pp. B1+; and Udayan Gupta, "Natural-Products Makers Discover Power of an Image," *The Wall Street Journal*, June 23, 1992, p. B2.
7. Bradley Johnson, "Abby Kohnstamn: IBM," *Advertising Age*, June 26, 1995, p. S-4.
8. Jamie Goldman, "Mike Provenzano: Olympic/Lucite," *Advertising Age*, June 26, 1995, p. S-21.
9. Ibid.
10. An excellent description of the past, present, and future of the Federal Trade Commission as well as the regulation of promotion in general can be found in Patrick E. Murphy and William L. Wilkie, *Marketing and Advertising Regulation*, University of Notre Dame Press, Notre Dame, IN, 1990.
11. *NAD Case Reports: Analysis of 1993 Closings*, National Advertising Division of Better Business Bureaus, Inc., January 1994, p. 105.
12. Emily DeNitto, "P&G's Aleve Quickly Joins Top Painkillers," *Advertising Age*, Dec. 5, 1994, pp. 3+; Pam Weisz, "J&J

Ups Dosage on Tylenol Ads for Aleve Relief," *Adweek's Marketing Week*, June 27, 1994, pp. 1+; and Emily DeNitto, "American Home Applies Legal Pain to P&G's Aleve," *Advertising Age*, Aug. 15, 1994, p. 4.

CHAPTER 17

1. Geoffrey Brewer, "Wheeler Dealers," *Sales & Marketing Management*, June 1995, pp. 38–44; "Agco Corp.," *Standard and Poor's Corporation Records*, Vol. 56, No. 13, July 1995, pp. 3483–3484; and Robert Luke, "Agco Reaps Again, Plants Seeds for '95," *The Atlanta Journal Constitution*, May 21, 1995, p. T-17.
2. Allison Lucas, "Portrait of a Salesperson," *Sales & Marketing Management*, June 1995, p. 13.
3. Calmetta Y. Coleman, "A Car Salesman's Bizarre Prank May End Up Backfiring in Court," *The Wall Street Journal*, May 2, 1995, p. B1.
4. Susan Greco, "Hands-on Sales & Marketing," *Inc.*, April 1995, p. 107.
5. Andy Cohen, "Practice Makes Profits," *Sales & Marketing Management*, July 1995, pp. 24–25.
6. "More Sales Pay Linked to Satisfied Customers," *Sales & Marketing Management*, June 1995, p. 37.
7. Brewer, loc. cit.

CHAPTER 18

1. Dorothy Giobbe, "Ad Shocks Its Way into the Spotlight," *Editor & Publisher*, Mar. 5, 1994, p. 24; Dagmar Mussey, "Benetton, German Retailers Squabble," *Advertising Age*, Feb. 6, 1995, p. 48; Jeanne Whalen, "U.S. Ads Take More Restrained Tone," *Advertising Age*, Feb. 6, 1995, p. 48; Bob Garfield, "Benetton, Lee Try New Ideas, but They End Up a Bad Fit," *Advertising Age*, Mar. 27, 1995, p. 3; John Rossant, "The Faded Colors of Benetton," *Business Week*, Apr. 10, 1995, pp. 87–88; and Bruce Horovitz, "Benetton Takes Conventional Turn," *USA Today*, Mar. 14, 1995, p. 1B.
2. If you examine an issue of your local newspaper, you will frequently notice competing retailers featuring the same item (such as La-Z-Boy recliners, 7-Up, or Kodak film). This is a good sign that co-op funds are being used.
3. Christine Blank, "Mags Are Best," *Progressive Grocer*, July 1995, p. 10.

4. Weld F. Royal, "Do Databases Really Work?" *Sales & Marketing Management*, October 1995, pp. 66–74.
5. For more information on some dramatic predictions for interactive media, see G. Pascal Zachery, "Advertisers Anticipate Interactive Media as Ingenious Means to Court Consumers," *The Wall Street Journal*, Aug. 17, 1994, p. B1; Cyndee Miller, "Marketers Find It's Hip to Be on the Internet," *Marketing News*, Feb. 27, 1995, p. 2; Cathy Taylor, "Z Factor," *Media Week*, Feb. 6, 1995, pp. IQ/14–IQ/18; and Michael Krantz, "The Mass Struggle," *Media Week*, Feb. 6, 1995, pp. IQ/20–IQ/23.
6. Scott Hume, "Trade Promos Devour Half of All Marketing $," *Advertising Age*, Apr. 13, 1992, p. 3.
7. Kate Fitzgerald, "AT&T, MCI Ringing Up Bigger Cash Lures," *Advertising Age*, May 8, 1995, p. 6.
8. Terry Lefton, "Try It You'll Like It," *Brandweek*, May 24, 1993, pp. 27–32.
9. Kelly Shermach, "Coupons, In-Store Promotions Motivate Consumer Purchasing," *Marketing News*, Oct. 9, 1995, p. 6.
10. Marcia Mogelonsky, "Counting Out Mexico," *Marketing Tools*, September 1995, pp. 30–32.
11. Kathleen Deveny and Richard Gibson, "Awash in Coupons? Some Firms Try to Stem the Tide," *The Wall Street Journal*, May 10, 1994, pp. B1+.
12. "Global Coupon Use Up; U.K., Belgium Tops in Europe," *Marketing News*, Aug. 15, 1991, p. 5.
13. Diane Crispell, "Unredeemed Coupons Pack a Big Sales Punch," *The Wall Street Journal*, Apr. 7, 1995, p. B1.
14. Deveny and Gibson, loc. cit.
15. Nancy Ten Kate, "And Now, a Word from Our Sponsor," *Marketing Tools*, June 1995, pp. 46–55.
16. Ibid.
17. William Dunn, "On with the Show," *Marketing Tools*, July/August 1995, pp. 46–55.
18. Ibid.
19. Ibid.
20. Fara Warner, "Why It's Getting Harder to Tell the Shows from the Ads," *The Wall Street Journal*, June 15, 1995, pp. B1+; and Kelly Shermach, "Casting Call Goes Out," *Marketing News*, July 31, 1995, pp. 1+.
21. Maria Mooshil, "Bank's $3 Teller Fee Has PR Pros Wondering," *Advertising Age*, May 15, 1995, p. 82.

22. Giobbe, loc. cit.; Mussey, loc. cit.; Whalen, loc. cit.; Garfield, loc. cit.; Rossant, loc. cit.; and Jennifer De-Coursey, "Benetton Illustrates New Battles on Ads," *Advertising Age*, July 24, 1995, p. 28.

CHAPTER 19

1. John DeMatteo, "The Company That Jack Built," *Forbes*, Oct. 15, 1990, pp. 108–112; Greg Burns, "It Only Hertz When Enterprise Laughs," *Business Week*, Dec. 12, 1994, p. 44; and Gabriella Stern, "If You Don't Feel Like Fetching the Rental Car, It Fetches You," *The Wall Street Journal*, June 9, 1995, pp. B1+.
2. Jyott Thottam, "Post Offices Nationwide to Undergo Redesign," *The Wall Street Journal*, Aug. 30, 1993, p. B1.
3. When an accounting firm entered into a partnership to operate a fashion mall on the Internet, one accountant observed that becoming involved in a form of direct marketing would lead to what had been perceived as a group of "learned professionals" being viewed by the public as "hucksters." Lee Berton, "This Accounting Firm Will Do Your Taxes, Help You Accessorize," *The Wall Street Journal*, Oct. 9, 1995, p. B1.
4. John A. Byrne, "Profiting from the Nonprofits," *Business Week*, Mar. 26, 1990, p. 66.
5. Pam Black, "Finally, Human Rights for Motorists," *Business Week*, May 1, 1995, p. 45.
6. Leonard L. Berry and Terry Clark, "Four Ways to Make Services More Tangible," *Business*, October–December 1986, p. 53.
7. Dana Milbank, "Airlines Are Plunging into Shower Wars," *The Wall Street Journal*, Mar. 31, 1995, p. B13.
8. Eleena de Lisser, "Banks Court Disenchanted Customers," *The Wall Street Journal*, Aug. 30, 1993, p. B1.
9. Allan C. Reedy, Bruce D. Buskirk, and Ajit Kaicker, "Tangibilizing the Intangibles: Some Strategies for Services Marketing," *Journal of Services Marketing*, Vol. 7, No. 3, 1993, pp. 13–17.
10. Jay Mathews and Peter Katel, "The Cost of Quality," *Newsweek*, Sept. 7, 1992, p. 48.
11. "A New Twist: Not-for-Profit," *International Herald Tribune*, Apr. 21, 1995, p. 16.
12. A. Ben Oumlil and C. P. Rao, "Services Marketing: Review and Synthesis of Critical Distribution Problems," *The Journal of Marketing Management*, Vol. 3, No. 2, 1993, pp. 6–16.
13. de Lisser, loc. cit.
14. Nancy Arnott, "Marketing with a Passion," *Sales & Marketing Management*, January 1994, pp. 64–71.
15. "Indiana College Asks 'Bob' to Help Market the School," *The Marketing News*, Oct. 9, 1995, p. 2.
16. Fara Warner, "Churches Develop Marketing Campaigns," *The Wall Street Journal*, Apr. 17, 1995, p. B4.
17. A case in point is the airline industry. See Thomas Petzinger, Jr., "Four Lessons Our Airlines Need to Learn," *The Wall Street Journal*, Nov. 6, 1995, pp. B1+.
18. For suggestions on restructuring, see Leonard A. Schlesinger and James L. Heskett, "The Service-Driven Service Company," *Harvard Business Review*, September–October 1991, pp. 71–81; and Stephen S. Roach, "Services under Siege—The Restructuring Imperative," *Harvard Business Review*, September–October 1991, pp. 82–91.
19. Roland T. Rust, Bala Subramanian, and Mark Wells, "Making Complaints a Management Tool," *Marketing Management*, Vol. 1, No. 3, 1992, pp. 41–45.
20. See, for example, Paul A. Bloom and Margaret P. Dalpe, "The Proactive Professional," *Marketing Management*, Vol. 2, No. 1, 1993, pp. 27–34.
21. DeMatteo, loc. cit.; Burns, loc. cit.; Stern, loc. cit.; and Carl Quintanilla, "Hertz Is a Little Wary about Putting You in the Driver's Seat," *The Wall Street Journal*, July 28, 1995, pp. A1+.

CHAPTER 20

1. Joseph Pereira, "Toys 'R' Us Grows Up, Finds Life Isn't All Fun, Games," *The Wall Street Journal*, Mar. 20, 1995, p. B6; Laura Liebeck, "Toys 'R' Us Leaps on Retail-tainment," *Discount Store News*, Oct. 2, 1995, pp. 1+; Laura Liebeck, "Toys 'R' Us Plans U.S. Refinement, International Expansion," *Discount Store News*, Feb. 6, 1995, pp. 23+; Kathryn Graven, "For Toys 'R' Us, Japan Isn't Child's Play," *The Wall Street Journal*, Feb. 7, 1990, pp. B1+; Annette Miller, Lourdes Rosado, Peter McKillop, and Don Kirk, "The World 'S' Ours," *Newsweek*, Mar. 23, 1992, pp. 46–47; Phil Davies, "Playing to Win," *Express Magazine*, Summer 1992, p. 14; and Kevin Cote, "Toys 'R' Us Grows in Europe," *Advertising Age*, Apr. 27, 1992, p. I16.
2. Andrew E. Serwer, "McDonald's Conquers the World," *Fortune*, Oct. 17, 1994, pp. 103–116.
3. Tara Parker-Pope, "Nonalcoholic Beer Hits the Spot in Mideast," *The Wall Street Journal*, Dec. 6, 1995, pp. B1+.
4. G. Pascal Zachery, "U.S. Companies Again Hold Wide Lead over Rivals in Direct Investment Abroad," *The Wall Street Journal*, Dec. 6, 1995, p. A2.
5. Laurel Wentz, "Rising International Brands to Change Buying Habits," *Advertising Age*, Sept. 18, 1995, pp. I33+.
6. "Mahindra and Ford Will Announce Soon Site of Plant in India," *The Wall Street Journal*, Nov. 15, 1995, p. B7A.
7. Emily DeNitto, "Pepsi, Coke Think International for Future Growth," *Advertising Age*, Oct. 3, 1994, p. 44.
8. Paula Dwyer, Andrea Rothman, Seth Payne, and Stewart Toy, "Air Raid: British Air's Bold Global Push," *Business Week*, Aug. 24, 1992, pp. 54–61.
9. Cacilie Rohwedder and Brandon Michener, "Mexican-Made VW Bugs Are Selling like Weiners at German Supermarket," *The Wall Street Journal*, Oct. 25, 1995, p. A17.
10. Rita Koselka, "Candy Wars," *Forbes*, Aug. 17, 1992, pp. 76–77.
11. DeNitto, loc. cit.
12. Bob Ortega, "Wal-Mart Is Slowed by Problems of Price and Culture in Mexico," *The Wall Street Journal*, July 29, 1994, p. A1.
13. Joan Warner, John Templeman, and Robert Horn, "The World Is Not Always Your Oyster," *Business Week*, Oct. 30, 1995, pp. 123–124.
14. Joann S. Lublin, "Slim Pickings: U.S. Food Firms Find Europe's Huge Market Hardly a Piece of Cake," *The Wall Street Journal*, May 15, 1990, pp. A1+.
15. Rick Arons, *EuroMarketing*, Probus, Chicago, 1991, p. 186.
16. "Toys 'R' Us Inc. Files Complaint in Japan over Rival's Hours," *The Wall Street Journal*, Nov. 24, 1995, p. A2.
17. Amy Borrus, Keith Naughton, and Laxmi Nakarmi, "Now Detroit's Heavy Artillery Is Trained on Seoul," *Business Week*, Sept. 25, 1995, p. 78.
18. Harvey D. Shapiro, "After NAFTA," *Hemisphere*, March 1995, pp. 74–79.
19. Kyle Pope, "EU Customs Union Would Pull Turkey Closer to West, Bolster

Shaky Economy," *The Wall Street Journal*, Dec. 12, 1995, p. A6.

20. Raf Casert, "7 Members of EU Drop Border Security," *South Bend Tribune*, Mar. 26, 1995, p. A9.

21. Arons, op. cit., p. 75.

22. Helene Cooper and Michael Williams, "U.S. Scales Down Hopes for APEC Talks," *The Wall Street Journal*, Nov. 16, 1995, p. A17.

23. William Flannery, "Fast-Growing Southeast Asia Is Land of Opportunity," *The St. Louis Post-Dispatch*, June 27, 1994, pp. 6BP+.

24. Mark M. Nelson and Brian Coleman, "U.S. and EU Sign Trade, Security Pact, Boosting Trans-Atlantic Cooperation," *The Wall Street Journal*, Dec. 4, 1995, p. A11.

25. Amy Borrus, Pete Engardio, and Dexter Roberts, "The New Trade Superpower," *Business Week*, Oct. 16, 1995, pp. 56–57.

26. Parker-Pope, loc. cit.

27. Keith Naughton, "Ford's Global Gladiator," *Business Week*, Dec. 11, 1995, pp. 116–117.

28. Christopher Knowlton, "Europe Cooks Up a Cereal Brawl," *Fortune*, June 3, 1991, pp. 175–179.

29. Paulette Thomas, "Cosmetic Makers Offer World's Women an All-American Look with Local Twist," *The Wall Street Journal*, May 8, 1995, pp. B1+.

30. Cyndee Miller, "Not Quite Global: Marketers 'Discover' the World but Still Have Much to Learn," *Marketing News*, July 3, 1995, pp. 1+.

31. William Echikson, "The Trick to Selling in Europe," *Fortune*, Sept. 20, 1993, p. 82.

32. Dana Milbank, "Made in America Becomes a Boast in Europe," *The Wall Street Journal*, Jan. 19, 1994, pp. B1+.

33. "Who Makes the Best Products?" *Business Week*, Mar. 14, 1994, p. 8.

34. Clay Chandler, "Why Cherokee Jeep Sales Slump in Japan," *The Wall Street Journal*, Jan. 14, 1992, p. A10.

35. Hermann Simon, "Pricing Problems in a Global Setting," *Marketing News*, Oct. 9, 1995, p. 4.

36. Arons, op. cit., p. 204.

37. "U.S. Steelmakers Continue to Fight Alleged Cartels in Europe and Japan," *New Steel*, February 1995, p. 9.

38. Steve Glain, "South Koreans Say Bribes Are Part of Life," *The Wall Street Journal*, Nov. 21, 1995, p. A15.

39. Veronica Byrd and Wendy Zellner, "The Avon Lady of the Amazon," *Business Week*, Oct. 24, 1994, pp. 93–95.

40. Lisa Bannon and Laura Bird, "Toyota Irritates Italians by Using Corruption Theme," *The Wall Street Journal Europe*, Jan. 24, 1994.

41. The issues and some empirical evidence are presented in Dennis M. Sandler and David Shani, "Brand Globally but Advertise Locally?" *Journal of Product & Brand Management*, Vol. 2, No. 2, 1993, pp. 59–71.

42. Ken Wells, "Selling to the World: Global Ad Campaigns, after Many Missteps, Finally Pay Dividends," *The Wall Street Journal*, Aug. 27, 1992, pp. A1+.

43. Ashish Banerjee, "Global Campaigns Don't Work; Multinationals Do," *Advertising Age*, Apr. 18, 1994, p. 23.

44. *Economic Indicators*, U.S. Government Printing Office, Washington, D.C., October 1995.

45. Pereira, loc. cit.; Liebeck, "Toys 'R' Us Leaps on . . . ," loc. cit.; Liebeck, "Toys 'R' Us Plans . . . ," loc. cit.; Graven, loc. cit.; Miller et al., loc. cit.; Davies, loc. cit.; and Cote, loc. cit.

CHAPTER 21

1. Nancy Brumback, "Muy Caliente: Mexican Food Is Hotter Than a Jalapeño as Segment Sales and Customer Traffic Continue to Climb," *Restaurant Business*, Nov. 1, 1995, pp. 152+; E. Scott Reckard, "Charge of the Light Brigade," *St. Louis Post-Dispatch*, June 15, 1995, p. 15C; Jeanne Whalen, "Taco Bell Cuts the Fat, Aims for Hefty Sales," *Advertising Age*, Feb. 13, 1995, p. 36; and Ronald Henkoff, "Service Is Everybody's Business," *Fortune*, June 27, 1994, p. 56.

2. For some guidelines to aid in identifying implementation difficulties and suggestions for remedying them, see Thomas V. Bonoma, "Enough about Strategy! Let's See Some Clever Executions," *Marketing News*, Feb. 13, 1989, p. 10; and Thomas V. Bonoma, "Making Your Marketing Strategy Work," *Harvard Business Review*, March–April 1984, pp. 69–76.

3. Bradley A. Stertz, "For LH Models, Chrysler Maps New Way to Sell," *The Wall Street Journal*, June 30, 1992, p. B1.

4. See, for example, Gail E. Schares, "The New Generation at Siemens," *Business Week*, Mar. 9, 1992, p. 46.

5. Seven elements of a horizontal organization are described in John A. Byrne, "The Horizontal Corporation," *Business Week*, Dec. 20, 1993, pp. 76–81.

6. The Modicon example is from ibid., p. 80. For a discussion of two new organizational forms—a marketing exchange company and a marketing coalition company—needed to cope with complex and dynamic business environments, see Ravi S. Achrol, "Evolution of the Marketing Organization: New Forms for Turbulent Environments," *Journal of Marketing*, October 1991, pp. 77–93.

7. See Jeen-Su Lim and David A. Reid, "Vital Cross-Functional Linkages with Marketing," *Industrial Marketing Management*, Spring 1992, pp. 159–165.

8. Melissa Campanelli, "A New Focus," *Sales & Marketing Management*, September 1995, pp. 56, 58.

9. J. Joseph Muller, "Three Key Issues in Consideration of Product Liability," *Mid-Missouri Business Journal*, Feb. 16–29, 1995, p. 22.

10. The Turbomeca S.A. example was reported in Michael Bradford, "Juries Send a $1.33 Billion Message," *Business Insurance*, Jan. 22, 1996, p. 3. The data on sizes of awards were drawn from Richard Waters, "Juries Cut Product Liability Awards," *Financial Times*, Jan. 8, 1996, p. 4.

11. For the description of a simulation model of product liability costs, see Conway Lackman and John Lanasa, "Product Liability Cost as a Marketing Tool," *Industrial Marketing Management*, May 1993, pp. 149–154.

12. Most of this paragraph is based on Ted Gest, "Product Paranoia," *U.S. News & World Report*, Feb. 24, 1992, pp. 67–69.

13. "Xerox Guarantees 'Total Satisfaction,'" *Marketing News*, Oct. 15, 1990, p. 2.

14. Daniel Pearl, "More Firms Pledge Guaranteed Service," *The Wall Street Journal*, July 17, 1991, p. B1.

15. "Road Test," *St. Louis Post-Dispatch*, Feb. 6, 1996, p. 6C.

16. John W. Verity, "The Gold Mine of Data in Customer Service," *Business Week*, Mar. 21, 1994, p. 114.

17. Jagdish N. Sheth and Rajendra S. Sisodia, "Feeling the Heat," *Marketing Management*, Fall 1995, p. 22; and Scott McCartney, "PC Makers Cure Customer Ills with Virtual House Calls," *The Wall Street Journal*, Mar. 21, 1995, p. B10.

18. Wendy Bounds, "Jury Finds Kodak Monopolized Markets in Services and Parts for Its Machines," *The Wall Street Journal*, Sept. 19, 1995, p. A4.

19. For useful recommendations, see Mary C. Gilly and Richard W. Hansen, "Consumer Complaint Handling as a Strategic Marketing Tool," *The Journal of Product and Brand Management,* Summer 1992, pp. 5–16. Also see Roland T. Rust, Bala Subramanian, and Mark Wells, "Making Complaints a Management Tool," *Marketing Management,* Vol. 1, No. 3, 1992, pp. 41–45.

20. For one of the early overviews of this technique, see Philip Kotler, William Gregor, and William Rodgers, "The Marketing Audit Comes of Age," *Sloan Management Review,* Winter 1977, pp. 25–43. A more recent, in-depth description can be found in D. T. Brownlie, "The Marketing Audit: A Metrology and Explanation," *Marketing Intelligence & Planning,* Vol. 11, No. 1, 1993, pp. 4–12.

21. Dale Terry, "How Does Your Bank's Marketing Size Up?" *Bank Marketing,* January 1995, pp. 53–58. For a similar view, see Douglas Brownlie, "The Conduct of Marketing Audits," *Industrial Marketing Management,* January 1996, pp. 11–22.

22. For the original discussion of the marketing audit, see Abe Schuchman, "The Marketing Audit: Its Nature, Purpose, and Problems," in *Analyzing and Improving Marketing Performance: "Marketing Audits" in Theory and Practice,* American Management Association, New York, Management Report No. 32, 1959, p. 14.

23. Reckard, loc. cit.; G. Pascal Zachary, "Restaurant Computers Speed Up Soup to Nuts," *The Wall Street Journal,* Oct. 25, 1995, p. B1; and Richard Martin, "Taco Bell Revamps Exec Team, Ends HQ Move Threat," *Nation's Restaurant News,* July 11, 1994, pp. 3, 119.

CHAPTER 22

1. Mark Maremont, "Blind Ambition," *Business Week,* Oct. 23, 1995, pp. 78–92; J. Leslie Sopko, "Besieged Bausch & Lomb CEO Retires," *USA Today,* Dec. 14, 1995, p. 4B; Myron Magnet, "Let's Go for Growth," *Fortune,* Mar. 7, 1994, pp. 60–62+; Jennifer Reingold, "Bausch & Lomb: Clouded Vision," *Financial World,* May 23, 1995, pp. 16+; and Mark Maremont, "Eyeway Robbery," *Business Week,* Feb. 27, 1995, p. 48.

2. Kathleen Deveny, "Anatomy of a Fad: How Clear Products Were Hot and Then Suddenly Were Not," *The Wall Street Journal,* Mar. 15, 1994, pp. B1+.

3. Betsy Morris and Peter Waldman, "The Death of Premier," *The Wall Street Journal,* Mar. 10, 1989, p. A1.

4. Joseph Weber and Sandra Dallas, "Cure? Well . . . Profit? Sure," *Business Week,* Oct. 23, 1995, pp. 58–59.

5. "Campbell to List Sodium Content in Its Soup Ads," *Marketing News,* Apr. 29, 1991, p. 7.

6. Jacquelyn A. Ottman, "When It Comes to Green Marketing, Companies Are Finally Getting It Right," *Brandweek,* Apr. 17, 1995, pp. 17+.

7. Betsy Weisendanger, "Significant Trends: Doing the Right Thing," *Sales & Marketing Management,* March 1991, pp. 82–83.

8. Mary L. Nicastro, "Infuse Business Ethics into Marketing Curriculum," *Marketing Educator,* Winter 1992, pp. 1+.

9. Laurie Grossman, "Desolate Housing Project Provides Profit and Lessons," *The Wall Street Journal,* Apr. 5, 1995, pp. B1+.

10. For more information on the magnitude of consumer fraud, see Kelley Holland, "Stalking the Credit-Card Scamsters," *Business Week,* Jan. 17, 1994, pp. 68–69; Vanessa O'Connell, "Fully 95% of Merchants Flunk Our Credit-Card Test," *Money,* April 1993, pp. 16+; "Average Firm Bilked of $117,000," *The Practical Accountant,* September 1994, p. 10; and Michael Hartnett, "Privacy vs. Security," *Stores,* January 1994, pp. 88+.

11. Philip Elmer-Dewitt, "Beyond a Place Called Hype," *Time,* Nov. 13, 1995, pp. TD24–TD25.

12. Julian Dibbell, "Nielsen Rates the Net," *Time,* Nov. 13, 1995, p. 121.

13. Lynn Beresford, Janean Chun, Heather Page, and Debra Phillips, "Trends," *Entrepreneur,* December 1995, pp. 110–125; and Heather Page, "Hot Stuff," *Entrepreneur,* December 1995, pp. 100–108.

14. Paul R. Campbell, *Population Projections for States, by Age, Sex, Race, and Hispanic Origin: 1993 to 2020,* U.S. Department of Commerce, Economics and Statistics Administration, Washington, D.C., 1994.

15. Yumiko Ono, "Kraft Hopes Hispanic Market Says Cheese," *The Wall Street Journal,* Dec. 13, 1995, p. B7.

16. John Stover, "The Latest Figures on World Population Growth," *Challenge,* July–August 1989, p. 56.

17. Several of the following points are adapted from David W. Cravens, "Marketing Management's Future Challenges," *Journal of Marketing Management,* Fall 1991, pp. 1–10.

18. Carla Rapoport and Justin Martin, "Retailers Go Global," *Fortune,* Feb. 20, 1995, pp. 102–108.

19. Amy Barrett, "It's a Small (Business) World," *Business Week,* Apr. 17, 1995, pp. 96–101.

20. Robert Frank, "Efficient UPS Tries to Increase Efficiency," *The Wall Street Journal,* May 24, 1995, pp. B1+.

21. Sandra Vandermerwe and Michael Oliff, "Corporate Challenges for an Age of Reconsumption," *Columbia Journal of World Business,* Fall 1991, pp. 23–28.

22. Weld F. Royal, "It's Not Easy Being Green," *Sales & Marketing Management,* July 1995, pp. 84–90.

23. Charles Laughlin, "The Missing Piece," *Link,* November/December 1993, pp. 15+.

24. Laura Litvan, "Going 'Green' in the '90s," *Nation's Business,* February 1995, pp. 30–32.

25. Michael J. McCarthy, "Marketers Zero In on Their Customers," *The Wall Street Journal,* Mar. 18, 1991, p. B1.

26. This section as well as the following example are based on Joseph Pine II, Don Peppers, and Martha Rogers, "Do You Want to Keep Your Customers Forever?" *Harvard Business Review,* March/April 1995, pp. 103–114.

27. Maremont, "Blind Ambition," loc. cit.; Sopko, loc. cit.; Magnet, loc. cit.; Reingold, loc. cit.; and Maremont, "Eyeway Robbery," loc. cit.

PHOTO CREDITS

GLOSSARY

A

accessory equipment Business goods that have substantial value and are used in an organization's operations.

activity indicator of buying power A market factor that is related to sales and expenditures and serves as an indirect estimate of purchasing power.

administered vertical marketing system An arrangement that coordinates distribution activities through the market and/or economic power of one channel member or the shared power of two channel members.

adoption process The set of successive decisions an individual or organization makes before accepting an innovation.

advertising All activities involved in presenting to an audience a nonpersonal, sponsor-identified, paid-for message about a product or an organization.

advertising agency An independent company that provides specialized advertising services and may also offer more general marketing assistance.

advertising campaign All the tasks involved in transforming a theme into a coordinated advertising program to accomplish a specific goal for a product or brand.

advertising media The communications vehicles (such as newspapers, radio, and television) that carry advertising as well as other information and entertainment.

agent middleman A firm that never actually takes title to (i.e., owns) products it helps market but does arrange the transfer of title.

agent wholesaling middleman An independent firm that engages primarily in wholesaling by actively negotiating the sale or purchase of products on behalf of other firms but does not take title to the products being distributed.

agribusiness Farms, food-processing firms, and other large-scale farming-related enterprises.

AIDA A sequence of steps in various forms of promotion, notably personal selling and advertising, consisting of attracting *A*ttention, holding *I*nterest, arousing *D*esire, and generating buyer *A*ction.

annual marketing plan A written document that presents the master blueprint for a year's marketing activity for a specified organizational division or major product.

Asia-Pacific Economic Cooperation forum (APEC) A trade pact among 18 Pacific Rim nations that seeks the elimination of major trade barriers.

Association of Southeast Asian Nations (ASEAN) An agreement creating a free-trade zone among Brunei, Indonesia, Malaysia, the Philippines, Singapore, and Thailand.

attitude A learned predisposition to respond to an object or class of objects in a consistently favorable or unfavorable way.

auction company An agent wholesaling middleman that helps assembled buyers and sellers complete their transactions by providing auctioneers who do the selling and physical facilities for displaying the sellers' products.

automatic vending A form of nonstore retailing where the products are sold through a machine with no personal contact between the buyer and seller.

average fixed cost The total fixed cost divided by the number of units produced.

average fixed cost curve A graph of average fixed cost levels showing a decline as output increases because the total of the fixed costs is spread over an increasing number of units.

average revenue The unit price at a given level of unit sales. It is calculated by dividing total revenue by the number of units sold.

average total cost The total cost divided by the number of units produced.

average total cost curve A graph of average total costs, which starts high, then declines to its lowest point, reflecting optimum output with respect to total costs (not variable costs), and then rises because of diminishing returns.

average variable cost The total variable cost divided by the number of units produced.

average variable cost curve A graph of average variable cost levels, which starts high, then declines to its lowest point, reflecting optimum output with respect to variable costs (not total costs), and then rises.

B

balance of payments The accounting record of all of a country's transactions with all the other nations of the world.

balance sheet A financial statement that summarizes the assets, liabilities, and net worth of a company at a given time.

barter The exchange of goods and/or services for other products.

base price The price of one unit of the product at its point of production or resale. Same as *list price*.

behavioral segmentation Market segmentation based on consumers' product-related behavior, typically the benefits desired from a product and the rate at which the consumer uses the product.

Boston Consulting Group (BCG) matrix A strategic planning model that classifies strategic business units or major products according to market shares and growth rates.

boycott A refusal to buy products from a particular company or country.

G-1

brand A name and/or mark intended to identify and differentiate the product of one seller or a group of sellers.

brand equity The value a brand adds to a product.

brand label The application of the brand name alone to a product or package.

brand licensing See *trademark licensing.*

brand manager See *product manager.*

brand mark The part of a brand that appears in the form of a symbol, design, or distinctive color or type of lettering.

brand name The part of a brand that can be vocalized—words, letters, and/or numbers.

breadth of product mix The number of product lines offered for sale by a firm.

break-even analysis A method of calculating the level of output at which total revenue equals total costs, assuming a certain selling price.

break-even point The level of output at which total revenue equals total costs, assuming a certain selling price.

broker An agent wholesaling middleman that brings buyers and sellers together and provides market information to either party and that ordinarily neither physically handles products being distributed nor works on a continuing basis with those sellers or buyers.

business analysis One stage in the new-product development process, consisting of several steps to expand a surviving idea into a concrete business proposal.

business cycle The three recurring stages in an economy, typically prosperity, recession, and recovery.

business format franchising An agreement, covering an entire method (or format) for operating a business, under which a successful business sells the right to operate the same business in different geographic areas.

business market The total of all business users.

business marketing The marketing of goods and services to business users, as contrasted to ultimate consumers.

business product A product that is intended for purchase and resale or for purchase and use in producing other products or for providing services in an organization.

business-to-business advertising Advertising that is directed at businesses.

business users Business, industrial, or institutional organizations that buy goods or services to use in their own organizations, to resell, or to make other products.

buy classes Three typical buying situations in the business market—namely new-task buying, modified rebuy, and straight rebuy.

buying center In an organization, all individuals or groups involved in the process of making a purchase decision.

buying-decision process The series of logical stages, which differ for consumers and organizations, that a prospective purchaser goes through when faced with a buying problem.

buying motive The reason why a person or an organization buys a specific product or makes purchases from a specific firm.

buying roles The users, influencers, deciders, gatekeepers, and buyers who make up a buying center.

C

campaign A coordinated series of promotional efforts built around a single theme and designed to reach a specific goal in a defined period of time.

cartel A group of companies that produce similar products and act collectively to restrain competition in manufacturing and marketing.

cash discount A deduction granted to buyers for paying their bills within a specified period.

category-killer store A type of retail institution that has a narrow but very deep assortment, low prices, and few to moderate customer services. It is designed to "destroy" all competition in a specific product category.

change agent In the process of diffusion, a person who seeks to accelerate the spread of a given innovation.

channel conflict A situation in which one channel member perceives another channel member to be acting in a way that prevents the first member from achieving its distribution objectives.

channel control The actions of a firm to regulate the behavior of other companies in its distribution channel.

channel power The ability of a firm to influence or determine the behavior of another channel member.

client market Individuals and/or organizations that are the recipients of a nonprofit organization's money or services. Same as *recipient market.*

commercial information environment As contrasted with the social information environment, all communications directed to consumers by organizations and individuals involved in marketing.

commission Compensation tied to a specific unit of accomplishment.

commission merchant An agent wholesaling middleman, used primarily in the marketing of agricultural products, that may physically handle the seller's products in central markets and has authority regarding prices and terms of sale.

communication The verbal or nonverbal transmission of information between someone wanting to express an idea and someone else expected or expecting to get that idea. The four elements are a message, a source of the message, a communication channel, and a receiver.

company sales branch See *manufacturer's sales branch.*

comparative advertising A form of selective-demand advertising in which an advertiser either directly (by naming a rival brand) or indirectly (through inference) points out the differences among competing brands.

competitive intelligence The process of gathering and analyzing publicly available information about the activities and plans of competitors.

concentration strategy See *single-segment strategy*.

Consolidated Metropolitan Statistical Area (CMSA) A giant urban center consisting of two or more adjacent Primary Metropolitan Statistical Areas.

consumer An individual or organizational unit that uses or consumes a product.

consumer advertising Advertising that is directed at consumers.

consumer product A product that is intended for purchase and use by household consumers for nonbusiness purposes.

Consumer Product Safety Act Federal legislation that created the Consumer Product Safety Commission (CPSC), which has authority to establish mandatory safety standards for many consumer products.

consumerism Consumers' protests against and attempts to remedy perceived injustices in the relationships between businesses and consumers.

containerization A cargo-handling system in which shipments of products are enclosed in large metal or wood receptacles that are then transported unopened from the time they leave the shipper's facilities until they reach their destination.

contract logistics An arrangement under which a firm outsources various physical distribution activities to one or more independent firms.

contract manufacturing An arrangement in which a firm in one country arranges for a firm in another country to produce the product in the foreign country.

contracting A legal relationship that allows a firm to enter a foreign market indirectly, quickly establish a market presence, and experience a limited amount of risk.

contractual vertical market system An arrangement under which independent firms—producers, wholesalers, and retailers—operate under contracts specifying how they will operate in order to improve their distribution efficiency and effectiveness.

contribution-margin approach In marketing cost analysis, an accounting method in which only direct expenses are allocated to each marketing unit being analyzed.

contributor market See *donor market*.

convenience goods A category of tangible consumer products that the consumer has prior knowledge of and purchases with minimum time and effort.

convenience store A type of retail institution that concentrates on convenience-oriented groceries and nonfoods, typically has higher prices than other grocery stores, and offers few customer services.

cooperative advertising Advertising promoting products of two or more firms that share its cost.

corporate chain An organization of two or more centrally owned and managed stores that generally handle the same lines of products.

corporate vertical marketing system An arrangement under which a firm at one level of a distribution channel owns the firms at the next level or owns the entire channel.

correlation analysis A statistical refinement of the direct-derivation method, an approach to demand forecasting that takes into account how close the association is between potential sales of the product and the market factor affecting its sales.

cost of goods sold A financial figure showing the value of the merchandise sold during a given period, calculated by adding the value of any merchandise on hand at the beginning of the period to the net cost of what is purchased during the period and then deducting the value of whatever remains at the end of the period.

cost per thousand (CPM) The media cost of gaining exposure to 1,000 persons with an ad.

cost-plus pricing A major method of price determination in which the price of a unit of a product is set at a level equal to the unit's total cost plus a desired profit on the unit.

countertrade An arrangement under which domestically made products are traded for imported goods.

creative sales person An individual who typically sells services, but sometimes goods, by designing a system to fit the needs of a particular customer.

culture A complex of symbols and artifacts created by a society and handed down from generation to generation as determinants and regulators of human behavior.

cumulative discount A quantity discount based on the total volume purchased over a specified period.

customer An individual or organization that has an existing or potential exchange relationship with a marketer.

customer specialization One method of organizing selling activities in which each sales person is assigned a specific group of customers, categorized by type of industry or channel of distribution, to which to sell. Same as *market specialization*.

D

database A set of related data that are organized, stored, and updated in a computer.

decision maker The individual or organizational unit that has the authority to commit to an exchange.

decision support system (DSS) A procedure that allows a manager to interact with data and methods of analysis to gather, analyze, and interpret information.

decline stage The fourth, and final, part of a product life cycle during which the sales of a generic product category drop and most competitors abandon the market.

Delphi method A forecasting technique, applicable to sales forecasting, in which a group of experts individually and anonymously assesses future sales, after which each member has the chance to offer a revised assessment as the group moves toward a consensus.

demand forecasting The process of estimating sales of a product during some future period.

demographic segmentation Subdividing markets into groups based on population factors such as size, age, and growth.

demographics The characteristics of human populations, including such factors as size, distribution, and growth.

department store A large-scale retail institution that has a very broad and deep product assortment, tries not to compete on the basis of price, and offers a wide array of customer services.

depth of product line The relative variety of sizes, colors, and models offered within a product line.

descriptive label The part of a product that gives information about its use, construction, care, performance, and/or other pertinent features.

desk jobber See *drop shipper*.

differential advantage Any feature of an organization or brand perceived by customers to be desirable and different from those of the competition.

differential disadvantage Any feature of an organization or brand perceived by customers to be undesirable and different from those of the competition.

diffusion A process by which an innovation spreads throughout a social system over time.

direct-action advertising Product advertising that seeks a quick response.

direct costs Separate expenses that are incurred totally in connection with one market segment or one unit of the sales organization. Same as *separable expenses*.

direct-derivation method An approach to demand forecasting that directly relates the behavior of a market factor to estimated demand.

direct distribution A channel consisting only of producer and final customer, with no middlemen providing assistance.

direct investment The actions of a company to build or acquire its own production facilities in a foreign country.

direct marketing A form of nonstore retailing that uses advertising to contact consumers who, in turn, purchase products without visiting a retail store.

direct selling A form of nonstore retailing in which personal contact between a sales person and a consumer occurs away from a retail store. Sometimes called *in-home selling*.

direct tests Measuring or predicting the sales volume attributable to a single ad or an entire advertising campaign.

discount house A large-scale retail institution that has a broad and shallow product assortment, low prices, and few customer services.

discount retailing A retailing approach that uses price as a major selling point by combining comparatively low prices and reduced costs of doing business.

distribution center A facility that has under one roof an efficient, fully integrated system for the flow of products—taking orders, filling them, and preparing them for delivery to customers.

distribution channel The set of people and firms involved in the transfer of title to a product as the product moves from producer to ultimate consumer or business user.

donor market Individuals and/or organizations that contribute money, labor, or materials to a nonprofit organization. Same as *contributor market*.

door-to-door selling One kind of direct selling, in which the personal contact between a sales person and an individual prospect occurs at the prospective customer's residence or business.

drop shipper A merchant wholesaler that does not physically handle the product being distributed, but instead sells merchandise for delivery directly from the producer to the customer. Same as *desk jobber*.

dumping The process of selling products in foreign markets at prices below the prices charged for these goods in their home market.

E

early adopters A group of consumers that includes opinion leaders, is respected, has much influence on its peers, and is the second group (following the innovators) to adopt an innovation.

early majority A group of fairly deliberate consumers that adopts an innovation just before the "average" adopter in a social system.

economic environment A set of factors, including the business cycle, inflation, and interest rates, that affect the marketing activities of an organization.

economic order quantity (EOQ) The optimal quantity for reorder when replenishing inventory stocks, as indicated by the volume at which the sum of inventory-carrying costs and order-processing costs are at a minimum.

80–20 principle A situation in which a large proportion of the total orders, customers, territories, or products account for only a small share of the company's sales or profit, and vice versa.

elastic demand A price-volume relationship such that a change of one unit on the price scale results in a change of more than one unit on the volume scale.

environmental monitoring The process of gathering information regarding a company's external environment, analyzing it, and forecasting the impact of whatever trends the analysis suggests. Same as *environmental scanning*.

environmental scanning See *environmental monitoring*.

ethics The rules and standards of moral behavior that are generally accepted by a society.

European Union (EU) A political and economic alliance among most of the countries of Western Europe that seeks to liberalize trade among its members.

evaluation The stage of the management process during which an organization determines how well it is achieving the goals set in its strategic planning.

everyday low pricing (EDLP) A pricing strategy that involves consistently low prices and few, if any, temporary price reductions.

exchange The act of voluntarily providing a person or organization something of value in order to acquire something else of value.

exclusive dealing The practice by which a manufacturer prohibits its dealers from carrying products of its competitors.

exclusive distribution A strategy in which a supplier agrees to sell its product only to a single wholesaling middleman and/or retailer in a given market.

exclusive-territory policy The practice by which a producer requires each middleman to sell only to customers located within an assigned territory.

executive judgment A method of sales forecasting that consists of obtaining opinions regarding future sales volume from one or more executives.

expected price The price at which customers consciously or unconsciously value a product—what they think the product is worth.

experiment A method of gathering primary data in which the researcher measures the results of changing one variable in a situation while holding all others constant.

export agent A middleman that operates either in a manufacturer's country or in the destination country and that negotiates the sale of the product in another country and may provide additional services such as arranging for international financing, shipping, and insurance on behalf of the manufacturer.

export merchant A middleman operating in a manufacturer's country that buys goods and exports them.

exporting The activities by which a firm sells its product in another country, either directly to foreign importers or through import-export middlemen.

express warranty A statement in written or spoken words regarding restitution from seller to customer if the seller's product does not perform up to reasonable expectations.

expropriation A situation in which a company's investment in a country is taken by the host government.

F

fabricating materials Business goods that have received some processing and will undergo further processing as they become part of another product.

fabricating parts Business goods that already have been processed to some extent and will be assembled in their present form (with no further change) as part of another product.

fad A product or style that becomes immensely popular nearly overnight and then falls out of favor with consumers almost as quickly.

family A group of two or more people related by blood, marriage, or adoption living together in a household.

family branding A strategy of using the company name for branding purposes.

family life cycle The series of life stages that a family goes through, starting with young single people, progressing through married stages with young and then older children, and ending with older married and single people.

family packaging A strategy of using either highly similar packages for all products or packages with a common and clearly noticeable feature.

fashion A style that is popularly accepted and purchased by successive groups of people over a reasonably long period of time.

fashion-adoption process A series of buying waves by which a style becomes popular in a market; similar to diffusion of an innovation.

fashion cycle Wavelike movements representing the introduction, rise, popular acceptance, and decline of the market's acceptance of a style.

fashion obsolescence See *style obsolescence*.

Federal Trade Commission Act A federal law, passed in 1914, prohibiting unfair competition and establishing the Federal Trade Commission.

field experiment An experiment in which the researcher has only limited control of the environment because the study is conducted in a real-world setting.

fixed cost A cost that remains constant regardless of how many items are produced or sold.

flexible-price strategy A pricing strategy under which a seller charges different prices to similar customers who buy identical quantities of a product. Same as *variable-price strategy*.

fluctuating demand A characteristic of a service indicating that the market for services shifts considerably by season, by day of the week, and by hour of the day.

FOB (free on board) factory pricing A geographic pricing strategy whereby the seller quotes the selling price at the point of production and the buyer selects the mode of transportation and pays all freight costs. Same as *FOB mill pricing*.

FOB mill pricing See *FOB factory pricing*.

focus group A preliminary data-gathering method involving an interactive interview of 4 to 10 people.

form utility The want-satisfying capability that is created when a good is produced.

forward dating A combination of a seasonal discount and a cash discount under which a buyer places an order and receives shipment during the off-season but does not have to pay the bill until after the season has started and some sales revenue has been generated.

franchising A type of contractual vertical marketing system that involves a continuing relationship in which a franchiser (the parent company) provides the right to use a trademark plus various management assistance in return for payments from a franchisee (the owner of the individual business unit).

freight absorption pricing A geographic pricing strategy whereby the seller pays for (absorbs) some of the freight charges in order to penetrate more distant markets.

freight forwarder A specialized marketing institution that serves firms by consolidating less-than-carload or less-than-truckload shipments into carload or truckload quantities and arranging for door-to-door shipping service.

freight in Freight charges paid by a buyer.

full-cost approach In marketing cost analysis, an accounting method in which all expenses—direct and indirect—are allocated to the marketing units being analyzed.

full-service wholesaler An independent merchant middleman that performs a full range of wholesaling functions (from creating assortments to warehousing).

functional discount See *trade discount*.

functional obsolescence See *technological obsolescence*.

G

General Agreement on Tariffs and Trade (GATT) An organization, formed in 1948 and now comprising over 100 countries, that seeks to develop fair-trade practices among its members.

General Electric (GE) business screen A planning model developed by General Electric that classifies strategic business units or major products based on two factors, market attractiveness and business position.

Generation X Those people in the U.S. who were born between approximately 1966 and 1976. Also called *baby busters, twentysomethings,* or *boomerangers.*

generic product A product that is packaged in a plain label, is sold with no advertising and without a brand name, and goes by its generic name, such as "tomatoes" or "paper towels."

geographic segmentation Subdividing markets into groups based on their locations.

geographic specialization One method of organizing selling activities, in which each sales person is assigned a specific geographic area—called a territory—in which to sell.

global marketing A strategy in which essentially the same marketing program is employed around the world.

global sales teams A type of personal selling where a team of sales people is responsible for all of its company's sales to an account anywhere in the world.

goal See *objective.*

government market The segment of the business market that includes federal, state, and local units buying for government institutions such as schools, offices, hospitals, and military bases.

grade label The part of a product that identifies the products judged quality (grade) by means of a letter, number, or word.

green marketing Any marketing activity of a firm that is intended to create a positive impact or lessen the negative impact of a product on the environment in order to capitalize on consumers' concerns about environmental issues.

gross margin The amount of money that is left after cost of goods sold is subtracted from net sales.

gross margin percentage The ratio of gross margin to net sales.

gross sales The total amount sold by an organization, stated in dollars.

growth stage The second part of a product life cycle during which the sales and profits of a generic product category rise and competitors enter the market, causing profits to decline near the end of this part of the cycle.

H

heterogeneity A characteristic of a service indicating that each unit is somewhat different from other units of the same service.

hierarchy of effects The stages a buyer goes through in moving toward a purchase, specifically awareness, knowledge, liking, preference, conviction, and purchase.

high-low pricing A pricing strategy that combines frequent price reductions and aggressive promotion to convey an image of very low prices.

horizontal business market A situation where a given product is usable in a wide variety of industries.

horizontal conflict A form of channel conflict occurring among middlemen (either of the same type or different types) at the same level of distribution.

household A single person, a family, or any group of unrelated persons who occupy a housing unit.

hypothesis A tentative supposition that if proven would suggest a possible solution to a problem.

I

iceberg principle A concept related to performance evaluation stating that the summary data (tip of the iceberg) regarding an activity may hide significant variations among segments of this activity.

image utility The want-satisfying capability that is associated with a product or brand because of the reputation or social standing of that product or brand; a special type of information utility.

implementation The stage of the management process during which an organization attempts to carry out its strategic plans.

implied warranty An intended but unstated assurance regarding restitution from seller to customer if the seller's product does not perform up to reasonable expectations.

import-export agent An agent wholesaling middleman that brings together sellers and buyers in different countries. Export agents work in the country in which the product is made; import agents work in the country in which the product will be sold.

import quota A limit on the amount of a particular product that can be brought into a country.

impulse buying A form of low-involvement decision making; purchases made with little or no advance planning.

income statement See *operating statement.*

independent retailer A company with a single retail store that is not affiliated with a contractual vertical marketing system.

indirect-action advertising Product advertising that is intended to inform or remind consumers that a product exists and to point out its benefits.

indirect costs Expenses that are incurred jointly for more than one marketing unit and therefore cannot be totally charged to one market segment.

indirect distribution A channel consisting of producer, final customer, and at least one level of middleman.

indirect tests Measuring or predicting the effects of advertising by using a factor other than sales volume.

inelastic demand A price-volume relationship such that a change of one unit on the price scale results in a change of less than one unit on the volume scale.

inflation A rise in the prices of goods and services.

influencer Those individuals or organizational units that affect the decisions of others because of their expertise, position, or power.

informal investigation The stage in a marketing research study at which preliminary, readily available data are gathered from people inside and outside the company—middlemen, competitors, advertising agencies, and consumers.

information utility The want-satisfying capability that is created by informing prospective buyers that a product exists.

infrastructure The country's levels and capabilities with respect to transportation, communications, and energy.

in-home selling See *direct selling*.

innovation adopter categories Groups of people differentiated according to when they accept a given innovation.

innovators A group of venturesome consumers that are the first to adopt an innovation.

inseparability A characteristic of a service indicating that it cannot be separated from the creator-seller of the service.

installations Manufactured products that are an organization's major, expensive, and long-lived equipment and that directly affect the scale of operations in an organization producing goods or services.

institutional advertising Advertising that presents information about the advertiser's business or tries to create a favorable impression—build goodwill—for the organization.

intangibility A characteristic of a service indicating that it has no physical attributes and, as a result, is impossible for customers to taste, feel, see, hear, or smell before they buy it.

integrated marketing communications A strategy in which each of the promotion-mix components is carefully coordinated.

intensity of distribution The number of middlemen used by a producer at the retail and wholesale levels in a particular territory.

intensive distribution A strategy in which a producer sells its product through every available outlet in a market where a consumer might reasonably look for it.

interest rates The percentage amounts either charged to lend money or paid to acquire money.

intermodal transportation The use of two or more modes of transportation to move a shipment of freight.

international market Sales, market potential, or sales potential in foreign (or nondomestic) areas.

international marketing The activities of an organization to market its products in two or more countries.

introduction stage The first part of a product life cycle during which a generic product category is launched into the market in a full-scale marketing program. Same as *pioneering stage*.

invention The development of an entirely new product.

inverse demand A price-volume relationship such that the higher the price, the greater the unit sales.

ISO 9000 quality standards The International Organization for Standardizations certification to assure that firms conform to specific standards in processes, procedures, operations, controls, and management.

J

joint venture A partnership arrangement in which a foreign operation is owned in part by a domestic company and in part by a foreign company.

just-in-time (JIT) A form of inventory control, purchasing, and production that involves buying parts and supplies in small quantities just in time for use in production and then producing in quantities just in time for sale.

K

kinked demand A condition in which total revenue declines when a product's price is increased or decreased in relation to the prevailing market level.

L

label The part of a product that carries information about the product and the seller.

laboratory experiment An experiment in which the researcher has complete control over the environment during the study but which, as a result, is unnatural and perhaps unrealistic.

laggards A group of tradition-bound consumers who are the last to adopt an innovation.

Landham Trademark Act A federal law passed in 1946 that made it illegal for organizations to make false claims about their own products.

late majority A group of skeptical consumers who are slow to adopt an innovation but eventually do so to save money or in response to social pressure from their peers.

leader In leader pricing, an item on which price is cut.

leader pricing A pricing and promotional strategy in which temporary price cuts are made on a few items to attract customers.

learning Changes in behavior resulting from observation and experience.

level of involvement The amount of effort that is expended in satisfying a need.

licensing A business arrangement whereby one firm sells to another firm (for a fee or royalty) the right to use the first company's brand, patents, or manufacturing processes.

life-style Habits that relate to a person's activities, interests, and opinions.

limited-line store A type of retail institution that has a narrow but deep product assortment and customer services that vary from store to store.

line extension One form of product-mix expansion in which a company adds a similar item to an existing product line with the same brand name.

list price See *base price.*

local-content law A regulation specifying the proportion of a finished product's components and labor that must be provided by the importing country.

logistics See *physical distribution.*

loss leader In leader pricing, an item on which price is cut to a level that is below the store's cost.

M

mail survey A method of gathering data by mailing a questionnaire to potential respondents, and asking them to complete it and return it by mail.

major-accounts organization A variation of customer specialization that usually involves team selling to better service key accounts.

management The process of planning, implementing, and evaluating the efforts of a group of people working toward a common goal.

manufacturers' agent An agent wholesaling middleman that sells part or all of a manufacturer's product mix in an assigned geographic territory. Same as *manufacturers' representative.*

manufacturers' representative See *manufacturers' agent.*

manufacturer's sales branch A manufacturer's sales facility that carries a stock of the product being sold. Same as *company sales branch.*

manufacturer's sales facility An establishment that engages primarily in wholesaling and is owned and operated by a manufacturer but is physically separated from manufacturing plants.

manufacturer's sales office A manufacturer's sales facility that does not carry a stock of the product being sold.

marginal cost The cost of producing and selling one more unit; that is, the cost of the last unit produced or sold.

marginal cost curve A graph of marginal cost levels, which slopes downward until marginal costs start to increase, at which point it rises.

marginal revenue The income derived from the sale of the last unit.

markdown A reduction from the original selling price.

markdown percentage The ratio of the total dollar markdowns to total net sales during a given period.

market People or organizations with wants to satisfy, money to spend, and the willingness to spend the money. Alternatively, any person or group with whom an individual or organization has an existing or potential exchange relationship.

market aggregation strategy A plan of action under which an organization treats its total market as a single segment—that is, as one mass market whose members are considered to be alike with respect to demand for the product—and thus develops a single marketing mix to reach most of the customers in the entire market. Same as *mass-market strategy* and *undifferentiated-market strategy.*

market factor An item or element that (1) exists in a market, (2) may be measured quantitatively, and (3) is related to the demand for a good or service.

market-factor analysis A sales forecasting method that assumes the future demand for a product is related to the behavior of certain market factors and, as a result, involves determining what these factors are and then measuring their relationships to sales activity.

market fragmentation The identification of smaller and smaller market segments.

market-penetration pricing A strategy in which the initial price of a product is set low in relation to the target market's range of expected prices.

market potential The total sales volume that all organizations selling a product during a stated time period in a specific market could expect to achieve under ideal conditions.

market-response system A form of inventory control in which a purchase by a final customer activates a process to produce and deliver a replacement item.

market segmentation The process of dividing the total market for a good or service into several smaller groups, such that the members of each group are similar with respect to the factors that influence demand.

market segments Within the same general market, groups of customers with different wants, buying preferences, or product-use behavior.

market share The proportion of total sales of a product during a stated time period in a specific market that is captured by a single firm.

market-share analysis A detailed analysis of the company's share of the market in total as well as by product line and market segment.

market-skimming pricing A strategy in which the initial price of a product is set high in relation to the target market's range of expected prices.

market specialization See *customer specialization.*

market tests One stage in the new-product development process, consisting of acquiring and analyzing actual consumers' reactions to proposed products.

marketer Any person or organization that desires to stimulate and facilitate exchanges.

marketing A total system of business activities designed to plan, price, promote, and distribute want-satisfying products to target markets to achieve organizational objectives.

marketing audit A comprehensive review and evaluation of the marketing function in an organization—its philosophy, environment, goals, strategies, organizational structure, human and financial resources, and performance.

marketing concept A philosophy of doing business that emphasizes customer orientation and coordination of marketing activities in order to achieve the organization's performance objectives.

marketing cost analysis A detailed study of the Operating Expenses section of a company's profit and loss statement.

marketing information system (MkIS) An ongoing, organized procedure to generate, analyze, disseminate, store, and retrieve information for use in making marketing decisions.

marketing intermediary An independent business organization that directly aids in the flow of products between a marketing organization and its markets.

marketing mix A combination of the four elements—product, pricing structure, distribution system, and promotional activities—used to satisfy the needs of an organization's target market(s) and, at the same time, achieve its marketing objectives.

marketing-orientation stage The third stage in the evolution of marketing management, in which a company focuses on the needs of its customers and carries out a broad range of marketing activities in order to satisfy them.

marketing research The development, interpretation, and communication of decision-oriented information to be used in the strategic marketing process.

markon See *markup*.

markup The amount added to the cost of a product to arrive at the price at which the seller would like to make a transaction. Alternatively, the difference between the selling price of an item and its cost. Same as *markon*.

Maslow's need hierarchy A structure of five need levels, arrayed in the order in which people seek to gratify them.

mass customization Developing, producing, and delivering affordable products with enough variety and uniqueness that nearly every potential customer can have exactly what he or she wants.

mass-market strategy See *market aggregation strategy*.

maturity stage The third part of a product life cycle during which the sales of a generic product category continue to increase (but at a decreasing rate), profits decline largely because of price competition, and some firms leave the market.

merchant middleman A firm that actually takes title to (i.e., owns) products it helps to market.

merchant wholesaler An independently owned firm that engages primarily in wholesaling and takes title to products being distributed. Sometimes called a *wholesaler*.

Metropolitan Statistical Area (MSA) An urban area in the U.S. with a center of population of at least 50,000 and a total MSA population of at least 100,000.

middleman A business firm that renders services directly related to the purchase and/or sale of a product as it flows from producer to consumer.

middleman's brand A brand owned by a retailer or a wholesaler.

misdirected marketing effort Marketing endeavors that do not produce results commensurate with the resources expended.

mission An organization's statement of what customers it serves, what needs it satisfies, and what types of products it offers.

mix extension One form of product-mix expansion in which a company adds a new product line to its present assortment.

modified rebuy In the business market, a purchasing situation between a new task and a straight rebuy in terms of time and people involved, information needed, and alternatives considered.

motive A need sufficiently stimulated to move an individual to seek satisfaction.

multinational corporation A truly worldwide enterprise, in which the foreign and the domestic operations are integrated and are not separately identified.

multiple-brand strategy A strategy in which a firm has more than one brand of essentially the same product, aimed either at the same target market or at distinct target markets.

multiple-distribution channels The use by a producer of more than one channel of distribution for reasons such as achieving broad market coverage or avoiding total dependence on a single arrangement.

multiple packaging The practice of placing several units of the same product in one container.

multiple-segment strategy A plan of action that involves selecting two or more different groups of potential customers as the firm's target markets.

N

net cost of delivered purchases A financial figure calculated by taking gross purchases at billed cost, deducting sales returns, sales allowances, and cash discounts for early payment, and adding freight in.

net profit The amount of revenue that remains after a firm pays the cost of merchandise and its operating expenses.

net profit percentage The ratio of net profit to net sales.

net sales The net amount of sales revenue, out of which the company will pay for the products and all its expenses.

new product A vague term that may refer to (1) really innovative, truly unique products, (2) replacement products that are significantly different from existing ones, or (3) imitative products that are new to a particular firm but are not new to the market.

new-product department An organizational structure for product planning and development that involves a small unit, consisting of five or fewer people, and that reports to the president.

new-product development process A set of six stages that a new product goes through, starting with idea generation and continuing through idea screening, business analysis, prototype development, market tests, and eventually commercialization (full-scale production and marketing).

new-product strategy A statement identifying the role a new product is expected to play in achieving corporate and marketing goals.

new-task buying In the business market, a purchasing situation in which a company for the first time considers buying a given item.

niche marketing A strategy in which goods and services are tailored to meet the needs of small market segments.

nonadopters Those consumers that never adopt an innovation.

nonbusiness market The total set of churches, colleges and universities, museums, hospitals and other health institutions, political parties, labor unions, and charitable organizations.

noncumulative discount A quantity discount based on the size of an individual order of one or more products.

nonprice competition A strategy in which a seller maintains stable prices and attempts to improve its market position by emphasizing other (nonprice) aspects of its marketing program.

nonstore retailing Retailing activities resulting in transactions that occur away from a retail store.

North American Free Trade Agreement (NAFTA) An agreement among the United States, Canada, and Mexico to eliminate tariffs between the countries.

nutrition labeling The part of a product that provides information about the amount of calories, fat, cholesterol, sodium, carbohydrates, and protein contained in the package's contents.

O

objective A desired outcome. Same as *goal*.

observation method A method of gathering primary data by observing the actions of a person without direct interaction.

odd pricing A psychological pricing strategy that consists of setting prices at uneven (or odd) amounts, such as $4.99, rather than at even amounts, such as $5, in the belief that these seemingly lower prices will result in larger sales volume.

off-price retailer A type of retail institution, often found in the areas of apparel and shoes, that has a narrow and deep product assortment, low prices, and few customer services.

oligopoly A market structure dominated by a few firms, each marketing similar products.

one-price strategy A pricing strategy under which a seller charges the same price to all similar customers who buy identical quantities of a product.

operating expense ratio Operating expenses divided by net sales.

operating expenses The marketing, administrative, and miscellaneous costs, but not the cost of goods purchased or manufactured, incurred by a firm.

operating statement A financial statement summarizing the firm's income, expenses, and profit or loss over a given period of time. Same as *income statement* and *profit and loss statement*.

operating supplies The "convenience" category of business goods, consisting of tangible products that are characterized by low dollar value per unit and a short life and that aid in an organization's operations without becoming part of the finished product.

organizational strategies Broad plans of action by which an organization intends to achieve its goals and fulfill its mission. These plans are for (1) the total organization in a small, single-product company or (2) each SBU in a large, multiproduct or multibusiness organization.

outside sales The kind of personal selling group in which sales people go to the customers, making contact by mail, telephone, or face-to-face.

P

packaging All the activities of designing and producing the container or wrapper for a product.

party-plan selling One kind of direct selling, in which a host or hostess invites some friends to a party at which a sales person makes a sales presentation.

past sales analysis A method of sales forecasting that applies a flat percentage increase to the volume achieved last year or to the average volume of the past few years.

patronage buying motives The reasons why a consumer chooses to shop at a particular store.

perception The process carried out by an individual to receive, organize, and assign meaning to stimuli detected by the five senses.

perfect competition A market structure in which product differentiation is absent, buyers and sellers are well informed, and the seller has no discernible control over the selling price.

perishability A characteristic of a service indicating that it is highly transitory and cannot be stored.

personal interview A face-to-face method of gathering data in a survey.

personal selling The personal communication of information to persuade somebody to buy something. Alternatively, the direct (face-to-face or over-the-phone) presentation of a product to a prospective customer by a representative of the organization selling it.

personal selling process The logical sequence of prospecting, preapproach, presenting, and postsale services that a sales person takes in dealing with a prospective buyer.

personality An individual's pattern of traits that influences behavioral responses.

physical distribution All the activities involved in the flow of products as they move physically from producer to consumer or industrial user. Same as *logistics*.

physical distribution management The development and operation of processes resulting in the effective and efficient physical flow of products.

physical facilities The building—including its location, design, and layout—that serves as a store for a retail firm.

piggyback service The transporting of loaded truck trailers on railroad flatcars.

pioneering stage See *introduction stage*.

place utility The want-satisfying capability that is created when a product is made readily accessible to potential customers.

planned obsolescence A strategy that is intended to make an existing product out of date and thus to increase the market for replacement products. There are two forms: technological and style.

planning The process of deciding now what we are going to do later, including when and how we are going to do it.

political and legal forces A set of factors, including monetary and fiscal policies, legislation, and regulations, that affect the marketing activities of an organization.

positioning A product's image in relation to directly competitive products as well as other products marketed by the same company. Alternatively, a firm's strategies and actions related to favorably distinguishing itself from competitors in the minds of selected groups of consumers. Same as *product positioning*.

possession utility The want-satisfying capability that is created when a customer buys the product—that is, when ownership is transferred to the buyer.

postage stamp pricing See *uniform delivered pricing*.

postpurchase behavior Efforts by a consumer to reduce the anxiety that often accompanies purchase decisions.

postpurchase cognitive dissonance The anxiety created by the fact that in most purchases the alternative selected has some negative features and the alternatives not selected have some positive features.

postsale activities The fourth and final stage in the personal selling process, in which a sales person follows up sales to ensure that no problems occur in delivery, financing, installation, employee training, and other areas that are important to customer satisfaction.

postsale service Maintenance and repairs as well as other services that are provided to customers in order to fulfill the terms of a firm's warranty and/or to augment the firm's revenues.

price The amount of money and/or other items with utility needed to acquire a product.

price competition A strategy in which a firm regularly offers products priced as low as possible, usually accompanied by a minimum of services.

price discrimination A situation in which different customers pay different prices for the same product.

price elasticity of demand The responsiveness of quantity demanded to price changes.

price lining A pricing strategy whereby a firm selects a limited number of prices at which it will sell related products.

price war A form of price competition that begins when one firm decreases its price in an effort to increase its sales volume and/or market share, the other firms retaliate by reducing prices on competing products, and additional price decreases by the original price cutter and/or its competitors usually follow.

pricing above competition One form of market-based pricing in which price is set above the prevailing market level.

pricing below competition One form of market-based pricing in which price is set below the level of your main competitors.

pricing objective The desired outcome that management seeks to achieve with its pricing structure and strategies.

pricing to meet competition A pricing method in which a firm ascertains what the market price is and, after allowing for customary markups for middlemen, arrives at its own selling price.

primary data New data gathered specifically for the project at hand.

primary-demand advertising Advertising that is designed to stimulate demand for a generic category of a product.

Primary Metropolitan Statistical Area (PMSA) A Metropolitan Statistical Area in the U.S. that has a population of at least 1 million.

private warehouse A warehouse that is owned and operated by the firm whose products are being stored and handled at the facility.

producer's brand A brand that is owned by a manufacturer or other producer.

product A set of tangible and intangible attributes, which may include packaging, color, price, quality, and brand, plus the seller's services and reputation. A product may be a good, service, place, person, or idea.

product abandonment A decision and subsequent action by a firm to drop a product that has insufficient and/or declining sales and lacks profits.

product adaptation Modifying a product that sells successfully in one market so as to suit the unique needs or requirements of other markets.

product advertising Advertising that focuses on a particular product or brand.

product alteration A strategy of improving an existing product.

product and trade name franchising A distribution agreement under which a supplier (the franchiser) authorizes a dealer (the franchisee) to sell a product line, using the parent company's trade name for promotional purposes.

product color The hue(s) given to a particular product, including its packaging.

product counterfeiting The unscrupulous placement of a brand name on a product without the legal right to do so.

product design The arrangement of elements that collectively form a good or service.

product differentiation A strategy in which a firm uses promotion to distinguish its product from competitive brands offered to the same aggregate market.

product liability A legal action alleging that an illness, accident, or death resulted from the named product because it was harmful, faulty, or inadequately labeled.

product life cycle The aggregate demand over an extended period of time for all brands comprising a generic product category.

product line A broad group of products intended for essentially similar uses and having similar physical characteristics.

product manager An organizational structure for product planning and development that makes one person responsible for planning new products as well as managing established products. Same as *brand manager*.

product-market growth matrix A planning model that consists of four alternative growth strategies based on whether an organization will be selling its present products or new products to its present markets or new markets.

product mix The set of all products offered for sale by a company.

product-mix contraction A strategy in which a firm either eliminates an entire line or simplifies the assortment within a line.

product-mix expansion A strategy in which a firm increases the depth within a particular line and/or the number of lines it offers to consumers.

product-planning committee An organizational structure for product planning and development that involves a joint effort among executives from major departments and, especially in small firms, the president and/or another top-level executive.

product positioning See *positioning*.

product quality See *quality*.

product specialization One method of organizing selling activities so that each sales person is assigned one or more product lines to sell.

production-orientation stage The first stage in the evolution of marketing management, in which the basic assumption is that making a good product will ensure business success.

profit and loss statement See *operating statement*.

promotion The element in an organization's marketing mix that serves to inform, persuade, and remind the market of a product and/or the organization selling it in the hope of influencing the recipients' feelings, beliefs, or behavior.

promotional allowance A price reduction granted by a seller as payment for promotional services performed by buyers.

promotional budgeting method The means used to determine the amount of dollars allocated to promotion in general and/or to specific forms of promotion.

promotional mix The combination of personal selling, advertising, sales promotion, public relations, and publicity that is intended to help an organization achieve its marketing objectives.

psychoanalytic theory Freudian theory that argues people have subconscious drives that cannot be satisfied in socially acceptable ways.

psychographic segmentation Subdividing markets into groups based on personality dimensions, life-style characteristics, and values.

psychological obsolescence See *style obsolescence*.

public relations Communications efforts that are designed to favorably influence attitudes toward an organization, its products, and its policies.

public warehouse An independent firm that provides for a fee storage and handling facilities for individuals or companies.

publicity A special form of public relations that involves any communication about an organization, its products, or its policies through the media that is not paid for by the sponsoring organization.

pull strategy Promotional effort directed primarily at end users so they will ask middlemen for the product.

purchaser The party who carries out a transaction.

push strategy Promotional efforts directed primarily at middlemen that are the next link forward in the distribution channel for a product.

Q

qualifying One task in the first step in the personal selling process, in which the sales person determines if a prospective customer has the necessary willingness, purchasing power, and authority to buy.

qualitative performance bases In sales-force evaluation, subjective criteria for appraising the performance of sales people.

quality The degree to which a product meets the expectations of the customer. Same as *product quality*.

quantitative performance bases In sales-force evaluation, specific, objective criteria for appraising the performance of sales people.

quantity discount A deduction from a seller's list price that is offered to a buyer when a large quantity of the product is purchased.

R

raw materials Business goods that become part of another tangible product prior to being processed in any way.

recipient market See *client market*.

reconsumption Making products so that the materials, components, and packages can be used longer and reused either in part or whole.

reference group A group of people who influence a person's attitudes, values, and behavior.

refusal to deal A situation in which a producer that desires to select and perhaps control its channels declines to sell to some middlemen.

relationship marketing An ongoing interaction between a buyer and a seller in which the seller continuously improves its understanding of the buyer's needs, and the buyer becomes increasingly loyal to the seller because its needs are being so well satisfied.

relationship selling An attempt by a sales person or organization to develop a deeper, longer-lasting relationship built on trust with key customers—usually larger accounts.

resale price maintenance A pricing policy whereby a manufacturer seeks to control the prices at which middlemen resell their products.

reseller market One segment of the business market, consisting of wholesaling and retailing middlemen that buy products for resale to other organizations or to consumers.

retail trade See *retailing*.

retailer A firm engaged primarily in retailing.

retailer cooperative A type of contractual vertical marketing system that is formed by a group of small retailers who agree to establish and operate a wholesale warehouse.

retailing The sale, and all activities directly related to the sale, of goods and services to ultimate consumers for personal, nonbusiness use. Same as *retail trade*.

return on investment A commonly used measure of managerial performance, calculated by dividing net profit by either total assets or equity.

Robinson-Patman Act A federal law passed in 1936 that was intended to curb price discrimination by large retailers and the granting by manufacturers of proportionally unequal promotional allowances to large retailers or wholesalers.

role ambiguity Confusion among sales people, usually occurring in the absence of company policies, about how much responsibility to assume in dealing with customers in various difficult situations.

role conflict The stress created for a sales person by the often contrary demands and expectations of an employer, customers, and family.

S

sales allowance A situation in which a customer who is dissatisfied with a product keeps it but is given a reduction from the selling price.

sales-force composite A method of forecasting sales that consists of collecting from all sales people estimates of sales for their territories during the future period of interest.

sales forecast An estimate of probable sales for one company's brand of a product during a stated time period in a specific market and assuming the use of a predetermined marketing plan.

sales-orientation stage The second stage in the evolution of marketing management, in which the emphasis is on using various promotional activities to sell whatever the organization produces.

sales potential The portion of market potential that a specific company could expect to achieve under ideal conditions.

sales promotion Demand-stimulating devices designed to supplement advertising and facilitate personal selling.

sales return A situation in which a customer returns merchandise and receives a refund equal to the full purchase price in cash or credit.

sales team See *selling center*.

sales-volume analysis A detailed study of the Net Sales section of a company's profit and loss statement.

satisfaction The consumer condition when experience with a product equals or exceeds expectations.

scrambled merchandising The main source of horizontal channel conflict, a strategy under which a middleman diversifies by adding product lines not traditionally carried by its type of business.

seasonal discount A deduction from the list price that is offered to a customer for placing an order during the seller's slack season.

secondary data Available data, already gathered for some other purpose.

selective-demand advertising Advertising that is intended to stimulate demand for individual brands.

selective distortion The phenomenon in which an individual compares new information with one's existing store of knowledge or frame of reference and then, in the case of an inconsistency, alters the new information to conform to the established beliefs.

selective distribution A strategy in which a producer sells its product through multiple, but not all possible, wholesalers and retailers in a market where a consumer might reasonably look for it.

selective perception The process of screening all the marketing stimuli to which an individual is exposed on a daily basis.

selective retention The phenomenon of retaining in memory only part of what is perceived.

self-concept The way a person sees himself/herself. Same as *self-image*.

self-image See *self-concept*.

selling agent An agent wholesaling middleman that essentially takes the place of a manufacturer's marketing department by marketing the manufacturer's entire output.

selling center A group of people representing a sales department as well as other functional areas in a firm (such as finance, production, and research and development) that work cooperatively to achieve a sale. Sometimes called a *sales team* or *team selling*.

separable expenses See *direct costs.*

service An identifiable, intangible activity that is the main object of a transaction designed to provide want-satisfaction to customers.

service encounter In services marketing, a customer's interaction with any service employee or with any tangible element, such as a service's physical surroundings.

service quality The degree to which an intangible offering meets the expectations of the customer.

services characteristics The four factors (intangibility, inseparability, heterogeneity, and perishability) that differentiate services from goods.

services market The set of all transportation carriers and public utilities, and the many financial, insurance, legal, and real estate firms.

shopping center A planned grouping of retail stores that lease space in a structure that is typically owned by a single organization and that can accommodate multiple tenants.

shopping goods A category of tangible consumer products that are purchased after the buyer has spent some time and effort comparing the price, quality, perhaps style, and/or other attributes of alternative products in several stores.

single-price strategy An extreme variation of a one-price strategy in which all items sold by a firm carry a single price.

single-segment strategy A plan of action that involves selecting one homogeneous segment from within a total market to be the firm's target market. Same as *concentration strategy.*

single-source data A data-gathering method in which exposure to television advertising and product purchases can be traced to individual households.

situation analysis The act of gathering and studying information pertaining to one or more specified aspects of an organization. Alternatively, a background investigation that helps in refining a research problem.

situational influences A temporary force, associated with the immediate purchase environment, that affects behavior.

slotting allowance A fee that some retailers charge a manufacturer in order to place its product on store shelves.

small-order problem A situation confronting many firms, in which revenue from an order is less than allocated expenses because several costs, such as billing and direct selling, are essentially the same regardless of order size.

social and cultural forces A set of factors, including lifestyles, social values, and beliefs, that affect the marketing activities of an organization.

social class A division of, or ranking within, society based on education, occupation, and type of residential neighborhood.

social information environment As contrasted with the commercial information environment, all communications among family members, friends, and acquaintances about products.

social responsibility The commitment on the part of a company to improve the well-being of society.

societal marketing concept A revised version of the marketing concept under which a company recognizes that it should be concerned about not only the buyers of its products but also other people directly affected by its operations and with not only tomorrow but also the long term.

specialty goods A category of tangible consumer products for which consumers have a strong brand preference and are willing to expend substantial time and effort in locating and then buying the desired brand.

specialty store A type of retail institution that has a very narrow and deep product assortment (often concentrating on a specialized product line or even part of a specialized product line), that usually strives to maintain manufacturers' suggested prices, and that typically provides at least standard customer services.

stages in the adoption process The six steps a prospective buyer goes through in deciding whether to purchase something new.

Standard Industrial Classification (SIC) system A coding system developed by the federal government that groups firms into similar types of businesses and thus enables a company to identify and analyze small segments of the business market.

stimulus-response theory The theory that learning occurs as a person (1) responds to some stimuli and (2) is rewarded with need satisfaction for a correct response or penalized for an incorrect one.

stockturn rate The number of times the average inventory is turned over, or sold, during the period under study.

straight rebuy In the business market, a routine, low-involvement purchase with minimal information needs and no great consideration of alternatives.

strategic alliance A formal, long-term agreement between firms to combine their capabilities and resources to accomplish global objectives.

strategic business unit (SBU) A separate division for a major product or market in a multiproduct or multibusiness organization.

strategic company planning The level of planning that consists of (1) defining the organization's mission, (2) analyzing the situation, (3) setting organizational objectives, and (4) selecting appropriate strategies to achieve these objectives.

strategic marketing planning The level of planning that consists of (1) conducting a situation analysis, (2) developing marketing objectives, (3) determining positioning and differential advantage, (4) selecting target markets and measuring market demand, and (5) designing a strategic marketing mix.

strategic planning The managerial process of matching a firm's resources with its market opportunities over the long run.

strategic window The limited amount of time in which a firm's resources coincide with a particular market opportunity.

strategy A broad plan of action by which an organization intends to reach its objectives.

style A distinctive manner of presentation or construction in any art, product, or endeavor.

style obsolescence A form of planned obsolescence in which superficial characteristics of a product are altered so that the new model is easily differentiated from the previous model and people become dissatisfied with it. Same as *fashion obsolescence* and *psychological obsolescence*.

subculture Groups in a culture that exhibit characteristic behavior patterns sufficient to distinguish them from other groups within the same culture.

suggested list price A pricing policy whereby a manufacturer recommends to retailers a final (retail) price that should provide them with their normal markups.

supercenter A combination of a discount house and a complete grocery store.

supermarket A type of retail institution that has a moderately broad and moderately deep product assortment spanning groceries and some nonfood lines, that offers relatively few customer services, and that ordinarily emphasizes price in either an offensive or defensive way.

supermarket retailing A retailing method that features several related product lines, a high degree of self-service, largely centralized checkout, and competitive prices.

suppliers The people or firms that supply the goods or services that an organization needs to produce what it sells.

survey A method of gathering primary data by interviewing people in person, by telephone, or by mail.

survey of buyer intentions A form of sales forecasting in which a firm asks a sample of current or potential customers how much of a particular product they would buy at a given price during a specified future period.

SWOT analysis Identifying and evaluating an organization's most significant strengths, weaknesses, opportunities, and threats.

systems approach to physical distribution The unification of individual physical distribution activities.

systems selling Providing a total package of related goods and services to solve a customer's problem (needs).

T

tactic A specific means by which a strategy is implemented.

target market A group of customers (people or organizations) for whom a seller designs a particular marketing mix.

tariff A tax imposed on a product entering a country.

team selling See *selling center*.

technological obsolescence A form of planned obsolescence in which significant technical improvements result in a more effective product. Same as *functional obsolescence*.

technology Applications of science for industrial and commercial purposes.

telemarketing A form of nonstore retailing in which a sales person initiates contact with a shopper and also closes the sale over the telephone.

telephone survey A method of gathering data by interviewing people over the telephone.

televised shopping One form of direct marketing, in which TV channels and shows sell consumer electronics, jewelry, and other products at relatively low prices.

test marketing A method of demand forecasting in which a firm markets its new product in a limited geographic area, measures the sales, and then—from this sample—projects the company's sales over a larger area. Alternatively, a marketing research technique that uses this same approach to judge consumers' responses to a strategy before committing to a major marketing effort.

time utility The want-satisfying capability that is created when a product is available to customers when they want it.

total cost The sum of total fixed cost and total variable cost for a specific quantity produced or sold.

total cost concept In physical distribution, the recognition that the best relationship between costs and profit must be established for the entire physical distribution system, rather than for individual activities.

total fixed cost The sum of all fixed costs.

total quality management (TQM) A philosophy as well as specific procedures, policies, and practices that commit an organization to continuous quality improvement in all of its activities.

total variable cost The sum of all variable costs.

trade balance In international business, the difference between the value of a nation's imports and the value of its exports.

trade discount A reduction from the list price that is offered by a seller to buyers in payment for marketing functions the buyers will perform. Same as *functional discount*.

trademark A brand that has been adopted by a seller and given legal protection.

Trademark Law Revision Act A federal law, passed in 1988, that broadened the Landham Trademark Act to encompass comparisons made in promotional activity.

trademark licensing A business arrangement in which the owner of a trademark grants permission to other firms to use the owner's brand name, logotype, and/or character on the licensee's products in return for a royalty on sales of those products. Same as *brand licensing*.

trading down A product-line strategy wherein a company adds a lower-priced product to a line to reach a market that cannot afford the higher-priced items or that see them as too expensive.

trading up A product-line strategy wherein a company adds a higher-priced product to a line in order to attract a broader market and, through its added prestige, helps the sale of its existing lower-priced products.

trend analysis A statistical method of forecasting sales over the long term by using regression analysis or over the short term by using a seasonal index of sales.

trickle-across theory In fashion adoption, a fashion cycle that moves horizontally and simultaneously within several socioeconomic levels.

trickle-down theory In fashion adoption, a fashion cycle that flows downward through several socioeconomic levels.

trickle-up theory In fashion adoption, a fashion cycle in which a style first becomes popular with lower socioeconomic levels and then flows upward to become popular among higher levels.

truck distributor See *truck jobber*.

truck jobber A merchant wholesaler that carries a selected line of perishable products and delivers them by truck to retail stores. Same as *truck distributor*.

tying contract The practice by which a manufacturer sells a product to a middleman only under the condition that the middleman also buy another (possibly unwanted) product from the manufacturer.

U

ultimate consumers People who buy goods or services for their own personal or household use in order to satisfy strictly nonbusiness wants.

undifferentiated-market strategy See *market aggregation strategy*.

unfair-practices acts State laws intended to regulate some forms of leader pricing that are intended to drive other products or companies out of business. Same as *unfair-sales acts*.

unfair-sales acts See *unfair-practices acts*.

uniform delivered pricing A geographic pricing strategy whereby the same delivered price is quoted to all buyers regardless of their locations. Same as *postage stamp pricing*.

universal design The design of products in such a way that they can be used by all consumers, including disabled individuals, senior citizens, and others needing special considerations.

unsought goods A category of consumer tangible products that consists of new products the consumer is not yet aware of or products the consumer is aware of but does not want right now.

utility The attribute in an item that makes it capable of satisfying human wants.

V

value The ratio of perceived benefits to price and any other incurred costs.

value added The dollar value of a firm's output minus the value of the inputs it purchased from other firms.

value marketing Activities that make significant improvements in a product in order to provide the customer with real benefits.

value pricing A form of price competition in which a firm seeks to improve the ratio of a product's benefits to its price and related costs.

values Intangible principles that are a reflection of people's needs, adjusted for the realities of the world in which they live.

variable cost A cost that changes directly in relation to the number of units produced or sold.

variable-price strategy See *flexible-price strategy*.

venture team An organizational structure for product planning and development that involves a small group, with representatives from engineering, production, finance, and marketing research, that operates like a separate small business, and that typically reports directly to top management.

vertical business market A situation where a given product is usable by virtually all the firms in only one or two industries.

vertical conflict A form of channel conflict occurring among firms at different levels of the same channel, typically producer versus wholesaler or producer versus retailer.

vertical marketing system (VMS) A tightly coordinated distribution channel designed to improve operating efficiency and marketing effectiveness.

voluntary chain A type of contractual vertical marketing system that is sponsored by a wholesaler who enters into a contract with interested retailers.

W

warehouse club A combined retailing and wholesaling institution that has a very broad but very shallow product assortment, very low prices, few customer services, and is open only to members. Same as *wholesale club*.

warning label The part of a product that tells consumers not to misuse the product and informs them of almost every conceivable danger associated with using it.

warranty An assurance given to buyers that they will be compensated in case the product does not perform up to reasonable expectations.

wheel of retailing A theory proposing a cyclical pattern of changes in retailing, whereby a new type of store enters the market as a low-cost, low-price store and over time takes business away from unchanging competitors, after which the successful new retailer trades up, incurring higher costs and higher prices and making itself vulnerable to a new type of retailer.

Wheeler-Lea Act A federal law, passed in 1938, that amended the Federal Trade Commission Act by strengthening the prohibition against unfair competition, especially false or misleading advertising.

wholesale club See *warehouse club*.

wholesale trade See *wholesaling*.

wholesaler See *merchant wholesaler*.

wholesaling The sale, and all activities directly related to the sale, of goods and services to businesses and other organizations for resale, use in producing other goods and services, or the operation of an organization.

wholesaling middleman A firm engaged primarily in wholesaling.

wholly owned subsidiary A business arrangement in foreign markets in which a company owns the foreign operation in order to gain maximum control over its marketing program and production operations.

Z

zone-delivered pricing A geographic pricing strategy whereby a seller divides its market into a limited number of broad geographic zones and then sets a uniform delivered price for each zone.

NAME INDEX

Note to the reader: An "N" number indicates the entry is to be found in the "Notes and References" section. A "B" numbered page indicates the entry is to be found in Appendix B. An italicized "*n*" indicates the entry is to be found in a source citation on that page.

SUBJECT INDEX